#18
class

LAW FOR BUSINESS

JOHN D. DONNELL, J.D., D.B.A.
Indiana University

A. JAMES BARNES, J.D.
Beveridge, Fairbanks, and Diamond

MICHAEL B. METZGER, J.D.
Indiana University

LAW FOR BUSINESS

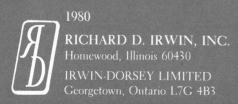

1980

RICHARD D. IRWIN, INC.
Homewood, Illinois 60430

IRWIN-DORSEY LIMITED
Georgetown, Ontario L7G 4B3

© RICHARD D. IRWIN, INC., 1980

All rights reserved. No part of this publication may be
reproduced, stored in a retrieval system, or transmitted,
in any form or by any means, electronic, mechanical,
photocopying, recording, or otherwise, without the prior
written permission of the publisher.

ISBN 0-256-02316-6
Library of Congress Catalog Card No. 79–90539
Printed in the United States of America

2 3 4 5 6 7 8 9 0 K 7 6 5 4 3 2 1

LEARNING SYSTEMS COMPANY—
a division of Richard D. Irwin, Inc.—has developed a
PROGRAMMED LEARNING AID
to accompany texts in this subject area.
Copies can be purchased through your bookstore
or by writing PLAIDS,
1818 Ridge Road, Homewood, Illinois 60430.

Preface

Business today operates in an increasingly "legalized" environment. In the last ten years a large number of federal statutes have influenced American business practices in important ways. A few examples include the Occupational Safety and Health Act, the Consumer Product Safety Act, and the Consumer Credit Protection Act. State legislatures have also recently enacted numerous laws affecting business. The courts too have played an active role in changing the law concerning business. Generally these changes have made it easier for customers, employees, and others affected by business operations to recover for injuries and losses resulting from those operations. *Fortune* magazine has called this a "legal explosion." It has changed the business practices and costs of doing business of both large and small firms.

These developments in the law have resulted in a major change in the nature of lawyers' work. The trend toward preventive law practice is discussed in Chapter 1. There we emphasize that lawyers alone cannot control these new costs. This requires cooperation between the business manager and the lawyer. The problem of dealing with the recent increase in the number and size of court awards in product liability cases is a good example. At least in a large manufacturing firm, handling this "legal problem" will involve a number of employees as well as one or more company lawyers. Product design, production, testing, advertising, and insurance people will all participate. To be able to make their maximum contribution to an effective response to product liability problems, they must have some understanding of the legal system, the way courts work, tort law, and sales law.

These areas of the law and others affecting business have all become more complex in recent years. For this reason we, as authors, have made a special effort to make this book as clear and simple as we can. We believe it is not only easier to read than other texts with similar coverage now available, but we have used more examples to clarify the principles and rules discussed. In addition, in selecting the actual court cases used in the text, we have looked for those involving people as consumers and employees as well as managers. We have also tried to select cases that teach something about business practices as well as the law. While trying to keep them brief we have tried to include enough of the facts to make both the business situation and the legal issues understandable.

We welcome comments from users of this book, both instructors and students. Our aim is to offer an authoritative yet easy to read text that provides broad coverage of the law applicable to business. We solicit your suggestions for improvement.

L. Thomas Bowers, Jane P. Mallor, Michael J. Phillips, and Eric L. Richards, all colleagues of ours at Indiana, have prepared a student workbook and an instructor's test manual for use with this text. We are indebted to them for this important contribution. An instructor's manual and test bank are also available to adopters from the publisher. These supplementary materials give the instructor a variety of teaching aids to use in structuring his or her course.

In preparing this text we have had a great deal of support and assistance from colleagues, friends, and students. It is impossible to recall and give credit to them all. We wish particularly to mention Byron Notter, Mitchel Posvner, Gregory Naples, Raymond Stark, Lyle Brenna, John di Stasio, Douglas Gordon, Marjorie Gilmore, Sanford Searleman, and William E. Ringle.

The manuscript was read by C. George Alvey, James W. Garlanger, David B. Michaels, John Miklos, and Gary L. Woods. We appreciate the thoughtful comments they made. While we followed many of their suggestions, we elected not to follow others. Whatever shortcomings remain in the book are, therefore, ours alone.

In addition, we wish to express appreciation to a number of people whose assistance was very valuable. Craig Benson, Wyman Bravard, and Philip Carey provided research assistance. Sarah Jane Hughes made a valuable contribution to Chapter 49. Chapters 2 and 32 benefited from the constructive comments of Andrew Mallor. Roberta Aubin, Kim Ellis, Katherine Leach, and Annette Panagakos prepared the manuscripts. Susan Marquet assisted in proofreading.

January 1980   John D. Donnell
                                                 A. James Barnes
                                                 Michael B. Metzger

Contents

PART ONE
Introduction to the Law

1. Law and Its Sources   3

Introduction: *Law in Business. Preventive Law. The Authors' Objectives.* The Nature of Law: *What Is Law? The Legal System. A Definition. A Limited Meaning. Functions of Law.* Classifications of Law: *Substantive and Procedural Law. Criminal and Civil Law.* The American Legal System: *Law and Government. Checks and Balances. Constitutional Powers. Constitutional Limitations. Fifty-One Legal Systems.* Sources of Law: *Federal and State Sources. Constitutions. Treaties. Statutes. Administrative Rules and Decisions. Executive Orders. Court Decisions.* How the Law Changes: *Predictability versus Adaptability. Predictability. Adaptability.* The Adversary System: *The Function of the Lawyers. The Function of the Judge. Advantages and Disadvantages.*

2. Dispute Settlement   18

Means of Dispute Settlement: *Negotiation. Mediation and Fact Finding. Arbitration. Other Alternatives to the Courts. The Courts. Confusion of Terminology.* Federal Courts: *Jurisdiction. District Court. Court of Appeals. The Supreme Court. Special Courts.* State Courts: *Jurisdiction. Inferior Courts. Trial Courts. Appeal Courts.* Procedure: *The Functions of Procedure. Summons. The Complaint. The Answer. Reply. Pleadings. Discovery. Pretrial Hearing.* Trial Procedure: *Setting the Case for Trial. Opening the Case. Presentation of Testimony. Closing the Case.* Appeal Procedure: *When an Appeal Is Possible. The Appeal. Oral Argument.*

3. Crimes and Intentional Torts   36

Crimes: *The Essentials of Crime. Criminal Procedure. Crime and People in Business.* Intentional Torts: *Interference with Personal Rights. Interference with Property Rights. Interference with Economic Relations.*

4. Negligence and Strict Liability   50

Negligence: *Duty. Breach. Causation. General Causation Rules. Defenses to Negligence. Recklessness. Strict Liability.*

PART TWO
Contracts

5. The Nature and Origins of Contracts   61

What Is a Contract? Why Have Contracts? How Has Contract Law Developed? Types of Contracts: *Unilateral and Bilateral Contracts. Valid, Unenforceable, Voidable, and Void Contracts. Express and Implied Contracts. Executed and Executory Contracts.* Quasi Contract. The Uniform Commercial Code.

6. Creating a Contract: Offers   69

Introduction. What Is an Offer? *Definiteness. Communication to the Offeree.* Special Problems with Offers: *Advertisements. Rewards. Auctions. Bids.* What Terms Are Included in Offers? How Long Do Offers Last? *Terms of the Offer. Lapse of Time. Revocation. Options. Estoppel. Revocation of Offers for Unilateral Contracts. The Effectiveness of Revocations. Rejection. Death or Insanity of Either Party. Destruction of Subject Matter. Intervening Illegality.*

7. Creating a Contract: Acceptances   82

What Is an Acceptance? *Accepting an Offer for a Unilateral Contract. Accepting an Offer for a Bilateral Contract. Silence as Acceptance.* Who Can Accept an Offer? Acceptance When a Writing Is Anticipated. Communication of Acceptance: *Manner of Communication. When Is Acceptance Communicated? Authorized Means of Communication. Stipulated Means of Communication.*

8. Voluntary Consent   93

Introduction: *The Need for Real Consent. The Parties' Duty of Care. The Remedy. Ratification.* Misrepresentation: *Knowledge of Falsity. Materiality. Fact versus Opinion. Justifiable Reliance. Detriment.* Fraud: *What Is a "Knowingly Made" Misstatement? Intent to Deceive. Fraud by Silence. The Remedy for Fraud.* Duress and Undue Influence: *General Nature. Duress. Undue Influence.* Mistake: *The Nature of Mistake. Mutual Mistake. Unilateral Mistake.*

9. Capacity to Contract   106

Minors' Contracts: *The Reason for Minors' Incapacity. The Age of Majority. The Right to Disaffirm. The Consequences of Disaffirming. Misrepresentation of Age by*

Minors. Ratification. Necessaries. Contracts of Insane and Drunken Persons: *Theory of Incapacity. The Test of Insanity. The Effect of Insanity. Necessaries. The Right to Disaffirm. Ratification.*

10. Consideration   115

The Idea of Consideration: *Legal Value. Bargained for and Given in Exchange.* Solving Consideration Problems. Rules of Consideration: *Preexisting Duties. Promises Not to Commit Crimes or Torts. Promises by Public Officials to Perform Official Duties. Promises to Perform Preexisting Contractual Duties. Promises to Discharge Debts for Part Payment. Composition Agreements. Past Consideration. Forbearance to Sue. Mutuality of Obligation. Adequacy of Consideration.* Exceptions to the Requirement of Consideration: *Promissory Estoppel. Charitable Subscriptions. Debts Barred by Bankruptcy Discharge or the Statute of Limitations. Promises to Perform a Conditional Duty.*

11. The Form and Meaning of Contracts   128

The Statutes of Frauds: *The Effect of Failure to Comply.* Contracts Covered by the Statutes of Frauds: *Executors' Agreements to Personally Pay Their Decedents' Debts. Contracts to Answer for the Debt of Another. Contracts Transferring an Interest in Land. Bilateral Contracts Not Capable of Being Performed within One Year. What Kind of Writing Is Required?* Interpreting Contracts: *The Necessity of Interpretation. Rules of Construction.* The Parol Evidence Rule: *The Purpose of the Rule. Exceptions to the Parol Evidence Rule.*

12. Illegality   140

Introduction: *Illegality. Types of Illegality. The Presumption of Legality.* The Effect of Illegality: *General Rule. Ignorance of Fact or Special Regulation. Rights of Protected Parties. Rescission before Performance of Illegal Act. Illegality and Divisible Contracts.* Contracts to Commit Illegal Acts: *Agreements to Commit Crimes. Agreements to Commit Torts.* Contracts Made Illegal by Statute: *Wagering Statutes. Statutes Declaring Bargains Void. Regulatory Statutes.* Contracts Contrary to Public Policy: *The Idea of Public Policy. Contracts Injurious to Public Service. Contracts to Influence Fiduciaries. Exculpatory Clauses. Contracts in Restraint of Trade. Unequal Bargains.*

13. Third Parties' Contract Rights   152

Assignment of Contracts: *Definition. What Contracts Are Assignable? Delegation of Duties.* The Consequences of Assignment: *The Rights and Duties of Assignees. The Duties of Assignors.* Third-Party Beneficiary Contracts: *Donee Beneficiaries. Creditor Beneficiaries. Incidental Beneficiaries.*

14. Performance and Remedies   160

Conditions: *Definitions. Types of Conditions. The Creation of Conditions.* Standards of Performance: *Complete or Satisfactory Performance. Substantial Performance. Material Breach. Special Performance Problems. The Time for Performance.* Excuses for Nonperformance: *Prevention. Impossibility.* Discharge: *The Nature of Discharge.*

Discharge by Agreement. Discharge by Waiver. Discharge by Alteration. Discharge by Statute of Limitations. Remedies: *The Theory of Remedies. Damages in Contracts Cases. The Duty to Mitigate Damages. Equitable Remedies.*

PART THREE
Sales

15. Introduction to Sales   177

When and How Does Article 2 Apply? How Does Article 2 Differ from Contract Law? The Creation of Sales Contracts. Offers and the Code: *Firm Offers.* Acceptance and the Code: *The Battle of the Forms. Manner and Medium of Acceptance. Acceptance by Shipment.* Consideration and the Code: *Modification of Sales Contracts.* Voluntary Consent and the Code: *Unconscionable Contracts.* Writing and the Code.

16. Title, Risk of Loss, and the Terms of Sales Contracts   194

The Terms of Sales Contracts: *Price Terms. Quantity Terms. Delivery Terms. Time Terms.* Title and the Code. Title and Third Parties: *Transfers of Voidable Title. Buyers in the Ordinary Course of Business. Entrusting Goods. Risk of Loss. The Terms of the Agreement. Shipment Contracts. Destination Contracts. Goods in the Possession of Third Parties. Risk Generally. Breach of Contract and Risk. Insurable Interest.* Sales on Trial: *Sale or Return. Sale on Approval. Sale on Consignment.* Bulk Transfers.

17. Product Liability   207

Introduction: *Expectations about Product Quality. Historical Development of the Law.* Warranties: *Warranties in General. Express Warranties. Creating an Express Warranty.* Implied Warranties: *Nature of Implied Warranties. Implied Warranty of Merchantability. Implied Warranty of Fitness for a Particular Purpose. Implied Warranty of Title.* Exclusions and Modifications of Warranties: *General Rules. Limitation of Express Warranties. Exclusion of Implied Warranties. Unconscionable Disclaimers.* Who Benefits from a Warranty? *Purchasers. Privity of Contract. Nonpurchasers.* Federal Trade Commission Warranty Rules: *Magnuson-Moss Warranty Act. Purpose of the Act. Requirement of the Act. Full Warranties. Limited Warranties. Availability of Warranties. Enforcement.* Negligence: *Product Liability in General. Negligence. Privity Not Required. Disclaimers.* Strict Liability: *Reasons for Development of Strict Liability. Elements of Strict Liability. State of the Art. Intended Use. Statutes of Repose. Possible Limitations on Strict Liability.*

18. Performance of Sales Contracts   227

General Rules: *Good Faith. Course of Dealing. Usage of Trade. Waiver. Assignment.* Delivery: *Basic Obligation. Place of Delivery. Seller's Duty of Delivery.* Inspection and Payment: *Buyer's Right of Inspection. Payment.* Acceptance, Revocation, and Rejection: *Acceptance. Effect of Acceptance. Revocation of Acceptance. Buyer's Rights on Improper Delivery. Rejection. Buyer's Duties after Rejection.* Assurance,

Repudiation, and Excuse: *Assurance. Anticipatory Repudiation. Excuse. Commercial Impracticability.*

19.   Remedies for Breach of Sales Contracts   239

Introduction: *Remedies in General. Agreements as to Remedies. Statute of Limitations.* Seller's Remedies: *Remedies Available to an Injured Seller. Cancelation and Withholding of Delivery. Resale of Goods. Recovery of the Purchase Price. Damages for Rejection or Repudiation. Seller's Remedies Where Buyer Is Insolvent.* Buyer's Remedies: *Buyer's Remedies in General. Buyer's Right to Cover. Incidental Damages. Consequential Damages. Damages for Defective Goods. Buyer's Right to Specific Performance. Buyer and Seller Agreements as to Remedies.*

PART FOUR
Agency and Employment

20.   Introduction to Agency and Employment   253

Overview: *Examples of Agents. Nature of Agency. Background.* Important Terms: *Agent. Professional Agent. Independent Contractor. General and Special Agents. Brokers. Franchisees. Attorney-in-Fact.* Capacity to Be Principal or Agent: *Who Can Be a Principal? Who Can Be an Agent?* Scope of Agency Law: *Basic Issues. Employment Law.*

21.   Agency Authority and Termination   261

Authority to Bind the Principal: *Liability of Principal. Express Authority. Implied Authority. Apparent Authority. Apparent Agent. Duty of Third Person to Determine Agent's Authority.* Ratification: *Nature of Ratification. Requirements for Ratification. Effect of Ratification.* Termination of Agent's Powers: *Termination by Will of Parties. Termination by Operation of Law. Damages. Agency Coupled with an Interest. Notice to Third Person.*

22.   Liability of Principals and Agents to Third Persons   270

Disclosed, Undisclosed, and Partially Disclosed Principals: *Disclosed Principal. Undisclosed Principal. Partially Disclosed Principal.* Liability of Agent: *Unauthorized Actions. Nonexistent or Incompetent Principal. Other Situations.* Liability of Principal: *Where the Agent Has Made Representations. Exculpatory Clauses. Where the Agent Has Given a Warranty. Payment to the Agent. Credit Contracts. Negotiable Instruments.* Notice to or Knowledge of Agent: *Effect of Notice. When There Is a Conflict of Interest.* Liability of Principal for Acts of Subagents: *Agent's Authority to Appoint Subagents. Agents May Have Employees. Liability for Acts of Subagents.* Liability for Torts—General: *General Rule as to Agents and Employees. General Rule as to Employers. Scope of Employment. Liability for Physical Torts of Professional Agents.* Liability for Certain Torts: *Liability of Agent for Deceit. Liability of Principal for Deceit of Agent. Liability for Conversion. Intentional Physical Acts. Liability for Negligence. Liability to Third Persons for Breach of Duty to Principal.* Liability for Crimes: *Liability of Agent or Employee. Liability of Employer.*

23. Duties of Principals and Agents to Each Other 283

Duties of Agents to Principals: *Duty of Loyalty. Dual Agency. Duty to Obey Instructions. Duty to Exercise Care and Skill. Duty to Communicate Information. Duty to Account.* Duties of Principals to Agents: *Sources of Duties. Duty to Compensate. Duty to Reimburse and Imdemnify. Duty to Keep Accounts. Duration of Employment.* Enforcement of Liabilities between Principals and Agents: *Breach of Duty by Agent. Breach of Duty by Principal.*

24. Employment Laws 295

Health and Safety Legislation: *State Legislation. OSHA. Workmen's Compensation.* Wages and Hours: *Fair Labor Standards Act. State Wage Statutes.* Collective Bargaining and Union Activities: *The Norris-LaGuardia Act. The National Labor Relations Act. The Labor Management Relations Act. Unfair Labor Practices.* Discrimination in Employment: *Title VII, The Civil Rights Act of 1964. The Equal Pay Act of 1963. Age Discrimination Act. State Legislation.* Employment Retirement and Income Security Act: *Coverage. Requirements. Pension Guaranty Corporation.*

PART FIVE
Business Organizations

25. Introduction to Business Organizations 313

Types of Business Organizations. Sole Proprietorship. Partnership: *Nature of a Partnership. Carrying on a Business. Co-ownership. Disputes on the Existence of a Partnership. A Partnership as an Entity. Limited Partnership.* Corporation: *Nature of a Corporation. Types of Corporations. "Piercing the Corporate Veil."* Franchising: *The Nature of Franchising. Advantages of Franchising. Franchisee Complaints. Franchisor Problems. Government Regulation.*

26. Formation and Operation of Partnerships 324

Formation of Partnerships: *No Formalities. Purpose. Name. Articles of Partnership.* Persons Represented to Be Partners: *Holding out as Partner. Requirements for Liability.* Capacity to Be a Partner: *Corporations. Minors and Insane Persons.* Management and Authority of Partners: *Voice in Management. Express Authority. Implied Authority. Apparent Authority. Trading and Nontrading Partnerships. Where Unanimous Consent Is Required.* Property of Partnerships: *What Is Partnership Property? Title to Partnership Property. Transfer of Title. Ownership and Possession. Creditors of Partners.* Compensation of Partners: *Right to Compensation. Profits and Losses.* Duties of Partners: *Duty of Loyalty and Good Faith. Duty of Care in Partnership Business. Duty to Inform. Duty to Account.* Enforcement of Partnership Rights and Liabilities: *Suits by and against Partnerships. Liability for Torts. Liability for Crimes.*

27. Dissolution of Partnerships 337

Introduction: *When Termination Occurs. Definitions.* Dissolution: *Dissolution without Violation of the Agreement. Dissolution in Violation of the Agreement. Dissolution by Operation of Law or Court Order. Dissolution after Assignment. Effect of Dissolution.* Winding up Partnership Business: *Right to Wind up. Powers during Winding up. Duties of Partners during Winding up. Compensation for Winding up.* When the Business Is Continued: *Continuation without Winding up. Liability for Prior Obligations. Liability for New Obligations. Rights of Noncontinuing Partner.* Distribution of Assets: *Solvent Partnerships. Insolvent Partnerships. Illustration of Distribution Rules. Individual and Partnership Creditors. Liabilities between Parties.*

28. Limited Partnerships and Related Forms   350

Limited Partnerships: *Definition. Purpose. Use of Limited Partnerships. Formalities.* Rights and Liabilities of Partners in Limited Partnerships: *General. Rights of Limited Partners. Liabilities of Limited Partners. 1976 Uniform Limited Partnership Act.* Dissolution of a Limited Partnership: *When the Certificate Must Be Canceled or Amended. Distribution of Assets.* Other Forms Related to Partnerships: *Joint Ventures. Mining Associations.*

29. Formation and Termination of Corporations   359

Relationship of Corporation and State: *The Charter or Articles of Incorporation. Powers of a Corporation. Domicile of the Corporation. Domestic and Foreign Corporations. Doing Business in a State. Jurisdiction of Courts. Taxation. Qualifying to Do Business. Means of Regulation of Corporations.* First Steps in Forming a Corporation: *Promoters. Liability of the Promoter to the Corporation. Liability of Corporation to Promoter. The Corporation's Liability on Promoter's Contracts. Liability of Promoter on Contracts.* Next Steps in Forming a Corporation: *A Certificate of Incorporation. The Model Business Corporation Act. Content of the Articles of Incorporation. Who May Be Incorporators? Organization Meeting. Bylaws.* Financing the Corporation: *Sources. Types of Securities. Common Stock. Preferred Stock. Warrants, Rights, and Options. Treasury Stock. Debt Securities.* Termination of the Corporation: *Dissolution by Agreement. Involuntary Dissolution.*

30. Management of the Corporate Business   374

Corporate Powers: *Sources of Powers. Limitations. The* Ultra Vires *Doctrine.* Management of the Corporation. The Board of Directors: *Powers and Duties. Powers and Rights of the Director as an Individual. Election of Directors. Removal of Directors. Directors Meetings. Compensation of Directors. Recent Changes in Board Operation.* Officers of the Corporation: *Powers. President or Chairman. Vice President. Corporate Secretary. Treasurer. Duties of Directors and Officers.* Liability for Torts and Crimes: *Torts. Crimes. Indemnification and Insurance.*

31. Shareholder Functions, Rights, and Liabilities   390

Introduction: *The Role of Shareholders. Functions of Shareholders.* Becoming a Shareholder: *Means of Acquiring Stock. The Federal Securities Acts. Antifraud Provisions of the Securities Acts. Blue Sky Laws.* Shareholder Meetings: *Annual Meeting. Special Meetings. Notice of Meetings. Shareholders Entitled to Vote. Proxy Voting. Conduct of the Meeting. Shareholder Proposals and Right to Speak. Cumulative Voting.* Right of Inspection and Preemptive Right: *The Shareholder's Right to Inspect. Preemptive*

Rights. Dividends: *Directors' Discretion to Pay Dividends. Types of Dividends. Legal Limits on Dividends. Stock Splits. Dividends on Preferred Stock. Effect of Dividend Declaration.* Shareholder Rights in Extraordinary Corporate Transactions: *Amendment of Articles. Other Extraordinary Transactions. Appraisal Rights.* Lawsuits by Shareholders: *Individual Actions. Class Actions. Derivative Actions.* Shareholder Liability: *Liability of Shares. Liability for Illegal Dividends. Transfer and Redemption of Shares.*

32. Which Form of Business Organization   **409**

Introduction: *Starting a New Business. Frequency.* Forms of Business Organization: *Individual Proprietorships. Partnerships. Corporations. Subchapter S Corporations. Other Less Common Types.* Factors to Consider in Choosing a Form of Business Organization: *Limited Liability. Taxation. Tax-Free Exchanges. Lack of Formalities. Financing. Management. Freeze-outs in Close Corporations. Life of the Business. Liquidity of Investment.* Making the Choice.

PART SIX
Property

33. Personal Property   **421**

Nature and Classification: *Property. Real and Personal Property. Tangible and Intangible Property. Public and Private Property.* Acquiring Ownership of Personal Property: *Possession. Production or Purchase. Lost and Mislaid Property. Gift. Confusion. Accession.* Co-ownership of Property. *Tenancy in Common. Joint Tenants. Tenancy by the Entirety. Community Property.*

34. Bailments   **432**

Nature of Bailments: *Elements of a Bailment. Delivery and Acceptance of Possession. Types of Bailments.* Rights and Duties: *Duties of the Bailee. Bailee's Duty of Care. Bailee's Duty to Return the Property. Limitations on Liability. Right to Compensation. Bailor's Liability for Defects in the Bailed Property.* Special Bailment Situations: *Common Carriers. Hotelkeepers. Safe-Deposit Boxes. Involuntary Bailments.*

35. Real Property   **444**

Fixtures: *Nature of Fixtures. Express Agreement. Attachment. Use with Real Property. Additions by Owners. Additions by Tenants.* Rights and Interests in Real Property: *Fee Simple. Life Estate. Leasehold. Easement. License. Private Restrictions.* Co-ownership of Real Property: *Forms of Co-ownership. Condominium Ownership. Cooperative Ownership.* Acquisition of Real Property: *Acquisition by Purchase. Acquisition by Gift. Acquisition by Will or Inheritance. Acquisition by Tax Sale. Acquisition by Adverse Possession.* Transfer by Sale: *Steps in a Sale. Real Estate Brokers. Contract for Sale. Financing the Purchase. Transfer by Deed. Recording Deeds. Warranties in the Sale of a House.* Public Controls on the Use of Land: *Societal Restraints. Nuisance Control. Zoning and Subdivision Ordinances. Eminent Domain.*

36. Landlord and Tenant   **468**

The Nature of Leases: *Landlord-Tenant Relationship. Term of the Lease. Execution of a Lease. Rights, Duties, and Liabilities of the Parties.* Rights, Duties, and Liabilities of the Landlord: *Landlord's Duties. Landlord's Rights. Habitability. Housing Codes. Protection of Tenants against Criminal Conduct. Security Deposits.* Rights, Duties, and Liabilities of the Tenant: *Rights of the Tenant. Duties of the Tenant. Liability for Injuries to Third Persons. Assignment and Subleasing.* Termination: *Termination of the Lease. Constructive Eviction. Abandonment. Eviction.*

37. Estates and Trusts   **479**

Introduction: *Estate Planning. Disposition of Property on Death of Owner. Dying Intestate. Example of Intestacy Law. Special Rules. Murder Disqualification. Simultaneous Death.* Wills: *Right of Disposition by Will. Execution of Will. Limitations on Disposition by Will. Revocation of Will. Codicils.* Administration of Estates: *Executor of Administrator. Steps in Administration.* Trusts: *Introduction. Definitions. Creation of Express Trusts. Creation of Implied Trusts. Transfer of the Beneficiary's Interest. Termination and Modifications of a Trust. Duties of a Trustee.*

PART SEVEN
Commercial Paper

38. Negotiable Instruments   **497**

Nature of Negotiable Instruments: *Introduction. Negotiability.* Kinds of Commercial Paper: *Promissory Notes. Certificates of Deposit. Draft. Checks.* Benefits of Negotiable Instruments: *Rights of an Assignee of a Contract. Rights of a Holder of a Negotiable Instrument.* Formal Requirements for Negotiability: *Basic Requirements. Importance of Form.* In Writing and Signed: *Writing. Signed.* Unconditional Promise or Order: *Requirement of a Promise or Order. Promise or Order Must Be Unconditional.* Sum Certain in Money: *Sum Certain. Payable in Money.* Payable on Demand or at a Definite Time. Payable to Order or Bearer. Special Terms: *Additional Terms. Ambiguous Terms.* Electronic Banking.

39. Negotiation and Holder in Due Course   **512**

Negotiation: *Nature of Negotiation. Formal Requirements for Negotiation. Nature of Indorsement.* Indorsements: *Effects of an Indorsement. Kinds of Indorsements.* Holder in Due Course: *General Requirements. Holder. For Value. Good Faith. Overdue and Dishonored. Notice of Defenses.* Rights of a Holder in Due Course: *Importance of Being a Holder in Due Course. Personal Defenses. Real Defenses.* Changes in the Holder in Due Course Rule: *Consumer Disadvantages. Changes by Some States. Federal Trade Commission Rules.*

40. Liability of Parties   **528**

Liability in General: *Introduction. Signing an Instrument. Signature by an Authorized Agent. Unauthorized Signature.* Contractual Liability: *Primary and Secondary Liabil-*

ity. *Contract of a Maker. Contract of Drawee. Contract of a Drawer. Contract of Indorsers. Contract of an Accommodation Party.* Contractual Liability in Operation: *Presentment of a Note. Presentment of a Check or Draft.* Warranties: *Transferor's Warranties. Presentment Warranties. Operation of Warranties.* Other Liability Rules: *Negligence. Impostor Rule. Fictitious Payee Rule. Conversion.* Discharge of Negotiable Instruments: *Discharge of Liability. Discharge by Cancelation. Discharge by Alteration.*

41. **Checks and Bank Collections**   **544**

The Drawer-Drawee Relationship: *The Bank's Duty to Pay. Stop Payment Order. Bank's Liability for Payment after Stop Payment Order.* The Drawee Bank: *Bank's Right to Charge to Customer's Account. Certified Checks. Cashier's Checks. Death or Incompetence of Customer.* Forged or Altered Checks: *Bank's Right to Charge Account. Customer's Duty to Report Forgeries and Alterations.*

PART EIGHT
Credit Transactions

42. **Introduction to Secured Transactions**   **555**

Introduction: *Nature of Credit. Unsecured Credit. Secured Credit. Security Interests in Personal Property and Fixtures.* Liens on Personal Property: *Common Law Liens. Statutory Liens. Characteristics of Liens. Foreclosure of Lien.* Security Interests in Real Property: *Real Estate Mortgage. Deed of Trust. Land Contracts. Mechanic's and Materialman's Liens.* Suretyship: *Sureties and Guarantors. Creation of Principal in a Surety Relationship. Defenses of a Surety. Creditor's Duties to Surety. Subrogation and Contribution.*

43. **Secured Consumer Transactions**   **571**

Introduction: *Article 9 of the Uniform Commercial Code. Security Interests in Consumer Goods.* Obtaining a Security Interest. Attachment of the Security Interest: *Attachment. The Security Agreement. Future Advances. After-Acquired Property. Proceeds. Assignment.* Perfecting the Security Interest: *Perfection. Perfection by Public Filing. Possession by Secured Party as Public Notice. Perfection by Attachment. Motor Vehicles. Fixtures.* Special Priority Rules: *Artisan's and Mechanic's Liens. Fixtures.* Default and Foreclosure: *Default. Right to Possession. Sale of the Collateral. Distribution of Proceeds. Liability of Creditor.*

44. **Secured Commercial Transactions**   **588**

Introduction: *Security Interests in Commercial Personal Property. Types of Collateral.* Obtaining a Security Interest: *Attachment. Future Advances. After-Acquired Property. Proceeds.* Perfecting the Security Interest: *Public Filing. Possession by the Secured Party. Removal of Collateral.* Priorities: *Importance of Determining Priority. Basic Priority Rule. Exceptions to General Priority Rule. Buyers in the Ordinary Course of Business. Fixtures.* Default and Foreclosure.

45.   Bankruptcy   **600**

Introduction: *The Bankruptcy Act.* Types of Bankruptcy Proceedings: *Straight Bankruptcy. Reorganizations. Consumer Debt Adjustments.* Straight Bankruptcy Proceedings: *Petitions. Involuntary Petitions. The Bankruptcy Courts. Appointment of Trustee. Duties of the Trustee. Exemptions. Other Duties of the Trustee. Provable Claims. Allowable Claims. Secured Claims. Priority Claims. Preferential Payments. Preferential Liens. Fraudulent Transfers. Discharge in Bankruptcy. Objections to Discharge. Acts That Bar Discharges. Reaffirmation Agreements. Nondischargeable Debts.* Reorganizations: *Relief for Businesses. Administration.* Consumer Debt Adjustments: *Relief for Individuals. Procedure. Discharge. Advantages of Chapter 13.*

46.   Insurance   **615**

Life Insurance Contracts: *Whole Life Insurance. Term Life Insurance.* Fire Insurance Contracts. Insurance Policies as Contracts: *Offer and Acceptance. Misrepresentation. Capacity. Form and Content. Interpreting Insurance Contracts. Third Parties and Insurance Contracts.* Insurable Interest: *Insurable Interest in Life Insurance. Insurable Interest in Fire Insurance.* Notice and Proof of Loss. Cancelation and Lapse: *Cancelation. Lapse.*

PART NINE
Government Regulation

47.   Government Regulation of Business   **629**

Introduction: *Early Regulation. The Growth of Regulation.* State Regulation of Business. Federal Regulation of Business. Administrative Agencies: *Rise of Agencies. Characteristics of Agencies. Limits on Agencies' Powers. Breadth of Agency Regulation.* The Federal Trade Commission Act.

48.   The Antitrust Laws   **640**

The Sherman Act: *Section 1—Restraints on Trade. Section 2—Monopolization.* The Clayton Act: *Section 3. Section 7. Section 8.* The Robinson-Patman Act: *Direct Price Discrimination. Indirect Price Discrimination. Buyer Inducements.* Antitrust Exceptions and Exemptions: *Regulated Industries. The Parker Doctrine. The Noerr Doctrine.*

49.   Consumer Protection Laws   **658**

Introduction: *The Federal Trade Commission Act.* Consumer Credit Laws: *Consumer Protection Act. Fair Credit Billing Act. Fair Credit Reporting Act. Equal Credit Opportunity Act. Fair Debt Collection Practices Act. FTC Holder in Due Course Rule.*

Uniform Commercial Code   **676**

Glossary of Legal Terms and Definitions   **803**

Index of Cases   **827**

General Index   **831**

Introduction to the Law

PART ONE

Law and Its Sources

1

A person who is involved in business is also involved in the law concerning business. Making contracts and using negotiable instruments—both of which are legal concepts—are the essence of business. Business and law were closely associated even when there were few lawyers and business managers spent relatively little time with them. The growing importance of law in business, however, is shown by the rapid increase in the use of lawyers by people in business. In recent years, the number of corporate counsel, the full-time lawyers who are employed by corporations, has been growing faster than the number in any other category of attorneys. Law firms that serve primarily business people have also been expanding at a great rate. Even the smallest businesses turn to lawyers frequently.

In the past quarter-century there has been a qualitative as well as a quantitative change in the concern of business managers with law. In earlier times, business managers generally employed lawyers only in emergencies. A lawyer might be engaged if a summons to appear in court was received, if a businessperson could not collect a debt that was due, or if a supplier's goods were defective and no settlement could be reached. Lawyers are still sought out when such things happen today. However, more and more, business managers employ lawyers to help them plan to avoid such emergencies and comply with a rapidly growing mass of legal rules imposed on business operations by government bodies. This use of lawyers by business people is called *preventive law*.[1]

---

[1] The term appears to have been coined by Louis M. Brown, a Beverly Hills, California, lawyer and a professor of law at the University of Southern California. His book, *Preventive Law*, was published in 1950 by Prentice-Hall. He has been very active in helping lawyers develop skills in counseling business people.

3

Preventive Law

The objectives of preventive law are to arrange business plans and methods to increase business profits by: (1) avoiding losses through fines and damage judgments, and (2) reaching business goals through enforceable contracts while avoiding government prohibitions. Preventive law involves seeking the advice of a lawyer in the business planning process rather than waiting until trouble develops. It looks for ways to change plans to reach an intended business objective with less legal risk. It further aims to minimize the possibility of failure if the business has to go to court to enforce its rights.

The Authors' Objectives

You cannot expect to "learn the law" from this book; it will not save you the cost of employing lawyers. Our objectives for you are both more modest and more ambitious.

Almost every business activity involves legal risks and consequences. To avoid costly court judgments and to get what they are entitled to under the law, people in business need to be generally familiar with the law applicable to their activities. Studying this book will aid in this, but it will not prepare you to be your own lawyer. Perhaps we can use an analogy from the field of medicine. There are times when you need a physician, but you still need a good knowledge of first aid, with which you can deal with the most common problems. Such knowledge also will help you to know when you should call a physician—or in this case a lawyer.

The practice of preventive law requires a knowledgeable client as well as a knowledgeable lawyer. The client needs to understand the legal system and the applicable law well enough to be able to communicate with the lawyer. As a client you need to know what information is relevant and necessary to the lawyer's opinion. Too often clients get in trouble because they have not fully informed their lawyers. A legal opinion is no better than the information upon which it is based. Clients also often apply legal advice to situations not comtemplated by the lawyer. This can lead to a lawsuit, or it may discourage the client from doing something that is clearly legal. This problem is especially likely to occur in applying a broad statute like the Sherman Act, which forbids certain anticompetitive trade practices.

Our other aim is broader. Law is an important part of the culture of any society. Like its language, law reflects the values, history, and current problems of a society. To learn something about law as an institution, how it functions in the society, and some of its basic concepts is essential to an understanding of the society. Ours is very much a business society; therefore, it cannot be understood without a knowledge of both law and business. We hope this book will help you to gain such an understanding.

THE NATURE OF LAW

What Is Law?

Trying to determine the nature of law is a bit like the fable of the blind men and the elephant. One of the blind men took hold of the leg and commented that an elephant is like a log, another grabbed the tail and believed it to be like a rope, and the third ran his hand over the elephant's ear and said he thought it like a fan. As for law, some people think of it as police officers; others as courts; still others as the product of a legislature, a statute. All these perceptions are at least partially accurate, all are part of a legal system, and all these and more are part of law as an institution in society.

The Legal System

Legal philosophers and legal scholars do not agree on a single definition of *the law*. The term is sometimes applied to *a legal system*, as when we speak of "the rule of law." Here we are referring to a political system in which all people within the system, including the most powerful rulers, are required to follow the rules called "the law." Furthermore, they are all answerable to a system of courts that applies that body of law. The U.S. Constitution is the foundation of this legal system.

A legal system involves processes for social control—the framework within which people carry on their activities. It also provides institutions such as legislatures, government agencies, courts, and police forces that provide rules of behavior and means for enforcing them and for settling disputes.

A Definition

More commonly when people speak of *law* they refer to the rules themselves. "The law says that you must . . ." is a phrase you often hear. This is the sense in which *the law* will generally be used in this book. Therefore, you may find the following definition of law useful: *The law is a set of principles, rules, and standards of conduct: (1) that have general application in the society, (2) that have been developed by an authority for that society, and (3) for the violation of which the society imposes a penalty.*

Law in a broader sense is seen in all societies. In a primitive society, where there is little change over time, the rules of behavior may not be consciously developed by the leader or representatives of the society; they may have been handed down as custom from earlier generations. But they apply to all the society or at least to all of a certain class of people within the society. The penalty for breaking the rule may be decided by the chief or a group of tribal leaders, and it may be carried out by one of them. However, perhaps the worst punishment of all in a primitive society is exclusion, in which the entire group serves as executioners by turning their backs to the violator.

A Limited Meaning

The term *a law* has a different and more limited meaning. The term is usually applied to a statute—a rule declared by a legislature. As we shall see, legislatures such as Congress are only one source of law. Examples of well-known federal statutes include the Sherman Act (mentioned above), the Magnuson-Moss Consumer Warranty Act, and the Occupational Safety and Health Act.

Functions of Law   The basic function of law is *keeping the peace*. Closely related functions are *enforcing standards of conduct* and *maintaining order* and the status quo. These were the functions of law in earlier societies; however, you can think of many statutes today that have different purposes. The tax laws, the antitrust laws, and the many consumer protection laws have quite different objectives. The tax laws seek not only to raise revenue for government expenditure but also to redistribute wealth by imposing higher inheritance and income taxes on wealthy people. The antitrust laws seek to prevent certain practices that might reduce competition and thus increase prices. Consumer laws have a wide range of purposes, from prohibiting the sale of unsafe products to providing more information to shoppers.

The function of these statutes is to *promote social justice* by protecting the disadvantaged. Courts, in applying the law, also seem to be seeking to balance the scales to benefit the "little guy" in dealing with big business, big labor, and big government. Helping the ordinary citizen in dealing with a very complex and quite impersonal economy is also the objective of the federal legislation establishing social security, welfare, housing, and medical programs.

Another function of law that is especially important to business is to *facilitate planning*. Contract and sales law are the best examples. In making the courts available to enforce contracts, the legal system assures that the parties to contracts will either carry out their promises or be liable for damages. Through contracts, a manufacturing company can count on either receiving the raw materials and machinery it has ordered or else getting money from the contracting supplier to cover the extra expense of buying substitutes.

CLASSIFICATIONS OF LAW

Substantive and Procedural Law   There are many ways to subdivide the law as we have just defined it. One way is to distinguish between substantive law and procedural law. *Substantive law* in itself involves three types of rules. Some establish duties, others privileges (or liberties), and others powers.

Duties tend to take the form of a command: "Do this!" or "Don't do that!" An example is the Civil Rights Act of 1964, as amended. In it Congress told employers that they must not discriminate among people in hiring and employment on the basis of race, color, religion, sex, or national origin.

Rules that grant *privileges* are less common. An example is the freedom of speech granted by the U.S. Constitution. Another is the right you have to defend yourself if physically attacked—the so-called right of self-defense. A slightly different example is the privilege of receiving food stamps if you meet the qualifications set up by Congress.

A third type of rule gives people a *power*. An example is the power you have as a prospective automobile buyer to make the seller an "offer."

Under contract law if you do make an offer, you at the same time also give the seller the power to accept your offer. If the seller does so, a contract is formed. Then both of you are under a legal duty to complete the sale. If either of you fails, the other party can go to court, and the court will then enforce the contract.

Procedural law establishes the rules under which you can enforce the substantive rules of law. Rules as to what cases a court can decide, how a trial is conducted, and how a judgment by a court is to be enforced are all part of procedural law.

Criminal and Civil Law

Another important distinction is between criminal and civil law. *Criminal law*, which is discussed in Chapter 3, defines breaches of duty to society at large. It is the society, through government employees called *public prosecutors* or *district attorneys*, that brings court action against violators. If you are found guilty of a crime, such as theft, you will be punished by imprisonment or a fine. When a fine is paid, the money goes to the state, not to the victim of the crime.

Duties owed by one person (including corporations) to another are established by *civil law*. For example, we have a duty to carry out our contractual promises. Tort law defines a host of duties people owe to each other. These are discussed in Chapters 3 and 4. One of the most common is a failure to exercise reasonable care with regard to others, which is the tort of negligence. Civil law also has another meaning that is not relevent here. It refers to the legal systems of most European and many other countries that are based on Roman law.

A court action seeking redress for the breach of a civil duty must be brought by the person wronged. Generally the court does not seek to punish the wrong but rather to make the wronged party whole through a money award called *damages*. For example, if someone carelessly runs a car into yours, that person has committed the civil wrong (tort) of negligence. If you have suffered a broken leg, you will be able to recover damages from him (or his insurance company). The damages will be an amount of money sufficient to repair your auto, to pay your medical bills, to pay for wages you have lost, and to give you something for any permanent disability like a limp. Sometimes a court awards additional damages for "pain and suffering."

Although generally the civil law does not aim to punish, there is an exception. If the behavior of someone who commits a tort against you is outrageous, you might ask the court to award *punitive damages* (also called *exemplary damages*). Unlike a fine paid in a criminal case, punitive damages go to the injured party.

THE AMERICAN LEGAL SYSTEM

Law and Government

Law is made and enforced by government. Law also defines and organizes the government. To understand the American legal system, you need to be familiar with the structure of American government, so perhaps a very brief review is appropriate here.

Checks and Balances

The founders of the United States feared government power, yet they realized that only a strong government could keep the freedom they had just won in the Revolutionary War. They wanted a federal as opposed to a national government. The original 13 colonies had become sovereign, independent states—nations—when they won independence from England. The people in each state were fearful that their state might be dominated by other states with different interests. Yet they knew that in order to be workable, the federal government had to have more power than had been given to the Continental Congress. So the founders set up a system of checks and balances between the powers of the states and those of the federal government. However, they also wrote the Supremacy Clause into the Constitution, which declares that where state and federal laws are in conflict, federal law shall be supreme.

The founders also devised a system of checks and balances within the federal government. They set up three equal branches of government: the legislative, executive, and judicial branches, which have different but complementary functions. The method of selection of the officers for each branch is different. To prevent the passage of statutes that might be ill advised, it is necessary that the President and both houses of Congress agree on any measure. A two-thirds majority is required in each house to override a veto by the President. Furthermore, Congress itself cannot enforce a statute; that is left to the executive and judicial branches. The initiative for enforcement must be taken by the executive branch—originally the attorney general. Now the regulatory agencies take the lead in enforcing certain statutes. However, the executive must go to the judicial branch to punish violations of a statute. Also it is this branch—the courts—that interprets statutes and other sources of law.

Constitutional Powers

Under the Constitution, laws passed by Congress are not effective unless they meet two conditions: It must be shown that the Constitution gives the power to Congress to pass such a law and that the Constitution does not prohibit the law's enactment. These requirements are part of the system of checks and balances.

Most federal regulations that affect business are based on power given by the *Commerce Clause*, which permits Congress to regulate interstate and foreign commerce. Supreme Court decisions since the 1930s have interpreted that power very broadly. For example, the Civil Rights Acts were passed under the Commerce Clause power; so also was the Clean Air Act. The regulatory power of the federal government is discussed more fully in Chapter 47.

The federal *taxing power* has also been used to regulate business. For example, high import duties can be used to shut off the importation of certain foreign goods. The income tax law (the Internal Revenue Code) is used to regulate business activity. Business is encouraged to make certain kinds of investments by being given tax credits. Other expenditures, such as bribes or political expenditures, are discouraged since they cannot be deducted as business expenses.

Constitutional Limitations

Many of the prohibitions against federal regulation are contained in the *Bill of Rights*—the first ten amendments to the Constitution, which were added as the Constitution was being ratified by the states. The prohibitions are guarantees of certain rights to the people, including the familiar rights of free speech, freedom of religion, and the privilege against unreasonable search and seizure. Although there were originally limits only on the power of the federal government, the fourteenth amendment has been interpreted as applying the most important parts of the Bill of Rights to the state governments as well. The rights established by these prohibitions are not limited to just individuals. For example, the Supreme Court has recently interpreted the first amendment to give the right of "commercial speech" to corporations. Although corporations are usually treated by the law as "persons," they do not have all the rights of individuals.

At one time the *Due Process Clause* of the fourteenth amendment was held by the courts to prohibit many types of business regulation by state governments. Its statement that a person's liberty shall not be taken without due process was interpreted to be a guarantee of almost total freedom of contract. The judges then went on to hold that regulatory statutes that they thought unreasonable were imposed without due process. Federal regulatory legislation was declared *unconstitutional* as violating the Due Process Clause of the fifth amendment on the same reasoning. Since the 1930s, however, no regulation of the economic activities of business has been held by the courts to be a violation of the Due Process Clause.

Fifty-One Legal Systems

An important feature of the American legal system is the fact that we really have 51 different legal systems. This is because we have a federal government with limited powers rather than a national government. It is also part of the concept of checks and balances. There is a federal system, and each state has its own system. The Supremacy Clause of the Constitution indicates that where there is conflict between the two systems, the federal system will prevail. This, of course, assumes that the federal government is acting under one of the powers granted to it by the Constitution.

SOURCES OF LAW

Federal and State Sources

There is a variety of sources of law in each of the 51 systems. Generally, there are similar sources in each system, but the exceptions will be pointed out as we discuss each source.

Constitutions

Each state has a constitution. These constitutions are similar to the U.S. Constitution in the design of the government that is provided. However, many of them are much more specific and detailed in their provisions. As a result, they are not as adaptable as the U.S. Constitution, and many have been completely rewritten one or more times. The U.S. Constitution, on the other hand, has had only 16 additional amendments in the nearly 200 years since the adoption of the Bill of Rights. Although state constitutions are subordinate to the U.S. Constitution, they are superior to law derived from other sources within the state; they are the fundamental law. The importance of this will become clear when the power of judicial review is discussed below.

Treaties

The Constitution declares that treaties that have been made by the President with heads of foreign governments and ratified by the Senate are "the Supreme Law of the Land." They therefore may override acts of Congress or state legislatures and other law that is inconsistent. Conflicts of this sort have seldom arisen, however. Ratification by the Senate requires a favorable vote by two thirds of the Senators. States have no government powers to deal with foreign countries, although they may enter into contracts with them as any person or entity might.

Statutes

Within each legal system, federal or state, statutes stand next in the hierarchy of sources of law. A statute is the product of the lawmaking of a legislature. Statutes may add details to the government framework, such as establishing a regulatory agency or an agency to provide a service to the public such as medical treatment. Or statutes may establish rules that govern certain kinds of activities, such as the use of automobiles on highways. Business people are particularly interested in statutes that regulate the way they do business.

Both Congress and the state legislatures enact a large number of statutes at every session. People tend to turn to Congress and/or the state legislatures to urge the passage of "a law" (statute) whenever they recognize a problem. This seems to be true whether it is primarily an economic problem such as the dwindling availability of petroleum or a moral problem such as sexual practices or the use of marijuana. The faith of voters and legislators in legislative solutions sometimes seems greater than results support. The entire criminal law, the law applicable to the sales of goods and to negotiable instruments, and almost all law limiting or regulating business activities is statutory law. Much of this is federal law, but most of the criminal law and the law applicable to sales of goods and negotiable instruments come from state statutes.

Administrative Rules and Decisions

By statute Congress and the state legislatures occasionally delegate some of their lawmaking power to a government agency. This is how much business regulation is handled. We shall discuss federal regulatory agencies here, but states have used this device also. The first federal regulatory agency was the Interstate Commerce Commission (ICC), which was organized by a statute passed in 1887. Congress has followed this model often in establishing other agencies. There are many of them, but the ones that will receive the most attention in this book are the National Labor Relations Board (NLRB), discussed in Chapter 24; the Federal Trade Commission (FTC), discussed in Chapter 47; and the Securities and Exchange Commission (SEC), discussed in Chapters 30 and 31. These are called *independent agencies* because they are not really part of the executive branch of the government; they are headed by a board or commission. Although the members are nominated by the President, approximately half of them must be from each major political party and their appointment is confirmed by the Senate for fixed terms.

This type of regulatory agency is given authority by Congress both to make rules and to enforce them. Congress grants rule-making power to the agency instead of establishing detailed rules in statutes. It was believed that the agency members and staff would have greater expertise than Congress and would develop it further through regulatory experience. In addition, it was believed that continuous regulatory supervision by the agency would be more adaptive to specific needs than reliance on legislation. An example of an agency that relies primarily on rule making is the SEC; the commission issues rules and may go to the federal courts to enforce them.

Valid rules issued by an agency have the same force as statutes passed by Congress. However, the Constitution has been interpreted as requiring Congress to provide standards or guidelines whenever it delegates its law-making power. Without such guidelines this delegation is unconstitutional and the rules of the agency are invalid and of no effect. However, some very broad delegations of rule-making power have been upheld that contained only quite vague guidelines.

A number of *agencies also make law by deciding cases*. Some of them, such as the FTC and the NLRB, regulate primarily on a case-by-case basis through their decisions. Here the agency performs a quasi-judicial function. It is also, in effect, the prosecutor, since the agency staff decides whether or not to begin an enforcement action. If the agency enforces one of its own rules, it is also performing an executive function. This concentration of functions in a single agency was much criticized until passage of the Administrative Procedures Act of 1946, which requires a separation of the functions within the agency. Now independent administrative law judges hear the evidence and make preliminary decisions. The agency board or commission then issues a final order. Their orders, however, must be enforced by the courts.

Executive Orders   Congress or a state legislature may also delegate rule-making power to the President or a governor. Again, guidelines must be furnished. An example of an important executive order was President Franklin D. Roosevelt's 1943 order requiring all contracts for war supplies to include a clause prohibiting discrimination on the basis of race. Like agency rules, these orders have the force of law if they are within the authority granted by statute.

Court Decisions

Courts make law in three ways: (1) they determine the meaning of statutes, administrative rules, executive orders, and even treaties and constitutions; (2) they "find" or determine the law in settling disputes where none of the other sources of law appears to supply an applicable rule; and (3) they review the constitutionality of the acts of the legislative and judicial branches.

Interpretation. Both federal and state courts make law by the first process, although many people would deny that this is "making law." The courts have the last word on what a legislature has said in a statute. Since many statutes—the Sherman Act, for example—are written in very broad and general language, the *power to interpret* is an important one. Of course, a court cannot say that the legislature meant to establish a 65-miles-per-hour speed limit when the statute says 55. However, as an example, when Congress in the Sherman Act prohibited any "attempt to monopolize," it did not define that term. The extent of the prohibition was then left to the courts.

In interpreting statutes *courts usually defer to the expertise of a government agency* that has been charged with its enforcement. If an agency has issued rules interpreting the statute, the court will try to uphold the rules so long as it considers them reasonable.

Common Law. The second manner in which courts make law is by "declaring" the common law. *Common law* or *decisional law* arises from the fact that courts must decide any dispute brought to the proper court—with a few exceptions that will be mentioned in the next chapter. If there is no statute or other type of law that provides a rule the court can apply to settle the dispute, the court is not excused from making a decision. It then follows the same process that courts in other English-speaking countries have used for centuries. The term *common law* comes from its origin. The Normans conquered England in 1066, and one of the principal devices William the Conqueror and his successors used to unite the country was to send royal judges around to hold court in the various cities. In this manner the varying customs and law of each locality were replaced by a uniform or "common" system. This body of law developed as the judges resolved the disputes brought to them. If the facts were similar to those of an earlier case, they tended to follow the earlier decision. Thus developed the rule of precedent or the *doctrine of stare decisis;* this Latin phrase means "let the decision stand." Over centuries during which thousands of disputes were settled, a large body of law was developed. This body of law was adopted by the American colonies when they won their freedom from England.

Much of the law discussed in this book is still basically common law, despite the fact that state legislatures grind out more and more statutes at every session. For example, tort law, contract law (except for certain kinds of contracts such as those involving the sale of goods), agency law, and much of property law are almost entirely based on common law rather than statutes.

There is, however, no federal common law, although in certain cases, federal courts apply state common law. Where the state courts have not developed a rule, the federal court will guess, based on past decisions in similar cases, how the highest court of that state would decide the case. There is a body of procedural law called *conflict of laws* that provides rules for a court to follow in deciding the law of which state is appropriate.

Another important source of decisional law was *equity*. The early English common law courts could determine title to land and could award money damages in settling disputes. Where someone wanted some other remedy, such as an order to the *defendant* (the party sued) not to do something he or she was about to do, that person's only recourse was to petition the king through the chancellor. The chancellor was usually the most influential member of the king's court. Eventually a new court, the court of chancery, took form. It provided different remedies than those of the common law courts, most notably the *injunction* and *specific performance*. Another difference was that procedures were less rigid. Also the court of chancery (or court of equity) sought fairness between the individual parties rather than following precedents from past cases. Almost all states have now abolished a separate court of chancery, but the remedies and the approach of the equity courts continue to be applicable in the kinds of disputes those courts were accustomed to handle.

Judicial Review. The third way a court makes law derives from its power to interpret a constitution. It has the power to declare that a decision of a lower court is inconsistent with the U.S. Constitution (or for a state court, inconsistent with the state constitution). The U.S. Supreme Court can declare unconstitutional a decision of the highest court of a state. In addition, courts have the power to declare unconstitutional statutes passed by the legislature and also acts of the executive branch. This last power, called the *power of judicial review*, was not specifically granted in the Constitution; however, it was claimed by Chief Justice John Marshall of the U.S. Supreme Court in 1803 in his decision in the famous case of *Marbury v. Madison*.[2] Courts in the United States have successfully followed this interpretation of the Constitution ever since. State courts can exercise the same judicial power with respect to state statutes and acts of state officials.

HOW THE LAW CHANGES

Predictability versus Adaptability

A legal system should be fair; the law should be just. In order to avoid punishment or loss for failing to act within the law, people must know the law. It must be predictable.

---

[2] 1 Cr. 137 (1803).

On the other hand, in a society where technological and social change is rapid, law must adapt to changing conditions. This is especially true where even basic values are also shifting. A famous judge, Benjamin N. Cardozo (later a U.S. Supreme Court justice), was faced with this problem. He said in a decision that changed the law sharply, "Precedents drawn from the days of travel by stage coach do not fit the conditions of travel today. The principle . . . does not change, but the things subject to the principle do change."[3] If that case did not change a broad legal principle, it certainly overturned the prior legal rule.

Predictability

There are several procedural requirements imposed by law on legislatures that help to make statutes knowable to the people. For example, all bills that are introduced are published so that citizens as well as the legislators can become aware of them. A bill is assigned to a committee, which may hold a public hearing on it. If reported out of the committee, the bill is discussed on the floor of the house that originated it. Amendments are likely both in committee and on the floor. The same process is then followed in the other house. If signed by the President (or the governor for state legislation) so the bill becomes law, it is then published in its final form. Frequently the new statute does not become effective for several months after passage.

Section IX(3) of Article I of the Constitution prohibits *ex post facto laws*. This means that the new statute applies only to transactions made or actions taken after the law becomes effective. Since one cannot adjust one's conduct to a law not yet passed, this requirement is essential to justice.

The Administrative Procedure Act requires federal rule-making agencies to publish in the *Federal Register* both notice of intent to issue regulations and the text of final ones. It also requires the agencies to hold a hearing or to consider comments from the public, including those who are to be regulated, on the proposed rules. The new rules are then printed in the *Code of Federal Regulations* (CFR), where all administrative rules are published.

The feature of decisional law that is most important in making it predictable is the doctrine of the English common law discussed above—*stare decisis*. This doctrine says that a court in making a decision must follow the *precedents* of prior cases that had similar facts. It is the decision—who wins on the basis of the facts before the court, plaintiff or defendant—that is the binding precedent. Statements the court makes about the law are not necessarily binding on a judge in a later case. A statement on a matter not necessary to the decision is called a *dictum*. Dicta are not binding on later courts.

Precedent is binding only within the same state. Each of the 50 state

[3] *MacPherson v. Buick Motor Co.*, 111 N.E. 1050 (Ct. App. N.Y. 1916).

court systems is independent. Although all states received the English common law, the common law decisions (hence the law) differ somewhat among states. A court in California may follow a precedent established by a court in Arizona. However, it is no more bound to do so than to follow a precedent of a Canadian court.

As suggested by the hierarchy of law discussed above, a legislature may change a common law rule by passing a statute. The rule established by the statute applies thereafter.

Adaptability

The doctrine of *stare decisis* is backward looking, but the common or judge-made law is not rigid and unchanging. To understand how flexibility in the common law is possible, one must understand more about the operation of the doctrine of *stare decisis*.

Three steps are involved in applying the doctrine of *stare decisis:* (1) finding an earlier case or cases in the same jurisdiction (state) that had similar facts, (2) deriving from the decision (for or against the *plaintiff*—the party bringing the lawsuit) a rule of law, and (3) applying that rule to the case presently before the court.

The judge, or a lawyer seeking to influence the judge's thinking, has considerable freedom in picking precedent cases. Seldom is a case exactly the same as an earlier case in all facts. The judge or lawyer can choose, therefore, within limits, which facts to emphasize and which to disregard in seeking precedent cases. Certainly a lawyer for the plaintiff will choose as precedent those cases in which the decision favored the plaintiff. He or she will seek to persuade the judge that they are the precedents that should be followed. There is also flexibility at the second step; the lawyer or judge can state the rule to be applied from the precedent cases broadly or narrowly. A difference of a few words in the way the rule is phrased may either include or exclude the case in dispute. The third step—application—follows the first two almost automatically. If the analysis appears acceptable in the first step and the induction of a rule seems reasonable in the second step, the third step will be convincing.

THE ADVERSARY SYSTEM

The Function of the Lawyers

American courts, following the British practice, operate on the *adversary system*—trial through a battle of words between two lawyers. Each acts as the advocate of his or her client.

It is the lawyer's job to present the client's view of the facts to the judge, or to the jury if one is used. The lawyer tries to persuade the judge or jury not only that the client's version is correct but also that the other party's view of the facts, to the extent it is inconsistent, is in error.

The lawyer likewise seeks to persuade the judge that the law favors the party he or she represents. Proposals are made to the judge for instructions to the jury that will put the law in the light most favorable to the lawyer's client. If there is no jury, the lawyer offers the judge a line of reasoning from the relevant legal concepts that will permit a decision favoring the client. Of course, dishonesty or trickery by a lawyer, although it does sometimes occur, is improper and may result in disbarment.

The Function of the Judge

The judge's role, under the adversary system, is viewed as not only unbiased but also essentially passive. The judge is to keep order in the court and, when a jury is present, to see that the lawyers do not use improper methods to influence the jury. Basically, the judge during a trial is an referee who makes a "call" when one lawyer claims the other is "off side." Generally, the judge stops questions from lawyers or orders witnesses to change their behavior only when asked to do so by one of the lawyers.

The judge does not have to be entirely passive, however. A judge may ask questions of a witness and may suggest to a lawyer the kind of evidence the judge believes should be presented. The judge is responsible for the correct application of the law to the facts of the case. Therefore, he or she may disregard the legal reasoning of the attorneys for both parties and base rulings and the decision on a personal study of the law. In some kinds of cases, especially divorces and other family disputes, the judge may assume the initiative and even engage in attempts at mediation.

Advantages and Disadvantages

The adversary system is based on the belief that both the facts and the law applicable to a dispute can best be determined through competition of lawyers before a judge. Truth can be most effectively told, it is thought, through permitting each lawyer to control the development of the client's "case" through witnesses. Likewise, deception and misperception are best exposed through cross-examination.

Critics argue that honest witnesses can be confused by hostile questioning. They say that the system does not work when the opposing lawyers are of unequal skill. This gives advantage to the wealthy who can hire better lawyers. Furthermore, it is argued that the competition to win encourages the suppression of unfavorable facts and overstatement, if not outright distortion, of the truth. On the other hand, the system makes it more difficult for a dishonest or biased judge to control the outcome of a case.

The adversary system is not followed on the European continent and in other jurisdictions that derive their law from Rome. Their judges have a duty to direct the search for truth rather than assuming that it will emerge from the efforts of the lawyers for the parties. Therefore, they assume a much more active role in directing proceedings in the court, in requesting certain evidence, and in questioning witnesses.

QUESTIONS AND PROBLEM CASES

1. Do primitive societies without a written language have law?

2. Does the concept of law include the rules of play on a private golf course?

3. What is the relationship between the federal and the state systems of law?

4. Are there any significant differences between the sources of federal law and those of state law?

5. Why are predictability and adaptability (which are opposites) both desirable in a body of law?

6. Describe how the doctrine of *stare decisis* is related to these conflicting objectives.

7. Would court decisions be more just if the questioning of witnesses were conducted by the trial judge rather than the attorneys for the parties? Should the judge direct the investigation of the facts prior to the trial of a lawsuit?

8. How is it possible for the lawyers for each of the opposing parties to find law supporting their clients?

Dispute Settlement

2

Negotiation

One cannot operate a business without getting into disputes. Customers are not always satisfied with the firm's products or services, suppliers do not always carry out their promises, and government regulators sometimes are unreasonable. The courts are the most visible and familiar vehicle for dispute settlement, but most disputes are, and should be, settled by negotiation.

In an earlier day most business people shunned lawyers and the courts. Typically, a lawsuit was filed only after there had been a "divorce" in the commercial relationship. The buyer-seller or debtor-creditor relationship had usually totally dissolved before a lawyer was even consulted. This is certainly not true today. Indeed, we are a more litigious society; many of us are quick to go to court. There are many more lawyers (attorneys), and business people call upon them frequently. As indicated in the preceding chapter, lawyers are often involved in business planning—in the practice of preventive law.

The cost of bringing or defending a lawsuit has been increasing rapidly. The fees of lawyers have increased; however, the big increases in costs have come because discovery procedures (discussed later in this chapter) and the trials themselves have become much more time-consuming. This involves the time of both business people and lawyers.

Settlement of disputes through negotiation is, therefore, even more attractive than it was earlier. If this can be done by the business people, good! However, many attorneys are skilled negotiators, and having a competent advocate speak as an intermediary is often more effective than speaking for oneself.

Negotiations should begin before a lawsuit is filed and continue after the filing. Many cases are not settled until the parties are "at the courthouse door." In a few, such as the public utility–Westinghouse Electric Company uranium suits, settlements take place after the trial but before the judge announces a damage award. In one recent, very complex patent suit (these are usually very long and expensive) the parties avoided the uncertainty and additional expense of a full trial before a judge in a very novel way. A "minitrial" was held before the chief executives of the two companies. They then negotiated a settlement after more fully understanding the issues and the relative strengths and weaknesses of the legal positions of their two companies.

Mediation and Fact Finding

A voluntary process that is sometimes used when negotiation seems to be failing is *mediation*. The parties to the dispute choose a third party to assist them in settling their dispute. This *mediator* often tries first to communicate the positions of the parties to each other. Frequently the areas of serious disagreement are narrower than the parties think. The mediator then usually proposes a basis or several bases for settlement. A mediator merely facilitates negotiation; no award or opinion on the merits of the dispute is given.

The Federal Mediation and Conciliation Service makes experienced mediators available to serve in labor disputes. When the President declares a "cooling off" period after finding that a strike endangers the national safety or health, the service is called in. It is available in other cases as well upon request of the union or the employer. Either arbitration or court action may follow unsuccessful mediation.

Under some dispute settlement statutes, *fact finding* follows mediation. Fact finders state publicly the positions of the parties to the dispute and the underlying facts. However, they do not make an award or recommend a particular settlement.

Arbitration

When negotiation and perhaps even mediation fail, *arbitration* is a widely used alternative to settling disputes in court. Most union-management contracts contain an arbitration clause, and many commercial contracts provide that in case of dispute, binding arbitration will be used. Arbitration clauses are typical in the contracts in certain industries such as the trading of securities and commodity contracts. Casualty insurance companies frequently use arbitration. Some of these cases involve claims against insurers by policyholders. Others arise from disputes between insurers as to their respective liabilities when two or more companies are involved in a single insured incident. From 1971 to 1977 the number of disputes settled by arbitration under the sponsorship of the American Arbitration Association increased from 22,459 to 47,066.[1]

---

[1] American Arbitration Association, 1977–1978 *Annual Report* (New York, N.Y.).

Advantages claimed for arbitration over a court trial include the following: (1) An arbitrator who is familiar with the technical or social setting of the dispute may be chosen. (This may be particularly important in an international trade dispute or a labor dispute.) (2) There is less delay in disposing of the dispute. (It may take several years to get to trial in some state courts.) (3) Less time is required of executives involved in the hearing. (It may be a few hours or days instead of weeks or even months in court.) (4) Since procedure is more informal than in court, the parties may choose not to be represented by lawyers. They often are, however. (5) Privacy can be maintained in both the arbitration hearing and the award.

Usually there is only one arbitrator. The parties may select the arbitrator in any way they desire. They may ask the American Arbitration Association to provide a list of available arbitrators. The parties can then alternate in eliminating names from that list until a single name remains. Sometimes a board of three arbitrators is chosen by having each party choose one person, with both arbitrators choosing the third.

Most states have passed the Uniform Arbitration Act, which makes both the agreement of parties to arbitrate and the *arbitration award* enforceable in court. A court will not review the wisdom of the decision of an arbitrator. It may, however, hold that the dispute was not arbitrable under the agreement or that the arbitrator exceeded his or her authority. The parties may or may not require an opinion (reasons for the award) from the arbitrator. Arbitration awards are usually not published, although some labor dispute awards have been.

Other Alternatives to the Courts

There have been a number of suggestions, including those of Chief Justice Burger and the American Bar Association, for other alternatives to court resolution of disputes. It is often said, "Justice delayed is justice denied." Despite the recent addition of more judges, especially in the federal courts, delay in the courts remains a major problem.

One proposal with numerous supporters is to use an administrative agency to determine compensation for injuries and damage in automobile accidents. This would be similar to workmen's compensation. Malpractice claims against physicians and other professionals and claims for defective products might also be decided in this manner. These cases clog the courts and result in awards to only a small proportion of those injured. The cost of bringing suit, including attorney's fees, often eats up more than half the damage award.

Other alternatives to court trials are being tried experimentally. One example is a storefront mediation service where a selected neighbor is available to help settle minor disputes.

The Courts

The dispute resolution mechanism of last resort (short of the use of force) is the courts. Either party to a dispute can bring the lawsuit, and no prior agreement is necessary. The court must decide the case unless it has no jurisdiction, that is, it is the wrong court. It cannot wait for the legislature to pass a statute or suggest that the parties go to a different or higher court. The jurisdiction of the various courts and how cases are processed by them will be discussed later in this chapter.

There are some general kinds of cases that American courts do not consider. Courts do not decide a case if the question is *moot.* A case is moot if a decision by the court is meaningless in a particular case because later events have made a decision unnecessary. An example was a case brought by a white applicant to a law school.[2] At first he was not admitted and claimed reverse racial discrimination; however, his admission came before his case had been decided on appeal to the U.S. Supreme Court. The Court refused to rule on the case because it was moot, even though other similar cases were being brought.

Federal courts and most state courts hear only real controversies—concrete disputes between actual parties. *They do not give advisory opinions, nor do they make rulings on hypothetical cases.* This saves the time of judges, and, consistent with the adversary system, it avoids the danger that the arguments for one side may not be vigorously pressed because no one as yet has been truly hurt.

Confusion of Terminology

Perhaps this is the place to clarify what is likely to be confusing later. The term *court* can be applied either to the institution or to an individual judge or group of judges. Lawyers usually say, "May it please the court," as they begin their cases in court. Here the court is a person—the judge presiding in the courtroom. A lawyer may also say, "I'll be in court tomorrow," in which *court* refers to the institution. The lawyer will be in either a courtroom or possibly a judge's *chambers* (office), perhaps to make a motion to *continue* (postpone) a case.

FEDERAL COURTS

Jurisdiction

The scope of the authority of a court to hear and determine disputes is referred to as its *jurisdiction.* Some courts have broad jurisdiction; they can deal with a wide variety of types of cases. Others have power to handle only a particular type of case, such as tax disputes. The jurisdiction of all courts is limited geographically.

The cases to be heard in the federal courts fall into one of two classes: They are either cases involving a *federal question* or cases where there is *diversity of citizenship* between the parties. Federal questions include cases in which a federal statute is involved, such as a violation of a crime defined by such a statute, or a violation of a right granted by the Constitution. Diversity cases are those in which the parties to the dispute are citizens of different states.

---

[2] *DeFunis v. Odegard,* 416 U.S. 312 (1974).

If the parties are from different states, the plaintiff may choose whether to bring the case in state or federal court. However, the amount involved must be $10,000 or more to qualify for federal court jurisdiction. If $10,000 is at stake, the defendant may *remove* the case to federal court if the plaintiff brings it in a state court. Federal judges tend to have more prestige, so the federal courts attract, on the average, more competent judges. Another common reason for choosing a federal court is to obtain certain procedural advantages that may be available. This may make it easier to get jurisdiction over the defendant and force witnesses to testify. Lack of local bias is also more certain in federal court.

Federal courts have exclusive jurisdiction over patents, copyrights, bankruptcy, crimes defined by federal statutes, and a few other matters. One of these areas involves maritime cases, which are decided under admiralty law. See Figure 2–1 for a diagram of the types of courts in the federal court system.

FIGURE 2–1
The Federal Court System

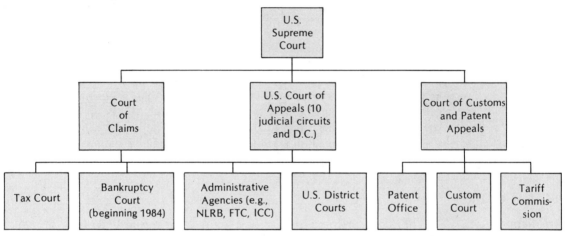

District Court   With few exceptions lawsuits brought in federal courts must be started in a district court. These are the trial courts; they hear the witnesses and decide questions of both fact and law. There is at least one U.S. district court in each state, and most states have two districts. The number of judges assigned to a district depends on the case load; some have only one judge. Almost all cases are heard by a single judge.

Court of Appeals   An appeal from a district court is taken to a U.S. court of appeals. To be able to appeal, a party must claim that the district court made an *error of law* or that the evidence in the trial did not support the trial court's decision. For example, if an attorney objects to a question asked of a witness by the other attorney, the judge must rule on it. If the attorney takes exception to the ruling at the time, he or she may later appeal on the basis that the judge's ruling was in error. Or the attorney might claim the judge had misstated the law in the instructions to a jury. No witnesses appear in the court of appeals, only the attorneys for the two parties.

There are 11 U.S. courts of appeal (see Figure 2–2). One serves the District of Columbia alone because so many appeals involving the federal government arise there. The others, as shown on the map, cover several states. Usually a case is heard by a panel of three judges, but some cases may be heard *en banc*, that is, by all the judges of that circuit.

FIGURE 2–2
The 11 Federal Judicial Circuits

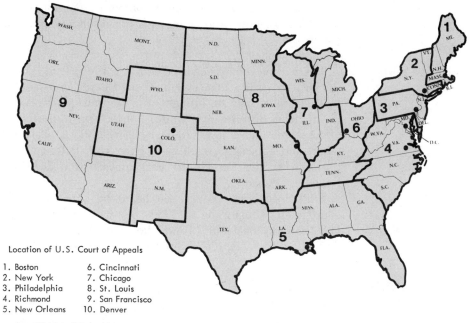

Location of U.S. Court of Appeals

1. Boston   6. Cincinnati
2. New York   7. Chicago
3. Philadelphia   8. St. Louis
4. Richmond   9. San Francisco
5. New Orleans   10. Denver

District of Columbia

Note: Hawaii and Alaska are in the 9th Circuit.

The Supreme Court

As the name implies, the U.S. Supreme Court is the highest court of the land. It has final responsibility for interpretation of the Constitution and federal statutes. However, the idea that a party who is dissatisfied with the decision of a lower court can "take it all the way to the Supreme Court" is erroneous.

There are two procedures by which a case may be reviewed by the Supreme Court. One is by right of *appeal*. Although said to be a right, the Supreme Court may merely affirm the lower court's decision or dismiss the appeal without a hearing. This right applies when a court of appeals holds that a state statute is unconstitutional and in certain other cases. These include decisions of the highest court of a state that either: (1) a federal statute or treaty is invalid, or (2) a state statute is valid against a claim by a party that it conflicts with the Constitution, a treaty, or a federal statute.

The second procedure is by *writ of certiorari*. Hearing such cases is entirely discretionary with the Court. The Court may take a case *on certiorari* where there have been conflicting decisions in similar cases by different courts of appeal. It may also take a case *on certiorari* from the highest court of a state where a right is claimed under the Constitution or where the validity of a federal statute is in question.

If the Court does hear a case, a long opinion is usually published. In most cases the justices do not all agree. Then there may be a *minority (dissenting) opinion* and even a *concurring opinion*. The latter states the reasoning of those who agree with the result but not the rationale of the majority.

Special Courts

There are several specialized courts in the federal court system. Although the district courts may also hear such cases, contract claims against the United States may be brought in a special Court of Claims. A Customs Court hears disputes over duties imposed on imported goods. The Court of Customs and Patent Appeals hears both appeals from the Customs Court and appeals from rulings of the U.S. Patent Office on patents and trademarks. The Tax Court hears appeals from decisions of the Internal Revenue Service.

Bankruptcy cases have been heard by bankruptcy referees or district court judges. Beginning in 1984 they will be heard exclusively by a new U.S. Bankruptcy Court. It will be divided into the same districts as the district courts. Chapter 45 discusses in greater detail the work of this court.

STATE COURTS

Jurisdiction

Except for cases involving federal statutes and other federal matters such as patents and bankruptcy, the state courts have jurisdiction to hear almost any sort of dispute. Most disputes between citizens of the state and disputes arising from events occurring within the state, such as automobile accidents, are tried in a state court.

The names of the various courts and the way jurisdiction is divided between them vary from state to state. We will use the courts of California as an example; they are typical of most states (see Figure 2–3).

Inferior Courts

Most minor criminal violations and civil disputes involving small amounts of money are handled by courts that keep no record (transcript) of the testimony or proceedings. They are, therefore, not *courts of record*. Without a record there can be no appeal. Usually a dissatisfied party claiming error

FIGURE 2–3
California Court System

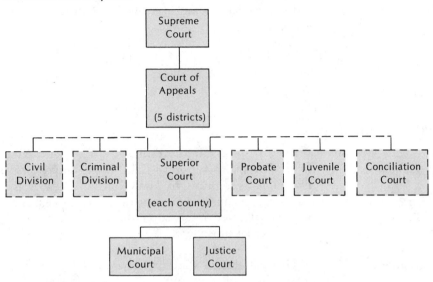

may have a new trial (a *trial de novo*) in a court of record. Inferior courts may be called *municipal courts* in urban areas. *Justice of the peace* courts once handled such matters in small towns and rural areas, but many states have now abolished such courts. Today in California justice courts operate in less populated counties. However, some small cases are brought in courts of record.

Small claims courts are often provided in cities. Disputes between landlord and tenant, buyer and seller, and others involving small amounts of money may be brought in these courts. The parties may represent themselves and avoid the expense of lawyers. The maximum amount involved is usually limited to a few hundred dollars. $1500

Trial Courts

The name of the trial court that has general jurisdiction varies greatly among states. They may be called circuit, superior, district, or county courts, and their geographic jurisdiction is often a county. In California they are called superior courts. These courts may be divided into those that hear criminal cases and those that hear only civil cases.

Where there is a large population within a state, specialized courts may be set up. There may be domestic relations courts (called conciliation courts in California) to hear divorce and child custody cases. Probate courts handle estates of deceased persons. Juvenile courts deal with law violators who are younger than a certain age.

Appeal Courts

Many states have only one court of appeals, usually called the supreme court. The more populous states usually have two levels for appeals. The intermediate court is frequently called the court of appeals. New York's terminology is confusing; the intermediate court is called the supreme court, and it even has a trial division. The highest New York court is the court of appeals.

Some types of cases may, under the state statutes, be appealable directly to the highest court, or the statute may require the case to go to the intermediate court. California and other states permit the supreme court to select the cases it wants to hear and assign others to the court of appeal.

PROCEDURE

The Functions of Procedure

Rules of procedure governing the filing and conduct of cases in court are complex and technical. The basic purpose of procedure is fairness. The nonlawyer needs to know only enough of this body of law to be able to understand the progress of a case through the courts. The procedure in criminal cases differs somewhat from that in civil cases. Here we will focus on civil procedure.

Summons

The first step in starting a lawsuit is the serving of a *summons* on the defendant. This gives notice to the defendant of the suit, informs him or her who the plaintiff is, and states a certain time before which the defendant must make an *appearance* in order to avoid a *default judgment* (see Figure 2–4). In most states the complaint, which is described below, must be served with the summons.

The rules relative to the service of the summons vary widely. Generally it is served by the sheriff or a deputy and only within the geographic limits of the court's jurisdiction. In state courts this is normally a county. Some statutes permit, in some types of cases, service by mail by leaving the summons at the defendant's residence or place of business.

The defendant must then make an appearance. This may be done by filing an *answer* to the complaint. At other times a defendant might make a motion, asking the court for additional time or claiming the court lacks jurisdiction. If the defendant fails to appear, the plaintiff is entitled to a default judgment. This has the same effect as if he or she had won in court everything requested in the complaint.

The Complaint

Complete information about the claim of the plaintiff must be included in the *complaint*, which is sometimes called a petition or a declaration. The remedy requested, usually damages of a certain amount, must also be stated. The complaint must set out in numbered paragraphs the legal facts, as distinguished from the evidence, upon which the claim is based (see Figure 2–5). No evidence will be permitted to be given at a trial that is not related to a material fact stated in the complaint.

The Answer

To avoid default, the defendant must submit an *answer* that responds to the complaint paragraph by paragraph. Each *allegation* (statement) of

FIGURE 2–4
Summons

UNITED STATES DISTRICT COURT
SOUTHERN DISTRICT OF INDIANA
INDIANAPOLIS DIVISION

JOHN SMITH   )
)
            Plaintiff   )
)
        vs.   )   CIVIL ACTION NO. 1P 79–53-C
)
WORLD PRESS, INC.,   )
and HERBERT MILLER   )
)
            Defendants   )

SUMMONS

To Above Named Defendants _____

You have been sued by the person(s) named "plaintiff" in the court stated above.

The nature of the suit against you is stated in the complaint which is attached to this document. It also states the demand which the plaintiff has made and wants from you.

You must answer the complaint in writing, by you or your attorney, within twenty (20) days, commencing the day after you receive this summons, or judgment will be entered against you for what the plaintiff has demanded. You have twenty-three (23) days to answer if this summons was received by mail. Such Answer Must Be Made in Court.

If you have a claim for relief against the plaintiff arising from the same transaction or occurrence, you must assert it in your written answer.

Date _____November 12, 1979_____   _Oliver M. Jones_____
                                                 Clerk (Seal)

_Quik and Bono_____
      Attorneys for Plaintiff

_____430 S. Walnut St._____

_____Bloomington, IN 47401_____

Telephone _____812-336-5202_____

FIGURE 2–5
Complaint

UNITED STATES DISTRICT COURT
SOUTHERN DISTRICT OF INDIANA
INDIANAPOLIS DIVISION

JOHN SMITH	)	
	)	
Plaintiff	)	
	)	
v.	)	CIVIL ACTION NO. IP 79–53–C
	)	
WORLD PRESS, INC.,	)	
and HERBERT MILLER	)	
	)	
Defendants	)	

PLAINTIFF'S COMPLAINT

Plaintiff, for his complaint states:

1. Plaintiff is a citizen of the State of Indiana. Defendant World Press, Inc., is a Delaware corporation incorporated under the laws of the State of Delaware having its principal place of business in New York, N.Y. Defendant Herbert Miller is the author of the book *40 Seconds and Death* and is a citizen of the State of New York. The matter in controversy exceeds, exclusive of interests and costs, Ten Thousand Dollars ($10,000.00). Jurisdiction is based upon diversity of citizenship.

2. Defendant World Press, Inc., owns, operates and publishes books under the name of World Press.

3. During 1979, defendant World Press, Inc., published without plaintiff's prior knowledge or consent, and expressly against plaintiff's permission in excess of one million copies of the book *40 Seconds and Death,* authored by defendant, Herbert Miller, which contained within Chapter Four (4) a section entitled "Weekend Tryst." This book unnecessarily exposed to the public the private affairs of the plaintiff, John Smith. A copy of said chapter is attached hereto as Exhibit One (1).

4. Said chapter disclosed private facts that would be offensive to a reasonable person and were not of legitimate public interest or concern. Defendant World Press, Inc., and defendant Herbert Miller knew that the plaintiff did not want the matters contained in the chapter to be exposed to the general public and published said chapter over the expressed warnings of the plaintiff.

5. Defendant Herbert Miller was personally told by the plaintiff that he did not want to be quoted by defendant Herbert Miller nor did plaintiff want any reference to plaintiff's family or relatives to appear in any publication. The matters published were culled from a private conversation and amount to an unwarranted intrusion into the plaintiff's private life.

FIGURE 2–5 *(continued)*

6. Defendant Herbert Miller misled the plaintiff to his detriment by publishing matters of a personal nature without securing the plaintiff's consent. The article exposed private matters concerning plaintiff's marital difficulties and his intimate relationships with family members.

7. The identity of the plaintiff was altered in the book, but the name used in the publication made the plaintiff's true identity readily apparent to neighbors, friends, relatives, business associates, and other members of the community who read the book.

8. As a direct and proximate result of the publication of said book the plaintiff has suffered great mental anguish and humiliation. Relatives of the plaintiff who had been purposely kept unaware of the marital difficulties existent between plaintiff and his wife were notified of same upon reading the book. The plaintiff has become the subject of public curiosity and gossip in his community and his business affairs have been adversely affected. The plaintiff is a reasonable person of ordinary sensibilities who has been justifiably aggrieved by virtue of having his private life exposed by this publication in a manner constituting an actionable invasion of privacy.

9. Defendant World Press, Inc., and defendant Herbert Miller maliciously intended to injure and aggrieve the plaintiff by thrusting on him unwarranted and undesirable publicity and notoriety, knowing that the plaintiff did not wish the matters contained in the chapter to be published. The plaintiff seeks punitive damages of Five Hundred Thousand Dollars ($500,000.00).

WHEREFORE, plaintiff prays for judgment against the defendants World Press, Inc., and Herbert Miller as follows:

1. General damages of One Million Dollars ($1,000,000.00);
2. Special damages as may hereafter be ascertained;
3. Punitive damages of Five Hundred Thousand Dollars ($500,000.00);
4. Costs of this action;
5. Compensation for reasonable attorney's fees;
6. Such other and further relief as the Court may deem proper in the premises.

QUIK & BONO

By *John P. Quik*

Attorneys for Plaintiff,
John Smith

the complaint is admitted or denied, or the defendant may disclaim knowledge and leave the plaintiff to prove the allegation (see Figure 2–6).

The defendant may also state an *affirmative defense.* For example, if the plaintiff seeks damages for breach of contract, the defendant might respond by admitting that a contract had been reached. However, he or she might defend on the ground that it had been induced by fraudulent

FIGURE 2–6
Answer

UNITED STATES DISTRICT COURT
SOUTHERN DISTRICT OF INDIANA
INDIANAPOLIS DIVISION

JOHN SMITH	)	
	)	
Plaintiff,	)	
	)	
v.	)	CIVIL ACTION NO. IP 79–53-C
	)	
WORLD PRESS, INC., and	)	
HERBERT MILLER	)	
	)	
Defendants	)	

DEFENDANTS' ANSWER

Defendants World Press, Inc., and Herbert Miller make the following answer to Complaint of plaintiff John Smith.

<u>First Defense</u>

1. They admit the allegations of paragraph 1, except they deny that Herbert Miller is a citizen of New York. He is a citizen of Maine.

2. They admit that World Press, Inc., publishes books under the name World Press. They deny all other allegations of paragraph 2.

3. They admit that during 1979 World Press, Inc., published a book entitled *40 Seconds and Death* authored by Herbert Miller and that the book contained in its Chapter 4 a section entitled "Weekend Tryst." They admit that Exhibit One (attached to plaintiff's Complaint) is a copy of that section of the book. They deny all other allegations of paragraph 3.

4, 5, 6. They deny the allegations of paragraphs 4, 5, and 6.

7. They admit that plaintiff's real name was not used in the book. They are without knowledge or information sufficient to form a belief as to the truth of the remaining allegations of paragraph 7.

8, 9. They deny the allegations of paragraphs 8 and 9.

<u>Second Defense</u>

Plaintiff John Smith consented to the publication of the information complained of.

2 / Dispute Settlement

FIGURE 2–6 *(continued)*

Third Defense

The information published by defendants relates to an event and topic of general and public interest. Defendants' publication of the information complained of was privileged by the First and Fourteenth Amendments to the United States Constitution and by Article I, Section 9, of the Indiana Constitution.

Fourth Defense

The information published by defendants is true or substantially true in all relevant respects.

WHEREFORE, defendants World Press, Inc., and Herbert Miller pray that plaintiff John Smith take nothing by his complaint, for their costs, and for all other proper relief.

Roger P. Rogers

Roger P. Rogers
Attorney for Defendants
World Press, Inc., and Herbert Miller

---

representations by the plaintiff. The defendant might then *counterclaim* that the fraud resulted in damages to the defendant for which the plaintiff should be liable. The defendant's affirmative defense must be supported by facts presented in the same manner as a complaint.

The defendant may make a *motion to dismiss* the case rather than give an answer. The grounds for such a motion might be that the facts given in the plaintiff's complaint are not legally sufficient to "state a cause of action"—that is, to permit the plaintiff to win even if he or she can prove the facts alleged.

Reply

If the defendant states an affirmative defense or counterclaim, then the plaintiff must respond with a *reply*. The reply answers paragraph by paragraph the affirmative defense or counterclaim of the defendant.

Pleadings

The complaint and answer (and reply, if any) are known as the *pleadings*. They serve two major functions: They inform the parties of their relative claims and they form the basis for a trial. Only those matters that are disputed in the pleadings are tried in court. If a fact material to the case has been omitted from the pleadings, a court may, during trial, permit a party to amend the pleading.

Discovery

Cases are sometimes won at the trial because material facts are withheld or come to light too late to permit the other party to prepare properly. In recent years, rules of procedure have been adopted to avoid this by permitting broad *discovery* before trial. This permits an attorney to request a copy of almost any relevant document, photograph, or other evidence that the opposite party might rely upon or that, if available, would help the lawyer's case. In a claim for physical injuries, the plaintiff can be required to undergo a medical examination. A party may also take depositions from the opposite party and key witnesses. A *deposition* is an examination under oath, much like the questioning at a trial, in the presence of the attorney for the other party. Or a party may be required to answer written questions called *interrogatories*.

The discovery procedure is sometimes abused. A lawyer may file suit for a client, wording the complaint in very general language. He or she then hopes through discovery to find the evidence needed to win the case. If successful, the complaint will be amended.

Pretrial Hearing

Another fairly recent procedural device is the *pretrial hearing*. Its purpose is to try to minimize trial time by reducing and narrowing the issues to be tried. The judge assigned to the case tries to get the parties to *stipulate to* (agree to) as many of the material facts as possible. The judge may find that, in spite of the appearance of the pleadings, there is no true disagreement on some important facts. For example, in an automobile accident case there may be no real question as to who ran into whom; the only real question may be whether the plaintiff has suffered permanent disability and what value should be put upon it. It saves much court time if the parties enter a *stipulation* to the facts about the collision.

The judge may also try to persuade the parties to settle the case before trial. By suggesting the difficulty of proving some of the facts alleged in the pleadings and the uncertainty of decision by a jury, the judge may get the parties to conclude that they would rather settle than fight in court.

The pretrial hearing is held in the judge's chambers. The parties themselves and their witnesses are not present because the hearing is likely to go better if the parties are represented by intermediaries.

TRIAL PROCEDURE

Setting the Case for Trial

Once the pleadings are complete, the case may be set for trial on the court calendar. Unfortunately, there may be a delay of several months or even years in some overcrowded courts. The court clerk sets a date for trial after conference with the judge assigned to the case. Frequently cases have to be *continued* (postponed) and another date set for any one of several reasons. It may be that another trial has lasted longer than expected or a necessary witness is unavailable.

If a jury is requested, arrangements must be made to have prospective jurors present at the time the trial is scheduled to begin. The jury list is drawn by chance from a list of eligible citizens. Judges differ as to the excuses they accept from prospective jurors for being excused from this duty of citizenship.

Opening the Case

The plaintiff's attorney opens the case after the jury, if any, is selected and sworn. First, normally, is an *opening statement* of the plaintiff's case. The nature of the case is usually described and the major facts to be proved through the plaintiff's witnesses are summarized. Then the defendant's attorney does the same. The opening statements are more elaborate and perhaps more dramatically presented if a jury is present than if the case is tried before only a judge.

Presentation of Testimony

The plaintiff's attorney then presents the plaintiff's evidence through witnesses. Each is sworn and then examined by the plaintiff's attorney; this is called *direct examination*. The defendant's attorney then may *cross-examine*. This is used to raise doubts about the credibility or trustworthiness of the witness. The plaintiff's attorney may then conduct a *redirect examination* to clarify the plaintiff's view of the facts and perhaps to minimize whatever negative effect was created in the cross-examination.

Following the end of testimony by witnesses for the plaintiff, the defendant's lawyer frequently makes a motion for a *directed verdict*. The judge grants the motion only if the plaintiff has offered no evidence to support a decision granting the requested remedy. If the motion is granted, the trial ends. Otherwise, the motion is denied and the trial continues. There is then direct examination of the defendant's witnesses by the defendant's attorney, followed by cross-examination.

Closing the Case

After the witnesses for both parties have been heard in a jury case, either or both attorneys may make a motion for a directed verdict. If granted, this takes the case away from the jury and the decision is made by the judge. Such a motion by an attorney is granted only when the judge believes that a jury would not be justified in finding for the opposing party on the evidence presented.

The attorneys then make closing arguments that sum up the case. Normally the defendant's attorney goes first. This gives the plaintiff, who has the *burden of proof*, the last word. The burden of proof is different for a criminal than a civil case. In a criminal case the state as plaintiff must convince the fact finder—jury or judge—*beyond a reasonable doubt* of the defendant's guilt. In a civil case the plaintiff need only have the *preponderance of the evidence* on his or her side.

If there is a jury, the judge instructs it on the law applicable to the case. The attorneys for the parties suggest instructions, tailoring them to the facts as they hope the jury will find them. The judge may determine the instructions alone if he or she chooses. Their purpose is to tell the jury what its decision should be according to the facts as determined.

After being instructed the jury goes to the jury room, where it discusses the case and takes ballots until a verdict is reached. In important criminal cases where there are much public interest and discussion, the jury may be *sequestered.* This means they are not permitted to leave the supervision of the court, day or night, until excused; this is to keep outside influences away. Once there is unanimous agreement (or whatever majority is required by law) on a verdict, the jury foreman reports this to the judge. If the jury cannot come to a verdict, there is a *hung jury.* Then a decision must be made by the plaintiff (or prosecutor in a criminal case) whether to bring the case to trial again.

Whichever way the jury finds, the losing party in a civil case can make a motion for *judgment notwithstanding the verdict (judgment n.o.v.).* The claim is that no reasonable jury could come to that verdict on the basis of the evidence presented at the trial. Such a motion is very rarely granted. A state cannot make such a motion if the defendant is acquitted in a criminal case.

APPEAL PROCEDURE

When an Appeal Is Possible

Being dissatisfied with the judgment of the court is not a sufficient ground for an appeal. The party must allege that the court made an error of law. An example of such an error is that the judge erred in instructing the jury, or it might be alleged that the judge made a wrong ruling on a motion by the party's attorney during the trial. In order to permit the judge to correct an error and avoid the possible expense of a retrial, the attorney must *take exception* to the judge's action at the time the alleged error was made. Another requirement for an appeal is that the error must have been material; that is, the result might have been different if the error had not been made.

The Appeal

A party who desires to appeal must file for an appeal with the proper appeal court within a certain period of time, which is established by statute. A *transcript* of the entire trial proceeding, including the testimony of all the witnesses and any discussions between the judge and the attorneys must be prepared and forwarded to the appeal court.

The attorney for each party (which may be a different person or firm than the one conducting the trial) submits a *brief,* which presents a written argument supporting the party's position on the proper rule of law and asks for the desired judgment. *Citations* (references) are made to precedent cases and perhaps to *treatises* (textbooks or articles written by legal scholars). When a number of groups other than the parties involved are interested in the outcome of a certain appeal, they may request to be permitted to file *amicus curiae* (friend of the court) briefs.

Oral Argument   Usually the attorneys for the parties ask to give oral argument to supplement the written briefs. The attorneys are given a limited amount of time for their oral arguments. The judges of the appeals court frequently ask questions of the attorneys. There are, however, no witnesses. The facts as found by the jury (or judge) at the trial are accepted as true. An exception occurs when it is claimed that there was no competent evidence to support a finding of fact or the granting or refusal of a motion. For example, an appeals (appellate) court would have to review the evidence presented at the trial when the error by the trial judge is alleged to be a failure to accept a motion to dismiss or a motion for a directed verdict. The transcript of the trial is used for this purpose. If there is doubt, it is assumed the trial judge who heard the witnesses made the correct assessment.

The appeals court may *affirm* (uphold) the judgment of the trial court, or it may merely *reverse*. Sometimes, as for example when the defendant's motion to dismiss was accepted by the judge at the end of the plaintiff's case, a court may *reverse and remand*. This sends the case back to the trial court for further proceedings, and a new trial is then required. It may be on a very narrow question of fact or it may be a complete repeat of the original trial. Frequently the parties settle their controversy at this point rather than going through another trial.

QUESTIONS AND PROBLEM CASES

1. Discuss the advantages and disadvantages of the various methods of dispute settlement.

2. Which, if any, of the dispute settlement methods are mutually inconsistent?

3. Discuss the meaning of the concept of jurisdiction.

4. Some people call the adversary system the "sporting theory of justice." Are discovery procedures consistent with that idea?

5. What functions do the pleadings in a lawsuit serve?

6. What requirements must be met before a party can appeal a case lost in the trial court?

7. Suppose Sally enters into a sales contract with Phillip. The contract has a provision stating that any dispute under the contract will be settled by arbitration. Phillip refuses to make the payments called for by the contract and Sally sues. Is the arbitration clause a good defense to the suit?

8. The automobiles of Andrew and Barry collided as a result of Barry's negligence. Andrew suffered bruises and two broken bones. His medical bills were $2,000 and he lost two weeks' pay at $500 each because of treatment and arranging to get his car fixed. The low estimate for repairing his automobile was $2,500. Barry suffered injuries that resulted in medical bills and lost time totaling $3,000 plus $2,000 damage to his automobile. The accident was in Illinois. Andrew is a resident of Colorado. Barry is a resident of Illinois. Could Andrew sue for his damages in a federal court? Would it make any difference if he also claimed $5,000 for pain and suffering?

Crimes and Intentional Torts

3

Crimes are *public wrongs*—acts prohibited by the *state*. Criminal prosecutions are brought by an agent of the state (the prosecutor) in the name of the state. Those who are convicted of committing criminal acts are subject to punishment imposed by society in the form of fines, imprisonment, or execution.

Crimes are usually classed as felonies or misdemeanors, depending on the seriousness of the offense. *Felonies* are serious offenses such as murder, rape, and arson that are generally punishable by confinement to a state penitentiary for substantial periods of time. Conviction of a felony may, in some cases, also result in *disenfranchisement* (loss of the right to vote) and bar a person from practicing certain professions, such as law or medicine. *Misdemeanors* are lesser crimes like traffic offenses or disorderly conduct that are punishable by fines or confinement in a city or county jail.

Whether a given act is classed as criminal or tort is a social question. Our definitions of criminal conduct change with time. Behavior that was once considered criminal (e.g., blasphemy) is no longer treated as such. Today we see many proposals to "decriminalize" certain kinds of behavior like gambling, prostitution, consensual sex, and various drug offenses. Those who argue for decriminalization maintain that attempts to treat such "victimless crimes" criminally are ineffective, cause corruption, overburden the courts and police, and cause a loss of respect for the law. Deciding how to treat such behavior is one of the more difficult problems facing society today.

The Essentials of Crime

In order for a person to be convicted of criminal behavior, the state must: (1) demonstrate a prior statutory prohibition of the act, (2) prove beyond a reasonable doubt that the defendant committed the criminal act, and (3) prove that the defendant had the capacity to form a criminal intent.

Prior Statutory Prohibition.   There are no common law crimes today. Before behavior can be treated as criminal, the legislature must have passed a statute making it criminal. Then only those who commit the prohibited act *after* passage of the statute may be prosecuted. The power of Congress and the state legislatures to make behavior criminal is constitutionally limited in two ways. They cannot make behavior criminal that is protected by the U.S. Constitution. For example, the exercise of free speech protected by the first amendment to the Constitution cannot be made criminal. Criminal statutes must also define the prohibited behavior clearly, so that an ordinary person would understand what behavior is prohibited. This requirement comes from the Due Process Clauses in the fifth and fourteenth amendments to the U.S. Constitution.

Coates v. City of Cincinnati
402 U.S. 611 (U.S. Sup. Ct. 1971)

FACTS   Coates was a student involved in a demonstration. He was arrested and convicted for violating a Cincinnati ordinance that made it a crime for "three or more persons to assemble . . . on any of the sidewalks . . . and there conduct themselves in a manner annoying to persons passing by. . . ." Coates appealed his conviction, arguing that the ordinance was unconstitutional.

ISSUE   Is the ordinance unconstitutional?

DECISION   Yes. The Court held that the ordinance was "unconstitutionally vague" because "men of common intelligence must necessarily guess at its meaning," since "conduct that annoys some people does not annoy others." Therefore the ordinance violates the Due Process Clause of the fourteenth amendment. The Court also found that the ordinance was "unconstitutionally broad," since it could be read as authorizing punishment for conduct (free speech and assembly) protected by the first amendment.

Proof beyond a Reasonable Doubt.   In view of the fact that in criminal cases we are dealing with the life and liberty of the accused person, the legal system places strong limits on the power of the state to convict a person of crime. Criminal defendants are *presumed innocent*. The state must overcome this presumption of innocence by proving every element of the offense charged against the defendant *beyond a reasonable doubt*. This means beyond any substantial doubt in fact or in law.

The state must prove its case within a framework of procedural safeguards, discussed later in this chapter, that are designed to protect the accused. The state's failure to prove any material element of its case results in the accused being acquitted, even though he or she may actually have committed the crime charged.

The Defendant's Capacity.   *Criminal intent* is an element of most serious crimes. Intent may be inferred from the nature of the defendant's acts, but the defendant must be capable of forming the required criminal intent. The basic idea behind requiring intent is that the criminal law seeks to punish *conscious* wrongdoers. The criminal law recognizes several kinds of incapacity: intoxication, infancy, and insanity.

Voluntary intoxication is generally not a complete defense to criminal liability. It can, in some cases, diminish the extent of a defendant's liability if it prevents the formation of a specific criminal intent. For example, many first-degree murder statutes require proof of *premeditation,* a conscious decision to kill. A highly intoxicated defendant may not be capable of premeditation and may therefore be convicted of only second-degree murder, which does not generally require premeditation. Involuntary intoxication may be a complete defense to criminal liability.

In common law, children under the age of 7 were incapable of forming a criminal intent, children between the ages of 7 and 14 were presumed incapable, and children between the ages of 14 and 21 were presumed capable. These presumptions relating to capacity were rebuttable by specific evidence about the intellectual and moral development of the accused. Most states today by statute treat defendants below a stated age (usually 16 or 17) differently than adult offenders, with special juvenile court systems and separate detention facilities. Juvenile law today focuses on rehabilitation rather than capacity. Repeated offenders, or those charged with very serious offenses, may be treated as adults.

Insanity on the part of a criminal defendant can affect a criminal trial in three ways. If the accused is incapable of assisting in the defense of the case, trial may be delayed until the accused regains sanity. An accused who becomes insane after trial but before sentencing is not sentenced until sanity has been regained. Insanity at the time the criminal act was committed absolves the defendant of criminal liability.

The states have adopted various insanity tests for criminal responsibility. These tests are legal tests designed to punish conscious, willful wrongdoers, not medical tests. A person may have been medically insane at the time of the criminal act, but still be legally responsible. An insanity test that is gaining some popularity today is the American Law Institute test, which says that the defendant is not criminally responsible if at the time the act was committed, and as a result of mental disease or defect, he or she lacked the substantial capacity to appreciate the wrongfulness of the act or to conform his or her conduct to the requirements of the law.

A criminal defendant is presumed to be sane. The defendant must introduce evidence that creates a reasonable doubt as to his or her sanity. Juries are often hostile toward insanity pleas, fearing that defendants attempt to avoid responsibility by pleading insanity.

**Criminal
Procedure**

In addition to the presumption of innocence, our legal system has several other built-in safeguards to protect the accused. These safeguards are designed to prevent innocent people from being convicted for crimes they did not commit, and they also represent an ideal of the proper role of government in a democracy. As Justice Oliver Wendell Holmes once said, "I think it less evil that some criminals should escape than that the government should play an ignoble part."

The following are some of the safeguards enjoyed by criminal defendants in our legal system.

1. Defendants who have been acquitted of a crime may not be tried again for the same offense by the same jurisdiction. This is known as the prohibition against *double jeopardy.*
2. Defendants in criminal cases have a right to remain silent and cannot be compelled to testify against themselves.
3. Illegally obtained evidence, that is, evidence resulting from "unreasonable searches and seizures" prohibited by the fourth amendment, may not be used by the state in criminal prosecutions.
4. Persons charged with crimes have a right to be represented by an attorney if imprisonment is a possible result of conviction.
5. Persons accused of crimes have the right to confront and cross-examine their accusers.
6. When the police take a person into custody, they must advise the person of the right to remain silent and the right to counsel. Confessions made in the absence of these warnings are inadmissible as evidence in court and cannot be used to convict a person.

In times of rising crime rates, we frequently hear the argument that the incidence of crime is somehow related to our treatment of criminal defendants. While there may be some truth in this assertion, attacking the root causes of criminal behavior might do more to reduce crime than any reformation of the criminal justice system.

**Crime and People
in Business**

People in business today are more likely than ever before to have some unpleasant contact with the criminal justice system. There is a trend today to make violations of regulatory statutes criminal offenses punishable by fines and/or imprisonment. Many prosecutors and judges are demonstrating a "get tough" attitude about white-collar crimes that have often been treated leniently in the past. They argue that personal liability for corporate executives is necessary to *deter* corporations from violating laws and viewing any fines imposed on the corporation as merely a cost of doing business.

This attitude on the part of government officials is probably the result of several factors. There has been a long-standing public outcry against the lenient treatment of white-collar crime. This has been aggravated by statistics indicating the tremendous cost of such crime (amounting to billions of dollars annually) and by the post-Watergate atmosphere of public hostility toward people in positions of power and authority. In addition to seeking jail sentences for corporate defendants, prosecutors are also using mail fraud, wire fraud, and conspiracy statutes to prosecute them.

An additional problem is created by the fact that some regulatory statutes, particularly in the area of public health and safety, seem to impose liability without proof of the level of intent traditionally required for criminal liability.

United States v. Park
421 U.S. 658 (U.S. Sup. Ct. 1975)

FACTS   John R. Park was the president of Acme Markets, Inc., a large national food chain. He was charged with violating the Federal Food, Drug, and Cosmetic Act by receiving food shipped in interstate commerce and storing it in a Baltimore warehouse where it was accessible to rodents and exposed to contamination by rodents. In 1970, federal investigators had notified Park of unsanitary conditions in Acme's Philadelphia warehouse. In late 1971, another investigation disclosed evidence of rodent activity and food contamination in Acme's Baltimore warehouse. When informed of this, Park conferred with Acme's vice president for legal affairs and was told that corrective action would be taken. A follow-up investigation in early 1972 showed some improvement, but still yielded evidence of rodent contamination. Park argued that he had delegated authority to his subordinates and that the government had to show some "wrongful action" on his part before he could be convicted.

ISSUE   Did these facts justify convicting Park?

DECISION   Yes. The court held that the fact that Park knew of the earlier Philadelphia violations should have put him on notice that he could not justifiably rely on delegating authority to his subordinates because that method of operation had proven ineffective to avoid violations. The court recognized that the act dispensed with the traditional requirement of "awareness of some wrongdoing" for criminal liability, but held that public policy justifies the imposition of liability on otherwise innocent persons who stand "in responsible relation to a public danger." The court concluded that a failure to act was enough for liability if the defendant had the power to prevent the violation.

INTENTIONAL TORTS

Torts are private (civil) wrongs against persons or property. Persons who are injured by the tortious act of another may file a civil suit for actual (compensatory) damages to compensate them for their injuries. In some cases, punitive damages in excess of the plaintiff's actual injuries may be recovered. Punitive damages are used to punish the defendant and deter the defendant and others from repeating behavior that is particularly offensive.

The same behavior may give rise to both civil (tort) and criminal liability. For example, a rapist is criminally liable for the crime of rape and is also civilly liable for the torts of assault and battery. The reason more victims of crimes do not file civil lawsuits against their attackers is simply that most criminal defendants are financially unable to pay a damage award.

The plaintiff's burden of proof in a tort case is the preponderance of the evidence. This simply means that when both sides have presented their evidence, the greater weight of the believable evidence must be on the plaintiff's side. This standard of proof is applied in all civil cases where only money is at stake, in contrast to criminal cases where the defendant's life or liberty may be at stake.

In tort law, society is engaged in a constant balancing act between individual rights and duties. What kinds of behavior should a person have to tolerate in his or her fellow citizens, and what kinds of behavior should be considered intolerable? Historically, our legal system seems to be expanding the grounds for tort liability. There are three bases for tort liability: intentional wrongdoing, negligence, and strict liability. Chapter 4 discusses negligence and strict liability. We will now look at the various kinds of intentional misbehavior that are considered tortious.

Interference with Personal Rights

Battery. The basic personal interest that any legal system can protect is a person's right to be free from injurious or unpleasant physical contacts with others. *Battery* is the intentional, harmful, or offensive touching of the plaintiff without the plaintiff's consent. The least touching can be a battery if it produces injury or would be considered offensive to a person of *ordinary sensibilities*. The defendant need not actually touch the plaintiff's body to be liable for battery if anything connected to the plaintiff's body was touched. For example, if Bob snatches Mary's purse off her shoulder, or kicks her dog while she is walking him on a leash, he is liable for battery even though he has not touched her body.

Consent must be freely and intelligently given to be a defense to battery. Consent may in some cases be inferred from a person's voluntary participation in an activity. For example, a boxer could hardly complain about normal injuries suffered in a fight. However, a quarterback who is knifed on the 50-yard line clearly has a battery claim. What about a hockey player who is hit by a hockey stick in a fight that erupts during a game? Should his claim be barred due to his voluntary participation in an admittedly violent sport? Such cases raise difficult issues about the scope of consent; there are no easy answers.

Assault. The tort of *assault* is designed to protect people from threats of battery. Any unlawful offer to touch the person of another in a rude or angry manner is an assault if it causes a well-grounded apprehension of imminent (immediate) battery in the plaintiff's mind. No contact is necessary for assault. Assault focuses on the apprehension in the mind of the plaintiff.

Would an ordinary person in the plaintiff's situation have thought that battery was imminent? Most courts say that "mere words are not enough" for assault and require some affirmative act, like a threatening gesture by the defendant. Threats of battery in the future ("I'll get you next week") or attempts at battery that the plaintiff is not aware of at the time, like a bullet fired from a great distance that misses the plaintiff, are not grounds for a civil assault suit.

False Imprisonment. The tort of false imprisonment protects both physical (freedom of movement) and mental (freedom from knowledge of confinement) interests. *False imprisonment* is the intentional confinement of a person for an appreciable time (a few minutes is enough) without the person's consent. *Confinement* occurs when a person substantially restricts another person's freedom of movement. A partial obstruction of a person's progress is not false imprisonment. Two examples of partial obstructions are standing in a person's path and locking the front door of a building a person is in without locking the back door.

If escape from confinement is possible but requires an unreasonable exposure of the plaintiff's person, false imprisonment has occurred. So, a person who would have to crawl through a sewer or walk a tightrope to escape has been confined. Traditionally, a person must know that he or she is confined, and any consent to confinement must be freely given. Consent given in the face of an implied or actual threat of force by the confiner or an assertion of legal authority by the confiner is not freely given.

Most false imprisonment cases today probably involve shoplifting. Under common law, the store owner who stopped a suspected shoplifter was liable in court for any torts committed in the process if the plaintiff was innocent of any wrongdoing. Today many states have passed statutes giving store owners a *conditional privilege* to stop persons they reasonably believe are shoplifting, as long as the owner acts in a reasonable manner and detains the suspect for only a reasonable length of time.

Southwest Drug Stores of Mississippi, Inc. v. Garner
195 So.2d 837 (Sup. Ct. Miss. 1967)

FACTS   Mrs. Garner was shopping in the Southwest's store in Laurel, Mississippi. While she was at the cosmetic counter looking for soap she was approached by Ratliff, the store manager, who asked if he could help her. She told him what she wanted and he had a salesperson wait on her. The salesperson helped her find the soap and went with her to the cashier, where she paid for it. When she left the store, Ratliff followed her and, in the presence of a number of people, said to her in a rude and loud manner, "Hey, wait there . . . You stop there, I want to see what you got in that little bag. You stole a bar of soap." She said: "You mean you're accusing me of stealing this soap?" He replied: "Yes, you stole the soap, and let's

> prove it, let's go back." Garner said the incident made her sick and she had to visit her doctor twice thereafter. She sued Southwest for slander and false imprisonment. Southwest relied on a conditional privilege statute as a defense.
>
> **ISSUE**   Was Ratliff's behavior privileged?
>
> **DECISION**   No. The court noted the existence of a conditional privilege, but concluded that "the privilege was lost by the manner in which it was exercised." The court said that: "Granting that Ratliff had reason to believe" that Garner had stolen some soap, "still he was careless . . . in his manner of ascertaining whether Mrs. Garner had paid for the soap."

Defamation.   Injury to a person's reputation can cause that person considerable anguish and harm. The torts of *libel* (written defamation) and *slander* (oral defamation) are designed to protect against injury to a person's reputation. The basis of both torts is the publication of a defamatory statement about a person. Communication to one person other than the defamed party is sufficient for publication. A defamatory statement is one that exposes a person to hatred, contempt, or ridicule. Whether a given statement is defamatory is usually a question for a jury to decide.

Damages are presumed in libel cases, unless the written statement is not defamatory on its face. For example, a statement that Bob married Sue is not defamatory on its face even though Bob was married to Mary at the time. A person may not recover for slander without proving actual damages, unless the nature of the defamatory statement is so serious that the law has classified it as *slander per se*. Classic forms of slander per se are statements that a person has a "loathsome" disease, has committed a serious crime, or is professionally incompetent or guilty of professional improprieties. To these three categories some courts have added charges that a woman is unchaste or that a person is a homosexual. All other slanderous statements are *slander per quod*, and cannot be a basis for recovery unless a person can prove actual damages as a result of the defamation.

Truth is a complete defense to a defamation suit. False statements may also not be the basis for a successful defamation suit if they are absolutely or conditionally privileged. The law recognizes that certain kinds of statements are socially necessary, even though they involve some risk to reputation. An *absolute privilege*, unlike a *conditional privilege*, is totally unqualified and cannot be defeated by a showing that the defamatory statement was made recklessly or in bad faith. Statements by members of Congress on the floor of Congress or by judges or lawyers during the trial of a lawsuit are absolutely privileged. Statements made in the furtherance of legitimate business interests or in credit reports may be conditionally privileged.

In a famous recent case, the U.S. Supreme Court held that a public official suing for false and defamatory statements must show *actual malice* (knowledge of falsity or reckless disregard for the truth) on the part of a media defendant in order to recover any damages.[1] The Court felt that the public interest in the "free and unfettered debate" of important social issues justified this limitation on a public official's rights. *Public figures* (private persons who are famous or have involved themselves in some public controversy) face a similar burden of proof for similar reasons.[2]

Jones v. Walsh
222 A.2d 830 (Sup. Ct. N.H. 1966)

FACTS   Dolores Jones was a waitress in John Walsh's restaurant. One day while Jones was operating the cash register, Walsh, in the presence of several customers, said to her: "You are not ringing the cash up in the cash register." Jones replied: "Are you accusing me of stealing?" Walsh said: "Well, you're not ringing in the cash." Jones filed a *slander per se* suit against Walsh, who argued that he had not defamed her and that his words were privileged.

ISSUE   Was Walsh liable for slander?

DECISION   Yes. The fact that Walsh did not accuse Jones of embezzlement in a technical or direct way does not mean that he did not slander her. It is possible to slander by innuendo. The proper test is whether an ordinary person overhearing Walsh's words would have understood that Jones was being charged with a criminal offense. The court concluded that this was so. The court recognized that Walsh had a conditional privilege to protect the receipts of his business, but observed that "the defamatory communication must be made to a person whose knowledge of the defamatory matter . . . is likely to prove useful in the protection of that interest." Walsh exceeded the scope of his privilege by allowing customers to overhear his statements to Jones.

Invasion of Privacy.   The recognition of a *right of privacy* is a relatively recent development in tort law. This area is still undergoing considerable development and has currently expanded to include several kinds of behavior that infringe on a person's "right to be let alone." Intrusion on a person's physical solitude is a widely recognized form of invasion of privacy. Phone harassment of debtors by creditors, illegal searches of a person or a person's property, and obscene calls are examples of this form of invasion of privacy. Publishing private facts about a person has also been held to be invasion of privacy. Acts like putting an ad in the paper saying that a person does not pay his or her bills, publishing embarrassing details of a person's illnesses, or publishing pictures of a parent's deformed child are examples of this

---

[1] *New York Times v. Sullivan,* 376 U.S. 254 (1964).

[2] *Curtis Publishing Co. v. Butts,* 388 U.S. 130 (1967).

form of invasion of privacy. Putting a person in a false light in the public eye by signing his or her name to a public letter or telegram or using his or her picture to illustrate an article with which that person has no real connection has also been held to be invasion of privacy. Finally, using a person's indorsement for commercial purposes without his consent by using his name or picture is a widely recognized form of invasion of privacy.

Students should note that the "publication of private facts" and "placing in a false light" forms of this tort are based on *publicity*. Therefore, some widespread dissemination of the information involved is necessary for liability. It should also be noted that truth is not a defense to "publication of private facts" and that "public figures" cannot complain about publicity that is reasonably related to their public activities.

Vogel v. W. T. Grant Co.
327 A.2d 133 (Sup. Ct. Penn. 1974)

FACTS   Vogel and other credit customers of Grant filed a class action invasion of privacy suit against Grant. They charged that Grant, in seeking to coerce payment of their overdue accounts, had violated their rights to privacy by notifying their employers and relatives about their debts.

ISSUE   Was Grant liable for invasion of privacy?

DECISION   No. The court said that "unreasonable publicity given to the existence of a debt has often been held to constitute an invasion of privacy." The court noted that "the crux of the tort" is "publicity," and cited the case of a mechanic who placed a five by eight foot notice in the window of his garage, calling attention to a customer's overdue account as an example of undue publicity. The court concluded that Vogel and the others had not shown sufficient publicity, holding that "notification of two or four third parties is not sufficient to constitute publication."

Infliction of Mental Distress.   The courts have traditionally been reluctant to grant recovery for purely mental injuries for fear of opening the door to fictitious claims. Developments in modern medicine have, however, made such injuries more provable. As a result, many courts are moving away from the traditional "impact" rule, which allowed recovery for mental injuries only if a battery had occurred, and are allowing recovery solely for severe emotional distress. Other courts still require some serious physical injury as a result of the emotional distress before they grant recovery. All courts require that the defendant's conduct be *outrageous*—that is, substantially certain to produce severe emotional distress in a person of ordinary sensibilities.

Interference with Property Rights

Property rights have traditionally occupied an important position in our legal system. Suits for tortious interference with property rights are generally brought by the party with the right to *possess* the property rather than its owner. Actions for *trespass* to land that has been leased to another may be brought by the owner if the owner's reversionary interests in the property are being damaged. Trespass to land, trespass to personal property, and conversion are the traditionally recognized torts against property.

Trespass to Land. Any entry by a person onto land in the possession of another is a trespass, unless the entry is done with the possessor's permission or is privileged. The same is true for causing anything to enter the land in the possession of another, or remaining on the land of another, as in the case of a tenant who stays after his or her lease has expired. The same is also true for allowing anything to remain on another's property, as in the case of a holdover tenant's property. No actual harm to the property is necessary for trespass. However, if no actual losses result, the plaintiff can recover only nominal damages.

Trespass to Personal Property. Intentional interference with personal property in the possession of another is a trespass if it: (1) harms the property, or (2) deprives the possessor of its use for an appreciable time. Consent and privilege are defenses to trespass to personal property.

Conversion. *Conversion* is the unlawful taking of or exercise of control over the personal property of another person. The essence of conversion is the wrongful deprivation of a person's personal property rights. One who unlawfully takes goods from the possession of another is liable for conversion even though the taker mistakenly believes he or she is entitled to possession. The same is true of those who wrongfully sell, mortgage, lease, or use the goods of another. The plaintiff in a lawsuit based on conversion has a right to recover the reasonable value of the property. Some courts reduce the plaintiff's damages when the property can be returned unharmed and the defendant's conversion was the result of an honest mistake.

Interference with Economic Relations

The tort law protecting persons against unreasonable interferences with their economic relations with others is a more recent development than the previously discussed areas. Three classic torts in this area are: disparagement, interference with contract, and interference with economic expectations.

Disparagement. False statements about the personal behavior of persons in business are covered by the tort of defamation. False statements about the quality of a seller's product or services, or the seller's ownership of goods offered for sale may give rise to the tort of disparagement. Proof of actual damage (e.g., lost sales or other opportunities) is necessary for a successful disparagement action.

Interference with Contract. One who actively induces a person to breach a contract with another may be liable in damages to the party deprived of the benefits of the contract. This tort seeks to protect the sanctity of private contractual relationships. Some courts do not hold a person liable whose conduct merely caused a breach of contract (as opposed to actively inducing the breach). Inducing a breach of contract may be justifiable in some cases. For example, the mother of a private school student who induced the school to exclude a diseased child would probably not be liable to the excluded child's parents for interference with contract.

Interference with Economic Expectations. Early examples of this tort involved the use of force to drive away a person's customers or employees. Today, liability has been broadened to include nonviolent forms of intentional interference as well.

Carolina Overall Corp. v. East Carolina Linen Supply, Inc.
174 S.E.2d 659 (Ct. App. N.C. 1970)

FACTS   Carolina Overall and East Carolina Linen were competitors in the industrial laundry business. East Carolina induced one of Carolina Overall's route salesmen to breach his employment contract and enter the employment of East Carolina. East Carolina, acting through the salesman and others, also solicited the business of 14 of Carolina Overall's customers and induced them to breach their contracts with Carolina Overall for laundry service. East Carolina argued that competition was a legal justification for interfering in the contract of a competitor and a third person.

ISSUE   Is East Carolina liable for interference with contract?

DECISION   Yes. The court said: "We see no valid reason for holding that a competitor is privileged to interfere wrongfully with contract rights. If contracts otherwise binding are not secure from wrongful interference by competitors, they offer little certainty in business relations, and it is security from competition that often gives them value." In order to make a case for tortious interference with contract, the plaintiff must show that: (1) he or she had a contract with a third person, (2) the defendant knew of the contract, (3) the defendant intentionally induced the third person not to perform his or her contract with the plaintiff, (4) the defendant acted without justification, and (5) the defendant's acts caused the plaintiff actual damages. The court concluded that Carolina Overall had proven all these elements.

QUESTIONS AND PROBLEM CASES

1. What limits does the U.S. Constitution place on the power of Congress and the state legislatures to make behavior criminal?

2. What competing social interests were the courts seeking to balance by creating the "public official" and the "public figure" doctrines?

3. Why were the courts historically reluctant to award damages for mental distress suffered in the absence of physical injury?

4. Rogers was convicted of violating a Columbus, Ohio, city ordinance prohibiting the public appearance of any person "in a dress not be-

longing to his or her sex, or in an indecent or lewd dress." He appealed, arguing that the ordinance was unconstitutionally vague under the Due Process Clause. Should his conviction be reversed?

5. Fabish purchased a new book at a book store and then entered Montgomery Ward in order to shop. An employee of Montgomery Ward thought she saw Fabish take the book off a shelf and Fabish was detained for about one hour before he was able to clear himself. Fabish repeatedly requested that he be allowed to call the store where he had purchased the book. These requests were denied. Fabish sued for false imprisonment and the jury awarded him $3,300 compensatory damages and $5,000 punitive damages. Montgomery Ward appealed, asking that the punitive damages be set aside for lack of evidence of willful or malicious conduct. Should the damages be reduced?

6. Mrs. Cantrell's husband was killed, along with 43 others, when a bridge collapsed. Five months later Forest City Publishing Co. sent a reporter to interview Mrs. Cantrell. The reporter instead interviewed four minor children of Mrs. Cantrell's at a time when she was not present. The reporter's article stated that Mrs. Cantrell would not talk of the accident and that she "wears the same mask of nonexpression she wore at the funeral," as well as other inaccuracies. Will Cantrell's suit for invasion of privacy prevail?

7. Neff, a private citizen, was in the dugout with a group of fans prior to a professional football game. A photographer for *Sports Illustrated* magazine was present, preparing to take pictures of the upcoming game. Upon hearing for whom the photographer worked, Neff and his group began to request the photographer to photograph them, which he did. All these fans, including Neff, made no objection to the picture taking. One rather embarrassing picture of Neff with his pants unzipped was published in a book, although Neff was not mentioned by name and the precise football game involved was not mentioned. Neff sued the owner of *Sports Illustrated*, claiming an invasion of his right of privacy due to the publication of his picture. Should he recover?

8. Mark and Mary Peth were engaged in the collection business and were employed by Dr. Lydic to collect a $197 debt that Joan Housh owed Lydic. The Peths called Housh on the telephone many times in the course of a day with regard to this collection and called her at her place of employment three times within 15 minutes on March 19, 1954. As a result, her employer told her on March 19, 1954, that unless this collection was "straightened up" on or before March 23, 1954, Housh would be discharged from her employment. The Peths also called the supervisor of music of the Dayton Public Schools and called the Housh's landlord regarding the collection, claiming that she did not pay her bills and inquiring about her earnings. Two weeks prior to filing her suit, the Peths called Housh at her place of residence eight or nine times a day for this collection, giving her notices and warnings, and called her as late as 11:45 P.M. Housh sued Lydic and the Peths, claiming that their conduct constituted an invasion of her right of privacy. Is Housh entitled to damages?

9. Van Dorn, an internationally known professional race car driver, brought suit against T. L. Parker Tobacco Co. for invasion of privacy, alleging that the defendant had misappropriated his "likeness" in a nationally televised advertisement. Parker legally obtained a "stock" photograph of Van Dorn seated in his automobile, which could be identified immediately by its number 7, its color, and its unique front pinstripes. In retouching the photograph, Parker changed "7" to "75" and added the name of its tobacco to the sides of the automobile. Although Van Dorn himself was unrecognizable in the final advertisement, the pinstripes and color of the automobile had not been removed or changed by Parker. The advertisement made no reference to Van Dorn by name. Will the court award damages to Van Dorn based on the alleged invasion of privacy by Parker through the misappropriation of his "likeness"?

10. "Black History: Stolen, Lost, or Strayed?" was a documentary produced and shown by the Columbia Broadcasting System and narrated by a well-known black entertainer, Bill Cosby. Cosby, in narrative commentary, said:

> The tradition of the lazy, stupid, crap-shooting, chicken-stealing idiot was popularized by an actor named Lincoln Boles. The cat made $2 million in five years in the middle 30s. It's too bad he was as good as he was. The character he played was planted in a lot of people's heads and they remember it the rest of their lives as clear as an auto accident.

In a suit against CBS, Boles claims that the reference to him was a defamation of character because he is neither "lazy" or "stupid" and because the characters he portrayed in movies were never crap shooters or chicken stealers. CBS claims that its commentary is fair and accurate. Can Boles win?

11. About July 18, 1971, Heuer and Wiese entered into an oral contract whereby Heuer agreed to sell and Wiese agreed to buy for $600 a clover crop then standing on Heuer's field. Heuer was to cut the crop when directed by Wiese. Heuer cut the crop on July 31, 1971. After Heuer had cut the crop, he notified Wiese by letter to remove the crop by August 10, 1971. Wiese failed to remove the crop by August 10, and a week later Heuer took possession of the cut crop and with a chopper cut the crop up on his field. On September 25, 1971, Heuer brought suit against Wiese to recover the unpaid balance of the purchase price of the crop and Wiese filed a counterclaim for damages for the conversion of the crop by Heuer. Who will prevail?

assuming

12. Herman Parker, a rhythm and blues singer known as "Little Junior," signed a contract with Sun Record Company giving Sun exclusive recording rights over Parker for two years. During the period of the contract, Parker also agreed to record for Robey. When confronted with the existence of the Sun contract, Robey continued to record Parker's music. Sun brought an action against Robey for wrongful interference with its contractual relationship with Parker. Is Robey liable?

No
singer is
Parker

Negligence and Strict Liability

4

The Industrial Revolution that began in the early part of the 19th century created serious problems for the law of torts. Railroads, machinery, and newly developed tools were contributing to a growing number of injuries to people and property that simply did not fit within the framework of intentional torts, since most of these injuries were unintended. The legal system was forced to develop a new set of rules to deal with these situations, and the result was the law of negligence.

Basically, *negligence* is an unintentional breach of duty by the defendant that results in harm to another. A plaintiff in a negligence suit must prove several things to recover: (1) that the defendant had a duty to not injure the plaintiff, (2) that the defendant breached that duty, and (3) that the defendant's breach of duty was the actual and legal (proximate) cause of the plaintiff's injuries. To be successful, the plaintiff must also overcome any defenses to negligence liability raised by the defendant. In some cases the plaintiff may be able to use a doctrine called *last clear chance* to overcome an otherwise valid defense.

Duty

The basic idea of negligence is that every member of society has a duty to conduct his or her affairs in a way that avoids injury to others. The law of negligence holds our behavior up to an objective standard of conduct; we must conduct ourselves like a "reasonable person of ordinary prudence in similar circumstances." This standard is *flexible*, since it allows consideration of all the circumstances surrounding a particular accident, but it is still *objective*, since the "reasonable person" is a hypothetical being, not an average individual.

Trout v. Bank of Belleville
343 N.E.2d 261 (Ct. App. Ill. 1976)

FACTS   Gilbert Trout and several of his friends were riding their motorcycles through town at 2:00 A.M. and decided to take a shortcut through an alley. Trout attempted to cut through the bank's parking lot and was killed when he hit a chain strung across the entrance. The lot was well lighted and several signs were posted on the chain, although there were none at the point where Trout crashed. Trout's mother filed a negligence suit against the bank.

ISSUE   Did the bank breach its duty to Gilbert Trout?

DECISION   No. A landowner owes a duty of reasonable care to invitees (those who are on his or her property by express or implied invitation for the purpose of furthering mutual interests or the interests of the landowner). To trespassers (those on the property without invitation or permission) or licensees (those on the property for personal purposes with the consent of the owner), however, the landowner only owes a duty to avoid "willfully and wantonly" injuring them and to use "ordinary care" to avoid injuring them once their presence in a place of danger becomes known. Trout was a trespasser and there was no evidence that the bank knew that anyone used the lot at night. The bank's conduct was not "willful or wanton," and it is therefore not liable for Trout's death.

Breach

A person is guilty of breach of duty if he or she exposes another person to a foreseeable, unreasonable risk of harm, something the "reasonable person" would never do. The courts ask whether the defendant did something the reasonable person would not have done, or failed to do something the reasonable person would have done. If the defendant guarded against all foreseeable harms and exercised reasonable care, he or she is not liable for any injury to the plaintiff. So, if Bob is carefully driving his car within the speed limit and a child darts into his path and is hit, Bob is not liable for the child's injuries.

Roberts v. American Brewed Coffee
319 N.E.2d 212 (Ct. App. Ohio 1973)

FACTS   American operated "Mister Softee" ice cream trucks. One of its trucks stopped in the middle of a block where there was no traffic light or crosswalk and began playing music to attract customers. Cheryl Roberts, age 4, ran across the street to buy ice cream and was struck by a car. Cheryl's mother filed a negligence suit on Cheryl's behalf against American.

ISSUE   Did American breach any duty it owed to Cheryl?

<blockquote>

DECISION   Yes. The court called street vendors "modern Pied Pipers." It held that those who park on busy streets, thereby requiring some children to cross the street to make a purchase, owe the children a duty to exercise reasonable care to protect them from the obvious danger posed by moving traffic. The court concluded that American had breached its duty by taking no steps to protect Cheryl, and that her injury was a foreseeable result of American's negligence.

</blockquote>

Negligence may, in some cases, be very difficult to prove. Plaintiffs in some negligence cases may be able to take advantage of two doctrines that can aid them in proving negligence: *negligence per se* and *res ipsa loquitur.*

Many states have recognized the doctrine of *negligence per se*. If the defendant violates a statute, something the "reasonable person" would not do, and if the harm the statute was designed to protect against results to a person the statute was designed to protect, breach of duty has been conclusively proven.

<blockquote>

Brockett v. Kitchen Boyd Motor Co.
100 Cal. Rptr. 752 (Ct. App. Cal. 1972)

FACTS   The Brocketts were injured when their car was hit by a car driven by Jimmie Huff, an employee of Kitchen Boyd Motor Company. The evidence indicated that Huff, a minor, had become intoxicated on liquor he was served at Kitchen Boyd's Christmas party. A state statute made it a misdemeanor to sell, furnish, or give alcoholic beverages to a minor.

ISSUE   Was Kitchen Boyd negligent in giving alcoholic beverages to Huff?

DECISION   Yes. The court noted that California had adopted the doctrine of negligence per se by statute. Therefore, although the common law negligence decisions exempted noncommercial furnishers of alcohol from liability for injuries caused by their guests, Kitchen Boyd was negligent per se in violating the statute that prohibits furnishing liquor to a minor. The Brocketts' injuries were among those the statute was designed to avoid and they were (along with minors themselves) members of the class of persons the statute sought to protect.

</blockquote>

In some cases negligence may be difficult to prove. The defendant has superior knowledge of the facts leading up to the plaintiff's injury because the defendant had exclusive control of the thing that caused the harm. If the defendant was in fact negligent, he or she understandably will be reluctant to disclose facts that prove liability. If the defendant had exclusive control and the injury that occurred would not ordinarily happen in the absence of negligence, the doctrine of *res ipsa loquitur* ("the thing speaks for itself") creates an inference of negligence. This forces the defendant to come forward and introduce evidence to rebut the inference of negligence. If the defendant fails to do so, he or she may be found liable. *Res ipsa* has been used frequently in plane crash cases where the cause of the crash may be difficult to prove because important evidence was destroyed in the crash itself.

Causation

Even if the defendant has breached a duty owed to the plaintiff, the plaintiff must convince the court that his or her injury was caused by that breach of duty. Courts often express this idea by saying things like: "There is no liability for negligence in the air." For example, Bob is speeding down the street, breaching his duty to those in the area, and Frank falls down the front steps of his house and breaks his leg. Bob was negligent, but since there is no causal connection between his breach of duty and Frank's injury, he is not liable for it.

In some cases a person's act may be the *cause in fact*—the actual or direct cause—of an incredible series of losses to numerous people. In intentional tort cases the courts have traditionally held people liable for all the consequences that directly result from their intentional wrongdoing, however bizarre and unforeseeable they may be.

With the creation of liability for negligence, the courts began to recognize that negligent wrongdoers (who were less at fault than intentional wrongdoers) should not necessarily be liable for every direct result of their negligence. This idea of placing a legal limit on the extent of a negligent person's liability came to be called *proximate cause*. So, a negligent person is liable for only the *proximate* results of his or her negligence.

The courts have not, however, reached agreement on the test that should be used for proximate cause. The proximate cause question is really one of social policy. In deciding which test to adopt, a court must weigh the possibility that negligent persons will be bankrupted by tremendous liability against the fact that some innocent victims may go uncompensated.

Some courts hold defendants liable for only the reasonably foreseeable results of their negligence. Others hold defendants liable for only injuries that are within *the scope* of the foreseeable risk. If the defendant could have reasonably foreseen some injury to the plaintiff, then the defendant is liable for every injury to the plaintiff that directly results from his or her negligence. The Restatement of Torts, recognizing the "after-the-fact" nature of proximate cause determinations, suggests that negligent defendants should not be liable for injuries that, looking backward after the accident, appear to be "highly extraordinary."

General Causation Rules

Regardless of what test for proximate cause the courts adopt, they generally agree on certain basic principles of causation. One such basic rule is that negligent defendants "take their victims as they find them." This means that if some physical peculiarity of a person aggravates his or her injuries, the defendant is liable for the full extent of the injuries. For example, Jim's head strikes the windshield of his car when Mary's negligently driven truck runs into him. Due to the fact that Jim's skull was abnormally thin he dies from the blow, which would have only slightly injured a normal person. Mary is liable for Jim's death. Likewise, negligent persons are generally held liable for diseases their victims contract while weakened by their injuries and for negligent medical care their victims receive for their injuries.

Negligent persons are also generally liable for injuries sustained by those who are injured while making reasonable attempts to avoid being injured by their negligent acts. So, if June dives out of the path of Steve's negligently driven car and breaks her arm in the process, Steve is liable for her injury. It is also commonly said that "negligence invites rescue," and that negligent persons should be liable to those who are injured while making a reasonable attempt to rescue someone endangered by their negligence.

Defenses to Negligence

The two traditional defenses that may be available to a negligent person are *contributory negligence* and *assumption of risk*. Every member of society has a duty to exercise reasonable care for his or her own safety. Persons who fail to exercise reasonable care for their own safety are barred from recovery if their contributory negligence is a substantial factor in producing their injuries. So, if John steps into the path of Fred's speeding car without checking to see whether any cars are coming, his contributory negligence will prevent him from receiving damages for his injuries from Fred.

Jiffy Markets, Inc. v. Vogel
340 F.2d 495 (8th Cir. 1965)

FACTS Vogel was injured when he walked through a large glass panel that formed the front of Jiffy Markets' supermarket. The evidence indicated that there were no signs or markings of any kind on the glass and that the glass was spotlessly clean. Vogel thought he was walking through an entrance to the store. When sued for negligence, Jiffy Markets raised the defense of contributory negligence.

ISSUE Was Vogel contributorily negligent?

DECISION No. The court said that a business proprietor has a duty to exercise reasonable care to keep the premises in a safe condition for invitees like Vogel and to warn them of any known dangerous places on the premises. The court noted a number of reported cases involving injuries to people from contact with glass doors and panels, and the testimony of a former employee of Jiffy that he had seen several persons "bounce off" the glass that injured Vogel. The court also noted the testimony of a safety engineer that the panel was a dangerous arrangement and that several methods could have been used to correct the lack of visibility of the glass. Therefore, the court concluded that there was ample evidence to support the jury's finding that Jiffy had breached its duty to Vogel and that Vogel had been exercising reasonable care for his own safety.

Contributory negligence can produce harsh results in some cases. Slightly negligent persons may be unable to recover anything for very serious injuries. As a result, some states have been adopting *comparative negligence* systems. Since they are statutory creations, comparative negligence systems differ in their details. Their basic idea, however, is to diminish the plaintiff's recovery according to the degree of his or her fault.

A number of courts also hold that a contributorily negligent plaintiff will not be barred from recovery if he or she can show that the defendant had the "last clear chance" to avoid the harm. The idea here is that, despite the contributory negligence of the plaintiff, if the accident could have been avoided by the exercise of reasonable care by the defendant, the defendant's superior opportunity to avoid the accident makes him more at fault.

There are some cases in which plaintiffs in negligence suits have voluntarily exposed themselves to a known danger created by another's negligence. For example, Mary voluntarily goes for a ride with Jim, who is obviously drunk. Such plaintiffs have assumed the risk of injury and are barred from recovery. The plaintiff must fully understand the nature and extent of the risk to be held to have assumed it.

Scott v. John H. Hampshire, Inc.
227 A.2d 751 (Ct. App. Md. 1967)

FACTS   Scott was working for a contractor at a library construction site. He noticed some of Hampshire's employees using a piece of chain to lengthen a steel cable they were using to unload steel. Scott knew this was dangerous and went to warn the workmen. His warning was ignored and the chain broke, striking Scott, who was standing about 20 feet away, in the head. Hampshire argued that Scott had assumed the risk of injury.

ISSUE   Did Scott assume the risk of injury by Hampshire's negligence?

DECISION   No. Assumption of risk does not apply where the defendant's negligence has created a situation that justifies an attempt to warn others to avoid harm to them. "Rescuers" like Scott are not barred from recovering for injuries suffered in their rescue attempts unless they were reckless in their attempt.

Recklessness

When a defendant's behavior indicates a "conscious disregard for a known high degree of probable harm to another," the defendant is guilty of *recklessness*. For example, Bob bets his friends he can drive down a crowded street blindfolded, and he strikes Tom. Recklessness is more morally objectionable than negligence (i.e., if Bob had been merely speeding) but less objectionable than intentional wrongdoing (i.e., if Bob had driven up on the curb after Tom). Therefore, contributory negligence is not a good defense to recklessness, but assumption of risk is a good defense. So, the fact that Tom did not look before stepping into Bob's path would not defeat his recovery, but evidence that Tom had bet Bob's friends he could run in front of Bob without being hit would bar any recovery by Tom.

STRICT LIABILITY

The most recently recognized basis for tort liability is the doctrine of strict liability. *Strict liability* means that a person who participates in certain kinds of activities is held responsible for any resulting harm to others, despite the use of the utmost care and caution. For this reason, strict liability is commonly described as "liability without fault." The basic idea behind strict liability is that, in some cases, social policy justifies imposing a loss on an innocent person whose actions caused the loss, rather than on an innocent person who has suffered the loss. Generally speaking, contributory negligence is not a good defense in strict liability suits, but assumption of risk is a good defense.

Strict liability was first applied to persons who kept animals that were "naturally dangerous." The owners of such animals were held strictly liable for any damage the animal caused, regardless of the precautions they took to avoid injury to others.

Strict liability was next extended to persons who participated in ultrahazardous activities, those that necessarily involve a risk of harm to others that cannot be eliminated by the utmost care. Examples of activities that have been classed as ultrahazardous are blasting, crop dusting, and stunt flying.

The most recent major application of strict liability is to the manufacturers of defective products that are "unreasonably dangerous"—that is, defective in a way that endangers life or property and is not readily apparent to buyers. This important topic is discussed in greater detail in Chapter 17.

Wood v. United Airlines, Inc.
223 N.Y.S.2d 692 (N.Y. Sup. Ct. Kings Cty. 1961)

FACTS Two commercial jets, belonging to United and Trans World Airlines, collided over New York City. Ms. Wood suffered physical injuries and damage to her property when the United plane fell into a building next to her apartment. She moved for a summary judgment against United, based on the theory of strict liability in tort.

ISSUE Is commercial aviation an ultrahazardous activity?

DECISION No. The court noted that earlier cases had recognized commercial aviation as an ultrahazardous activity, but said that "in the light of the technical progress achieved in the design, construction, operation and maintenance of aircraft generally, . . . flying should no longer be deemed to be an ultrahazardous activity." The court noted that more recent decisions had recognized that the art of flying had reached the point where "aircraft do not generally meet disaster in the absence of some negligence." Therefore, the court concluded that Wood was entitled to rely on *res ipsa loquitur* to help prove a negligence case against United, but was not entitled to a summary judgment based on strict liability.

QUESTIONS AND PROBLEM CASES

1. What factors are responsible for the development of negligence law?

2. What is the difference between contributory negligence and assumption of risk?

3. What is the doctrine of *res ipsa loquitur*, and when does it apply to a negligence case?

4. On November 23, Mrs. Enos and her daughter and daughter-in-law were shopping in Grant's department store. The store was more crowded than usual and the patrons included both adults and children. While ascending the stairway leading from the basement to the ground floor, Enos was bumped by a young girl who was running up the stairs. As a result she lost her balance and fell to the floor. Enos sued Grant. What will be the result?

5. Mick had been a customer of Kroger for several years. During this period Kroger had maintained a carry-out service for its customers. One particular day Mick was informed that no one was available to help her take groceries to her car. She then lifted a 30-pound bag, carried it outside, and fell while stepping off the sidewalk onto the parking lot pavement. She sued Kroger for the resulting injuries and won a jury verdict for $4,000. A lower appellate court upheld the judgment on the theory that a jury could find that Kroger's duty of reasonable care included assisting customers in carrying large packages of groceries. Should the judgment be sustained by the state supreme court?

6. Franc was crossing a railroad bridge on foot when she fell through a hole in the floor of the bridge due to a missing plank and sustained serious personal injuries. The gap was covered by snow and had been in the bridge for three weeks. Although the bridge was the private property of the Pennsylvania Railroad, the public had used the bridge for many years with the knowledge of the railroad. The railroad had in the past maintained the bridge, but argued that Franc was a trespasser, and as such could not recover damages. Is the railroad liable to Franc for the injuries she sustained by her fall?

7. Quinlivan parked his car in a parking lot of a supermarket, intending to make purchases in the store. The parking lot was covered with snow and ice, although snow had not fallen for several days. Quinlivan fell due to these conditions, suffering physical and mental disablement. Quinlivan alleged that the supermarket was negligent in permitting a dangerous icy condition to exist in the parking lot area. The supermarket responded by alleging that no duty was owed to Quinlivan, an invitee, with respect to hazards arising from natural accumulations of ice and snow. Who will prevail?

8. While on the premises of Griffeth Brothers Tire Company having his automobile repaired, Boggs fell and sustained injury due to a step-down between the yard and office area. Boggs sued Griffeth Brothers, alleging injury due to their failure to exercise ordinary care in keeping the premises and approaches safe. Boggs introduced evidence showing that there were two step-downs, each approximately six inches, and no warning signs. Furthermore, Boggs alleged that decals plastered on the glass door of entry interfered with the vision of one opening the door and that the colors of the floors inside the office and on the steps blended into each other. The trial court directed a verdict for Griffeth Brothers, stating that the evidence did not show any defect in the condition of the premises that would be sufficient to make Griffeth Brothers liable to Boggs for whatever injuries he had sustained. On appeal, should Boggs be granted a trial on the merits of his negligence suit?

9. Miles and his wife were watching Ace Van Lines move their furniture out. The first of two tables was removed by a process of lowering it, with the use of a rope, over the railing of the second-story porch to the ground below. This was accomplished without participation or comment by Miles. As the second table was being lowered, Miles, without comment or invitation, leaned out over the railing to help free the table from an obstacle and fell to the ground when the railing broke. The trial court jury found that both Miles and Ace Van Lines had been negligent, but that only the negligence of Ace Van Lines was the cause of Miles's injuries. Should this case be reversed?

10. Cities Service Company operated a phosphate rock mine in Florida. On December 3, 1971, a dam restraining a settling pond broke, allowing approximately one billion gallons of phosphate slimes to enter Peace River and causing a gigantic fish kill and other substantial damage. The state sued to enjoin Cities Service's activities and for compensatory damages. Cities Service defended against strict liability on the basis that this use is the natural method of mining phosphate rock and hence not ultrahazardous activity. Will this defense prevail?

Contracts

PART
TWO

The Nature and Origins
of Contracts

5

A *contract* is a *legally enforceable promise* or set of promises. However, not all promises are contracts. If Bill promises to take Mary
to the movies on Saturday night but takes Judy instead, can Mary successfully sue Bill for breaking his promise? No. If Bill buys a car from Friendly
Motors and promises to pay for it in monthly installments, can Friendly
Motors force Bill to honor his promise if he stops making payments? Yes.
What is the difference between these two promises?

Over the years the common law courts developed a number of requirements that a promise had to meet before it would be considered a contract:

1. An agreement (an *offer* and an *acceptance* of the offer)
2. voluntarily entered into
3. by parties having capacity to contract
4. supported by consideration (with some exceptions)
5. to do a legal act or acts.

In addition to these elements, the courts required *written* evidence of
some kinds of contracts. Chapters 5–12 will discuss each of these elements.
When you fully understand each element, you will be able to differentiate
a contract from an unenforceable promise.

WHY HAVE CONTRACTS?

Contracts are probably a necessary device in any kind of market economy
where goods and services are exchanged by people acting in their own

interest. People might not enter into agreements that call for some future performance unless they know some means exist (the law) to force other people to honor their promises. For example, a small, weak person might be afraid to sell a large, strong person a horse today in return for the strong person's promise to pay for the horse next month, unless the weak person knows he will have outside help to force the strong one to pay. Similarly, a weak person might not be willing to pay a strong person today for goods to be delivered next week unless the weak person knows she will have outside help getting her money back if the goods are not delivered, or if the goods delivered are not what was agreed to.

It is also true that it would probably be impossible to have an industrialized, market economy without contracts. A manufacturer would be unable to do the kind of planning necessary to run a business if he could not rely on agreements with suppliers to furnish the raw materials he needs to make the products. Similarly, a manufacturer might not be willing to commit herself to buy raw materials or hire employees if she could not rely on buyers' promises to buy her products.

It is not surprising, then, that the contract was accepted as the basis for business transactions at a very early point in history. Egyptians and Mesopotamians recognized and enforced contracts thousands of years before Christ. By 1603 the common law courts of England recognized the enforceability of simple contracts. To fully understand why our contract law took its present shape, we must look briefly at its historical roots.

HOW HAS CONTRACT LAW DEVELOPED?

Many of the rules of contract law you will study in later chapters were first created in the 18th and 19th centuries. The social conditions existing at that time played a strong role in shaping contract law.

Most contracts people entered into in the 18th century and the early 19th century fit a typical mold. People dealt with each other on a face-to-face basis; the parties often knew each other personally, or at least knew each other's reputation for fair dealing. The kinds of things people bought and sold were relatively simple and the odds were that the buyer knew enough about the purchase to make an intelligent choice.

The 19th century also saw *laissez-faire* (free market) economic theories treated as a highly important part of public policy. The courts were unwilling to interfere with peoples' private agreements or to do anything that might interfere with the country's growing industrialization. "Freedom of contract" was the rule of the day. This "hands-off" policy made contracts an ideal device for business. People in business were able to do the kinds of economic planning that increasing industrialization required. They were also able to limit or shift many of their economic risks by placing clauses in their contracts that they could be sure the courts would enforce. For example, manufacturers were commonly allowed to *disclaim* (avoid responsibility for) any liability for injuries caused by their products.

The result of these factors was what may appear to the student to be a "hard-nosed" attitude on the part of the courts. As long as a person voluntarily entered into a contract (within the broad limits discussed in Chapter 8), the courts would generally enforce it against him, even if the results were grossly unfair. It was not uncommon for courts to say things like: "It is not the business of the courts to relieve fools of the consequences of their folly." The courts were also generally unwilling to consider the argument that a party did not freely enter a contract because the other party had superior bargaining power and used that power to force the weaker party to accept "unfair" contract terms.

The Industrial Revolution that modernized America also changed many of the basic assumptions underlying contract law. The things people bought and sold became more and more complex. Buyers often had little or no knowledge about the goods they bought. People were buying products manufactured hundreds of miles from their homes, from sellers they often did not know.

An increasingly large percentage of agreements were based on "form contracts." Frequently, people did not sit down and bargain about the terms of their agreement; instead, they used a form contract written before their agreement, often doing little more than filling in the blanks. Any student who has signed a lease or bought a car on time has had experience with form contracts. Some people argued that many parts of our economy in fact had "imperfect" or "monopolistic" competition and that "free market" theories were no longer the correct basis for public policy in modern society.

The legal system began to respond to these changes in our way of life, changing contract law in the process. Many important contractual relationships that had earlier been left to private bargaining began to be controlled to some degree by legislation. Think for a minute about all the state and federal laws that govern employment contracts: minimum wages, maximum hours, workmen's compensation, unemployment and retirement benefits, and so on. The legislatures have also, for example, passed statutes that make manufacturers more responsible for the products they produce. Often, this public interference in private contracts is justified as an attempt to protect those who lack the power to protect themselves by bargaining for fair contract terms.

Many courts also began to shift their emphasis from protecting business and promoting industrialization to protecting consumers and workers. Courts today are generally willing to consider defenses based on inequality of bargaining power between the parties, and they may refuse to enforce or even rewrite such contracts to avoid injustice. Most modern courts also, for example, tend to view with great suspicion attempts by manufacturers to limit their responsibility for their products by contract. This is particularly so when the buyer is a consumer. It is probably safe to say that the trend toward more public inputs into private contracts will continue for some time to come. Despite this trend, however, the idea that a contract is an agreement freely entered into by the parties is still the basis for enforcing most private contracts today.

TYPES OF CONTRACTS

Several terms are used to describe the different kinds of contracts our legal system recognizes. These terms will be used throughout the following chapters.

Unilateral and Bilateral Contracts

Contracts are called either unilateral or bilateral depending on whether one or both of the parties made a promise. In a *unilateral contract* only *one* of the parties makes a promise. A unilateral contract may be *a promise for an act* or *an act for a promise*. For example, Mary runs an ad in the paper offering a $5 reward for the return of her lost dog, Sparky. Mary has made a promise to pay the person who performs the act of returning Sparky. On the other hand, Bill loans Frank $10 today in return for Frank's promise to pay Bill back at the end of the month. Bill has performed the act of giving Frank the money in return for Frank's promise to pay him back.

In a *bilateral contract, both* parties make a promise. For example, Sue Smith, the owner of Hi-Fi Heaven, orders 100 stereo receivers from Steve Jones, a salesman for Slick Sound Manufacturing Company. Sue has made a promise to pay for the receivers in exchange for Slick Sound's promise to deliver them. In the next chapter you will learn that unilateral contracts create some special problems in the areas of offer and acceptance. This fact causes the courts to treat a contract as bilateral whenever it is possible to do so.

Valid, Unenforceable, Voidable, and Void Contracts

A *valid contract* is one that meets all the legal requirements for a contract. Valid contracts are therefore enforceable in court.

An *unenforceable contract* is one that meets the basic legal requirements for a contract but will not be enforced due to some other legal rule. For example, in Chapter 11 we will see that the law says some kinds of contracts must be in writing to be enforceable. Contracts for the sale of real estate are one example of a contract required to be in writing. So, Bob may agree to sell his house to Mary and every basic requirement for a contract may be present (a voluntary agreement to do a legal act by parties with the capacity to contract, supported by consideration), but if the agreement is not in writing the contract will not be enforceable.

A *voidable contract* is one that may be canceled by one or both of the parties. It is enforceable against both parties unless a party with the right to cancel the contract has done so. For example, in Chapter 9 we will see that minors have the legal right to cancel their contracts. So, if Frank buys a used car from Honest Bob's Used Cars and Frank is a minor, the parties have a voidable contract. It is binding and enforceable against both parties unless Frank decides to cancel the contract.

The *void contract* lacks one or more of the basic requirements for a contract. Such an agreement has no legal force or effect. An example is an agreement to steal a car. One of the basic requirements for a valid contract is that the thing the parties have agreed to do is legal. Stealing a car is illegal; therefore, such an agreement would be considered void.

Express and Implied Contracts

A contract is *express* when the parties have directly stated its terms at the time the contract was formed. They may have done this orally or in writing. So, when Bill tells Joe: "I'll sell you my 1976 Chevy Blazer for $4,500," and Joe replies: "You've got a deal," an express contract has been created.

There are many cases, however, in which the parties have clearly reached an agreement, even though they have not expressly stated its terms. When the surrounding facts and circumstances indicate that an agreement has in fact been reached, an *implied contract* is created. Suppose you go to your dentist for treatment. Ordinarily you would not expressly state the terms of your mutual agreement beforehand, although it is clear that you do, in fact, have an agreement. A court would infer a promise on the part of your dentist to use reasonable care in treating you and a promise on your part to pay a reasonable fee for his or her services.

Executed and Executory Contracts

A contract is *executed* when all the parties have fully performed their duties under the contract. A contract is *executory* as long as it has not been fully performed.

It is possible to describe any contract by using one or more of the above terms. Consider this contract: Martha's Beauty Salon sends Hair Affair Manufacturing Company an order for ten cases of hairspray at $50 a case. Hair Affair sends Martha's an acknowledgment form accepting the order. The parties have a *valid, express, bilateral* contract. The contract will be executory until Hair Affair has delivered the goods and Martha's has paid for them.

QUASI CONTRACT

As you saw in Chapter 1, the common law as it initially developed was a fairly rigid, inflexible way of dealing with many problems. One aspect of this rigidity was that the courts insisted that all the elements of a contract be present before the courts would find a legally binding agreement between the parties. This attitude caused an injustice in some cases. Sometimes a person may have done something that benefited another person, but there are no facts from which a court could infer an agreement between the parties. In such a case the party who received the benefit may be *unjustly enriched* at the expense of the other party. This unfair result could be avoided if a court implied a promise by the benefited party to pay the reasonable value of the benefit.

Since there was no factual basis for implying a promise to pay, as we have in an implied contract case, the courts began to imply a promise to pay as a matter of law, even though the parties did not really have a contract. This idea was called *quasi contract*. It is impossible to list all the kinds of cases that may create a liability based on quasi contract. The basic idea is that quasi contract applies where one of the parties has received a benefit from the other party under circumstances that make it unfair to keep the benefit without paying for it. A person is generally not held liable under quasi contract for benefits he or she received unknowingly, or for benefits he or she reasonably believed were given as a gift.

For example, Fred's Painting Company has a contract to paint Walter's house at 525 East Third Street. Fred's painters arrive by mistake at Bob's house at 325 East Third Street and begin painting. Bob sees Fred's painters but does not say anything because his house needs painting. Bob later refuses to pay for the paint job, arguing that the parties have no contract. There are clearly no facts here to justify implying an agreement between Fred's and Bob. However, the courts would probably hold Bob liable to Fred's on a quasi contract basis. On the other hand, if Bob had come home from vacation to find his home mistakenly painted, he would not be liable to Fred's, since he did not knowingly accept the paint job.

Gebhardt Brothers, Inc. v. Brimmel
143 N.W.2d 479 (Sup. Ct. Wis. 1966)

FACTS Gebhardt had a subcontract with Semrow (a general contractor) to supply fill dirt for a construction job Semrow was doing on Brimmel's land. Brimmel paid Semrow for all the work done, but Semrow failed to pay Gebhardt. Gebhardt then sued Brimmel in quasi contract for the value of the fill dirt.

ISSUE Is Brimmel liable for the value of the fill dirt?

DECISION No. The court said that there may be circumstances when it is unjust for one party to fail to pay for the goods or services furnished by another even though there is no contract between the parties. A plaintiff must prove three things to show unjust enrichment: (1) the plaintiff conferred a benefit upon the defendant, (2) an appreciation or knowledge of the benefit by the defendant, and (3) acceptance or retention of the benefit by the defendant under circumstances that make it unfair for the defendant to keep the benefit without paying for it. Applying this test to the facts, the court held that Gebhardt had failed to prove the third element. This was so because Brimmel had already paid Semrow for fill and was therefore not unjustly enriched by it.

THE UNIFORM COMMERCIAL CODE

The Uniform Commercial Code was created by the American Law Institute and the National Conference of Commissioners on Uniform State Laws. All the states except Louisiana (which has adopted only part of the Code) have adopted the Code. The District of Columbia and the Virgin Islands have also adopted it. The Code is divided into ten articles that deal with many of the problems that might ordinarily arise in a commercial transaction. Most of these articles are discussed in Parts Three, Seven, and Eight of this book.

The drafters of the Code had several purposes in mind. The most obvious was to establish a uniform law to govern commercial transactions that often are conducted across state lines. Complete uniformity has not been achieved, however, despite the Code's widespread adoption. This is so for several reasons. Some sections of the Code were drafted with alternatives, giving adopting states two or three versions of a section to choose from. Some states later amended various sections of the Code, and some sections of the Code have been interpreted differently by different state courts.

The drafters of the Code also tried to create rules that would deal realistically with common problems that occur in everyday commercial transactions. They also tried to promote fair dealing and higher standards of behavior in the marketplace. They attempted to do this in several ways (the numbers in parentheses refer to specific Code sections):

1. Every contract and duty under the Code imposes a duty to act in *good faith* on all the parties (1–203).
2. Some sections of the Code impose a higher standard of behavior on "merchants" (defined in 2–104 [1]) than on nonmerchants.
3. The Code expressly recognizes the concept of an *unconscionable contract* (2–302), one that is grossly unfair or one-sided, and gives the courts broad powers to remedy such unfairness.
4. The Code has several sections that deal with the problems created by *form contracts* (e.g., 2–207, 2–205, 2–209 [2]).
5. The Code imposes certain standards of quality on sellers of goods as a matter of law. These are called *implied warranties* (2–314, 2–315). The Code also limits the power of the seller to contractually deny (disclaim) responsibility for his goods (2–316, 2–302).

Although there are many kinds of contracts that are not specifically covered by the Code, the Code plays an influential role in shaping other areas of law because some courts apply Code concepts by analogy to contracts not specifically covered by the Code. For example, you will see in Part Three that Article 2 of the Code applies only to contracts for the sale of "goods" (2–102 and 2–105). Contracts for the sale of real estate and contracts to provide services are not covered. In several cases, however, courts have imposed implied warranties in real estate and service situations.

QUESTIONS AND PROBLEM CASES

1. Define a contract.

2. What is the difference between a unilateral and a bilateral contract?

3. What is the difference between an unenforceable and a voidable contract?

4. Were the drafters of the Uniform Commercial Code successful in achieving total uniformity in the laws that govern commercial transactions? Explain.

states inter brl

5. Hanks was charged with burglary and filed a false statement claiming he could not afford to hire an attorney to defend him. A public defender was appointed to represent him free of charge. After the trial it was discovered that Hanks had more than $28,000 in assets. The state of Illinois sued him in quasi contract to recover the reasonable value of the legal services rendered. A trial court awarded the state a judgment for $2,000. Is this correct?

yes

knew

Creating a Contract: Offers

6

INTRODUCTION

When a dispute arises between the parties to a contract, there are two basic questions the courts often have to answer: Did the parties in fact have a contract? If they did, what are its terms? The way the court answers these questions is very important in shaping its decision.

The main thing a court looks for in deciding whether the parties entered into a contract is an *agreement*, or "meeting of the minds" between the parties. This is so because the whole of contract law is based on the idea of enforcing agreements that the parties made freely. At a very early point in the development of contract law, the courts created the basic formula for a contract:

Offer + Acceptance (and other legal requirements) = Contract

Did one of the parties indicate to the other party that he or she was willing to enter into an agreement on certain terms and conditions? Did the other party indicate that he or she was willing to agree to those terms and conditions? If so, and if the other requirements for a binding contract that will be discussed in later chapters are met, the parties have a contract.

There are two things that you should bear in mind while studying contracts. The first is that the courts do not concern themselves with what the parties *actually* (subjectively) intended, because we can never know what the parties actually intended and, after a dispute has arisen, we do not want to rely on what they say they intended. Instead, the courts look at the *objective* intent of the parties. Would a reasonable person who knew all the circumstances surrounding the agreement believe that the parties intended to enter into an agreement?

The second thing the student should bear in mind is that when courts use the words *offer* and *acceptance*, they are using them in their technical, legal sense. This can cause confusion in two ways. *Offer* and *accept* have everyday meanings that are not necessarily the same as their legal meanings. Also, the parties to a dispute may have used these words in their everyday sense, being unaware of their legal meaning. This can lead to the potentially confusing situation where a party says "I accept" but the courts find that he or she, in fact, made an "offer." Therefore, it is very important that you understand the legal meaning of *offer* and *acceptance*.

WHAT IS AN OFFER?

The question of what amounts to an offer is important for several reasons. If there is no offer, there is nothing to accept and a contract cannot be created. A person who has made an offer (the *offeror*) has given the party to whom he or she has made the offer (the *offeree*) the power to create a binding contract by accepting. It is also important to know what is included in the terms of the offer, since the offer often contains all the terms of the contract. This is so because all the offeree does in most cases is indicate acceptance of the offer.

The basic thing the courts require for the creation of an offer is a present intent to contract on the part of the offeror. When all the circumstances surrounding the parties' dealings are considered, did the offeror ever, in effect, say: "This is it, agree and we have a contract on these terms"? The two main things a court looks for in answering this question are how *definite* the supposed offer is and whether the offeror has *communicated* it to the offeree.

Definiteness

Did the offeror specifically state what he was willing to do and what he wanted the offeree to agree to do in return? If not, his behavior will probably be classed as an "invitation to offer" or an "invitation to negotiate," and will have no legal effect. If the offeror said: "If we're going to trade cars, you'll have to give me some money in addition to your car," this clearly was not an offer. The parties are still negotiating and may never reach a mutually satisfactory agreement. On the other hand, if the offeror said: "I'll trade you my car for your car and $500," this looks like an offer. If the offeree accepts, both parties are bound to a contract.

Definiteness is also important because the offer is usually the entire text of the agreement and the courts traditionally have been reluctant to enforce indefinite agreements. The terms of the offer need not be absolutely clear, but they must be clear enough so that the court can determine the parties' intent and fairly enforce the agreement.

Communication to the Offeree

An important factor in determining whether an offeror had the required intent to contract is whether she communicated her offer to the offeree. The act of communicating the offer indicates that the offeror is willing to be bound by its terms. On the other hand, an uncommunicated offer may be evidence that the offeror has not yet decided to enter into a binding agreement. For example, Bill has been discussing the possibility of selling his house to Joan. Bill tells Frank, a mutual friend, that he intends to offer the house to Joan for $35,000. Frank calls Joan and tells her of his conversation with Bill. Joan then calls Bill and says: "I accept your offer." Is this a contract? No, since Bill had not communicated his proposal to Joan, there was no offer for Joan to accept.

SPECIAL PROBLEMS WITH OFFERS

There are several common problems for students when they attempt to determine whether an offer exists. These involve situations where the courts have applied special rules to certain types of behavior, or where there are difficult problems of interpretation.

Advertisements

The courts have generally held that ads for the sale of goods at a specified price are not offers; instead, they are treated as invitations to negotiate or offer. The same rule is generally applied to catalogs, price lists, price quotations, and goods displayed in stores. This rule probably fairly reflects the intent of the sellers involved, since they probably have only a limited number of items to sell and do not intend to give everyone who sees their ad the power to bind them to a contract. It causes problems for would-be buyers, however, who may believe they have legal right to the goods they attempt to buy. In reality, such a buyer is making an offer to purchase the goods, which the seller (as offeree) is free to accept or reject. This is so because the buyer has indicated a present intent to contract on definite terms (the advertised goods and price), and there is no offer for him or her to accept.

In a few cases, however, courts have held that particular ads were offers. These cases generally involve ads that are highly specific about the goods that are offered and what is requested in return. However, it is probably accurate to say that specific terms standing alone are not enough to make an ad an offer. Most of the ads that have been treated as offers require the buyer to do something extraordinary to accept. The great potential for unfairness to the offeree in such cases is probably the true basis for the courts' holdings that ads of this sort are offers.

O'Keefe v. Lee Calan Imports, Inc.
262 N.E.2d 758 (Ct. App. Ill. 1970)

FACTS Lee Calan Imports advertised a 1964 Volvo station wagon in the *Chicago Sun-Times*. Calan told the paper to set the price at $1,795, but the paper mistakenly advertised the car at $1,095. O'Brien saw the ad, went to Calan's, and tried to buy the car for $1,095. When the mistake was discovered, Calan refused to sell the car. O'Brien filed a suit, arguing that he had accepted Calan's offer and was entitled to the car. O'Brien died and O'Keefe, the administrator of his estate, was substituted for him as the plaintiff in the lawsuit.

ISSUE Was Lee Calan's ad an offer?

DECISION No. The court said that most ads are merely invitations to negotiate, not offers, unless "special circumstances" are present. There was no "meeting of the minds" between the parties because the ad did not discuss how the automobile was equipped or what warranties would accompany its sale, and it was therefore too indefinite and incomplete to be an offer. The court pointed to an earlier case, *Johnson v. Capital City Ford*, in which a car advertisement had been held to create an offer. In that case Capital City had advertised that those purchasing a 1954 Ford could trade it in for a 1955 Ford at no additional cost. Johnson bought a 1954 Ford and Capital refused to allow him to trade. The difference between Capital City's ad and Lee Calan's, the court said, was that Capital City's ad had required "the performance of an act" (purchasing the earlier model car), while Lee Calan's ad "did not call for any performance by the plaintiff" and therefore was not an offer.

Rewards

Ads for rewards for the return of lost property, for information, or for the capture of criminals are generally held to be offers for unilateral contracts. The offeree must perform the requested act to accept—that is, return the lost property, supply the requested information, or capture the wanted criminal.

Auctions

Sellers at auctions are generally held to be making an invitation to offer. Therefore, bidders at such auctions are treated as offerors, making offers the seller is free to accept or reject. Acceptance occurs when the auctioneer strikes the goods off to the highest bidder. Only when the auction is advertised as being "without reserve" is the seller held to have made an offer to sell to the highest bidder. Section 2–328 of the Uniform Commercial Code contains the rules of law that govern an auction of goods.

Bids

The bidding process in construction work is a source of many legal disputes. People who advertise for such bids (the owner of the project or a general contractor who wants to farm out a portion of a large job to a subcontractor, for example) are generally held to have made an invitation to offer. Those who submit bids are treated as offerors. This causes particular problems in disputes between general contractors and subcontractors.

A general contractor may rely on a subcontractor's bid by using the subcontractor's figures in arriving at the total amount of his bid. Later, the subcontractor may find that the price of the materials or labor needed to do the job has risen, and he may wish to revoke the bid. Unfortunately, the subcontractor may find that he will not be allowed to revoke (see the section on estoppel later in this chapter). The subcontractor may then be especially disturbed to find that when the general contractor's bid is accepted, the general contractor does not have to award him the job. This is because the courts usually hold that the general contractor's use of the subcontractor's bid in computing his own is not an acceptance of that bid.[1]

This treatment of subcontractors is probably not so unfair as it seems at first glance. A general contractor whose bid is accepted is bound by contract to do the job at the bid price. If the subcontractor is allowed to revoke, the general contractor may not be able to get anyone else to do the subcontractor's job for the price of the subcontractor's bid. The general contractor's profit on the job will then be reduced, and she may even have to do the job at a loss. On the other hand, the subcontractor who does not get the job has only lost the cost of computing the bid, a normal business expense.

WHAT TERMS ARE INCLUDED IN OFFERS?

Once a court decides that an offer existed, it must then decide what terms were included in the offer so it can determine the terms of the parties' agreement. Another way of asking this question is to ask what the offeree agreed to. Is a person going to the movies bound by the fine print on the ticket? How about fine print or clauses on the back of a contract?

There are no easy answers to these problems. The courts have generally held that if the offeree actually reads the terms, or if a reasonable person should have been on notice of them, the offeree is bound by them.

Cutler Corp. v. Latshaw
97 A.2d 234 (Sup. Ct. Pa. 1954)

FACTS   Jennie Latshaw hired Cutler Corporation to do some repair work to her home in Philadelphia. She signed a standard form contract provided by Cutler that contained a confession of judgment clause in the fine print on its reverse side. A confession of judgment clause is an antiquated legal device (held unenforceable as contrary

---

[1] See *Southern California Acoustics Co. v. C. V. Holder, Inc.* in Chapter 7.

ISSUE | Is Jennie Latshaw bound by the confession of judgment clause?

DECISION | No. The court noted the drastic nature of a confession of judgment clause, saying that signing such a clause was "equivalent to a warrior of old entering a combat by discarding his shield and breaking his sword." There was no evidence Latshaw was aware of the clause, and "the mere physical inclusion" of the clause "in a mass of fine-type verbiage on each reverse sheet does not itself make it part of the contract."

to public policy in many states) that gives one party to the contract the power to enter a judgment against the other party if a dispute arises. Latshaw was unhappy with the work Cutler was doing, a dispute arose between the parties, and Cutler confessed judgment against her. Latshaw appealed.

A closely related problem is technical legal language on form contracts like insurance policies and loan agreements that is not truly understandable to the average person. The courts have traditionally enforced such terms on the theory that a reasonable person does not enter agreements he or she does not understand. This is probably unrealistic and may in fact encourage technically worded contracts. This unfairness is responsible for some recent arguments for legislation to ensure clearly worded consumer contracts.

Steinberg v. Chicago Medical School
371 N.E.2d 634 (Sup. Ct. Ill. 1977)

FACTS | Robert Steinberg applied for admission to the Chicago Medical School. The bulletin Steinberg received from the school said students would be selected on the basis of "scholarship, character, and motivation." Steinberg was denied admission and filed a breach of contract suit. He argued that students were in fact selected on their ability to pledge or pay large sums of money to the school.

ISSUE | Could the school be held to have contracted to judge applicants on the criteria stated in the bulletin?

DECISION | Yes. The court likened the school's bulletin to a merchant advertising goods at a fixed price. The ad is not an offer but is an invitation to offer on the terms of the ad. Here the bulletin description was an invitation to offer and Steinberg's application and payment of the application fee were an offer. Acceptance of the application and fee could be viewed as an acceptance of the offer under the criteria the school had established.

HOW LONG DO OFFERS LAST?

Once you know that an offer existed and what its terms were, you must then decide how long the offer was in effect. This is important because if an offer has been terminated for some reason, the offeree no longer has the power to create a contract by accepting. In fact, an offeree who attempts to accept after an offer has terminated is himself making an offer because he is indicating a present intent to contract on the terms of the original offer. The original offeror is free to accept or reject this new offer.

Terms of the Offer

The offer itself may include terms that limit its life. These may be specific terms like "this offer good for ten days" or "you must accept by October 4, 1978," or more general terms like "by return mail," "for immediate acceptance," or "prompt wire acceptance." Obviously, the more general terms can cause difficult problems for courts in trying to decide whether an offeree accepted in time. This is also true of more specific terms like "this offer good for ten days" if the offer does not specify whether the ten-day period begins when the offer is sent or when the offeree receives it. The courts do not agree on this point. It should be clear that wise offerors will protect themselves by being as specific as possible in stating when their offers end.

Lapse of Time

If the offer does not state a time for acceptance, it is valid for a "reasonable time," which depends on the circumstances surrounding the offer.

If an offer covers items that have rapidly changing prices, like stocks and bonds or commodities, a reasonable time may be measured in minutes. If the offer covers goods that may spoil, like produce, a reasonable time for acceptance is also fairly short. On the other hand, a reasonable time for the acceptance of an offer to sell real estate may be several days.

If the parties have dealt with each other on a regular basis, the timing of their prior dealings is highly relevant in measuring a reasonable time for acceptance.

Revocation

Offerors generally have the power to revoke their offers at any time prior to acceptance even if they have promised not to revoke for a stated period of time. However, there are several exceptions to the general rule that can take away an offeror's power to revoke.

Options

If the offeree gives the offeror something of value in exchange for a promise not to revoke the offer for a stated period of time, an option contract has been created. An *option* is a separate contract for the limited purpose of holding the offer open. The offeree, as with any other offer, is free to accept or reject the offer; he or she has simply purchased the right to accept or reject within the stated period.

Board of Control of Eastern Michigan University v. Burgess
206 N.W.2d 256 (Ct. App. Mich. 1973)

FACTS   On February 15, 1966, Burgess signed a document that appeared to grant Eastern Michigan University a 60-day option to purchase her home. The document said that Burgess had received "One and no/100 Dollar ($1.00) and other valuable consideration" in return for the option. The university admitted it had not paid Burgess anything for the agreement. On April 14, 1966, the university gave Burgess written notice that it intended to exercise the option. Burgess refused to deliver a deed on the closing date, and the university filed a lawsuit against her.

ISSUE   Was a valid option created by the agreement Burgess signed?

DECISION   No. The court of appeals held that a promise to hold an offer open must be supported by consideration to be an option. The fact that the document acknowledged receipt of consideration merely created a rebuttable presumption that consideration had, in fact, been paid. Since the university admitted it had paid nothing, no option was created.

     The basic issue, then, was whether Burgess had revoked her offer before the university's attempt to accept on April 14, 1966. The parties' testimony conflicted on this point. Burgess had testified that she had told the university's agent she would not sell at the option price within hours after signing the option, and again when he delivered the April 14, 1966, notice. The university's agent denied receiving any notice of Burgess' dissatisfaction until sometime in July. The court remanded the case so the trial court could decide who was telling the truth, noting that: "If defendant is telling the truth, she effectively revoked her offer several weeks before plaintiff accepted that offer, and no contract of sale was created. If plaintiff's agent is telling the truth, defendant's offer was still open when plaintiff accepted that offer, and an enforceable contract was created."

Estoppel

     Strictly following any legal rule can sometimes produce an unfair result, so the courts have often created exceptions to a general rule in order to avoid unfairness. One such situation occurs when the offeror makes her offer in such a way that the offeree might reasonably expect her not to revoke it. If the offeree in fact does reasonably rely on the offer in such a way that he will suffer some loss (detriment) if the offeror is allowed to revoke, a court may say she is *estopped* from revoking. This means that the court will deny the offeror the power to revoke in order to avoid unjustly injuring the offeree. The doctrine of *promissory estoppel* is usually defined as including three elements:

1. A statement calculated to produce reliance by one party.
2. Reasonable reliance on the statement by the other party.
3. Detriment (harm) to the relying party.

If any one of the three elements is missing, estoppel does not apply.

Consider the subcontractor-contractor dispute discussed earlier in the chapter. Estoppel is frequently applied to such cases. Smith Electrical Supply (a subcontractor) submits a bid of $100,000 to Evans Construction Company (a general contractor) for the electrical work in the new Acme Building. Smith's bid is the lowest Evans receives and Evans knows Smith to be a reliable firm, so Evans uses Smith's $100,000 figure in computing its bid for the total job. Due to rising costs of electric wiring and conduit, Smith decides it cannot profitably do the job and tries to revoke. Evans is awarded the contract and cannot get anyone to do the electric work for less than $120,000. Smith will be estopped from revoking. Smith knew Evans was likely to rely on its bid (in fact, it hoped Evans would). Evans relied on Smith's bid by making an offer to perform based, in part, on Smith's price. Evans will lose $20,000 if Smith is allowed to revoke.

What if Evans could get Walters Electric to do the job for $100,000? In this case estoppel would not apply since Evans suffers no harm (detriment) if Smith is allowed to revoke

Revocation of Offers for Unilateral Contracts

The general rule that the offeror can revoke at any time prior to acceptance causes special problems when the offer is for a unilateral contract. The common law traditionally held that the offeree must fully perform the requested act to accept an offer for a unilateral contract. What if the offeree intends to accept and starts to perform, but the offeror revokes before the performance is complete?

If the offeror benefited from the offeree's attempted performance, the courts will allow the offeror to revoke but require him or her to pay the offeree the reasonable value of the performance under a quasi contract theory. Suppose Bob says to Frank: "I'll give you $800 to plow my 40 acres," and Frank begins to plow, intending to accept. After Frank has plowed 15 acres, Bob says: "I've changed my mind; I revoke." Bob is allowed to revoke but is liable to Frank for the reasonable value of plowing 15 acres.

If the offeror did not benefit from the offeree's attempted performance, the courts hold that the offeree has a reasonable time to complete the performance and that the offeror cannot revoke for that reasonable time. So, if Betty offered Frank a commission for finding her a $10,000 loan at a 9 percent annual rate and Frank has begun to contact lenders about the loan, Frank will have a reasonable time to get a loan commitment. During this time Betty is not allowed to revoke. This rule prevents unfairness to Frank but may result in unfairness to Betty. If Frank's attempted performance is half-hearted or ineffective, Betty must wait for a reasonable period before making her offer to someone else.

To avoid these kinds of problems, the courts hold a contract to be bilateral whenever possible, and some courts, like the one in the next case, are developing new ways of dealing with unilateral contracts.

Sunshine v. Manos
496 S.W.2d 195 (Ct. App. Tex. 1973)

FACTS On April 12, 1972, Manos offered to pay Sunshine, a loan broker, a commission of 1 percent if Sunshine could get Manos a mortgage loan on specified terms and conditions. Sunshine began to contact lenders, trying to get the loan. On April 18, 1972, Sunshine called Manos to tell him that he thought he could get a loan on suitable terms. Manos told Sunshine to quit trying to get the loan and, on the following day, sent him a letter saying the same thing.

ISSUE Could Manos legally revoke his offer?

DECISION No. The court noted that Manos's offer proposed the creation of a unilateral contract. The court then said that the central issue in the case was "whether the acts and conduct of Sunshine constituted part performance amounting to an acceptance of the offer and a sufficient consideration to make the offer irrevocable, or turn it into a bilateral contract." Applying principles previously applied only to real estate brokerage contracts, the court held that Sunshine had expended enough time and effort to make a unilateral contract binding and irrevocable. Therefore, the court held that "the unilateral offer in this instance ripened into a binding contract."

The Effectiveness of Revocations

Difficult problems of timing can result when an offeror is trying to revoke and an offeree is attempting to accept. The general rule is that a revocation is not effective until it is *actually received* by the offeree. So, if the offeree accepts before he or she has received a mailed revocation, a contract results. A few states hold that a revocation is effective when it is sent, however.

A major exception to the general rule involves offers made to the general public in newspapers and on radio and television. Since it would be impossible in most cases to reach every offeree with a revocation, the courts have held that a revocation made in the same manner as the offer is effective when published without proof of communication to the offeree.

Rejection

An offer is terminated when it is rejected by the offeree. An offeree may *expressly reject* an offer by stating that he will not accept it or by giving some other indication that he does not intend to accept the offer.

An offeree may *impliedly reject* an offer by making a *counteroffer*. Any attempt by the offeree to change the terms of the offer or to add new terms to the offer is treated as a counteroffer. This is so because the common law required that the acceptance be the "mirror image" of the offer. If an offeree merely asks about the terms of the offer without indicating a rejection of it (an *inquiry regarding terms*) or accepts but complains about the terms (a *grumbling acceptance*), a rejection is not implied. Determining whether an offeree has made a counteroffer, an inquiry regarding terms, or a grumbling acceptance is sometimes a difficult matter, to be decided on the facts of each case.

The general rule on effectiveness of rejections is that rejections, like revocations, must be actually received by the offeror to be effective. This means that an offeree who has mailed a rejection can change her mind and accept if she communicates her acceptance to the offeror before the rejection arrives.

Jaybe Construction Co. v. Beco, Inc.
216 A.2d 208 (Ct. App. Conn. 1965)

FACTS Jaybe (a general contractor) submitted a bid to the state of Connecticut for a job renovating a state school. Jaybe used a bid submitted by Beco (a subcontractor bidding on certain plumbing equipment needed for the renovation) in computing the amount of its bid. Jaybe received the contract from the state and called Beco on the phone to tell Beco that Jaybe had gotten the contract and that it had used Beco's $14,450 bid. Jaybe stated that a formal contract would be sent for Beco's signature, and requested that Beco "shave" its bid if possible. Beco refused to perform at the quoted price and Jaybe had to pay another subcontractor $15,450 to supply the needed equipment. Jaybe sued for $1,000 damages.

ISSUE Was Jaybe's request that Beco "shave" its bid a counteroffer?

DECISION No. The court held that Beco's bid was an offer, not merely a price quote, and noted that when Jaybe used Beco's figure in computing its own bid, it bound itself to perform in reliance in Beco's price. Beco was bound to realize the substantial possibility that its bid would be the lowest and that it would be included by Jaybe in its bid. Jaybe's phone call was an acceptance of Beco's offer and Jaybe's request that Beco "shave" its bid was an inquiry regarding terms, which did not amount to a rejection.

Death or Insanity of Either Party

The death or insanity of either party to an offer automatically (without notice) terminates the offer. This is so because no "meeting of the minds" is possible when one of the parties has died or become insane.

Destruction of Subject Matter

If the subject matter of a proposed contract is destroyed without the knowledge or fault of either party, after the making of an offer but before its acceptance, the offer is terminated. So, if Joan offers to sell Ralph a stack of hay but lightning destroys the hay before Ralph accepts, the offer was terminated when the hay burned.

Intervening Illegality

If the performance of a proposed contract becomes illegal after the offer is made but before it is accepted, the offer is terminated. So, if Johnson Farms has offered to sell its wheat crop to an agent of the Soviet

Union, but two days later, before Johnson's offer has been accepted, Congress places an embargo on all grain sales to the Soviet Union, the offer is terminated by the embargo.

QUESTIONS AND PROBLEM CASES

1. What is the primary thing a court will look for in determining whether a party made an offer?

2. What is the general rule concerning offerors' power to revoke their offers?

3. What is the legal effect on an offer of the death of the offeror?

4. On Thursday, Surplus Store published the following advertisement in the newspaper: "Saturday 9 A.M. Sharp—3 Brand New Fur Coats—Worth to $100—First Come, First Served—$1 Each." The following Thursday, Surplus Store again published an advertisement in the same paper as follows: "Saturday 9 A.M.—2 Brand New Pastel Mink 3-Skin Scarfs—Selling for $89.50—Out they go—Saturday Each . . . $1—1 Black Lapin Stole—Beautiful, worth $139.50 . . . $1—First Come, First Served." On each Saturday following publication Lefkowitz was the first one to present himself at Surplus Store and attempt to buy the advertised items. On both occasions, Surplus refused to sell, stating on the first occasion that by a "house rule" the offer was intended for women only, and on the second that Lefkowitz knew Surplus's house rules. Lefkowitz sued Surplus for breach of contract. Is Surplus entitled to a judgment in its favor?

5. Giarraputo gave the Willmotts a six-month option to buy property. The option agreement described the property, the price, and the amount of the purchase-money mortgage, but the mortgage terms provided that "the payment of interest and amortization of principal shall be mutually agreed upon at the time of entering into a more formal contract." When the Willmotts elected to exercise the option, Giarraputo's lawyer submitted a contract to them, which they declined to sign because it did not contain a prepayment term. Their lawyer then modified the contract by inserting a prepayment term, and they signed and returned it to Giarraputo, who refused to sign the modified contract. The Willmotts then filed suit against Giarraputo. Should they win?

6. Wescoat, for a valuable consideration, gave Ryder an option to purchase a 120-acre farm upon which Wescoat had an option. Ryder's option was to expire on September 1; but on August 20, Ryder told Wescoat that he (Ryder) was going to "pass" on the option. Wescoat then talked to a bank about financing so that he could exercise his option. Wescoat also talked to a bulldozer operator about doing some work on the farm and investigated the possibility of getting some liming done. On August 30 Ryder offered Wescoat a signed agreement, picking up Ryder's option along with the down payment as originally agreed. Wescoat refused to sign the agreement or accept the money. Can Ryder pick up the option after once passing it?

7. Ramsey offered to sell certain real estate to Herndon and gave him until January 15, 1965, to accept the offer. He knew that Herndon was attempting to arrange a loan so that he could purchase the property, but Herndon did not complete the arrangements for his loan by January 15, and Ramsey sold the property to Armstrong. Herndon completed the arrangements for his loan on January 17, 1965, and tendered performance to Ramsey, who then informed him of the sale to Armstrong. Herndon brought suit against Ramsey for damages for breach of contract. Is Herndon entitled to a judgment?

8. Erickson offered to sell a building to Podnay. The offer was "a continuing option to purchase the building for the consideration of

$20,000 in cash." Podnay, intending to accept the offer, wrote Erickson: "Notice is hereby given that I accept your offer to purchase your property for $20,000 cash. Will you please furnish me with abstract brought down to date so that I may have the title examined before completing the transaction and paying the money?" Was this an unconditional acceptance of the offer?

9. Beach offered to contribute $2,000 to a church building fund on condition that the church first raise $8,000. Before the church had raised $8,000, Beach was adjudged insane and committed to an asylum. Later the church raised $8,000, but the conservator of Beach's estate refused to pay the promised $2,000. The church sued to recover a judgment for $2,000. Is the church entitled to a judgment?

10. On September 21, 1942, Gentry executed to New Headley Tobacco Warehouse Company (Warehouse Co.) a lease of property in Lexington for a term of 21 years and 6 months. The lease contained no provision for renewal or extension. On March 24, 1952, Gentry addressed the following letter to Warehouse Co.

   In the event you build within the next five years (from March 1, 1952) an addition to your warehouse at cost of not less than $25,000.00 on the property you have under lease from me, I agree,

   First, to extend your present lease so you will have a total term of twenty-two years (22 years) from March 1 of the year the addition is built.

   Second, the extended term of lease shall carry a net rental to me of Sixteen Hundred Dollars ($1,600.00) per annum instead of the present net rental of Twelve Hundred Dollars per annum.

   Third, in all other respects the terms and conditions of the extended lease shall be the same as the present lease.

Warehouse Co. had not made any response or started construction of the building before Gentry died on September 29, 1955. On April 16, 1956, Warehouse Co. communicated its acceptance of Gentry's offer to the executor of Gentry's estate. The executor refused to extend the lease, and Warehouse Co. brought an action to force the executor to extend the lease. Does Warehouse have a lease?

11. On December 15, Patrick wrote Kleine concerning a lot owned by her: "If you have not sold, I, of course, am the logical purchaser, as it is worth more to me than anybody else. . . . I hope I shall have the pleasure of hearing from you shortly." On December 16, Kleine acknowledged Patrick's letter and wrote: "If you should be interested in this (my lot) would be glad to hear from you. Size of lot 20 × 100, Price $1,000 (one-thousand dollars)." The next day, the following letter was written to Kleine by Patrick: "Enclosed you will find contracts in the usual form and also my check for $100 as an evidence of good faith, and will you please sign and return one copy to me, so that the title company can institute search?" On December 23, Kleine returned the contract and check and advised Patrick that the lot had been sold. Patrick filed suit against Kleine. Can Patrick get the property?

Creating a Contract: Acceptances

7

WHAT IS AN ACCEPTANCE?

Once the court has found that one of the parties to a dispute made an *offer*, the next thing it looks for to determine whether a contract resulted is whether the offeree *accepted* the offer. The court looks for the same present intent to contract on the part of the offeree that it earlier looked for on the part of the offeror. When all the circumstances surrounding the parties' dealings with each other are considered, did the offeree ever, in effect, say: "I'm willing to enter into a binding contract on the terms of your offer?" If so, the offer has been accepted.

The offeree may indicate assent expressly or impliedly. The offeree must, however, accept the offer on the offeror's terms. As you saw in the preceding chapter, any attempt by the offeree to materially alter the terms of the offer is treated as a counteroffer and terminates the offer. What is necessary for acceptance depends to some extent on the type of contract offered.

Accepting an Offer for a Unilateral Contract

As you saw in Chapter 5, a unilateral contract is a promise for an act or an act for a promise. To accept an offer to enter into such a contract, the offeree must perform the requested act or make the requested promise. So, if Mary tells Sue: "I'll give you $100 (the promise) if you find my lost dog Sparky (the requested act)" Sue must find the dog to accept Mary's offer. If Bill says to Frank: "I'll loan you $100 today (the act) if you'll pay me back $102 next Friday (the requested promise)" and Frank takes the money, he has accepted Bill's offer and is bound to pay him $102 on Friday.

Accepting an Offer for a Bilateral Contract

The courts, if possible, interpret an offer as proposing a bilateral contract. A bilateral contract is a promise for a promise, and the offeree must make the promise requested in the offer. So, if Tom hands Betty a detailed offer for the purchase of Betty's house and Betty signs the offer without changing any of its terms, both parties are bound on the terms of the offer. Betty has promised to deliver a deed on the agreed upon closing date in exchange for Tom's promise to pay the agreed upon price on that date.

Reilly v. Rogers Park Prudential Savings & Loan Association
377 N.E.2d 1135 (Ct. App. Ill. 1978)

FACTS
The Reillys intended to purchase real estate from the Bisluks. The Reillys applied for a first-mortgage loan from Rogers Park, filling out Rogers Park's printed loan application form. The form provided, among other things, that a service charge of $2,310 would be due if Rogers Park gave the Reillys a loan commitment and the Reillys did not complete the loan within 30 days. The sale of the real estate was never completed. The Reillys sued Rogers Park for the return of a $500 loan standby fee minus any actual expenses Rogers Park incurred. Rogers Park counterclaimed, arguing that it was entitled to the $2,310 service charge less the $500 it had received from the Reillys.

ISSUE
Is Rogers Park entitled to the service charge?

DECISION
Yes. The court held that the loan agreement the Reillys signed was an offer for a bilateral contract that Rogers Park had accepted by issuing a loan commitment. The Reillys had made a promise to pay the service charge in exchange for Rogers Park's promise to commit a specified sum of money for the Reillys use for a specified time. When Reilly breached the agreement to borrow the money thus committed, Rogers Park was entitled to demand payment of the service charge.

An offeree may expressly accept the offer, as Betty did in the preceding example, or may impliedly accept by doing something that objectively indicates agreement. For example, James, a farmer, leaves three bushels of tomatoes with Roger, the owner of a grocery store. James says: "Look these over. If you want them, they're $3 a bushel." Roger sells the tomatoes to his customers. By treating them as if he owned them, he has impliedly accepted James's offer.

> ### *Chase Manhattan Bank v. Hobbs*
> ### 405 N.Y.S.2d 967 (Civ. Ct. N.Y. City 1978)
>
> **FACTS**   Chase Manhattan issued several credit cards to Hobbs. Each card was accompanied by a "retail installment credit agreement" executed by the bank that stated that the agreement would become effective when the cardholder signed a sales slip evidencing a purchase and that the cardholder was liable for attorney's fees of up to 20 percent of any past due amount referred to any attorney for collection. Hobbs used the cards to make $1,861.74 in purchases he never paid for. The bank sued for that amount, plus $372.34 in attorney's fees. Hobbs argued he had no agreement with the bank obligating him to pay attorney's fees.
>
> **ISSUE**   Is Hobbs liable for attorney's fees?
>
> **DECISION**   Yes. The court held that when the bank issued the cards to Hobbs, it had made an offer to do business under the terms of the accompanying "retail installment credit agreement." Therefore, the court held that Hobbs's use of the credit cards issued to him by Chase Manhattan was an implied acceptance of the credit agreement and all the terms it contained. The court entered a judgment for the bank in the amount of $2,234.08.

Silence as Acceptance

Since the basis of contract law is the voluntary agreement of the parties, the law generally requires some affirmative indication of assent from offerees before it binds them to the terms of their offers. This generally means that an offeror is not allowed to word his or her offer so that the offeree must act to avoid being bound to a contract. An offer that said: "If you do not object within ten days, we have a contract" imposes no legal duty on the offeree to respond. It also means that mere silence on the part of the offeree is generally not acceptance.

On the other hand, you must always bear in mind that the ultimate question of the courts in acceptance cases is: Did the offeree objectively indicate an intent to be bound by the terms of the offer? Sometimes the circumstances of the case impose on the offeree a duty to reject an offer or be bound by it. In such a case the offeree's silence constitutes an acceptance and a contract is created. If the parties have dealt with each other before and silence signaled acceptance in their prior dealings, the offeree who remains silent in the face of an offer may be held to have accepted.

Return to the example of the farmer and the grocer. Assume that for the last two years James has regularly sent Roger certain produce items and Roger always promptly returned those items he did not want. James sends Roger ten bushels of green beans and Roger does not return them. At the end of the month, as is his usual practice, James bills Roger for the beans. Roger sends back the bill, saying: "I don't want the beans; come to the store and pick them up." Was there a contract? Most courts would probably say that, due to the prior dealings between the parties, Roger accepted the beans by failing to reject them. A similar situation could arise due to trade usage, where the parties are both members of a trade in which failure to reject promptly customarily indicates acceptance.

Southern California Acoustics Co. v. C. V. Holder, Inc.
79 Cal. Rptr. 319 (Sup. Ct. Cal. 1969)

FACTS Southern California Acoustics, a subcontractor, submitted a bid to C. V. Holder, a general contractor, for part of a public construction job Holder was bidding on. Holder submitted a bid on the project and listed Southern California as the acoustical tile subcontractor (a California statute requires general contractors to list all subcontractors who would perform work on the project valued over one half of 1 percent of the total bid). A local trade newspaper reported that Holder had been awarded the job and included Southern California's name as a subcontractor listed in Holder's bid. Southern read the report and refrained from bidding on other jobs to remain within its bonding limits. Holder later got permission from the contracting authority to substitute another subcontractor for Southern California on the grounds that Southern had been listed by mistake. Southern sued, arguing breach of contract.

ISSUE Did Holder have a duty to award the subcontract to Southern?

DECISION No. The court held that there was *no contract* between the parties, since Holder never accepted Southern's offer. Silence in the face of an offer is not an acceptance unless there is a relationship between the parties or a previous course of dealing pursuant to which silence would be understood as acceptance. The court further held that Holder had not accepted the bid by using it in presenting its own bid and that listing Southern as a subcontractor he intended to use was also not an acceptance, since it was done in response to a statutory command. Estoppel was also not available to Southern, the court held, since Holder had made no *promise* on which Southern could rely.

Who Can Accept an Offer?

The only person with the legal power to accept an offer and create a contract is the original offeree. An attempt to accept by anyone other than the offeree is, therefore, treated as a legal *offer*, since the party attempting to accept is indicating a willingness to contract on the terms of the original offer. The original offeror is free to accept or reject this new offer. For example, Mary offers to sell her business to Jane. Jane tells Mike about the offer and Mike sends Mary a letter attempting to accept her offer. No contract is created; since Mike is not the offeree, he has merely made an offer that Mary is free to accept or reject.

Acceptance When a Writing Is Anticipated

Often the parties who are negotiating a contract prepare a written draft of the agreement for both parties to sign. This is a good idea because then there is written evidence of the terms of their agreement if a dispute arises at a later date. If a dispute arises before the writing is signed, however, there may be a question about when or whether the parties in fact reached agreement. One of the parties may want to back out and argue that the parties did not intend a contract to result until the writing was signed. The other party may argue that a contract was created before the writing was signed and that the writing was merely intended to record on paper the agreement the parties had already reached.

The courts determine the intent of the parties on this point by applying the objective test of what a reasonable person familiar with the circumstances would be justified in believing the parties intended. If it appears that the parties concluded their negotiations and reached agreement on all the material aspects of the transaction, the courts will probably conclude that a contract resulted at the time when agreement was reached. The failure of the parties to sign the writing is therefore unimportant. If, on the other hand, it appears that the parties were still in the process of negotiation at the time the dispute arose, the courts will probably find no contract was created. The same would be true when the parties have clearly indicated an intent not to be bound until both sign the writing.

COMMUNICATION OF ACCEPTANCE

To accept an offer for some unilateral contracts (the promise for an act type), the offeree must perform the act requested by the offeror. When the act is completed, the contract is created. Notice of this type of acceptance is not necessary for the creation of the contract unless the offer specifically requires notice. In order to accept offers for other unilateral contracts (the act for a promise type) and all bilateral contracts, however, the offeree must make the requested promise. The general rule is that such promises must be communicated in order to be effective and create a contract.

Manner of Communication

The offeror may specify *(stipulate)* in the offer the time, place, or method of communicating acceptance. In such a case the offeree must comply fully with the offeror's stipulations. Any deviation makes the attempt to accept ineffective.

Town of Lindsay v. Cooke County Electric Cooperative
502 S.W.2d 117 (Sup. Ct. Tex. 1973)

FACTS Lindsay, Texas, was incorporated as a town in 1959. The cooperative had been serving the area since 1938, and submitted to the town council a proposed ordinance granting the cooperative a 50-year franchise to provide electric power to the town. The council enacted the ordinance on March 24, 1960. The final section of the ordinance required the cooperative to accept the franchise in writing within 30 days after the passage of the ordinance and provided that the ordinance would not be effective until such acceptance. Shortly after the ordinance was passed, the cooperative gave the town a check for 2 percent of its gross profits on the sale of electricity within the corporate limits for the previous year as required by the ordinance. The board of directors of the cooperative unanimously approved the franchise and directed its attorney to file the formal written acceptance, but he failed to do so. After the 30-day period expired, the town refunded the amount it received for gross profits and repealed the ordinance. Under Texas law, the cooperative was entitled to continue its operations for ten years after the town's incorporation without a franchise. When the ten-year period had passed, the town filed suit to force the cooperative to remove its poles and lines.

ISSUE   Did the cooperative effectively accept the franchise?

DECISION   No. The court said: "Where, as here an offer prescribes the time and manner of acceptance, its terms in this respect must be complied with to create a contract. The use of a different method of acceptance by the offeree will not be effectual unless the original offeror thereafter manifests his assent to the other party." The court went on to say that if the ordinance had not required written acceptance, the cooperative's payment of the gross receipts tax might have been an implied acceptance of the franchise. The court found nothing in the facts of the case to indicate the town agreed to the cooperative's attempt to accept by paying the tax.

If the offer merely suggests a method or place of communication, or is silent on these points, the offeree may accept within a reasonable time by any reasonable means of communication.

When Is Acceptance Communicated?

When acceptance is effective is critically important in some contract cases. The offeror has the power to revoke the offer at any time before acceptance. The offeror may be seeking to revoke an offer that the offeree is desperately trying to accept. A mailed or telegraphed acceptance may get lost and never be actually received by the offeror. The time limit for accepting the offer may be rapidly approaching. Was the offer accepted before a revocation was received or before the offer expired? Does a lost acceptance create a contract when it is dispatched, or is it totally ineffective?

If the parties are dealing face to face or the offeree is accepting by telephone, these problems are minimized. As soon as the offeree has said: "I accept," or words to that effect, a contract is created (assuming the offer is still in existence). For example, Mary offered to sell Chuck her 1965 Mustang for $500. While talking on the phone to Bruce, she mentions her offer. Bruce tells her that old Mustangs are in big demand and her car is worth at least $1,500. When she hangs up the phone she looks out the window and sees Chuck walking up her driveway. She opens the window and yells: "I revoke!" The startled Chuck then yells: "I accept!"

Is there a contract? Clearly not, since Mary revoked her offer before Chuck accepted.

Problems with the timing of acceptances multiply when the offeree is using a means of communication that creates a time lag between dispatching the acceptance and its actual receipt by the offeror. The offeror can minimize these problems since he or she has the power to control the conditions under which the offer can be accepted. The offeror need only state in the offer that he or she must *actually receive* the acceptance for it to be effective. This is clearly the best thing for an offeror to do since it affords the offeror the maximum amount of protection. It gives the offeror the most time to revoke and assures that he or she will never be bound to a contract by an acceptance that is not received.

The offeror who does not use the power to require actual receipt of the acceptance will find that the law has developed rules that make some acceptances effective at the moment they are dispatched, regardless of whether the offeror ever actually receives them. These rules generally apply when the offeror has made the offer under circumstances that might reasonably lead the offeree to believe that acceptance by some means other than telephone or face-to-face communication is acceptable.

Authorized Means of Communication

As a general rule, an acceptance is effective *when dispatched* (delivered to the communicating agency) if the offeree uses the *authorized means* of communication. The offeror may expressly authorize a particular means of communication by saying, in effect: "You may accept by mail (telegram, etc.)." In such a case, a contract is created at the moment the acceptance was mailed, even if it was lost and the offeror never received it. Any attempt by the offeror to revoke after the letter was mailed (for example, by a letter of revocation mailed before the acceptance but received after it was mailed) would be ineffective.

A given means of communication may also be impliedly authorized in one of two ways. First, if the offer or circumstances do not indicate otherwise, the means the offeror used to communicate the offer is the impliedly authorized means for accepting. So, mailed offers impliedly authorize mailed acceptances, telegraphed offers impliedly authorize telegraphed acceptances, and so on. Trade usage may also impliedly authorize a given means of acceptance. If both the parties are members of a trade in which acceptances are customarily made by a particular means of communication, the courts assume the offeree is impliedly authorized to accept by that means unless the offer indicates to the contrary.

If an authorized means of acceptance is expressly or impliedly present, any attempt by the offeree to accept by a *nonauthorized means* is not effective until the acceptance is *actually received* by the offeror. The following example illustrates these principles: On May 1, 1979, Bob received a telegram from Ralph offering to build Bob a resort cottage for $50,000. On May 5, 1979, at 10:00 A.M. Ralph sends Bob a telegram attempting to revoke the offer. At 11:00 A.M. on the same day, Bob mails Ralph a letter attempting to accept the offer. At 11:30 A.M. Bob receives Ralph's revocation. Do the parties have a contract? The answer depends on several factors:

1. Assume Ralph's telegraphed offer said: "Acceptance by mail is advisable." If so, the parties have a contract because Ralph expressly authorized acceptance by mail. Therefore Bob's mailed acceptance would be effective when dispatched at 11:00 A.M. and a contract would be created at that time. Ralph's revocation would be ineffective, since it was not actually received (as revocations must be) before the contract was created.

2. Assume Ralph's offer was silent on the question of what means Bob could use to accept. If so, the parties would not have a contract because the impliedly authorized means of communication in this instance was telegram (the means Ralph used to communicate the offer). Bob attempted to accept by a nonauthorized means (mail), so his acceptance would not be effective until Ralph actually received it. Ralph, however, has effectively revoked the offer before receiving Bob's acceptance.

3. Assume Bob and Ralph are both construction contractors and the custom in the construction business is to offer by telegram and accept by mail. In this instance the parties would have a contract because Bob used the means of communication impliedly authorized by trade usage. His acceptance would be effective when mailed, creating a contract before Ralph's revocation was received.

Pribil v. Ruther
262 N.W.2d 460 (Sup. Ct. Neb. 1978)

FACTS   On April 12, 1976, Lawrence Pribil made a written offer to purchase Bertha Ruther's land. Bertha and her husband signed the owners' acceptance blanks in the offer and handed it to their real estate broker, John Thor. Thor asked his secretary to send a copy of the agreement to Pribil, which she did by a letter dated April 14, 1976, and postmarked "April 15, 1976, P.M." Pribil received the letter on April 16, 1976. Bertha Ruther became dissatisfied with the transaction the day after she signed the acceptance when she found out a test well had been drilled on the property at Pribil's request. She also learned that the driller had estimated the well would produce 500 to 800 gallons of water a minute. She testified that on April 13, 1976, she called Pribil's home and told his wife she would not sell the property. Pribil's wife said the conversation did not occur until ten days later. Ruther also testified that she called Thor on April 14, 1976, and told him she was going to "terminate the contract." Thor said this took place on the morning of April 15, 1976, and that he immediately called Pribil and told him the deal was off. Pribil sued for breach of contract.

ISSUE   Did Ruther effectively reject Pribil's offer before her acceptance was communicated to him?

> **DECISION**   Yes. The court held that Ruther's signing of the acceptance did not make the contract effective, since there had been no communication of the acceptance to Pribil. Communication generally requires some irrevocable element such as depositing the acceptance in the mail so that it is placed beyond the power or control of the sender. Delivery of the signed acceptance to Thor was not delivery to Pribil since Thor was Ruther's agent and the acceptance was therefore not beyond her control. The court noted that the deposit of the acceptance in the mail could satisfy the requirement that the acceptance be communicated, but concluded that: "If we assume that transmission by mail was authorized in this case, there is no evidence to show that the acceptance was deposited in the mail before the defendant's call to Thor, and Thor's call to the plaintiff notifying him that the defendant had rejected his offer."

Stipulated Means of Communication

Some courts have distinguished a *stipulated* means of communication from an *authorized* means. The offeror stipulates a given means of communication when the offer says, in effect: "You must accept by mail (telegram, etc.)." If the offeree uses the stipulated means, the acceptance is effective upon dispatch. If the offeree attempts to use some nonstipulated means to accept, however, the attempted acceptance will never be effective to create a contract and might arguably be considered a counteroffer (since it contradicts a term in the offer).

QUESTIONS AND PROBLEM CASES

1. How must an offeree accept an offer for a unilateral contract?

2. Can an offeree's silence ever be acceptance?

3. What is the effect of using a nonauthorized means of communication in attempting to accept an offer?

4. Chalkley Metals Company had contracted to supply the U.S. Navy with 500,000 pounds of copper ingot. Because the Navy needed more copper, Hoover, a Navy procurement officer, telephoned Chalkley and inquired whether Chalkley could supply another 600,000 pounds of copper. Hoover and Chalkley discussed the terms of the new agreement, and Hoover said, "It's practically in the bag, but I'll need formal approval from the top brass. I seldom get turned down on contracts like this." Chalkley purchased 600,000 pounds of copper from primary sources and then learned that Hoover's agreement had been unacceptable to the Navy. After the new copper was sold at less than the Hoover agreement anticipated, Chalkley sued for breach of contract to recover the balance. The Navy claimed that there was no new contract. Is the Navy correct?

5. The Rio Grande Pickle Co. offered Fujimoto an employment contract under which he would receive a bonus of 10 percent of the company's profits for each fiscal year. The written offer was made in order to prevent Fujimoto from terminating his employment with the company. Fujimoto signed the contract and continued to work for the company for another 14 months, but he failed to return the contract to the company. The company

argued that by his failure to return the contract, Fujimoto had failed to accept the offer. Can Fujimoto bind the company to the terms of the contract?

6. Dohman offered his residence for sale. Sullivan was interested and offered to buy the property for $10,250 cash. Dohman was in Florida and negotiations were carried on by letter and telegrams. When negotiations were completed, Dohman sent his broker a contract embodying the terms agreed upon. Sullivan signed the contract and it was returned to Dohman for his signature. Dohman refused to sign and refused to convey the residence to Sullivan. Sullivan brought suit asking specific performance of the contract. Dohman set up a defense that he had not signed the formal contract. Is the defense good?

7. Mr. and Mrs. Colburn filed suit against Mid-States Homes, Inc., to restrain a mortgage foreclosure sale of their property. The Colburns argued that the mortgage was "null, void, and of no effect" because they never realized at the time of signing that they were signing a mortgage document. The signatures were properly notarized, and no fraud was alleged. Assuming the Colburns' ignorance about the mortgage was correct, does Mid-State hold a valid mortgage?

8. Swingle was vice president of a Tucson Savings and Loan Association. Myerson, while lunching with Swingle, remarked that it was too bad that Swingle's firm was not interested in buying another savings and loan company that he knew was available for acquisition. Swingle then told Myerson that although his firm would not be interested, he was. Later, he told Myerson that he would consider purchasing the stock of the other savings and loan company if a Tucson branch could be established and if he could own 51 percent of its stock. Myerson then put Swingle in contact with the savings and loan company and mentioned that he expected to be compensated for his efforts if the transaction was effected. Swingle bought the company, but refused to pay Myerson. Can Myerson recover a "finder's fee" against Swingle?

9. James obtained a contract to lay sewer lines. He then subcontracted to Price the related paving work. Price wrote James stating the terms of the subcontract. James, after some delay, said he would not accept these terms and wrote new ones which he gave to Price. Price said that he could not accept James's terms, but that he would attach a supplement and sign James's terms with the supplement. The supplement provided that James would pay Price for any repair due to trench settlement. James received the signed terms and supplement but never indicated his acceptance of the supplement. Price proceeded with the work and incurred additional costs for repaving the subsequent settlement from tamped trenches. Price sued James for this cost and won a judgment. Should the judgment be upheld on appeal?

10. Brooks hired Conkey to construct an apartment building according to the specifications set forth by Ratner, his architect. Brooks had given Ratner the authority to change the plans of construction and to grant extensions in completion deadlines, limited only by Brooks's "express disapproval." When the apartment building was not completed according to schedule, Brooks sued Conkey for damages. In his defense, Conkey stated that on several occasions he had requested that Ratner give him an extension of time and that Ratner had not replied but had encouraged him to continue work. Conkey said he had relied on Ratner's acquiescence since Brooks had made no express disapproval. Is this a good defense?

11. Duckett had an automobile insurance policy with Reserve Insurance Company, whose agent was Davis. In accordance with the usual practice, Davis sent Duckett a letter 30 days prior to the expiration of the Reserve policy with a request for payment of a renewal premium, enclosing self-addressed envelopes for Duckett's use in making payment. Duckett was uncertain about the exact time he mailed the money order for the premium, but he said that he had done so "four or five days" before the expiration date. September 6 was the policy expiration date and on September 7 Duckett had an accident. On September 8 a policy

identical with the original one was issued to Duckett, marked "renewal." Reserve Insurance Company refused to pay Duckett's accident claim, alleging that his coverage was nonexistent at the time of the accident. Duckett sued, arguing that the renewal notice from Davis was an offer from Reserve that he had accepted by paying the renewal premium, which gave rise to a binding contract between Reserve and Duckett to issue an insurance policy. Was the offer properly accepted?

Voluntary Consent

8

INTRODUCTION

The Need for Real Consent

Even if the facts and circumstances surrounding a case indicate that the parties reached an agreement, that agreement must be *voluntary* to be enforceable. This is so because the idea that a contract is a voluntary agreement between the parties is the basis of contract law. The common law came to recognize several kinds of behavior that could operate to take away a person's ability to freely enter into a contract: misrepresentation, fraud, duress, and undue influence. The courts also came to recognize that a mistake of fact on the part of one or both of the parties could sometimes prevent a true agreement from being reached.

The Parties' Duty of Care

People who enter into contracts are required to exercise reasonable caution and judgment. The rules requiring voluntary consent are designed to protect a party to a contract from innocent errors on his or her own part and from unacceptable behavior by the other party to the agreement. A person should use reasonable care to discover everything relevant to the contract he or she is about to enter. Rarely do the courts allow a party to avoid responsibility for a carelessly made promise.

The Remedy

Contracts entered into as a result of misrepresentation, fraud, duress, undue influence, and mistake are *voidable*. The injured party (or parties) may *rescind* (cancel) the contract. The injured person returns what he or she has received and recovers what he or she has given under the contract. If no performance has yet been rendered when the grounds for rescission are discovered, the injured party may notify the other party that he or she *disaffirms* (denies the validity of) the contract. If the other party sues for breach of contract, the injured party can use lack of voluntary consent as a defense.

Ratification

Those who discover that they have been the victim of misrepresentation, fraud, duress, undue influence, or mistake must act promptly to rescind or disaffirm their contracts. The person who waits for an unreasonable time after discovery to complain may be held to have *ratified* the contract and lose the power to rescind. The idea behind the doctrine of ratification is simple: One who waits too long to complain has indicated satisfaction with the agreement despite the initial lack of true consent.

MISREPRESENTATION

The basic idea of misrepresentation is that one of the parties to a contract created in the mind of the other party a mistaken impression about an important fact or facts about the subject of the contract. Acting in reliance upon this mistaken belief, the victimized party entered into a contract he or she would not otherwise have entered if the full truth had been known. The elements of *misrepresentation* are ordinarily given as: *misrepresentation* of a *material fact justifiably relied upon* to the *detriment* of (causing harm to) the person relying.

Knowledge of Falsity

You should first note that none of the elements listed above requires any proof that persons guilty of the misrepresentation know that their statement is untrue. Misrepresentation can result from an honest mistake or negligence on the part of the misrepresenter. This is so because of the long-standing equitable principle that one who makes a statement bears the risk of its truth.

Materiality

A *material fact* is one that would contribute to a reasonable person's decision to enter the contract. Materiality is determined by the circumstances of each particular case. For example, assume that Bob, who was living in Illinois, bought real estate by mail through Fran, a Florida realtor. Fran sent Bob several pictures of the house and a general description of the house and its neighborhood. Included in the description was the statement that the house was "within easy walking distance of schools, churches, and shopping centers." After moving in, Bob discovers that the closest school is four miles away. Is this misrepresentation sufficiently material to justify rescission?

The answer depends on who Bob is. If Bob is a retired, childless widower, it is hard to see how the misrepresentation could be judged material. On the other hand, if Bob has a child in school, the nearness of schools could well be considered material.

Fact versus Opinion

In addition to being material, an actionable misrepresentation must concern a present or past fact; this is another way of saying that the subject of the misrepresentation must be *knowable*. Statements about future events ("This stock will double in price in the next two years") or statements of opinion ("This is the most attractive house in the neighborhood") do not serve as a basis for rescission, although people may, in fact, rely on them. One of the constant problems in this area is whether a given statement was mere "puffing" (a term used to indicate sales talk) or amounted to an actionable misstatement of material fact. For example, the seller who says: "This is a good car" is probably "puffing," whereas the seller who says: "This car was owned by a little old lady who only drove it twice a week" is probably guilty of misrepresentation if the car was actually used by a drag racer.

Justifiable Reliance

There are basically two ideas behind making justifiable reliance on element of misrepresentation. The first is the idea that there should be some *causal connection* between a misrepresentation and the complaining party's entry into the contract. If the complaining party knew the truth, or for some other reason did not in fact rely on the misrepresentation, why should it be a basis for canceling the contract? The second idea behind justifiable reliance is that parties who enter a contract must take reasonable steps to discover the facts about the contracts they enter into. So, if the facts are readily discoverable by either party (e.g., by reasonable inspection or because they are a matter of public record), a party is not allowed to rely on the other party's statements about them.

Morton v. Young
311 So.2d 755 (Ct. App. Fla. 1975)

FACTS   Emil Morton and Henry Young were casual acquaintances who played in a weekly poker game, occasionally lunched together, and had some minor business dealings with one another. Young offered to sell Morton some unregistered corporate stock. Morton asked whether the stock would be registered in the future, and Young, in the presence of Morton's secretary, said it would be registered within 18 months. Morton bought 4,000 shares at $12 a share. When the stock was not registered, Morton filed suit to rescind the agreement.

ISSUE   Could Morton justifiably rely on Young's statement that the stock would be registered?

DECISION   No. The court disagreed with Morton's argument that he and Young had a fiduciary relationship. It found instead that the transaction was an "arm's-length" one and Young owed no special duty to Morton. The court then said, "Every person must use reasonable diligence for his own protection." The court noted that Morton was an experienced businessman with accountants, lawyers, and stockbrokers at his disposal, but he had failed to consult anyone before buying. Young, on the other hand was merely a minority shareholder in the corporation and held no corporate office. The court noted that Morton's lawyers could have told him that a minority

> shareholder had no power to have stock registered, and that any attempt at registration would have to be approved by the Securities and Exchange Commission. "Morton having failed to make any independent investigation," the court said, "he now cannot be heard to say that he was deceived by defendant's alleged misrepresentation."

Detriment

The courts do not allow a person who claims to have been victimized by a misrepresentation to cancel the contract unless he or she can show some *detriment* (injury) as a result of the misrepresentation. Ordinarily, however, if one can prove the other elements of misrepresentation (particularly the "material fact" element), it is fairly easy to show injury. All that must be shown is that the complaining party would be in a better position if things were as they had been represented.

FRAUD

In some cases the complaining party may be able to prove that the party who made the misstatement knew or should have known that it was untrue. *Fraud* is intentional misrepresentation. To prove fraud, one must prove all the elements of misrepresentation plus two additional elements: that the misrepresentation was *knowingly* made with the *intent to deceive* (technically called *scienter*).

What Is a "Knowingly Made" Misstatement?

Clearly, if it can be shown that a defendant actually knew that what he or she said was untrue, a "knowing" misstatement has been proven. It is also sufficient to show that the defendant possessed enough information so that he should have known the truth, even if he actually did not. So, if Bob tells Mary that the net receipts from his business average $500 a week and Mary buys the business in reliance on this statement, proof by Mary that Bob's records show an average profit of only $200 a week would satisfy this element. Bob either knew or should have known the truth. Mary could also satisfy this element by showing that Bob made the statement *recklessly* (without sufficient information to believe it was true). So, if Mary could show that Bob's records were so inadequate that he could not really know how the business was doing, that would probably also be sufficient.

Intent to Deceive

Scienter refers to the mental state of the defendant. The courts generally infer an intent to deceive from the fact that the defendant made a knowing misstatement to a plaintiff who was likely to rely on it. The defendant's motivation is irrelevant; she may actually believe that she is doing the plaintiff a favor. For example, Beth is trying to sell her friend Mike a car. Beth thinks the car is a good one and that the price is a real bargain. Beth knows, however, that the car's odometer was disconnected for a year and that the car has much higher mileage on it than the odometer indicates. She tells Mike that the car "has only 20,000 miles on it" (the figure the odometer shows). Beth is guilty of fraud.

Fraud by Silence

Does a party to a contract have a duty to disclose all the material facts he or she knows about the subject of the contract to the other party? The original common law position on this issue was *caveat emptor* (let the buyer beware). The seller could remain silent without fear of being found guilty of fraud. Only actual statements by the seller could serve as a basis for fraud. The duty therefore was placed on buyers to ask the right questions of the seller, forcing the seller to make statements about the subject of the sale.

Many courts today, however, recognize that *caveat emptor* often produced unfair results. Some buyers simply do not know enough to ask the right questions about the subject of the sale, so many courts are recognizing a limited duty to disclose material facts on the part of the seller. Generally this duty is limited to material facts that the buyer could not have discovered by reasonable inspection of the subject of the sale.

personal

Griffith v. Byers Construction Co.
510 P.2d 198 (Sup. Ct. Kan. 1973)

FACTS Byers developed land and sold lots to builders who built houses on the lots and sold to buyers. The Griffiths bought a house from one of the builders and then discovered that the soil on their lot was defective due to a high salt content. They sued Byers for damages for fraud.

ISSUE Did Byers have a duty to disclose the nature of the soil to the Griffiths?

DECISION Yes. The court noted that in an earlier case it had held that builders who sold homes they had built had a duty to disclose to buyers any defects that were not discoverable by reasonable inspection. The court said that it saw no reason why this rule should not be extended to cover a developer like Byers. The court concluded that Byers knew about the salt content of the soil of the lots, and that after the grading and development of the lots the defect was not reasonably discoverable by the Griffiths. The court held that Byers's silence was "actionable fraudulent concealment."

The Remedy for Fraud

The buyer who can prove fraudulent misstatements or failure to disclose on the part of the seller has a choice of remedies. He or she may *rescind* the contract, like the buyer who can only prove misrepresentation. Such a buyer has the option, however, of *affirming* the contract and suing in tort for damages resulting from the fraud. This is so because the elements of fraud are the same as the elements for the tort of *deceit*. The buyer could recover actual damages resulting from the fraud (usually the difference between the true value of what the buyer bought and its represented value). So, if Bob bought a car from Frank for $500 and Frank told him it was in excellent condition, knowing its transmission was bad, Bob can choose his remedies. He could rescind the contract, return the car, and get back his $500, or keep the car and sue for $100 (the difference between the purchase price and the true value of the car with a defective transmission). Bob might also be able to get punitive damages since fraud is intentional wrongdoing.

DURESS AND UNDUE INFLUENCE

General Nature

Duress and *undue influence* are terms used to describe situations in which one party to the agreement interfered with the other party's ability to resist entering into an agreement. The basic idea of *duress* is that one of the parties, by making some *threat of harm*, forced the other party to enter an agreement he or she would not otherwise have entered. *Undue influence* is closely related to duress, but it exists only when the parties had some confidential relationship at the time of the contract. The basic idea of undue influence is that the dominant person in a confidential relationship took advantage of the other party to the relationship by getting the other party to enter into an unfavorable agreement.

Contracts made under duress and undue influence are *voidable* because the injured party has been deprived of his or her ability to make a free choice. Such a promise is not a voluntary one as required by contract law.

Duress

The common law courts originally required a threat of physical injury before they would find duress. Modern courts require only that the threat be a "wrongful" one, however.

A threat of criminal prosecution may be wrongful if the person making the threat is attempting to gain some unfair advantage by making the threat, even if there is a factual basis for prosecution. Clearly, an unfounded threat of prosecution is wrongful.

The courts have generally held that the threat of a well-founded civil suit is not duress. If this were not so, every party who settled a suit out of court could later argue duress. If, however, the threat is used to force the party to enter an unfair transaction that is unrelated to the rights involved in the threatened suit, this can be duress. For example, a husband in the process of divorcing his wife may threaten to sue for custody of their children (something he has a legal right to do) unless she gives him stock she owns in his company. The threat of an unfounded civil suit could also constitute duress if the resulting fear of the expense of defending the suit forced the threatened party to enter an agreement against his or her will.

As the following case shows, the unjustified withholding of a person's goods for the purpose of forcing him to pay an unreasonable charge can also amount to duress.

Austin Instrument, Inc. v. Loral Corporation
272 N.E.2d 533 (Ct. App. N.Y. 1971)

FACTS In July 1965, Loral was awarded a government contract to produce radar sets. The contract included a penalty provision for late deliveries and a cancellation clause in the event of Loral's default. Loral solicited bids for the production of 40 precision gears needed to produce the sets, and Austin's bids were accepted for 23 of the gears. In May 1966, Loral was awarded another similar government contract. Austin bid on all 40 gears but was only accepted on those gears on which its bids were the lowest. Austin said it would only accept an order for all 40 gears and that it would breach the first subcontract unless it was granted the second subcontract for all 40 gears, plus a price increase on the first contract. Loral could not get anyone else to supply the gears in time, so it accepted Austin's conditions. Loral withheld payment on some of the gears Austin delivered and when Austin sued for the amount owing, Loral counterclaimed for the price increases it had been forced to pay.

ISSUE Did Austin's threat to withhold the gears amount to duress?

DECISION Yes. The court said that duress may be proven by showing that one party to a contract has threatened to breach the agreement by withholding goods unless the other party agrees to some further demand. Such a threat standing alone would not be enough to show duress unless the threatened party could not obtain the goods from another source of supply and the ordinary remedy of an action for breach of contract would not be adequate. Since Loral had been unable to get the gears elsewhere, and since it would still have to get the gears even if it had sued Austin for breach of contract, both these conditions were met. Loral therefore had no choice when Austin raised its prices but to take the gears at the coerced prices and then sue to get the excess back.

Whether a given "wrongful" act amounted to duress in a particular case depends on the facts and circumstances of that case. The basic question the courts ask is whether the wrongful act of one of the parties effectively deprived the other party of his or her ability to resist entering the agreement.

Undue Influence   The basic idea behind undue influence is to protect the old, the timid, and the physically or mentally weak from those who gain their confidence and attempt to take advantage of them. Victims of undue influence must have the mental capacity to contract but lack the ability to adequately protect themselves against unscrupulous persons who gain their confidence.

Most of the cases in which undue influence is charged involve relatives, friends, or long-time advisors (like lawyers or bankers) of an old or sick person who are alleged to have gotten the victim to make gifts or sales at unfair prices. For example, Marge Johnson, age 84, spent her last five years living with her daughter Joan. Marge had been in poor health and was unable to care for herself. When Marge died, her other heirs discovered that two weeks before her death Marge sold her house to Joan for $35,000. The market value of the house at the time of the sale was $60,000. The other heirs may attempt to have the sale set aside, arguing it is the product of undue influence. Joan will probably argue that Marge knew the true value of the house but sold it to her at the lower price as a reward for taking care of her for so many years. Whether this was, in fact, undue influence depends on Marge's mental state, Joan's behavior, and Marge's knowledge of the value of the property.

Methodist Mission Home of Texas v. N_. A_. B_.
451 S.W.2d 539 (Civ. App. Tex. 1970)

FACTS   The plaintiff (whose name was not given in the court's opinion) was a former resident of the Methodist home for unwed mothers. Before she had her child, she had expressed an intention to give the child up for adoption. After having the child, however, she changed her mind and announced her intention to keep it. At this point she was subjected to a five-day series of interviews with a counselor (Mrs. Burns) employed by the home, who repeatedly urged her to give up the child. She testified that as a result of her discussions with Mrs. Burns she felt "trapped" and that she finally consented to the adoption of her child to avoid further harassment. She later filed suit to rescind her consent to the adoption, arguing it was the product of undue influence.

ISSUE   Was there sufficient evidence to support a finding of undue influence?

DECISION   Yes. The court said that undue influence exists only "where the actor's free agency and will have been destroyed and subverted to the extent that his act, instead of expressing his own will, expresses the will of the person exerting the influence." The plaintiff was a shy person, she had been emotionally upset at the time, and she had been subjected to a campaign designed to convince her to give up the child. She had been falsely told she had no right to keep the child, and that she was selfish for wanting to do so. She was told her parents, who accepted her decision to keep the child, were "putting something over" on her. This pressure, the court observed, "came from a person to whom plaintiff was encouraged to look for guidance, a member of an organization to which plaintiff was undoubtedly indebted and on which . . . she was dependent for help in finding her employment and a place to live." All these facts were sufficient to support a finding of undue influence.

MISTAKE

The Nature of Mistake

The term *mistake* is used in contract law to describe the situation in which one or both of the parties to an agreement acted under an untrue belief about the existence or nonexistence of a *material fact*. In mistake cases, unlike fraud and misrepresentation cases where the victim is also acting under a mistaken belief about the facts, the mistaken belief about the facts is not the product of a misstatement by the other party. Mistake in this sense does not include errors of judgment, ignorance, or a party's mistaken belief that he or she will be able to fulfill certain obligations under a contract. The things that were said about materiality and fact in the section on misrepresentation hold true in mistake cases.

The reason behind the idea of mistake is that mistake may prevent the "meeting of the minds" required by contract law. In deciding mistake cases, courts often seem to be trying more obviously to "do justice" than in other kinds of cases. This is why decisions in mistake cases sometimes seem to depart from the announced rules of law dealing with mistake.

Mutual Mistake

Mistake cases are classed as *mutual* or *unilateral*, depending on whether both or only one of the parties was acting under a mistaken belief about a material fact. Mutual mistake is always a basis for granting rescission of the contract at the request of either party. Clearly, no "meeting of the minds" took place and therefore no true contract was ever formed.

Mutual mistake can arise in many different ways. The parties may unintentionally use a term in their agreement that is *ambiguous*—capable of being honestly understood in two different ways. For example, on August 5, 1979, Apex Imports, Inc., of New York City orders a shipment of oriental rugs from Bristol Carpets, Ltd., of Bristol, England. Apex requests that the carpets be shipped on the China Seas, a ship scheduled to leave Liverpool, England, on August 15, 1979, for New York. Bristol accepts Apex's order, thinking Apex means another ship with the same name scheduled to leave Liverpool on December 1, 1979. Since Apex was unaware of the second ship, its order did not specify a shipment date. Neither party to the agreement is at fault and either may elect to rescind the agreement. The test for determining the existence of a mutual mistake is, however, an *objective* one. As the following case shows, this means that objective factors may remove what first looks like ambiguity.

First Regional Securities, Inc. v. Villella
377 N.Y.S.2d 424 (Civ. Ct. N.Y.C. 1975)

FACTS   Mr. Villella's son, who had authority to trade for him, visited First Regional Securities' brokerage office. He noticed that General Energy Corporation's stock was listed on the daily stock quotations ("pink sheets") at $7.00 a share. He placed an order to sell 2,000 shares at that price. When Villella delivered the certificates, it was discovered that he had General Energy Corporation of Arizona, a stock that had no public market, not General Energy Corporation of Delaware, the stock listed on the "pink sheet." First Regional had to buy 2,000 shares of General Energy of Delaware to cover Villella's sale order and filed suit to recover the $2,735.50 it lost in the process. Villella argued mistake of fact and negligence by First Regional as defenses.

ISSUE Can Villella rescind his sale order due to mistake of fact?

DECISION No. The court found no mutual mistake of fact. It said that the First Regional had been asked to sell the General Energy Corporation stock that was then selling for $7.00 a share on the over-the-counter market, which it did. "The defendant might well have thought and indeed intended to sell the stock in his possession," the court said, "however, the test is an objective one and the fact is that he requested to sell the stock of the Delaware corporation." The court found no negligence on First Regional's part, since the Arizona stock had not been purchased through First Regional. The court also refused to allow Villella to rescind on the basis of unilateral mistake, since First Regional had no notice that Villella was mistaken and would suffer a loss if Villella was allowed to rescind.

The parties may also be mistaken about the subject matter of their agreement. For example, Kathy owns a Mercedes and a Porsche. Bob has always wanted a Porsche and knows Kathy owns one. Kathy decides to sell her Mercedes and buy a BMW. A mutual friend of Bob and Kathy tells Bob, "Kathy's selling her car." Thinking Kathy is selling the Porsche (he does not know she also has a Mercedes), Bob calls Kathy and says "I'll give you $9,500 for your car." Kathy, thinking Bob is talking about the Mercedes, says "You've got a deal." Obviously, there was no "meeting of the minds" in this case.

Unilateral Mistake The basic rule is that if only one of the parties to the agreement is acting under a mistaken belief, this is not grounds for rescission. The reasoning behind the rule is that the law does not want to give all people who want to get out of a contract an easy exit by allowing them to argue mistake. It also wants to encourage people to exercise reasonable care to find out all the facts when entering their agreements. Therefore it is often said that if a person's own negligence is the cause of his or her mistake, relief will not be granted.

However, when one looks at the cases involving unilateral mistake, it appears that the courts often grant rescission if they are convinced that a person was truly mistaken and that a serious injustice will result from enforcing the agreement. This is sometimes true even when the mistaken party was slightly negligent.

Other factors the courts weigh when deciding whether to grant relief are: whether relief can be granted without causing the other party to suffer a material loss and whether the nonmistaken party knew or should have known of the mistake. If the nonmistaken party will not be hurt by allowing rescission, the courts are more inclined to do so. If someone must bear a loss as a result of the agreement, the courts are inclined to impose the loss on the mistaken party by not granting rescission unless it appears that the other party should have known of the mistake. In such a case the courts are likely to grant rescission rather than allow one party to take advantage of the other's mistake. This is so even if the nonmistaken party must bear a loss as a result of rescission, since he or she could have avoided the loss by acting in good faith (by informing the mistaken party of the error) or by exercising reasonable care (to discover the mistake when the facts should have indicated that the other party was mistaken).

Reed's Photo Mart v. Monarch Marking System Co.
475 S.W.2d 356 (Civ. App. Tex. 1971)

FACTS   Monarch sued Reed for the price of 4 million labels Reed ordered from Monarch. Reed's order was for "4 MM" labels ("M" is the roman numeral for 1,000 and was commonly used in the label industry). Monarch and Reed had dealt together for several years and Reed had never before ordered more than 4,000 of any type labels at any given time. The price of 4 million labels was $2,680; the price of 4,000 was $13. Monarch's salesman, when transferring order information from Reed's purchase order to the Monarch order form, changed the shipping instructions from "parcel post" and "ship at once" to "best way" and "as soon as possible."

ISSUE   Should Reed be allowed to rescind its order due to its unilateral mistake?

DECISION   Yes. The court said that several things should have made Monarch aware of the fact that Reed did not intend to order 4 million labels: the fact that in their prior dealings Reed had never ordered more than 4,000 of any type of label at any time; the fact that Reed's shipping instructions were only appropriate for a small order; and the fact that Monarch's salesman had never before received such a large order from any customer. An offeree is not permitted to snap up an offer that is too good to be true. Monarch knew or should have known of Reed's mistake.

QUESTIONS AND PROBLEM CASES

1. Discuss the differences between misrepresentation and fraud.

2. What does the term *scienter* mean?

3. Can threatening to file a civil suit ever amount to duress?

4. Is it true that unilateral mistake is never grounds for rescission?

5. Kennedy contracted to sell his business for 4,000 shares of Flo-Tronics stock with a market value of $8.50 per share. Under the con-

tract, Kennedy was obliged to retire the $17,500 in debts the business then owed. Kennedy claimed that he was induced to enter the contract by the assurance of Flo-Tronics that the price of its stock would rise to $25 a share within a year. The stock increased to $17 within three months, but under SEC regulation Kennedy was required to hold the stock for six months. The stock subsequently dropped to $3 a share, causing severe financial problems for Kennedy. Is he entitled to rescission on the grounds of misrepresentation?

6. Welsh was engaged in the business of selling automobile tires and accessories at retail. In 1970, he entered into a written contract with Kelly-Springfield Tire Company, whereby Welsh agreed to purchase all his tires, tubes, and other automobile accessories from Kelly. This contract contained a provision permitting Welsh, in the event of the termination of the contract, to return for credit at invoice price all goods purchased from Kelly. Similar contracts were executed by the parties in subsequent years. On January 2, 1973, Welsh executed a contract with Kelly, but the contract did not include the clause providing for the return of goods in the event of termination. The contract was terminated, and Kelly refused to accept the returned goods. Kelly brought suit to recover an unpaid balance for goods sold to Welsh. Welsh claimed credit for goods on hand, but Kelly refused to accept them. No specific representations were made. Welsh did not read the contract, and Kelly did not point out to him the change in the contract. Is Welsh entitled to credit for goods on hand? *No*

7. Stone contracted to build a home for Batey. During the construction Batey closely supervised the work, although there were periods of up to two or three weeks at a time when he was not present. After completion of the home and payment under the contract, Batey discovered several defects and sued Stone for fraud. Evidence at the trial revealed that Stone, the contractor, was aware of defective waterproofing, which he had concealed with dirt and paneling; that the driveway had less than the stipulated thickness and base in some

areas; that some beams had sagged because of inadequate size; that the paint and other finishes were improperly and inadequately applied; that portions of the house had sunk as much as three inches and had cracked and malfunctioned due to fill dirt underneath; and that these defects were not apparent until after Batey had occupied the house. In his defense Stone alleged that his duties were defined solely by the contract, that he had fulfilled them as such, and that no fraud had been perpetrated. Is this a valid defense to Batey's allegation of fraud?

8. Anderson advertised in a magazine a dredge specially designed and built for cutting narrow trenches underwater through submerged stumps, rocks, and so forth. O'Meara wanted a dredge capable of digging wide channels for access to offshore well sites. He saw the advertisement and sent a representative, who was an expert on engines but knew nothing of dredges, to examine it. After checking the dredge engines and talking by telephone with O'Meara, the representative signed an agreement on behalf of O'Meara to buy the dredge. Upon delivery it soon became obvious that it would require serious modification for O'Meara's need. After Anderson refused to contribute toward the cost of the modifications, O'Meara sued for rescission, alleging mutual mistake. Is rescission appropriate?

9. Anna Voboril's husband owed International Harvester Company for machinery purchased. The account was past due, and an agent of the company told Anna that if she did not agree to be personally responsible for paying her husband's debt, the company would have her husband arrested and put in jail. Anna was an uneducated foreigner who knew nothing about court procedure, and she did not know that her husband could not be imprisoned for debt. Anna executed notes covering the debt and, on the due date, refused to pay them. When sued on the notes, she set up duress as a defense. Is the defense good?

10. Curran submitted a bid of $102,171.98 to build an addition to a campus building at Plymouth State Teachers College. The bid had been computed on a hand-operated, ten-

key adding machine by an experienced employee. When the bids were opened on July 23, 1964, Curran's bid was more than $55,000 less than the next lowest bid. Realizing the possibility that a mistake had been made, Curran totaled the bids again that evening and discovered that the adding machine used would not add over $99,999.99 and thus omitted $100,000.00 in the cost estimates. On July 24, Curran notified the state of error and asked that his bid be canceled. Curran was then informed that he would be held to his bid. Curran sued to rescind the contract. Should Curran win? *Yes -*

reasonable time

misrepresentation
duress

Capacity to Contract

9

The law uses the word *capacity* to describe the ability of a person to do a legally valid act. Certain classes of persons have traditionally been treated as having a limited capacity to contract because the law sought to protect them in their contractual relations with others. Three major classes of persons are given this special protection: minors, insane persons, and drunken persons.

If either party entering a contract lacked the capacity to contract, the contract is *void* or *voidable*, depending on the kind of incapacity involved. Capacity to contract, however, is *presumed*, which means that the party who claims incapacity must prove it.

MINORS' CONTRACTS

The Reason for Minors' Incapacity

The idea behind minors' incapacity is that a minor (a person who is not old enough to be held to adult responsibilities) may not be able to bargain effectively with older, more experienced persons. The courts have responded to this idea by making minors' contracts *voidable*, which means that a minor has the right to *disaffirm* (cancel) his or her contracts. The right to disaffirm belongs exclusively to the minor; adults who contract with minors are bound to the agreement unless the minor chooses to disaffirm.

The Age of Majority

Under common law a person legally became an adult at 21 years of age (the age of majority). Many states, however, have lowered the age of majority to 18 years. Some states have lowered the age of majority for women but not men. Others have stated that married minors have the capacity to contract.

**The Right
to Disaffirm**

As a general rule, minors may disaffirm their contracts at any time during their minority. The only exception to this rule is that a minor must attain majority before he or she is allowed to disaffirm a contract involving title to real estate. No one but the minor or the minor's personal representative (the minor's guardian or the administrator of a deceased minor's estate) may exercise the right to disaffirm. Minors also have a reasonable time to disaffirm after they have attained majority. What constitutes a "reasonable time" depends on the facts and circumstances of each case. The minor who does not disaffirm within a reasonable time after attaining majority may be held to have *ratified* the contract and therefore loses the right to disaffirm. Generally, a minor may disaffirm by doing anything that clearly indicates to the other party an intent not to be bound by the terms of the contract.

**The
Consequences of
Disaffirming**

Minors who disaffirm a contract are entitled to the return of any consideration they have given the adult party to the contract. In return, minors are obligated to return to the adult any consideration they received from the adult that is still in their possession.

A difficult problem arises when the minor is no longer in possession of the consideration the adult gave, or when the consideration has been partially consumed, damaged, or otherwise declined in value. For example, Bob (age 17) bought a 1969 Plymouth Roadrunner from Happy Harry's Motors. Two months later Bob totally wrecks the car. He then calls Happy Harry and says he is disaffirming the contract and wants back his $300 down payment, plus the two $125 monthly payments he has made. The question is: Must Bob place Harry *in statu quo* (the position Harry would be in if the contract had never come into existence) by paying the reasonable value of the car? The traditional common law answer is that the minor who no longer has the consideration the adult gave does not have any duty to place the adult *in statu quo*.

This rule places severe hardship on adults in some cases, and it was probably adopted as a deterrent. What was to prevent adults from contracting with minors if the worst thing that could happen if the minor disaffirmed was that adults would get back whatever consideration they gave under the contract? Some courts today are reacting against the harshness of this rule by requiring the disaffirming minor to place the adult *in statu quo* in some circumstances. Some states have gone even further by passing statutes denying minors the right to disaffirm certain kinds of contracts. These statutes typically involve things like contracts for medical care, life insurance, bank accounts, and loans for college tuition.

**Misrepresentation
of Age by Minors**

Often an adult faced with a minor's attempt to disaffirm a contract argues that the minor misrepresented his or her age. If the adult can prove this charge to the court's satisfaction, a question arises about what effect the misrepresentation should have on the minor's right to disaffirm. In theory, the right to disaffirm should not be affected, since one who lacks capacity cannot acquire it merely by claiming to have capacity.

In reality, however, the minor who misrepresents his or her age is not allowed to defraud adults by doing so. The courts have used several different methods to achieve this result. Some courts allow the minor to disaffirm but require the minor to place the adult *in statu quo.* Others hold that the minor is *estopped* from raising the defense of minority and is therefore bound by the terms of the agreement. Many states allow the minor to disaffirm, but hold the minor liable to the adult in tort for *deceit.*

Haydocy Pontiac, Inc. v. Lee
250 N.E.2d 898 (Ct. App. Ohio 1969)

FACTS Jennifer Lee, saying that she was 21 years old, bought a car from Haydocy Pontiac while she was 20 years old. She traded in a car worth $150 and signed a promissory note for $2,016.36. She loaned the car to John Roberts, who in turn sold it to another auto dealer, Consolidated Holdings. Jennifer made no payments on the car, and when Haydocy filed suit on the note, she sought to disaffirm the contract on the grounds of minority. At the time of the trial, Roberts's whereabouts were unknown and Consolidated was insolvent. Neither Jennifer nor Haydocy had been able to recover the car.

ISSUE Can Jennifer disaffirm without placing Haydocy *in statu quo?*

DECISION No. The court noted that Jennifer had misrepresented her age when she purchased the car. Where the consideration received by the minor cannot be returned upon disaffirmance because it has been disposed of, the minor must account for the value of it, not in excess of the purchase price, where the other party is free from any fraud or bad faith and where the contract has been induced by a false representation of the age of the minor. The court concluded that Jennifer was estopped from pleading minority as a defense because to allow her to do so would be to give her a "weapon of injustice."

Ratification

The idea behind ratification is that an adult who indicates an intent to be bound by a contract he or she entered while still a minor should be bound to the contract and denied the right to disaffirm thereafter. As we have already seen, the minor who fails to disaffirm within a reasonable time after attaining majority may be held to have ratified the contract.

Terrace Company v. Calhoun
347 N.E.2d 315 (Ct. App. Ill. 1976)

FACTS   On December 27, 1967, Marilyn Calhoun's mother, her father's cousin, and L. C. Wesley, the owner of the L. C. Wesley Funeral Home, came to the apartment where Marilyn was baby-sitting. Wesley told Marilyn, who was 13 at the time, that her father (who was divorced from her mother) had been found dead, that his body was decomposing, and that her signature was needed on some documents before his body could be picked up. Wesley covered the written portion of the documents with his hand and Marilyn signed them. No one told Marilyn that the documents were a note for $1,977.72 for a funeral service for her father and an assignment of $1,977.72 of her interest in the proceeds of her father's life insurance. The next day Wesley assigned the documents to Terrace for $1,799.14. Eight months later Terrace confessed judgment on the note against Marilyn. Marilyn attained majority on July 7, 1972. A year later, when a prospective employer told her that her credit record was impaired, Marilyn first learned of the confessed judgment. On September 13, 1973, she filed suit to open the judgment, seeking to disaffirm the note and insurance assignment.

ISSUE   Did Marilyn wait too long to disaffirm the note and assignment?

DECISION   No. The obligations of a minor are voidable and may be ratified upon majority if the minor fails to disaffirm the obligation within a reasonable time after reaching majority. What constitutes a reasonable time is a question of fact to be determined by the circumstances of a particular case. Marilyn did not learn the true nature of the documents she signed until after she had attained majority, and she had filed suit two months later. The court concluded that she had disaffirmed within a reasonable time. The court also rejected Terrace's argument that Marilyn could not disaffirm without placing Terrace *in statu quo*. While a minor is under an obligation to make restitution upon disaffirmance, a minor who no longer has the consideration need not return it. The court concluded that: "What plaintiff is asking defendant to return is a funeral service, an intangible which is incapable of being returned."

Any words or conduct on the part of a minor after reaching majority that clearly indicate an intent to be bound by the contract are enough for ratification. If the minor, after attaining majority, sells or gives away the consideration he or she received under the agreement, this is probably enough for ratification. If the minor performs part of the contract or accepts some performance under the contract after attaining majority, this may also be treated as evidence of an intent to ratify. Some states require a formal statement by the minor before they find ratification. However, minors should decide whether or not to disaffirm their contracts fairly quickly after attaining majority and avoid doing anything that could be treated as ratifying the contract before deciding.

Robertson v. Robertson
229 So.2d 642 (Ct. App. Fla. 1969)

FACTS Robertson, while a minor, agreed to borrow money from his father for a college education. His father mortgaged his home and took out loans against his life insurance policies to get some of the money he loaned his son, who ultimately graduated from dental school. Two years after graduation Robertson's father asked him to begin paying back the amount of $30,000 at $400 per month. Robertson later agreed to pay $24,000 at $100 per month. He did this for three years before stopping the payments. His father sued for the balance owing.

ISSUE Did Robertson ratify his agreement to repay his father?

DECISION Yes. The court said there was ample evidence to support a finding of ratification. Robertson had continued to accept money from his father for four years after attaining majority. He had agreed orally and in writing to repay the debt after reaching adulthood and he had made payments for three years. All this was enough to show ratification.

Necessaries

Necessaries are generally defined as those things that are essential to a minor's continued existence and general welfare. Things that have traditionally been treated as necessaries include food, clothing, shelter, medical care, basic educational and/or vocational training, and the tools of a minor's trade. Minors are generally held liable on a *quasi-contract* basis for the *reasonable value* of necessaries furnished to them. This is so because penalizing adults who supply minors with necessaries would not only produce an unfair result but also discourage other adults from supplying minors with necessaries.

There are several important points about a minor's liability for necessaries. First, since minors are liable for only the reasonable value of necessaries they actually receive, they are not liable for the contract price of necessaries if it is greater than their reasonable value. They also are not liable for the value of necessaries they have purchased under the contract, but that they have not received at the time they disaffirm. For example, Mary Smith, a minor, rented an apartment in Tudor Village for $300 a month. She signed a one-year lease. After living there three months, Mary decided to move to another apartment complex. Mary can disaffirm her lease because she lacked capacity to contract. She is liable for the reasonable value of three months' rent at Tudor Village, but she is not liable for the remaining nine months' rent (she has not actually received any benefits from the remainder of the lease). If she could convince the court that the reasonable value of living at Tudor Village was less than the $300 a month the lease called for, she would only be liable for the lesser amount.

Whether a given item is considered a necessary depends on the facts of the particular case. The minor's age, station in life, and personal circumstances are all relevant to this issue. The adult has the burden of proving that an item is a necessary.

Fisher v. Cattani
278 N.Y.S.2d 420 (Dist. Ct. Nassau Cty. N.Y. 1966)

FACTS   Elaine Cattani, while 19 years of age, entered a contract with Fisher's employment agency. Fisher got her a job, but she did not like it and quit after one month. She sent Fisher a notice of disaffirmance by registered mail. Fisher filed suit for the employment fee provided in the contract, arguing, among other things, that the employment service was a necessary.

ISSUE   Is Cattani liable for the fee as a necessary?

DECISION   No. Elaine was a minor when she signed the contract and she had effectively disaffirmed the contract. A minor cannot disaffirm an agreement for necessaries, but necessaries must be measured against both the infant's standard of living and the ability and willingness of the infant's guardian, if any, to supply the needed services or articles. Fisher did not introduce any proof relevant to these issues. The court said that after a full presentation of the facts about Elaine's need to work to support herself, an employment agency contract might be regarded as a necessary, but in the absence of any proof by Fisher, she should be allowed to disaffirm.

CONTRACTS OF INSANE AND DRUNKEN PERSONS

Theory of Incapacity

The basic reason for holding that insane persons lack the capacity to contract is that we presume such persons are unable to bargain effectively with those who do not share their disability. Many states treat drunken persons like insane persons if, at the time they entered the agreement, they were so drunk that they were unable to understand the nature of the business at hand.

The Test of Insanity

The test usually applied in contract law is whether a party, at the time the contract was entered into, had sufficient mental capacity to understand the nature and effect of the contract. A person could be medically insane (e.g., suffering from paranoid delusions) but still have the legal capacity to contract. A person could be periodically insane but enter a binding contract during a lucid moment. A person could be senile, of less than ordinary intelligence, or highly neurotic but still be able to understand the nature of the transaction.

The Effect of Insanity

If a court later finds that a person was insane at the time the contract was entered into, the contract is *voidable* at the election of the insane party (or his or her guardian or the administrator of his or her estate). A distinction is made between such agreements and those made by persons who had been adjudicated insane before entering the agreement. *Adjudication* in this context means that a general hearing was held on the person's mental competency and the court determined that the person was of unsound mind and appointed a guardian or conservator of the person's estate. In most states the agreements of persons who have been adjudicated insane are *void*.

Krasner v. Berk
319 N.E.2d 897 (Sup. Ct. Mass. 1974)

FACTS   Krasner and Berk were doctors who had shared a suite of offices for several years and split the rent. In 1969 they renewed their agreement for three years. The written contract called for continued rent payments even if one of the parties became disabled. Professional testimony at trial indicated that Berk began suffering from premature senility in 1967 and that prior to signing the agreement Mrs. Berk had discussed her husband's condition with Krasner. Two months after signing the agreement, Berk went to a brain surgeon and, within six months, he had given up his practice. Krasner filed suit to enforce the agreement.

ISSUE   Did Berk have the mental capacity to enter a binding contract?

DECISION   No. The court said that insanity is a valid defense to a contract suit, and an inability to realize the true purport of the matter on hand is equivalent to mental incapacity. The court added: "Even where there is sufficient understanding, a contract may in some circumstances be voidable by reason of failure of will or judgment, where the person contracting, by reason of mental illness or defect, is unable to act in a reasonable manner in relation to the transaction and the other party has reason to know of his condition." The evidence at trial, the court concluded, indicated that Berk lacked capacity at the time of the contract and that Krasner was on notice of this fact.

Necessaries

Insane persons are liable for the *reasonable value* of necessaries on the same basis and for the same reasons as minors.

The Right to Disaffirm

Like minors, insane persons can disaffirm their contracts. Must insane persons who disaffirm place the other party *in statu quo?* Insane persons who disaffirm must always return any consideration they received that they still have. If the consideration has been lost, destroyed, damaged, or consumed, however, the insane person's duty to place the other party *in statu quo* depends on whether the other party was on notice of the insane party's lack of capacity. If the sane party had no reason to know of the other party's insanity, the insane party is not allowed to disaffirm without placing the other party *in statu quo*. If, on the other hand, the sane party knew or should have known of the other party's insanity, the insane party is allowed to disaffirm without placing the sane party *in statu quo*. This rule punishes those who may try to take advantage of an insane person, but protects those who have no such intent.

Ratification

Insane persons who regain their sanity can ratify their contracts just like a minor who attains majority. If the insane person dies or is adjudicated insane, his or her personal representative may ratify the contract. Ratification has the same effects in this context that it does in minors' contracts.

QUESTIONS AND PROBLEM CASES

1. When can minors disaffirm their contracts?

2. Discuss the concept of ratification and its application to minors' contracts.

3. Are minors liable for the contract price of necessaries? Explain. *reasonable values* No

4. Kabler, a minor, was killed while driving a Simco, Inc., truck under a lease agreement whereby Kabler used the truck to sell ice cream products supplied to him by Simco. Byrne, the administratrix of Kabler's estate, filed suit, charging Simco with failure to maintain the truck in safe operating condition. Simco set up as a defense the written contract between it and Kabler, in which Kabler agreed to hold Simco harmless for any injury suffered by him arising from the use of the truck. Byrne argued that since Kabler was a minor, the contract was not binding and that Simco's defense is not valid. Is the provision in the contract binding on Kabler or his estate? No

5. Bell, a minor, went to work as an employee of the Pankas Beauty Parlor. As a condition of employment, Bell agreed that if he left the employ of Pankas, he would not work in or run a beauty parlor business within a ten-mile radius of downtown Pittsburgh for a two-year period. Bell eventually quit the Pankas Beauty Parlor and immediately opened a shop of his own three blocks away from Pankas, violating his agreement not to compete. Pankas sues to enforce the noncompetition agreement. Bell claims that as a minor he is not bound by the terms of the covenant. Can Pankas prevent Bell from competing? Yes/No *Beneficiary*

6. Heiman had been actively involved in various business enterprises since his 17th birthday. While still a minor, Heiman issued several personal checks to Eastern Airlines in payment for airline tickets in 1963 and through February 1964. On April 21, 1964, several months after attaining majority, he wrote Eastern Airlines a letter disaffirming these personal checks. Heiman was sued by Eastern airlines and he set up his minority and letter of disaffirmance as a defense. Is this a good defense? No *Estopped or br*

7. Hurley and his grandmother, Price, inherited as co-owners 575 shares of the common stock of Edison Company. At the time of inheritance, Hurley was a minor of the age of 20 years and lived with his grandmother. On December 11, 1955, the grandmother requested Hurley to sign a dividend order authorizing Edison Co. to pay all dividends due on the shares of stock to her. Hurley signed the dividend orders without receiving any consideration for doing so and without knowing the nature of the document. Price died on December 27, 1970, and it was not until March 18, 1971, that Hurley first learned that he was co-owner of the stock. On March 30, 1971, Hurley gave notice to Edison Co. that he disaffirmed the dividend order which he had signed earlier and demanded that the Edison Co. pay him half of all dividends paid on the stock since he became co-owner of it.

The Edison Co. refused to pay and Hurley brought suit. Edison Co. contends that Hurley did not disaffirm within a reasonable time after he became of age. Does Hurley have the right to disaffirm the contract?

8. On August 8, 1953, Rotondo purchased a diamond ring from Kay Jewelry Company. He told Kay that he was a minor 19 years of age and that he was buying it as an engagement ring. He made a part payment of $94.49 on the ring and on that same day presented the ring to his fiancée. On April 10, 1954, the engagement was terminated but the ring was not returned. Rotondo testified that he asked Kay to repossess the ring shortly after the engagement was broken, but there was no evidence that the ring was repossessed. Rotondo sought to disaffirm the contract for the ring, and Kay argued that he could not do so without returning the ring. Can Rotondo disaffirm?

9. In an earlier criminal proceeding, Davis had been found not guilty on the grounds of insanity. He was committed to a hospital for the criminally insane, but in a later mental health proceeding he was not declared to be insane. He escaped from the hospital five years before bringing this suit. During that time he had married and established a trucking business. In connection with the trucking business, he had bought equipment from the Colorado Kenworth Corporation (Kenworth) as follows: Kenworth tractor, $15,000—paid on purchase price $9,058.90; trailer—paid $8,693.74; refrigerator unit—purchase price $17,450; tires—$1,125, paid $242.50. Davis sold his business, including this equipment for $1,600, the value of his equity in the equipment. Notice of disaffirmance was given, but no offer was made to place Kenworth *in statu quo*. Davis contends that since he was found to be insane in the criminal proceedings, all his contracts are void. Is Davis right?

Consideration

10

At a fairly early point in the development of contract law, the common law courts decided not to enforce gratuitous (free) promises. Simply put, this means that the courts generally do not enforce a promise against the person who made it (the *promisor*), unless the person the promise was made to (the *promisee*) has given up something in exchange for the promise. In effect, the requirement of consideration requires a promisee to pay the "price" the promisor asked for in order to gain the right to enforce the promisor's promise. So, if Mary (the promisor) promises to give Bob (the promisee) a diamond ring and Bob has done nothing in return for her promise, Bob will not be able to enforce Mary's promise against her, since it was *not supported by consideration*. A useful definition of *consideration* is *legal value, bargained for and given in exchange for an act or promise.*

Legal Value

A promisee's consideration may be an *act* (in the case of some unilateral contracts) or a *promise* (in the case of some unilateral contracts and all bilateral contracts). Consideration can have legal value in one of two ways. If the promisee does or agrees to do something he or she had no prior legal duty to do in exchange for the promisor's promise, that provides legal value. If the promisee agrees not to do something he or she has a legal right to do in exchange for the promisor's promise, that also provides legal value.

Under this definition many things can have *legal* value without having *monetary* (economic) value. So, if Frank's grandmother promises to pay Frank $500 if he will quit smoking for one year and Frank quits, he can enforce her promise against her. He has given legal value (by not doing something he had a right to do) in exchange for her promise, despite the fact that his quitting smoking has no everyday value in dollars and cents.

Bargained for and Given in Exchange   Saying consideration must be bargained for means that, in addition to having legal value, the consideration given by the promisee must be the consideration the promisor *requested in exchange for making his or her promise.* The courts are saying, in effect: "If you (the promisor) got your 'price' for making your promise, we will enforce your promise against you."

SOLVING CONSIDERATION PROBLEMS

Students often have difficulty with the concept of consideration. One reason is that most disputes about consideration involve *bilateral contracts* (a promise for a promise). This causes confusion in two ways. First, since bilateral contracts by definition include two promises, each party is both a promisor (on the promise he or she made to the other party) and a promisee (on the promise the other party made in return). Second, students often forget that *merely making the requested promise* is enough for consideration in bilateral contracts cases.

Here is a simple problem-sovling method to help you in determining whether consideration has been given in a case. Ask yourself:

1. *Which promise is at issue?* This ordinarily is the promise that a court is trying to decide whether to enforce.
2. *Who is the promisee of that promise?* This is the party seeking to enforce the promise.
3. *Has the promisee given consideration?* If so, and the other elements of a binding contract are present, the promise is enforceable.

If you understand the definition of consideration and use this method, you will be able to work most consideration problems with ease. Take a simple bilateral contract situation and see how this problem-solving method works.

Facts.   On May 1, 1980, Mary enters into an agreement with Apex Painting Company to have Apex paint her house before June 1, 1980, for the sum of $1,000.

Alternative Case A.   On May 5, 1980, Mary calls Apex and tells it the deal is off, since Ralph's Painting Company has agreed to paint her house for $800. Apex sues Mary and she argues lack of consideration as a defense.

1. The promise at issue is Mary's promise to pay Apex for painting her house.
2. The promisee on this promise is Apex.
3. Apex has given consideration. Apex agreed to do something it had no

prior duty to do—paint Mary's house—in exchange for her promise. Apex can enforce Mary's promise against her.

Alternative Case B.   On May 5, 1980, Apex calls Mary and tells her it will not be able to paint her house because it just got a very profitable job painting a new apartment complex. Mary sues Apex and it argues lack of consideration as a defense.

1. The promise at issue is Apex's promise to paint Mary's house.
2. Mary is the promisee on this promise.
3. Mary has given consideration. She agreed to do something she had no prior duty to do—hire and pay Apex for painting her house—in exchange for Apex's promise. She can enforce Apex's promise against it.

Now that you understand the meaning of consideration and have a method to help you solve consideration problems, you are ready to learn some of the traditional rules about consideration. These are mostly statements about how the requirement of consideration works in various kinds of situations.

RULES OF CONSIDERATION

Preexisting Duties   As a general rule, performing or agreeing to perform a preexisting duty is not consideration. This makes sense when you remember the definition of consideration. In order to have given *legal value*, the promisee must either have done (or agreed to do) something he had no duty to do or have agreed not to do something he had a right to do. If the promisee already had a duty to do what he has done or promised to do, the promisee has not given legal value. The same is clearly true if the promisee agreed not to do something he had no right to do. The following are several examples of how this rule applies.

Promises Not to Commit Crimes or Torts   Every member of society has a duty to obey the law and not commit crimes or torts. Therefore, a promisee's promise not to commit such an act can never be consideration. For example, Bill promises to pay Mike, the school bully, $2 a week for "protection" in exchange for Mike's promise not to beat Bill up. Bill refuses to pay. Bill's promise is unenforceable because it is not supported by consideration.

Promises by Public Officials to Perform Official Duties   Public officials obviously are bound to perform their official duties, so promises by public officials to perform their duties are not consideration. For example, Harry owns a liquor store that has been robbed several times. He promises to pay Fran, a police officer whose beat includes Harry's store,

$50 a week to "keep an eye on the store" while walking her beat. Harry's promise is unenforceable, since it was not supported by consideration.

By far the greatest number of preexisting duty cases involve *contractual* duties. These cases usually occur when the parties attempt to modify an existing contract, but no new consideration is furnished to support the agreement to modify.

For example, Ralph enters into a contract with Toptex Construction Company to build a new house for him for $50,000. When the construction is partially completed, Nancy Jones, the owner of Toptex, calls Ralph and says that due to the rising cost of building materials Toptex will have to stop work unless Ralph pays an extra $5,000. Ralph agrees, but later refuses to pay more than the $50,000 originally agreed upon. Toptex sues for $5,000. The promise at issue is Ralph's promise to pay the extra $5,000. Toptex cannot enforce Ralph's promise, because Toptex has not given consideration. All Toptex has done is build the house, something it already had a legal duty to do under the parties' original contract.

Of course, if *new consideration* is provided to support a modification, it is enforceable. So, if Ralph had asked Toptex to add a room that was not called for in the original plans and promised to pay an extra $5,000 for the new room, Ralph's promise to pay more would be enforceable against him. Toptex in this case has done something it had no legal duty to do in exchange for Ralph's promise.

Generally speaking, a court enforces a modification that is not supported by new consideration only when a contracting party has run into *unforeseeable difficulties* that make his or her performance impossible or highly impracticable. In this situation the party who has run into trouble is neither a bad person trying to take advantage of the promisor nor an imprudent person trying to escape the consequences of a bad bargain. Therefore, the courts enforce the modification in the interest of fairness, although technically no new consideration has been given. You should note, however, that strikes, increases in the costs of raw materials, and bad weather are not considered unforeseeable. An example of a truly unforeseeable difficulty that would justify exception to the general rule would be the case of a building contractor who, in excavating the foundation of a new building, strikes bedrock in an area where bedrock formations are not usually found so close to the surface.

The parties to a contract can always terminate their old contract and enter into a new one by mutual agreement, even if the obligations of one party remain the same, while the obligations of the other party are increased. The courts, however, are very suspicious of these situations, asking, in effect: Who would voluntarily agree to pay more for what they have a right to for less? Therefore, the courts require clear and convincing evidence that the termination of the old contract and the creation of the new one were free of any elements of coercion or fraud.

Trisko v. Vignola Furniture
299 N.E.2d 421 (Ct. App. Ill. 1973)

FACTS   Stephen Trisko bought a pair of love seats from Vignola Furniture. When he discovered the love seats were defective, Trisko filed suit against Vignola. Vignola failed to answer Trisko's complaint, and a default judgment was entered in his favor. Later Vignola moved to set aside the default judgment, arguing that it had a "meritorious defense" to Trisko's claim; namely, that he had orally agreed not to file suit in exchange for Vignola's promise to repair the love seats.

ISSUE   Is Trisko's promise not to file suit supported by consideration?

DECISION   No. Vignola's argument overlooked the fact that Vignola had sold Trisko defective goods and that Trisko had given Vignola prompt notice of the defect. On these facts Vignola was under a legal duty to repair the defective goods. Therefore, Trisko's promise was unenforceable, since a promise to do what one is already legally obligated to do is not consideration.

Promises to Discharge Debts for Part Payment

In many cases a debtor offers to pay a creditor a sum less than the creditor is demanding in exchange for the creditor's promise to accept the part payment as full payment of the debt. If the creditor later sues for the balance of the original debt, is the creditor's promise to take less enforceable? The answer depends on the nature of the debt and the circumstances of the debtor's part payment.

Liquidated Debts.   The general rule is that a promise to discharge a *liquidated debt* for part payment of the debt at or after its due date is unenforceable due to lack of consideration. A liquidated debt is one that is *due* and *certain*, which means that there is no dispute about the existence or the amount of the debt. If a debtor does nothing more than agree to pay less than an amount clearly owed, how can that be valid consideration for the creditor's promise to take less? The debtor has actually done less than he or she already had a duty to do, namely, to pay the full amount of the debt.

For example, Beth borrows $2,000 from the First City Bank, payable in six months. When the time for payment arrives, Beth sends the bank a check for $1,800 marked: "In full payment for any and all claims First City has against me." First City cashes the check (impliedly promising to accept it as full payment by cashing it) and later sues Beth for $200. First City can recover the $200, since Beth has given no consideration to support its implied promise to accept $1,800 as full payment.

On the other hand, if Beth had done something she had no duty to do in exchange for First City's promise, she could enforce First City's promise against it and avoid paying the $200. If Beth had *paid early* (before the loan contract called for payment), or *at a different place* than that called for in the loan contract, or in a *different medium of exchange* than that called for in the loan contract (e.g., a car worth $1,800), in exchange for First City's promise, she has given consideration and can enforce the promise.

Unliquidated Debts. An honest dispute about the existence or amount of a debt makes the debt an *unliquidated* one. Assume Tom and Mark are involved in an automobile accident. Tom claims Mark is at fault and that his total losses from the accident are $9,500. Mark denies responsibility for the accident and also argues that Tom's losses are far less than $9,500. There are only two ways to finally settle this dispute: Allow a court to determine the nature and extent of the parties' liabilities or reach a private settlement agreement. If Mark offers to pay Tom $2,000 in full payment of all claims Tom has against him and Tom accepts, Tom has entered a binding *accord and satisfaction*—the legal term for settling a disputed claim. Both Mark and Tom have given up their right to have a court decide their liability in exchange for the other's promise to settle their dispute for a definite amount. Therefore, their mutual promises are supported by consideration and enforceable.

Garcia v. Villarreal
478 S.W.2d 830 (Ct. App. Tex. 1972)

FACTS Dora Garcia was injured in an automobile accident caused by Margarita Villarreal. At the time of the accident Garcia was driving a car owned by her employer, H. A. Ahrens. The car was slightly damaged, and Farmers Insurance Group, Villarreal's insurance company, negotiated a settlement with Ahrens in the amount of $53.06. Farmers gave Ahrens a release form and a bank draft for $53.06 and told him that both he and Garcia had to sign the release and draft. Ahrens told Garcia the release was a formality to enable him to collect for damage to the car. Garcia signed the release, but refused to sign the draft, saying she intended to file a claim for her injuries. Ahrens told this to Farmers Insurance and they eventually gave him a draft in his name alone. When Garcia filed suit, Farmers raised the release as a defense.

ISSUE Is Garcia bound by the release?

DECISION No. Before a release can be enforceable, there must be a "meeting of the minds" between the parties and the promise sought to be enforced must be supported by consideration. The court said that the facts indicated that Garcia had signed the release as accommodation to her employer and derived no personal benefit from signing. The insurance company knew of her refusal to sign the draft and her initial refusal to be a party to the release. Therefore no accord and satisfaction resulted.

Composition Agreements

Compositions are agreements between a debtor and two or more creditors who agree to accept a stated percentage of their liquidated claims against the debtor, at or after the due date, in full satisfaction of their claims. They are generally treated as binding on the parties to the agreement, despite the fact that doing so appears to be contrary to the general rule on liquidated debts. Creditors usually enter compositions when they believe that failure to do so may result in the debtor's bankruptcy, in which case they might ultimately recover a smaller percentage of their claims than that agreed to in the composition.

Past Consideration

The courts generally hold that past consideration is no consideration. This rule of consideration basically focuses on the "bargained for and given in exchange" part of our definition of consideration. If a promisee's performance was rendered *before* the promisor's promise was made, then it can never serve as consideration, even though it may meet the "legal value" part of the test. This is so because it was not "bargained for and given in exchange" for the promisee's promise. Return to our earlier example with Frank and his grandmother, but assume that in this case Frank's grandmother says to him: "I'm glad you quit smoking last year, so I'll give you $500 for your birthday." If she later refuses to pay, can Frank enforce her promise? No, he has not given consideration because he did not quit smoking in exchange for her promise.

Arrow Employment Agency, Inc. v. Seides
311 N.Y.S.2d 182 (Dist. Ct. Nassau Cty. N.Y. 1970)

FACTS Arrow Employment sent Arthur Seides to a job interview with Futuronics Corporation. Seides was told that the job was a "fee paid" position and that Futuronics would pay the 10 percent recruiting fee. Futuronics refused to pay the full 10 percent fee and paid only 5 percent. Seides took the job and agreed to pay the remaining 5 percent but later refused to pay. Arrow filed suit and Seides moved to dismiss, arguing lack of consideration.

ISSUE Was Seides's promise to pay part of the fee supported by consideration?

DECISION No. Present consideration is generally necessary to the validity of contract, and past consideration is no consideration. Arrow's act of introducing Seides to Futuronics was performed with the express understanding that Seides would not have to pay. Therefore, Arrow's act of introducing Seides to Futuronics constituted past consideration for his promise to pay a 5 percent fee and, as such, was no consideration.

Forbearance to Sue

If the promisee agrees not to file suit against the promisor in exchange for the promisor's promise (usually to pay a certain sum of money), this can be valid consideration to support the promisor's promise. The promisee has agreed not to do something he or she has a legal right to do (file suit), and that constitutes legal value. There are, however, some qualifications on this rule.

The courts clearly do not want to sanction extortion by allowing people to threaten to file spurious (unfounded) claims in the hope that others will agree to some payment to avoid the expense or embarrassment of suit. On the other hand, we have a strong public policy favoring private settlement of disputes and do not want to require people to second-guess the courts. Therefore, it is generally said that in order for forbearance to be valid consideration, the promisee must *reasonably believe* he or she has a valid claim.

Frasier v. Carter
437 P.2d 32 (Sup. Ct. Idaho 1968)

FACTS   Lena Frasier's husband died, leaving her specific property in his will. The will provided that she had to waive her statutory rights to the community property she had owned with her husband in order to get the more valuable property left to her in the will. Carter, Lena's attorney, failed to have her execute the waiver required by the will and the probate court refused to grant her more than her statutory share. Carter signed an agreement promising to pay Lena the difference in value between the specific property and her statutory share if the probate court's decision were affirmed on appeal. It was, and Carter refused to pay, arguing that his promise was not supported by consideration.

ISSUE   Was Carter's promise supported by consideration?

DECISION   Yes. Mere forbearance, without any request or agreement to forbear, is not consideration. However, an agreement to forbear may be inferred from the facts and circumstances of the case. The facts in this case supported Frasier's argument that Carter's promise to pay was made to prevent her from suing him for negligence.

Mutuality of Obligation

It is generally said that a bilateral contract that lacks mutuality is unenforceable due to lack of consideration. As you learned earlier, in a bilateral contract the mutual promises of the parties form the consideration for the agreement. However, the fact that a party made a promise in exchange for the other party's promise is, in itself, not enough to provide consideration. The promise made must also meet the "legal value" part of our consideration definition. The parties must have bound themselves to do something they had no duty to do, or not to do something they had a right to do.

This issue is raised in some cases because what first looks like a binding promise, upon closer inspection turns out to be an *illusory promise.* Illusory promises are worded in a way that allows the promisor to decide whether or not to perform the promise. A promise to "buy all the wheat I want" or to "paint as much of your house as I feel like painting" is illusory. A bilateral agreement based on an illusory promise is said to be unenforceable due to lack of mutuality. All this really means is that an illusory promise cannot serve as consideration.

Hillman v. Hodag Chemical Corporation
238 N.E.2d 145 (Ct. App. Ill. 1968)

FACTS William Hillman was an employee of Hodag Chemical. He was fired after approximately four months on the job. Hillman filed suit claiming Hodag had breached its employment contract, which provided for two years' employment. The contract was evidenced by the following letter:

December 28, 1961

Mr. William P. Hillman, Jr.
195 Boulevard
Mountain Lakes, N.J.

Dear Mr. Hillman:

This letter will confirm my conversation with you today.

Hodag Chemical Corporation of Skokie, Illinois, will employ you to perform such functions as assigned for two years minimum and at $15,400 per year.

This employment begins today.

Very truly yours,
Hodag Chemical Corporation
(s) Sheldon E. Kent
Sheldon E. Kent, President

Agreed:
(s) 12/28/61   (s) William P. Hillman, Jr.
                          William P. Hillman, Jr.

Hodag argued that the agreement lacked mutuality since, by merely signing "Agreed," Hillman was not obligated to work for Hodag for any definite period.

ISSUE Does the agreement lack mutuality?

DECISION No. Mutuality of obligation is necessary to establish a valid employment contract. A contract must be binding upon both parties at the same time if it is to be treated as valid and enforceable against either party. However, mutuality is determined by looking at the language the parties used in their contract, and mutuality may be implied as well as expressed in the parties' agreement. Looking at the written agreement, the court said: "In the contract here the word 'Agreed' preceded the plaintiff's signature. When we accord to that word its ordinary and accepted meaning, it was the equivalent of a promise on the part of the plaintiff to obligate himself for a minimum of two years employment with defendant." Therefore, the court concluded that the contract imposed mutual obligations and was enforceable against Hodag.

Adequacy of Consideration

As long as the consideration given by the parties to an agreement passes the test of our definition of consideration, the courts generally do not concern themselves with whether parties to a contract received any actual value in exchange for their promises, or whether the promises or performances exchanged were of relatively equal value. Freedom of contract is the freedom to make bad bargains as well as good ones, so promisors' promises are enforceable if they "got what they asked for" in exchange for making their promises, even if "what they asked for" is not nearly so valuable in worldly terms as what they promised in return.

Several qualifications must be made to this general rule. First, if the inadequacy of consideration is apparent *on the face of the agreement,* no contract results. A contract to pay $5 for $10 with no other terms or conditions is therefore unenforceable.

Also, gross inadequacy of consideration may give rise to an inference of fraud, duress, lack of capacity, and so on. Inadequacy of consideration standing alone, however, is not enough to prove lack of reality or capacity.

Courts may refuse to grant *equitable* remedies to those who seek to enforce grossly inadequate bargains on the grounds that such persons are not entitled to the special treatment equity affords. So, if Bob agrees to sell Mary his house (worth $55,000) for $35,000, Mary can probably recover damages for breach of contract if Bob refuses to perform, but she probably will not be able to get an order for the specific performance of Bob's promise (ordering Bob to give Mary a deed to his house).

Finally, some agreements recite "$1.00" or "$1.00 and other valuable consideration" as the consideration for a promise; this is called *nominal consideration.* A minority of courts enforce such agreements, but the majority enforce them only if the nominal consideration was in fact *truly bargained for.* If not, the promise is a disguised gift, and unenforceable.

EXCEPTIONS TO THE REQUIREMENT OF CONSIDERATION

Promissory Estoppel

This doctrine, which was discussed earlier in the case of promises to hold offers open, may also be applied to enforce other kinds of promises that are not supported by consideration. If the three elements required for estoppel are present (*representation, reliance,* and *detriment*), the promisor may be *estopped* from raising the defense of lack of consideration. For example, a tenant tells her landlord that she is considering remodeling her apartment and asks if he intends to allow her to renew her lease. He says yes but later refuses to honor his promise. If the tenant has actually spent a substantial sum remodeling in reliance on the landlord's promise, his promise is probably enforceable against him.

> ### Hunter v. Hayes
> ### 533 P.2d 952 (Ct. App. Colo. 1975)
>
> **FACTS**   Hunter was working for the telephone company when Hayes promised her a job as a flag girl on a construction project. She was told to quit her job, which she did. Hayes then refused to hire her and she filed suit to recover lost wages while unemployed. Hayes argued that his promise was not supported by consideration.
>
> **ISSUE**   Is Hayes's promise enforceable despite the absence of consideration?
>
> **DECISION**   Yes. The court cited section 90 of the Restatement of Contracts, which provides: "A promise which the promisor should reasonably expect to induce action or forbearance of a definite and substantial character on the part of the promisee and which does induce such action or forbearance is binding if injustice can be avoided only by enforcement of the promise." The court noted that Hunter had quit her job in reliance on Hayes's promise, that Hayes should have foreseen she would do so, and that she was out of work for two months as a result.

Charitable Subscriptions

A promise to make a gift for a charitable or educational purpose is unenforceable unless and until the institution to which the promise was made incurs obligations by *relying* on the promise. This exception is usually justified on the basis of either estoppel or public policy.

Other promises because of your promise create consideration

Debts Barred by Bankruptcy Discharge or the Statute of Limitations

Once a bankrupt debtor is granted a discharge (bankruptcy is discussed in Chapter 45), creditors no longer have a legal right to collect the discharged debts. Similarly, a creditor who fails to file suit to collect a debt within the time limit set by the appropriate statute of limitations loses the right to collect it. However, many states enforce *new promises* by debtors to pay these kinds of debts even though technically they are not supported by consideration, since the creditors have no rights to give up in exchange for the debtors' new promises. This is a source of great potential danger to debtors and great temptation for creditors. Many states recognize this fact by requiring such promises to be in writing to be enforceable.

Promises to Perform a Conditional Duty

If a promisor's duty to perform depends on the occurrence of some condition, a later promise to perform is enforceable even if the condition has not occurred. So, if Mike agrees to sell Tim his stock in Zipco Corporation if the price reaches $8.00 a share, and later Mike agrees to sell at $7.50 a share, his promise is enforceable against him.

QUESTIONS AND PROBLEM CASES

1. What must a promisee do to give "legal value" in exchange for a promisor's promise?

2. What is the difference between a liquidated debt and an unliquidated debt?

3. Baehr owned a gas station, which he leased to Kemp. Kemp had severe financial problems and was heavily indebted to Penn-O-Tex Oil Corporation. Later, Kemp transferred his rights to receive payments on all his claims to Penn-O-Tex. He eventually defaulted in his rent payments to Baehr. Baehr, knowing of the Kemp–Penn-O-Tex transfer agreement, complained to the corporation. Penn-O-Tex gave Baehr its unqualified assurance that the overdue rent would be paid. The rent was not paid, and Baehr sued Penn-O-Tex. Is Penn-O-Tex liable on its promise to pay Baehr the rent?

4. Signs was employed by an insurance company as a selling agent. The contract of employment set out in detail the commissions to be paid to Signs on business he produced, and it provided that the stipulated commissions were "full and complete compensation" for all business produced. In December, the insurance company put out a bulletin stating that the company would distribute $1 million to deserving agents, and that agents who sell $20,000 worth of life insurance during the month of December would receive $10,000. Signs sold more than $20,000 during the month of December but the company refused to pay him a bonus. He brought suit against the company to recover a judgment for $10,000. The company set up lack of consideration as a defense. Is the defense good?

5. On September 1, 1967, Monroe entered into a written contract to sell a house and lot to Bixby for $4,000. A payment of $60 was made at the time the contract was signed, and the balance, with interest at the rate of 6 percent per year, was to be paid in monthly installments of $30 or more per month the first year and $35 or more each month thereafter until the contract price was paid in full. Sometime later Bixby asked to have the monthly payments reduced, and Monroe agreed to accept $30 per month and to reduce the total sale price to $2,500. Bixby made payments until January 25, 1970, when she refused to make further payments on the ground that she had paid $2,500 and was entitled to a deed, and that she was under no obligation to pay the balance of the $4,000. Monroe claimed that there was an unpaid balance of $1,178.08 due on the original contract. Is Monroe right?

6. Hardy, an attorney, was employed by Murphy, president of CPC Corporation, to draft several documents relating to Gregory becoming the major shareholder and chief executive officer of CPC Corporation. Murphy was the present chief executive officer of CPC and was relinquishing control to Gregory upon Gregory's arranging for a loan for CPC. Hardy drew up the required documents for Murphy and then later requested payment for his services from Gregory, who had then become the chief executive officer for CPC. Gregory promised Hardy that he would be paid for his services. Later, Hardy sent a bill for his services to CPC and was denied payment by Gregory, who argued that the work Hardy performed was for Murphy, and therefore the oral promise to pay his debt was without consideration. Is Gregory correct? Yes 3rd party

7. Dr. Browning contracted to purchase the equipment and the practice of Dr. Johnson. Shortly thereafter, Browning decided not to buy and wanted to be released from the contract, but Johnson refused to cancel unless Browning paid him $40,000. Browning agreed. When payment became due, Browning refused to tender Johnson the $40,000. Johnson sued Browning, arguing that there was a lack of consideration on his part to pay Johnson $40,000. Can Johnson recover? Yes

8. Finley contracted with an insurance company to sell life insurance. He was to receive 50 percent of the initial net premium and, in addition, contingent commissions during the life of the policy on all insurance he sold. After

illusory promise

five years he stopped selling for the company. The company then wrote him, saying that although they believed under the contract that his contingent commissions should cease as of the date he terminated writing policies for them, they were sending him the contingent commissions for the balance of that year "in full and final settlement for contingent commissions due under our contract." They enclosed a check that on its face read: "Received as full payment of all money due as contingent commission under the contract between Finley and Insurance Co." Finley cashed the check. Can the company successfully raise accord and satisfaction as a defense to a suit by Finley to recover the balance of the contingent commissions accruing on his policies?

9. Lipsey managed a co-op for 31 years. In 1958 the directors of the co-op decided to relieve him of his duties and promised to pay him retirement benefits for 30 months, provided he cooperated with the directors and the new management. Lipsey somewhat reluctantly accepted the offer and did not encourage opposition from his friends who were co-op members. He spent some time each day for two months aiding the new manager. The co-op terminated the retirement payments after five months, arguing the promises were without consideration. Is the co-op correct? *No*

10. Portland Gasoline Company entered into a contract with Superior Marketing Company, Inc. Superior agreed to market all of the butane-propane gas mixture produced by Portland at its natural-gas processing plant. Superior failed and refused to market all the butane-propane gas mix produced by Portland, and Portland brought suit to recover damages for breach of contract. Superior set up lack of consideration as a defense. Is this a good defense? *Yes*

No consideration

No, implied (court) promised to supply mixture

The Form and Meaning
of Contracts

11

Many people mistakenly believe that oral contracts are not binding and enforceable. How many times have you heard someone say: "I agreed, but they didn't get it in writing"? The truth of the matter is that oral contracts are generally every bit as binding and enforceable as written ones.

There are, however, some exceptions to this general rule. As you will see later in this chapter, all states have *statutes of frauds* that require certain kinds of contracts to be evidenced by writing to be enforceable.

Even if a contract is not one of those that the statute of frauds requires to be in writing, written contracts are more desirable than oral contracts for several reasons. The parties are less likely to misunderstand the terms of their agreement if they have reduced it to written form. If a dispute about the parties' obligations should arise at a later date, the writing is better evidence of the terms of their agreement than their memories, which may fail or be distorted by wishful thinking. Likewise, the existence of a written agreement may provide protection against intentional misstatements about the terms of the agreement.

Parties who put their contracts in writing should try to make the writing as complete and unambiguous (clear) as possible. This reduces the potential for later disagreement and makes it easier for a court to construe (interpret) the agreement if a dispute arises. A court that is called upon to interpret an ambiguous (unclear) agreement relies on rules of construction (interpretation) that the law has created for this purpose. These will be discussed later in this chapter.

The parties to a written agreement should also be sure that the writing is complete and covers all the important terms of their agreement for another important reason. As you will see in a later part of this chapter, a rule of evidence called the *parol evidence rule* often prevents a party to a written contract from trying to prove terms that were left out of the writing.

THE STATUTES OF FRAUDS

The statutes of frauds adopted by the states are patterned after the original statute of frauds adopted in England in 1677. The basic purpose of the statutes is indicated by their name: to prevent frauds. The statutes of frauds are essentially saying that in some cases the law will require more evidence (a writing) that the parties had an agreement than the oral testimony of the party claiming that a contract existed. Fraud is, of course, possible in any kind of contract, but the statute of frauds traditionally focused only on contracts in which the potential for fraud was great or the consequences of fraud were especially serious (due to the nature of the subject matter of the contract).

Among those classes of contracts traditionally included in the statutes of frauds are: (1) contracts by the executor or administrator of a deceased person's estate to be personally liable for a debt of the deceased person, (2) contracts by one person to answer for the debt or default of another, (3) contracts for the transfer of an interest in land, and (4) bilateral contracts that have not been fully performed by either party and are not capable of being performed within a year of their formation.

Several additional classes of contracts have been added to the traditional categories covered by the statutes. In the section of the text on sales, for example, you will learn that the Uniform Commercial Code requires contracts for the sale of goods for the price of $500 or more to be evidenced by a writing, with some exceptions. Many states also require contracts to pay debts barred by a bankruptcy discharge or the statute of limitations to be evidenced by a writing. In addition, many states require contracts to pay a commission on the sale of real estate to be evidenced by a writing.

The Effect of Failure to Comply

In general, the statutes of frauds make oral contracts that come within their provisions *unenforceable*, not void or voidable (some state statutes are exceptions to this rule). This means several things. If the parties to such an oral contract have both fully performed their obligations, neither is allowed to rescind the contract. Their mutual performance is ample evidence that a contract in fact existed. If one of the parties to an executory oral contract files suit to enforce the contract and the other party does not raise the statute of frauds as a defense, the court will enforce the agreement.

If one of the parties to an unenforceable oral contract has rendered some performance under the contract, conferring benefits on the other party, he or she can recover the reasonable value of the performance in a *quasi-contract* suit. In some instances that will be discussed later, part performance of a contract is sufficient to take the contract outside the scope of the statute or to satisfy the statute's requirement of some extra element of proof of a contract's existence beyond the mere oral testimony of a party.

In a recent important development, some states have begun to use the equitable doctrine of *estoppel* to allow some parties to recover under oral contracts that the statutes of frauds would ordinarily render unenforceable. If the plaintiff has *materially relied* on the oral promise and will suffer *serious losses* if the promise is not enforced, courts in these states hold that the other party is *estopped* from raising the statute of frauds as a defense.

Lucas v. Whittaker Corp.
470 F.2d 326 (10th Cir. 1972)

FACTS Whittaker Corporation orally offered Lucas a two-year employment contract. To take the job Lucas left a secure job with a company he had been employed by for nine years (giving up numerous job benefits in the process), left a new home he had had built only eight months before, and moved from California to Colorado. Whittaker fired Lucas after 13 months on the job and, when Lucas filed suit, raised the statute of frauds as a defense. The trial court held that the doctrine of equitable estoppel prevented Whittaker from raising the statute of frauds defense.

ISSUE Is Whittaker estopped from raising the statute of frauds as a defense?

DECISION Yes. The court held that, since the contract was created in California, Colorado law required that California law be applied to test its validity. The contract in question would ordinarily have to be evidenced by a writing since it was not capable of being performed within one year. The court further noted, however, that: "In California the doctrine of equitable estoppel to assert the statute of frauds is applied to prevent fraud that would result from refusal to enforce an oral contract." Estoppel applies when denying enforcement of the contract would produce an unconscionable result because one party has been induced by the other to seriously change his position in reliance on the contract. The court agreed with the trial court's conclusion that Lucas gave up more to accept the job with Whittaker than would normally be suffered in an ordinary change of jobs.

CONTRACTS COVERED BY THE STATUTES OF FRAUDS

**Executors'
Agreements to
Personally Pay
Their Decedents'
Debts**

When a person dies, an executor or administrator is appointed by the probate court to settle the deceased person's (the decedent's) estate. Basically, this involves paying all outstanding claims against the estate and distributing the remainder, if any, to the decedent's heirs. The executor or administrator is often a relative or close friend of the decedent.

Creditors of the decedent who fear that the decedent's estate will not be great enough to cover their claims may try to get the executor to agree to be personally responsible for the decedent's debts. Executors who are relatives or close friends may feel morally obligated to make such promises, although they have no legal obligation to do so. In extreme cases, creditors who would otherwise suffer a great loss may be tempted to lie and claim the executor made such a promise. To prevent such frauds and to guard against ill-considered promises by executors, such promises must be in writing to be enforceable.

Contracts to Answer for the Debt of Another

In addition to the executor's contracts just discussed, there are many other common situations in which one person agrees to be responsible for the debts or default of another. Such contracts are called *collateral* or *guaranty contracts*. The essence of such contracts is that a third person (the *guarantor*) agrees to perform the contractual duties another person (the *obligor*) owes under another contract, in the event that the obligor defaults. The person to whom the obligor and the guarantor are contractually liable is called the *obligee*.

If, for example, a clothing store (the obligee) that has entered a credit account with Mike, a college student (the obligor), gets Mike's older brother Tom (the guarantor) to agree to pay the amount owed on the account if Mike fails to do so, this is a guaranty contract. Such contracts must be in writing to be enforceable.

Many three-party transactions are not guaranty contracts, but are instead *original contracts* of the third party. The distinction between an original contract and a guaranty contract is important because original contracts do not need to be evidenced by a writing to be enforceable. The major difference between the two is that a party to an original contract is *primarily* liable (absolutely liable under the terms of the contract) to perform his or her contractual duties, while a guarantor is only *secondarily* liable (liable only if the obligor does not perform).

For example, Bob and Joe agree to buy a television set from Frank's T.V. Service for $189.95, payable over 24 months. Bob and Joe are *co-obligors* on the sales agreement and are both *primarily* liable to make the payments. Frank's T.V. can collect the amount due under the agreement from *either* Bob or Joe without first showing a demand for payment from the other. Bob and Joe's promises are therefore *original* ones and need not be evidenced by a writing to be enforceable.

> ### *Pravel, Wilson & Matthews v. Voss*
> ### 471 F.2d 1186 (5th Cir. 1973)
>
> **FACTS** Pravel, Wilson & Matthews, a law firm, was hired to bring a patent infringement suit for V & S Ice Machine Company. Upon learning that V & S was a shell corporation organized for the sole purpose of holding the patent and conducting the suit, the law firm sought assurances from Voss, a principal stockholder of V & S, that the firm would be paid for its services. Voss on several occasions assured the firm he would pay, at one point telling Wilson he saw the suit as an "investment" that could yield several times the fee. V & S lost the suit and when the firm's $14,000 bill went unpaid, suit was filed against Voss, who raised the defense of statute of frauds.
>
> **ISSUE** Was the agreement between Voss and Pravel, Wilson & Matthews a guaranty contract within the scope of the statute of frauds?
>
> **DECISION** No. The court said that there was nothing in the record to support Voss's claim that he had promised to answer for a debt owed by the corporation. Instead, the court said that: "Voss clearly and repeatedly promised the lawyers that he personally would pay their fee. Thus, the statute of frauds is simply inapplicable to this case on its facts." Even if the record indicated that Voss had promised to pay a corporate debt, the court said that the firm could recover a quasi-contract judgment for the reasonable value of their services.

Contracts Transferring an Interest in Land

Our legal system has historically treated land as being more important than other forms of property. This special treatment stems from the time when land was the primary basis of wealth. As a result of this special status, contracts transferring an interest in land must be evidenced by a writing to be enforceable. Therefore, oral contracts to sell or mortgage real estate, to permit the mining and removal of minerals from land, and to grant easement rights to land are generally unenforceable. Most states have a separate statute of frauds covering leases. Generally, these statutes require a writing only for long-term leases (e.g., for leases of a year or longer).

In some cases, *part performance* of a contract for the sale of land takes the contract out of the coverage of the statute. In order for part performance to have this effect, it must clearly indicate the existence of a contract of sale and not be consistent with any other interpretation. Ordinarily, this requires that the buyer either has made substantial improvements to the property or has taken possession of the property and paid part or all of the purchase price. The only other instance where part performance has this effect is in the case of sales contracts under the Uniform Commercial Code. This exception will be discussed in Chapter 15.

> ### *Uscian v. Blacconeri*
> ### 340 N.E.2d 618 (Ct. App. Ill. 1975)
>
> **FACTS** Uscian entered into a written contract to sell Blacconeri a piece of real estate. The contract was conditioned on Uscian's obtaining city approval to subdivide the property. Uscian failed to get approval and the parties later orally agreed to the sale without the subdivision condition. Uscian later refused to sell the property and, when Blacconeri sued for specific performance, he raised the statute of frauds as a defense.
>
> **ISSUE** Is the parties' agreement within the scope of the statute of frauds?
>
> **DECISION** Yes. The statute of frauds requires that contracts to convey land be evidenced by a writing. The parties' earlier written contract had terminated due to Uscian's inability to get permission to subdivide. Therefore, the later oral agreement was a new contract and was unenforceable since it was not evidenced by a writing.

Bilateral Contracts Not Capable of Being Performed within One Year

Long-term bilateral contracts must be in writing because contracts that call for performance over a considerable period of time increase the risk of faulty or willfully inaccurate recollection of their terms in subsequent disputes. Unfortunately, attempts at line-drawing such as this all too often produce apparently silly results in many cases. The following are examples of how the courts have applied this rule.

The first thing to note is that these statutes are generally worded to include only *executory* bilateral contracts "not to be performed within one year" or "not capable of being performed within one year." This means that if it is *possible* for the contract to be performed within a year, it need not be evidenced by a writing, despite the fact that performance *is not likely to be* or *is not in fact* completed within a year.

The one-year period is computed from the time the contract comes into existence, not from the time performance is to begin. Most states begin counting on the day after the contract comes into existence (parts of days are not counted). A few states start on the day the contract is entered.

When a contract states an indefinite time for performance, it need not be evidenced by a writing if it is possible to perform the contract within one year. So, oral contracts to perform "for life" are generally enforceable, since one of the parties concerned could die within a year and have thereby fully performed.

What Kind of Writing Is Required?

While the statutes of frauds of all the states are not the same, most states require only a *memorandum* of the parties' agreement; they do not require that the entire contract be in writing. The memorandum may consist of several documents, so long as it is clear that they all relate to the same agreement. It can be in any form, including letters, telegrams, receipts, or any other writing indicating that the parties had a contract.

Although there is a general trend away from requiring complete writings to satisfy the statute of frauds, an adequate memorandum must still contain several things. The identity of the parties to the contract must be indicated in some way, and the subject matter of the contract must be identified with reasonable certainty. This latter requirement causes particular problems in contracts for the sale of land, since many states require a fairly detailed description of the property to be sold. The statutes of the states vary on whether the memorandum must state the consideration agreed to by the parties.

McDaniel v. Silvernail
346 N.E.2d 382 (Ct. App. Ill. 1976)

FACTS George McDaniel was a tenant of Alfreda Silvernail's. Alfreda signed the following document, agreeing to sell McDaniel *part* of her property:

> 2/14/72
>
> I agree to sell to George McDaniel the house on R. R. 2, in which he now lives, plus two acres for $6,000 to be agreed.
>
> (s) Alfreda Silvernail
>
> Rent of $70 monthly to be applied as purchase price—less taxes and insurance.

Silvernail refused to convey a deed and McDaniel filed suit for specific performance.

ISSUE Does the statute of frauds bar enforcement of the parties' agreement?

DECISION Yes. The court said that the writing was insufficient to satisfy the statute of frauds because it did not contain "a description of the property which is sufficiently certain so that it can be identified." The court found the property description inadequate because it could not locate the boundaries of the property to be conveyed from the language of the document. The court refused to allow proof of part performance by McDaniel, because part performance cannot exist unless the parties have a contract and have fully agreed on all its essential terms.

One point on which the states generally agree is that the memorandum needs to be signed only by the party to be bound (or his or her agent). This means that both parties' signatures do not have to appear in the writing. The idea here simply is that it is the defendant who needs protection against fraud, so it is his or her signature that is required to satisfy the statute. It is, however, in the best interests of both parties for both signatures to appear on the writing; otherwise, the contract evidenced by the writing is enforceable only against the signing party.

INTERPRETING CONTRACTS

The Necessity of Interpretation

Many times the parties to a contract disagree about the meaning of one or more terms of their agreement. When this occurs, the courts must interpret or construe the contract to determine the rights and duties of the parties. The interpretation of uncertain or ambiguous terms is generally a question for the jury. The basic standard of interpretation is objective: The courts attempt to give the agreement the meaning that the parties would be expected to give it in the light of the surrounding facts and circumstances.

Rules of Construction

The courts have created certain basic rules to guide them in interpreting contracts. Most of these are simply matters of common sense. The first thing a court does is attempt to determine the *principal objective* of the parties. Every clause of the contract is then determined in the light of this principal objective. Ordinary words are given their usual meaning and technical words their technical meaning unless a different meaning was clearly intended.

If the parties used a form contract, or the contract is partly printed and partly written, the *written terms control the printed terms* if the two conflict. If one of the parties drafted the contract, ambiguities are resolved *against the party who drafted the contract.*

If the parties are both members of the same trade, profession, or community in which certain words are commonly given a particular meaning (this is called *usage*), the courts presume the parties intended the meaning that usage gives to the terms they use. Usage can also add provisions to the parties' agreement. If the court finds that a certain practice is a matter of common usage in the trade, profession, or community of the parties, the court assumes that the parties intended to include that practice in their agreement. Parties who are members of a common business, profession, or community and intend not to be bound by usage should specifically say so in their agreement.

Stender v. Twin City Foods, Inc.
510 P.2d 221 (Sup. Ct. Wash. 1977)

FACTS Twin City Foods, a food processor, entered a contract with Stender, a grower, obligating Twin City to harvest and vine Stender's pea crop at maturity and pay Stender a specified price. The contract gave Twin City the right to divert (at a lower price) to seed or feed purposes as much of Stender's crop as quality ". . . of salvage might dictate in the event of *adverse weather conditions that might delay harvest of pea crop beyond optimum maturity for processing.*"Weather conditions resulted in an early maturation of Stender's entire crop. Twin City claimed the right to divert Stender's crop under the adverse weather clause, arguing that the custom in the pea industry was to plant peas in a staggered manner to avoid the entire crop maturing at once.

ISSUE   Did the adverse weather clause give Twin City the right to divert Stender's crop?

DECISION   Yes. The intent of the contracting parties must be determined by viewing the contract as a whole and all the circumstances surrounding its making. Both parties had long experience in the industry, and therefore the contract should be construed in light of the usages of the pea industry in existence when the contract was executed. In his trial testimony Stender had admitted knowing of the custom of staggered planting, and the facts indicated that Twin City bypassed Stender's crop because weather conditions increased the size of crops ready for processing beyond any reasonable expectations. Therefore, the court concluded that the phrase "adverse weather conditions" included "unusual temperature fluctuations resulting in an unexpected maturation of the entire pea crop which has been systematically planted with the objective of partial maturation over a period of time to allow for orderly harvesting."

THE PAROL EVIDENCE RULE

The Purpose of the Rule

The basic idea behind the parol evidence rule is that when the parties to an agreement have expressed their agreement in a complete, unambiguous writing, the writing is the best evidence of their intent. This is generally true since the terms of the writing are known and irrefutable, whereas oral statements by the parties after a dispute has arisen may be affected by faulty memory, wishful thinking, or outright bad intent. So, the *parol evidence rule* says that a party cannot vary the terms of a written contract by introducing evidence of oral terms allegedly agreed upon prior to, or contemporaneous with (at the same time as), the writing.

The parol evidence rule is a potential source of danger for parties who reduce their agreements to written form, since it can operate to prevent proof of oral terms that the parties did in fact agree to. For example, Bob buys a house from Susan. They orally agree that Susan will pay for any major repairs the house needs for the first year Bob owns it. The written contract of sale, however, does not include this term, and when the furnace breaks down three months after the sale, Susan refuses to pay the cost of repair. If the written contract is complete and unambiguous, Bob will probably be barred from proving the oral repair term.

The lesson to be learned from this example is that parties who put their agreements in writing should make sure that all the terms of their agreement are included in the writing.

Exceptions to the Parol Evidence Rule

There are many situations where the writing is not the best evidence of the agreement between the parties. These are the bases of the following exceptions to the rule.

Lack of Voluntary Consent.   A party is always allowed to introduce oral proof that the contract the writing represents was entered into as the result of fraud, misrepresentation, duress, undue influence, or mistake. This sort of proof is allowed because it does not seek to contradict the terms of the writing and because of our strong public policy against enforcing such agreements. For the same reasons, oral testimony that attempts to show that the contract is illegal is also allowed.

Ambiguous Contracts.   If the terms of the writing are unclear, oral testimony can be introduced to aid the court in interpreting the writing. A party can introduce testimony about the facts and circumstances surrounding the agreement without contradicting its terms.

Incomplete Writings.   If the writing is clearly incomplete, a party can introduce proof of *consistent* oral terms that "fill in the gaps" in the writing. A party is never allowed, however, to use this exception to alter, vary, or contradict the written terms of the contract.

Subsequent Oral Contracts.   A party can always introduce proof of an oral agreement made *after* the writing was created. A writing made on the fifth of the month is plainly not the best evidence of an agreement made on the tenth of the month. You should note, however, that subsequent oral modifications of contracts may sometimes be unenforceable due to lack of consideration or failure to comply with the statute of frauds.

Conditions Precedent.   If the written agreement is silent about the date it is to take effect or about any conditions that must occur before it becomes effective, oral testimony can be introduced to prove these facts. Such proof merely elaborates upon, but does not contradict, the terms of the writing.

Estrada v. Darling-Crose Machine Company, Inc.
80 Cal. Rptr. 266 (Ct. App. Cal. 1969)

FACTS   Richard Estrada was a sales engineer for Darling-Crose, a distributor of machine tools. He and Darling-Crose had a written agreement providing that Estrada would get a 35 percent commission on all "sales" he made plus expenses. Estrada quit his job with Darling-Crose, and Darling-Crose refused to pay more than half of his normal commissions on those items he sold that were delivered to customers after he quit. At trial, Darling-Crose attempted to prove that the custom in the machine tool industry was to pay half the normal commission on orders solicited by a sales engineer before quitting but delivered after quitting. They argued that a sales engineer normally performs important and time-consuming functions after delivery, like installation and adjustment of the machinery. The trial court held that the parol evidence rule barred Darling-Crose's proof of custom. Darling-Crose appealed.

ISSUE   Should Darling-Crose have been allowed to introduce proof of custom in the machine tool industry?

> **DECISION** Yes. When the parties to a writing intend it as an *integration*, a complete and final embodiment of the terms of the agreement, parol evidence cannot be used to add to or vary its terms. However, when the agreement was not an integration, parol evidence can be used to prove elements of the agreement that were not reduced to writing. The writing in this case did not discuss how commissions were to be paid on orders like those in question, when delivery was made after Estrada's employment had ceased. Under these circumstances, the interpretation of the term "sale" must be implied from the nature of the contract and the circumstances surrounding it. Whether the matter of the duration of the 35 percent commission provision is viewed as an omission or as an ambiguity in the term "sale" (i.e., whether the sale took place when the order was obtained or on the delivery and installation), Darling-Crose's evidence of custom should have been considered.

QUESTIONS AND PROBLEM CASES

1. What is the effect of failure to comply with the statute of frauds?
2. Why doesn't the parol evidence rule bar the introduction of proof of oral agreements made subsequent to a writing?
3. Weitnauer agreed to act as a purchasing agent for Annis's company and to guaranty to creditors the payment of the company's orders. This agreement provided that Annis was to be personally liable to Weitnauer for the amount of the orders up to $100,000. Subsequently, the orders exceeded $100,000 and Weitnauer requested an additional $50,000 personal guaranty from Annis to cover these increases, which Annis orally promised to do. Annis later sent several signed letters to Weitnauer in which he admitted entering the new guaranty agreement. Eventually Weitnauer had to pay creditors on these accounts and sued Annis to collect on these personal guaranties. Annis set up the statute of frauds as his defense. Will Annis prevail?
4. Hartford issued a three-year term fire insurance policy to Gillespie Co. through its agent, Frontier. The policy contained a provision that it could be canceled at any time at the request of Gillespie. Later Gillespie expanded to a second location and Frontier orally contracted with Hartford to modify the original contract to provide coverage at the new location. A fire occurred at the new location, resulting in a loss of $107,000. Hartford refused to pay the claim, arguing that the oral contract was unenforceable under the statute of frauds since it was a contract not to be performed within one year. Is this a valid defense?
5. Powless responded over the telephone to an advertisement offering employment. Pawtucket Screw Company's plant manager allegedly made an oral wage offer that was higher than Powless subsequently received for working. Powless continued to work for five years, but no specified length of time for Powless to remain employed had been discussed in the telephone conversation. Powless sued for back-pay due under the oral agreement. Is Powless's claim barred by the statute of frauds?
6. Tradeways, Inc., brought an action for breach of contract against Chrysler Corporation. Tradeways offered to conduct an advertising campaign for Chrysler, with payment to be made in one of two alternative ways. First, Chrysler would pay $130,000 cash, or second, each Chrysler dealer could be assessed $180. The services would be rendered over a two-year period. Chrysler stated that it wanted the offer

reduced to writing, and Blount, Chrysler's representative, later told Tradeways over the phone that it had been "selected" by Chrysler. Chrysler later refused to go ahead with the deal. Can Tradeways collect damages?

7. In April 1973, Lyle orally offered to sell Farmers Elevator 20,000 bushels of corn for $1.22 per bushel for May delivery. Farmers Elevator accepted the offer and entered a note to this effect in the company ledger and then, according to customary trade practice, began to sell various amounts of corn to buyers for future delivery. When Lyle refused to deliver corn in May, Farmers Elevator had to cover the deficiency in its inventory by buying elsewhere at prices averaging about $1.80 per bushel. When sued, Lyle set up the statute of frauds as a defense. Will Lyle prevail?

8. Ranch, Inc., contracted in writing with Washington Tent & Awning Co. to manufacture and install a canopy in front of Ranch's restaurant. It was orally understood that Ranch needed the permission of its landlord for the installation of the canopy. The canopy was installed and Ranch now refused to pay for it, contending it never received the landlord's permission. Washington argued that the admission of the evidence concerning the term requiring the landlord's permission was barred by the parol evidence rule. Will the court permit Ranch to prove that the written agreement was conditioned on the approval of the landlord?

Illegality

12

Illegality

The parties to an agreement may have met every other requirement for a valid contract, but their agreement is unenforceable if either its formation or its performance is illegal or contrary to the public interest. The public welfare is simply more important than the right of individuals to bargain freely. No sensible legal system would enforce bargains that undermine its authority or its basic objectives.

Types of Illegality

An agreement is illegal if it calls for behavior that violates a statute or a rule of common law. Also, certain kinds of agreements are themselves made illegal by statutes. An agreement that is contrary to a general rule of public policy is also illegal.

The Presumption of Legality

When determining the legality of an agreement, the courts presume the parties intended a legal result and interpret their agreement accordingly. All doubts are resolved in favor of the legality of the agreement unless the parties clearly intended an illegal bargain.

THE EFFECT OF ILLEGALITY

General Rule

Hands off illegal agreements is the general position taken by the courts. A court will not enforce illegal agreements but will leave the parties where it finds them. This means that a party to an illegal agreement generally cannot recover damages for breach of the agreement, recover consideration given to the other party, or recover in quasi contract for benefits conferred on the other party. The basic reason for this rule is to further the public

140

interest, not to punish the parties to an illegal agreement. In some cases, however, the public interest may be best served by allowing some recovery. In such cases exceptions are made to the hands-off approach.

Ignorance of Fact or Special Regulation

Even though it is often said that ignorance is no excuse, the courts have sometimes allowed recovery if one or both of the parties to an illegal bargain are ignorant of the facts that made the bargain illegal. Recovery is allowed only for performance rendered before the parties learned of the illegality, and only if the illegality does not involve immoral behavior. The same is true where one of the parties to a contract is unaware of the fact that the contract is illegal due to a violation of a special statute regulating the other party's business. For example, Frank enters a contract to perform in a play at Martha's theater. Frank does not know that Martha does not have the license to operate a theater as required by statute. Frank can recover the wages provided in the agreement for work he performs before he knows of the violation.

One of the main reasons for refusing to enforce illegal contracts is to deter people from entering such contracts. A court is therefore not likely to be disturbed when a person who has knowingly entered such a contract is hurt by the hands-off approach. The same is not true where a party unknowingly enters such a contract, and this accounts for the above exceptions. Similarly, exceptions to the general rule are usually made on behalf of those who have entered illegal agreements due to misrepresentation, fraud, duress, or undue influence.

Rights of Protected Parties

Many regulatory statutes attempt to protect certain classes of the public. In cases where a person whom a statute seeks to protect enters into an agreement in violation of the statute, the protected person is allowed to enforce the agreement, or at least recover any consideration he or she has parted with. The obvious reason for this exception to the hands-off rule is that public policy is not well served if courts punish the person a statute seeks to protect by following the general rule. For example, most states require foreign corporations (those incorporated outside the state) to get a license before doing business in the state. These statutes often specifically provide that an unlicensed corporation cannot enforce contracts it enters into with citizens of the state. Citizens of the licensing state, however, are generally allowed to enforce their contracts with the unlicensed foreign corporation.

Rescission before Performance of Illegal Act

Public policy is clearly served best by any rule that encourages people not to commit illegal acts. Parties who have fully or partially performed their part of an illegal contract have little incentive to raise the question of illegality if they know that they will be unable to recover what they have given due to the hands-off approach to illegal contracts. To encourage such people to cancel illegal agreements, the courts allow one who rescinds the contract before any illegal act has been performed to recover any consideration given. For example, John, the owner of a restaurant, offers Bob, an employee of a competitor's restaurant, $1,000 for some of his competitor's secret recipes. He gives Bob $500 in advance. If John has second thoughts and tells Bob the deal is off before receiving any recipes, he can recover the $500.

Illegality and Divisible Contracts

A contract may call for the performance of several promises, some legal and some illegal. If the contract is *divisible*, that is, if the legal parts can be separated from the illegal parts, the courts enforce the legal parts of the contract. If the contract is not divisible, the illegal part "taints" the entire contract, making it unenforceable.

Similarly, if the main purpose of a contract can be achieved without enforcing an illegal part of the contract, a court enforces the main part of the agreement. For example, Barbara agrees to buy Kathy's beauty shop and the agreement bars Kathy from operating as a beautician for the rest of her life. The sale is enforceable, but the agreement not to compete is not enforced for reasons discussed later in this chapter.

CONTRACTS TO COMMIT ILLEGAL ACTS

Agreements to Commit Crimes

An agreement that calls for the commission of a crime is illegal. If Alice hires Bob to burn down Tom's place of business, such an agreement would be unenforceable, and Alice would be unable to recover any money she paid Bob to do the job. An agreement may be illegal if its net effect is criminal, even though the acts called for are individually lawful. For example, the only newspapers in a city may form a joint agency to sell subscriptions and advertising, acts that are legal in themselves. However, the effect of these acts may be to fix the price of these items, which, as you will see in Chapter 48, is a violation of the antitrust laws.

Allen v. Jordanos', Inc.
125 Cal. Rptr. 31 (Ct. App. Cal. 1975)

FACTS   Allen was an employee of Jordanos'. Jordanos' suspected him of theft but could not prove it. Allen, as a union member, was entitled to an arbitration of Jordanos' charges. The union negotiated an agreement with Jordanos' that called for Allen to accept a permanent layoff from Jordanos' in exchange for Jordanos' agreement not to disclose the reason for the layoff. State law provided that anyone who voluntarily left work without good cause or was discharged for misconduct was not eligible to receive unemployment benefits. State law also made it a misdemeanor for an employer to willfully withhold or fail to report information in an attempt to aid a discharged employee in obtaining unemployment benefits. Jordanos' informed the state unemployment bureau of the reasons for Allen's layoff, and Allen was denied unemployment benefits. He filed suit for breach of contract.

ISSUE   Is Jordanos' contract with Allen unenforceable due to illegality?

DECISION   Yes. The court observed that: "Allen was bargaining for an act that was illegal by definition—to withhold information from or give false information to the state bureau." Illegal nondisclosure was not a minor or indirect part of the contract, but a major and substantial consideration of the agreement. A contract calling for such illegal consideration is unenforceable.

Agreements to Commit Torts

A contract that cannot be performed without committing a tort is illegal. So, if Mary hires John to throw a pie in her business law professor's face, their agreement is illegal, since John would have to commit the tort of battery (and probably assault) to perform his side of the contract.

CONTRACTS MADE ILLEGAL BY STATUTE

Wagering Statutes

All states have statutes that either prohibit or regulate gambling. Agreements in violation of these statutes are illegal. A recurring problem in this area is how to tell an illegal *wagering* contract from legal *risk-shifting* and *speculative bargaining* agreements.

When the parties create a new risk for the sole purpose of bearing it, that is an illegal wager. If, however, the parties agree who shall bear an existing risk, that is a legal risk-shifting agreement. Property insurance contracts are classic examples of risk-shifting agreements. The owner of the property pays the insurance company a fee in return for the company's agreement to bear the risk that the property will be damaged or destroyed. If, however, the person who takes out the policy had no legitimate economic interest in the insured property (called an *insurable interest* in insurance law), the agreement is an illegal wager.

Stock and commodity market transactions are good examples of speculative bargains that are legal. In both cases the purchasers are obviously hoping their purchases will increase in value and the sellers believe they will not. The difference between these transactions and wagers lies in the fact that the parties to stock and commodities transactions are legally bound to the purchase agreement (although the purchaser may never intend to actually take delivery of the stock or commodity). In an illegal wager, no purchase is involved, for example, a bet on the future performance of a stock or commodity.

Statutes Declaring Bargains Void

Many states have passed statutes making certain kinds of agreements void or voidable. Two examples of such statutes are usury laws and Sunday laws.

Usury laws prohibit charging more than a stated amount of interest for the use of money. The penalty for violation ranges from forfeiture of excess interest, through forfeiture of all interest, to forfeiture of interest and principal, depending on the state. In several states usury laws do not apply to loans to corporations, and many states allow a higher price to be charged for credit sales than cash sales without counting the price difference as interest.

Sunday laws prohibit the performance of certain work and the transaction of certain business on Sunday, depending on the provisions of the statute.

Regulatory Statutes

Congress and the state legislatures have passed a variety of statutes regulating numerous kinds of activities. The most common kind of regulatory statute requires persons, partnerships, or corporations to acquire a license before engaging in a regulated activity. The basic purpose of such statutes is to protect the public from dishonest or unskilled persons. Lawyers, doctors, dentists, and other professionals are required to pass examinations to become licensed to practice. In many states real estate brokers, stockbrokers, and insurance agents may also be required to pass an examination and prove they are of good character before being granted a license.

Barbers, beauty operators, building contractors, electricians, plumbers, and others who perform skilled services may also be required to obtain licenses. The same is true for pawnbrokers, retailers and wholesalers of liquor and tobacco, and sellers of other special items.

It is generally held that agreements by unlicensed persons to perform regulated services or engage in regulated businesses are illegal and therefore unenforceable. For example, an unlicensed person who acts as a real estate broker and sells a house would be unable to recover the agreed upon commission for the sale.

One major exception to this general rule that must be noted is the case of *revenue-raising statutes.* The failure to obtain a license required by a statute whose sole purpose is to raise revenue does not affect the legality of unlicensed persons' agreements. Whether a statute is classed as *regulatory* or *revenue-raising* depends on the intent of the legislature, which may not always be clearly expressed. As a general rule, statutes that require proof of character and skill and impose a penalty for violation are considered regulatory. Those that impose a significant license fee and allow anyone who pays the fee to obtain a license are classed as revenue-raising.

The reason for making the distinction between the two types of statutes is that the strong public interest in protecting the public against fraud and incompetence may justify the sometimes harsh measure of denying recovery for services rendered to those who violate regulatory statutes. This strong public interest is absent where the statute violated is merely aimed at raising revenue, and such statutes ordinarily impose a substantial fine for violation in any event.

You should also note that the courts may not deny recovery in every case even where regulatory statutes are violated. If the amount forfeited would be great and the unlicensed party is neither dishonest nor incompetent, a court may not feel that the public interest is best served by allowing the other party to the agreement to be unjustly enriched at the expense of the unlicensed party.

Wilson v. Kealakekua Ranch, Ltd.
551 P.2d 525 (Sup. Ct. Hawaii 1976)

FACTS Wilson was a licensed architect who had failed to pay the annual $15 registration fee required by the licensing statute. He had done $33,900 of work for Kealakekua Ranch, which refused to pay. He sued for his fee and Kealakekua raised the defense of illegality.

ISSUE Did Wilson's failure to pay the annual registration fee make his contract with Kealakekua illegal?

DECISION No. When a statute does not state whether a violation deprives the parties of their right to sue on the contract, a distinction is made between revenue-raising statutes and those whose purpose is to protect the public against incompetence and fraud. There is no relationship between the payment of annual fees and the competence or character of an architect. The provision requiring renewal by way of payment of a $15 fee was, therefore, not for public protection but for raising revenue.

CONTRACTS CONTRARY TO PUBLIC POLICY

The Idea of Public Policy

Public policy is a broad concept that is impossible to define precisely. Perhaps the only realistic way to define it is to say that a court's view of public policy is determined by what the court feels is in the best interests of society. Public policy may change with the times; changing social and economic conditions may make behavior that was acceptable in an earlier time unacceptable today, or vice versa.

There is therefore no simple rule for determining when a particular bargain is contrary to public policy and illegal. Public policy includes immoral and unethical agreements, even though they may not call for the performance of an illegal act. The courts have broad discretion in ruling on questions of public policy, and this discretion can provide the legal system with a degree of healthy flexibility. However, the courts may differ in their views of what constitutes desirable public policy—a difference that can make a contract legal in one state and illegal in another. The following are examples of contracts that the courts have found to be contrary to public policy.

Contracts Injurious to Public Service

The public interest is best served when public officials fully and faithfully perform their duties. It should come as no surprise, then, that agreements that induce public servants to deviate from their duty are illegal. For example, agreements to pay public employees more or less than their lawful salary are unlawful. Also, agreements that create a conflict between a public employee's personal interests and public duties are also illegal. A good example of this kind of case would be an agreement between a state highway department employee and a real estate speculator who pays the public employee for advance notice of the planned routes of new highway construction. Agreements to pay public servants to influence their decision making are also illegal.

Troutman v. Southern Railway Co.
441 F.2d 586 (5th Cir. 1971)

FACTS The Interstate Commerce Commission issued an order in 1963 requiring Southern to increase freight rates on grain shipments from the Midwest to the Southeast by approximately 16 percent. Compliance with the order would have caused significant losses on investments and in future revenues. Southern hired Troutman, an attorney with no experience in ICC matters, but who was known to be a personal friend and political ally of President John F. Kennedy. Southern planned to file suit to enjoin the ICC order, and Troutman was instructed to persuade the President and the Department of Justice (headed by Robert F. Kennedy) to "ditch" the ICC and enter the case on Southern's side. Troutman's efforts were successful, but Southern refused to pay his legal fees. The trial court awarded Troutman $175,000 and Southern appealed.

ISSUE Was Troutman's contract with Southern an illegal contract to influence a public official's exercise of his duties?

DECISION No. A contract to influence a public official in the exercise of his duties is illegal and unenforceable when that contract contemplates the use of personal or political influence rather than appeal to the judgment of the official on the merits of the case. However, all citizens have the right to petition the government for redress of grievances and one can employ an agent or attorney to use his or her influence to gain access to a public official. Only elements of personal influence and sinister means would make such a contract illegal. Southern had the burden of proving such illegality and apparently failed to do so, since the jury found that Troutman had been hired to use his influence merely to gain access to the President and present to him the merits of Southern's case.

Contracts to Influence Fiduciaries

Any agreement that tends to induce a *fiduciary* (a person in a position of trust or confidence like a trustee, agent, or partner) to breach his or her fiduciary duties is illegal. This is so because such an agreement operates as a fraud upon the principal or beneficiary who is entitled to the fiduciary's loyalty. This applies to agreements by fiduciaries that favor the interests of a third person at the expense of their principals' interests, and agreements that produce a conflict between fiduciaries' personal interests and their principals' interests. The only way a fiduciary may lawfully enter such an agreement is by fully and fairly disclosing the conflict to his or her principal or beneficiary in advance. *need consent of party*

Exculpatory Clauses

An *exculpatory clause* is a provision in a contract that attempts to relieve one party to the contract from liability for the consequences of his or her own negligence. Public policy generally favors holding people responsible for their own behavior. On the other hand, if no duty to the public is involved and the parties have freely and knowingly agreed, the exculpatory clause may be enforceable. Exculpatory clauses that seek to avoid liability for willful misconduct or fraud, however, are generally held to be illegal.

Hy-Grade Oil Co. v. New Jersey Bank
350 A.2d 279 (Super. Ct. N.J. 1975)

FACTS Hy-Grade filed suit against New Jersey Bank due to the bank's refusal to credit Hy-Grade's account with an amount Hy-Grade claimed to have deposited in the bank's night depository box. In defense, the bank pointed to a clause in its "night depository agreement" with Hy-Grade that provided that "the use of night depository facilities shall be at the sole risk of the customer."

ISSUE Is the exculpatory clause in the night depository agreement enforceable against Hy-Grade?

DECISION No. Where a party to an agreement is under a public duty entailing the exercise of care, he may not relieve himself of liability for negligence. Either unequal bargaining power or the existence of a public interest may be a basis for rejection of such clauses. The court noted that the majority of states tend to enforce exculpatory clauses in night deposit contracts due to fear of dishonest claims being presented by customers, but concluded that: "In New Jersey we have rejected such a thesis in other situations and have held that the possibility of fraudulent or collusive litigation does not justify immunity from liability for negligence."

Contracts in Restraint of Trade

One of the basic assumptions underlying our economic system is that the public interest is, in most cases, best served by free competition. On the other hand, the courts have recognized that there are some situations where limited restrictions on competition are justifiable. The courts therefore look very closely at agreements that attempt to limit competition to see whether the restraint imposed is reasonable or should be stricken down for violating public policy. In Chapter 48 you will also learn that some agreements in restraint of trade are specifically made illegal by the antitrust laws.

Agreements whose *sole* purpose is to restrain trade are illegal. However, a restraint that is merely *ancillary to* (supplementary to) a contract may be legal if it is designed to protect interests created by the contract and is no broader than is reasonably necessary to protect those interests. For example, it is common for a contract for the sale of a business to provide that the seller will not compete with the buyer for a specified period of time after the sale. If the restriction covers a reasonable geographic area and a reasonable time period, it will probably be upheld. Similarly, employment contracts sometimes provide that employees will not compete with or work for a competitor of their employer after they have ceased their employment. If such a restriction is reasonably necessary to prevent an employee from disclosing trade secrets or taking away the employer's customers, and it is reasonably limited geographically and in time, it is also likely to be upheld.

The courts do not agree on how to treat a restriction that is unreasonably broad. Some courts enforce the restraint for a reasonable period of time and within a reasonable geographic area. Others strike the entire restriction and refuse to grant the buyer or employer any protection.

Central Credit Collection Control Corp. v. Grayson
499 P.2d 57 (Ct. App. Wash. 1972)

FACTS Central, a debt collection agency operating in Pierce County and surrounding counties, hired Grayson under a six-year employment contract. The contract contained a clause prohibiting Grayson from working in the debt collection business in Pierce County or any bordering county for two years after termination of his employment. Within a month after his employment had ceased, Grayson had opened a competing collection business 73 yards from Central's office, taking over several accounts formerly serviced by Central. Central sued to enforce the restrictive clause.

ISSUE Is the restrictive clause legally enforceable?

DECISION Yes. Covenants not to compete upon termination of employment are valid but should not be greater than reasonably necessary to protect the business or goodwill of the employer. The court did not decide whether the clause in Grayson's contract was reasonable as to time and area, noting that if either were unreasonably broad it would enforce the clause for a reasonable time and area. The court concluded that Grayson's acts would clearly have violated any reasonable restrictions.

It has been traditionally held that agreements restricting the free *alienation* (sale) of land are contrary to public policy, which favors a free market in land.

Unequal Bargains

As you saw in Chapter 5, the courts were historically unwilling to consider arguments that a contract was the product of unequal bargaining power. As long as all the legal elements of a contract were present and the agreement was free from misrepresentation, fraud, duress, undue influence, or mistake, the common law courts would enforce it, despite the fact that its terms might be grossly unfair to one of the parties. This was justified by the doctrine of *freedom of contract.*

The changing nature of our society, however, has produced many contract situations in which the bargaining power of the parties may be grossly unequal. This may make it possible for one of the parties to effectively dictate the terms of the agreement, and to take advantage of this power by dictating terms that are unfair to the other party. The legal system has responded to these changes in two major ways.

First, there has been an increasing "public" input through legislation into many previously private contract situations. Wage and hour laws, workmen's compensation laws, usury laws, and model lease laws are just a few of the many kinds of statutes aimed at placing limits on the exercise of private bargaining power.

Second, today's courts are responding to the problem by recognizing the idea of *unconscionable contracts* and *contracts of adhesion*—contracts where the only choice for one of the parties is between "adhering" to the terms dictated by the other party or not contracting at all. A court may refuse to enforce such an agreement as contrary to public policy. Clauses in fine print or in such technical language that an ordinary person would not understand their meaning have also been stricken on this basis. Unequal bargaining power standing alone is not enough to justify unenforceability, however. It must also appear that the party with superior power used it to take unfair advantage of the other party to the agreement. The courts are especially likely to find such inequality in cases involving consumer contracts with businesses, although there are also numerous cases where contracts between small companies and large industrial giants have been held to be adhesion contracts.

In Chapter 15 on sales we will see that the Uniform Commercial Code has specifically recognized the *unconscionable* contract concept and given the courts broad power to deal with such contracts.

W. T. Grant Co. v. Walsh
241 A.2d 46 (Dist. Ct., Middlesex Cty., N.J. 1968)

FACTS Janet Walsh was shopping at Grant's when she was approached by a salesperson and asked if she wanted to open a charge account. She refused at first, but agreed after the salesperson pleaded with her, saying that she needed points for a contest. Walsh was given a book of coupons totaling $200.00, and told that she would be charged only for the coupons she used. In reality, the agreement she signed was an installment sales contract, obligating her to pay a total of $246.01 over a 24-month period at $10.00 per month. When she failed to make the first payment, Grant's filed suit. Walsh argued the agreement was usurious and contrary to public policy.

ISSUE Is the agreement illegal?

DECISION Yes. Grant's argued that the agreement was not usurious because the interest charged was within allowable limits set by a state statute on retail installment sales. The court disagreed, noting that the statute applied only to sales of goods and that Walsh had not received any goods, only coupons. The transaction was held to violate the general usury statute, which set the maximum interest rate at 6 percent. The court also noted that Grant's may have been guilty of fraud for deceiving Walsh about the true nature of the agreement. Finally, the court found the plan to be contrary to public policy, saying: "It is difficult to imagine a more one-sided scheme for the enrichment of a commercial establishment at the expense of a potential customer." The plan charged Walsh interest on her account before she made any purchases and Grant's could recover the full value of the coupons, even if they were stolen, lost, or destroyed before being used.

QUESTIONS AND PROBLEM CASES

1. Why do courts make an exception to the hands-off rule in situations where a party to an illegal contract rescinds before performing an illegal act?

2. What is the difference between a legal risk-shifting contract and an illegal wagering contract?

3. Tovar, a Kansas physician, sought employment in an Illinois hospital as a resident physician. Terms of employment were agreed upon and Tovar signed a contract. After two weeks of employment with the Illinois hospital, Tovar was summarily dismissed on the grounds that he did not have a valid Illinois medical license. Tovar sues the hospital for wrongful termination of his employment contract, claiming that the license is not necessary to the fulfillment of the terms of the contract. Is the hospital liable on the contract?

4. Kennedy brought an action against Smith for damages for personal injuries consisting of burns on her neck, head, and back suffered while she was receiving a permanent wave. Kennedy had signed a "hold harmless agreement" with the Student Operator Beauty School operated by Smith, purporting to absolve the school of any liability for negligence. The student operator misjudged the amount of solution necessary for

a permanent, and Kennedy suffered second-degree chemical burns when the chemicals ran down her neck. Is Smith liable to Kennedy?

5. Aztec, Inc., borrowed $50,000 from Union Planters Bank, executing in return a promissory note and agreeing to repay the principal "in constant United States Dollars adjusted for inflation (deflation)," and the stated interest, which was set at the maximum legal rate. The adjusted principal was to be calculated by dividing the consumer price index at maturity by the consumer price index at the date of borrowing. Aztec seeks to avoid the payment of the adjustment on the basis that payment of such additional money is contrary to the usury law. Will Aztec prevail?

6. An unwed pregnant woman agreed to release the alleged father from liability in a pending paternity action. The father acknowledged paternity and agreed to pay the mother $500 for dropping the paternity suit. After the birth of the child, the mother reinstituted paternity proceedings. The father raised the release as a defense. Is this a good defense?

7. Bridgeman took part in a prison riot and escape attempt, during which time several hostages, including Corrections Director Hardy, were assaulted and brutalized. Bridgeman pleads immunity from criminal charges based on an oral contract he claims he entered with Hardy during the riot. Hardy promised Bridgeman immunity from prosecution if he would stop all acts of violence. Is this a valid defense?

8. International Dairy Queen negotiated an irrevocable letter of credit with the Bank of Wadley that was in excess of 20 percent of the bank's capital. The bank refused to perform on the contract and defended against the action brought by Dairy Queen on the basis that such a contract was void and unenforceable as a violation of statute. The statute stated "no bank shall lend to any one corporation more than 20 percent of its capital. . . ." Is this a good defense?

Third Parties' Contract Rights

13

Up to this point our discussion of contracts has focused on the rights and duties of the original parties to the contract. There are, however, two kinds of situations in which persons who were not originally parties to a contract may claim some interest in it: These concern assignments of contracts and third-party beneficiaries of contracts.

ASSIGNMENT OF CONTRACTS

Definition

A party to a contract may wish to *assign* (transfer) his or her rights under the contract to a third party. The person who makes an assignment is called the *assignor*, and the person who accepts the assignment is called the *assignee*. The basic idea of an assignment is that the assignee is entitled to whatever performance the assignor had a right to under the original contract. The other original party to the contract (called the *promisor* or *obligor*) must render all performance to the assignee. For example, Bill owes Frank $100, payable in six months. Frank, who needs money today, assigns his rights under the contract to Mary for $80. Bill (the promisor or obligor) must now pay to Mary (the assignee) the money he previously owed a duty to pay to Frank (the assignor). Although this particular assignment is supported by consideration, assignments generally do not need to be supported by consideration to be enforceable.

What Contracts Are Assignable?

Not all contracts are assignable over the objection of the promisor. Any assignment that would *materially alter* the duties of the promisor is unenforceable, since the promisor cannot be required to do something more than, or different from, what he or she originally agreed to do. So, if Acme Sugar Company has entered a "requirements" contract to supply all the sugar requirements of Goody Candy Company, a small candy manufacturer, Goody could not assign its contract rights to Yummy Candy Corporation, a much larger candy manufacturer. Clearly, Yummy's sugar requirements would be much greater than Goody's.

Contracts involving *personal rights* are also generally nonassignable. These are contracts in which some element of personal skill, character, or judgment is an essential part of the agreement. In such a case, the substitution of the assignee for the assignor would materially change the nature of the performance required of the promisor. Employment contracts are therefore generally held nonassignable.

Contracts that *expressly forbid assignment* are also generally nonassignable. Some states refuse to enforce such clauses where the rights assigned would otherwise be assignable.

Assignments of future wages are prohibited by statute in some states. Others allow such assignments, but regulate them in various ways, such as limiting the amount that may be assigned.

Generally, all other kinds of assignments that do not involve personal relationships or increase the promisor's burden are enforceable. Promises to pay money, deliver goods, or sell land are generally assignable. Contracts not to compete with a buyer of a business or an employer are also generally assignable with the sale of the business. The purpose of such contracts is to protect the *goodwill* of the business (the value of the business as a going concern), an asset that can be sold with the business.

Munchak Corp. v. Cunningham
457 F.2d 721 (4th Cir. 1972)

FACTS Cunningham signed a three-year contract to play basketball for the Carolina Cougars professional basketball team. His contract contained a clause prohibiting its assignment to any other "club" without his consent. Southern Sports Corporation, the owner of the Cougars at the time Cunningham joined the team, later assigned the Cougars and Cunningham's contract to Munchak Corporation. Cunningham refused to play for the new owners, claiming his contract had been illegally assigned. Munchak sued to enjoin him from playing for any other team.

ISSUE Was Cunningham's contract assignable?

DECISION Yes. A personal service contract requiring special skills and based on the personal relationship between the parties generally cannot be assigned without the promisor's consent. However, some such contracts can be assigned when the nature of the performance and the obligation will not be changed. Cunningham was not obligated to perform any differently for Munchak than he was for Southern Sports. There is therefore no reason why the contract should not be assignable.

Delegation of Duties

The courts have generally held that a promisor cannot assign his or her duties to perform under a contract. A promisor may, in some cases, however, *delegate* the performance of duties to another person. If the duty to be performed could be performed fully by many different persons, it is delegable. If performance is dependent on the personal skill, character, or judgment of the promisor, however, it may not be delegated.

The promisor who delegates his or her duties is still liable to the promisee if the party to whom the duties were delegated fails to satisfactorily perform them. This rule is necessary to make contracts truly binding; otherwise, a promisor could practically avoid all liability by merely delegating duties he or she did not want to perform. The only exception to this rule is when the parties enter into a novation. A *novation* is a new, separate agreement by the promisee to release the original promisor from liability in exchange for a third party's agreement to assume the promisor's duties.

THE CONSEQUENCES OF ASSIGNMENT

The Rights and Duties of Assignees

An assignee is entitled to all the rights his or her assignor had under the assigned contract. An assignee cannot acquire any greater rights than the assignor has. Therefore, if the promisor has a good defense against the assignor (e.g., fraud, lack of consideration, lack of capacity, etc.), that defense is also good against the assignee.

Assignees should promptly notify the promisor of the assignment. This is necessary because the promisor who renders performance to the assignor without notice of the assignment has no further liability under the contract.

General Factors, Inc. v. Beck
409 P.2d 40 (Sup. Ct. Ariz. 1965)

FACTS Beck bought some construction materials from Tempe Gravel Company. Tempe sent invoices for Beck's purchases to General Factors under an assignment and factoring agreement. General paid Tempe for the invoices and then mailed them to Beck's place of business. General attached a sticker to the invoices giving notice of the assignment and directing payment to General. There was also a stamped notice from Tempe on the invoices directing payment to General. Beck's bookkeeper opened the letters containing the invoices and merely checked the amounts. Beck did not actually see the invoices. He paid Tempe, which was in financial difficulty. General sued for the amount due under the invoices.

ISSUE Did Beck have notice of Tempe's assignment to General?

DECISION Yes. An Arizona statute provides that debtors who pay assignors "without actual notice" of the assignment are not liable to assignees for the amount paid. *Actual notice* is distinguishable from *actual knowledge*. Actual notice includes notice to an authorized agent as well as the communication of any information that would allow the person receiving it to acquire actual knowledge by exercising reasonable diligence. Notice was sent to Beck at his place of business, and received and opened by one of his employees. This is enough for actual notice.

Notice to the promisor may be important in one other situation. If the assignor later wrongfully assigns the contract to a second assignee who pays for it without notice of the first assignment, a question of priority results. Who is entitled to the promisor's performance and who is stuck with a lawsuit against the assignor? In states that follow the *American rule*, the first assignee has priority. Some states, however, follow the *English rule*, which gives priority to the first assignee to give notice of assignment. In both types of states, a potential assignee should contact the promisor before taking the assignment.

A more difficult question concerns the assignee's duties to the promisor. Does an assignment of the assignor's rights carry with it an implied delegation of the assignor's duties under the contract? Unless the assignment agreement clearly indicates a contrary intent, courts today tend to interpret assignments as including a delegation of the assignor's duties. A promise on the part of the assignee to perform these duties is implied, and this implied promise is enforceable by *either* the promisor or the assignor.

Rose v. Vulcan Materials Co.
194 S.E.2d 521 (Sup. Ct. N.C. 1973)

FACTS   Rose owned a stone quarry and a ready-mix cement business, using stone from the quarry in the cement business. Dooley contracted to buy Rose's rock crushing business and lease his quarry for ten years. The terms of the agreement obligated Dooley to supply Rose with enough stone to meet his business needs for ten years at favorable prices. Dooley sold his business to Vulcan and assigned his rights under the contract with Rose to Vulcan. Vulcan later told Rose that the prices for stone would have to be increased over those listed in his contract with Dooley. Rose paid the higher prices under protest and then sued Vulcan for breach of contract.

ISSUE   When Vulcan took Dooley's rights by assignment, did it also assume Dooley's duties to Rose?

DECISION   Yes. Some states hold that the assignee of a bilateral contract does not assume the assignor's duties unless the assignee expressly promises the assignor or the promisee to perform them. However, North Carolina and several other states hold that the assignee of an executory bilateral contract under a general assignment becomes not only the assignee of the rights of the assignor, but also the delegatee of his duties. When there is no showing of contrary intent, the assignee impliedly promises the assignor that he will perform the delegated duties. The other party to the original contract may therefore sue the assignee as a third-party beneficiary of this implied promise of performance.

The Duties of Assignors

As you have already learned, unless the parties enter into a novation, the assignor remains liable to the promisor under the original contract for any duties the assignee fails to perform. Assignors who are *paid* for making an assignment are also potentially liable to assignees for certain *implied guarantees.* These guarantees are imposed by law unless the assignment agreement clearly indicates to the contrary. They are:

1. The assigned claim is valid, which means that:
   a. The promisor has capacity to contract.
   b. The contract is not illegal.
   c. The contract is not voidable for any other reason known to the assignor (like fraud or misrepresentation).
   d. The contract has not been discharged prior to assignment.
2. The assignor has good title to the rights assigned.
3. The assignor will not do anything to impair the value of the assignment.
4. Any written instrument representing the assigned claim is genuine.

The assignor does not impliedly warrant the solvency of the promisor.

Assignors who accept performance from the promisor after the assignment hold any benefits they receive as trustees for their assignees. Assignors who wrongfully assign the same claim more than once are liable to the assignee who is later held to have acquired no rights against the promisor.

THIRD-PARTY BENEFICIARY CONTRACTS

Generally, those who are not parties to a contract have no rights in the contract. However, when the parties to the contract intended to benefit a third party, the third party can enforce the contract. Third parties who benefit from the performance of other people's contracts are called *third-party beneficiaries*. Once a third-party beneficiary has accepted the contract, or relied upon it, the original parties cannot cancel or modify the contract without the third party's consent, unless the original contract gives them the right to do so. There are three classes of third-party beneficiaries: donee beneficiaries, creditor beneficiaries, and incidental beneficiaries.

Donee Beneficiaries

A third person is a *donee beneficiary* if the promisee's *primary purpose* in contracting was to make a *gift* of the contracted performance to the third party. Either the promisee or the donee beneficiary can sue the promisor for not performing the promise. The beneficiary can recover the value of the promised performance, while the promisee can recover damages resulting from nonperformance (usually only nominal damages).

Life insurance contracts are a common form of donee beneficiary contract. The insurance company (the promisor), in return for payment of a premium, contracts with the owner of the policy (the promisee) to pay benefits to a beneficiary on the death of the insured (who may or may not be the promisee). If the insured dies and the company does not pay, the beneficiary can sue for the policy amount.

Creditor Beneficiaries

If the promisor's performance will *satisfy a legal duty* that the promisee owes a third party, the third party is a *creditor beneficiary*. The duty owed can be any kind of legal duty and need not necessarily be the payment of money.

For example, Bill buys a car on time from Honest Bob's Motors. Bill then sells the car to Mary, who agrees to make the remaining payments Bill owes Honest Bob's. Honest Bob's is a creditor beneficiary of Bill (the promisee) and Mary's (the promisor) contract and can recover the balance due from either Bill or Mary.

Incidental Beneficiaries

Occasionally, the performance of a contract intended solely for the benefit of the promisee would also incidentally benefit a third person. Such third persons are called *incidental beneficiaries*. They acquire no rights under the contract and so cannot sue for nonperformance.

For example, John's house is in bad condition. He hires Ace Construction Company to paint and re-roof the house. John's neighbor Frank would benefit from this contract, since John's house is an eyesore that may affect the value of Frank's property. Frank, however, is an incidental beneficiary of John's contract with Ace and has no right to sue Ace if it breaches the contract. Members of the general public are also generally held to be incidental beneficiaries of contracts like street repair contracts entered into by municipalities or other government units.

Brown v. Wichita State University
540 P.2d 66 (Sup. Ct. Kan. 1975)

FACTS   In July of 1970 Wichita State University (WSU) entered into a contract (an "Aviation Service Agreement") with Golden Eagle to provide a qualified flight crew to fly members of the WSU football team to away games on leased aircraft. WSU was required to lease the planes and provide passenger liability insurance as required by federal regulations. On October 2, 1970, two leased planes carrying members of the WSU team, faculty, and team supporters left Wichita for a game with Utah State University. One of the planes crashed into a mountain in Colorado due to excess takeoff weight. WSU had failed to purchase the insurance required by the service agreement, and the survivors of the crash and the estates of those who were killed filed suit.

ISSUE   Were the plaintiffs third-party beneficiaries of the aviation service agreement?

DECISION Yes. It is an established principle of contract law that a person may avail himself or herself of a promise made by a second party to a third party for the benefit of the first party, although the first was not a party to the contract and had no knowledge of it when made. Under the circumstances of the case, the court concluded that the plane's passengers were third-party beneficiaries of the service agreement and could enforce it as such.

QUESTIONS AND PROBLEM CASES

1. What implied guarantees does an assignor for pay make to an assignee?

2. What is the difference between a donee and a creditor beneficiary?

3. Davis owned a tract of land that contained mineral deposits, which he sold to Basalt Rock Co. As part of the consideration for the conveyance of the land to it, Basalt agreed that over a period of 60 years it would sell to Davis "as he may require, such amount of basalt of any size for plastering purposes" at an agreed upon price. The contract further provided that "the price is based on a blend of basalt in accordance with the formula attached." The contract gave Davis the right to change the formula and provided for price adjustments to compensate for the changes. Davis assigned the contract to Soule, and Basalt refused to recognize the assignment and to make deliveries to Soule. Soule sued Basalt for damages for breach of contract, and Basalt set up as a defense that the contract was not assignable. Is the contract assignable?

4. Newman contracted to sell all of the eggs he produced to Sunrise Eggs Co. Newman then gave Crosby a written assignment of the proceeds of this contract. Sunrise knew of the assignment, but ignored it and made payments directly to Newman. Newman failed to pay $17,000 of the assigned proceeds delivered by Sunrise. Crosby sued Sunrise for this amount. Can Crosby collect? yes

5. Smith, owner of an apartment complex, was converting the complex to a cooperative by selling individual units. Each purchaser was required to pay Smith an extra $15 per month for utilities, taxes, and insurance. Smith sold all his rights to the complex to Roberts and assigned the purchasers' contracts to him. Roberts failed to pay the applicable property tax, and Radley, a purchasing tenant, sued him to compel payment of the tax. Roberts argued that in purchasing Smith's interests, all he bought was the right to collect the payments made by tenants and that he assumed no duties. Is Roberts liable for the property tax?

6. Murray contracted with the McDonald Construction Co. to build an addition to his building. The contract required McDonald to build the addition within 75 days. It took 239 days to finish the project. Queen Ann News, Inc., the would-be tenant in the new addition, sued McDonald for damages resulting from the delay. Assuming that McDonald was aware that Queen Ann was going to be the tenant in the addition at the time the contract was signed, should it be liable for damages to Queen Ann? No

7. Wiscombe Painting and Sandblasting Co. was a member of the Decorating Association of America, which had signed a collective bargaining agreement with the Decorators and Paperhangers of America, Local 77. Wiscombe was bound by Section V of the contract to make

contributions to an apprenticeship trust fund on behalf of its employees. Section I of the agreement provided:

> The Association recognizes the Union as the bargaining representative of all the employees employed by its contractor members wherever such employees are performing work covered by this agreement.

Wiscombe contributed to the trust only on behalf of its employees who belonged to Local 77. To force Wiscombe to contribute to the trust for its nonunion employees also, the trustee of the fund brought suit against Wiscombe, claiming a breach of Sections I and V of the contract. Wiscombe's defense is that only Local 77, not the trustee, can attempt to enforce the contract. Is he correct? *No*

8. Bilich, a contractor, entered into a contract with Reliable Trucking Co., whereby he agreed to install designated sewer lines for Reliable. Reliable agreed that it would have Barnett prepare survey lines and grade sheets covering the work that was to be done by Bilich. Barnett prepared survey lines and grade sheets and submitted them to Bilich. The grade sheets were negligently prepared and were an inaccurate representation of the grade lines on the property. Bilich relied on the grade sheets and discovered, on the completion of the grading, that the excavation was not as it should have been according to plans and specifications. As a result of the errors, Bilich was required to fill in part of the excavation and incur additional expenditures of $382. Bilich sued Barnett to recover a judgment of $382 on the theory that Bilich was a third-party beneficiary of the contract between Reliable Trucking Co. and Barnett. Is Bilich a third-party beneficiary of the contract? *yes*

Performance and Remedies

14

I n the introductory chapter to this part of the text (chapter 5) we defined contracts as *legally enforceable agreements.* If an agreement meets all the requirements we have discussed in previous chapters, it is a contract and therefore enforceable. In the majority of contract situations, issues of enforceability never even arise because the parties perform their duties voluntarily and fully.

If a dispute arises between the parties to a contract, however, several important questions may be raised. Many of these questions deal with the parties' duties of performance under the contract. Are there any *conditions* in the contract that affect the parties' duties? If so, have these conditions been met? Have parties who have rendered performance under the contract satisfied their contractual duties, or is their performance so defective that it amounts to a *material breach* of the contract? Does a party who has failed to perform satisfactorily have some legal *excuse* for not performing, or has his or her duty to perform been *discharged* in some way?

Even if it is clear that one of the parties has materially breached the contract, a dispute may still arise about the *remedies* to which the other party is entitled. The answers to these questions can be very important in determining the rights of the parties.

CONDITIONS

Definition

Generally, a party's contractual duty to perform arises at the time the contract is formed, even though the time for performing is set for a future date. The parties may, however, provide that a party's duty to perform is qualified by the happening of some event, or *condition*.

Types of Conditions

If the event must occur before a party's duty to perform arises, this is called a _condition precedent._ For example, Tom promises to buy Mary's race car for $250,000 *if* the car wins the 1980 Indianapolis 500 race. The car's winning the race is a condition precedent to Tom's duty to buy. If the car does not win, a *failure of condition* has occurred, and Tom has no duty to buy the car.

If the happening of a condition discharges an existing duty to perform, this is called a *condition subsequent*. For example, Joan and Mike enter a contract requiring Joan to paint a portrait of Mike by March 1, 1980. The contract also provides that if Joan breaches the contract, Mike must file suit within 30 days to preserve his rights. Joan breaches her duty to perform, but Mike does not sue until May 5, 1980. Joan's duties under the contract were discharged by Mike's failure to sue within 30 days.

If the contract calls for the parties to perform their duties at the same time, each party's duty to perform is conditioned upon the other party's performance. These conditions are called *concurrent conditions*. Neither party can enforce the other party's promise without performing, or *tendering* (offering) performance.

The Creation of Conditions

Conditions may be expressly or impliedly created. *Express conditions* are created by the express language of the contract. No special words are necessary to create an express condition, but they are often created by words like "provided that," "on condition that," "if," "when," "while," "after," and "as soon as."

The nature of the parties' contract may also lead the courts to imply a *constructive (implied) condition* on the parties' duties of performance. For example, in bilateral contracts that call for an exchange of performances at the same date or do not state a time for performance, the law infers that each party's performance is a *constructive concurrent condition* of the other party's duty to perform. So, in a contract between Mike and Joan for the sale of a car, Mike's duty to pay for the car is conditioned upon Joan's delivery of the car, and Joan's duty to deliver is conditioned upon Mike's tender of the purchase price. If, however, their contract had called for Joan to deliver the car on a stated date and Mike to pay for the car two weeks later, Joan's delivery would be a *constructive condition precedent* of Mike's duty to pay.

Clarkson v. Wirth
481 P.2d 920 (Ct. App. Wash. 1971)

FACTS   Wirth signed an exclusive listing contract giving Clarkson, a real estate broker, the right to sell a piece of real estate owned by Wirth. Clarkson produced the Grimnes brothers, who made an offer to purchase the property. Wirth accepted the offer which contained the following provision:

> This offer to purchase is made subject to purchasers' disposing of certain properties upon which deals are now pending and said deals to be closed prior to the closing of this deal. Legal description of these properties will be furnished sellers upon request. Sale to be closed no later than October 1st, 1965.

The Grimnes brothers were unable to sell their properties by October 1, 1965, and the sale of Wirth's property was not completed. In April 1966, the Grimnes brothers and two other men bought Wirth's property without dealing through Clarkson. Clarkson sued Wirth for a commission on the sale.

ISSUE   Is Clarkson entitled to a commission on the sale?

DECISION   No. A real estate broker is entitled to a commission when he or she produces a buyer who enters a binding contract to purchase the property. In this case the Grimnes's promise to purchase was subject to two conditions precedent: the prior sale of their other properties and closing of the sale before October 1, 1965. Since neither of these conditions was satisfied, Wirth could not enforce the first agreement against the Grimnes brothers. Therefore, Clarkson was not entitled to any commission.

STANDARDS OF PERFORMANCE

A common source of dispute between contracting parties is whether the parties have fulfilled their duties of performance under the contract. Promisors must perform their contractual duties in the manner they have promised to perform them. The courts have attempted to create practical, commonsense standards for evaluating the parties' performance. They recognize three basic degrees of performance: complete or satisfactory performance, substantial performance, and material breach of contract.

Complete or Satisfactory Performance

Some kinds of contractual duties can be completely and perfectly performed. The payment of money, the delivery of a deed, and, in some cases, the delivery of goods are all duties that can be performed to a high degree of perfection. Promisors who completely perform such duties are entitled to receive the full contract price in return.

Substantial Performance

Some kinds of contractual duties cannot be performed perfectly due to their nature and the limits of human ability. Examples of these are found in construction projects, agricultural contracts, and many contracts for personal or professional services. Such duties are, however, capable of being substantially performed in most cases. *Substantial performance* is slightly less perfect than complete or satisfactory performance. Promisors may make an honest attempt to perform, but due to lack of ability or factors beyond their control, they may fall short of complete performance. If the nature of their performance is such that it cannot be returned to them, they will be held to have substantially performed their duties. An example of substantial performance is a building that deviates slightly from the contract's specifications. What constitutes substantial performance depends on the circumstances of each case. The promisor who substantially performs is generally entitled to the contract price less any damage the other party has suffered as a result of the defective performance.

Material Breach   The promisor is guilty of material breach of contract if his or her performance fails to reach the degree of perfection the other party is justified in expecting under the circumstances. Such a promisor has no right of action under the contract and is liable to the other party for damages resulting from the breach. If the promisor's defective performance conveyed some benefits to the party that cannot be returned, the promisor may, under a quasi contract theory, be able to recover the reasonable value of benefits conferred from the other party.

A promisor may also be held to have breached the contract under the doctrine of *anticipatory repudiation* or *anticipatory breach*. If the promisor, prior to the time for performance, indicates an intent not to perform his or her duties under the contract, the other party may treat the contract as breached. Anticipatory repudiation may take the form of an express statement by the promisor, or it may be implied from actions by the promisor that indicate an intent not to perform. Implied anticipatory repudiation is the case when Mike, who has contracted to sell a car to Bill, sells the car to Mary two weeks before the delivery date set by his contract with Bill.

Special Performance Problems   There are two special problem areas relating to performance that should be discussed in detail. These are contracts where the promisor agrees to perform to the *personal satisfaction* of the promisee, and construction contracts that condition the promisee's payment on the promisor's obtaining an *architect's or engineer's certificate* of satisfactory performance by the promisor.

When the promisor agrees to perform to the promisee's personal satisfaction in contracts involving matters of personal taste, comfort, or judgment, the promisor who is honestly dissatisfied may reject the performance without liability, even if doing so is unreasonable. If, on the other hand, the contract involves issues of mechanical fitness, utility, or marketability, most courts require the promisee to accept performance that would satisfy a reasonable person.

Contractors who are unable to produce a required architect's or engineer's certificate cannot recover under the contract unless their failure is excused. This may be done by showing that the named architect or engineer is dead, ill, or insane; that the architect or engineer is acting in bad faith; or that the other party has prevented the issuance of the certificate. If the architect or engineer who denies certification is acting in good faith, even if he or she is being unreasonable in doing so, the majority of courts do not excuse the builder's failure to produce the certificate. A minority of courts recognize unreasonable refusal as an excuse where the contract has been substantially performed.

The Time for Performance

If the contract does not expressly or impliedly state a time for performance, performance must be completed within a reasonable time. What constitutes a "reasonable time" depends on the circumstances of each case. Failure to perform on time is a breach of the contract and, in some cases, may be serious enough to constitute a material breach of the contract. In such cases it is said that *time is of the essence* of the contract.

The contract may expressly provide that time is of the essence of the contract. If so, the courts enforce this provision unless doing so would impose an unjust penalty on the promisor. The courts may also imply that time is of the essence if late performance is of little or no value to the promisee. For example, Ted contracts with the *Morning Tribune* to run an ad for Christmas trees from December 21, 1980, to December 24, 1980, but the *Morning Tribune* does not start running Ted's ad until December 26, 1980. Clearly, time is of the essence in this contract and the *Morning Tribune* has materially breached.

If time is not of the essence of a contract, the promisee must accept late performance rendered within a reasonable time of when performance was due. The promisee is then entitled to deduct or set off from the contract price any losses suffered due to the delay.

Kole v. Parker Yale Development Co.
536 P.2d 848 (Ct. App. Colo. 1975)

FACTS Kole entered a contract to have Parker Yale construct a condominium unit for him. The contract provided for completion of the unit in 180 days and gave Kole the right to make changes in the plans and specifications during construction. The unit was not completed within the 180-day period, and Kole brought suit to rescind the contract.

ISSUE Was time of the essence in the parties' contract?

DECISION No. Rescission is appropriate where a contract has been materially breached, or breach has caused irreparable injury, or damages would be inadequate or difficult to assess. Rescission would not be a proper remedy for a mere variance from the terms of the contract. Time is not of the essence of a contract unless it is made so by express provisions in the contract or by the facts of the case. A completion requirement in a building contract is ordinarily construed as providing the buyer with a remedy in damages for breach of contract if the builder renders late performance. The parties' contract did not contain a "time is of the essence" provision and Kole's right to change the plans is evidence that time was not of the essence. Kole introduced no evidence of material breach or of any damages or injury caused by delay.

EXCUSES FOR NONPERFORMANCE

Promisors who fail to satisfactorily perform may be able to avoid liability for breach of contract if they can show some *legal excuse* for their failure. Prevention of performance and impossibility of performance are the two traditionally accepted forms of excuse.

Prevention

The basic idea of prevention is that the promisee who causes the promisor's failure of performance cannot complain about the failure. Promisees owe promisors a duty of cooperation in the performance of a contract. Promisees who breach this duty by failing to cooperate or actively hindering or delaying performance are *themselves* guilty of a material breach of the contract. This relieves the promisor of any duty of further performance under the contract.

Impossibility

If it becomes impossible for a promisor to perform his or her contractual duties, the duty to perform is discharged and the promisor is not liable for material breach. *Impossibility* in the legal sense of the word, however, means "It cannot be done," not "I cannot do it." Promisors who find they have agreed to perform duties that are beyond their capabilities, or that have become unprofitable or difficult to perform are generally not excused from their duty to perform. The courts have traditionally recognized three kinds of impossibility: incapacitating illness or death of the promisor, intervening illegality, and destruction of the subject matter essential to performance. Some courts today also recognize a fourth kind of impossibility called *commercial impracticability* or *commerical frustration*.

Illness or Death of Promisor.   Personal service contracts are the only contracts that the promisor's death terminates. For example, if Tom contracts to sell his house to Mary and dies before the closing date, Mary can enforce the contract against Tom's estate. However, if Tom, a concert pianist, dies before giving a concert he has agreed to perform, his estate is not liable for breach of contract.

Illness may also excuse the promisor's failure to perform, if the nature of the required performance and the seriousness and duration of the illness make it impossible for the promisor to substantially perform.

Intervening Illegality. If a statute or government regulation enacted after a contract's creation makes performance of a party's contractual duties illegal, the promisor is excused from performing. Statutes or regulations that merely make performance more difficult or less profitable do not excuse nonperformance.

Destruction of Subject Matter. If, through no fault of the promisor, something that is essential to the promisor's performance is destroyed, the promisor is excused from performing. The destruction of items the promisor intends to use in performing do not excuse nonperformance if substitutes are available, even though securing them makes performance more difficult or less profitable.

La Gasse Pool Const. Co. v. City of Fort Lauderdale
288 So.2d 273 (Dist. Ct. App. Fla. 1974)

FACTS La Gasse contracted to repair and renovate a city swimming pool. One night, after most of the work had been done, vandals damaged the pool and a large part of the work had to be redone. La Gasse filed suit for the value of the extra work.

ISSUE Is La Gasse entitled to compensation for its extra efforts?

DECISION No. Under an indivisible contract to build an entire structure, liability for loss or damage to the structure during construction falls upon the builder. The reason for this rule is that the builder is bound to build an entire structure, and that he or she is still able to perform by rebuilding the damaged or destroyed part. In contracts to do repair work on existing structures, the general rule is that total destruction of the subject matter of the contract, without fault of either the builder or owner, excuses performance by the builder and entitles him or her to recover for the value of the work done. This is so because an implied condition of the contract is that the structure remain in existence so the builder can perform. Destruction makes performance impossible and excuses nonperformance. In this case, the pool was not destroyed and performance was still possible. Therefore, La Gasse must perform the contract and is not entitled to recover the value of its extra work.

Commercial Impracticability. Some courts are relaxing the strict common law position on impossibility of performance by recognizing as an excuse for nonperformance circumstances that do not amount to impossibility. These courts recognize commerical *impracticability* or *frustration* as an excuse. Frustration occurs when unforeseeable developments make performance highly impracticable or unreasonably expensive, or of little value to the promisee. The Code has adopted an impracticability standard for contracts that fall within its provisions.

> ### American Trading and Production Corp. v. Shell International Marine, Ltd.
> #### 453 F.2d 939 (2d Cir. 1972)
>
> **FACTS** On March 23, 1967, Shell hired American's oil tanker, *Washington Trader*, to deliver a cargo of lube oil from Texas to Bombay, India. On June 5, 1967, the Suez Canal was closed due to war breaking out in the Middle East. This forced the ship to go to Bombay via the Cape of Good Hope, more than 8,000 miles farther than the route through the Suez. American sued for $131,978.44 as extra compensation for the extended trip.
>
> **ISSUE** Did the closing of the Suez Canal amount to impossibility or commercial impracticability?
>
> **DECISION** No. American argued that passage through the Suez Canal was the specified means of performance and that closing made performance impossible, discharging their duty to perform and entitling them to recovery in quasi contract for the extra cost of performing. The court disagreed, saying that while it was likely that both parties contemplated that the canal would be the probable route, this is not the same thing as an agreement that it be the exclusive method of performance. Some U.S. courts have recognized commercial impracticability as an excuse for nonperformance where performance can be achieved only with extreme and unreasonable difficulty, expense, injury or loss. American's case here basically rests on the element of additional expense involved, an increase of less than one-third more than the agreed upon $417,327.36 charter fee. Such an increase is not enough to constitute commercial impracticability.

DISCHARGE

The Nature of Discharge

Parties who have been released from their obligations under a contract are said to be *discharged.* Normally, both parties to a contract are discharged when they have completely performed their contractual duties. There are, however, several other things that can operate to discharge a party's duty of performance.

Earlier in this chapter you saw several situations where a party's duty to perform may be discharged. These were: the occurrence of a condition subsequent, the nonoccurrence of a condition precedent, material breach by the other party, and where the party has an excuse for nonperformance. There are several other ways discharge can occur.

Discharge by Agreement

Since contracts are created by mutual agreement, they may also be discharged by *mutual agreement.* An agreement to discharge must be supported by consideration to be enforceable.

Discharge by Waiver

A party to a contract may *waive* his or her right to insist on complete performance. Waiver occurs when a party accepts incomplete performance without objection, knowing that the defects in performance will not be remedied. In order to avoid waiving their rights, parties who receive incomplete performance should give the other party prompt notice that they expect complete performance and will seek damages if defects are not corrected.

Discharge by Alteration

If the parties' agreement is represented by a written instrument, an *intentional alteration* of the instrument by one of the parties discharges the other party. If a party consents to an alteration or does not object to it after learning of it, he or she is not discharged. Alterations by third parties without the knowledge or consent of either contracting party do not affect the parties' rights.

Discharge by Statute of Limitations

One who has breached a contractual duty may be discharged from liability for breach if the other party does not bring suit within the time specified by the appropriate *statute of limitations*. The time period for enforcing contracts varies from state to state, and many states distinguish between oral and written agreements. The statutory period ordinarily begins to run from the date of the breach and may be delayed if the party with the right to sue is incapacitated (e.g., insane) or beyond the jurisdiction of the court.

REMEDIES

The Theory of Remedies

A court that awards a remedy for breach of contract tries to put the injured party in the same position he or she would be in if the contract had been performed. Ordinarily this may be done by awarding the injured person a judgment for money damages.

If the loser in the suit does not pay the judgment, the winner is entitled to the court's help in enforcing it. The court issues either a writ of execution or a writ of garnishment. A *writ of execution* orders the sheriff to seize and sell enough of the defendant's property to satisfy the judgment. All states have *exemption laws* that exempt certain classes and amounts of a debtor's property from execution. A *writ of garnishment* is designed to reach things belonging to the debtor that are in the hands of third parties, such as wages, bank accounts, and accounts receivable. Garnishment proceedings, like execution sales, are highly regulated by statute.

Damages in Contracts Cases

There are several kinds of damages that may be recoverable in contracts cases. The amount and kind of damages that may be recovered in a given dispute depend on the circumstances of the case.

Compensatory Damages. A party suing for breach of contract who has suffered actual losses as a result of the breach is entitled to recover *compensatory damages*. These damages are designed to place the plaintiff in the same position as if the contract had been performed. Compensatory damages ordinarily include such things as the cost of securing substitute performance, lost profits on the contract, and incidental losses suffered due to delayed or imperfect performance. They are normally limited to losses that would ordinarily occur as a result of breaching the contract.

Consequential Damages. In some cases the special circumstances of the plaintiff cause him or her to suffer losses that would not ordinarily be foreseeable as a result of the breach. Normally, such *consequential damages* are not recoverable unless the defendant had reason to foresee them at the time the contract was created. Generally this means the defendant must have known of the special circumstances that caused the loss. So, if Speedy Trucking Company contracts to deliver parts to Apex Manufacturing's plant without knowing that Apex is shut down waiting for the part, Speedy is not liable for the consequential damages Apex suffers as a result of late delivery of the parts.

Nominal Damages. *Nominal damages* are very small damage awards that are made when a technical breach of contract has occurred without causing any actual loss.

Liquidated Damages. The parties to a contract may provide in advance that a specific sum shall be recoverable if the contract is breached. Such provisions are called *liquidated damage* provisions. If the amount specified is reasonable and if the nature of the contract is such that actual damages would be difficult to determine, liquidated damage provisions are enforced. If the amount specified is unreasonably great in relation to the loss or injury suffered, or if the amount of damages could be determined easily in the event of breach, the courts declare the provision to be a *penalty* and refuse to enforce it.

Punitive Damages. Ordinarily *punitive damages* are not recoverable for breach of contract. They are recoverable only when extreme circumstances justify penalizing the defendant or they are specifically authorized by statute, as is the case with some consumer protection statutes.

Vernon Fire and Casualty Insurance Co. v. Sharp
349 N.E.2d 173 (Sup. Ct. Ind. 1976)

FACTS Sharp's corporation carried a fire insurance policy with Vernon. His business was destroyed by fire and he filed a claim for recovery under the policy. The parties disagreed about the exact amount due Sharp, but Vernon admitted it owed at least $23,000. Vernon, knowing Sharp desperately needed money to rebuild, refused to pay Sharp anything unless he settled a third-party lawsuit against him arising out of the fire. Vernon was arguably liable to the third party, but the terms of the policy did not require Sharp to settle. The trial court awarded Sharp compensatory damages and $17,000 punitive damages. Vernon appealed.

ISSUE	Was the punitive damage award to Sharp justified?
DECISION	Yes. Vernon claimed its conduct was nothing more than a legitimate exercise of an insurer's right to disagree about the amount of recovery due under a policy. The court said, however, that Sharp had introduced enough evidence to show that Vernon had acted in an intentional and wanton manner in refusing to pay his claim unless he settled the third-party suit. This evidence indicated that Vernon wrongfully attempted to use its superior position to exact additional consideration from Sharp before performing its obligations under the contract. The court then concluded that public policy allowed the recovery of punitive damages under these circumstances.

The Duty to Mitigate Damages

Plaintiffs who have been injured by a breach of contract have a duty to *mitigate* (avoid or minimize) the damages they suffer if they can do so without undue risk, expense, or humiliation. They are not able to recover damages for injuries they could have easily avoided. For example, an employee who has been wrongfully fired would be entitled to damages equal to his or her wages for the remainder of the employment period. Such an employee, however, has a duty to make reasonable efforts to seek a similar job elsewhere and minimize damages.

Parker v. Twentieth Century-Fox Film Corp.
474 P.2d 688 (Sup. Ct. Cal. 1970)

FACTS	Shirley MacLaine Parker had a $750,000 contract with Fox to do a film called "Bloomer Girl," a musical to be filmed in Los Angeles. Fox decided not to produce the picture and told Parker they would not honor their obligations to her under the contract. Instead, Fox offered Parker the lead in "Big Country, Big Man," a dramatic "western type" film to be produced in Australia. The compensation offered was identical, but Parker was not to be given the same director and screenplay approval rights she had under the "Bloomer Girl" contract. Parker refused to accept and brought suit for $750,000. Fox argued that Parker had unreasonably refused to mitigate damages by refusing the "Big Country" part.
ISSUE	Did Parker have a duty to mitigate damages by accepting the substitute part?
DECISION	No. A wrongfully discharged employee is generally entitled to recover the amount of salary agreed upon, less any amount that the employer can prove the employee has earned or with reasonable effort could have earned from other employment. The employer must show that the other employment was comparable or substantially similar to the employment provided by the breached contract. An employee's rejection of or failure to seek other available employment of a different or inferior kind cannot be resorted to in order to mitigate damages. The court concluded that the "Big Country" lead was "both different and inferior" due to its nature, location, and the lesser degree of production control afforded Parker.

**Equitable
Remedies**

If the legal remedies for breach of contract are not adequate to fully remedy a party's injuries, a court has the discretionary right to grant an *equitable remedy*. Whether equitable relief is granted depends on the equities of a particular case. By applying "maxims" of equity like "He who seeks equity must do equity" and "He who comes to equity must come with clean hands," the courts grant equitable relief only when justice is served by doing so. The two most common equitable remedies are specific performance and injunction.

Specific Performance. If the subject matter of a contract is *unique*, so that a money damage award will not adequately compensate a buyer whose seller has refused to perform, a court may order the seller to *specifically perform* the contract. Real estate traditionally has been treated as unique and is the most common subject of specific performance decrees. For example, Frank enters a contract to sell his house to Dorothy for $45,000. When he learns that the market value of the house is $50,000, Frank decides not to go through with the sale. Dorothy sues Frank for breach of contract. Her normal legal remedy would be her lost profit on the sale (the market price less the contract price: $5,000 in this example). However, since real estate is generally treated as unique, Dorothy could get the court to order Frank to specifically perform his duties under their contract by giving her a deed to the property.

Personal property is generally not considered unique, but antiques, heirlooms, and works of art may merit specific performance.

Injunctions. *Injunctions* are available when a breach of contract threatens to produce an *irreparable injury*. A court can order a party to do certain acts (a *mandatory* injuction) or to refrain from doing certain acts (a *prohibitory* injunction). For example, an employee with special skills who has agreed not to work for a competitor may be *enjoined* from breaching his or her contract.

QUESTIONS AND PROBLEM CASES

1. What is the difference between a condition precedent and a condition subsequent?
2. When will a "time is of the essence" clause be part of the parties' contract?
3. What is the basic aim of compensatory damages?
4. Leach signed an agreement with Cahill to purchase a house for $18,000 and paid a deposit of $1,000. The contract contained the following provisions: "This agreement is contingent upon buyer being able to obtain a mortgage of $12,000 on the premises and have immediate occupancy of the property." Leach made an honest effort to borrow $12,000 on the security of the house but was unable to do so. Cahill refused to repay the $1,000 deposit and Leach brought suit to recover a judgment for the $1,000. Can Leach recover the deposit?
5. Herbert contracted to build a house for Dewey according to designated plans and specifications. Three payments were to be made during the course of the work and all payments were

to be made on the production of the architect's certificate. The architect gave his certificate for the first three payments but refused to give a certificate for the final payment. Herbert sued Dewey to recover a judgment for the final payment, claiming that the work was done in a workmanlike manner and in accordance with the plans and specifications. Dewey set up as a defense Herbert's failure to get the architect's certificate. Is the defense good?

6. Cramer contracted to remodel a house for Essivein. In performing the contract, Cramer installed only seven radiators instead of eight as specified in the contract, leaving the bathroom without a radiator. He also installed a used bathtub and a used washbasin in the bathroom where the contract required that both be new. Essivein refused to pay Cramer, who brought suit on the contract to recover the contract price for work and material. Is Cramer entitled to a judgment under the doctrine of substantial performance?

7. On October 30, 1966, Wasserman Theatrical Enterprises, Inc., entered into a contract with Jed Harris whereby Harris agreed to present Walter Huston in a theatrical performance entitled *The Apple of His Eye* at Worcester, Massachusetts, on the night of December 16, 1966. On December 12, 1966, Harris canceled the performance due to Huston's illness. Prior to that time Wasserman had spent considerable money in advertising the performance and in preparing the theater for the performance. Wasserman brought suit to recover for money expended in preparation for the show and for loss of profits. Harris set up as a defense that Huston was the chief artist and essential performer in the production, and that by reason of his illness performance of the contract on December 16, 1966, was rendered impossible. Is Harris liable for breach of contract?

8. Kennedy entered into a contract with Reese whereby Kennedy was to drill a 12-inch well to an estimated depth of 400 feet and case it with 6-inch casing, with the bottom half perforated and packed with gravel. Kennedy selected the site on Reese's land and drilled to a depth of 130 feet where he struck rock. Reese got permission for Kennedy to drill on neighboring land at a site selected by Kennedy. Kennedy drilled to a depth of 270 feet and again struck rock. He then abandoned work without Reese's permission. Evidence was offered at the trial to the effect that the rock encountered was brittle and that it could have been drilled through. Kennedy sued to recover for labor performed and set up impossibility as a defense to Reese's counterclaim for breach of contract. Is this a good defense to the counterclaim?

9. Vector, Inc., contracted with the Department of Housing and Urban Development (HUD) to construct low-cost housing in Puerto Rico. The agreement specified that Vector would construct 396 dwelling units, which it would sell to HUD for $7 million. No guaranteed profitability clause appeared in the written contract. When subcontracting major portions of the project, Vector learned that because of increased costs the expenditures it would have to make were in excess of $8 million. Vector tried to renegotiate the contract with HUD, but HUD refused. Vector then refused to proceed with construction. In a suit by HUD for specific performance of the contract, Vector claims that to perform would entail a loss of at least $500,000. Must Vector perform the contract?

10. Otinger contracted with the city water board to construct a pump and water station on Catona Creek. Due in part to flood conditions on the Catona, Otinger went over the time specified for completion. The contract contained a provision stating that time was of the essence and authorizing the city to withhold $50 per day for every day, including Sundays and holidays, that the work remained uncompleted beyond the date specified. The $50 was stated to represent not liquidated but actual stipulated damage that the city would have sustained. The total amount of the contract was $120,000. Otinger maintained that the city waived the time limit when, in reply to his letter requesting an extension, they in-

structed him to "proceed with the unfinished work with reasonable and continual progress until completion" and stated that upon completion they "would gladly have you appear for a review of the delay and assure you of full consideration of the circumstances."

Otinger sued for a balance due on the contract and the city counterclaimed for overpayment because the amount of the stipulated damages had exceeded this balance. Who should prevail?

Sales

PART
THREE

Introduction to Sales

15

The common law contract rules you studied in the preceding chapters were significantly influenced by the historical setting which they developed. On the whole, they were well suited to the tasks they were called upon to perform. However, in some cases the common law rules produced results that were contrary to the parties' intentions. In addition, the changes in the ways goods are sold today, which were discussed in Chapter 5, sometimes produced situations where applying traditional contract rules produced seemingly unfair or absurd results. This was particularly true in cases involving contracts for the sale of goods. Consider the following everyday contract situations and the effect of applying traditional contract law rules to them:

1. Frank is interested in buying Joan's lawn mower. He talks to Joan, who finally agrees to sell it to him for $150. Their entire negotiations dealt only with the price of the lawn mower. A week passes, and Frank asks Joan to deliver the lawn mower to his home and tells Joan he will give her $50 down and pay the balance of the price in monthly installments of $25. When Joan refuses, Frank files suit for breach of contract. Joan defends by arguing that no contract resulted from their negotiations because they never agreed on important terms like delivery and how the sale price was to be paid. A court applying common law principles might well side with Joan and hold that the parties' agreement was too "indefinite" to result in a contract.

2. Modern Manufacturing Corporation, in response to an inquiry from Thompson's Cleaners, sends Thompson's a letter offering to sell Thompson's ten washing machines for $2,500. Modern's offer says: "You have two weeks to accept this offer." The following day Thompson's arranges to

borrow the money for the washing machines, but before it can send Modern a letter of acceptance, Modern's sales manager phones and attempts to revoke the offer. A court applying common law principles would hold that since Modern's promise to hold the offer open was not supported by consideration, Modern could revoke its offer at any time before Thompson's accepted.

3. Goody Candy Company sends General Sugar Corporation a purchase order for 5,000 pounds of granulated sugar at $0.25 a pound. Goody's purchase order was on a standard form drafted by its attorney and provided, among other things, that payment would be made within ten days after delivery. General receives Goody's order and responds by sending its standard "acknowledgment of order" form agreeing to supply the sugar. General's form includes provisions that require payment within five days of delivery and provide that all disputes are to be arbitrated. Goody's purchasing officer does not read all of General's form and makes no response to it, thinking they have a contract. The market price for sugar soars to $0.40 a pound and General refuses to send the sugar to Goody. Because General's acknowledgment form contained terms that materially varied Goody's offer, a court applying common law principles would probably hold that General's acknowledgment was a counteroffer that Goody failed to accept. Therefore, General would not be obligated to supply the sugar at the agreed upon price.

4. Steve's Steak House regularly buys its meat from Apex Meats, Inc. Steve's normally picks up the meat it buys at Apex's packing plant, which is 75 miles from Steve's restaurant. Steve's truck breaks down and its manager calls Apex and asks if Apex would deliver Steve's latest order. Apex's vice president, wanting to keep a good customer happy, agrees to deliver the meat at no charge. Due to other commitments, Apex fails to deliver the meat on time and Steve's has to buy meat from a local butcher at a higher price. A court applying common law principles would hold that Apex was not bound to deliver the meat, since Steve's gave no new consideration to support Apex's promise to deliver.

In each of these examples the original intentions or expectations of one or both of the parties are frustrated by the application of common law contract rules. One of the major forces behind the creation of the Uniform Commercial Code[1] was the need to develop a set of rules to deal fairly and realistically with modern commercial transactions. Article 2 of the Code has made some significant changes in the law of contracts governing the sale of "goods." In each of the preceding examples, applying Code principles produces a dramatically different result than applying contract principles. So, it is very important for you to learn *when* to apply the Code and *how* it applies.

---

[1] See the discussion of the Code at the end of Chapter 5.

WHEN AND HOW DOES ARTICLE 2 APPLY?

Article 2 applies to *all contracts for the sale of goods* (2–102).[2] Although the Code contains a somewhat complicated definition of *goods* (2–105), the most important thing for you to understand is that the term *goods* means *tangible personal property.* This means that contracts for the sale of things like motor vehicles, books, appliances, and clothing are covered by Article 2. Article 2 does not apply to contracts for the sale of real estate or stocks and bonds and other intangibles.

Article 2 also does not apply to service contracts. This can cause confusion because, while contracts for employment or other services are clearly not covered, many contracts involve elements of both goods and services. The test the courts most frequently use to determine whether Article 2 applies to a particular contract is to ask which element, goods or services, *predominates* in the contract.

Basically, this means that any agreement calling for services that involve significant elements of personal skill and judgment is probably not governed by Article 2. For example, Lucy suffers an injury due to impurities in a permanent lotion. Can she sue for breach of warranty under the Code, or must she sue on some other theory? If Lucy bought the lotion ("goods") at a drugstore and applied it herself, the Code is applicable. If, however, the lotion was applied at a beauty shop (the application by a trained professional is a substantial service element), a court would probably not refer to the Code. Construction contracts, remodeling contracts, and auto repair contracts are other examples of mixed goods and services contracts that may be considered outside the scope of the Code.

So, the first question you should ask when faced with a contracts problem is: Is this a contract for the sale of goods? If it is not, apply the principles of contract law you have already learned. If it is, apply the Code rule, *if there is one.* The Code has modified only some of the basic rules of contract law. If there is no specific Code rule governing the problem, apply the relevant contract law rule.

HOW DOES ARTICLE 2 DIFFER FROM CONTRACT LAW?

Article 2 reflects an attitude about contracts that is fundamentally different from the common law. The Code is more concerned with rewarding people's legitimate expectations than with technical rules, so it is generally more flexible than contract law. A court that applies the Code is more likely to find the parties had a contract than a court that applies contract law (2–204). In some cases, the Code gives less weight to technical requirements like consideration than is the case in contract law (2–205 and 2–209).

---

[2] The numbers in parentheses refer to sections of the Uniform Commercial Code, which is reproduced in the Appendix of this book.

The drafters of the Code sought to create practical rules to deal with what people actually do in today's marketplace. We live in the day of the form contract, so some of the Code rules try to deal fairly with that fact.[3] Throughout the Code the words *reasonable, commercially reasonable,* and *seasonably* (within a reasonable time) are found. This reasonableness standard is different in *kind* from the hypothetical "reasonable person" standard you encountered in tort and contract law. A court that tries to decide what is "reasonable" under the Code is more likely to be concerned with what people really do in the marketplace rather than what a nonexistent "reasonable person" would do.

The drafters of the Code wanted to promote fair dealing and higher standards in the marketplace, so they imposed a *duty of good faith* (1–203) in the performance and enforcement of every contract under the Code. *Good faith* means "honesty in fact" and "the observance of reasonable commercial standards of fair dealing" (2–103[1][b]). The parties cannot alter this duty of good faith by agreement (1–102[3]).

The Code also recognizes that buyers tend to place more reliance on professional sellers and that professionals are generally more knowledgeable and better able to protect themselves than nonprofessionals. So, the Code distinguishes between merchants and nonmerchants by holding merchants to a higher standard in some cases.[4] The Code defines *merchant* (2–104[1]) on a case-by-case basis. If a person regularly deals in the kind of goods being sold, or pretends to have some special knowledge about the goods, or employed an agent in the sale who fits either of these two descriptions, that person is a "merchant" for the purposes of the contract in question. So, if you buy a used car from a used-car dealer, the dealer is a merchant for the purposes of your contract. But, if you buy a refrigerator from a used-car dealer, the dealer is probably not a merchant.

THE CREATION OF SALES CONTRACTS

No part of Article 2 is a better indication of the Code's desire to dispense with technicalities and protect people's expectations than its general rules governing the creation of sales contracts (2–204). A sales contract can be created "in any manner sufficient to show agreement, including conduct by both parties which recognizes the existence of a contract" (2–204[1]). So, if the parties are *acting* like they have a contract (by delivering or accepting goods or payment, for example), this is enough to create a binding agreement, even if it is impossible to point to a particular moment in time when the contract was created (2–204[2]).

Nor does the fact that the parties did not expressly agree on all the

---

[3] See, for example, U.C.C. Sections 2–205, 2–207, 2–209, and 2–302.

[4] See, for example U.C.C. Sections 2–201(2), 2–205, 2–207(2), and 2–314.

terms of their contract prevent its creation. A sales contract does not fail due to "indefiniteness" if the court finds that the parties *intended* to make a contract and that their agreement is complete enough to allow the court to reach a fair settlement of their dispute ("a reasonably certain basis for giving an appropriate remedy," 2–204[3]).In Chapter 16 you will learn that the Code contains several gap-filling rules to fill in the blanks the parties left in their agreement.[5] Of course, if the facts indicate that a term was left out because the parties were *unable* to reach an agreement about it, this would probably mean that the intent to contract is absent, and no contract was created.

Paloukos v. Intermountain Chevrolet Co.
588 P.2d 939 (Sup. Ct. Idaho 1978)

FACTS   Gust Paloukos visited the showrooms of Glen's Chevrolet (the business name of Intermountain Chevrolet Co.) and agreed to purchase a 1974 ¾-ton Chevrolet pickup from George Rowe, one of Glen's salesmen. Rowe filled out a form headed: "WORK SHEET—This is NOT a Purchase Order" in bold print. The form indicated Paloukos's name and address and described the truck as a new yellow or green 1974 ¾-ton four-wheel drive vehicle with a radio, V-8 engine, and automatic transmission at a purchase price of $3,650. Rowe printed his name in a space provided for the salesman's name and Paloukos signed at the bottom of the form (no signature line was provided). Glen's sales manager approved the sale, Paloukos paid a $120 deposit and was told the truck would be ordered. Five months later Glen's sent Paloukos a letter stating that, due to "a product shortage," Glen's would be unable to deliver the truck and returned his deposit. Paloukos filed suit for breach of contract. Intermountain argued that the work sheet was too indefinite to create a contract.

ISSUE   Did Paloukos have a contract with Intermountain?

DECISION   Yes. Intermountain argued that the work sheet failed to specify the specific shade of green or yellow, engine size, and the size and style of the pickup bed. The court said that the Code does not require a document itemizing all the specific terms of the agreement to create an enforceable contract. The Code merely requires that the parties' conduct be "sufficient to show agreement" [quoting from 2–204(1)]. Under Section 2–204(3), the fact that some terms are undetermined does not prevent a contract from being formed if the parties "intended to make a contract and there is a reasonably certain basis for giving an appropriate remedy." Looking at the facts of the case, the court concluded that "We do not believe that the paucity of the vehicle description in the work sheet, as a matter of law, precludes the court from concluding that a contract was formed."

---

[5] For example, see U.C.C. Sections 2–305, 2–307, 2–308, and 2–309.

OFFERS AND THE CODE

The major change the Code has made in the law that governs offers is in the area of the offeror's power to revoke the offer. Under common law, the offeror can revoke the offer at any time prior to acceptance, even if he or she promised not to revoke. The only exceptions to this general rule are options, estoppel, and some offers for unilateral contracts.

The drafters of the Code knew that offerors often promise to hold their offers open and that offerees who receive such offers are often ignorant of the law and believe them to be irrevocable. So the Code protects the expectations of offerees in some cases by recognizing the idea of a *firm offer* (2–205).

Firm Offers

A firm offer is irrevocable, even though the offeree has given no consideration to support the offeror's promise to hold the offer open. For an offer to sell goods to be a firm offer, it must meet three basic requirements:

1. It must have been made in a *signed writing* (no oral firm offers).
2. The offeror must be a *merchant* (nonmerchants cannot make firm offers).
3. It must contain *assurances* that it will be held open (some indication that it will not be revoked).

If any one of these requirements is missing, the common law applies, allowing the offeror to revoke at any time prior to acceptance.

Firm offers are irrevocable for the period of time stated in the offer. If none is stated, they are irrevocable for a reasonable time, as determined by the circumstances of the case. The outer limit on the period of irrevocability for firm offers is three months, whatever the terms of the offer may say. So, the offeror who makes a firm offer and promises to hold it open for six months could revoke after three, assuming the offeree has not accepted.

The drafters of the Code were afraid that some offerees who in reality controlled the form of their offeror's orders (by providing preprinted purchase order blanks or order forms in catalogs, etc.) would try to take advantage of their offerors by including an "assurances" term in their order forms. A merchant offeror who used such a preprinted order form might unknowingly be making a firm offer, which would allow the offeree to await market developments before deciding whether to accept the offer. To avoid this result, the Code requires that the offeror *separately sign* an assurance term on a form provided by the offeree before the offeror will be held to have made a firm offer.

E. A. Coronis Associates v. M. Gordon Construction Co.
216 A.2d 246 (Sup. Ct. N.J. 1966)

FACTS   Coronis, a subcontractor specializing in the construction of structural steel, submitted a bid of $155,413.50 to Gordon, a general contractor, for the structural steel portion of two buildings to be constructed at the Port of New York Authority's Elizabeth piers. Gordon used Coronis's figure for computing its own bid, which was accepted by the Port Authority. Before Gordon accepted Coronis's offer, Coronis sent a telegram attempting to revoke it. Gordon had to pay another company $208,000 to do the structural steel work. When sued by Coronis on three other contracts, Gordon counterclaimed on the subcontract, arguing that Coronis's bid was irrevocable either as a firm offer or due to estoppel.

ISSUE   Could Coronis revoke its bid?

DECISION   No. Before the Code was enacted, an offer that was not supported by consideration could be revoked at any time prior to acceptance. The Code, however, changed this rule in some cases because it was contrary to modern business practice and in some cases produced unjust results. The court concluded that Coronis's offer did not come within the provisions of U.C.C. Section 2–205 because it did not contain any terms of assurance that it would be held open. Therefore, the court felt it was not necessary to decide whether Coronis's offer was for the sale of "goods" and the Code would therefore apply to the case. (You should note, however, that since the offer included the delivery and *erection* of the steel, some courts would probably treat it as a "services" contract that is outside the scope of the Code.) The court concluded that Gordon could recover on the theory of estoppel if it could prove all the elements of that doctrine.

ACCEPTANCE AND THE CODE

The Code made two major kinds of changes in the common law rules that govern acceptances. In a controversial section that is often called the "Battle of the Forms" section (2–207), the Code changed the common law "mirror image" rule for acceptances. It also made some important changes in the *way* in which certain kinds of offers could be accepted (2–206[1][b]) and in the *time* when an acceptance is effective to create a contract (2–206[1][a]).

The Battle of the Forms

The common law rule holds that attempted acceptances that are not the "mirror image" of the offer are counteroffers. The drafters of the Code realized that, since many commercial transactions are carried out by using preprinted forms, acceptance forms in many cases would not be the "mirror image" of offer forms. The offeror would be using a standard order form drafted by his or her lawyer, while the offeree would be using a standard acceptance form drafted by another attorney. In reality, the parties might not even read each other's forms except for such crucial provisions as the kinds of goods ordered, their price, and the date of delivery called for. Both parties would, nonetheless, think they had a contract.

Applying the "mirror image" rule to these cases would often frustrate the parties' original intent. If a dispute arose before the parties started to perform, a court applying the "mirror image" rule would hold that the parties did not have a contract. If a dispute arose after the parties had started to perform, the court would probably hold that the offeror had impliedly accepted the offeree's counteroffer and was bound by its terms. Neither of these results was very satisfactory.

The Code changes the common law rule by saying that a timely *expression of acceptance* creates a contract even if it includes terms that are *different* from those stated in the offer or states *additional* terms on points the offer did not address (2–207[1]). The only exception to this rule occurs when the attempted acceptance is *expressly conditional* on the offeror's agreement to the terms of the acceptance (2–207[1]). In that case no contract is created.

What are the terms of the resulting contract? This has been the subject of considerable disagreement among the courts and legal scholars. The Code clearly says that if the parties are both merchants, the additional terms are included in the agreement unless: (1) the offer *expressly* limited acceptance to its own terms, (2) the new terms would *materially alter* the nature of the offer, or (3) the offeror gives *notice of objection* to the new terms within a reasonable time after receiving the acceptance (2–207[2]).

The major disagreement centers around what happens to any different terms (those that contradict a term in the offer). The Code is silent on this point. Clearly the terms do not become part of the agreement, but is the offeree bound by terms in the offer that the acceptance plainly shows he or she objects to? Some commentators say yes, but others argue that the different terms should cancel out conflicting terms in the offer.

This is clearly what happens when the acceptance is made expressly conditional on agreement to the new terms, or when the offeree clearly is making a counteroffer by expressly rejecting the offer. The Code (2–207[3]) in this case says that if the parties begin performance (or do something else that "recognizes the existence of a contract"), a contract is created. The terms of this contract are those on which the writings of the parties *agree*, supplemented by appropriate gap-filling provisions of the Code.

Uniroyal, Inc. v. Chambers Gasket & Mfg. Co.
380 N.E.2d 571 (Ct. App. Ind. 1978)

FACTS   Chambers mailed a purchase order to Uniroyal for certain raw material for use in gasket fabrication. Chamber's order form specified merely the quantity, price, and shipment date for the material. Uniroyal responded by sending an "Order Acknowledgement" form that included the phrase:

> OUR ACCEPTANCE OF THE ORDER IS CONDITIONAL ON THE BUYER'S ACCEPTANCE OF THE CONDITIONS OF SALE PRINTED UPON THE REVERSE SIDE HEREOF. IF THE BUYER DOES NOT ACCEPT THESE CONDITIONS OF SALE, HE SHALL NOTIFY SELLER IN WRITING WITHIN SEVEN (7) DAYS AFTER RECEIPT OF THIS ACKNOWLEDGEMENT.

Among the "conditions" of sale on the reverse side of the acknowledgement were clauses disclaiming implied warranties, limiting the buyer's remedy for breach to a refund of the purchase price, and requiring any claim for breach to be filed within 30 days of delivery. Chambers did not respond to the acknowledgement and accepted and paid for the goods. Chambers later filed suit, arguing that the goods were defective.

ISSUE   Were the disclaimer and limitation of warranty clauses on Uniroyal's acknowledgement form part of the parties' contract?

DECISION   No. U.C.C. Section 2–207 was specifically designed to alter the common law mirror-image rule by allowing the creation of a contract despite discrepancies between the offer and acceptance, if this can be done without binding either party to a material term that has not been agreed to. The drafters of the Code made this change because they knew that in commercial practice, especially after the advent of printed forms, the terms of the offer and acceptance are seldom the same. Under Section 2–207(1) no contract results if the acceptance is expressly conditioned on the offeror's assent to the new terms as Uniroyal's was. A contract may still be found under Section 2–207(3) if the parties' conduct recognizes the existence of a contract. Since Uniroyal and Chambers had performed the agreement before the dispute arose, the court found that the parties had a contract, whose terms under Section 2–207(3) "are those on which the writings of the parties agree, together with supplemental provisions of the Code." Therefore, the disclaimer and limitation provisions on Uniroyal's acknowledgement did not become a part of the parties' agreement, and the implied warranty of merchantability should apply to this case.

Manner and Medium of Acceptance

Offerors under the Code can still limit their offerees' power to bind them to a contract by specifying the manner in which their offerees may accept and the means their offerees must use to communicate acceptance. Offerors who do not exercise this power, however, are held to have *impliedly authorized acceptance* "in any manner and by any medium reasonable under the circumstances" (2–206[1][a]).

This expands the common law "mailbox" rules and means that an acceptance dispatched by a "reasonable means" is effective to create a contract under the Code at the *moment of dispatch*. This is so despite the fact that the means used was neither expressly authorized by the offeror nor impliedly authorized by the offeror's use of it to communicate the offer or by trade usage. So, a telegraphed acceptance of a mailed offer could create a contract under the Code when delivered to Western Union if telegraph was a "reasonable means" to use to accept the offer.

Acceptance by Shipment

The Code also expressly deals with another problem that frequently arises in commercial transactions: attempts to accept by *shipping ordered goods*. The Code says that an order requesting "prompt" or "current" shipment of goods impliedly invites acceptance by either a *prompt promise to ship* or a *prompt shipment of the goods* (2–206[1][b]). For example, Mary's Office Supply sends Bob's Business Machines an order for 25 Royal typewriters, to be shipped "as soon as possible." The day Bob receives Mary's order he ships the typewriters. Later that day Mary phones Bob and tries to revoke her offer. She cannot revoke, since a contract was created when Bob shipped the typewriters.

What if Bob did not have 25 Royals in stock and shipped 15 Royals and 10 IBM typewriters? The Code says that the seller who ships "nonconforming goods" (something different from what was ordered) has *accepted and breached the contract*, unless the seller seasonably notifies the buyer that such a shipment is intended as an "accommodation" to the buyer. In such a case, shipment is in effect a counteroffer that the buyer is free to accept or reject (2–206[1][b]).

Village of Woodridge v. Bohnen International, Inc.
377 N.E.2d 121 (Ct. App. Ill. 1978)

FACTS The Village of Woodridge advertised for bids to supply the village with three trucks and attached equipment. Bohnen International submitted the lowest bid. The specifications for bids called for the price bid to remain firm for "60 days after the bid opening." The bids were opened on May 20, 1974. On June 6, 1974, the Woodridge Board of Trustees voted "to recommend to the Mayor and Board of Trustees" that Bohnen's bid be accepted. No notice of acceptance was given to Bohnen by any Woodridge official during the 60-day period after May 20, 1974. Bohnen refused to supply the trucks and Woodridge filed suit for breach of contract.

ISSUE Was the vote of the board of trustees to "recommend" acceptance in legal effect an acceptance of Bohnen's bid?

DECISION No. The board of trustees' motion was not sufficient to create a contract. A contract for the sale of goods may be made in any manner sufficient to show agreement

(2–204), but there must be a meeting of the minds. Under Code Section 2–206 a written bid need not be effectively accepted only by a written acceptance, but it may be accepted in any manner and by any medium reasonable under the circumstances. It still must be accepted, however, and here it was not; acceptance was only recommended.

CONSIDERATION AND THE CODE

As you have already learned, the Code dispenses with the common law requirement of consideration in the case of firm offers. The Code has also made one other major change in traditional rules on consideration in the case of agreements to modify existing contracts. In Chapter 10 you learned that agreements to modify contracts generally have to be supported by some new consideration to be binding. However, people often freely agree to modify their agreements and believe that such modifications are binding. The Code chose to reward people's expectations by providing that agreements to modify contracts for the sale of goods *need no consideration* to be binding (2–209[1]).

Modification of Sales Contracts

To illustrate how this section works, suppose Bill agrees to buy 50 pairs of leather-lined boots from John. Bill later asks John if he can change the order to fur-lined boots at the same price and John agrees. If John later refuses to deliver fur-lined boots, can Bill enforce the modification against him? Under the common law rule, Bill could not enforce John's promise to deliver fur-lined boots, since Bill has not agreed to do anything he did not already have a *preexisting contractual duty* to do (pay the original contract price) in exchange for the new promise. Under the Code, however, the agreement to modify the original contract is enforceable, since no consideration is necessary (2–209[1]).

You should understand several things about the way this section of the Code operates. First, there is no *duty* to agree to a modification, so John could have refused to agree to Bill's order change and enforced the original contract against Bill. Second, the Code contains two provisions to protect people from fictitious claims that an agreement has been modified. If the original agreement requires any modification to be in writing, an oral modification is unenforceable (2–209[2]). Regardless of what the original contract says, if the price of the goods in the modified agreement is $500 or more, the modification is not enforceable unless the requirements of the Code's statute of frauds section (2–201) are satisfied (2–209[3]).

> **Ruble Forest Products, Inc. v. Lancer Mobile Homes, Inc.**
> **524 P.2d 1204 (Sup. Ct. Ore. 1974)**
>
> **FACTS**   Ruble, a lumber broker, sent Lancer 11 truckloads of lumber between August 10 and September 28, 1971, for a total price of $31,091.24. When Lancer did not pay promptly for the lumber, Ruble complained and was told by Lancer's manager that since 1969 Lancer had received "about $5,000" worth of defective lumber from Ruble and that some kind of compromise would have to be made before Lancer would pay any part of the amount owed. Ruble, who was having financial problems at the time, later sent Lancer a letter agreeing to give Lancer a $2,500 "credit" against the amount owed. Lancer then paid the balance due. Ruble later filed suit for the $2,500, claiming that the lumber had not been defective, that the debt was a liquidated one, and, therefore, that the "credit" was not supported by consideration and that the settlement was coerced by Lancer in bad faith.
>
> **ISSUE**   Is Ruble's agreement to give Lancer a "credit" enforceable?
>
> **DECISION**   Yes. Under common law an agreement to take less than the whole amount of a liquidated claim is without consideration and unenforceable. The court concluded, however, that enough evidence had been introduced at trial to show the existence of a bona fide dispute and a binding accord and satisfaction. In addition, the court observed that the agreement between the parties was covered by the Code, which in Section 2–209(1) dispensed with the requirement of consideration for agreements to modify contracts within the scope of the Code. The court noted that Comment 2 to Section 2–209 requires that all modifications meet the "test of good faith" imposed by Section 1–203, but concluded that there was ample evidence to support a finding by the trial court that Lancer did not act in bad faith with an intent to coerce Ruble.

VOLUNTARY CONSENT AND THE CODE

One of the most important and controversial sections of the Code is Section 2–302, which recognizes the idea of an *unconscionable contract.* The drafters of the Code knew that many contracts today are not truly consensual, even though the classic forms of lack of voluntary consent (like fraud, duress, undue influence, and mistake) are not present.

Many contracts today are the products of unequal bargaining power between the parties.[6] Many consumer contracts are created on preprinted forms drawn by one party's attorney. These form contracts sometimes contain provisions that are unreasonably favorable to the party whose attorney drafted them. These contracts are sometimes also so filled with "legalese" (technical legal wording) that consumers in reality do not understand the nature of the contract they have signed.

---

[6] See the discussion of unequal bargains in Chapter 12.

The Code gives the courts considerable power to deal with these problems by giving them freedom to remedy unconscionable contracts. If a court finds a contract to be unconscionable, it can refuse to enforce it entirely, enforce it without any unconscionable clause, or enforce it in a way that avoids an unconscionable result.

Unconscionable Contracts

When is a contract unconscionable? The Code does not define the term, leaving it instead for the courts to define. In doing so, the courts have tended to follow the path charted by those earlier courts that refused to enforce "adhesion contracts" on the grounds that they were contrary to public policy.[7] Unconscionable contracts are often described as those that are so unfair that they "shock the conscience of the court." This unfairness may result from the fact that one of the parties did not either notice or truly understand a clause of the contract (because it was too technically worded, in fine print, on the back of the contract, etc.). It can also result when a party with superior bargaining power imposed unfair terms on the other party. One famous case described this sort of unconscionability as "the absence of meaningful choice on the part of one of the parties together with contract terms which are unreasonably favorable to the other party."[8]

Unconscionability will probably not apply to any terms of an agreement that were truly bargained for, even though one of the parties made a "bad deal." Consumers who are dealing with merchants are generally more successful in arguing unconscionability than merchants who are dealing with other merchants because the courts are more likely to assume that merchants have more bargaining power, better access to legal advice, and more knowledge than consumers about the nature of the transactions they enter. In those few cases where merchants have successfully argued unconscionability, they were usually small businesspeople (who in reality had no more bargaining power than a consumer) dealing with large corporations.

Bunge Corp. v. Williams
359 N.E.2d 844 (Ct. App. Ill. 1977)

FACTS   Bunge Corporation operated a grain elevator in Cairo, Illinois. Bunge entered into its standard-form soybean purchase contracts with Marion Williams and two other local farmers. The farmers failed to deliver the soybeans and refused to pay Bunge the damages it sought for breach of contract. Bunge started arbitration proceedings,

---

[7] See the discussion of unequal bargains in Chapter 12.

[8] *Williams v. Walker-Thomas Furniture Co.*, 350 F.2d 145 (D.C. Cir. 1965); see Problem Case 8 at the end of the chapter.

but the farmers refused to arbitrate, arguing that they were not on notice of the arbitration provisions on the backs of their contracts and that the provisions were unconscionable. Bunge filed suit to compel arbitration.

ISSUE   Are the farmers bound by the arbitration provisions?

DECISION   Yes. The farmers claimed they had not read the arbitration provisions, had never heard of arbitration, and had no intent to agree to arbitration when they signed the contracts. The court, however, did not find this argument convincing. It noted that a clause in large bold-faced capital letters that called attention to the terms on the back of the page was on the contract only one-quarter inch above where the farmers had signed. The court noted that the defendants were experienced farmers, each of whom had entered at least one prior contract with Bunge on identical forms. It concluded that the farmers had an ample opportunity to read the contracts and to know their terms and that there was nothing inherently unconscionable about an arbitration clause.

WRITING AND THE CODE

The Code has its own statute of frauds section (2–201), which applies to contracts for the sale of goods for $500 or more. The unique thing about the Code's approach to the statute of frauds issue is that the Code recognizes that the basic purpose of the statute of frauds (to provide more evidence that a contract existed than the mere oral testimony of one of the parties) can be satisfied by several kinds of things *other than a writing*.

The basic Code writing requirement (2–201[1]) is that there be evidence of the parties' contract in the form of a written memorandum that indicates the existence of a contract between the parties, indicates the quantity of goods sold, and is signed by the party to be charged. So, a letter that said:

> I agree to sell to John Smith 200 wrenches.
>
> Signed,
> Steve Jones

would be sufficient to satisfy the Code's writing requirement against Steve.

In most cases, however, John Smith would have a good statute of frauds defense against Steve because John did not sign the writing. The Code provides, however, that if John is a merchant and he receives this writing from Steve and does not object within ten days after receiving it, he loses his statute of frauds defense (2–201[2]). Steve still must convince the court that the parties had a contract, but he is not prevented by the statute of frauds from trying to do so. The idea behind this subsection of the Code is that the natural response to such a writing of a person who did not have a contract would be to object. John's failure to object satisfies the statute's requirement of some extra proof (beyond Steve's oral testimony) that a contract existed.

Several other things also satisfy the statute. If the goods are "specially manufactured for the buyer" and "not suitable for sale to others in the normal course of the seller's business," and the seller has made a substantial beginning in manufacturing them or entered a binding agreement to acquire them for the buyer before learning that the buyer is denying the existence of a contract, the buyer loses the statute of frauds defense (2–201[3][a]).

If a party being sued on a contract *admits the existence of the contract* in his or her testimony in court or in any of the pleadings he or she files during the course of the lawsuit, that satisfies the statute (2–201[3][b]). Finally, if a party accepts goods or accepts payment for goods, the statute of frauds is satisfied *to the extent of the payment made or the goods accepted* (2–201[3][c]). For example, Mary and John have an oral contract for the sale of 100 pairs of boots at $10 a pair. If Mary delivers the boots and John accepts them, or if John pays for the boots and Mary accepts payment, neither can raise the statute of frauds as a defense. If, however, only part of the boots are delivered (50 pairs) or only a partial payment is made ($500), the *remainder* of the agreement is unenforceable.

Thomaier v. Hoffman Chevrolet, Inc.
410 N.Y.S.2d 645 (Sup. Ct. N.Y., App. Div. 1978)

FACTS On January 4, 1978, Ray Thomaier ordered a 1978 Limited Edition Corvette Coupe from Hoffman Chevrolet. Thomaier signed an order form and gave Hoffman a $1,000 check as a deposit. Hoffman cashed the check and placed a written order for the car with General Motors, listing Thomaier as "customer" and the type of order as "sold" (rather than "stock" for inventory). Limited Edition Corvettes became a subject of intense market speculation, selling in some cases for more than $20,000. On April 9, 1978, Hoffman sent Thomaier a letter saying that "market conditions" had made his "offer" unacceptable and that his $1,000 was being returned. Hoffman raised the statute of frauds as a defense.

ISSUE Does Hoffman have a good statute of frauds defense?

DECISION No. The order form Hoffman sent to General Motors, either by itself or when read in conjunction with Thomaier's "purchase order," is a sufficient note or memorandum to satisfy U.C.C. Section 2–201(1). Nothing in the statute prevents a writing directed to a third party from satisfying the statute's requirements. In any event, Thomaier's part payment of $1,000 would satisfy U.C.C. Section 2–201(3)(c). Although the effect of part payment on a contract for the sale of a single, indivisible item is not specifically covered by the Code, the weight of authority is clearly to the effect that such a payment renders an indivisible oral contract enforceable.

QUESTIONS AND PROBLEM CASES

1. What kinds of contracts are covered by the Code?

2. Give two examples of the fact that the Code sometimes holds "merchants" to a higher standard of behavior.

3. Under what circumstances will a freely agreed to, oral modification of a sales contract fail under the Code?

4. Suchy Funeral Home brought suit against Waldenmaier to recover the contracted price for a funeral, including the providing of a casket. Waldenmaier claimed that the lawsuit was commenced more than four years after the funeral and thus was barred by the Code's four-year statute of limitation's (2–725). Suchy contended that the Code's statute of limitations did not apply because no "sale of goods" was involved. Should the court apply the Code provisions to this contract?

5. Apex Parts Company sent its salesperson Nelson to solicit parts orders from Green Distributing Company. Green placed an order for $5,000 and signed the order form provided by Nelson. The order form contained many terms, but one stated, "All orders are subject to approval by home office and buyer agrees this order will remain firm for 30 days from date placed." Green signed the form at the bottom. Ten days later Green wrote Apex asking that the order be canceled. Apex immediately notified Green that the parts were being shipped. Green refused to accept delivery and Apex sued for breach of contract, contending that Green had made a firm offer. Is Apex right?

6. In 1970, the University of Wisconsin invited bids from contractors for the construction of water transmission lines. Janke, intending to bid on the job, obtained price quotations from several suppliers. One such supplier, Vulcan, gave Janke a quotation over the phone. Since Vulcan's quotation was the lowest, Janke used it in the bid; subsequently Janke was awarded the contract. Later a dispute arose over the type of pipe to be used in the project and Vulcan ultimately refused to furnish the type of pipe requested by Janke. Janke sued Vulcan for breach of contract, contending that a valid offer and acceptance occurred when he used Vulcan's price quotation in his bid. Is Janke correct?

7. Doughboy, Inc., sent a purchase order for film to Pantasote Co. Pantasote immediately mailed back an acknowledgment form and subsequently delivered the film. The acknowledgment form conflicted with Doughboy's purchase form; it contained a general arbitration clause for disputes while the Doughboy purchase form did not, and it provided that a failure to object in writing to the acknowledgment was acceptance of all its terms. Doughboy's purchase form said that no term could be changed without its written approval. Doughboy never objected to the terms of the Pantasote acknowledgment. A dispute has arisen which Pantasote wishes to settle by arbitration, but Doughboy wants court litigation. Pantasote sues to require that Doughboy submit to arbitration. Must Doughboy arbitrate?

8. Owens successfully bid on a job of installing a plastic water pipe system for a small Alabama community. Clow Corporation orally agreed to supply pipe as needed by Owens and sent Owens an invoice describing the amount of pipe and prices for the pipe. Neither the proposal nor the invoice prescribed times for delivery, although Clow orally agreed to attempt to supply a truckload of pipe per day. After satisfactorily delivering pipe for three days, Clow fell behind in delivery and Owens was forced to buy from an alternative supplier at a higher price. Can Owens recover damages from Clow if Clow can prove that the agreed price exceeded $500 and raises the defense of the statute of frauds?

9. Starting in December 1957, Mrs. Williams bought several items worth more than $1,400 on time from the Walker-Thomas Furniture Company. On April 17, 1962, she bought a stereo on time. Later she defaulted in her payments, owing $164 on the stereo. Walker-Thomas tried to repossess everything she had

ever purchased from them, pointing to a very complicated clause in their sales contract that said that all items purchased were leased until every item had been paid for. Williams's attorney argued that this provision was unconscionable. Was the lawyer correct?

10. Gardner bought a $400 sewing machine on time from Singer Company. Then Gardner bought three $70 vacuum cleaners from Singer on time. After paying a total of $200, Gardner defaulted. Singer tried to repossess all the items, since none of them had been fully paid for. Was Gardner's attorney correct in arguing that allowing Singer to repossess all the items would be unconscionable?

11. Lewis and Hughes entered an oral contract for the sale of a mobile home. Hughes later refused to go through with the sale. Lewis sued and Hughes raised the statute of frauds as a defense. In his testimony at the trial, Hughes repeatedly admitted the existence of the oral contract. Does the statute of frauds bar Lewis's claim?

12. Wright, a grain elevator operator, entered an oral contract to buy corn for the Augustin Brothers Company. The Augustin Brothers were to repurchase the corn from Wright at his cost plus a four cents per bushel handling charge. Wright bought corn for four months, and then the market price for corn dropped sharply. The Augustin Brothers, having made a prepayment to Wright of $27,882.24, refused to honor the oral contract. Wright filed suit for the $64,187.95 owed under the oral agreement. Can the Augustin Brothers use the statute of frauds as a defense?

Title, Risk of Loss, and the Terms of Sales Contracts

16

I n their attempt to create a comprehensive set of rules to govern the everyday problems that can arise in the sale of goods, the drafters of the Code were faced with several serious problems. Since, as you saw in the preceding chapter, they had decided to enforce sales contracts in some cases even though the parties never fully agreed on all the terms of their agreement (2–204[3] and 2–207[3]), what terms would be used to fill in the blanks left by the parties? Their response was to create several gap-filling rules to supplement the parties' agreement.

The Code also had to deal with many important questions about the *ownership (title)* of the goods in sales contracts. This is important for several reasons. If the goods are lost, stolen, damaged, or destroyed, who must bear the *risk of loss,* the seller or the buyer? Whose creditors (the seller's or the buyer's) have the legal right to seize the goods to satisfy their claims? What are the rights of those who buy goods that are subject to the claims of *third parties* (their rightful owner, secured creditors, etc.)? Who has the *insurable interest* that the law requires before a party can purchase insurance protection for the goods?

Prior to the adoption of the Code, most of these questions were answered by determining who had title to the goods. This was a highly technical question and produced a great deal of litigation and uncertainty. The drafters of the Code changed the common law rules in many cases by attempting to provide clarity and fairness in the process.

THE TERMS OF SALES CONTRACTS

The Code recognizes the fact that parties to sales contracts frequently omit terms from their agreements or state terms in an indefinite or unclear manner. The Code deals with these cases by filling in the blanks with common trade practices, or by giving commonly used terms a specific meaning that is applied unless the parties' agreement clearly indicates a contrary intent.

Price Terms

A fixed price is not essential to the creation of a binding sales contract. Of course, if price has been the subject of a dispute between the parties that has never been resolved, no contract is created because a "meeting of the minds" never occurred. However, if the parties omitted a price term or left the price to be determined at a future date or by some external means, the Code supplies a price term (2–305). Under common law such contracts would have failed due to "indefiniteness."

If a price term is simply omitted, or if the parties agreed to agree on price at a later date but cannot, or if the parties agreed that price would be set by some external agency (like a particular market or trade journal) that fails to set the price, the Code says the price is a *reasonable price at the time for delivery* (2–305[1]). If the agreement gives either party the power to fix the price, that party must do so *in good faith* (2–305[2]). If the surrounding circumstances clearly indicate that the parties did not intend to be bound in the event that the price is not determined in the agreed upon manner, no contract results (2–305[4]).

Quantity Terms

In some cases the parties may state the quantity of goods covered by their sales contract in an indefinite way. Contracts that obligate a buyer to purchase a seller's *output* of a certain item or all the buyer's *requirements* of a certain item are commonly encountered. These contracts caused frequent problems in common law because of the indefiniteness of the parties' obligations. If the seller decided to double its output, did the buyer have to accept the entire amount? If the market price of the item soared much higher than the contract price, could the buyer double or triple its demands?

The Code limits quantity in such cases to "such actual output or requirements as may occur in good faith" (2–306[1]). Even good faith amounts may not be tendered or demanded if they are "unreasonably disproportionate" to any stated estimate in the contract or to "normal" prior output or requirements if no estimate is stated (2–306[1]).

The Code takes a similar approach to *exclusive dealing* contracts that obligate dealers to deal only in one manufacturer's product line. Under common law these contracts were sources of difficulty due to the indefinite nature of the parties' duties. Did the dealer have to make any effort to sell the manufacturer's products, and did the manufacturer have any duty to supply the dealer? The Code says that unless the parties agree to the contrary, the seller has a duty to use his or her "best efforts" to supply the buyer, who has a duty to use "best efforts" to sell the goods (2–306[2]).

Delivery Terms

Unless the parties agree to the contrary, the Code says that the goods ordered are to be delivered in a *single-lot shipment* (2–307). If the contract is silent about the place for delivery, the goods are to be delivered at the *seller's place of business* (2–308[a]). The only exception to this rule is in the case of contracts dealing with identified goods that both parties at the time of contracting know are located someplace besides the seller's place of business. In such a case, the *site of the goods* is the place for delivery (2–308[b]).

Time Terms

The Code takes the same position as the common law when the parties' contract is silent about the time for performance. Performance in such cases must be tendered within a *reasonable time* (2–309[1]). If the parties' contract calls for a number of performances over an indefinite period of time (e.g., an open-ended requirements contract), the contract is valid for a *reasonable time* but may be terminated at any time by either party after giving *reasonable notice* (2–309[2] and [3]).

Finally, unless the parties agreed to the contrary, payment for the goods is due at the "time and place at which the buyer is to receive the goods" (2–310[a]).

Southwest Engineering Co. v. Martin Tractor Co.
473 P.2d 18 (Sup. Ct. Kan. 1970)

FACTS   Southwest Engineering wanted to submit a bid for the construction of runway lighting facilities at an Air Force base in Wichita, Kansas. Southwest called Martin Tractor for a price quote on a standby generator and accessory equipment. Martin quoted a price of $18,500 and later confirmed that price over the phone. Southwest used the $18,500 figure in its bid and was ultimately awarded the job. Representatives of the two firms then met, and Martin told Southwest it wanted $21,500 for the generator. Southwest agreed to the change and a written memorandum was drawn to reflect this agreement. Martin refused to supply the generator and Southwest bought one from another source for $27,541. Southwest filed suit for $6,041, and Martin argued that since the parties had failed to reach a definite agreement on the time and method of payment, no contract existed.

ISSUE   Did Southwest and Martin have a contract?

DECISION   Yes. The court noted that under Section 2–204(3) of the Code the parties' failure to reach agreement on payment terms was not necessarily fatal to their agreement. The court concluded that under Section 2–310(a) of the Code payment was due at the time and place set for delivery of the generator.

TITLE AND THE CODE

Under common law most problems concerning risk of loss, insurable interest, and the rights of various third parties to the goods were answered by determining who had title to the goods. The Code, in an attempt to clarify these questions, has specific rules that do not generally depend on who has title.

The Code does have a general title section. It provides that title passes to the buyer when the seller has completely performed his or her duties concerning *physical delivery* of the goods (2–401[2]). So, if the contract merely requires the seller to *ship* the goods, title passes to the buyer when the seller delivers the goods to the carrier. If the contract requires *delivery* of the goods by the seller, title passes to the buyer when the goods are delivered and tendered to the buyer.

If delivery is to be made without moving the goods, title passes at the *time and place of contracting*, if the goods have been identified to the contract. *Identification* occurs when the surrounding circumstances make it clear that the goods are those "to which the contract refers" (2–501). This may result from the contract description of the goods (if they are unique from other goods in the seller's possession) or from actions of the seller like setting aside or marking the goods.

If the contract calls for the seller to deliver a negotiable document of title to the goods (like a warehouse receipt or a bill of lading) to the buyer, title passes when the document of title is delivered.

If the buyer rejects tender of the goods, this automatically revests title in the seller.

State of Alabama v. Delta Airlines, Inc.
356 So.2d 1205 (Ct. App. Ala. 1978)

FACTS The Alabama Department of Revenue assessed Delta for $57,178.30 in sales tax for meals and snacks Delta provided to passengers who bought airline tickets in Alabama. The Revenue Department argued that the sale of the meals and snacks occurred when the passengers purchased their tickets in Alabama. All of Delta's flights were interstate and none of the snacks or meals was served while its aircraft were in Alabama airspace. Either Delta or the passenger could cancel the ticket sale, and the ticket price was the same whether or not a meal was served. If for some reason no meal was served, passengers had no right to a refund.

ISSUE Did the sale of the meals to passengers occur when they purchased their tickets?

DECISION No. Alabama sales tax applies only to sales that are "closed" within the state. Under Section 2–401(2) title to goods passes, unless otherwise agreed, when the seller completes delivery of the goods. Under the facts of this case, delivery occurs outside Alabama and title passes at that time. The sale is therefore not subject to Alabama sales tax.

TITLE AND THIRD PARTIES

A basic rule of property law is that a buyer can never receive better title to the goods than the seller had. So if Bob steals a stereo from Mary and sells it to Mike, Mike has no title to the stereo and Mary could recover it from him. The Code makes three major exceptions to this rule that are designed to protect innocent buyers.

Transfers of Voidable Title

A seller who had voidable title can pass good title to a *good faith purchaser for value* (2–403[1]). Sellers may obtain voidable title by impersonating another person when acquiring the goods from their rightful owner, paying for the goods with a bad check, failing to pay for goods sold on a "cash sale" basis, or obtaining the goods in some other fraudulent manner. *Good faith* means "honesty in fact in the transaction concerned" (1–201[19]), and a buyer has given "value" if he or she has given any consideration sufficient to support a simple contract (1–201[44]).

The primary reason for this exception is to place the burden of loss on the party who had the best opportunity to avoid the harm. Good faith purchasers can do nothing to avoid injury. However, the rightful owners of goods at least have the opportunity to protect themselves by taking steps to assure themselves of the buyer's identity, accepting only cash or certified checks, refusing to part with the goods until they have cash in hand, or taking steps to discover fraud before parting with the goods. In view of their greater relative fault, the Code requires the original owners of the goods to bear the burden of collecting from their fraudulent buyers.

Buyers in the Ordinary Course of Business

A "buyer in the ordinary course of business" is one who, in good faith, buys goods from a person dealing in goods of that type without knowing that the sale violates the ownership rights of any third party (1–201[9]). Under the Code, buyers in the ordinary course take the goods free of any security interest in the goods their seller may have given a third party (9–307).

For example, Art's Jeep Sales borrows money from First Financial Services and gives First Financial a security interest in all its inventory. The security interest gives First Financial the right to seize Art's inventory if it defaults on the loan. If Bob buys a new Jeep from Art's, he takes the Jeep free and clear of First Financial's security interest if he is a "buyer in the ordinary course." The basic purpose of this exception is to protect those who innocently buy from merchants and thereby promote confidence in such commercial transactions. Security interests and the rights of buyers in the ordinary course of business are discussed in more detail in Chapters 42 and 43.

Entrusting Goods

The Code's third major exception to the general common law rule on title is the "entrusting rule" (2–403[2] and [3]). Anyone who entrusts goods to a merchant who regularly deals in such goods gives that merchant the power to give good title to a "buyer in the ordinary course." So, if Mary takes her watch to Precious Jewelers, Inc., for repair, Precious could give good title to a buyer in the ordinary course who buys the watch. In such a case, Mary would have to sue Precious for conversion of the watch; she could not get her watch back from the buyer. The purpose of this exception is to promote commerce by giving buyers the knowledge that they will get good title to goods they purchase in the ordinary course of their sellers' business.

Fuqua Homes, Inc. v. Evanston Building & Loan Co.
370 N.E.2d 780 (Ct. App. Ohio 1977)

FACTS   Kenneth and Wilma Ryan borrowed money from the Evanston Building & Loan Company to buy a "modular home" manufactured by Fuqua Homes, Inc. They bought the home from MMM, a partnership acting as a middleman-dealer for Fuqua. The partners behind MMM disappeared after receiving the proceeds of the sale to the Ryans without making any payment to Fuqua. Fuqua filed suit, claiming that since it had not been paid and was still the holder of the certificate of origin of the modular home, it had title to the home.

ISSUE   Does Fuqua have title to the modular home?

DECISION   No. The Ryans should win on the grounds of the public policy that when one of two innocent persons must suffer from the fraud of a third, the one who made it possible for the fraud to be committed should bear the loss. Section 2–403(2) of the Code applies to the case, since MMM was a merchant who dealt in modular homes and the Ryans were buyers in the ordinary course of business. Therefore, the sale by MMM to the Ryans transferred all of Fuqua's rights in the modular home to them.

RISK OF LOSS

The transportation of goods from sellers to buyers is a risky business. The carrier of the goods may lose, damage, or destroy them; floods, tornados, and other natural catastrophes may take their toll; thieves may steal all or part of the goods. If neither party is at fault for the loss, who should bear the risk? If the buyer has the risk when the goods are damaged or lost, the buyer is liable for the contract price. If the seller has the risk, he or she is liable for damages unless substitute performance can be tendered.

The common law placed the risk on the party who had technical title at the time of the loss. The Code rejects this approach and provides specific rules governing risk of loss that are designed to provide certainty and place the risk on the party best able to protect against loss and most likely to be insured against it. Risk of loss under the Code depends on the terms of the parties' agreement, the moment the loss occurs, and whether one of the parties was in breach of contract when the loss occurred.

The Terms of the Agreement

The parties have the power to control who has the risk of loss by specifically saying so in their agreement (2–509[4]). This they may do directly or by using certain commonly accepted shipping terms in their contract. In addition, the Code has certain general rules on risk of loss that amplify specific shipping terms and control risk of loss in cases where specific terms are not used (2–509).

Shipment Contracts

If the contract requires the seller to ship the goods by carrier but does not require their delivery to a specific destination, the risk passes to the buyer when the goods are delivered to the carrier (2–509[1][a]). The following are commonly used shipping terms that create *shipment contracts:*

1. *F.O.B. (free on board)*—This term calls for the seller to deliver the goods free of expense and at the seller's risk to the place designated. So, if the contract term is "F.O.B. Chicago" or some other place of *shipment*, the seller bears the risk and expense of delivering the goods *to the carrier* (2–319[1][a]). If the term is "F.O.B. vessel, car, or other vehicle," the seller must *load* the goods on board at his or her own risk and expense (2–319[1][c]).
2. *F.A.S. (free alongside)*—This term is commonly used in maritime contracts and is normally accompanied by the name of a specific vessel and port. The seller must deliver the goods alongside the vessel at his or her own risk and expense (2–319[2]).
3. *C.I.F. (cost, insurance, and freight)*—This term means that the price of the goods includes the cost of shipping and insuring them. The seller bears this expense and the risk of loading the goods (2–320).
4. *C.&F.*—This term is the same as C.I.F., except that the seller is not obligated to *insure* the goods.

Destination Contracts

If the contract requires the seller to deliver the goods to a specific destination, the seller bears the risk and expense of delivery to that destination (2–509[1][b]). The following are commonly used shipping terms that create *destination contracts:*

1. *F.O.B. destination*—An F.O.B. term coupled with the place of destination of the goods puts the expense and risk of delivering the goods to that destination on the seller (2–319[1][b]).
2. *Ex-ship*—This term does not specify a particular ship, but places the expense and risk on the seller until the goods are *unloaded* from whatever ship is used (2–322).

3. *No arrival, no sale*—This term places the expense and risk during shipment on the seller. If the goods fail to arrive through no fault of the seller, the seller has no further liability to the buyer (2–324).

Ninth Street East, Ltd. v. Harrison
259 A.2d 772 (Cir. Ct. Conn. 1968)

FACTS Ninth Street East, a Los Angeles, California, manufacturer of men's clothing, and Harrison, the owner of a clothing store, entered four sales contracts for goods totaling $2,216. Ninth Street East delivered the goods to Denver-Chicago Trucking Company, Inc., and sent Harrison four invoices noting that shipment had been made "F.O.B. Los Angeles" and "via Denver-Chicago," and including the statement: "Goods Shipped at Purchaser's Risk." The goods were shipped "collect" (at Harrison's expense). Denver transferred the goods to Old Colony Transportation Company. When Old Colony tried to deliver the goods to Harrison, a dispute arose. Old Colony kept the goods but later lost them. Ninth Street East filed suit against Harrison for the price of the goods.

ISSUE Did Harrison have the risk of loss of the goods?

DECISION Yes. The court found that the parties originally agreed that the goods were to be shipped by common carrier F.O.B. Los Angeles, as the place of shipment. The use of "F.O.B." in this context made this a "shipment" contract under Section 2–319(1)(a) of the Code. Therefore, under Section 2–509(1)(a) the risk of loss passed to Harrison when the goods were delivered to Denver-Chicago.

Goods in the Possession of Third Parties

When, at the time of contracting, the goods are in the hands of a third-party bailee (like a carrier or warehouseman) and are to be delivered without being moved, the risk passes to the buyer when the buyer *has the power to take possession* of the goods (2–509[2]). If the goods are covered by a document of title (negotiable or nonnegotiable), risk passes when the buyer *receives the document of title.* When no document of title is involved, the risk passes when the bailee *acknowledges the buyer's right to possession.*

Risk Generally

If none of the special rules that have just been discussed applies, risk passes to the buyer on receipt of the goods if the seller is a merchant. If the seller is not a merchant, the risk passes to the buyer when the seller tenders (offers) delivery of the goods (2–509[3]). For example, Frank offers to sell Susan a car, and Susan sends a telegram accepting Frank's offer. When he receives the telegram, Frank calls Susan and tells her she can "pick up the car anytime." That night the car is destroyed by fire. If Frank is a used-car salesman, he must bear the loss. If Frank is an accountant, Susan must bear the loss.

Ramos v. Wheel Sports Center
409 N.Y.S.2d 505 (Civ. Ct. N.Y.C. 1978)

FACTS   In June, Ramos entered into a contract to buy a motorcycle from Wheel Sports Center. He paid the purchase price of $893 and was given the papers necessary to register the cycle and get insurance on it. Ramos registered the cycle but had not attached the license plates to the cycle. He left on a vacation and told the salesman for Wheel Sports Center that he would pick the cycle up on his return. While Ramos was on vaction there was an electric power blackout in New York City and the cycle was stolen by looters. Ramos then sued Wheel Sports Center to get back his $893.

ISSUE   Did Wheel Sports Center have the risk of loss of the motorcycle?

DECISION   Yes. Where the seller is a merchant dealing in goods of the kind sold, the risk of loss passes to the buyer on his receipt of the goods under U.C.C. Section 2–509(3). Here the seller was a merchant and still had possession of the goods when they were stolen. Under these conditions, Wheel Sports Center was still responsible for the motorcycle.

Breach of Contract and Risk

The Code follows the trend set by earlier law of placing the risk of loss on a party who is in breach of contract. There is no necessary reason why a party in breach should bear the risk, however. In fact, shifting the risk to parties in breach sometimes produces results contrary to some of the basic policies underlying the Code's general rules on risk by placing the risk on the party who does not have possession or control of the goods.

When the seller tenders goods that the buyer could lawfully reject because they do not conform to the contract description, the risk of loss remains on the seller until the defect is cured or the buyer accepts the goods (2–510[1]). When a buyer rightfully revokes acceptance of the goods, the risk of loss is on the seller to the extent that it is not covered by the buyer's insurance (2–510[2]).

Buyers who repudiate a contract for identified, conforming goods before risk of loss has passed to them are liable for a commercially reasonable time for any damage to the goods that is not covered by the seller's insurance (2–510[3]). For example, Trendy Shoe Stores contracts to buy 100 pairs of shoes from Acme Shoe Manufacturing Company. Acme crates the shoes and stores them in its warehouse pending delivery to Trendy. Trendy then tells Acme it will not honor its contract for the shoes and they are destroyed by a fire in Acme's warehouse shortly thereafter. If Acme's insurance covers only part of the loss, Trendy is liable for the balance.

Insurable Interest

The Code rules that govern risk of loss are supplemented by rules that give the parties an *insurable interest* in the goods, which allows them to insure themselves against most of the risks they must bear. Buyers may protect their interest in goods before they obtain title to them, since they have an insurable interest in goods at the moment the goods are *identified to the contract* (2–501[1]). Sellers have an insurable interest in their goods as long as they have title to the goods or a security interest in them (2–501[2]).

SALES ON TRIAL

There are several common commercial situations in which a seller entrusts goods to another person. This may be done to give a potential buyer the chance to decide whether or not to buy the goods, or to give the other party a chance to sell the goods to a third party. These cases present difficult questions about who has the risk of loss of the goods and whose creditors may attach the goods. The Code provides specific rules to answer these questions depending on the nature of the parties' agreement.

Sale or Return

In a *sale or return contract* the goods are delivered to the buyer primarily for resale with the understanding that the buyer has the right to return them (2–326[1][b]). Unless the parties agreed to the contrary, title and risk of loss rest with the buyer. Return of the goods is at the buyer's risk and expense (2–327[2][b]), and the buyer's creditors can attach the goods while they are in the buyer's possession (2–326[2]). Placing the risk on the buyer in these cases recognizes the fact that sale or return contracts are generally *commercial* transactions.

Sale on Approval

In a *sale on approval* the goods are delivered to the buyer primarily for the buyer's use (2–326[1][a]). The buyer is given the opportunity to examine or try the goods to decide whether to accept them. Risk of loss and title to the goods do not pass to the buyer until the buyer accepts the goods (2–327[1][a]). Any use of the goods that is consistent with a trial of the goods is not an acceptance, but the buyer who fails to give reasonable notice of an intent to return the goods may be held to have accepted (2–327[1][b]).

The buyer's creditors cannot reach goods held on approval (2–326[2]), and return of the goods is at the seller's risk and expense (2–327[1][c]). These provisions recognize the fact that sales on approval are primarily *consumer* transactions.

Sale on Consignment

Frequently a seller (a consignor) places goods in the hands of a merchant (a consignee) who has agreed to act as the seller's agent in selling the goods. These are called *sales on consignment* or *sales on memorandum*. Since consigned goods still belong to the consignor, the consignor has title to and risk of loss of the goods. One potential danger in such cases is that the consignee's creditors may incorrectly assume that the consigned goods belong to the consignee and extend credit on that basis. Accordingly, the Code gives the consignee's creditors the power to attach consigned goods unless the consignor takes steps to notify them of his or her interest in the goods (2–326[3]).

Consignors may do this by either prominently posting a sign at the consignee's place of business indicating their interest in the goods, or filing a financing statement covering the goods pursuant to Article 9 of the Code. Consignors who fail to take either of these steps may defeat a consignee's creditors' claims by proving that the consignee "is generally known by his creditors to be substantially engaged in selling the goods of others" (2–326[3][b]).

Collier v. B & B Sales, Inc.
471 S.W.2d 151 (Ct. App. Tex. 1971)

FACTS Collier, a retail store operator, accepted a delivery of stereo tapes, cartridges, and equipment from B & B Sales. The invoice noted that the goods had been "sold to" Collier and said: "Terms 30–60–90 this equipment will be picked up if not sold in 90 days." Shortly thereafter Collier's store was burglarized and all the merchandise was stolen. B & B filed suit, claiming that the transaction was a sale and Collier was liable to pay for the merchandise. Collier argued that the transaction was a consignment and that B & B had the risk of loss.

ISSUE Did Collier have the risk of loss of the goods?

DECISION Yes. The transaction was a "sale or return" under Section 2–326(1)(b) of the Code because the language on the invoice indicated that a sale had occurred but that B & B would take back unsold goods after 90 days. Accordingly, Collier had title to and the risk of loss of the goods while they were in his possession.

BULK TRANSFERS

There is one other major situation where the creditors of a party to a sales contract may claim an interest (other than an Article 9 security interest) in the goods. This is in the case of a *bulk transfer* as covered by Article 6 of the Code. A bulk transfer occurs when a person whose main business is selling goods from stock (a retailer, wholesaler, and, in some cases, a manufacturer) sells a major part of the materials, supplies, merchandise, or other inventory of the business *in bulk and not in the ordinary course of business* (6–102).

The danger in such cases is that financially troubled sellers may secretly dispose of their assets, pocket the proceeds, and disappear. In order to protect such a seller's creditors from being defrauded in this manner, Article 6 is designed to give them notice of the sale and enable them to file any claims they may have against the goods. The seller must give the buyer a sworn list of the seller's creditors and a schedule of the property to be transferred (6–104). The buyer must keep this list available for inspection and copying by the seller's creditors for six months after the sale (6–104).

The buyer must notify all known creditors of the sale at least ten days before taking possession of the goods (6–105). Failure to comply with the requirements of the law means that the buyer holds the goods *in trust* for the seller's creditors. In some states (Pennsylvania, for example) an optional provision of the Code has been enacted requiring that the proceeds of the bulk transfer be paid to the seller's creditors (6–106).

Creditors only have six months from the time the transfer took place to file suit to enforce their rights under Article 6, unless the transfer was concealed from them. In such a case they have six months after the transfer was discovered (6–111).

QUESTIONS AND PROBLEM CASES

1. Are there any limits on the quantity of goods a buyer can demand under a requirements contract? *reasonable or normal*

2. Discuss the concept of voidable title under the Code.

3. What is the basic purpose underlying the bulk transfer rules of Article 6? *seller / evade / creditors* *protect*

4. On August 3, 1974, a Chevrolet Corvette was stolen from its owner, Location Gallop Leasing of Quebec, Canada. At about the same time, blank registration forms were stolen from the Department of Motor Vehicles in Montreal and used to complete the transfer of the Corvette to a certain Richard Dooust in New York state, which issued a certificate of title for the vehicle. The auto was then transferred by Dooust to Julian LaDuke, another member of the auto theft ring. Thereafter, Patrick D. Elmer, an innocent buyer, purchased the car from LaDuke sometime in early 1975. Then on May 16, 1975, Johnny Dell, an automobile dealer purchased the Corvette from Elmer for the sum of $5,425. On that date Johnny Dell took physical possession of the automobile, and the New York state registration to the vehicle and the certificate of title to it were transferred to Dell. On June 30, 1975, the

New York State Police impounded the vehicle. Johnny Dell then sued the New York State Police for the return of the car. Is Dell entitled to possession of the car? *Yes Buyer ordinary course* *No.*

5. Samuel Higgonbottom sold his Mercedes-Benz to Katrina Walters in exchange for a check for $13,500 made out to Walters and gave her the title to the vehicle indorsed over to her. Walters transferred ownership to the vehicle, together with the ownership papers, to an automobile dealership, Benzel-Busch, which in turn sold it to a company known as A-Leet. Higgonbottom discovered that the check given to him was originally issued in the sum of $13.50 and had been fraudulently raised by Walters. Neither Benzel-Busch nor A-Leet was aware of the fraud. Higgonbottom sued A-Leet to recover possession of the vehicle. Is he entitled to recover? *Yes No*

6. Eberhard Manufacturing Company entered into a contract to sell certain truck parts to Brown with the parts to be "shipped to" Brown's place of business in Birmingham, Alabama. Eberhard packaged the parts and placed them on board a common carrier with instructions to deliver the goods to Brown. The parts were lost while in transit. The parties did not

expressly agree as to who had the risk of loss and the contract did not contain an F.O.B. term. Between Eberhard and Brown, who had the risk of loss? Brown

7. White Motor Company, a truck manufacturer, delivered an Autocar truck ordered by Bronx Trucks. White received a signed receipt from the manager of Bronx Trucks for the delivery and also invoiced Bronx Trucks for the agreed purchase price. After the truck had been delivered and invoiced, it was stolen from Bronx Truck's garage. The title papers to the truck were not delivered to Bronx Truck until after the truck was stolen. White sued Bronx Truck for the purchase price of the truck, and Bronx Truck defended on the grounds that it did not have title to the truck when it was stolen and thus White was still the owner of it and had the risk of loss. Is Bronx Truck responsible for paying the purchase price to White? Yes

8. The Federal Republic of Germany purchased a sophisticated rocket system and parts from a private munitions manufacturer through the U.S. government. The delivery terms were "F.O.B. VESSEL." After some of the systems and parts had been loaded on the ship that was to transport them to Germany, fire broke out on the ship, partially destroying the system. Had the risk of loss passed to the Federal Republic of Germany? Yes

9. General Electric Company delivered a stock of large lamps to Pettingell Supply Company "as agent to sell or distribute such lamps." Under the agency contract, Pettingell could sell the lamps directly to certain customers for their own use or resale; it was also authorized to make deliveries of lamps under contracts of sale entered into by General Electric and the purchasers as well as to make deliveries to other retail agents of General Electric. About 20 percent of Pettingell's sales of General Electric lamps were direct sales to its own customers. Pettingell also wholesaled other electric supplies, hardware, and housewares. The lamps were its only consignment business, however. Pettingell had financial difficulties and entered into an assignment for the benefit of the creditors. Those creditors claimed the stock of G.E. lamps, while G.E. claimed the lamps were its property because it had a principal-agency relationship with Pettingell. Who is entitled to the lamps? GE creditors

10. Trend House sold its entire business, including stock of merchandise on hand, to Erving's, who failed to obtain a list of creditors of Trend House and failed to give the prescribed notice of sale to the creditors. The state in which the bulk transfer was made had adopted the "Pennsylvania Plan" (U.C.C. Section 6–106), under which the proceeds of the sale are required to be distributed to the transferor's creditors. Darby, as trustee in bankruptcy for Trend House, brought an action against Erving's to recover the value of transferred merchandise. Can Erving's be held personally liable for the value of the property transferred in the bulk sale? Yes

Product Liability

When you buy a product from a merchant, you have certain expectations concerning that product. These expectations usually relate to the quality of the product as well as the use that can safely be made of it. For example, if you buy a new Ford car from a Ford dealer, you might have the following expectations:

1. After discounting certain of the statements the salesperson made to you as sales talk, the car will perform as well as that person promised you it would perform.
2. The car will perform as well as the manufacturer—Ford—said it would in its advertisements on television and in magazines and newspapers.
3. The car will conform to any written guarantees that were made by the manufacturer or dealer; for example, Ford may have advertised a one-year, 12,000 mile warranty on certain parts.
4. The car will be suitable for driving on the highway and its quality will be similar to that of other cars.
5. The car has been properly designed and manufactured.
6. The car does not have any dangerous defects or unusual problems of which you have not been warned.
7. You will be the owner of the car once you have paid the dealer for it.

Suppose as you are driving the new car home from the dealership, the steering mechanism breaks. The car suddenly turns to the right and smashes into a wall. The car is badly damaged. You are injured in the crash and so is a person who was walking along the sidewalk in front of the wall.

This accident raises a number of legal questions. Who is responsible for the accident and for the damages that have been sustained to your car, to you, and to the pedestrian? Who must bear the cost—you, the dealer, or the manufacturer?

If it can be shown that the automobile was defective at the time you purchased it, liability might be placed on the dealer or the manufacturer based on one or more of a number of legal theories: (1) express warranty, (2) implied warranties that are imposed by law, (3) negligence, or (4) strict liability. In this chapter we will explore the legal rules for holding manufacturers and sellers liable for the quality of their products. This area of the law is called *product liability*.

Historical
Development
of the Law

Prior to 1900, the sale of goods was commonly made in a face-to-face negotiation between the buyer and the seller. Frequently, the seller was a peddler who would leave for parts unknown as soon as he had sold his wares. The sale was often looked upon as a test of wits; the seller did his best to drive a sharp bargain. Similarly, the buyer did everything possible to get a good buy. In this situation, neither the buyer nor the seller placed much faith in the statements of the other. The statements made by the seller were taken by the buyer to be sales talk. These statements were not binding on the seller unless he clearly assumed responsibility for the quality of goods he was selling.

Business methods have changed over time. Today sales to business people are frequently made by a salesperson calling on the customer. The salesperson either describes the goods or displays samples of the goods that the seller is offering for sale. Selling of many kinds of consumer goods is done through advertising on television or in newspapers and magazines. Manufacturers and sellers are now held much more accountable for the quality and safety of the goods they sell. This is in part because of these changes in the way sales of goods are made and also because of changes in society's concept of who can best bear the responsibility for the quality of goods.

WARRANTIES

Warranties
in General

In general, a *warranty* is the assumption of responsibility by the seller for the quality, character, or suitability of the goods he or she has sold. The seller may assume this responsibility by agreement with the buyer. In this case the warranty is created by contract, and the rights of the buyer and the liabilities of the seller are contractual in nature. Such a warranty is called an *express warranty*. In addition, certain responsibilities for the quality of goods sold are imposed on the seller by the Uniform Commercial Code (Code). These warranties arise whether or not the seller has made express promises as to the quality of the goods. The warranties imposed by law are known as *implied warranties*.

Express
Warranties

Suppose you go to an appliance dealer to buy a new television set. The dealer points to a sign on which is printed:

> Guarantee: All TV sets we sell are guaranteed against defects in material or workmanship for 12 months. If a set fails to give satisfactory service under the terms of this guarantee, return it to us and we will either repair or replace the set.

This guarantee is also included in the sales contract you sign, so you decide to purchase a television set from the dealer. This guarantee is an *express warranty* that becomes part of the contract of sale between you and the dealer. If the television set does not conform to the promises in the guarantee, you have a right to claim breach of contract.

Creating an Express Warranty

In order to create an express warranty, it does not matter whether the seller uses the words *warranty* or *guarantee* or whether the seller *intends* to make a warranty. The critical elements for creation of an express warranty are: a *statement of fact or a promise* made by the seller to the buyer *concerning the goods* that *becomes part of the bargain* between the buyer and seller (2–313[1][a]).[1] Sellers who merely give an opinion or recommend the goods do not create an express warranty. Thus sellers are not considered to have made an express warranty if they confine their statements to "sales talk." Some examples of sales talk are "It is a good buy," "These goods are high class," or "You should be happy with this." Similarly, a statement as to the value of the goods, for example, "This car is worth $2,500," is not an express warranty.

Whether a statement made by a seller is interpreted as an opinion or as an express warranty often depends on the relative experience and knowledge of the buyer and seller. If the seller deals in the type of goods he or she is selling and the buyer does not deal in such goods and knows little about them, a statement by the seller about the quality or character of the goods might be interpreted as a warranty. On the other hand, if the buyer is a dealer in such goods and has had experience and knowledge similar to that of the seller, the same statements might be interpreted as an expression of an opinion.

For example, if a used-car salesperson who is very familiar with the mechanical operation of cars is selling a car to a person who is not knowledgeable about cars, the salesperson's statements about the condition of the car and its performance are likely to be treated as statements of fact or promises. Such statements are likely to create express warranties. However, if that same salesperson is selling a car to another dealer who is equally knowledgeable about cars, the seller's statements are less likely to be treated as promises on which the dealer would rely in deciding to purchase the car.

In negotiating a sale, a seller may use descriptive terms to convey to the buyer an idea of the quality or characteristics of the goods; for example, Brand X is "a skin cream for oily skin." Similarly a seller might use pictures,

---

[1] The numbers in parentheses refer to the sections of the Uniform Commercial Code; 1972, which is reprinted in the Appendix.

drawings, blueprints, or technical specifications, or in some cases the seller might use a sample or model. When a seller uses descriptive terms on which the buyer relies, the seller has expressly warranted that the goods he or she delivers will meet that description. If a sample or model is part of the basis of a bargain of a contract, the seller has expressly warranted that the goods delivered will conform to the sample or model (2–313[1][b],[c]).

McCarty v. E. J. Korvette, Inc.
347 A.2d 253 (Ct. Spec. App. Md. 1975)

FACTS   McCarty bought four tires from Korvette. The sales invoice for the tires contained the following clause:

> The tires identified hereon are guaranteed for the number of miles designated (36,000) against all road hazards including stone bruises, impact bruises, blowout, tread separation, glass cuts, and fabric breaks, only when used in normal, noncommercial passenger car service. If a tire fails to give satisfactory service under the terms of this guarantee, return it to the nearest Korvette Tire Center. We will replace the tire, charging only its proportionate part of the sale price for mileage used from the date of purchase.

McCarty was involved in an accident when the right rear tire on his car had a blowout. The car swerved off the road and turned over. McCarty and his wife were injured and the car was damaged.

ISSUE   Was the guarantee an express warranty against blowouts?

DECISION   Yes. The court held that the guarantee clause constituted an express warranty that the tires would not blow out during the first 36,000 miles of use. It found it to be an affirmation that the tires are of such quality as to make them capable of being driven for 36,000 miles without blowing out.

IMPLIED WARRANTIES

Nature of Implied Warranties

Under present methods of merchandising, the buyer commonly has little or no opportunity to examine goods carefully before making a decision to purchase them. In addition, because of the complexity and nature of many of the goods that are sold today, buyers are often not in a position to test the goods adequately to determine their quality prior to buying them. The merchant dealing in the goods or the manufacturer of such goods is in a much better position than the buyer to make a thorough examination of the goods or to make tests to determine their adequacy and quality. Therefore, in the interest of promoting higher standards in the marketplace, the law imposes certain responsibilities on the seller for the quality, character, and suitability of the goods sold. This is particularly true where the seller is a merchant dealing in goods of that kind.

Implied warranties imposed by law are not absolute. They arise only under certain circumstances, and the seller may include a clause in the contract that excludes implied warranties. The courts, however, favor implied warranties. If the seller wishes to be relieved from the responsibility for implied warranties, the sales contract must clearly provide that the parties did not intend the implied warranties to become part of the contract.

There are two implied warranties of quality imposed under the Code: (1) the implied warranty of merchantability and (2) the implied warranty of fitness for particular purpose. These two warranties overlap, and under some circumstances the seller may be held liable for breach of both warranties.

Implied Warranty of Merchantability

If the seller is a merchant who deals in the kind of goods sold, there is an *implied warranty* that the goods are *merchantable*. If the person who sells the goods does not deal in goods of that kind, the implied warranty of merchantability is not involved. For example, if your occupation is selling clothing and you sell your used 1975 Chevrolet to a neighbor, there is no implied warranty that the car is merchantable.

Under the Code, the selling of food or drink is a sale. Thus if food or drink sold in a restaurant is not wholesome, the seller may be held liable for breach of the implied warranty of merchantability. Prior to the adoption of the Code, some courts had held that serving food in a restaurant was the sale of a service, not the sale of goods. These courts then refused to imply that the food served was wholesome. The Code specifically rejects this idea and implies a warranty of merchantability in the sale of food (2–314[1]).

The common test for *merchantability* is whether the goods are *fit for the ordinary purpose* for which such goods are used (2–314[2][c]). Thus a person who buys a chair should be able to expect that it will be suitable for sitting in and will not collapse under the weight of a normal person who sits down in it. Similarly, a buyer should be able to expect that a baby shampoo can safely be used to shampoo a baby's hair, and the buyer of a can of soup should be able to assume it is wholesome and edible.

The other tests of merchantability are:

1. The goods conform to any promises or statements of fact made on the container or label.
2. The goods are adequately packaged and labeled.
3. The goods are of the same kind, quality, and quantity within each unit (case, package, carton).
4. Fungible goods (such as grain and coal) are of average quality for the kind of goods described in the contract.
5. The goods conform closely enough to the description in the contract to be acceptable to others in the trade or business (2–314[2]).

It should be noted that not each of these tests applies to every sales contract.

Hunt v. Ferguson-Paulus Enterprises
415 P.2d 13 (Sup. Ct. Ore. 1966)

FACTS Hunt purchased a cherry pie from a vending machine owned and operated by Ferguson-Paulus. When Hunt bit into the pie, he broke a tooth on a cherry pit in the pie.

ISSUE Did the presence of a cherry pit in a cherry pie constitute a breach of the implied warranty of merchantability that accompanied the sale of the pie?

DECISION No. The court held that there was no breach of the implied warranty of merchantability. It noted that most courts have used one of two different tests for determining whether food is unfit for consumption and thus in breach of the implied warranty of merchantability: (1) the foreign-natural test, and (2) the reasonable-expectation test. Under the *foreign-natural test* the court looks to see whether there was a foreign substance in the food or whether the condition of the food was impure or noxious. For example, is there glass, stones, wire, or nails in the food, or is the food tainted, diseased, or infected? Under the foreign-natural test, however, there is no liability for a fish dish that contains a fish bone, a chicken sandwich that contains a chicken bone, or a cherry pie that contains a cherry stone. Under the *reasonable-expectation test,* the question is what might reasonably be expected in the food served, and not what is natural to the food prior to its preparation. The court found that a consumer would reasonably expect that he or she might find a cherry pit in a cherry pie.

Implied Warranty of Fitness for a Particular Purpose

At times, the seller may know the *particular purpose* for which the buyer needs the goods and that the buyer is *relying* on the seller to select goods suitable for that purpose. If these two conditions are met, then the seller makes an *implied warranty* that goods sold will be *fit for the particular purpose of the buyer* (2–315).

For example, a farmer goes to a feed store and tells the clerk that he needs a pesticide that will kill corn borers. If the clerk knows the farmer is depending on her to pick a suitable pesticide, there is an implied warranty that the product selected will be fit for the farmer's needs. If, when properly used, the product selected kills the farmer's corn or is ineffective against corn borers, there is a breach of the implied warranty of fitness for a particular purpose.

It should be noted that the implied warranty of merchantability focuses on whether the goods are fit for the ordinary purposes for which such goods are used. The implied warranty of fitness for a particular purpose focuses on the buyer's individual purpose.

If the buyer gives the seller technical specifications of the goods he or she wishes to buy or clearly indicates the particular goods desired, there is no implied warranty of fitness for a particular purpose. Under these circumstances there is no evidence that the buyer is relying on the seller's judgment or expertise; thus there is no implied warranty. The seller does not have to be a merchant dealing in goods of that kind in order to make an implied warranty of fitness for a particular purpose.

Filler v. Rayex Corp.
435 F.2d 336 (7th Cir. 1970)

FACTS Beck, a high school baseball coach, ordered six pairs of flip-type baseball sunglasses from Rayex Corp. Rayex had advertised the sunglasses as baseball sunglasses that would give "instant eye protection." While one of his baseball players, Michael Filler, was using a pair of the glasses, they were hit by a flyball. The glasses shattered and as a result Filler lost his right eye. Filler then brought a lawsuit against Rayex claiming, among other things, a breach of the implied warranty of fitness for a particular purpose.

ISSUE Was the manufacturer liable for breach of the implied warranty of fitness for a particular purpose?

DECISION Yes. The court held that there was a breach of implied warranty of fitness for a particular purpose. The glasses were advertised as suitable for use by baseball players and were bought and used for that purpose. In fact, they were not fit for that purpose. Here the buyer was relying on the seller's assurance that the glasses were suitable for use by baseball players.

Implied Warranty of Title

The *implied warranty of title* differs from other warranties in that it protects the buyer in his or her ownership of the goods bought. In contrast, the other warranties discussed in this chapter relate to the quality of the goods sold. The general rule is that in any contract for the sale of goods, the seller warrants to the buyer that he or she has the right to sell them (2–312). If, for example, the seller had stolen the goods, the seller does not have good title to them, and the warranty of title is breached when he or she sells them to the buyer.

Under the implied warranty of title, the seller also warrants that the goods are *free of any liens or claims of other parties* unless the buyer was given notice of the liens or claims at the time the contract was made (2–312). Suppose John puts his used automobile up for sale. John originally borrowed the money to buy the automobile from his bank, and the bank took a security interest or lien on it to secure John's repayment of the loan. If John still owes $600 to the bank at the time he sells the car to Ann, John must either pay off the bank before he transfers title to Ann or specifically provide in his agreement with Ann that the automobile is being sold subject to the bank's lien.

The implied warranty of title also covers a claim by a third party that the sale or use of the goods infringes a patent held by that third party.

EXCLUSIONS AND MODIFICATIONS OF WARRANTIES

General Rules

Under the Code, the parties to a contract have, within certain limits, the right to agree to relieve the seller from all or part of the liability for express or implied warranties. Frequently, sellers try to exclude or limit their responsibility for these warranties; however, such exclusions and modifications are not looked on with favor by the courts. The seller must satisfy a number of strict requirements in order to be successful in excluding or modifying an express or implied warranty. These requirements are designed to make sure that the buyer is likely to be aware of the clause modifying or excluding the warranty and freely consents to it. In a dispute, the courts consider the reasonableness of the particular exclusion or modification and may refuse to enforce an exclusion it finds to be unreasonable or unconscionable (2–302).

Limitation of Express Warranties

If sellers do not want to be liable for express warranties, they should try to avoid making any. This is difficult, however, because the seller is likely to make statements about the goods or use models or samples. A seller who makes an express warranty and who also tries to disclaim all express warranties by including a disclaimer clause in the contract is not likely to succeed. The disclaimer will probably be disregarded on the grounds that it is inconsistent with the express warranty (2–316[1]).

Sellers may try to limit their liability for breach of the express warranty. For example, the seller might agree to be responsible for only repairing or replacing a product that is not as it is warranted to be. Such a limitation may be enforced unless a court finds that it is *unconscionable* or that the limitation causes the warranty to *fail of its essential purpose*. A court is most likely to find a failure of essential purpose where a defect in a small part causes serious injury to a consumer and the seller is claiming that his responsibility is only to replace the defective part.

Exclusion of Implied Warranties

In order to exclude the implied warranty of merchantability, the seller must specifically mention *merchantability* in the exclusion. The exclusion does not have to be in writing, but if it is in writing, the clause that excludes all or part of the warranty of merchantability must be *conspicuous* (2–316[2]). Thus the exclusion clause must be printed or written into the contract in large type or letters or an ink of a different color so that the person reading the contract is not likely to overlook it. If the seller is particularly concerned that the exclusion clause be enforced, the seller should have the buyer separately initial the exclusion clause.

To exclude the implied warranty of fitness for a particular purpose, the exclusion must be in *writing* and it must be *conspicuous* (2–316[2]).

Language such as "as is" or "with all faults" is sufficient to exclude both the implied warranty of merchantability and the implied warranty of fitness for a particular purpose. Either phrase calls the buyer's attention to the exclusion of the warranty and makes it clear that there are no warranties (2–316[3][a]).

A seller can also limit both implied warranties by making goods available for examination and demanding that the buyer examine the goods before taking them. Then there is no implied warranty with regard to defects that the buyer should have discovered by inspecting the goods (2–316[3][b]).

Unconscionable Disclaimers

Generally under the Code the buyer and seller are given considerable freedom as to the terms they may include in the contract. As discussed previously in this chapter, the Code specifically provides means for excluding and limiting warranties. In addition, the Code gives the court the authority to refuse to enforce a particular clause or even an entire contract if it finds the clause or contract *unconscionable* at the time that it was made (2–302). The Code requirement that disclaimers of warranty be conspicuous makes unenforceable disclaimers that the buyer is not likely to have seen.

A court may also refuse to enforce a disclaimer of warranty as unconscionable if there is a great disparity of bargaining power between the buyer and the seller and if the court feels the disclaimer was forced on the buyer with no chance to bargain over its form. A court is most likely to find a disclaimer unconscionable in the case of a personally injured consumer, and somewhat less likely when the consumer has suffered only property damage or economic loss. It is least likely to find the disclaimer unconscionable where the plaintiff is a merchant trying to recover for property damage or economic loss.

Henningsen v. Bloomfield Motors
161 A.2d 69 (Sup. Ct. N.J. 1960)

FACTS   Claus Henningsen purchased a new Plymouth manufactured by Chrysler Corporation from Bloomfield Motors. At the time he bought the car, he signed a purchase order provided by the dealer. The purchase order contained an express warranty against defects in material and workmanship, but it limited Chrysler's responsibility to replacing any defective parts. The warranty clause also stated that this express warranty was "in lieu of all other warranties express or implied and all other liabilities" on its part. This clause was contained in fine print as one of ten clauses on the back of the purchase order. While the car was being driven, the steering mechanism snapped. The car veered sharply to the right and crashed into a brick wall. Henningsen brought a lawsuit against the dealer and Chrysler to recover for injuries sustained as well as for damage to the car. Chrysler claimed that its responsibility was only to replace the defective part and that it had effectively disclaimed any other liability for implied warranties.

ISSUE   Could Chrysler enforce its disclaimer of the implied warranty of merchantability?

DECISION   No. The court refused to enforce Chrysler's attempt to disclaim the implied warranty of merchantability. The court noted that the disclaimer was not conspicuous or likely to be noticed by the buyer. In addition, the court held that the disclaimer clause was unconscionable. The clause was imposed on the automobile consumer without an opportunity for the buyer to bargain over it. There is also a great inequality of bargaining power between the manufacturer and the buyer. At the time this case was decided, the same warranty clause was used by all U.S. automobile manufacturers so there was no opportunity for a buyer to get a more favorable warranty.

WHO BENEFITS FROM A WARRANTY?

Purchasers

When a product is defective and injures someone, the question arises as to whether the injured person can benefit from the warranty and recover from the seller or manufacturer for breach of warranty. For example, supppose Molly buys an electric table saw for her husband Joe as a birthday present. She purchases the saw at Ace Hardware. The saw had been made by the Blake Manufacturing Company. While Joe is using this saw, the blade flies off, severely injuring Joe's arm. This happened because the saw had been improperly designed. The saw came with a warranty that it was guaranteed against defects in material and workmanship for a period of 90 days.

Suppose Joe tries to sue Ace Hardware, claiming breach of an express warranty or breach of the implied warranty of merchantability. The hardware store might try to claim that Joe should not be able to sue it for breach of warranty because he did not purchase this saw from the hardware store. Remember that warranties arise as part of a contract, and the contract in this case was between Molly and the hardware store.

A similar problem could arise if either Joe or Molly tried to sue Blake to recover from the injuries on the grounds that the manufacturer had breached either an express warranty or the implied warranty of merchantability. The manufacturer might claim that it had sold the saw to the hardware store but that it had not dealt with either Joe or Molly. The manufacturer would say it had no contract or warranty responsibility to either of them.

Privity of Contract

In the past, the courts applied the general rule of contract law that a person who is not a party to the contract has no right to enforce it. A person had to be in *privity of contract* to enforce the contract. Unless a person had purchased the defective goods, he or she had no cause of action for breach of warranty. Furthermore, even the purchaser of defective goods was able to sue only the immediate seller and not the manufacturer with whom there had been no contract.

Today most courts allow an injured purchaser to recover directly from the manufacturer of the goods. This is true even thought the version of the Code adopted in some states does not expressly authorize a suit against the manufacturer unless the purchaser bought directly from the manufacturer. In most cases the manufacturer had control over the condition of the product when it reached the buyer's hands and should be held liable for any defects in it. The fact that the consumer may bring suit against the manufacturer in no way relieves the retailer of its responsibility for the fitness or merchantability of the goods. In most states the buyer is permitted to sue both the retailer and the manufacturer in the same suit. This is true both for implied warranties and for express warranties that may have been made by the manufacturer.

Nonpurchasers

The Code also extends some of the benefits of warranties to persons who did not themselves purchase the particular defective goods. The Code extends warranty protection to *"any natural person who is in the family or household of the buyer or who is a guest in his house* if it is reasonable to expect that such person may use, consume or be affected by the goods and who is injured in his person by breach of warranty" (2–318). Thus in the example involving the table saw, the Code would allow Joe to sue for breach of warranty because he is a member of the buyer's household.

A more difficult question is raised when the injured person is an employee of the buyer of the goods or a bystander. The decisions concerning bystanders and employees are not consistent among all states; however, there is a growing tendency for the courts to allow persons who have been injured as a result of breach of warranties of goods to claim the benefit of the warranties. Persons who could reasonably be expected to use the goods are then allowed to sue if they were injured as a result of the breach of warranty. It is important to note that under the Code, a seller is not permitted to exclude or limit liability to members of the buyer's household or guests of the buyer for breaches of express or implied warranties that the seller has made (2–318).

Alternative versions of the Code that have been adopted in some states explicitly extend warranty coverage to bystanders and employees. In addition some specifically authorize direct suits against manufacturers.

FEDERAL TRADE COMMISSION WARRANTY RULES

Magnuson-Moss Warranty Act

In the late 1960s and early 1970s Congress conducted a number of investigations into consumer product warranties and their terms. It concluded that the warranties were frequently confusing, misleading, and frustrating to consumers and that the law governing warranties should be changed to encourage manufacturers to market more reliable products for competitive reasons. Congress based its findings in part on the fact that consumer products are typically sold with a form contract dictated by the seller, that the consumer cannot bargain with the seller over terms, and that the remedies stated in these contracts are sometimes not useful to the consumer. For these reasons, Congress passed the Magnuson-Moss Warranty Act, which became effective on January 4, 1975.

Purpose of the Act

The Magnuson-Moss Warranty Act is intended to: (1) provide minimum warranty protection for consumers, (2) increase consumer understanding of warranties, (3) insure warranty performance by providing useful remedies, and (4) encourage better product reliability by making it easier for consumers to choose among products on the basis of their likely reliability. The act applies to all sellers of a "consumer product" that costs more than $5[2] who give the consumer a written warranty. It does not require the seller to make a warranty, however; in fact, it may have led to fewer warranties being made.

Requirements of the Act

Under the act and the FTC's warranty regulations, the seller is not required to give a written warranty. If the seller does give a warranty, however, it must comply with the act and the regulations. The seller must disclose in a single document in simple and understandable language the following items of information:

1. The persons who can enforce or use the warranty (for example, the original purchaser or any subsequent owner of the item during the term of the warranty).
2. A clear description of the products, parts, components, characteristics, and properties covered by the warranty, and, if necessary, the items excluded from the warranty.
3. A statement of what the maker of the warranty will do and what items or services will be paid for if the product is defective, malfunctions, or does not conform to the warranty, and (if needed for clarity) a statement of what the warrantor will not pay for.
4. The time the warranty begins (if it begins on a date other than the purchase date) and its duration.
5. A step-by-step explanation of how to obtain warranty service and information about any *informal dispute settlement mechanisms* (for example, arbitration) made available by the seller.
6. Any limitations on the duration of implied warranties and any exclusions or limitations on relief, such as consequential or incidental damages (for example, not paying to drain the basement after the water heater

---

[2] The act covers consumer products that cost more than $5, but the regulations adopted by the Federal Trade Commission to implement the act cover only products that cost more than $15.

breaks), and an explanation that under some state laws those exclusions or limitations may not be allowed.

7. A statement that the consumer has certain legal rights under the warranty as well as other rights that may vary from state to state.

Full Warranties

The maker of the warranty must state whether the warranty is a *full warranty* or a *limited warranty*. A full warranty means:

1. The warrantor will fix or replace any defective product, including removal and reinstallation if necessary, free of charge.
2. It is not limited in time (say, to one or two years).
3. It does not either exclude or limit payment for consequential damages unless the exclusion or limitation is printed conspicuously on the face of the written warranty.
4. If the product cannot be repaired or has not been repaired after a reasonable number of efforts to repair it, the consumer may choose between a refund and a replacement.
5. The warrantor cannot impose duties on the consumer except reasonable duties (the warranty cannot require the consumer to ship a piano to the factory) or a duty not to modify the product.
6. The warrantor is not required to fulfill the warranty terms if the problem was caused by damage to the product by unreasonable use.

A full warranty does not have to cover the whole product. It may cover only part of the product, such as the picture tube of a television set. Also, anyone who owns the product during the warranty period may invoke or use the warranty.

Limited Warranties

A limited warranty is any other warranty covered by the act that does not meet the standards for a full warranty. For example, a limited warranty may cover only parts, not labor, or may require the purchaser to return a heavy product to the seller or service representative for service. It may also require the purchaser to pay for handling or allow only a pro rata refund or credit, depending on the length of time since the product was purchased. Often, a limited warranty protects only the first purchaser.

Availability of Warranties

The act requires the seller to make the written warranty terms available to the prospective buyer before the sale. For example, the text of the warranty might be displayed next to the product, or on the package in which the product is enclosed. Warranty terms can also be collected in notebooks in the department that sells the goods and may even be microfilmed, so long as the prospective buyer can readily use the microfilm reader. The maker of the warranty is required to make the text of the warranty available to sellers in forms that sellers can readily use, such as providing copies of the written warranty with each product, or on a tag, sticker, label, or other attachment to the product, or on a sign or poster. These warranty requirements also cover catalog and door-to-door sales.

Enforcement

The Federal Trade Commission enforces the disclosure provisions of the warranty act and regulations; for example, it enforces the seller's obligation to make the terms available before the sale and the format requirements imposed on all makers of warranties (manufacturers or sellers). Consumers have the right to sue the maker for failure to fulfill the terms of the warranty. Consumers can sue the manufacturer if the manufacturer offers the warranty or the retailer if the retailer grants the warranty.

NEGLIGENCE

Product Liability in General

Liability of a seller based on breach of warranty is only one of the theories of liability that courts have used to impose liability on the manufacturer or seller of goods for personal injury or property damage that results from the use of the goods. Two other legal bases for product liability are negligence and strict liability.

Negligence

In Chapter 4, you studied the general rules concerning negligence. The basic rule is that a person owes a *duty of care* to avoid *foreseeable injury* to other persons that may be caused if the person does not use reasonable care in his or her actions. As long ago as 1916, courts held that a manufacturer can be liable to a consumer of a defective product on the grounds that the manufacturer was negligent in not adequately *inspecting* the product so that a person would be protected from injury. Subsequently, courts have held manufacturers liable for negligence not only for failing to inspect but also for:

1. *Misrepresenting* the character of goods or their fitness for a particular purpose.
2. Failing to *disclose known defects* or to *warn about known dangers.*
3. Failing to use *due care in designing and preparing goods for sale.*

Privity Not Required

Because liability based on negligence does not involve a contractual relationship, it does not matter whether or not the buyer dealt directly with the manufacturer. The manufacturer's duty of care extends to all persons who might foreseeably be injured if the manufacturer does not exercise its duty of care. It is foreseeable that the ultimate consumer of goods or an employee, guest, or member of the family of the purchaser—or even a bystander—might be hurt if goods are not properly designed or built.

Disclaimers

Disclaimers in contracts are usually not effective to shield a manufacturer or seller against liability for negligence.

Larsen v. General Motors
391 F.2d 495 (8th Cir. 1968)

FACTS Larsen was driving a 1963 Chevrolet Corvair when it was involved in a head-on collision. The collision forced the steering mechanism back into Larsen's head, and he was severely injured. Larsen brought a lawsuit against General Motors, claiming that the steering mechanism was negligently designed. He claimed that other cars were designed so that the steering mechanism would not be pushed so far back if the car was hit head-on. Larsen contended that because of this design defect, he was injured more severely than he otherwise would have been. He also claimed that General Motors should have warned him about this dangerous condition. General Motors took the position that it did not have a duty to design and make a car that would be safe in an accident.

ISSUE Can a manufacturer be held liable for negligent design if its product is unusually dangerous to the user when it is involved in an accident?

DECISION Yes. The court held that General Motors was liable for design negligence. It said that a manufacturer must use reasonable care to design an automobile to make it safe to the user for its foreseeable use. The court found that it was reasonable to expect that cars would be involved in accidents. In view of this, the manufacturer should use reasonable care in designing the car to make sure it will not be unduly dangerous to the user. The design of the steering mechanism was a hidden defect that the court found was unreasonably dangerous to the user.

STRICT LIABILITY

Reasons for Development of Strict Liability

Persons who are injured by defective products are not always able to recover for their injuries if they must rely on negligence or breach of warranty. Under common law *contributory negligence* on the part of the plaintiff completely barred recovery for injuries sustained as a result of negligence on the part of the defendant. While more than 30 states have adopted at least a modified form of *comparative negligence*, an injured plaintiff, even in one of these states, may be partially or completely barred from recovery if his or her own negligence was a significant factor in causing the injury. This can make it difficult for a person who is injured by a defective product to recover on the grounds of manufacturer *negligence* if there was any improper use on his or her part.

Similarly, as you have seen, a person who is injured by a defective product may have trouble bringing a successful lawsuit based on *breach of warranty* if he or she was not the buyer or a member of the buyer's family or household or a guest in the buyer's home. Bystanders and employees who are injured by products purchased by others are typically barred by their *lack of privity* from recovering for breach of warranty.

In the mid-1960s, courts increasingly took note of the limitations inherent in both breach of warranty and negligence as a means for redressing injuries caused by defective products. They began to apply strict liability in tort to product liability cases. As discussed in Chapter 4, strict liability was originally imposed on persons who were engaged in ultradangerous activities. Thus a person was held liable if he used dynamite and caused damage to another person's property or if he kept wild animals that escaped and caused injury to people or property.

Sellers are now commonly held strictly liable in tort when products they place on the market and know will be used without inspection for defects turn out to have defects that cause injuries to people. The purpose of such liability is to insure that the costs of injuries from defective products are borne by the seller who put the products on the market, rather than by the injured person. Sellers are held liable regardless of whether they exercised reasonable care. When strict liability is imposed, sellers are made, in effect, the virtual insurer of their products. Strict liability is now more frequently the basis on which injured persons recover for defective products than breach of warranty or negligence.

Elements of Strict Liability

The essential elements for strict liability are:

1. A product has been sold in a *defective condition* and is *unreasonably dangerous* to the user or consumer.
2. The seller is engaged in the business of selling such a product.
3. The product is expected to and does reach the consumer without substantial change in the condition in which it is sold.
4. The consumer or other person sustains physical harm because of the defective condition.

It does not matter whether or not the user or consumer bought the product directly from the seller or had any contractual relationship with the seller. Similarly it is not a defense on the seller's part that he or she exercised all possible care in the preparation and sale of the product. If the product is inherently dangerous so that no amount of due care could make it safe, then the manufacturer is required to give the user notice of the unreasonable danger.

Borel v. Fibreboard Paper Products Corp.
493 F.2d 1076 (5th Cir. 1973)

FACTS Between 1936 and 1969 Borel was employed as an industrial insulation worker. In the course of his job, he was exposed to heavy concentrations of asbestos dust caused by insulation materials. Borel became disabled from the disease known as asbestosis. He then brought a lawsuit to recover for his injuries against the companies that manufactured the insulation materials he had used.

ISSUE   Were the manufacturers strictly liable to Borel because they did not warn him of the dangers of exposure to asbestos dust?

DECISION   Yes. The courts found the manufacturers were liable to Borel on the basis of strict liability. If a product—such as asbestos—cannot be made safe regardless of the amount of care used by the manufacturer, the manufacturer is under an obligation to warn the user of known dangers involved in using the product. Then the user has the right to decide whether or not to expose himself to the danger of which he has been advised. The dangers of exposure to asbestos have been known since the mid-1930s.

Strict liability is currently accepted by most states, but it is not consistently applied to all types of products and all types of defects. Over time it has been extended to a wide variety of products that can prove to be unreasonably dangerous because of their defective condition. In addition, some states have applied it to situations involving the sale of services, used merchandise, and real estate. As presently applied, strict liability can be used against retailers as well as manufacturers of such defective products. Disclaimers of liability in contracts of sale are generally not effective to shield the seller or manufacturer against strict liability.

State of the Art   In determining whether a product is *inherently dangerous* or has been *defectively designed*, the courts look to the "state of the art" in existence at the time of manufacture. Under the decisions in most states, this does not mean simply what other companies in the industry are doing; rather the focus is on whether anything else could have been done to make the product safer, given the practical and technological limitations of the time. In some instances, design changes or improvements made subsequently by a manufacturer have been used as evidence of what the manufacturer should have done earlier.

LaGorga v. Kroger Co.
275 F.Supp. 373 (W.D.Pa. 1967)

FACTS   Mildred Lettieri purchased a boy's jacket for $2.98 from a Kroger food store and sent it to her nephew, John LaGorga, as a Christmas present. The jacket was not labeled, there was no identity of the fabrics used in the jacket, and there was no warning that it had not been treated with flame retardant. While John and some companions were playing around a refuse barrel in a schoolyard, the jacket was ignited by a spark. It was rapidly consumed by fire and efforts by rescuers to free John from the jacket were impeded by a defective zipper. John suffered severe burns over about 80 percent of his body. The burning characteristics of the jacket were that it ignited easily, burned rapidly, burned with a high heat intensity and was difficult to extinguish. It was agreed by the parties that the jacket conformed to, or at least was not in violation of the Federal Flammable Fabrics Act. However, there was evidence introduced at the trial that 80–90 percent of cotton fabric is treated with flame retardant but that the outer shell of the jacket had not been so treated. There was also evidence presented that treatment of the outer shells with flame retardant would add only a few cents to their cost and would not impair their usefulness.

ISSUE   Should Kroger be held strictly liable for the injuries sustained by the wearer of the jacket?

DECISION   Yes. The court upheld a jury verdict in favor of John LaGorga. The court held that the burning characteristics of the jacket made it unreasonably dangerous and thus the seller could be held strictly liable for injuries sustained because of its defective condition.

Intended Use

Courts in about half the states that use strict liability allow the injured party to recover only if the injuries resulted from the *intended use* of the product. However, other courts have imposed strict liability even where the product was being used in a way that was not intended or foreseeable by the seller. Thus some persons have recovered on the basis of strict liability even though they misused the product or disregarded the seller's instructions and were injured as a result. Sellers have also been held strictly liable in a few instances for products that were altered by a user after they left the manufacturer.

Statutes of Repose

The four-year statute of limitations in the Code requires that lawsuits for breach of warranty be brought within four years of the time the breach occurs (usually when the goods are delivered). This limitation does not apply to claims based on strict liability. As a result, such suits can be and have been brought many years after the sale of the goods. For example, a worker may be injured while using industrial machinery made decades earlier. Rather than utilizing workmen's compensation with its limited benefits, the worker sues the manufacturer of the machinery on the grounds of strict liability. More than a dozen states have now passed so-called *statues of repose*, which set a statute of limitations on actions for strict liability. These limitations generally range between 6 and 12 years from the date the product is first sold.

Possible Limitations on Strict Liability

The broad expansion of seller's liability for defective products, primarily through the application of strict liability, has generated claims that the law has gone too far. Some manufacturers and insurance companies contend that product liability law now so favors the consumer that it is stifling the development of new products and putting unreasonable cost burdens on manufacturers—and, in turn, on consumers. As a result, Congress and many state legislatures have been considering or have passed proposals to limit certain aspects of strict liability. Frequently these proposals focus on: (1) defining what is state of the art, (2) protecting a manufacturer if its products meet government safety standards, and (3) using comparative fault to reduce a damage award if the plaintiff contributed to his or her own injury.

QUESTIONS AND PROBLEM CASES

1. What is the difference between an express warranty and an implied warranty?

2. Mrs. Carpenter went to the City Drug Store to buy some hair dye. While looking over the more than 20 products that the store carried, she was offered assistance by a sales clerk. The clerk stated that she and several of her friends used a particular brand and that their hair came out "very nice" and "very natural." The clerk also told Carpenter that "she would get very fine results." Carpenter bought the recommended product. After using it, she developed a skin reaction. She then filed suit against the drug store for breach of an express warranty. Can she recover for breach of an express warranty? Yes

3. Kruger acquired a 1955 Chevrolet Corvette from Bibi for $2,800. Sometime later Kruger learns that a prior owner had placed a $3,600 lien on the automobile. Does Kruger have any legal grounds for suing Bibi? Yes

4. Mrs. Maze purchased three cans of purple hull peas canned by Bush Brothers & Co. at Liberty Cash Grocery. Several days later she opened a can and placed its contents in a saucepan on the stove. While stirring the peas a large green object came to the surface. While at first she believed it to be a stem, upon closer examination she found it to be a green worm. She became nauseated and sick and remained so for several days. She also remained upset over the thought that she had almost served the peas to her children. She then filed suit against Liberty Cash Grocery. Can she recover?

5. Mr. Hochberg, while dining at O'Donnell's Restaurant, ordered a martini. When it arrived it contained an olive. Hochberg removed the olive and after noticing a hole in one end, bit down on it. He broke his tooth on an olive pit. He then filed suit for a breach of an implied warranty of merchantability by O'Donnell's Restaurant. Can he recover? No

6. Dr. Gates, wishing to purchase a Christmas present for his wife, went to Penelope's, a women's specialty shop. Although he did not know what size his wife wore, he knew that she frequently shopped there and was well known to the sales personnel. He was waited on by the owner of the store, who sold him three pants suits and told him that she was certain that the suits would fit his wife. He was told if there is any problem he could return them. The clothing turned out to be too large for Mrs. Gates and she attempted to exchange it. She could not find anything that was suitable and asked for a refund of the purchase price. She was refused. Dr. Gates then filed a lawsuit against Penelope's in a small claims court, claiming breach of the implied warranty of fitness for a particular purpose. What are his chances of success? Pretty good

7. Mr. Williams bought a five-year-old used car from College Dodge, Inc. As part of the sale he was required to fill out a "vehicle buyer's order" form. This was used to apply for a

change of title for the car and required a considerable amount of information. On the back of this form, together with still more printing but set in larger type, was this sentence "No implied warranties are made, either of merchantability or fitness for particular purpose." After Williams took the car, he began to have serious problems with the engine. After returning it to College Dodge three times, with no results, he rescinded the contract, claiming a breach of an implied warranty of merchantability. Is he on sound legal grounds? Yes

8. Glenn Gray bought a new 1971 Mach I Mustang automobile manufactured by the Ford Motor Company from Pettigrew Motor Company. While Gray's wife Nancy was driving the automobile, the right front wheel collapsed, causing it to crash and to injure Nancy's mother, Mrs. Browder. Browder filed suit against the Ford Motor Company, alleging breach of express and implied warranties and claiming she was a third-party beneficiary of the warranties. Ford Motor Company defended on the ground that there was no privity of contract between Browder and Ford. Is privity a defense to Ford in this case? No

9. Mrs. Hanberry, a frequent reader of *Good Housekeeping* magazine, was well acquainted with the Good Housekeeping Seal and the guarantee that accompanied it. This guarantee provided that products bearing it had been tested and found to be good and safe for the use intended. She purchased a pair of shoes that was both advertised in the magazine and bearing the seal. The shoes were defectively designed, which caused them not to grip adequately on vinyl floors. Hanberry, while wearing the shoes, slipped on her vinyl kitchen floor and was severely injured. She then filed suit against *Good Housekeeping* magazine for negligent misrepresentation. Should Hanberry recover on this claim?

10. Mr. Klimas, an electrician, was testing various fuses with a standard tester. He had not purchased any of the fuses but had been supplied them by his employer. While testing a Royal Crystal fuse manufactured by International Telephone and Telegraph Corp., the fuse exploded and injured his eye, blinding him. Upon later examination it was discovered that the fuse had been defective. Klimas filed an action against IT&T Corp. based on strict liability and on the implied warranty of fitness for a particular purpose under the Code. Discuss the relative merits of each claim. Include in your discussion whether IT&T can defend against Klimas claiming lack of privity.

Performance of Sales Contracts

18

GENERAL RULES

The parties to a contract for the sale of goods are obligated to perform the contract according to its terms. The Code gives the parties great flexibility to decide between themselves how a contract will be performed. The practices in the trade or business as well as any past dealings between the parties are used to supplement or explain the contract. The Code provides both buyer and seller with certain rights. It also sets out what is expected of the buyer and seller on points the parties did not deal with in their contract. You should keep in mind that the Code changes basic contract law in a number of respects.

Good Faith

The buyer and seller must act in "good faith" in the performance of a sales contract (1–203).[1] *Good faith* is defined to mean "honesty in fact" in performing the duties assumed in the contract or in carrying out the transaction (1–201[19]). Thus, if the seller is required by the contract to select an assortment of goods for the buyer, the selection must be made in good faith; the seller should pick out a reasonable assortment (2–311). It would not, for example, be good faith to include only unusual sizes or colors.

---

[1] The numbers in parentheses refer to the sections of the Uniform Commercial Code, 1972 which is reprinted in the Appendix.

Umlas v. Acey Oldsmobile
310 N.Y.S.2d 147 (Civ. Ct. N.Y. 1970)

FACTS Umlas signed a contract to purchase a 1970 Oldsmobile from Acey Oldsmobile. The contract provided that Umlas would receive $650 for trading in his old car and allowed him to continue to drive it until his new car was delivered. Another clause in the contract provided that Acey could reappraise the used car when the new car was delivered. When Umlas brought his trade-in to the dealer to exchange for his new car, an employee of Acey took it for a test drive. The employee told Umlas it was worth $300 to $400. Acey told Umlas that his trade-in had been reappraised at $50. Umlas refused to go through with the sale and bought a car from another dealer. That dealer gave him $400 for trading in his old car. Umlas then sued Acey for breach of contract.

ISSUE Did Acey breach the contract by not acting in "good faith" in its reappraisal of the car?

DECISION Yes. The court held that Acey had breached the contract. The contract did give Acey the right to reappraise the trade-in at the time it was delivered to the dealer. However, the Code requires that a person must act in good faith in exercising rights in a contract. Here dropping the appraisal to less than 10 percent of the original appraisal ($650) was not acting in good faith.

Course of Dealing

The terms in the contract between the parties are the primary means for determining the obligations of the buyer and seller. The meaning of those terms may be explained by looking at any performance that has already taken place. For example, a contract may call for periodic deliveries of goods. If a number of deliveries have been made by the buyer without objection by the seller, the way the deliveries were made shows how the parties intended them to be made. Similarly, if there were any past contracts between the parties, the way they interpreted those contracts is relevant to the interpretation of the present one. If there is a conflict between the express terms of the contract and the past course of dealing between the parties, the express terms of the contract prevail (2–208[2]).

Usage of Trade

In many kinds of businesses there are customs and practices of the trade that are known by people in the business. These customs and practices are usually assumed by parties to a contract for goods of that type. Under the Code these trade customs and practices can be used in interpreting a contract (1–205). If there is a conflict between the express terms of the contract and trade usage, the express terms prevail (2–208[2]).

Waiver

In a contract where there are a number of instances of partial performance (such as deliveries or payments) by one party, the other party must be careful to object to any late deliveries or payments. If the other party does not object, it may be waiving its right to cancel the contract if other deliveries or payments are late (208[3], 209[4]).

For example, a contract calls for a fish market to deliver fish to a supermarket every Thursday and for the supermarket to pay on delivery. If the fish market regularly delivers the fish on Friday and the supermarket does not object, it will be unable later to cancel the contract for that reason. Similarly, if the supermarket does not pay cash but rather sends a check the following week, then the fish market must object if it may want to rely on the late payment as grounds for later canceling the contract.

A party who has waived rights to a portion of the contract not yet performed may *retract the waiver* by giving reasonable notice to the other party that strict performance will be required. The retraction of the waiver is effective unless it would be unjust because of a *material change* of position by the other party in *reliance* on the waiver (2–209[5]).

Assignment

Under the Code, the duties of either the buyer or the seller generally may be delegated to someone else. If there is a strong reason for having the original party perform the acts, such as if the quality of the performance might be different, then duties cannot be delegated. Also, if the parties agree in the contract that there is to be no assignment, then duties cannot be delegated. However, the right to receive performance—such as to receive goods or payment—can be delegated (2–210).

DELIVERY

Basic Obligation

The basic duty of the seller is to *deliver* the goods called for by the contract. The basic duty of the buyer is to *accept and pay for the goods* if they conform to the contract (2–301). The buyer and seller may agree that the goods are to be delivered in several lots or installments. If there is no agreement for delivery in installments, then all the goods must be delivered to the buyer in a single delivery.

Place of Delivery

The buyer and seller may agree on the place where the goods will be delivered. If no such agreement is made, then the goods are to be delivered at the seller's place of business. If the seller does not have a place of business, then delivery is to be made at his or her home. These rules do not apply if the goods are located somewhere other than the seller's place of business or home. In those cases, the place for delivery is the place where the goods are located.

Seller's Duty of Delivery

The seller's basic obligation is to tender delivery of goods that conform to the contract with the buyer. *Tender of delivery* means that the seller must make the goods available to the buyer. This must be done during reasonable hours and for a reasonable period of time so that the buyer can take possession of the goods (2–503).

The contract of sale may require the seller merely to ship the goods to the buyer but not to deliver the goods to the buyer's place of business. If it does, the seller must put the goods into the possession of a carrier, such as a trucking company or a railroad. The seller must also make a *reasonable contract* with the carrier to take the goods to the buyer. Then the seller is required to *notify* the buyer that the goods have been shipped.

If the seller does not make a reasonable contract for delivery or notify the buyer and a material delay or loss results, the buyer has the right to reject the shipment. For example, suppose the goods are perishable, such as fresh produce, and the seller does not have them shipped in a refrigerated truck or railroad car. If the produce deteriorates in transit, the buyer can reject the produce on the grounds that the seller did not make a reasonable contract for shipment of it (2–504).

In some situations the goods sold may be in the possession of a bailee such as a warehouse. If the goods are covered by a negotiable warehouse receipt, the seller must indorse the receipt and give it to the buyer (2–503[4][a]). This enables the buyer to obtain the goods from the warehouse. An example of this type of situation is when grain being sold is stored at a grain elevator. If the goods are with a bailee but no negotiable warehouse receipt was issued, the seller must notify the bailee of the sale. The seller must then obtain the bailee's agreement to hold the goods for the buyer or the seller must have the goods released to the buyer (2–503[4][b]).

INSPECTION AND PAYMENT

Buyer's Right of Inspection

Normally the buyer has the right to inspect the goods before he or she accepts or pays for them. The buyer and seller may agree on the time, place, and manner in which inspection will be made. If no agreement is made, then the buyer may inspect the goods at any reasonable time and place and in any reasonable manner (2–513[1]).

If the shipping terms are *cash on delivery (C.O.D.)*, then the buyer must pay for the goods before inspecting them unless they are marked "Inspection Allowed." However, if it is obvious even without inspection that the goods do not conform to the contract, the buyer may reject them without paying for them first (2–512[1][a]). For example, if a farmer contracted to buy a bull and the seller delivered a cow, the farmer would not have to pay for it. The fact that a buyer may have to pay for goods before inspecting them does not deprive the buyer of remedies against the seller if the goods do not conform to the contract (2–512[2]).

Payment

The buyer and seller may agree in their contract that the price of the goods is to be paid in money or in other goods, services, or real property. If all or part of the price of goods is payable in real property, then only the transfer of goods is covered by the law of sales of goods. The transfer of the real property is covered by the law of real property (2–304).

The contract may provide that the goods are sold on credit to the buyer and that the buyer has a period of time to pay for them. If there is no agreement for extending credit to the buyer, the buyer must pay for them on delivery. The buyer can usually inspect them before payment except where the goods are shipped C.O.D., in which case the buyer must pay for them before inspecting them.

Unless the seller demands cash, the buyer may make payment by personal check or by any other method used in the ordinary course of business. If the seller demands cash, the seller must give the buyer a reasonable amount of time to obtain it. If payment is made by check, the payment is conditional on the check being honored by the bank when it is presented for payment (2–511[3]). If the bank refuses to pay the check, the buyer has not satisfied the duty to pay for them. In that case, the buyer does not have the right to retain the goods and must give them back to the seller.

ACCEPTANCE, REVOCATION, AND REJECTION

Acceptance

Acceptance of goods occurs when a buyer, after having a reasonable opportunity to inspect the goods, either indicates he will take them or fails to reject them. To *reject* goods, the buyer must *notify* the seller of the rejection and *specify* the defect or nonconformity. If a buyer treats the goods as if he owns them, the buyer is considered to have accepted them (2–606).

For example, Ace Appliance delivers a new color television set to Beth. Beth has accepted the set if, after trying it and finding it to be in working order, she says nothing to Ace or tells Ace that she will keep it. Even if the set is defective, Beth is considered to have accepted it if she does not give Ace timely notice that she does not want to keep it because it is not in working order. If she takes the set on a long trip with her even though she knows it does not work properly, this also is an acceptance. In the latter case, the use of the television would be inconsistent with the rejection of it and the return of ownership to the seller.

If a buyer accepts any part of a *commercial unit* of goods, he or she is considered to have accepted the whole unit (2–606[2]). A *commercial unit* is any unit of goods that is treated by commercial usage as a single whole. It can be a single article (such as a machine), a set of articles (such as a dozen, bale, gross, or carload), or any other unit treated as a single whole (2–105[6]). Thus if a bushel of apples is a commercial unit, then a buyer purchasing ten bushels of apples who accepts eight and one-half bushels is considered to have accepted nine bushels.

Miron v. Yonkers Raceway, Inc.
400 F.2d 112 (2d Cir. 1968)

FACTS On the afternoon of October 19, Finkelstein bought a racehorse at an auction. The horse was sold with a warranty that it was "sound." Finkelstein paid $32,000 for the horse. He took possession of the horse at 3 P.M. and transported it to his stables at a different track near New York City. He did not inspect the horse at that time. The next morning the horse was taken out for exercise and it was noticed that the horse was limping and its foreleg was swollen. At 11:30 A.M. he notified the auction people that the horse was "lame and not sound." Finkelstein wanted to reject the horse. It was later learned that the horse had a fractured leg. There was some dispute as to when the fracture occurred.

ISSUE Did the buyer try to reject the horse within a reasonable time after taking delivery of it?

DECISION No. The court held that by 11:30 A.M. the buyer had already "accepted" the horse. It said, "We conclude that rejection did not take place within a reasonable time after delivery and the buyer thus accepted the horse." The court felt that this kind of defect should have been noticed sooner if it were present in the horse when delivered and rejection attempted at that time. The buyer should have inspected it when he took delivery and immediately called any defects to the seller's attention.

Effect of Acceptance

Once a buyer has accepted goods, he or she cannot later reject them unless, at the time they were accepted, the buyer had reason to believe that the nonconformity would be cured. By accepting goods, the buyer does not forfeit or waive remedies against the seller for any nonconformities in the goods. However, if the buyer wishes to hold the seller responsible, he or she must give the seller *timely notice* that the goods are nonconforming.

The buyer is obligated to pay for goods that are accepted. If the buyer accepts all the goods sold, he or she is, of course, responsible for the full purchase price. If only part of the goods are accepted, the buyer must pay for that part at the contract rate. (2–607[1]).

Revocation of Acceptance

Under certain circumstances a buyer is permitted to *revoke* or undo the acceptance. A buyer may revoke acceptance of nonconforming goods where (1) the nonconformity *substantially impairs the value* of the goods and (2) the buyer accepted them *without knowledge* of the nonconformity due to the difficulty of discovering the nonconformity or the buyer accepted the goods because of *assurances* by the seller (2–608[1]).

The right to revoke acceptance must be exercised within a reasonable time after the buyer discovers or should have discovered the nonconformity. Revocation is not effective until the buyer notifies the seller of the intention to revoke acceptance. After a buyer revokes acceptance, he or she has the same rights as if the goods had been rejected when delivery was offered (2–608).

The right to revoke acceptance could arise, for example, where Arnold buys a new car from a dealer. While driving it home, Arnold discovers that the car has a seriously defective transmission. When he returns it to the dealer; he promises to repair it, so Arnold decides to keep the car. If the dealer does not fix the transmission after repeated efforts to do so, Arnold could revoke his acceptance on the grounds that the nonconformity substantially impairs the value of the car, he took delivery of the car without knowledge of the nonconformity, and his acceptance was based on the dealer's assurances that he would fix it. Similarly, revocation of acceptance might be involved where a serious problem with the car that was not discoverable by inspection shows up during the first month's use.

Revocation must be invoked prior to any *substantial change in the goods*, however, such as serious damage in an accident or wear and tear from using it for a period of time. What constitutes a "substantial impairment in value" and when there has been a "substantial change in the goods" are questions that courts frequently have to decide when an attempted revocation of acceptance results in a lawsuit.

Murray v. Holiday Rambler, Inc.
265 N.W.2d 513 (Sup. Ct. Wis. 1978)

FACTS   In January 1974, the Murrays bought a 22-foot Avenger motorhome manufactured by Holiday Rambler for $11,000. The Murrays had problems with the motorhome from the day they took delivery of it. By July it had been returned to the dealer nine or ten times for various repairs and adjustments. These repairs were paid for by Holiday Rambler. In July the Murrays took a trip to Colorado in the motorhome and had repeated problems. These included problems with the gas tanks, suspension system, brakes, short-circuited lights, noncharging generator, exposed wiring, furnace, refrigerator, fuel tank gauge that registered full when empty, oven door, uncoupling water lines, and the folding seats. For example, the motorhome stalled while climbing a mountain, the brakes failed while going down a mountain, the electric system caught on fire, and fumes from the gas tank drove the Murrays from the vehicle. Somehow they got it back to Wisconsin and back to the dealer. Holiday Rambler offered to make further free repairs. The Murrays wanted to revoke their acceptance of the motorhome. At the time they had driven it 3,650 miles, including 2,200 miles on the trip to Colorado.

ISSUE   Where a product is not satisfactorily repaired by the manufacturer after repeated efforts, does the buyer have to give the manufacturer additional opportunities to repair or can the buyer revoke acceptance?

DECISION   The court held that the manufacturer had had a reasonable time and opportunity to repair the motorhome and to provide the Murrays with a safe and substantially nondefective motorhome. The court found that the Murrays were trying to revoke within a reasonable time in view of their efforts to get it repaired. It also found that the revocation came before there had been a substantial change in the condition of the motorhome.

Buyer's Rights on Improper Delivery

If the goods delivered by the seller do not conform to the contract, the buyer has several options. The buyer can (1) reject all of the goods, (2) accept all of them, or (3) accept any commercial units and reject the rest (2–601). The buyer, however, cannot accept only part of a commercial unit and reject the rest. The buyer must pay for the units accepted at the price per unit provided in the contract.

Where the contract calls for delivery of the goods in separate installments, the buyer's options are more limited. The buyer may reject an installment delivery only if the nonconformity *substantially affects the value* of that delivery and *cannot be corrected* by the seller. If the defect or nonconformity is relatively minor, the buyer must accept the installment. The seller may offer to replace the defective goods or give the buyer an allowance in the price to make up for the nonconformity (2–612).

Rejection

If a buyer has a basis for rejecting a delivery of goods, the buyer must act within a reasonable time after delivery. The buyer must also give the seller notice of the rejection, preferably in writing (2–602). The buyer should be careful to state all the defects on which he or she is basing the rejection, including all that a reasonable inspection would disclose. This is particularly important if the defect is one that the seller might cure (remedy) and the time for delivery has not expired. In that case the seller may notify the buyer that he intends to redeliver conforming goods.

If the seller had some reason to believe the buyer would accept nonconforming goods, then the seller can take a reasonable time to reship conforming goods. The seller has this opportunity even if the original time for delivery has expired. For example, Ace Manufacturing contracts to sell 200 red baseball hats to Sam's Sporting Goods with delivery to be made by April 1. On March 1, Sam's receives a package from Ace containing 200 blue baseball hats and refuses to accept them. Ace can notify Sam's that it intends to cure the improper delivery by supplying 200 red hats and has until April 1 to deliver the red hats to Sam's. If Ace thought Sam's would accept the blue hats because on past shipments it did not object to the substitution of blue hats for red, then Ace has a reasonable time even after April 1 to deliver the red hats.

Buyer's Duties after Rejection

If the buyer is a merchant, then the buyer owes certain duties concerning the goods that he or she rejects. First, the buyer must follow any reasonable instructions the seller gives concerning disposition of the goods. The seller, for example, might request that the rejected goods be shipped back to the seller. If the goods are perishable or may deteriorate rapidly, then the buyer must make a reasonable effort to sell the goods. The seller must reimburse the buyer for any expenses the buyer incurs in carrying out the seller's instructions or in trying to resell perishable goods. In reselling goods, the buyer must act reasonably and in good faith (2–603).

If the rejected goods are not perishable or the seller does not give the buyer instructions, then the buyer has several options. First, the buyer can store the goods for the seller. Second, the buyer can reship them to the seller. Third, the buyer can resell them for the seller's benefit. If the buyer resells them, the buyer may keep his expenses and a reasonable commission on the sale. Where the buyer stores the goods, the buyer should exercise care in handling the goods. The buyer must also give the seller a reasonable time to remove the goods (2–604).

If the buyer is not a merchant, then his obligation after rejection is to hold the goods with reasonable care to give the seller an opportunity to remove them. The buyer is not obligated to ship them back to the seller (2–602).

Traynor v. Walters
342 F.Supp. 455 (M.D. Pa. 1972)

FACTS   Walters, a grower of Christmas trees, contracted to supply Traynor with "top-quality trees." When the shipment arrived and was inspected, Traynor discovered that some of the trees were not "top quality." Within 24 hours, Traynor notified Walters that he was rejecting the trees that were not top quality. Walters did not have a place of business or an agent in the town where Traynor was. Christmas was only a short time away. The trees were perishable and would decline in value to zero by Christmas Eve. Walters did not give Traynor any instructions, so Traynor sold the trees for Walters's account. Traynor then tried to recover from Walters the expenses he incurred in caring for and selling the trees.

ISSUE   Did the buyer act properly in rejecting the trees and reselling them for the seller?

DECISION   Yes. The court held that Traynor had acted exactly as he should have when he received the shipment of trees that did not conform to the contract. Traynor inspected them, gave prompt notice of rejection to the seller, awaited the seller's instructions, and then acted to prevent further loss to perishable goods by selling them. Traynor was entitled to recover his expenses of caring for and selling the trees, including rental of a lot and wages for a night watchman and salesman.

ASSURANCE, REPUDIATION, AND EXCEP

Assurance   The buyer or seller may become concerned that the other party may not be able to perform his or her contract obligations. If there is a reasonable basis for that concern, the buyer or seller can demand *assurance* from the other party that the contract will be performed. If such assurances are not given within 30 days, then the party is considered to have repudiated the contract (2–609).

For example, a farmer contracts to sell 1,000 bushels of apples to a canner with delivery to be made in September. In March, the canner learns that a severe frost has damaged many of the apple blossoms in the farmer's area and that 50 percent of the crop has been lost. The canner has the right, in writing, to demand assurances from the farmer that he will be able to fulfill his obligation in light of the frost. The farmer must provide those assurances within 30 days. For example, he might advise the canner that his crop sustained only relatively light damage or that he had made commitments to sell only a small percentage of his total crop and expects to be able to fill his obligations. If the farmer does not provide such assurances in a timely manner, then he is considered to have repudiated the contract. The canner then has certain remedies against the farmer for breach of contract. These remedies are discussed in the next chapter.

Anticipatory Repudiation

Sometimes one of the parties to a contract repudiates the contract by advising the other party that he or she does not intend to perform her obligations. When one party repudiates the contract, the other party may suspend his performance. In addition, he may either await performance for a reasonable time or use the remedies for breach of contract that are discussed in the next chapter (2–610).

Suppose the party who repudiated the contract changes his or her mind. Repudiation can be withdrawn by clearly indicating that the person intends to perform his or her obligations. The repudiating party must do this before the other party has canceled the contract or materially changed position by, for example, buying the goods elsewhere (2–611).

Excuse

Unforeseen events may make it difficult or impossible for a person to perform his or her contractual obligations. The Code rules for determining when a person is excused from performing are similar to the general contract rules. General contract law uses the test of *impossibility*. However, in most situations the Code uses the test of *commercial impracticability*. If the goods required for the performance of a contract are destroyed without fault of either party prior to the time the risk of loss passed to the buyer, then the contract is voided (2–613).

Suppose Jones agrees to sell and deliver an antique table to Brown. The table is damaged when Jones's antique store is struck by lightning and catches fire. The specific table covered by the contract was damaged without fault of either party prior to the time the risk of loss was to pass to Brown. Under the Code, Brown has the option of either canceling the contract or accepting the table with an allowance in the purchase price to compensate for the damaged condition (2–613).

Commercial Impracticability

If unforeseen conditions cause a delay or inability to make delivery of the goods (make performance *impracticable*), the seller is excused from making delivery. However, if a seller's capacity to deliver is only partially affected, then the seller may allocate production among his customers. If the seller chooses to allocate production, notice must be given to the buyers.

When a buyer receives this notice, the buyer may either terminate the contract or agree to accept the allocation (2–615).

For example, United Nuclear contracts to sell certain quantities of fuel rods for nuclear power plants to a number of electric utilities. If the federal government limits the amount of uranium United has access to so that United is unable to fill all its contracts, United is excused from full performance on the grounds of commercial impracticability. However, United may allocate its production of fuel rods among its customers and give them notice of the allocation. Then each utility can decide whether to cancel the contract or accept the partial allocation of fuel rods.

Colley v. Bi-State, Inc.
586 P.2d 908 (Ct. App. Wash. 1978)

FACTS Ray Colley was an experienced wheat farmer. In the spring of 1974 he planted 1,200 acres of wheat. In April 1974, he contracted with Bi-State, a grain dealer, to deliver 25,000 bushels of wheat in July or August. The contract price was $4.10 per bushel. In reliance on its contract with Colley, Bi-State contracted to sell 25,000 bushels to a grain exporter. June 1974 was particularly hot and dry. In early July Colley told Bi-State that as a result of the weather conditions, he was going to be short of wheat. After Colley harvested his wheat in August, he was able to deliver to Bi-State only 5,000 of the 25,000 bushels of wheat. Bi-State had to purchase wheat elsewhere to fill its contracts and then sued Colley for breach of contract.

ISSUE Was Colley excused from delivering the wheat because of the adverse weather conditions?

DECISION No. The court held that Colley was not excused from performing the contract because of the adverse weather conditions. A seller can be excused from performing a contract if performance becomes impracticable because of conditions the buyer and seller did not foresee. Colley's duty to deliver 25,000 bushels of wheat was not limited to wheat grown on his land. If it had been limited to wheat grown on his land, he might have been excused when his crop failed. Here, Colley still had the option of obtaining the wheat from some other source to fill his contract with Bi-State.

QUESTIONS AND PROBLEM CASES

1. What is meant by the term *usage of trade*?

2. If one party to a contract has good reason to question whether or not the other party intends to perform its obligation, what should he do?

3. Spada, an Oregon corporation, agreed to sell Belson, who operates a business in Chicago, two carloads of potatoes at $4.40 per sack, F.O.B. Oregon shipping point." Spada had the potatoes put aboard the railroad cars; however, he did not have floor racks used in the cars under the potatoes as is customary during winter months. As a result there was no warm air

238

circulating and the potatoes froze while in transit. Spada claims that his obligations ended with the delivery to the carrier and that the risk of loss was on Belson. What argument would you make for Belson?

4. Alpirn contracted to purchase from Williams 40,000 feet of ½-inch new steel pipe. The pipe was not to be plugged. Shipment was C.O.D. When the pipe arrived, Alpirn's foreman permitted the truck driver to unload about 50 pieces of pipe, at which time he discovered that the pipe was plugged. Alpirn refused to accept the pipe. Williams contended that since the shipment was C.O.D., Alpirn was obligated to accept and pay for the pipe. Was Alpirn obligated to accept and pay for the pipe?

5. Government Hospital ordered 275 pounds of raw shrimp from Mazur Brothers. Mazur Brothers had the shrimp federally inspected, packed in ice, and delivered to the hospital. The shrimp were kept refrigerated until the next day when they were put in steam kettles. The cook testified that there appeared to be nothing wrong with the shrimp in their raw state, but after they had boiled for five minutes they had an unwholesome odor and were discolored. The shrimp were not served to patients and were kept refrigerated for four days pending reinspection by the Department of the Interior. Six days after delivery, the hospital informed Mazur Brothers that it wanted to reject the shrimp. Could it reject the shrimp at that time?

6. Mrs. Shea purchased a new Rambler automobile from Menard & Holmberg Rambler, Inc. As part of the deal, she traded in her old car. Upon taking delivery her new car continually stalled so she returned it to the dealer who replaced the carburetor. The car continued to stall and would not move in reverse. On the fourth day after delivery she returned the car to the dealer, told him the sale was off, and drove off in her old car. He called her and offered to replace the transmission in the new car but she refused. The dealer then brought a lawsuit against Shea for the price of the new car and the return of the old car. Can the dealer recover from Shea? No

7. Dade purchased a new 1970 Jaguar automobile from Orange Motors, Inc. Almost immediately after delivery Dade had problems with the car. The power steering was stiff, the air-conditioner leaked and rattled, the doors did not close properly, and the steering column almost fell off. The car was in the shop for half of the three months Dade had it. Dade then filed a lawsuit seeking to revoke his acceptance of the car and to rescind the sales contract. Orange Motors claimed that it should be required only to repair the car. Is Orange Motors' contention correct?

8. Dewey, a paint store owner, decided to open a toy department for the Christmas trade. He contracted with Hays Merchandise Company to buy toys for an inventory for $3,500. Several small shipments were made, but the number of toys he received fell far below his expectations. He made several calls to Hays to complain and was told that the toys were back-ordered. When less than half the goods that he had ordered had been delivered by December 1, Dewey called Hays and said that he wanted no more toys and was sending back those that he had received. Hays then filed suit for the entire $3,500. What must Dewey show in order to win? Will he be successful?

9. Whelan ordered fuel oil from Griffith to be delivered at his farm home, which was located on a country road. The oil was to be delivered C.O.D. Griffith made two attempts to deliver the oil but each time no one was found at home. The morning after a night of heavy snowfall, the heaviest in more than 20 years, Griffith equipped the truck with chains and made a third attempt to deliver oil but found on arrival at Whelan's house that the driveway was impassable due to snowdrifts approximately six feet high. When Griffith's driver drove past the house and attempted to turn around, the truck became stuck in the snow and had to be towed back to the main highway. Whelan ran out of oil and as a result of having no fuel, the heating plant froze, causing substantial damage to it. Whelan sued Griffith to recover for the damage to the heating plant, claiming its breach of contract to deliver oil was the cause of the loss. Should Griffith be held liable?

Remedies for Breach
of Sales Contracts

19

Remedies in General

Usually both parties to a contract for the sale of goods perform the obligations they agreed to in the contract. Occasionally, however, one of the parties to a contract fails to perform his or her obligations. When this happens, the injured party has a variety of remedies for breach of contract. The objective of these remedies is to put the injured person in the *same position as if the contract had been performed*. The remedies that are made available to the injured party by the Uniform Commercial Code are discussed in this chapter.

Agreements as to Remedies

The buyer and seller may provide their own remedies to be applied in the event that one of the parties fails to perform. They can also limit either the remedies that the law makes available or the damages that can be recovered (2–719[1]).[1] If the parties agree on the amount of damages that will be paid to the injured party, this amount is known as *liquidated damages*. An agreement for liquidated damages is enforced if the amount is reasonable and if actual damages would be difficult to prove in the event of a breach of the contract. The amount is considered reasonable if it is not so large as to be a penalty or so small as to be unconscionable (2–718[1]).

For example, Carl Carpenter contracts to sell a display booth for $1,000 to Hank Hawker for Hawker to use at the state fair. Delivery is to be

---

[1] The numbers in parentheses refer to sections of the Uniform Commercial Code, 1972, which is reprinted in the Appendix.

made to Hawker by September 1. If the booth is not delivered on time, Hawker will not be able to sell his wares at the fair. Carpenter and Hawker might agree that if delivery is not made by September 1, Carpenter will pay Hawker $750 as liquidated damages. The actual sales Hawker might lose without a booth would be very hard to prove so Hawker and Carpenter can provide some certainty through the liquidated damages agreement. Carpenter then knows what he will be liable for if he does not perform his obligation. Similarly, Hawker knows what he can recover if the booth is not delivered on time. The amount ($750) is probably reasonable. If it were $50,000, it would be void as a penalty because it would be way out of line with the purchase price. And if the amount were too small, say $1, it might be considered unconscionable and therefore not enforceable. If a liquidated damages clause is not enforceable because it is a penalty or unconscionable, then the injured party can recover actual damages that were suffered.

Liability for *consequential damages* resulting from a breach of contract (such as lost profits or damage to property) may also be limited or excluded by agreement. The limitation or exclusion is not enforced if it would be unconscionable. Any attempt to limit consequential damages for injury caused to a person by consumer goods is considered unconscionable (2–719[3]). Suppose an automobile manufacturer makes a warranty as to the quality of the automobile. Then it tries to disclaim responsibility for any person injured if the car does not conform to the warranty and to limit its liability to replacing any defective parts. The disclaimer of consequential injuries in this case would be unconscionable and therefore not enforced.

Statute of Limitations

The Code provides that a lawsuit for breach of a sales contract must be filed within four years after the breach occurs. The parties to a contract may shorten this period to one year, but they may not extend it for longer than four years (2–725). A breach of warranty normally is considered to have occurred when the goods are delivered to the buyer. However, if the warranty covers future performance of goods (for example, four years or 40,000 miles), then the breach occurs at the time the buyer should have discovered the defect in the product.

Hoeflich v. William S. Merrell Co.
288 F.Supp. 659 (E.D. Pa. 1968)

FACTS In 1960 Hoeflich went to his family doctor. Because of a high cholesterol count, he was given a prescription for a drug (MER/29) manufactured by Merrell Co. Hoeflich took the drug for the period of time directed by his doctor. He stopped using it in 1960 as instructed by his doctor when his cholesterol count returned to normal. Starting in 1961 and continuing through 1964, Hoeflich was bothered by his skin breaking out, loss of hair, and finally cataracts. In 1966 he discovered that these problems were caused by the Merrell drug he had taken in 1960. Hoeflich then brought suit against Merrell Co. One of his claims was for breach of the warranty of merchantability of the drug.

ISSUE   Was the breach of warranty claim barred by the statute of limitations?

DECISION   Yes. The court held that the four-year statute of limitations began to run when the drug was sold to Hoeflich. The breach of warranty occurred at that time. Because he filed his lawsuit more than four years later, he was too late to claim breach of warranty. The court ruled that under Pennsylvania law it made no difference that Hoeflich did not know of the breach at the time he bought the drug. It also made no difference that the "accident" that caused his injury happened later.

SELLER'S REMEDIES

Remedies Available to an Injured Seller

A buyer may breach a contract in a number of ways; the most common are: (1) by wrongfully refusing to accept goods, (2) by wrongfully returning goods, (3) by failing to pay for the goods when payment is due, and (4) by indicating an unwillingness to go ahead with the contract.

When a buyer breaches a contract, the seller has a number of remedies under the Code, including the right to:

1. Cancel the contract.
2. Withhold delivery of any undelivered goods.
3. Resell the goods covered by contract and recover damages from the buyer.
4. Recover from the buyer the profit the seller would have made on the sale or the damages the seller sustained.
5. Recover the purchase price of goods delivered to or accepted by the buyer.

Cancellation and Withholding of Delivery

When a buyer breaches a contract, the seller has the right to cancel the contract and to hold up his or her own performance of the contract. The seller may then set aside any goods that were intended to fill the seller's obligations under the contract (2–704).

If the seller is in the process of manufacturing the goods, the seller has two choices. The seller may complete manufacture of the goods, or stop manufacturing and sell the uncompleted goods for their scrap or salvage value. In choosing between these two alternatives, the seller should choose the one that will minimize the loss (2–704[2]). Thus the seller would be justified in completing the manufacture of goods that could be resold readily at the contract price. However, a seller would not be justified in completing specially manufactured goods that could not be sold to anyone other than the buyer who ordered them. The purpose of this rule is to permit the seller to follow a reasonable course of action to *mitigate* (minimize) the damages.

Resale of Goods   If the seller sets aside the goods intended for the contract or completes the manufacture of such goods, the seller is not obligated to try to resell the goods to someone else. However, the seller may resell them and recover damages. The seller must make any resale in *good faith* and in a *reasonable commercial manner.* If the seller does so, the seller is entitled to recover from the buyer as damages the *difference* between the *resale price* and the *price the buyer agreed to pay* in the contract (2–706).

If the seller resells, he or she may also recover incidental damages but must give the buyer credit for any expenses the seller saved because of the buyer's breach of contract. *Incidental damages* include storage charges and sales commissions paid when the goods were resold. Expenses saved might be the cost of packaging and/or shipping the goods to the buyer (2–710).

If the seller intends to resell the goods in a private sale to another buyer, the seller must give the first buyer reasonable notice of the proposed resale. If the resale will be at a public sale such as an auction, the seller generally must give the buyer notice of the time and place of the auction. The seller may make a profit at the resale if the goods bring more than the contract price. If the seller makes a profit, the seller may keep it and does not have to give the profit to the buyer (2–706).

Cohn v. Fisher
287 A.2d 222 (Super. Ct. N.J. 1972)

FACTS   Cohn advertised a 30-foot sailboat for sale in the *New York Times.* Fisher saw the ad, inspected the sailboat, and offered Cohn $4,650 for the boat. Cohn accepted the offer. Fisher gave Cohn a check for $2,535 as a deposit on the boat. He wrote on the check "Deposit on aux sloop, D'arc Wind, full amount $4,650." Fisher later refused to go through with the purchase and stopped payment on the deposit check. Cohn readvertised the boat and sold it for the highest offer he received, which was $3,000. Cohn then sued Fisher for breach of contract. He asked for damages of $1,679.50. This represented the $1,650 difference between the contract price and the sales price plus $29.50 in incidental expenses in reselling the boat.

ISSUE   Was Cohn entitled to recover the difference between the contract price and the resale price plus his incidental expenses?

DECISION   Yes. The court awarded Cohn $1,679.50 as damages. The court held that the resale was made in good faith and in a commercially reasonable manner after giving notice of it to Fisher. Under these circumstances the seller is entitled to recover from the defaulting buyer the difference between the contract price and the resale price together with incidental damages.

**Recovery of the
Purchase Price**

In the normal performance of a contract, the seller delivers conforming goods (goods that meet the contract specifications) to the buyer. The buyer accepts the goods and pays for them. The seller is entitled to the purchase price of all goods *accepted* by the buyer. The seller is also entitled to the purchase price of all goods that *conformed* to the contract and were *lost or damaged after the buyer assumed the risk for their loss* (2–709). For example, a contract calls for Frank, a farmer, to ship 1,000 dozen eggs to Susan, a grocer, with shipment "F.O.B. Frank's Farm." If the eggs are lost or damaged while on their way to Susan, she is responsible for paying Frank for them.

In one other situation the seller may recover the purchase or contract price from the buyer. This is where the seller has made an honest effort to resell the goods and was unsuccessful or if it is apparent that any such effort to resell would be unsuccessful. This might happen where the seller manufactured goods especially for the buyer and the goods are not usable by anyone else. Assume Sally's Supermarket sponsors a bowling team. It orders six green and red bowling shirts to be embroidered with "Sally's Supermarket" on the back and the names of the team members on the pocket. After the shirts are completed, Sally's wrongfully refuses to accept them. The manufacturer will be able to recover the agreed purchase price if it cannot sell the shirts to someone else.

If the seller sues the buyer for the contract price of the goods, the seller must hold the goods for the buyer. Then the seller must turn the goods over to the buyer if the buyer pays for them. However, if resale becomes possible prior to the time the buyer pays for the goods, the seller may resell them. Then the seller must give the buyer credit for the proceeds of the resale (2–709[2]).

Bacon Estate
5 U.C.C. Rep. 486 (Orphans' Ct. Pa. 1968)

FACTS   Dubrow, a widower, was engaged to be married. In October he placed a large order with a furniture store for delivery the following January. The order included rugs cut to special sizes for the prospective couple's new house and many pieces of furniture for various rooms in the house. One week later Dubrow died. When the order was delivered, the furniture and carpeting were refused by his only heir, his daughter. The furniture store then sued his estate to recover the full purchase price. It had not tried to resell the furniture and carpeting to anyone else.

ISSUE   Under the circumstances, was the seller entitled to recover the purchase price of the goods?

DECISION   No. The court held that the furniture store was not entitled to recover the purchase price. First, it had to show that it had tried to resell the furniture and rugs to someone else but had been unable to do so or that it would be fruitless to try. The court said it was not convinced that the goods could not be resold if the price were marked down.

Damages for Rejection or Repudiation

When the buyer refuses to accept goods that conform to the contract or repudiates the contract, the seller does not have to resell the goods. The seller has two other ways of determining the damages the buyer is liable for because of the buyer's breach of contract: (1) the difference between the contract price and the market price at which the goods are currently selling, and (2) the "profit" the seller lost when the buyer did not go through with the contract (2–708).

The seller may recover as damages the *difference* between the *contract price* and the *market price* at the time and place the goods were to be delivered to the buyer. The seller may also recover any incidental damages but must give the buyer credit for any expenses the seller has saved (2–708[1]). This measure of damages is most commonly sought by a seller when the market price of the goods dropped substantially between the time the contract was made and the time the buyer repudiated the contract.

For example, on January 1, Toy Maker, Inc., contracts with the Red Balloon Toy Shop to sell the shop 100,000 hula hoops at $1.50 each, with delivery to be made in Boston on June 1. By June 1 the hula hoop fad has passed and they are selling for $1.00 each in Boston. If the shop repudiates the contract on June 1 and refuses to accept delivery of the 100,000 hula hoops, Toy Maker is entitled to the difference between the contract price of $150,000 and the June 1 market price in Boston of $100,000. Thus Toy Maker could recover $50,000 in damages plus any incidental expenses but less any expenses saved by it in not having to ship the hula hoops to the Toy Shop.

If getting the difference between the contract price and the market price would not put the seller in as good a financial position as if the contract had been performed, the seller may choose an alternative measure of damages based on the *lost profit and overhead* the seller would have made if the sale had gone through. The seller can recover this lost profit and overhead plus any incidental expenses. However, the seller must give the buyer credit for any expenses saved as a result of the buyer's breach of contract (2–708[2]).

Using the hula hoop example, assume that the direct labor and material cost to Toy Maker of making the hoops was $0.55 each. Toy Maker could recover as damages from the Toy Shop the profit Toy Maker lost when the shop defaulted on the contract. Toy Maker would be entitled to the difference between the contract price of $150,000 and its direct cost of $55,000. Thus Toy Maker could recover $95,000 plus any incidental expenses and less any expenses saved.

Seller's Remedies Where Buyer Is Insolvent

Unless the seller has agreed to extend credit to the buyer, the buyer must pay for the goods at the time they are delivered. When the seller is ready to make delivery of the goods, the seller may withhold delivery until the payment is made (2–511[1]).

Suppose a seller has agreed to extend credit to a buyer and then before making delivery the seller discovers the buyer is insolvent. A buyer is insolvent if he cannot pay his bills when they become due. The seller then has the right to withhold delivery until the buyer pays cash for the goods and for any goods previously delivered for which payment has not been made. The seller also has the right to require the buyer to return any goods the insolvent buyer obtained from the seller within the previous ten days. If the buyer told the seller she was solvent any time in the previous three months—and in fact she was not solvent—the seller can reclaim goods received by the buyer even earlier than the last ten days (2–702).

If a seller discovers a buyer is insolvent, the seller has the right to stop delivery of any goods that are being shipped to the buyer. This would involve notifying the carrier, for example, the trucker or airline, in time to prevent delivery to the buyer (2–705).

BUYER'S REMEDIES

Buyer's Remedies in General

A seller may breach a contract in a number of different ways. The most common are: (1) failing to make an agreed delivery, (2) delivering goods that do not conform to the contract, and (3) indicating that he or she does not intend to fulfill the obligations under the contract.

A buyer whose seller breaks the contract is given a number of remedies. These include:

1. Buying other goods ("covering") and recovering damages from the seller based on any additional expense the buyer incurs in obtaining the goods.
2. Recovering damages based on the difference between the contract price and the current market price of the goods.
3. Recovering damages for any nonconforming goods accepted by the buyer based on the difference in value between what the buyer got and what he or she should have gotten.
4. Obtaining specific performance of the contract where the goods are unique and cannot be obtained elsewhere.

In addition the buyer can in some cases recover consequential damages (such as lost profits) and incidental damages (such as expenses incurred in buying substitute goods).

Buyer's Right to Cover

If the seller fails or refuses to deliver the goods called for in the contract, the buyer can purchase substitute goods; this is known as *cover*. If the buyer does purchase substitute goods, the buyer can recover as damages from the seller the *difference* between the *contract price* and the *cost of the substitute goods* (2–712). For example, Frank Farmer agrees to sell Ann's Cider Mill 1,000 bushels of apples at $3.00 a bushel. Farmer then refuses to deliver the apples. Cider Mill can purchase 1,000 bushels of similar apples, and if it has to pay $3.50 a bushel, it can recover the difference ($0.50 a bushel) between what it paid ($3.50) and the contract price ($3.00). Thus Cider Mill could recover $500 from Frank.

The buyer can also recover any incidental damages sustained but must give the seller credit for any expenses saved. In addition, the buyer may be able to obtain consequential damages. The buyer is not required to cover, however. If the buyer does not cover, the other remedies under the Code are still available (2–712[3]).

Incidental Damages

Incidental damages include expenses the buyer incurs in receiving, inspecting, transporting, and storing goods shipped by the seller that do not conform with those called for in the contract. Incidental damages also include any reasonable expenses or charges the buyer has to pay in obtaining substitute goods (2–715[1]).

Consequential Damages

In certain situations an injured buyer is able to recover *consequential damages*, such as the buyer's lost profits caused by the seller's breach of contract. The buyer must be able to show that the seller knew or should have known at the time the contract was made that the buyer would suffer special damages if the seller did not perform his obligations. The buyer must also show that he could not have prevented the damage by obtaining substitute goods (2–715[2]).

Suppose Knitting Mill promises to deliver 1,000 yards of a special fabric to Dora by September 1. Knitting Mill knows that Dora wants to acquire the material to make garments suitable for the Christmas season. Knitting Mill also knows that in reliance on the contract with Knitting Mill, Dora will enter into contracts with department stores to deliver the finished garments by October 1. If Knitting Mill delivers the fabric after September 1 or fails completely to deliver it, it may be liable to Dora for any consequential damages she sustains if she is unable to acquire the same material elsewhere in time to fulfill her October 1 contracts.

Consequential damages can also include an injury to a person or property caused by a breach of warranty. For example, an electric saw is defectively made. Hank purchases the saw and while he is using it, the blade comes off and severely cuts his arm. The injury to Hank is consequential damage resulting from a nonconforming or defective product.

De La Hoya v. Slim's Gun Shop
146 Cal. Rptr. 68 (Super. Ct. Cal. 1978)

FACTS   De La Hoya bought a used handgun for $140 from Slim's Gun Shop, a licensed firearm's dealer. At the time neither De La Hoya nor Slim's knew that the gun had been stolen prior to the time Slim's bought it. While De La Hoya was using the gun for target shooting, he was questioned by a police officer. The officer traced the serial number of the gun, determined that it had been stolen, and arrested De La Hoya. De La Hoya had to hire an attorney to defend himself against the criminal charges. De La Hoya then brought a lawsuit against Slim's Gun Shop for breach of warranty of title. He sought to recover the purchase price of the gun plus $8,001, the amount of his attorney's fees, as "consequential damages."

ISSUE   Can a buyer who does not get good title to the goods he purchased recover from the seller consequential damages caused by the breach of warranty of title?

DECISION   Yes. The court awarded De La Hoya damages covering both the purchase price of the gun and the attorney's fees. The court held that De La Hoya was entitled to recover the difference between the value of the gun he received ($0 because he had to give it back to the real owner) and what he paid ($140) plus "incidental and consequential damages." The court felt that the attorney's fees were a direct and natural consequence of the breach of warranty and that they could not have been prevented by "cover."

Damages for Nondelivery

If the seller fails or refuses to deliver the goods called for by the contract, the buyer has the option of recovering damages for the nondelivery. Thus, instead of covering, the buyer can get the *difference* between the *contract price* of the goods and their *market price* at the time the buyer learns of the seller's breach. In addition, the buyer may recover any incidental damages and consequential damages but must give the seller credit for any expenses saved (2–713).

Suppose Bill agreed on June 1 to sell and deliver 500 bushels of wheat to a grain elevator on September 1 for $7 per bushel and then refused to deliver on September 1 because the market price was then $8 per bushel. The grain elevator could recover $500 damages from Bill, plus incidental damages that could not have been prevented by cover.

Damages for Defective Goods

If a buyer accepts defective goods and wants to hold the seller liable, the buyer must give the seller *notice* of the defect within a *reasonable time* after the buyer discovers the defect (2–607[3]). Where goods are defective or not as warranted and the buyer gives the required notice, the buyer can recover damages. The buyer is entitled to recover the *difference* between the *value of the goods received* and the *value the goods would have had if they had been as warranted*. The buyer may also be entitled to incidental and consequential damages (2–714).

For example, Al's Auto Store sells Anne an automobile tire, warranting it to be four-ply construction. The tire goes flat when it is punctured by a nail, and Anne discovers that the tire is really only two-ply. If Anne gives the store prompt notice of the breach, she can keep the tire and recover from Al's the difference in value between a two-ply and a four-ply tire.

Buyer's Right to Specific Performance

Sometimes the goods covered by a contract are *unique* and it is not possible for a buyer to obtain substitute goods. When this is the case, the buyer is entitled to specific performance of the contract. *Specific performance* means that the buyer can require the seller to give the buyer the goods covered by the contract (2–716). Thus the buyer of an antique automobile such as a 1910 Ford might have a court order the seller to deliver the specified automobile to the buyer because it was one of a kind. On the other hand, the buyer of grain in a particular storage bin could not get specific performance if he could buy the same kind of grain elsewhere.

Schweber v. Rallye Motors, Inc.
12 U.C.C. Rep. 1154 (Sup. Ct. N.Y. 1973)

FACTS   In 1972 Schweber contracted to purchase a certain black 1973 Rolls Royce Corniche automobile from Rallye Motors. He made a $3,500 deposit on the car. Rallye later returned his deposit to him and told him the car was not available. However, Schweber learned that the automobile was available to the dealer and was being sold to another customer. The dealer then offered to sell Schweber a similar car but with a different interior design. Schweber brought a lawsuit against the dealer to prevent it from selling the Rolls Corniche to anyone else and to require that it be sold to him. Rallye Motors claimed that he could get only damages and not specific performance. Approximately 100 Rolls Royce Corniches were being sold each year in the United States but none of the others would have the specific features and detail of this one.

ISSUE   Was the remedy of specific performance available to Schweber?

DECISION   The court held that Schweber could get specific performance if he could show a breach of contract by Rallye Motors. Under the Code, specific performance may be granted "where the goods are unique or in other proper circumstances."

Buyer and Seller Agreements as to Remedies

As mentioned earlier in this chapter, the parties to a contract may provide for additional remedies or substitute remedies for those expressly provided in the Code (2–719). For example, the buyer's remedies may be limited by the contract to the return of the goods and the repayment of the price or to the replacement of nonconforming goods or parts. However, a court looks to see whether such a limitation was freely agreed to or whether it is unconscionable. In those cases, the court does not enforce the limitation and the buyer has all the rights given to an injured buyer by the Code.

QUESTIONS AND PROBLEM CASES

1. What is the objective of the remedies that the Code makes available to a party to a contract who has been injured when the other party breached its obligations?

2. Under what circumstances will a court enforce a liquidated damages clause?

3. Kohn ordered a suit from Meledani Tailors. A few days later before much work had been completed, Kohn told the tailors that he did not want the suit. They therefore stopped its manufacture and filed suit for the entire contract price. Is Kohn liable for the full purchase price?

4. Schutt, acting as an agent for Reed, purchased 180 steers in Arkansas for $27,846. After the steers had been shipped, the seller called Reed with regard to the draft given him by Schutt in payment. Reed refused to pay the draft. The steers were sold upon their arrival at their destination, Kansas City, for $22,663 through a sale barn. The seller then sued Reed for the difference between the contract price and the resale price. Can he recover this amount?

5. Miles sold a dining room table and four chairs to Lyons for $100. She told Lyons that the table and chairs were hers, but in reality they belonged to her relatives. The value of the set at the time of the sale was $275. After the table and chairs were reclaimed by their rightful owners, Lyons instituted an action against Miles. What amount can he claim in damages?

6. Dennler, an experienced livestock feeder, informed W&W Livestock Enterprises that he was in the market for about 400 good pigs. W&W sold him 408 of what they claimed to be "real good head." A few days after delivery, it became evident that some of the pigs were ill. Over time many of the pigs became seriously diseased and 191 of the 408 died before they could be marketed. Dennler brought an action against W&W Livestock Enterprises, claiming as his damages (1) a sum equal to the difference between the value of the pigs at delivery and their value if they had been as warranted, (2) the total sum expended by him on veterinary services and medicines, and (3) the total value of the feed consumed by the pigs that died and the extra feed consumed by the other pigs because of their illness. Are these elements of damages recoverable under the Code?

7. In November 1969, Sorenson Orchard Company contracted with Michigan Sugar Company for 800 bags of sugar to be used in processing frozen diced apples. Of the 800 bags, Sorenson returned 68 bags to Michigan Sugar because there was excessive "pan scale" in the bags, and the 68 were replaced by Michigan Sugar. Although Sorenson's inspection noticed some "pan scale" in the remaining 732 bags, Sorenson used the bags anyway. Sorenson completed packing the apples for its customers, the apples were put in cold storage, and Sorenson was paid for them. In the spring, Sorenson's customers began using the apples and rejected the batch after finding specks of "pan scale" in the apples. Over the next three years Sorenson sold the frozen apples at a great loss. Michigan Sugar sued Sorenson to recover the contract price of the sugar, and Sorenson counterclaimed for breach of warranty, seeking as consequential damages the profits it lost because of its customers' rejection of the frozen apples. Is Sorenson entitled to consequential damages?

8. Myers purchased a new car from Thompson Chrysler-Plymouth Inc. The price he paid included $3,695.00 for the car, $55.45 for sales tax, $88.87 for life insurance, and $574.72 for finance charges, for a total of $4,414.04. From the outset the car was faulty. Many of the car's features malfunctioned or did not work at all. After several return trips to the dealer, all of which failed to remedy the problems, it became evident that Myers had a valid claim for a breach of an implied warranty. He therefore filed an action against the dealer for $4,414.04. The dealer admitted liability but only for $3,695.00, the cash price of the car. Is the dealer liable for the $4,414.04?

9. The Carpels contracted with Saget Studios to take black-and-white photographs of their wedding for $110. Because of carelessness on the part of Saget Studios, the pictures were never delivered. The Carpels brought a lawsuit claiming they were entitled to consequential damages in excess of $10,000 because of the breach of contract. They contended that the damages should include the cost to restage the wedding and photograph it, loss of sentimental value by the failure to perform timely, emotional distress caused by the failure to perform, and punitive damages. Should the Carpels be allowed to recover for these damages?

10. Voth purchased a new Chrysler automobile on August 8, 1969. Chrysler warranted the vehicle against defects in material or workmanship for 12 months or 12,000 miles and stated that it would, without charge, repair or replace any part of the car defective under the warranty. While driving the vehicle, Voth began experiencing nausea, headaches, vertigo, and other physical difficulties in the course of which he incurred substantial medical expenses. Voth had contracted lead poisoning which was attributed to gasoline fumes he inhaled. On July 2, 1970, he discovered that a defective gasoline vent tube was causing gasoline fumes to be gathered and dispersed in the car by the air-conditioning system. On June 27, 1974, Voth brought a lawsuit for breach of warranty against Chrysler. Chrysler defended on the grounds that the action was barred by the statute of limitations in the Code. Is Voth's suit barred by the statute of limitations?

Agency and Employment

Introduction to Agency and Employment

20

OVERVIEW

Examples of
Agents

Y ou have no doubt been involved in agency relationships a number of times. You may have assisted a friend by making a purchase for him on your trip to a shopping center. While doing so you were acting as his agent. If you have ever employed an attorney to represent you in court or to negotiate a claim against someone whose car smashed into yours, the attorney has acted as your agent. If you weave or practice some other handicraft and send your products to a shop to sell for you, the shop becomes your agent for the sale of your goods.

Agency is a legal device that allows you to transact business in several places at once, like selling your weaving in several cities at the same time. It permits you to do things that require skills or memberships you do not have, such as appearing in court or buying securities on a stock exchange. When you are engaged in business, it allows you to expand your activities far beyond the limits of your time and the geographic limits of easy travel. Without the use of agents, business activity would be mostly face to face and our standard of living would be much lower.

Nature of Agency

An agency relationship arises when two people agree that one (the agent) shall act for the benefit of the other (the principal) and under the principal's direction. Agency relationships usually are formed by contract; however, consideration is not essential to establish an agency relationship. In fact, a court may find that there is an agency relationship even though the parties have expressly agreed that they do not intend to create one. For

253

example, a manufacturer may control the selling activities of a franchised retailer so closely that the retailer is treated as the agent of the manufacturer. A statement in the franchise agreement declaring that the retailer is not an agent of the manufacturer is not binding on a court.

Fair v. Hamersmith Distributing Co.
203 S.E.2d 120 (Sup. Ct. Va. 1974)

FACTS A loaded tractor-trailer truck operated by Hamersmith Distributing Co. hit a pillar on a bridge on Interstate 95 in Virginia. The driver was killed. C. E. Seymour, a state trooper, investigated the accident. He phoned the head office of the company and talked with a man who said he was Joe Hamersmith, president. The trooper told Hamersmith that the wreckage was spread over the traveled part of the highway and into a ravine. He told Hamersmith that the State Highway Department wanted the wreckage removed from the right-of-way, including the ravine. Hamersmith told him to have someone remove it.

Charles Fair, trading as Powerline Shell Service, was called by the trooper to remove the wreckage. He did this and sent a bill to Distributing Co. for $3,557, which was not paid. An expert in the wreck removal business testified that the bill was reasonable.

ISSUE Was Seymour, the trooper, an agent of Distributing Co. so as to bind it on the oral contract to remove the wreckage?

DECISION Yes. The court said that in telling Seymour to go ahead and have someone remove the wreckage, Hamersmith gave him authority to act as agent for the Distributing Co. to get Fair to do the job. In this way Distributing Co. assumed payment for the reasonable cost of the removal.

Background

The body of the law called *agency law* is an outgrowth of the law of master and servant. The earliest agents were members of the households of kings and nobles. These households, of course, included many people carrying on the activities of and arranging for the comfort of the king or noble and his family. Only a few of the most trusted were allowed to make contracts, but all were known as servants. As a result, agency law covers the relations between masters (today called *employers*) and servants *(employees)* and *third persons* who may be affected by the acts of the servants. It especially focuses on the relations between *principals* and *agents* and the *third persons* with whom the agent deals in making contracts on behalf of the principal. This body of law has developed primarily from the decisions of courts; it is common law.

It is this background that leads to a confusing use of the term *agent* in agency law. Some definitions may be helpful to try to minimize this confusion.

IMPORTANT TERMS

Agent

In this book the term *agent* refers to a person who *represents and acts for another person in a transaction*. Frequently the agent is empowered to enter into a contract on behalf of that other person (the principal). For the historical reason given above, courts often use the term *agent* in a broader sense to include any *employee* (formerly "servant"). In the sense that *agent* is used here, it includes both employees who transact business for their employers and those who perform similar acts but who are not employees. For example, all salespersons are agents; they may be employees who sell on a full-time basis for a single employer, or they may be in business for themselves making sales for several sellers.

Professional Agent

A person whose occupation is to serve others as an agent is a *professional agent*. He or she is not an employee of the person being served. The firm or person employing a professional agent (the principal) informs the agent about the purpose of the agency. However, the principal has *no right to control the details* of the work the professional does to accomplish that purpose. For example, one common type of professional agent is a manufacturer's representative. A manufacturer's representative sells the products of several different firms, usually on a straight commission. He or she may drive a Cadillac or a Chevette, start early or late, or take the day off. Other professional agents include real estate brokers, stockbrokers, auctioneers, and attorneys. The professional agent may be likened to an independent contractor.

Independent Contractor

Independent contractors are persons or firms that contract to do work according to their own methods. They are under the *control* of the employer as to the *result* to be obtained but not the means used to accomplish that result.

Employees, on the other hand, are under the control of the employer as to both the objective of their work and the means used to achieve it. Employers may give detailed directions to employees about their physical activities on the job. In effect, the employer is buying the time of the employee. This is, of course, much less true for high-level managers and those with professional training, such as accountants and attorneys, than for blue-collar employees.

For example, James, a delivery truck driver for a retail shop, may be told when to start work, in what order to make deliveries, what routes to use, and how long to take for lunch. On the other hand, the retailer may choose to employ Bill, a local deliveryman who is in the business of delivering goods. He may be told where and about when the deliveries for the retailer are to be made. However, the starting time, the routes to be used, and the order of delivery are left to Bill's choice.

The distinction between an employee and an independent contractor (or a professional agent) becomes important when a tort is committed. An employer, under agency law, is usually liable for torts committed by an employee. He or she is not liable for torts committed by an independent contractor or a professional agent, however.

The factor that distinguishes an employee from an independent contractor is the *degree of control* of the employer. Since right to control is not always clearly expressed in the employment agreement, disputes about liability for torts committed on the job are frequent. Even if there is an agreement that there is no right of control, if the employer is actually directing the work at the time a tort is committed, the employer is liable.

When the right to control and even the degree of actual control are unclear, courts look to other factors to determine whether the person committing the tort is an independent contractor. Some of these factors are whether the one employed is engaged in a distinct occupation or business, the degree of skill required, who furnishes the equipment used, and whether the work in the locality is usually done by independent contractors. Not infrequently, some factors point toward finding that an employee has committed the tort and some toward finding an independent contractor relationship. This makes a decision difficult for the trier of facts—the judge or jury.

Massey v. Tube Art Display, Inc.
551 P.2d 1387 (Ct. App. Wash. 1976)

FACTS Redford owned and operated a backhoe. He spent 90 percent of his working time digging holes for Tube Art Display, Inc., a sign company. He had no employees, was not registered as a subcontractor, was not the one who obtained the permits required for the jobs he did, and did not receive the fringe benefits available to other Tube Art employees. He did pay his own business taxes. He was directed by Tube Art's service manager to dig a hole six feet deep where the service manager marked off in yellow paint a four-by-four foot square. He started the work in the evening, and at 9:30 P.M. he struck a small natural gas pipeline. He examined the pipe. Finding no evidence of a leak, he concluded that the pipe was not in use and left the worksite. At 2:00 A.M. an explosion and fire destroyed the building to which the pipe ran. Massey, a tenant in the building, sought to recover from Tube Art for loss of business and an inventory of goods.

ISSUE Was Redford an employee?

DECISION Yes. Redford was an employee rather than an independent contractor. Tube Art had the right to control Redford's physical conduct. It also made the most important decisions—the size and location of the hole.

General and Special Agents

A *general agent* is a person who acts for the principal in a number of transactions over a period of time. Two examples of general agencies may clarify the term. Henry, a retailer, may delegate responsibility for the operation of a certain store to Clara as manager. Or a manufacturer may give Tony as a purchasing agent authority to purchase all parts needed in assembling its products.

A *special agent* is authorized by the principal to do a specific act or handle one or a few of a certain type of business transaction. For example, if you employed a stockbroker to buy for you 100 shares of General Motors stock, the stockbroker is a special agent. His or her authority to act is limited to that transaction.

Brokers

Most brokers, including stockbrokers, actually enter contracts on behalf of their principals. When the agent is dealing in merchandise, a distinction is made between a *broker* and a *factor*. The broker is not given possession of the principal's goods, while the factor is. Real estate brokers and *finders* are generally employed merely to find a buyer or seller for the principal to contract with. In this latter case they are middlemen rather than agents with authority to buy or sell.

Franchisees

The terms *agent* and *agency* are sometimes used in franchise relationships where the business is acting as an independent contractor rather than as an agent. A dealer for Ford Motor Company is often referred to as having an agency. However, the business is likely to be an independent contractor that has a franchise to sell Ford products.[1]

Attorney-in-Fact

An *attorney-in-fact* is an agent who has his or her authority as agent in writing. Suppose Jane plans to be in Europe for the summer and wishes to sell her automobile. She may appoint Sue as her attorney-in-fact to sign the necessary papers on her behalf. The power given to Sue is called a *power of attorney*.

CAPACITY TO BE PRINCIPAL OR AGENT

Who Can Be a Principal?

Generally, a person may do anything through an agent that the person could legally do personally. The legal effect of the agent's action on behalf of the principal is usually the same as if the principal had done the act. Minors and insane persons are bound on contracts made by their agents only to the extent they would have been bound by taking the action in person. This is true even though the agent has full capacity to contract.

Business organizations and groups of people can also act through an agent. Each partner is an agent of the other partner(s) in carrying on partnership business. A corporation is viewed by the courts as a legal entity.

---

[1] See discussion of franchise arrangements in Chapter 25.

It can act only through agents. An unincorporated association, such as a club or neighborhood association, is not viewed as a legal entity. Although its members may appoint an agent and will be bound by the agent's acts, the association itself does not become a party to a contract made by an agent. However, by statute many states have made the assets of unincorporated associations subject to suit.

Who Can Be an Agent?

A person may have capacity to act as an agent although he or she does not have the legal capacity to contract. For example, Helen, a minor, may as an agent make a contract that is binding on William, her principal. Partnerships as well as corporations may act as agents. Marriage alone does not establish an agency relationship; therefore, a check made out to both husband and wife must be indorsed by both. However, a person may be appointed an agent by his or her spouse. Also a husband may be liable for the value of "necessaries" furnished to his wife.

Alphonse Brenner Company, Inc. v. Dickerson
283 So.2d 849 (Ct. App. La. 1973)

FACTS In August Mrs. Dickerson ordered $2,380 worth of carpeting from Brenner Company. The store opened an account in Mr. Dickerson's name. He paid the bill. Mrs. Dickerson then bought $370 worth of furniture and later ordered draperies at $1,133. In October she ordered $3,352 worth of custom-made draperies and bedspreads, and Brenner started work on them. In November she had the game room completely redecorated. Mr. Dickerson was not pleased with that furniture and it was returned for full credit. After the furniture was returned, Mr. Dickerson wrote Brenner saying, "Please, in the future do not work at my house unless you have my written approval." Sometime after this, the custom-made draperies and bedspreads were delivered. Mr. Dickerson refused to pay for them, saying he had no knowledge of the purchase. The Dickersons were separated by this time.

ISSUE Can Brenner Company recover from Mr. Dickerson on the ground that Mrs. Dickerson was his agent?

DECISION Yes. The store did not claim that Mrs. Dickerson was an agent by virtue of her relationship as wife. Rather, it argued that by paying for earlier purchases charged to the account, Mr. Dickerson gave her apparent authority (discussed in Chapter 21) to act as his agent to buy goods and services from Brenner. The court agreed and held Mr. Dickerson liable. It said that the attempt to terminate that authority by letter came too late. Work had already been nearly completed on the custom-made draperies and bedspreads.

SCOPE OF AGENCY LAW

Basic Issues

Agency law addresses three basic questions: (1) When is the dominant person (principal) liable on contracts made by the subordinate person (agent)? (2) When is the dominant person (employer) liable for the torts of the subordinate person (employee)? (3) What duties do the principal (or employer) and agent (or employee) owe to each other?

A typical instance where the first question would arise occurs when a salesman gives an unauthorized guarantee of performance on a product he sells. Is the principal liable if the product does not perform as promised? The second question might arise when a saleswoman is driving to a customer's plant and negligently runs into a pedestrian in the street. Is the principal or employer liable to the pedestrian? The third type of question would be raised if a real estate broker arranged to sell to his own brother a house listed for sale with the broker.

The next two chapters discuss the first two questions; Chapter 23 discusses the third problem.

Employment Law

In the past century Congress and the state legislatures have enacted many laws dealing with the responsibilities employers have to their employees. These supplement the duties that agency law imposes on principals and employers, and therefore, they are included in this part of the book.

This body of law is generally called *employment law*. These statutes are so numerous and varied that only the more important ones can be mentioned. They regulate almost every aspect of the employment relationship. Subjects covered include hiring, minimum rates of pay, when wages must be paid, hours of work, health and safety protection, pay for work-related illness and injury, retirement, union activity, and many others. The general aim of employment law has been to establish minimum standards to protect the interests of employees and to strengthen their position in dealing with their employers. This body of law is discussed in Chapter 24.

QUESTIONS AND PROBLEM CASES

1. How would the American economy be different if agency relationships were illegal?

2. What is the most important factor in determining whether one is an employee or an independent contractor?

3. What other factors may be used to distinguish an employee from an independent contractor?

4. In what kind of situations may it be important to distinguish between a general and a special agent?

5. Crouch owned a truck and welding equipment. He had operated under the name of Crouch Welding Co. for 15 years. Since the business of Parker Drilling Co. "kept him busy," he had stopped doing work for others. Crouch supplied his own welding materials and maintained his own insurance coverage. He worked from sketches furnished by Parker in reinforcing drilling derricks. He kept his own time records and billed Parker monthly at an agreed upon hourly rate. He employed other welders and signed time records for them but they were paid directly by Parker. A derrick reinforced by a welder hired by Crouch collapsed, killing Flick. Flick's widow sued Crouch. His defense was that he was an employee of Parker rather than an independent contractor responsible for the

work of the people he hired. Is this a good defense?

6. Mr. and Mrs. Kuchta wanted an outdoor living area like they had seen built onto a neighbor's house in Orange County, California. According to a sign on the lawn, the builder was Allied Builders Corporation. They phoned the Allied number in Los Angeles. They were told by Allied's vice president to contact the nearest Allied branch, which was in Anaheim, and he gave them Weiner's phone number. Weiner represented that he was from Allied. He looked at the Kuchtas' house and later submitted plans to them, which they approved. They then entered into a contract with Allied. It stated that the franchisee would, as contractor, furnish all labor and materials for $5,671 and that construction would conform to local and state codes. It also provided that Allied would obtain necessary building permits.

The original plans were not approved by the building department of Orange County because the planned structure would come too close to the property line. Without the knowledge of the Kuchtas, Weiner submitted alternate plans that called for only a concrete slab; however, he built the supports and roof according to the original plans. Later the Kuchtas were required to tear down the addition because it violated the building code. They then sued Allied Builders Corporation. Allied's defense was that Weiner was an independent contractor. Allied's franchise agreement with Weiner said that Weiner was not an employee or agent of Allied. It also gave Allied the right to regulate the quality of goods used or sold, to control the standards of construction, to approve the design, and to inspect all construction. Is Allied liable for Weiner's fraud?

Agency Authority and Termination

21

AUTHORITY TO BIND THE PRINCIPAL

Liability of Principal

A principal is bound by a contract entered into for him or her by an agent if the person who is acting as agent had authority to act for the principal. Authority may be either actual or apparent. *Actual authority* is true authority; it may be *express authority* or *implied authority*. Even if no actual authority has been given, the principal may be held liable because he or she either appeared to give authority or has ratified the act of the agent (or one posing as an agent).

Express Authority

A principal may appoint an agent by specifically stating the authority granted. Generally, this may be oral. By statute, however, most states require the authority of an agent who is to buy or sell land to be in writing. Otherwise, the agent cannot enforce his claim to a commission.

Implied Authority

The principal can seldom foresee every circumstance in which the agent may need to act. Often express authority is incomplete. Therefore, an agent has *implied authority* to do whatever else is reasonably necessary to accomplish the objectives of the agency. Implied authority also includes what is *customary* for agents to do in the particular business of the principal or for agents in similar transactions in the community. However, implied authority is limited by any specific prohibitions or other indications of the wishes of the principal.

The test used by a court in determining the extent of the agent's implied authority is the *justifiable belief of the agent*. Suppose Herb is left in charge of Joe's store while Joe is camping in a wilderness area. Joe says nothing about the arrival of merchandise. Herb would have implied authority to sign a delivery receipt for goods that he could determine from store records had been ordered. He would also have implied authority, based on custom for retail store managers, to employ someone to replace a store clerk who quit.[1]

Agents also have implied power to act in emergencies, although this is sometimes called *inherent agency power*. If a tornado breaks the windows and tears off part of the roof of the store, Herb has implied authority to make necessary repairs if he cannot reach Joe. This is true even though Joe told Herb not to make purchases of any kind.

Pacific Guano Company v. Ellis
315 P.2d 866 (Sup. Ct. Ariz. 1957)

FACTS Corbus was a fertilizer salesman for Pacific Guano Company. He sold fertilizer to George Ellis and arranged with Crumbaker to apply it to Ellis's cotton crop. Corbus had previously arranged with Crumbaker to apply fertilizer he had sold to other customers, and Pacific Guano was aware of this. Its practice was to pay Crumbaker and bill the customer for his services as well as for the fertilizer. The fertilizer was improperly applied to Ellis's cotton and he did not pay the bill. When Pacific Guano sued, Ellis filed a counterclaim for damages to his crop. Pacific Guano's defense to the counterclaim was that Corbus had exceeded his authority in arranging to apply the fertilizer. The written contract between Corbus and Pacific Guano neither expressly authorized application of fertilizer nor prohibited it.

ISSUE Did Corbus have implied authority to arrange for application of fertilizer so as to make Pacific Guano liable when it was done improperly?

DECISION Yes. Corbus had made similar arrangements for application before; Pacific Guano was aware of this and had made no objection. Therefore, Corbus had implied authority to arrange for application as a part of a sale of fertilizer.

---

[1] The *Brown v. Wichita State University* airplane crash case appearing on page 157 is an example of the use of the implied authority of an agent. The athletic director had been told by the president of the university that he could make contracts to transport the Wichita State University athletic teams. However, such contracts were to be made through a nonprofit corporation, PEC. PEC had been formed to make arrangements for the university's interschool athletic program. The court found that the university had controlled the activities of PEC on several occasions. Therefore, PEC (through which the contract was actually made) was an agent of the university. The athletic director, as an officer of the agent, had implied authority to bind the university in contracting with Golden Eagle Aviation. This made the university liable for the negligence of the athletic director in not buying insurance as he had promised Golden Eagle he would do.

**Apparent
Authority**

Apparent authority arises from the *appearance* of authority in the agent *created by the principal.* The source is the principal, just as it is for express and implied authority. Words or acts of an agent cannot alone create apparent authority. The test used for determining the extent of an agent's apparent authority is the *justifiable belief of a third party* dealing with the agent. The test is not the actual belief of the third person. This type of authority is also sometimes called *ostensible authority.*

Apparent authority is often found when a principal has, to the knowledge of the third person or others generally, permitted the agent to do certain acts. Suppose, in our earlier example, Joe had told Herb not to hire anyone for more than a day at a time. However, Joe had said nothing to anyone else when Herb had hired clerks for indefinite periods. Herb would have apparent authority to employ a clerk. Joe has given apparent authority to Herb by failing to act.

Apparent authority may also arise from customs in the trade. For example, assume it is customary for managers of this kind of store to have authority to purchase goods for stock. Herb has apparent authority to do so unless Joe advises his suppliers that Herb has not been given that authority. Forbidding Herb to buy only cuts off implied authority.

Apparent Agent

One may have apparent authority to act as an agent although he or she has never been appointed an agent by the principal. Again the apparent authority arises from an act or failure to act by the principal. As an example, suppose Jane, a retailer, loans Phillip her delivery truck containing merchandise already addressed for delivery. The truck bears Jane's name. Phillip delivers the merchandise to Jane's customers who have ordered it and he collects. Phillip has authority to collect even though he has never been employed by Jane.

**Duty of Third
Person to
Determine
Agent's Authority**

Generally people who deal with an agent or purported agent have a duty to determine the extent, if any, of the agent's authority. The fact that an agent may have some implied or apparent authority does not end the inquiry. The specific question is whether the agent or purported agent had implied or apparent authority to make the particular agreement in question. However, courts are tending more and more to allow the jury to decide whether or not there was implied or apparent authority to enter into a particular agreement. Juries are often inclined to find such authority.

**Dudley v. Dumont
526 S.W.2d 839 (Ct. App. Mo. 1975)**

FACTS   Carl Dudley and his son went to a State Farm Insurance office to buy liability insurance for an automobile. Because the car was to be driven by the son, State Farm would not write the policy. However, Ken Gainey, the State Farm agent, often referred "high-risk" clients to John Dumont, an agent for Prudent Mutual Insurance Co. Gainey had a set of forms with the name, "John T. Dumont, Jr., Insurance," printed on it. He filled out the form to show receipt for $131.50 from Dudley "for liab 10/20/5 on '56 Ply.—Effective date 12/20/65." Gainey told Dudley the car was covered. The son had an accident with the car on December 23, 1965, and this was reported to Dumont. Dumont could find no record of insurance for Dudley and sent no claim forms.

Dudley sued Dumont for losses from the accident. At the trial there was evidence that Gainey had made a phone call prior to completing the receipt form. There was no evidence of the subject of the call or to whom it was made.

ISSUE Did Gainey have apparent authority as Dumont's agent to tell Dudley that the car was insured?

DECISION No. The court said that the party claiming the existence of an agency has the burden of proof. Dudley failed to make this proof. To find apparent agency, the appearance of authority must have been created by the principal. Possession of printed forms does not prove an agency. It may indicate only authority to take orders instead of authority to make contracts.

RATIFICATION

Nature of Ratification

One may become liable through *ratification* for an unauthorized act that was done by an agent. Ratification may be of either an act of an agent who has exceeded the authority given or an act by someone who had not been appointed an agent at all For example, suppose Alex is a buyer for Polly's furniture store, Scandinavian Importers. While in Norway Alex finds a classic MG sports car for sale. Although his authority is limited to buying furniture, he contracts to buy it as an agent for Polly, who is a collector of antique cars. She, not Alex, is liable on the contract if she ratifies it by instructing the seller to ship the car.

Any act that the principal could have authorized at the time the act was done may be ratified. Generally, the effect of ratification is the same as if the act had been authorized in the first place.

Ratification is basically a question of the *intent* of the principal. However, the principal need not express intent; it may be *implied* by his acts or failure to act. Often ratification is inferred by a court from the fact that the principal accepted the benefits of an unauthorized contract. It may also be inferred from the principal's failure to repudiate an unauthorized contract after he or she becomes aware of it

Requirements for Ratification

For ratification to be effective, the agent or purported agent must have *acted on behalf of the principal*. The principal must have had *capacity* to do the act both at the time it was done in the principal's name by the agent and when ratification occurs. Thus there can be no ratification of an act done in the name of a corporation that was not in existence when the act was done. Only the *entire act* of the agent can be ratified; the principal may not ratify what is beneficial and deny what is burdensome. Ratification of a contract must be done before cancellation by the third person. Before ratification, however, the third person may usually withdraw from an unauthorized transaction. A requirement that frequently causes disputes is that the principal must have had *knowledge of all material facts* at the time of ratification. It is not necessary, however, that the principal fully understand the legal meaning of those facts.

Effect of Ratification

Ratification releases the agent from liability for having exceeded his or her authority both to the principal and to third persons. It also gives the agent the same right to compensation as if there had been prior authorization (and the principal the right to the full benefit of the contract). Likewise, the principal is bound in the same manner and to the same extent as if the agent had originally been authorized.

Wing v. Lederer
222 N.E.2d 535 (Ct. App. Ill. 1966)

FACTS Jacob Wing, a licensed tree surgeon, sued Lederer to recover $500 for services rendered. Novera was a part-time yard man at the Lederer residence. In court Wing claimed that in June, Novera, as agent for Lederer, had shown him a maple tree that needed care. According to Wing, Novera told him to go ahead and do the work necessary. Wing sprayed, then later pruned and root-fed several trees. He returned in September to do more spraying and root-feeding. He did not talk to either Lederer or his wife. Wing sent his bill in November. Lederer refused to pay it, claiming that Novera had authority only to recommend someone to care for the maple tree. Wing sued. Mrs. Lederer testified that she had discussed whether the maple tree needed care with Novera in early spring. He had suggested pruning and said he knew a man in the business. She claimed she told Novera to send him to her. Novera testified that he had told Wing to talk to the lady of the house about the tree.

ISSUE Did Novera have apparent authority to order the work? Did Lederer ratify his action by accepting the benefits?

DECISION No on both issues. Neither of the Lederers had done or failed to do anything that would justify Wing in believing that Novera had authority to hire Wing to do whatever he thought proper to the Lederers' trees. Therefore, Novera did not have apparent authority. It was impossible for the Lederers to return the services rendered. Therefore, their retention did not show an intent to ratify any act of Novera as their agent. Lederer is not bound.

TERMINATION OF AGENT'S POWERS

Termination by Will of Parties

Since the agency relationship is based on mutual consent, either party may terminate the agency at any time. No reason need be given, and any reason may be used except one made unlawful by statute, such as race or religion. Although either party has the *power* to terminate, there may be no *right* to do so. For example, suppose the contract appointing the agent provides that the agency will continue for five years. Either the agent or the principal can end it before then—say, in two years. However, then the other party is entitled to damages for breach of contract.

Most agency relationships are the result of a contract. It is desirable for the parties to agree in the contract as to when or how the agency is to end. The agency terminates at the time or upon the happening of an event stated in the contract. For example, the agency may be for one year, or the principal and agent may agree that the agency is to last until the principal's new plant is complete and ready to operate. If no time or event is specified, then the agency ends when the result for which the agency was created has been accomplished. Also the parties may agree to end the relationship before a time or event stated in the original agreement.

Termination by Operation of Law

The law terminates an agency if certain events occur. Among these are the death or insanity of either party, and the bankruptcy of either party, if it affects the agency. Where an agent's credit does not affect the agency (for example, a salesperson in a retail store), the agency is not terminated by bankruptcy.

Termination also occurs if the objective of the agency becomes impossible or illegal or if the subject matter of the agency is lost or destroyed. For example, a real estate broker may be hired as a rental agent for a house. If the house burns down, however, the agency ends.

A substantial change in market values or business conditions that affect the subject of the agency ends it if a reasonable agent would believe that termination is desired by the principal. For example, assume a broker is authorized to sell a large block of stock in McDonnell Douglas Corporation at a fixed price. War breaks out in the Middle East and the President announces a large increase in aircraft purchases that would greatly benefit McDonnell Douglas. The agency authority would terminate.

Damages

A principal or agent who terminates an agency when there is no right to do so is liable for any damages suffered by the other party. Of course, there is no liability when the agency is terminated by operation of law.

Agency Coupled with an Interest

There is an exception to the general rule that either party has the power to terminate an agency. An *agency coupled with an interest* is one in which the agency power is given as a security. It is irrevocable without the consent of the agent.

A common example of such an agency is where one is authorized to sell property pledged as security for a loan in case of default by the debtor. Suppose Joan borrows $1,000 from John. She gives John authority as her agent to sell a diamond ring if she does not pay the loan back as promised. Joan cannot revoke John's power to sell the ring. Even her death does not terminate the agency so long as the debt is unpaid.

Notice to Third Person

An agent may have apparent authority to bind the principal after termination of the agency; this is particularly true of a general agency. To avoid being bound by acts of the agent after termination, the principal should give individual notice to those who have dealt with the former agent. A written notice is desirable because it is easy to prove. A notice in a newspaper of general circulation in the area is normally sufficient for other persons. For example, suppose a husband has permitted his wife to charge things to his account at several stores. He then publishes an advertisement in the local newspaper: "After November 1, I shall no longer accept responsibility for debts incurred by my wife." This would be effective against stores that had not yet charged to him goods bought by his wife, but he should send letters to stores where he has paid bills incurred by his wife.

Wall v. Ayrshire Corporation
352 S.W.2d 496 (Civ. App. Tex. 1961)

FACTS   Ayrshire Corporation bought a 215-acre tract of unimproved land which it planned to subdivide and plot into city lots. In February 1946 Wall entered a contract with Ayrshire that gave him an exclusive agency to sell the lots. Wall was to be paid a 5 percent commission on all lots sold. In 1957 Ayrshire gave Wall notice of termination of the contract. Wall sold several lots after this notice and sued Ayrshire for the commission on these lots.

ISSUE   Was the agency terminated before the last lots were sold?

DECISION   Yes. The court found that no time had been established for the termination of the agency. An agency that is of indefinite duration may be terminated at any time by the principal. The court said the result would have been different if the agent had made substantial expenditures but was given no reasonable chance to perform the contract. It also held that this was not an agency coupled with an interest as argued by Wall. The agent has no present ownership interest in the property; he has an interest only in a part of the proceeds from future sales of the lots.

QUESTIONS AND PROBLEM CASES

1. Distinguish among express, implied, and apparent authority. State the tests for implied authority and for apparent authority.

2. What are the requirements for an effective ratification of an unauthorized act of an agent?

3. Distinguish between a *right* to terminate an agency and the *power* to do so. When does a principal have the right to terminate the agency?

4. What acts and events terminate an agency?

5. Burkhiser, manager of the building services department of Gulf Oil Co., was asked by Gulf's president to review Gulf's office arrangements in New York City. Consolidation of several scattered offices was being considered. Burkhiser employed Studley, a real estate broker, to help him find space. He told Studley not to give any information to other Gulf employees at that time. Studley showed Burkhiser several buildings, including Sperry Rand. Later, when Gulf's senior New York manager learned of the consolidation plans, he contacted another real estate broker and told Burkhiser to leave the arrangements to him. The other real estate broker arranged space in the Sperry Rand Building and was paid the commission. Studley then claimed he was entitled to the commission. Can he recover a commission from Gulf?

6. Solomon Antar bought an air tour through Peters, who was just beginning to operate a travel business in New York City under the name "The Wonderful World of Travel." Antar ordered six, 30-day all-expense tours to Israel at a very low price of $1,353 each. Peters prepared six tickets for the air transportation on TWA and gave them to Antar when he paid for the entire trip. Peters said the hotel arrangements would be confirmed shortly. Then Peters disappeared. When Antar contacted TWA, he was advised the airline would not honor the tickets. It said that although Peters had once been its agent in California, this relationship had been terminated by TWA. He had never been its agent in New York. Is TWA liable for the $8,118 paid by Antar to Peters?

7. Weingart drove his Cadillac to the door of the Directoire Restaurant in New York City. He gave the keys to the car to Douglas, who was standing in front of the restaurant in a doorman's uniform. He asked Douglas to park the car and gave him a $1 tip. Weingart had done this previously when he ate at the restaurant. Douglas could not find the car when Weingart finished about 45 minutes later. Weingart then sued the Directoire Restaurant for its value, since Douglas was judgment proof. The defense of the restaurant was that Douglas was not its employee. He furnished his own uniform and parked customers' cars for several restaurants on the block. The manager of the restaurant was aware of Douglas's activities and had not objected to them. Is the Directoire Restaurant liable for the value of the car?

8. Fendler parked her Chrysler Imperial in front of a "No Parking" sign and next to a shop in the Chris-Town shopping center. Her car and two others parked next to it were towed away at the request of Chris-Town by Charles Swinford, who operated a towing service in connection with his Texaco station. Fendler sued Texaco for conversion, alleging that Swinford was its apparent agent because of the signs and other indications that Texaco was operating the station and the tow truck. If Swinford did wrongfully remove the auto, could Texaco be liable under the doctrine of apparent authority?

9. Larry Wilks traded a Plymouth to Stone, an auto dealer, in part payment for a Chevrolet convertible. He also gave a check for $1,695. Stone claimed that Larry represented that he was acting for his mother, Hazel Wilks. The check was returned marked "no account." Stone discussed the check with Hazel. He alleges that she told him she knew of the "deal" and that "the matter would be straightened out and completed." Hazel denies that Larry

was acting as her agent or that she had indicated that she would make good on the check. Stone sues Hazel for the amount of the check. Is Hazel liable?

10. McBride and Pogue were the principal shareholders of Delta Lumber Company, which was having financial difficulties. In order to keep the business going so it could complete certain contracts, they entered into a credit agreement for Delta with Village Bank. McBride and Pogue appointed each other as attorney-in-fact to execute notes to the bank under the credit agreement. The credit agreement could be terminated by any party on ten days' notice. Delta became insolvent about a year and a half after the credit agreement was entered into. McBride had refused to sign the last note; however, Pogue had signed it for him under the power of attorney given in the credit agreement. McBride argued that he was not liable to the bank on the note. Is he?

Liability of Principals and Agents to Third Persons

22

Usually a person who is dealing with an agent is aware of the fact and knows for whom the agent is acting. If a salesperson comes to your door and announces that "Avon is calling," you know that the person is an agent for a principal, which is Avon Products, Inc. Avon Products in such a case is a *disclosed principal.*

However, sometimes principals do not want their identities known to those who deal with their agents. A common example is when a large and well-known corporation wants to acquire a plot of ground, perhaps for a new plant. If it were known that General Motors Corporation wanted to buy 160 acres on the edge of a city, owners of suitable land would probably expect a higher price than if some local individual or small company were interested. If plots owned by several different people are desired, GM would be even more likely to have to pay more than its normal value for the last plot. The owner would think GM would be willing to pay a high price to complete the purchases. To avoid the extra cost, GM is likely to ask a local person to act as its agent but to pretend to be buying for himself or herself. If several plots are to be purchased, GM is likely to purchase through several agents, each purporting to be buying personally. In such cases General Motors is an *undisclosed principal.*

A principal is *partially disclosed* when the third person knows he or she is dealing with an agent but does not know the identity of the principal. This is likely to occur when there is a possible failure to keep the principal undisclosed.

Disclosed Principal

Rights and Liabilities of Agent.   When the principal is disclosed, all parties intend the contract to be between the principal and the third party. In ordering from the Avon agent, both you and the agent intend that you contract with Avon, not the agent. Therefore, the agent is not a party to the contract. If the agent has acted within his or her authority, the agent has no liability on the contract.

Generally agents for disclosed principals cannot bring suit on contracts they make for principals. There are a few exceptions, however. For example, only the agent can bring an action on a negotiable instrument payable to him unless indorsed to the principal. By custom an auctioneer is permitted to sue the buyer for breach of contract.

Rights and Liabilities of Principal.   Since the principal rather than the agent is the intended party to the contract, the principal may enforce it, and the principal rather than the agent is liable upon the contract. Suppose goods you have ordered from the Avon agent are shipped and you fail to pay. Avon, and normally not the agent, can sue you. If Avon fails to deliver, you may recover from Avon, not from the agent.

Undisclosed Principal

Rights and Liabilities of Agent.   When the principal is undisclosed, the third party who deals with the agent believes the agent is acting personally, and the third party expects the agent to be a party to the contract. Therefore, the agent is held liable on contracts entered into on behalf of an undisclosed principal. The agent is also permitted to sue upon such a contract as a party to it.

Rights and Liabilities of Principal.   Since the contract was made for his or her benefit, an undisclosed principal is also permitted to enforce it. The principal is entitled to the rights under the contract; however, the principal is subject to whatever claims the third person has against the agent. For example, if the agent had made a misrepresentation, the principal would be liable for the resulting damages.

The principal is also liable upon the contract. If the third person learns of the principal's identity, he or she may elect to sue the principal instead of the agent. The third person cannot, of course, gain damages from both the agent and the principal.

Lagniappe of New Orleans, Ltd. v. Denmark
330 So.2d 626 (Ct. App. La. 1976)

FACTS Mr. and Mrs. Denmark operated the Courtyard Curio Shoppe as a partnership for several years. They then formed a corporation to operate it. They did not change their sign to indicate the incorporation. They ordered merchandise from a representative of Lagniappe, which did not know that the business was incorporated. Shortly thereafter the business failed. Although the word "Inc." was imprinted after the name of the shop on its checks, Lagniappe had only received one check shortly before the business failed.

ISSUE Were the Denmarks personally liable to Lagniappe for the goods they purchased for the business?

DECISION Yes. The court said that if a person acting on behalf of a corporation wishes to avoid personal liability, he or she must disclose the agency and identify the corporation. It added that it is up to the agent to prove that he had disclosed the principal. Mere receipt of a corporate check is not sufficient notice that one is dealing with a corporation.

Partially Disclosed Principal

The rights and duties of the parties when the principal is partially disclosed are the same as when the principal is undisclosed. If the principal is unknown, the third person must rely on the credit and trustworthiness of the agent. Therefore, the agent is held liable on the contract.

The third party may make an agreement with the agent to relieve the agent from liability. This would leave only one party bound, so such a contract is unenforceable for lack of consideration. The agreement protects the agent from liability, however, if the third party performs but the principal fails to do so.

LIABILITY OF AGENT

Unauthorized Actions

A person who represents that he or she is making a contract on behalf of a principal but who has no authority to do so does not bind the principal. Therefore, the agent is liable to the third person for damages suffered because the principal refuses to perform the contract. The same is true whenever agents exceed their authority—express, implied, and apparent.

Liability is imposed on an agent who has exceeded his or her authority on the basis of an *implied warranty of authority*. The agent is treated as if she had guaranteed to the third party that she had authority to make the contract. Suppose you are employed as a sales agent for Acme Machine Tool Manufacturing Co. and guarantee that a machine you sell to a customer will eliminate the need for three employees. If you have no authority from Acme to make such a guarantee (and such a guarantee is not common in the machine tool industry), then you, and not Acme, will be liable to the customer if the machine fails to replace the employees.

The intent, knowledge, and good faith of the agent are immaterial in deciding whether the implied warranty of authority applies. If the person acting as an agent exceeds his or her authority, liability results—unless the principal ratifies the act. Knowledge on the part of the third person that the agent is not authorized also relieves the agent of liability.

Nonexistent or Incompetent Principal

A person who acts as an agent for a principal that is not in existence is personally liable on the contract. Therefore, if an agent acts for a corporation that is not yet formed or for an entity, such as an unincorporated association, that has no legal existence, the agent is liable.

Assume that the Grant County Community College Jogging Club makes arrangements to hold a marathon run. One of its members makes contracts for renting certain equipment and for an award banquet at a hotel. If the club is not incorporated, she is an agent for a nonexistent principal. If the contracts are not performed by the club, she will be personally liable on them.

The same is true if the principal has been judged insane or is a minor. The law imposes an *implied warranty* by the agent that the principal has the *capacity* to be bound. However, if the third person is aware of the lack of capacity of the principal, the agent is protected.

Other Situations

Of course, an agent may make a contract in his or her own name while being employed as an agent. An agent may also become a party to a contract along with the principal, thus assuming joint liability. Or an agent may guarantee a contract made for the principal, in which case the agent becomes liable as a surety—that is, liable if the principal defaults.

To avoid liability because of confusion as to whether or not an agent is acting for himself or for a principal, an agent should sign all documents carefully. If he intends to act for a principal, the agent should use the form:

I, Maria Sanchez, . . .
(Signed) *Maria Sanchez*
By James Archer, her agent.

LIABILITY OF PRINCIPAL

Where the Agent Has Made Representations

The principal is, of course, bound by representations he or she has expressly authorized. The principal is also bound by representations that are reasonably necessary for the agent to make to accomplish the purpose of the agency; the agent has *implied authority* to make them. In addition, the principal is bound on representations that are customary in the kind of business being transacted by the agent; the agent has *apparent authority* to make such statements. If the representation is a usual one, the principal is bound even though he or she has told the agent not to make such a statement. This is not true, of course, if the third person knows that the agent had no such authority.

As stated earlier, agents cannot give themselves apparent authority. A third party cannot rely on a statement by the agent that he or she has authority from the principal.

A person who is induced to enter a contract by the misrepresentation of an agent has the same remedies as if he or she had contracted directly with a person who had made a misrepresentation. As you learned in the contracts part of this text, the remedy of rescission is available.

When the agent induces a third person to contract, the person who entered the contract relying on a misrepresentation may rescind the contract. If the representation is considered to be a warranty or guarantee, the principal is liable for damages if the product or service is not as represented. If the representation was made by the agent with the intent to deceive, this is a tort, which is discussed later in this chapter.

Exculpatory Clauses

To give notice of lack of authority in the agent, sellers often use an *exculpatory clause* in the printed offer forms they furnish their sales people. The form has a provision that says in effect, "It is understood and agreed that salespersons have no authority to make any representation other than those printed herein and that none has been made in connection with this sale." Most courts permit a third person to rescind a contract when the person has relied on a misrepresentation by the agent even though the contract contains an exculpatory clause.

The use of printed offer forms is itself a device used by sellers to control the contracts made by their sales agents. This is done by arranging the transaction so that the salesperson merely solicits an order that is, by its terms, "subject to approval of the home office." There is no contract then until the seller has received the written offer and decided to accept it. The printed form makes it clear that the salesperson is only taking an order (offer). It also usually contains an exculpatory clause about the salesperson's authority.

Killinger v. Iest
428 P.2d 490 (Sup. Ct. Idaho 1967)

FACTS   Iest owned a farm and Tadlock was his tenant under an oral lease. Tadlock telephoned Killinger to ask him to come to repair an irrigation pump on the farm. Killinger took it to his shop and found it would need extensive repairs. Tadlock inspected it there and decided that a new, more efficient pump should be installed immediately. Tadlock told Killinger that he was Iest's tenant, that he had authority to buy a new pump, and that Iest would pay for it. Killinger installed the new pump and sent the bill for $2,048 to Iest. Iest refused to pay it and denied that Tadlock had authority to buy the pump. A major irrigation improvement installed earlier had been ordered personally and paid for by Iest. Tadlock had once had a repair made on Iest's tractor but Tadlock paid for it himself without consulting Iest.

ISSUE   Are either Iest or Tadlock liable for the cost of the pump ordered by Tadlock?

DECISION   Iest is not liable. The court held that the existence of an agency cannot be proved by the statements of the agent. The fact that the pump was installed at Iest's farm and used there does not amount to ratification by Iest of Tadlock's purchase without proof that Iest had benefited. Tadlock failed to prove any direct benefit to Iest from the purchase. Tadlock is liable because he represented falsely that he had authority from Iest to buy the pump. Killinger acted in good faith and relied on Tadlock's false statement.

Where the Agent Has Given a Warranty

Principals are liable for unauthorized warranties given by agents if such warranties are usually given in that type of business. This liability is based on apparent authority. Principals are not liable on unusual warranties.

Payment to the Agent

Payment of a debt to an agent of the principal who has express, implied, or apparent authority to receive payment discharges the debt. This is true even if the agent steals the money. An agent who makes over-the-counter sales is viewed as having apparent authority to collect for the goods. The same is true of a selling agent who is given possession of the goods for delivery. However, these agents do not have apparent authority to collect on account for goods sold earlier. Other salespersons generally have no authority to collect unless it is expressly or impliedly given to them. An agent who has negotiated a loan or sold property, and has been permitted by the principal to keep a negotiable instrument payable to the principal, has apparent authority to receive payment on that instrument.

Credit Contracts

Unless the principal has held an agent out as having authority to borrow or purchase on credit for the principal, the principal is not usually liable. A *general agent* may have *implied authority to borrow or purchase on credit* if the purpose of the agency requires it. If an agent is asked to purchase goods for the principal but is given no money, authority to buy on credit is implied.

Negotiable Instruments

Authority of agents to sign or indorse negotiable instruments is not readily implied by courts. Nor do they often find that an agent has apparent authority to sign checks or drafts. Even officers of corporations, such as the president or treasurer, are not viewed as having authority to do this merely by virtue of their position. Third persons who have not previously had dealings with them should seek evidence of their authority from the principal.

NOTICE TO OR KNOWLEDGE OF AGENT

Effect of Notice

Generally, notice to the agent is notice to the principal if it relates to the business of the agency, since the agent has a duty to inform the principal. If the information is not related to the agency, the principal is bound by the notice only if he or she actually receives it from the agent. The principal is held to have knowledge of any information that comes to the agent while acting within the scope of the agency. Information coming to an employee that may affect his or her employer but that is not related to the employee's work does not bind the employer. For example, Gomez has a standing order to purchase fresh fish for his restaurant from Lee, a fish supplier. He tells a janitor at Lee's office that he is terminating the order. This is not binding upon Lee.

When There Is a Conflict of Interest

Sometimes an agent does not inform the principal of knowledge gained while acting within the scope of the agency because it is to the agent's advantage not to do so. If this is the case, the principal may be held not to be bound. This is definitely true if the agent colludes with the third person to withhold knowledge from the principal. This problem is perhaps most common when the third party is seeking an insurance policy. For example, an agent may be told or learn of facts that would prevent the issuance of a policy, and he may decide not to inform those responsible for issuing policies. Whether the information is withheld to help a friend or to earn a commission does not matter. The principal is not held to have that knowledge. Therefore, the issuer can cancel the policy when it learns of the fraudulent application.

Southern Farm Bureau Casualty Ins. Co. v. Allen
388 F.2d 126 (5th Cir. 1967)

FACTS   Southern Farm Bureau Casualty Insurance Co. had turned down an application by Joe Jezisek for a policy on his car. Joe was a minor and his record included an accident and two "moving violations." Southern's agent suggested that title to the car be transferred to Joe's brother, who was carrying insurance with Southern. The insurance application showed that the car would be kept in the town where Joe lived rather than where his brother lived several hundred miles away. The policy was issued to Joe's brother, but Joe paid the premium. Three months later Joe was driving the car when he was involved in an accident resulting in the death of Cecil Allen. Southern sought to have the policy declared void.

ISSUE   Is the knowledge of Southern's agent imputed to Southern so that it cannot void the policy for fraud?

DECISION   No. Generally notice to the agent is notice to the principal if the agent is acting within his authority. However, if the agent is acting against the interests of the principal and for his own or a third party's benefit, the principal is not bound by notice to the agent. Here Joe joined with the agent to mislead Southern; therefore, Southern is not bound by its agent's knowledge of the fraud.

LIABILITY OF PRINCIPAL FOR ACTS OF SUBAGENTS

Agent's Authority to Appoint Subagents

A *subagent* is an agent of the agent. When a corporation is made an agent, of necessity the principal is served by subagents and such authority is implied. Otherwise, authority of an agent to employ subagents to whom the agent may delegate his work for the principal may be given expressly or it may be implied or apparent. If the agent is found to have such authority, both the principal and the agent are bound to a third party by acts of the subagent. Between the agent and the principal, however, it is the agent who is liable for the acts of the subagent.

Some agents are given authority to employ agents for the principal. For example, a sales manager for a corporation would probably have authority to hire sales agents for the corporation. Such agents are not subagents; they are only agents of the corporation. The sales manager is not bound by their acts.

Agents May Have Employees

Agents may delegate to employees acts for the principal that involve no judgment or discretion. These are called *ministerial acts*. The principal is normally not bound by acts of employees of agents unless these employees are also subagents whose appointment by the agent is authorized. A principal also is not liable for torts, such as negligence in driving an automobile or fraud upon someone seeking to do business with the principal, when committed by an employee of an agent.

Liability for Acts of Subagents

If an agent has acted within his or her authority in appointing an agent or employee of the principal, the principal is liable for the agent's or employee's acts as if he or she were appointed by the principal. This is true whether the authority is express, implied, or apparent. The appointing agent is not liable to third persons for their acts. However, the appointing agent could be liable to the principal for failure to use reasonable care and skill in selecting agents.

LIABILITY FOR TORTS—GENERAL

General Rule as to Agents and Employees

The fact that an agent or employee is acting within his authority normally does not relieve the agent from personal liability for a tort he has committed. This is true even if the agent or employee acts at the direction of the principal or employer. An agent or employee has no duty to comply if the principal directs him to commit a tort. If he does commit a tort, the fact that the principal or employer may also be liable does not reduce the agent's liability.

Of course, a third party who is injured by a tort can get only one recovery. The injured party is more likely to be able to recover from the employer, who probably will have liability insurance. Therefore, she may choose to sue only the employer, although both could be sued.

General Rule as to Employers

Employers are liable to third persons injured by torts of their employees under the doctrine of *respondent superior*, which means "let the master answer." This doctrine does not apply to principals of agents who are independent contractors or professional agents. It imposes liability upon employers without fault on their part. Employers cannot escape liability by showing that they carefully selected and trained their employees. Even proof that an employee violated specific instructions of the employer in committing the tort is not a good defense.

Scope of Employment

The employer is liable only if the tort of the employee was committed *within the scope of employment*. Whether a tort committed by an employee was done within the scope of employment is often difficult to ascertain. Several factors are looked at in making the decision. One is whether the tort was committed within the time and space limits of the employment. If an act is done during off-hours or at a distance from the work, it is not within the scope of employment. A second factor is whether the employee intended to serve the employer in doing the act. If the act is directed at some personal objective such as settling a personal dispute, the employer is not liable. A third factor is whether the act is of the same general nature as (or incidental to) the authorized conduct. For example, a tavern that employs a bouncer is likely to be held responsible for any assault or battery the bouncer commits upon a customer.

Courts distinguish between a situation when an employee temporarily abandons his or her employment and a mere deviation. For example, if Elvis, a truck driver for United Parcel Service, takes a one- or two-block detour while making deliveries to stop briefly at the home of a friend, it is a mere deviation. In such a case UPS, the employer, would be liable for damages suffered by a pedestrian injured by the negligence of Elvis just before he reached his friend's house. However, if the friends decide to go fishing and the pedestrian is struck after Elvis leaves his friend's house on the way to a lake, UPS would not be liable.

Courts disagree as to when an employee has returned to his or her employment after a temporary abandonment. In the fishing trip example, some courts would impose liability upon the employer for negligence of the trucker as soon as he started toward his next delivery. Others would make the employer liable only if the trucker were at or near a point on his original route when the injury occurred.

Liability for Physical Torts of Professional Agents

Principals are not liable for the physical torts of agents who are not employees. Whether the torts of professional agents, such as manufacturers' representatives or lawyers, are intentional or negligent, principals are not liable. Of course, the principals would be liable if they directed or participated in a tort.

LIABILITY FOR CERTAIN TORTS

Liability of Agent for Deceit

Any agent, whether or not an employee, who knowingly makes misrepresentations in doing business for the principal is liable for deceit. The same is true if the agent knowingly assists the principal or other agents of the principal in defrauding a third person. However, if the agent is innocent and merely repeats in good faith statements made to her by the principal, then she is not liable for deceit. Suppose Paul employs Agnes to find a buyer for his house. He tells her that the house is fully insulated with rock wool even though it is not. Agnes would not discover this fact by an ordinary inspection. She repeats this to Terry, who buys the house relying on this statement. Agnes is not liable to Terry, although Paul is.

If Agnes were aware that the house was uninsulated but told Terry it was, Agnes would be liable along with Paul. If Agnes were an employee of Priscilla, a real estate broker, the doctrine of *respondeat superior* would apply; Priscilla would also be liable.

Liability of Principal for Deceit of Agent

The employer may be held liable for fraudulent representations of even a professional agent. The trend of court decisions is toward holding the principal liable when it is usual in that business for agents to make representations. There would then be apparent authority in the agent.

A number of cases have held banks liable to customers for fraudulent schemes of their officers, such as the sale of stolen negotiable bonds. In some of these cases the bank had no connection with the scheme except for the position of the officer and the use of its name.

The principal may ratify an unauthorized transaction in which a tort was committed by the agent. The principal then becomes liable for the tort if he or she had knowledge of it.

Liability for Conversion

An agent (or employee) who is acting for the principal (or employer) may be liable for the tort of conversion when he takes possession of goods of another even if he reasonably believes the principal is entitled to them. That is because the intent to steal is not a necessary element of this tort. If Phillip tells Axel, his employee, to get his car from a certain parking lot and Axel gets Thomas's car by mistake, Axel is liable to Thomas. However, if Phillip were present and directed Axel to take a specific car to Phillip's garage, then Axel would not be liable to Thomas because Phillip selected the car. If Thomas saw Axel driving the car and demanded it, then carrying out Phillip's instructions to drive it to Phillip's garage would make Axel liable to Thomas. If an agent or employee is given notice of a third person's right to goods, he is liable if he fails to give them to the proper person.

Intentional Physical Acts

In the past, courts seldom held an employer liable for an intentional physical act of an employee, such as striking or shooting a third person. Unless the act was encouraged by the employer, the courts tended to find that it was committed outside the scope of employment. Today, however, courts are much more likely to find the employer liable. If the use of force is foreseeable by the employer, this is generally enough to find liability.

Lange v. National Biscuit Co.
211 N.W.2d 783 (Sup. Ct. Minn. 1973)

FACTS   Lange was the manager of a small grocery store. Lynch was a new cookie salesman for Nabisco. Nabisco had received a number of complaints from grocers on Lynch's route that he was too aggressive and that he was taking shelf space from competing cookie companies. While Lynch was stocking Lange's shelves, he and Lange got into an argument over Lynch's activities in the store. Lynch became angry and started swearing. Lange told him either to stop swearing or leave the store, as children were present. Lynch's anger then increased. He said to Lange: "I ought to break your neck." He went behind the counter and dared Lange to fight. Lange refused. Lynch then beat him, threw merchandise around the store, and left.

ISSUE   Is Nabisco liable for Lange's injuries?

DECISION   Yes. The court decided to change its basis for determining when the *respondeat superior* doctrine applies. Previously the court had looked at the motive of the employee, whether it was to further the business of the employer or merely involved a personal dislike. Here the court held that the employer is liable for an assault by an employee if the source of the attack is related to the duties of the employee and it occurs within work-related limits of time and place. Thus the court found the employer liable. The assault took place in a store on Lynch's route during his working hours, and the argument grew out of the way he was doing his work.

Liability for Negligence

As indicated in the example of Elvis the truck driver, if an employee negligently injures a third person in the scope of his or her employment, the employer is liable. So, of course, is the employee. A breach of duty against the third person is the basis of liability.

Liability to Third Persons for Breach of Duty to Principal

Courts have difficulty with cases that involve an agent's breach of duty to the principal that results in injury to a third person. For example, a prospective purchaser of an apartment house may employ a consulting engineer to inspect the building. Suppose the engineer negligently fails to discover certain structural defects. If the building collapses and injures a tenant, is the structural engineer liable to the tenant? Courts have tended to impose liability on professional agents who cause physical injury to third parties through failure to perform their duties to their principal. They have been less willing when the injury has involved only a loss of money.

A number of cases have involved accountants employed to audit the books of a business. If the accountants are negligent in making the audit, then those who rely on the audited financial statements may suffer loss. Early cases found no liability to third parties, such as banks that had loaned money to the business because they relied on audited statements prepared for the owners of the business. Later, liability was imposed upon accountants only if they had been grossly negligent. More recently a few courts have gone further. They have held accountants or other professional agents liable for their negligence to anyone who relies on their work and is in the class of persons for whose benefit or guidance the work was performed.

For example, suppose Jones & Smith Candies, a manufacturer, wants to borrow money. Susan Rogers, a CPA, is engaged to audit the partnership books. She is told that the bank requires the audited financial statements. She is negligent in making the audit, and the bank, relying upon her statements, makes a loan. If Smith and Jones, as well as their partnership, become bankrupt and the bank is not repaid, Susan is liable to the bank for its loss.

Accountants may also be held liable to third parties for failure to disclose information under the federal securities laws. They have even been found guilty of crimes for their auditing errors under these laws.

LIABILITY FOR CRIMES

Liability of Agent or Employee

A person who commits a crime under instructions from his or her principal or employer is guilty of that crime. The agent or employee's duty to society overrides the duty to follow the direction of the principal or employer.[1]

Liability of Employer

It was once difficult to convict the employer for a crime committed by an employee. The view was that the commission of a crime was generally outside the scope of employment unless directed by or participated in by the employer. Employers were held liable for nonphysical crimes defined by statute, such as price-fixing under the Sherman Act. However, they were generally not found guilty of common law crimes such as assault and battery. Newly revised criminal codes impose liability on the employer even for criminal physical acts when committed by an employee with decision-making power while involved in his or her work. Here, as in tort cases, courts have broadened what is considered to be within the scope of employment.

---

[1] Refer to Chapter 3 for a discussion of criminal law.

QUESTIONS AND PROBLEM CASES

1. Suggest at least two situations when a principal might properly want to remain undisclosed.

2. Discuss the liability of an agent on a contract entered into on behalf of an undisclosed principal. How does this differ from the agent's liability if the principal is partially disclosed or fully disclosed?

3. Under what theory, if any, is an agent liable to a third party when the agent exceeds his or her authority?

4. Under what circumstances is a principal liable for a tort that was committed by an agent but not authorized by the principal?

5. While Bob Harvey was employed as a laboratory technician by Magnolia Health Center, he ordered some testing services from Bio-Chem Medical Laboratories, Inc. He did not inform Bio-Chem that he was acting as an agent for Magnolia. Magnolia did not pay the bill and Bio-Chem sued Harvey. Is Harvey liable?

6. The Council of Long Island Educators, Inc., arranged a tour to Israel through a travel tour wholesaler. The council's travel brochure made several representations about the arrangements to be enjoyed on the tour. In the brochure, the council disclaimed any responsibility for the conduct of the tour; however, it made contrary statements orally. The wholesaler that made the arrangements was not identified by the council in the brochure or otherwise. Ten of the tour members sued the council in small claims court for $218 each for a failure to provide three days of tours in Israel and other misrepresentations. Is the council, which was only an agent, liable?

7. Kjome was a sales agent for Arntson. He sold 200 gallons of Shell Oil Company's Weed Killer #20 to Start, who was a commercial grower of lily bulbs. Start had told Kjome that he wanted the weed killer to use on a field of lily bulblets, and Kjome told him that the weed killer would be safe for that purpose. However, when applied, it killed most of the bulblets. Start sued Arntson for damages for breach of warranty. Arntson's defense was that Kjome had no authority to warrant the product. Is Arntson liable?

8. State Capital Life Insurance Co. issued a policy on the life of Roney D. Boykin without a medical examination. Boykin died three months later, and Capital Life refused to pay on the policy. Material statements about Boykin's health that were false were made in the application. Boykin had given correct information, but the Capital Life agent had filled in incorrect answers. This was known to Boykin when he signed the application. Is Capital Life liable on the policy?

9. Davis was a cattle buyer for Prairie Livestock Co. He went to a public livestock auction to buy for Prairie. The bleachers were crowded, but he thought he saw a vacant seat on the far side of Crenshaw, an acquaintance. When he got there he found there was no seat and playfully sat down on Crenshaw's lap. Mitchell, another cattle buyer, was sitting behind Crenshaw. Just as Davis sat on Crenshaw, Mitchell "goosed" Crenshaw. Crenshaw jumped up and this hurled Davis down onto Chandler, who was several rows below. Chandler sued Prairie for his injuries. Prairie's defense was that Davis was not acting within the scope of his employment. Should the jury verdict for $10,000 against Prairie be reversed?

Duties of Principals and Agents to Each Other

23

DUTIES OF AGENTS TO PRINCIPALS

The duties of an agent to the principal (or employee to employer) normally derive from two sources: (1) the contract, if any, between them, and (2) those duties implied by law. Most agency relationships arise out of contract. However, the contract, especially if it is oral, may state little more than the general purpose of the agency. For example, Archie may merely tell Perry to sell Archie's car after Archie goes in the Army.

Even if nothing is said in the employment agreement, the agent owes several duties imposed by law. The most important is the fiduciary duty of loyalty to the principal. A *fiduciary* is one who is trusted to act on behalf of another person. The law also imposes upon the agent the duties of care and obedience. These duties may be reduced by agreement, but the duty of loyalty cannot be eliminated. Courts hesitate to interpret an agreement even to diminish this duty.

Duty of Loyalty

The agent or employee owes the *duty of loyalty* to the principal. This requires complete honesty from the agent in all dealings with the principal. Further, the duty requires either avoidance of conflicts between the interests of the agent and those of the principal or disclosure of any such conflict to the principal. This includes full disclosure of all compensation to be received by the agent from transactions for the principal.

283

> ### *Rushing v. Stephanus*
> #### 393 P.2d 281 (Sup. Ct. Wash. 1964)
>
> **FACTS** Eugene Rushing was a sewer contractor with a fifth-grade education. He wanted to borrow $1,800 to use in his business. Stephanus, a mortgage loan broker, promised to obtain for Rushing a first-mortgage loan that would refinance the existing mortgage on his home and provide $1,800 in cash. He asked Rushing and his wife to sign a stack of papers. He said they were several copies of the loan application, which was on top. In fact, the Rushings signed a note, a mortgage, and a hold-harmless agreement as well as the loan application. Stephanus later filled in the application to show the loan amount as $6,600.
>
> Stephanus did not obtain the loan promptly although he could have done so. After a month Rushing expressed concern. Stephanus told him there was a problem with the title to the home. He suggested a $1,000 interim loan. The Rushings again signed a number of papers in blank. When a savings and loan finally accepted the original loan, Stephanus claimed that he held a recorded mortgage on the home with an unpaid balance of $6,600. This was the commission Stephanus charged on the loan. He had already charged $160 on the interim loan. From these transactions Rushing received $1,560 and increased the debt on his house from $3,200 to $6,600. Rushing sued Stephanus to recover the $820 in commissions and $85 in closing and other fees he had received.
>
> **ISSUE** Was Stephanus liable for breach of his fiduciary duty of loyalty to Rushing?
>
> **DECISION** Yes. The court said, "The broker must fully reveal the nature and extent of his fees to the client for whom he acts, and failure to do so will render him liable." It held that because of his deliberate breach of his duty of loyalty, he was entitled to no compensation even for properly performed services.

Agents breach their duty of loyalty by buying for the principal from themselves except with the principal's permission. The same is true of sales to agents. Such sales or purchases may be rescinded by the principal. Suppose Bill authorizes Alice, who is going to an antique car rally, to buy a car for him if she finds a bargain. She learns of a very good buy but takes it for herself instead of buying it for Bill. Alice has breached her fiduciary duty of loyalty. Bill would be able to get the car from Alice for her cost. If Alice sold it to her sister Theresa, Bill could recover damages for the loss of the bargain.

Desfosses v. Notis
332 A.2d 83 (Sup. Ct. Me. 1975)

FACTS   Desfosses was a mobile home park developer. He employed Notis, a real estate broker, at a weekly salary to acquire land suitable for mobile home parks. Notis told Desfosses about a tract of land that was available at $32,400. Since Desfosses did not want to appear to be the purchaser, he asked Notis to take title in his name and then convey the property to him. He gave Notis the purchase price. Later Desfosses learned that Notis had actually purchased the land for $15,476.62 before being employed by Desfosses. Desfosses sued Notis for $16,926, the amount of Notis's secret profit. Notis contended that the only remedy is rescission.

ISSUE   Can Desfosses recover the secret profit from Notis, the agent?

DECISION   Yes. Notis had a duty to inform Desfosses that he was the owner of the land he recommended and of the price he had paid for it. Since he did not do that, Desfosses may recover the secret profit. (Desfosses could have rescinded the purchase instead if he decided that he did not want the property.)

If the agent sells the principal's property to himself, the fact that this was the best price obtainable does not bar the principal from rescinding the sale. Even if the principal agrees to the sale to the agent, it is not binding on the principal unless the agent fully discloses all the facts. Suppose Patricia agrees that Andrew, her real state agent, may himself purchase the acreage she listed with him. If he did not tell her that a new highway was planned that would run beside it, she could recover the acreage. This would be true even though no other offer for the property had been received.

An agent is not permitted to make a secret profit from the agency. If Alfred is a purchasing agent for General Electric and receives kickbacks or secret gifts from suppliers from whom he purchases goods for GE, the company is entitled to those gifts.

Dual Agency

Usually one cannot serve as agent for both parties to a transaction; however, the parties may consent to the double role if they are both informed. Suppose Pamela employs Allen as real estate broker to find a buyer for her residence. Polly wants to buy some houses as rental property and has agreed to pay Allen a commission on those she buys through him. Allen arranges a sale of Pamela's house to Polly. If he has not informed both of them of his dual role, he is not entitled to a commission from either. If only Polly is aware of and approves the arrangement, Allen may collect a commission from her but not from Pamela. A party who was not informed of Allen's dual role can rescind the sale.

Courts make an exception when the dual agent is employed merely to find a buyer for one party and a seller for the other and the parties intend to and do negotiate their own transaction. If neither party relies on the agent for advice or negotiation, there is no breach of loyalty.

Another aspect of the duty of loyalty is the duty of agents to avoid disclosing or using the principal's secrets. Agents breach this duty if they either disclose confidential information to others or use it to benefit themselves. Trade secrets such as formulas, processes, and mechanisms are included within this duty; so also are customer lists, special selling techniques, and sales manuals. However, agents may use the general knowledge and skills they have learned while employed by their principal. This is true even when the agent is competing with the former principal. The agent is not allowed to compete with the principal while the agency relationship continues unless this is permitted by an express or implied agreement.

Duty to Obey Instructions

The principal has a right to instruct the agent or employee in how the agent is to perform services for the principal. The agent has a duty to follow all instructions, and he or she will be liable for any loss to the principal caused by failure to follow such instructions. Suppose Joe instructs Alma, a clerk in his store, to sell goods only for cash except to those who have previously established accounts. While Joe is gone, Alma sells goods on credit to a very well-dressed customer. Later Joe is unable to collect. Alma is liable to Joe for the price of the goods. The fact that Alma thought Joe would benefit from her action is not a defense.

There are a few situations where the agent may act contrary to instructions without liability. In the tornado example on page 262, Joe would be liable for the roof repairs even if he had told Herb not to obligate him for any goods or services. Herb would have implied authority. It would be reasonable for Herb to believe that, in the emergency and despite the instructions, Joe would have wanted him to have the repairs made.

An agent or employee is not entitled to substitute personal judgment for that of the principal, however. The agent may not ignore instructions just because he thinks them unwise or not truly in the best interest of the principal. If no instruction is given, the agent should exercise best judgment to further the interests of the principal.

Duty to Exercise Care and Skill

Unless changed by agreement, the agent has the duty to act with ordinary care and with the skill common in the community for the kind of work he or she is employed to do. There is a trend, which is likely to continue, to shift from a local to a national standard of skill for professionals. This is because of the widespread availability of continuing education and training programs as well as specialized informative journals for physicians, lawyers, accountants, and other professional agents.

If the agent is acting without pay—a *gratuitous agent*—that fact is taken into account by the courts. The standard of care and skill required is likely to be less than when the agent is to be compensated.

An agent is bound by any representation he or she makes as to skill. Also an agent may warrant results, guaranteeing satisfaction or successful results. For example, an art broker might guarantee that the painting he buys for you will double in value within two years. In the absence of such a warranty, the agent does not assume the risk of success or satisfaction with his or her performance.

An agent or employee who is authorized to receive goods or to make collections has a duty to use customary practices to keep them safely. An agent who makes loans is not an insurer of their collectability. The agent, however, must use care to investigate the credit standing of borrowers. If it is usual to require security, the agent must investigate the adequacy of the security.

Duty to Communicate Information

When notice is given an agent while transacting the principal's business, the principal is bound by the notice. Also the principal is bound by information relevant to the agency that comes to the agent while transacting the principal's business. Therefore the law requires the agent to advise the principal promptly of such information. For example, if Alan, a salesman for Pratt Co., learns that a customer is unable to pay her debts, he has a duty to tell Pratt Co. If Alan fails to do so, he could be liable for any resulting loss to Pratt Co.

Duty to Account

An agent is frequently given money or property, such as tools, an automobile, or samples, by the principal. If so, the agent has a duty to return them or to account for them upon request by the principal. If the job of the agent includes receiving payments or operating a farm or business for the principal, the agent must periodically give the principal an accurate record of receipts and expenditures. The contract that establishes the agency normally states when such records are due. It may be as often as each day or it may be only once a year.

The agent, upon request of the principal, must also participate in an *accounting*. An accounting involves more than just giving the principal a record of receipts and expenditure. It also involves an agreement, express or implied, between the agent and the principal that the record is correct.

The principal may ask a court for a formal accounting if he or she is dissatisfied with the records of the agent. The court will then settle the disputed items.

Bain v. Pulley
111 S.E.2d 287 (Sup. Ct. Va. 1959)

FACTS   Douglas Pulley was employed by the trustees of the estate of Thomas Bain, deceased, to manage the business and farms of the estate. Pulley served as manager for 20 years. Pulley kept handwritten records concerning the properties and business operations. Substantial profits from the operations were paid to the trustees, and Pulley provided the trustees with an annual income report. These reports were not verified or checked with the records of the estates by the trustees, the beneficiaries of the trust, or any accountant. When Pulley resigned as manager, an accountant found his records to be incomplete. The trustees brought an action in court for an accounting. Pulley's defense was that since he made annual reports that were not questioned, the trustees were not entitled to an accounting.

ISSUE Must Pulley render an accounting to the trustees when he has regularly provided annual reports of income from the estate?

DECISION Yes. The court said that, in an action for an accounting, the agent has the burden of proving that he or she has paid to the principal or otherwise properly disposed of whatever has been received from the principal. The annual income report was not an accounting. There had been no reconciliation of the income and expense items with the amount of cash in the bank or with the records of the estate. Nor had there been any agreement by the trustees or beneficiaries that the annual income reports were final accountings.

The principal or employer is entitled to anything of value that comes to the agent or employee because of his position, such as the gifts in the previous GE example. The duty to account requires the agent to turn over to GE any kickback as well as other funds coming to him because of his position.

An agent or employee has a duty to keep the principal's and his property separate. If the agent fails to do this, he is liable for any loss to the principal. If the agent *commingles* goods that are fungible, that is, mixes goods that are identical and cannot be separated, then the agent bears the risk of any loss. For example, suppose Amy is carrying $1,000 in expense money that belongs to RCA Corporation, her employer, in a billfold. Mixed with it is $500 of her own money. She is robbed. Later the bandit is caught with $900 left. RCA will be entitled to the $900 if Amy cannot identify which bills were stolen.

An agent has the duty to deposit funds of the principal in a separate bank account. The account should be either in the principal's name or in a special account in the form "Ames, in trust for Parker." Professional agents who serve a number of clients often maintain an account in the form "Ames's Clients' Trust Fund."

Agents are often given property of the principal for use in the principal's business. If the agent takes the property with the intent to deprive the principal of it, the agent is guilty of the crime of *embezzlement*. Whether or not it is wrongfully used, the agent must return the property of the principal or be liable for its value in an action for *conversion*.

If an agent uses the money of the principal for the agent's purpose, the principal may choose either to sue for the money or to obtain whatever was purchased with it. Suppose Axel as agent is paid $5,000 owed by a debtor of Perkins, Axel's principal. Instead of giving it immediately to Perkins, Axel invests it in the stock of Golden Mining Co. Luckily, the market price of the shares rises to $10,000 before Perkins learns of Axel's wrongdoing. Perkins can get a court to order Axel to transfer the stock to him despite its increased value. If instead the price has decreased, Perkins could recover $5,000.

DUTIES OF PRINCIPALS TO AGENTS

Sources of Duties The agency contract should set out the duties of the principal to the agent. If it does not, the law implies certain duties, including the duty to compensate, the duty to reimburse for money spent for the principal, and the duty to indemnify for losses suffered by the agent. Even in a gratuitous agency the principal has the last two duties.

Duty to Compensate Normally, a duty to pay the agent is implied, as when you employ a stockbroker or a lawyer. Special circumstances or the relationship of the parties, however, may suggest that a *gratuitous agency* was intended.

The agency agreement should specify the amount of compensation due the agent or employee and when it has been earned. Many disputes arise because no clear agreement is reached. In the absence of agreement, the agent or employee is entitled to the customary or reasonable value of the services performed. Custom is sometimes quite clear; for example, in most communities real estate brokers all charge the same commission rate. If there is no clear custom and the amount is in dispute, expert witnesses may testify as to what a reasonable amount would be.

Contingent Compensation. Compensation is often made contingent upon results. Sales agents are frequently paid an agreed upon percentage of the value of the sales they make. Stockbrokers are also usually paid on a commission basis. Lawyers in the United States, especially when serving plaintiffs in tort actions such as automobile accident claims, often agree to contingent fees. If they win the case for the plaintiff, they get some share, often one-third, of the recovery. The plaintiff has only expenses and court costs to pay if there is no recovery.

An agent is entitled to be paid if the agreed upon result is obtained even though the principal does not benefit. For example, Albert is employed by Pierce Manufacturing Co. as a salesman. His compensation is to be a commission on all orders accepted by the company. As a result of material shortages, Pierce is unable to produce and ship several large orders taken by Albert and accepted by Pierce. Albert is entitled to his commission on those orders. However, if Pierce had informed Albert of the shortage and stopped approving orders he sent in, Pierce would have no liability to Albert.

It is common to give agents who are compensated on a commission basis a monthly or weekly "draw" against commission to be earned. This gives the agent money for living expenses. At some longer interval, such as quarterly or once a year, the agent is paid the amount that the commissions exceed the draw. If it is not clear from the employment contract whether the agent must reimburse the principal if the draw exceeds the commissions, courts generally hold that overpayments cannot be recovered.

Generally, agents are not entitled to commissions on transactions that occur after termination of the agency even if the customer was found by the agent. However, where the agent was the primary factor in the purchase or sale, called the *effective cause* or *procuring cause*, he or she may be entitled to the agreed upon compensation.

Floyd v. Morristown European Motors, Inc.
351 A.2d 791 (Super. Ct. N.J. 1976)

FACTS Michael Floyd was employed by an oral contract with Morristown European Motors, Inc., to sell new automobiles. He was given a "draw" of $100 per week against commissions of 25 percent of the net profit to Motors. Nothing was said as to when the commissions would become earned. In January and February, Floyd took orders for three automobiles prior to the new models being in stock. Prices on them had not been set, but the buyers paid 10 percent of the expected purchase price. The deposits were said to be refundable.

Floyd took a leave of absence in March. He was gone when the cars arrived and the buyers took delivery. He claimed $721.25 in commissions on the sales. Motors claimed he was not entitled to any commission on the sales because the orders he took were not binding. Furthermore, he was not an employee when the cars were shown to and delivered to the customers. Floyd brought suit.

ISSUE Was Floyd entitled to the commissions?

DECISION Yes. The court found that Floyd was "the procuring cause of the sale." Since he had effectively produced the sale, he was entitled to the commissions even though the sale was completed by another agent or the principal personally.

Real Estate Commissions.   A real estate broker who represents a seller normally earns the commission when he or she finds a buyer "ready, willing, and able" to make the purchase on the offered terms. "Able," of course, means the buyer has or can borrow the asking price for the property. If the seller has not given the broker specific terms of price, closing date, or other important terms, then the commission is not earned until a contract of purchase has been made. Sometimes, a broker is employed to obtain a net price to the seller. If a contract at the agreed upon net price is not made, no commission is earned.

Axilbund v. McAllister
180 A.2d 244 (Sup. Ct. Pa. 1962)

FACTS   Jacob Axilbund, a real estate broker, learned that McAllister wished to sell his building. McAllister promised Axilbund that if he "produced a purchaser for the premises for $300,000 net, the usual brokerage commission would be paid." Axilbund showed Gross the building. He told Gross the building was available at $315,000 and provided him with additional information. He talked with Gross about the building several times on the telephone over several months, even after Gross said he was not interested. Later Axilbund learned that Gross had purchased the building directly from McAllister for $295,000. Axilbund sued McAllister for a commission.

ISSUE   Was McAllister liable for a commission on the sale?

DECISION   No. The court held that the commission was contingent upon a sale being made that would net McAllister $300,000. The completed sale was not in accord with those terms. Unless McAllister had acted in bad faith, he was not liable to Axilbund for a commission.

Whether a commission has been earned sometimes depends on the type of listing (contract of agency). There are four general types: open or general, exclusive right to sell, exclusive agency, and multiple listing.

The *open or general listing* makes the real estate broker an agent of the owner merely to seek a buyer for the property. The owner may enter into such an agreement with several such agents. The first one to find a buyer ready, willing, and able to buy gets the commission. However, the owner may avoid the commission by making the sale first or by terminating the agency.

At the other extreme is the *exclusive right to sell agency*. In this type, the real estate agent gets the commission upon the sale of the property without regard to who finds the buyer. Even if the owner finds the buyer and makes the sale without help from the agent, the agent is assured the commission.

An *exclusive agency* (also called an exclusive listing) does not prevent the owner from finding a buyer and completing the sale personally so as to avoid payment of the commission. It does prevent the owner from appointing other agents.

A *multiple listing* occurs when the listing agent is a member of a group of agents who have an agreement to exchange listings. Usually the listing broker obtains an exclusive right to sell, but other agents in the group are permitted to show the property to prospective buyers. If another agent makes the sale, he or she is entitled to a prearranged share of the listing agent's commission.

Insurance Commissions.   In the life insurance business it is customary for the company to pay the agent a commission on all premiums paid on the insurance contracts sold. This encourages the agent to provide continued service to policyholders as well as recognizing the fact that the value of the sale is greater than the first payment. In other lines of business, including casualty insurance, the agent is paid a commission on renewals by or repeated transactions with a customer first sold by the agent. Such agreements should clearly state whether the agent or his or her representative is entitled to such payments after the agent's death or termination of employment.

Duty to Reimburse and Indemnify

Sometimes agents make advances from their own funds in conducting the principal's business. If the agent is acting within the scope of his or her authority, the principal has a duty to reimburse the agent for expenses incurred for the principal. Also if the agent suffers losses while acting for the principal within the scope of the agent's authority, the principal has a duty to indemnify the agent.

For example, suppose Abby is a salesperson for Pierce Manufacturing Co. She is in Cleveland when she is asked by Pierce to go to a foreign exposition. She uses her own funds to pay workers to set up the booth. In order to ship the exhibit back to Pierce, she is required to pay a $500 export fee, again from her own funds. Pierce has the duty to reimburse her for her expenses and indemnify her for the fee she was required to pay.

If fault of the agent was the cause of a loss, the principal need not indemnify the agent; nor is the principal liable for unauthorized expenses incurred by an agent.

Duty to Keep Accounts

The employer has the duty to keep records from which it can be determined the compensation due the agent. This duty is reinforced by the tax laws. For example, an employer must keep and make available to a salesperson a record of the sales on which commissions are earned.

Duration of Employment

Sometimes the agreement between principal and agent or employee does not specify the duration of the employment. Then, as indicated in Chapter 21, either party can terminate it at any time without liability for breach. The pay period—week or month—does not necessarily imply a promise to employ for that period. It may, however, be accepted as evidence of such intent. If an agent or employee is hired for a month (or a year) and continues beyond that period, it is usually inferred that the agreement has been renewed on the same terms.

An agent may be expected to incur substantial expense that he or she is to recoup through a commission upon completion of the agency. When no duration is agreed upon and the agent has made the expenditures, a court may hold that the principal cannot terminate the agency until after the agent has had a reasonable time to try to earn the expected commission. Suppose Ralph, a real estate broker, is given an exclusive right to sell residential lots by a developer. It is customary for brokers to use extensive advertising and to establish an office in the subdivision. Ralph does this even though the agreement with the developer does not specify its duration. The developer cannot cancel the contract until Ralph has had a reasonable opportunity to recover his costs.

ENFORCEMENT OF LIABILITIES BETWEEN PRINCIPALS AND AGENTS

Breach of Duty by Agent

When an agent breaches a duty that causes harm to the principal, the principal may deduct the loss from the amount due the agent. If no compensation is due the agent, the principal can bring an action in court. If the breach of duty is serious enough, the principal may have no duty to compensate the agent even though no harm can be proven. The agent may even be discharged without liability in spite of an unexpired contract. For example, an agent who takes kickbacks while serving the principal could be fired and perhaps even be denied compensation for the period in which she acted disloyally.

Breach of Duty by Principal

In most situations an agent who is in lawful possession of property that belongs to the principal has a lien upon it for the compensation due him related to the agency. For example, if a stockbroker has purchased a security for a client, she may hold the certificate until being paid. Likewise, an attorney has a lien on the documents of the client. Of course, a lawsuit may be brought by agents who have been injured by a breach of duty by the principal.

QUESTIONS AND PROBLEM CASES

1. In the absence of agreement between them, what duties does the agent owe to the principal?

2. Give examples of acts by an agent that are a breach of the duty of loyalty to the principal.

3. When two real estate brokers each claim a commission on the same sale, which broker is entitled to it?

4. It is often expensive to bring a lawsuit. Describe what other means an agent may be able to use to get the compensation due. What device, if any, does a principal have to protect his or her interests against an agent who has breached a duty?

5. Dr. Becker was a physician without experience in the real estate business. He asked Capwell, a real estate broker, to assist him in investing in real estate. Capwell informed him of an available piece of property and made a favorable analysis of its investment potential. Becker bought it. Later he learned that Capwell had entered into a contract to purchase the land prior to talking with Becker. The price to Capwell was much less than the sale price to Becker. Can Becker recover the difference between what Capwell paid and what Becker paid for the property?

6. Merkley employed MacPherson, a real estate broker, to find a buyer for Merkley's apartments. MacPherson found a buyer, and Merkley signed the purchase contract. It said that MacPherson had received from the buyer and was holding earnest money in the form of a demand note for $2,700. It provided that, if

the buyer did not complete the purchase, the earnest money would be divided equally between Merkley and MacPherson. The buyer forfeited the earnest money. However, Mac-Pherson had failed to get the note from the buyer. Merkley sued MacPherson for half the value of the note. Will Merkley win?

7. McQueen was a contractor building a house for sale. Jarrell sold certain appliances for the house to McQueen. Dallas Title Co. was financing the project, and it promised Jarrell that it would withhold and pay to Jarrell, when the house was sold, the amount due on the appliances. When the house was sold, Dallas Title failed to withhold the funds to pay Jarrell. Jarrell was unable to collect from McQueen or the buyer and sues Dallas Title. Is its defense that it is a gratuitous agent a good one?

8. Want was employed by Century Supply Co. as a salesperson. He was to pay his own expenses and receive a 5 percent commission on sales made. Century terminated the contract after seven months. Want had averaged $10,000 in sales per month and had incurred expenses of $3,600. Want sues to recover the share of his expenses that was connected with soliciting business not yet completed and on which no commissions had been paid. Will he win?

9. Rotella listed his restaurant for sale with Lange, a real estate broker. The offering price was $9,000 cash. The listing agreement said that Rotella had a three-year lease on the building in which the restaurant was operated. Lange obtained an offer from Armstrong for $9,000, part in monthly payments secured by a security agreement. Rotella refused both this offer and a later one for $7,000 cash from Armstrong. Then Armstrong offered $9,000 cash subject to a provision which said, ". . . the offer to be binding only if Armstrong can obtain an A.B.C. license, a health permit, and a five-year lease." Rotella again rejected the offer, although this provision was in the two earlier offers and Rotella had not objected to it before. Lange claims he has found a buyer ready, willing, and able to buy on the terms stated in the listing. Can Lange recover his commission?

Employment Laws

24

If you operate a business that employs even one person outside your own family, you must comply with a myriad of statutes. Some of these require that you make a variety of reports to both state and federal agencies. These laws impose duties on employers that supplement and greatly increase the duties imposed by the common law of agency just discussed.

There have long been some statutes to govern the employment relation. The objective of the early statutes in both England and the United States was to *control and restrict workers*. For example, the earliest statutes on wages set maximums rather than minimums. A statute of Edward VI in 1549 prohibited joint actions such as strikes or the formation of unions by workers.

The Industrial Revolution changed the nature and conditions of work. As more power machinery was used and the size of mining, manufacturing, and processing activities grew, accidents and industrial disease killed and disabled many workers. Women and children as well as men were drawn off the farms to work in factories. Hours were long—often 14 hours a day, six days a week.

Beginning soon after the Civil War, a number of states passed statutes whose aim was to protect workers. Massachusetts established a system of state safety inspection of factories in 1867. It and other states soon passed laws setting ten hours as the maximum workday for women. Employment of young children in mining and manufacturing was prohibited by other statutes. Some of this early protective legislation was declared unconstitutional by the U.S. Supreme Court, which held that such statutes interfered with freedom of contract as guaranteed by the Due Process Clause of the fourteenth amendment of the U.S. Constitution.

Today, as discussed in Chapter 47, the Constitution is interpreted to put few limits on the power of both state and federal governments to regulate business. The regulation of the employment relationship itself is an important part of such regulation. Following is a brief description of some of the most important of these statutes.

HEALTH AND SAFETY LEGISLATION

State Legislation

Most states passed factory inspection laws before 1900. A Massachusetts statute passed in 1877 required employers to install safety devices on their machinery. Few of these statutes were vigorously enforced, however.

Emphasis on industrial safety by employers was stimulated by the passage of workmen's compensation statutes (discussed later in this chapter). Most employers insure their risks under these statutes. Premiums vary by industry and individual employer experience. Despite this fact and the efforts to promote safety in the workplace by insurance companies and some employers, many employers tolerated unsafe practices by workers and their workplaces were often hazardous.

OSHA

The first federal safety statute that applied to all types of business was the *Occupational Safety and Health Act (OSHA)* of 1970. It applies to all businesses that affect interstate commerce, even those with only one employee. It seeks to protect the safety and health of employees in two ways. It imposes a general duty on covered employers to *prevent workplace hazards* that may cause death or serious physical harm. It also delegates to the Secretary of Labor authority to establish detailed *health and safety standards* that must be complied with by employers. In carrying out this second function, the secretary has set maximum levels of exposure for certain hazardous substances such as asbestos and lead.

Employers are required to report on-the-job fatalities and injuries that require hospitalization to the Secretary of Labor within 48 hours. Employers with more than ten employees are required to keep a log of all work-related deaths, injuries, and illness.

Enforcement of the act is in the hands of the Occupational Safety and Health Administration, a division of the Department of Labor. Inspectors may enter any place of employment at any reasonable time and without advance notice. However, if an employer objects to the inspection, the inspector can be forced to obtain a search warrant from a court. Inspectors usually check workplaces after fatalities have occurred, often in response to complaints of workers, and occasionally on just a random basis.

Representatives of the union and employer are entitled to accompany the inspector. On-site construction is also available to encourage voluntary compliance with the act. If the inspection is requested, no penalties are imposed unless the employer fails to correct conditions found by the consultant that might result in death or serious injury.

A compliance officer may issue a citation that carries a penalty of as much as $1,000 for each violation. A penalty is mandatory for any violation where the employer knew or should have known that a substantial probability of death or serious harm was present. Willful or repeated violations are subject to a civil penalty of up to $10,000. Criminal penalties of a fine of up to $10,000 and/or six months in prison may be imposed for willful violations that cause death.

If an employer wishes to contest a citation, the case is first heard by a judge of the Occupational Safety and Health Review Commission. An appeal may be taken to a panel of the commission itself. The U.S. Court of Appeals hears appeals from the decisions of the commission.

The statute permits states to develop and enforce their own health and safety programs. Such programs must provide protection to employees at least as great as that established by OSHA. OSHA has approved the programs of at least 21 states.

REA Express, Inc. v. Brennan
495 F.2d 822 (D.C. Cir. 1974)

FACTS A conveyer belt in an REA shipping terminal failed to operate because of a short circuit. The local manager called Traugott, a licensed electrical contractor. Coy, REA's maintenance supervisor, was in the circuit breaker room when Traugott arrived. The floor was wet and he was using sawdust to try to soak up the water. After cutting some cables, Coy threw the switch to energize them again. Traugott, believing they carried 600 volts rather than 15,000, then tested one for voltage. This caused a blinding flash that electrocuted Coy who was standing on the wet floor four or five feet away. Traugott was standing on a wooden platform and he was burned and knocked unconscious. The Occupational Safety and Health Review Commission imposed a fine of $1,000 on REA Express for failure to furnish a place of employment free from recognized hazards. REA Express asked the court to review the decision.

ISSUE Is either assumption of the risk or contributory negligence by an independent contractor or employee a good defense to an action for violation of OSHA?

DECISION No. There may be a violation of OSHA even though no accident or injury occurs. The intent of the act is to set new standards of industrial safety. Therefore, the court said, defenses to a personal injury action by an employee are not relevant in defense of an OSHA action. The court said, however, that the act does not impose strict liability. Some hazards may not be preventable. An employee's conduct may be so reckless or so unusual that the employer could not reasonably prevent the hazard his conduct creates.

Workmen's Compensation

In the 19th century it was very hard for an employee who was injured on the job to recover damages from the employer. This was true although the common law and some state statutes imposed a duty on the employer to furnish a reasonably safe workplace. It was difficult to prove that the employer had been negligent. Even if negligence could be proven, the common law defenses of *contributory negligence* and *assumption of risk* by the employee usually barred recovery. In addition the employer could claim the *fellow-servant rule* as a defense. This rule declared that if the injury was the result of negligence by another worker, the employer had no liability.

In the period between 1911 and 1925 most states enacted workmen's compensation laws. These put *liability* for injuries occurring within the scope of employment on the employer *without regard to fault*. The three common law defenses could not be raised. The cost and uncertainty of law suits were largely eliminated, and disability from industrial diseases was also covered.

Disputes as to the employer's liability are heard by an administrative board rather than a court. The statutes require the employer to furnish the employee with medical treatment and a fixed level of income during disability. Scheduled amounts are awarded for death or loss of limb. Generally they also include some rehabilitation services. Disability income payments tend to be low. Although many statutes specify a rate of two thirds of wages, they also establish a maximum, which, because of inflation, has become quite low.

Employers with three or fewer employees are frequently exempted. Employees in certain types of employment, such as farming, charitable organizations, and household service, are also often excluded. Disability caused by certain work-related diseases is not covered by some statutes. Merit rating (varying the amount to be paid by the employer into the state compensation fund) is often provided. Insurance coverage of workmen's compensation liability or self-insurance by large employers is also provided in many states.

Electro-Voice, Inc. v. O'Dell
519 S.W.2d 395 (Sup. Ct. Tenn. 1975)

FACTS While at work on an assembly line, Gladys O'Dell was stung by a bee. As a result she had swelling all over her body and was hospitalized for a week. After the general swelling went down, she continued to have stiffness, numbness, and localized swelling, especially in her legs. Gladys won a trial court verdict under the Tennessee Workmen's Compensation Act. She was given temporary total disability from the date of the bee sting to the date of the trial. Electro-Voice, Inc., appealed the decision.

ISSUE Was the injury one that arose "out of and in the course of employment"?

DECISION Yes. The court said that an injury is "in the course of" employment if it happens while the employee is doing work he or she is employed to do. It is an injury "arising out of" employment if caused by a hazard incident to the job. The court said there was no doubt that the employee was on duty. It is a hazard incident to the employment if there is a cause-and-effect connection between the conditions under which the work is required to be done and the injury. Here the bees were part of the environment on the assembly line. Therefore, they were a risk of Gladys O'Dell's job.

There is no federal law requiring injury compensation that applies to employers generally. Railroads and mining are covered by such federal legislation, however. Because of rather substantial differences in coverage and benefits under various state workmen's compensation statutes, mandatory federal standards have often been proposed to Congress.

WAGES AND HOURS

Fair Labor Standards Act

In 1938 Congress passed the *Fair Labor Standards Act (FLSA),* which requires covered employers to pay their employees a minimum hourly wage and to pay time and one-half for hours worked in excess of 40 in one week. The minimum wage has been increased several times. It was $3.10 as of 1980.

Coverage under the act has also been expanded from time to time. Generally employers are covered if they are engaged in interstate commerce or their annual gross sales exceed $250,000 and their business affects interstate commerce. Covered employers must keep certain records. The act is administered by the Wage and Hour Division of the Department of Labor.

State Wage Statutes

A number of states have minimum wage and overtime statutes. These have become less important as coverage under the FLSA has increased. Other state statutes specify how soon after wages are earned they must be paid to the employee. For example, the California statute requires the employer to pay off a discharged employee immediately. It also provides that in most types of employment, employees must be paid every two weeks and within seven days following the last day of the pay period.

Most states also have statutes dealing with the garnishment of wages. *Garnishment* is a court order that makes money or property held by a debtor (the *garnishee*) subject to the claim of a creditor.[1] The statutes usually limit the amount of wages subject to garnishment. For example, Illinois limits attachment to 15 percent of gross wages. It also prohibits the firing of employees because their wages have become subject to garnishment.

---

[1] See Chapter 42 for further discussion of garnishment.

COLLECTIVE BARGAINING AND UNION ACTIVITIES

The first recorded organized action by workers in America was a strike for a $6-per-week wage by printers in Philadelphia in 1786. Workers in certain trades, including shoemakers, weavers, and tailors, organized unions in the early years of the 19th century to seek higher wages and shorter hours. Employers were able to get some of these workers prosecuted for conspiracy; the courts held that such activities were criminal because they restrained trade.

Although later they were unable to get criminal actions brought against union activity, most employers remained strongly opposed to unions. One device they developed was the "yellow dog" contract, which required a worker taking a job to promise not to join a union. Courts were often quick to enjoin a strike if the employer could show that there might be violence or that other persons' interests would be hurt. Perhaps the greatest obstacle to the growth and power of unions, however, was periodic economic depressions.

The Norris-LaGuardia Act

In 1932, when union membership and influence had been hurt severely by the Great Depression, Congress passed the *Norris-LaGuardia Act* to help unions offset some of the advantage held by employers. It prohibited the federal courts from issuing injunctions against lawful strikes, picketing, and certain other union activities. Unlawful acts that might result in irreparable harm could still be enjoined. It also prohibited the enforcement of "yellow dog" contracts.

The National Labor Relations Act

The right of workers to organize and bargain collectively was expressly recognized in the *National Labor Relations Act (Wagner Act)* in 1935. The act also prohibited certain actions by employers that were thought to deter union organizing and bargaining. These were declared to be unfair labor practices. It established the National Labor Relations Board (NLRB) to administer the act. Its major functions are to conduct elections of employees for choosing a union to represent them and to hear charges of unfair labor practices.

An election is held after a petition is filed with the board by a group of employees, a labor union, or an employer. Sometimes more than one union is on the ballot. The board determines what group of employees will be allowed to vote. This becomes the *bargaining unit*. If the bargaining unit is subject to dispute, the board will hold a hearing before defining it. A board representative supervises the election. If a union receives a majority of the votes of the employees who vote, the board certifies it as the exclusive bargaining representative for the unit. It then represents all employees in the unit whether or not they voted for or belong to the union.

Union membership and power grew rapidly as World War II approached.

After the war (1947), Congress amended the Wagner Act by the *Taft-Hartley Act* to limit what was then believed to be the excessive power of unions. It declared certain union practices to be unfair labor practices. It also provided for an 80-day "cooling-off" period in strikes that the President finds likely to harm national safety or health. During this period employees must return to work or continue working. It also created a Federal Mediation and Conciliation Service, whose function is to provide skilled people to help unions and employers in their bargaining so as to prevent strikes or lockouts. A *lockout* is when the employer discontinues operations during a labor dispute.

The Labor Management Relations Act

The present statute is known as the *Labor Management Relations Act (LMRA)*. It is also called the Taft-Hartley Act. Coverage of the act is very broad. For NLRB jurisdiction out-of-state purchases or sales of goods and services must equal $50,000. Federal, state, and local government employees are excluded, as are agricultural laborers and household employees.

The *Labor Management Reporting and Disclosure Act (Landrum-Griffin Act)* was passed in 1959 to promote honesty and democracy in running the internal affairs of the union. It requires a union to have a constitution and bylaws, and it sets forth a "bill of rights" for union members. It also requires certain reports to the Secretary of Labor. These reports must disclose a great deal about the financial situation of the union and its internal procedures. The procedures disclosed include those involved in holding elections, determining bargaining demands, and deciding whether to strike.

Unfair Labor Practices

Under the Labor Management Relations Act the NLRB processes unfair practice charges against unions as well as employers. The following practices by employers are declared to be unfair:

1. Interfering with the right of employees to form or join a labor union or to engage in concerted activities for their mutual aid or protection.
2. Establishing or dominating a labor union.
3. Discriminating against employees who have filed charges with the NLRB.
5. Refusing to bargain collectively with a union that represents the employees.

H. K. Porter Co. v. NLRB
397 U.S. 99 (U.S. Sup. Ct. 1970)

FACTS   The NLRB certified the United Steelworkers of America as the bargaining agent for certain employees of H. K. Porter Co. at its plant in Danville, Virginia. Negotiations for a contract continued for the next eight years. The primary dispute was over the union's demand for a "checkoff." An employer who agrees to a checkoff must deduct union dues from the pay of employees who are union members and pay them to the union. Although the company made deductions for insurance and contributions to certain charities like the United Appeal, it said it was "not going to aid and comfort the union." The NLRB ordered the company to cease and desist from refusing to bargain because of its unwillingness to agree to the checkoff.

ISSUE Is the refusal to agree to the checkoff an unfair labor practice?

DECISION No. The effect of the board's order would be to compel agreement on the checkoff issue. Section 8(d) of the National Labor Relations Act prohibits the board from finding bad faith bargaining solely on evidence of a refusal to agree. The purpose of the act is to require bargaining (meeting and considering the demands and offers of the other party) without compulsion as to the actual terms of a labor contract.

Unfair labor practices by unions include the following:

1. Coercing an employee to join a union and coercing an employer in the selection of representatives for collective bargaining.
2. Coercing an employer to discriminate against an employee who is not a union member, except for failure to pay union dues under a union shop agreement.
3. Refusing to bargain collectively with the employer.
4. Picketing or conducting a secondary boycott or strike (that is, against someone other than the employer with whom the union has a dispute) for an illegal purpose.
5. Setting excessive initiation fees under a union shop agreement.
6. Forcing an employer to pay for work not performed ("featherbedding").
7. Picketing to require an employer to recognize or bargain with a union that has not been certified as the bargaining agent.

Also the LMRA prohibits an employer and union from agreeing that the employer will refrain from dealing in the products of another employer who is considered to be unfair to the union. Such contracts are called *hot-cargo agreements*.

If the board finds that the employer or union charged has committed an unfair labor practice, it orders the offending party to "cease and desist." It may also order affirmative action to remedy the harm caused by the violation. Suppose Jacob was discharged because he was trying to get fellow employees to join a union. The employer would be ordered to reinstate him with back-pay. An employer who has committed an unfair practice by making threats or promises before an election might be required to mail an NLRB notice to the employees, and a new election might be directed.

An employer or union that wishes to contest an order of the NLRB has two choices: It may appeal the order directly to the U.S. Court of

Appeals or it may wait for the NLRB to apply to that court for enforcement of its order.

Advance Industries Div. v. NLRB
540 F.2d 878 (7th Cir. 1976)

FACTS About 80 out of 150 employees of the Advance Industries Division of Overhead Door Corporation participated in a strike to attempt to force Advance Industries to bargain with the United Brotherhood of Carpenters. The strike failed. The company refused to take back employees who were involved in misconduct during and just after the strike. The first two acts occurred during the strike. Darlene Romenesko was fired for drawing a handgun from under her coat and shooting out a light in the company parking lot. Betty Koester was fired for pounding on a nonstriker's car and shaking, though not damaging, a post in the plant driveway. Five other employees were discharged for refusing to leave the plant after being told their work had ended for the day. This occurred on the second shift the day the plant reopened after the strike. Although they had normally worked until midnight, their supervisor told them their work would end when they finished 40 hours for the week at 10 P.M. They complained to other supervisors and to their union business agent. The business agent advised them to "stay working even though they turn the lights off." After further conversations between the employees and supervisors, the police was called and arrested the employees for refusing to leave. The NLRB ordered that the employees be reinstated.

ISSUE Did Advance Industries commit an unfair labor practice in firing the employees? (If the activities for which the employees were fired were proper concerted activities for their mutual aid and protection, the firings would be an unfair labor practice.)

DECISION The court reinstated only Koester. It said: "Trivial rough incidents or moments of animal exuberance must be distinguished from misconduct so violent or of such a serious character as to render the employee unfit for further service." It held that Darlene Romenesko's conduct was sufficiently serious to justify refusal to rehire her. The bringing to the plant and use of a gun could have a strong coercive effect on nonstrikers. However, it held that Betty Koester's acts were not serious enough to justify refusal to reinstate her. The court said that employees have a right to make limited use of their employer's property in exercising their rights under the NLRA. However, here they failed to use the established grievance procedure to process their complaint. Instead they abused their employer's property rights by refusing to leave at the end of their shift when ordered to do so. This prevented the employer from closing the plant for the night.

DISCRIMINATION IN EMPLOYMENT

Title VII, The Civil Rights Act of 1964   As amended extensively in 1972, this act prohibits discrimination by employers on the basis of race, color, religion, sex, or national origin. The employer cannot use any of these human differences to make distinctions for purposes of hiring, firing, promoting, fixing pay rates, or other terms and conditions of employment such as "fringe benefits" like pensions and medical insurance.

Discrimination based on religion, sex, or national origin is permitted where one of these characteristics is a *bona fide occupational qualification (BFOQ)*. A Christian church would not have to consider a Moslem as an applicant for choir director. A country club could limit its employment of attendants in its men's locker room to men. The courts have given a narrow interpretation to this exception, however. No BFOQ exception is permitted with respect to discrimination based on race or color.

Diaz v. Pan American World Airways
442 F.2d 385 (5th Cir. 1971)

FACTS   Celio Diaz applied for a job as a cabin attendant with Pan American World Airways. He was rejected because Pan Am had a policy of restricting its hiring for that position to women. Diaz sued for violation of Title VII. Pan Am testified that its policy was based on long experience with both male and female flight attendants. It had found that on the average, women were better than men in reassuring anxious passengers and in giving courteous, personalized service. Most Pan Am passengers had said they preferred female flight attendants. A psychologist testified that a plane in flight is a unique environment where passengers have special psychological needs that are better attended to by women. The trial court had held for Pan Am. It found that women on the average were better able to perform the nonmechanical functions of the flight attendant's job.

ISSUE   Is being a woman a bona fide occupational qualification (BFOQ) for flight attendants?

DECISION   No. The appeals court reversed, declaring that the primary function of an airline is to transport passengers safely from one point to another; a pleasant environment is secondary. Pan Am may consider the ability of individuals to perform the nonmechanical functions of the job in its hiring. However, it cannot exclude all men just because most men may not perform adequately.

The act applies to employers engaged in interstate commerce who have 15 or more employees on each working day of 20 or more calendar weeks in the current or the preceding calendar year. It applies also to state and local government positions.

Administration of the act is by the *Equal Employment Opportunity Commission (EEOC)*, which can act on its own or in response to complaints of discrimination by applicants or employees. If attempts at settlement fail, it may bring an action in the federal courts to require steps to correct discrimination that is found to exist. This may involve money awards to those discriminated against, "affirmative action" hiring or promotion plans, or other remedial action. Lawsuits by persons who claim discrimination are also permitted.

The U.S. Supreme Court recently upheld voluntary *affirmative action plans*.[2] This ruling permits employers and unions, even where there has been no previous discrimination, to agree to give preference to members of minority groups until their numbers in certain jobs approximate those in the local mix of the population.

Griggs v. Duke Power Co.
401 U.S. 424 (U.S. Sup. Ct. 1971)

FACTS   Prior to 1965, Duke Power Co. had openly discriminated against blacks in hiring and assigning employees in its Dan River plant. It later had required a high school education for assignment to its three "inside" departments. After Title VII became effective, it began requiring scores at about the national median for high school students on a certain intelligence test and on an aptitude test. To assist employees who lacked a good education, it began paying two thirds of the cost of high school training courses. The company had no proof that employees who passed these tests were better able to perform the inside jobs. Employees who had neither completed high school nor taken the tests continued to perform satisfactorily in the inside departments. A smaller proportion of blacks than whites who took the test passed it.

ISSUE   Is the use of a test that cannot be shown to be related to on-the-job performance a violation of Title VII of the Civil Rights Act when performance on it varies between races?

DECISION   Yes. The U.S. Supreme Court said, "The act proscribes not only overt discrimination but also practices that are fair in form, but discriminatory in operation. . . . If an employment practice which operates to exclude Negroes cannot be shown to be related to job performance the practice is prohibited."

The Equal Pay Act of 1963

This act requires employers covered by the statute to pay employees of both sexes equally for jobs that require equal skill, effort, and responsibility. The result is to raise the lower rate. Different rates of pay are permitted under seniority and merit systems as well as under piecework or other incentive systems. The courts require only that jobs that are comparable be substantially equal; they need not be identical. The act is administered by the Wage and Hour Division of the Labor Department. The employers covered are the same as those covered by the Wage and Hour Act.

---

[2] *Weber v. Kaiser Aluminum & Chemical Corp.*, 47 USLW 4851 (1979).

Hodgson v. Security National Bank
460 F.2d 57 (8th Cir. 1972)

FACTS The Security National Bank of Sioux City hired both men and women to work as paying and receiving tellers. All of the men were paid higher salaries than any of the women. Some of the women had more banking experience and more education than some of the men who were paid more while doing the same work. The bank claimed that the pay differential was permitted in the Equal Pay Act because it was based upon a "factor other than sex."

It claimed that all of the men were in the bank's management training program and that they rotated between different teller windows for 18 to 24 months to gain experience. The bank also claimed that the women who had college training and previous banking experience were not considered for management training because of pregnancy or the likelihood that their husbands would be transferred out of Sioux City. The rotation of the men did not follow the specific plan described in the written management training program. The rotation of both men and women tellers was random and appeared to be geared to the bank's personnel needs, not to training benefits.

ISSUE Was the pay differential between men and women justified under the Equal Pay Act?

DECISION No. The court held that the bank violated the act. It said that the bank's excuse for excluding women from its management training program was not acceptable. It indicates an outmoded, traditional notion that women, because of their principal roles as wives and mothers, must occupy a status second to men outside the home.

Age Discrimination Act

This act prohibits covered employers from refusing to hire, paying less to, or discharging or otherwise discriminating against employees because of their age. Labor unions are also prohibited from excluding from their membership or otherwise discriminating against persons because of age. Employment agency activities are also covered by the act. The protection given is to persons 40 through 69 years of age. Like the Equal Pay Act, the statute is enforced by the Wage and Hour Division of the Labor Department.

A BFOQ exemption is provided. For example, a drama company would be able to limit its casting for a teenager's part to young people.

State Legislation

Thirty-five states and some cities and counties have statutes that prohibit discrimination in employment on the basis of race, religion, sex, or national origin. Under Title VII of the act, EEOC defers to them for investigation of complaints even against firms engaged in interstate commerce.

EMPLOYMENT RETIREMENT AND INCOME SECURITY ACT

In 1974 Congress passed the *Employment Retirement and Income Security Act (ERISA)*. Its purpose is to avoid in the future certain problems that have occurred with pension plans for employees. The problems included underfunding, dishonest or careless management of funds, and the loss of benefits by long-service employees who change employers, who are fired, or whose employers go out of business.

Coverage

The act covers both employer and union-sponsored pension plans. It does not require that employers have a pension plan. In fact, many plans were terminated because it was felt by their sponsors that the requirements of the act would be too difficult to meet.

Requirements

Under the act, existing and new plans must comply with certain standards. These include:

1. Heavy responsibilities are placed on the pension fund manager and others who make decisions about the investments and operation of a fund.
2. Certain information must be given to covered employees and to the Secretary of Labor.
3. Participation in the plan must begin within one year of employment unless 100 percent "vesting" is immediate. (*Vesting* occurs when contributions become credited to an individual employee's account. Many plans had no vesting, and the result was that if the employee quit or was fired he lost his claim to the retirement fund.)
4. Partial vesting must begin no later than after 10 years of employment and full vesting in no more than 15 years.
5. Credits for current service of employees must be fully funded.
6. Funding of credits for service of employees before the plan was established (past service) must be completed within 30 years for single-employer plans.

Pension Guaranty Corporation

A Pension Benefit Guaranty Corporation was formed by the act to provide insurance for plans whose total assets are insufficient to pay promised benefits. This might occur because of termination of the employer's business or certain other causes. The corporation is funded by a small premium for each covered employee, paid by the pension plan.

The Department of Labor and the Internal Revenue Service share in enforcing the act. Violations are subject to criminal and civil penalties.

QUESTIONS AND PROBLEM CASES

1. Contrast the purposes of the Occupational Safety and Health Act (OSHA) and workmen's compensation laws? Are they state or federal legislation?

2. What is the purpose of defining in the Labor Management Relations Act a group of prohibited unfair labor practices for both employers and labor unions? What punishment can be applied and how?

3. Under what circumstances might BFOQ be a defense to a charge of discrimination in employment against an employer?

4. Does the Employment Retirement and Income Security Act require employers to grant pensions to employees? Does it forbid vesting of pension benefits?

5. Southern Contractors was hired to disassemble a missile launching tower at Cape Kennedy. An employee fell to his death from an exposed beam. OSHA conducted an investigation and issued a citation because no safety device was in use. OSHA had previously issued the following regulation:

   > A safety net should be provided when workplaces are more than 25 feet above [the surface] where the use of ladders, scaffolds, . . . or safety belts is impractical.

   The citation was contested by Southern. A safety specialist testified at the hearing that only a safety belt with a lanyard would provide the worker with enough mobility. The Administrative Law Judge ruled that because a safety net was impractical there was no violation. Did Southern violate OSHA?

6. Etha Schillinger was purchasing agent for Swiss Colony, Inc. The firm's business that she was responsible for expanded from $2 to $13 million in ten years while she held this position. This created many pressures on her, although at the end of the ten years she had three employees working under her supervision. In addition, her immediate supervisor was brusque and belittling to her on all occasions. She began to suffer physical and mental problems and was hospital-

ized on several occasions. Finally she had to take a different job with the firm at reduced pay because of these conditions. She applied for workmen's compensation for the mental injury that she claimed arose from her employment. Is she entitled to it?

7. The Otsego Ski Club operated a resort hotel and restaurant. Its employees went on strike. Seven of the striking employees were fired for misconduct during the strike. The NLRB ordered that four of these be reinstated. One of these had spread nails on the main driveway into the resort. Two of the others had served as "lookouts" in this incident. The fourth was discharged for throwing an egg at the windshield of a nonstriker. The administrative law judge had accepted this striker's uncorroborated denial despite the testimony of two Pinkerton guards that they had seen her do it. Were the discharges unfair labor practices?

8. Gregory was offered employment by Litton Systems, Inc., as a sheet metal mechanic. As part of the hiring procedure he completed a form called "Preliminary Security Information." It required a listing of all arrests other than for minor traffic violations. Gregory listed 14 such arrests, none resulting in conviction. Only one arrest had occurred in the last nine years. Following its policy, Litton withdrew the offer of employment. Gregory brought an action under Title VII, claiming discrimination on the basis of race. Litton followed its policy without regard to race. However, evidence at the trial showed that although blacks comprise 11 percent of the population, they account for 27 percent of arrests. They also account for 45 percent of the arrests reported as "suspicious arrests." There was also evidence that as a group there was no difference in efficiency and honesty between those who had been arrested but not convicted and those who had not been arrested. Is the Litton policy, as applied, a violation of Title VII?

9. Betty J. Moses had served as secretary to Griesedieck, an officer of Falstaff Brewing Corporation, for 22 years. She was discharged when

he retired as chairman of the board. She was told the position as secretary to Griesedieck had been eliminated, and this was consistent with Falstaff's policy. Secretaries of executive officers remained with them as they changed positions within Falstaff. The position was eliminated when they left the company. Moses was 48 when discharged. Older women remained at work as secretaries. She brought suit for age discrimination under Title VII. Was Title VII violated?

Business Organizations

PART FIVE

Introduction to Business Organizations

25

TYPES OF BUSINESS ORGANIZATIONS

I f you wish to start a business you have a variety of legal types from which to choose. The most common types are sole proprietorship, partnership (including limited partnership), and corporation. A few other seldom used types will be discussed in Chapter 32. There are advantages and disadvantages to each form of business organization; these will be discussed in Chapter 32. First, however, you need to know some of the basic characteristics of each form and the legal rules that apply to their operation. These will be discussed in the next few chapters.

Many businesses are conducted as part of a franchise system. This is not a "type of business organization" as the term is used here. A franchised business may be operated by any of the types of organizations just mentioned.

SOLE PROPRIETORSHIP

A *sole proprietorship* is merely an extension of the individual owner. The business is literally *his* or *her* business. Agents and employees may be hired, but the owner has all the responsibility; all profit, or loss, is the owner's.

The business may be conducted under a trade name. For example, Jeffrey Miller might open a restaurant and call it "The Red Door." Suppose a customer choked on a bone in the fish chowder and sued Miller. The complaint would probably be addressed in the following manner: "Jeffrey

Miller, d/b/a/ The Red Door," *d/b/a/* being an abbreviation for "doing business as." The complaint describes the business although the suit is brought against Jeffrey Miller as an individual.

PARTNERSHIP

Nature of a Partnership

The Uniform Partnership Act (UPA) is in effect in 48 states. It declares: *"A partnership is an association of two or more persons to carry on as co-owners a business for profit."* If one receives a share of the profits from a business, he or she is likely to be treated as a partner, and the UPA says that this is prima facie evidence of a partnership. However, sometimes people in other relationships are given shares in the profits of a business. The UPA mentions five such situations: (1) payment on a debt, (2) wages or rent, (3) an annuity to a widow or representative of a deceased partner, (4) interest on a loan, and (5) consideration for the sale of the goodwill of a business (that is, a sale of a going business). If you are going to share in the profits of a business and do not want to have the liabilities of a partner, it is important to have a written agreement clearly stating your relationship to the business.

Carrying on a Business

Any trade, occupation, or profession is treated as a business in determining the existence of a partnership; however, the *objective* must be to make a *profit*. People who are involved in a nonprofit association are not partners.

For example, a group of people may form a club or association to promote understanding of China. It may sell books and pamphlets on China to its members and others. If those who sell books and administer the affairs of the association are paid salaries but no one is entitled to share in any surplus, none of the members would be a partner. The same is true of a food-buying cooperative. If the purpose is to reduce the food costs of the members, this is not a partnership.

Co-ownership

For there to be a partnership there must be *co-ownership*, which means ownership of the business as such. It does not require that the property used in the business be owned by the partnership or in equal shares by the partners. In fact, the property and capital used in the business of a partnership can be supplied entirely by a single partner. Or the property may be leased from others and the working capital borrowed.

The term *co-ownership* in the UPA really means *a community of interest*. In a partnership there is a community of interest in the property of the partnership, even if the only property is undivided profits. There is also a community of interest or sharing in the management of the business.

Disputes on the Existence of a Partnership

There are often disputes as to whether or not there is or has been a partnership. Lawsuits tend to arise in two situations: (1) creditors may allege the existence of a partnership when a business fails if someone who had a right to share in the profits has enough assets to pay the debt, and (2) associates in a successful business may claim they were partners in order to share in the profits.

A clearly expressed intent not to share losses is evidence that the business relationship is not a partnership. A failure to agree on sharing losses has little meaning, however. Few people who enter business expect losses. Lawsuits raising the question of whether or not there is a partnership usually arise where arrangements have been casual. Disputes are more likely when there are no written articles of partnership.

Rosenberger v. Herbst
232 A.2d 634 (Sup. Ct. Pa. 1967)

FACTS Parzych operated a farm owned by Herbst under a written agreement. The contract gave Parzych the use of the farm and acknowledged his debt to Herbst in the amount of $6,000, at 5 percent interest. Herbst and Parzych were to share equally in profits and losses. The contract stated that the farming operations were to be "under the full control of Parzych." It also said: "The parties do not intend by this agreement to establish a partnership, but rather the relation of Debtor and Creditor and Landlord and Tenant." Parzych bought farm supplies from Rosenberger. When they were not paid for, Rosenberger demanded payment from Herbst. Parzych had told Rosenberger that he was a partner of Herbst, and Rosenberger had relied upon that statement. Herbst was unaware of this statement.

ISSUE Was Herbst liable for the supplies either because he was a partner of Parzych or because he had been represented as a partner?

DECISION No. The contract clearly stated the intent that the sharing of profits was to be considered rental payments. Therefore, Herbst was not a partner. Although Parzych said Herbst was his partner, there is no evidence that Herbst himself had said anything to Rosenberger or done anything that would be a representation to this effect, nor did he consent to Parzych's statement.

One who *shares in the management* of the business as well as in the profits is more likely to be considered a partner. However, a creditor can be given veto power and the right to be consulted on major decisions without being held a partner. On the other hand, one or a few of the partners may be in charge of the day-to-day management of the business without danger to its status as a partnership.

In short, a court that is forced to determine whether a business is a partnership must look at all the facts. If, overall, there appears to be a *community of interest*, a partnership is found. Usually a sharing in both the profits and making the important management decisions results in a partnership. The decisions suggest that courts are less likely to find partnerships in disputes that involve farming and ranching operations than in similar cases in other types of business.

Grissum v. Reesman
505 S.W.2d 81 (Sup. Ct. Mo. 1974)

FACTS Nora Grissum lived on a farm with her brother, Elwood Grissum, for 30 years. Title to the farm was in the name of Elwood. All proceeds from the farming operation except for their living expenses were reinvested in additional land, livestock, and equipment. Nora was the housekeeper, kept the accounts, fed livestock, and did other heavy farm work. She was consulted by her brother concerning the purchase and sale of land as well as livestock. She usually went with him to buy or sell livestock. Elwood had placed a sign on one of the buildings, visible from the highway, that read, "Elwood & Nora Grissum—Boonville, Mo." There was a similar sign on the farm truck. Elwood had told a number of people in Nora's presence that they were 50–50 partners.

The farm insurance was applied for and issued in both names. However, Elwood filed individual tax returns and alone signed all notes for borrowed money. The bank account was in his name until 1967 when it was changed to a joint account. Elwood died in 1970. Nora claimed her share of the farm, the farm equipment, livestock, and feed.

ISSUE Was Nora Grissum a partner with equal ownership of all the property?

DECISION Yes. The court said it should not be expected that people like the Grissums would know the usual or legal requirements and incidents of a partnership. The fact that some aspects of the partnership business were conducted in the individual name of Elwood Grissum was not controlling. Nora was not an employee or wife, so the court was convinced she was a partner.

Associates who fail to carry out an intention to incorporate a business are likely to be found to be partners. Suppose you and a friend intend to start a corporation, and the friend makes several contracts in the name of the proposed corporation. You will be held liable as a partner on those contracts.

A Partnership as an Entity

The UPA treats a partnership as an entity separate from the partners for some purposes. For other purposes it is viewed as an aggregate of the individual partners. For example, a partnership may own and transfer property in the firm name. Accounting is between the firm and the partners rather than merely among partners. Firm creditors are given priority in firm assets. In each of these cases the partnership is treated as separate from the partners. On the other hand, there is no provision for suits in the firm name. (The firm name can be used in some states under other statutes.) If the restaurant, "The Red Door," is operated by a partnership, a suit might be brought against it in the name: "Jeffrey Miller and Janet Miller, d/b/a/ The Red Door."

Limited Partnership

The limited partnership, a variation of the ordinary or general partnership is discussed in Chapter 28. It permits investors who do not engage in management to share in the profits of the business without becoming personally liable for its debts.

CORPORATION

Nature of a Corporation

The concept of a corporation developed in early law. Its advantage was that it permitted property to be held over long periods of time. This is because the *corporation* is treated by the law as an *intangible being* that is separate from its members; its life is not affected by their death.

Other powers early came to be associated with the corporate form of organization. It can acquire, hold, and convey property in its own name. It can also sue and be sued in its own name. It has a right to have a seal, which was the symbol used to validate documents in earlier times when few people could write. Today the corporate seal is kept by the corporate secretary and is used on important documents such as deeds. Corporations also have the right to make bylaws to govern the relations of the members of the corporation with each other.

These powers are held by corporations today. The principal reason to incorporate a business today, however, is the *limited liability* of its shareholders. Ordinarily, the owners of a corporation are not liable for its debts. Their loss is limited to their investment.

The early corporations were municipalities, churches, and the guilds of tradesmen in the Middle Ages. The business corporation is a much later development. In English-American law it had its beginning with the large joint-stock trading companies chartered by the king or queen beginning in 1600. These companies were given an exclusive right to establish settlements and to trade in a certain part of the world. Their powers were governmental as well as commercial. They were given the right to have a military force and sometimes even to coin money. One of these, the Hudson's Bay Company, still operates in Canada.

Types of Corporations

Today three types of corporations are recognized. The first is a *governmental corporation*, often called a *municipal corporation*. Examples are a city, a school corporation, and a sewage district. They usually have the power to tax. Other government corporations have no taxing power, however. Often they operate much like a business corporation except that they do not seek to make a profit. Examples are the Tennessee Valley Authority and the Federal Home Loan Bank.

The second type, *nonprofit corporations*, are similar to nontaxing governmental corporations; however they are formed and operated by private persons. They include hospitals, clubs, and some very large businesses like Blue Cross and Blue Shield. Their founders and members are not permitted to make a profit from the operation of the corporation, although, of course, their officers as well as employees are paid salaries. All states have a special statute under which not-for-profit corporations are formed.

The third type, the *for-profit corporation*, is the most common. The aim of such corporations is usually to make a profit that may be distributed to the shareholders as dividends. Sometimes, however, most or all of the profits are reinvested to make the business grow. At a later time shareholders may sell their stock or the entire business may be sold. In this way the shareholders pay only the lower capital gains tax rather than an income tax on the retained profits.

From here on in this book we shall discuss only the for-profit corporation. However, many of the legal principles and rules are the same for all corporations.

For-profit corporations are often divided into publicly held and close corporations. The stock of a *close* (privately held) *corporation* is held by a family or a small group of people who know each other. Usually some or all of them intend to be active in the management and operation of the business. An example is a family owned and operated retail shop. A *publicly held corporation* sells shares to people who may have little interest in it except as investors. General Motors Corporation is a good example. Of course, most publicly held corporations are much smaller. In general, however, the largest corporations are publicly held. Sometimes an individual or a family controls even very large corporations. An example is the Ford Motor Company. In a large corporation with the stock owned by many scattered shareholders, ownership of less than 10 percent of the shares may be enough for control.

A *Subchapter S corporation* is a for-profit corporation that is taxed as a partnership under the Internal Revenue Code. The principal limitation is that the corporation must have no more than 15 shareholders.

"Piercing the Corporate Veil"

Normally shareholders in corporations are not personally liable for debts of the corporation. Sometimes a creditor is able to persuade a court to disregard this separateness between shareholder and corporation, however. If so, it is said that the court has "pierced the corporate veil." This is done by a court to give the creditor a judgment against one or more of the shareholders. The shareholders held liable are usually only those who are active in the management of the business.

There are several situations in which such a court judgment may be made. One situation is when the corporation is given so few assets by its promoters that it could not be expected to pay its debts. Starting a corporation "on a shoestring" (called a "thin incorportion" or "thin capitalization") is not unlawful; however, it may amount to fraud if the objective seems to be to operate a risky business while avoiding the claims of creditors.

A number of cases have held shareholders personally liable where they mixed their personal business dealings and corporate transactions as if all were personal. The corporation is then viewed as the *alter ego* of the shareholder-manager. Sometimes courts call it a "mere instrumentality." The danger is greater if corporate formalities such as holding shareholder and directors meetings are not observed.

Similar principles are followed by courts in dealing with suits against corporations that operate a part of their business through a subsidiary corporation. If the subsidiary is given few assets and most decisions are made by the parent, the parent may be held liable for the subsidiary's debts.

Kilpatrick Bros., Inc. v. Poynter
473 P.2d 33 (Sup. Ct. Kan. 1970)

FACTS   W. R. Poynter operated a Ford dealership through a corporation. All its share were registered in Mrs. Poynter's name. He became interested in building portable motel rooms. He leased in his own name a portion of a building. He then incorporated Economotels, Inc., to manufacture these units in the leased space. He was the only shareholder. The articles showed a paid-up capital of $1,000. Economotels built units for seven months and then ceased activity, owing $93,726 to unsecured creditors.

Standard Buildings, Inc., was then incorporated with Mrs. Poynter as the only shareholder. It built mobile classrooms in the leased space for about a year. It ceased operations, owing unsecured creditors $66,218. It was followed by Modern Structures, which manufactured mobile classrooms in the same space for eight months. The equipment, supplies, and materials remaining were sold and the proceeds went to pay loans personally guaranteed by Mr. and Mrs. Poynter.

W. R. Poynter was president of all three corporations. No board of directors meetings were held. Each corporation took over the equipment and supplies of its predecessor without a formal sale or a price being established. Funds were shifted between the three corporations and Poynter Motors. Suppliers to all three corporations seek to hold W. R. Poynter personally liable

ISSUE   Should the corporate veil be pierced to hold Poynter personally liable?

DECISION   Yes. The court said that Poynter seemed to consider the funds and assets as his own in shifting them back and forth between corporations. The *alter ego* doctrine puts liability on a person who uses a corporation merely as an instrumentality to conduct his or her own personal business. Since Poynter disregarded the fact that the corporations were separate from himself, so should the court.

FRANCHISING

Franchising has become one of the most common ways of conducting business in the United States. It is estimated that franchise outlets sold more than $100 billion of goods and services through approximately 400,000 outlets in 1979.

Automobiles, gasoline, and certain home appliances like refrigerators and washing machines have long been sold through franchise arrangements. The great growth of franchising, however, has come in the last quarter-century. It has become the most common arrangement in providing certain services. This is particularly true in the fast-food industry (for example, McDonald's) and motels (Holiday Inns), but franchises are also used in many other fields. A few examples include Century 21 real estate brokerage firms, Culligan water softeners, H & R Block tax preparing services, and Muzak sound systems.

The franchising relationship is contractual. The franchisor has developed a product or service or a particular pattern of marketing it, and the franchisee becomes an outlet in what appears to be a regional or national (or even international) chain. The franchisor may conduct its business as a sole proprietorship, partnership, or corporation; so may the franchisee. Typically the franchisor is a corporation, and often the franchisee forms a corporation to own and operate the franchised business.

Franchising may combine the advantages of a small business managed by its owner and the resources, especially marketing impact, available only to large firms. The franchisee may be interested mainly in securing the privilege of selling a highly advertised product. Usually one of the most important advantages of a franchise to the franchisee is the right to use a trademark owned by the franchisor that is well known and/or highly advertised. In addition, many franchisors have developed a standardized and tested method of conducting the business, whether it is producing hamburgers, conducting an employment service, or replacing automobile mufflers, that will be adopted by the franchisee.

From the franchisee's standpoint, especially if he or she has had little or no experience in the business being franchised, the most important services of the franchisor are likely to be advertising, training in the business, and advice after the business is under way. Some franchisors also assist with financing. They may build and equip the place of business and lease it to the franchise—a so-called "turnkey operation."

One of the major advantages of franchising for the franchisor, however, is the possibility of rapid expansion by using the financial resources of the franchisees. Through franchising, the franchisor can gain considerable control over the distribution of its products or services without owning the retail outlets. By carefully controlling the number and location of outlets, the franchisor can reduce competition among them and perhaps encourage them not to carry competitive products. This may make the franchise organization's competition against similar products (or services) more effective by encouraging bigger investments and more aggressive marketing by franchisees. Efforts may also be made to influence prices charged by the franchisee. Where the franchisee prepares a product, such as food, or offers a service, the franchisor usually maintains a high degree of control over operations to standardize quality.

Franchisee Complaints

Although many franchisees have been very successful, some have quickly lost their life savings. Of course, there are risks in any business; not all McDonald's franchisees have been successful. However, some franchisors have grossly misrepresented the opportunities for success of their franchisees and the assistance that the franchisor will actually provide. All franchise contracts are typical "contracts of adhesion" as discussed in Chapter 12. Some contain terms that may bring hardship to franchisees who are acting in good faith and performing reasonably well under the contract. Termination clauses frequently give broad discretion to the franchisor. The term of the contract may be short—only a year for the typical service station contract—with no assurance of the right to renew or to transfer a going business to another. Some contracts even prohibit franchisees from joining franchisee associations.

Franchisor Problems

In an attempt to control distribution to maximize its profits and perhaps those of its franchisees, franchisors run the risk of violation of federal and state antitrust laws. Attempts to require franchisees to buy products, equipment, and supplies exclusively from the franchisor may violate the prohibition in the Clayton Act against tie-in sales. Attempts to require adherence to prices set by the franchisor and prohibitions against sales to customers outside an assigned sales territory may violate the Sherman Act. These risks can better be understood after studying Chapter 48.

Franchise contracts usually declare that the franchisee is an independent contractor and is not an agent or employee of the franchisor. However, in an effort to maintain the quality of the product or service offered by the franchisee, and thus the value of its trademark, the franchisor often exerts considerable control over many aspects of the franchisee's operations. This control has been sufficient in many cases to cause courts to hold that the franchisee is not an independent contractor. Thus the franchisor becomes liable for torts committed by the franchisee as discussed in Chapter 22.[1] Although insurance can cover this risk in most cases, lawsuits against the franchisor can be damaging to reputation as well as a time-consuming diversion for the franchisor's executives.

Government Regulation

After a number of persons who were inexperienced in business had been ruined financially by believing extravagant claims of the wealth-building

---

[1] See also Problem Case 6, Chapter 20.

potential of franchises or had suffered unfair terminations, federal and state governments began to regulate franchisors. A majority of the states have statutes that limit franchisors' power to terminate, control the advertising of franchisors, and/or prohibit certain other practices and certain franchise contract provisions thought to be unfair to franchisees.

At the federal level, the Automobile Dealer's Day in Court Act was passed in 1956. It aims to protect dealers from coercive practices, including abrupt terminations, by automobile manufacturers. A later federal statute gives some protection to service station operators. After a long study, the Federal Trade Commission issued rules under Section 5 of the Federal Trade Commission Act aimed primarily at giving prospective franchisees more information. These became effective in October 1979. They require franchisors to explain termination, cancellation, and renewal provisions of the franchise contract. Franchisors must disclose the number of franchisees terminated in the past year and the reasons for termination. All restrictions on franchisees must be included in the agreement, which makes them more vulnerable to attack under the antitrust laws. All representations made to prospective franchisees must have a "reasonable basis." Violations are subject to a $10,000 per day civil penalty and the FTC can sue on behalf of injured purchasers. State laws vary widely in their provisions.

QUESTIONS AND PROBLEM CASES

1. Does the requirement of co-ownership necessary for a partnership mean that property used by a partnership is co-owned by the partners?

2. What does the term "piercing the corporate veil" mean? Under what circumstances does this occur?

3. Discuss the relationship between franchising and sole proprietorships, partnerships, and corporations.

4. Discuss briefly the objectives of the federal statutes and rules regulating franchising.

5. Johnson and McNaughton jointly leased a parcel of land. Johnson paid the cost of erecting a building on it. McNaughton operated a package liquor store in the building. Their agreement was that McNaughton would receive $60 per week in salary and pay 50 percent of the balance of net profits to Johnson. Johnson loaned McNaughton the funds to stock the store but this was repaid. The business was carried on in McNaughton's name, who managed the business and its finances. The business ran into financial difficulty. Escoe sued Johnson on dishonored checks given by McNaughton, alleging a partnership. Did a partnership exist?

6. When Charlie Borum died, he left his home to his wife for life and the remainder to his four children. After the wife died, the children continued to live in the home. They shared equally the cost of taxes, insurance, and repairs and improvements on the home. They also shared living expenses, but each bought his or her own clothing. Was this a partnership?

7. Plesko invited Shain to join him in buying a tavern. Shain agreed but said he did not want to work in it. He arranged with Bengston, an employee in Shain's pawnshop, to work in the tavern. Plesko put $16,000 and Shain $6,000 into the partnership. Bengston continued to work in the pawnshop from 10:15 A.M. to 4:00 P.M. and was paid the same salary as

before. He worked in the tavern from 4:00 until closing. Neither Shain nor Bengston drew any money from the tavern. The tavern was quite profitable. About six months after the purchase, Shain told Bengston to run the pawnshop for him and that Shain would work in the daytime and Plesko at night in the tavern. Shain then told Bengston he did not consider him a partner. Bengston brought suit, seeking dissolution of the partnership and an accounting. He claimed that Plesko owned a one-half interest and he and Shain each one-quarter interest. At the trial there was conflict between the statements of Shain and Bengston as to their conversations about Bengston's participation in the business. A CPA employed by Plesko and Shain had made an audit report showing Bengston as a partner. The liquor license had been taken out in the names of all three. Was Bengston a partner?

8. Olson was in the real estate business. He controlled and his family owned the stock of several corporations. All the corporations used the same office and employed the same bookeeper. Olson hired Zaist to clear and grade for shopping centers several parcels of land in three cities owned by these corporations. Zaist was told to send the bills, which eventually amounted to nearly $200,000, to East Haven, Inc., one of Olson's corporations. East Haven operated as a general contractor. It had its own checking account, separate corporate and financial records, and a number of employees. None of the parcels of land was held in the name of East Haven. They were owned by and transferred from time to time between Olson and the other corporations. Olson's operations got into financial trouble, and the interests in the lands graded by Zaist were sold. East Haven became insolvent, owing Zaist $23,000. Zaist sued Olson personally. He alleged that East Haven was a mere instrumentality and "the corporate veil should be pierced." Is Olson personally liable?

9. Carlton organized and was the principal shareholder in ten corporations. Each owned and operated two taxicabs in New York City. Each corporation carried the minimum liability insurance required by state statute. The vehicles, the only assets other than the taxi licenses of each corporation, were mortgaged. The 20 cabs were operated more or less as one business with respect to employees, repairs, and supplies. Walkovszky was severely injured when run over by one of the taxis. He sues Carlton personally. Should the "corporate veil be pierced?"

10. George Arnott moved from Minneapolis to Sioux Falls, South Dakota, in 1972 after leasing an Amoco service station on an interstate highway. The lease required the station to remain open 24 hours per day. He was given a copy of an Amoco Statement of Policy that declared that dealers were free to stock competing brands of motor oils, tires, batteries, and accessories as well as those offered by Amoco. It also said that dealers had a right to set their own resale prices.

In practice Amoco representatives threatened not to renew Arnott's lease on several occasions for not adhering to the resale prices desired by Amoco and once for carrying competing tires. Amoco retained Arnott's copy of a one-year renewal of the lease for several months, telling him he was on probation for not being cooperative. Amoco established an allocation system during the oil embargo of 1973. Although he put a limit on sales of gasoline to his customers, Arnott frequently ran out of gasoline. Amoco wanted him to keep the station open 24 hours but to put up "out of gas" signs during the day to send customers to downtown stations. This was highly unprofitable because gasoline was his primary source of revenue. He informed Amoco that he was closing down from 10:00 P.M. to 6:00 A.M. Amoco told him this was a violation of his lease. Shortly thereafter Amoco cancelled the lease. Arnott brought suit alleging that Amoco had breached its duty by terminating the lease without good cause and not dealing with him in good faith. Is Arnott entitled to damages?

Formation and Operation of Partnerships

26

FORMATION OF PARTNERSHIPS

No Formalities

I f you and a friend decide to form a partnership, no written agreement nor government filing is required. In fact, you and your friend, as indicated in the preceding chapter, might find yourselves treated by a court as partners even without any such intent. Moreover, occasionally courts find partnerships where those involved in a joint project have expressly agreed that they will not be partners.

Partnership is a voluntary relationship. It cannot be forced upon one; nor is a person made a partner by gift or by inheriting property jointly with others. It is the result of at least an implied agreement between the partners to carry on a business together.

Purpose

A partnership can be formed to carry on any lawful business. It can widen its scope of business or shift to a different kind of business whenever its partners all agree to do so.

Name

A partnership is not required to adopt a firm name. Property may be held in the names of the partners, e.g., Joan Smith, Robert Brown, and Jessica Goldberg. The firm may adopt a name using one or more of the surnames of the partners, or it may adopt a fictitious trade name such as "The Wheelery" for a bicycle shop. A fictitious name must be registered under the state's assumed name statute. This often requires filing in each county in which the partnership does business. (An individual proprietorship is also required to file if it uses a name other than that of the owner.) The purpose is to disclose to the public the persons who are actually carrying on the business.

Articles of Partnership

Although not required, it is highly desirable to have written *articles of partnership*. A written contract tends to minimize misunderstanding and disagreement. The process of preparing such an agreement is likely to cause the parties to provide for contingencies they might not otherwise consider. This is especially true if a lawyer is called upon who is experienced in drafting partnership agreements.

Articles of partnership usually state how profits and losses are to be shared. They should provide a means for continuing the business upon the death or disability of a partner. Other matters usually included in articles of partnership are: name of the firm, the business to be carried on, the term for which the partnership is to exist, salary and drawing accounts, the authority of the partners to bind the firm, and provisions for withdrawal of partners.

Unless otherwise stated in the agreement, a partnership agreement can be modified only by consent of all partners.

PERSONS REPRESENTED TO BE PARTNERS

Holding out as Partner

You can be held liable as a partner without being a partner. If you go with a friend to a bank to borrow money and tell the banker that you and the friend are partners in a business, the banker can hold you liable as a partner. The same result would occur if the friend stated that you were his partner and you failed to correct the statement. However, if the friend went alone to the bank and told the banker you were his partner, you would not be liable.

Requirements for Liability

Some courts have held that persons who are aware that they have been held out as partners have a duty to correct a wrong impression. Otherwise they will be liable as partners. The Uniform Partnership Act (UPA) says that a person will not be held liable as a partner without consenting to the holding out. Standing by while one is described as a partner is considered implied consent. However, mere knowledge that one has been held out as a partner does not, under the UPA, require the person to correct the wrong impression.

The legal concept that is applicable is *estoppel*. The person who seeks to hold another liable as a partner must prove that he or she relied upon the holding out or consent. The reliance must be justifiable and must result in loss to the person who sold goods or otherwise relied upon the credit of the person held out as a partner. If reliance is justifiable, the defendant is *estopped* from claiming that there was, in fact, no partnership.

Wisconsin Telephone Co. v. Lehmann
80 N.W.2d 267 (Sup. Ct. Wis. 1957)

FACTS   Walter R. Lehmann had been in business with his son, Wayne, under the name, W. R. Lehmann and Son. Wayne withdrew from the business to become a dealer in calves. He operated this business out of a barn on his father's farm. On the barn was a sign, "W. R. Lehmann & Son—Dairy Cattle." The phone in the barn was listed in Wayne's name, and he paid the phone bills by his own checks. A year later Wayne requested the phone company to list the telephone under the name of W. R. Lehmann & Son. Bills were sent so addressed and paid by checks signed by Wayne. The December bill for $1,261.16 was not paid. This came a year and a half after this method of billing began. The telephone company then tried to collect from W. R. Lehmann. There was no proof that W. R. Lehmann knew that Wayne had listed the telephone in the name of W. R. Lehmann & Son. No bill was sent to Walter R. Lehmann until after Wayne had not paid the December bill.

ISSUE   Was Walter R. Lehmann liable for the bill?

DECISION   No. Under the UPA, Walter R. Lehmann would be liable only if the telephone company had given credit in reliance upon a representation that he was a partner. The telephone company must also prove that Walter R. Lehmann represented by words or conduct that he was a partner or consented to being represented as a partner. There was no such proof.

CAPACITY TO BE A PARTNER

Corporations

     The UPA includes corporations as persons who may form partnerships. The Model Business Corporation Act expressly authorizes corporations to enter partnerships. It is common for a corporation to be a partner, especially in limited partnerships that are tax shelters.

Minors and Insane Persons

     A minor may become a member of a partnership. He or she may withdraw at any time, however, by disaffirming the contract that established the partnership. The fact that a minor is a partner does not permit the partnership to disaffirm the contracts of the partnership. The minor cannot get back the capital he brought to the partnership unless all the creditors of the partnership can be paid.

     The UPA permits any partner to dissolve a partnership without penalty if one of the partners is adjudged insane. However, until a court has declared a person insane, that person is able to enter a partnership and function as a partner. He or she can withdraw by pleading insanity, just as a minor can withdraw.

MANAGEMENT AND AUTHORITY OF PARTNERS

Voice in Management

Each partner normally has an equal voice in managing the business. A vote of the majority prevails if there are more than two partners. This may be changed by agreement, however. One or a group of partners may, by agreement of the partners, be granted authority to make the day-to-day operating decisions of the business. This might include making usual contracts for goods and services and hiring and firing employees.

Unanimous agreement is required to act contrary to the partnership agreement. Such agreement is also necessary to change the nature of the business. Assume you are a member of a retail partnership. You decide that it would be a good investment to buy a nearby residence to put up for rent. Approval of all the partners is necessary. Such approval would also be required to authorize a sale of the entire inventory or the building in which the business is conducted.

When a certain action is proposed and there is an even split among the partners, the action cannot be taken. If it is an important matter and the deadlock continues, it may be impossible to continue the business. In such case, any partner may petition a court for dissolution of the partnership.

Authority to act for a partnership may be of three types: express, implied, and apparent. These concepts have the same meaning as under agency law, and the tests for implied and apparent authority are the same. Both implied and apparent authority are influenced by customs and usages of the particular partnership and those of similar businesses in the area.

Express Authority

A partner has express authority to do whatever he or she is authorized to do by the articles of partnership. In addition, express authority stems from any other agreement of the partners.

Implied Authority

The UPA states: "Every partner is an agent of the partnership for the purpose of its business." He or she can bind the partnership on contracts that are usually appropriate to that business. For example, if your partnership runs a ladies' ready-to-wear clothing store, any partner has the authority to buy dresses for resale. This implied authority may be abolished or limited by agreement of the partners, however.

Apparent Authority

When the agency authority of a partner is abolished or limited by agreement, the partner may still have apparent authority. Suppose, in the above example, that you and your partners, Roger and Jane, have agreed that all merchandise buying will be done by Jane. Suppose further, as is likely, that it is customary for all partners in this type of business to give merchandise orders. A manufacturer takes and fills an order given by Roger. If the manufacturer is unaware of the restriction, the partnership and ultimately you are bound.

A partner who has apparent authority to purchase goods for a partnership may purchase on credit. The partnership is liable even if the partner keeps the goods for his or her own use. In making sales the partner may bind the partnership with a warranty to the extent any agent can.

Trading and Nontrading Partnerships

In determining implied and apparent authority, courts often distinguish between trading and nontrading partnerships. The UPA does not expressly recognize this distinction. *A trading partnership is engaged in buying and selling for profit.* It may be in retailing, wholesaling, importing, or exporting. Other businesses that require substantial working capital, such as commercial farming, general contracting, and manufacturing, are treated as trading activities also. *Nontrading partnerships are generally those that provide a service.* The practice of medicine or accounting and the carrying on of a real estate brokerage or insurance business are treated as nontrading activities.

This distinction is made most often when a question of a partner's authority to borrow money is raised. Courts that make the distinction hold trading partnerships liable for money borrowed by a partner in the name of the partnership. A nontrading partnership may also be liable on apparent authority when the partners or those in other similar firms have previously borrowed money.

Of course, disputes as to authority arise only when the partnership claims the partner who borrowed had no authority to do so. If authority to borrow is found, the partnership is liable even if the partner converts the money to his or her own use. On the other hand, if money is borrowed by a partner in his or her own name, there is no partnership liability even if the money is used for partnership purposes.

If a partner has authority to borrow, he or she may sign negotiable instruments such as notes in the firm's name. If it is normal for such loans to be secured, the partner has power to pledge the firm's assets.

Holloway v. Smith
88 S.E.2d 909 (Sup. Ct. Va. 1955)

FACTS   Warren Ten Brook had an opportunity to purchase an automobile dealership. He did not have sufficient funds. Milton Smith and his wife, Maude, agreed to join him in a partnership to buy and operate the business. The capital was to be contributed equally; however, Ten Brook was to pay his share from the profits of the business. He was to devote full time to the business and serve as general manager. Either of the Smiths would sign all checks. Maude Smith kept the books and handled the partnership money. The business was short of operating funds. Mrs. Holloway, an acquaintance of Ten Brook, agreed to loan the firm $6,000. She made out the check to the partnership. It was deposited by one of the Smiths in the firm's bank account and was used to buy automobiles for resale. Unknown to the Smiths, Ten Brook gave her a note paying interest at 5 percent. He signed this for the partnership. The note was not paid. Mrs. Holloway brought an action on the note against Milton and Maude Smith and Ten Brook as partners d/b/a Greenwood Sales & Service. The Smiths argued that it was a loan to Ten Brook personally and that it was a capital contribution by him.

ISSUE   Were the Smiths liable on the note?

DECISION   Yes. In the absence of a limit on his authority known to Mrs. Holloway, Ten Brook had the same power to bind the partnership as his partners had. He got the loan apparently for carrying on in the usual way the business of the firm. The loan was made to the partnership.

Where Unanimous Consent Is Required

Agreement by all the partners is necessary to bind the partnership on certain actions. One of these is an act that would make it impossible to carry on the business of the partnership. To illustrate, an individual partner cannot sell the business or its goodwill. Nor can an individual make an assignment of the firm's property for the benefit of creditors.

The UPA also requires unanimous consent to submit a dispute involving the firm to arbitration. Today this seems strange, but arbitration was not viewed with much favor when the act was drafted. The UPA also prohibits a confession of judgment. This permits a third party with a claim against the firm to admit on behalf of the firm the propriety of the claim. It would prevent the other partners from contesting the claim.

An agreement of the firm to guarantee the debt of another, such as that of a partner, also requires unanimous consent. This is true of any contract of suretyship or indemnity that does not directly benefit the firm.

PROPERTY OF PARTNERSHIPS

What Is Partnership Property?

Disputes often arise as to what property is partnership property. As pointed out in Chapter 25, a partnership can get started without any partnership property. However, both nontrading and trading partnerships are likely to acquire at least some personal property.

All property that was originally contributed to the partnership by the partners is partnership property; so is property purchased then or later for the partnership. In addition, any property acquired with partnership funds is partnership property unless a contrary intent is clearly shown. The fact that property is used in the business does not make it partnership property. Assets that appear on the account books of the partnership are presumed to be partnership property. The payment of taxes or insurance on property may suggest but is not conclusive evidence that the property is owned by the partnership. The same is true if improvements are made on the property by the partnership.

Title to Partnership Property

It is not necessary to hold title in partnership property in the firm name. However, this is desirable because it is presumed that property so held belongs to the partnership. There is more likely to be a dispute if partnership property is held in the name of one or more but less than all of the partners.

Transfer of Title

Real property held in the name of the partnership may be conveyed by any partner authorized by the partners to do so. The deed must be in the name of the partnership and signed by the partner. If the partner was not authorized to give the deed, then the transferee must return the property if he did not pay value for it or know it was firm property. If the partner merely uses his own name on the deed, only an equitable title is transferred. The transferee then has a right to a properly prepared deed.

If real property of a partnership is held in the name of one or more, but not all, of the partners and they sign a deed, there is a problem. An innocent purchaser for value would get title good against the partnership. However, someone who knew that it was partnership property would not.

Partnership property may be held in the names of all the partners. A deed signed by all partners passes all their rights in the property.

Ownership and Possession

Partnership property is held by the partners as *tenants in partnership*. Partners have no separate interest in partnership property. They have no right to sell, mortgage, or devise to an heir any individual item of the firm's property.

A partner has a right to take possession of the firm's property for partnership purposes but not for personal use. For example, if you are a partner, you have no right to use the firm's automobile for your vacation. Permission of a majority of the partners would be required.

Creditors of Partners

A creditor of a partner may not attach any of the property owned by the partnership; however, a partner may assign her partnership interest to a creditor or to anyone else. This entitles the assignee to receive that partner's share of the profits. It does not give the assignee a right to any information about partnership affairs or a right to look at its books.

A creditor who gets a judgment against a partner may get from the court a *charging order* against the partner's interest in the firm. The court may appoint a receiver to look after the creditor's interests. If profits are insufficient to pay off the creditor, the court may order that the partner's interest be sold. The purchaser may dissolve the partnership if it is to exist for an indefinite time. If it is for a term of years that has not expired, the partnership will continue as originally agreed. *The purchaser will not be a partner,* nor can he or she exercise any of the partner's rights except to receive that share of the profits. The partnership or any partner may purchase the debtor's partnership interest by paying the debt.

COMPENSATION OF PARTNERS

Right to Compensation

A partner is not ordinarily entitled to salary or wages. The compensation is presumed to be the partner's share of profits. This is true even if one partner spends much more time than another on partnership business. The same principle applies to rent to a partner for use of the partner's property and to interest on a capital contribution. An exception is made by the UPA when a partner dies. Then any surviving partner is entitled to reasonable compensation for winding up partnership affairs.

Of course, the partners may agree that one or more of them is to be paid salary, rent, interest, or wages in addition to sharing in profits. Often drawing accounts for all partners are agreed on, or perhaps regular monthly payments are made. These are then deducted from the partner's share of profits when year-end settlements are made.

Disputes often arise over compensation. Therefore, it is advisable for the partners to discuss it and reach agreement. If the agreement is clearly stated in the articles of partnership, dispute will be minimized.

Profits and Losses

In the absence of a contrary agreement, profits are shared equally even if capital contributions are unequal. The sharing of losses is the same as the sharing of profits unless there is a different agreement.

DUTIES OF PARTNERS

The duties of partners to each other are substantially the same as those that agents owe to their principals. However, lawsuits against a partner for breaches of duty to the partnership are not usually permitted while the partnership exists. The remedy is through an action for an accounting supervised by a court. To permit lawsuits between partners would undermine the trust and confidence essential to a successful partnership.

Duty of Loyalty and Good Faith

Not only must partners be honest, but they also must not permit self-interest to come before duty to the partnership. Partners may buy from or sell to the partnership. However, if they do, they must make full disclosure of any facts relevant to the deal that are not known to the other partners. Partners may not make secret profits from their position as a member of a partnership.

<hr>

Liggett v. Lester
390 P.2d 351 (Sup. Ct. Ore. 1964)

FACTS   Odell Lester was a distributor of oil products. He and George Liggett formed a partnership to operate a service station. They expected that Lester's ability to purchase oil products at the distributors' discount would be an advantage to the partnership. Shortly after forming the partnership, Lester obtained a bulk plant. This entitled him to an additional one and a half cents per gallon discount on his purchases of oil products. He did not tell Liggett of this and did not pass it on to the partnership. When Liggett learned of the additional discount received by Lester, he claimed the partnership should have it. The service station was closed as a result of the dispute. Liggett then sued Lester for the profit made on the partnership purchases.

ISSUE   Was Liggett entitled to half of the jobbers' discount on purchases by the partnership?

DECISION   Yes. Lester breached the duty of loyalty and good faith one partner owes to another. He wrongfully withheld a secret profit from his partner.

<hr>

In the absence of a contrary understanding, each partner owes a duty to devote full time and his or her best efforts to the affairs of the partnership. A partner must not engage in activities that are in competition with or otherwise likely to injure the partnership. For example, suppose you join with a friend in forming a real estate brokerage partnership. If your partner accepts commissions for arranging sales of property not listed with the firm, the partnership is entitled to those commissions. A partner is also liable to the partnership for the value of partnership property he or she uses for individual purposes.

Duty of Care in Partnership Business

Partners have a duty to exercise reasonable care and skill in transacting business for the partnership. A further duty is not to exceed the authority granted to them by the partnership. Partners are liable for their negligence while acting for the partnership but not for honest errors of judgment.

Duty to Inform

Partners owe a duty to pass on to the other partners all information coming to them that may be important to the operation of the partnership. This is because a notice by a third person to any partner is treated as having been given to the partnership. Of course, this is not true if the third person has been told that all notices must be given to a certain partner.

A partner has a right to inspect the partnership books. It is presumed that all partners know what is in them. Failure to inform one's partners about such information is, therefore, not a breach of duty.

Duty to Account

Partners have a duty to account for any expenditure they make of partnership funds. They must also account for the sale or other disposal of partnership property. The same is true for any benefit or profit coming to them as partners. They also have a right to be reimbursed by the partnership for expenses on its behalf.

The duty of keeping the account books is usually assigned to one partner. He or she then has a duty to keep them accurately. If the records do not show a proper application of the funds coming to the firm, the partner will be liable for them.

The UPA establishes several situations in which a partner has a right to demand an *accounting*. An accounting is a formal statement of the partnership books. It shows the capital accounts of each partner and his or her share of undivided profits as well as partnership assets. It includes an accurate income statement for the appropriate period. A partner has the right to an accounting when excluded from the partnership business or from proper use of its property. The right also exists when there have been benefits or profits received by a partner without the consent of the other partners.

An accounting assumes agreement by all the partners that the statements prepared are correct. If a partner is dissatisfied, he or she may bring an *action for an accounting*, which asks a court to supervise the preparation of correct statements.

ENFORCEMENT OF PARTNERSHIP RIGHTS AND LIABILITIES

Suits by and against Partnerships

Partnerships were not considered a legal entity in common law. They could not sue or be sued in the firm name, rather all partners had to be joined as plaintiffs or defendants. This requirement of joinder (naming and serving all parties as defendants or naming all as plantiffs) made it hard for creditors to sue on partnership contracts. Under the UPA, *the firm is primarily liable if a contract is made by a partner* or other agent who has express, implied, or apparent authority. If the partnership does not pay off the liability, then the partners become *jointly liable*. When liability is joint, all those liable must be sued in the same suit at common law. However, at common law any partner is liable for the entire debt if the other partners are dead, beyond the jurisdiction of the court, or judgment proof (without property that can be seized for debt).

Horn's Crane Service v. Prior
152 N.W.2d 421 (Sup. Ct. Neb. 1967)

FACTS   Wendell Prior, Orie Cook, and C. E. Piper formed a partnership to operate a rock quarry and rock crushing business. Horn's Crane Service furnished supplies and services to the partnership. Piper, the manager of the partnership, lived in Colorado.

When Horn's Crane Service was not paid, it brought an action against Prior and Cook and each of them individually to recover the amount due. Piper was not joined. There was no claim in Horn's complaint that partnership assets were not sufficient to pay the debt.

ISSUE   May a creditor of a partnership recover against a partner individually on a partnership debt without alleging that partnership assets are not enough to pay the debt?

DECISION   No. The court said that the partners have a right to require a creditor to exhaust partnership assets before going against those of individual partners.

Most states today have a *common name statute* that permits suits against a partnership in the name under which it commonly does business. These statutes eliminate the common law requirement to get personal service on (to deliver the summons to) each partner. Common name statutes permit a plaintiff who is suing on a partnership contract to get a judgment if one or more of the partners is served. Common name statutes differ from *assumed name statutes*, which are intended merely to give notice who the real persons in the firm are.

Liability for Torts   The doctrine of *respondeat superior* imposes liability on the partnership for torts committed by any partner or employee of the firm while engaged in partnership business. The principles of agency law apply in determining whether a tort is committed within the scope and during the course of the partnership business. If the partnership funds are insufficient, the liability of the partners for partnership torts is *joint and several.* This permits the injured person to sue any partner individually or all of them together.

A partner who commits a tort against another partner is, of course, liable for the resulting injury. However, the other partners who had not participated in any way in the tort are not liable.

Vrabel v. Acri
103 N.E.2d 564 (Sup. Ct. Ohio 1952)

FACTS   Florence and Michael Acri owned and operated a cafe as partners. They had problems with their marriage and Florence sued for divorce. After the divorce action was filed, Michael operated the cafe alone. While Vrabel and a friend were drinking at the bar, Michael Acri shot and killed the friend and seriously wounded Vrabel. Michael shot without provocation, was convicted of murder, and was sentenced to life in prison. Vrabel sued Florence Acri to recover damages for his injuries.

ISSUE   Was Florence liable as a partner for Michael's tort?

> **DECISION**　No. Michael made an intentional attack on Vrabel for his own reasons. The attack was not related to the operation of the partnership. It was outside the actual and apparent scope of the business. Although Florence remained a partner, she did not participate in the tort in any way.

Liability for Crimes

A partnership may commit a crime by the manner in which it carries on its business, for example, violating antitrust laws, failing to obtain a necessary business license, or discharging a prohibited pollutant. The firm, or the individual partners if the firm's assets are not enough, is liable for resulting fines.

The other partners are not subject to imprisonment for a crime committed by a partner. This is true even if the crime were committed while he or she was acting for the partnership. Some direct participation or encouragement would be necessary for liability.

QUESTIONS AND PROBLEM CASES

1. Under what circumstances may one who is not truly a partner be held liable as one?

2. What proportion of the partners must agree when making management decisions in a partnership?

3. What is the distinction between trading and nontrading partnerships? Under what circumstances is the difference important?

4. What alternatives are available to partnerships in choosing how to hold title to real property? What are the advantages and disadvantages of each?

5. Ben and Arthur Schaefer operated an automobile dealership as partners. They also were real estate operators. They maintained a bank account titled, "Ben G. Schaefer and Arthur E. Schaefer, Real Estate Trust Account, Partnership." This account was drawn upon in purchasing 13 parcels of real estate. On the deeds for nine of the parcels, the grantees appeared merely as the two Schaefers; on three, they were shown as tenants in common; and one deed referred to them as partners. In leasing property, sometimes one partner and sometimes the other would sign the lease. Some were signed by both. Some were signed by both men and their wives. In selling real estate, some deeds were signed by all four. Tax returns were uniformly filed on a partnership form. When Arthur Schaefer died, his wife claimed that he had been a tenant in common in each parcel of property not deeded to Arthur and Ben as partners. Was she correct?

6. Gloria Harestad, a licensed real estate broker, and Victor Weitzel, a licensed salesperson, made an oral agreement to become partners. They opened an office with a sign reading, "Harestad & Co.—Realty." Each contributed $1,250 and they opened a bank account under the name, "Harestad & Co. Realty." Soon after this, Weitzel purchased a five-acre parcel in his own name and with his own funds. He made arrangements for financing and building an apartment complex on the land. Harestad participated in meetings with city officials and architects and in the selection of carpeting and appliances for the apartments. Many checks for expenses on the project were drawn on the partnership account. Also certain payments were deposited in the account in July 1971, including

the down payment for its sale—a check for $629,332. At that time both Harestad and Weitzel drew checks for themselves of $7,500 each on the account. The 1971 partnership tax return did not refer to the apartment project; however, each showed deductions on their individual returns indicating a 50 percent interest in it. The partnership was dissolved and Harestad claimed a 50 percent share in the profit on the apartment project. Is she entitled to it?

7. Four brothers operated a dairy farm under the name "Bender Bros." Two of the brothers as individuals borrowed money from Klein and gave security interests (mortgages) in specific items of partnership property. The two brothers were also indebted to Windom Bank. The bank obtained a judgment against them and a charging order against their interest in the partnership. The bank contends that the security interest given to Klein is void. Is it?

8. Koenig and Huber entered into a written partnership agreement to operate a plumbing and heating business. The agreement stated that the partners would "at all times diligently employ themselves in the business." After six and one-half years, Koenig asked a court for dissolution and an accounting. The court appointed a CPA to prepare the accounts. He found that Koenig had withdrawn $6,528 more than Huber in cash from the partnership. Koenig argued that this should be treated as proper compensation for his "extra time" in the business. Huber had operated an oil station for more than a year. He had also served as a deputy sheriff for a year during the existence of the partnership. Is Koenig entitled to this extra compensation?

9. Sims and Alexander had been partners in a retail jewelry business. Sims became ill and underwent surgery. The operation disclosed cancer in an advanced stage, but Sims was not told. Learning of Sim's condition, Alexander had a new partnership agreement prepared. It provided that, upon the death of a partner, all the partnership assets would become the sole property of the surviving partner. Sims signed it, and the next day she learned of her condition. A few months later Sims asked for a copy of the partnership agreement and then executed a will that left her interest in the partnership to her parents. After her death, her executor sued to get the value of her interest in the partnership. Did the interest pass to Alexander upon the death of Sims?

Dissolution of Partnerships

27

INTRODUCTION

When Termination Occurs

Assume you have formed a partnership. How long will it exist? Can it continue perpetually like a corporation? The answer is that the business of a partnership may continue for an indefinite period. However, a particular partnership comes to an end when any one of the partners dies or otherwise terminates his or her participation as partner. Understanding how this occurs requires that you know some important terms.

Definitions

Dissolution occurs, according to the Uniform Partnership Act (UPA), *when any partner ceases to be associated in the carrying on of the business.* This may happen in a number of ways, including death and retirement. Dissolution does not terminate the business, however. In fact, the business may be carried on without a break in any one of several ways: It may be continued by the remaining partners or by some of them with one or more new partners; it may be continued as a sole proprietorship by one of the partners; or it may be continued by a corporation formed by all or some of the partners.

The UPA gives any partner a right to insist on liquidation of the partnership assets upon dissolution. This right can be, and usually should be, modified in the partnership agreement because most partnership businesses are worth more alive than dead. A going business is often worth more than the sum of its assets because of the *goodwill* the business has developed. Goodwill is the favorable view of a business, or perhaps only habit, that causes customers or clients to do business with it. Much of this can be preserved if the business is continued rather than liquidated. Liquidation involves turning the assets into cash. This is often done by public auction if no ready buyer is found.

The UPA uses the word *termination* to describe the state when all the partnership affairs have been brought to an end. *Winding up* is the process of settling partnership affairs; it comes between the dissolution and the termination of the partnership. A partnership may be dissolved without any violation of the partnership agreement, it may be dissolved in violation of that agreement (wrongful dissolution), or it may be dissolved automatically by law or by court decree.

DISSOLUTION

Dissolution without Violation of the Agreement

A partnership established for a certain period of time dissolves at the end of that period. This is also true when a partnership is formed for a certain objective, such as to subdivide a certain plot of ground and then to develop and sell residential lots. When the lots have all been sold, the partnership is automatically dissolved. In addition, of course, the partners can at any time unanimously agree, despite an earlier agreement fixing a time, to dissolve the partnership. Where no period of time or specific undertaking is agreed upon, the partnership is a *partnership at will*. Such a partnership may be dissolved at any time by any partner. All that is necessary is for the partner to notify the other partners.

Cox v. Jones
412 S.W.2d 143 (Sup. Ct. Mo. 1966)

FACTS   William Cox and Charles Jones were partners in a medical practice. They had a series of disagreements, and Dr. Jones told Dr. Cox that he was leaving the partnership as of October 1. Before October 1, Jones informed Cox that he had changed his mind. Cox then wrote Jones a letter requesting him to depart as of December 3. He said that if Jones did not, Cox would leave as of February 15. The partnership agreement provided that a withdrawing partner's capital investment could be purchased by the remaining partner at book value. Then for six months following withdrawal, all collections of accounts receivable would be divided. After six months the remaining accounts receivable would become the property of the remaining partner. Cox claimed that Jones was the withdrawing partner so that Cox was entitled to the remaining accounts receivable.

ISSUE   Was Jones the withdrawing partner?

DECISION   No. The court held that since Cox had not accepted Jones's offer to withdraw and Jones had withdrawn his notice before it became effective on October 1, Jones did not withdraw. Therefore, Cox was the withdrawing partner, and Jones is entitled to the remaining accounts receivable.

In the partnership agreement the partners may also provide for expelling a partner. If so, and if the agreed upon procedure is followed, a partner may be forced out without violation of the agreement. This eliminates the right the expulsed partner would otherwise have to insist on liquidation.

Dissolution in Violation of the Agreement

A partner has the *power* to dissolve a partnership even though he or she does not have the *right* to do so. If a partner causes a *wrongful dissolution*, he loses the right to require liquidation. In addition, the innocent partners are given the right by the UPA to continue the business by themselves or with a new partner or partners. If this is done, the partner who breaches the agreement must still be paid the value of his interest less damages for the breach. As an alternative, which is often necessary when the partnership or remaining partners do not have enough cash, the partnership must secure a bond to assure that the departing partner will be paid off and *indemnified* (protected) against partnership liabilities. The wrongdoing partner is not entitled to anything for goodwill in computing the value of his partnership share.

Refusal by partners to carry out their obligations under a partnership agreement is usually treated as causing a dissolution in violation of the agreement. So if a partner fails to pay the capital or furnish the services agreed upon, the other partners are permitted to carry on the business.

Dissolution by Operation of Law or Court Order

The death or bankruptcy of any partner automatically dissolves the partnership. The same is true if the conduct of the partnership business becomes illegal, as it would for example, in time of war if one of the partners is an enemy alien. It also occurs if a member of the partnership loses her license to practice the profession or carry on the business of the partnership.

A court may also dissolve a partnership by judicial degree. This usually occurs upon petition by one or more partners. Several grounds for such action are given by the UPA: *insanity* of a partner, *permanent disability* of a partner, and *willful or continuing breach* of the partnership agreement. Mere personal friction or antagonism is usually not considered a basis for dissolution when the business continues to be profitable. A partner who seeks dissolution by a court is viewed as voluntarily dissolving the partnership. However, the prospect of long-continuing losses may be a sufficient ground for court dissolution even if there is no wrongdoing or inability to work together.

Clark v. Allen
333 P.2d 1100 (Sup. Ct. Ore. 1959)

FACTS   Justin Clark, Gordon Allen, and John Truhan formed a partnership to operate a radio station. Allen was an engineer. He was assigned responsibility for obtaining the FCC license and for building the facilities and installing the equipment after a license was obtained. There were numerous delays in getting the license and getting the equipment ready for operation. During this time Clark was highly critical of Allen's efforts, and Clark continued to be uncooperative after broadcasting began. About six months after broadcasting started, Clark brought a lawsuit seeking dissolution of the partnership and an accounting. Clark claimed that Allen had breached the partnership agreement. Allen and Truhan claimed the right to purchase Clark's interest in the business under a provision of the partnership agreement that said, "Upon voluntary dissolution of the partnership by any partner . . . the remaining parties shall have the first right to purchase the interest of such partner . . . by paying the value of such interest as determined by current accounting and inventory."

ISSUE Was the filing of the lawsuit a notice of voluntary dissolution?

DECISION Yes. The court said it found no justifiable grounds for Clark to seek a judicial dissolution. Therefore, his action was a "voluntary dissolution."* Under the partnership agreement, this gave Allen and Truhan the right to purchase his interest and to continue the business.

* Presumably a "voluntary dissolution," as the term was used in the agreement, might be either a wrongful dissolution or one without violation of the agreement.

Dissolution after Assignment

If one partner assigns her partnership interest or a court imposes a charging order on her interest, the other partners have a right, by unanimous agreement among themselves, to dissolve the partnership. This would not be a wrongful dissolution. An assignee or beneficiary of a charging order may petition a court for dissolution of a partnership at will. The effects of assignments and charging orders were discussed in Chapter 26.

Effect of Dissolution

Dissolution has no effect on the existing liabilities of the partnership, and contracts of the partnership are usually not affected. However, contracts that call for the personal services of individual partners must, of course, be discharged. Obligations under other contracts must be either completed or settled by negotiation during the winding-up process.

WINDING UP PARTNERSHIP BUSINESS

Right to Wind up

Normally the partners themselves wind up—that is, liquidate the assets of the business—after dissolution. If the partnership is dissolved by the death or bankruptcy of a partner, the remaining partners have the right to wind up. If a partnership has been dissolved in violation of the partnership agreement, the innocent partners have the right to liquidate the partnership assets. These rights to wind up, which are granted by the UPA, may be modified by the partnership agreement.

Where dissolution is by court order, the court usually appoints a representative as *receiver* to wind up the business. When disputes arise during any winding up, a partner may ask a court to appoint a receiver.

Powers during Winding up

The purpose of the winding up is to *liquidate the assets* at their highest value by bringing the affairs of the partnership to an end promptly. This may involve completing partnership contracts. For example, in a partnership involved in the construction business, it may be desirable to finish contracts for constructing large buildings that may take two or three years. To complete these contracts, the winding-up partners have the power to enter into new contracts with subcontractors, with suppliers of material, and, of course, with workers. In addition, completion of the contracts is likely to require borrowing money in the name of the partnership.

State v. Ed Cox and Son
132 N.W.2d 282 (Sup. Ct. S.D. 1965)

FACTS   Ed Cox and Son was a partnership of Ed Cox and William Cox. It had a contract with the state of South Dakota for highway construction. The partnership had borrowed money for operating expenses. Ed Cox died and William Cox, as surviving partner, borrowed further sums of money to pay for labor and materials for the highway. The partnership was unable to repay the bank. The bank sued an insurance company that had executed a performance bond assuring completion by the partnership of the highway project. The defense of the bonding company was that William Cox had acted without authority in borrowing additional money after dissolution of the partnership.

ISSUE   Did William Cox have authority to borrow money to finish the construction contract after dissolution?

DECISION   Yes. The court emphasized that although the death of Ed Cox dissolved the partnership, it did not terminate it. William Cox continued to have authority to wind up partnership affairs, including completing contracts already begun.

The winding-up partners have no power to enter contracts for new business. In the above case, if William Cox had bid on new construction jobs, the bonding company would not be liable.

Disputes may arise between partners on whether it is desirable to assign these fairly long-term contracts to other contractors or to continue the business long enough to complete them. As between a wrongdoing partner or the representative of a deceased partner and the partners winding up, the good faith judgment of the latter is usually accepted if the dispute gets to a court.

King v. Stoddard
104 Cal. Rptr. 903 (App. Ct. 1972)

FACTS Lyman Stoddard, Alda Stoddard, and their son, Lyman, Jr., were partners in a newspaper business. Alda died and a year later Lyman died. The business was continued by Lyman Stoddard, Jr. It was eventually discontinued because of insolvency four years after Lyman Stoddard's death. Harley King had provided accounting services to the partnership before Alda's death and went on doing the same kind of work while the business was continued. In settling a dispute with his brother, Lyman, Jr., agreed to be responsible for all debts of the business. King brought suit against the estates of Alda and Lyman Stoddard for the accounting services he provided after their death.

ISSUE Were the services provided in connection with the winding up of the partnership so that the estates of the deceased partners were liable?

DECISION No. The court found that the accounting services were not related to a winding up of the affairs of the partnership. They were in the ordinary course of operating the business. Although it might be appropriate to continue it for a time in order to be able to sell a going business, Lyman, Jr., continued it despite the insistence of the executor that it be liquidated. Therefore, the estates were not liable.

Except for actions necessary to wind up partnership affairs, dissolution terminates the actual authority of the partners. However, after dissolution the partners retain apparent authority to bind the partnership *except against someone with knowledge of its dissolution.* This power can be cut off by giving notice as specified in the UPA. The UPA requires *actual notice* to creditors of the former partnership. Actual notice is either personal notice to the creditor or written notice properly sent to the creditor at his residence or place of business. Notice to noncreditors who had done business with or had previous knowledge of the existence of the partnership is effective if it is published in a newspaper of general circulation in each place where the partnership had regularly conducted its business. This is called *constructive notice.* No notice needs to be given to those persons who were not aware of the partnership.

When a partner dies, the surviving partner or partners can pass title to partnership property. A representative of the deceased partner need not participate in such transfers.

Duties of Partners during Winding up

Partners continue to have fiduciary duties to their copartners during winding up. A partner who is entitled to participate in the winding up cannot be excluded, nor can a partner claim specific partnership property without the agreement of the others.

> ### Lavin v. Ehrlich
> ### 363 N.Y.S.2d 50 (Sup. Ct. N.Y. 1974)
>
> **FACTS** Alexander Lavin, Robert Dillworth, and Ben Ehrlich were partners in a storefront tax-preparing business. It was a partnership at will. Ehrlich managed the business, and Lavin and Dillworth were little more than investors. By letter Ehrlich announced his immediate withdrawal from and the dissolution of the partnership. Later the same month he made a contract to buy the storefront property from its owner. He had started the negotiations before the dissolution, and he told his partners that as owner he would not make a new lease of the building with the partnership. Lavin and Dillworth sued to have the building treated as an asset of the partnership and asked the court to order the sale of all assets.
>
> **ISSUE** Was the building an asset of the partnership?
>
> **DECISION** Yes. The court pointed out that such a storefront business depends on clients returning to the same place year after year. It said that the opportunity to purchase the building and thereby to insure continued possession of the goodwill should have been offered to the partnership. Ehrlich breached his fiduciary duty to his partners in trying to take this for himself. This fiduciary duty of the partner does not end immediately upon dissolution, especially where, as here, he had even begun negotiations before dissolution.

Compensation for Winding up

Under the UPA the partners who wind up a partnership business are not entitled to be paid for that work. They are limited to their share of the profits. However, surviving partners are entitled to reasonable compensation when the winding up follows the death of a partner. The partnership agreement may provide for compensation.

WHEN THE BUSINESS IS CONTINUED

Continuation without Winding up

Some courts take the view that there is an automatic dissolution of the partnership upon the withdrawal or death of a partner. However, many partnership agreements declare that there will be no dissolution at such an event even if a new partner or partners come into the partnership. This is usually beneficial to all concerned because it preserves the value of the going business. Whether or not there has been a technical dissolution, courts enforce partnership agreements that provide for a continuation of the business. There is then no winding up or termination. Such agreements seek to specify a plan to protect the financial interests of the partners who are leaving (and those entering, if any) the partnership. These are called *buyout agreements*. Usually life insurance is bought to fund the purchase of the interests of partners who die.

Liability for Prior Obligations

The continuing partnership becomes liable for the debts incurred by the original partnership. A withdrawing partner or the representative of a deceased partner remains liable for those debts if the continuing partnership does not or cannot pay them.

Usually the continuing partners agree to relieve the withdrawing partners of liability on the debts of the old partnership. However, such agreements are not binding upon creditors unless they have joined in a *novation*. This involves an agreement by the creditor with both the withdrawing partners (or representatives of deceased partners) and the continuing partners, by which the continuing partners agree to assume the obligation and the creditor agrees to hold only them liable and to release the withdrawing partners or their representatives.

A novation is sometimes inferred by courts from the conduct of the creditor of the original partnership. Acceptance of a check or other negotiable instrument from a continuing partner has been held to be a novation if it is in full settlement of the claim and the creditor had knowledge of the change of membership. This would not apply to a partial payment.

White v. Brown
292 F.2d 725 (D.C. Cir. 1961)

FACTS John White withdrew as a partner in an architectural firm. The two continuing partners agreed to assume responsibility for partnership debts. At the time White left, the partnership owed William Brown $20,695 for services as a consulting engineer. Brown was given notice of the withdrawal agreement. Five months later Brown accepted on the debt a series of 12 promissory notes from the continuing partners. One note was payable with interest each month. None of the notes was paid and the partnership shortly became insolvent. Brown sued White on the partnership debt.

ISSUE Did the acceptance of notes from the continuing partners discharge White from the partnership debt?

DECISION Yes. The court held that acceptance of the notes by Brown in full knowledge of both the dissolution of the partnership and the assumption of its debts by the continuing partners was a novation. It therefore discharged the partnership debt.

A person who joins an existing partnership becomes liable for all previous obligations of the partnership as if he or she had been a partner. However, liability is limited to the partnership assets.

Liability for New Obligations

Former partners or their estates remain liable for the new obligations of a continuing partnership where there is apparent authority. Both partners in the original partnership and the partners who are continuing the business may have apparent authority to make contracts appropriate to the business. Withdrawing partners can protect themselves by giving the notice specified in the UPA as indicated above.

Credit Bureaus of Merced County, Inc. v. Shipman
334 P.2d 1036 (Sup. Ct. Cal. 1959)

FACTS   The partnership of Donald Davis and Russell Shipman was dissolved by written agreement. Under the agreement Shipman continued the business and was to assume and pay all partnership debts. A notice of the dissolution was published in the local newspaper. Laird Welding Works had extended credit to the partnership. After dissolution it continued to do repair work for the business. Shipman was unable to pay for the repair work and Welding Works sued Davis. Davis's defenses were that he was not a partner and that the newspaper notice was sufficient.

ISSUE   Was Davis liable?

DECISION   Yes. The court said that the burden of proof was on Davis to prove that Welding Works was aware of the dissolution. Mere publication in a newspaper is not sufficient against a creditor of the prior partnership. The former partner remains liable in the absence of actual notice or knowledge.

Rights of Noncontinuing Partner

The noncontinuing partner (or his or her estate) becomes a creditor of a continuing partnership. The obligations to the noncontinuing partner are subordinate to those of other creditors. So if a person withdraws from a partnership business that continues, he would get what the business owes him only if the partnership can pay all other debts first. The value of the partnership interest of the noncontinuing partner is determined as of the time he leaves the partnership.

In the absence of a provision in the partnership agreement, the UPA gives a retiring partner or the representative of a deceased partner an option. The noncontinuing partner can take either the partnership interest at the time of dissolution plus interest or the partnership interest plus her share of profits gained from the use of her property. The choice need not be made until after an accounting. At that time it can be determined which choice is more favorable.

The UPA gives the other partners a right to continue the business (with or without additional partners) when a partner decides to withdraw before its agreed term or objective has been reached. The withdrawal, of course, would be a breach of the partnership agreement. In this case the remaining partners have two options; they must either pay the breaching partner his or her interest promptly or continue the business only for the agreed upon term and then settle with all partners during winding up.

DISTRIBUTION OF ASSETS

**Solvent
Partnerships**

The final act of winding up a partnership is the distribution of assets. If the partnership business has been profitable, there is no problem; creditors and partners will be paid in full. Partners may choose to distribute items of partnership property instead of selling all assets to raise cash.

Where there have been losses, creditors of the firm must be paid first. Then, under the UPA, the partners are entitled to share the remaining assets according to the following priorities:

1. Debts owed to a partner either for loans or advances made to the firm or for liabilities of the firm paid by the partner are payable first.
2. Return of each partner's capital contribution comes second.
3. Finally, the remaining assets are divided as profits according to the partnership agreement.

A distinction is made between money or property loaned to the firm by a partner and that which is contributed as capital. In winding up, the loans from partners are paid after debts due other creditors. It is only after all debts are paid that the partners are entitled to the return of their capital investment. Therefore, if a partner makes a loan, it is important that the firm's account books clearly show this.

Unless the agreement specifies that a certain value has been placed on a partner's labor, a partner who has contributed no cash or other property would normally receive nothing under step 2. However, a value may by agreement be put on a nonproperty contribution of a partner and set up as capital on the firm's books. For example, a partner may have spent a great deal of time developing the basic ideas on which the business operates. Or he or she may have the friendships or other contacts on which the business is dependent. Special knowledge or skill in operating the partnership business might also be recognized in this way.

The order of distribution between partners, stated in the three rules above, can be varied by agreement between the partners. However, creditors of the firm who are not partners must always be paid first.

**Insolvent
Partnerships**

If the partnership has suffered losses that have reduced capital, then the order of distribution set out above becomes more important. If the partnership is insolvent, it will be unable to pay all of its creditors. Then the burden of paying off the creditors may make one or more of the partners individually insolvent. The Bankruptcy Act of 1978 permits partnership creditors to share (through the trustee in bankruptcy for the partnership) in the individual assets of a general partner who is also bankrupt. This is a change from prior law, which gave individual creditors first claim to individual assets of a bankrupt partner.

**Illustration of
Distribution Rules**

Suppose Andy, Betty, and Charles have organized a partnership to run a retail shop. Andy contributed a stock of merchandise, the lease of a small building in which he had been carrying on a business as a sole proprietorship, and the business itself. The partners agreed on a value of $55,000 for this. The partnership also assumed Andy's business debts of $20,000. This gave Andy a capital contribution of $35,000. Betty contributed $50,000 in cash. Charles contributed no capital. Because of early losses and the need for more working capital, Betty loaned the firm an additional $10,000.

The firm operated for two years. Betty was unwilling to loan more money, so the partnership was dissolved by mutual agreement. A closing-out sale was held, and then the remaining merchandise and the store fixtures were sold at very low prices to a similar firm in another city. Cash accumulated through the liquidation of the assets was $40,000. Debts of the firm are $35,000 to suppliers, the landlord, and other creditors plus the $10,000 loaned by Betty.

The partnership paid very low salaries to the partners and had no profits to distribute. Therefore, both Andy and Charles ran up substantial debts. The accounts of the individual partners are as follows:

	Capital Contributed to Partnership	Individual Assets	Individual Liabilities
Andy	$35,000	$10,000	$ 8,000
Betty	50,000	40,000	10,000
Charles	0	2,000	10,000

The $40,000 in cash will first be used to pay off the creditors other than Betty. Next, $5,000 will be paid to Betty, leaving $5,000 unpaid.

Individual and Partnership Creditors

Individual creditors are entitled to recover from the partners' personal assets before partnership creditors may share in personal assets. Andy will be able to pay off his personal creditors, leaving only $2,000 available to firm creditors. Betty will have $35,000 after paying her individual creditors. Charles is insolvent. His creditors will receive only 20 cents on each dollar of claim.

Total losses from the operation of the partnership are $90,000. This is the capital investment of $85,000 plus the unpaid debts of $5,000 after all assets have been distributed. There was no agreement on sharing losses. Profits were to be shared equally. Therefore, the partners are equally liable for the partnership losses, or $30,000 each. Their capital accounts will be reduced by that amount as follows:

	Capital Contributed to Partnership	Share of Loss	Balance in Capital Account
Andy	$35,000	$30,000	$ 5,000
Betty	50,000	30,000	20,000
Charles	0	30,000	−30,000

Liabilities between Parties

Charles owes the firm $30,000 but can pay nothing. In order to pay Betty the additional $5,000 owed her as a creditor of the firm, Andy must pay what he can. That is $2,000. He will then have a claim against Charles for that amount plus the $5,000 return of capital to which he is entitled. Betty will have a claim against Charles for the $3,000 debt unpaid plus what she is owed for the return of $20,000 of her capital.

If Charles chooses to declare bankruptcy, these claims will be cut off. If not, and if Andy and Betty get judgments from a court on their claims, they may be collectible if Charles later acquires property that can be attached.

QUESTIONS AND PROBLEM CASES

1. Distinguish between dissolution and termination of a partnership?

2. How does the power of a partner to bind the partnership differ during winding up from the ordinary operation of the partnership?

3. What obligations does a retiring partner have to partnership creditors? How can he or she minimize these obligations?

4. List the order in which creditors and partners participate in the assets of a partnership upon liquidation.

5. Drs. Langdon, Hurdle, and Hoffman established a partnership for the practice of medicine. Langdon died four years later and Hurdle and Hoffman continued the practice. However, disagreements arose and Hoffman left and set up a separate practice. Hurdle sued for an accounting, claiming damages against Hoffman for leaving the partnership. The partnership agreement contained no provision as to how long the partnership was to continue. Will Hurdle win damages?

6. Charles and his brother Thomas Smith entered into a partnership with Kennebeck. A year later Thomas Smith and Kennebeck informed Charles by letter that they were dissolving the partnership and forming a corporation to operate the business. Charles was offered the same 25 percent share in the corporation that he had in the partnership. Charles declined the offer. Kennebeck and Thomas continued the business and the assets passed into the corpora-tion. The corporation then completed the work that was in progress before dissolution of the partnership. Charles Smith brought an action seeking a winding up of the partnership, an accounting, and a determination of the value of his interest. What are his rights?

7. Cooper and Isaacs were partners in a janitorial supplies business. They did business as Lesco Associated. The written partnership agreement stated that the partnership would continue "until terminated as herein provided." The specific provisions covered sale of the business, mutual consent, retirement, death, and incompetency of a partner. After eight years of operation Cooper brought suit seeking dissolution of the partnership because of irreconcilable differences. Isaacs filed a counterclaim saying that Cooper's action in suing constituted a wrongful dissolution of the partnership. Therefore, he claimed, he was entitled to continue the business under the partnership name. Is Isaacs right?

8. Dr. Settle was a radiologist. In 1958 he took his assistant, Dr. Berg, in as a partner. Berg agreed to purchase a 45 percent interest in the business, including x-ray and other equipment, for $40,500. In effect, this valued the business at $90,000. In 1960, when a third partner was to be taken in, the business was valued at $100,000. This transaction was not completed, however. In 1962 Berg withdrew from the partnership and Settle continued the business in

the same hospitals. Berg sued for his partnership interest. He claimed it should be 45 percent of the fair market value rather than of the book value. Book value of the partnership was $40,000. Is he entitled to his share of market value?

9. Fielder and Lohman entered a partnership to construct and operate a trailer park. They borrowed $6,600 from First Bank. The partnership name was not included on the note they both signed, but the proceeds of the loan were used by the partnership. Fielder died. Both the partnership and his personal estate were insolvent, their assets not being sufficient to pay creditors. First Bank filed a claim against Fielder's personal estate. Is the bank entitled to participate in his personal assets?

Limited Partnerships and Related Forms

28

LIMITED PARTNERSHIPS

Definition

L imited partnership has one or more general partners and one or more limited partners. Normally limited partners have no obligation for the debts of the partnership. Management of the business of the partnership is in the hands of the general partner or partners. Limited liability is a privilege given by the state; therefore, limited partnerships can be created only under a state statute. All states have such statutes. In all but Louisiana it is the Uniform Limited Partnership Act (ULPA) or the Revised Uniform Limited Partnership Act of 1976 (RULPA).

Lowe v. Arizona Power & Light
427 P.2d 366 (Ct. App. Ariz. 1967)

FACTS Blomquist Electric Co. operated under a "Certificate of Limited Partnership." It stated that Blomquist and Preston were general partners and Lowe a limited partner. Preston left the partnership. A new certificate was filed that did not designate Lowe as a limited partner. Power & Light extended credit to the business both before and after Preston left. Power & Light sued both Preston and Lowe for the unpaid bills.

ISSUE Was either Preston or Lowe liable for partnership debts?

DECISION Preston, as a general partner, is liable for debts incurred by the original limited partnership. He is not liable for debts under the new certificate of partnership if Power & Light had actual notice of the change. Lowe, as a limited partner, is not

---

> liable for debts of the original partnership. However, to obtain protection as a limited partner, the partnership must comply with the requirements of the limited partnership statute. If not, the partners are liable as general partners. Therefore, Lowe is liable for debts incurred after the new certificate was filed.

Purpose

The purpose of the limited partnership form of business organization is to permit some partnership investors to have limited liability. The limited partner gives up the right to participate in the management of the partnership business in return for limited liability. Like a corporate shareholder, the limited partner may lose his investment but no more.

Use of Limited Partnerships

This form of business organization is chosen when taxation as a partnership is desired but investors want limited liability. It is often used in real estate investment activities, in oil and gas drilling, and other "tax shelter" ventures. Such limited partnership interests are treated as securities. Their offering and sales are regulated under the federal and state securities laws. See Chapter 32 for further discussion of the advantages and disadvantages of the limited partnership.

Formalities

The statutory formalities must be complied with to form a limited partnership. A certificate must be filed with the appropriate government official. The certificate (see Figure 28–1) must describe the nature of the business,

FIGURE 28–1

LIMITED PARTNERSHIP CERTIFICATE

I. The name of the Limited Partnership is Sunset Acres Estates, Ltd.
II. The business of the Limited Partnership shall be the development and operation of a mobile home park in Monroe County, Indiana.
III. The location of the principal place of business of the Limited Partnership shall be at 400 North Walnut Street, Bloomington, IN 47401, or wherever the General Partner may from time to time designate.
IV. The name and address of each Partner are as follows:
    A. The name of the General Partner is Bloomington Realty, Inc., 400 North Walnut Street, Bloomington, IN 47401.
    B. The names and residences of the Limited Partners are:
       George E. Ash, 4210 Saratoga Avenue, Bloomington, IN 47401
       Helen V. Brown, 4203 E. 3rd Street, Bloomington, IN 47401
       Alice A. Jones, 468 Elm Street, Bloomington, IN 47401
       Roger S. Smith, 1807 E. 2d Street, Bloomington, IN 47401
V. The Limited Partnership shall continue until dissolved by any one of the following events:
    A. The mutual consent of all Partners,
    B. The sale of the Partnership business,

FIGURE 28–1 *(continued)*

  C. The adjudication that the General Partner is bankrupt or the filing of a voluntary petition of bankruptcy or an admission by the General Partner that it is unable to pay its debts,

  D. Or in any event, at midnight December 31, 1999.

VI. The initial capital contribution of the General Partner is $20,000, the agreed value of its services in acquiring the tract to be developed by the Partnership. The initial contribution of each of the Limited Partners is $50,000 in cash.

VII. Each Limited Partner agrees to contribute an additional $30,000 on or before May 1, 1979, and an additional $20,000 on or before May 1, 1980. In addition, each Limited Partner agrees to make an additional capital contribution not to exceed $20,000 on or before May 1, 1981, if in the sole discretion of the General Partner additional capital is needed for the proper development, maintenance, or sale of the property.

VIII. The capital contribution of the Partners shall be repaid upon dissolution and winding up of the Partnership.

IX. The net profits and net losses of the Partnership for any calendar year shall be allocated among the Partners in the same proportion as their capital contributions. However, the profit, if any, from the sale of the property shall be divided equally among the General Partner and the Limited Partners. If any Limited Partner has failed to make any of the capital contributions called for in Articles VI or VII, his share shall be proportionately reduced and reallocated to the other Partners.

X. A Limited Partner or his legal representative may assign his partnership interest at any time and substitute the assignee as a Limited Partner upon notification to the General Partner and all Limited Partners, with a copy of the assignment furnished to the General Partner.

XI. Additional Limited Partners may be added upon the approval of the General Partner and a majority of the then-existing Limited Partners.

XII. No Limited Partner shall have priority over any other Limited Partner as to the return of his capital contributions.

  IN WITNESS WHEREOF, the Partners have executed this Certificate this 5th day of January, 1978.

LIMITED PARTNERS:

George E. Ash
George E. Ash

Helen V. Brown
Helen V. Brown

Alice A. Jones
Alice A. Jones

Roger S. Smith
Roger S. Smith

GENERAL PARTNER:

Bloomington Realty, Inc.

by *William Glass*, President

its location, and the term of its existence. It must also give the names and addresses of all partners and their capital contributions. A description and a statement of the agreed value of contributions in property other than cash must be included. Certain other information must be provided, such as whether the partners may admit additional partners and whether limited partners may assign their interests to others. The ULPA does not require that the firm name include any word or words to indicate that it is a limited partnership. However, the firm name may not include the last name of a limited partner unless it is also the name of a general partner.

In most cases the certificate serves as the articles of partnership; however, the partners often enter into a more detailed written agreement.

RIGHTS AND LIABILITIES OF PARTNERS IN LIMITED PARTNERSHIPS

General

Partnership law applies to limited partnerships except to the extent changed by the applicable limited partnership statutes. There are several ULPA provisions that deal with the rights and liabilities of limited partners. Those of general partners are essentially the same as those of partners in an ordinary partnership. However, without the approval of all the limited partners, the general partners cannot admit other general partners and may not add other limited partners unless this right is given in the certificate.

Rights of Limited Partners

A limited partner has the same rights as a partner in an ordinary partnership to inspect the partnership books, to have an accounting of partnership affairs, and to obtain a dissolution and winding up by a court. Unless a time is stated in the certificate, she may get her capital contribution to the partnership back by giving six months written notice to all the other partners. The return of any property other than cash contributed may not be claimed unless this is stated in the certificate; the right is to receive cash only.

The right to receive a return of capital or a share of partnership income is limited by the rights of creditors. Neither kind of payment can be made unless afterwards partnership assets will exceed all partnership liabilities except for liabilities to general partners and the capital contributions of limited partners.

For example, suppose Paul and Peter are general partners and Pamela and Polly are limited partners in Good Vibes Recordings, Ltd. Undistributed net income for the year is $15,000, which, according to the certificate, is to be distributed equally. Pamela and Polly each contributed $15,000 to capital. Peter and Paul made no capital contribution. Polly later loaned the firm another $10,000. The partnership has $12,000 in the bank but has debts of $20,000 besides that owed to Polly and it has inventory of $22,000 and fixtures and equipment of $8,000. It can distribute only $12,000 of the earnings to the partners. If Polly were to convert $3,000 or more of her loan to a capital contribution, the entire $15,000 profit could be distributed.

Liabilities of Limited Partners

A limited partner is liable to the partnership for any part of the capital contribution stated in the certificate that he has not paid. The same is true if the certificate states that a later contribution is to be made and has not been. In addition, a limited partner is liable for any amounts paid to him that should not have been paid. Even when all or part of the capital contribution has been rightfully returned, a limited partner is liable for any part of it that is necessary to pay off partnership creditors whose claims arose before the return of capital.

A limited partner who takes part in the control of the business becomes liable like a general partner to partnership creditors. However, a person who mistakenly thinks she is only a limited partner and does not join in management is not held liable for partnership debts. To avoid such liability, the person must promptly give up any claim to share in the profits as soon as she learns of the mistake.

Holzman v. de Escamilla
195 P.2d 833 (Ct. App. Cal. 1948)

FACTS Hacienda Farms, Limited, was organized as a limited partnership. Ricardo de Escamilla was the general partner. James Russell and H. W. Andrews were the limited partners. De Escamilla was raising beans when the partnership was formed. The partnership continued to raise vegetables. Most of the produce was marketed through a business controlled by Andrews. Partnership checks had to be signed by two of the partners. Russell and Andrews visited the farm about twice a week and discussed with de Escamilla the crops to be planted. The latter did not want to plant peppers or eggplants. However, Russell and Andrews overruled him. The same was true of watermelons. Finally, Russell and Andrews requested de Escamilla to resign as manager, which he did. He was replaced, but the partnership went into bankruptcy soon afterward. The trustee in bankruptcy claimed that Russell and Andrews became liable for partnership debts by taking part in control of the business.

ISSUE Were Russell and Andrews liable as general partners?

DECISION Yes. The court held that they had taken part in control of the business. The arrangement on the checks gave control over de Escamilla to either Russell or Andrews. They not only had dictated the crops to be planted but had actually ousted him as manager.

1976 Uniform Limited Partnership Act

A new uniform limited partnership statute has been drafted. It clarifies some of the uncertainties under the present act. It defines the kinds of management activities that limited partners are allowed to perform without becoming liable for partnership debts. It also requires the use of the term "limited partnership" in the name of the firm. It states what formalities are required to protect the limited partnership status of firms that operate outside their home state; this is not covered by the present act. It requires less information in the certificate, and therefore it must be amended less often. It assumes the preparation of separate articles of partnership.

Only Connecticut and Arkansas had adopted the new uniform act as of late 1979. Delay was due in part to uncertainty as to whether the Internal Revenue Service would treat as a partnership for income tax purposes those businesses formed under the new act. The IRS has now clarified its position, and several other states are likely to adopt the act at their next legislative session. California is currently considering a variant of the new act.

DISSOLUTION OF A LIMITED PARTNERSHIP

When the Certificate Must Be Canceled or Amended

The death or bankruptcy of a limited partner does not result in dissolution; neither does the addition or substitution of a limited partner. The certificate must be canceled when all limited partners have died or withdrawn. The retirement, death, or insanity of a general partner usually dissolves a limited partnership. Dissolution can be avoided, however, if the right to continue is granted in the certificate or all other general and limited partners agree.

The certificate must be amended whenever the business is continued after the death, retirement, or insanity of a general partner or when another is admitted as a general partner. The substitution or addition of a limited partner also requires an amendment. It is not necessary upon the death or withdrawal of a limited partner. Amendment is required also when there is a change in the nature of the business of the partnership, the time stated in the certificate for dissolution, or other statements made in the certificate.

Distribution of Assets

The order in which the liabilities of the partnership are to be paid after dissolution is different from that of an ordinary partnership. It is as follows:

1. Firm creditors other than limited partners as to their capital contributions.
2. Limited partners as to their share of profits.
3. Limited partners as to their capital contribution.
4. General partners as to loans and other debts.
5. General partners as to profits.
6. General partners as to capital contributions.

Between partners (general and limited), the order of distribution may be changed in the certificate.

OTHER FORMS RELATED TO PARTNERSHIPS

Joint Ventures

Courts distinguish joint ventures from partnerships. These business undertakings may also be called *syndicates, joint enterprises,* or *joint adventures*. They differ from partnerships primarily in that they have a more limited business objective; they may involve only a single project rather than an ongoing business with many transactions.

An example is an agreement to buy and resell for profit a single tract of real estate. The undertaking might involve holding the land for several years and even improving it by grading. If the participants are going to develop the tract into a residential subdivision, installing streets, sewers, and water mains and then selling a large number of lots individually, the undertaking is more likely to be considered a partnership. Corporate promoters who enter contracts prior to incorporation are often treated as joint adventurers.

Generally, courts require a profit-seeking purpose for a joint venture. However, some courts find a "joint enterprise" when people join together to share expenses on an automobile trip where savings rather than profit is the goal.

The line between partnership and joint venture is not clear and sharp. This makes little difference, however, because the rules applied when disputes arise are generally those of partnership law. All participants in the venture are personally liable for debts arising from it. The parties owe each other fiduciary duties like partners. A joint venturer, like a partner, is entitled to an accounting. Tax treatment is like that for partnerships. The principal difference is that courts are less likely to find that a joint venturer has bound the enterprise on the basis of apparent rather than actual authority.

Florida Tomato Packers, Inc. v. Wilson
296 So.2d 536 (Ct. App. Fla. 1974)

FACTS George Lytton was a farmer who grew tomatoes. He had a contract with Florida Tomato Packers, Inc., under which it had furnished funds to market the tomatoes grown by Lytton. It placed $100,000 in a checking account under the name of L & D Farms. All Lytton's farming expenses were paid for by checks on this account written by the manager of Packers. Lytton was to deliver the crop to Packers' warehouse. After the tomatoes were sold, all growing, shipping, and selling expenses were deducted from the proceeds. Any profits were to be equally divided between Lytton and Packers. A farm vehicle owned by Lytton and driven by his employee was involved in an accident that injured Willie Floyd Wilson. Wilson sought to hold Packers liable as a member of a joint venture.

ISSUE Were Lytton and Packers involved in a joint venture?

DECISION Yes. The court found that Lytton and Packers were seeking a profit jointly from raising tomatoes. It held that a corporation can be a member of a joint venture. It said that both members of a joint venture are liable for the torts of the other committed within the scope of the undertaking. They are both liable for losses arising out of the joint venture.

Most states today permit corporations to become partners. In earlier times when this was generally not true, courts treated joint undertakings between corporations as joint ventures. Undertakings between corporations still tend to be called "joint ventures" even when the joint business is conducted by a corporation with the parent corporations owning the shares.

Mining Associations

Miners often associate together in developing a mining claim. This can be done through a corporation, a partnership, or other form of business organization. Where the parties appear to intend joint development, the association is treated as a *mining partnership*. This is true of oil and gas operations as well as the mining of minerals like coal or silver ore.

The associates in a mining partnership are tenants in common (or sometimes joint tenants—with ownership passing to the survivors when an associate dies) of the real estate. They owe each other a fiduciary duty with respect to their joint claim but not with respect to other claims. Each associate has the power to bind the others for expenses in connection with reasonable development of the claim. They have tort liability like that of partners. However, because of the more limited scope of the business, contract liability in both the mining partnership and the joint venture is narrower than in a partnership.

A major distinction compared with general partnerships is that a mining partner may sell his or her interest in a claim to another without the permission of the associates. The new owner then becomes a tenant in common with the others. The mining partnership also continues after the death of a partner.

Misco-United Supply, Inc. v. Petroleum Corporation
462 F.2d 75 (5th Cir. 1972)

FACTS   Petroleum Corporation (Petco) entered into an agreement with C. J. Pinner to drill an oil well. Pinner was to conduct the drilling. Petco agreed to put up $82,000 toward drilling expenses to an agreed upon depth. This was subject to several conditions. One required Pinner to give Petco 60 days' notice and evidence of good title before drilling. Pinner ordered supplies in his own name from Misco-United Supply in the amount of $141,716. They were used in the well drilling. Misco learned that Petco had been involved, so when Pinner could not pay, Misco sued Petco as a mining partner.

ISSUE   Was Petco liable as a mining partner?

DECISION   No. The jury found that Petco did not intend to enter a mining partnership. Pinner had not complied with either the notice to Petco or the title provisions of the contract. Whether a mining partnership or joint venture exists is a matter of intent. Such a partnership goes into effect only after the conditions agreed upon have been met.

QUESTIONS AND PROBLEM CASES

1. What formalities, if any, are required to give a limited partner liability limited to his or her investment?

2. What are the rights of a limited partner with respect to the partnership?

3. Does the addition, substitution, or withdrawal of one or all limited or general partners require cancellation or amendment of the limited partnership certificate?

4. To what extent do the rules of partnership law apply to joint ventures?

5. Robert Davis and James Davis were partners in a trucking business, although not related. They had signed a limited partnership certificate showing Robert as a limited partner; however, it had never been filed. The business was operated under the name "Davis Company, Oreg., Ltd." The business was profitable and grew. Both men had made equal contributions to the capital of the firm and shared equally in the profits. Although both had been active in operating the business, Robert had actually spent more time at it. After dissolution, James claimed that Robert, as a limited partner, is entitled only to the return of his original investment plus his share of undistributed profits. Robert then sued for an equal share in the partnership assets. Will he win?

6. LNP was a limited partnership. It provided engineering advice relating to the use of liquified natural gas. Petsinger was the general partner, and there were ten limited partners, who were furnished periodic reports on the business. Some of them attended meetings where additional information was provided by Petsinger. Some of them also attended meetings for the purpose of raising additional capital. Two of the limited partners were employed by the partnership as project managers and served as consultants on certain LNP projects. The written

partnership agreement provided that management and control of the partnership would rest exclusively with the general partner. Are any of the limited partners liable to partnership creditors because they had participated in control?

7. Dewees, Duley, Herring, and another formed a joint venture to purchase and develop a 14.6-acre tract of land. Duley died while holding a 25 percent interest. Dewees and Herring tried to interest Offutt in buying part of Duley's share. They represented that a 24.5 percent interest could be purchased for $25,000. Offutt agreed to buy a 10 percent interest for $10,000. Dewees and Herring then bought Duley's 25 percent interest for $14,000. They sold two fifths of it to Offutt. Five years later Offutt learned the true facts. He then sued Dewees and Herring for breach of fiduciary duty. Will he win?

8. Auld, Stark, and Estridge entered a joint venture to conduct a woodworking business. They agreed to share proceeds when the business was liquidated. Auld, who lived in Haiti, was to supervise production in Haiti; Stark was to handle selling; and Estridge was to furnish financing. The venture was unsuccessful. Estridge looked for a buyer for the business. He traded the business for 60,000 unregistered shares in Allen Electronics Industries. He also received 60,000 shares in Calculator Computer Leasing Corp. when Allen shortly thereafter "spun off" to its shareholders it shares in this subsidiary corporation. Estridge met Auld in New York. He told him he had made a good deal and that Auld would receive 5,000 shares of Allen, worth $25,000. He said nothing about the Calculator stock or why Auld was not entitled to 20,000 shares of Allen. Auld later learned the facts and sued. Is Estridge liable?

Formation and Termination of Corporations

29

Today it is easy to form a corporation. If you plan to form a new business, you may very well decide that it should be a corporation. As indicated in Chapter 32, all business corporations are not huge economic entities; most of them are small businesses. In many states they can be formed with as little as $1,000 capital. The purpose of this chapter is to describe how corporations are formed, how they are financed, and how they are terminated.

RELATIONSHIP OF CORPORATION AND STATE

The Charter or Articles of Incorporation

All business corporations derive their existence from the state in which they are incorporated. The earliest business corporations in America obtained *charters* from the King of England, since the colonies were governed by the English monarch. The Constitutional Convention of 1787 considered giving this power to the federal government; however, no such power was included. Therefore, it was left to the states. To form a corporation the promoters had to find a legislator who was willing to introduce a bill. The legislature then decided whether to grant a charter.

Early legislators feared the growth of corporate power. Charters, therefore, tended to be for short terms. The powers granted and the amount of capital involved were generally rather limited. Most of the earliest corporations were formed to supply public facilities, such as bridges, toll roads, and waterworks. A few, however, were mining and manufacturing businesses.

As commercial and industrial development progressed in America, legislators were impressed by the benefits brought to the people and they wanted to encourage corporations. There was also a growth of egalitarian belief. These factors resulted in the passage of *general incorporation laws*, which made it a right, instead of a legislative privilege, to establish a corporation. Under these statutes all that is necessary to form a corporation is to prepare *articles of incorporation* that comply with the state's incorporation statute. If they do, a state official—usually the secretary of state—has a duty to issue a *certificate of incorporation*.

Powers of a Corporation

The *certificate of incorporation* serves the same function as a charter. It is rather like a constitution: It is the basic document of the corporation and a major source of its powers. However, today the general incorporation statute of the state of incorporation, rather than the certificate of incorporation, spells out most of the powers of the corporation. Such statutes usually set forth the powers that corporations have had from the earliest days, such as holding property in its own name and making bylaws. In addition they grant many other powers that earlier business corporations did not have. One of these is the power to hold stock in other corporations, which permits holding companies to control subsidiary corporations by owning all or a substantial part of their stock. Other powers granted today that were earlier denied corporations include making donations to educational and charitable organizations and paying pensions and giving stock options to corporate directors, officers, and employees.

Domicile of the Corporation

The corporation has its own *domicile* separate from its shareholders. It is in the state in which it is incorporated and in the place within that state where it has its registered office. The registered office need not be its principal office, however. For example, General Motors is incorporated in Delaware although its headquarters office is in Detroit, Michigan.

Domestic and Foreign Corporations

A corporation is a *domestic* corporation in the state in which it is incorporated; it is a *foreign* corporation in all other states, territories, and countries. A corporation has a right to engage in *interstate* commerce in any of the United States. For example, it may sell by mail or telephone and ship its goods to customers in any state. Under the Commerce Clause of the U.S. Constitution, a state may not exclude or discriminate against a corporation chartered in another of the United States that is engaged only in interstate commerce. In contrast, however, a corporation has no right to engage in *intrastate* business in any state except the one in which it is domiciled.

Doing Business in a State

The activities that constitute "doing business" within a state differ depending on the purpose of the determination. There are three such purposes:

(1) to determine whether a corporation is subject to a lawsuit in the state courts, (2) to determine whether the corporation's activities are subject to taxation by the state, and (3) to determine whether the corporation must *qualify*, that is, be granted permission by the state to carry on its activities there. The courts have held that fewer activities within a state are necessary to subject a foreign corporation to a lawsuit in the state than are necessary to permit its activities within the state to be taxed. Before a state can require a foreign corporation to qualify, it must be carrying on additional activities within the state beyond those required for taxation.

Jurisdiction of Courts

The U.S. Supreme Court has held that a foreign (not qualified in the state) corporation may be hailed into court in a state in connection with almost any activity engaged in by it within that state. The only requirement is that subjecting the corporation to suit cannot offend "traditional notions of fair play and substantial justice." Requiring it to defend a suit within the state must not be too inconvenient. The corporation must have certain "minimum contacts" with the state; however, even an isolated event may be sufficient. For example, sending a truck across the state permits a suit against the owner corporation for a tort committed in connection with the trip.

Inpaco, Inc. v. McDonald's Corp.
413 F.Supp. 415 (E.D. Pa. 1976)

FACTS McDonald's Corporation made a contract with Inpaco, Inc., to design and manufacture a machine for dispensing food sauces. The work was to be done at Inpaco's plant in Allentown, Pennsylvania. McDonald's employees went to Allentown from McDonald's offices in Oak Brook, Illinois, to discuss the development of the machine. McDonald's, which was incorporated in Delaware, was not licensed to do business in Pennsylvania. It operated its fast-food restaurants in Pennsylvania through a subsidiary. A dispute arose over the development of the machine. Inpaco sued McDonald's in Pennsylvania for breach of the contract. McDonald's argued that it was not doing business in Pennsylvania and, therefore, could not be sued there.

ISSUE Was having machinery designed and built for it in Pennsylvania sufficient "doing business" to make McDonald's subject to suit?

DECISION Yes. The court said that the corporation had intentionally conducted activities within the state that had an economic impact on Pennsylvania. There is nothing unfair about requiring it to defend a suit in Pennsylvania growing out of its activities there.

Taxation

A corporation's property is taxable in any state in which it is located. However, it is taxable on its transactions within the state only if it is "doing business" in the sense that this term is applied in tax jurisdiction cases.[1] Courts have held that a manufacturer who maintains a sales office in a state is subject to a state corporate income tax even if the goods sold are prepared and shipped from outside. However, under the Federal Interstate Income Tax Act, using an independent agent such as a manufacturer's representative to sell goods that are prepared and shipped from outside the state does not subject the manufacturer to taxation. A truck line that regularly carries goods into the state in interstate commerce has also been held subject to taxation.

Qualifying to Do Business

Conducting an intrastate business within a state requires the "foreign" corporation to *qualify to do business.* Maintaining a stock of goods within a state from which to fill orders, even if the orders are taken or accepted outside, is "doing business." Carrying on service activities such as machinery repair and construction work are also "doing business." Taking orders for acceptance and filling them from outside the state is not "doing business" even if the salesperson lives in the state. "One-time" transactions such as the sale of a building or an entire stock of goods are not "doing business"; nor is mere ownership of real or personal property.

Qualification requires compliance with a statute. The corporation must give information similar to that required of a domestic corporation in applying for a charter. It must maintain a registered office and an agent within the state upon whom those bringing suit against the corporation may serve a complaint. A license fee and an annual franchise tax must be paid. These are usually related to the value of the corporation's property and to its income within the state.

Doing intrastate business within the state without qualifying usually subjects the foreign corporation to a fine. Many states also deny such a corporation the right to bring suits in the courts of the state. This may make it very difficult to collect from customers within the state.

Means of Regulation of Corporations

State regulation of the activities of corporations today does not come through limitations in their charters or articles of incorporation. Activities of corporations are usually regulated by specific statutes that cover all types of businesses. For example, safety regulations in factories, limitations on air and water pollution, and credit regulations all apply to sole proprietorships and partnerships as well as to corporations.

Federal regulation also generally applies to all types of business organizations. Ralph Nader and others have proposed requiring the very largest corporations, perhaps the top 500–1,000, to obtain federal charters. The

---

[1] The limited activities of McDonald's in the *Inpaco, Inc.,* case would not subject McDonald's Corporation to taxation by Pennsylvania. Of course, its subsidiary operating restaurants in Pennsylvania would be subject to tax.

idea is to subject such corporations to more thorough and detailed regulation than other businesses through the Securities and Exchange Commission or some new agency. So far there has been little enthusiasm in Congress for doing this. Nor has Congress shown much interest in a proposal that would establish minimum standards for state incorporation statutes.

FIRST STEPS IN FORMING A CORPORATION

Promoters

Promoters are people who bring a corporation into being. Promotion is a vital activity in a free enterprise system, and it is too bad that a few "fast buck" operators have given the term a bad name. The promoter is the person who has the idea for a business. He or she finds people who are willing to finance it—to buy shares of stock and/or to lend money and credit. Contracts must be made for building or leasing space, buying or renting equipment, hiring employees, buying supplies and advertising, and whatever else is required for the early operation of the business. Most state incorporation statutes permit reserving a name for a proposed corporation. This is also done by the promoter. The promoter must arrange for the filing of the legal papers to incorporate the business. The promoter usually guides the corporation through the critical early months and perhaps years before the new company is a "going concern."

A person who takes a leading part in converting to a corporation a going business that is an individual proprietorship or a partnership is also a promoter. Sometimes there is a small group of promoters rather than a single person or corporation.

Liability of the Promoter to the Corporation

The relation of promoters to the corporation, to its shareholders, and to those with whom they contract is unique. Promoters are not agents of the corporation prior to its incorporation, since it is not in existence. Promoters are not agents of the persons who are interested in the venture, since the promoters were not appointed by them and are not under their control.

Nevertheless, promoters owe a *fiduciary duty* to the corporation and to the persons interested in it. This includes the duties of full disclosure, good faith, and absolute honesty to the corporation and to the original shareholders. It would be a breach of duty to use money received on stock subscriptions to pay the expenses of forming the corporation unless this intent were disclosed. It would also violate fiduciary duty if the promoters were to take a secret profit.

Krause v. Mason
537 P.2d 105 (Sup. Ct. Ore. 1975)

FACTS   Mr. and Mrs. Donald Mason had been in the carpet business in Oregon for several years. They operated a business called Mason Custom Carpets. They proposed to Mr. and Mrs. Randall Krause that the Krauses join them to sell "area carpets" (carpets cut and bound rather than wall-to-wall). They were issued a certificate of incorporation as Golden Age Distributors, Inc. Each of the four individuals was to be issued 5,000 common shares in Golden Age. Each of the Krauses was to pay $5,000, and each of the Masons was to contribute 1,000 carpets that have a value of $5,000. Just after the certificate of incorporation was issued and before a bank account was opened, Donald Mason informed the Krauses that he was flying to Georgia to buy carpets for Golden Age. For this purpose the Krauses gave him $7,900 as part payment for their shares. Mason used some of this money for carpets for Mason Custom Carpets, selling these carpets at a profit. Later Mason bought an equivalent value of carpets for Golden Age. The Krauses brought suit on behalf of Golden Age for the profits made on the carpets sold by the Masons.

ISSUE   Were the Masons liable for the profits because they breached their fiduciary duty as promoters?

DECISION   Yes. Promoters are liable for any gain they may realize from their breach of fiduciary duty. The fact that the Masons later replaced the corporation's supply of carpets with similar ones does not entitle them to keep the profits they made by their wrongful conduct.

A promoter often takes an option on or purchases property for the corporation. If he or she misrepresents the price paid or to be paid, the corporation may recover the secret profit made by the promoter. However, if the promoter makes a full disclosure of the expected profit to an independent board of directors, the corporation cannot recover. If the board of directors is under the control of the promoter, the corporation could rescind the contract or recover damages.

Park City Corp. v. Watchie
439 P.2d 587 (Sup. Ct. Ore. 1968)

FACTS   H. R. Watchie, a Seattle real estate broker and developer, took options to purchase 965 acres of land near Portland, Oregon. A group of Seattle investors put up the cost of $729,000. Watchie took title as trustee. He was paid a commission on the purchase but did not participate in the investment. It was agreed that the land would be held until it could be resold at double the cost. Two years later Watchie formed a publicly owned corporation, Park City Corporation, to acquire the land at $1,458,000. The stock subscription agreement described the development plans in detail. It also stated that the property would be acquired by the corporation at cost plus "a commission" to Watchie. The corporation was unsuccessful financially and Watchie resigned as president. New directors and officers were elected. They caused the corporation to sue Watchie to recover secret profits. The suit was based on the fact that the land had been sold at twice what Watchie had originally paid for it without disclosing this to the subscribers. Watchie was paid a commission on the sale to Park City Corporation.

ISSUE
Was Watchie liable to the corporation for secret profits?

DECISION
Yes. The court held that Watchie was liable for the commission he made on the original purchase because it had not been disclosed to the subscribers. However, he was not liable for the difference between the selling price to the original investors and their price to the corporation. Although he held title, he received no profit from that sale. Liability comes from the ambiguity concerning the cost to Watchie for the land. Was it the cost less the first commission? The court resolved the ambiguity against Watchie because of his lack of full disclosure.

Liability of Corporation to Promoter

There is nothing illegal or wrong if promoters are paid for their services. Profit to the promoters is illegal only if it is not disclosed. After formation of the corporation, the corporation may agree to pay the promoters not only for their expenses but also for their services. Frequently promoters are issued shares of the stock of the new corporation for their services.

The Securities Act of 1933 requires that promotional expenses and profits going to promoters be disclosed in the registration statement and prospectus for the new issue of securities. State "blue sky" laws (so-called because securities sellers were said to be selling blue sky) also require such disclosures.

The Corporation's Liability on Promoter's Contracts

When the corporation comes into existence it is not automatically liable on the contracts made by the promoter. As indicated above, the corporation cannot be liable as principal since it was not in existence. The same fact prevents the corporation from ratifying the promoter's contracts; ratification requires capacity to contract at the time the contract was made.

Nevertheless, all American courts except those of Massachusetts have held corporations liable if, after incorporation, *the board acts to adopt the contract* (adoption is similar to ratification). Even acceptance of the benefits of the contract is generally sufficient. Massachusetts requires an express agreement among the corporation after it is formed, the third party, and the promoter (a novation).

Liability of Promoter on Contracts

Promoters are generally held liable on contracts they make on behalf of corporations not yet formed. If the corporation is not formed or fails to adopt the agreement, the promoters are liable. This is based on agency law: An agent who makes a contract for a nonexistent principal is personally liable on it. A promoter may escape this danger by having the third party agree, when the agreement is made, that the promoter is not to be liable. However, under contract law this would make it impossible for the promoter or corporation to enforce the agreement against the third party. This results from the rule for bilateral contracts that if one party is not bound, neither is the other. Such contracts lack mutuality.

Vodopich v. Collier County Developers, Inc.
319 So.2d 43 (Ct. App. Fla. 1975)

FACTS Charles Vodopich, a real estate broker, sold some land to Basil Mulley and others who were acting as promoters of a land development corporation. He agreed, rather than taking his commission of $31,500 in cash, to accept the exclusive right to resell the developed lots. The agreement was entered into in the name of the corporation, Collier County Developers, Inc. Vodopich knew at that time that the corporation was not in existence. When the corporation was properly incorporated, it took title to the property and later resold several parcels. Vodopich several times demanded an exclusive listing with him of the properties to be sold as agreed with Mulley. This was refused. Vodopich sued Mulley for the $70,710 in commissions he claimed due under the agreement.

ISSUE Was Mulley personally liable on the contract made by him on behalf of the corporation?

DECISION Yes. The court said the general rule is that a promoter is liable on a contract entered into on behalf of a corporation he or she is organizing. An exception applies where the other party knows that the promoter does not intend to be personally liable on it. But it must be shown that the parties agreed to bind the corporation alone. The trial court erred in instructing the jury that mere knowledge of the third party that the corporation is not in existence relieves the promoter from liability.

NEXT STEPS IN FORMING A CORPORATION

A Certificate of Incorporation

After the promoter's preliminary activities, the next step in forming a corporation is to obtain a certificate of incorporation. The *articles of incorporation* are prepared for the corporation, usually by a lawyer. Most state statutes prescribe the general form of the articles. It is usually unwise merely to copy a standard form for this important document.

If the responsible state official finds that the articles meet the requirements of the statute, they will be approved. The official will then return a certificate of incorporation or mark the articles as accepted.

**The Model
Business
Corporation Act**

The Model Business Corporation Act (MBCA), prepared by the Corporation, Banking, and Business Law Section of the American Bar Association, is followed in a number of states. It has been used as a basis for the statutes of 28 states and has greatly influenced those of 10 more. It will be used in this book as representative of state law.

**Content of the
Articles of
Incorporation**

The content of the articles of incorporation required by the MBCA includes:

1. The name of the corporation, which must not be deceptively similar to any other corporation registered earlier. (It must contain the words "corporation," "incorporated," "company," "limited," or an abbreviation.)
2. The duration of the corporation, which may be and usually is perpetual.
3. The purposes of the corporation. (Frequently this is stated very broadly, such as to "engage in any lawful activity.")
4. The number of shares of capital stock that the corporation shall have authority to issue and their par value. (It may be stated that the shares have no par value. Also the capital stock may be divided into classes; if so, they must be described.)
5. Preemptive rights of shareholders, if granted.[2]
6. The address of the initial registered office of the corporation and the name of its registered agent.
7. The number and names of the initial board of directors.
8. The name and address of each incorporator.

Figure 29–1 is a simple certificate of incorporation that would satisfy the requirements of the MBCA.

**Who May Be
Incorporators?**

Some states require that three natural persons who are adults serve as incorporators. The MBCA now permits a single person or a corporation to be an incorporator.

**Organization
Meeting**

The MBCA requires an *organization meeting* of the board of directors. Some statutes require that the incorporators hold the organization meeting. The MBCA specifies that bylaws shall be adopted and officers elected at the organization meeting. Usually a corporate seal is adopted, the form of stock certificates is approved, stock subscriptions are accepted, and issuance of stock is authorized. Other business may include adoption of the promoter's contracts, authorization of payment of or reimbursement for expenses of incorporation, and determination of the salaries of officers.

Bylaws

The function of *bylaws* is to establish rules for the conduct of the internal affairs of the corporation. They usually set out the duties and authority

---

[2] See discussion of preemptive rights in Chapter 31.

FIGURE 29–1

CERTIFICATE OF INCORPORATION OF
UNIVERSAL ENTERPRISES, INC.

ARTICLE I.   The name of the Corporation is Universal Enterprises, Inc.

ARTICLE II.   The purpose of the Corporation is to engage in any lawful activity for which corporations may be organized under the Domestic Corporations for Profit Act of Indiana.

ARTICLE III.   The term of existence of the Corporation shall be perpetual.

ARTICLE IV.   The post office address of the principal office of the Corporation is 205 North College Avenue, Bloomington, IN 47401. The name of its Resident Agent is Charles Smith, 205 North College Avenue, Bloomington, IN 47401.

ARTICLE V.   The total number of authorized shares shall be 1,000 common shares, each with a par value of $100.

ARTICLE VI.   The shares may be issued in one (1) or more classes. Each class shall have such relative rights, preferences, and limitations, and shall bear such designations as shall be determined by resolution of the Board of Directors prior to the issuance of any shares of such classes.

ARTICLE VII.   (a) Each share shall be entitled to one (1) vote on all matters.
(b) Cumulative voting shall not be permitted on any matter.

ARTICLE VIII.   The Corporation will not commence business until at least $1,000 has been received for the issuance of shares.

ARTICLE IX.   (a) The initial Board of Directors of the Corporation shall be composed of three members. The number of Directors may from time to time be fixed by the Bylaws of the Corporation at any number not less than three (3). In the absence of a Bylaw, the number shall be three (3).

(b) Directors need not be shareholders of the Corporation.

ARTICLE X.   The initial Board of Directors of the Corporation and their post office addresses are as follows:

Alvin B. Cortwright, 1234 Saratoga Drive, Bloomington, IN 47401

Douglas E. Fenske, 567 East 9th Street, Bloomington, IN 47401

Gordon H. Inskeep, 8910 East 10th Street, Bloomington, IN 47401

ARTICLE XI.   The name and post office address of the Incorporator is:

P. D. Quick, 1112 North Walnut Street, Bloomington, IN 47401

ARTICLE XII.   Provisions for the conduct of the affairs of the Corporation shall be contained in the Bylaws. The Bylaws may be amended from time to time by the affirmative vote of the majority of the Board of Directors.

IN WITNESS WHEREOF, the undersigned, being the Incorporator designated in Article XI, has executed these Articles of Incorporation and certifies to the truth of the facts above stated, this 12th day of November, 1979.

P. D. Quick

P. D. Quick

of the officers and the conduct of meetings. This would include the time and place of the annual shareholders' meeting and how special meetings of shareholders are to be called. They establish the quorum necessary for the meetings and how elections to the board of directors shall be conducted. The bylaws also provide for the organization of directors into committees if desired and for the frequency and conduct of board meetings. They also usually set up the procedures for the transfer of shares, for the keeping of stock records, and for declaring and paying dividends.

To be valid, bylaws must be consistent with state law and the articles of incorporation. Directors, officers, and shareholders of the corporation are bound by bylaws properly adopted. Others, including corporate employees, are not bound by them unless they have notice or knowledge of them. The MBCA gives the power to adopt the initial bylaws to the directors. Some statutes give this power to the incorporators or the initial shareholders. The MBCA and most statutes give the power of amendment and repeal to the directors; however, shareholders have an inherent right to make bylaws. If they choose to do so, they may amend or repeal the bylaws adopted by the directors.

FINANCING THE CORPORATION

Sources

The initial funds and property for a corporation come from the promoters or from other investors. They furnish money or property or settle claims for services they have furnished to the corporation in exchange for its stock or other securities. Bank loans usually form at least part of the operating funds for the corporation. Often the promoters or major shareholders are required to cosign the notes. Sometimes a customer or supplier lends money.

Shares of stock can generally be issued in exchange for money, property, or services already performed for the corporation. Promissory notes and future services are not permitted as consideration for shares in most states. Where the value of property or services is less than the par value (or stated value, which is the value placed by the corporation on no-par shares for the purpose of establishing the amount of paid in capital), it is said that the stock is "watered." *Watered stock* is illegal, and those persons who establish the illegal value may be liable to creditors or to the corporation for damages resulting from overvaluation. However, today the various disclosure statutes have almost eliminated what was earlier a serious problem.

Other securities, such as debentures, bonds, and notes, are called *debt securities*. They will be discussed after equity securities are taken up.

Types of Securities

A corporation must issue some common stock. It may also, if authorized by its articles, issue preferred stock. Both kinds of stock are known as *equity securities*. Certificates are issued to represent the shares of stock, but they are not the stock; they are merely evidence of ownership.

Common Stock

If a corporation has only one class of stock, it is *common stock*. If there is more than one class, the common shareholders usually bear the major risks of the business and will benefit most from success. They receive what is left over after the preferences of other classes have been satisfied. This is usually true both for income available for dividends and for net assets upon liquidation. Common stock usually carries voting rights. There may be more than one class of common stock, however, such as Class A and Class B. One class may have no right to vote.

Preferred Stock

Any stock that has a preference over other classes of stock is called *preferred stock*. Usually preferred shareholders have a preference as to dividends and the distribution of assets when the corporation is dissolved. Dividends on *cumulative preferred* stock, if not paid in any year, will be payable later when funds are available. Dividends on *noncumulative preferred* stock need not be paid later if they are not earned and paid in the year due. Sometimes *participating preferred* stock is issued. Holders of such stock get their usual dividend. Then after the common shareholders receive a prescribed "normal" dividend, the preferred shareholders participate with the common shareholders in income available for dividends. Of course, if there are no funds available for dividends, none will be paid to either class.

Preferred stock may be made convertible into common stock. Sometimes preferred stockholders are given voting rights. Usually the right to vote is granted only in the event that dividends due are not paid.

Preferred stock can be *redeemed*, that is, paid off and canceled by the corporation, if the articles permit. Under the MBCA, the redemption price must be stated in the articles. Redemption permits the corporation to buy back the shares even if the holders do not wish to sell. Redemption is not permitted if the cost would make the corporation insolvent. A sinking fund may be, although seldom is, provided.

Warrants, Rights, and Options

The MBCA expressly permits directors to issue *options* to purchase shares of the corporation. These may be given in connection with the sale of other securities or they may be issued to high-level managerial employees as an incentive to increase profitability in order to maximize the market value of the corporation's stock. Shareholder approval is required under the MBCA for employee and director stock option plans.

Options that are represented by certificates are known as *warrants*. They are sometimes part of a package of securities sold as a unit; for example, they may be given along with notes, bonds, or even shares. The term *rights* is usually applied to short-term and often nonnegotiable options. Rights are used to give present security holders a right to subscribe to some proportional quantity of the same or a different security of the corporation. Often they are given in connection with a preemptive right requirement.

Treasury Stock

A corporation may purchase its securities from any willing seller. It does not need specific authority to do so in its articles. However, the MBCA permits such purchases only out of unrestricted earned surplus. Capital surplus may be used only upon a two-thirds vote of shareholders. Repurchased shares become *treasury shares*. They cannot be voted in elections, and they can be resold without regard to par value or original issue price.

Debt Securities

Corporations have the power to borrow money necessary for their operations. Debt securities are of several types. Short-term debt instruments are called *notes*, a longer-term unsecured debt is called a *debenture*, and a long-term secured debt is called a *bond*. In the event of liquidation, the claims on assets of note and debenture holders are paid pro rata (proportionately) with those of general creditors. Bondholders have priority as to assets securing the loan. The security may be real property such as a building or personal property such as machinery, raw materials, or even accounts due from customers.

Interest on debt securities is due according to the contract. Usually a fixed rate of interest is promised, although occasionally a debt holder may share in the net profits or have payments limited to them.

A convertible bond or debenture may be exchanged by the holder for an equity security, usually common stock. This permits the debt security holder to benefit from a rise in the price of common stock. If the price of the common stock rises compared with that of the debt security, the holder may exchange on the basis prescribed in the contract. Frequently, a sinking fund is provided to pay off an issue of debt securities.

TERMINATION OF THE CORPORATION

Dissolution by Agreement

Since the corporation is an entity created by the state, it must have the state's consent to dissolve. If the articles of incorporation provide for a limited rather than an indefinite life, the corporation automatically terminates at the end of the designated time. This is so rare that the MBCA does not even make clear whether any statement must be filed with the secretary of state after such automatic dissolution.

Incorporation statutes establish procedures for other situations where termination is voluntary. The MBCA provides for dissolution by a majority of the incorporators if the corporation has not begun business or issued any shares. The corporation may also be dissolved by written consent of all shareholders. The MBCA authorizes the board of directors to propose dissolution and hold a shareholder meeting. Dissolution results if a majority of the shareholders entitled to vote do so in favor of the proposal. Corporations with more than one class of shareholders sometimes provide for voting on dissolution and other matters by class. In such a case, the majority of each class must vote in favor of dissolution.

A corporation that merges into another is dissolved. If two corporations consolidate into a new corporation, both of the old ones are dissolved.

Involuntary Dissolution

A corporation may be dissolved by a judgment of a court. Under the MBCA the attorney general of the state may file an action for dissolution. Grounds for dissolution include failure to pay the annual franchise tax or to file its annual report with the secretary of state. Failure to appoint or maintain a registered agent in the state is another ground.

A shareholder may ask a court to dissolve a corporation. The MBCA allows this where the directors are in conflict, their deadlock cannot be broken by the shareholders, and the corporation faces ruin as a result. If directors are acting illegally or are being very unfair to shareholders, a court may dissolve the corporation. Misapplication or waste of corporate assets is another ground. A creditor may be able to get a court to dissolve a corporation if it is insolvent and cannot pay its bills.

Levant v. Kowal
86 N.W.2d 336 (Sup. Ct. Mich. 1957)

FACTS   The Keywell family owned half the shares of Barlum Hotels, Inc. The Kowal family owned the other half. The bylaws set a quorum for shareholder meetings (the number required to be represented for business to be conducted) of all the shares. The quorum for directors meetings was set at 12, the total number. The two families got into a bitter dispute. Arguments were often carried on in the lobby of the hotel in front of the guests. One argument had ended in fisticuffs. No shareholder or directors meetings were held for five years. No profits had been paid in dividends for six years. The corporation began to operate at a loss. Members of the Keywell family brought suit, asking for appointment of a receiver and the dissolution and liquidation of the corporation.

ISSUE   Were the circumstances appropriate for a court to dissolve the corporation and distribute its assets?

DECISION   Yes. A court may dissolve even a solvent corporation. If the directors are ruining the corporation from purely selfish motives, are freezing out minority shareholders, or are engaged in extreme mismanagement, a court may act to protect shareholders from abuses. To this end a court may appoint a temporary receiver. If there is no chance of eliminating the problem, the court may dissolve the corporation.

QUESTIONS AND PROBLEM CASES

1. What are the functions of a promoter of a corporation?

2. What liabilities does a promoter have?

3. What are the purposes of the articles of incorporation and the bylaws? How are they related to each other?

4. What is the basic difference between equity and debt securities?

5. Describe the differences among cumulative, noncumulative, and cumulative-to-the-extent-earned preferred stock.

6. Mr. and Mrs. Gullett were residents of Nashville, Tennessee. They planned a trip to Australia. A Nashville travel agency issued the tickets. The flight from California to Australia was on Qantas Airways. Mr. Gullett's mother died in Nashville while they were stopping in Nandi, Fiji Islands. A relative phoned Qantas there, requesting them to notify the Gulletts. The message was not delivered until after the Qantas plane had taken off for Australia, a five and one-half hour flight. Then it said only that they faced a grave emergency. The Gulletts sued Qantas in Nashville for $75,000 damages for extra expenses and emotional distress caused by its negligence. Qantas's defense was that it could not be sued in Tennessee because it did no business there and the claim arose elsewhere. Qantas had a listed toll-free phone number in both Memphis and Knoxville. Magazines carrying its advertising were distributed in Tennessee. Is Qantas subject to suit in Tennessee?

7. Dunnet and his associates acquired two oil royalty contracts. They paid $18,000 for one and

$2,500 for the other. They formed a corporation and transferred the contracts to it in exchange for its entire authorized stock—200,000 shares. Dunnet then donated back 80,000 shares to the corporation. All shareholders were aware of these transactions. Later Arn bought some of this stock at $3.50 per share. At this time the corporation had no assets other than the royalty contracts. The price of oil dropped and the corporation got into financial trouble. Arn sued to have Dunnet's stock and that of his associates canceled. Should the court cancel the stock?

8. Lord planned to form a corporation to take over a group of root beer drive-ins. He made a five-year contract with McCrillis to employ him as general manager. The corporation later received its charter. McCrillis was employed for 18 months and then discharged. McCrillis sued the corporation for breach of the contract. Its defense was that the contract was made before the corporation was formed. Is this a good defense?

9. Robert Bowers was an incorporator and promoter of Rio Grande Investment Company. He spent a good deal of time over a two-year period promoting the corporation. For these efforts the directors of the corporation gave him an option to buy 18,000 $1 par value shares of the corporation for $4,800. Bowers exercised the option. After a change of management, the corporation sued Bowers for the difference between the par value and what he had paid in cash. Is Bowers liable?

Management of the Corporate Business

30

CORPORATE POWERS

Sources of Powers

Corporations and their managers have legal power to do many things. This is true regardless of the amount of economic power the business itself may have, whether it is General Motors or Mom & Pop's Used Furniture. As indicated in the preceding chapter, a corporation gets its legal powers from the state in which it is incorporated. They come from the corporation statute, its articles of incorporation, and the court decisions of that state.

Limitations

Most promoters and incorporators try to give the corporation as broad a range of powers as the statute permits. Many corporations state their corporate purpose as broadly as possible. This clause in the articles may say "to transact any lawful business." However, sometimes the incorporators want to limit the business to a field in which they and/or the shareholders are experienced. They do not want to permit the directors to enter different businesses that might involve greater risks. Then the purpose clause may say something like, "to engage in the business of mining and sale of coal."

A few states limit or prohibit the acquisition of agricultural land by corporations and by trust departments of banks. It has been only recently that most states have permitted those engaged in professions such as medicine, dentistry, and law to use the corporate form. They can now incorporate as "professional associations" (P.A.s) or "professional corporations" (P.C.s). This allows them to take advantage of federal tax laws that encourage corporations to offer retirement plans to their employees. Incorporation does not, however, permit them to limit their liability for professional malpractice.

The *Ultra Vires* Doctrine

For many years courts took the view that acts done by corporations that were beyond the authority given them by either the state of incorporation or their articles were void and of no effect. A transaction that was beyond the corporation's powers was said to be *ultra vires*. The state (through the proper official), or a shareholder, or the corporation itself could prevent the enforcement of an *ultra vires* contract. This view was often used by the corporation to avoid a contract that later looked unattractive because of a change of conditions; unfairness to the other party to the contract was often the result.

For example, suppose the articles of the Clark Corporation stated that its purpose was to engage in the retail furniture business. Its shareholders had invested in the corporation and its banker had loaned it money because its principal directors and officers were experienced in this business. However, the directors later decided to extend the activities of the corporation to real estate development. The real estate activities would be *ultra vires*.

Assume Clark Corporation buys on contract 40 acres of land, contracts to have an engineer lay out streets and lots, and hires a contractor to put in sewers and pave. If the market for building lots slows down because of high interest rates, the shareholders stand to lose a great deal of money. If a court were to release the corporation from these contracts because they are *ultra vires*, the loss would fall on the other parties. This is clearly unfair.

Courts have not all agreed in handling these cases. Most of them have refused to enforce wholly executory contracts but let stand those that had been performed by both parties. Contracts that had been partially executed were most difficult for the courts. The majority of courts have held that such a contract is enforceable if one of the parties has received a benefit.

The Model Business Corporation Act (MBCA) has eliminated the use of *ultra vires* as a defense to the enforcement of a contract. However, it permits a shareholder to seek a court injunction to stop a corporation from carrying out a proposed action beyond its powers. It also permits the corporation itself, a shareholder, or a receiver in bankruptcy to bring a suit for damages to the corporation against the officers and/or directors who entered into an *ultra vires* contract. The state's attorney general is also permitted to enjoin the corporation from entering into unauthorized transactions.

Marsili v. Pacific Gas and Electric Co.
124 Cal. Rptr. 313 (Ct. App. Cal. 1975)

FACTS   Proposition T was on the ballot in the 1971 city election in San Francisco. It would require advance approval by the voters of any new building more than 72 feet high. A citizens group that opposed Proposition T asked Pacific Gas and Electric Co. to contribute to its campaign. The management determined that if this proposal were passed, it would have to redesign and buy more land for a planned substation. It estimated that PG&E's property taxes might be raised by as much as $1,135,000 per year over ten years. The executive committee of the board of directors authorized a donation of $10,000 to the campaign. It was properly reported to the California Public Utilities Commission. It was not treated as an operating expense for rate-making purposes, nor was it claimed as an income tax deduction.

Mr. and Mrs. Marsili and other shareholders sued the directors to recover for the corporation the amount of the donation. Neither PG&E's articles nor the corporate statute authorized corporations to make political expenditures.

ISSUE   Was the donation made to defeat Proposition T *ultra vires?*

DECISION   No. The court said that corporations have implied powers to do acts that are reasonably necessary to carry out their express powers. In the absence of an express restriction, a corporation may enter transactions that are reasonably related to the attainment of its corporate purposes. California statutes do not prohibit political activity by corporations, and the corporation's articles do not prohibit the directors from participating in political activities where the corporation has a legitimate concern. The directors reasonably concluded that adoption of Proposition T would adversely affect the business of the corporation.

MANAGEMENT OF THE CORPORATION

The shareholders are the owners of the corporation. They can affect the way the business is run through their power to elect directors and to amend the articles of incorporation. They do not, however, have the power to make management decisions. All statutes of incorporation give that power to the directors. The directors, in turn, usually delegate the making of at least the day-to-day operating decisions to the officers.

If the shareholders are dissatisfied with those decisions, they can replace the directors, who in turn will probably replace the officers. The shareholders generally have no right, however, to instruct the directors or the officers on the operating decisions they should make.

Shareholders must approve certain extraordinary corporate transactions such as a merger, a sale or lease of substantial assets of the corporation, or the dissolution of the corporation. However, the MBCA requires that the proposal for these actions come from the board of directors.

THE BOARD OF DIRECTORS

Powers and Duties

Most state incorporation statutes declare that *the business of the corporation shall be managed by a board of directors.* Of course, in a large corporation, especially where a number of the directors have full-time jobs elsewhere, this is impossible. The directors tend to ratify management decisions made by the top executives rather than to take the initiative in making the decisions. Recognizing this, the MBCA now says: "All corporate powers shall be exercised by or under the authority of, and the business and affairs of a corporation shall be managed under the direction of, a board of directors."

Certain corporate actions can be taken only after authorization by the board of directors. Statutes of the states vary on this. Among the actions for which director approval is required under the MBCA are: declaring a dividend; establishing the price for the sale of shares of stock; electing and removing officers; filling vacancies on the board of directors; and selling, leasing, and mortgaging assets of the corporation outside the normal course of its business.

Powers and Rights of the Director as an Individual

A director is not an agent for the corporation by virtue of that office. He or she has power to act for the corporation *only as a part of the board,* not as an individual. A director might, of course, be appointed by the board as an employee or an agent of the corporation.

A director has the right to inspect the corporate books and records. This right is necessary to carry out the director's duty of overseeing the management. The right to inspect can be denied where it can be shown that the director has an interest that conflicts with that of the corporation. Such an adverse interest would probably be a reason for removal of the director.

Election of Directors

Some states require corporations to have a minimum of three directors. The MBCA requires only one, recognizing that it would be superfluous to have more than one director when a single individual or another corporation owns all the stock. The MBCA allows the number of directors to be fixed in either the articles or the bylaws. If it is fixed in the bylaws, the directors can easily vary the number as conditions change. It is not necessary to go to the trouble and expense to amend the articles when a director dies or resigns and the directors are not ready to nominate a successor.

A few state statutes require directors to be shareholders. Some require that a certain percentage of the directors be citizens of the state of incorporation or of the United States. Qualifications for directors can be set out in the articles if desired.

Directors are elected by the shareholders at their annual meeting. Usually they are nominated by the current directors; however, nominations can be made from the floor during the shareholder meeting. This is not likely to have any effect in a large corporation that solicits proxies, as is discussed in Chapter 31.

Directors normally hold office only until the next annual meeting, or until a successor has been elected and qualified. The MBCA permits corporations to provide for staggered terms in their articles. A corporation that has a board of nine or more members may establish either two or three nearly equal *classes of directors*. Then only one class of directors is elected at each annual meeting unless there are vacancies. Staggered terms are said to assure that experienced directors remain on the board; however, they are usually adopted to make a corporate takeover more difficult.

Vacancies on the board can be filled only by vote of the shareholders unless the state statute, the articles, or the bylaws give this power to the board itself. The MBCA permits a majority of the remaining directors, even though less than a quorum, to elect directors to serve out unexpired terms. It also permits the board to increase the size of the board and then to elect a director to the vacancy created. Such a director may serve only until the next shareholder meeting.

Removal of Directors

A director may not be removed without cause unless this is permitted by statute or by articles or bylaws adopted prior to the director's election. The MBCA permits shareholders to remove directors with or without cause. A director who has failed to or is unable to attend and participate in directors meetings or who has acted contrary to the interests of the corporation can be removed for cause. Shareholders can remove a director for cause at any time even though the power of removal has been given by the articles or bylaws to the directors. Before being removed for cause, a director must be given notice and a hearing.

Directors Meetings

Boards of directors usually schedule regular meetings. Today boards of large corporations typically meet monthly; however, some corporations have regular meetings only quarterly. Small corporations in which most of the directors are active in the business have only an annual meeting of the directors.

Reasonable notice must be given for special meetings. If all directors attend a meeting, this cures any defect in or failure to give notice. However, a director who has not received a proper notice may attend solely to complain of the notice. In this case, he or she would not be held to have been in attendance. Directors may also cure a defect in the notice by waiving notice. The corporate secretary usually prepares and gets such a waiver signed if notice is late or otherwise defective. Under common law a waiver of notice has to be signed by all directors either before or during the meeting. The MBCA permits the waiver to be signed after the meeting.

Grossman v. Liberty Leasing Co., Inc.
295 A.2d 749 (Ch. Ct. Del. 1972)

FACTS The stock of Liberty Leasing Co. was publicly held. The Grossman and Gross families owned about 20 percent of it. Grossman was president and treasurer. Gross was executive vice president and secretary. Although the bylaws called for five, there were only four directors for more than a year. This was because of lack of agreement among board members. They finally agreed on three additional members. In December, with all four directors present, they amended the bylaws accordingly and elected the new directors.

A board meeting was held in February. It was attended by all seven directors. The board, with Grossman and Gross opposing, voted to sell immediately a division of the company. In a March meeting the board voted to oust Grossman and Gross as officers. Again, theirs were the only negative votes.

Grossman and Gross then asked the court to void the election of new directors in December. They argued that Liberty Leasing's bylaws require the filling of vacancies and the newly created directorships "at a special meeting called for the purpose." No notice of such a purpose had been given the directors. Therefore, they argued, the March elections were also void.

ISSUE Were the actions taken in the December and March meetings binding?

DECISION Yes. The court said the bylaw requiring notice is enforceable. However, the Delaware statute provides that any director may waive notice of any meeting. It also provides that attendance is a waiver unless it is only to object to transaction of business. Since all directors, including Grossman and Gross, attended the meetings, they waived any defect in the notice of meeting.

Under common law directors could act only when properly convened as a board and could not vote by proxy. This rule is based on the belief in the value of mutual counsel and collective judgment. The MBCA permits directors to act without a meeting if all directors consent in writing to the action taken. It also permits a director to attend a meeting through the use of a telephone hookup so that she or he can hear and be heard by the other directors.

Directors each have only one vote regardless of their shareholdings. Actions taken by a board are ineffective unless a *quorum* is present. Normally a quorum is a majority of the number of directors fixed by the articles or bylaws. The articles or bylaws may set the quorum at a higher figure. If there is a quorum present, the vote of a majority of directors present is the act of the board.

Compensation of Directors

Under common law directors had no power to fix their own salaries, and they were not entitled to compensation for their ordinary duties as a director. The MBCA permits directors to fix their compensation unless this is prohibited by the articles. Outside directors (those who are not employees of the corporation) are paid rather modest fees even in the largest corporations. However, directors' fees have been rising rapidly in recent years as their duties and liabilities have become greater. A study in 1978 found that among the largest 1,000 corporations, the average compensation was $10,499, with 46 percent paying between $6,000 and $12,000 per year.[1]

Recent Changes in Board Operation

Corporate Governance.   Recently there has been a good deal of discussion of what has been called "corporate governance." Several events triggered this concern. One was the failure of several large businesses, notably the Penn Central Railroad. Another was the fact that more than 400 large corporations admitted they had paid bribes to try to attain business objectives or had made illegal political contributions or both. In many of these cases it appeared that board members, or at least the outside directors, were not well informed. In some cases, such as the Penn Central, they were not even aware of the company's financial condition.

Courts had long recognized that boards of directors in large companies do not actually manage the corporation. However, it was widely believed that boards selected the top officers, determined major company policies, evaluated executive performance, and probed into company operations by asking discerning questions.

An extensive study of boards published in 1972 found that in many corporations this concept of the board was a myth.[2] It was concluded that board members serve as advisors to management rather than as business decision makers. They often act to replace the chief executive only when he or she is dead or disabled. They are usually slow to act when the company is doing poorly. However, it was found that the requirement of making reports to a board did provide some discipline for management.

In fact, most directors were selected by the top management they were supposed to supervise. This was accomplished through the proxy system of electing directors, which will be discussed in the next chapter. This was true of the outside directors as well as the inside directors (those who are full-time executives of the corporation). Frequently, nearly the entire board was made up of inside directors.

Changes.   It appears that recently most boards of directors have become more independent from top management, devote more time to their duties as directors, and make a greater effort than formerly to see that the company is well managed.

There have been several causes of these changes. There has been a great increase in the number of lawsuits brought by shareholders and the

---

[1] Heidrick and Struggles, "The Changing Board," *Directors & Boards*, vol. 4, no. 4, Winter 1979, p. 63.

[2] Myles L. Mace, "The President and the Board of Directors," *Harvard Business Review*, March–April 1972, p. 37.

Securities and Exchange Commission (SEC) against directors who allegedly breach their duties. Quite a number of these have resulted in settlements, although few in actual court judgments against directors. There has been a good deal of public criticism of board practices and their lack of accountability by the SEC, by professors, and by people such as Ralph Nader. The passage of the Foreign Corrupt Practices Act in 1977 was also a stimulus. It imposes a duty on directors to see that the corporation has an effective record-keeping system as well as forbidding payments to officials of foreign governments.

Committees of the Board. The boards of directors of large corporations are using committees of the board more and more. This permits a small group from the board to give considerable attention to a specific responsibility and then to make recommendations to the entire board. Expertise and experience of board members can thus be better used and the time demands of board duties reduced.

The bylaws of most large corporations set up an *executive committee*, which is often given full authority to act for the board between meetings. Members of the committee are often inside directors and/or board members who can easily come to a meeting. In the past many corporations used such committees to avoid taking some matters to the entire board or to make recommendations to the whole board on complex or important matters. Today they are more likely to be used only on routine matters that require immediate board approval such as approval of the sale of a piece of property.

Under pressure from the SEC, the New York Stock Exchange now requires all corporations whose stock it lists to set up *audit committees* composed of outside directors. Principal functions usually include recommending to the board the outside auditing firm, serving as the board contact with that firm, and overseeing for the board the auditing function within the company. Most publicly held corporations, even those not listed on any exchange, now have such committees.

Recently, a number of the larger publicly held corporations have established *nominating committees* of the board. Their duties usually are to nominate new directors and to recommend to the whole board the selection of the top officers of the corporation. Such a committee can be effective in the development of a board that is not dominated by the chief executive.

Other common board committees in large corporations include a *finance committee* and a *compensation committee*. The compensation committee is concerned with the compensation of the officers of the corporation. It is usually composed of a majority of outside directors because the top officers are usually directors.

In 1978 the SEC issued rules requiring a corporation that makes reports to it to disclose whether it has audit, nominating, and compensation committees of the board. It must describe committee functions and identify their members. It must also name any director who attends less than 75 percent of the board meetings plus the meetings of committees on which he or she sits.

OFFICERS OF THE CORPORATION

Powers

The MBCA provides that a corporation shall have a president, one or more vice presidents (as stated in the bylaws), a secretary, and a treasurer. Any two or more offices may be held by the same person except the offices of president and secretary. This permits dual signatures on corporate documents. Many corporations have established the office of chairman of the board; this person may be the chief executive of the corporation. Occasionally it is only a part-time position.

President or Chairman

The power of the officers to bind the corporation on contracts they make on its behalf is the same as that of any agent. In addition to their express authority, they have implied and apparent authority. Certain officers may also have *ex officio* authority, that is, authority by virtue of their offices. This, however, is more restricted than is generally believed. The president or chairman of the board has no power to bind the corporation solely because of his position. However, if he is also the chief executive, then broad authority is implied to make contracts and do other acts appropriate to the ordinary business of the firm. A corporate officer is liable to the corporation for resulting losses if he acts beyond his authority.

Belcher v. Birmingham Trust Nat'l. Bank
348 F.Supp. 61 (N. D. Ala. 1968)

FACTS The W. E. Belcher Lumber Co. was a family-owned business. Brady Belcher, son of the founder, was president. He had slightly more shares in the corporation than each of the families of his four brothers and sisters. Brady Belcher organized a subsidiary corporation to exploit a timber contract to log certain public lands in Costa Rica. This required an investment in road building of $400,000. It required an additional capital investment after depreciation of $200,000 per year for ten years. Brady took these actions without discussing them with the board of directors. Those directors who were active in the business were aware of the investments. The project was not profitable. A member of the family who was not a director sued to require Brady to indemnify the corporation for its losses.

ISSUE Was Brady Belcher personally liable for the losses?

DECISION Yes. The court found that the project was not in the ordinary course of the corporation's business. Brady, therefore, acted beyond the scope of his authority as president. An unusual project involving the investment of large sums of money, especially in a foreign country, required action by the board of directors. This is true even though timber operations were the corporation's business.

Vice President

A vice president has no authority by virtue of that office. However, if the title indicates that the person is the principal officer of some area of the business, he or she has considerable implied authority. For example, the vice president of marketing has implied authority to do those acts normally done by a manager of sales.

Corporate Secretary

The corporate secretary (called "clerk" in some states) keeps the minutes of meetings of the shareholders and directors and other general corporate records such as stockholder records. The office gives the secretary no authority to bind the corporation on contracts. However, there is a presumption that a document to which the secretary has affixed the corporate seal has been properly authorized.

Treasurer

The treasurer has charge of the funds of the corporation. He or she has power to pay out corporate funds for proper purposes and is the person who receives payments to the corporation. The treasurer binds the corporation on receipts, checks, and indorsements. However, the treasurer does not have authority by virtue of the office alone to borrow money or issue negotiable instruments.

Like any principal, a corporation may ratify an unauthorized act by its officers or other agents. This may be done through a resolution of the board of directors or of the shareholders. It may also be implied from acceptance of benefits from the unauthorized act.

Duties of Directors and Officers

Although directors and officers are not agents of the corporation, they have the same fiduciary duties any agent owes the principal. These include: (1) to act within one's authority and within the powers of the corporation, (2) to act diligently and with due care in conducting the affairs of the corporation, and (3) to act with loyalty and good faith for the benefit of the corporation.

The recent trend has been to raise the standard of conduct required of directors and officers. This has been done through the SEC and the federal securities laws it administers. It has also been done by courts in interpreting the common law. The corporation has a right of action against directors and officers who breach their duties to it. If the same directors are still in control, they are unlikely to bring a suit, but a shareholder can bring the suit on behalf of the corporation. Shareholder suits are discussed in the next chapter.

Acting within Authority. Directors and officers must act within the authority given to them and to the corporation by statute, the articles, and the bylaws. However, if they enter an *ultra vires* transaction, justifiably believing it to be within the scope of the corporation's business, they are not held liable.

Due Care and Diligence. The standard of care required of directors is stated differently by various statutes and courts. The MBCA requires that they act with "such care as an ordinarily prudent person in a like position would use under similar circumstances." They are not liable for mere errors of judgment if they act with care and good faith. This is the *business judgment rule*. The courts do not second-guess decisions intended to benefit the corporation. Directors and officers are liable for negligence, both for their actions and for their failures to take appropriate action. This includes negligence in selecting and supervising officers and employees of the corporation.

Loyalty and Good Faith.   Directors and officers must act for the best interests of the corporation. They breach their duty if they try to profit personally at the expense of the corporation.

Directors and officers are not prohibited from entering into transactions with the corporation. At one time courts held that such deals were voidable by the corporation, but today the majority of courts hold them voidable only if unfair to the corporation. However, before a director (or another business organization in which he or she has a major interest) enters a contract with the corporation, the director should make a *full disclosure* of his or her interest. If the board is to vote on the transaction, the director should not vote or even participate in the discussion preceding the vote.

Directors and officers may not *usurp a corporate opportunity*. If a business opportunity comes to them in their job and it falls within the corporation's normal scope of business, they cannot take it for themselves. For example, directors may not buy land near the corporation's plant and then sell it to the firm at a profit. Nor may they buy the right to sell a product that would fit into the corporation's line of goods. If the corporation is financially unable to take the opportunity or if a noninterested majority of directors votes against it, then a director or officer may take it. However, this is not true if the result would be competitive injury to the corporation.

Guth v. Loft, Inc.
5 A.2d 503 (Sup. Ct. Del. 1939)

FACTS   Loft, Inc., was a manufacturer of candy, beverages, and food products. It also had a large number of retail stores and did a wholesale business. Guth became general manager of Loft. Loft was selling large amounts of Coca-Cola in its retail stores, and Guth unsuccessfully tried to negotiate a jobber's discount. He learned that Pepsi-Cola could be purchased for about one-third less. While Guth was considering the purchase of Pepsi-Cola, then little-known, that company went bankrupt. Guth assisted the man who controlled Pepsi-Cola to form a new corporation to take over its trademark, secret formula, and business. Guth eventually came to hold most of the stock.

Loft became Pepsi-Cola's chief customer, but profits of its retail stores were estimated to have dropped by $300,000 because it discarded Coca-Cola. Guth used

Loft's working capital, plant, and equipment in Pepsi-Cola's business. He claimed the Loft directors had decided not to acquire Pepsi-Cola and had authorized the use of Loft facilities, money, and credit. However, the minutes of their meetings did not record any such actions and there was no other evidence.

Pepsi-Cola became profitable and the stock very valuable. Loft brought suit to force Guth to give his shares in Pepsi-Cola to Loft.

ISSUE   Did Guth breach his duty of loyalty to Loft by usurping a corporate opportunity in developing Pepsi-Cola?

DECISION   Yes. The court directed Guth to turn over the stock to Loft, Inc. It found that he had not given Loft a chance to acquire Pepsi-Cola. He had used Loft's assets for the benefit of himself. It said, "He thrust upon Loft the hazard, while he reaped the benefit."

There have been many lawsuits in which minority shareholders complain that they have been unfairly treated by the directors. Usually these involve close corporations. The suits may claim oppression of minority shareholders or an attempt to "freeze" them out. Some of these allege refusal to pay dividends even though the corporation is able to do so. Others allege that unreasonably high salaries have been paid to controlling shareholders and their friends. Others involve purchases by or sales of assets to controlling shareholders where the price is said to be unfair. Usually minority shareholders win such suits only where the acts of directors have clearly been in bad faith or clearly abuse the discretion given them under the business judgment rule.

SEC Actions against Stock Traders.   Buying or selling the corporation's stock may be a breach of duty. Rule 10b-5 of the SEC has been interpreted to prohibit an officer or director who has material information concerning the corporation that has not been given to the public from buying or selling its stock. Information is material if it is likely to affect the desire of an investor or potential investor to buy, sell, or hold the stock.

SEC v. Texas Gulf Sulphur Co.
401 F.2d 833 (2d Cir. 1968)

FACTS   Texas Gulf Sulphur Co. (TGS) obtained a drill core that was fabulously rich in minerals while test drilling near Timmons, Ontario. It stopped further drilling until it could buy mineral rights on nearby land, and it tried to maintain secrecy both within and outside the company. During this period several company directors, officers, and employees who were aware of the results of the first drilling purchased shares of TGS stock through brokers on the New York Stock Exchange. Some other employees were given stock options by a committee of corporate directors who were not aware of the find. The Securities and Exchange Commission brought an action alleging violations of SEC Rule 10b–5.

ISSUE   Did those who bought stock and accepted options before TGS fully disclosed the nature of the discovery violate Rule 10b–5?

DECISION   Yes. The court held that the information was material even though the extent of the ore body was uncertain when the purchases were made. The information, if known, might well have affected the price of TGS stock. It would be important to an investor in deciding whether to buy, sell, or hold TGS stock. Anyone in possession of material "inside" information must either disclose it to the investing public or abstain from trading in or recommending the securities while the information remains undisclosed.

Under Section 16b of the Securities Exchange Act of 1934 a director or officer who makes a "short-swing" profit in the company's stock must give the profit to the corporation. A profit is "short-swing" if it occurs when a purchase and an offsetting sale (or a sale and purchase) are made within six months.

Other Securities Act Violations.   Directors and officers can be held liable for other violations of the federal securities acts. The Securities Act of 1933 makes directors liable for anything false or misleading in the registration statement for a security issued by the corporation. Registration with the SEC is required of securities offered for sale to the public.[3] Even omissions of information necessary to make accurate disclosures imposes liability.

Directors and officers may also become liable for violation of several antifraud provisions of the securities acts. Any statement about a security that is misleading made orally as well as in writing is a violation. A *security* includes not only stocks and bonds but other investment contracts as well. These have been interpreted as including limited partnerships and franchises. The test is whether the business is one in which profits are expected to come primarily from the efforts of the promoter rather than the investor. The acts impose criminal penalties and give the SEC the right to seek injunctions. Private damage actions by those injured by violations are also permitted.

LIABILITY FOR TORTS AND CRIMES

Torts

A corporation is liable for all torts committed by its employees while acting in the course of and within the scope of their employment. This

---

[3] See Chapter 31 for a further discussion of registration with the SEC.

may be true even when the corporation has instructed the employee to avoid the act. Directors and officers who have not personally participated in or authorized the tort have no individual liability; only the corporation and the person committing the tort are liable. The fact that the corporation rather than the employee benefited from the tort is no defense in an action against an officer or employee of a corporation.

McGlynn v. Schultz
231 A.2d 386 (Super. Ct. App. Div. N.J. 1967)

FACTS Office Buildings of America (OBA) was engaged in the business of syndicating real estate. It would enter a contract to purchase an income-producing property and then sell it to a limited partnership. It would lease back the property, usually guaranteeing a return of 9 percent on the partners' investment.

OBA contracted to buy the Neptune City Shopping Center. It then organized Neptune Center Associates (NCA), a limited partnership, and sold partnership interests to the public. The partnership agreement provided for a separate bank account but none was opened. Instead the sum of $414,900 collected from the limited partners was deposited in OBA's account. Before title to the shopping center was transferred to NCA, OBA was declared bankrupt.

A receiver for NCA, the partnership, sued the officer-directors of OBA for damages due to their conversion of trust funds belonging to NCA. None of the funds went to them personally. They had been advised by a lawyer that there was no statute requiring that the funds be put in escrow.

ISSUE Were the officer-directors who participated in the misappropriation of the funds liable for conversion when they received no benefit?

DECISION Yes. A director or officer who instigates or assists in a conversion by his corporation is personally liable. Good faith is not a defense to an action for conversion. Therefore, good faith reliance on a lawyer's opinion is no defense. In any case, the officers knew of the serious shortage of cash of OBA. They took a chance in using the funds they held in trust for NCA. Unfortunately, their belief that they would be able to repay them was unfounded.

Courts are becoming more willing to find negligence on the part of corporate directors and officers. Where corporate activities have caused injury or economic damage to others, the officer in charge, or even the directors, may be held liable.

Crimes Many criminal statutes clearly are intended to apply to corporations. Examples besides the securities acts include the Sherman Act and various laws relating to employment, such as OSHA. The traditional view was that a corporation could not be guilty of a crime involving intent. However, modern penal codes make corporations responsible for crimes committed by a high-level manager within the scope of employment.

Directors and officers may be held individually guilty of crimes even if their only motive is to benefit the corporation. They are also guilty if they request, authorize, or assist in some way the commission of a crime by an employee. As the *Park* case in Chapter 3 indicates, they may also be held criminally liable in some instances where they have failed in their supervisory duties.

Indemnification and Insurance

The cost of defending and/or settling a suit or criminal charge brought against a director, officer, or employee may be very high. Some court decisions have not permitted a corporation to pay these costs or indemnify the defendant even though the act was done in what the defendant thought to be the interests of the corporation. The MBCA permits the corporation to indemnify that person for costs, judgments, and fines if he acted in good faith in a manner "he reasonably believed to be in or not opposed to the best interests of the corporation." In a criminal case the defendant must further show that he had "no reasonable cause to believe his conduct was unlawful." The SEC has opposed the application of such statutes to violations of the securities laws.

Many corporations take out directors' and officers' (D&O) liability insurance to protect them in case of such legal actions. Typically, both the liability of the corporation to indemnify and the direct liability of the director and officer are insured under these policies.

QUESTIONS AND PROBLEM CASES

1. Explain the meaning of the *ultra vires* doctrine. Who can claim a corporate transaction is *ultra vires*?

2. What powers and what rights does a corporate director have as an individual?

3. Discuss the nature of recent criticism of boards of directors of large publicly held corporations. What changes in board operation have been made to deal with some of this criticism?

4. Discuss the meaning and application of the business judgment rule.

5. Give two examples of acts by officers or directors that might be held to be usurpation of a corporate opportunity.

6. Capital Service, Inc., was incorporated under the general incorporation statute of Wiscon-

sin. Education institutions were required to incorporate under another statute. Capital's articles stated its purpose: "To . . . assist and advise . . . persons seeking employment . . . , to provide information relating to employment with governmental agencies, to print, . . . sell, and distribute pamphlets and letters relating to employment with governmental agencies, and to manufacture, sell . . . books, . . . examination papers, . . . and school supplies of every class and description." Capital prepared and sold a two-year course of study involving study materials, lessons to be submitted, and giving and grading examinations. The attorney general brought suit to cancel Capital's charter. He claimed it was operating as an education institution in excess of the powers given in its charter. Will he win?

7. The articles of incorporation of Automatic Steel Products, Inc., provided for staggered terms with three classes of two directors each. It further provided that each director would hold office for three years or until his or her death or resignation. A bylaw provided that a director might be removed, with or without cause, at any time by the vote of a majority of shareholders. Three of the six directors were removed without cause by a majority vote of the shareholders. A shareholder brought suit, claiming their removal was invalid as contrary to the articles of incorporation. Is the removal valid?

8. Phx.-Scotts. Sports Company was incorporated to operate retail sporting goods departments in two department stores. The stores were operated by Govway Corporation in Phoenix and Scottsdale, Arizona. Frank Farella and Doris Kadish each owned 50 percent of the voting stock of the corporation. Farella was in the wholesale sporting goods business. He was named president of Phx.-Scotts. Doris Kadish was secretary-treasurer and was also the active manager. Her husband, Moses Kadish, was a director as well as being president and principal shareholder in Govway Corporation. He also was a 50 percent shareholder in both Esskay Corp. and Kemco, Inc. Both Moses and Doris Kadish were authorized to sign checks on the Phx.-Scotts. bank account. Two months after the formation of Phx.-Scotts., Moses drew a check for $29,000 payable to himself. Another check signed by Moses for $2,600 was made payable to Govway and one to Esskay for $8,000 signed by Doris. The checks were not authorized by the board of directors. Mr. and Mrs. Kadish contend that the checks were for a valid business purpose. Govway was having financial difficulties and they were necessary to keep Phx.-Scotts.'s advantageous position in the Govway stores. Were the acts of preparing the checks wrongful so the liability to repay would not be cut off by the bankruptcy discharge of both Moses and Doris Kadish?

9. The J. H. Cox Manufacturing Co. was a wholesale supplier of drapery material. The corporation was controlled by Cox. Engdahl was an assistant to Cox and a shareholder. Engdahl also held 10 percent of the shares of Aero Drapery of Kentucky, which was a drapery wholesaler controlled by Cox. Engdahl, who lived in Indianapolis, visited Aero twice a week. Engdahl learned that Aero's manager was dissatisfied with his job. He and the manager decided to open a competing business. They were joined by both Aero's workroom manager and its top salesperson. Space was rented, goods purchased, and a yellow pages listing purchased. Then Engdahl gave notice of quitting and sold his stock back to Cox. Cox Manufacturing Co. brought a suit for damages against Engdahl. Is he liable?

10. The manager of the television department of a W. T. Grant store in Santa Barbara sold used television sets as new. W. T. Grant was charged with grand theft. Its defense was that it could not be guilty unless a higher-level executive was aware of the practice. Is this a good defense?

Shareholder Functions, Rights, and Liabilities

31

INTRODUCTION

The Role of Shareholders

If you are not already the owner of shares of stock in a corporation, you may wish to become one. No large investment is necessary. Many shares sell for less than $10 per share, although those of companies with good financial prospects usually sell for more. Although you will find in this chapter that shareholders have a number of rights, most shareholders are interested in only one—the right to share in the profits of the corporation.

Functions of Shareholders

Although owners of the corporation, shareholders have few functions and in most corporations exercise little influence. Normally, their principal function is the election of the directors. In large corporations the proxy system of voting and the tendency of most shareholders to follow the recommendations of management usually result in the election of persons nominated by management.

Shareholders are also required to approve unusual or extraordinary corporate transactions such as a merger, sale of substantially all corporate assets, or a voluntary dissolution. In addition, their favorable vote is necessary to amend the corporate articles. Some states require shareholder approval for other matters as well. For example, the Model Business Corporation Act (MBCA) requires shareholder approval of stock option plans for corporate officers and other managers. It also requires approval of loans to officers by the corporation.

These functions are performed at shareholder meetings. The meetings may be either the regular annual meeting or special meetings.

BECOMING A SHAREHOLDER

Means of Acquiring Stock

One can become a shareholder by several means. One is by subscribing to shares in a new corporation being formed. Another is by subscribing for shares that are being issued by an existing corporation. More common is to buy newly issued shares that have been underwritten by an investment banker and sold through a stockbroker. (An underwriter of a stock issue agrees to market it to investors and usually guarantees to sell the entire issue.) The most common way of becoming a shareholder is by buying previously issued shares from a former owner, either directly or through a broker.

Subscriptions to buy stock in a corporation that is not yet in existence are usually treated as offers until incorporation is completed. The MBCA makes such subscriptions irrevocable for six months. Many statutes provide that the issuance of the certificate of incorporation amounts to an acceptance. *At that time the subscriber becomes a shareholder.*

A subscription for unissued shares in an existing corporation is usually treated as an offer. A contract is formed and *the subscriber becomes a shareholder when the corporation accepts the offer.* The making of the subscription contract is called "issuing stock." The stock certificate cannot, under the MBCA, be issued until the shares are fully paid for.

The Federal Securities Acts

Congress passed the Securities Act of 1933 and the Securities Exchange Act of 1934 to protect investors in securities. They have two basic aims. The first is to require disclosure of enough information to permit the investor to evaluate the merits of a security and its issuer. The second is to prohibit unfair, deceptive, and manipulative practices in the issuance, distribution, and sale of securities. The Securities and Exchange Commission (SEC) was established to interpret and enforce these acts.

For the purpose of the acts, the term *security* includes a much broader range of investments than just shares of stock and corporate bonds. Any investment contract involving an enterprise in which the investor is led to expect profits primarily from the efforts of the promoter or some other person rather than the investor's efforts is treated as a security. Limited partnerships and some franchises have been held to be securities covered by the acts.

The 1933 act requires corporations that intend to make a public offering of stock or other securities to file a *registration statement* with the SEC. It also requires the filing of a *prospectus* with the SEC. The prospectus includes most of the information about the company and the stock issue that is required in the registration statement. The prospectus must be furnished to any purchaser of the security. Resales after the security issue has been distributed need not be accompanied by a prospectus. The purpose of the registration statement and prospectus is to provide information. The SEC does not approve the security itself or its soundness as an investment.

Purely intrastate offerings and small offerings totaling no more than $1.5 million are exempted from the requirement of the registration with the SEC. Another exemption is given to *private offerings*. Under this exemption sales must be limited to 35 purchasers or less who are experienced investors and who are able to assume the economic risk. The purchasers in private offerings are restricted in their right to resell the securities.

If there are any false or misleading statements or omissions in the registration statement and prospectus, the corporation will be liable. The directors, certain corporate officers, and experts such as accountants who have prepared material included in these documents will also be liable.

Corporations that have registered securities with the SEC and those that have total assets exceeding $1 million and 500 shareholders must file quarterly and annual reports with the SEC. These reports must include not only income statements and balance sheets but also other information necessary to bring the registration statement up to date.

Antifraud Provisions of the Securities Acts

The prohibition in the securities acts against making false and misleading statements and using deceptive schemes applies to offers or sales of any security by anyone. One who makes such statements in offering to sell shares in a small, local corporation is in violation if the mail or even the telephone is used.

Escott v. BarChris Construction Corp.
283 F.Supp. 643 (S.D.N.Y. 1968)

FACTS Escott and other investors brought suit to recover the loss of their investment in debentures issued by BarChris Construction Corporation. BarChris built bowling alleys. It became bankrupt when the owners could not meet payments due on the alleys. Defendants were those who had signed the registration statement filed with the SEC. In its prospectus for the debentures, BarChris had overstated sales and earnings and its current assets. It also understated its contingent liabilities on some of its sales contracts and failed to disclose that a large part of the proceeds from the sale of the debentures would be used to pay off old debts. It also failed to disclose that it was in the business of operating bowling alleys. It had begun operating some of the alleys whose owners were in default on their payments. Some of the defendants were unaware of the misleading statements and omissions. Auslander was an outside director who had just joined the board before the debentures were registered and had not read the registration statement. Another defendant was Peat, Marwick, Mitchell & Co., the public accounting firm. Trilling, a junior officer who was controller, also claimed he was unaware of the falsity.

ISSUE Were those who signed the registration statement liable because of misleading statements and omissions even if they were unaware of them?

DECISION Yes. The Securities Act of 1933 provides a "due diligence" defense. The court held that this defense requires some sort of an investigation by the defendant to determine whether what is in the registration statement is true and complete. The court concluded that Trilling did not believe in the accuracy of the prospectus because he should have known of some of the inaccuracies. It held Auslander liable because he merely accepted the word of top management officials. Peat, Marwick was held liable because its review of the accounts should have alerted it to make a more thorough investigation.

Rule 10b–5 of the Securities and Exchange Commission has been the basis of recovery most often used by investors for misleading statements in connection with purchases or sales of securities. It has been used in suits against corporate directors and officers, accountants, lawyers, security salespeople, and many others as well as corporations.

The securities acts and SEC rules do not always permit an investor who loses money to recover the loss. However, lawyers for unfortunate investors often seek to find some failure to disclose or a misleading disclosure that could be the basis of a lawsuit. Criminal penalties are also provided.

Myzel v. Fields
386 F.2d 718 (8th Cir. 1967)

FACTS Harry Fields purchased 30 shares of stock at $50 per share in Lakeside Plastics and Engraving Co. when it was founded. It was a close corporation. He made the investment on the advice of his friend, Benn Myzel. Myzel was a financial advisor of the company, and he also had served several terms as a director. The small company struggled to sell its advertising signs for five years but built up deficits. Myzel used both the telephone and personal meetings to buy the stock of Fields and three other shareholders at prices ranging from $6.67 to $45.00 per share. He told them the company was not making money and that he was "going to get out."

At this time Myzel knew the company had made a large and potentially very profitable contract with Blatz Brewing Co. He later sold these shares and his own at a big profit to one of the other shareholders, who then took over control. Fields and the other sellers sued Myzel.

ISSUE Did Myzel violate SEC Rule 10b–5 so as to be liable for damages?

DECISION Yes. He had used the telephone, which is "an instrumentality of interstate commerce," making the 1934 act applicable. A misrepresentation is not necessary under Rule 10b–5. It applies to omissions to give material information as well as to untruths.

Blue Sky Laws

All states have statutes to protect investors. These are called "blue sky" laws because they aim to stop extravagant claims about the securities being offered. Frequently they exempt from state registration any security registered with the SEC. The major thrust of most state statutes, like the federal ones, is to require disclosure and prohibit deception. However, a few give the state securities commissioner power to deny the registration of securities that are found to be of little investment value. Many require securities sales people to be licensed. Criminal penalties are provided.

SHAREHOLDER MEETINGS

Annual Meeting

All state laws except Delaware's require corporations formed in the state to have an annual meeting. A Delaware corporation can use a mail ballot instead of holding a meeting. The main purpose of the annual meeting is the election of directors. Many larger corporations ask the shareholders to approve the selection of public auditors. There may be other proposals by management for shareholder approval, such as an executive stock option or profit-sharing plan or an amendment to the articles of incorporation. There may also be resolutions proposed by shareholders to be voted upon. It is customary for the chief executive and perhaps other officers to give brief reports on the corporation's operations during the past year and the prospects for the current year. Shareholders may ask questions of the top officers, usually during a question period scheduled to follow the officer reports.

Only a few states require those businesses incorporated by them to hold their shareholder meetings within the state. Most large corporations hold their annual meetings in the city where their headquarters office is located. A few rotate their meetings between major cities to give more shareholders a chance to attend an occasional meeting. Some publicly held corporations hold their meetings in their state of incorporation even though (and probably because) it is inconvenient for many shareholders to attend. Companies that wish to encourage shareholder attendance often provide refreshments or, if appropriate, a small gift of company products. Even so, it is uncommon for more than 1,000 shareholders to attend an annual meeting of even the largest corporation. For example, in May 1979, 753 shareholders out of a total of 1,269,778 (.06 percent) attended General Motors Corporation's annual meeting. However, 714,795 shareholders (56.29 percent) were represented at the meeting either in person or by proxy.[1]

Special Meetings

Special meetings of shareholders are quite rare in most corporations. One is called when shareholder approval of a corporate action is necessary between annual meetings. The most common purpose is probably to get approval of a proposal by the directors to merge with another corporation.

---

[1] From the June 9, 1979, communication to shareholders accompanying the quarterly dividend check.

The MBCA provides that a special meeting may be called by the president, the board of directors, or the holders of one tenth or more of the shares entitled to vote at the meeting. Under the MBCA the bylaws may provide that other officers or persons (such as the chairman of the board) may call a special meeting of shareholders.

Notice of Meetings

The MBCA requires notice of all shareholder meetings to be given not less than 10 or more than 50 days before the meeting. The notice must give the place, day, and hour of the meeting. For special meetings, the purpose of the meeting must be given. If an extraordinary corporate transaction such as a merger is to be voted on, notice of the proposal must be given to *all* shareholders, even if there are shareholders who own a class of stock not usually entitled to vote. Those shareholders entitled to notice are those *of record*. They are the people whose names appear on the stock-transfer book of the corporation.

If the required notice is not given, actions taken at a meeting are of no effect. However, shareholders who did not get proper notice may *waive notice*. As in the case of directors meetings, attendance at the meeting is an automatic *waiver*. However, there is no waiver if the shareholder attends only to object to the holding of the meeting. Waiver is effective only if all shareholders either attend or waive in writing.

Darvin v. Belmont Industries, Inc.
199 N.W.2d 542 (Ct. App. Mich. 1972)

FACTS Frank Darvin owned one fourth of the shares in Belmont Industries, Inc., a small corporation. There were four other shareholders. Darvin and three others were the officers and employees of the corporation. They also were the directors. A dispute over management arose between Darvin and Underwood, the president of the company. The other three directors decided they no longer wanted Darvin in the company.

A special shareholder meeting and a directors meeting were scheduled for September 12. Darvin received notice of the shareholder meeting on September 11. He and his attorney attended and at the beginning objected to the lack of adequate notice. The board of directors was reduced to three members and Darvin was not elected. He did not vote his stock. At the directors meeting that followed, Darvin was not elected an officer. He was later fired as an employee. The bylaws of the corporation called for notice of shareholder meetings at least ten days in advance.

ISSUE Did Darvin's attendance at the shareholder meeting amount to a waiver of the defect in the notice of the meeting?

DECISION No. The purpose of the requirement of notice at a certain time before a meeting is to allow the shareholder time to prepare for it. The court held that attendance at the meeting without participation is not a waiver of defective notice. Darvin had attended only to object to the lack of timely notice.

Shareholders Entitled to Vote

If you are a shareholder, your right to vote at a shareholder meeting depends on the incorporation statute and the articles and bylaws of the corporation. If you own common stock and have it listed in your name, you probably have a right to vote.

Owners of a nonvoting class of stock have a right to vote only under certain circumstances. The MBCA gives holders of such stock the right to vote on extraordinary corporate transactions, which are discussed later in this chapter.

The person who has legal title to the stock is the one usually entitled to vote. Directors of publicly held corporations usually establish a *record date* prior to each shareholder meeting. Those who are *shareholders of record* on that date are allowed to vote. Those who are owners of shares held in the name of another, such as a stockbroker, may obtain a proxy from the record holder. SEC rules require brokers to mail proxy material to customers for whom they hold shares.

Neither a corporation nor its subsidiary may vote *treasury shares*. Treasury shares are those that are issued and then later reacquired by the corporation. Unissued stock, of course, carries no vote.

Proxy Voting

As a shareholder you may appoint another person, known as a *proxy*, to vote for you. The MBCA requires a written document appointing the proxy as an agent to vote for you. This document is also, rather confusingly, called a *proxy*. Some states permit an oral proxy. A proxy may generally be revoked at any time; it is automatically revoked if you later give another proxy.

As indicated above, usually in publicly held corporations only a small proportion of the shares are owned by persons who attend shareholder meetings. Management then solicits proxies. It asks the shareholders who do not expect to attend to appoint, as their proxy, one or more of the directors or some other person friendly to management. Most shareholders sign and return their proxies.

The proxy document, under SEC rules, must permit the shareholder to vote yes or no for the election of directors and any resolutions that have been proposed. Shareholders usually follow the recommendations of management in their voting or merely sign the proxy without voting. The proxy also usually gives management authority to vote the shares on any other matter coming before the meeting. The effect, of course, is to determine the outcome of the meeting before it is held. Argument made for or against a resolution at the meeting can only affect the votes of those present. A resolution made from the floor has no chance of passing unless the management votes its proxies in favor of it.

It is control of the proxy system, of course, that permits management to control the corporation without owning many shares itself. The corporation pays for the preparation and mailing of a proxy statement. If someone else or a group wants to nominate directors, that group must bear the expense of soliciting proxies. A proxy battle tends to be very expensive, and relatively few challengers win. If they do, they are entitled to be reimbursed by the corporation for their expenses because it is assumed from the shareholder support that the corporation has benefited.

The SEC has power under the 1934 act to make rules about proxy statements. The *proxy statement* must give certain information. For example, if directors are to be elected, information must be given about any employment contract and pension or stock option benefits and any material transaction between a nominee and the corporation. An annual statement must be mailed with or before the proxy statement for an annual meeting.

SEC rules require corporations subject to them to furnish a shareholder list to any shareholder who desires to solicit proxies. As an alternative, the corporation may mail the proxy material for the soliciting shareholder.

Conduct of the Meeting

Before any voting can be done at a meeting, a quorum must be present either in person or by proxy. This is the reason managements in publicly held corporations solicit proxies. The MBCA defines a quorum as a majority of the *shares* (not of the *shareholders*). It permits the bylaws to set the quorum at a different percentage. Some states require the quorum to be at least one third of outstanding shares.

The bylaws usually state who is to preside at shareholder meetings. It is usually the chairman of the board if there is such a person; otherwise, the president is given this task. The minutes of the meetings are usually prepared by the secretary of the corporation. Although not required by the statutes of most states, these records may be very important if questions arise as to what happened in a meeting.

Shareholder Proposals and Right to Speak

Shareholders have the right in shareholder meetings both to ask questions and to propose resolutions. The first right is that of an owner to be informed about his or her investment. The second is the right of an owner to participate in establishing the framework within which the directors exercise their powers of management. It is related to the shareholders' right to make bylaws.

In recent years shareholder activists have submitted resolutions at the annual meetings of quite a number of the largest corporations. They fall generally into two types. One type aims to protect or enhance the interests of small shareholders. Proposals to amend the corporate articles to permit cumulative voting for directors (discussed in the next section), to put ceilings on salaries of top executives, and to limit corporate gifts to charitable and education organizations are of this type. The other type had its beginnings about 1970. These proposals are usually offered by groups that have goals of social or political change or that oppose certain corporate activities. A few shares may be purchased solely to permit making the proposal. Other such groups, particularly church groups, may have owned quite a few shares as an investment for some time.

One of the earliest resolutions seeking a change in corporate policy asked the directors of Dow Chemical Company to stop selling napalm for use against people in Vietnam. This was proposed in 1968. The SEC ruled that Dow did not need to include the resolution in its proxy statement. After a rather inconclusive court decision, the SEC liberalized its proxy rules as outlined below. Other such resolutions have asked corporations to withdraw from South Africa until apartheid has ended. Some merely have asked the corporation to publicize certain information withheld as confidential, such as statistics on minority employment.

The present SEC Rule 14a–8 defines the type of resolution that a corporation need not include in proxy statements. Management may omit proposals relating to personal claims or grievances and proposals that are beyond the power of the corporation to put into effect. Since they would infringe on the right of management given to the directors, proposals relating to the conduct of the ordinary business of the firm may be omitted. The rule also excludes proposals that are not proper subjects of shareholder action under the law of the state of incorporation. It permits management to omit a proposal that was defeated by shareholder vote in a recent meeting. To be eligible for another vote, it must have received a certain percentage of the vote the last time it was presented. The percentage varies from 3 to 10, depending on how often it has been presented to shareholders. Few resolutions draw 10 percent unless supported by management.

Therefore, if you are an employee and own ten shares in General Motors, you cannot use a shareholder resolution at the annual meeting to try to obtain a raise. This is a personal grievance, and setting salaries and wages is part of the conduct of the ordinary business of the firm. Nor can you ask the shareholders to vote on whether they favor a reduction in the federal income tax. You can, however, propose that GM nominate a Hispanic person to its board of directors. This resolution and a 200-word statement supporting it would have to be included in GM's proxy statement. If 3 percent of the shares vote in favor of the resolution, you could submit it again the following year.

Cumulative Voting

Most corporations elect directors on the basis that each share is entitled to one vote for each director. Many corporations, however, permit shareholders to cumulate their votes. By using all their votes to support one director, a group of minority shareholders may be able to elect one director. If they spread their votes among all nominees, on the other hand, they would not be able to elect any.

A number of states require businesses incorporated in that state to permit shareholders to cumulate their votes for directors; therefore, few large publicly held corporations are incorporated in these states. The purpose of cumulative voting is to give minority shareholders an opportunity to be represented on the board. Opponents say this is likely to be devisive and cause friction among board members that will damage the firm.

The formula for determining the number of shares, X, required to elect one director under cumulative voting is:

$$X = \frac{S}{D+1} + 1$$

where S is the number of shares voting and D is the total number of directors to be elected. Clearly, the fewer directors to be elected, the greater the number of shares required to elect one director. Dividing directors into three classes, one class to be elected each year, makes it more difficult for minority shareholders to attain representation on the board.

RIGHT OF INSPECTION AND PREEMPTIVE RIGHT

The Shareholder's Right to Inspect

The MBCA requires a corporation to send its latest financial statements to any shareholder on request. It also requires the corporation to permit a shareholder, on written request, to examine in person, or through an agent such as a lawyer or accountant, its "relevant books and records of account, minutes, and record of shareholders." The shareholder or agent may make extracts from these records.

The shareholder must have a proper purpose for examining the records. To learn business secrets or to gain a competitive advantage is not a proper purpose. To determine the value of one's shares or to identify fellow shareholders in order to communicate with them concerning corporate affairs is a proper purpose. It is a proper purpose to make a copy of the shareholder list in order to wage a proxy contest to unseat present management.

The MBCA gives shareholders an absolute right to inspect the shareholder list. In order to discourage the denial of proper demands to inspect, the MBCA makes a corporate official who denies a proper demand liable for a penalty of 10 percent of the value of the shares of the demanding shareholder. Many state statutes have no such penalty provision and denials are common.

State ex rel.* Pillsbury v. Honeywell, Inc.
191 N.W.2d 406 (Sup. Ct. Minn. 1971)

FACTS   Pillsbury went to a meeting in 1969 of persons opposed to American involvement in Vietnam. He learned there that Honeywell, Inc., was producing antipersonnel fragmentation bombs for use in Vietnam. He was upset by this information about a company he respected that was located in his own community. He then bought 100 shares of Honeywell stock solely to gain a chance to persuade Honeywell to

Ex rel. means upon information. Here the state of Minnesota brought the action upon information from Pillsbury.

cease producing weapons. He wrote the corporation asking to see the shareholder list and all corporate records dealing with weapon manufacture. The company refused. He then brought an action to compel the company to make them available.

ISSUE Must Honeywell let him see these records?

DECISION No. The court held that Pillsbury did not have a proper purpose. It said that a shareholder concerned with the long- or short-term economic effect on Honeywell of making weapons of war would have a right of inspection. However, Pillsbury was not concerned with the value of his shares. His sole purpose was to get the company to adopt his social and political views.

Preemptive Rights

A number of states require their corporations that issue additional shares to give their current shareholders an option to purchase their proportionate share of the new issue. This enables the shareholder to maintain the same relative interest in the corporation as before.

Granting such a preemptive right creates difficult problems in large corporations that have several classes of stock. Generally, courts do not apply preemptive rights to treasury shares, shares issued in connection with a merger or consolidation, or shares issued in exchange for property or past services. The statutes of many states permit a corporation to avoid preemptive rights by including an appropriate provision in its articles.

DIVIDENDS

Directors' Discretion to Pay Dividends

Before the time of high income taxes, the primary objective of shareholders was high dividends. Today it is not unusual for some corporations to reinvest all their earnings in the business rather than pay any dividends. This may be attractive to investors in the upper income tax brackets if the value of the shares increases, because such an increase is a capital gain for the shareholder. Such gains are taxed at a lower rate, and taxation is postponed until disposal of the shares.

Shareholders have a right to share in the net income of the corporation; however, *the declaration of dividends is subject to the business judgment of the board of directors.* They may not pile up unneeded cash in the treasury or pay it out in unreasonably high salaries to management. However, the burden of proof is on the shareholder to show that the directors have abused their discretion.

Gay v. Gay's Super Markets, Inc.
383 A.2d 577 (Sup. Ct. Me. 1975)

FACTS Lawrence Gay and his brother, Carroll Gay, each owned 24.5 percent of the common stock of Gay's Super Markets, Inc. Hannaford Brothers Co., a food wholesaler, owned 51 percent. Carroll Gay was president and general manager of the corporation. Lawrence was manager of one of its retail stores. Lawrence was dismissed as manager of the Machias, Maine, store. No dividend was declared for that year, although the corporation had $125,000 in cash. Lawrence brought an action to compel payment of a dividend. The defense was that because of increased competition, the corporation planned to improve and expand its store in Machias. It was also planning to open a new store in Calais, Maine. Carroll Gay testified that there would be start-up costs and losses were expected in these stores for a year or two. The minutes of the board of directors meeting showed that the matter of a dividend had been discussed. They stated that none had been declared because of "the anticipated needs of the corporation, particularly in Calais."

ISSUE Should the court direct the payment of a dividend?

DECISION No. The court said that Lawrence Gay had the burden of proof. He must show bad faith, breach of fiduciary duty, or abuse of discretion by the directors in order to get the court to order the declaration of a dividend. If, as here, there are plausible reasons for the board's decision, a court will not interfere.

Types of Dividends

Dividends are usually paid in cash; however, assets of the corporation, such as shares in another corporation, may be distributed.

Distributions of shares in the corporation itself are called *stock dividends*. They are usually paid when management wants to retain all or an unusually high proportion of earnings for reinvestment. A large stock dividend may have as its main purpose a reduction in the market price per share to encourage greater investor interest in the stock. Stock dividends payable in the same class of shares do not change a shareholder's stake in the corporation. The proportion of shares owned remains the same; the shareholder just has a higher number of shares. However, the *par value* or *stated value* of the shares distributed must be transferred from a surplus account to the capital stock account on the balance sheet of the corporation. The account reduced might be either capital surplus or earned surplus. *Capital surplus* arises from the sales of stock at more than its par value; *earned surplus (retained earnings)* is the sum of previous net earnings that has not been paid out in dividends. There is no change in surplus if the shares distributed are treasury shares.

For example, on May 31, 1979, Philip Morris Incorporated distributed to shareholders a 100 percent stock dividend that had been approved by shareholders at the annual meeting held April 26. Suppose you owned 200 shares on April 27, the record date. This would give you a total of

400 shares. The quarterly dividend rate had been 62.5 cents per share. The rate paid on the next regular dividend date was 31.25 cents per share, so you would receive no increase in dividends. Philip Morris reduced its capital surplus account by $1 per share, the par value of the shares, and transferred this to the capital stock account. The market price per share went down, of course, to approximately half the former price.

Legal Limits on Dividends

Incorporation statutes all put limits on the dividends a corporation may pay. *The MBCA permits paying dividends only out of retained earnings.* It also prohibits the payment of a dividend that would make the corporation insolvent. A business is insolvent when it cannot pay its debts as they become due.

Stock Splits

A *stock split* is not a dividend; it changes merely the par value or stated value of the shares and the number outstanding, not the retained earnings account. A stock split increases the number of shares; a reverse stock split reduces the number of shares outstanding. The reason for either action is to adjust the price of the stock to one that the management of the corporation believes is more appropriate. Brokers' commissions tend to be lower on 100-share lots. If the stock price is high, this may discourage investors from buying it. If it is too low, it may appear to be less than a sound investment.

An amendment of the articles of incorporation is necessary to make a stock split. Therefore, there must be a favorable vote of shareholders. Only the vote of the directors is necessary for a stock dividend unless additional shares must be authorized. An amendment of the articles of incorporation is required to increase the number of authorized shares. A recent well-known example of a stock split was a 4–1 split by International Business Machines Corporation in 1979. This had the effect of reducing the par value of the stock from $5.00 to $1.25 per share. The market price was reduced from approximately $300 to about $75 per share. The reason given by IBM for the change was to make the price competitive with shares of "other quality companies."

Dividends on Preferred Stock

The contract with preferred shareholders usually gives them a preference in dividends over common shareholders. A fixed rate of dividend is specified. For example, Textron Inc. has a Series B $1.40 convertible preferred stock. It is convertible at the option of the shareholder into 0.9 share of common stock. If you bought 100 shares, you would expect to get $140 per year in dividends. Even if company earnings should fall substantially, so that common stock dividends were discontinued, you would still expect to receive your $140 per year.

However, suppose earnings were so small that the payment of any dividend would be illegal; or suppose the directors believe that although legal, a payment would endanger the corporation's ability to remain in business.

If the dividend is omitted or "passed," will you have a right to the dividend later if earnings improve? The answer depends on the shareholder contract.

If the stock you bought is *cumulative preferred*, you have a right to receive the omitted dividend before a dividend could be paid in the future to common shareholders. If the stock is *noncumulative*, the corporation could pay a common stock dividend in any fiscal year in which it paid the preferred dividends due in that period. If the preference is *cumulative-to-the-extent earned*, you have a right to be paid, before common shareholders receive any dividends, all dividends that were not declared when earned in prior fiscal years. In the case of Textron Series B preferred, it was provided when the stock was issued that accrued but unpaid dividends must be paid upon liquidation. Of course, all creditors would have to be paid first.

<table>
<tr><td>

Effect of Dividend Declaration

</td><td>

Once the directors have voted to pay a lawful dividend, it becomes a debt of the corporation. It may treat as the shareholder the persons registered as such on its records; therefore, directors usually set a *record date*. If a sale of the stock is made on a stock exchange, the purchaser is entitled to the dividend unless the sale occurs after the *ex dividend* date, which is five business days before the record date for the dividend.

</td></tr>
</table>

SHAREHOLDER RIGHTS IN EXTRAORDINARY CORPORATE TRANSACTIONS

<table>
<tr><td>

Amendment of Articles

</td><td>

Any amendment to the articles of incorporation must be approved by the shareholders. The MBCA requires approval by a majority of the shares entitled to vote but permits the articles of incorporation to impose a higher requirement. If the amendment would affect the rights of a class of shares, then shareholders of that class have a right to vote as a class even though those shareholders normally have no vote. For example, if the proposal is to eliminate a provision for cumulative dividends on a class of preferred stock, a majority of the shares of that class must approve.

</td></tr>
</table>

Bove v. Community Hotel Corp.
249 A.2d 89 (Sup. Ct. R.I. 1969)

FACTS   Community Hotel Corporation had paid no dividend on its preferred stock for 24 years. The arrearage totaled $645,000, or about $149 per share. It wanted to be able to obtain additional capital. In order to do this, it incorporated a subsidiary corporation, Newport Hotel Corp. It then proposed merging with the subsidiary under a plan that would eliminate the arrearage. It proposed converting each preferred share into five shares of common stock in Newport. Under the Rhode Island statute, the merger could be accomplished if two thirds of each class of stockholders voted in favor of it. To amend the articles, on the other hand, required a unanimous vote of each class. Bove and some other preferred shareholders sought to enjoin the merger. The trial court dismissed the suit.

ISSUE	Can Community Hotel eliminate the arrearage on the preferred stock through a merger with a subsidiary approved by less than all shareholders?
DECISION	Yes. The court said that the language of the Rhode Island statute was "clear, all-embracing, and unqualified." It pointed to words in the statute that allow the merger agreement to prescribe under what terms the shares of the corporations involved are to be converted into shares of the surviving corporation. It declared that nothing in the statute even suggested that the legislature was concerned about the underlying purpose of the merger.

Other Extraordinary Transactions

Under the MBCA, approval of all classes of shares is required for a merger or consolidation. A *merger* is when one corporation is absorbed into another existing corporation. A *consolidation* occurs when two or more corporations become part of a new corporation. A sale of most of the corporation's assets or a voluntary dissolution of the corporation also requires the favorable vote of the shareholders.

Appraisal Rights

The statutes in many states give appraisal rights to shareholders who vote against some of these transactions. Suppose you vote against a proposal to merge your corporation with another, but the majority supports the merger. If you have an appraisal right, you may demand that the corporation pay you the fair value of your shares. If you cannot agree with the corporation on the value, you may ask a court to determine ("appraise") their value. Under the MBCA this right applies in cases of mergers, consolidations, or a sale of most of the corporate assets.

Santee Oil Co., Inc. v. Cox
217 S.E.2d 789 (Sup. Ct. S.C. 1975)

FACTS	Marsden Cox owned 37.5 percent of the stock in Santee Oil Co., a closely held family corporation. He held the same percentage interest in another corporation, Services, Inc. He had duly objected to a merger of Services, Inc., into Santee. The trial court had established the fair value of both corporations to be $1,032,214 and Cox's interest at $387,080. It had used net asset value in arriving at this figure. Cox was dissatisfied and appealed.
ISSUE	Was the trial court's decision of the value correct?
DECISION	Yes. The Supreme Court said that the job was to determine "the fair market value of the corporate property as . . . a going business." It held that the proper method was to consider three bases for valuation: value of net assets, market value, and the earnings or investment value of the stock.

The Supreme Court took for net asset value the average estimate of three appraisers who had testified at the trial. This figure was $1,122,666. Approximately nine months prior to the merger, 10 percent of the shares of both corporations had been sold. The court used this price to determine that the market value of the company stock was $931,603. It determined from testimony that oil stocks had been selling at a price/earnings ratio of no more than 12/1. It averaged the earnings for the last three years and multiplied it by 12, the price/earnings ratio. This resulted in a figure for capitalized earnings of $644,976. It then determined that net asset value should be given the greatest weight. It then made the following calculation:

Value Factor	Value	Weight (percent)	Total
Net asset value	$1,122,666	70	$ 785,866
Market value	931,603	15	139,740
Capitalization earnings	644,976	15	96,746
Total value of corporation stock			$1,022,352

The court then noted that its valuation was within $10,000 of that of the trial court. Therefore, it affirmed that valuation.

LAWSUITS BY SHAREHOLDERS

Individual Actions

Shareholders may sue the corporation for a breach of their *shareholder contract*, the basis for the relationship between the corporation and the shareholder. The contract is a product of the corporate articles and bylaws and any board of directors resolution applicable to the particular stock issue, as well as the corporation statute. It is not a document signed by the shareholder and the corporation. Suppose you are a shareholder and other shareholders of the same class are paid a dividend but you are not. You as an *individual* could sue the corporation to get the same dividend on your shares because you have not received a benefit to which you are entitled as a shareholder.

Class Actions

When a number of people have a right or claim against the same defendant growing out of essentially the same set of facts, a *class action* may be brought by any one of them. For example, if the corporation did not pay a preferred dividend that was due, you could bring a suit demanding that the dividend be paid. If you win, the corporation would have to pay the dividend to all preferred shareholders of the class. You would then be able to recover from the corporation your expenses in bringing suit. If you lose there would be no reimbursement.

Derivative Actions

Shareholders are not usually able to sue to enforce a right of the corporation. Suppose an officer of the corporation has breached his duty by setting up a business to compete with the corporation and has made $1 million at the expense of the corporation. A shareholder could not sue him to recover the proportionate share of that loss. This is because the corporation is a legal entity separate from the shareholders.

However, under certain conditions a shareholder is permitted to sue as a *representative of the corporation*. There are two basic requirements: first, the shareholder must have owned shares at the time of the wrong, and second, the shareholder must urge the directors and, if appropriate, the other shareholders to direct that such a suit be brought by the corporation. A shareholder is permitted to bring suit only if they refuse or have a conflict of interest that is likely to keep them from suing. If the shareholder wins, the damages normally go to the corporation, not to the shareholder directly. However, as in the case of a successful class action, the shareholder will be reimbursed for her expenses in bringing the suit.

SHAREHOLDER LIABILITY

Liability on Shares   If a person buys stock that was fully paid for when issued, he or she normally has no further liability to the corporation or its creditors. The same is true of subsequent buyers of the stock regardless of the price paid. However, a shareholder who did not pay the full subscription price for newly issued shares is liable for the balance due. This would include "watered stock" situations where property exchanged for shares is overvalued. However, under the MBCA the evaluation of the board of directors is conclusive in the absence of fraud.

The shareholder is also liable if the consideration given for the shares is not lawful payment under the incorporation statute. The MBCA permits property or services actually performed to be exchanged for stock. It does not permit the exchange of a promissory note or the promise of future services for stock.

Liability for Illegal Dividends   A dividend that was paid illegally may be recovered from a shareholder who receives it knowing it is illegal. If the corporation is insolvent at the time, the shareholder is liable even if unaware of the illegality.

TRANSFER AND REDEMPTION OF SHARES

A shareholder has a right to sell or give away her shares unless there is a valid restriction. Under SEC rules sale may be restricted because the shares were part of a private offering. In close corporations the original shareholders may not want to have to deal with strangers. An agreement by all of them to require any shareholder who desires to sell to give the corporation or the other shareholders a first right to purchase the shares would be upheld by courts. Notice of a restriction on the right of sale must be conspicuously placed on the stock certificate to be effective against a purchaser who is unaware of it.

To transfer the stock, the owner indorses the assignment form usually printed on the back of the stock certificate. An assignment may also be made by the use of a separate document called a *stock power*. Banks usually use such assignment forms when stock is put up as collateral for a loan. If no transferee is named, the certificate and the shares it represents are transferable by mere delivery. Sending such a certificate through the mails would then be risky because the Uniform Commercial Code makes a stock certificate negotiable.

The corporation has a duty to record the transfer of its stock and its other registered securities. It is liable to the transferee if it refuses to do so. Such duty depends, of course, on proper indorsement of the certificate and assumes there is no valid restriction.

Ling and Co. v. Trinity Savings & Loan Ass'n.
482 S.W.2d 841 (Sup. Ct. Tex. 1972)

FACTS   Bruce Bowman borrowed money from Trinity Savings & Loan. As security for the loan, he assigned 1,500 shares of Ling and Co. common stock. When Bowman defaulted on the loan, Trinity brought an action to get Ling and Co. to transfer the stock. The articles of incorporation of Ling and Co. required shareholders who wanted to transfer their shares to notify all other shareholders and give them a ten-day option to buy them. On the front of the certificate, it stated in small print that the shares were subject to the provisions of the articles of incorporation, which were available from the corporation. It also stated that references to provisions setting forth preferences and restrictions were on the back of the certificate. On the back in small print appeared a summary of the restriction on transfer of shares.

ISSUE   Was Trinity Savings & Loan entitled to have the shares transferred without giving an option to buy to the other shareholders?

DECISION   Yes, if it were unaware of the restriction. The Uniform Commercial Code Section 8–204 requires that a restriction on transferability be "noted conspicuously on the security." It excepts people who have knowledge of the restriction. There had been no finding by the trial court on whether Trinity had knowledge. Therefore, the Supreme Court sent the case back for further proceedings.

QUESTIONS AND PROBLEM CASES

1. Does the Securities and Exchange Commission try to prevent the sale of securities that are worthless or very risky?

2. What is the effect of tardy notice of a shareholder meeting? How, if at all, can this effect be overcome?

3. Why do corporations solicit proxies? Why is the SEC interested in the information in proxy statements and the form of proxy cards?

4. What is the difference between a stock split and a stock dividend?

5. Describe a situation in which an individual shareholder's action, a class action, and a derivative action would each be appropriate.

6. LaForce was a corporation involved in the invention and marketing of an improved engine and carburetor. Webster was a former stockbroker who was an assistant to the president of LaForce. Webster sold 25,000 shares of LaForce stock to approximately 80 persons at $5 per share. Shimer invested $11,500. He demanded stock certificates, but he was told that there was some difficulty with the SEC and that he would receive the certificates after the stock was registered the following January. The certificates were finally delivered almost three years later, but by then the stock was practically worthless. Shimer sued Webster to rescind his purchase. He alleged a violation of the Securities Act of 1933 because no registration statement was filed. Webster's defense was that the sale was exempt as a private offering. Is this a good defense?

7. The bylaws of Tank Cleaners, Inc., stated that the annual meeting of shareholders would be held on October 27 of each year. It also said that notice of the meeting should be sent to shareholders "ten days prior thereto." Shannon, the president, ordered the meeting to be held on October 8. Notice was mailed on September 30. The meeting was attended by all shareholders and chaired by Shannon. Shannon was replaced as a director by vote at the meeting. At the directors meeting held immediately afterward he was replaced as president. Shannon brought suit to have the meeting declared void because it was not on October 27 and proper notice was not given. Was it illegal?

8. Miles, a shareholder, was dissatisfied with the management of the Bank of Heflin. He wrote to the bank requesting that his accountant be permitted to review the books and records of the bank. He said he wanted "to ascertain whether any action had been taken contrary to the best interests of the stockholders, such as misuse of corporate funds . . . or favoring certain customers of the Bank because of personal connections with officers or directors of the Bank." The bank refused his request. Miles sued. Will a court direct the bank to permit the inspection?

9. Fuller and Krogh were the sole shareholders in Cormier Corporation, which was formed to build and own an industrial building. It was undercapitalized and the contractor quit because Cormier was unable to make the monthly progress payments to him. Krogh then took over responsibility for finishing the building. Prior to that time the parties had invested equal amounts and had each been issued 218 shares of stock. Krogh accepted additional shares for the additional expenses on the building that he paid. As president of the corporation, Fuller signed the certificates. A year later Krogh owned 527 shares and Fuller 244. Fuller sued Krogh, claiming a preemptive right to purchase enough shares to equalize ownership. Does he have this right?

10. Mr. Steak issued 2,400 shares of stock to Price, an employee. The stock was not registered and its sale was restricted. It was issued for investment purposes only; however, there was no notation of the restriction on the stock certificate. Price pledged the shares to Edina State Bank as security for a loan. The bank asked Price if the stock was restricted, and he said no. Later the bank sold 1,000 shares to protect its loan. The transfer agent refused to register the transfer on advice from Mr. Steak. Edina State Bank sued Mr. Steak. Will it recover its loss?

Which Form of Business Organization?

32

INTRODUCTION

Starting a New Business

If you are one of the many people who plan to start your own business, one of the decisions you will need to make is the legal form of the organization. Today there is a tendency to equate corporations and business. You might assume, particularly if you will need the help of other investors to finance the business, that the corporation is the form to use. It may not be the most advantageous form, however. Other forms to consider are the individual proprietorship, the general partnership, the limited partnership, and the Subchapter S corporation. A person faced with this choice would like to know what form other similar businesses are using. Nevertheless, the needs of the particular business and its owners are the principal factors that should determine the choice.

Frequency

Table 32–1 shows the relative numbers of businesses operated under each of three forms in various industries: sole proprietorship, partnership, and corporation. The figures on business receipts and net income give an idea of relative economic impact.

Many sole proprietorships operate in the fields of agriculture, forestry, and fishing. They also are very numerous in the service industry and in retail trade. However, both the business receipts and the net income of corporations are much greater in both the service industry and retail trade.

Table 32–2 better shows the extent to which small businesses are operated as sole proprietorships and large businesses as corporations.

409

TABLE 32–1

Proprietorships, Partnerships, and Corporations—Number, Receipts, and Net Income by Industry, 1975

Industry	Number (000)			Business Receipts ($ billions)			Net Income (less debit) ($ billions)		
	Proprietorships	Active Partnerships	Active Corporations	Proprietorships	Active Partnerships	Active Corporations	Proprietorships	Active Partnerships	Active Corporations
Total	10,881	1,073	2,024	339.2	146.0	3,120.4	44.6	7.7	142.6
Agriculture, forestry, and fishing	3,367	123	56	69.3	12.6	26.6	5.6	0.9	0.7
Mining.........................	56	16	14	3.5	4.0	63.7	0.3	−0.5	23.6
Construction	892	61	191	31.0	12.3	143.4	4.4	0.8	2.2
Manufacturing	222	29	217	8.7	6.8	1,258.3	1.0	0.3	68.4
Transportation, public utilities	355	17	81	10.0	2.5	234.7	1.3	—	10.1
Wholesale and retail trade	2,193	193	615	148.3	45.2	951.5	9.9	2.7	22.5
Wholesale	336	31	220	33.3	16.0	502.0	2.9	0.8	13.9
Retail	1,765	162	395	112.5	29.1	449.3	6.7	1.8	8.6
Finance, insurance, real estate......	744	434	412	12.1	32.4	315.8	3.8	−3.7	11.7
Services......................	3,034	199	436	56.0	30.2	125.7	18.4	7.2	3.4

Source: U.S. Bureau of the Census, *Statistical Abstract of the United States: 1978*, p. 561. Data from U.S. Internal Revenue Service, preliminary reports, *Statistics of Income, Business Income Tax Returns*, annual, and *Statistics of Income, Corporation Income Tax Returns*, annual.

TABLE 32–2

Proprietorships, Partnerships, and Corporations—Number and Business Receipts by Size of Receipts, 1974

Size Class of Receipts	Total		Number (000)			Receipts ($ billions)		
	Number (000)	Receipts ($ billions)	Proprietorships	Partnerships	Corporations	Proprietorships	Partnerships	Corporations
Total	13,902	3,320	10,874	1,062	1,966	328.3	137.2	2,854.8
Under $25,000	9,141	54	8,136	538	467	48.2	3.8	2.2
$25,000–$49,999	1,506	52	1,185	139	182	42.2	5.0	5.2
$50,000–$99,999	1,228	85	833	137	258	58.6	9.9	16.8
$100,000–$199,999	} 1,512	} 315	454	117 }	} 639	62.7	16.7 }	} 146.0
$200,000–$499,999			213	89 }		62.8	27.0 }	
$500,000–$999,999	241	163	37	25	179	25.0	17.3	120.4
$1,000,000 or more	273	2,651	14	17	242	28.8	57.5	2,564.2
			Percent Distribution					
Under $25,000	65.8	1.6	74.8	50.7	23.8	14.7	2.8	0.1
$25,000–$49,999	10.8	1.6	10.9	13.1	9.3	12.8	3.6	0.2
$50,000–$99,999	8.8	2.6	7.7	12.9	13.1	17.9	7.2	0.6
$100,000–$199,999	} 10.9	} 9.5	4.2	11.0 }	} 32.5	19.1	12.2 }	} 5.1
$200,000–$499,999			2.0	8.4 }		19.1	19.7 }	
$500,000–$999,999	1.7	4.9	0.3	2.4	9.1	7.6	12.6	4.2
$1,000,000 or more	2.0	79.8	0.1	1.6	12.3	8.8	41.9	89.8

Source: U.S. Bureau of the Census, *Statistical Abstract of the United States: 1978*, p. 562. Data from U.S. Internal Revenue Service, *Statistics of Income, Business Income Tax Returns*, annual, and *Statistics of Income, Corporation Income Tax Returns*, annual.

FORMS OF BUSINESS ORGANIZATION

Individual Proprietorships

An individual proprietorship is a business operated by a person as his or her own personal property. For example, one might conduct a computer service business as an individual proprietorship. It would be very much like buying a house as an investment and renting it out. The person operating the business need not use his or her own name as the name of the business; it may be operated under an assumed or trade name such as the Data Experts Company. Such a trade name would have to be registered with the proper state or local official, however. Employees of the business are the personal employees of the owner. Legally they are no different from a household employee except for income tax purposes. The salaries and wages paid to employees of the business and other business expenses are deductible in determining taxable income.

Partnerships

The nature of a *general partnership* was discussed in Chapter 25. The limited partnership was covered in Chapter 28. There is no need to expand on these discussions here.

Corporations

The nature of corporations was discussed in Chapter 25.

Subchapter S Corporations

This is an important variant of the corporation that should be considered if a business is to be owned by 15 shareholders or less. A Subchapter S corporation is a corporation that is taxed very much like a partnership. This is its advantage over ordinary corporations. Several requirements must be maintained or the Subchapter S corporation loses its tax status. Only a few will be mentioned here. There can initially be no more than 15 shareholders, they must all be individuals or estates, and they must consent in writing to having the corporation taxed as a partnership. Not more than 20 percent of the corporation's income can come from sources other than sales of products and services by the corporation.

Other Less Common Types

Two other forms of business organizations should be mentioned. Both are taxed as corporations. The *business trust* was originally developed in Massachusetts at a time when corporations were not permitted to own real property. The trustees held title to the assets of the business. Investors were free from personal liability for debts of the business but were not permitted to have any voice in the management of the business. Control of the business was left to the trustees. The trust certificates that indicated ownership were often called shares. This form of organization was also used to avoid the prohibition in early corporation statutes against corporations holding stock in other corporations. John D. Rockefeller, for example, used this device to gain control of a number of oil companies. The trustees issued certificates to owners of the acquired corporations in exchange for their shares.

Although relatively rare, this form of organization is still used today.

Its greatest disadvantage is that limited liability of shareholders is uncertain in some states. A similar concentration of control can be accomplished in a corporation through a *voting trust.*

The *joint-stock association* is a form of partnership; however, it has most of the characteristics of a corporation. These include free transferability of shares, continuing existence despite transfers of shares, and delegation of management decision-making power by the owners. The board is usually called the board of governors. Shareholders generally remain personally liable for the debts of the corporation. This was the business form used by the express companies connected with the railroads.

FACTORS TO CONSIDER IN CHOOSING A FORM OF BUSINESS ORGANIZATION

Limited Liability

Safety is a prime consideration for most investors, particularly when they are not major participants in the enterprise. Limited partners who do not participate in management and shareholders in a corporation may lose their investment if the business fails. However, there is no further liability to creditors of the business or to victims of torts that are attributable to the business. In contrast, partners in a general partnership not only may lose their investment but may also be required to pay partnership debts from personal assets. Of course, sole proprietors have the same risk.

Credit to a small corporation, especially a new one that does not have a strong earnings record, may be granted only if the debt is guaranteed by one or more of the shareholders. Lending banks often require shareholders to cosign corporate notes. Suppliers may require shareholders to guarantee accounts. These acts are seldom demanded of limited partners because the general partners are liable. Potential tort claimants are almost never able to get shareholders to agree to protect them. For example, a victim of the negligence of an employee in driving the corporation's delivery truck cannot get the wealthiest shareholder to agree to assume liability after an accident. Therefore, from a risk standpoint, a shareholder or limited partner is better off than a general partner.

Taxation

The wealth-increasing potential of an investment in a business is greatly affected by the income tax laws. These laws change from time to time; however, the basic principles tend to remain constant. Changes in rates of taxation may shift the tax advantage between the partnership and corporate forms in certain circumstances. Since earnings projections for a business are also uncertain, the possibility of rate changes seldom changes the final choice of the form of organization.

The basic difference is between taxation as a partnership and taxation as a corporation. A corporation is a taxable entity. It pays income taxes on its own income, and its shareholders pay income taxes on dividends from the corporation although they are paid out of income already taxed to the corporation. On the other hand, a partnership is not treated as a taxable entity. Income (or loss) is passed through pro rata to the partners and taxed to them. As noted above, a Subchapter S corporation is taxed like a partnership.

Taxation as a corporation can be an advantage. The income tax rate on the first $25,000 in earnings (17 percent in 1979) is usually well below the same rate if earned by a single individual. The maximum rate (46 percent in 1979) is usually well below the maximum rate for individuals on dividend income (70 percent in 1979). If corporate profits are reinvested in expansion of the business rather than paid out in dividends, the corporation can serve as a tax shelter. The shareholder's interest in the retained earnings is not taxed until the stock is sold or the corporation is dissolved. Then the shareholder is taxed at a capital gains rate, which is lower than the ordinary income rate applied to dividends, on the difference between the tax basis (usually cost) and the selling or liquidation value.

Tax savings for shareholders as compared with partners can also be realized in a corporation involved in a business that has wide swings in income by keeping the dividend rate constant. The tax rates for partners are much higher in very profitable years. On the other hand, there may be tax as well as income advantages to shareholders if they cause the corporation to pay dividends when their other income is low. However, such advantages cannot be gained unless all shareholders have similar financial situations.

The corporation offers another tax advantage if the owners are active in the operation of the business. Fringe benefits such as a pension plan and health insurance can be provided to shareholder employees if furnished to other employees. The cost can be deducted by the corporation and there is no immediate taxation to the employees of the value to them of the plans. In contrast, partners are not treated as employees. Their benefits, as well as their drawings or salary, are viewed as distributions of partnership profits.

Tax-Free Exchanges

Another tax advantage of corporations may be realized when the business is sold. A tax-free transaction is possible when the shares of a corporation are exchanged for shares of another corporation. The shareholders of the acquired corporation then become shareholders of the acquiring corporation without being required to pay a capital gains tax at that time. On the other hand, a sale of the business of a sole proprietorship or of a partnership is usually a taxable transaction. If the sale is for an amount greater than the net book value of the business, an immediate capital gain tax will be due.

If losses are anticipated in the early years of a business and the owners have other income, the partnership form will save taxes during that period. The owners can reduce their tax liability on their other income by the amount of the partnership losses.

Partnerships and individual proprietorships are not required to pay corporate franchise taxes. Usually taxes on their operations (other than income taxes) are set at a lower level than those on corporations. Also they do not need to pay privilege taxes to do intrastate business in another state.

Lack of Formalities

An individual proprietorship or general partnership can be formed without the formalities required of a corporation or limited partnership; no filing with a government official is necessary. The same is true at termination. Cancellation of the certificate is necessary for limited partnerships.

Less is required also when proprietorships and partnerships operate in other states. A corporation must be qualified if it wants to do intrastate business in any state except where it is incorporated. For example, if a corporation wanted to operate a retail shop in another state, it would have to file its articles of incorporation in the new state, appoint a local representative to accept legal papers for the corporation, and pay annual privilege or franchise taxes as well as pay for the privilege of qualification. None of this is required of an individual proprietorship or a general partnership.

Although not required, a limited partnership should probably file its articles in whatever counties it does an intrastate business. This will avoid the possibility of its limited partners being held liable for its debts. The recently approved Uniform Limited Partnership Act requires registration only with the secretary of state in such instances.

Financing

For larger businesses the corporate form makes financing easier. The wide variety of equity and debt securities that may be designed gives flexibility. Limited liability and the tendency of investors to relate corporate securities to familiar "blue chip" companies make them appear safer. For small corporations the continuity factor may make it easier for the business to borrow money from a bank. If the principal shareholders put up their stock as collateral, the loan may be more acceptable. This would give the lender a chance to take control of the management or to sell the corporation as a going business rather than be forced to liquidate if the loan becomes uncollectible.

Management

The corporation is most flexible in management arrangements. Day-to-day operating management can be given to one or more officers, while the board of directors retains general policy control. Shareholders who are not directors have a very limited voice in corporate decision making; however, they do not risk liability by participating in management.

A limited partner cannot participate in management at all without losing limited liability. A general partner can delegate routine management decisions to one or more partners. Nevertheless, all general partners are likely to have apparent authority to bind the partnership. Partners seldom give up their right to participate in management. As a result decisions may be delayed by time-consuming consultation, and deadlocks may occur.

The close corporation is no freer of serious problems than a partnership when owners cannot agree on management. Since it is more traditional in the corporate form to assign everyday management to a chief executive officer, it may be that conflicts and disputes arise less often under that form.

Freeze-outs in Close Corporations

A minority shareholder in a close corporation has little power, and he or she may be "frozen out" by the majority. This may include a reduction or elimination of dividends as well as a loss of employment. The business judgment rule makes it an uphill battle to fight such a freeze-out in court. Even if no attempt at freeze-out is made, without power to terminate the corporation, the minority shareholder is at best "locked in" to the investment.

Various kinds of agreements may be used to give protection to minority shareholders. There may be shareholder agreements guaranteeing employment, requiring dividends except in certain situations, or establishing separate classes of stock each of which is entitled to elect a director. Buy-out agreements may require purchase of the shares if a shareholder wants out as well as protecting other shareholders from having an unwanted shareholder imposed upon them by a sale of shares.

The difficulty with such agreements is that they reduce the flexibility inherent in the corporate form of business. In trying to avoid one undesirable contingency, an agreement may make another more likely to occur. For example, attempts to avoid the possibility of freezing a shareholder out of employment may result in giving an ineffective employee a lifetime sinecure. An effort to assure the continuation of dividends may, particularly in a period of inflation, bleed the company of the funds necessary to grow or even maintain its business.

Life of the Business

Although the life of many businesses is short, it may be very beneficial to owners of successful businesses to keep them going for many years. Of course, the business of a partnership may be continued when a partner dies, becomes insolvent, or wishes to retire. Nevertheless, the law treats the partnership as dissolved. Special agreements to keep the business operating must be made in advance of these events or it may be difficult to attain agreement to form a new partnership. A partner can terminate an ordinary partnership at will. If the partnership agreement provides for a term of years, termination in advance will subject the partner who terminates to liability for damages. The threat of using this power, however, can be used to protect that partner; of course, it can also be used wrongfully.

The success of an individual proprietorship is usually dependent on its owner. Therefore, successful continuation of the business by a widow, widower, son, or daughter is less likely than in a partnership.

Legally a corporation is not affected by the death or insolvency of a shareholder. Of course, if the knowledge or skill of the deceased had been the principal reason for the corporation's success, it may not remain profitable very long. A great advantage of the corporation in providing continuity is in the ease of transferring ownership of the shares. Ownership of a family or other close corporation can be shifted gradually by gift or sale of shares to those who will succeed the present managers. This may minimize the tax consequences at death that would require selling the business. Those who will not participate as employees can be given a claim to income through dividends. Two or more classes of stock can be established to separate the major share of ownership from control.

Generally it is easier to preserve goodwill in a corporation as owners change than it is in a partnership. This results from the continuity of the corporation, which may be very important in a business that serves the public.

Liquidity of Investment

The ease of selling one's investment in a publicly held corporation is one of the major advantages of the corporation form. However, although theoretically the minority shareholders in a close corporation can sell their shares, unless at least a seat on the board of directors can be obtained through cumulative voting, there may be little that is attractive to a potential buyer. Shareholders of the corporation have little incentive to buy out the minority interest because of the freeze-out potential that was discussed earlier. Shareholders in close corporations are often restricted in the sale of their stock. This may also make the investment less marketable or liquid.

General partners can sell their partnership interests, but the purchaser does not become a partner unless accepted unanimously by the other general partners into what is essentially a new partnership. A general partner who wants to sell out before the end of the agreed upon term of the partnership is in a weak bargaining position. Unless the partnership agreement changes the UPA rules, a general partner is not entitled to force the partnership business to be liquidated. Nor is a partner entitled to share in the goodwill value of the business if the other partners exercise their right to continue it.

Limited partnership interests can be sold without such adverse effects; however, there is no public market such as a stock exchange where they can be sold. Publicly offered partnership interests are designed to serve as tax shelters for the original purchasers during the early years of ownership. Under current Internal Revenue Service recapture provisions, this makes the limited partnership rather unattractive from a tax standpoint during the later years when the owner may wish to sell.

MAKING THE CHOICE

Rarely do all these factors point toward the choice of one form of business organization. Each factor needs to be analyzed separately and then all the advantages and disadvantages weighed together.

It is possible that a single factor such as limited liability will be so important as to outweigh other factors. However, if the business involves little risk or the owners have few other assets, this factor should be given no weight.

Likewise, in starting a small business, financing a corporation will be no easier than financing a partnership or an individual proprietorship. If several years of substantial losses are expected and the owners have other income that can be offset by the losses, being taxed as a partnership may be the primary factor. The partnership can be changed to a corporation later when profits are assured. Then pension plans and other employee fringe benefits for owners and reinvestment of profits in the business will probably result in minimizing taxes through the corporate form.

It is wise to consult a public accountant and a lawyer who have had experience with businesses faced with these choices and who are familiar with the latest IRS rules. Certainly this should be done if the business is beyond minimal size or capitalization before forming a corporation. There are likely to be adverse tax consequences from liquidating a corporation or selling its assets to another form of business.

QUESTIONS AND PROBLEM CASES

1. What are the most common reasons people use the corporate form of business organization?

2. Under what circumstances might it be advantageous to use a sole proprietorship rather than a corporation to operate a business?

3. Under what circumstances might it be advantageous to use a partnership rather than a corporation to operate a business?

4. Under what circumstances might it be advantageous to use a limited partnership rather than an ordinary partnership?

5. What are the principal disadvantages of being a limited partner rather than a shareholder in a corporation?

6. Herb Jones started making tooled leather belts as a hobby. Later he learned how to cast bronze belt buckles. He had little trouble selling them to friends. He was taking some art classes and was seeking a certificate in business at the local college. His belts, which he sold on weekends at craft shows, paid his tuition and provided spending money. He has been able to get a few men's clothing stores to stock his belts on a consignment basis. Demand has now increased beyond his ability to fill it. As he com-

pletes his program at the college, he decides he would like to go into the business of making and selling belts and other leather goods. He learns of the availability of a small shop location in a popular shopping mall. A friend, Bill Williams, who has another year to go at the college, is willing to help him in his spare time. Suburban Bank and Trust Co. is willing to loan Herb $8,000, the amount he thinks he needs to pay rent for one year, to buy a stock of leather and brass from which to make the belts, and to pay Bill to work weekends for three months. The loan is conditional on Herb's father cosigning the note. Herb's Uncle Joe, who works for a large corporation, suggests that Herb should incorporate the business. Do you agree?

7. Assume that the business has been operating for a year and has made a profit. Herb has expanded by purchasing other leather products to sell. All profit has been reinvested in the business. He has, however, paid off $2,000 of the loan to the bank. The bank is willing to renew the loan and even to increase it to $10,000 if Herb's father cosigns again. Bill Williams would like to join the firm full-time but has no money or credit to contribute. They

think that if they had a salesman to visit men's clothing shops and perhaps other retailers they could increase their sales substantially. A mutual friend, George Robbins, has had sales experience and would be willing to join the business. He could invest $10,000. The workshop in the back of the shop is already too small. Herb would like to rent a loft or other low-rent space for belt production where there would be no interruptions and enough space for several workers. Herb would like to have Bill supervise this operation. Herb estimates that minimum capital of $40,000 is necessary. What he owns in equipment, supplies, and inventory is worth $10,000 at cost and he believes the value of the going business is at least $10,000 in addition. His father is willing to invest $5,000 but wants no further liability. Uncle Joe is also willing to invest $5,000 on the same basis. What form of business organization is appropriate? How should it be capitalized?

8. Roger Smith and Tom Billings are physicians. Their medical specialty is anesthesiology. Their annual earnings exceed $80,000 each. Tom's hobby is electronics. Roger and Tom have been developing an electronic machine to monitor and control the administration of anesthetics to surgical patients. They have had the part-time help of an experienced tool and die maker, Fred Walmsley, who is regularly employed by a large corporation. Fred spends most of his income. His only assets besides his home are his savings to supplement his company pension. Roger and Tom would like to form a business to manufacture the machines and bring in Fred on a full-time basis. The machines will be high-priced and carry a large margin of profit, but it is expected that demonstration and advertising costs will be high. There will also be substantial additional development costs. Tom has an idea for another machine he would like to develop also. The accountant for Roger and Tom believes that the business is likely to show substantial losses for at least two years or more. Would a corporation or partnership be the better form of business organization for their venture?

9. Assume you have a business idea that you believe will permit you to build a large, profitable business that could continue to grow over many years. You think it will be easy to sell either limited partnership interests or stock in the enterprise. What are the advantages and disadvantages of the two forms of organization in this case?

Property

PART SIX

Personal Property

33

NATURE AND CLASSIFICATION

A fox hunter on horseback named Pierson and his foxhounds are chasing a fox across a piece of land owned by the state of New York. Just as Pierson is about to catch the fox, Post steps out from behind some bushes and shoots the fox. When Post tries to carry the fox away, Pierson objects. Post claims that he owns the fox and has the right to keep it. Pierson says the fox is his property and that Post should give it to him.

This situation, which happened many years ago, raises a number of questions that are important to us today. First, what does the term *property* mean? Second, what do we mean by *ownership* of property. Finally, how can a person obtain ownership of property? This chapter will focus on the answers to these questions.

Property

The word *property* has a variety of meanings. It may refer to an object, such as a building, or it may refer to legal rights connected with an object, such as the lease of a building, which gives the tenant the right to occupy and use the building. However, the word *property* can also refer to legal rights that have economic value but are not connected with an object. A patent is an example of this kind of property.

When we talk about *ownership* of property, we are talking about a bundle of legal rights that are recognized and enforced by society. For example, ownership of a building includes the exclusive right to use, enjoy, sell, mortgage, or rent the building. If someone else tries to use the property without your consent, you can use the courts and legal procedures to eject the person. Ownership of a patent includes the rights to sell it, to license others to use it, or to produce the patented article personally.

421

In the United States private ownership of property is very important and is protected by the Constitution. It provides that no person shall be deprived by the state of "life, liberty or property without due process of law." We recognize and encourage the right of individuals to acquire, enjoy, and use property. These rights, however, are not unlimited. For example, a person cannot use the property in an unreasonable manner to the injury of others. Also, the state has the "police power" to impose reasonable regulations on the use of property, to tax it, and to take it for public use by paying compensation for it to the owner.

Real and Personal Property

Property can be divided into different classes based on its characteristics. The same piece of property may fall into more than one class. The most important classification is that of real property and personal property. *Real property* is the earth's crust and all things firmly attached to it. *Personal property* includes all other objects and rights that can be owned.

Real property can be turned into personal property if it is detached from the earth. Similarly, personal property can be attached to the earth and become real property. For example, marble in the ground is real property. When the marble is quarried it becomes personal property, but if it is used in constructing a building, it becomes real property again. Perennial vegetation, such as trees, shrubs, and grass, that does not have to be seeded every year is usually treated as part of the real property. When trees and shrubs are severed from the land, they become personal property. Crops, such as corn, oats, and potatoes, which must be planted each year are usually treated as personal property. However, if the real property on which they are growing is sold, the new owner of the real property also becomes the owner of the crops.

Tangible and Intangible Property

Tangible property has a physical existence; land, buildings, and furniture are examples. Property that has no physical existence is called *intangible property;* patent rights, easements, and bonds are intangible property.

The distinction between tangible and intangible property is important primarily for tax and estate planning purposes. Generally, tangible property is subject to tax in the state in which it is located, whereas intangible property is usually taxable in the state where its owner lives.

Public and Private Property

Property is also classifed as public or private based on the ownership of the property. If the property is owned by the government or a government unit, it is classified as *public property;* but if the property is owned by an individual, a group of individuals, a corporation, or some other business organization, it is *private property.*

ACQUIRING OWNERSHIP OF PERSONAL PROPERTY

Possession

In very early times, the most common way of obtaining ownership of personal property was simply by taking possession of unowned property.

For example, the first person to take possession of a wild animal became its owner. Today, we still recognize the right to ownership of unowned property by taking possession of it. Wildlife and abandoned property are classified as *unowned property*. The first person to take possession of wildlife or abandoned property becomes the owner.

To acquire ownership of a wild animal by taking possession, a person must obtain enough control over it to deprive it of its freedom. If a person fatally wounds an animal, the person becomes the owner. Animals caught in a trap or fish caught in a net are usually considered to be the property of the person who set the trap or net. If a captured animal escapes and is caught by another person, that person generally becomes the owner. However, if the person knows the animal is an escaped animal and that the prior owner is chasing it to recapture it, then the person does not become the owner.

If property is *abandoned* by the owner, it becomes unowned property. For example, if a television set is taken to the city dump and left there, the first person who takes possession of it with the intention of claiming ownership becomes the new owner.

Production or Purchase

The most common ways of obtaining ownership of property are by producing it and purchasing it. A person owns the property he or she makes unless the person has agreed to do the work for someone else. In that case the employer is the owner of the product of the work. For example, if you create a painting or knit a sweater, you are the owner unless you have been hired by someone to do the painting or knit the sweater.

The other major way of acquiring property is by purchase. The law of sale of goods was discussed in Chapters 15–19.

Lost and Mislaid Property

Suppose Barbara's camera falls out of her handbag while she is walking down the street. Laura later finds the camera in the grass where it fell. Leslie then steals the camera from Laura's house. What rights to the camera do Barbara, Laura, and Leslie have? Barbara is still the owner of the camera. She has the right to have it returned to her if she discovers where it is— or if Laura knows that it belongs to Barbara. As the finder of lost property, Laura has a better right to the camera than anyone else except its true owner (Barbara). This means she would have the right to require Leslie to return it to her if she finds out that Leslie has it.

If the finder of lost property knows who the owner of it is and refuses to return it, the finder is guilty of *larceny*. If the finder does not know who the true owner is or cannot easily find out, the finder must still return the property if the real owner shows up and asks for the property. If the finder does not return it, he or she is liable for *conversion* and must pay the owner the fair value of the property.

Some states have a statute that allows finders of property to clear their title to the property. The statutes generally provide that the person must give public notice of the fact that the property has been found, perhaps by putting an ad in a local newspaper. All states have what are called *statutes of limitations.* They require the true owner of property to claim it or bring a legal action to recover possession of it within a certain number of years. A person who keeps possession of lost or unclaimed property for longer than that period of time will become the owner of it.

Lieber v. Mohawk Arms, Inc.
314 N.Y.S.2d 510 (Sup. Ct. N.Y. 1970)

FACTS In 1945 Lieber was serving in the U.S. Army. He was one of the first soldiers to occupy Munich, Germany. He and some other soldiers entered Adolph Hitler's apartment and removed various items of his personal belongings. Lieber brought his share to his home in Louisiana. It included Hitler's uniform jacket and cap and some of his decorations and personal jewelry. Lieber's possession of these items was well known. There were several feature articles about them, and they were occasionally displayed to the public. In 1968 Lieber's chauffeur stole the collection and sold it to a dealer of historical material in New York. The dealer sold it to the Mohawk Arms Company, which had no knowledge it had been stolen. Lieber learned that Mohawk Arms had the collection and demanded that it return the collection. Mohawk Arms claimed that it did not have to return the collection to Lieber because it properly belonged to the occupational military authority or to the Bavarian government and not to Lieber.

ISSUE Was Lieber entitled to the return of the collection that had been stolen from him?

DECISION Yes. The court held that Mohawk Arms had to return the collection to Lieber. Mohawk Arms did not have good title to the collection because it had obtained it through a thief. The court did not allow Mohawk Arms to use the claim that someone else had a better title than Lieber. Between Lieber and Mohawk Arms, Lieber had the better right to the collection. In addition, in Louisiana, the statute of limitations for the recovery of personal property is ten years. Lieber held possession of the collection for more than ten years. Anyone who felt they had a better claim to the collection had to sue him during that time to have it returned. Once the ten years passed, Lieber was recognized as the owner of the collection.

The courts have made a distinction between lost property and mislaid property. If Julia, while shopping in Vicky's store, drops her wallet in the aisle, the wallet is generally considered *lost property;* but if she lays it on the counter and, forgetting it, leaves the store, it is considered *mislaid property.* If the wallet is mislaid, Vicky becomes the *bailee* of it. If Dick finds the wallet in the aisle, he has the right to take possession of it. If Dick discovers the wallet on the counter, Vicky has the right to take possession of it.

The distinction between lost and mislaid property was developed to increase the chance the property would be returned to its real owner where its owner knowingly placed it down but had forgotten to pick it up. In that case, the owner might well be expected to remember later where the property had been left and return for it. Sometimes, it is very difficult to distinguish between lost property and misplaced property. As a result, the courts are not always consistent in the way they make the distinction.

Jackson v. Steinberg
200 P.2d 37 (Sup. Ct. Ore. 1948)

FACTS Laura Jackson was a maid in a hotel owned by Steinberg. She found eight $100 bills under the paper lining in a dresser in a guest room. She turned the money over to Steinberg. Steinberg tried to locate the true owner by sending a letter to everyone who had occupied the room over the last three months. However, no one claimed it. Jackson demanded that the money be returned to her, but Steinberg refused.

ISSUE Was Jackson entitled to the money she found in the dresser drawer in Steinberg's hotel?

DECISION No. The court held that Jackson was not entitled to have the money returned to her. It said that the natural assumption was that the money had been left by a guest at the hotel. Its value and the way it was concealed indicated that the person did it to protect the money and that he or she intended to reclaim it. The bills should be classified as misplaced or forgotten property rather than lost property. The owner of the premises on which mislaid property is found has the right and duty to take it into his possession. He then holds the property as a gratuitous bailee for the true owner. (Bailments are discussed in Chapter 34.)

Gift

Title to personal property can be obtained by gift. A *gift* is a voluntary transfer of property without the donor getting any consideration in return. To have a valid gift: (1) the donor must *intend* to make a gift, (2) the donor must *make delivery* of the gift, and (3) the donee must *accept* the gift. The most critical requirement is delivery. The person who makes the gift must actually give up possession and control of the property to either the *donee* (the person who receives the gift) or a third person to hold it for the donee. Delivery is important because it makes clear to the donor that he or she is voluntarily giving up ownership without getting something in exchange. A promise to make a gift is usually not enforceable; the person must actually part with the property. In some cases the delivery may be symbolic. For example, handing over the key to a strongbox can be symbolic delivery of the property in the strongbox.

There are two kinds of gifts: gifts *inter vivos* and gifts *causa mortis*. A *gift inter vivos* is a gift between two living persons; a *gift causa mortis* is a gift made in contemplation of death. For example, Uncle Ernie is about to undergo a serious heart operation. Ernie gives his watch to his nephew Ted and tells Ted he wants him to have it if he does not survive the operation. A gift *causa mortis* is a conditional gift. It is not effective if: (1) the donor recovers from the peril or sickness under fear of which the gift was made, (2) the donor revokes or withdraws the gift before he or she dies, or (3) the donee dies before the donor. If one of these events takes place, ownership of the property goes back to the donor.

Ownership can also be transferred when the owner dies. The property may pass under the terms of a will if the will was validly executed. If there is no valid will, the property is transferred to the heirs of the owner according to state laws. Transfer of property at the death of the owner will be discussed in Chapter 37.

Taylor v. Smith
102 S.E.2d 160 (Sup. Ct. Va. 1958)

FACTS Hunter Taylor lived with Hattie Smith. Taylor rented a safe-deposit box at the Crown Center Bank in the name of Hattie Smith and gave her both keys to the box. Smith signed a card that authorized and directed the bank to allow Hunter Taylor to enter "my box" at any time. On several occasions, Taylor borrowed the keys to the box without explanation and then returned them to her. Smith claimed that Taylor told her he had put money in the box for her. Smith did not see Taylor put any money in the box and none was put in the day the box was rented. Taylor was murdered, and at the time of the murder he had both of the keys to the box in his possession. Smith had the box opened by the bank and $8,000 was found in it. The administrator of Taylor's estate claimed the money for the estate. Smith claimed the money was a gift to her.

ISSUE Had Taylor made a valid gift of the money to Smith?

DECISION No. The court held that Taylor had not made a valid gift of the money to Smith. To be effective, there must be an intent by the donor to make a gift. There must also be an actual or constructive delivery of the gift whereby the donor gives up all dominion and control over the gift. Here the money was not in the box when it was rented. Taylor always had access to the keys to the box and could put money in or take it out at will. He never gave up all control over the contents of the box. Smith never knew how much it contained. Under these circumstances, Taylor did not intend to part with ownership to the contents. Also, periodic delivery of the keys meant that he had not been divested of control so there was not an effective delivery to Smith. Thus, there was not a valid gift to Smith.

Confusion

Title to personal property can be obtained by confusion. *Confusion* is the intermixing of goods that belong to different owners in a way that they cannot later be separated. For example, suppose wheat belonging to several different people is mixed in a grain elevator. If the mixing was by agreement or if it resulted from an accident without negligence on anyone's part, then each person owns his or her proportionate share of the entire quantity of wheat.

However, a different result would be reached if the wheat was wrongfully or negligently mixed together. Suppose a thief steals a truckload of Grade #1 wheat worth $4.50 a bushel that belongs to a farmer. The thief dumps the wheat into a storage bin that contains a lower-grade wheat worth $2.50 a bushel. Once mixed, the wheat cannot be separated into the two grades, so it is worth only $2.50 a bushel. The farmer becomes the owner of the mixture to the extent it is necessary to protect his interest. The thief, or any other person whose intentional or negligent act results in confusion of goods, must bear any loss caused by the confusion.

Accession

Title to personal property can also be obtained by accession. *Accession* means increasing the value of property by adding materials and/or labor. As a general rule, the owner of the original property becomes the owner of the improvements. For example, Harry takes his GTO to a shop which replaces the engine with a larger engine and puts in a new four-speed transmission. Harry is still the owner of the GTO as well as the owner of the parts added by the auto shop.

Problems can arise if materials are added or work is done on personal property without the consent of the owner. If property is stolen from one person and improved by the thief, the original owner can get it back and does not have to reimburse the thief for the work or materials in improving it. For example, a thief steals Ralph's used car, puts a new engine in it, replaces the tires, and repairs the muffler. Ralph is entitled to get his car back from the thief and does not have to pay him for the engine, tires, or muffler.

The problem is more difficult if property is mistakenly improved in good faith by someone who believes he or she is the owner of the property. Then two innocent parties—the original owner and the person who improved the property—are involved. Usually the person who improved the property in good faith is entitled to recover the cost of the improvement made to the property. Alternatively, the improver can keep the property and pay the original owner the value of the property as of the time he or she obtained it. Whether the original owner has the right to recover the property after paying for the improvements depends on several factors. First, what is the relative increase in value? Second, has the form or identity of the property been changed? Third, can the improvements be separated from the original property?

Ochoa v. Rogers
234 S.W. 693 (Ct. Civ. App. Tex. 1921)

FACTS   Ochoa's Studebaker automobile was stolen. Eleven months later the automobile somehow found its way into the hands of the U.S. government, which sold it at a "junk" auction for $85 to Rogers. At the time it was purchased by Rogers, no part of the car was intact. It had no top except a part of the frame; it had no steering wheel, tires, rims, cushions, or battery; the motor, radiator, and gears were out of the car; one wheel was gone, as was one axle; the fenders were partly gone; and the frame was broken. It was no longer an automobile but a pile of broken and dismantled parts of what was once Ochoa's car.

Having purchased these parts, Rogers used them in the construction of a delivery truck at an expense of approximately $800. When the truck was completed, he put it in use in his furniture business. Several months later, Ochoa was passing Rogers's place of business and recognized the machine from a mark on the hood and another on the radiator. He discovered that the serial and engine numbers matched those on the car he had owned. Ochoa demanded the car from Rogers, who refused to surrender it. Ochoa brought suit to recover possession of the property. In the alternative, he asked for the value at the time of the suit, which he alleged to be $1,000, and for the value of the use of the car at the rate of $5 per day from the time Rogers purchased it from the government.

ISSUE   Was Ochoa entitled to recover possession of his property, which Rogers had substantially improved?

DECISION   No. The court gave judgment to Rogers and said that he was only liable to Ochoa for the market value of Ochoa's property at the time he obtained it. If Ochoa had found his car in the hands of the thief, he would have been able to recover it from him. This would be true even if the thief had spent money to improve it and had increased its value. The thief would be out the money he spent. It would also be true of anyone who bought it from the thief knowing that it was stolen property. Here, however, Rogers was an innocent trespasser who substantially improved the value of the car. His improvements exceeded the value of Ochoa's property and he became the owner of the improved product by accession.

CO-OWNERSHIP OF PROPERTY

Ownership of personal property as well as real property can be shared by two or more people. The four major forms of co-ownership of real and personal property are: (1) tenancy in common, (2) joint tenancy, (3) tenancy by the entirety, and (4) community property.

Tenancy in Common

Where property is transferred to two or more people and no provision is made as to how they will own it, they are *tenants in common*. For example, if Mary Post wills her cottage at the beach to her two daughters, they will own it as tenants in common. The shares of a tenant in common do not have to be equal. Thus, one tenant could own two-thirds and the other tenant could have a one-third interest.

The distinguishing feature of a tenancy in common is that on the death of one of the owners, his interest passes to his heirs or the person(s) specified by will. For example, Brenda and Ruth each have a half-interest in a farm as tenants in common. If Ruth dies, she could will her one-half interest to her son Rick. Rick and Brenda then would be tenants in common. A tenant in common may also sell or mortgage her interest in the property. Each tenant in common has the right to possess and use the property. However, she cannot exclude the other tenants in common from also possessing and using the property. If the property is rented, each tenant in common has the right to share in the income in proportion to the tenant's interest in the property. Similarly, each tenant in common must pay his or her proportionate share of the taxes and repairs to the property.

Tenants in common may divide up the property by agreement. If they cannot agree, any one tenant has the right to ask a court to *partition* the property. The court will physically divide the property if that is practicable. Then each co-tenant gets his or her proportionate share. If the property cannot easily be divided, the court will order that it be sold and the proceeds divided.

Joint Tenants

A *joint tenancy* is created when equal interests in real property are conveyed to two or more people by a single document that specifies they are to hold it as joint tenants. The most significant feature of a joint tenancy is what is called *right of survivorship*. This means that on the death of one of the joint tenants, that person's interest in the property passes to the surviving joint tenant(s). A joint tenant cannot will his interest to someone else. This feature makes it easy to convey property at death without the need for a will. For example, a grandfather opens a savings account with his grandson. The account specifies that the two are joint tenants. The grandfather can add money to the account from time to time, and on his death, the money in the account will belong to the grandson.

If one of the joint tenants sells or conveys his or her interest to someone else, the joint tenancy is broken as to the share sold. The new person comes into the joint ownership as a tenant in common rather than as part of a joint tenancy. The rights of use, possession, contribution, and partition of joint tenants are the same as those of tenants in common. Some states, however, do not permit joint tenancies.

Tenancy by the Entirety

Tenants by the entirety must be husband and wife. A tenancy by the entirety is basically a joint tenancy. It can be created only by a conveyance of property to persons who are husband and wife at the time of the conveyance. A tenancy by the entirety cannot be broken by the act of only one of the parties. For example, neither can transfer the property unless the other person also signs the deed. Similarly, neither person can convey the property by will. On the death of the husband or wife, the entire property belongs to the surviving spouse.

Naccash v. Naccash
188 S.E.2d 83 (Sup. Ct. Va. 1972)

FACTS   In 1961, Dr. Edward Naccash and his wife Mary purchased an office building as tenants by the entirety. They converted it into office space for three doctors. In 1967, the Naccashes were divorced. Under Virginia law the tenancy by the entirety was converted into a tenancy in common. At that time, Dr. Naccash was occupying one of the suites but the other two were vacant. In 1969 he was able to rent one of the suites for a short period of time. His wife made no effort to try to rent the vacant offices. Dr. Naccash brought a lawsuit against his former wife to partition the property they owned as tenants in common. She claimed she was entitled to half of the rental value of the property during the time Dr. Naccash occupied it.

ISSUE   What is the obligation of a cotenant to account to his cotenant for his use and rental of property they own as tenants in common?

DECISION   The court held that Mrs. Naccash was entitled to half the rental value of the space Dr. Naccash occupied after their divorce and half the rent paid to him in 1969. Mrs. Naccash was not entitled to half the rental value of the entire property because Dr. Naccash only occupied or benefited from a portion of it.

Community Property

Some states have a community property system. In such states, any property that is acquired by a husband or wife during their marriage and as a result of their efforts becomes common or *community property*. Each has an equal interest in the property regardless of who produced or earned it. In addition, a husband or wife may own what is called *separate property*. Generally, separate property is property that was owned prior to the marriage or that is obtained by gift or inheritance during the marriage. It also includes any property received in exchange for separate property.

QUESTIONS AND PROBLEM CASES

1. How do we distinguish real property from personal property?

2. What is the primary difference between a tenancy in common and a joint tenancy?

3. An oil company holds oil leases on land located in the state of Illinois that the state taxes as tangible property. The company contends that the oil leases are intangible property since they convey only the right to drill for oil and gas and to take oil and gas if discovered. Are the oil and gas leases tangible or intangible property?

4. Liesner shot and mortally wounded a previously wounded wolf. Before Liesner could reach the

wolf, Warnie, with his gun pointed within three feet of the wolf, fired the finishing shot. Liesner had the wolf in such condition that escape was improbable if not impossible. Who owned the wolf, Liesner or Warnie?

5. Blanchard, who worked in a hotel owned by Hamaker, found three $20 bills on the floor in the public lobby of the hotel. She turned them over to Hamaker on his representation that he knew the guest who had lost them. Actually, he did not know who had lost the bills, and they were not reclaimed. Hamaker refused to return the bills to Blanchard. Is Blanchard entitled to the return of the bills?

6. Faulke, a passenger on a train, saw on the seat opposite him a package that had been left by a passenger who had left the train. Faulke picked up the package, examined it, found no name or mark on it, and took the package with him when he disembarked. Was the package lost property?

7. Richard Rothchild was engaged to marry Carol Sue Cohen and gave her a diamond engagement ring valued at $1,000. Richard was killed in an automobile accident shortly before the wedding date. Richard's estate brought a lawsuit to recover the ring from Carol on the grounds that it was a conditional gift. She claimed she was entitled to retain it even if it was a conditional gift because she had not performed any act that would prevent the marriage. Who should get the ring?

8. Henry Blandy desired to make some provisions for the support of his daughter Amanda. He purchased and set apart as a "gift" to her $2,000 worth of U.S. bonds. The bonds were never delivered to Amanda, who lived some distance away, and she never had actual possession of them. Rather, by her request and assent, they were left under the dominion and control of her father for safekeeping. Each year he collected and sent to her the interest that had accrued on the bonds. Blandy became interested in the cashmere coat business and decided that such an investment would be more profitable to his daughter. So he sold the bonds and invested money in that business. He then wrote Amanda, telling her that if she did not accept the new investment, he would pay to her, in place of the bonds, $2,000 plus interest. Blandy died and Amanda claimed she was entitled to $2,000 because her father had made a valid gift to her of the bonds. Did he make a valid gift?

9. On January 18, 1905, Sarah Hume executed a will that provided in part:

> Sixth. I will, devise and bequeath to Phillip Russell Hume and Robert Cumberland Hume my farm of one hundred (100) acres, if said farm is not sold by me before my death, but in event of death of either one of them it is to go to the surviving one.

She died in 1909 and her will was probated. Phillip and Robert Hume were her grandsons and were teenagers at the time the will was executed. The brothers held the farm of 100 acres until the death in 1961 of Phillip, who left his interest in the land to his daughter Louise. Louise claims she is entitled to a half-interest, and Robert claims he is entitled to the entire property. What is the basis for each party's claim? How should the court decide the case?

Bailments

34

You take your car to a parking garage where the attendant gives you a claim check and then drives the car down the ramp to park it. Charlie borrows his neighbor's lawn mower to cut his grass. Ann asks Kathy, who lives in the next apartment, to take care of her cat while she goes on a vacation. These are everyday situations that involve bailments. This chapter will focus on the legal aspects of bailments. For example, what are your rights if your car is damaged while it is parked in the parking garage? How effective are the signs you may see near checkrooms that say "Not responsible for loss or damages to property"?

Elements of a Bailment

A *bailment* is the delivery of personal property by one person (the *bailor*) to another person (the *bailee*) who accepts it and is under an express or implied agreement to return it to the bailor or to someone designated by the bailor. The essential elements are: (1) the bailor has title to or the right to possess the item of property, (2) possession and temporary control of the property must be given to the bailee, and (3) the bailee must owe a duty to return the property as directed by the bailor.

Delivery and Acceptance of Possession

A critical requirement is whether the person to whom the property was delivered *intended to assume possession and control* over the property. Suppose you go into a restaurant and hang your hat and coat on an unattended rack. It is unlikely that this created a bailment because the restaurant owner never assumed control over the hat and coat. However, if there is a checkroom and you check your hat and coat with the attendant, a bailment will arise.

432

If you park your car in a parking lot, keep the keys, and can drive the car out yourself whenever you wish, a bailment has not been created. The courts treat this situation as a lease of space. Suppose you take your car to a parking garage where an attendant gives you a claim check and then parks the car. In this case there is a bailment of your car since the parking garage has accepted delivery and possession of your car. However, a distinction is made between the car and some packages locked in the trunk. If the parking garage was not aware of the packages, it would probably not be a bailee of them as it did not knowingly accept possession of them.

Hallman v. Federal Parking Services, Inc.
134 A.2d 382 (Ct. App. D.C. 1957)

FACTS Hallman and his family were taking an automobile trip to Florida. They stopped at the New Colonial Hotel to spend the night. Hallman asked the registration clerk if the hotel had parking facilities. He was told that the bellboy would take care of the car. The bellboy took the luggage needed by the Hallmans from the car and put it in their room. Then he took the car to a nearby parking lot that was not owned by the hotel. The bellboy left the car with the attendant, who locked it and kept the keys. When the car was taken to the lot, it still contained some luggage in the rear seat and several garments hung on racks. When the bellboy returned to the hotel, he gave Hallman a claim check bearing the name of the parking lot and the stamped name "New Colonial." The next morning Hallman went to pick up his car and discovered the side window was broken. Personal property worth $557 had been stolen from the car. Hallman then sued the hotel to recover for the personal property and for repairing the damage to his car.

ISSUE Was the hotel the bailee of the car?

DECISION Yes. The court held that the hotel was the bailee of the car and its contents and was liable to Hallman for the loss and damage to his property. When the bellboy, with the authority of the hotel, took the keys and the car, the hotel had accepted custody of the car and its contents. It had physical control and the intent to control the property. Thus a bailment relationship was created. Responsibility for the contents of the car depends on whether the hotel had notice of the contents. The hotel knew Hallman was a traveler and was likely to leave belongings in his car. In addition, the items were clearly visible to the hotel's employee. The result could be different if the goods were not in plain view so that the hotel was not aware of them.

A distinction is made between delivering *possession* of goods and merely giving *custody* of goods. If a shopkeeper entrusts goods to a clerk in the store, the shopkeeper is considered to have given the clerk custody of the goods but to have retained possession. Because the shopkeeper has retained legal possession, there has not been a bailment of goods to the clerk.

Types of Bailments

Bailments are commonly divided into three different classes: (1) bailments for the sole benefit of the bailor, (2) bailments for the sole benefit of the bailee, and (3) mutual benefit bailments. The type of bailment may be important in determining the liability of the bailee for loss of or damages to the property. However, some courts no longer rely on these distinctions for this purpose.

Bailments for Benefit of Bailor. A bailment for the sole benefit of the bailor is one in which the bailee renders some service but does not receive a benefit in return. For example, you allow your neighbor to park her car in your garage while she is on vacation and she does not pay you anything for the privilege. Your neighbor (bailor) has received a benefit from you (bailee), but you have not received a benefit in return.

Bailments for Benefit of Bailee. A bailment for the sole benefit of the bailee is one in which the owner of the goods allows someone else to use them free of charge. For example, you loan your lawn mower to your neighbor so he can cut his grass.

Mutual Benefit Bailments. If both the bailee and the bailor receive benefits from the bailment, it is a mutual benefit bailment. For example, you rent a U-Haul trailer from a store. You, the bailee, benefit by being able to use the trailer, while the store benefits from your payment of the rental charge. Similarly, if you store some furniture at a commercial warehouse, it is a mutual benefit bailment. You get the benefit of having your goods cared for, while the storage company benefits from the storage charge you pay. On some occasions, the benefit to the bailee is less tangible. Suppose you check your coat at an attended coatroom at a restaurant. Even if no charge is made for the service, it is likely to be treated as a mutual benefit bailment because the restaurant is benefiting from your patronage.

RIGHTS AND DUTIES

Duties of the Bailee

The bailee has two basic duties: (1) to take reasonable care of the property that has been entrusted to him or her and (2) to return the property at the termination of the bailment.

Bailee's Duty of Care

The bailee is responsible for using reasonable care to protect the property during the time he or she has possession of it. If the bailee does not exercise reasonable care and the property is lost or damaged, the bailee is liable for negligence. Thus the bailee would have to reimburse the bailor for the amount of loss or damage. If the property is lost or damaged without the fault or negligence of the bailee, the bailee is not liable to the bailor.

Whether the care exercised by the bailee in a particular case was *reasonable* depends in part on who is benefiting from the bailment. If it is a mutual benefit bailment, then the bailee must use ordinary care, which is the same kind of care a reasonable person would use to protect his or her own property in that situation. If the bailee is a professional that holds itself out as a professional bailee—such as a warehouse—it must use the degree of care a person in that profession would use. This is likely to be more care than the ordinary person would use. In addition, there is usually a duty on a professional bailee to explain any loss or damage to property, that is, to show it was not negligent. If it cannot do so, it will be liable to the bailor.

If the bailment is solely for the benefit of the bailor, then the bailee may be held to a somewhat lower degree of care. If the bailee is doing you a favor, it is not reasonable to expect him to be as careful as when you are paying the bailee for keeping your goods. On the other hand, if the bailment is for the sole benefit of the bailee, it is reasonable to expect that the bailee will use a higher degree of care. If you loan your sailboat to your neighbor, you probably expect her to be even more careful with it than you would be.

Who benefits from the bailment is one consideration in determining what is reasonable care. Other factors include: the nature and value of the property, how easily it can be damaged or stolen, whether the bailment was paid for or free, and the experience of the bailee. Using reasonable care includes using the property only as was agreed between the parties. For example, you loan your lawn mower to your neighbor to cut his lawn. However, if he uses it to cut the weeds on a trash-filled vacant lot and the mower is damaged, he would be liable because he was exceeding the agreed purpose for the bailment—that is, to cut his lawn.

Axelrod v. Wardrobe Cleaners, Inc.
289 So.2d 847 (Ct. App. La. 1974)

FACTS   George Pringle, the head of the drapery department at Wardrobe Cleaners, went to the home of Dr. Arthur Axelrod to inspect some dining room draperies for dry-cleaning purposes. He spent about 30 minutes looking at the drapes and inspected both the drapes and the lining. He pointed out some roach spots on the lining that could not be removed by cleaning, but this was not of concern to the Axelrods. He did not indicate to them that the fabric had deteriorated from sunburn, age, dust, or air-conditioning so as to make it unsuitable for dry-cleaning. He took the drapes and had them dry-cleaned. When the drapes were returned they were unfit for use. The fabric had been a gold floral design on an eggshell-white background. When returned, it was a blotchy gold. Wardrobe Cleaners stated that it was difficult to predict how imported fabrics would respond to the dry-cleaning process and the company was not equipped to pretest the fabric to see if it was colorfast. The Axelrods sued Wardrobe Cleaners for $1,000, the replacement value of the drapes.

ISSUE	Was the cleaner liable for the damage caused to the drapes during the dry-cleaning process?
DECISION	Yes. The court awarded $1,000 damages to the Axelrods. When the cleaner accepted the drapes for cleaning, a bailment for hire was created. As bailee, the cleaner made an implied assurance that the drapes could withstand the cleaning process when it accepted the drapes. There was a *prima facie* case of negligence by the cleaner when the drapes were damaged while in its custody. The cleaner then had the burden of showing it used due care. If there was doubt as to whether the drapes would be suitable to be dry-cleaned, it should have either done further tests before dry-cleaning them or refused to accept them.

Bailee's Duty to Return the Property

One of the essential elements for a bailment is the duty of the bailee to return the property at the termination of the bailment. The bailee must return the goods in an undamaged condition to the bailor or to someone designated by the bailor. If the goods have been damaged or lost, the bailee may excuse the failure to return undamaged goods by showing that the goods were lost or damaged without negligence on his part.

In most instances the bailee must return the identical property that was bailed. If you loan your 1979 Volkswagen Rabbit to your friend, you expect to have that particular car returned to you. In some cases, the bailor does not expect the identical goods back. For example, if a farmer stores 1,500 bushels of wheat at a local grain elevator, that farmer expects to get back 1,500 bushels of similar wheat when the bailment is terminated.

The bailee is also liable to the bailor if she misdelivers the bailed property at the termination of the bailment. The property must be returned to the bailor or to someone specified by the bailor.

Limitations on Liability

Bailees may try to limit or relieve themselves of liability for the bailed property. Common examples include the signs near checkrooms, "Not responsible for loss or damage to checked property," and *disclaimers* on claim checks, "Goods left at owner's risk." Any attempt by the bailee to be relieved of liability for intentional wrongful acts is against public policy and will not be enforced.

A bailee's ability to be relieved of liability for negligence is also limited. The courts look to see whether the disclaimer or limitation of liability was *communicated* to the bailor. Did the attendant point out the sign near the checkroom to the person when the coat was checked? Did the parking lot attendant call the person's attention to the disclaimer on the back of the claim check? If not, the court may hold that it was not communicated to the bailee and did not become part of the bailment contract. Even if the bailee was aware of the disclaimer, it still may not be enforced on the grounds that it is contrary to public policy.

Courts do not look with favor on efforts by a person to be relieved of liability for negligence. We expect people to use reasonable care and to be liable if they do not and if someone or something is injured as a result. If the disclaimer was offered on a take-it-or-leave-it basis and was not the subject of arm's-length bargaining, it is not likely to be enforced. A bailee may be able to limit liability to a certain amount. Ideally the bailee will give the bailor a chance to declare a higher value and to pay an additional charge to be protected up to the declared value of the goods. Common carriers like railroads and trucking companies often take this approach.

Carter v. Reichlin Furriers
386 A2d647 (Sup. Ct. Conn. 1977)

FACTS   On April 18, 1973, Mrs. Carter brought her fur coat to Reichlin Furriers for cleaning, glazing, and storage until the next winter season. She was given a printed form of receipt, upon the front of which an employee of the Furrier had written $100 as the valuation of the coat. There was no discussion of the value of the coat and Carter did not realize that such a value had been written on the receipt, which she did not read at the time. A space for the customer's signature on the front of the receipt was left blank. Below this space in prominent type appeared a notice to "see reverse side for terms and conditions." The other side of the receipt stated that it was a storage contract and that by its acceptance the customer would be deemed to have agreed to its terms unless notice to the contrary was given within ten days. Fifteen conditions were listed. One of the conditions was as follows: "Storage charges are based upon valuation herein declared by the depositor and amount recoverable for loss or damage to the article shall not exceed its actual value or the cost of repair or replacement with materials of like kind and quality or the depositor's valuation appearing in this receipt, whichever is less."

In the fall of the year, after Carter had paid the bill for storage and other services on the coat, Furrier informed her that the coat was lost. The fair market value of the coat at the time was $450. Carter sued Furrier for loss of the coat and sought $450 damages. Furrier claimed its liability was limited to $100.

ISSUE   Was the limitation of liability on the claim check effective to limit Furrier's liability?

DECISION   No. The court held that the limitation of liability was not effective and that Carter was entitled to recover $450. The court noted first that a warehouseman could limit his liability in case of loss or damage by a term in a warehouse receipt or storage agreement. Here, however, there was a question as to whether the limitation of liability ever became part of the contract between Carter and Furrier. It is not enough to hand a bailor a receipt containing a limitation of liability. In this case there was no evidence that Carter read the notice, that the inserted valuation was discussed with her, or that she had signed the receipt. Thus the court concluded that she had never consented to the limitation of liability.

Right to Compensation

Whether or not the bailee gets paid for keeping the property or must pay for having the right to use it depends on the bailment contract or the understanding of the parties. If the bailment is made as a favor, then the bailee is not entitled to compensation even though the bailment is for the sole benefit of the bailor. If the bailment is the rental of property, then the bailee must pay the agreed upon rental rate. If the bailment is for the storage or repair of property, then the bailee is entitled to the contract price for the storage or repair services. If there is no price agreed upon, then the bailee gets the reasonable value of the services provided.

In many instances the bailee will have a *lien* on the bailed property for the reasonable value of the services. Suppose you take a chair to an upholsterer to have it recovered. This is a mutual benefit bailment. When the chair has been recovered, the upholsterer has the right to keep it until you pay the agreed price or—if no price was set—the reasonable value of the work.

Bailor's Liability for Defects in the Bailed Property

When personal property is rented or loaned, the bailor makes an *implied warranty* that there are no hidden defects in the property that make it unsafe for use. If the bailment is for the sole benefit of the bailee, then the bailor is liable for injuries that result from defects in the bailed property only if the bailor knew about the defect and did not tell the bailee. For example, Paul loans his car, which has bad brakes, to Sally. If Paul does not tell Sally about the bad brakes and if Sally is injured in an accident because the brakes fail, Paul is liable for Sally's injuries.

If the bailmnent is a mutual benefit bailment, then the bailor has a larger obligation. The bailor must use reasonable care in inspecting the property and seeing that it is safe for the purpose for which it is rented. The bailor is liable for injuries suffered by the bailee by defects that the bailor either knew about or should have discovered by reasonable inspection. For example, Frank's Rent-All rents trailers. Suppose Frank's does not inspect the trailers after they come back from being rented. A wheel has come loose on a trailer that Frank's rents to Harold. If the wheel comes off while Harold is using it and the goods Harold is carrying in it are damaged, Frank's is liable to Harold.

In addition, if goods are rented to someone (mutual benefit bailment) for his or her personal use, there may be an *implied warranty* that the goods are fit for the purpose for which they are rented. Liability does not depend on whether the bailor knew about or should have discovered the defect. The only question is whether the property was fit for the purpose for which it was rented. Some courts have also imposed *strict liability* on lessors/bailors of goods that turn out to be more dangerous than the lessee/bailee would have expected. This liability is imposed regardless of whether the lessor was negligent or at fault.

> ### Cintrone v. Hertz Truck Leasing & Rental Service
> ### 212 A.2d 769 (Sup. Ct. N.J. 1965)
>
> **FACTS**   Hertz Truck Leasing & Rental Service leased a truck to Contract Packers. Francisco Cintrone was a driver-helper for Contract Packers. One day while Cintrone was on a delivery, the brakes on the truck failed. He was injured when the truck hit a trestle bridge when it could not be stopped by the brakes. He sued Hertz to recover for his injuries.
>
> **ISSUE**   Was Hertz liable for injuries suffered by a third person because of the defect in the bailed property?
>
> **DECISION**   Yes. The court held that Cintrone could recover from Hertz. It said that when Hertz rented the truck, it made an implied warranty that the truck would be fit to be used by Contract Packers during the term of the lease. The court held that Hertz was strictly liable for any flaws or defects in the goods it rents regardless of whether the defect could be discovered by reasonable inspection or testing.

SPECIAL BAILMENT SITUATIONS

Common Carriers

Bailees who are common carriers are held to a higher level of responsibility than those who are private carriers. *Common carriers* are persons who are licensed by government agencies to carry the property of anyone who requests the service. Airlines licensed by the Civil Aeronautics Board (CAB) and trucks and buses licensed by the Interstate Commerce Commission (ICC) are examples of common carriers. The rates and terms under which a common carrier will carry property are normally subject to approval of these government agencies. *Private contract carriers* are persons who carry goods only for persons selected by the carrier.

Both common carriers and private contract carriers are bailees. However, the law makes the common carrier an *absolute insurer* of the goods it carries. The common carrier is responsible for any loss or damage to goods entrusted to it. The common carrier can avoid responsibility only if it can show that the loss or damage was caused by: (1) an act of God, (2) an act of a public enemy, (3) an act or order of the government, (4) an act of the person who shipped the goods, or (5) the nature of the goods themselves.

The common carrier is liable if goods entrusted to it are stolen by some unknown person but not if the goods are destroyed when a tornado hits its warehouse. If the shipper improperly packages or crates the goods and this results in them being damaged, then the carrier is not liable. Similarly, if perishable goods are not in suitable condition to be shipped and deteriorate in the course of shipment, the carrier is not liable so long as it used reasonable care in handling them.

Common carriers are usually permitted to limit their liability to a stated value unless the bailor declares a higher value for the property and pays an additional fee.

Hotelkeepers

Hotelkeepers are engaged in the business of offering food and/or lodging to transient persons. They hold themselves out to serve the public and are obligated to do so. Like the common carrier, the hotelkeeper is held to a higher standard of care than the ordinary bailee.

The hotelkeeper is not a bailee in the strict sense of the word. The guest does not usually surrender the exclusive possession of his or her property to the hotelkeeper. However, the hotelkeeper is treated as the virtual insurer of the guest's property. The hotelkeeper is not liable for loss of or damage to property if he can show that it was caused by: (1) an act of God, (2) an act of a public enemy, (3) an act of government authority, (4) the fault of a member of the guest's party, or (5) the nature of the goods.

Most states have passed laws that limit the hotelkeeper's liability. Commonly they require the hotel owner to post a notice advising guests that any valuables should be checked into the hotel vault. The hotelkeeper's liability is then limited for valuables that are not so checked.

Wallinga v. Johnson
131 N.W.2d 216 (Sup. Ct. Minn. 1964)

FACTS Marie Wallinga was staying at the Commodore Hotel. She had her son take her two diamond rings to the hotel clerk for safekeeping. The rings were shown to the clerk and then placed in a "safety deposit envelope," which was sealed. The son received a depositor's check stub, which had a number corresponding to the number on the envelope. He also signed his name on the safety deposit envelope. Both the stub and his signature were necessary to get the envelope back. The envelopes were kept in a safe located in the hotel's front office, which was four to five feet behind the reception desk. The safe was used to keep cash for use in the hotel as well as the valuables of guests. The safe was equipped with a combination lock, but for many years it had never been locked. A clerk was always on duty at the reception desk. One night at 3:30 A.M. the hotel was robbed by two armed men and Wallinga's rings were taken. She sued the hotel for the value of the rings. The hotel claimed that the robbery relieved it of liability for them.

ISSUE Was the hotelkeeper liable for the theft of property left with it for safekeeping?

DECISION Yes. The court held the hotel liable for the value of the rings. When the rings were left with the hotel for safekeeping, a bailment relationship was created. Here the purpose of the bailment was to protect against theft. The robbery was not an event that relieved the hotel of liability. The failure to lock the safe, at least at night, was negligence on its part.

Safe-Deposit Boxes

If you rent a safe-deposit box at a local bank and place some property in the box, the box and the property are in the manual possession of the bank. However, it takes both your key and the key held by the bank to open the box, and in most cases the bank does not know the nature, amount, or value of the goods in your box. Although a few courts have held the rental of a safe-deposit box not to be a bailment, most courts have found that the renter of the box is a bailor and the bank is a bailee.

Involuntary Bailments

Suppose you own a cottage on a beach. After a violent storm, you find a sailboat washed up on your beach. You may be considered the *involuntary bailee* of the sailboat. This relationship may arise when you find yourself in possession of property that belongs to someone else without having agreed to accept possession.

The duties of the involuntary bailee are not well defined. The bailee does not have the right to destroy the property or to use it. If the true owner shows up, the property must be returned to the owner. Under some circumstances, the involuntary bailee may be under an obligation to assume control of the property and/or to take some minimal steps to ascertain who the owner is.

QUESTIONS AND PROBLEM CASES

1. What are the basic duties of a bailee?
2. Why are hotelkeepers and common carriers treated as the virtual insurers of goods entrusted to them?
3. Grana worked as a waitress in the Mid-Top Restaurant and was required to wear a Mid-Top waitress uniform. She and the other waitresses were provided with a locker room adjacent to the dining room where they could change into the uniforms and ready themselves for work. In the middle of the locker room was a large rack and on one wall were several small metal lockers. Grana was assigned one of the lockers and was provided with one key to it; Mid-Top also retained a key to the locker. Street clothes and other items were generally hung on the rack or placed under it and smaller items were placed in the lockers, which on some occasions were left open. Employees of Mid-Top, other than waitresses, cleaned the locker room, which could be entered only through a single door that was left unlocked. The restaurant was destroyed by fire as were all of the personal belongings of the waitresses in the locker room. Was Mid-Top the bailee of their clothes and personal belongings left in the locker room?

4. Simkins owned a thoroughbred racehorse named Cider Dave. Because she was unable to train or race Cider Dave, she sent him to the Ritters on the understanding that Cider Dave was to be returned to Simkins when he was finished racing. The Ritters were to pay the entire cost of Cider Dave's upkeep and in return they were to retain all of his earnings. Simkins sent the Ritters the jockey club certificate of registration, which she had signed in blank. Kate Ritter placed her name on Cider Dave's registration as the transferee and inserted the date of transfer as June 8, 1970. Simkins contended that the transfer of foal registration is frequently done in the racing business to allow someone else to race a horse. Was this transaction a sale or a bailment?

5. Pond owned and operated a parking lot. Rehling parked his automobile on Pond's lot, which was near Crosley Field, and proceeded with others to a night baseball game. Rehling paid $1 to the parking lot attendant, for which he received a "claim check." Before leaving his automobile, Rehling turned the ignition switch to neutral, rolled up the windows, locked the doors, and took the keys with him. When he returned after the ballgame to get his automobile, it was gone. The parking lot attendants testified that during about the third inning of the ball game, they saw a person walk directly to Rehling's automobile, get in, back up, and drive away. There was no showing that the claim check was ever used for anything but identification in case a patron was unable to find his automobile on the lot. Is Pond liable as bailee for the loss of the automobile?

6. Wells rented a trailer from Brown and agreed to return the trailer clean and in the same condition as when rented. The trailer was damaged when a tree was blown across it during a violent windstorm. The damage was caused solely by the violence of the storm and without any negligence or fault on the part of Wells. Brown sued Wells to recover for the damage done to the trailer. Can he recover?

7. Hightower delivered his Cadillac automobile to Auto Auction for sale and, while on Auto Auction's lot, the car was damaged. At the trial Hightower offered evidence of the delivery of the Cadillac automobile to Auto Auction's lot in good condition and its subsequent damaged condition. Auto Auction contended (1) that no bailment was created, (2) that Hightower did not prove that the damage to his Cadillac automobile was caused by the negligent acts of Auto Auction, and (3) that the damage was caused by the negligence of a third party. Mrs. Tune had driven her automobile on Auto Auction's lot to sell it and parked it as directed by the attendant in charge of the lot. When Tune stepped out of her automobile, it started to roll down an incline on the lot. Although she attempted to stop it, she was knocked down and the automobile continued to roll down the incline and struck Hightower's Cadillac broadside and damaged it. Is Auto Auction liable to Hightower for the damage to his Cadillac automobile?

8. An equipment company was negotiating the sale of a crane to a lumber company, and during the negotiations it let the lumber company have the crane for trial and inspection. Roy, an employee of the lumber company who was experienced in the operation of cranes, was assigned the duty of operating the crane and inspecting it. While doing so, he slipped, fell, and was injured. The circumstances were as follows. There was a catwalk 12 or 13 inches wide around the sides and rear of the crane, and a grab handle at the door of the cab. The flow of fuel into the engine for the purpose of operating the crane was regulated by a throttle located high inside the cab. There was a place in the cab for the operator to stand or he could sit, and, in operating the crane, he would reach for the throttle over his head with his right hand. When Roy was injured, he was trying to reach for the throttle from where he was standing on the catwalk. He was holding the door jamb with his left hand and was reaching into the cab for the throttle with his right. It had been raining up to about an hour before, and the catwalk was wet. Roy's feet slipped, causing him to fall backward and sustain his injuries. Roy sued the equipment company, claiming that it had not used reasonable care to see that the crane was reasonably safe for use in the manner and for a purpose reasonably to be anticipated. Is the equipment company liable to Roy?

9. Mrs. Olson asked Security Van Lines to store a Persian rug for her while Security was in the process of moving the Olsons to a smaller home. She signed a document authorizing Security to prepare the rug for storage and to store it for her. The document had no clauses relating to Security's liability. Some ten days after the rug was left with Security, Olson was sent a warehouse receipt that limited Security's liability for damage to $50 and excluded liability for moth damage. The rug was extensively damaged by moths and Olson sued to

recover the value of it, $3,053. Security claimed its liability was limited to $50. Is this claim correct?

10. Dovax had been shipping goods with Delivery Company for more than a year. On November 1, 1966, Dovax gave Delivery Company goods valued at $1,799.95 for delivery to three different consignees. Delivery Company kept the goods in one of its trucks overnight, but the next morning the truck was discovered stolen along with the goods. On the bills of lading given to Dovax was the legend "Liability limited to $50 unless greater value is declared and paid for." Dovax claims he should recover $1,799.95 for the loss; Delivery Company wants to pay only $150. Who is correct?

35

Real Property

Real property includes not only land but also things that are firmly attached to it or embedded under it. Thus, buildings and other permanent structures, trees and shrubs, as well as coal and oil in the earth are considered to be part of real property. As a businessperson, investor, or consumer, it is likely that you will acquire an interest in real property at some time during your life. In this chapter we will look at: (1) the kinds of interests you might acquire in real property, (2) the different ways you might acquire the interest, (3) the various steps and aspects involved in purchasing real property, and (4) the controls that society places on a person's ability to use his or her property.

Before addressing these topics, the initial focus will be on the law of fixtures. *Fixtures* are items of personal property that may be treated as a part of real property because of their use with or attachment to that real property.

FIXTURES

Nature of Fixtures

Suppose you are renting an apartment. You install some drapery rods, attach a bookcase to the wall, and put down wall-to-wall carpeting. Will you be able to take the rods, bookcase, and carpeting with you when you leave the apartment or will they belong to the landlord? Similarly, suppose you are buying a house. Will the refrigerator, the screen and storm windows, and the shrubbery be left when the seller vacates the property or will the seller be able to take them. Problems like these may also come up if real estate is mortgaged. The lender (mortgagee) may claim that its lien covers items like appliances in a building, while the appliance store from which the appliances were purchased on credit may claim that it has a priority lien on them. The answers to these questions come from the law regarding fixtures.

As mentioned, a fixture is personal property that is so attached to or used with real property that it is considered to be part of the real property. Normally whether a particular item has become a fixture is determined by looking at the *intent* of the parties who own the real property and/or who attached or are using the personal property with it. In making this determination, the relationship of the parties, when and how the personal property was attached, and the suitability of the personal property to use with this particular real property are considered.

Express Agreement

Within limits the parties, such as landlord and tenant or buyer and seller, can agree on whether or not a particular item is to be considered a fixture. Their agreement makes their intent clear. They cannot go so far as to agree that a piece of land is to be treated as personal property. However, a landlord can agree that a tenant may attach certain property—such as a bookcase or wall-to-wall carpeting—to the rental house or apartment and remove it when he or she leaves. Similarly, the buyer of a house could agree to allow the seller to take a chandelier or shrubbery that is attached to the real property.

Attachment

The way that an item of personal property is *attached* or *annexed* to real property is important in determining whether it was intended to become a fixture. If bricks are cemented into a building so that they become an integral part of it, they are considered to be part of the real property. The bricks have lost their character as personal property regardless of any agreement by the parties. If personal property is firmly attached to real property and its removal would damage the real propery, then it is likely to be treated as a fixture.

On the other hand, if personal property can be removed with little or no injury, then it is less likely to be treated as a fixture. For example, if a redwood tub containing a shrub could be removed from a patio without damage to the patio, it is not likely to be considered a fixture. An article attached to land only by gravity can become a fixture. Courts have found a building sitting on cement blocks and a statue weighing several tons to be fixtures.

Use with Real Property

Some attachment to real property is usually necessary for an article to become a fixture. However, some unattached articles are considered fixtures where they would be of little value except for use with a particular piece of property. For example, keys and custom-sized storm windows and screens have been held to be fixtures. Similarly, refrigerators, stoves, and cabinets in an apartment house were held to be fixtures when the apartment house was sold. This conclusion was reached even though they were attached in a way that they could easily be removed. The court focused on the suitability of these items for use with that particular real property.

Additions by Owners

If the owner of real property improves it by attaching personal property, there is a presumption that he intended it to become part of the real property. Thus, if the owner sells or mortgages the real property, he must reserve the right to keep the attached property if he wants to do so. Otherwise the buyer or mortgagee will be able to claim it as fixtures. For example, Margo owns an old Victorian-style house. She buys several Tiffany chandeliers and installs them in her house. Suppose Margo wants to sell the house but wants to keep the chandeliers. She should either replace them before the house is shown to prospective purchasers or make it clear in the contract of sale that they will not be included. Otherwise the buyer can claim they were fixtures and part of the house he bought.

Special rules apply to personal property that is subject to a lien or security interest at the time it is attached to real property. For example, you buy a dishwasher on a time-payment plan from an appliance store and have it built into your kitchen. The rules concerning security interests in consumer goods that will become fixtures will be covered in Chapter 43.

Additions by Tenants

A distinction is made between tenants who attach property for business purposes and those who do it for residential or agricultural purposes. The usual fixture tests are applied to the attachment of personal property by residential and agricultural tenants. However, if personal property is brought onto premises leased for business purposes for the use of carrying on the business, it is called a *trade fixture*. Trade fixtures remain the personal property of the tenant regardless of the manner of attachment. Only if such business property is so built into the real property that removing it would weaken the structure will it be considered a permanent fixture.

Where a tenant has added trade fixtures or has brought other personal property onto the premises, the tenant must remove the property before the expiration of a lease for a fixed period. If the business tenant does not remove the trade fixtures by the end of the lease period, they become the property of the landlord. If the lease is for an indefinite period, such as a tenancy at will, the tenant has a reasonable amount of time after the lease expires to remove the property. Where there is an express agreement between landlord and tenant that certain items attached by the tenant may be removed, the tenant has a reasonable time after the term of the lease to remove the articles.

Roberts v. Yancy
165 S.E.2d 399 (Sup. Ct. Va. 1969)

FACTS   Yancy rented a building to Roberts who operated a restaurant on the first floor and converted the second floor into apartments. The lease contained a provision permitting Roberts to remove from the second floor any fixtures he furnished provided that such removal did not injure the real estate. Shortly before the lease was to expire, Roberts began to remove property from the building and to move it to a new building. He removed booths, stools, sinks, dishwashers, refrigerators, and other items of equipment used in his restaurant business. He also took various lighting fixtures, paneling and sheetrock from the walls, and canopies and false ceilings from over the booths. The lighting fixtures were replacements for ones on the premises when Roberts took possession. The paneling was nailed to wooden strips nailed to sheetrock and in turn to the wooden walls. The false ceilings were made of 2-by-4's nailed to the walls and covered by paneling and celotex. On the second floor, Roberts was preparing to take plumbing fixtures, hot water heaters, shower stalls, commodes, lighting fixtures, the heating system, and other items he had installed. Yancy filed a lawsuit against Roberts seeking damages for injuries caused to the property and to enjoin him from removing "permanent improvements, fixtures, and attachments from the property."

ISSUE   Which of these items of property was Roberts entitled to take and which did he have to leave when he vacated the property?

DECISION   The removal of the booths, stools, sinks, dishwashers, refrigerators, and other equipment used in the restaurant business was proper. These items were *trade fixtures,* which Roberts was entitled to remove. The lighting fixtures could not be removed because they were replacements for ones that were there when the premises was rented. To remove them would not leave the premises in the same position as when rented. The paneling, sheetrock, and false ceilings could not be removed without materially damaging the premises and thus Yancey was entitled to recover damages because they were removed. The items Roberts wanted to remove from the second floor were not trade fixtures and could not be removed even though installed by Roberts. Their removal would damage the property to which they were attached.

RIGHTS AND INTERESTS IN REAL PROPERTY

When you think of ownership of real property, you normally think of somebody owning all the rights in a particular piece of land. However, there are a variety of different interests that can be created in a particular piece of land and it is possible that those various interests may be divided among a number of people. These interests include leases, licenses, easements, life estates, and mineral or timber rights.

Fee Simple

The *fee simple* is the basic land ownership interest in the United States. If a person owns real property in fee simple, he or she has the right to the entire property for an unlimited period of time and the unconditional power to dispose of it either during the owner's lifetime or upon his or her death. If the person does not make a will, the land will automatically pass to the person's heirs on his or her death. A person who owns land in fee simple may grant many rights to others without giving up the ownership of his or her fee simple interest.

For example, Arnold, who has a fee simple interest in land, may give Bob a mortgage on the land, grant Cindy an easement of right-of-way across the land, and lease the land to a farmer for a period of time. Arnold has granted rights to Bob, Cindy, and the farmer, but Arnold still owns the land in fee simple. When the rights of Bob, Cindy, and the farmer terminate, they pass back to Arnold and again become part of his bundle of ownership rights.

Life Estate

Sometimes a person has the right to use property only for his or her own lifetime or for a time that is measured by the lifetime of somebody else. In this case the interest in land is known as a *life estate*. A person who has a life estate in a piece of real property has the right to use the property but does not have the right to do acts that will result in permanent injury to the property.

Hawkins v. Kourlias
282 N.E.2d 551 (Sup. Ct. Ind. 1972)

FACTS James Kourlias, a 75-year-old retired fruit peddler, offered his home for sale. The asking price was $15,000. Roland Hawkins, an engineer, offered Kourlias $10,000 plus the use of an upstairs room and kitchen privileges in the property "free of charge for as long as Kourlias lives or cares to stay there." Kourlias accepted the offer. Hawkins was given a deed granting Hawkins a fee simple interest but reserving Koulias's continued interest in the property. Four months later, Hawkins demanded that Kourlias pay him rent for the use of the upstairs apartment. Kourlias refused and Hawkins then brought a lawsuit to eject Kourlias from the premises. Kourlias filed a counterclaim for damages.

ISSUE What kind of an interest did Kourlias have in the property, and to what damages was he entitled if the property interest was taken from him?

DECISION The court held that Kourlias had reserved a life estate in the property he sold. If it was taken from him, he was entitled to damages. The parties had agreed that he had a life expectancy of 7.77 years. The court found that the value to Kourlias of his life estate in the property was $14,923.67 and gave him judgment for this amount against Hawkins.

Leasehold

A *lease* gives the tenant the right to occupy and use a particular piece of property. This right may be for a fixed period of time such as a month or year. If no time period is specified, then it is known as a *tenancy at will*. Under a tenancy at will, either the landlord or the tenant can terminate the leasehold after giving notice to the other person of his or her intention to do so. The law of landlord and tenant will be discussed in Chapter 36.

Easement

A person may have the right to use or enjoy the land of another person but not to actually occupy it on a long-term basis; this is known as an *easement.* An easement can be either an affirmative or a negative easement. An *affirmative easement* is the right to make certain uses of the land of another. The right to drive across another person's property to reach your property, to run a sewer line across it, or to drill for oil and gas on the land of another person is an affirmative easement.

A *negative easement* is the right to have someone who owns an adjoining piece of property refrain from making certain uses of his or her land. The right to have your neighbor refrain from erecting a building on his property that would cut off light and air from your building is a negative easement.

Easements may be acquired in a number of different ways. They may be bought or sold or they may be held back when the owner of a piece of property sells other rights to the property. Sometimes an easement is implied even though the parties did not specifically grant or purchase an easement. For example, Arthur owns 80 acres of land fronting on a dirt road and bounded on the other three sides by a limited-access highway. If Arthur sells the back 40 acres to Byron, Byron will get an easement by *necessity* across Arthur's remaining property because that would be the only way he could get to his property. An easement can also be created by *adverse possession* (prescription). Obtaining a property interest by adverse possession is discussed later in this chapter. As an example, if someone uses a shortcut across a corner of your property openly for the statutory period of time, that person will obtain an easement. She will have a continuing right to engage in that activity. The true owner of the property must assert his rights during that period and stop the other person or end up losing an interest in his property.

License

A license is similar in some ways to an easement; however, it is not considered to be an interest in land and usually does not have to be in writing to be enforceable. It may be created orally. A common example of a license is obtaining permission to hunt or fish on another person's land. A *license* is usually a temporary right to use another person's land for a limited and specific purpose.

Private Restrictions

Within certain limits a person who sells real estate may obtain the agreement of the buyer to certain restrictions on the subsequent use of the land. Similarly, the owner of real estate may, by agreement or by a declaration in trust, impose restrictions on the use that will be made of that property.

For example, Frank owns two adjacent lots. He sells one to Rose but gets Rose to promise not to operate any business involving the sale of liquor on the property. This commitment is included in the deed Frank gives to Rose along with a statement that the property is to revert back to Frank if the commitment is broken. Similarly, suppose that a developer sells lots in a subdivision and puts a restriction in each deed concerning the minimum size and cost of houses that can be built on the property. He might also restrict the types of design. Alternatively, the restrictions may be put in the plat for the subdivision that is filed in the local land records office.

The validity and enforceability of such private restrictions on the use of real property depend on the *purpose, nature,* and *scope* of the restriction. If a restraint is so great that it effectively prevents the sale or transfer of the property to anyone else, it is not enforceable. If a restriction is reasonable and its purpose is not against public policy, it is enforceable. For example, a restriction that prohibits future sale of the property to a non-Caucasian is not enforceable. However, restrictions that relate to the minimum size of lots, maintenance of the area as a residential community, or cost, size, and design of buildings are frequently enforceable.

These restrictions are usually enforceable by the parties to the agreement or by persons who are intended to benefit by them. If the restriction is contained in a subdivision plat in the form of a general building scheme, other property owners in the subdivision may be able to enforce it. Restrictions can be waived, the right to enforce them can be lost by abandonment, or they can terminate by their own terms. If a restriction is invalid, waived, or abandoned, the basic deed remains valid but it is treated as if the restriction had been stricken from the deed.

Carter v. Conroy
544 P.2d 258 (Ct. App. Ariz. 1976)

FACTS William and Alice Carter purchased two lots in a subdivision called Payson Ranchos in Payson, Arizona. Each lot in the subdivision had a restriction in the deed that prohibited the use of house trailers on the lots except for a period of up to 90 days during the time a house was being constructed on the lot. The Carters moved a trailer onto one of their lots. They removed the tongue and wheels and set the trailer up on concrete blocks. They also connected it to a septic tank and attached power and water lines. A number of the Carters' neighbors brought a lawsuit to require them to remove the trailer because it was in violation of the deed restriction.

The Carters claimed that the restriction did not apply because their home was no longer a trailer. They also claimed that other neighbors were violating other deed restrictions concerning erection of fences so they should not be able to enforce the trailer restriction against the Carters.

ISSUE   Could the restriction against trailers be used to force the Carters to remove their trailer?

DECISION Yes. The court held that the Carters had to remove the trailer. The court found that trailers—whether on wheels or blocks—were intended to be forbidden by the deed restriction. The restriction could be enforced by their neighbors who were the beneficiaries of the restriction. The right to enforce this restriction was not affected by the fact that other restrictions were being violated by those same neighbors.

CO-OWNERSHIP OF REAL PROPERTY

Forms of Co-ownership

Co-ownership of property exists when two or more persons own an undivided interest in such property. A number of forms of co-ownership of property that are common to both real and personal property were discussed in Chapter 33: (1) tenancy in common; (2) joint tenancy; (3) tenancy by the entirety; and (4) community property. There are two other forms of joint ownership that are unique to real property: condominiums and cooperatives.

Condominium Ownership

In resort and urban areas the form of ownership known as condominium has come into extensive use. In a *condominium*, the purchaser gets title to the apartment or townhouse unit he or she occupies and also becomes a tenant in common of the facilities shared in common with the other owners such as hallways, elevator and utility shafts, swimming pools, and parking areas. The condominium owner pays property taxes on his individual unit, he can take out a mortgage on his unit, and he is generally able to sell the unit without having the prospective buyer approved by the other owners. He also makes a monthly payment to cover the maintenance of the common areas. For federal income tax purposes he is treated like the owner of a single-family home and is allowed to deduct his property taxes and mortgage interest expenses.

Cooperative Ownership

In a *cooperative*, the entire building is owned by a group of people or by a corporation. Usually the buyer of a unit buys stock in the corporation and holds his apartment under a long-term lease that he can renew. Frequently the cooperative owner must obtain the approval of the other owners in order to sell or sublease his or her unit.

ACQUISITION OF REAL PROPERTY

Among the different methods of obtaining title to real property are: (1) purchase, (2) gift, (3) will or inheritance, (4) tax sale, and (5) adverse possession. Original title to land in the United States was acquired either from the federal government or from a country that held the land prior to its acquisition by the United States. The land in the 13 original colonies had been granted by the King of England either to the colonies or to certain individuals. The land in the Northwest Territory was ceded by the states to the federal government, which in turn issued grants or patents of land. Original ownership of much of the land in Florida and in the Southwest came by grants from the rulers of Spain.

Acquisition by Purchase

A basic ownership right is the right to sell the property. In fact, any restriction on the right of an owner to sell his or her property is usually considered to be against public policy and is not enforced. Most people who own real property acquired title by buying it from someone else. Each state sets the requirements for transferring a piece of real property located in that state. The various elements of selling and buying real property, including broker agreements, contracts to buy real estate, and deeds, will be covered in the next section of this chapter.

Acquisition by Gift

Ownership of real property may be acquired by *gift*. For such a gift to be valid, the donor must *deliver* a properly executed deed to the property to the donee or to some third person to hold it for the donee. It is not necessary that the donee or the third person take possession of the property. The essential element of the gift is the delivery of the deed. Suppose a man makes out a deed to the family farm and leaves it in a safe-deposit box for delivery to his son when he dies. The attempted gift will not be valid because there was no delivery of the gift during the donor's lifetime.

Acquisition by Will or Inheritance

The owner of real property generally has the right to dispose of that property by *will*. The requirements for making a valid will be discussed in Chapter 37. If the owner of real property dies without making a valid will, the property will go to his or her heirs as determined under the laws of the state in which the real property is located.

Acquisition by Tax Sale

If the taxes assessed on real property are not paid, they become a lien on the property. This lien has priority over all other claims of other persons to the land. If the taxes remain unpaid for a period of time, the government sells the land at a tax sale, and the purchaser at the tax sale acquires title to the property. However, in some states the original owner has the option for a limited time (perhaps a year) to buy it from the purchaser at the tax sale for his or her cost plus interest.

Acquisition by Adverse Possession

Each state has a statute of limitations that provides an owner of land only a fixed number of years to bring a lawsuit to regain possession of his or her land from someone who is trespassing on it. This time period generally varies between 5 and 20 years, depending on the state. Thus if someone else moves onto your land and acts as if he is the owner, you must take steps to have the person ejected from your land. If you do not do so during the statutory period, you will lose your right to do so. The person who stayed in possession of your property for the statutory period will be treated as the owner. He will have acquired title to it by *adverse possession* or *prescription*.

To acquire title by adverse possession, there must be actual occupancy that is hostile to the real owner's title, with an open claim to title (not with the owner's persmission) continuously for the statutory period. In some states the person in possession of land who is claiming the right to be there must also pay the taxes. It is not necessary that the same person occupy your land for the statutory period; however, the possession must be continuous for the necessary time.

Adverse possession can take place in some fairly common situations. For example, Buzz Miller and Claire Alton own adjoining lots on which they have built houses. In 1955, Alton builds a fence to separate the two lots; however, she erects it about four feet onto Miller's land. She also builds a driveway that extends into the four-foot strip even though Miller did not give her permission to do so. He does not take steps to have the fence moved to its rightful position on the line between their lots. For ten years Alton acts as if she owns the four-foot strip. Then she sells her lot to Edgar Gray, who also uses it and acts as if he is the owner. If the statute of limitations in that state is 20 years, in 1976 Gray will be the owner of the four-foot strip by adverse possession.

William T. Burton Industries, Inc. v. Cook
322 So.2d 880 (App. Ct. La. 1976)

FACTS   In 1922 Ivey Cook bought an 80-acre farm. It was located next to a 40-acre tract owned by Burton Industries. In 1924 Cook and his family moved to the farm. At that time, they rebuilt a fence around the Cook farm. Enclosed within the fence were about 4.7 acres of land belonging to Burton. Over the next 50 years Cook cultivated part of the 4.7 acres and used the remainder of the land as pasture for his horses, cattle, and hogs. He also cut timber from the property and maintained the fence in good repair. In 1975 Burton Industries brought a lawsuit against the Cooks to establish its title to the 4.7 acres. Cook claimed he owned it by adverse possession. The Louisiana law provides that possession of real property for 30 years gives the possessor ownership. The possession is required to be "continuous, uninterrupted, public and unequivocal."

ISSUE	Was Cook the owner of the 4.7 acres through adverse possession?
DECISION	Yes. The court held Cook was the owner of the property. Because the land was best suited for agriculture and timber, the acts of Cook in farming and timbering it were possession of it. The building of the fence indicated the area he was claiming. The fence was notice to the public and to the true owner of Cook's possession of it. The possession was continuous for a period of more than 30 years.

TRANSFER BY SALE

Steps in a Sale

The major steps normally involved in the sale and purchase of real property are: (1) contracting with a real estate broker to sell the property or to locate suitable property for sale, (2) negotiating and signing a contract to sell the property, (3) arranging for the financing of the purchase and satisfaction of other contingencies such as a survey or acquisition of title insurance, (4) closing the sale, at which time the purchase price is paid and the deed is signed and delivered, and (5) recordation of the deed.

Real Estate Brokers

Although it is not necessary to engage a broker, a prospective seller of real estate commonly enters into a listing agreement with a real estate broker. The broker's job is to locate a buyer ready, willing, and able to buy the property on the seller's terms. The listing agreement should be in writing, specify the length of the listing period, and provide for the amount or percentage of the commission. Generally a seller must pay the commission as long as the broker produces a *ready, willing, and able buyer*, even if the seller decides not to go through with the sale. However, a few courts have held that the commission was not due where the sale was not consummated.

Hollaway v. Forshee
491 P.2d 556 (Sup. Ct. Kan. 1971)

FACTS	On February 7, 1969, C. L. Hollaway, a real estate broker, obtained an open listing to sell Forshee's residence. The property was listed for sale at $55,000 and Hollaway was to receive a 6 percent commission if he sold the property. On May 17, Elaine Sparks, a real estate agent who worked for Hollaway, showed the Forshee property to Mr. and Mrs. Corris Bell. She told the Bells where Forshee lived. She also offered to help the Bells find financing but was told they were doing it themselves. On May 23, Sparks learned that the Forshee property had been sold to the Bells. Hollaway then brought a lawsuit against Forshee to recover a commission.

ISSUE   Was Hollaway entitled to a commission on the grounds that his sales agent had been the effective procuring cause of the sale?

DECISION   Yes. The court held that Forshee had to pay a commission to Hollaway. A real estate broker is normally entitled to a commission if he produces a buyer ready, willing, and able to buy on terms acceptable to the seller and if he is the procuring cause of a consummated deal. It is not required that the broker bring the parties together personally or that he actually procure the binding contract. Here Hollaway's agent procured the buyer, who shortly thereafter entered into an agreement. Under these circumstances, Forshee could not avoid paying a commission by closing the deal himself.

Contract for Sale

The agreement between the seller and the buyer to purchase real property should be in writing to be enforceable under the statute of frauds. The agreement commonly spells out such things as the purchase price, the type of deed the purchaser will get, and what items of personal property such as applicances and carpets are included. It may also make the "closing" of the sale contingent on the buyer being able to obtain financing at a specified rate of interest and the seller's procurement of a survey, title insurance, and termite insurance.

Financing the Purchase

The various arrangements for financing the purchase of real property such as mortgages, land contracts, and deeds of trust will be discussed in Chapter 42.

Federal Disclosure Laws

The federal *Real Estate Settlement Procedures Act* (RESPA) requires that a buyer receive advance disclosure of the settlement costs that will be incurred in settlement. RESPA also requires that a record be kept of the actual settlement charges in all real estate transactions involving federally related loans, such as Veterans Administration and Federal Housing Administration loans. The required settlement/disclosure statement itemizes each settlement cost charged to the buyer and each charged to the seller (see Figure 35–1). These settlement charges commonly include: (1) real estate broker's commissions, (2) loan origination fees, (3) loan discount points, (4) appraisal fees, (5) credit report fees, (6) lender's inspection fees, (7) insurance premiums, (8) settlement closing/escrow fees, (9) prepaid interest and taxes, (10) title search fees, (11) notary's and/or attorney's fees, (12) survey fees, (13) title insurance premiums, and (14) transfer and recording fees.

Among the purposes of the settlement statement are to give the buyer notice of the cash needed at settlement and to give the buyer an opportunity to engage in "comparison shopping" of settlement terms so that the buyer can arrange the most favorable terms.

RESPA prohibits a number of practices including kickbacks or payments for referral of business to title companies. It also prohibits any requirement by the seller that title insurance be purchased from any particular company.

In response to fraud and misrepresentations made by some sellers of land, particularly retirement and vacation properties, Congress enacted the *Interstate Land Sales Full Disclosure Act.* The act generally applies to developers who subdivide property into 50 or more lots and who use interstate means, such as the mail and telephone, to sell the property. The act requires that a "property report" be prepared disclosing certain kinds of information about the property and the developer's plans regarding it. The report is filed with the U.S. Department of Housing and Urban Development and

FIGURE 35–1

Example of a Closing or Settlement Statement

```
                            CLOSING STATEMENT

                                            Dated____February 15,__19 80

SALE/MORTGAGE LOAN made by____Michael A. Watson.
to____Kenneth R. Hansen
Property____195 Main Street, Annapolis, MD____Adjustments made to____February__15_19_80

CREDIT TO SELLER OR MORTGAGOR                                    $  210,000 00
19 79/80 Taxes paid in advance              4    months    14    days       654 68
19 ____ Taxes paid in advance                    months    ____ days
Accruing Ground Rent                             months    ____ days
19 ____ Sewer, Water, Sanitary charges paid in advance   months  ____ days
19 ____ Maintenance charges paid in advance
Interest on $
                                                 months    ____ days
Water/Sewer paid in advance                 1    month     25    days        24 41

DEDUCT FROM SELLER                                              210,679 09
Cash paid on account                         $   5,000.00
19 ____ Taxes (current) ____ months ____ days
19 ____ Taxes (current) ____ months ____ days
Ground Rent ____ months ____ days
House Rent ____ months ____ days
½ State Documentary Stamps                       735.00
½ State Transfer Tax and 1/2 County transfer tax   1,575.00
FNB mortgage assumed                             115,719.38
2nd mortgage to seller                           55,000.00
Total Deductions                             $   178,029.38   $ 178,029 38
                NET AMOUNT DUE SELLER BY PURCHASER             $  32,649 71

COST OF TRANSFER
Fee for Title Examination and Title Insurance    $  1,090.00
Fee for Preparing Papers Deed, assumption agreement 2nd mortgage  90.00
Settlement Fee                                   55.00
Notary Fees  3.50   Judge Reports ____ Lien Certificate  10.00  13.50
                TOTAL COST OF TRANSFER

Taxes for 19
Tax Accrual 19____ Mos. @
Ground Rent Accrual ____ Mos. @
FHA Insurance Accrual ____ Mos. @
Insurance
Interest to
Service Charge
Appraisal ____ Credit Report  13.00   Photos
Survey  Record Assumption Agreement             13.00
State Documentary Stamps  1470.00   Transfer Tax 2100. + $1050.  4,620.00
Recording, Deed,  12.00   2nd Mortg.  15.00      27.00
Total Cost of Transfer and Accruals          $   5,908.50   $  5,908 50

                        Gross Amount Due By Purchaser          $  38,558 21

Amount of Mortgage Loan by                                     $

                Balance Paid to/or by Borrower or Purchaser    $
                Net Amount Due Seller by Purchaser   $ 32,649.71

                                                    (CONTINUED)
```

FIGURE 35–1 *(continued)*

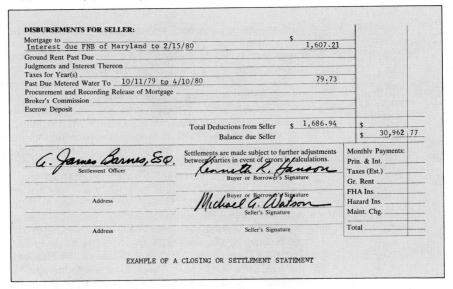

EXAMPLE OF A CLOSING OR SETTLEMENT STATEMENT

must be made available to prospective buyers. Developers who do not comply with the law are subject to civil and criminal penalties.

Transfer by Deed

Each state has enacted statutes that set out the formalities for transferring land located within its borders. As a general rule the transfer of land is accomplished by the execution and delivery of a deed. A *deed* is an instrument in writing whereby the owner of an interest in real property (the *grantor*) conveys to another (the *grantee*) some right, title, or interest in that real property.

Quitclaim and Warranty Deeds. Two types of deeds are in general use in the United States: the quitclaim deed and the warranty deed. When

FIGURE 35–2
Example of a Quitclaim Deed

QUITCLAIM DEED

THIS DEED, made the 15th day of August, 1980, BETWEEN Frances B. Pearce, a married woman, of No. 150 Oaklawn Street, City of Baltimore, State of Maryland, party of the first part, and Kathleen M. Sparks, a single woman, of No. 300 Maryland Avenue, City of Annapolis, State of Maryland, party of the second part.

WITNESSETH, that the party of the first part, in consideration of One Hundred Dollars ($100.00) lawful money of the United States, paid by the party of the second part, does hereby release and quitclaim unto the party of the second

FIGURE 35–2 *(continued)*

part, the heirs, successors and assigns of the party of the second part forever.

ALL that certain plot, piece or parcel of land, with the buildings and improvements thereon erected, situate and lying in the City of Annapolis, Anne Arundel County, State of Maryland, described as follows:

BEGINNING for the same at the northeast corner of the building numbered 197 Main Street on the Southwest side of Main Street (formerly Church Street) and running thence with the partition wall between the building hereby conveyed and that of Mary J. Moss, et al., Liber S. H. 15, folio 97; (1) South 15° 09' 11" West 30.67 feet to the junction of the partition walls; thence with the division line between the lot hereby conveyed and that of before mentioned Mary J. Moss; (2) South 18° 13' 02" West 66.70 feet to a fence corner; thence with the fence line; (3) North 68° 01' 58" West 18.75 feet to an iron pipe found; thence (4) North 27° 42' 20" East 10.79 feet to a fence corner; thence with a fence line (5) North 71° 34' 50" West 7.75 feet to an iron pipe found; thence with a fence line (6) North 12° 42' 30" East 23.67 feet to the Southeast corner of the building numbered 199 Main Street; thence with the partition wall between the building hereby conveyed and No. 199 Main Street (7) North 14° 57' 30" East 60.33 feet to the Northwest corner of the building hereby conveyed and the southwest side of Main Street; thence with the Southwest side of Main Street (8) South 75° 02' 30" East 28.79 feet to the place of beginning. Containing 2,537 square feet of land, more or less, as surveyed by C. D. Meekins and Associates, Annapolis, Maryland.

TOGETHER with all right, title and interest, if any, of the party of the first part in and to any streets and roads abutting the above described premises to the center lines thereof; together with the appurtenances and all the estate and rights of the party of the first part in and to said premises.

TO HAVE AND TO HOLD the premises herein granted unto the party of the second part, the heirs or successors and assigns of the party of the second part forever.

IN WITNESS WHEREOF, the party of the first part has duly executed this deed the day and year first above written.

In Presence of:

Charles S. Reinhart   _Frances B. Pearce_
Witness   Grantor

ACKNOWLEDGEMENT OF DEED
State of Maryland   )
) ss
County of Anne Arundel)

I, an officer authorized to take acknowledgements according to the laws of the State of Maryland, duly qualified and acting, HEREBY CERTIFY that Frances B. Pearce to me personally known, this day personally appeared and acknowledged before me that she executed the foregoing Deed, and I further certify that I know the said person making said acknowledgement to be the individual described in and who executed the said Deed.

Edward A. Smith
Edward A. Smith
Notary Public

the grantor conveys by a *quitclaim deed*, he conveys to the grantee whatever title he has at the time he executes the deed. However, in a quitclaim deed, the grantor does not claim to have good title or, in fact, any title. If the title proves to be defective or if the grantor has no title, the grantee has no right to sue the grantor under the quitclaim deed. Quitclaim deeds are frequently used to cure a technical defect in the chain of title to property. In such a case the grantor may not be claiming any right, title, or interest in the property. See Figure 35–2 for an example of a quitclaim deed.

A *warranty deed* contains covenants of warranty; that is, the grantor, in addition to conveying title to the property, guarantees to make good any defects in the title he has conveyed (see Figure 35–3). A warranty deed may be a deed of general warranty or of special warranty. In a *general warranty deed*, the grantor warrants against all defects in the title and all encumbrances (such as liens and easements). In a *special warranty deed*, the grantor warrants against only those defects in the title or those encumbrances that arose after he acquired the property. If the property conveyed is mortgaged or subject to some other encumbrance, such as an easement or long-term lease, it is a common practice to give a special warranty deed that contains a provision excepting those specific encumbrances from the warranty.

Form and Execution of Deed. Some states have enacted statutes setting out the form of deed that may be used in that state. However, a deed may be valid even though it does not follow the statutory form. The statutory requirements of the different states for the execution of deeds are not uniform, but they do follow a similar pattern. As a general rule, a deed states the name of the grantee, contains a recitation of consideration and a description of the property conveyed, and is signed by the grantor. In most states the deed, to be eligible for recording, must be *acknowledged* by the grantor before a notary public or other officer authorized to take an acknowledgment.

No technical words of conveyance are necessary. Any language is sufficient that indicates with reasonable certainty an intent to transfer the ownership of the property. The phrases "give, grant, bargain, and sell" and "convey and warrant" are in common use.

A consideration is recited in a deed for historical reasons. The consideration recited is not necessarily the purchase price of the real property. It is sometimes stated to be "one dollar and other valuable consideration."

The property conveyed must be described in such a manner that it can be identified. In urban areas, descriptions are as a general rule given by lot, block, and plat. In rural areas the land, if it has been surveyed by the government, is usually described by reference to the government survey; otherwise, it is described by metes and bounds, which is a surveyor's description using distances and angles measured in the survey (see Figure 35–2).

A deed must be delivered to be valid. Suppose a woman executes a

FIGURE 35–3
Example of a Warranty Deed

WARRANTY DEED

THIS DEED, made in the City of Washington, District of Columbia, on the 8th day of September, nineteen hundred and eighty,

BETWEEN William S. Clark, an unmarried man, party of the first part, and Samuel D. Butler, party of the second part.

WITNESSETH, that the party of the first part, in consideration of Eighty-seven Thousand Five Hundred Dollars ($87,500.00) lawful money of the United States, paid by the party of the second part, does hereby grant and release unto the party of the second part, his heirs and assigns forever,

ALL that certain plot, piece or parcel of land located in the District of Columbia and known and described as Lot numbered Thirty-nine (39) in William D. Green's subdivision of part of Lot numbered Twenty-two (22) in Square numbered Twelve Hundred Nineteen (1219), as per plat recorded in the Office of the Surveyor for the District of Columbia in Liber 30 at folio 32, together with the buildings and improvements thereon and all the estate and rights of the party of the first part in and to said property.

TO HAVE AND TO HOLD the premises herein granted unto the party of the second part, his heirs and assigns forever.

And the party of the first part covenants as follows:

FIRST—That the party of the first part is seized of the said premises in fee simple, and has good right to convey the same.

SECOND—That the party of the second part shall quietly enjoy the said premises.

THIRD—That the premises are free of encumbrances.

FOURTH—That the party of the first part will execute or procure any further necessary assurances of the title to said premises.

FIFTH—That the party of the first part will forever warrant the title to said premises.

IN WITNESS WHEREOF, the party of the first part has set his hand and seal the day and year above written.

In presence of:

Millicent A. Fenton
Millicent A. Fenton

William S Clark (SEAL)
William S. Clark

ACKNOWLEDGEMENT OF DEED
District of Columbia, ss:

I, an officer authorized to take acknowledgements according to the laws of the District of Columbia, duly qualified and acting, HEREBY CERTIFY that William S. Clark to me personally known, this day personally appeared and acknowledged before me that he executed the foregoing Deed and I further certify that I know the said person making said acknowledgement to be the individual described in and who executed the said Deed.

Kathryn R. Cole
Kathryn R. Cole
Notary Public

deed to her home and puts it in her safe-deposit box together with a note directing that the deed be delivered to her son after her death. The deed is not effective to pass title after the woman's death. A deed, to be valid, must be delivered in the lifetime of the grantor.

Recording Deeds   Each state has a recording statute that establishes a system for the recording of all transactions that affect the ownership of real property. The statutes are not uniform in their provisions. In general, they provide for the recording of all deeds, mortgages, and other such documents, and declare that an unrecorded transfer is void as against an innocent purchaser or mortgagee for value. Under this system, it is customary in some states for the seller to give the buyer an *abstract of title* certified to the date of closing. The abstract is a history of the passage of title of the real property according to the records and is not a guarantee of title. The buyer, for his or her own protection, should have the abstract examined by a competent attorney who will give an opinion as to the title held by the grantor. The opinion will state whether or not the grantor has a *merchantable title* to the property. A merchantable title is one that is readily salable and not subject to objection because of defects in it. If the title is defective, the nature of the defects will be stated in the title opinion.

In many states the buyer obtains protection against defects in the title by acquiring *title insurance*. This insurance is designed to reimburse the buyer for loss if the title turns out to be defective. Where the purchase of the property is being financed by a third party, the lender often requires that a policy of title insurance be obtained for the lender's protection.

Several of the states have adopted the "Torrens system." Under this system the person who owns the land in fee simple obtains a certificate of title. When the real property is sold, the grantor delivers a deed and certificate of title to the grantee. The grantee then delivers the deed and certificate of title to the designated government official and receives a new certificate of title. All liens and encumbrances against the property are noted on the certificate of title, and the purchaser is assured that the title is good except as to the liens and encumbrances noted on it. However, it should be noted that some claims or encumbrances like adverse possession or easements by prescription do not appear on the records. They must be discovered by making an *inspection* of the property. In some states, certain encumbrances, such as liens for taxes, short-term leases, and highway rights, are good against the purchaser even though they do not appear on the certificate.

Warranties in the   Traditionally, unless there was an express warranty of the habitability
Sale of a House   or condition of a house, or unless there was some fraud or misrepresentation involved, the purchaser of a house was subject to the doctrine of *caveat emptor* (that the buyer must beware at his own risk). This was based on the fact that buyer and seller dealt at arm's length and the buyer had

the opportunity to become acquainted with the condition and quality of the property he was acquiring. Thus, the buyer has a choice: either obtain an express warranty from the seller as to the quality of the property or take the property at his own risk.

A number of courts have abandoned the *caveat emptor* doctrine in the sale of new homes by builder-sellers. Where latent or undiscoverable defects are involved, they have adopted the doctrine of *caveat venditor* (that the responsibility is on the seller). This tends to put the buyer of a new home in roughly the same position as the buyer of goods. The buyer gets an *implied warranty of habitability* (or merchantable fitness) of the house. Most court decisions to date have not dealt with the quality of the land itself, but rather with that of the new home, which they have treated like any other manufactured product.

Other courts have imposed a duty on sellers of property to disclose any known defects in the premises that are not discoverable by reasonable inspection by the buyer. If the seller does not make such disclosure, such silence may be held to constitute *misrepresentation*. In a few states the courts have gone even further and protected buyers where the seller of a used house was not aware of a defect. For example, the buyers of a used house in Louisiana discovered extensive termite infestation after they bought the house. The termite problem was not readily apparent to the naked eye and the sellers were not aware of it. The court said the buyers could recover the cost of repairing the hidden defects where the defect was so serious that the purchasers would not have bought the house had it be known.

Elmore v. Blume
334 N.E.2d 431 (Ct. App. Ill. 1975)

FACTS David and Patricia Elmore purchased a newly constructed home from Robert Blume, a builder. When they looked at the house prior to purchasing it, there was water standing in the basement. Blume told them that the water was due to the fact the gutters and windows had not been installed. Blume said that after the "rainy season" the basement would be dry. The Elmores also advised Blume that they planned to carpet the basement to use as a recreation room. After taking possession of the house, the Elmores had repeated problems with water entering the basement. Blume furnished waterproof paint, installed a sump pump, and built a trench around the house. These measures reduced the quantity of water entering the basement but did not eliminate the problem. The Elmores filed a lawsuit against Blume, claiming breach of implied warranty of habitability and breach of the express warranty of intended use.

ISSUE Can the Elmores recover for breach of warranty because of the faulty construction of their house?

> **DECISION** Yes. The court held that there is an implied warranty of habitability in a contract for the sale of a new house. There is a violation of the implied warranty where the house sustains water damage caused by faulty construction. A seller also creates an express warranty if he affirms a fact or makes a promise—as opposed to merely stating an opinion. Here the court found that Blume had expressly warranted that the house would be suitable for the Elmores to use the basement for a recreation room.

PUBLIC CONTROLS ON THE USE OF LAND

Societal Restraints   While the owner of an interest in real property may generally make such use of his or her property as he or she desires, the owner does not have an unlimited right to do so. Society places a number of restraints on the owner of real property: (1) the owner cannot use the property in such a way as to unduly injure others, (2) through the use of the "police power," government units have the right to impose reasonable regulations on the use of property, and (3) the government has the right to take the property through the power of eminent domain.

Nuisance Control   When different uses are made of separate parcels of land, those uses may conflict and one or more of the users may become very unhappy. For example, the owner of a grove of orange trees might find that the dust from a nearby cement mill is forming a crust on the oranges. The owner of a drive-in movie might find that the spotlights at an auto racetrack are interfering with the customers' enjoyment of the movies. Similarly, a homeowner might find that the noise from planes using an airport is interfering with her peace of mind. In some cases the courts have granted damages and injunctive relief to the affected persons on the grounds that the use being made of the other property constitutes a nuisance. A *nuisance* is an unjustified and unreasonable interference with someone's right to enjoy and use his or her property.

Nuisances may be divided into private and public. A *private nuisance* is created when a landowner's use or enjoyment of her land is substantially interfered with due to unjustifiable conduct by another person. A *public nuisance* involves a broader class of affected parties, and the action to stop it usually must be brought in the name of the public by the government. Private parties can sue to stop a public nuisance only where they can show a unique harm different from that suffered by the public in general.

The conduct that creates the nuisance may be either intentional or negligent. In a few situations liability may be imposed for extra hazardous activity even though neither intent nor negligence is present. The fact that the use of land by a neighbor hinders an owner from putting his own land to a special or "delicate use" does not mean the hindered owner can enjoin the conduct. Nuisance actions involve a balancing of the various interests and rights involved. For example, the courts may weigh the social utility of the objectionable conduct and the burden of stopping it against the degree to which the conduct is infringing on the rights of other property owners.

Spur Industries, Inc. v. Del Webb Development Co.
4 Envir. Rep. Cases 1052 (Sup. Ct. Ariz. 1972)

FACTS In 1956 Spur's predecessor began operating a small cattle-feeding operating of some 6,000 to 7,000 head in an area that included about 25 cattle pens within a seven-mile radius. About one-and-a-half miles away was the city of Youngstown, a retirement community appealing primarily to senior citizens. In 1959 Del Webb acquired some 20,000 acres, a portion of which was located between Youngstown and Spur's predecessor's property, and began to build Sun City, a retirement community. In 1960 Spur acquired the feedlot and began expanding the acreage from 35 to 114 acres and by 1967 was feeding between 20,000 and 30,000 head of cattle. Del Webb in the meantime had acquired additional property between its original acreage and the Spur operation which Webb intended to sell as residential lots. There was considerable sales resistance to about 1,300 lots in the area closest to the Spur operation. Del Webb then brought suit against the Spur feeding operation, complaining that it constituted a public nuisance because of the flies and the odors that drifted or were blown over onto the Webb property. Webb contended that even with good feedlot management the citizens of Sun City were unable to enjoy the outdoor living they had been promised, and that the feedlot should be enjoined.

ISSUE Should the operation of the feedlot be enjoined on the grounds it constitutes a nuisance?

DECISION Yes. The court held that the Spur feedlot was a public nuisance that unreasonably interfered with the right of the residents of Sun City to enjoy their property. The court said that if the inconveniences were minor, then it would give the affected landowners only money damages. Here it felt the inconvenience to the residents was substantial and they were entitled to an injunction. However, Spur was operating in this area first and Del Webb encouraged people to move there and buy homes. Accordingly, the court required Del Webb to reimburse the costs Spur would incur in either moving to another location or shutting down the operation.

Zoning and Subdivision Ordinances

State legislatures commonly delegate to counties, cities, towns, and other local governments the *police power* to impose reasonable regulations designed to promote the public health, safety, morals, and general welfare of the community. *Zoning ordinances* are an exercise of such a power to regulate. Generally, zoning ordinances divide the area into a number of districts, specify or limit the use to which property in those districts can be put, and restrict improvements on and use of the land.

Such restrictions and controls may be of four basic types:

1. *Control of use.*   The activity on the land may be regulated or limited, for example, to single-family dwellings, multifamily dwellings, commercial, light industry or heavy industry.
2. *Control of height and bulk.*   The regulation may control the height of buildings; the setback from front, side, and rear lot lines; and the portion of a lot that can be covered by a building.
3. *Control of population density.*   The regulation may provide how much living space must be provided for each person and may specify the maximum number of persons who can be housed in a given area.
4. *Control of aesthetics.*   These regulations are commonly used to control billboards, but also may be used to enforce similarity and dissimilarity of buildings as well as to preserve historic areas.

When zoning ordinances are passed they have only a prospective effect, so existing uses and buildings are permitted to continue. However, the ordinance may provide for the gradual phasing-out of such uses and buildings that do not conform to the general zoning plan. If a property owner later wants to use the property in a way other than that which is permitted by the zoning ordinance, the owner must try to have the ordinance amended. To do this the owner must show that the proposed changes are in accordance with the overall plan or try to obtain a *variance* on the ground that the ordinance creates an undue hardship by depriving him of the opportunity to make a reasonable use of the land. Such attempts to obtain amendments or variances often conflict with the interests of other nearby property owners who have a vested interest in the zoning status quo. These conflicts sometimes produce heated battles before the zoning authorities.

Many local governments also have ordinances that deal with proposed subdivisions. The ordinances often require that the developer meet certain requirements as to lot size, street and sidewalk layout, and sewers and water. The ordinances commonly require city approval of the proposed development before it can be started. In some cases the developer may be required to dedicate land to the city for streets, parks, and schools. The purpose of such ordinances is to protect the would-be purchasers in the subdivision as well as the city population as a whole by ensuring that minimum standards are met by the developer.

Some urban planners feel that it is undesirable to segregate totally the living, working, shopping, and entertainment areas as is commonly done with a zoning scheme. They argue that a more livable environment is one that combines these uses so as to insure the vitality of an area for the vast part of each day. In response to this philosophy, cities and counties are allowing "planned unit developments" and "new towns" that mix such uses so long as the plans are submitted to the authorities and approved pursuant to general guidelines established for such developments.

People are also becoming more aware of the shortcomings of making land-use decisions on a piecemeal basis at the local level. Airports, major shopping centers, highways, and new towns require a regional rather than a local planning focus. Moreover, sensitive ecological areas, such as marshes, can be destroyed readily if encroached upon in a piecemeal manner. Accordingly, a number of states and the federal government have passed, or are considering, legislation to put some land-use planning on a regional or a statewide basis.

Eminent Domain

The Constitution provides that private property shall not be taken for public use without just compensation. Implicit in this statement is the power of the state to take property for public use by paying "just compensation" to the owner of the property. This power of *eminent domain* makes possible our highways, water control projects, municipal and civic centers, public housing, and urban renewal.

Currently, there are several major problems inherent in the use of the eminent domain power. The first is what is meant by "just compensation." The property owner now receives the "fair market value" of the property. Some people feel that this falls short of reimbursing the owner for what is lost because it does not cover the lost goodwill of a business or the emotional attachment a person may have to his or her home.

A second problem is deciding when a "taking" has occurred. The answer is easy where the owner is completely dispossessed by a government unit. It is much more difficult where (1) the zoning power has been utilized to restrict the permissible use of a given piece of property only for a narrow publicly beneficial use, such as a parking lot, or (2) the government uses nearby land in such a way as to almost completely destroy the usefulness of adjoining privately owned land as sometimes occurs in the case of municipal airports.

A third problem is determining when the eminent domain power is properly exercised. Clearly where the government unit itself uses the property, as in the case of a municipal building or a public highway, the use of the power is proper. However, as in the case of urban renewal, where condemned property may be resold to a private developer or the condemned property is not substandard, the use of the power is not so clearly justified.

QUESTIONS AND PROBLEM CASES

1. If you hire a real estate broker to sell your house, what normally must the broker do to earn a commission?

2. What is the difference between a general warranty deed and a special warranty deed?

3. What is the power of eminent domain?

4. Kelm owned a building that he leased to Timper. The first floor of the building had always been used as a tavern. The upper floor of the building was a rooming house. When Timper

originally leased the building, an old-fashioned bar was situated against one wall of the building. Timper, without the knowledge or consent of Kelm, removed this old bar and installed a new 60-foot circular bar in the center of the room. By removing the new bar, there would be left in the floor 12 holes differing in diameter from one to six inches. These holes were made so that the bar could have the necessary electric, water, and sewage facilities and so that the beer could be piped from the basement. A bottle chute had also been installed. Should the new bar be considered a fixture?

5. William D. Robinson left a will in which he gave his real estate as follows: "I give all of my real estate to my wife, Lela S. Robinson, and at her death it goes to Frank M. Robinson, and at his death to his two boys, David Robinson and Richard Robinson." Does Lela have a *fee simple* interest in the property or a *life estate?*

6. Sewell and Reilly owned adjoining lots. They entered into a written agreement whereby each agreed to allow the other to use the south ten feet of his lot for alley purposes "for so long as the alley" over the other party's lot remained open. Did this agreement create an *easement* or a *license?*

7. Flynn and Korsalk own adjoining lots, and a strip of land 11 to 12 feet wide separates the houses on the lots. The distance from Flynn's house to the boundary is 7½ feet. Flynn's prodecessor in title, Mrs. Brewer, and her husband owned automobiles from 1927 and 1949 and drove them on the strip, including the portion owned by their neighbors, because it could not be avoided and because it was impossible to tell where the lot line was. Flynn purchased the property from the Brewers in 1949 and continued to drive across the strip. Korsalk purchased the other lot in 1948. In 1952 Korsalk began to protest Flynn's driving on his land, and in 1954 he erected a chain link fence on the lot line which effectively prevented Flynn from driving his car across the strip

to get to his garage. Flynn seeks an injunction ordering Korsalk to remove the fence and other obstructions in the driveway and to enjoin him from placing obstructions in the future. Should the injunction be granted?

8. Bridges and Neighbors owned houses that were separated by a vacant lot owned by Bridges. Bridges allowed debris to accumulate and weeds to grow on the property. Over a 20-year period Neighbors cleaned up the vacant lot on numerous occasions. Neighbors claims that he has become the owner of Bridge's vacant lot by taking care of it for the statutory period (20 years). Should Neighbors be considered to have acquired title to the lot by *adverse possession?*

9. The Schlemeyers purchased a frame apartment house in 1954 and discovered shortly after the purchase that there was substantial termite infestation. They undertook some of the steps suggested by a specialist in pest control but did not take all the measures he indicated would be necessary to make sure of success. In 1960 the Schlemeyers sold the apartment house to Fred Obde but did not advise him of the termite condition. When Obde later discovered the termite infestation, he brought a lawsuit for damages against the Schlemeyers, contending that they fraudulently concealed the infestation from him and were under a duty to disclose it. Can Obde recover?

10. Hobbs kept two horses in the backyard of her home in a residential section of Jefferson County, Colorado. The local zoning ordinance permitted the keeping of two horses on property in this area. Hobbs used reasonable skill and care in maintaining the horses, and no health regulations were violated. However, the horses did attract flies to the general area and noxious smells also permeated the area. Smith, who owns the adjoining property, sues Hobbs, claiming the horses constitute a nuisance that should be abated. What arguments will Hobbs and Smith each make? How should the court rule?

Landlord and Tenant

36

Landlord-Tenant Relationship

In recent years there has been considerable change in landlord and tenant law. In England and in early America, farms were the most common subjects of leases. The primary object was to lease land on which crops could be grown or cattle grazed. Any buildings on the leased property were frequently of secondary importance to the land itself, and they generally were rather simple structures built without such modern conveniences as plumbing and wiring. The tenant would have control over the entire property and would be responsible for its upkeep. The landlord and the tenant would normally have similar knowledge of the condition of the property at the time the lease was entered. Accordingly, traditional landlord-tenant law looked at a lease mainly as a conveyance of land and gave relatively little attention to its contractual aspects.

Today the landlord-tenant relationship is typified by the lease of an apartment in a building located in an urban area. The tenant occupies only a small portion of the total property. He is likely to have signed a form lease dictated by the landlord. The tenant is less likely than his grandparents to be adept at making the kind of repairs that might be required in the apartment. In the rundown sections of cities, the tenant's situation is commonly made worse by the presence of rats and filth and by his relatively meager economic status.

The law was slow to recognize the changed nature of the landlord-tenant relationship. However, exceptions were made to the rule of *caveat emptor* (that the buyer must beware at his own risk), and the emphasis has gradually changed from focusing on the lease as a conveyance of land to focusing on its contractual aspects. In recent years, the courts, state legislatures, and city councils have provided a number of new rules to govern the relationship. In this chapter we will be concerned not only with the time-developed common law of landlord and tenant but also with recent statutory and case law developments.

Term of the Lease

A lease can be: (1) for a fixed or stated period of time, (2) on a periodic basis such as year to year or month to month, (3) at the will of both parties, or (4) at the sufferance of the landlord. In many leases of property, the landlord and tenant agree on the duration of the lease and fix the date on which the tenant must surrender the property back to the landlord.

In some cases there is no explicit agreement between the landlord and the tenant as to how long the lease will last. For example, the tenant may pay rent a month at a time; this is a tenancy from month to month. If the tenant pays a year at a time, it is a tenancy from year to year. These are known as *periodic tenancies*. In most states, a landlord or tenant must give a certain amount of notice to the other party if he intends to terminate a periodic tenancy. Suppose you are renting an apartment on a month-to-month basis. Most states require you to give the landlord at least a month's notice that you intend to terminate the lease.

In a *tenancy at will*, property is leased for an indefinite period of time and either the landlord alone or both of the parties acting together may terminate it at their option. For example, Sam tells his friends Sid and Kathy that they may move into a house owned by Sam and rent it until they find a home to buy. In most states some advance notice must be given to the tenant if the landlord decides to terminate the tenancy at will.

In a *tenancy at sufferance*, a tenant remains in possession of the property after the expiration of a lease. The landlord may decide to treat the tenant as a trespasser or may continue to treat the person as a tenant. Until the landlord decides, the tenant is a tenant by sufferance.

Execution of a Lease

A lease is a contract. In most states, if the lease is for a term of more than one year from the date it is made, it must be in writing or it is not enforceable. In a few states, however, only leases for a term of more than three years have to be in writing to be enforceable.

In the leasing of real estate, good business practice demands that the landlord and tenant execute a carefully drafted lease that defines their respective rights. The lease normally contains provisions covering such essential matters as the uses the tenant can make of the property, who shall make repairs, the landlord's right to enter the premises, the purposes for which the landlord may enter, the rent to be paid, warranties as to the condition of the property, whether or not the tenant may assign the lease or sublet the property, and the term of the lease.

Rights, Duties, and Liabilities of the Parties

The rights, duties, and liabilities of the landlord as well as the tenant must be considered in three different situations: (1) where there is no applicable and enforceable lease clause, (2) where there is an applicable and enforceable lease clause, and (3) where there is an applicable statute. The discussion in this section of the text relates primarily to the law that applies in the absence of a lease clause or statute. It should be kept in mind that a lease clause or statute may replace the common law rule in any given situation.

RIGHTS, DUTIES, AND LIABILITIES OF THE LANDLORD

Landlord's Duties

When a landlord leases certain premises, the landlord impliedly warrants that he or she will give the tenant possession of the premises, or at least that the tenant will have the right to possession for the term of the lease. The landlord also warrants that the tenant's possession will not be interfered with as the result of any act or omission on the part of the landlord. In the absence of covenants in the lease to the contrary, the landlord has no right to enter the premises during the term of the lease; if the landlord does, he or she is a trespasser.

Landlord's Rights

The landlord is entitled to the agreed rent for the term of the lease. At the expiration of the term of the lease, the landlord has the right to the return of the premises in as good condition as when leased except for normal wear and tear and any destruction by the weather or act of God.

Habitability

Under traditional law, the landlord did not warrant the condition of the premises, or that the premises were suitable for the purpose of the tenant. The tenant took the premises as he found them. Because the landlord had no duty as to the condition of the premises, the landlord was not liable to the tenant or his family for injuries or property damage due to obvious defects or disrepair.

To this general rule, the courts created some very important exceptions: (1) the landlord is liable to use due care for those common areas of a building in which he or she retains control; (2) the landlord is liable for injury from known concealed defects unless disclosed to the tenant or discoverable on a reasonable inspection by the tenant; (3) the landlord remains liable for the consequences of any negligently made repairs, even though he or she was not obligated to make them; and (4) the landlord who rents a fully furnished dwelling for a short time impliedly warrants that the premises are safe and habitable.

Over time many courts have moved away from the traditional rule. Many courts now hold that an *implied warranty of habitability* is made in the lease of premises for residential use.

Pines v. Perssion
111 N.W.2d 409 (Sup. Ct. Wisc. 1961)

FACTS   Pines was a student at the University of Wisconsin. In May 1959 he and some other students asked Perssion if he had a house they could rent for the next school year. He showed them a house that was in filthy condition. Perssion said he would clean and fix up the house, provide the necessary furniture, and have it in good condition by September. Pines agreed to rent the house. When Pines and the other tenants arrived in the fall, it was still filthy and there were no student furnishings. They began to clean up the house themselves and to paint it using some paint supplied by Perssion. However they became discouraged with their progress. They contacted an attorney who advised them to request the city building inspector to check the building. The inspector found numerous violations of the building code, including inadequate electric wiring, the kitchen sink and the toilet in need of repair, a broken furnace, a broken handrail on the stairs, and no screen doors or windows. The inspector gave Perssion two weeks to make the repairs. Pines and the other tenants moved out of the house. They then sued Perssion to get their deposit returned to them along with payment for the work they did cleaning the house.

ISSUE   Was there an implied warranty of habitability in the lease of the house that was breached?

DECISION   Yes. The court held that in this case there was an implied warranty that the premises were habitable and that the warranty was breached. The court noted that the general rule is that there are no implied warranties that the premises are inhabitable. The tenant is responsible for inspecting them before entering the lease or for getting an express warranty as to the condition the premises will be in. The tenant is not normally entitled to abandon the premises on the grounds of uninhabitability.

However, the court said that legislatures have now imposed certain duties on landlords as to the condition in which they must keep their property. To follow the old rule that there is no implied warranty of habitability would be inconsistent with these new housing standards. Thus the court said there would be a warranty of habitability. In this case the warranty was breached. The house was not in a condition decently fit to live in. The tenants were entitled to move out and were responsible for paying only the "reasonable value" of the premises during the time they occupied it. They could get the rest of their deposit back plus an amount for their labor in fixing the property up.

Housing Codes   Many cities and states have enacted housing codes that impose duties on a property owner with respect to the condition of premises that are rented to others. Typical of these provisions is Section 2304 of the District of Columbia Housing Code, which provides that: "No person shall rent or offer to rent any habitation or the furnishing thereof unless such habitation and its furnishings are in a clean, safe and sanitary condition, in repair and free from rodents or vermin." Such codes also commonly call for certain minimum temperatures to be maintained in the building; for minimum bathroom and kitchen facilities to be provided along with water and heating; for a minimum amount of space per tenant; for certain lighting, ventilation, and maintenance to be provided; for stairways, windows, doors, floors, and screens to be in repair; for minimum ceiling heights; for keys and locks to meet certain specifications; for the property to be kept painted and free of lead paint; and for the landlord to issue written receipts for rent payments. The codes may prohibit landlords from retaliating against a tenant who complains to city authorities about conditions in the premises. Buildings of a certain size may be required to have resident custodial care. Some cities have adopted rent-control ordinances that limit the amount of rent tenants can be charged by landlords.

Failure of a landlord to conform to the housing code may result in the landlord losing part or all of his or her claim to the agreed upon rent. The landlord who does not make the repairs required by the housing code may be subject to fines and liable for injuries that result from the disrepair. Under a few statutes, the tenant has the right to withhold the rent until the repairs are made and may have the right to move out.

Garcia v. Freeland Realty, Inc.
314 N.Y.S.2d 215 (Civ. Ct. N.Y.C. 1970)

FACTS Garcia rented an apartment from Freeland Realty under an oral lease. There was no agreement as to who would make repairs to the property. Garcia had two small children, and he discovered that the children were eating paint and plaster that was flaking off the walls in two rooms in the apartment. Garcia complained about the situation to the landlord. When the landlord did not fix the problem, Garcia purchased some paint and plaster. He repaired the walls and then sued the landlord to recover for the work. He claimed $29.35 for materials and $1.60 an hour (the minimum wage) for each of the ten hours he spent doing the work. Under the "Multiple Dwelling Law" in New York City a landlord is obligated to keep his property repaired and painted. However, the law gives only the city—not the tenant—the right to force the landlord to obey this law.

ISSUE Could the tenant recover the cost of making these repairs from the landlord where the lease did not require the landlord to make repairs?

DECISION Yes. The court allowed Garcia to recover the cost of making the repairs. The court noted that normally a landlord does not have a duty to make repairs unless he agrees to do so in the lease. Here the city requires the landlord to make repairs. This duty can be enforced only by the city and not by the tenant. However, if the landlord does not make the repairs he is obligated to make under city law, the landlord is liable for injuries suffered by a tenant or his family because of the landlord's failure to repair. Here the landlord would have been liable if Garcia's children had gotten lead poisoning from eating the paint. Garcia's actions in repairing the walls prevented this from happening. There was a threat to the health and safety of the tenant's children that was corrected by the tenant. He had given the landlord notice to fix it. Because the tenant corrected the threat to health, which was the landlord's responsibility, Garcia was allowed to collect the cost of the repairs.

Protection of Tenants against Criminal Conduct

A growing trend of the law is the imposition of a duty on a landlord to safeguard tenants against foreseeable criminal conduct. Thus landlords have been found liable for injuries sustained by tenants because the landlord failed to maintain sufficient security control over access to an apartment building and for failure to provide sufficient lighting outside a building in a high-crime area. While the landlord is not an insurer of tenants' saftey, he or she must take reasonable precautions to safeguard tenants. This means providing proper locks and lighting. For larger buildings or ones in high-crime areas, security guards and alarm systems may have to be provided.

Trentacost v. Brussel
395 A.2d 540 (Sup. Ct. N.J. 1978)

FACTS Florence Trentacost, who was 61 years old, was "mugged" in the hallway of the apartment house where she was a tenant. The incident happened about 4:00 o'clock in the afternoon about 25 feet into the building at the foot of some stairs. She suffered a number of injuries including a dislocated shoulder, broken leg, broken ankle, and several other fractures and cuts. She sued the landlord to recover for her personal injuries. She claimed that the landlord had been negligent by failing to maintain the safety of the common areas of the building and by failing to have a lock on the front door entrance to the building. The apartment building was located in an area where there had been civil disturbances in 1969–71, and the neighborhood was considered by the police to be a high-crime area. Unauthorized persons had previously been seen in the building and reported to the landlord.

ISSUE Was the landlord liable to the tenant for the injuries she sustained when she was mugged in the apartment house?

DECISION Yes. The court allowed the tenant to recover from the landlord. The court noted that in order to recover from the landlord for the crimes of third persons, the tenant must show that the landlord was negligent in the particular case. There is no general duty on the part of landlords to protect tenants against crimes by third persons. However, where such crimes are clearly foreseeable, the landlord does have a duty to take reasonable steps to protect tenants. If his failure to provide a lock for the front door was the proximate cause of the injury, she could recover. Here the court focused on whether the failure to provide a lock made it easier for an intruder to injure a tenant. It felt a jury could reasonably conclude that the lack of a lock would make it easier for such an attack to occur.

Security Deposits

Security deposits or advance payments of rent are commonly required by landlords. Some states and cities limit the amount that can be required to be deposited in advance and require that deposits on leases for more than minimal lengths of time be placed in interest-bearing accounts. They also require landlords to account to tenants for the deposit within a specified period of time—say, 30 days—from the termination of the lease. Failure of the landlord to do so may result in the imposition of a penalty on the landlord.

RIGHTS, DUTIES, AND LIABILITIES OF THE TENANT

Rights of the Tenant

The tenant may use the leased property for any lawful purpose that is reasonable and appropriate, unless the purpose for which it may be used is expressly limited in the lease. Under the common law rule, the tenant has the exclusive right to the possession and use of the premises during the term of the lease. If the landlord comes onto the premises without the consent of the tenant, the landlord is guilty of trespassing.

Duties of the Tenant

The tenant is fully responsible for the care and upkeep of the property. Traditionally the tenant owed a duty to make all ordinary repairs so that the premises would be returned in the same condition as rented except for normal wear and tear. This duty for the upkeep of residential property has been changed by statute in many places and put on the landlord. The tenant has no duty to make major repairs except where he or she is negligent. However, the tenant must take steps to prevent further damage from the elements, as when a window breaks or a roof leaks.

Liability for Injuries to Third Persons

The landlord is responsible for keeping the common areas—such as walks, lobby, hallways, stairs, and elevators—in repair and in a safe condition for the tenants and visitors to the property. If the landlord fails to fulfill this duty, he can be liable to a person who is injured as a result. For example, if the light bulbs in the stairwell burn out and the landlord does not replace them in a reasonable time, he could be responsible if one night someone trips and falls on the stairs.

The tenant is normally liable to persons injured or property damaged because of the tenant's negligence on that part of the property over which he or she has control.

Filipczak v. I.B.E.W.
197 N.W.2d 433 (Sup. Ct. Minn. 1972)

FACTS   Local 110 of the International Brotherhood of Electrical Workers occupied a building in St. Paul, Minnesota. On the first floor of the building was a kitchen and bar. The second floor was a lodge hall with an asphalt tile floor suitable for dancing.

Local 110 leased the hall to Rosemary Naudauer for a wedding reception. Under the lease, Local 110 furnished a bartender. Naudauer hired a caterer and a band. Frances Filipczak, a guest at the wedding, was sitting at a table on the second floor watching people dancing. When the band played a polka, she and her sister began to dance. They got about a third of the way around the floor before they fell on what appeared to be freshly spilled pop. Filipczak broke her leg as a result of the fall. She then sued Local 110 to recover for her injuries.

ISSUE Was the landlord liable for the injuries that were sustained while the tenant was in control of the premises?

DECISION No. The court held that Filipczak could not recover from the landlord, Local 110. When Local 110 turned the premises over to Naudauer for the reception, it knew they would be used for purposes of admitting the public. Thus it was obligated to warn her of any dangerous conditions of which it was aware. Here there was no evidence of any dangerous condition existing when possession was given to the tenant. However, once it turned over control of the premises to the tenant, it is not liable for the tenant's negligence in maintaining the premises.

Assignment and Subleasing

The tenant has a property interest in the leased premises that may be transferred to another person by the assignment of the lease unless the lease expressly provides that it shall not be assigned. However, total prohibitions against assignment are generally considered void as against public policy. Most leases contain a clause that requires the landlord's consent to any assignment and provides that such consent will not be unreasonably withheld.

A tenant who assigns the lease is not relieved from any contractual obligations under the lease. However, the tenant does give up his interest in the leased property. The tenant may sublease the property or part of it. If the tenant subleases the property, the tenant does not give up his property interest, and the tenant remains liable to the landlord for the commitments in the lease. For example, if the subtenant does not pay the rent, the tenant is liable to pay it to the landlord. The tenant's relation to the sublessee is that of landlord. The tenant cannot grant to a sublessee greater rights than he has under the original lease. If the original lease contains a provision denying the tenant the right to sublease the premises, it usually is enforceable.

TERMINATION

Termination of the Lease

Normally, a lease is ended by *surrender* of the property by the tenant to the landlord and *acceptance* of the property by the landlord. However, sometimes the tenant may be forced out by the landlord prior to the end of the lease period, or the tenant may vacate the property before the end of the lease period.

Constructive Eviction

If the premises become uninhabitable because of the acts of the landlord, then under the doctrine of *constructive eviction* the tenant may, after giving the landlord a reasonable opportunity to correct the defect, vacate (move out) and incur no further liability for rent. The tenant must move out within a reasonable amount of time. For example, if the furnace breaks down in the middle of the winter and the apartment is without heat for February and March, the tenant cannot use this as an excuse for breaking the lease in August.

Abandoment

If the tenant abandons the premises before the end of the lease, the consequences vary from state to state. In some states the landlord is under an obligation to mitigate damages. The landlord must attempt to rerent or he or she will lose any claim for further rent against the original tenant. In other states, the landlord may continue to collect rent from the tenant without rerenting, but loses the right if he or she does rerent. As a result, many leases contain a clause that maintains the landlord's right to the rent whether or not the landlord tries to rerent and continues the tenant's liability for any difference in rents if the landlord does rerent.

Eviction

A landlord who desires to evict a tenant for nonpayment of rent or breach of a lease agreement should be careful to comply with any applicable state or city regulations governing evictions. Such regulations may forbid forcible entry to change locks or other self-help measures on the part of landlords. Under landlord lien statutes, the landlord may be entitled to remove and hold belongings of a defaulting tenant as security for the rent payment. However, pursuant to the Due Process Clause the tenant must be given notice of the lien and an opportunity to defend and protect his or her belongings before they can be sold to satisfy the lien.

Parkin v. Fitzgerald
240 N.W.2d 828 (Sup. Ct. Minn. 1976)

FACTS On March 1, 1974, Sharon Fitzgerald entered into an oral lease of a house owned by Parkin. The lease was on a month-to-month basis and rent was set at $290 per month. Parkin also agreed to make certain repairs to the house. On July 1, Fitzgerald notified Parkin by mail of the repairs that needed to be made. These included leaky pipes, the kitchen ceiling, and the back porch. She also said she would withhold rent if the repairs were not made within 30 days. On July 18, Fitzgerald had the premises inspected by a city housing inspector who found eight violations of the city code. Parkin was given notice of these violations. On July 29 Parkin served Fitzgerald with a formally correct notice to vacate the premises within 30 days. In September he brought a lawsuit to have Fitzgerald evicted. A Minnesota statute gives a tenant a defense to an eviction action if the eviction is in retaliation for the reporting of a housing violation in good faith to city officials.

ISSUE	Could the landlord evict the tenant from the house under these circumstances?
DECISION	No. The court held that Parkin did not have the right to evict Fitzgerald. Where the notice of eviction came so close to the report to the city, the landlord has to show he is not acting in retaliation or to penalize the tenant. Here he was not able to do so. The fact that the inspector found violations of the city code showed the tenant had acted in good faith.

QUESTIONS AND PROBLEM CASES

1. Does a lease have to be in writing to be enforceable? Explain.

2. What is a warranty of habitability?

3. Remedco leased a building on West 121st Street in New York City to the Bryn Mawr Hotel, which used the building to operate a hotel. The multiyear lease contained a clause which required that the building not be used "for any business or purpose deemed disreputable." Over a long period of time the hotel rented rooms to anyone who applied and who paid a week's rent in advance even though it had some reason to believe its rooms were being used for various illegal purposes. The premises were marked by the police as a focal point for various types of crimes and they made repeated arrests of roomer-occupants for narcotics addiction, prostitution, and assorted other crimes. Remedco brought suit to terminate the lease at a time it still had 13 years to run because of the long pattern of conduct by the roomers. Should the court allow Remedco to end the lease?

4. A tenant rented an apartment from the landlord pursuant to a lease that required her to surrender the premises in "as good a state and condition as reasonable use and wear and tear will permit" and also required her to make a refundable security deposit. After the lease was executed, the landlord notified the tenants in the building that no tenant was to shampoo the wall-to-wall carpet on surrender of the lease because the landlord had retained a professional carpet cleaner to do it. The cost of the carpet cleaner's services was to be automatically deducted from the security deposit. When the tenant left the building, a portion of her security deposit was withheld to cover carpet cleaning and she sued for a refund of the full deposit. Is the tenant entitled to a refund?

5. The toilet bowl in a tenant's apartment had a defective seat. The tenant notified the landlord of the problem but the landlord did not respond in a timely fashion. The tenant tried to fix it by using wire to hold the seat in place; however, the tenant was injured when she fell off when the seat broke. She sued the landlord to recover damages for her injuries. The landlord claimed he was not liable because the tenant had assumed the risk or had been contributorily negligent. Should the tenant be barred from recovering?

6. On April 2 Ireland entered into a one-year lease for an apartment in a two-family duplex owned by Marini for a monthly rental of $95. The lease did not include a specific clause covering responsibility for repairs. On June 25, Ireland discovered that the toilet in the apartment was cracked, and water was leaking onto the bathroom floor. Ireland tried unsuccessfully to notify Marini of the problem and then on June 27 hired a plumber to repair the toilet. Ireland paid the plumber $85.72 for this work and deducted it from her next rent payment. Marini sought to have Ireland dispossessed for nonpayment of rent since Ireland refused to pay the $85.72 she offset. What argument

will Marini make? What argument will Ireland make? What result should the court reach?

7. In 1965, Miss Kline moved into an apartment house in Washington, D.C. At the time she signed the lease, a doorman was on duty at the main entrance 24 hours a day, at least one employee was at a desk in the lobby from which all persons entering the elevators could be observed, and attendants were stationed at the entrance of the garage. By mid-1966, the main entrance had no doorman, the lobby desk was unattended much of the time, and the garage entrances were generally unlocked and unattended. This was true despite the fact that an increasing number of assaults and robberies were being perpetrated against tenants in the hallways of the apartment. At 10:00 P.M. on November 17, 1966, Kline was assaulted and robbed just outside her apartment of the 535-unit apartment building. Two months before, another tenant had been similarly attacked in the same hallway. Kline sued the landlord because of injuries she sustained in the assault. What arguments will Kline and the landlord make? What result should the court reach?

8. Bailey rented an apartment in a building owned by Zlotnick. One of the provisions of the lease was that Bailey would not sublease or assign the lease without the permission of the landlord. One day Bailey was injured by plaster that fell from the ceiling of her kitchen shortly after a new hot water heating system had been installed in the building. Bailey brought a lawsuit against Zlotnick to recover for her injuries. Zlotnick defended on the grounds that Bailey was in violation of her lease because she was renting rooms in her apartment to others. This fact had been known to Zlotnick's agents for some time but he continued to accept rent from her. Should the court hold that Bailey was not rightfully in possession because of the breach and thus barred from any recovery?

9. On October 1, Zankman entered into a two-year lease with a landlord for rental of an apartment that he intended to use not only as a residence but also as a place to make and receive business calls and correspondence. The lease was executed not only in Zankman's name but also in the name of New Jersey Steel Products. He paid his October and November rent but on December 1 notified the landlord that he would be late with his December rent payment. On December 29 he received a telegram advising him that unless his rent was paid by 11 A.M. the next day his apartment would be padlocked. On December 30, Zankman left to go to the drugstore to have a prescription filled and when he returned, his apartment had been padlocked. He was not allowed to remove his belongings until January 8. A New Jersey statute provides that "with regard to any property occupied solely as a residence by the party in possession, such entry shall not be made in any manner without the consent of the party in possession unless the entry and detention is made pursuant to legal process." Zankman claimed the entry to his apartment to padlock it was unlawful. What conclusion would a court reach?

10. Winslow rented an apartment and signed a lease that provided, in part, that "Landlord or Landlord's agents shall not be responsible for the presence of bugs, vermin, or insects, if any, in the premises, nor shall their presence affect this lease." Some mice appeared in Winslow's apartment and, despite efforts to get rid of them, they remained in the apartment. Winslow moved out, claiming constructive eviction. He cited Section 227 of the Real Property Law of New York, which provides: "Where any building, which is leased or occupied, is destroyed or so injured by the elements or any other cause as to be untenable, and unfit for occupancy, and no express agreement to the contrary has been made in writing, the lessee or occupant may if the destruction or injury occurred without his fault or neglect, quit and surrender possession of the leasehold premises . . . and he is not liable to pay to the lessor or owner, rent for the time subsequent to the surrender." The landlord sued Winslow for rent for the unexpired portion of the lease. Is Winslow liable for the remaining rent?

Estates and Trusts

37

INTRODUCTION

Estate Planning

During your lifetime you may accumulate a sizable amount of property. This commonly includes real property, such as a home, and a variety of kinds of personal property such as a car, furniture, clothes, cash, and stocks and bonds. You may also develop a number of obligations—either legal or self-created—to others such as a husband or wife, children, parents, and other family members or close friends and even to institutions such as churches, colleges, and charities. During your life you may dispose of some of your property to meet these obligations. You may make gifts of property or establish trusts to benefit those individuals or institutions. On your death it is desirable that your property go, to the extent possible, to the individuals and institutions of your choosing. In this chapter, we will discuss the disposition of property at death as well as the law of trusts.

This area of the law is commonly known as *estate planning* or *estates and trusts*. State and federal tax laws are an important factor in this area but will not be discussed in detail. There are also many state statutes that affect estate planning. While this chapter will outline some of the considerations involved, it is important that you develop your estate plan with a competent attorney who is familiar with federal tax laws and the laws of the state where you reside or your property is located.

Disposition of Property on Death of Owner

When a person dies, the law provides for the payment of his or her debts and the distribution of any remaining property in the estate to those who are entitled to it. The administration of a person's estate is generally handled under the supervision of a specialized court known as the *probate court*. If a deceased person did not make a will, his or her property will

479

be distributed according to state laws known as statutes of *descent and distribution* or *intestate succession.* However, if a person makes a valid will, that document generally controls the distribution of his or her property when the person dies.

Dying Intestate

If a person dies without having made a will, or if the will is invalid, then the person is said to have died *intestate.* In that case his or her real property is distributed according to the statutes of the state in which it is located. His or her personal property is distributed according to the statutes of the state in which he or she lived. Generally any debts must be satisfied out of the personal property before it is distributed to the heirs.

The laws that provide for distribution of an intestate's estate differ from state to state. Theoretically, the rationale of the intestate laws is to distribute the property in a way that reflects the desire of the deceased, that is, to distribute it to those persons most closely related to him or her. In general, the statutes look first to see whether the deceased person was survived by a husband, wife, children, or grandchildren and then provide for at least some, if not total, distribution of the estate to them. The next focus is on any *lineal* (blood) *descendants* such as a mother, father, brother, sister, niece, or nephew. If no such relatives are living at this level, the property goes to what are called *collateral relatives.* Collateral relatives are not direct descendants of the deceased person but are related through a common ancestor, for example, aunts, uncles, grandfathers, grandmothers, and cousins. Generally persons who are related to the same degree to the deceased person take equal shares. If the entire property is not distributed according to the statutory formula, the property that remains *escheats* (goes) to the state.

Example of Intestacy Law

Suppose that Carlos Hernandez, who lives in the District of Columbia, dies leaving a wife and two children. Under the laws of the District, his wife is entitled to one third of his estate and the two children are entitled to split the remaining two thirds. If Carlos were survived by a wife, a mother, and a father but not by any children, then his wife would get half of his estate and his mother and father would split the other half. If Carlos dies leaving only two brothers and a sister, each of them would get one third of his estate. While the exact portion of the estate to which a surviving spouse, child, or other family member is entitled varies somewhat from state to state, the basic concept is the same in each state.

Special Rules

Under the intestacy laws, a person must have a blood relationship to the deceased person in order to inherit part or all of his or her estate. "In-laws"—or persons related through marriage other than as husband or wife—are not entitled to share in the estate. State law commonly extends the definition of "children" to include adopted children and treats them the same as natural children. Half-brothers or half-sisters are frequently treated the same as those related by whole blood. Illegitimate children may inherit from their mother the same as legitimate children. Usually they do not inherit from their father unless their paternity has been either acknowledged or established in a legal proceeding.

Generally a person must be alive at the time the decedent dies in order to claim his or her statutory share of that person's estate. An exception may be made for children or descendants who are born after the person's death. If a person who is entitled to a share of another estate dies after the holder of that estate dies but before receiving his share of it, his share in that estate becomes part of his own estate.

Murder Disqualification

Many states provide that a person who is convicted of the homicide (murder or manslaughter) of another person may not inherit any of that person's property. Similarly, a person usually cannot share in the insurance proceeds on the life of a person he has murdered.

Simultaneous Death

A statute known as the *Uniform Simultaneous Death Act* provides that where two persons, such as husband and wife, die under circumstances that make it difficult or impossible to determine who died first, each person's property is to be distributed as though he or she survived. This means, for example, that the husband's property will go to his relatives and the wife's property to her relatives.

WILLS

Right of Disposition by Will

A will is a document in which a person provides for the disposition of his or her property at death. The right to dispose of property by will is based on statutes. Under the feudal system in England, the King was the owner of all the land. The lords and knights only had the right to use the land for their lifetimes. On the death of a landholder, the rights in the land he held terminated, and no rights in the land descended to his heirs. In 1215 the King granted to the nobility the right to pass their interest in the land they held to their heirs.

Today we recognize the theory of basic ownership by the state. The fact that unclaimed property escheats to the state is an example of this. On the basis of this theory, the courts have upheld the right of the state and the federal government to tax the estate of a deceased person and to tax an inheritance. The state also can establish the formalities that must be complied with to pass property by will.

Execution of Will

A man who makes a will is known as a *testator* and a woman who makes one is a *testatrix*. Although the statutes concerning wills are not uniform in the various states, all are similar in their basic requirements. The courts have been strict in interpreting these statutes. They declare a will to be void unless all the requirements of the statute have been complied with in the execution of the will. If a will is declared void, the property

FIGURE 37–1
Example of a Will

LAST WILL AND TESTAMENT
OF
WILLIAM R. FOLGER

I, WILLIAM R. FOLGER, of McLean, County of Fairfax, Commonwealth of Virginia, being of sound and disposing mind and memory, do make this to be my Last Will and Testament, hereby revoking all former wills and codicils made by me.

FIRST. I direct that the expenses of my funeral and burial, including a grave site, grave stone and perpetual care, be paid out of my estate in such amount as my Executrix may deem proper and without regard to any limitation in the applicable law as to the amount of such expenses and without necessity of prior Court approval.

SECOND. I direct that all estate, inheritance, succession and other death taxes and duties occasioned by my death, whether incurred with respect to property passing by this Will or otherwise, shall be paid by my Executrix out of the principal of my residuary estate with no right of reimbursement from any recipient of any such property.

THIRD. I further direct my Executrix to pay all of my legal obligations and debts (exclusive of any debt or debts secured by a deed of trust or mortgage on real estate, not due at the time of my death or becoming due during the period of administration of my estate). In determining what are my obligations and debts, I direct my Executrix to avail herself of every legal defense that would have been available to me.

FOURTH. I hereby confirm my intention that the beneficial interest in all property, real or personal, tangible or intangible (including joint checking or savings accounts in any bank or savings and loan association), which is registered or held, at the time of my death, jointly in the names of myself and any other person (including tenancy by the entireties, but, excluding any tenancy in common), shall pass by right of survivorship or operation of law and outside of the terms of this Will to such other person, if he or she survives me. To the extent that my intention may be defeated by any rule of law, I give, devise and bequeath all such jointly held property to such other person or persons who shall survive me.

FIFTH. I give my tangible personal property, including furniture, clothing, automobiles and their equipment, and articles of personal or household use or ornament, but not including money, securities or the like, to my wife Kristin A. Folger, if she survives me by thirty (30) days, and if she does not so survive me, I give the same absolutely to my issue who so survive me, such issue to take *per stirpes*.

William R. Folger

FIGURE 37–1 *(continued)*

I express the hope that my wife or my issue will dispose of my tangible personal property according to my wishes, however my wishes may be known to her or to them, but I expressly declare that I do not intend to create any trust in law or in equity with respect to my tangible personal property.

SIXTH.   I give the sum of $1,500 to St. Christopher's Church, McLean, Virginia, for its unrestricted use.

SEVENTH.   I give, bequeath and devise all the rest and residue of my estate, of whatsoever nature and wheresoever situated, to my wife Kristin A. Folger, if she survives me by more than thirty (30) days. If she does not so survive me, I give the same absolutely to my issue who so survive me, such issue to take *per stirpes*.

EIGHTH.   I nominate, constitute and appoint my wife Kristin A. Folger, to be the Executrix of this my Last Will and Testament. My Executrix shall have full power in her discretion to do any and all things necessary for the complete administration of my estate, including the power to sell at public or private sale, and without order of court, any real or personal property belonging to my estate, and to compound, compromise or otherwise to settle or adjust any and all claims, charges, debts and demands whatsoever against or in favor of my estate, as fully as I could do if living.

NINTH.   I direct that no bond or other security be required of my Executrix appointed hereunder in any jurisdiction, any provision of law to the contrary notwithstanding.

IN WITNESS WHEREOF, I have hereunto set my hand and seal to this Last Will and Testament, typewritten upon two (2) pages, each one of which has been signed by me this 15th day of August, 1980 at McLean, Virginia.

William R. Folger (SEAL)
William R. Folger

The foregoing instrument consisting of two (2) typewritten pages was signed, published and declared by the testator to be his Last Will and Testament in the presence of us, who, at his request, in his presence, and in the presence of each other, have hereunto subscribed our names as witnesses this 15th day of August, 1980.

Carole H. Carson of *McLean, Virginia*

Robert R. Carson of *McLean, Virginia*

Sandra N. Somers of *Falls Church, Virginia*

of the deceased person is distributed according to the statutes of descent and distribution.

Only persons of *sound mind* and of *legal age* are permitted to dispose of property by will. Persons who execute a will must have the mental capacity to understand the nature and character of their property and to realize that they are making a will. They should also know who the persons are who would naturally be the beneficiaries of their affection. People do not have to be in perfect mental health, however. Because people are sometimes in ill health when they make a will, the law does not expect them to possess even the same level of mental capacity as is required to execute a contract.

The required formalities vary from state to state, and the laws of the states that may affect a will should be consulted before a will is executed. Formalities required by many states are: (1) the will must be in *writing;* (2) it must be *witnessed* by two or three "disinterested" witnesses—persons who do not stand to take any property under the will; (3) it must be *signed* by the testator or at his direction; (4) it must be *published* by the testator—as a general rule, all that is required for publication is a declaration by the testator, at the time of signing, that the instrument is his will; (5) the testator must sign *in the presence* and *in the sight* of the witnesses; and (6) the witnesses must sign in the presence and in the sight of the testator and in the presence and in the sight of each other. If the statutory formalities are not all complied with, the will is not valid. As a general rule, an *attestation clause*, stating the formalities that have been followed in the execution of the will, is written following the testator's signature. See Figure 37–1 for an example of a will.

A will procured by fraud or undue influence is not accepted as a valid will. *Lack of testamentary capacity* and *undue influence* are the most common grounds for challenging a will. In assessing a claim of undue influence, the court looks to see whether a bequest appears to be made on the basis of natural affection or on some improper influence. The actions of fiduciaries such as attorneys are scrutinized carefully, particularly for improper influence. This is especially true if they are not related to the deceased person, were made a beneficiary, and had a critical role in preparing the will.

In Re Estate of Weir
475 F.2d 988 (D.C. Cir. 1972)

FACTS   Paul Weir was a lifelong bachelor. Shortly after World War II he met Elizabeth Holmstead, a widow, who was about his age. They became close friends until Weir died on February 19, 1971. Although they had separate apartments, they traveled together, ate their meals together, and were constant companions. In February 1956 Weir executed a will that left a life estate to Holmstead and the remainder to his brother or, if his brother was dead, to his brother's children. In 1965 Weir's brother died. Then in June 1966 Weir executed a new will that left $10,000 each to his niece and nephew and the remainder of his estate to Holmstead. When Weir died, his niece Margaret challenged the 1966 will. She claimed that Weir did not have testamentary capacity and that he had been unduly influenced by Holmstead. Margaret said that Weir dressed conservatively, was occasionally forgetful, was sometimes untidy (he left his socks on the floor), and had some strange habits like picking dust up from the floor and inspecting it.

ISSUE   Was Weir's 1965 will invalid on the grounds of lack of capacity and undue influence?

DECISION   No. The will was valid. In order to make a will, the maker must be "of sound and disposing mind and capable of executing a deed or contract." He has to know the nature and character of his estate and who the persons are who would be the natural beneficiaries. The court found that the evidence as to Weir's mental state was not sufficient to show incapacity. Similarly, the court said there was no evidence of undue influence. It said that Holmstead's influence was not improper because it was gained by years of mutual affection. Undue influence is influence gained by improper means.

Some states recognize the validity of holographic wills, and some recognize the validity of nuncupative wills. A *holographic will* is one that is entirely written and signed in the testator's or testatrix's own handwriting. A few states recognize these wills as valid without formal execution or attestation. A *nuncupative will* is an oral will. In many states the oral wills made by sailors at sea or by soldiers in military service are recognized as valid for the purpose of disposing of the personal property that is in the actual possession of the person at the time the will is made.

Chambers v. Young
399 S.W.2d 655 (Sup. Ct. Ark. 1966)

FACTS   After Boyd Ruff died, his wife found in his wallet a blank check on the back of which was written "I Boyd Ruff reqest that all I own in the way of personal or real estate property go to my wife Modene, Boyd Ruff." Ruff had a serious coronary condition which he knew could be fatal at any time. He executed the document shortly before his death and just after a serious heart attack. Ruff was survived by his wife, three brothers, and a sister, but left no children. Modene Ruff filed a petition in probate court to admit the document as a will. Ruff's sister, Lois, filed a petition to set the will aside on the grounds: (1) that on its fact it was not a valid holographic will and (2) that it did not show a valid intent to make a will.

ISSUE   Was the document a valid will?

> **DECISION** Yes. Under Arkansas law, a holographic will entirely in the handwriting of the testator along with his signature is valid despite the lack of witnesses. The testator's handwriting and signature must be established by three credible disinterested witnesses. The court held that the document was a valid holographic will. Ruff knew death was imminent and that his wife was a natural person to receive the benefit of his estate. Thus, the court found that the document was executed with the necessary testamentary intent that it control the disposition of his property on his death.

Limitations on Disposition by Will

A person who takes property by will takes it subject to all outstanding claims against the property. For example, if real property is subject to a mortgage or a lien, the beneficiary who takes the real property gets it subject to the mortgage or lien. Also, the rights of creditors are superior to the rights of a beneficiary under the will. Thus if the deceased person is insolvent (his debts exceed his assets), persons named as beneficiaries do not receive any property by virtue of the will.

Under the laws of most states the widow or widower of the deceased has statutory rights in the property of the deceased spouse that cannot be defeated by will. This means the husband cannot effectively disinherit his wife. As a general rule a widow is given the right to claim certain personal property of the deceased husband. She is also given the right to use their home for a stated period, usually a year (the *homestead right*) and is given a portion of her husband's real estate or a life estate in a portion of his real estate. In many states the widow's share in the husband's real property is a one-third interest or a life estate in one third of his real property. Under common law this was known as her *dower right*. A number of states have changed it by statute to give the surviving wife a one-third interest in fee simple in her deceased husband's real property.

In some states the husband of a deceased wife is given an interest in her property, and this right cannot be defeated by will. This is known as the *right of curtesy*. In the community property states, each spouse has a one-half interest in community property from their marriage and the rights of the surviving spouse cannot be defeated by will.

Revocation of Will

One important feature of a will is that it conveys no interest in the maker's property until he or she dies and the will has been probated. All wills are *revocable* at the option of the maker. A will, at the time it is executed, does not confer any present rights in the property devised or bequeathed. A person may revoke his or her will by destroying or canceling it or by making a later will, duly executed, in which he or she expressly states that all former wills are thereby revoked. Under state statutes, certain changes in relationship may operate as a revocation of a will. In some states the marriage of a man or a woman revokes a will made by the person while single. Similarly, a divorce and property settlement may revoke gifts made to the divorced spouse in a will prior to the divorce. The birth of a child after the execution of a will may, under the laws of some states, revoke a will or operate as a partial revocation of a will.

Codicils

A person may amend a will without executing an entire new will. This is done by executing a *codicil* to the earlier will with the same formalities that are required for the execution of a will.

ADMINISTRATION OF ESTATES

When a person dies, an orderly procedure is needed to collect the property, settle the debts, and distribute any remaining property to those who are entitled to it. If the deceased person did not own any property at the time of death, or if the property was jointly owned with right of survivorship so that it all passed automatically by operation of law, there is no estate to administer. In addition, summary (simple) procedures are sometimes available where the estate is relatively small, for example, where it has assets of less than $2,500.

Executor or Administrator

The first step is to determine whether or not the deceased person left a will. This may require a search of the deceased person's personal papers and safe-deposit box if he or she had one. It may also involve discussions with his or her attorney or any other person who may know whether a will was made. If there is a will, the deceased has likely exercised his or her right to name the person who will administer the estate. This person is known as the *executor* if the designee is a man or *executrix* if the designee is a woman. The executor might, for example, be the spouse of the deceased person, a close friend, an attorney, or the trust department of a bank.

If there is no will, or if the will fails to name an executor, the court will name an *administrator* (man) or an *administratrix* (woman) to administer the estate. A surviving spouse or child usually has a statutory right to be appointed as administrator. A grandchild, a father or mother, a brother or sister, or other next of kin also has a preferential right to be appointed as administrator. If no relative is available and qualified to serve, a creditor or other person may be appointed by the court.

Both the federal and state governments impose estate or inheritance taxes on estates of a certain size. The administrator is responsible for filing estate tax returns. The federal tax is a tax on the deceased's estate, with provision for deducting debts, expenses of administration, and charitable gifts. In addition, an amount equal to the greater of $250,000 or half of the adjusted gross estate may be deducted if at least that amount has been left to the surviving spouse. State inheritance taxes are imposed on the person who receives a gift or statutory share from an estate. However, it it common for a person to include a provision in his or her will that the estate will pay all taxes, including inheritance taxes, so that the beneficiaries will not have to do so.

When the debts, expenses, and taxes are taken care of, the remainder is distributed to the designated beneficiaries. Special rules apply when the estate is too small to satisfy all the bequests or when some or all of the designated beneficiaries are no longer alive.

Most states require that the executor or administrator post a bond in an amount in excess of the estimated value of the estate to insure that he or she will properly and faithfully perform his duties. However, in drawing a will, a person may direct that the executor need not post a bond and the court will usually accept the exemption.

Kaufman v. Kaufman's Administrator
166 S.W.2d 860 (Sup. Ct. Ky. 1942)

FACTS When Peter Kaufman died, his son William reluctantly qualified to become the administrator of his father's estate. William was a farmer with relatively little schooling or experience in financial matters. He agreed to serve as administrator only on the understanding that he could hire an attorney who would do most of the work. William Kaufman retained W. L. Doolan as the attorney and put the management of the estate entirely in his hands. Doolan was a highly respected lawyer with a good reputation. Over a period of five years, Doolan systematically embezzled money from the estate. When the embezzlement was discovered, Doolan was insolvent and unable to repay the money. While Kaufman checked with Doolan about once a week, he never demanded an accounting from him. A new administrator was appointed for the estate, and he sued William Kaufman to hold him liable for the amount of the embezzlement.

ISSUE Was the administrator of an estate liable where an agent he appointed embezzled money entrusted to him that belonged to the estate?

DECISION Yes. The court held that William Kaufman was personally liable in this case. An administrator is not personally liable for his lawyer's misconduct if the administrator used due care in selecting the attorney. However, where the administrator surrenders all his duties and delegates all his functions to someone else, the administrator is liable to the beneficiaries of the estate for any loss sustained.

Steps in Administration

If the deceased person left a will, it must be *proved* in order to be admitted to probate. Proving the will involves testimony by the witnesses, if they are still alive, as to the mental capacity of the deceased at the time the will was executed, that the document was intended to control the disposition of his property, and the circumstances of execution of the will. If the witnesses are no longer alive, the signatures of the deceased and the witnesses have to be otherwise established.

Whether or not there is a will, the identity of the heirs of the deceased must be established by testimony of witnesses. If the deceased person did not make a will, the heirs must be identified so that the estate can be distributed pursuant to the intestacy laws. If there is a will, the notification of heirs is necessary so that they can protect their interests. For some heirs this may mean defending a will that provides for them. Other heirs may want to try to claim a statutory share in the estate or to otherwise challenge the will.

The executor or administrator must also see that an inventory is taken of the estate and that the assets are appraised. Notice must be given to creditors or potential claimants against the estate for them to file and prove their claims within a specified time. Generally, a widow of a deceased is entitled to be paid an allowance during the time the estate is being settled. This allowance has priority over other debts of the estate. The executor must see that any properly payable funeral or burial expenses are paid and that the creditors' claims are satisfied. Provision must be made for filing an income tax return and for paying any income tax due for the period prior to the deceased person's death.

TRUSTS

Introduction

A *trust* arises when a person who has legal rights to property also has the duty to hold it for the use or benefit of another person. The person benefited by a trust is considered to have "equitable title" to the property because it is being maintained for his benefit. This means he or she is regarded as the real owner even though the trustee has the legal title in his or her name. A trust may be created in a number of different ways:

1. The owner of the property may declare that he or she is holding certain property in trust; for example, a mother might state that she is holding 100 shares of General Motors stock in trust for her daughter.
2. The owner of property may transfer property to another person with the expressed intent that person is not to have the use of it but rather is to hold it for the benefit of either the original owner-donor or a third person; for example, Arthur transfers certain stock to First Trust Bank with instructions to pay the income to Arthur's daughter during her lifetime, and after her death to distribute the stock to her children.
3. A trust may be created by operation of law; for example, where a lawyer who represents a client injured in an automobile accident receives a settlement payment from an insurance company, the lawyer holds the settlement as trustee for his client.

Definitions

A person who creates a trust is known as the *donor* or the *settlor*. The person who holds the property in trust is known as the *trustee*. The person for whose benefit the property is held is known as the *beneficiary*. A single person may occupy more than one of these positions. However, if there is only one beneficiary, he cannot be the sole trustee. The property held is sometimes called the *corpus* or *res* and a distinction is made between the property in trust, which is known as the *principal*, and the *income* that is produced by the principal.

A trust that is established and made effective during the donor's lifetime is known as an *inter vivos* (or living) *trust*. If a trust is established by a will and takes effect on the donor's death, it is known as a *testamentary trust*.

Creation of Express Trusts

Five basic elements are required for the creation of an express trust:

1. The donor must have the *legal capacity* to convey property. This means the donor must have the capacity needed to make a contract in the case of a trust created by contract or the testamentary capacity to make a will in the case of a trust created by will.
2. The donor must *intend* to create a trust at the present time and to impose enforceable duties on the trustee. The donor must do it with the *required formalities*. In the case of a trust of land, the trust must be created in writing to comply with the statute of frauds. A trust created by a will must satisfy the formal requirements for wills.
3. The trust must involve *specific property*, which the donor has the right to convey.
4. The beneficiary must be sufficiently *identified* so that he or she can be ascertained.
5. The trust must be created for a proper purpose; that is, it cannot be created for a reason contrary to public policy such as the commission of a crime.

Special and somewhat less restrictive rules govern the establishment of *charitable trusts*.

If the settlor does not name a trustee for a validly created trust, the court will appoint one. Similarly, a court will replace a trustee who resigns, is incompetent, or refuses to act.

Creation of Implied Trusts

The law recognizes certain trusts, known as *resulting trusts*, that are based on the implied or presumed intent of a person to create a trust. For example, if Ann transfers property to Arthur, intending that he be a trustee of it, but if she fails to satisfy the requirements for creating a valid express trust, then Arthur will not be permitted to retain the property for his own use. He holds the property in a *resulting trust* for Ann or her successors in interest.

Another example of a resulting trust would be where Sam transfers property to Ellen to provide for the needs of Grandfather out of the principal and income, but Grandfather dies before the trust funds are exhausted. Ellen then holds the trust property for the benefit of Sam or his successors.

A *constructive trust* is another type of trust created by operation of law. It imposes on the constructive trustee a duty to convey property held by him to another person on the grounds that the trustee would be unjustly enriched if he were allowed to retain it. For example, if Sally obtained the transfer of property to her by a fraudulent misrepresentation or duress, she becomes a constructive trustee. As such, she is under an obligation to return the property to the original owner.

Transfer of the Beneficiary's Interest

Generally the beneficiary of a trust may voluntarily assign his or her right to the principal or income from a trust to another person. Similarly, those rights are subject to the claims of his or her creditors. However, trusts sometimes contain what are known as *spendthrift clauses*, whereby the settlor restricts the voluntary or involuntary transfer of a beneficiary's interest. Such clauses are generally enforced and preclude assignees or creditors from compelling a trustee to recognize their claim to the trust.

There are several exceptions: (1) a person cannot put his own property beyond the claims of his own creditors, and thus a spendthrift clause is not effective in a trust where the settlor makes himself a beneficiary; (2) divorced wives and minor children can compel payment for alimony and child support; (3) creditors who have furnished necessaries to a beneficiary can compel payment; and (4) once the trustee distributes property to a beneficiary, it can be subject to valid claims of others.

A trust may give the trustee *discretion* as to the amount of principal or income paid to a beneficiary. In such a case the beneficiary cannot require the trustee to exercise discretion as desired by the beneficiary.

Termination and Modifications of a Trust

Normally a donor cannot revoke or modify a trust unless he or she reserves the power to do so at the time the trust is established. However, a trust may be modified or terminated with the consent of the donor and all the beneficiaries. Where the donor is dead or otherwise unable to consent, a trust can be modified or terminated by the consent of all persons who have a beneficial interest only where it would not frustrate a material purpose of the trust. Because trusts are under the supervisory jurisdiction of the court, the court can permit a deviation from the terms of a trust when unanticipated changes in circumstances threaten accomplishment of the donor's purpose.

Duties of a Trustee

A trustee must use a reasonable degree of skill, judgment, and care in the exercise of his or her duties unless he or she holds himself out as having a greater degree of skill. In that case he or she is held to the higher standard. A trustee may not commingle the property he or she holds in trust with his or her own property or with that of another trust. A trustee owes a *duty of loyalty*, which means he or she must administer the trust for the benefit of the beneficiaries and must avoid any *conflict of interest* between his interests and that of the trust. For example, if

Amy is a trustee she cannot do business with a trust she administers. A trustee must not prefer one beneficiary's interest to another; she must account to the beneficiaries for all transactions; and, unless the trust agreement provides otherwise, she must make the trust productive. A trustee may not delegate *discretionary duties* to someone else to perform, such as the duty to select investments. However, the trustee may delegate the performance of *ministerial duties* such as the preparation of statements of account.

Cross v. Cross
246 S.W.2d 801 (Sup. Ct. Mo. 1952)

FACTS In his will, Carl Cross left a sum of money to his brother, Sam, in trust for Sam's lifetime. On Sam's death, it was to go to Marvin Cross in trust for Marvin's lifetime. On Marvin's death, it was to be divided among Carl's brothers and sisters. Sam took the money left to him and bought some property in the name of himself and his wife, Maggie Cross, as tenants by the entirety. Maggie did not contribute any funds of her own and was aware that trust funds were being used to pay the purchase price. When Sam died, Sam's interest in the property passed to Maggie. Marvin and the other beneficiaries of the Carl Cross trust then sued Maggie, seeking a judgment for the amount of the trust funds and to obtain a lien on the property.

ISSUE Were Marvin and the other beneficiaries entitled to recover the trust property that Sam commingled with his own?

DECISION Yes. The court allowed Marvin and the other beneficiaries to recover the trust funds from Maggie. She was aware of Sam's breach of trust in commingling the trust funds with his property. She was also aware that Sam was placing the title so that it would go to her and would leave nothing in his estate to restore the trust fund. When a trustee wrongfully disposes of trust funds and acquires other property with it, the beneficiary can follow the trust property into the new property and enforce a constructive trust.

The powers of a trustee may be defined by the trust agreement; if they are not, the trustee has all the powers reasonably necessary to carry out the trust. The trustee is personally liable on all contracts made on behalf of a trust unless the contract specifically provides otherwise. However, he or she is entitled to reimbursement from the trust property for all legitimate expenditures.

QUESTIONS AND PROBLEM CASES

1. If a person dies without leaving a will, who will be entitled to his or her property?

2. What is the difference between a nuncupative will and a holographic will?

3. Under what circumstances can an administrator or executor of an estate become liable for the acts of those he employs to carry out his fiduciary responsibilities?

4. Explain the duty of loyalty owed by the trustee of a trust.

5. Floyd, 84 years of age, was suffering from incurable cancer and was confined to his bed at the time he executed his will. He conversed for about one-half hour with the two men who witnessed the will, talking about their families and other topics. The will was read to him topic by topic and he approved each item as read. At the conclusion of the reading, he said that that was the way he wanted his property distributed. He had left a life estate in all his property to his wife, and the fee simple to his grandson and his grandson's wife. They had cared for Floyd during his last illness. Objections were filed to the probate of the will on the ground of lack of mental incapacity to make a will. Should the will be admitted to probate?

6. For 36 years Ward Duchett lived in Washington, D.C., with his sister Mary in her home. On numerous occasions Mary had promised Ward she would leave him her real estate if he remained single and continued to live with her. At age 60 Mary became seriously ill and was put in a hospital. Three weeks later, her sister Maude, who was a nurse in Philadelphia, came to Washington and took Mary home even though her doctors advised against it and she did not ask to be taken home. Maude took complete charge of Mary, repeatedly prevented other relatives, including Ward, from seeing Mary, and told them she was doing it on doctor's orders. That statement was false. Mary was in a very weak physical condition, sometimes could recognize people only by their voices, and could not sit up or carry on a conversation. Maude secretly arranged for a lawyer to come and prepare a will, which was quickly executed. It left everything to Maude in "consideration of her kindness, untiring devotion and personal service to me during my illness when no other relative offered or came to do for me, and without hope of reward." The will was witnessed by the lawyer and by a cousin who was very close to Maude. Mary died the next day. There was no evidence that Mary had previously felt any ill will toward any of her relatives. Ward moves to set the will aside. Should the will be set aside?

7. In 1937, a testator died leaving a will executed in 1928 in which the bulk of his estate was in trust. The will provided that the trust was to continue during the lifetime of his two sons, Orin Byers and Clifford W. Byers. On the death of either son, if they were survived "by children lawfully begotten of their bodies," the children were to share equally their father's share. If a son died without "leaving surviving children begotten of his body," the trust was to be kept intact until the death of the other son and then divided "among children of said sons who survive him." Orin died in 1941. Clifford died in 1961 leaving a legitimate daughter, Guineveve, and an illegitimate son, Raymond. Both were living when the testator died. Raymond brought an action claiming he was entitled to a half interest in trust. Should his claim be granted?

Commercial Paper

PART SEVEN

Negotiable Instruments

38

Introduction

W hen you go to a store to buy a television set and give the merchant a check drawn on your checking account, you are using a form of negotiable commercial paper. Similarly, you might go to a bank or a credit union to borrow money and sign a promissory note agreeing to pay the money back in 90 days. Again, you are using a form of negotiable commercial paper.

Commercial paper is basically a *contract for the payment of money*. It commonly is used as a substitute for money and can also be used as a means of extending credit. When you buy a television set by giving the merchant a check, you are using the check as a substitute for money. The use of commercial paper as a means of extending credit is illustrated in the other example where you borrow money by signing a promissory note. There the credit union is willing to give you money now in exchange for your promise to repay it later on certain terms.

There are two basic types of commercial paper: *promises* to pay money and *orders* to pay money. *Notes* and *certificates of deposit* issued by banks are promises to pay someone a sum of money. *Drafts and checks* are orders to another person to pay a sum of money to a third person. A check is an order directed to a bank to pay money from a person's account to a third person.

The law of commercial paper is covered in Article 3 (Commercial Paper) and Article 4 (Bank Deposits and Collections) of the Uniform Commercial Code.

Negotiability

Commercial paper that is *negotiable* or a *negotiable instrument* is a special kind of commercial paper. If commercial paper is negotiable, it can pass readily through our financial system and be accepted in place of money. This has many advantages.

For example, Sam, the owner of a clothing store in New York, contracts with Amanda, a swimsuit manufacturer in Los Angeles, for $10,000 worth of swimsuits. If negotiable instruments did not exist, Sam would have to send or carry $10,000 across the country, which would be inconvenient and risky as well. If the money were stolen along the way, Sam would lose the $10,000 unless he could locate the thief. By using a check in which Sam orders his bank to pay $10,000 from his account to Amanda, or to someone designated by Amanda, Sam can make the payment in a very convenient manner. He has sent only a single piece of paper to Amanda. If the check is properly prepared and sent, it is less risky than sending money. If it is stolen along the way, Sam's bank may not pay it to anyone but Amanda or someone authorized by Amanda. And because Amanda has the right to either collect the $10,000 or transfer the right to collect it to someone else, the check is a practical substitute for cash to Amanda as well.

In this chapter, and in the three chapters that follow, we will discuss the requirements that are necessary for a contract to qualify as a negotiable instrument. We will also explain the features that distinguish a negotiable instrument from a contract and lead to its widespread use as a substitute for money.

KINDS OF COMMERCIAL PAPER

Promissory Notes

The *promissory note* is the simplest form of commercial paper; it is simply a promise to pay money. In a promissory note, one person (known as the *maker*) makes an unconditional promise in writing to pay another person (the *payee*), or a person specified by the payee, a specified sum of money either on demand or at some particular time in the future (see Figure 38–1).

FIGURE 38–1
Example of a Promissory Note

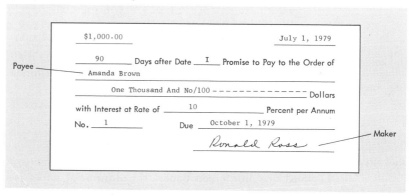

FIGURE 38–2

Example of a Promissory Note (Consumer Loan Note)

The National BANK OF WASHINGTON

CONSUMER LOAN NOTE

Date November 21 , 19 80

The words I and me mean all borrowers who signed this note. The word bank means The National Bank of Washington.

Promise to Pay

30 months from today, I promise to pay to The National Bank of Washington Seventy-Eight Hundred Seventy-Five and no/100 -------------- dollars ($ 7,875.00).

Responsibility

Although this note may be signed below by more than one person, I understand that we are each as individuals responsible for paying back the full amount.

Breakdown of Loan

This is what I will pay:

Amount of loan	1.$	6,800.00
Credit Life Insurance (optional)	2.$	100.00
Other (describe)	3.$	-0-
Amount Financed (Add 1 and 2 and 3)	4.$	6,900.00
FINANCE CHARGE	5.$	975.00
Total of Payments (Add 4 and 5)	$	7,875.00

ANNUAL PERCENTAGE RATE 10.5 %

Repayment

This is how I will repay:
I will repay the amount of this note in 30 equal uninterrupted monthly installments of $ 262.50 each on the 1st day of each month starting on the 1st day of December , 19 80 , and ending on May 1, , 19 83 .

Prepayment

I have the right to prepay the whole outstanding amount of this note at any time. If I do, or if this loan is refinanced—that is, replaced by a new note—you will refund the unearned finance charge, figured by the rule of 78—a commonly used formula for figuring rebates on installment loans.

Late Charge

Any installment not paid within ten days of its due date shall be subject to a late charge of 5% of the payment, not to exceed $5.00 for any such late installment.

Security

To protect The National Bank of Washington, I give what is known as a security interest in my auto and/or other: (Describe) Ford Thunderbird
Serial #115117-12-11974

See the security agreement.

Credit Life Insurance

Credit life insurance is not required to obtain this loan. The bank need not provide it and I do not need to buy it unless I sign immediately below. The cost of credit life insurance is $ 100.00 for the term of the loan.

Signed: A. J. Smith

Date: November 21,1980

Default

If for any reason I fail to make any payment on time, I shall be in default. The bank can then demand immediate payment of the entire remaining unpaid balance of this loan, without giving anyone further notice. If I have not paid the full amount of the loan when the final payment is due, the bank will charge me interest on the unpaid balance at six percent (6%) per year.

Right of Offset

If this loan becomes past due, the bank will have the right to pay this loan from any deposit or security I have at this bank without telling me ahead of time. Even if the bank gives me an extension of time to pay this loan, I still must repay the entire loan.

Collection Fees

If this note is placed with an attorney for collection, then I agree to pay an attorney's fee of fifteen percent (15%) of the unpaid balance. This fee will be added to the unpaid balance of the loan.

Co-borrowers

If I am signing this note as a co-borrower, I agree to be equally responsible with the borrower for this loan. The bank does not have to notify me that this note has not been paid. The bank can change the terms of payment and release any security without notifying or releasing me from responsibility for this loan.

Copy Received

I received a completely filled in copy of this note. If I have signed for Credit Life Insurance, I received a copy of the Credit Life Insurance certificate.

Borrower: A. J. Smith
A. J. Smith
3412 Brookdale, S.W., Washington, DC
Address
Co-borrower: Andrea H. Smith
Andrea H. Smith
3412 Brookdale, S.W., Washington, DC
Address
Co-borrower:

Address

CONSUMER CREDIT HOTLINE: If you have any questions, please call us immediately at (202) 624-3450.

NBW437 (Rev. 11-78)

1-Bank's copy   2-File copy   3-Customer's copy

The promissory note is primarily a *credit* instrument. It is used in a wide variety of transactions in which credit is extended. For example, if you purchase an automobile on credit, the dealer will probably have you sign a promissory note for the unpaid balance of the purchase price. Similarly, if you buy a house, the lender who takes a mortgage on the house will have you sign a promissory note for the amount due on the mortgage. The note will probably have a notation on it that it is secured by a mortgage. The terms of payment of your note should correspond with the terms of your sales contract for the purchase of the car or the house. Figure 38–2 shows an example of a consumer loan note.

Certificates of Deposit

The *certificate of deposit* that your bank or savings and loan association may give you when you make a deposit of money is a form of commercial paper. Like the promissory note, the certificate of deposit is a *promise to pay money*. When a bank issues a certificate of deposit (CD), it acknowledges that it has received a deposit of a specific sum of money. It also agrees to pay the owner of the certificate the sum of money plus a stated rate of interest at some time in the future (see Figure 38–3).

FIGURE 38–3
Example of a Certificate of Deposit

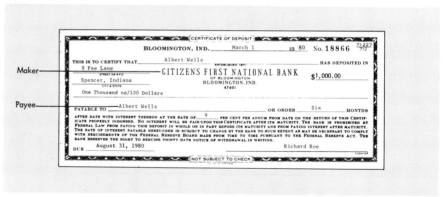

Draft

A *draft* is a form of commercial paper that involves an order to pay money rather than a promise to pay money. The most common example of a draft is a check. A draft has three parties to it: One person (known as the *drawer*) orders a second person (the *drawee*) to pay a certain sum of money to a third person (the *payee*) (see Figure 38–4). Drafts other than checks are used in a variety of commercial transactions. However, they are used much less frequently than checks and our focus in this textbook is primarily on checks.

FIGURE 38–4
Example of a Draft

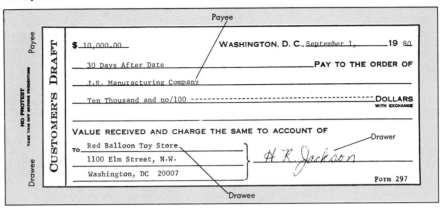

A *check* is a draft on which the *drawee* is always a bank and which is payable *on demand*. It is the most widely used form of commercial paper. By issuing a check, you are ordering the bank at which you maintain an account to pay a specified person, or someone designated by that person, a certain sum of money from your account (see Figure 38–5). For example, Elizabeth Brown has a checking account at the First National Bank. Elizabeth goes to Sears and agrees to buy a washing machine priced at $259.95. If she writes a check to pay for it, she is the drawer of the check, First National Bank is the drawee, and Sears is the payee. By writing the check, Elizabeth is ordering her bank to pay $259.95 from her account to Sears or to whomever Sears asks it to pay the money.

Checks

FIGURE 38–5
Example of a Check

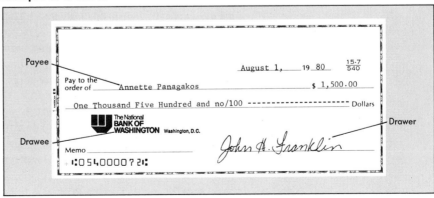

BENEFITS OF NEGOTIABLE INSTRUMENTS

Rights of an Assignee of a Contract

As you may recall from Chapter 13, which discussed the assignment of contracts, the assignee of a contract can obtain no greater rights than the assignor had at the time of the assignment. For example, Mary and Joe enter into a contract which provides that Joe will provide Mary with a dozen fresh eggs a week for a year and Mary will pay Joe $40 at the end of the year. If at the end of the year Joe assigns his right under the contract, including the right to collect the money from Mary, to Sam, then Sam has whatever rights Joe has at that time. If Joe has delivered all the eggs to Mary as he promised, then Joe would be entitled to $40 and Sam would obtain that right from him. However, if Joe had not delivered all the eggs he had promised, or if they were not fresh, then Mary might have a valid "defense" or reason to refuse to pay the full $40. In that case, Sam would have only what rights Joe had and would also be subject to the "defense" Mary has against full payment.

Thus, taking an assignment of a contract involves assuming certain risks. The assignee (Sam) may not be aware of the nature and extent of any defenses the party liable on the contract (Mary) might have against the assignor (Joe). If the assignee does not know for sure what rights he is getting, or what risks he is assuming, he may be reluctant to take an assignment of the contract.

Rights of a Holder of a Negotiable Instrument

The object of commercial paper (a contract for the payment of money) is to have it be accepted readily as a substitute for money. In order for a person to accept it readily, the person must be able to take it free of many of the kinds of risks assumed by the assignee of a regular contract. Under the law of negotiable instruments, this is possible if two conditions are met: (1) the contract for the payment of money must be in the proper form so as to qualify as a "negotiable instrument," and (2) the person who is acquiring the instrument must qualify as a "holder in due course." Basically, a *holder in due course* is a person who has good title to the instrument, paid value for it, acquired it in good faith, and had no notice of any claims or defenses against it.

The proper form for a negotiable instrument will be discussed in the next section of this chapter. The requirements a person must meet to qualify as a holder in due course will be discussed in Chapter 39.

A holder in due course of a negotiable instrument takes the instrument free of all defenses and claims to the instrument except those that concern its validity. For example, a holder in due course of a note given in payment for goods does not have to worry if the buyer is claiming that the seller breached a warranty. However, if a note was written under duress (such as a threat of force) or if the maker of a note was a minor, then even a holder in due course who acquires the note is subject to the defenses of duress or lack of capacity. The person who holds the note could not obtain the payment from the maker but would have to try to recover from the person from whom he or she got the note.

The Federal Trade Commission has adopted some regulations that alter the holder in due course situation. These are designed to allow a *consumer* who gives a negotiable instrument to use *any* defenses against payment of the instrument against even a holder in due course. Similarly some states have enacted the Uniform Consumer Credit Code (U.C.C.C.), which produces a similar result. The rights of a holder in due course will be discussed in more detail in the next chapter.

FORMAL REQUIREMENTS FOR NEGOTIABILITY

Basic Requirements

An instrument, such as a check or a note, must meet certain formal requirements in order to be a "negotiable instrument." If the instrument does not meet these requirements, it is nonnegotiable; that is, it is treated as a simple contract and not as a negotiable instrument. A primary purpose for these formal requirements is so that prospective purchasers of the instrument, particularly financial institutions such as banks, will be willing to accept the instrument as a substitute for money.

For a promissory note or a certificate of deposit to be negotiable, it must:

1. Be in *writing.*
2. Be *signed* by the *maker.*
3. Contain an *unconditional promise* to pay a *sum certain in money.*
4. Be *payable on demand or at a definite time.*
5. Be *payable to order or to bearer.* (3–104).[1]

For a check or a draft to be negotiable, it must:

1. Be in *writing.*
2. Be *signed* by the *drawer.*
3. Contain an *unconditional order* to pay a *sum certain in money.*
4. Be *payable on demand or at a definite time.*
5. Be *payable to order or to bearer.* (3–104).

Importance of Form

Whether or not an instrument is drafted so that it satisfies these formal requirements is important for only one purpose, that is, for determining whether the instrument is negotiable or nonnegotiable. Negotiability should not be confused with validity or collectibility. If the instrument is negotiable, the law of negotiable instruments in the Code controls in determining the rights and liabilities of the parties to the instrument. If the instrument is nonnegotiable, the general rules of contract law control. The purpose of determining negotiability is to determine whether a possessor of the instrument can become a holder in due course.

---

[1] The numbers in parentheses refer to the sections of the Uniform Commercial Code, 1972, which is reproduced in the Appendix.

An instrument that fills all the formal requirements is a negotiable instrument even though it is void, voidable, unenforceable, or uncollectible. Negotiability is a matter of form and nothing else. Suppose a person gives an instrument in payment of a gambling debt in a state that has a statute declaring that any instrument or promise given in payment of a gambling debt is null and void. The instrument is a negotiable instrument if it is negotiable in form even though it is absolutely void. Also, an instrument that is negotiable in form is a negotiable instrument even though it is signed by a minor. The instrument is voidable at the option of the minor, but it is negotiable.

IN WRITING AND SIGNED

Writing

To be negotiable, an instrument must be in *writing* and must be *signed* by the maker or the drawer. An instrument that is handwritten, typed, or printed is considered to be in writing (1–201[46]). The writing does not have to be on any particular material; all that is required is that the instrument be in writing. A person could draw a negotiable instrument in pencil on a piece of wrapping paper. It would be poor business practice to do so, but it would meet the statutory requirement that it be in writing.

Signed

An instrument has been signed if the maker or drawer has put a *symbol* on it with the *intention of validating* it (3–401). Normally the maker or drawer signs it by writing his or her name on it; however, this is not required. A person or company may authorize an agent to sign instruments for it. A typed or rubber-stamped signature is sufficient if it was put on the instrument to validate it. A person who cannot write his or her name might make an "X" and have it witnessed by someone else.

UNCONDITIONAL PROMISE OR ORDER

Requirement of a Promise or Order

If an instrument is a note or a certificate of deposit, it must contain an *unconditional promise* to pay or else it cannot be negotiable. Merely acknowledging a debt is not sufficient. For example, indicating "I owe you $100" does not constitute a promise to pay. An IOU in this form is not a negotiable instrument.

If an instrument is a check or a draft, it must contain an *unconditional order*. A simple request to pay as a favor is not sufficient; however, a politely phrased demand can meet the requirement. The language "Pay to the order of _____" is commonly used on checks. This satisfies the requirement that the check contains an order to pay.

Promise or Order Must Be Unconditional

An instrument is not negotiable unless the promise or order is unconditional. For example, a note that provides "I promise to pay to the order of Karl Adams $100 if he replaces the roof on my garage" is not negotiable because it is payable on a condition.

To be negotiable, an instrument must be written so that a person can tell from reading it what the obligations of the parties are. If a note contains a statement, "Payment is subject to the terms of a mortgage dated August 30, 1979," it is not negotiable. In order to determine the rights of the parties on the note, another document—the mortgage—would have to be examined. However, it would not affect the negotiability of a note if it stated simply, "This note is secured by a mortgage dated August 30, 1979." In the latter case, the rights and duties of the parties to the note are not affected by the mortgage. It would not be necessary to examine the mortgage document to determine the rights of the parties to the note.

A check may contain a notation as to the account to be debited without making the check nonnegotiable. For example, a check could contain the notation "payroll account" or "petty cash." On the other hand, if a check states that it is payable only out of a specific fund, it is generally not negotiable. In this case the check is conditioned on there being sufficient funds in the account. Thus it would not be unconditional and could not qualify as a negotiable instrument. This rule does not apply to instruments issued by a government or a government agency. It is permissible for their instruments to contain a provision saying they are payable only out of a particular fund (3–105).

SUM CERTAIN IN MONEY

Sum Certain   The promise or order in an instrument must be to pay a *sum certain in money*. The sum is certain if a person can compute from the information in the instrument the amount that is required to discharge—or pay off—the instrument at any given time.

Sometimes notes contain a clause that provides for the payment of collection fees or attorney's fees in the event of a default on the note. Even though this would make the amount due on default uncertain until the collection or attorney's fees were determined, such a clause does not make the note nonnegotiable (3–106). Business practice justifies the inclusion of such a clause in the instrument.

A. Alport & Sons, Inc. v. Hotel Evans, Inc.
317 N.Y.S.2d 937 (Sup. Ct. N.Y. 1970)

FACTS   Hotel Evans was the maker on a promissory note that contained a promise to pay $1,600 with "interest at bank rates." The holder of the note, A. Alport & Sons, brought a lawsuit to collect on the note. Hotel Evans claimed that the note was not negotiable because it contained an indefinite interest rate.

ISSUE   Was the promissory note that provided for "interest at bank rates" a negotiable instrument?

DECISION	No. The court held that the promissory note was not negotiable. To be negotiable it must contain an unconditional promise to pay a sum certain. Because the note provides for interest at bank rates, the amount due on the note cannot be readily determined and does not qualify as a sum certain.

Payable in Money

The amount specified in the instrument must be payable in *money*, which is a medium of exchange authorized or adopted by a government as part of its currency (1–201[24]). If the person obligated to pay an instrument can do something other than pay money, the instrument is not negotiable. For example, if a note reads "I promise to pay to the order of Sarah Smith, at my option, ten dollars or five bushels of apples, John Jones," the note is not negotiable.

PAYABLE ON DEMAND OR AT A DEFINITE TIME

To be negotiable, an instrument must be payable either on *demand* or at a *specified time* in the future. This is so that the time the instrument will be payable can be determined with some certainty. An instrument that is payable on the happening of some uncertain event is not negotiable (3–109). Thus, a note payable "when my son graduates from college" is not negotiable.

If no time for payment is stated in an instrument, it is considered to be payable on demand. For example, if you forget to state when a note is payable, it is payable immediately at the request of the holder of the note. Because no time for payment is stated on a common check, it is considered to be payable on demand (3–108). However, a postdated check is treated as a "draft" and is not properly payable until the day it is dated. An instrument can be negotiable even though it is undated, postdated, or antedated (3–114).

Under the Code, an instrument may contain a clause permitting the time for payment to be accelerated at the option of the maker. Similarly, it can contain a clause allowing an extension of time at the option of the holder. Both kinds of clauses are allowed as long as the time for payment can be determined with certainty (3–109).

	Smith v. Gentilotti **356 N.E. 2d 953 (Sup. Jud. Ct. Mass. 1977)**
FACTS	In 1964 S. Gentilotti wrote a check for $20,000 payable to the order of his son, Edward J. Gentilotti. He postdated the check November 4, 1984, which would be his son's twentieth birthday. The father also wrote on the check that it should be

paid from his estate if he died prior to November 4, 1984. The father then gave the check to Edward's mother for safekeeping. On May 31, 1972, the father died. The check was then presented for payment but the bank refused to pay it. The mother and the son then brought a lawsuit against the executor of the father's estate to require payment. The executor claimed that the check was not a valid negotiable instrument because it had been postdated.

ISSUE   Can a check be a negotiable instrument if it is postdated 20 years?

DECISION Yes. The court held that the check was a negotiable instrument. The fact a check is postdated does not affect its negotiability. The check is simply payable on the stated date. The words added by the father accelerated the due date and also made it directly payable from his estate.

PAYABLE TO ORDER OR BEARER

To be negotiable an instrument must be payable *to order* or *to bearer*. A check that provides "Pay to the order of Sarah Smith" or "Pay to Sarah Smith or bearer" is negotiable; however, one that provides "Pay to Sarah Smith" is not. The words "Pay to the order of" or "to bearer" show that the drawer of the check (or the maker of a note) intends to issue a negotiable instrument. The drawer or maker is not restricting payment of the instrument to just Sarah Smith but is willing to pay someone else designated by Sarah Smith. This is the essence of negotiability. The original payee of a check or a note can transfer the right to receive payment to someone else. By making the instrument payable "to the order of" or "to bearer," the drawer or maker is giving the payee the chance to negotiate it to another person and to cut off certain defenses the drawer or maker may have against payment of the instrument.

A check that is payable to the order of someone is known as *order paper*. A check payable to bearer is known as *bearer paper*. A check made payable "to the order of cash" is considered to be payable to bearer and is also known as *bearer paper* (3–111). Bearer paper can be negotiated or transferred without indorsement.

An instrument can be made payable to two or more payees. For example, a check could be drawn payable "to the order of John Jones and Henry Smith." Then both John and Henry have to be involved in negotiating it or enforcing payment of it. An instrument can also be payable in the alternative, for example, "to Susan Clark or Betsy Brown." In this case either Susan or Betsy could negotiate or enforce payment of it.

SPECIAL TERMS

Additional Terms   Banks and other businesses sometimes use forms of commercial paper that have been drafted to meet their particular needs. These forms may include terms that do not affect the negotiability of an instrument. Thus a note form may provide for a place of payment without affecting the negotiability. Similarly, insurance reimbursement checks frequently contain a clause on the back stating that the payee, by indorsing or cashing the check, acknowledges full payment of the claim. This clause does not affect the negotiability of the check (3–112).

Ambiguous Terms

Occasionally, you may write a check or receive a check on which the amount written in figures differs from the amount written in words. Or, a note might have conflicting terms or an ambiguous term. Where there is a conflict or an ambiguous term, there are general rules of interpretation applied to resolve the conflict or ambiguity. If there is a conflict between words and figures, the words control the figures. If there is a conflict, the handwritten terms prevail over the printed and typewritten terms, and the typed terms prevail over printed terms (3–118).

If a note provides for the payment of interest, but no interest rate is spelled out, then interest is payable at the judgment rate (the rate of interest imposed on court awards until they are paid by the losing party) at the place of payment.

Newman v. Manufacturer's National Bank
152 N.W.2d 564 (Ct. App. Mich. 1967)

FACTS   In 1955 Newman wrote two checks totaling $1,200 payable to Belle Epstein. There was a printed dateline on the checks which read "Detroit, Michigan _____ 195___" but Newman never filled it in. Newman claimed that over the next four years he paid Belle Epstein all but $400 of the $1,200 he owed her. He also claimed that Epstein told him she had destroyed the checks. However, on April 17, 1964, the checks were cashed after having been indorsed in the name of Belle Epstein. Someone had written in the date "April 16, 1964" but the printed figures "_____ 195___" remained clearly visible. Newman objected to having his checking account charged with the two checks.

ISSUE   Was the bank justified in paying the checks and charging them to Newman's account?

DECISION   Yes. The court held that the bank could charge the checks to Newman's account. A bank may charge a customer's account with any item that is properly payable from the account. When an instrument is dated, the date is presumed to be correct. Here the handwritten date "April 16, 1964" prevails over the printed date "_____ 195___." The bank was justified in believing that the check was dated currently with the day it paid it.

ELECTRONIC BANKING

As a result of computer technology, many banks are encouraging their customers to transfer funds electronically through the use of computers rather than by the use of paper drafts and checks. You may have a specially coded card that can be used at terminals provided by your bank to make deposits to your account, to transfer money from one account (checking or savings) to another, to pay bills, or to withdraw cash from your account.

These new forms of transferring money have raised questions about the legal rules that will be applied to them, and the questions are only beginning to be resolved. In at least one recent court decision, *State of Illinois v. Continental Illinois National Bank*, the court held that a customer's withdrawal from a checking account by using a bank card at an electronic terminal should be treated the same as cashing a check.

State of Illinois v. Continental Illinois National Bank
536 F.2d 176 (7th Cir. 1976)

FACTS Continental Illinois National Bank operated several so-called Customer Bank Communications Terminals (CBCTs), which were unmanned terminals connected directly with Continental's main-office computer. Customers of the bank insert a specially coded card into the terminal, enter an identification number, and then, using keys on the transaction keyboard, indicate the type and amounts of the transactions they wish to conduct. The customers may:

1. Withdraw cash (in the amount of $25 or any multiple thereof, up to $100) from their savings, checking, or credit card accounts.
2. Deposit checks or currency in a checking or savings account. At the time of the transaction, the customer is given a receipt at the CBCT indicating the amount and date of the deposit; it is not credited to his account and he may not draw on it until it is received and verified at the main banking premises.
3. Transfer funds between accounts: checking to savings, credit card to checking, or savings to checking.
4. Make payments on Continental Illinois National Bank installment loans or credit card charges.

When the transactions are completed, the customer receives a receipt and, if he has withdrawn cash from his account, he receives packets containing the cash. A copy of the receipt is retained in the machine and the transactions are later verified by bank employees.

The Illinois State Banking Commissioner brought a lawsuit against Continental seeking a declaratory judgment that the unmanned terminals were branch banks. One issue in the case was whether use of the machine to withdraw money constituted cashing of a check.

ISSUE Does the use of an electronic funds transfer system to withdraw money from an account constitute the cashing of a check?

DECISION Yes. The court held that it was the same as cashing a check. It said that the use of the card in the machine serves the same purpose as a check and is an order to the bank. Any order to pay that is properly executed by the customer, whether it be check, card, or electronic device, should be recognized as the same.

Just as a transfer of funds by cable or telegraph is in law a check, despite the non-negotiability of the cable, the card here for the purpose of withdrawing cash is a check. What must be remembered is that the foundation of the relationship between the bank and its customer is the former's agreement to pay out the customer's money according to the latter's order. There are many ways in which an order may be given and one way of late is by computer.

QUESTIONS AND PROBLEM CASES

1. What is the difference between a check and a promissory note?
2. Is the following instrument a note, a check, or a draft? Why? If it is not a check, how would you have to change it to make it a check?

> TO: Arthur Adams   January 1, 1974
> TEN DAYS AFTER DATE PAY TO THE ORDER OF: Bernie Brown
> THE SUM OF: Ten and no/100 Dollars.
> SIGNED: Carl Clark

3. Sarah sells $5,000 worth of toys to Ralph. Ralph offers to either sign a contract obligating him to pay Sarah $5,000 or sign a negotiable promissory note for $5,000 payable to the order of Sarah. Would you advise Sarah to ask for the contract or the promissory note? Explain.
4. Wiley, Tate & Irby, buyers and sellers of used cars, sold several autos to Houston Auto Sales. Houston wrote out the order for payment for each group of cars on the outside of several envelopes. He signed them and they were drawn on his bank, Peoples Bank & Trust Co., to be paid on the demand of Wiley, Tate & Irby. Can the envelopes qualify as negotiable instruments?
5. Is the following a negotiable instrument?

> I.O.U. A. Gay, the sum of seventeen 5/100 dollars for value received.
> John R. Rooke

6. Is the following a negotiable instrument?

> February 26, 1973
> Subject to Approval of Title
> Pay to the Order of Vernon Butterfield $1,997.90.
> The Culver Company
> By A. M. Culver

7. Is the following instrument negotiable?

> Marshall, Ill., July 18, 1968 No. 112
> The Dulaney National Bank 70–559
> Pay to the order of C. A. Libs $9,200.00
> Nine Thousand Two Hundred Dollars
> Agent's disbursing account.
> Roy F. Keown

8. Sylvia signed a note dated May 25, 1963, obligating her to pay to Ferri or to his order $3,000 "within ten (10) years after date." Is this a negotiable instrument?
9. Nation-Wide Check Corporation sold money orders to drugstores. The money orders contained the statement "Payable to" followed by a blank. Can the money order qualify as a negotiable instrument?
10. Louis Canino signed the following instrument:

> No. 922B.   INSTALLMENT NOTE
>
> $27,000.   March 11, 1970
> LOUIS G. CANINO for value received, does promise to pay to the order of CARL

MEES the sum of Two Hundred Twenty-Five . . . Dollars at Lakewood, Colorado, said principal payable on the first day of each and every month commencing April 1, 1970 with interest at the rate of 8 percent per annum.

/s/ Louis G. Canino

When Mees sued Canino on the note, Canino argued that the word "Two Hundred Twenty-Five Dollars" should control the figures "$27,000" and that he was obligated to pay only $225. Is this a valid argument?

Negotiation and Holder in Due Course

39

Nature of Negotiation

When you write your name on the back of a check made out to you and cash it at the grocery store, you have negotiated the check to the grocery store. Your signature on the back of the check is called an *indorsement*. *Negotiation* is the transfer of an instrument in such a way that the person who receives it becomes a holder. A *holder* is a person who is in *possession* of an instrument (1) that was *issued to him*, (2) that has been *indorsed to him or to his order*, or (3) that is *payable to bearer* (1–201[20]).[1]

Formal Requirements for Negotiation

The formal requirements for negotiation are very simple. If an instrument is payable to order, it is called *order paper* and it can be negotiated by delivery of the instrument after any necessary indorsements are added to it (3–202[1]). For example, if Rachel's father gives her a check payable "to the order of Rachel Stern," then Rachel can negotiate the check by indorsing her name on the back of the check and giving it to the person to whom she wants to transfer it.

If an instrument is payable to bearer or to cash, it is called *bearer paper* and negotiating it is even simpler. If someone gives you a check that is made payable "to the order of cash," it can be negotiated simply by giving

---

[1] The numbers in parentheses refer to the sections of the Uniform Commercial Code, 1972, which is reproduced in the Appendix.

it to the person to whom you wish to transfer it. No indorsement is necessary to negotiate an instrument payable to bearer. However, the person who takes the instrument may ask for an indorsement for his or her protection. By indorsing the check, you agree to be liable for its payment to that person if it is not paid by the drawee bank when it is presented for payment. This liability will be discussed in the next chapter.

Nature of Indorsement

An indorsement is made by adding the signature of the holder of the instrument to the instrument, usually on the back of it (3–202[2]). The signature can be put there either by the holder or by someone who is authorized to sign on behalf of the holder. For example, a check payable to "H&H Meat Market" might be indorsed "H&H Meat Market by Jane Frank, President" if Jane is authorized to do this on behalf of the market.

Wrong or Misspelled Name. When you indorse an instrument, you should spell your name the same way as it appears on the instrument. If your name is misspelled or wrong, then legally you can indorse either in your name or in the name that is on the instrument. However, any person who pays the instrument or otherwise gives you something of value for it may require you to sign both names (3–203).

Suppose Joan Ash is issued a check payable to the order of "Joanne Ashe." She may indorse the check as either "Joan Ash" or "Joanne Ashe." However, if she takes the check to a bank to cash, the bank may require her to sign both "Joanne Ashe" and "Joan Ash."

Agaliotis v. Agaliotis
247 S.E.2d 28 (Ct. App. N.C. 1978)

FACTS Louis Agaliotis took out a policy of insurance on his son, Robert. Louis paid all the premiums on the policy and under the terms of the policy was entitled to any refunds on the premiums. The insurance company sent a refund check for $1,852 to Louis. By mistake the check was made payable to "Robert L. Agaliotis." Louis indorsed the check "Robert L. Agaliotis" and cashed it. His son Robert then sued Louis to get the $1,852.

ISSUE Was Louis entitled to sign his son's name to the check and to keep the money he got when he cashed it?

DECISION Yes. The court held that Louis properly indorsed the check and kept the proceeds. Under the terms of the insurance policy, he was entitled to the refund. The insurance company made a mistake in making the check payable to Robert rather than to Louis. When a check is made out to a person with a misspelled or incorrect name, the person may indorse the check (1) in the incorrect or misspelled name, (2) in his own name, or (3) in both names. Here Louis indorsed the check in the incorrect name, which he was entitled to do.

Indorsements by a Depositary Bank. When a customer deposits a check to his or her account with a bank and forgets to indorse the check, the bank normally has the right to supply the customer's indorsement (4–205). The only time the bank does not have the right to put the customer's indorsement on a check the customer has deposited is when the check specifically requires the payee's signature. Insurance and government checks commonly require the payee's signature. Instead of actually signing the customer's name to the check as the indorsement, the bank may just stamp on it that it was deposited by the customer or credited to his or her account.

INDORSEMENTS

Effects of an Indorsement

There are two aspects to an indorsement. First, an indorsement is necessary in order for there to be a negotiation of an instrument that is payable to the order of someone. Thus, if a check is payable to the order of James Lee, James must indorse it before it can be negotiated. The form of the indorsement James uses will also affect future attempts to negotiate the instrument. For example, if James indorses it "Pay to the order of Sarah Hill," Sarah must indorse it before it can be negotiated further.

The second aspect of an indorsement is that it generally makes a person liable on the instrument. By indorsing an instrument, a person makes a contractual promise to pay the instrument if the person primarily liable on it (for example, the "maker" of a note) does not pay it. The contractual liability of indorsers will be discussed in Chapter 40. In this chapter the discussion will be limited to the effect of an indorsement on further negotiation of an instrument.

Kinds of Indorsements

There are four basic kinds of indorsements: (1) special, (2) blank, (3) restrictive, and (4) qualified.

Special Indorsement. A *special indorsement* contains the signature of the indorser along with words indicating to whom, or to whose order,

FIGURE 39–1
Example of a Special Indorsement

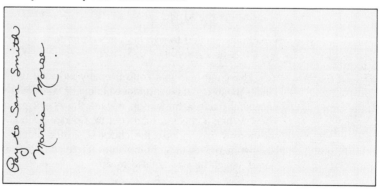

the instrument is payable. For example, if a check drawn "Pay to the Order of Marcia Morse" is indorsed by Marcia "Pay to the Order of Sam Smith, Marcia Morse" or "Pay to Sam Smith, Marcia Morse," it has been indorsed with a special indorsement (see Figure 39–1). An instrument that is indorsed with a special indorsement remains order paper. It can be negotiated only with the indorsement of the person specified (3–204[1]). In this example, Sam Smith must indorse the check before it can be negotiated to someone else.

Blank Indorsement.   If an indorser merely signs his or her name and does not specify to whom the instrument is payable, the instrument has been indorsed *in blank.* For example, if a check drawn "Pay to the Order of Natalie Owens" is indorsed "Natalie Owens" by Natalie, it has been indorsed in blank (see Figure 39–2). An instrument indorsed in blank is payable to the bearer (person in possession of it). As you should recall, this means the check is bearer paper. As such, it can be negotiated by delivery alone and no further indorsement is necessary for negotiation (3–204[2]).

If Natalie indorsed the check in blank and gave it to Kevin Foley, Kevin would have the right to convert the blank indorsement into a special indorsement (3–204[3]). He could do this by writing the words "Pay to the Order of Kevin Foley" over Natalie's indorsement. Then the check would have to be indorsed by Kevin before it could be further negotiated.

If you take a check indorsed in blank to a bank and present it for payment or for collection, the bank normally asks you to indorse the check. It does this not because it needs an indorsement for the check to be negotiated to it; the check indorsed in blank can be negotiated merely by delivering it to the bank cashier. Rather, the bank asks for your indorsement because it wants to make you liable on the check if it is not paid when the bank sends it to the drawee bank for payment. The liability of indorsers will be discussed in the next chapter.

FIGURE 39–2
Example of a Blank Indorsement

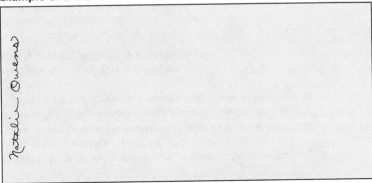

Restrictive Indorsement.   A restrictive indorsement is one that specifies the purpose of the indorsement or specifies the use to be made of the instrument. The most common example of a restrictive indorsement is when you indorse a check "For Deposit Only" or "For Deposit to My Account at _____ Bank" (see Figure 39–3). Other examples include: "Pay to Arthur Attorney in Trust for Mark Minor," "Pay to Carl Clark Only," and "Pay to Bernard Builder Only If He Completes Construction on My House by November 1, 1982." A similar restriction by a maker or drawer would destroy the negotiability of the instrument; however, indorsers are permitted to so limit payment.

A restrictive indorsement does not prevent further negotiation of an instrument (3–206[1]). However, the person who takes an instrument with a restrictive indorsement must pay or apply any money or other thing of value he or she gives for the instrument consistently with the indorsement. Suppose a person takes a check payable to "Arthur Attorney in trust for Mark Minor." The money given for the check should be put in Mark Minor's trust account. A person would not be justified in taking the check in exchange for a television set he knew Attorney was acquiring for his own—rather than Minor's—use.

FIGURE 39–3
Example of a Restrictive Indorsement

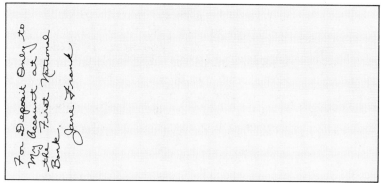

O.K. Moving & Storage Co. v. Elgin National Bank
363 So.2d 160 (Dist. Ct. App. Fla. 1978)

FACTS   Raye Walker was a bookkeeper for O.K. Moving & Storage Co. She opened a checking account in her name at Elgin National Bank. She then took checks that were made payable to O.K. Moving & Storage and indorsed them "For Deposit Only, O.K. Moving & Storage Co., 80 Carson Drive, N.E., Fort Walton, Florida" and deposited them in her individual account at Elgin National Bank. In a period of one year she deposited, and Elgin Bank accepted for deposit to her account, checks totaling $19,356.01. When O.K. Moving & Storage discovered this, it sued Elgin Bank for $19,356.01 for conversion of its checks.

ISSUE   Could checks restrictively indorsed "For Deposit Only" to a corporation's account be deposited to an individual account?

DECISION   No. The court held that Elgin Bank had to repay O.K. Moving & Storage for all the restrictively indorsed checks payable to it which the bank had deposited to Raye Walker's account. The bank has a duty to pay the check only as ordered by the payee. Here the payee—O.K. Moving & Storage—had authorized payment of the money as a deposit to its account. Elgin Bank did not follow these instructions.

Qualified Indorsement. A qualified indorsement is one where the indorser disclaims his or her liability to make the instrument good if the maker or drawer defaults on it. Words such as "Without Recourse" are used to qualify an indorsement (see Figure 39–4). They can be used with either a blank or a special indorsement and thus make it a qualified blank or a qualified special indorsement. The use of a qualified indorsement does not change the negotiable nature of the instrument. Its effect is to eliminate the contractual liability of the indorser. This liability will be discussed in Chapter 40.

FIGURE 39–4
Example of a Qualified Indorsement

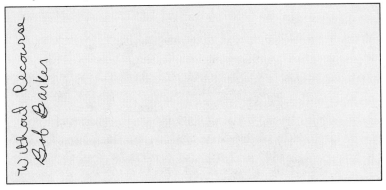

HOLDER IN DUE COURSE

A person who qualifies as a holder in due course of a negotiable instrument gets special rights. Normally, the transferee of an instrument—like the assignee of a contract—gets only those rights in the instrument that the person has from whom he or she got the instrument. But a holder in due course can get better rights. Before going further into the advantages of being a holder in due course, we will develop the requirements for becoming a holder in due course.

General Requirements

In order to become a *holder in due course*, a person who takes a negotiable instrument must be a *holder*, and take the instrument for *value*, in *good faith*, *without notice* that is *overdue* or has been *dishonored*, and *without notice* of any *defense against it* or *claim to it* (3–302). If a person who takes a negotiable instrument does not meet these requirements, he or she is not a holder in due course. Then the person is in the same position as an assignee of a contract.

Holder

To be a *holder* of a negotiable instrument, a person must have possession of an instrument that is properly indorsed and delivered to him or her. For example, if Teresa Gonzales is given a check by her grandmother that is made payable "to the order of Teresa Gonzales," Teresa is a holder of the check because it is made out to her. If Teresa indorses the check "Pay to the order of Ames Grocery, Teresa Gonzales" and gives it to Ames Grocery in payment for some groceries, then Ames Grocery is the holder of the check. Ames Grocery is a holder because it is in possession of a check that is indorsed to its order. If Ames Grocery indorses the check "Ames Grocery" and deposits it in its account at First National Bank, the bank becomes the holder. The bank is in possession of an instrument that is indorsed in blank.

It is important that all indorsements on the instrument at the time it is payable to the order of someone are *authorized indorsements*. A forged indorsement is not an effective indorsement and prevents a person from becoming a holder.

To be a holder, a person must have a complete chain of authorized indorsements. Suppose the U.S. government mails an income tax refund check made out to Robert Washington to him. Tom Turner steals the check from Washington's mailbox, signs (indorses) "Robert Washington" on the back of the check, and cashes it at a shoe store. The shoe store could not be a holder of the check because it does not have a good chain of authorized indorsements. The check has to be indorsed by Robert Washington in order for there to be a valid chain of indorsements. The signature by Turner is not effective for this purpose because Washington did not authorize him to sign Washington's name to the check.

Watkins v. Sheriff of Clark County
453 P.2d 611 (Sup. Ct. Nev. 1969)

FACTS   Mrs. Reggie Bluiett worked at the Silver Slipper Gambling Hall and Saloon. She received her weekly paycheck made out to her from the Silver Slipper. She indorsed the check in blank and left it on her dresser at home. Freddie Watkins broke into Reggie's house and stole the check. Freddie took the check to the local auto store, where he bought two tires at a cost of $71.21. He obtained the balance of the check in cash.

ISSUE   Could the auto store qualify as a holder of the check?

DECISION   Yes. The court held that the auto store could qualify as a holder. Because Mrs. Bluiett had indorsed the check in blank, it was bearer paper and could be negotiated merely by delivery. When the check was delivered to the auto store it became a holder. It was in possession of an instrument payable to bearer.

For Value

To qualify as a holder in due course of a negotiable instrument, a person must give *value* for it. A person who gets a check as a gift or merely makes an executory promise has not given value for it and thus cannot qualify as a holder in due course. If, for example, Ace Appliance takes a check in payment for a refrigerator and delivers the refrigerator to the person who gave it the check, Ace has given value for the check.

Good Faith

To qualify as a holder in due course of a negotiable instrument, a person must take it in *good faith*, which means that the person obtained it honestly (1–201[19]). If a person obtains a check by trickery or with knowledge that it has been stolen, the person has not obtained the check in good faith and cannot be a holder in due course. A person who pays too little for an instrument, perhaps because he or she suspects something may be wrong with the way it was obtained, may have trouble meeting the good faith test. Suppose a finance company works closely with a door-to-door sales company that engages in shoddy practices. If the finance company buys the consumers' notes from the sales company, it will not be able to meet the good faith test and qualify as a holder in due course of the notes.

Overdue and Dishonored

In order to qualify as a holder in due course, a person must take a negotiable instrument before he or she has notice that it either is *overdue* or has been *dishonored*. The reason for this is that obligations are generally performed when they are due. If a negotiable instrument is not paid when it is due, this is considered to put the person taking it on notice that there may be defenses to the payment of it.

If a negotiable instrument due on a certain date is not paid by that day, then it is overdue at the beginning of the next day after the due date. For example, if a promissory note dated January 1 is payable "30 days after date," it is due on January 31. If it is not paid by January 31, it is overdue beginning on February 1.

If a negotiable instrument is payable on demand, a person must acquire it within a reasonable time after it was issued. A reasonable time for presenting a check is presumed to be 30 days (3–304[3][c]). Thus, a person who acquires a check 60 days after the date it is dated is probably taking it after it is overdue.

In determining when a demand note is overdue, business practices and the facts of the particular case must be considered. In a farming community, the normal period for loans to farmers may be six months. A demand note might be outstanding for six or seven months before it is considered overdue. On the other hand, a demand note issued in an industrial city where the normal period of such loans is 30 to 60 days would be considered overdue in a much shorter period of time.

To be a holder in due course, a person not only must take a negotiable instrument before he has notice that it is overdue but must also take it before it has been dishonored. A negotiable instrument has been *dishonored* when it has been presented for payment and payment has been refused.

For example, Susan writes a check on her account at First National Bank that is payable "to the order of Sven Sorensen." Sven takes the check to First National Bank to cash it but the bank refuses to pay it because Susan has insufficient funds in her account to cover it. The check has been dishonored. If Sven then takes Susan's check to Harry's Hardware and uses it to pay for some paint, Harry's could not be a holder in due course of the check if it is on notice that it had been dishonored. It would have such notice if First National stamped it "Payment Refused NSF" (not sufficient funds).

Similarly, suppose Carol Carson signs a 30-day note payable to Ace Appliance for $100 and gives it to Ace as payment for a stereo set. When Ace asks Carol for payment, she refuses to pay because the stereo does not work properly. If Ace negotiates the note to First National Bank, First National cannot be a holder in due course if it knows about Carol's refusal to pay.

Notice of Defenses

To qualify as a holder in due course, a person must also acquire a negotiable instrument without notice that there are any defenses or adverse claims to it. For example, you cannot be a holder in due course of a check (or other negotiable instrument) if some important or *material term* is blank. If someone gives you a check that has been signed but the space where the amount of the check is to be written has been left blank, then you cannot be a holder in due course of that check. The fact that a material term is blank puts you on notice that the drawer may have a defense to payment of it. To be material, the omitted term must be one that affects the legal obligation of the parties to the negotiable instrument. Material terms include the amount of the instrument and the name of the payee. If a negotiable instrument is completed after it was signed but before you acquire it, you can qualify as a holder in due course if you had no knowledge about the completion.

If there is something apparently wrong with a negotiable instrument, such as an obvious alteration in the amount, then it is considered to be *irregular paper*. If you take an irregular instrument, you are considered to be on notice of any possible defenses to it. For example, Kevin writes a check for "one dollar" payable to Karen. Karen inserts the word "hundred" in the amount, changes the figure "$1" to "$100," and gives it to a druggist in exchange for a purchase of goods. If the alterations in the amount should be obvious to the druggist, perhaps because there are erasures, different handwriting, or different ink, then the druggist cannot be a holder in due course. She would have taken irregular paper and would be considered to be on notice that there might be defenses to it. These defenses include Kevin's defense that he is liable for only $1 because that is the amount for which he made the check out.

Nationwide Acceptance Corp. v. Henne
194 So.2d 434 (App. Ct. La. 1967)

FACTS Two smooth-talking salesmen for the Rich Plan of New Orleans called on Leona and George Henne at their home. They sold the Hennes a home food plan. One of the salesmen suggested that the Hennes sign a blank promissory note. The Hennes refused. The salesman then wrote in ink "$100" as the amount and "4" as the number of installments in which the note was to be paid. The Hennes then signed the note. Several days later the Hennes received a payment book from Nationwide Acceptance. The payment book showed that a total of $843.38 was due, payable in 36 monthly installments. Rich Plan had erased the "$100" and "4" on the note and typed in the figures "$843.38" and "36." The erasures were cleverly done but were visible to the naked eye. Rich Plan then negotiated the Hennes' note to Nationwide Acceptance. The Hennes refused to pay the note. Nationwide claimed that it was a holder in due course and was entitled to receive payment.

ISSUE Was Nationwide Acceptance a holder in due course?

DECISION No. The court ruled that Nationwide was not a holder in due course. The note was not regular on its face because of the obvious alteration. The note was irregular paper. A person who takes a negotiable instrument that is irregular cannot be a holder in due course.

A person cannot qualify as a holder in due course of a negotiable instrument if he or she is aware that the obligation of a party to it is voidable. Thus if you know that a signature on the instrument was obtained by fraud, misrepresentation, or duress, you cannot be a holder in due course. If you know that the instrument has already been paid, you cannot become a holder in due course. Of course, the best way for the person who is liable on an instrument to be protected is to mark it "paid" or "canceled" when he or she pays it.

One other situation in which a person may be considered to be on notice of defenses is if he or she is taking a negotiable instrument from a fiduciary such as a trustee. If a negotiable instrument is payable to a person as a trustee or an attorney for someone, then any attempt by that person to negotiate it for his own behalf or for his or her use (or benefit) puts the person on notice that the beneficiary of the trust may have a claim (3–304[2]).

For example, a check is drawn "Pay to the order of Arthur Adams, Trustee for Mary Minor." Adams takes the check to Ace Appliance Store, indorses his name to it, and uses it to purchase a television set for himself. Ace Appliance cannot be a holder in due course because it should know that the negotiation of the check is in violation of the fiduciary duty Adams owes to Mary Minor. Ace should know this because Adams is negotiating the check for his own benefit, not Mary's.

RIGHTS OF A HOLDER IN DUE COURSE

Importance of Being a Holder in Due Course

In the preceding chapter, you learned that the advantage of negotiable instruments over other kinds of contracts is that they are accepted as substitutes for money. People are willing to accept them as substitutes for money because generally they can take them free of claims or defenses to payment between the original parties to the instrument. On the other hand, a person who takes an assignment of a simple contract gets only the same rights as the person had who assigned the contract.

There are two qualifications to the ability of a person who acquires a negotiable instrument to be free of claims or defenses between the original parties. First, the person who acquires the negotiable instrument must be a holder in due course. If the person is not, then he or she is subject to all claims or defenses to payment that any party to it has. Second, the only claims or defenses the holder in due course has to worry about are so-called *real defenses*—those that affect the validity of the instrument. For example, if the maker or drawer did not have legal capacity because she was a minor, the maker or drawer has a real defense. The holder in due course does not have to worry about so-called personal defenses.

Personal Defenses

The basic rule of negotiable instruments law is that a holder in due course of a negotiable instrument is not subject to any personal (or limited) defenses or claims that may exist between the original parties to the instrument (3–305). *Personal defenses* include things like breach of warranty, misrepresentation, fraud in the inducement of any underlying contract, or any failure of consideration.

The type of fraud that is a personal defense is known as *fraud in the inducement.* For example, an art dealer sells a lithograph to Cheryl, telling her that it is a Picasso, and takes Cheryl's check for $500 in payment. The art dealer knows the lithograph is not a genuine Picasso but rather is a forgery. Cheryl has been induced to make the purchase and to give her check by the art dealer's fraudulent representation. Because of this fraud, Cheryl has a personal defense against having to honor her check to the art dealer.

The following example illustrates the limited extent to which a maker or drawer can use personal defenses as a reason for not paying a negotiable instrument he signed. Suppose Trent Tucker bought a used truck from Honest Harry's and gave Harry a 60-day promissory note for $750 in payment for the truck. Honest Harry's "guaranteed" the truck to be in "good working condition," but in fact the truck had a cracked engine block. If Harry tries to collect the $750 from Trent, Trent could claim breach of warranty as a reason for not paying Harry the full $750 because Harry is not a holder in due course. However, if Harry negotiated the note to First National Bank and the bank was a holder in due course, the situation would be changed. If the bank tried to collect the $750 from Trent, Trent would have to pay the bank. Trent's defense or claim of breach of warranty cannot be used as a reason for not paying a holder in due course. It is a personal defense and cannot be used against the bank. Trent must pay the bank the $750 and then pursue his breach of warranty claim against Harry.

The rule that a holder in due course takes a negotiable instrument free of any personal defenses or claims to it has been modified to some extent, particularly in relation to instruments given by consumers. These modifications will be discussed in the next section of this chapter.

Real Defenses

There are some claims and defenses to payment of an instrument that apply to the validity of the instrument. These claims and defenses are known as *real* (or universal) *defenses.* They can be used as reasons against payment of a negotiable instrument even if the person who requests payment is a holder in due course.

Two common examples of real defenses are (1) incapacity of a person to execute a negotiable instrument, and (2) duress or any other illegality that nullifies the obligation of a party liable to pay the instrument. If Mark Miller, age 17, signs a promissory note as maker, he can use his lack of capacity to contract as a defense against paying it even to a holder in due course. Similarly, if Harold points a gun at his grandmother and forces her to execute a promissory note, the grandmother can use duress as a defense against paying it even to a holder in due course.

Another example of a real defense is *fraud in the essence*. This occurs where a person signs a negotiable instrument without knowing or having a reasonable chance to realize that it is a negotiable instrument. For example, Amy Jones is an illiterate person who lives alone. She signs a document that is actually a promissory note but she is told it is a grant of permission for a television set to be left in her house on a trial basis. Amy has a real defense against payment on the note. She does not have to pay the note to even a holder in due course. Fraud in the essence is distinguished from fraud in the inducement discussed earlier, which is only a personal defense.

Real defenses can be asserted even against a holder in due course of a negotiable instrument because it is more desirable to protect people who have signed negotiable instruments in these situations than it is to protect persons who have taken negotiable instruments in the ordinary course of business.

Reading Trust Co. v. Hutchinson
35 Pa. D&C.2d 790 (Ct. of Common Pleas Pa. 1964)

FACTS   A representative of Gracious Living, Inc., called on the Hutchinsons and identified himself as a "demonstrator" of water-softening equipment. After explaining the cost of the equipment, he told the Hutchinsons that Gracious Living would install it for a four-month trial. In return the Hutchinsons were to give him a list of their friends and neighbors and permit a demonstration in their house. They were to receive a bonus if sales were made to any of their friends and neighbors. The Hutchinsons claimed that the man "asked them to sign a form which he could show to his boss to prove he had made the demonstration and also as a bond to cover the unit while it was on the Hutchinson's property." They signed the form.

Later the Hutchinsons received a payment book from the Reading Trust Company. They then realized they had been tricked into signing a contract and a note. Hutchinson was a high school graduate and his wife had completed her junior year in high school. Both could read and write the English language. Reading Trust had obtained the note from Gracious Living. It had no notice of Gracious Living's business practice and was a holder in due course. The Hutchinsons refused to pay the note and Reading Trust sued them to collect on it.

ISSUE   Did the Hutchinsons have a "real defense" they could use against the Reading Trust Company even though it was a holder in due course?

DECISION   No. The court held that the Hutchinsons did not have a valid real defense. The court said this was not the kind of situation where a person could justify being "tricked" into signing a negotiable instrument in a belief that it was another document. The court said the ignorance was not excusable in this case. The court felt the Hutchinsons were capable of reading the documents and should have done so before signing them.

CHANGES IN THE HOLDER IN DUE COURSE RULE

Consumer Disadvantages

The rule that a holder in due course of a negotiable instrument is not subject to personal defenses between the original parties to it makes negotiable instruments a readily accepted substitute for money. This rule can also result in serious disadvantages to consumers. Consumers sometimes buy goods or services on credit and give the seller a negotiable instrument, such as a promissory note. They often do this without knowing the consequences of their signing a negotiable instrument. If the goods or services are defective or not delivered, the consumer would like to withhold payment of the note until the seller corrects the problem or makes the delivery. Where the note is still held by the seller, the consumer can do this because any defenses of breach of warranty or nonperformance are good against the seller.

However, the seller may have negotiated the note at a discount to a third party such as a bank. If the bank qualifies as a holder in due course, the consumer must pay the note in full to the bank. The consumer's personal defenses are not valid against a holder in due course. The consumer must pay the holder in due course and then try to get his or her money back from the seller. This may be difficult if the seller cannot be found or will not accept responsibility. The consumer would be in a much stronger position if he or she could just withhold payment, even against the bank, until the goods or services are delivered or the performance is corrected.

Changes by Some States

Some state legislatures and courts have limited the holder in due course rule, particularly as it affects consumers. Some states prohibit a seller from taking a negotiable instrument other than a check from a consumer in payment for consumer goods and services. Other states require promissory notes given by consumers in payment for goods and services to carry the words "consumer paper." Instruments with the legend "consumer paper" are declared to be nonnegotiable. A few states have virtually abolished the holder in due course rule. Thus the rights of a consumer who has signed a negotiable instrument vary from state to state. However, the trend is toward protecting the consumer against even a holder in due course.

Federal Trade Commission Rules

The Federal Trade Commission (FTC) has promulgated a regulation designed to protect consumers against operation of the holder in due course rule. The FTC rule applies to persons who sell to consumers on credit and have the consumer sign a note or an installment sale contract. The seller must put a notice in the note or the contract that reads as follows:

ANY HOLDER OF THIS CONSUMER CREDIT CONTRACT IS SUBJECT TO ALL CLAIMS AND DEFENSES WHICH THE DEBTOR COULD ASSERT AGAINST THE SELLER OF THE GOODS OR SERVICES OBTAINED PURSUANT HERETO OR

WITH THE PROCEEDS HEREOF. RECOVERY HEREUNDER BY THE DEBTOR SHALL NOT EXCEED AMOUNTS PAID BY THE DEBTOR HEREUNDER.

The effect of the notice is to make a potential holder of the note or contract subject to all claims and defenses of the consumer. If the notice is not put in a note or contract where it is required, the consumer does not gain any rights he or she would not otherwise have under state law. Thus if the notice is not put in the note or contract, the subsequent holder might qualify as a holder in due course. However, the FTC does have the right to seek a fine of as much as $10,000 against the seller who failed to include the notice.

QUESTIONS AND PROBLEM CASES

1. What is the difference between a blank and a special endorsement?

2. What is the difference between a real defense and a personal defense to a negotiable instrument?

3. Why have some states and the Federal Trade Commission taken action to limit the rights of a holder in due course of negotiable instruments issued by consumers?

4. A bank cashed the checks of its customer, Dental Supply, Inc., presented to the bank by an employee of Dental Supply named Wilson. The checks were indorsed in blank with a rubber stamp of Dental Supply, Inc. Wilson had been stealing the checks by taking cash rather than depositing them to the Dental Supply, Inc.'s account. What could Dental Supply have done to avoid this situation?

5. Davy Crockett Inn purchased a cashier's check payable to "Investments Universal" from the Bank of New Braunfels. Investments Universal was supposed to hold the check until it did certain work for Davy Crockett Inn. However, without performing that work, it deposited the check, without indorsement, in its account at the Main Bank. The Main Bank credited the check to Investment Universal's account, stamped the check "credited to account of within named payee, absence of indorsement guaranteed," and sent it to the Bank of New Braunfels where it was paid. Davy Crockett Inn brought a lawsuit against the bank, claiming the check was improperly paid without Investments Universal's indorsement. Is Davy Crockett's contention correct?

6. Williams signed a contract with Peerless and Reynolds whereby Peerless agreed to make certain improvements on Williams's home. Williams promised to pay $3,200 in monthly installments. Subsequent to the execution of the contract, Williams signed a promissory note payable to Reynolds in the amount of $6,399.60 representing principal and interest over a ten-year period. Reynolds negotiated the note to Financial Credit Corporation as part of a purchase of 480 notes. Financial paid $704 for the Williams's note. Financial later sued Williams on the note, and Williams sought to impose a fraud defense, claiming that Financial was not a holder in due course. There was testimony at the trial that "every Marylander knew" from the newspapers about Reynolds's fraudulent activities. Could Financial qualify as a holder in due course?

7. On March 2, 1960, Radio Sales drew a negotiable check payable to the order of Black. Black negotiated the check to Alexander, who deposited it in the Citizens Bank on March 10, 1960. The next day the check was presented to the drawee bank for collection, and payment was refused. Radio Sales had stopped payment on the check. Alexander sued Radio

Sales on the check, and it set up lack of consideration as a defense. Radio Sales claims that since Alexander did not take the check until March 10, 1960, he is not a holder in due course because the check was overdue before he took it. Is Alexander a holder in due course of the check?

8. Greenwald brought suit as the indorsee of a negotiable promissory note signed by Frank M. and Rose Manzon. The Manzons claimed that the note was incomplete and irregular on its face since the place of payment was not specified in the space provided on the printed form and since the blanks on the printed form appeared to have been filled in by different persons using different colored inks. They also claimed the instrument was irregular because the indorsements on the back were not in the same order as they were signed. Are these valid claims?

9. Kamensky gave a note for $19,000 to his brother. The sum of $1,000 was payable on February 15, 1965, and a like amount on the 15th day of each month for the next 19 months. On January 17, 1967, after it was past due, Kamensky's brother indorsed the note to Scrochi. He knew that the note was overdue. Scrochi brought a lawsuit against Kamensky to collect on the note. Kamensky tried to assert some personal defenses against payment. Can personal defenses be asserted against Scrochi?

10. Nickerson signed a promissory note marked "consumer note" to cover the cost of having his house covered with aluminum siding. The note was negotiated to a finance company, which claimed to be a holder in due course of the note. When the finance company tried to collect the note from Nickerson, he tried to defend against payment on the grounds that the aluminum siding was defective. A Massachusetts statute requires any note for the retail sale of consumer goods to be labeled "consumer note" and makes it nonnegotiable. Can Nickerson use the defense of breach of warranty against the finance company even if it is a holder in due course?

Liability of Parties

40

Introduction

When you sign a promissory note, you expect that you will be liable for paying the note on the day it is due. Similarly, when you sign a check and mail it off to pay a bill, you expect that it will be paid by the drawee bank out of your checking account and that if there are not sufficient funds in your account to cover it, you will have to make it good out of other funds you have. The liability of the maker of a note and of the drawer of a check is commonly understood.

However, there are other ways a person can become liable on a negotiable instrument. When you indorse a paycheck, you are assuming liability on it; and a bank that cashes a check with a forged indorsement on it is liable for *conversion* of the check. This chapter will discuss the liabilities of the various parties to a negotiable instrument. It will also cover what happens when the instrument is not paid when it is supposed to be paid. For example, a check may not be paid if there are insufficient funds in the drawer's account or if the instrument has been forged.

Liability may be based on the fact that a person has signed a negotiable instrument or authorized someone else to sign it. In that case the liability depends on the capacity in which the person has signed the instrument. Liability can also be based on certain warranties that are made when an instrument is transferred or presented for payment, improper payment, or negligence.

Signing an Instrument

No person is liable on a negotiable instrument unless his or her signature appears on the instrument. A "signature" can be any name, word, or mark used in place of a written signature (3–401).[1] A negotiable instrument can be signed either by a person or by an authorized agent.

The capacity in which a person signs a negotiable instrument affects that person's liability. This will be discussed in the next section of this chapter. In determining the capacity in which a person has signed a negotiable instrument, the position of the signature is important. If a person signs a check in the lower right-hand corner, the presumption is that he or she signed it as the *drawer*. If a person signs a promissory note in the lower right-hand corner, the presumption is that he or she signed it as the *maker*. A signature on the back of a negotiable instrument is presumed to be an *indorsement* (3–402).

Signature by an Authorized Agent

A negotiable instrument can be signed by an authorized agent. If Sandra Smith authorized her attorney to sign checks as her agent, then Sandra is liable on any checks properly signed by the attorney as her agent. All negotiable instruments signed by corporations have to be signed by an agent of the corporation. The agent is usually an officer of the corporation who is authorized to sign negotiable instruments.

If an agent or a representative signs a negotiable instrument on behalf of someone else, the agent should clearly indicate that he or she is signing as the representative of someone else. For example, Kim Darby, the president of Swimwear, Inc., is authorized to sign negotiable instruments for the company. If Swimwear borrows money from the bank and is given a 90-day promissory note to sign, Kim should sign it either "Swimwear, Inc. by Kim Darby, President" or "Kim Darby, President for Swimwear, Inc." Similarly, if Arthur Anderson, an attorney, is authorized to sign checks for Clara Carson, he should sign them "Clara Carson by Arthur Anderson, Agent." Otherwise, he risks being personally liable on them.

The agents or representatives who sign negotiable instruments are personally liable if they do not indicate that they are signing in a representative capacity or do not state the name of the person on whose behalf they are signing (3–403). Thus if Kim Darby signed the promissory note merely "Kim Darby," she would be personally liable on the note. To protect herself and to insure that the corporation will be the person liable, Kim should sign the name of the company and her title or office as well as her signature.

---

[1] Numbers in parentheses refer to the sections of the Uniform Commercial Code, 1972, which is reproduced in the Appendix.

Rotuba Extruders, Inc. v. Ceppos
385 N.E.2d 1068 (Ct. App. N.Y. 1978)

FACTS   Rotuba Extruders sold and delivered some goods to Kenbert Lighting Industries. Kenbert Lighting gave Rotuba seven promissory notes totaling $33,898.80 in payment for the goods. The first note was as follows:

$3,000.00   February 11, 1976

May 25, 1976   after date we promise to pay to

the order of Rotuba Extruders, Inc.

The Sum of $3,000 dols 00 cents   Dollars

at Chemical Bank Randall and Faile Sts. Bronx New York 10474

Value received   No interest   Kenbert Lighting Ind. Inc.

No.   Due 5/25/76   Kenneth Ceppos

Except for different dates and amounts, each of the other six notes was essentially a duplicate of this note. Kenneth Ceppos was the president and a major owner of Kenbert. When the first note was presented for payment, Kenbert did not pay it. Shortly afterward, Kenbert filed for bankruptcy. Rotuba then brought suit against Ceppos, claiming that he was liable for payment of the note. Rotuba claimed that he had signed as a comaker or guarantor and was personally liable for payment. Ceppos claimed he had signed only as the representative of Kenbert.

ISSUE   Was Ceppos liable as a maker of the note?

DECISION   Yes. The court held that Ceppos was liable as an individual for payment of the note. There was no indication that Ceppos had signed only as a representative for Kenbert. There were no words like "by" or "for" to indicate that he was signing for the company. Nor was there any designation of any office that Ceppos held with Kenbert such as "President" or "Treasurer." A person is personally obligated on a negotiable instrument if he does not indicate that he is signing in a representative capacity.

Unauthorized Signature

If a person's name is signed to a negotiable instrument without that person's authorization or approval, the person is not bound by the signature. For example, if Tom Thorne steals Ben Brown's checkbook and signs Brown's name to a check, Brown is not liable on the check because Thorne was not authorized to sign Brown's name. Thorne is liable on the check, however, because he did sign it, even though he did not sign it in his own name (3–404).

CONTRACTUAL LIABILITY

When a person signs a negotiable instrument, whether as maker, drawer, indorser, or some other capacity, he or she generally becomes contractually liable on the instrument. This contractual liability depends on the capacity in which the person signed the instrument. The terms of the contract of the parties to a negotiable instrument are not written out on the instrument; rather, they are supplied by Article 3 of the Uniform Commercial Code (Commercial Paper). So the terms of the contract are provided by law and are as much a part of the instrument as if they were written on it.

Primary and Secondary Liability

A party to a negotiable instrument may be either primarily liable or secondarily liable for payment of it. A person who is *primarily liable* has agreed to pay the negotiable instrument. For example, the maker of a promissory note is the person primarily liable on the note. A person who is *secondarily liable* is like a surety on a contract. The person who is secondarily liable is required to pay the negotiable instrument only if the person who is primarily liable to pay defaults on that obligation.

Contract of a Maker

The maker of a promissory note is primarily liable for payment of it. The maker has made an unconditional promise to pay a sum certain and is responsible for making good on that promise. The contract of the maker is that he will pay the negotiable instrument according to its terms at the time he or she signs it (3–413). If the material terms of the note are not complete when the maker signs it, then the maker's contract is that he will pay the note as it is completed, provided the terms filled in are as authorized.

Contract of a Drawee

At the time a check (or other draft) is written, no party is primarily liable on it. Usually a check is paid by the drawee bank when it is presented for payment and no person becomes primarily liable. However, the drawee bank may be asked by the drawer or by a holder of the check to *certify* the check. If it certifies the check, the drawee bank debits (takes the money out of) the drawer's account and holds the money to pay the check. If the drawee bank certifies the check, it becomes primarily (absolutely) liable for paying the check as it reads at the time it is certified (3–413).

A drawee has no liability on a check (or other draft) unless it certifies or accepts (agrees to be liable) it. However, a drawee bank that refuses to pay a check when it is presented for payment may be liable to the drawer for wrongfully refusing payment if the drawer had sufficient funds in his or her checking account to cover it. This liability of a drawee bank will be discussed in the next chapter.

Contract of a Drawer

The drawer of a check (or other draft) is *secondarily liable* on it. The drawer's contract is that if the check (or draft) is dishonored and if the drawer is given notice of the dishonor, he will pay the amount of the check (or draft) to the holder or to any indorser who takes it back (3-413[2]). For example, Janis draws a check on his account at First National Bank payable to the order of Colleen. If First National does not pay the check when it is presented for payment by Colleen, then Janis is liable to Colleen on the basis of her secondary liability.

Because a drawer is secondarily liable on a draft or check, he may disclaim this liability by drawing *without recourse* (3–413[2]).

Bank of Wyandotte v. Woodrow v. Durbin
394 F.Supp. 550 (W.D. Mo. 1975)

FACTS Durban bought some cattle through Woodrow, a livestock agent. In payment for the cattle, Durbin made three checks totaling $48,772 payable to Woodrow. When the checks were presented to the drawee bank for payment, the bank refused to pay the checks because Durbin did not have sufficient funds on deposit to cover the checks. The checks were returned unpaid to Woodrow by the drawee bank marked "Drawn on Uncollected Funds." Woodrow then brought suit against Durbin to collect the full amount of the checks.

ISSUE When these checks were dishonored by the drawee bank, did the payee have the right to hold the drawer of the checks liable for payment of them?

DECISION Yes. The court held that Durbin was liable to pay the amount of the checks to Woodrow. The drawer of a check makes a contractual promise that if the check is dishonored he will make it good. The holder of a check has the right to enforce this promise against the drawer. The drawer can avoid liability only if he has a good defense against payment. In this case Durbin did not have a good defense. He had received the cattle and was obligated to pay for them.

Contract of Indorsers

A person who indorses a negotiable instrument is usually *secondarily liable*. Unless the indorsement is qualified, the indorser agrees that if the instrument is not paid by the person who is primarily liable, then the indorser will make it good to the holder or to any later indorser who had to pay it (3–414). The indorser can avoid this liability only by putting a qualified indorsement, such as *"without recourse"* on the instrument when he indorses it.

Indorsers are liable to each other in the order in which they indorsed, from the last indorser back to the first. Suppose Mark Maker gives a promissory note to Paul Payee. Payee indorses it and negotiates it to Fred First, who indorses it and negotiates it to Shirley Second. If Maker does not pay the note when Shirley takes it to him for payment, then Shirley can require Fred to pay it to her. Fred is secondarily liable on the basis of his indorsement. Fred, in turn, can require Payee to pay him because

Payee also became secondarily liable when he indorsed it. Then Payee is left to try to collect the note from Maker. Shirley could also have skipped over Fred and gone directly against Payee on his indorsement.

Contract of an Accommodation Party

An accommodation party is a person who signs a negotiable instrument for the purpose of lending his or her name to another party to the instrument. For example, a bank might be reluctant to loan money to and to take a note from Paul because of Paul's shaky financial condition. However, the bank may be willing to loan money to Paul if he signs the note and has a friend or a relative also sign the note as an *accommodation maker*.

The contractual liability of an accommodation party depends on the capacity in which the party signs the instrument. If Paul has his brother Sam sign the note as an accommodation maker, then Sam has the same contractual liability as a maker. Sam is primarily liable on the note. However, if Sam pays the note to the bank, he has the right to recover his payment from Paul—the person on whose behalf he signed (3–415).

Similarly, if a person signs a check as an accommodation indorser, his or her contractual liability is that of an indorser. If the accommodation indorser has to make good on that liability, he or she can collect in turn from the person on whose behalf he or she signed.

CONTRACTUAL LIABILITY IN OPERATION

To bring the contractual liability of the various parties to a negotiable instrument into play, it generally is necessary that the instrument be *presented for payment*. In addition, to hold the parties that are secondarily liable on the instrument to their contractual liability, it is generally necessary that the instrument be *presented for payment* and *dishonored*.

Presentment of a Note

The maker of a note is primarily liable to pay it when it is due. Normally the holder takes the note to the maker at the time it is due and asks the maker to pay it. Sometimes the maker sends the payment to the holder at the due date. If the maker pays the note, the maker is entitled to have the note marked *paid* or *canceled* or to have it returned so that it can be destroyed.

If the maker does not pay a note when it is presented at its due date, the note has been *dishonored* (3–507). If the note is dishonored, then the holder can seek payment from any persons who indorsed the note before the holder took it. The basis for going after the indorsers is that they are secondarily liable on it. To hold the indorsers to their contractual liability, the holder must give *notice* of the dishonor. The notice can be either written or oral (3–508).

For example, Susan borrows $100 from Jack and gives him a promissory note for $100 at 9 percent annual interest payable in 90 days. Jack indorses the note "Pay to the order of Ralph Smith" and negotiates the note to

Ralph Smith. At the end of the 90 days, Ralph takes the note to Susan and presents it for payment. If Susan pays Ralph the $100 and accrued interest, she can have Ralph mark it paid and give it back to her. If Susan does not pay the note to Ralph when he presents it for payment, then the note has been dishonored. Ralph should give notice of the dishonor to Jack and advise him that he intends to hold Jack secondarily liable on his indorsement. Ralph is entitled to collect payment of the note from Jack. Jack, after making the note good to Ralph, can try to collect the note from Susan on the grounds that she defaulted on the contract she made as maker of the note.

Presentment of a Check or a Draft

A check or draft should be *presented* to the drawee. The presentment can be either for *payment* or for *acceptance* (certification) of the check or draft. No one is primarily liable on a check or draft and the drawee is not liable on a check or draft unless it accepts (certifies) it.

A drawer who writes a check is issuing an order to the drawee to pay a certain amount out of the drawer's account to the payee (or to someone authorized by the payee). This order is not an assignment of the funds in the drawer's account (3–409). The drawee bank does not have an obligation to the payee to pay the check unless it has certified the check. However, the drawee bank usually does have a contractual obligation to the drawer to pay any properly payable checks for which funds are available in the drawer's account.

For example, Janet has $100 in a checking account at First National Bank and writes a check for $10 drawn on First National and payable to Ralph Smith. The writing of the check is the issuance of an order by Janet to First National to pay $10 from her account to Ralph or to whomever Ralph requests it be paid. First National owes no obligation to Ralph to pay the $10 unless it has *certified* the check. However, if Ralph presents the check for payment and First National refuses to pay it even though there are sufficient funds in Janet's account, then First National is liable to Janet for breaching its contractual obligation to her to pay items properly payable from existing funds in her account. The liability of a bank for wrongful dishonor of checks will be discussed in more detail in Chapter 41.

If the drawee bank does not pay or certify a check when it is presented for payment or acceptance (certification), it has been dishonored (3–507). The holder of the check can then proceed against either the drawer of the check or any indorsers on their secondary liability. To do so the holder must give them notice of the dishonor.

If you want to hold an indorser liable, you should present the check for payment within seven days after the indorser signed the check. If you wait longer than that without a valid excuse, the indorsers are relieved of their secondary liability and your only recourse is against the drawer.

Suppose that Matt draws a check for $100 on his account at a bank payable to the order of Bill. Bill indorses the check "Pay to the order of Clark, Bill" and negotiates it to Clark. When Clark takes the check to the bank, it refuses to pay the check because there are insufficient funds in Matt's account to cover the check. The check has been presented and dishonored. Clark has two options: He can proceed against Bill on Bill's secondary liability as an indorser because by putting an unqualified indorsement on the check, Bill contracted to make the check good if it was not honored by the drawee. Or, Clark can proceed against Matt on his drawer's contractual liability because in drawing the check Matt promised to make it good to any holder if it was dishonored and he was given notice. Because Clark dealt with Bill, Clark is probably more likely to return it to Bill for payment. Bill then will have to go against Matt on Matt's contractual liability as drawer.

WARRANTIES

Whether or not a person signs a negotiable instrument, a person who transfers an instrument or presents it for payment may incur liability on the basis of certain implied warranties. These warranties are of two types: (1) *transferor's warranties*, which are made by persons who transfer negotiable instruments, and (2) *presentment warranties*, which are made by persons who present negotiable instruments for payment or acceptance (certification).

Transferor's Warranties

A person who transfers a negotiable instrument to someone else and receives something of value in exchange makes five warranties:

1. That the person has *good title* to the instrument or is authorized to obtain payment by someone who has good title.
2. That all *signatures* on the instrument are *genuine or authorized*.
3. That the instrument has *not been materially altered*.
4. That *no party* to the instrument *has a valid defense* against the person who is transferring it.
5. That the person transferring the instrument has *no knowledge* of any insolvencey proceedings against the maker, drawer, or acceptor (3–417[2]).

While secondary liability often furnishes a sufficient basis for suing a transferor when the party primarily liable does not pay, warranties are still important. First, they apply even when the transferor did not indorse. Second, unlike secondary liability, they do not depend on presentment, dishonor, and notice, but may be utilized before presentment has been made or after the time for giving notice has expired. Third, it may be easier to return the instrument to a transferor on the grounds of breach of warranty than to prove one's status as a holder in due course against a maker or drawer.

Presentment Warranties

A person who presents a negotiable instrument for payment or a check to be certified makes a different set of warranties. Normally the person to whom a negotiable instrument is presented for payment does not pay it unless he or she either is obligated to do so or is entitled to credit or payment from someone else if the person does pay. For example, a drawee bank does not normally pay a check unless there are funds in the drawer's account. And, it should know whether the signature on the check is that of its customer—the drawer of the check. If a drawee bank pays the check to a holder in due course, it cannot later get the money back from the holder in due course if it discovers there are insufficient funds in the drawer's account. Payment is usually final in favor of a holder in due course unless one of the three presentment warranties is broken.

The three warranties that are made by a person who is presenting an instrument for payment are:

1. That the presenter has *good title* to the instrument or is authorized to obtain payment by someone who has good title.
2. That the presenter has *no knowledge* that the *signature of the maker or drawer is unauthorized.*
3. That the instrument has *not been materially altered* (3–417[1]).

A holder in due course who presents a note to a maker does not warrant that the signature of the maker is valid or that the note has not been materially altered. The maker should recognize whether the signature on the note is his or her signature and whether or not the note has been altered. Similarly, a holder in due course does not make these warranties to the drawer of a check who should also recognize his or her signature and whether or not the check has been altered.

County Trust Co. v. Cobb
522 F.2d 728 (2nd Cir. 1975)

FACTS   Willard Cobb operated an insurance agency in Brattleboro, Vermont. Cobb received a check dated March 17, 1968, in the amount of $13,750 issued by the Hartford Insurance Company and payable to R. A. McQuaide Milk Transport. The check was issued in payment of a property loss incurred by McQuaide under a policy issued by Hartford Insurance through Cobb's agency. Willard Cobb, without authorization from McQuaide, fraudulently indorsed McQuaide's name to the check. He then added his own indorsement "For Deposit Only—Franklin County Trust Co., Willard D. Cobb." He gave the check to his brother Leon to deposit at Franklin County Trust in a new partnership account they had opened in the name of "Econo Car Rental Center." The bank credited the partnership account with the money. Willard took the money from the account and left town. The bank had to pay Hartford Insurance back for the check it had wrongfully paid to Willard and Leon rather than to McQuaide. Then it sued Willard and Leon Cobb to recover the money from them.

ISSUE   Were Leon and Willard liable to the bank on the grounds that they breached the warranty of good title?

DECISION   Yes. The court held that Willard and Leon were liable to the bank for breach of the warranty of title. When the partnership took the check for deposit to its account, it warranted to the bank that it had good title to the check. The partnership did not have good title to this check because the payee's indorsement had been forged. Accordingly, the warranty of title was breached and the partnership is liable to the bank. Leon, as Willard's partner, had to repay the bank.

Operation of Warranties

Following are some examples that show how the transferor's and present-ment warranties shift the liability back to a wrongdoer or to the person who dealt immediately with a wrongdoer and thus was in the best position to avert the wrongdoing.

Arthur makes a promissory note for $100 payable to the order of Betsy. Carl steals the note from Betsy, indorses her name on the back, and gives it to David in exchange for a television set. David negotiates the note for value to Earl, who presents the note to Arthur for payment. Assume Arthur refuses to pay the note because he has been advised by Betsy that it has been stolen. Earl can then proceed to recover the face amount of the note from David on the grounds that as a transferor David warranted that he had good title to the note and that all signatures were genuine. David, in turn, can proceed against Carl on the same basis—if he can find Carl. If he cannot, then David must bear the loss caused by Carl's wrongdoing. David was in the best position to ascertain whether Carl was the owner of the note and whether the indorsement of Betsy was genuine. Of course, even though Arthur did not have to pay the note to Earl, Arthur remains liable to his underlying obligation to Betsy.

Andrea draws a check for $10 on her checking account at First Bank payable to the order of Brown. Brown cleverly raises the check to $100, indorses it, and negotiates it to Carol. Carol then presents the check for payment to First Bank, which pays her $100 and charges Andrea's account for $100. Andrea then asks the bank to recredit her account for the altered check and it does so. The bank can proceed against Carol for breach of the presentment warranty that the instrument has not been materially altered, which she impliedly made to the bank when she presented the check for payment. Carol in turn can proceed against Brown for breach of his transferor's warranty that the check had not been materially altered—if she can find him.

Bates steals Albert's checkbook and forges Albert's signature to a check for $10 payable to "cash," which he uses to buy $10 worth of groceries from a grocer. The grocer presents the check to Albert's bank, which pays the amount of the check to the grocer and charges Albert's account. Albert then demands that the bank recredit his account. The bank can recover against the grocer only if the grocer knew the signature of Albert had been forged. Otherwise the bank must look for Bates. The bank had the responsibility to recognize the true signature of its drawer, Albert, and not to pay the check that contained an unauthorized signature.

OTHER LIABILITY RULES

Normally a check that has a forged indorsement of the payee may not be charged to the drawer's checking account. Similarly, a maker does not have to pay a note to the person who currently possesses the note if the payee's signature has been forged. And, if a check or note has been materially altered, for example, if the amount has been raised, the maker or drawer is usually liable only for the instrument as it was originally written.

Negligence

A person can be so negligent in writing or signing a negotiable instrument that he or she in effect invites an alteration or an unauthorized signature on it. If a person is negligent, he or she is not able to use the alteration or lack of authorization as a reason for not paying a holder in due course. A person is also not able to use the alteration or lack of authorization to claim that a payment was improperly made by a bank if the bank paid the item in good faith and in accordance with reasonable commercial standards (3–406).

Suppose Diane Drawer makes out a check for $1 in such a way that someone could easily alter it to read $101. The check is so altered and is negotiated to Kathy Smith, who can qualify as a holder in due course. Kathy will be able to collect $101 from Diane. Diane will not be able to claim alteration as a defense to paying it because of her negligence in making it possible. Diane then has to find the person who "raised" her check and try to collect the $100 from him or her.

Fred Meyer Inc. v. Temco Metal Products
516 P.2d 80 (Sup. Ct. Ore. 1973)

FACTS Temco kept its blank checks in an unlocked cabinet behind its bookkeeper's desk. It also kept a check "protectograph" machine, which was used to print the amount on checks, in the bookkeeper's unlocked desk. On Friday night, a burglar broke into Temco's factory through a skylight, kicked open a locked door to its offices, and entered the bookkeeper's office. The burglar took 30 blank checks, used the protectograph to make each check out for $186.34, and forged the name of Temco's bookkeeper, Lee Adams, who was authorized to sign checks for the company. The checks were made payable to either "Randall Lees" or "Anthony Hawes." The next day, Fred Meyer discovered that several identical checks had been cashed at its stores in the area that day. It contacted officials at Temco who discovered the burglary and loss of the checks. Temco refused to pay the checks on the grounds that they were forgeries. Fred Meyer sued to collect on the checks, claiming that Temco's negligence had contributed to the forgeries.

ISSUE   Was Temco barred from claiming the signatures were unauthorized on the grounds that it had been negligent in not keeping the checks and protectograph in safekeeping?

DECISION   No. The court held that Temco had not been negligent in a way that substantially contributed to the making of the forged checks. Thus it was able to claim they had been forged and did not have to pay Fred Meyer for them. The court said the company had locked the building and had security devices to protect against outside entry. Here the checks still had to be signed after they were stolen. However, the court suggested that the result would have been different if Temco had left a signature stamp or other automatic signing device accessible to unauthorized persons. In that case its negligence could be considered to have substantially contributed to a forgery.

Impostor Rule

The Code establishes special rules for checks made payable to *impostors* and to *fictitious persons*. An *impostor* is a person who poses as someone else and convinces a drawer to make a check payable to the person being impersonated. When this happens, the Code makes any indorsement in the name of the impersonated person effective (3–405[1][a]). For example, suppose that Art steals Paul's automobile. Art finds the certificate of title in the automobile and then, representing himself to be Paul, sells the automobile to Berger Used Car Company. The car company draws its check payable to Paul for the agreed purchase price of the automobile and delivers the check to Art. Any person can negotiate the check by indorsing it in the name of Paul.

The rationale for the *impostor rule* is to put the responsibility for determining the true identity of the payee on the drawer of a check. The drawer is in a better position to do this than some later holder of the check who may be entirely innocent. The impostor rule allows that later holder to have good title to the check by making the payee's signature valid, even though it is a forgery. It forces the drawer to go after the wrongdoer who tricked him into signing the check.

Fictitious Payee Rule

A *fictitious payee* commonly arises in the following situation. A dishonest employee draws checks payable to someone who does not exist or to a person who does business with his employer. If the employee has the authority to do so, he may sign the check himself. If he does not have such authority, he presents the check for signature to his employer for signature and represents that the employer owes money to the person to whom the check is made payable. The dishonest employee then takes the check, indorses it in the name of the payee, presents it for payment, and pockets the money. The employee may be in a position to cover up the wrongdoing by intercepting the canceled checks and/or juggling the company's books.

The Code allows any indorsement in the name of the fictitious payee to be effective as the payee's indorsement (3–405[1][b] and [c]). For example, suppose that Ann, who is employed by the Moore Corporation as an accountant in charge of accounts payable, prepares a false invoice naming Parks, Inc., a supplier of the Moore Corporation, as having supplied Moore Corporation with goods and draws a check payable to Parks, Inc., for the amount of the invoice. She then presents it to Temple, treasurer of Moore Corporation, together with other checks with invoices attached, for Temple's signature, all of which Temple signs and returns to Ann for mailing. Ann then withdraws the check payable to Parks, Inc. Anyone can negotiate the check by indorsing it in the name of Parks, Inc.

The rationale for the fictitious payee rule is similar to that for the impostor rule. If someone has a dishonest employee or agent who is responsible for the forgery of some checks, the immediate loss of those checks should rest on the employer of the wrongdoer rather than on some other innocent party. In turn the employer must locate the unfaithful employee or agent and try to recover from him or her.

Conversion

If a check that contains a forged indorsement is paid by a bank, the bank has *converted* the check by wrongfully paying it. The bank then becomes liable for the face amount of the check to the person whose indorsement was forged (3–419). For example, Art Able draws a check for $50 on his account at First Bank payable to the order of Bernard Barker. Carol Collins steals the check, forges Barker's indorsement on it, and cashes it at First Bank. First Bank has *converted* Barker's property because it had no right to pay the check without Barker's valid indorsement. First Bank must pay Barker $50, and then it can try to locate Collins to get the $50 back from her.

DISCHARGE OF NEGOTIABLE INSTRUMENTS

Discharge of Liability

Generally all parties to a negotiable instrument are *discharged* (relieved from liability) when the person who is primarily liable on it pays the amount in full to a holder of the instrument. Any person is discharged of his or her liability to the extent the person pays the holder of the instrument (3–603). For example, Ann makes a check for $75 payable to the order of Bruce. Bruce indorses the check "Pay to the order of Caroline, Bruce" and negotiates it to Caroline. Caroline takes it to Ann's bank, presents it for payment, and is paid $75 by the bank. The payment to Caroline discharges Bruce's secondary liability as indorser and Ann's secondary liability as drawer.

A person is not discharged of liability if he or she pays someone who acquired the instrument by theft or from someone who had stolen it (3–603[1][a]). Also, if a negotiable instrument has been restrictively indorsed, the person who pays must comply with the restrictive indorsement in order to be discharged (3–603[1][b]). Suppose Arthur makes a note of $100 payable to the order of Bryan. Bryan indorses the note "Pay to the order of my account no. 16154 at First Bank, Bryan." Bryan then gives the note to his employee, Clark, to take to the bank. Clark takes the note to Arthur, who pays Clark the $100. Clark then runs off with the money. Arthur is not discharged of his primary liability on the note because he did not make his payment consistent with the restrictive indorsement. In order to be discharged, Arthur had to pay the $100 into Bryan's account at First Bank.

Discharge by Cancelation

The holder of a negotiable instrument may discharge the liability of the parties to the instrument by canceling it. If the holder mutilates or destroys a negotiable instrument with the intent that it no longer evidences an obligation to pay money, it has been canceled (3–605). For example, a grandfather loans $1,000 to his grandson Gerald for Gerald's college expenses. Gerald gives his grandfather a promissory note for $1,000. If the grandfather later tears up the note with the intent that Gerald no longer owes him $1,000, the note has been canceled.

An accidental destruction or mutilation of a negotiable instrument is not a cancellation and does not discharge the parties to it. If an instrument is lost or accidentally mutilated or destroyed, the holder can still enforce it. In such a case the holder must prove that it existed and that he or she was the holder of it when it was lost, destroyed, or mutilated (3–804).

Discharge by Alteration

Generally, a *fraudulent and material change* in a negotiable instrument discharges any party whose contract is changed (3–407[2]).

An alteration of an instrument is *material* if it changes the contract of any of the parties to the instrument. For example, if the amount due on a note is raised from $10 to $10,000, the contract of the maker has been changed. The maker promised to pay $10, but after the change is made, he would be promising to pay much more. A change that does not affect the contract of one of the parties, such as dotting an "i" or correcting the grammar, is not material.

Assume Anne signs a promissory note for $100 payable to Bonnie. Bonnie indorses the note "Pay to the order of Connie, Bonnie" and negotiates it to Connie. Connie changes the $100 to read $100,000. Connie's change is unauthorized, fraudulent, and material. As a result, Anne is discharged from her primary liability as maker of the note and Bonnie is discharged from her secondary liability as indorser. Neither of them has to pay Connie. The contracts of both Anne and Bonnie were changed because the amount they had agreed to be liable for had been altered.

There are exceptions to the general rule that a fraudulent and material alteration discharges parties whose contracts are changed. First, if in the example above Anne was so *negligent* in writing the note that it could easily be altered, she cannot claim the alteration against a holder in due course of the note. Assume Connie indorsed the note "Connie" and negotiated it to Darlene, who qualifies as a holder in due course. If Darlene was not aware of the alteration and it was not obvious, she could collect the $100,000 from Anne. Anne's only recourse would be to track down Connie to try to get the difference between $100 and $100,000.

Second, a holder in due course who takes an instrument after it has been altered can enforce it for the original amount. When an incomplete instrument is completed after it leaves the drawer's or maker's hands, a holder in due course can enforce it as completed. For example, Sam draws a check payable to Frank's Nursery, leaving the amount blank. He gives it to his gardener with instructions to purchase some fertilizer at Frank's and to fill in the purchase price of the fertilizer when it is known. The gardener fills in the check for $100 and gives it to Frank's in exchange for the fertilizer ($7.25) and the difference in cash ($92.75). The gardener then leaves town with the cash. If Frank's had no knowledge of the unauthorized completion, it could enforce the check for $100 against Sam.

QUESTIONS AND PROBLEM CASES

1. Does a person have to personally sign his or her name to a negotiable instrument in order to be liable on it?

2. What is the difference between the contractual liability of the maker of a promissory note and the contractual liability of an indorser of a promissory note?

3. Janota's signature appeared on a note under the name of a corporation, acknowledging a $1,000 debt. No other wording appeared other than Janota's name and the corporate name. The holder of the note sues Janota on the note. What will Janota argue and what will the result be?

4. If certain checks are drawn by "McCann Industries, Inc., Payroll Account, (signed) J. Y. McCann" and the checks are not paid, who is liable—the individual or the corporation?

5. Wilson was presented with a check payable to Jones and Brown and drawn on merchant's Bank. The check was indorsed by Brown alone. Wilson accepted the check, indorsed it, and submitted it to Merchant's Bank for payment. Merchant's paid Wilson. Does Merchant's Bank have any liability to Jones?

6. A check was drawn on First National Bank and made payable to Mr. Howard. It came into the possession of Mr. Carson, who forged

Howard's indorsement and cashed it at Merchant's Bank. Merchant's Bank then indorsed it and collected from First National. Assuming that Carson is nowhere to be found, who bears the loss caused by Carson's forgery?

7. A construction company's superintendent wrote out several checks to the company's creditors and thereafter converted them to his own use by forging the indorsements of the creditors and cashing the checks at First National Bank. In an action by the company against the bank to have its account recredited for the value of the checks, is the bank liable?

8. Moore, a stockbroker, drew a check on his account at Morgan Guaranty Trust payable to Abraham. The check was stolen and Abraham's indorsement was forged on the check. The check was cashed at Bankers Trust, which paid the presenter and then forwarded the check for collection to Morgan Guaranty for payment. When the forgery was discovered, Morgan Guaranty recredited Moore's account for the amount of the check and sought repayment from Bankers. Is Bankers liable to Morgan Guaranty?

9. Hutcheson held a note made to him by Herron that left blank the rate of interest and date of payment. Hutcheson inserted the interest rate and date of payment they had previously agreed upon. Does this constitute a material alteration so as to discharge Herron's liability on the note?

10. Terry and Jones were partners in a barber shop and had a partnershp checking account with National Bank on which both signatures were required. An employee of the barber shop obtained some of the checks and forged Terry's and Jones's names. National Bank honored and cashed the checks. During the four-month period during which this went on, the employee also intercepted the monthly bank statements and canceled checks, but Terry and Jones never inquired about them. The blank checks were left in an unlocked drawer in the barber shop. The signatures on the checks were skillful forgeries that could not easily be detected as wrongful. In an action to recover the monies paid by the bank from Terry and Jones's account, will Terry and Jones prevail?

Checks and Bank Collections

41

When you deposit money in your account at the bank, you are a creditor of the bank and the bank becomes your debtor. If the deposit is made to a checking account, then the bank also becomes your agent. The obligations of the bank under banking law are set out in Article 4 of the Uniform Commercial Code (Bank Deposits and Collections). The bank as your *agent* owes a *duty* to you to follow your *reasonable instructions* concerning payments from your account.

The Bank's Duty to Pay

When a bank receives a properly drawn and payable check on your account and there are sufficient funds to cover the check, it is under a duty to pay it. If you have sufficient funds in your account and the bank refuses to pay (dishonors) the check, the bank is liable to you for damages caused by its wrongful dishonor (4–402).[1] If the bank can show it rejected the check by mistake, then you can hold the bank liable only for any actual damages you suffered. These damages can include both direct and consequential damages.

For example, Donald Dodson writes a check for $1,500 to Ames Auto Sales in payment for a used car. At the time Ames Auto presents it for payment at Dodson's bank, First National Bank, Dodson has $1,800 in his account. However, a teller, by mistake, refuses to pay the check and

---

[1] The number in parentheses refer to the sections of the Uniform Commercial Code, 1972, which is reproduced in the Appendix.

stamps it NSF (not sufficient funds). Ames Auto then goes to the local prosecutor and signs a complaint against Dodson for writing a bad check. Dodson is then arrested. Dodson can recover from First National the damages he sustained because his check was wrongfully dishonored, including those involved in his arrest such as his attorney's fees.

Stop Payment Order

A *stop payment order* is a request made by the drawer of a check to the drawee bank asking it not to pay or certify the check. As the drawer's agent in the payment of checks, the drawee bank must follow the reasonable orders of the drawer as to payments made on the drawer's behalf. To be effective, a stop payment order must be received in time to give the drawee bank a reasonable opportunity to act on it. This means the stop payment order must be given to the bank before it has paid or certified the check. The stop payment order must also come soon enough for the bank to have time to give instructions to its tellers and other employees that they should not pay the check (4–403[1]).

A stop payment order can be given orally to the bank. An oral stop payment is valid for only 14 days unless it is confirmed in writing during that time. Banks normally require such written confirmation. A written stop payment order is valid for six months. The written stop payment order can be extended for an additional six months by giving the bank instructions in writing to continue the order (4–403[2]).

Sherrill v. Frank Morris Pontiac-Buick-GMC, Inc.
366 So.2d 251 (Sup. Ct. Ala. 1978)

FACTS   Dr. Sherrill purchased a Buick Skylark from Frank Morris Buick. He gave a check for $4,860.61 drawn on his account at First Alabama Bank. The check was dated 2/6/1976, was payable "to the order of Frank Morris Buick," and was not numbered. After he bought the Skylark, Sherrill became concerned about whether he had gotten valid title to it. The day after he gave the dealer the check, he called in an oral stop payment order on the check. He later confirmed the stop payment order in writing. In the stop payment order, Sherrill stated that the check was not numbered, was payable to "Walter Morris Buick," was dated 6/3/76, and was in the amount of $4,860.61. The bank paid the check when it was presented for payment. Sherrill then claimed that the bank should recredit his account for $4,860.61 because it paid the check over a valid stop payment order.

ISSUE   Did the stop payment order describe the check accurately enough to constitute a valid stop payment order?

DECISION   No. The court held that the stop payment order did not give the bank enough accurate information about the check to give the bank a reasonable opportunity to act on the stop payment order. Because the check was not numbered, only three elements were involved in the description given to the bank: amount, payee, and date. Of these elements, only the amount was correct. The payee was mistakenly named as "Walter Morris Buick." Sherrill claimed that by dating the check 2/6/76, he really meant June 2, 1976. Even if that explanation was accepted, the stop payment order listed the date as 6/3/76. The court felt that these mistakes in the stop payment order meant the bank should not be liable for paying the check over the stop payment order.

Bank's Liability for Payment after Stop Payment Order

The drawee bank is liable to the drawer of a check that it pays while a stop payment order is in effect for any loss the drawer suffers by reason by such payment. However, the drawer has the burden of establishing the amount of the loss. To show a loss the drawer must establish that if the drawee bank had honored the stop payment order so that the holder of the instrument had to seek payment from the drawer, the drawer had a valid defense to payment that could have been asserted successfully against that holder of the instrument. To the extent the drawer had such a defense, he or she has suffered a loss due to the drawee's failure to honor the stop payment order.

For example, Brown buys what is represented to be a new car from Foster Ford and gives Foster his check for $5,280 drawn on First Bank. Brown then discovers that the car is in fact a used demonstrator model and calls First Bank, ordering it to stop payment on the check. If Foster Ford presents the check for payment the following day and First Bank pays the check despite the stop payment order, Brown can require the bank to recredit his account. Brown had a valid defense (misrepresentation) that he could have asserted against Foster Ford if it had sued him on the check. However, assume that Foster Ford negotiated the check to Sam Smith and Sam qualified as a holder in due course. Then if the bank paid the check to Sam over the stop payment order, Brown would not be able to have his account recredited. The reason for this is that Brown could not show that he sustained any loss. If the bank had refused to pay the check so that Smith came against Brown on his drawer's liability, Brown's personal defense of misrepresentation could not be used as a reason for not paying Smith. Brown's only recourse would be to go directly against Foster Ford on his misrepresentation claim.

The bank may ask the customer to sign a form in which the bank tries to disclaim or limit its liability for the stop payment order. However, the bank is not permitted to disclaim its responsibility for its failure to act in good faith or to exercise ordinary care in paying a check over a stop payment order. Similarly the bank cannot limit the measure of damages for such lack of good faith or failure to use ordinary care (4–103). Such attempted disclaimers or limitations are not enforced by the courts.

If the bank pays a check after it is given a stop payment order, it acquires all the rights of the person to whom it made payment, including rights based on the transaction on which the check was based (4–407). In the example above involving Brown and Foster Ford, assume that Brown was able to have his account recredited because First Bank had paid the check to Foster Ford over his stop payment order. Then the bank would have any rights that Brown had against Foster Ford for the misrepresentation.

If you stop payment on a check and the bank honors the stop payment order, you may still be liable to the holder of the check. Suppose you write a check for $450 to Ace Auto Repair in payment for repairs to your automobile. While driving the car home, you conclude that the car was not properly repaired. You call your bank and stop payment on the check. Ace Auto negotiated the check to Sam's Auto Parts, which took the check as a holder in due course. When Sam's takes the check to your bank, payment is refused because of the stop payment order. Sam's then comes after you on your drawer's liability. All you have is a personal defense against payment, which is not good against a holder in due course. So you must pay Sam's the $450 and pursue your claim separately against Ace. If Ace was still the holder of the check, however, the situation would be different. Your personal defense concerning the faulty work could be used against Ace to reduce or possibly cancel your obligation to pay for the check.

THE DRAWEE BANK

Bank's Right to Charge to Customer's Account

The bank has the right to charge any properly payable check to the customer's (drawer's) account. The bank has this right even where payment of the check will create an overdraft in the account (4–401). If an account is overdrawn, the customer owes the bank the amount of the overdraft. The bank may take the amount out of the next deposit the customer makes. Alternatively, the bank might seek to collect the amount directly from its customer.

A bank does not owe a duty to its customer to pay any checks out of the account that are more than six months old. Such checks are called *stale checks*. However, the bank may in good faith pay a check that is more than six months old and charge it to the customer's (drawer's) account (4–404).

Continental Bank v. Fitting
559 P.2d 218 (Ariz. Sup. Ct. 1977)

FACTS Fitting wrote a check for $800 and gave it to the payee. She then had second thoughts about the check. She contacted the bank at which she had her checking account about the possibility of stopping payment on the check. A bank employee told her she could not file a stop payment order until the bank opened the next morning. The next morning Fitting did not file a stop payment order. Instead she withdrew money from her account so that less than $800 remained in it. She believed the bank would not pay the $800 check if there were not sufficient funds in the account to cover it. However, the bank paid the check and created an overdraft in Fitting's account. The bank then sued Fitting to recover the amount of the overdraft.

ISSUE Can a bank pay a customer's check even if it creates an overdraft in the customer's checking account?

DECISION Yes. The court held that a drawee bank could pay a properly written check and charge it to the customer's account even though it creates an overdraft. The check authorizes the payment of the money from the customer's account and carries an implied promise to reimburse the drawee bank if there are not sufficient funds in the account to cover the check.

Certified Checks

Normally a drawee bank is not obligated to certify a check. When a drawee bank does certify a check, it becomes primarily liable for payment of the check. At the time a check is certified, the bank usually debits the customer's account (takes the money out of the account) and sets the money aside in a special account at the bank. The holder of a certified check looks to the drawee bank for payment.

If a check is certified by the drawee bank at the request of the drawer, the drawer remains secondarily liable on the check. However, if a check is certified by the drawee bank at the request of a holder of the check, then the drawer and any persons who have already indorsed the check are discharged of their secondary liability on the check (3–411). If the holder of a check chooses to have it certified, rather than seeking to have it paid at that time, the holder has made a conscious decision to look to the certifying bank for payment and is no longer relying on the drawer or the indorsers to make it good.

Cashier's Checks

A cashier's check should be distinguished from a certified check. A check on which a bank is both the drawer and the drawee is a *cashier's check*. The bank is primarily liable on the cashier's check.

Death or Incompetence of Customer

Under the general principles of agency law, the death or incompetence of the principal terminates the agent's authority to act for the principal. However, slightly different rules apply to the authority of a bank to pay checks out of the account of a deceased or incompetent person. The bank has the right to pay the checks of an incompetent person until it has notice that a court has determined the person is incompetent. Once it learns of this fact, the bank is no longer authorized to pay that person's checks.

Similarly, the bank has the right to pay the checks of a deceased person until it has notice of the customer's death. Even if the bank knows of the customer's death, for a period of ten days after the customer's death it can pay checks written by the customer prior to his or her death. However, the deceased person's heirs or other interested persons can order the bank to stop payment (4–405).

Russello v. Highland National Bank
392 N.Y.S.2d 439 (Sup. Ct. N.Y. 1977)

FACTS   John Doe had a checking account at Highland National Bank in New York. Two days after John Doe died in Florida, but before Highland National knew of his death, John's sister appeared at the bank. She had a check signed by John Doe but with the amount and name of the payee left blank. She told the bank her brother wanted to close his account. She asked how much was in the account, filled the check in for that amount, and made the check payable to herself. The bank checked her identification and verified the signature of John Doe. Then it paid the check to the sister. The executor of John Doe's estate later sued Highland National Bank to recover the amount of money that was in John's account on the day he died. The executor claimed that the bank had no authority to pay checks from John Doe's account after his death.

ISSUE   May a bank pay checks drawn on the account of a deceased customer?

DECISION   The court held that the bank was authorized to pay the check. A bank can charge the account of a customer for checks it pays in good faith. This is true even though the bank knows the item was completed after the drawer signed it, unless it knows the completion is unauthorized. A bank can pay checks for ten days after the death of a customer.

FORGED AND ALTERED CHECKS

Bank's Right to Charge Account

A check that has a forged signature of the drawer or payee is generally not properly chargeable to the customer's account. Similarly, a check that was altered after the drawer made it out, for example by increasing the amount of the check, is generally not properly chargeable to the customer's account. However, if the drawer is negligent and contributes to the forgery or alteration, he may be barred from claiming it as the reason that a particular check should not be charged to his account.

For example, Barbara makes a check for $1 in a way that makes it possible for someone to easily alter it to read $101, and it is so altered. If a person who qualifies as a holder in due course takes the check, he can collect the $101 from Barbara or her account if Barbara's negligence contributed to the alteration. Similarly, if a company uses a mechanical checkwriter to write checks, it must use reasonable care to see that unauthorized persons do not have access to blank checks and to the checkwriter.

If a check has been obviously altered, the bank should note that fact and refuse to pay it when it is presented for payment. Occasionally a check may have been so skillfully altered that the bank cannot detect the alteration. In that case the bank is allowed to charge the amount the check was originally written for to the account. The bank is also expected to be familiar with the authorized signature of its customer. It normally cannot charge the customer's account with checks on which the drawer's signature has been forged.

Customer's Duty to Report Forgeries and Alterations

The canceled checks drawn by a customer together with a statement of account are usually returned by the bank to the customer once a month. The customer, on receiving the checks and statement, owes a duty to examine them to discover if any signatures on the checks are forgeries or unauthorized or if any of the checks have been altered (4–406[1]).

If the customer fails to examine the checks and statement within a reasonable time, he or she cannot hold the bank responsible for the payment of the checks on which there are forgeries, unauthorized signings, or alterations if the bank can show it suffered a loss because of the customer's failure (4–406[2][a]). For example, the bank might show that the forger absconded during that time.

A different rule applies if there are a series of unauthorized drawer's signatures or alterations made by the same wrongdoer. The customer cannot hold the bank responsible for paying any such checks in good faith after the first check that had been altered or signed on behalf of the drawer without authority was available to the customer for a reasonable period not exceeding 14 calendar days and before the bank received notification from the customer of any such unauthorized signature or alteration (4–406[2][b]).

Thus checks forged or altered by the same person more than 14 days after the first forged check was available to the customer are the customer's problem—not the bank's. The customer can hold the bank liable for such forgeries or alterations only if he can establish a lack of due care on the part of the bank in paying any item (4–406[3]). The customer might show that the bank did not use due care if the alterations were very obvious.

Suppose that Ann employs Fred as an accountant and over a period of three months Fred forges Ann's signature to ten checks and cashes them. One of the forged checks is included in the checks returned to Ann at the end of the first month. Within 14 calendar days after the return of these checks, Fred forges two more checks and cashes them. Ann does not examine the return checks until a lapse of three months after the checks that included the first forged check were returned to her. The bank would be responsible for the first forged check and the two checks forged and cashed within the 14-day period after it sent the first statement and the canceled checks (unless the bank proves it suffered a loss because of the customer's failure to do so more promptly). It would not be liable for the seven forged checks cashed after the expiration of the 14-day period.

In any event a customer must discover and report to the bank any forgery of her signature, any unauthorized signature, or any alteration within *one year* from the time the checks are made available to him or her. If the customer does not do so, he or she cannot require the bank to recredit her account for such checks. Similarly, a customer has *three years* from the time his or her checks are made available to discover and report any unauthorized indorsement. If the customer does not discover the unauthorized indorsement within three years, he or she cannot require the bank to recredit his or her account for the amount of the check (4–406[4]).

George Whalley Co. v. National City Bank of Cleveland
55 Ohio App.2d 205 (Ct. App. Ohio 1977)

FACTS   In December 1971 Whalley Co. hired Nancy Cherauka as its bookkeeper. Her duties included preparing checks, taking deposits to the bank, and reconciling the monthly checking account statements. She was not authorized to sign or cash checks. Between January 24, 1972, and May 31, 1972, Cherauka forged 49 checks on the Whalley Co. account at National City Bank. Each month National City Bank sent Whalley Co. a statement and the canceled checks (including the forgeries) it had paid the previous month. The president of Whalley Co. looked at the statement to see the balance in the account but he did not look at the individual checks. Then he gave the statement and checks to the bookkeeper. The January 24 forged check was sent to Whalley Co. on February 3. In June 1972 Whalley Co. discovered that Cherauka was forging checks and fired her. It then brought a lawsuit against National City Bank to force it to recredit Whalley Co.'s account with the total amount of the 49 checks. Whalley claimed that the checks were not properly payable from the account.

ISSUE   If a customer does not promptly discover and report to its bank that someone is forging checks on its account, can it require the bank to recredit its account?

DECISION   No. The court held that Whalley Co. could only require its account to be recredited for the checks forged before Whalley Co. received the February statement containing the first forged check or 14 days after that. A customer has a duty to exercise reasonable care to promptly examine its statement and canceled checks. The customer must promptly notify the bank of any unauthorized signatures (forgeries) on any of the canceled checks. When Whalley Co. did not notify the bank of the forgery within 14 days of the time it received the first forged check back, it lost its right to have later forgeries by the same person credited back to its account.

QUESTIONS AND PROBLEM CASES

1. What duty does the drawee bank owe to a customer who maintains a checking account at the bank?

2. What is the difference between a cashier's check and a certified check?

3. May a drawee bank pay the checks of a drawer who is deceased? Explain.

4. Under what circumstances can a check that has been altered (raised) be charged to a customer's account?

5. J. E. B. Stewart received a check in the amount of $185.48 in payment of a fee from a client. Stewart presented the check, properly indorsed, to the Citizen's & Southern Bank. The bank refused to cash the check even though there were sufficient funds in the drawer's account. Stewart then sued the bank for actual damages of $185.48 and for punitive damages of $50,000 for its failure to cash a valid check drawn against a solvent account in the bank. Does Stewart have a good cause of action against the bank?

6. Skov sold fish to hotels and restaurants. He acquired his fish under an agreement whereby the supplier stored the fish that Skov had purchased for future delivery and no payment was made until such delivery. Following delivery of one shipment, Skov gave his supplier a check drawn on First National Bank. The bank erroneously refused to honor the check and the supplier canceled the agreement. Can Skov recover damages from the bank for the loss of this agreement?

7. Mullinax issued a check payable to Brown for the purchase price of an automobile. Mullinax discovered that the automobile had been stolen and he telephoned Rubin, the vice president of the Roswell branch of American Bank on which the check was drawn, and told him to stop payment on the check. The stop payment order was received at 11:05 A.M., and Rubin immediately called other branches of the bank, informing them of the stop payment order. The calls were completed by 11:15 A.M. The check was cashed by the bank at 11:45 A.M. Is the bank liable to Mullinax for cashing the check?

8. Keleher issued a check payable to the order of O'Keefe, who had the check certified. Later, Keleher issued a stop payment order to the bank before the check was presented for payment. Keleher has a valid defense if sued on the check. Should the bank pay the check to O'Keefe?

9. In January of 1970, Mrs. Baker began forging her husband's checks. In June of 1971, Mr. Baker notified the bank that he had not been receiving his checking account statements. The missing statements were then personally delivered to Mr. Baker. Mr. Baker balanced his account statements in February 1973. In March of 1973, he notified the bank that 25 of the checks that it had cashed were forgeries. Does the bank or Mr. Baker bear the liability of the forgeries?

10. An employee of Lawrence Fashions Co. had forged 250 of the company's checks over a period extending from November 1965 to May 1968. The company did not discover the forgeries until May of 1968. It then filed an action against the bank to recover the amount paid on these instruments. Is the bank liable?

Credit Transactions

PART
EIGHT

Introduction to
Secured Transactions

42

CREDIT

Nature of Credit

In the United States a substantial portion of business transactions involve the extension of credit. The term credit has many meanings. In this chapter, *credit* will be used to mean a transaction in which goods are sold, services are rendered, or money is loaned in exchange for a promise to pay for them at some future date.

Unsecured Credit

Many common transactions are based on unsecured credit. For example, you may have a charge account at a department store or a Master Charge account. If you buy a sweater and charge it to your charge account or Master Charge account, unsecured credit has been extended to you. You have received goods in return for your unsecured promise to pay for them later. Similarly, if you go to a dentist to have a tooth filled and he sends you a bill payable by the end of the month, services have been rendered on the basis of unsecured credit. Consumers are not the only people who use unsecured credit. Many transactions between business people utilize it. For example, a retailer buys merchandise or a manufacturer buys raw materials, promising to pay for the merchandise or materials within 30 days after receipt.

This type of credit transaction involves a maximum of risk to the creditor—the person who extends the credit. When goods are delivered, services rendered, or money loaned on unsecured credit, the creditor gives up all rights in the goods, services, or money. In return the creditor gets a promise by the debtor to pay or to perform the requested act. If the debtor does not pay or keep the promise, the creditor's only course of action is to bring a lawsuit against the debtor and obtain a judgment. The creditor may then have the sheriff execute the judgment on any property owned by the debtor that is subject to execution. The creditor might also try to garnish the wages or other moneys to which the debtor is entitled. However, the debtor might be *judgment proof.* For example, the debtor may not have any property subject to execution or may not have a steady job. Under these circumstances execution or garnishment would be of little aid to the creditor in collecting the judgment.

A businessperson may obtain credit insurance to stabilize the credit risk of doing business on an unsecured credit basis. However, the costs to the business of the insurance, or of the unsecured credit losses it sustains, are passed on to the consumer. The consumer pays a higher price for goods or services purchased, or a higher interest rate on any money borrowed, from a business that has high credit losses.

Secured Credit

To minimize his or her credit risk, a creditor can contract for *security.* The creditor may require the debtor to convey to the creditor a *security interest* or lien on the debtor's property. Suppose you borrow $1,000 from a credit union. It might require that you put up your car as security for the loan. The creditor might also ask that some other person agree to be liable if the debtor defaults. For example, if a student who does not have a regular job goes to a bank to borrow money, the bank might ask that the student's father or mother cosign the note for the loan.

When the creditor has security for the credit he extends and the debtor defaults, the creditor can go against the security to collect the obligation. Assume you borrow $8,000 from a bank to buy a new car and the bank takes a security interest (lien) on the car. If you fail to make your monthly payments, the bank has the right to repossess the car and have it sold so it can recover its money. Similarly, if your father cosigned for the car loan and you default, the bank can sue your father to collect the balance due on the loan.

Security Interests in Personal Property and Fixtures

Chapters 43 and 44 will discuss how a creditor can obtain a security interest in the personal property or fixtures of a debtor. They will also explain the rights of the creditor, the debtor, and other creditors of the debtors to the property. These security interests are covered by Article 9 of the Uniform Commercial Code, which sets out a comprehensive scheme for regulating security interests in personal property and fixtures. Article 9 does not deal with security interests in real estate or the liens that landlords, artisans, and materialmen are given by statute. These security interests will be covered in this chapter.

LIENS ON PERSONAL PROPERTY

Common Law Liens

Under the common—or judge-made—law, artisans, inkeepers, and common carriers (such as airlines and trucking companies) were entitled to liens to secure the reasonable value of services they performed. An artisan, such as a furniture upholsterer or an auto mechanic, uses his or her labor and/or materials to improve personal property that belongs to someone else. The improvement becomes part of the property and belongs to the owner of the property. Therefore, the artisan who made the improvement is given a *lien* on the property until he or she is paid. For example, the upholsterer who recovers a sofa for you is entitled to a lien on the sofa.

The innkeeper and common carrier are in business to serve the public and are required by law to do so. Under the common law, the innkeeper was allowed to claim a lien on the guest's property brought to the hotel or inn to secure payment for the innkeeper's reasonable charges for food and lodging. Similarly, the common carrier, such as a trucking company, was allowed to claim a lien on the goods carried for the reasonable charges for the service. The justification for these liens was that because the innkeeper and common carrier were required by law to provide the service to anyone seeking it, they were entitled to the protection of a lien.

Statutory Liens

While common law liens are generally recognized today, many states have incorporated this concept in statutes. Some of the state statutes have created additional liens, while others have modified the common law liens to some extent. The statutes commonly provide a procedure for foreclosing the lien. *Foreclosure* is the method by which a court authorizes the sale of the personal property subject to the lien so that the creditor can obtain the money to which he or she is entitled.

Characteristics of Liens

The common law lien and most of the statutory liens are known as *possessory liens.* They give the artisan or other lienholder the right to keep possession of the debtor's property until the reasonable charges for services have been paid. For the lien to come into play, possession of the goods has to have been entrusted to the artisan. Suppose you take a chair to an upholsterer to have it repaired. She can keep possession of it until you pay the reasonable value of the repair work. However, if the upholsterer comes to your home to make the repair, she would not have a lien on the chair as you did not give up possession of it.

The two essential elements of the lien are: (1) *possession by the improver or provider of services,* and (2) a *debt* created by the improvement or provision of services concerning the goods. If the artisan or other lienholder gives up the goods voluntarily, he loses the lien. For example, if you have a new engine put in your car and the mechanic gives the car back to you before you pay for the engine, the mechanic loses the lien on the car to secure your payment for the work and materials. However, if the debtor regains possession by fraud or other illegal act, the lien is not lost. Once the debt is paid, the lien is terminated and the artisan or other lienholder no longer has the right to retain the goods. If the artisan keeps the goods after the debt has been paid, or keeps the goods without the right to a lien, he is liable for conversion or unlawful detention of goods.

Foreclosure of Lien

The right of a lienholder to possess goods does not automatically give the lienholder the right to sell the property or to claim ownership if his charges are not paid. Commonly there is a procedure provided by statute for selling the property once it has been held for a certain period of time. The lienholder is required to give notice to the debtor and to advertise the proposed sale by posting or publishing notices. If there is no statutory procedure, the lienholder must first bring a lawsuit against the debtor. After obtaining a judgment for his charges, the lienholder can have the sheriff seize the property and have it sold at a judicial sale.

Younger v. Plunkett
395 F.Supp. 702 (E.D. Pa. 1975)

FACTS During May and June, John Shumate regularly parked his automobile on a vacant lot in downtown Philadelphia. During that time there were no signs posted prohibiting parking or indicating that vehicles parked there without authorization would be towed. On July 7 he again left his car there. When he returned two days later it was gone and the lot was posted with signs warning that parking was prohibited. Shumate learned that his car had been towed away by Ruffie's Towing Service and that his car was being held by Ruffie's at its place of business. Ruffie's refused to release the car until Shumate paid a towing fee of $44.50 plus $4.00 per day storage charges. Shumate refused to pay the fee and Ruffie's kept possession of the car.

ISSUE Did Ruffie's have a common law possessory lien on the car?

DECISION No. The court held that common law liens are fundamentally consensual in nature. They arise from some express or implied agreement between the owner of goods and his bailee who renders some service with respect to those goods. The common law lien is limited to those circumstances where the creditor undertakes to render his services on the implied promise or consent of the debtor to pay him. Here there was no consent by the owner of the car to the services, and thus no common law lien could arise.

SECURITY INTERESTS IN REAL PROPERTY

There are three basic contract devices for using real estate as security for an obligation: (1) the real estate mortgage, (2) the deed of trust, and

(3) the land contract. In addition, the states have enacted statutes giving mechanics, such as carpenters and plumbers, and materialmen, such as lumberyards, a right to a lien on real property into which their labor or materials are incorporated. Some states give the right to a lien only to prime contractors while other states also extend it to subcontractors.

Real Estate Mortgage

A *mortgage* is a security interest in real property or a deed to real property that is given by the owner (the *mortgagor*) as security for a debt owed to the creditor (the *mortgagee*). Because the real estate mortgage conveys an interest in real property, it must be executed with the same formality as a deed. Unless it is executed with the required formalities, it will not be eligible for recording in the local land records. Recordation of the mortgage does not affect its validity as between the mortgagor and the mortgagee. However, if it is not recorded, it will not be effective against subsequent purchasers of the property or creditors, including other mortgagees, who have no notice of the earlier mortgage. It is important to the mortgagee that the mortgage be recorded so that the world will be on notice of the mortgagee's interest in that property. See Figure 42–1 for an example of a mortgage.

The owner (mortgagor) of property subject to a mortgage can sell the interest in the property without the consent of the mortgagee. However, the sale does not affect the mortgagee's interest in the property or claim against the mortgagor.

For example, Eric Smith owns a lot on a lake. Eric wants to build a cottage on the land so he borrows $35,000 from First National Bank. Eric signs a note for $35,000 and gives the bank a $35,000 mortgage on the land and cottage as security for his repayment of the loan. Several years later, Eric sells his land and cottage to Melinda Mason. The mortgage he gave First National might make the unpaid balance due on the mortgage payable on sale. If it does not, Eric can sell the property with the mortgage on it. If Melinda defaults on making the mortgage payments, the bank can foreclose on the mortgage. If at the foreclosure sale the property does not bring enough money to cover the costs, interest, and balance due on the mortgage, First National is entitled to a deficiency judgment against Eric. However, some courts are reluctant to give deficiency judgments where real property is used as security for a debt. If on foreclosure the property sells for more than the debt, Melinda is entitled to the surplus.

A purchaser of mortaged property can buy it "subject to the mortgage" or may "assume the mortgage." If she buys *subject to* the mortgage and there is a default and foreclosure, the purchaser is not personally liable for any deficiency. The property is liable for the mortgage debt and can be sold to satisfy it in case of default. If the buyer *assumes* the mortgage, then she becomes personally liable for the debt and for any deficiency on default and foreclosure.

FIGURE 42–1
Example of a Mortgage

MORTGAGE

THIS INDENTURE, made this 18th day of October, A.D. 1980, BETWEEN Raymond A. Dole and Deborah H. Dole, hereinafter called the Mortgagor, and First Federal Savings and Loan Association, hereinafter called the Mortgagee,

WITNESSETH, That the said Mortgagor, for and in consideration of the sum of One Dollar, to us in hand paid by the said Mortgagee, the receipt whereof is hereby acknowledged, have granted, bargained and sold to the said Mortgagee, its heirs and assigns forever, the following described land situate, lying and being in the County of Genesee, State of Michigan, to wit:

All that certain plot, piece or parcel of land located in the County of Genesee, State of Michigan and known and described as Lot numbered Thirty-nine (39) in William D. Green's subdivision of part of Lot numbered Twenty-two (22) in Square numbered Twelve Hundred Nineteen (1219), as per plat recorded in the Office of the Surveyor for the County of Genesee in Liber 30 at folio 32, together with the buildings and improvements thereon, and the said Mortgagor does hereby fully warrant the title to said land, and will defend the same against the lawful claims of all persons whomsoever.

PROVIDED ALWAYS, That if said Mortgagor, their heirs, legal representatives or assigns shall pay unto the said Mortgagee, its legal representatives or assigns, a certain promissory note dated the 18th day of October, A.D. 1980, for the sum of Thirty-eight Thousand Dollars ($38,000.00), payable in monthly installments of Three Hundred Fifteen Dollars ($315.00) with interest at ten percent (10%) beginning on November 18, 1980 and signed by Raymond A. Dole and Deborah H. Dole and shall perform, comply with and abide by this mortgage, and shall pay all taxes which may accrue on said land and all costs and expenses said Mortgagee may be put to in collecting said promissory note by foreclosure of this mortgage or otherwise, including a reasonable attorney's fee, then this mortgage and the estate hereby created shall cease and be null and void.

IN WITNESS WHEREOF, the said Mortgagor hereunto set their hands and seals the day and year first above written. Signed, sealed and delivered in presence of us:

John R. Bacon	)	*Raymond A. Dole* (SEAL)
	)	
James J. Brown	)	*Deborah H. Dole* (SEAL)

ACKNOWLEDGMENT OF MORTGAGE
State of Michigan) ss
County of Genesee)

I, an officer authorized to take acknowledgements according to the laws of the State of Michigan, duly qualified and acting, HEREBY CERTIFY that Raymond A. Dole and Deborah H. Dole to me personally known, this day personally appeared and acknowledged before me that they executed the foregoing Mortgage, and I further certify that I know the said persons making said acknowledgement to be the individuals described in and who executed the said Mortgage.

Susan B. Clark
Susan B. Clark
Notary Public

City Mortgage Investment Club v. Beh
334 A.2d 183 (Ct. App. D.C. 1973)

FACTS   Philip and Edith Beh purchased some property from Alfred M. Gromer and his wife. Sometime earlier the Gromers had borrowed money from City Mortgage. They had signed a note and had given City Mortgage a second deed of trust on the property. There was also a first deed of trust on the property at the time the Behs purchased it. In the contract of sale between the Behs and the Gromers, the Behs promised to "assume" the second deed of trust of approximately $5,000 at 6 percent interest. The Behs later defaulted on the first deed of trust on the property. Foreclosure was held on the first deed of trust, but the proceeds of the sale left nothing for City Mortgage on its second deed of trust. City Mortgage then brought a lawsuit against the Behs to collect the balance due on the second trust.

ISSUE   When the Behs "assumed" the second trust, did they become personally liable for it?

DECISION   Yes. The court held that the Behs were personally liable for the second trust. When they purchased the property, they agreed to assume the Gromer's obligation to pay the second trust to City Mortgage. City Mortgage was the third-party creditor beneficiary of that promise. Accordingly, City Mortgage could enforce that promise directly against the Behs.

The creditor (mortgagee) may assign his or her interest in the mortgaged property. To do this, the mortgagee must assign the mortgage as well as the debt for which the mortgage is security.

Foreclosure is the process by which any rights of the mortgagor or the current property owner are cut off. Foreclosure proceedings are regulated by statute in the state in which the property is located. The sale commonly takes place under the supervision of a court, but in a few states no court action is required. In the latter case, the mortgagee must give notice of the proposed sale to the mortgagor and advertise to the public, with the actual sale taking place by auction. If the property is sold at a foreclosure sale and not redeemed by the owner, then the proceeds of the sale are used to pay the foreclosure costs, interest, and the debt. Any surplus from the sale is returned to the owner of the property. Commonly the states provide a period of time (usually six months to a year) after default on the debt during which the owner or other person with an interest in the property can *redeem* it by paying off the mortgage.

A small number of states permit what is called *strict foreclosure*. The creditor keeps the property in satisfaction of the debt and the owner's rights are cut off. This means that the creditor has no right to a deficiency and the debtor has no right to any surplus. Strict foreclosure is normally limited to situations where the amount of the debt exceeds the value of the property.

Deed of Trust

There are three parties to a deed of trust: (1) the owner of the property who borrows the money, (2) the trustee who holds legal title to the property put up as security, and (3) the lender who is the beneficiary of the trust. The purpose of the deed of trust is to make it easy for the security to be liquidated. However, most states treat the deed of trust like a mortgage in giving the borrower a relatively long period of time to redeem the property, thereby defeating this rationale for the arrangement.

In a deed of trust transaction, the borrower deeds to the trustee the property that is to be put up as security (see Figure 42–2). The trust agreement usually gives the trustee the right to foreclose or sell the property if the borrower fails to make a required payment on the debt. Normally

FIGURE 42–2
Example of a Deed of Trust

DEED OF TRUST

THIS DEED made this 14th day of August, 1980, by and between Harold R. Holmes, grantor, party of the first part, and Frederick B. Cannon, trustee, party of the second part, and Sarah A. Miles, party of the third part,

WITNESSETH:

The party of the first part does hereby grant unto the party of the second part, the following described property located in the District of Columbia and known as Lot numbered One Hundred Fourteen (114) in James B. Nicholson's subdivision in Square numbered Twelve Hundred Forty-seven (1247), formerly Square numbered Seventy-seven (77), "Georgetown," as per plat recorded in the Office of the Surveyor for the District of Columbia in Liber Georgetown 2 at folio 34, in trust, however, to secure the balance only of the purchase price of the above described premises, evidenced by the following described obligation:

Promissory note executed by the party of the first part, payable to the party of the third part and dated August 14, 1980, in the principal sum of Sixty-four Thousand Dollars ($64,000.00) bearing interest at the rate of nine percent (9%) per annum until paid. Said principal and interest are payable in monthly installments of Five Hundred Thirty-five Dollars ($535.00) on the 14th day of each and every month beginning September 14, 1980, and continuing every month thereafter, with the unpaid balance of said principal and interest due and payable in full on August 14, 1990.

IN WITNESS WHEREOF, the party of the first part has hereunto set his hand and seal this the day and year first above written.

Harold R. Holmes
(SEAL)

Acknowledgement
This Deed of Trust accepted this 14th day of August, 1980.

Frederick B. Cannon
Trustee

the trustee does not sell the property until the lender notifies him that the borrower is in default and demands that the property be sold. The trustee then sells the property, usually at a public sale. The proceeds are applied to the costs of the foreclosure, interest, and debt. If there is a surplus, it is paid to the borrower. If there is a deficiency, the lender has to sue the borrower on the debt and recover a judgment.

Land Contracts

The *land contract* is a device for securing the balance due the seller on the purchase price of real estate (see Figure 42–3). The buyer agrees to pay the purchase price over a period of time. The seller agrees to convey title to the property to the buyer when the full price is paid. Usually the buyer takes possession of the property, pays the taxes, insures the property, and assumes the other obligations of an owner. However, the seller keeps legal title and does not turn over the deed until the purchase price is paid. If the buyer defaults, the seller has the right to declare a forfeiture and take over possession of the property. The buyer's rights to the property are cut off at that point. Most states give the buyer on a land contract a limited period of time to redeem his or her interest. Generally, the procedure for declaring a forfeiture and recovering property sold on a land contract is simpler and less time-consuming than foreclosure of a mortgage. In most states the procedure in case of default is set out by statute. Purchases of farm property are commonly financed through the use of land contracts.

Miller v. American Wonderlands, Inc.
275 N.W.2d 399 (Sup. Ct. Iowa 1979)

FACTS In October 1972 Verda Miller sold her 107-acre farm for $30,000 to Donald Kimball, who was acting on behalf of his own closely held corporation, American Wonderlands. Under the agreement Miller retained title and Kimball was given possession pending full payment of all installments of the purchase price. The contract provided that Kimball was to pay all real estate taxes. If he did not pay them, Miller could discharge them and either add the amounts to the unpaid principal or demand immediate payment of the delinquencies plus interest. Miller also had the right to declare a forfeiture of the contract and regain possession if the terms of the agreement were not met.

In 1975 Miller had to pay the real estate taxes on the property in the amount of $672.78. She demanded payment of this amount plus interest from Kimball. She also served a notice of forfeiture on him that he had 30 days to pay. Kimball paid the taxes but refused to pay interest of $10.48. Miller made continued demands on Kimball for two months, then filed notice of forfeiture with the county recorder in August 1975. She also advised Kimball of this.

ISSUE Was Miller justified in declaring a forfeiture and taking back possession of the land?

DECISION Yes. The court said that Miller was within her rights under the land contract even though only a trifling amount was involved. She had given Kimball numerous chances to pay the sum and he stubbornly refused to do so.

FIGURE 42–3
Example of a Land Contract

LAND CONTRACT

THIS AGREEMENT, made this 15th day of September, A.D. 1980, between Sarah A. Collins, a single woman, hereinafter designated "Vendor," and Robert H. Bowen, a single man, hereinafter designated "Vendee," in the manner following: The Vendor hereby agrees to sell and the Vendee agrees to buy all that certain piece or parcel of land being in the Township of Fenton, County of Genesee and State of Michigan, and more particularly described as follows:

Part of the Northeast ¼ of the Northwest ¼ of Section 20, Township 5 North, Range 5 East, described as follows: Beginning at a point on the North line of said Section 20, which is West along said North line, 797.72 feet from the North ¼ corner of said Section 20; thence continuing West along said North line, 522.72 feet; thence South 0 degrees, 18 minutes 12 seconds East along the West ⅛ line of said Section 1000 feet; thence East parallel to the North line of said Section, 522.72 feet; thence North 0 degrees, 18 minutes, 12 seconds West parallel to said West ⅛ line; 1000.0 feet to the point of beginning, containing 12.0 acres of land, more or less, and known as 1135 Long Lake Road.

Subject to all easements, laws, ordinances, reservations applying to this property.

For the sum of Sixty-four Thousand Nine Hundred Dollars ($64,900.00), payable as follows: Ten Thousand Dollars ($10,000.00), cash in hand, receipt of which is hereby acknowledged before the signing of this contract and the balance payable as follows: Three Hundred Dollars ($300.00) or more payable on the 1st day of November, 1980, and a like amount on the 1st day of each and every month thereafter until the full sum both interest and principal has been paid in full. Interest at the rate of nine percent (9%) per annum, starting October 1, 1980, shall be deducted from each and every monthly payment and the balance applied on the principal. The entire balance, both principal and interest, to be paid in full on or before 5 years from date of closing. It is understood and agreed that the above monthly payment includes taxes and insurance which may become due and payable subsequent to the date of this contract; said amounts to be paid by Vendor and added to the principal balance.

Vendee also agrees to pay all taxes and assessments extraordinary as well as ordinary that may be levied thereon, including taxes for the year 1981, and also deferred payments on special assessments which shall become due and payable after the date thereof to be prorated to date.

The Vendee agrees to keep the buildings upon or to be placed upon the premises insured against damage by fire and wind, in such company and amount as is approved by the Vendor, for the benefit of all parties in interest; such policies shall be delivered to and held by the Vendor.

And Vendee agrees to keep the buildings and other improvements on the premises in good repair. In case the Vendee shall fail to pay taxes, effect insurance, or make necessary repairs, the Vendor may do any or all of these things and the amount paid therefore by the Vendor shall be deemed a part of the principal sum under this contract and become payable immediately with interest at the rate of seven percent per annum until paid.

Figure 42–3 *(continued)*

> The Vendor on receiving payment in full of the principal and interest, and of all other sums chargeable under the contract, agrees, at his own proper cost and expense, to execute and deliver to the Vendee, or to his assigns, upon surrender of this contract, a good and sufficient conveyance in fee simple of the above described premises, free and clear of all liens and encumbrances, except such as may have accrued thereon subsequent to the date of this contract by or through the acts or negligences of others than the Vendor, and at the option of the Vendor furnish the Vendee an abstract of title or a policy of title insurance in an amount equal to the purchase price under this contract. The Vendor hereby reserves the right to mortgage said premises at any time in an amount not in excess of the amount then due on this contract, and the Vendee agrees that the said mortgage shall be a first lien on the premises.
>
> It is mutually agreed that the Vendee shall have possession of said premises from and after October 1, 1980.
>
> If the Vendee shall fail to comply with the terms of this contract, the Vendor may take possession of the property and all the improvements on it and treat the Vendee as a tenant holding over without permission and remove him therefrom and retain any money paid hereon as stipulated damages for nonperformance of this contract. It is hereby expressly understood and declared that time is and shall be taken as of the very essence of this contract. Notice of said forfeiture may be given by depositing the notice in post office, addressed to Vendee at his last known address.
>
> It is agreed that the stipulations contained in this contract are to apply to and bind the heirs, executors, administrators and assigns of the respective parties to this contract.
>
> In witness whereof, the said parties have set their hands and seals the day and year first above written.
>
> Signed, sealed and delivered in presence of:
>
> *Harriet Greene*)   *Sarah A. Collins*   (SEAL)
>   Sarah A. Collins
>
> *Samuel A. Gross*)   *Robert H. Bowen*   (SEAL)
>   Robert H. Bowen

Mechanic's and Materialman's Liens

Each state has a statute that permits persons who contract to furnish labor or materials to improve real estate to claim a lien on the property until they are paid. There are many differences among states as to exactly who can claim such a lien and the requirements that must be met to do so. In some states the rights of all subcontractors and furnishers of materials are based on whatever rights the general contractor has and cannot exceed the amount of money due to the general contractor. In other states subcontractors and materialmen, such as lumberyards, have the right to a direct lien for the full value of the work they did or materials they furnished.

The work and materials must be furnished for the improvement of a particular property or building. If they are sold generally without reference to a particular property, the provider of materials or labor is not entitled to a lien.

To obtain a lien, the person who furnishes labor or materials must comply strictly with the statutory requirements that cover the form, content, and time of notice of the lien. A mechanic's or materialman's lien is foreclosed in the same manner as a court foreclosure of a real estate mortgage. Under the provisions of some statutes, the right to a mechanic's lien can be waived by the supplier in the contract to make the improvement. Before the person who is having improvements made to his property makes final payment, he may require the contractor to sign an affidavit that all materialmen and subcontractors have been paid.

Bowen v. Collins
217 S.E.2d 193 (Ct. App. Ga. 1975)

FACTS Bowen-Rodgers Hardware Company was engaged in the business of furnishing materials for the construction of buildings. They delivered a quantity of materials to property owned by Ronald and Carol Collins. The materials were for the use of a contractor who was building a home for the Collins as well as several other houses in the area. The hardware company was not paid for the materials by the contractor and it sought to obtain a mechanic's lien against the Collins's property. The Collins claimed that even though the materials were delivered to their home, they were actually used to build other houses in the area.

ISSUE Was the Collins's property subject to a mechanic's lien because payment had not been made for materials delivered to it?

DECISION No. The court held that the Collins's property was not subject to a mechanic's lien. A person claiming a lien must clearly show he has complied with the statutory requirements. A materialman must show that materials he furnished went into construction of a building on the property pursuant to a contract. Here the materialman could not show that the materials were used in the Collins's house and thus he was not entitled to a lien.

SURETYSHIP

Sureties and Guarantors

A *surety* is a person who is liable for the payment of another person's debt or for the performance of another person's duty. The surety joins with the person who is primarily liable in promising to make the payment or to perform the duty. For example, Kathleen, who is 17 years old, buys a used car on credit from Harry's Used Cars. She signs a promissory note, agreeing to pay $50 a month on the note until the note is paid in full. Harry's has Kathleen's father cosign the note; thus her father is a surety.

Similarly, the city of Chicago hires the B&B Construction Company to build a new sewage treatment plant. The city will probably require B&B to have a surety agree to be liable for B&B's performance of its contract. There are insurance companies that, for a fee, will agree to be a surety for a company like B&B on its contract. If the person who is primarily liable (the principal) defaults, the surety is liable to pay or perform. Then the surety is entitled to be reimbursed by the principal.

A *guarantor* does not join in making a promise; rather, a guarantor makes a separate promise and agrees to be liable on the happening of a certain event. For example, a father tells a merchant, "I will guarantee payment of my son Richard's debt to you if he does not pay it," or "In the event Richard becomes bankrupt, I will guarantee payment of his debt to you." A guarantor's promise must be made in writing to be enforceable under the statute of frauds.

The rights and liabilities of the surety and the guarantor are substantially the same. No distinction will be made between them in this chapter except where the distinction is of basic importance.

Creation of Principal and Surety Relationship

The relationship of principal and surety, or that of principal and guarantor, is created by contract. The basic rules of contract law apply in determining the existence and nature of the relationship as well as the rights and duties of the parties.

Defenses of a Surety

Suppose that Jeff's father agrees to be a surety for Jeff on his purchase of a motorcycle on credit from a dealer. If the motorcycle was defectively made and Jeff refuses to make further payments on it, the dealer might try to collect the balance due from Jeff's father. As a surety, Jeff's father can use any defenses against the dealer that Jeff has if they go the merits of the primary contract. Thus, if Jeff has a valid defense of breach of warranty against the dealer, his father can use it as a basis for not paying the dealer.

Other defenses that go to the merits include (1) lack or failure of consideration, (2) inducement of the contract by fraud or duress, and (3) breach of contract by the other party. The personal defenses of the principal cannot be used by the surety. These personal defenses include lack of capacity, such as minority or insanity, and bankruptcy. Thus, if Jeff is only 17 years old, the fact he is a minor cannot be used by Jeff's father to defend against the dealer. This defense of Jeff's lack of capacity to contract does not go the merits of the contract between Jeff and the dealer and cannot be used by Jeff's father.

A surety contracts to be responsible for the performance of the principal's obligation. If the principal and the creditor change that obligation by agreement, the surety is relieved of responsibility unless the surety agrees to the change. This is because the surety's obligation cannot be changed without his or her consent.

For example, Fred cosigns a note for his friend Kathy, which she has given to Credit Union to secure a loan. Suppose the note was originally for $500 and payable in 12 months with interest at 11 percent a year. Credit Union and Kathy later agree that Kathy will have 24 months to repay the note but the interest will be 13 percent per year. Unless Fred consents to this change, he is discharged from his responsibility as surety. The obligation he agreed to assume was altered by the changes in the repayment period and interest rate.

The most common kind of change affecting a surety is an extension of time to perform the contract. If the creditor merely allows the principal more time without the surety's consent, it does not relieve the surety of responsibility. The surety's consent is required only where there is an agreement between the creditor and the principal as to the extension of time. In addition, the courts usually make a distinction between accommodation sureties and compensated sureties. An *accommodation surety* is a person who acts as a surety without compensation, such as a friend who cosigns a note as a favor. A *compensated surety* is a person, usually a professional such as a bonding company, who is paid for serving as a surety.

The courts are more protective of accommodation sureties. They are relieved of liability unless they consent to an extension of time. Compensated sureties, on the other hand, must show that they will be harmed by an extension of time before they are relieved of responsibility because of an unconsented extension of time.

Creditor's Duties to Surety

The creditor is required to disclose any material facts about the risk involved to the surety. If he does not do so, the surety is relieved of liability. For example, a bank (creditor) knows that an employee, Arthur, has been guilty of criminal conduct in the past. If the bank applies to a bonding company to obtain a bond on Arthur, the bank must disclose the information it knows about Arthur. Similarly, suppose the bank has an employee, Alice, covered by a bond and discovers that Alice is embezzling money. If the bank agrees to give Alice another chance but does not report her actions to the bonding company, the bonding company is relieved of responsibility for further wrongful acts by Alice.

If the principal posts security for the performance of an obligation, the creditor must not surrender the security without the consent of the surety. If the creditor does so, the surety is relieved of liability to the extent of the value surrendered.

Beneficial Finance Co. v. Marshall
551 P.2d 315 (Ct. App. Okla. 1976)

FACTS   Mr. and Mrs. Marshall went to Beneficial Finance to borrow money but were deemed by Beneficial's office manager, Puckett, to be bad credit risks. The Marshalls stated their friend Garren would be willing to cosign a note for them if necessary. Puckett advised Garren not to cosign because the Marshalls were bad credit risks. This did not dissuade Garren from cosigning a note for $480, but it prompted him to ask Beneficial to take a lien or security interest in Marshall's custom-built Harley Davidson motorcycle, then worth over $1,000. Beneficial took and perfected a security interest in the motorcycle. Marshall defaulted on the first payment. Beneficial gave notice of the default to Garren and advised him that it was looking to him for payment. Garren then discovered that Beneficial and Marshall had reached an agreement whereby Marshall would sell his motorcycle for $700; he was to receive $345 immediately, which was to be applied to the loan, and he promised to pay the balance of the loan from his pocket. Marshall paid Beneficial $89.50 and left town without giving the proceeds of the sale to Beneficial. Because Beneficial was unable to get the proceeds from Marshall, it brought suit against Garren on his obligation as surety.

ISSUE   When Beneficial released the security for the loan (the motorcycle) without Garren's consent, was Garren relieved of his obligation as surety for repayment of the loan?

DECISION   Yes. The court noted that the release of the security greatly increased Garren's risk as surety. The law traditionally has held that when the creditor engages in conduct that increases the surety's risk, the surety is discharged. Here the value of the security greatly exceeded the value of the debt, so Garren was totally discharged.

Subrogation and Contribution

If the surety has to perform or pay the principal's obligation, then the surety acquires all the rights the creditor had against the principal. This is known as the surety's *right of subrogation*. For example, Amanda cosigns a promissory note for $250 at the credit union for her friend Anne. Anne defaults on the note and the credit union collects $250 from Amanda on her suretyship obligation. Amanda then gets the credit union's right against Anne, that is, the right to collect $250 from Anne.

Suppose several persons (Tom, Dick, and Harry) are cosureties of their friend Sam. When Sam defaults, Tom pays the whole obligation. Tom is entitled to collect one-third from both Dick and Harry since he paid more than his prorated share. This is known as the cosurety's *right to contribution*.

QUESTIONS AND PROBLEM CASES

1. What is the difference between secured credit and unsecured credit?

2. What are the essential elements of a common law lien?

3. What is the difference between purchasing real property subject to a mortgage and assuming a mortgage?

4. What are the distinguishing characteristics of a land contract?

5. Maxwell owned the timber on a certain tract of land. He hired Fitzgerald to cut the timber into logs and to put the logs in Maxwell's mill pond. Fitzgerald had the logs cut and put on the back of the mill pond, where they were levied on by a judgment creditor of Maxwell's. Fitzgerald was not paid for his work. He claimed a common law lien on the logs for his labor in cutting and hauling them. Is Fitzgerald entitled to a common law lien on the logs?

6. On July 18, Anna Parker coveyed certain land to Benjamin Coombs and took back a mortgage to secure the payment of $1,616, which was the balance due on the purchase price. The mortgage was recorded on November 11 of that year. Several days earlier, on October 30, Coombs executed a mortgage to Mayham on that same property to secure the payment of $1,269. Mayham recorded his mortgage on October 30. Coombs defaulted on the Mayham mortgage and Mayham brought suit to foreclose it. Parker contended that her mortgage had priority over Mayham's because Mayham knew of it at the time he received his mortgage. The state law provides that mortgages "shall take effect from the time they are recorded." Which mortgage has priority?

7. Brown hired a contractor to build a house for him, and the contractor hired the Electric Con-

tracting Company to do the electric work. All the electric work was completed by March 10, except a certain type of ground clamp required by a city ordinance was not then available. The city inspector permitted a different type of clamp to be installed at that time. On April 25, Electric Contracting replaced the clamp with the required type. When Electric Contracting was not paid by the contractor, it filed a materialman's lien on June 13 and then brought suit against Brown to recover for its work. Brown claimed that the lien was not enforceable because it was not filed within 60 days of the time the work was completed as required by state law. Should the court accept Brown's contention?

8. Bayer was the general contractor on a Massachusetts state highway contract. He hired Deschenes as a subcontractor to do certain excavation work. Deschenes was to start the job by November 24, 1958, and to complete it on or before March 1, 1959. Deschenes was required to furnish a bond of $91,000 to assure his faithful performance of the subcontract, and he purchased such a bond from Aetna Insurance Co. Deschenes began the work on December 1, 1958, and quit on June 22, 1959, after completing only about half the work. Bayer had made numerous efforts to get Deschenes to do the work and then completed the job himself when Deschenes walked off the job. Bayer then brought a lawsuit against Aetna on the bond, and Aetna claimed it was discharged by the extension of time given to Deschenes. Should Bayer recover on the bond?

Secured Consumer Transactions

43

INTRODUCTION

Article 9 of the Uniform Commercial Code

Today a large portion of our economy involves the extension of credit. In many credit transactions, the creditor takes a security interest (or lien) in personal property belonging to the debtor in order to protect his investment. The law covering security interests in personal property is contained in Article 9 of the Uniform Commercial Code. Article 9, entitled Secured Transactions, applies to situations that consumers and business people commonly face, for example, the financing of an automobile, the purchase of a refrigerator on a time-payment plan, and the financing of business inventory.

If a creditor wants to obtain a security interest in the personal property of the debtor, he also wants to be sure that his interest will be superior to the claims of other creditors. To do so the creditor must carefully comply with Article 9. In Part Three, Sales, it was pointed out that business persons sometimes leave out necessary terms in a contract or insert vague terms to be worked out later. Such looseness is a luxury that is not permitted when it comes to secured transactions. If a debtor gets into financial difficulties and cannot meet his obligations, it is important to the creditor that he carefully complied with Article 9. Even a minor noncompliance may result in the creditor losing his preferred claim to the personal property of the debtor. If a creditor loses his secured interest, he will be only a general creditor of the debtor if the debtor is declared bankrupt. As a general creditor in bankruptcy proceedings, he may have little chance of recovering the money owed by the debtor because of the relatively low priority of such claims. This will be covered in detail in Chapter 45.

Article 9 has not been adopted in exactly the same form in every state. Each state law must be examined carefully to determine the procedure for obtaining a secured interest in that state and the rights of creditors and debtors. However, the general concepts are the same in each state and will be the basis of our discussion. This chapter will focus on secured consumer transactions; Chapter 44 will cover secured transactions in which the debtors are business persons.

Security Interests in Consumer Goods

Basic to a discussion of secured consumer transactions is the term security interest. A *security interest* is an interest in personal property or fixtures that a creditor obtains to secure payment or performance of an obligation (1–201[37]).[1] For example, when you borrow money from the bank to buy a new car, the bank takes a security interest (puts a lien) on your car until the loan is repaid. If you default on the loan, the bank can repossess the car and have it sold to cover the unpaid balance on the loan.

Under Article 9, a creditor can take a security interest in a wide range of personal property, including such categories as inventory, accounts receivable, equipment, and consumer goods. An item such as a stove could in different situations be classified as inventory, equipment, and consumer goods. In the hands of the manufacturer or an appliance store, the stove is *inventory* goods. If it is being used in a restaurant, it is *equipment*. In a home, it is classified as *consumer goods.*

In this chapter our focus will be on security interests in consumer goods. *Consumer goods* are goods bought or used primarily for personal, family, or household use such as automobiles furniture, and appliances (9–109[1]).

Obtaining a Security Interest

The goal of a creditor is to obtain a security interest in certain personal property that will be good against (1) the debtor, (2) other creditors of the debtor, and (3) a person who might purchase the property from the debtor. In case the debtor defaults on the debt, the creditor wants to have a better right to claim the property than anyone else. Obtaining an enforceable security interest is a two-step process consisting of *attachment* and *perfection.*

ATTACHMENT OF THE SECURITY INTEREST

Attachment

A security interest is not legally enforceable against a debtor until it is attached to a particular item or items of the debtor's property. The attachment of the security interest takes place in a legal sense rather than in a

---

[1] The numbers in parentheses refer to the sections of the Uniform Commercial Code, 1972, which is reproduced in the Appendix.

physical sense. There are two basic requirements for a security interest to be attached to the goods of a debtor (9–203). First, there must be an *agreement* by the debtor granting the creditor a security interest in particular property *(collateral)* in which the debtor has an interest. Second, the creditor must give something of value to the debtor. The creditor must, for example, loan money or advance goods on credit to the debtor. Unless the debtor owes a *debt* to the creditor, there can be no security interest. The purpose of obtaining the security interest is to secure a debt.

The Security Agreement

The agreement in which a debtor grants a creditor a security interest in the debtor's property generally must be in *writing* and *signed by the debtor*. A written agreement is required in all cases except where the creditor has *possession* of the collateral (9–203). Suppose you borrow $50 from a friend and give him your wristwatch as security for the loan. Your agreement whereby you put up your watch as collateral does not have to be in writing to be enforceable. Because the creditor (your friend) is in possession of the collateral, an oral agreement is sufficient.

The security agreement must *clearly describe the collateral* so that it can readily be identified. For example, the year, make, and serial number of an automobile should be listed. The security agreement usually goes on to spell out the terms of the arrangement between the creditor and the debtor. Also it normally contains a promise by the debtor to pay certain amounts of money in a certain way. It will specify what events, such as nonpayment by the buyer, will constitute a default. In addition, it may contain provisions the creditor feels are necessary to protect his security interest. For example, the debtor may be required to keep the collateral insured and/or not to move it without the creditor's consent (see Figure 43–1).

Future Advances

A security agreement may cover extensions of credit to be made in the future (9–204[3]). A later extension of credit is known as a *future advance*. A future advance is involved where a credit union agrees to give you a line of credit of $10,000 to buy and restore an antique car, but initially gives you only $1,500 to buy the car. As you draw additional money against the line of credit, you have received a future advance. The security interest the creditor obtained earlier also covers these later advances of money to you.

After-Acquired Property

A security agreement may be drafted to grant a creditor a security interest in the "after-acquired" property of the debtor. *After-acquired property* is property that the debtor does not currently own or have rights in, but that he or she may acquire in the future. However, the security interest does not attach until the debtor actually obtains some rights to the new property (9–204). For example, a finance company might loan you $2,500 now to buy some new furniture for your living room over the next three

574

FIGURE 43–1

Example of a Security Agreement

BUYER ~~Mr. and Mrs.~~ ~~Mrs.~~ Miss CHERYL COLE
ADDRESS 542 OAKDALE
CITY CHICAGO, ILL   TEL. NO. 828-0250
DELIVER TO: 542 OAKDALE

Account No.

C-1005

Date

SECURITY AGREEMENT
ACE APPLIANCE

THIS AGREEMENT, executed between Ace Appliance, as Secured Party ("Seller"), and Buyer named above, as Debtor ("Buyer"):

Seller agrees to sell and Buyer agrees to purchase, subject to the terms, conditions and agreements herein stated, the goods described below (hereinafter referred to as the "Collateral"), Seller reserving and Buyer granting a purchase money security interest in the Collateral to secure the payment of the balance owed (Item 7) and all other present and future obligations of Buyer to Seller.

Quan.	Article	Unit Price	Total		TERMS	
1	REFRIG.	425 —	425	00	(1) Cash Price	800 00
1	STOVE	375 —	375	00	(2) Down Payment	100 00
					Trade-in	
					Unpaid Principal	
					(3) Balance Owed	700 00
					(4) Finance Charge	100 00
					Time Balance	
					(5) Owed	800 00
					(6) Sales Tax	40 00
					(7) Balance Owed	840 00

DESCRIPTION OF COLLATERAL

Buyer agrees to pay Seller, without relief from valuation and appraisement laws, the balance owed (Item 7) of $840 00 in 11 successive ~~weekly~~ monthly installments of $70 00 each and a final installment of $70 00, commencing on JAN 1, 1981, and continuing thereafter on the same day of each ~~week~~ month until paid, together with all delinquent charges, costs of repossession, collection, disposition, maintenance and other like charges, allowed by law, and reasonable attorneys' fees.

This sale is made subject to the terms, conditions and agreements stated above and on the reverse side hereof. Buyer hereby represents that the correct name and address of Buyer is as stated above, and that all statements made by Buyer as to financial condition and credit information are true.

Buyer hereby acknowledges delivery by Seller to Buyer of a copy of this agreement.

Buyer warrants and represents that the Collateral will be kept at Buyer's address unless otherwise specified as follows: _____

_____; and will be used or is purchased for use primarily for: (check one) family or household purposes ☒ business use ☐; farming operations ☐. The Collateral will not be affixed to real estate unless checked here ☐. If the Collateral is to be affixed to real estate, a description of the real estate is as follows: _____

FIGURE 43–1 *(continued)*

and the name of the record owner is _____
_____.

IN WITNESS WHEREOF, the parties hereto have executed this agreement on this
_1 st_ day of _DEC._, 19_80_.

BUYER'S SIGNATURE   (Ace Appliance) Seller, (as Secured Party)

Cheryl Cole   By *Frank Singer*
_____   _____
            (as Debtor)

TERMS, CONDITIONS AND AGREEMENTS

1. The security interest of Seller shall extend to all replacements, proceeds (including tort claims and insurance), and accessories, and shall continue until full performance by Buyer of all conditions and obligations hereunder.

2. Buyer shall maintain the Collateral in good repair, pay all taxes and other charges levied upon the Collateral when due, and shall defend the Collateral against any claims. Buyer shall not permit the Collateral to be removed from the place where kept without the prior written consent of Seller. Buyer shall give prompt written notice to Seller of any transfer, pledge, assignment, or any other process or action taken or pending, voluntary or involuntary, whereby a third party is to obtain or is attempting to obtain possession of or any interest in the Collateral. Seller shall have the right to inspect the Collateral at all reasonable times. At its option, but without obligation to Buyer and without relieving Buyer from any default, Seller may discharge any taxes, liens or other encumbrances levied or placed upon the Collateral for which Buyer agrees to reimburse Seller upon demand.

3. If the Collateral is damaged or destroyed in any manner, the entire balance remaining unpaid under this agreement (hereinafter referred to as the ''Agreement Balance'') shall immediately become due and payable and Buyer shall first apply any insurance or other receipts compensating for such loss to the Agreement Balance. Buyer shall fully insure the Collateral, for the benefit of both Seller and Buyer, against loss by fire, theft and other casualties by comprehensive extended coverage insurance in an amount equal to the balance owed hereunder.

4. Buyer shall pay all amounts payable hereunder when due at the store of Seller from which this sale is made or at Seller's principal office in _GARY_, Indiana, and upon default shall pay the maximum delinquent charges permitted by law. Upon prepayment of the Agreement Balance, Seller shall allow the minimum discount permitted by law.

5. Time is of the essence of this agreement. Buyer agrees that the following shall constitute an event of default under this Security Agreement: *(a)* the failure of Buyer to perform any condition or obligation contained herein; *(b)* when any statement, representation or warranty made herein by Buyer shall be found to have been untrue in any material respect when made; or *(c)* if Seller in good faith believes that the prospect of payment or performance is impaired. Upon a default, Seller, at its option and without notice or demand to Buyer, shall be entitled to declare the Agreement Balance immediately due and payable, take immediate possession of the Collateral and enter the premises at which the Collateral is located for such purpose or to render the Collateral unusable. Upon request, Buyer shall assemble and make the Collateral available to Seller at a place to be designated by Seller which is reasonably convenient to both parties. Upon repossession, Seller may retain or dispose of any or all of the Collateral in the manner prescribed by the Indiana Uniform Commercial Code and the proceeds of any such disposition shall be first applied in the following order: *(a)* to the reasonable expenses of retaking, holding, preparing for sale, selling and the like; *(b)* to the reasonable attorneys' fees and legal expenses incurred by Seller; and *(c)* to the satisfaction of the indebtedness secured by this security interest. Buyer covenants to release and hold harmless Seller from any and all claims arising out of the repossession of the Collateral. No waiver of any default or any failure or delay to exercise any right or remedy by Seller shall operate as a waiver of any other default or of the same default in the future or as a waiver of any right or remedy with respect to the same or any other occurrence.

FIGURE 43–1 *(concluded)*

6. All rights and remedies of Seller herein specified are cumulative and are in addition to, and shall not exclude, any rights and remedies Seller may have by law.

7. Seller shall not be liable for any damages, including special or consequential damages, for failure to deliver the Collateral or for any delay in delivery of the Collateral to Buyer.

8. Buyer agrees that Seller may carry this agreement, together with any other agreements and accounts, with Buyer in one account upon its records and unless otherwise instructed in writing by Buyer, any payment of less than all amounts then due on all agreements and accounts shall be applied to any accrued delinquent charges, costs of collection and maintenance, and to the balances owing under all agreements or accounts in such order as Seller in its discretion shall determine.

9. Buyer authorizes Seller to execute and file financing statements signed only by Seller covering the Collateral described.

10. Any notice required by this agreement shall be deemed sufficient when mailed to Seller (state Seller's address), or to Buyer at the address at which the Collateral is kept.

11. Buyer shall have the benefit of manufacturers' warranties, if any; however, Seller makes no express warranties (except a warranty of title) and no implied warranties, including any warranty of MERCHANTABILITY or FITNESS. Buyer agrees that there are no promises or agreements between the parties not contained herein. Any modification or rescission of this agreement shall be ineffective unless in writing and signed by both Seller and Buyer.

12. ANY HOLDER OF THIS CONSUMER CREDIT CONTRACT IS SUBJECT TO ALL CLAIMS AND DEFENSES WHICH THE DEBTOR COULD ASSERT AGAINST THE SELLER OF GOODS OR SERVICES OBTAINED WITH THE PROCEEDS HEREOF. RECOVERY HEREUNDER BY THE DEBTOR SHALL NOT EXCEED AMOUNTS PAID BY THE DEBTOR HEREUNDER.

months and take a security interest in the furniture to secure the loan. As you buy the individual pieces of furniture, the finance company's security interest attaches to each new piece.

Proceeds

A security agreement may also provide that it covers not only the collateral described in the agreement but also any proceeds from the sale of the collateral by the debtor (9–203). Assume Anne buys a television set from Ace Appliance on a time-payment plan. The security agreement may provide that Ace Appliance has a security interest in the television set and in any money or other proceeds Anne gets if she sells the set to someone else.

Assignment

In the past installment sales contracts and security agreements commonly included a provision that the buyer would not assert against the assignee of a sales contract any claims or defenses the buyer has against the seller. Such clauses made it easier for a retailer to assign its installment sales contracts (security agreements) to a financial institution such as a bank. The bank knew that it could collect from the buyer without having to worry about any claims the buyer had against the retailer, such as for breach of warranty. The waiver clauses were usually presented to the buyer on a take-it-or-leave-it basis.

Such clauses can operate to the disadvantage of the buyer. For example,

Harriet Horn agrees to buy some storm windows from Ace Home Improvement Company. She signs an installment sales contract (security agreement) promising to pay $50 a month for 24 months and giving the company a security interest in the windows. The contract contains a waiver of defenses clause. Ace assigns the contract to First Bank and goes out of business. If the storm windows were of a poorer quality than called for by the contract, Harriet would have a claim of breach of warranty against Ace. She would not have to pay Ace the full amount if it tried to collect from her. However, under these circumstances, Harriet has to pay the full amount to the bank and then can try to collect from Ace for breach of warranty. Here Harriet might be out of luck.

While waiver of defenses clauses in commercial contracts can generally be enforced, their use in consumer contracts has been severely restricted (9–206). Some states have enacted legislation that abolishes the waiver of defenses clause in consumer contracts; other states have limited the use of such clauses. In addition the Federal Trade Commission (FTC) has adopted some rules that apply to situations where a buyer signs an installment sales contract. The FTC requires that the seller insert a specified clause in the installment sales contract and all direct loan agreements. The clause states that any assignee of the contract will be subject to any claims or defenses that the buyer-debtor could assert against the seller of the goods. The FTC rules are discussed in Chapter 49.

PERFECTING THE SECURITY INTEREST

Perfection

Attachment of a security interest to collateral owned by the debtor gives the creditor rights vis-à-vis the debtor. However, a creditor is also concerned about making sure he will have a better right to the collateral than any other creditor in the event the debtor defaults. A creditor may also be concerned about protecting his interest in the collateral if the debtor sells it to someone else. The creditor gets protection against other creditors or purchasers of the collateral by *perfecting* his security interest.

Under the Code there are three main ways of perfecting a security interest.

1. By filing a *public notice* of the security interest.
2. By the creditor taking *possession* of the collateral.
3. In certain kinds of transactions, by mere *attachment* of the security interest (automatic perfection).

Perfection by Public Filing

The most common way of perfecting a security interest is by filing a *financing statement* in the appropriate public office. The financing statement serves as constructive notice to the world that the creditor claims an interest in collateral that belongs to a certain named debtor. The financing statement usually consists of a multicopy form that is available from the state secretary of state's office (see Figure 43–2). However, the security agreement can

FIGURE 43-2
Example of a Financing Statement

UNIFORM COMMERCIAL CODE	STATE OF INDIANA FINANCING STATEMENT	FORM UCC-1

INSTRUCTIONS
1. Please type this form. Fold only along perforation for mailing.
2. Remove Secured Party and Debtor copies and send other three copies with interleaved carbon paper to the filing officer. Enclose filing fee of $1.00 (plus $.50 if collateral is or is to become a fixture).
3. When filing is to be with more than one office, Form UCC-2 may be placed over this set to avoid double-typing.
4. If the space provided for any item(s) is inadequate, the item(s) may be continued on additional sheets, preferably 5"x 8" or sizes convenient to secured party in case of long schedules, indentures, etc. Only one sheet is required. Extra names of debtors may be continued below box "1" in space for description of property.
5. If the collateral is crops or goods which are or are to become fixtures, describe the goods and also the real estate with the name of the record owner if he is other than the debtor.
6. Persons filing a security agreement (as distinguished from a financing statement) are urged to complete this form with or without signature and send with security agreement.
7. If collateral is goods which are or are to become fixtures, use Form UCC-1a over this Form to avoid double-typing, and enclose regular fee plus $.50.
8. The filing officer will return the third page of this Form as an acknowledgment. Secured party at a later time may use third page as a Termination Statement by dating and signing the termination legend on that page.

This Financing Statement is presented to Filing Officer for filing pursuant to the UCC:

3 Maturity Date (if any):

1 Debtor(s) (Last Name First) and Address(es)	2 Secured Party(ies) and Address(es)	For Filing Officer (Date, Time, Number, and Filing Office)

4 This financing statement covers the following types (or items) of property (also describe realty where collateral is crops or fixtures):

Assignee of Secured Party

This statement is filed without the debtor's signature to perfect a security interest in collateral (check [X] if so)

☐ under a security agreement signed by debtor authorizing secured party to file this statement, or

☐ already subject to a security interest in another jurisdiction when it was brought into this state, or

☐ which is proceeds of the following described original collateral which was perfected:

Check [X] if covered: ☐ Proceeds of Collateral are also covered ☐ Products of Collateral are also covered. No. of additional Sheets presented:

Filed with: ☐ Secretary of State ☐ Recorder of_____County

By:_____
Signature(s) of Debtor(s)

By:_____
Signature(s) of Secured Party(ies)

(1) Filing Officer Copy—Alphabetical
FORM UCC-1—INDIANA UNIFORM COMMERCIAL CODE

Approved by: *Charles O. Hendricks*
Secretary of State

be filed as the financing statement if it contains the required information and has been signed by the debtor.

To be sufficient, the financing statement must (1) contain the names of the debtor and of the secured party (the creditor), (2) be signed by the debtor, (3) give an address of the secured party from which additional information about the security interest can be obtained, (4) give a mailing address for the debtor, and (5) contain a statement of the types, or a description, of the collateral. If the financing statement covers goods that are to become fixtures, a description of the real estate must be included.

Each state specifies by statute where the financing statement has to be filed. In all states a financing statement that covers fixtures must be filed in the office where a mortgage on real estate would be filed (9-401).

If no maturity date is stated in the financing statement it is valid for five years. A *continuation statement* may be filed within six months before the maturity date of a financing statement. A continuation statement is also valid for five years, unless a shorter time is specified in it (9-403).

When all the debts of the debtor that are secured by a financing statement are completely satisfied, the debtor is entitled to a *termination statement* signed by the secured party. If the secured party does not furnish one on request, he is liable for a fine and any damages suffered by the debtor (9–404).

Possession by Secured Party as Public Notice

The purpose of public filing of a security interest is to put any interested members of the public on notice of the security interest. A potential creditor of the debtor or potential buyer of the collateral can check the records to see whether anyone else claims an interest in the debtor's collateral. The same objective can be reached if the debtor gives up *possession* of the collateral to the creditor or to a third person who holds the collateral for the creditor. If a debtor does not have possession of collateral he claims to own, then a potential creditor or debtor is on notice that someone else may claim an interest in it. Thus, change of possession of collateral from the debtor to the creditor/secured party, or his agent, perfects the security interest (9–302[1][a]).

For example, Sam borrows $50 from a pawnbroker and puts up his guitar as collateral for the loan. The pawnbroker's security interest in the guitar is perfected by virtue of his possession of the guitar. However, change of possession is not a common or convenient way for perfecting most security interests in consumer goods.

In Re Burnett
Little v. Regency East
21 U.C.C. Rep. 1471 (D.C. R.I. 1977)

FACTS   Robert Burnett was a tenant at the Regency East Apartments in Providence, Rhode Island. He was behind in his rent payments and Regency East obtained a judgment against him for the back rent. Burnett and the manager of Regency East then signed an agreement. The agreement read as follows:

> October 14, 1975
> As collateral on the $600.00 owed by Mr. Robert Burnett I have received one (1) 1811 Five Dollar Gold Piece to be kept until 12 Noon on Thursday, October 16 or until said rent is paid in full, whichever comes first.

Burnett filed for bankruptcy. One of the questions in the bankruptcy proceeding was whether Regency East had a security interest in Burnett's gold piece.

ISSUE   Did Regency East have a perfected security interest in the gold piece it had in its possession?

DECISION   Yes. A gold piece is "goods." The agreement between Burnett and Regency East gave Regency East a security interest in the gold piece. A security interest in goods is perfected when the creditor takes possession of the collateral. Regency East had possession of the gold piece, and thus it had a perfected security interest in it.

Perfection by Attachment

A creditor who sells goods to a consumer on credit, or who loans money to enable a consumer to buy goods, can obtain limited perfection of a security interest merely by attaching the security interest to the goods (9–307). A creditor under these circumstances has what is called a *purchase money security interest* in consumer goods. For example, an appliance store sells a television set to Margaret Morse on a conditional sales contract (time-payment plan). The store does not have to file its purchase money security interest in the television. The security interest is considered perfected just by virtue of its attachment to the set in the hands of the consumer.

In Re Nicolosi
4 U.C.C. Rep. 111 (S.D. Ohio 1966)

FACTS   Nicolosi bought a diamond ring on credit from Rike-Kumber as an engagement present for his fiancée. He signed a purchase money security agreement giving Rike-Kumber a security interest in the ring until it was paid for. Rike-Kumber did not file a financing statement covering its security interest. Nicolosi filed for bankruptcy. The bankruptcy trustee claimed that the diamond ring was part of the bankruptcy estate because Rike-Kumber did not perfect its security interest. Rike-Kumber claimed that it had a perfected security interest in the ring.

ISSUE   Did Rike-Kumber have to file a financing statement to perfect its security interest in the diamond ring?

DECISION   No. The court held that Rike-Kumber had a perfected security interest in the ring. It found that the ring was "consumer goods" even though it was bought to be a gift. The court said that this was a purchase for "personal, family or household use." As the diamond was a consumer good, Rike-Kumber obtained a perfected security interest in the ring when it attached its interest to the ring. This happened when Rike-Kumber and Nicolosi signed the security agreement and Rike-Kumber extended credit to Nicolosi.

Perfection by attachment is not effective if the consumer goods are either fixtures or motor vehicles for which the state issues certificates of titles (9–302). The special rules that cover these kinds of collateral will be discussed below.

There is also one major limitation to the perfection by attachment principle. A retailer of consumer goods who relies on attachment of a security interest to perfect it prevails over other creditors of the debtor/buyer. However, the retailer does not prevail over someone who buys the collateral from the debtor if the buyer (1) has no knowledge of the security interest, (2) gives value for the goods, and (3) buys them for his or her own personal, family, or household use (9–307[2]).

For example, an appliance store sells a television set to Arthur for $750 on a conditional sales contract, reserving a security interest in the television until Arthur has paid for it. The store does not file a financing statement but relies on attachment for perfection. Arthur later borrows money from a credit union and gives a security interest in the television set. If Arthur defaults on his loans and the credit union tries to claim the television, he appliance store has a better claim to the television than the credit union. The credit union then has the rights of an unsecured creditor against Arthur.

Now suppose Arthur sells the television for $500 to his neighbor Annette. Annette is not aware that Arthur still owes money on the television to the appliance store. Annette buys it to use in her home. If Arthur defaults on his obligation to the store, it cannot recover the television from Annette. To be protected against such a purchaser from its debtor, the appliance store must file a financing statement rather than relying on attachment for perfection.

Mahaley v. Colonial Trading Co.
6 U.C.C. Rep. 746 (Ct. Common Pleas Pa. 1969)

FACTS   Glatfelter purchased a stereo set under a purchase money security agreement from Mahaley's Store. This agreement was not perfected by filing. She sold the set to Colonial Trading Company, which in turn resold it. When Glatfelter did not meet her obligations, Mahaley's sued Colonial Trading for conversion of the stereo set in which it claimed a security interest.

ISSUE   Is Colonial Trading liable for selling the stereo set in which Mahaley has a security interest?

DECISION   Yes. Mahaley was able to recover damages from Colonial Trading. Mahaley had a purchase money security interest in consumer goods. A financing statement did not have to be filed to perfect the security interest. Because Colonial Trading did not purchase the stereo for its own use, it did not come within the exception to perfection by attachment. The set was subject to Mahaley's security interest when Colonial acquired it, and it wrongfully sold the stereo in violation of Mahaley's rights in it.

Motor Vehicles   If state law requires a certificate of title for motor vehicles, then a creditor who takes a security interest in a vehicle must have the security interest noted on the title (9–302). Suppose a credit union loans money to Carlos to buy a new car in a state that requires certificates of title for cars. The credit union cannot rely on attachment of its security interest in the car to perfect it; rather, it must have its security interest noted on the certificate of title.

This requirement protects the would-be buyer of the car or another creditor who might extend credit based on Carlos's ownership of the car. By checking the certificate of title to Carlos's car, a potential buyer or creditor would learn about the credit union's security interest in the car. If no security interest is noted on the certificate of title, the buyer can buy—or the creditor can extend credit—with confidence that there are no undisclosed security interests.

Fixtures

The Code also provides special rules for perfecting security interests in consumer goods that will become *fixtures* by virtue of their attachment to or use with real property. A financing statement must be filed with the real estate records to perfect a security interest in fixtures (9–401[1][a]). Suppose a hardware store takes a security interest in some storm windows purchased on credit by a homeowner. Because the storm windows are likely to become fixtures through their use with the homeowner's home, the hardward store cannot rely merely on attachment to perfect its security interest. It must file a financing statement to perfect the security interest.

This rule helps protect a person who is interested in buying the real property or a person who is considering loaning money based on the real property. By checking the real estate records, the potential buyer or creditor would learn of the hardware store's security interest in the storm windows.

SPECIAL PRIORITY RULES

Artisan's and Mechanic's Liens

Sometimes more than one creditor claims an interest in the same collateral. The rules for resolving these conflicting claims are the *priority* rules. The Code provides that certain liens that arise by operation of law (such as artisan's liens) have priority over even perfected security interests in collateral (9–310). This keeps the Article 9 secured creditor from being unfairly enriched by the artisan's work on the collateral. Suppose First Bank has a perfected security interest in Mary's car. Mary takes the car to Frank's Garage to have it repaired. Under common law or statutory law, Frank may have a lien on the car to secure payment for his repair work. The lien permits him to keep the car until he receives payment for his work. If Mary defaults on her loan to the bank and refuses to pay Frank for the repairs, the car is sold to satisfy the liens. Frank is entitled to his share of the proceeds of the sale to pay his bill before the bank gets anything.

Magnavox Employees Credit Union v. Benson
331 N.E.2d 46 (Ct. App. Ind. 1975)

FACTS   On April 10, 1969, Benson purchased a new Ford Thunderbird automobile. She traded in her old automobile and financed the balance of $4,326 through the Magnavox Employees Credit Union, which took a security interest in the Thunderbird. In July 1969 the Thunderbird was involved in two accidents and sustained major damage. It was taken to ACM for repairs, which took seven months to make and resulted in charges of $2,139.54. Benson was unable to pay the charges and ACM claimed a garageman's lien.

ISSUE   Does Magnavox Credit Union's lien or ACM's lien have priority?

DECISION   ACM's lien has priority. ACM has a common law lien because it furnished services and materials that were incorporated into the car. Under the Code a common law lien has priority over other security interests in the collateral.

Fixtures

The Code provides special priority rules for creditors who claim an interest in consumer goods that are fixtures. These will be discussed in Chapter 44.

DEFAULT AND FORECLOSURE

Default

Usually the creditor and debtor state in their agreement what events constitute a default by the buyer. The Code does not define what constitutes default. It is left to the parties' agreement, subject to the Code requirement that the parties act in "good faith" in doing so. If the debtor defaults, the secured creditor in a consumer goods transaction has several options: (1) forget the collateral and sue the debtor on his note or promise to pay; (2) repossess the collateral and use strict foreclosure (in some cases) to keep collateral in satisfaction of the remaining debt; or (3) repossess and foreclose on the collateral, then depending on the circumstances either sue for any deficiency or return the surplus to the debtor.

Right to Possession

The agreement between the creditor and the debtor may authorize the creditor to repossess the collateral in case of default. If the debtor does default, the creditor is entitled under the Code to possession of the collateral. If the creditor can obtain possession peaceably, he may do so. If the collateral is in the possession of the debtor and cannot be obtained without disturbing the peace, then the creditor must take court action to repossess the collateral (9–503).

Raffa v. Dania Bank
321 S.2d 83 (Dist. Ct. App. Fla. 1975)

FACTS   Nancy Raffa purchased a 1970 Cadillac Eldorado and signed a "Retail Installment Contract" whereby she was to pay for the automobile over a period of 36 months. The contract was assigned to the Dania Bank by the seller of the automobile. Raffa was periodically late with her monthly payments and was more than a month overdue on her 16th payment. The bank authorized a private investigator, who it designated as a "collection agent," to repossess the Cadillac. On September 27, 1972, while Raffa and her husband were entertaining friends, the Cadillac was parked unlocked with keys in the ignition, in the driveway of her home. The collection agent walked onto the premises, got into the car, and then drove it away.

The Retail Installment Contract provided that upon default "seller may without notice or demand for performance, lawfully enter any premises where the motor vehicle may be found and take possession of it." Raffa paid off the remainder of the loan and recovered her Cadillac. Then she sued the bank for unlawfully repossessing her automobile.

ISSUE   Does Raffa have a valid claim that her car was illegally repossessed?

DECISION   No. The court held that the repossession was proper. Under the Code, a secured creditor may retake its security if it can be done without a breach of peace. Even though there was a trespass onto Raffa's property, the court said it had been consented to in the contract.

Sale of the Collateral

If the creditor has a security interest in consumer goods and the debtor has paid 60 percent or more of the purchase price or debt (and has not agreed in writing to a strict foreclosure), the creditor must sell the repossessed collateral. If less than 60 percent of the purchase price or debt has been paid, the creditor may propose to the debtor that the seller will keep the collateral in satisfaction of the debt. The consumer-debtor has 21 days to object in writing. If the consumer objects, the creditor must sell the collateral. Otherwise, the creditor may keep the collateral in satisfaction of the debt.

In disposing of the collateral, the creditor must try to produce the greatest benefit both to him and to the debtor. The method of disposal must be *commercially reasonable*. If the creditor decides to sell the collateral at a public sale, such as an auction, then the creditor must give the debtor notice of the time and place of the public sale. Similarly, if the creditor proposes to make a private resale of the collateral, notice must be given to the debtor. This gives the debtor a chance to object or to otherwise protect his or her interests (9–504).

Until the collateral is actually disposed of by the creditor, the buyer has the right to *redeem* it. This means the buyer can pay off the debt and recover the collateral from the creditor (9–506).

Distribution of Proceeds

The Code sets out the order in which any proceeds of sale of collateral by the creditor are to be distributed. First, any expenses of repossessing the collateral, storing it, and selling it, including reasonable attorney's fees, are paid. Second, the proceeds are used to satisfy the debt. Third, any other junior liens are paid. Finally, if any proceeds remain, the debtor is entitled to them. If the proceeds are not sufficient to satisfy the debt, then the creditor is usually entitled to a *deficiency judgment*. This means the debtor remains personally liable for any debt remaining after the sale of the collateral (9–504).

For example, suppose that a loan company loans Chris $5,000 to purchase a new car and takes a security interest. After making several payments and reducing the debt to $4,800, Chris defaults. The loan company pays $50 to have the car repossessed and then has it sold at an auction, incurring a sales commission of 10 percent ($450) and attorney's fees of $150. The car sells for $4,500 at the auction. From the $4,500 proceeds, the repossession charges, sales commission, and attorney's fees totaling $650 are paid first. The remaining $3,850 is applied to the $4,800 debt, leaving a balance due of $950. Chris remains liable to the loan company for the $950.

Liability of Creditor

A creditor who holds a security interest in collateral must be careful to comply with the provisions of Article 9 of the Code. If the creditor acts improperly in repossessing collateral or in the foreclosure and sale of it, he or she is liable to parties injured. Thus a creditor can be liable to a debtor if he or she acts improperly in repossessing or selling collateral (9–507).

Gibson v. Hagberg
11 U.C.C. Rep. 655 (Dist. Ct. N. Mex. 1972)

FACTS   Mr. Gibson, a collector of rare old Indian jewelry, took two of his pieces to Mr. Hagberg, a pawnbroker. The two pieces, a silver belt and a silver necklace, were worth $500 each. Hagberg loaned only $45 on the belt and $50 on the necklace. Gibson defaulted on both loans, and immediately and without notice the belt was sold for $240. A short time later the necklace was sold for $80. At the time of their sale, Gibson owed interest on the loans of $22. Gibson sued Hagberg to recover damages for improperly disposing of the collateral.

ISSUE   Was Gibson entitled to damages because of Hagberg's actions in disposing of the collateral?

DECISION Yes. The court awarded Gibson the difference between the reasonable value of the items he pawned and the amount he owed on the loan. Hagberg violated the Code's repossession provisions when he sold the items without giving the required notice to Gibson. In addition, because this type of jewelry is not normally sold by a pawnshop, the court felt that Hagberg had not made a commercially reasonable sale. Accordingly, he was liable to Gibson for the damages Gibson sustained when Hagberg improperly disposed of his property.

QUESTIONS AND PROBLEM CASES

1. What is the purpose of a financing statement?

2. Does the seller of consumer goods have to file a financing statement to perfect a security interest in those goods? Explain.

3. The Donnellys purchased a color television set from D.V.M. Advertising at a price of $1,210.95 on a retail installment sales contract in which D.V.M. retained a security interest until the balance due on the set was paid. The contract required D.V.M. to service the set and contained a waiver of defenses clause in which the Donnellys agreed to pursue any defenses or claims they had against D.V.M. directly against D.V.M. and not to assert them against the assignee of the contract. D.V.M. assigned the contract to Fairchild Credit Corp. and disappeared. The television set was not serviced as D.V.M. had contracted to do, and the Donnellys stopped making payments. When Fairchild sued for the balance due, the Donnellys tried to assert their claim of breach of the service contract as a defense. Fairchild claimed they had waived the defense. Should the court enforce the waiver of defenses clause?

4. In May 1969 Associates Loan Corp. loaned Dave Hodgin $2,376 to finance the purchase of a 1969 Toyota automobile, serial number KF 16201585. It had Hodgin sign a security agreement granting Associates a security interest on the Toyota. Associates then filed a financing statement covering a "1969 Fiat." On September 8, 1969, Hodgin filed a voluntary petition in bankruptcy. The bankruptcy trustee claimed he was entitled to sell the Toyota because Associates had not properly perfected its security interest. Is the trustee correct?

5. On March 5, 1965, the Princeton Bank filed a financing statement with the New Jersey secretary of state perfecting the bank's security interest in the inventory of new and used automobiles owned by Callahan Motors as well as in the proceeds of the sale of automobiles in inventory. On December 29, 1967, the bank filed a *continuation statement* along with the appropriate filing fee and was given a copy of the statement marked "filed" by the secretary of state's office. On February 23, 1973, Callahan Motors filed a bankruptcy petition. The bank contends that it has a perfected security in those vehicles in the bankrupt Callahan Motors' inventory, which had been purchased from funds advanced by the bank. Does the bank have a perfected security interest?

6. The Spragues bought a house trailer from Sydney Trailer Court on a retail installment contract pursuant to which the seller retained a security interest in the trailer until the Spragues paid the purchase price. A financing statement was not filed. Under New York law, a trailer is considered to be a motor vehicle and is required to be registered by the state. The Spragues were declared bankrupt. The seller claimed it had a perfected security interest because the trailer was "consumer goods" and no filing was required. The bankruptcy trustee claimed that the security interest had not been properly perfected. Who is correct?

7. James Rafferty purchased a 1962 International tractor truck. GMAC financed the purchase and took a perfected security interest in the truck. In April 1969, Rafferty took the truck to Colwell Diesel Service & Garage to be repaired. The repair amounted to $450. Rafferty failed to pay the repair bill and Colwell retained possession of the truck, claiming a mechanic's lien. Does GMAC's or Colwell's lien take priority?

8. The Franklin State Bank held a security in an automobile owned by Parker. Parker fell behind in his payments and the bank had the automobile repossessed on June 20, 1974, by towing it from Parker's garage. The automobile was not operational at that time because Parker was giving the car a tune-up and had removed the spark plugs, condensor, and air filter. On June 26, 1974, Parker received notice that a private sale of the secured automobile would occur on June 29, 1974, at a designated time and place. Carteret Auto Parts, Inc., was the only party that appeared at the sale and submitted a bid of $50. The bank, feeling that this bid was low, held the automobile until October 1, 1974, waiting for additional bids. Not having received further bids, the bank sold the automobile to Carteret Auto Parts, Inc., for $50. At no time before or after the repossession did the bank make any attempts to determine, by inspection or otherwise, why the automobile was not mechanically operational. After the bank repossessed the automobile on June 20, 1974, Parker inquired of the bank if he could buy the automobile. The essence of the bank's response was that Parker could not buy the automobile at the private sale. The bank sued Parker for the deficiency due after the sale of the automobile. Parker defended on the ground that the notice of the sale was improper and that the sale was not made in a commercially reasonable manner. Should the bank be awarded a deficiency judgment?

Secured Commercial Transactions

44

Security Interests in Commercial Personal Property

Chapter 43 covered the basic elements of security interests in consumer goods. In this chapter, the focus is on security interests in personal property other than consumer goods. This includes such things as equipment, inventory, farm products, bonds, and warehouse receipts. The basic elements for obtaining security interests in these kinds of collateral are the same as they were for consumer goods; that is, the creditor who wants to obtain a security interest in such collateral must *attach* the security interest and then *perfect* it to gain protection against other creditors of the debtor. However, there are some more detailed rules that control which of the competing creditors will prevail.

Types of Collateral

One usually thinks of goods being put up as collateral. Article 9 of the Code actually covers security interests in a much broader grouping of personal property. The Code breaks personal property down into a number of different classifications, which are important in determining how a creditor gets an enforceable security interest in a particular kind of collateral. The Code classifications are:

1. *Instruments.* This includes checks, notes, drafts, stocks, bonds, and other investment securities (9–105[1][i]).
2. *Documents of title.* This includes bills of lading, dock warrants, dock receipts, and warehouse receipts (9–105[1][f]).
3. *Accounts.* This includes rights to payment for goods sold or leased or for services rendered that are not evidenced by instruments or chattel paper but rather are carried on open account. "Accounts" include such

rights to payment whether or not they have been earned by performance (9–106).

4. *Chattel paper.* This includes written documents that evidence both an obligation to pay money and a security interest in specific goods (9–105[1][b]). A typical example of chattel paper is what is commonly known as a conditional sales contract. This is the type of contract a consumer might sign when he or she buys a large appliance such as a refrigerator on a time-payment plan from an appliance store.

5. *General intangibles.* This is a catchall category that includes, among other things, patents, copyrights, literary royalty rights, franchises, and money (9–106).

6. *Goods.* Goods are divided into several classes; the same item of collateral may fall into different classes at different times, depending on its use.

   a. *Consumer goods.* Goods used or bought for primarily personal, family, or household use such as automobiles, furniture, and appliances (9–109[1]).

   b. *Equipment.* Goods used or bought for use primarily in business, including farming or a profession (9–109[2]).

   c. *Farm products.* Crops, livestock, or supplies used or produced in farming operations as long as they are still in the possession of a debtor who is engaged in farming (9–109[3]).

   d. *Inventory.* Goods held for sale or lease or to be used under contracts of service as well as raw materials, work in process, or materials used or consumed in a business (9–109[4]).

   e. *Fixtures.* Goods that will be so affixed to real property that they are considered a part of the real property (9–313[1]).

In Re Symons
5 U.C.C. Rep. 262 (E.D. Mich. 1967)

FACTS   Mr. Symons, a full-time insurance salesman, bought a set of drums and cymbals from Grinnel Brothers, Inc. A security agreement was executed between them but was never filed. Symons purchased the drums to supplement his income by playing with a band. He had done this before and his income from the two jobs was about equal. He also played several other instruments. Symons became bankrupt and the trustee tried to acquire the drums as part of his bankruptcy estate. Grinnel's claimed that the drums and cymbals were consumer goods and thus it had a perfected security interest merely by attachment of the security interest.

ISSUE   Were the drums and cymbals consumer goods?

DECISION   No. The court held that the drums and cymbals were business equipment and not consumer goods. Symons was a professional musician and used these items in his work with the band. They would be considered consumer goods only if they had been acquired solely for his personal, as opposed to business, use.

OBTAINING A SECURITY INTEREST

Attachment

To obtain a security interest in personal property other than consumer goods, the creditor must *attach* the security interest to the collateral. This requires (1) a *security agreement* with the debtor in which the debtor grants the creditor a security interest in the collateral and (2) a *debt* owing from the debtor to the creditor (9–203). In a secured commercial transaction—as opposed to a secured consumer transaction—future advances, after-acquired property, and proceeds are more likely to be important aspects of the security agreement.

Future Advances

Future advances are frequently covered in a commercial security agreement because the creditor may be extending a line of credit to the debtor. The debtor may draw little or none of the credit at the time the agreement is entered. However, as the business needs of the debtor require additional cash, he or she will draw on the line of credit. By covering future advances in the security agreement, the creditor can use the collateral to protect his or her interest in repayment of the money advanced to the debtor at a later time.

After-Acquired Property

A security agreement may also be drafted to grant a creditor a security interest in *after-acquired property* of the debtor, that is, property that the debtor does not currently own (or have rights in) but that he or she may acquire in the future. However, the security interest in the after-acquired property cannot attach to that property until the debtor obtains some property rights in the new property (9–204). For example, Dan's Diner borrows $5,000 from the bank and gives it a security interest in all the restaurant equipment it currently has as well as all that it may "hereafter acquire." If at the time Dan's owns only a stove, then the bank has a security interest only in the stove. However, if a month later Dan's buys a refrigerator, the bank's security interest attaches to the refrigerator at the time Dan's acquires some rights to it.

Proceeds

The security agreement may provide that the security interest not only will cover the collateral described in the agreement but also will attach to the *proceeds* on the disposal of the collateral by the debtor. If a bank loans money to a dealer to enable him to finance an inventory of new automobiles and the bank takes a security interest in the inventory as well as in the proceeds of the inventory, then the bank has a security interest in the cash proceeds obtained by the dealer when the automobiles are sold to customers. To create a security interest in proceeds, all that is necessary is to add the word "proceeds" to the description of the collateral in the security agreement. Under the amendments to Article 9 that were proposed in 1972, proceeds are automatically covered unless the security agreement specifically excludes them (9–203).

PERFECTING THE SECURITY INTEREST

A creditor protects his or her security interest in commercial collateral against other creditors of the debtor by *perfecting* the security interest. The two major ways to perfect a security interest in commercial collateral are public filing and possession of the collateral by the creditor.

Public Filing

Perfection of a security interest by public notice is accomplished by filing a *financing statement*. Financing statements were discussed in detail in Chapter 43 and the same principles apply to financing statements that cover collateral in commercial transactions. The only aspect that may be different is where the financing statement has to be filed. In the case of consumer goods or fixtures, the financing statement is usually filed in an office in the locality where the debtor lives or the property is located. Each state law specifies whether financing statements that concern commercial collateral are to be filed locally and/or in a central state file, usually in the state secretary of state's office. Some states require central filing for collateral other than fixtures. Most states, however, require local filing where the transaction is local in nature. Thus, where the collateral is equipment used in farm operations or farm products, local filing is required. If you are a creditor taking a security interest, it is important to check the law in your state to determine where to file the financing statement (9–401).

Possession by the Secured Party

Possession of the collateral by the creditor is another way he or she can perfect her security interest (9–302). This method of perfection is normally not workable for consumer goods; however, it is more practicable for perfecting security interests in commercial collateral. In fact, it is the only way to perfect a security interest in checks and promissory notes. If the creditor does not obtain possession of a check or note in which he or she has a security interest, the debtor might negotiate it to someone else. If that person were a holder in due course, the creditor would not be able to enforce his or her claim to the check or note against the holder in due course (see Chapter 39).

Possession of collateral by the creditor is often the best way to perfect a security interest in chattel paper, money, and negotiable documents of title. Possession is also a possible way of perfecting a security interest in inventory. This is sometimes done through a *field warehousing arrangement*. For example, a finance company makes a large loan to a peanut warehouse to enable it to buy peanuts from local farmers. The finance company takes a security interest in the inventory of peanuts. It sets up a field warehousing arrangement whereby a representative of the finance company takes physical control over the peanuts. This representative might actually fence off the peanut storage area and control access to it. When the peanut warehouse wants to sell part of the inventory to a food processor, it must make a payment to the finance company. Then the finance company's representative will allow the peanut warehouse to take some of the peanuts out of the fenced-off area and deliver them to the processor. In this way, the finance company controls the collateral in which it has a security interest until the loan is repaid.

Possession by the creditor is usually not a practicable way of perfecting a security interest in equipment or farm products. In the case of equipment, the debtor needs to use it in the business. For example, if a creditor kept possession of a stove that was sold on credit to a restaurant, it would defeat the purpose for which the restaurant was buying the stove, that is, to use it in its business.

Removal of Collateral

Even where a creditor has a perfected security interest in the collateral of a debtor, he needs to be concerned about the possibility that the debtor will remove the collateral from the state where the creditor has filed on it. The debtor might take the collateral to another state where the creditor does not have his claim filed on the public record. Commonly the security agreement between the creditor and the debtor provides where the collateral is to be kept and that it will not be moved without the debtor giving notice to and/or obtaining the permission of the creditor. There is, however, no absolute assurance that the debtor will be faithful to such an agreement.

Under the Code a secured creditor who has perfected his security interest generally has four months after the collateral is brought into the new state to perfect his security interest in that state. If the creditor does not perfect within four months, his security interest becomes unperfected and he could lose the collateral to a person who purchases it, or takes an interest in it, after it is removed. If the creditor has not perfected his security interest by the time collateral is removed, or within the time the creditor has to perfect in the former location of the collateral, then his interest is unperfected and he does not obtain the advantage of the four-month grace period (9–103).

The Code rules that govern the removal of collateral covered by the state certificate of title, such as an automobile, are more complicated. If an automobile that is covered by a certificate of title issued in one state on which a security interest is noted is moved to another state, the perfected secured interest is perfected for four months in the new state, or until the automobile is registered in the new state. If the original state did not require that security interests be noted on the title, and if a new title is issued in the second state without notation of the security interest, then under certain circumstances a buyer of the automobile can take it free of the original security interest. To qualify, the buyer must not be in the business of buying and selling automobiles and must (1) give value, (2) take delivery after issuance of the new title, and (3) buy without notice of the security interest (9–103).

PRIORITIES

Importance of Determining Priority

Because several creditors may claim a security interest in the same collateral of a debtor, the Code establishes a set of rules for determining which of the conflicting security interests has priority. Determining which creditor has the priority or the best claim takes on particular importance in bankruptcy cases. Unless a creditor has a preferred secured interest in collateral that fully protects the obligation owed to him, the creditor may realize only a few cents on each dollar he or she is owed by the bankrupt debtor.

Basic Priority Rule

The basic rule established by the Code is that when more than one security interest in the same collateral has been filed (or otherwise perfected), the first security interest to be filed (or perfected) has priority over any that is filed (or perfected) later. If only one security interest has been perfected, for example by filing, then that security interest has priority. However, if none of the conflicting security interests has been perfected, then the first security interest to be attached to the collateral has priority (9–312[5]).

Thus, if Bank A filed a financing statement covering a retailer's inventory on February 1, 1969, and Bank B filed such a financing statement on March 1, 1969, covering that same inventory, Bank A would have priority over Bank B. This is true even though Bank B might have made its loan and attached its security interest to the inventory prior to the time Bank A did so. However, if Bank A neglected to perfect its security interest by filing and Bank B did perfect, then Bank B would prevail as it has the only perfected security interest in the inventory.

If both neglected to perfect their security interest, then the first security interest that attached would have priority. For example, if Loan Company Y has a security agreement covering a dealer's equipment on June 1, 1978, and advances money to the dealer on that date, whereas Bank Z does not obtain a security agreement covering that equipment or advance money to the dealer until July 1, 1978, then Loan Company Y has priority over Bank Z. In connection with the last situation, it is important to note that unperfected secured creditors do not enjoy a preferred position in bankruptcy proceedings, thus giving additional importance to filing or otherwise perfecting a security interest.

Exceptions to General Priority Rule

There are several very important exceptions to the general rule, which are best discussed in the context of hypothetical situations. First, assume that Bank A takes and perfects a security interest in all present and after-acquired inventory of a debtor. Then the debtor acquires some additional inventory from a wholesaler, who retains a security interest in the inventory until the debtor pays for it. The wholesaler perfects this security interest. The wholesaler has a *purchase money security interest* in inventory goods and will have priority over the prior secured creditor (Bank A) if the wholesaler has perfected the security interest by the time the collateral reaches the debtor and if the wholesaler sends notice of his purchase money security interest to Bank A before the wholesaler ships the goods. Thus to protect itself, the wholesaler must check the public records to see whether any of the debtor's creditors are claiming an interest in the debtor's inventory. When it discovers that some are claiming an interest, it should file its own security interest and give notice of it to the existing creditors (9–312[3]).

Second, assume that Bank B takes and perfects a security interest in all the present and after-acquired equipment belonging to a debtor. Then a supplier sells some equipment to the debtor, reserving a security interest in the equipment until it is paid for. If the supplier perfects the purchase money security interest by filing by the time the debtor obtains the collateral or within ten days thereafter, it has priority over Bank B. A purchase money security interest in noninventory collateral prevails over a prior perfected security interest if the purchase money security interest is perfected at the time the debtor takes possession or within ten days afterward (9–312[4]).

The preference given to purchase money security interests, provided that their holders comply with the statutory procedure in a timely manner, serves several purposes. First, it prevents a single creditor from closing off all other sources of credit to a particular debtor and thus possibly preventing the debtor from obtaining additional inventory or equipment needed to maintain its business. The preference also makes it possible for a supplier of inventory or equipment to have first claim on it until it is paid for, at which time it may become subject to the after-acquired property clause of another creditor's security agreement. By requiring that the first perfected creditor be given notice of a purchase money security interest at the time the new inventory comes into the debtor's inventory, the Code alerts the first creditor to the fact that some of the inventory on which it may be relying for security is subject to a prior secured interest until it is fully paid.

National Cash Register v. Firestone
191 N.E.2d 471 (Sup. Jud. Ct. Mass. 1963)

FACTS   On November 18, 1960, Firestone Co., Inc. made a loan to Edmund Carroll doing business as Kozy Kitchen. To secure the loan a security agreement was executed, which listed the items of property included and concluded as follows: "together with all property and articles now, and which may hereafter be, used or mixed with, added or attached to, and/or substituted for any of the described property."

A financing statement that included all the items listed in the security agreement was filed with the town clerk on November 18, 1960, and with the secretary of state on November 22, 1960.

On November 25, 1960, National Cash Register Company delivered a cash register to Carroll on a conditional sales contract. National filed a financing statement on the cash register with the town clerk on December 20, and with the secretary of state on December 21, 1960. Carroll defaulted in his payments to both Firestone and National. Firestone repossessed all of Carroll's fixtures and equipment covered by its security agreement, including the cash register, and then sold it. National claimed that it was the title owner of the cash register and brought suit for its conversion.

ISSUE Did Firestone or National Cash Register have the better right to the cash register?

DECISION The court held that Firestone had the best right to the cash register. Firestone had a perfected security interest in Carroll's equipment and fixtures, including any "after-acquired property." The cash register was after-acquired equipment and was covered by Firestone's security agreement and financing statement. National Cash Register failed to protect its interest in the cash register. To do so it should have filed its security interest within ten days of the time it delivered the cash register to Carroll. Then, as the holder of a perfected purchase money security interest, it would have prevailed over Firestone.

Buyers in the Ordinary Course of Business

A *buyer in the ordinary course of business* (other than a person buying farm products from a person engaged in farming operations) takes free from a security interest created by his seller even though the security interest is perfected and even though the buyer knows of its existence (9–307[1]). For example, a bank loans money to a dealership to finance the dealership's inventory of new automobiles and takes a security interest in the inventory, which it perfects by filing. Then the dealership sells an automobile out of inventory to a customer. The customer takes the automobile free of the bank's security interest even though the dealership may be in default on its loan agreement. As long as the customer is a buyer in the ordinary course of business, that is, buys from someone in the business of buying and selling automobiles, the customer is protected. The reasons for this rule are that the bank really expects to be paid from the proceeds of the sale of the automobiles and the rule is necessary to the smooth conduct of commerce. Customers would be very reluctant to buy goods if they could not be sure they were getting clear title to them from the merchants from whom they buy.

Sterling Acceptance Co. v. Grimes
168 A.2d 600 (Super. Ct. Pa. 1961)

FACTS Grimes purchased a new Dodge car from Hornish, a franchised Dodge dealer. The sale was made in the ordinary course of Hornish's business. Grimes paid Hornish the purchase price of the car at the time of the sale. Hornish had borrowed money from Sterling Acceptance and had given it a perfected security interest in its inventory, including the car Grimes bought. Hornish defaulted on its loan. Sterling then tried to recover the Dodge from Grimes.

ISSUE Was the car Grimes bought still subject to Sterling Acceptance's security interest?

DECISION No. The court held that Grimes was a buyer in the ordinary course of business. As such, Grimes bought the car free of Sterling Acceptance's security interest. The court said that a creditor that has a security interest in a merchant's inventory expects the debtor to make sales from the inventory. The creditor is looking for the merchant to turn the inventory into cash to repay the loan. Thus the creditor must look to the merchant for repayment and not to the car in the hands of Grimes.

Fixtures

A separate set of problems is raised when the collateral is goods that become fixtures by being so related to particular real estate that an interest in them arises under real estate law. Determining the priorities among a secured party with an interest in the fixtures, subsequent purchasers of the real estate, and those persons who have a secured interest, such as a mortgage, on the real property can involve both real estate law and the Code. However, the Code does set out a number of rules for determining when the holder of a perfected security interest in fixtures has priority over a lienholder or owner of the real estate. Some of the Code priority rules are as follows.

First, the holder of the secured interest in a fixture has priority if: (1) the interest is a *purchase money security interest* that was obtained *prior* to the time the goods become fixtures; (2) the security interest is *perfected by fixture filing* (that is, by filing in the recording office where a mortgage on the real estate would be filed) *prior to, or within ten days of,* the time when the goods become fixtures; and (3) the debtor has a recorded interest in the real estate or is in possession of it (9–313[4][a]).

For example, Restaurant Supply sells Arnie's Diner a new stove on a conditional sales contract, reserving a security interest until it is paid for. The stove is to be installed in a restaurant where Arnie's is in possession under a ten-year lease. Restaurant Supply can assure that its security interest in the stove will have priority over any claims to it by the owner of the restaurant and anyone holding a mortgage on it if it (1) enters into a security agreement with Arnie's prior to the time the stove is delivered to him, and (2) perfects its security interest by fixture filing before the stove is hooked up by a plumber or within ten days of that time.

Second, the secured party whose interest in fixtures is perfected will have priority where: (1) the fixtures are removable factory or office machines or readily removable replacements of domestic appliances that are consumer goods, and (2) the security interest is perfected prior to the time the goods become fixtures. Suppose Harriet's dishwasher breaks down and she contracts with an appliance store to buy a new one on a time-payment plan. The mortgage on Harriet's house provides that it covers the real property along with all kitchen appliances or their replacements. The appliance store's security interest will have priority on the dishwasher against the holder of the mortgage if it perfects its security interest prior to the time the new dishwasher is installed in Harriet's home (9–313[4]).

Once a secured party has filed his security interest as a fixture filing, he has priority over purchasers or encumbrancers whose interests are filed after that of the secured party (9–313[4][d]).

Where the secured party has priority over all owners and encumbrancers of the real estate, he generally has the right on default to remove the collateral from the real estate. However, the creditor must reimburse for the cost of any physical injury caused to the property by the removal (9–313[8]).

State Bank of Albany v. Kahn
296 N.Y.S.2d 391 (Sup. Ct. N.Y. 1969)

FACTS   State Bank held a mortgage on some land owned by Kahn. Kahn applied for and obtained approval for a loan from Union National Bank to construct an in-ground swimming pool on the land. After the pool was constructed, Union National gave Kahn the money with which he paid the contractor. Union National then perfected its security interest in the pool by filing a financing statement. Kahn defaulted on his mortgage loan from State Bank and it attempted to foreclose on the mortgage. Union National claimed that it had a priority security interest for the value of the pool.

ISSUE   Did the Union National Bank's security interest in the pool have priority over State Bank's mortgage on the real property?

DECISION   No. State Bank's mortgage has priority. The in-ground swimming pool was a fixture. In order for State Bank's security interest to have priority, it would have to attach to the pool prior to the time it became a fixture and then be perfected within ten days after the pool became a fixture. Here the security interest was not attached to the pool until after it was installed and had become a fixture. The attachment occurred when State Bank gave the money to Kahn and thus created the debt that is necessary for attachment of a security interest.

DEFAULT AND FORECLOSURE

With one exception, the creditor's rights on the debtor's default on a secured commercial transaction are the same as in a secured consumer transaction. The creditor has the right to possess the collateral and to dispose of it after appropriate notice to the debtor. The same priority is used for the distribution of proceeds from a sale or other distribution. If the proceeds are not sufficient to satisfy the debt, the creditor can obtain a deficiency judgment. The difference is that with consumer goods the creditor must sell repossessed collateral if more than 60 percent of the purchase price or debt has been paid. This requirement is not imposed on a creditor with a security interest in commercial collateral. The creditor can propose to the debtor to keep the collateral in satisfaction of the debt regardless of how much of the debt has been paid by the debtor (9–505).

QUESTIONS AND PROBLEM CASES

1. Is possession of collateral as a means of perfecting a security interest more likely to be utilized for consumer goods or for business inventory? Explain.

2. On April 12, 1973, ESIC Capital, a finance company, loaned Magnum Opus Electronics, Inc., $100,000 Under a signed security agreement, ESIC took a security interest in "all present and future Accounts and Contract Rights, including all related documents, instruments and chattel papers, and *all General Intangibles. . . .*" A financing statement was properly filed. Magnum defaulted on the agreement. The question then arose whether the name "Magnum Opus," which was a trademark used to identify goods made and sold by Magnum Opus Electronics and which it used in its advertising, was to be considered a "general intangible" and thus an asset in which ESIC had a security interest. Does the trademark come within the category of "general intangibles"?

3. Weiners Men's Apparel, Inc., filed a copy of a financing statement describing property subject to a security agreement given to Dutchess Associates Co. The financing statement included as property covered "inventory, fixtures, improvements, equipment, accounts and ac-

counts receivable." The security agreement itself was much shorter and listed merely "the premises" of Weiners' store as the collateral. Weiners becomes bankrupt and the trustee seeks to exclude the inventory and accounts receivable from the security agreement. Are the inventory and accounts receivable covered by the security agreement?

4. Car Color entered into a security agreement with PPG whereby PPG obtained a security interest in all Car Color's equipment and inventory as well as in the proceeds of the inventory. A financing statement was properly filed. The security agreement required Car Color to insure the equipment and inventory for the benefit of PPG, which it did. Car Color's premises were destroyed by fire and it ceased doing business. PPG claimed it was entitled to the payment from the insurance company as "proceeds" from the collateral. Is this claim correct?

5. Thompson & Son, a partnership, owned and operated a service station. On November 19, 1965, they placed an order with National Cash Register Co. for a new cash register. On December 13, 1965, they executed a security agreement with American Bank and Trust which included, in part, "all equipment, cash registers,

machinery and tools used in the operation of the service station." The agreement also contained an after-acquired property clause. It was perfected by filing on December 27, 1965. On April 20, 1966, National delivered the new register. In return it received a purchase money security interest, which was perfected by filing on August 2, 1966. Thompson & Son defaulted to both parties. Who has priority rights to the new register?

6. Mr. Burrows purchased a Utah ranch from Mr. and Mrs. Wilson. The Wilsons retained a purchase money security interest in the livestock involved in the sale. This was perfected by filing a financing statement seven months after the sale. Burrows borrowed $80,000 from Walker Bank immediately after he purchased the ranch. At that time the bank obtained a security interest from Burrows, which covered the livestock at the ranch. The bank filed its financing statement two days later. Burrows defaulted on his obligations to both the Wilsons and the bank. Who has priority to the disputed livestock?

7. Galway Funding Corp. loaned $225,000 to Sanray Floor Covering Corp. to build a new store. A mortgage was given and duly recorded. It provided that "fixtures of every kind used in the operation of the building" were included. A similar financing statement was filed by Galway on June 6, 1966. Sanray Corp. purchased $16,000 of air-conditioning equipment from Center Electric Co. to be installed in the store. They gave Center Electric a purchase money security interest in this amount. The installation was completed on November 30, 1966. Center Electric perfected on February 27, 1967. Sanray Floor became insolvent. Between Galway and Center, who has priority to the air conditioning equipment?

8. Mr. Stroman purchased a car from a used-car dealer. Although he took the car, he did not receive a title certificate but relied on the dealer to have a certificate processed. The dealer, however, took the title and used it to obtain a loan from a bank. When the dealer defaulted on the loan, the bank attempted to get the car from Stroman. Is the bank entitled to recover the car from Stroman?

9. Hempstead Bank financed the purchase of cars by Andy's Rental Car System. The bank took a security interest in those cars and perfected the security interest by filing a financing statement. Andy's sold a number of its used cars to a dealer, who in turn resold them to a variety of customers. The bank claimed that those cars were still subject to Hempstead Bank's security interest. The dealer claimed that it was a buyer in the ordinary course of business from Andy's and thus took the cars free of the bank's security interest. Is the dealer correct?

Bankruptcy

45

INTRODUCTION

When an individual, partnership, or corporation is unable to pay its debts to its creditors, a number of problems can arise. Some creditors may demand security for past debts or start court actions on their claims in an effort to protect themselves. Such actions may adversely affect other creditors by depriving them of their fair share of the debtor's assets. In addition, quick depletion of the debtor's assets may effectively prevent a debtor who needs additional time to pay off his or her debts from having an opportunity to do so.

At the same time, creditors need to be protected against the actions that a debtor who is in financial difficulty might be tempted to take that would be to their detriment. For example, the debtor might run off with his or her remaining assets or might use them to pay certain favored creditors, leaving nothing for the other creditors.

Finally, a means is needed by which a debtor can get a fresh start financially and not continue to be saddled with debts beyond his or her ability to pay.

The Bankruptcy Act

The Bankruptcy Act is a federal law that provides an organized procedure under the supervision of a federal court for dealing with insolvent debtors. Debtors are considered insolvent if they are unable or fail to pay their debts as they become due. The power of Congress to enact bankruptcy legislation is provided in the Constitution. Through the years there have been many amendments to the Bankruptcy Act and in 1978 Congress completely revised it. Among other things, this revision established a new Bankruptcy Court and made significant changes in the basic bankruptcy proceedings.

There are several major purposes to the Bankruptcy Act. One is to assure that the debtor's property is fairly distributed to the creditors and that some of the creditors do not obtain unfair advantage over the others. At the same time, the act is designed to protect all the creditors against actions by the debtor that would unreasonably diminish the debtor's assets to which they are entitled. The act also provides the honest debtor with a measure of protection against the demands for payment by creditors. Under some circumstances the debtor is given additional time to pay the creditors free of pressures that the creditors might otherwise exert. If a debtor makes a full and honest accounting of his or her assets and liabilities and deals fairly with the creditors, the debtor may have most, if not all, of the debts discharged and thus have a fresh start.

At one time bankruptcy carried a strong stigma for those debtors who became involved in it. Today this is less true. It is still desirable that a person conduct his or her financial affairs in a responsible manner; however, there is a greater understanding that some events such as accidents, natural disasters, illness, divorce, and severe economic dislocations are often beyond the ability of individuals to control and may lead to financial difficulty and bankruptcy.

TYPES OF BANKRUPTCY PROCEEDINGS

The Bankruptcy Act covers several types of bankruptcy proceedings. In this chapter our focus will be on (1) straight bankruptcy (liquidation), (2) reorganizations, and (3) consumer debt adjustments. The Bankruptcy Act also contains provisions that cover municipal bankruptcies, but these will not be covered here.

Straight Bankruptcy

A straight bankruptcy (liquidation) proceeding is brought under Chapter 7 of the Bankruptcy Act. The debtor must disclose all the property he or she owns (the bankruptcy estate) and surrender it to the *bankruptcy trustee*. The trustee separates out certain property that the debtor is permitted to keep and then administers, liquidates, and distributes the remainder of the bankrupt debtor's estate. There is a mechanism for determining the relative rights of the creditors, for recovering any preferential payments made to creditors, and for disallowing any preferential liens obtained by creditors. If the bankrupt person has been honest in his or her business transactions and in the bankruptcy proceedings, he or she is usually given a *discharge* (relieved) of his or her debts.

Reorganizations

Chapter 11 of the Bankruptcy Act provides a proceeding whereby a debtor who is engaged in business can work out a plan to try to solve financial problems under the supervisions of a federal court. A reorganization plan is essentially a contract between a debtor and creditors. The proceeding is intended for debtors, particularly businesses, whose financial problems may be solvable if they are given some time and guidance and if they are relieved of some pressure from creditors.

Consumer Debt Adjustments

Chapter 13 of the Bankruptcy Act sets out a special procedure for individuals with regular income who are in financial difficulty to develop a plan under court supervision to satisfy their creditors. Chapter 13 permits compositions (reductions) of debts and/or extensions of time to pay debts out of the debtor's future earnings.

STRAIGHT BANKRUPTCY PROCEEDINGS

Petitions

All bankruptcy proceedings, including regular bankruptcy (liquidation) proceedings, are begun by the filing of a petition. The petition may be either a voluntary petition filed by the debtor or an involuntary petition filed by a creditor or creditors of the debtor. A *voluntary petition* in bankruptcy may be filed by an individual, a partnership, or a corporation. However, municipal, railroad, insurance and banking corporations, and savings and loan associations are not permitted to file for straight bankruptcy proceedings. It is not necessary that a person who files a voluntary petition be *insolvent*, that is, unable to pay his debts as they become due. However, the person must be able to allege that he or she has debts. The primary purpose for filing a voluntary petition is to obtain a discharge from some or all of the debts.

Involuntary Petitions

An *involuntary petition* is a petition filed by creditors of a debtor. By filing it, they seek to have the debtor declared bankrupt and his or her assets distributed to the creditors. Involuntary petitions may be filed against many kinds of debtors; however, involuntary petitions in straight bankruptcy cannot be filed against (1) farmers; (2) ranchers; (3) nonprofit organizations; (4) municipal, railroad, insurance, and banking corporations; (5) credit unions; and (6) savings and loan associations. If a debtor has 12 or more creditors, an involuntary petition to declare him or her bankrupt must be signed by at least three creditors. If there are fewer than 12 creditors, an involuntary petition can be filed by a single creditor. The creditor or creditors must have valid claims against the debtor that exceed by $5,000 or more the value of any security they hold.

If an involuntary petition is filed against a debtor who is engaged in business, the debtor may be permitted to continue to operate the business. However, an *interim trustee* may be appointed by the court if it is necessary to preserve the bankruptcy estate or to prevent loss of the estate. A creditor who suspects that a debtor may dismantle his or her business or dispose of its assets at less than fair value may apply to the court for protection.

Automatic Stay Provisions

The filing of a bankruptcy petition operates as an *automatic stay* of (holds in abeyance) various forms of creditor action against a debtor or his property. These actions include: (1) beginning or continuing judicial proceedings against the debtor; (2) actions to obtain possession of the debtor's property; (3) actions to create, perfect, or enforce a lien against the debtor's property; and (4) setoff of indebtedness owed to the debtor that arose before commencement of the bankruptcy proceeding. A court may give a creditor relief from the stay if the creditor can show it does not give him or her "adequate protection" and jeopardizes his or her interest in certain property. The relief to the creditor might take the form of periodic cash payments or the granting of a replacement lien or an additional lien on property.

The Bankruptcy Courts

The 1978 revision of the Bankruptcy Act created a *U.S. Bankruptcy Court* in each federal judicial district. The President was given the authority, with the advice and consent of the Senate, to appoint bankruptcy judges who hold office for 14 years. This new court system takes effect April 1, 1984. As a five-year experimental program, the attorney general is required to appoint U.S. Trustees in certain bankruptcy courts. The duties of the trustees will include acting as a trustee in bankruptcy cases where required to do so and supervising the administration of bankruptcy cases and private trustees.

Order of Relief

Once a bankruptcy petition has been filed, the first step is a court determination that relief should be ordered. If a voluntary petition was filed by the debtor or if the debtor does not contest an involuntary petition, this step is automatic. If the debtor contests an involuntary petition, then a trial is held on the question of whether the court should order relief. The court orders relief only if (1) the debtor is generally not paying his or her debts as they become due, or (2) within four months of the filing of the petition a custodian was appointed or took possession of the debtor's property. The court also appoints an interim trustee pending election of a trustee by the creditors.

Election of Trustee

The bankrupt person is required to file a list of his or her assets, liabilities, and creditors and a statement of his or her financial affairs. Then a meeting of creditors is called by the court. The creditors may elect a creditor's committee. The creditors also elect a *trustee*, who, if approved by the judge, takes over administration of the bankrupt's estate. The trustee represents the creditors in handling the estate. At the meeting the creditors have a chance to ask the debtor questions about his or her assets, liabilities, and financial difficulties. The questions are commonly focused on whether the debtor has concealed or improperly disposed of assets.

Duties of the Trustee

The trustee takes possession of the debtor's property and has it appraised. The debtor must also turn over his or her records to the trustee. For a time the trustee may operate the debtor's business. The trustee also sets aside the items of property that a debtor is permitted to keep under state exemption statutes or under federal law.

In Re Cohen
276 F.Supp. 889 (N.D. Calif. 1967)

FACTS Cohen entered into a contract to serve as a high school teacher for "the school year 1966–1967." The contract proviced that Cohen's services were to begin on August 20, 1966, and the school year was scheduled to end on June 13, 1967. Although the services under the contract were to be performed during the nine and one-half months of the school year, Cohen's salary was payable in 12 equal monthly installments. Cohen was declared bankrupt as of February 23, 1967, and on May 5, 1967, the trustee filed an application for a turnover order for amounts due Cohen under the employment contract as of the date of bankruptcy. The trustee claims accrued earnings of the amount of $684 were due Cohen as of that date, based on a pro rata computation of payments to be made during the two and one-half months of summer vacation.

ISSUE Should the amounts that Cohen was scheduled to receive during the summer months be turned over to the trustee as a current asset of Cohen?

DECISION Yes. Because the contract provided for the services to be performed during the school year, the money was already earned, even though the money was to be paid later in the summer. Because the bankrupt had already earned the money, the trustee was entitled to have it turned over to him.

Exemptions

Under the new Bankruptcy Act, the debtor may choose to keep either certain items of property that are exempted by state law or certain items that are exempt under federal law—unless state law specifically forbids use of the federal exemption. However, any such property that has been concealed or fraudulently transferred by the debtor may not be retained.

The specific items that are exempt under state statutes vary from state to state. Some states provide fairly liberal exemptions and are considered to be "debtors' havens." Items that are commonly made exempt from sale to pay debts owed to creditors include the family Bible, tools or books of the debtor's trade, life insurance policies, health aids (such as wheelchairs and hearing aids), personal and household goods, and jewelry, furniture, and motor vehicles worth up to a certain amount.

There are 11 categories of property exempt under the federal exemption that the debtor may elect in lieu of the state exemption. The federal exemptions include: (1) the debtor's interest (not to exceed $7,500 in value) in real property or personal property that the debtor or a dependent of the debtor uses as a residence; (2) the debtor's interest (not to exceed $1,200 in value) in one motor vehicle; (3) the debtor's interest (not to exceed $200 in value for any particular item) in household furnishings, household goods, wearing apparel, appliances, books, animals, crops, or musical instruments that are held primarily for the personal, family, or household use of the debtor or a dependent of the debtor; (4) the debtor's aggregate interest (not to exceed $500 in value) in jewelry held primarily for the personal, family, or household use of the debtor or a dependent of the debtor; and (5) the debtor's aggregate interest (not to exceed $750 in value) in any implements, professional books, or tools of the trade; (6) life insurance contracts; (7) professionally prescribed health aids; and (8) social security, disability, alimony, and other benefits reasonably necessary for the support of the debtor or his dependents. The term *value* means "fair market value as of the date of the filing of the petition." In determining the debtor's interest in property, the amount of any liens against the property must be deducted.

The exemptions permit the bankrupt person to retain a minimum amount of assets considered necessary to life and to the ability to continue to earn a living. They are part of the "fresh start" philosophy that is one of the purposes of the Bankruptcy Act. The general effect of the federal exemption is to provide a minimum exemption available to debtors in all states. States that wish to be more generous to debtors can provide more liberal exemptions.

The debtor is also permitted to *void* certain liens against exempt properties that *impair* his or her exemptions. The liens that can be avoided on this basis are judicial liens or nonpossessory, nonpurchase money security interests in: (1) household furnishings, household goods, wearing apparel, appliances, books, animals, crops, musical instruments, and jewelry that are held primarily for the personal, family, or household use of the debtor or a dependent of the debtor; (2) implements, professional books, and tools of trade of the debtor or the trade of a dependent of the debtor; and (3) professionally prescribed health aids for the debtor or a dependent of the debtor. Debtors are also permitted to *redeem* exempt property from secured creditors by paying them the *value* of the collateral. Then the creditor is an unsecured creditor to any remaining debt owed by the debtor.

Other Duties of Trustee

The trustee examines the claims that have been filed by various creditors and objects to those that are improper in any way. The trustee separates the unsecured property from the secured and otherwise exempt property. The trustee also sells the bankrupt's nonexempt property as soon as is possible and consistent with the best interest of the creditors.

The trustee is required to keep an accurate account of all property and money he or she receives and to promptly deposit moneys into the estate's account. At the final meeting of the creditors, the trustee presents a detailed statement of the administration of the bankruptcy estate.

Provable Claims

If creditors wish to participate in the estate of a bankrupt debtor, they must file a proof of claim in the estate within a certain time (usually six months) after the first meeting of creditors. If a claim is *provable*, it is the basis of that creditor's right to share in the bankruptcy estate. *Provable claims* are *rights to payment* whether or not they liquidated (where the amount is certain and not in dispute), unliquidated (where the amount is not certain), disputed, fixed, or contingent. Thus a claim might be an account receivable, damages alleged to be due because of a negligent act committed by the bankrupt, a liability on an unexpired lease (limited to a one year claim for rent) or a contingent debt or liability.

Allowable Claims

The fact that a claim is provable does not assure that a creditor can participate in the distribution of the assets of the bankruptcy estate. The claim must also be *allowed*. If the trustee has a valid defense to the claim, he or she can use the defense to disallow the claim or to reduce it. All the defenses that would have been available to the bankrupt person are available to the trustee.

Secured Claims

The trustee must also determine whether a creditor has a lien or secured interest to secure an allowable claim. If the debtor's property is subject to a secured claim of a creditor, that creditor has first claim to it. The property is available to satisfy claims of other creditors only to the extent that its value exceeds the amount of the debt secured.

Priority Claims

The Bankruptcy Act declares certain claims to have *priority* over other claims. These include: (1) expenses and fees incurred in administering the bankruptcy estate, (2) unsecured claims for wages of employees up to $2,000 per individual earned within 90 days before the petition was filed, (3) contributions to employee benefit plans, (4) claims up to $900 each by individuals for deposits made on goods or services for personal use that were not delivered or provided, and (5) taxes. These claims are paid *after* secured creditors realize on their security but *before* other unsecured claims are paid. Unsecured creditors frequently receive little or nothing on their claims. Secured claims, trustee's fees, and other priority claims often consume a large part of the bankruptcy estate.

In Re Pacific Oil and Metal Co.
24 F.Supp. 767 (S.D. Cal. 1938)

FACTS Hart was the secretary-treasurer as well as a director and stockholder of the Pacific Oil and Metal Company, a bankrupt corporation. In a corporate reorganization pursuant to the Bankruptcy Act, Hart filed a claim for $1,556.81 for compensation owed him under his contract as secretary-treasurer of the company and contended that he was entitled to a priority payment of $600 as wages earned by a "clerk" within three months prior to commencement of bankruptcy proceedings. A creditor objected to allowance of the priority payment.

ISSUE	Is the $600 claim for wages entitled to priority status?
DECISION	No. The court sustained the objection and rejected the priority claim. It said Hart was really claiming as a corporate officer. The Bankruptcy Act was designed to benefit those who are dependent on their wages for a living and lose their job by reason of the bankruptcy.

Special rules are set out in the Bankruptcy Act for distribution of the property of a bankrupt stockbroker or commodities broker.

Preferential Payments

A *preferential payment* is a payment made by an insolvent debtor within 90 days of the filing of the bankruptcy petition that enables the creditor receiving the payment to obtain a greater percentage of a preexisting debt than other similar creditors of the debtor receive. The trustee has the right to recover for the benefit of the bankruptcy estate all preferential payments made by the bankrupt person.

For example, Fred has $850 in cash and no other assets. He owes $500 to his friend Bob, $1,500 to the credit union, and $2,000 to the finance company. If Fred pays $500 to Bob and then files for bankruptcy, he has made a preferential payment to Bob. Bob has obtained his debt paid in full, whereas only $350 is left to satisfy the $3,500 owed to the credit union and the finance company. They stand to recover only 10 cents on each dollar Fred owes to them. The trustee has the right to get the $500 back from Bob.

If the favored creditor is an "insider"—a relative of an individual debtor or an officer, director, or related party of a company—then a preferential payment made up to one year prior to filing of the petition can be recovered. The trustee must show that the insider had reasonable grounds to believe the debtor was insolvent when he or she received the payment.

A major purpose of the Bankruptcy Act is to assure equal treatment for all the creditors of an insolvent debtor. It also seeks to prevent an insolvent debtor from distributing his or her assets to a few favored creditors to the detriment of the other creditors. This is the reason the trustee can recover preferential payments.

Preferential Liens

Preferential liens are treated in a similar manner. A creditor might try to obtain an advantage over other creditors by obtaining a lien on the debtor's property to secure an existing debt. The creditor might seek to get the debtor's consent to a lien or to obtain it by legal process. Such liens are considered *preferential* and are invalid if they are obtained on property of an insolvent debtor within 90 days of the filing of a bankruptcy petition and the lien is to secure a preexisting debt. A preferential lien obtained by an insider within one year of the bankruptcy can be avoided if the creditor had reasonable grounds to believe the debtor was insolvent when he or she obtained the lien.

The provisions of the Bankruptcy Act that negate preferential payments and liens do not prevent a debtor from engaging in current business transactions. For example, George, a grocer, is insolvent. George is permitted to purchase new inventory, such as produce and meat, for cash without it being considered a preferential payment. George's assets have not been reduced; he simply has traded money for goods to be sold in his business. Similarly, George could buy a new display counter and give the seller a security interest in the counter until he has paid for it. This is not a preferential lien. The seller of the counter has not gained an unfair advantage over other creditors and George's assets have not been reduced by the transaction. The unfair advantage comes where an existing creditor tries to take a lien or obtain a payment of more than his or her share. Then the creditor has obtained a preference and it will be disallowed.

Saperstein v. Holland, McGill & Pasker
496 P.2d 896 (Sup. Ct. Utah 1972)

FACTS Burger-in-the-Round, Inc., was a restaurant that owed $5,711.35 to a creditor, Holland, McGill & Pasker. The creditor sued Burger-in-the-Round to obtain a judgment for the amount due. The creditor then garnished funds in this amount that were in Burger-in-the-Round's bank account. The attorney for the restaurant told the creditor that the garnishment had tied up its funds so that it could not operate. He asked that the garnishment be released. He also said that the restaurant was going to file for bankruptcy shortly. The garnishment was issued and satisfied at that time. Five days later the bankruptcy petition was filed. The bankruptcy trustee then sued to recover as a preference the amount the creditor had taken by judgment and garnishment.

ISSUE Could the trustee recover the $5,711.35 as a preferential payment?

DECISION Yes. The court held that the payment was a voidable preferential payment and could be recovered by the trustee. It was made days before the bankruptcy petition was filed and thus was within the statutory period. The creditor knew or had reason to believe that Burger-in-the-Round was insolvent at the time it received the money. The garnishment enabled the creditor to obtain a greater percentage of its debt than other creditors of the same class would receive.

Fraudulent Transfers

If a debtor transfers property or incurs an obligation with *intent to hinder, delay, or defraud creditors*, the transfer is voidable. Similarly, transfers of property for less than reasonable value are voidable by the trustee.

Suppose Kathleen is in financial difficulty. She "sells" her $5,000 car to her mother for $100 so that her creditors cannot claim it. Kathleen did not receive fair consideration for this transfer. It could be declared void by a trustee if made within a year before the filing of a bankruptcy petition against Kathleen. The provisions of law concerning fraudulent transfers are designed to prevent a debtor from concealing or disposing of his or her property in fraud of creditors.

Discharge in Bankruptcy

A bankrupt person who has not been guilty of certain dishonest acts and who has fulfilled his duties as a bankrupt is entitled to a *discharge* in bankruptcy. A discharge relieves the bankrupt person of further responsibility for those debts that are dischargeable and gives the person a fresh start. A person may file a written waiver of his or her right to a discharge. An individual may not be granted a discharge if he or she had obtained one within the previous six years. A corporation is not eligible for a discharge in bankruptcy.

Objections to Discharge

After the bankrupt has paid all the required fees, the court gives creditors and others a chance to file objections to the discharge of the bankrupt. Objections may be filed by the trustee, a creditor, or the U.S. attorney. If objections are filed, the court holds a hearing to listen to them. At the hearing, the court must determine whether the bankrupt person has committed any acts that would bar discharge. If the bankrupt has not committed such an act, the court grants the discharge. If he or she committed an act that is a bar to discharge, the discharge is denied. It is also denied if the bankrupt fails to appear at the hearing on objections or refused earlier to submit to the questioning of the creditors.

Acts That Bar Discharges

Discharges in bankruptcy are intended for honest debtors. Therefore, there are a number of acts that will bar a debtor from being discharged. These acts include: (1) unjustified falsifying, concealing, or destroying of records; (2) making false statements as to the debtor's financial conditions in the course of obtaining credit or extensions of credit; (3) transferring, removing, or concealing property in order to hinder, delay, or defraud creditors; (4) failing to account satisfactorily for any assets; and (5) failing to obey court orders or to answer questions approved by the court.

Reaffirmation Agreements

Sometimes creditors put pressure on debtors to reaffirm (agree to pay) debts that have been discharged in bankruptcy. When the 1978 amendments to the Bankruptcy Act were under consideration, some individuals urged Congress to prohibit such agreements. They argued that reaffirmation agreements are inconsistent with the fresh-start philosophy of the Bankruptcy Act. Congress did not agree to a total prohibition, but it set up a rather elaborate procedure for a creditor to go through to get a debt reaffirmed. Essentially, the creditor must do so *before* the discharge is granted, the court must approve it, and the debtor must have 30 days to rescind the reaffirmation after he or she agrees to it.

In Re Barnhart
91 F.Supp. 453 (N.D. Ohio 1950)

FACTS   Barnhart had borrowed money from Credit Plan and was behind in her payments. She applied for a new loan, with which she intended to pay the existing loan and the interest on it. At the time of the granting of the new loan, the agent of Credit Plan prepared a financial statement that showed that Barnhart owed $837.50. In fact she owed approximately $1,800. The agent was a schoolmate of Barnhart's and was familiar with her financial affairs. At the time the statement was prepared, Barnhart talked to the agent about her other debts. She signed the statement without reading it. Credit Plan filed objections to Barnhart's discharge on the ground that she obtained credit on a materially false credit statement in writing.

ISSUE   Should Barnhart be denied a discharge on the grounds that she obtained credit by filing a materially false financial statement?

DECISION   No. The court granted Barnhart a discharge. It said there was no evidence that the financial statement was a material part of the transaction or that Credit Plan placed any reliance on it. Here Credit Plan was a beneficiary of the new loan because it covered the interest due on the old loan.

Nondischargeable Debts   Certain debts are not affected by the discharge of a bankrupt debtor. The Bankruptcy Act provides that a discharge in bankruptcy releases a debtor from all provable debts except those that: (1) are due as a *tax* or *fine* to the United States or any state or local unit of government; (2) result from liabilities for obtaining money by false pretense or false representations; (3) are due for willful or malicious injury to a person or his property; (4) are due for *alimony* or *child support;* (5) were created by the larceny or embezzlement by the debtor or fraud while acting in a fiduciary capacity; (6) are certain kinds of educational loans; or (7) were not scheduled in time for proof and allowance because the creditor did not have notification of the proceeding even though the debtor was aware that he owed money to that creditor.

All these nondischargeable debts are provable debts. The creditor who owns these debts can participate in the distribution of the bankrupt's estate. However, the creditor has an additional advantage: His or her right to recover the unpaid balance is not cut off by the bankrupt's discharge. All other provable debts are dischargeable; that is, the right to recover them is cut off by the bankrupt's discharge.

Airo Supply Co. v. Page
119 N.E.2d 400 (Ill. Sup. Ct. 1954)

FACTS   Tom Page was employed by Airo Supply Company as its only bookkeeper. Over a three-year period he appropriated $14,775.77 of Airo Supply's money to his own use. Airo Supply discovered the embezzlement and obtained a civil judgment against Page for $14,775.77. Page then filed a voluntary petition in bankruptcy and his discharge was granted. Page obtained new employment, and Airo Supply instituted proceedings to garnish his wages. Page defended on the grounds that Airo Supply's judgment had been discharged in bankruptcy.

ISSUE   Was Page's debt to Airo Supply discharged as part of his discharge in bankruptcy?

DECISION   No. The Bankruptcy Act excludes from discharge those debts created by fraud or embezzlement while acting in a fiduciary capacity. Page was acting in a position of trust in handling Airo Supply funds, a position he violated by his embezzlement. He is not the honest debtor the Bankruptcy Act is designed to help and thus his debt is not dischargeable.

REORGANIZATIONS

Relief for Businesses

Sometimes creditors benefit more from a continuation of a bankrupt debtor's business than from a liquidation of the debtor's property. Chapter 11 of the Bankruptcy Act provides a proceeding whereby the debtor's financial affairs can be reorganized, rather than liquidated, under the supervision of the Bankruptcy Court. Chapter 11 proceedings are available to virtually all business enterprises, including individual proprietorships, partnerships, and corporations (except banks, savings and loan associations, insurance companies, commodities brokers, and stockbrokers). Petitions for reorganization proceedings can be filed either voluntarily by the debtor or involuntarily by its creditors.

Administration

Once a petition for a reorganization proceeding is filed and relief is ordered, the court usually appoints a committee of creditors who hold unsecured claims, a committee of equity security holders (shareholders), and a trustee. The trustee may be given the responsibility for running the debtor's business. He or she also is usually responsible for developing a plan for how the various claims of creditors and interests of persons (such as shareholders) are to be handled. The reorganization plan is essentially a contract between a debtor and its creditors. It may involve recapitalizing a debtor corporation and/or giving creditors some equity (shares) in the corporation in exchange for part or all of the debt owed to them. The plan must (1) divide the creditors into classes, (2) set forth how each creditor will be satisfied, (3) state which claims are impaired or adversely affected by the plan, and (4) treat all creditors in a given class the same (unless the creditors in that class consent to different treatment).

The plan is then submitted to the creditors for approval. Approval generally requires that creditors who hold two-thirds in amount and one-half in number of each class of claims impaired by the plan must accept it. Once approved, the plan goes before the court for confirmation. If the plan is confirmed, the debtor is responsible for carrying it out.

CONSUMER DEBT ADJUSTMENTS

Relief for Individuals

Chapter 13 (Adjustments of Debts for Individuals) of the Bankruptcy Act provides a way for individuals who do not want to be declared bankrupt to be given an opportunity to pay their debts in installments under the protection of a federal court. Under Chapter 13, debtors have this opportunity free of such problems as garnishments and attachment of their property by creditors. Only individuals with regular incomes (including sole proprietors of businesses) who owe individually (or with their spouse) liquidated, unsecured debts of less than $100,000 and secured debts of less than $350,000 are eligible to file under Chapter 13. Under the pre-1978 Bankruptcy Act, Chapter 13 proceedings were known as "wage earner plans." The 1978 amendments to the Bankruptcy Act expanded the coverage of these proceedings.

Procedure

Chapter 13 proceedings are initiated by the voluntary petition of a debtor filed in the bankruptcy court. Creditors of the debtor may *not* file an involuntary petition for a Chapter 13 proceeding. The debtor in the petition states that he or she is insolvent or unable to pay his or her debts as they mature and that he or she desires to effect a composition or an extension, or both, out of future earnings or income. A *composition of debts* is an arrangement whereby the amount the person owes is reduced, whereas an *extension* provides the person a longer period of time to pay them. Commonly the debtor files at the same time a list of his or her creditors as well as his or her assets, liabilities, and executory contracts.

Following the filing of the petition, the court calls a meeting of creditors, at which time proofs of claims are received and allowed or disallowed. The debtor is examined, and he or she submits a plan of payment. The plan is submitted to the secured creditors for acceptance. If they accept it and the court is satisfied that it is proposed in good faith, meets the legal requirements, and is in the interest of the creditors, the court approves the plan. The court then appoints a trustee to carry out the plan. The plan must provide for payments over a period of three years or less, unless the court approves a longer period (up to five years).

Suppose Curtis Brown has a monthly take-home pay of $700 and a few assets. He owes $1,500 to the credit union for the purchase of furniture on which he is supposed to pay $75 per month. He owes $1,800 to the finance company on the purchase of a used car, which he is supposed to repay at $90 a month. He also has run up charges of $1,200 on a Master Charge account primarily for emergency repairs to his car; he must repay this at $60 per month. His rent is $250 per month, and food and other living expenses cost him another $300 per month.

Curtis was laid off from his job for a month and fell behind on his payments to his creditors. He then filed a Chapter 13 petition. In his plan he might, for example, offer to repay the credit union $50 a month, the finance company $60 a month, and Master Charge $40 a month, with the payments spread over three years rather than the shorter time for which they are currently scheduled.

Discharge

When the debtor has completed his or her performance of the plan, the court issues an order that discharges her from the debts covered by the plan. The debtor may also be discharged even though he or she did not complete her payments within the three years if the court is satisfied the failure is due to circumstances for which the debtor cannot justly be held accountable. An active Chapter 13 proceeding *stays* (holds in abeyance) any straight bankruptcy proceedings and any actions by creditors to collect consumer debts. However, if the Chapter 13 proceeding is dismissed (for example, because the debtor fails to file an acceptable plan or defaults on an accepted plan), straight bankruptcy proceedings may proceed.

Thompson v. Ford Motor Co.
475 F.2d 1217 (5th Cir. 1973)

FACTS On December 8, 1971, Thomas Thompson filed a petition under Chapter 13 to pay his debts through a wage earner plan. After the notice to creditors, Ford Motor Credit Company, a secured creditor to whom Thompson was indebted for payments on a 1970 Ford, filed a proof of claim and rejected the plan. The plan was confirmed over Ford's objections and provided for payments to Ford of $22.90 a week, equivalent to the same rate and adding up to the same total as in the original sales contract, and enjoined Ford from foreclosing on the automobile. In 1972 Thompson was injured at work and was able to work only part-time. He then fell behind in his payments to Ford, even though he was regularly submitting his disability checks to the trustee. Ford then filed a petition to reclaim the car, alleging that Thompson had failed to make the payments due on the car.

ISSUE Should Ford be permitted to have the plan disregarded so that it can foreclose its security interest on the car?

DECISION No. The court rejected Ford's petition. It said that the plan did not impair the security of the lien and did not require Ford to accept less than the full amount due. When a plan is confirmed, creditors are enjoined from foreclosing on the lien while the debtor is carrying out the plan in good faith. The injunction is necessary to preserve the debtor's estate and give him a chance to carry out the plan. Thompson had fallen behind in his payments due to circumstances beyond his control and acted in good faith in submitting his disability check. Under the Bankruptcy Act, the debtor can even be discharged after three years where the failure to complete payment is due to circumstances beyond the debtor's control.

Advantages of Chapter 13

A debtor may choose to file under Chapter 13 to try to avoid the stigma of bankruptcy or to try to retain more of his or her property than is exempt from bankruptcy under state law. Chapter 13 can provide some financial discipline to a debtor as well as an opportunity to get his or her financial affairs back in good shape. It also gives relief from the pressures of individual creditors so long as payments are made as called for by the plan. The debtor's creditors stand to benefit by possibly being able to recover a greater percentage of the debt owed to them than they would in straight bankruptcy proceedings.

QUESTIONS AND PROBLEM CASES

1. What are the primary purposes of the Bankruptcy Act?

2. Under what circumstances can the creditors of a debtor force the debtor into bankruptcy proceedings?

3. If an involuntary petition for bankruptcy is filed against an individual debtor, is all of the debtor's property sold to satisfy his or her creditors' claims? Explain.

4. Why are preferential payments and preferential liens voidable by the bankruptcy trustee?

5. Suppose you are a creditor of a debtor who is involved in straight bankruptcy (liquidation) proceedings. Would you be best off if your claim is *(a)* covered by a perfected security interest in collateral of the debtor, *(b)* based on a claim for wages, or *(c)* unsecured? Explain.

6. Suppose a friend of yours is insolvent and asks for your assistance in choosing between filing for straight bankruptcy (liquidation) or filing under Chapter 13. What would you tell your friend are the major differences between the two kinds of proceedings?

7. On November 2, 1964, Shainman was adjudicated a bankrupt upon the filing of a voluntary petition. In October 1963, Shear's of Affton had loaned Shainman $10,000 secured, at least in part, by inventory. Shear's objected to the discharge of Shainman on the grounds that Shainman had issued a false inventory statement as of January 31, 1964, wherein his inventory was valued at more than $800,000 when actual value as established by a physical inventory was less than $175,000. Shear's alleged that this false statement had been relied on by Receivables Finance Company in extending business loans to Shainman. Should the discharge be denied because of Shear's objections based on false financial statements issued to another creditor?

Insurance

46

Throughout this book, you have seen many situations in which the law requires a person to bear the risk of damage to property or the loss of property. Generally the owners of property must bear the risk of loss to their own property. If the damage is caused by the intentional or negligent act of another person, however, the wrongdoer is responsible in tort for the resulting loss. As we saw in Chapter 16, in some cases the buyers of goods may be responsible for losses involving goods that they do not technically own.

The purpose of insurance contracts is to allow people to shift a risk of loss that they would ordinarily have to bear to another. The essence of an insurance contract is that the *insurer*, in exchange for the payment of consideration (called the *premium*), agrees to reimburse the *insured* for losses that are caused by specific events (*perils*).

A distinction is made between valid insurance contracts and wagering contracts. A wagering contract *creates* a new risk that did not previously exist and is illegal as contrary to public policy. Insurance contracts *transfer* existing risks.

This chapter will discuss two major types of insurance contracts: life insurance contracts and fire insurance contracts. Two other important types of insurance you may be familiar with are health and disability insurance and automobile insurance.

LIFE INSURANCE CONTRACTS

A life insurance contract is not a contract of indemnity like a fire insurance contract. In life insurance contracts the insurer is bound to pay a certain sum when a certain event (the death of the insured) occurs. Only the time that the event occurs is uncertain. The amount paid is based on the amount of the premiums paid to the insurer, since it would be difficult to establish the value of the insured's life. There are two basic kinds of insurance: whole life and term life.

Whole Life Insurance

This kind of life insurance policy, also called *ordinary* or *straight life* insurance, normally binds the insurer to pay the *face value* of the policy on the death of the insured. The insured must pay the specified premium for the duration of his or her life. In addition to its risk-shifting character, a whole life insurance policy has an important *savings* feature. As premiums are paid on the policy, it develops a *cash surrender value* that the insured can recover if the policy is terminated. In the same way, whole life policies develop a *loan value*. This increases with the age of the policy and enables the insured to borrow money from the insurer at relatively low interest rates.

Term Life Insurance

A term life insurance contract only obligates the insurer to pay the face amount of the policy if the insured dies within a specified period of time—the term of the policy. The insured is obligated to pay premiums for the term of the policy. Term contracts, unlike whole life contracts, do not build up any cash surrender value or loan value. Many term contracts have a *guaranteed renewability* feature that allows the insured to renew the policy for additional terms up to a stated age without proving insurability (good health). However, the premium rate for additional terms is likely to be higher than that for the original term. Many term contracts also contain a *guaranteed convertibility* feature that allows the insured to convert the policy to a whole life policy.

FIRE INSURANCE CONTRACTS

Fire insurance contracts are indemnity contracts. The insurer is obligated to reimburse the insured for any actual losses the insured suffered due to damage to the insured property. The loss must occur during the period of time when the policy is in force. The amount that the insured may recover is limited to the extent of the loss sustained so long as it does not exceed the amount of coverage the insured purchased.

Fire insurance contracts generally cover losses only from *hostile* fires—those that burn where no fire is intended to be, like fires caused by lightning, outside sources, or electrical shorts, or fires that escape from places where they are intended to be, like a *friendly* fire in a fireplace that spreads. Fire insurance policies generally cover more than direct damage caused by the fire. They also cover indirect damage caused by smoke and heat, and the damage caused by the efforts of firefighters to put out the fire.

Youse v. Employers' Fire Insurance Co.
238 P.2d 472 (Sup. Ct. Kan. 1951)

FACTS   Mrs. Youse was carrying a valuable sapphire ring wrapped in a handkerchief in her purse. When she got home, she placed the handkerchief containing the ring on the dresser in her bedroom along with some paper tissues. A servant mistakenly put the tissues and the ring in a wastebasket and they were subsequently put in a trash burner at the rear of the Youse property. The ring was found in the trash burner a week later and had suffered $900 in damage. Youse filed a claim against Employers' Insurance under her fire insurance policy, which insured household goods and personal property "against all direct loss or damage by fire."

ISSUE   Is the damage to the ring covered by the fire insurance policy?

DECISION   No. The term *fire* as used in fire insurance policies means a hostile fire. A *hostile* fire is one that is "unexpected, unintended, not anticipated, in a place not intended for it to be and where fire is not ordinarily maintained" or "which has escaped from a place where it was intended to be." A *friendly* fire is one "lighted and contained in a usual place for fire." The court concluded that the fire that damaged Youse's ring was a friendly fire that was not covered by her policy.

Some fire insurance contracts are called *valued policies* because, in the event the property is totally destroyed, the insured can recover an amount stated in the policy regardless of the fair market value of the building. Most fire insurance policies are *open policies*. These allow the insured to recover the fair market value of the property at the time it was destroyed, up to the limits stated in the policy. Some policies give the insurer the option of replacing or restoring the damaged property instead of paying its fair market value.

Some fire insurance policies also contain a *coinsurance clause* that can operate to limit the insured's right to recovery. Coinsurance clauses require the insured to insure the property up to a stated percentage of the fair market value before the face amount of the policy can be recovered. For example, ABC Manufacturing Company has a fire insurance policy on its warehouse with Friendly Mutual Insurance Group. The policy has a 75 percent coinsurance clause. ABC's warehouse is damaged by a fire that does $33,000 damage. At the time of the fire, it had a fair market value of $100,000. Therefore, ABC was required by the coinsurance clause to carry at least $75,000 in insurance protection. ABC's policy with Friendly Mutual has only a face value of $50,000. ABC can recover only $22,000 from Friendly (the amount of the insurance carried [$50,000] divided by the amount of insurance required [$75,000] times the loss [$33,000]).

INSURANCE POLICIES AS CONTRACTS

Since the relationship between the insured and the insurer is basically a *contractual* one, insurance contracts must satisfy all the elements required for a binding contract.

Offer and Acceptance

The standard practice in insurance is to have the potential insured make an *offer* to enter an insurance contract by completing an *application* provided by the insurer's agent, and submitting it and the *premium* to the insurer, who either accepts or rejects it. What constitutes *acceptance* depends on the kind of insurance requested and the language of the application. It is very important to know the time when an offer to create an insurance contract is accepted. Any losses suffered prior to this point must be borne by the insured, not the insurer.

Applications for life insurance often provide that acceptance does not occur until the insurer delivers the policy to the insured. Most courts hold that delivery occurs when the insurer has executed and mailed the policy. A few courts, to avoid hardship, have held that delivery occurred when the policy was executed, even though it was still in the insurer's hands. If the application calls for the policy to be delivered to an agent of the insured, delivery to the agent constitutes acceptance, unless the agent has discretionary power not to deliver the policy.

Metropolitan Life Insurance Co. v. Wood
302 F.2d 802 (9th Cir. 1962)

FACTS Jean L. Wood delivered an application for a life insurance policy and a check for the first premium to an agent of Metropolitan Life. His wife Constance was designated as his beneficiary. The application contained language that could be read as saying that applicants who submitted the premium with their applications were covered by temporary insurance until Metropolitan acted on their applications. Five days later Jean Wood died, having been examined by Metropolitan's physician earlier in the day. Metropolitan rejected the application and offered to return the premium. Mrs. Wood sued to recover the amount of the policy.

ISSUE Was Mr. Wood's life insured at the time of his death?

DECISION Yes. The language of the application determines whether an applicant is entitled to insurance protection while his or her application is pending. The court cited two earlier cases where it had held that the language in Metropolitan's application could reasonably be read by an applicant as meaning: "pay the portion of the premium required in advance and in consideration thereof you will have protection until your application is accepted or rejected." The court further held that any ambiguity in the language of the application should be resolved against Metropolitan, which had drafted it.

In fire insurance contracts the application may be worded so that insurance coverage begins when the insured signs the application. This can provide temporary coverage until the insurer either accepts or rejects the policy. The same result may also be achieved by the use of a *binder,* an agreement for temporary insurance pending the insurer's decision to accept or reject the risk. Acceptance in fire insurance contracts generally occurs when the insurer (or agent, if authorized to do so) indicates to the insured an intent to accept the application.

A common problem that occurs in insurance law is the effect of the *insurer's delay* in acting on the application. If the applicant suffers a loss after applying, but before the insured formally accepts, who must bear the loss? As a general rule, the insurer's delay does not constitute acceptance. Some states, however, have held that an insurer's retention of the premium for an unreasonable time constitutes an acceptance. Others have allowed tort suits against insurers for negligent delay in acting on an application. The theory of these cases is that insurance companies, as licensees of the state, have a public duty to insure qualified applicants. Unreasonable delay prevents applicants from obtaining insurance protection from some other source. A few states have also enacted statutes holding that insurers who fail to give notice of rejection within a specified time are bound to the contract applied for.

Locke v. Prudence Mutual Casualty Co.
172 So.2d 351 (Ct. App. La. 1965)

FACTS Louise Locke's husband applied for a life insurance policy with Prudence Mutual and sent a check for the first year's premium. Five days after applying for the policy, Mr. Locke became ill and was admitted to the hospital. He died two months later. Seventeen days after his death, Prudence Mutual refunded the premium. The application contained a clause that read: "No obligation is incurred by the Company unless said application is approved by the Company at its Home Office and a contract is issued and delivered during the lifetime and good health of the applicant." Mrs. Locke, as administrator of her husband's estate, filed suit against Prudence Mutual for negligent delay in failing to act on her husband's application.

ISSUE Was Prudence Mutual negligent in failing to act on Mr. Locke's application?

DECISION No. The "good health" clause in the application relieved Prudence Mutual of any obligation to deliver the policy after the onset of Mr. Locke's illness. In order to show negligence on Prudence Mutual's part, Mrs. Locke would have to show that the company delayed acting on the application for an unreasonable length of time during the good health of Mr. Locke. The policy was applied for in New Orleans and the company's home office was in Chicago. Under these facts, a five-day delay could not be considered negligence.

Misrepresentation   Applicants for insurance have a duty to reveal fully to insurers all the material facts about the nature of the risk so the insurer can make an intelligent decision about whether to accept the risk. Misrepresentation of material facts or failure to disclose such facts generally has the same effect in insurance cases that it does in other contracts cases; it makes the contract *voidable at the election of the insurer.*

There are, however, two common provisions in life insurance policies that help to offset the potentially harsh effects that could otherwise result from strictly applying the general rule. It is common for life insurance policies to contain a *misstatement of age* clause. Such clauses allow the insurer, in cases where the insured has misstated his or her age, to adjust the benefits payable on the insured's death to reflect the amount of protection the insured's premiums would have purchased for a person of the insured's true age. For example, Bob buys a $50,000 life insurance policy from Friendly Mutual Insurance and states his age at 35. When Bob dies, Friendly Mutual finds out that Bot was in fact 40 when he took out the policy. Since premium rates increase with the insured's age at the time the policy is taken out, Bob's premiums would have bought only $40,000 in coverage at the correct rate. Bob's estate is therefore entitled to only $40,000.

Another common clause in life insurance policies is an *incontestable clause.* This clause bars the insurer from contesting its liability on the policy on the basis of the insured's misrepresentations if the policy has been in force for a specified period of time (often two years). Incontestable clauses do not bar the insurer from objecting on the basis of absence of insurable interest, an impostor taking the required physical exam in the insured's place, or the purchase of the policy with the intent to murder the insured.

Capacity   Generally speaking, both parties to a contract must have the capacity to contract for the agreement to be enforceable. Therefore, an insurance policy taken out by a minor would be voidable at the election of the minor. Many states, however, are making minors' insurance contracts enforceable against them by statute.

Form and Content   Most states require that life insurance contracts be in writing. Fire insurance contracts may not necessarily be required to be in writing, but wisdom dictates that the parties reduce their agreement to written form.

The insurance business is highly regulated. This is due partly to the important nature of the interests protected by insurance and partly to the states' recognition of the difference in bargaining power that often exists between insurers and their insureds. Many states, in an attempt to remedy this imbalance, require the inclusion of certain standard clauses in insurance policies. They may also regulate things like the size and style of print used in insurance policies.

Interpreting Insurance Contracts

Modern courts realize that many people who buy insurance do not have the training to fully understand the technical language contained in many policies. As a result, such courts interpret provisions in insurance contracts as they would be understood by an average person. Any ambiguities in insurance contracts are generally interpreted *against the insurer* who drafted the contract.[1]

Third Parties and Insurance Contracts

As a general rule, contracts are assignable only when the assignment will not materially alter the promisor's burden of performance. Applying this rule to life insurance policies leads to the conclusion that a life insurance contract should be assignable because assignment will not increase the risk of the insurer, since the identity of the insured will remain unchanged. If, however, the named *beneficiary* (the person to whom proceeds are payable) of the policy has been irrevocably designated because no right to change beneficiaries has been reserved in the policy, the policy may not be assigned without the beneficiary's consent. It is also common for the policy's terms to limit assignability. Many policies require notice to the insurer of any assignment. Failure to comply with such requirements renders an attempted assignment void.

An important element of the risk in fire insurance policies is the character of the insured. Therefore, such policies are generally nonassignable. Those who purchase property from the insured get no interest in any policy the insured owned covering the purchased property. After a loss has occurred, however, the insured can assign the right to receive benefits under the policy, since no change in the insurer's risk is involved.

INSURABLE INTEREST

In order for an insurance contract not to be considered an illegal wagering contract, the person who purchases the policy must have an insurable interest in the life or property being insured. A person who will suffer a financial loss from the destruction of the insured property or the death of the insured person has the required insurable interest. If no insurable interest is present, the policy is void.

Insurable Interest in Life Insurance

In life insurance contracts the required insurable interest must exist at the time the policy was issued. It need not exist at the time of the insured's death. Those who have a legitimate interest in the continuation of the insured's life have the required insurable interest.

In addition to the insured, the insured's spouse, parents, children, and any other persons who are dependents of the insured have an insurable interest in the insured's life. The insured's business associates like partners, employer, and fellow shareholders in a closely held corporation may also

---

[1] Refer back to *Metropolitan Life Insurance Co. v. Wood* earlier in this chapter.

have the required insurable interest. Likewise, the insured's creditors have an insurable interest to the extent of the debt owed them by the insured.

Insurable Interest in Fire Insurance

Those who have an insurable interest in property must have that interest at the time the loss occurs. This means that, in addition to the legal owner of the insured property, any other person who has a legal or equitable interest in the insured property when the loss occurs has the required insurable interest. So, life tenants, lessees, secured creditors (mortgagees or lienholders), and those holding reversionary or remainder interests in the insured property all have the required insurable interest. The extent of a person's insurable interest in property is limited to the value of his or her interest in the property.

Atlantic Insurance Co. v. Massey
381 F.2d 520 (10th Cir. 1967)

FACTS Bill Massey hired a contractor to build him a home. The terms of their agreement provided that the contractor retained title to the house until it was completed. The builder took out a builder's risk policy with Fireman's Fund Insurance Company. The policy provided that it only covered losses in excess of any other insurance coverage of the structure. Massey was allowed to move into the house prior to its completion and was issued a homeowner's policy by Atlantic before moving in. Three days after Massey moved in, the house was damaged by an explosion and fire. Fireman's Fund paid the contractor $14,223, which was applied to the contract price due from Massey. Massey bought the remains of the house from the contractor and had it rebuilt. Massey claimed he had suffered an additional $1,250 loss due to work he had done on the property himself. In exchange for Fireman's payment to the contractor, Massey assigned to Fireman's his claim against Atlantic for the $14,233. Massey filed suit against Atlantic for his $1,250 personal loss and Fireman's sued as Massey's assignee, claiming that its builder's policy was excess insurance and it should be reimbursed by Atlantic for the $14,223.

ISSUE Was Atlantic obligated to pay the total amount of the damage to Massey's house under his homeowner's policy?

DECISION No. The insurable interests of the contractor and Massey were separate and distinct. Both parties had insurance policies covering their respective interests, and their policies could not cover more than their interests. The contractor's insurable interest at the time of the loss was the value of the labor and materials the contractor had contributed, and Massey's insurable interest was the amount he had put into the house during its construction. Therefore, Atlantic was liable to Massey only for the $1,250 loss he suffered. It had no duty to pay the contractor's losses and Massey had no claim to assign to Fireman's beyond his insurable interest.

NOTICE AND PROOF OF LOSS

A person who seeks to recover benefits under an insurance policy must notify the insurer that a loss covered by the policy has occurred and furnish proof of loss. In life insurance contracts, the beneficiary is probably required to complete and return a proof-of-death form and may be required to furnish a certified copy of the insured's death certificate. Fire insurance policies ordinarily require the insured to furnish a sworn statement of loss.

It is common for insurance policies to specify that notice and proof of loss must be given within a specified time. The policy may state that compliance with these requirements is a *condition* of the insured's recovery and that failure to comply *terminates* the insurer's obligation. Some policies, however, merely provide that failure to comply *suspends* the insurer's duty to pay until proper compliance is made. Some courts require the insurer to prove it has been injured by the insured's failure to give notice before they allow the insurer to avoid liability on the grounds of tardy notice.

CANCELATION AND LAPSE

Cancelation of an insurance policy occurs when a party that has the power to terminate the policy (extinguish all rights under the policy) has exercised that power. *Lapse* occurs when the policy is permitted to expire by failure to renew it after its term has run, or by some default on the part of the insured.

Cancelation

Ordinarily, the insurer cannot cancel a life insurance contract. Allowing insurers to do so would be unfair to insureds since insurers would be tempted to terminate old or seriously ill insureds to avoid paying benefits. The insured can cancel a life insurance policy by surrendering the policy to the insurer. The insured who surrenders a whole life policy is generally allowed under the policy provisions to recover the accumulated cash surrender value of the policy, or to purchase a paid-up or extended insurance policy. A *paid-up* policy provides the insured with a fully paid policy in the amount that his or her cash surrender value will purchase at his or her age. An *extended* policy is a term policy with the same face value as the insured's original policy; the length of the term is determined by the cash surrender value of the original policy.

Generally, either party may cancel a fire insurance contract after giving notice to the other party. The amount and form of the notice required may be specified in the policy or regulated by state statute. Insurers who cancel must return the unearned portion of any premiums paid by the insured. Insureds who terminate are entitled to a return of the premium on a short-rate basis, which means that the insurer may compute the premiums owed for the time the policy was in effect at a slightly higher rate than the rate that would apply to the full term of the policy.

Property insurance policies frequently contain clauses that terminate the insurer's liability if the insured does anything that materially increases the insurer's risk. They may also specifically list certain kinds of behavior that will cause termination. Common examples of such behavior are keeping flammable or explosive material and allowing the premises to remain vacant for a stated period of time.

Standard Marine Insurance Co. v. Peck
342 P.2d 661 (Sup. Ct. Colo. 1959)

FACTS
The Pecks owned a lawn and garden supply store. Standard Marine was the insurer of the store and its contents. The Pecks placed a fireworks display in the store, where it was subsequently set off by a young boy. A fire resulted, which damaged or destroyed much of the Pecks' merchandise. Standard Marine refused to reimburse the Pecks for their loss, citing a clause in the policy that read: "The Company shall not be liable for loss occurring while the hazard is increased by any means within the control or knowledge of the insured."

ISSUE
Is Standard Marine liable for the Pecks' loss?

DECISION
No. The evidence clearly established that the fireworks were explosive and flammable in nature and increased the risk borne by Standard Marine. The Pecks' ordinary stock consisted of lawn and garden tools, lawn mowers, and so forth. The court concluded by observing that if stocking and displaying fireworks "was not an increase in the ordinary hazards of a hardware store, it is difficult to conceive what would be."

Lapse

Insurance policies that are written for a stated period of time (fire insurance contracts and term life insurance contracts) *lapse* at the expiration of the policy term. The insured's failure to pay premiums also causes a policy to lapse. The insured who allows a whole life insurance policy to lapse generally has the same rights to cash surrender value, paid-up, or extended term insurance as the insured who surrenders such a policy.

Many states have passed statutes that give the insured who fails to pay a life insurance premium a grace period, usually 30 or 31 days after the date the premium was due, to pay the overdue premium and prevent policy lapse. In addition, some life insurance contracts contain a reinstatement clause that allows an insured to reinstate a lapsed policy that has not been surrendered for its cash surrender value by requesting reinstatement within a specified period after default. To secure reinstatement the insured must pay all past-due premiums and a stated amount of interest and furnish proof of insurability (good health).

QUESTIONS AND PROBLEM CASES

1. Distinguish between a valid insurance contract and an illegal wagering contract.

2. Explain the operation of a coinsurance clause.

3. Why is it critically important in some cases to determine when an insurance contract came into existence?

4. Wright signed an application for a $10,000 life insurance policy with double indemnity for accidental death. Pilot Life's agent issued Wright a "conditional receipt" showing his advance premium payment. It stated that if the application were approved without restriction, the insurance would be in effect "from the date of this application." The reverse side of the printed form of the receipt was for signature by those, unlike Wright, who did not pay an advance premium. It stated, "Although the agent has explained to me how I may make settlement under this application, thereby placing it immediately in full force and effect . . . provided that I am insurable, it is not my desire to take advantage of this opportunity." Within the period covered by the prepaid premium, Wright was killed in an accident. Is Pilot Life liable on the risk?

5. Marshall signed an application and paid an initial premium on an accidental injury policy sold by an agent of Life and Casualty Co. The agent assured him that the coverage went into effect immediately and that there was no problem about the company accepting it because no physical examination was required. The application provided, "Policy hereby applied for will not take effect until it is issued by the Company . . . and the Company is not bound by any knowledge of, or statements made by, or to any agent, unless set forth herein." It also stated, ". . . accidents, incurred before date of issue of the policy by the Company . . . ARE NOT INSURED." Marshall signed below a statement that he had read the application and that he understood the first statement, it having been read to him by the agent. He was injured before a policy was issued, and Life and Casualty Co. refuses to pay benefits. Marshall claims that he has a valid agreement for temporary insurance. Is he correct?

6. Mrs. Hardy purchased an automobile on March 1, 1962, on an installment purchase contract and applied for credit life insurance to secure the balance due. The purchase was jointly in the names of Mr. Hardy, who was then a terminal cancer patient in a veterans' hospital, and Mrs. Hardy. Mr. Hardy was listed as the insured in the policy, which was to be effective until March 1, 1965. The top of the insurance certificate bore the following statement: "This certificate is null and void unless the insured is between the ages of 18 and 65 and in good health on the effective date hereof." The automobile salesman, who also served as agent of the insurance company, had sold the Hardys another auto a year earlier and at that time took the installment sales contract to the hospital for Mr. Hardy to sign. He did not inquire as to Mr. Hardy's health at the time of the 1962 purchase. Mr. Hardy died on May 8, 1962 and the insurer refused payment, claiming that Hardy was not in good health when the policy was issued. Is the insurer liable on the policy?

7. Alderson purchased a mobile home and executed a security agreement on it to Credit Corp. to secure a note. The note was further secured by a life insurance policy on Alderson's life, with Credit Corp. listed as beneficiary. Alderson sold the mobile home to Kincaid, who agreed to pay the unpaid balance to Credit Corp. Alderson died and the insurer paid the balance of the note to Credit Corp. Kincaid claims that since the note has been paid, he is entitled to a bill of sale to the mobile home. Credit Corp. argues that it, but not Kincaid, has an insurable interest in Alderson's life. Is it correct?

8. Mrs. Dennison purchased from Liberty National a $1,500 life insurance policy on the life of the two-year-old daughter of her husband's sister. Mrs. Dennison was listed as beneficiary. A few months later the girl died from poisoning and Mrs. Dennison was convicted

of murder. Weldon, the girl's father, sued Liberty National for negligence in issuing the policy to one who had no insurable interest. In the trial court, judgment was given to Weldon in the amount of $75,000. Liberty National appealed, claiming that Mrs. Dennison did have an insurable interest and that it had no duty to use care to avoid issuing the policy to one who does not have such an interest. Is Liberty National correct?

9. Radio Foods Corp. suffered a small fire that activated a sprinkler system, causing water to seep through its floor to the premises of Salvage Shoe Co. below. Adjusters of Radio Foods' and Salvage Shoe's insurance carriers examined the premises. The day after the fire, an attorney for an insurer of Salvage Shoe wrote a letter requesting Radio Foods not to move or affect the condition of a large refrigerator whose compressor had ignited at the time of the fire, but nothing was said in the letter or in various conversations between Salvage Shoe personnel or their insurers and Radio Foods managers to suggest that Radio Foods' employees had been negligent. More than four months later the attorney wrote another letter, in which he did claim that the fire resulted from negligence. This letter was forwarded to the agent of the company that carried the fire insurance for Radio Foods, who returned it. A few days later a complaint was served on Radio Foods, which then promptly sent all papers to the agent of Consolidated Mutual, Radio Foods' liability insurer. The liability insurer denies liability because of failure to notify it "as soon as practicable." Is this defense good?

10. Mr. Wisley purchased a life insurance policy from National Reserve Life Insurance Company, naming his wife Sarah as beneficiary and his father Rufus as beneficiary in the event of Sarah's death. Two years later the Wisleys were divorced and Sarah remarried. When Mr. Wisley died, both Sarah and Rufus claimed to be entitled to the proceeds of the policy. Rufus claimed that Sarah no longer had an insurable interest in his son's life. Was he right?

Government Regulation

Government
Regulation of Business

47

Early Regulation

Contrary to popular belief, government regulation of business is not a new phenomenon on the American scene. Even in colonial times, government regulation was a common factor in the everyday life of business. Businesses that performed public services, while privately owned, were regulated in the public interest. For example, the rates charged by the owners of toll bridges, ferries, grist mills, and inns and taverns were controlled by colonial regulators. The volume of production, quality, and price of essential commodities like bread and tobacco were also subjects of colonial regulation.

The major differences between early efforts at regulating business and contemporary government regulation lie in the breadth and volume of regulation and the source of regulation. Early regulation took place on a local or state level and was limited in scope. The last century, however, has seen a virtual explosion of regulation, particularly on the federal level.

The Growth of Regulation

The Industrial Revolution changed the nature of American society. Before the Civil War, more than 80 percent of Americans were self-employed, and the small proprietorship was the dominant form of business organization. Many forms of organization were objects of public distrust. Labor unions were treated as criminal conspiracies, and even corporations were viewed with some suspicion.

The growth of corporate power and the activities of the large industrial combines and trusts after the Civil War became subjects of major public

629

concern, producing a public outcry for federal action. Congress responded by passing the Interstate Commerce Act in 1887 and the Sherman Antitrust Act (discussed in detail in the next chapter) in 1890.

In addition, life was simply becoming more complex. New forms of human activity that presented a need for regulation were (and are today) arising on an almost daily basis. Ever-expanding scientific knowledge also continued to increase our understanding of the effects of our behavior on each other and on the environment.

This tremendous growth of government regulation, while it has no doubt produced many positive social benefits, has also produced considerable public dissatisfaction. We all regularly hear complaints about government "red tape" and bureaucratic inefficiency. Some commentators argue that the *costs* associated with complying with government regulations are a major contributor to spiraling inflation. Others complain that operating a business is becoming increasingly difficult in an environment of increasing and sometimes conflicting regulations. Regulatory agencies are criticized as being inefficient and overzealous on the one hand and "captive" tools of industry on the other.

Despite current popular disenchantment with regulation, however, it is probably fair to say that regulation is here to stay. Some areas of social activity may merit deregulation, and in other areas conflicting or overlapping regulations may need to be reworked, but nonetheless, as long as the United States is the kind of highly complex, industrialized society it is today, regulation will continue to be an important fact of life.

STATE REGULATION OF BUSINESS

State governments have very broad powers. They have the power to tax, to own and operate businesses, and to take private property for public purposes by the power of eminent domain. They also have broad police powers to legislate to promote the health, safety, and general welfare of their citizens.

The states also have the exclusive power to regulate *intrastate commerce*—economic activities that have no significant effect on commerce outside their own borders. The states' power to regulate *interstate commerce* (commerce among the states) is limited. The *Commerce Clause* of the U.S. Constitution gives the federal government the power to regulate commerce "with foreign nations" and "among the several states." This, combined with the *Supremacy Clause* of the Constitution, which holds federal laws superior to state laws in cases of conflict, restricts the states' powers.

The federal government has the exclusive right to regulate all *foreign commerce* of the United States, and all aspects of interstate commerce where there is an essential need for nationwide regulation. The federal government also has the exclusive right to regulate areas of interstate commerce that it has *preempted* by enacting inclusive federal regulatory schemes.

Burbank v. Lockheed Air Terminal, Inc.
411 U.S. 624 (U.S. Sup. Ct. 1973)

FACTS   The Burbank City Council passed an ordinance that prohibited "pure jet" aircraft from taking off from the Hollywood-Burbank Airport between 11 P.M. of one day and 7 A.M. of the next. Lockheed, the operator of the airport, brought suit to enjoin the enforcement of the ordinance, claiming it was unconstitutional under the Commerce Clause and the Supremacy Clause. The only regularly scheduled flight affected by the ordinance was an intrastate flight on Pacific Airlines that departed for San Diego every Sunday night at 11:30 P.M.

ISSUE   Did existing federal regulation preempt state regulation of aircraft noise?

DECISION   Yes. The Federal Aviation Act of 1958 gave the Federal Aviation Administration (FAA) broad authority to regulate the use of airspace, and the Noise Control Act of 1972 obligated the FAA and EPA to develop a comprehensive scheme of federal control of the aircraft noise problem. The Court said that the fact that the 1972 act did not contain an express preemption provision was not decisive, and noted that the pervasive control vested in the EPA and FAA "seems to us to leave no room for local curfews or other local controls." Upholding the Burbank ordinance could lead to "fractionalized control of the timing of takeoffs and landings" that would "severely limit the flexibility of the FAA in controlling air traffic flow." Therefore, the Court concluded that a uniform and exclusive system of federal regulation was necessary if the congressional objectives underlying the Federal Aviation Act were to be fulfilled.

The states are free to regulate other aspects of interstate commerce so long as their efforts do not unreasonably obstruct or interfere with interstate commerce, or conflict with any existing federal regulation.

Great Atlantic and Pacific Tea Co., Inc. v. Cottrell
424 U.S. 366 (U.S. Sup. Ct. 1976)

FACTS   A&P filed suit to challenge the constitutionality of a Mississippi statute that prohibited the sale of milk and milk products from another state unless the other state accepted milk produced and processed in Mississippi on a reciprocal basis. A state court ordered A&P not to distribute in Mississippi milk processed in A&P's Louisiana plant. Mississippi argued that the statute was a reasonable "police power" exercise designed to assure the distribution of healthful milk products to its citizens.

ISSUE   Is the Mississippi statute an unreasonable burden on interstate commerce?

DECISION   Yes. The Court stated that "the very purpose of the Commerce Clause was to create an area of free trade among the several states" and that "even without implementing legislation by Congress," it is a "limitation on the power of the States." The Court noted that the states retain broad powers to legislate for the protection of their citizens, and that local action is not necessarily invalid because it has some effect on the flow of interstate commerce. The Court, however, characterized Mississippi's argument that the reciprocity clause served its vital interests as "frivolous," since Mississippi would accept milk below its own domestic standards if the producing state would do the same. So, the Court concluded that the burden the statute imposed on interstate commerce was "clearly excessive" in relation to the local benefits.

FEDERAL REGULATION OF BUSINESS

Early interpretations of the Commerce Clause primarily focused on its negative power to restrict state regulation of interstate commerce. For example, in the landmark case of *Gibbons v. Ogden*,[1] the U.S. Supreme court held that New York could not grant Ogden a monopoly to operate coastal steamboats between New York and New Jersey, since Gibbons, a competitor, had acquired a federal license to operate in the same waters. Even after the increase in federal regulation that followed the Civil War, the courts tended to interpret the Commerce Clause narrowly, thereby limiting the federal government's power to regulate business. In 1918, for example, the Supreme Court struck down the Child Labor Act as an unconstitutional exercise of federal power.[2]

Later decisions took a broader view of the Commerce Clause, recognizing federal power to regulate activities that have a "substantial relationship" to interstate commerce. In 1937, for example, the Supreme Court upheld the National Labor Relations Act's application to labor organizing within a single plant.[3] The Court noted that the defendant was a large corporation with widespread operations, and said that the effect of its unfair labor practices on interstate commerce would be more than indirect and remote. In today's highly interdependent economy, most important economic activity is within the reach of federal regulation under the present expansive view of the Commerce Clause.

Wickard v. Filburn
317 U.S. 111 (U.S. Sup. Ct. 1942)

FACTS   In 1938 Congress passed the Agricultural Adjustment Act in an attempt to stabilize agricultural production and assure farmers of reasonable minimum prices for their produce. Wickard, the Secretary of Agriculture, announced annually a national acre-

---

[1] Wheat. 1 (1824).

[2] *Hammer v. Dagenhart*, 247 U.S. 251 (1918).

[3] *NLRB v. Jones & Laughlin Corp.*, 301 U.S. 1 (1937).

age allotment for various farm products like wheat, which was apportioned to the states and, ultimately, to individual farms. Filburn was a small farmer who kept dairy cattle and chickens and raised a small amount of winter wheat. He sold some of the wheat but used most of it on his farm as livestock feed and for family use. His 1941 allotment was 11.1 acres, but he sowed and harvested 23 acres. When the Department of Agriculture assessed a $117.11 penalty against him, he filed suit to enjoin its enforcement.

ISSUE   Does Congress have the power under the Commerce Clause to regulate local wheat production?

DECISION   Yes. The Court said that even if Filburn's activity was local and could not be classed as "commerce," it could still be reached by Congress if it exerted "a substantial economic effect on interstate commerce." The Court said that the effect of the consumption of home-grown wheat on interstate commerce is due to the fact that it constitutes "the most variable factor in the disappearance of the wheat crop." The Court noted that one of the primary purposes of the act was to increase the market price for wheat by limiting the volume that could affect the market. The Court therefore concluded that the volume of home-consumed wheat could have a substantial influence on the price of wheat sold in the market.

ADMINISTRATIVE AGENCIES

Rise of Agencies

The explosion of government regulation in this century has been accompanied, and in part aided, by another social phenomenon of great importance: the creation and widespread use on both the federal and state levels of administrative agencies. There are several reasons for this development, which some legal scholars have argued is the single most important legal development of this century. Many people who favored increased regulation of business felt that the courts and legislatures were not well suited to deal with many of the complex problems that were arising in our rapidly changing environment. They argued for the creation of specialized administrative bodies to develop a reservoir of expertise in various areas of regulation. This, it was argued, would permit the continuous and rapid development of regulatory policy without resorting to the slower, case-by-case approach followed by the courts and legislatures. Allowing such agencies to hear and judge disputes would speed up problem solving and reduce the burdens placed on our already overworked judicial system.

Characteristics of Agencies

Administrative agencies are unique in our legal system, since they are in theory part of the executive branch of government, but they also perform legislative and judicial functions. In addition to investigating and prosecuting violations of statutes and their own regulations, agencies generally have the power to issue regulations that have the force of law. They also have the power to adjudicate disputes involving alleged violations of their regulations and the statutes they are charged with enforcing.

Agency hearings are much less formal than court trials, since they never involve juries and rules of evidence are less strictly observed. Those who are unhappy with an agency's decision must exhaust all administrative remedies before appealing the decision to a court of law. On appeal, the scope of judicial review of administrative agencies' actions is fairly limited.

Limits on Agencies' Powers

Agencies must conduct their affairs in accordance with basic constitutional guarantees and the various administrative procedure acts designed to restrict their actions. *Due process* requires that those who will be affected by agency action have advance notice of agency proceedings and the opportunity to appear at a hearing and present their views. The enabling statute that created the agency may be attacked as an unconstitutional delegation of legislative power if it does not set out adequate guidelines for agency action. In some cases, agency actions may be attacked as being outside the jurisdiction of the agency as defined by the enabling statute.

The courts generally do not substitute their judgment for that of an agency, even if they believe an agency's actions to be unwise. Only agency decisions that are "arbitrary and capricious" are overturned by the courts. The fact that agencies have such broad powers and are subject to such limited control is very disturbing to many people. Many people may never enter a court in their entire lifetime, but the actions of administrative agencies directly affect all our lives on a daily basis.

Butz v. Glover Livestock Commission Co., Inc.
411 U.S. 182 (U.S. Sup. Ct. 1973)

FACTS The Department of Agriculture (Butz was the Secretary of Agriculture) instituted a proceeding against Glover, a registered livestock market agency, under Section 303 of the Packers and Stockyards Act. Glover was charged with intentionally underweighing livestock that had been cosigned to it for sale, a practice it had been formally warned against on three occasions during a five-year period before the proceedings were filed. The administrative hearing examiner recommended a cease-and-desist order, an order to henceforth keep correct records, and a 30-day suspension of Glover's registration. This recommendation was reviewed by the department's judicial officer, who reduced the suspension to 20 days and adopted the rest of the recommendation. The U.S. Court of Appeals reversed the suspension order as "unconscionable."

ISSUE Did the Court of Appeals act correctly in reversing the suspension order?

DECISION No. The Court of Appeals reversed the department's suspension order because it felt suspension was contrary to a policy of achieving uniformity of sanctions for similar violations (in four previous suspension decisions, the Secretary had imposed suspensions only in cases of "intentional and flagrant" violations, not merely negligent ones), and because it felt that the cease-and-desist order and the damaging publicity surrounding it were adequate punishment to deter the acts the department objected to. The Supreme Court, however, said that the Court of Appeals could not overturn the department's choice of sanction unless it was "unwarranted in law" or "without justification in fact." Nothing in the act confines suspension to cases of intentional misconduct, and an agency's use of a sanction in a particular case is not invalidated "because it is more severe than sanctions imposed in other cases." Therefore, the Court concluded that there was no evidence that the suspension was "unwarranted in law," and that, in view of Glover's disregard of the prior warnings, there was ample factual evidence to support the department's action.

Breadth of Agency Regulation

As consumers, the products we purchase, the advertising of those products, the interest rates we pay on loans, the rates we pay for utilities, and the availability and cost of public transportation are only a few of the many aspects of our lives that are regulated by administrative agencies. In the workplace, agencies regulate wages and hours of work, working conditions, unemployment and retirement benefits, and workmen's compensation. These regulations were discussed in detail in Chapter 24. Chapters 30 and 31 in part discussed the regulation of securities by the Securities and Exchange Commission.

In the marketplace, the behavior of competing firms is subject to comprehensive regulation. Chapter 48 will discuss the antitrust laws in detail. The Federal Trade Commission Act, which created one of the most active and controversial federal administrative agencies and gave it broad powers to regulate a wide variety of competitive activity, is a good example of the federal government's extensive regulation of business.

THE FEDERAL TRADE COMMISSION ACT

In 1914 Congress was disappointed with the efforts under the Sherman Act to control anticompetitive practices and tendencies in the American economy. One of Congress' responses to this situation was the passage of the Federal Trade Commission Act (it also passed the Clayton Act, which will be discussed in the next chapter). The act created the Federal Trade Commission (FTC), a bipartisan administrative agency, which was designed to provide expert and continuing enforcement of federal antitrust policies and to prevent unfair competitive practices in the marketplace.

The FTC is a large and vigorous federal agency. In 1977 it had an annual budget of $52 million, a staff of 1,700, and 759 investigations under way, including proceedings against major firms like Exxon, General Motors, Sears, Kellogg, and General Foods. Despite its size, the commission is still not adequately equipped to handle the flood of complaints it receives daily from the public.

Section 5 of the FTC Act gives the commission broad powers to deal with "unfair methods of competition" and "unfair or deceptive acts or practices in commerce." The FTC Act is technically not part of the antitrust laws, although restraints of trade that would violate Section 1 of the Sherman Act (discussed in the next chapter) are clearly also illegal under the FTC Act as "unfair methods of competition." The FTC Act also attacks behavior that is outside the scope of the antitrust laws. "Unfair methods of competition" include many anticompetitive practices that would not violate the letter of the antitrust laws.

FTC v. Texaco, Inc.
393 U.S. 223 (U.S. Sup. Ct. 1968)

FACTS Texaco had an agreement with Goodrich entitling Texaco to a 10 percent commission on all purchases of Goodrich tires, batteries, and accessories (TBA) by Texaco dealers, in exchange for "promoting" the sale of Goodrich products to Texaco dealers. Texaco constantly reminded the dealers of its desire that they stock Goodrich TBA, and it had earned over $22 million in commissions on $245 million in Goodrich sales to Texaco dealers during the five-year period of the FTC's study. Many of Texaco's dealers leased their stations from Texaco on a yearly basis. The leases were terminable on ten days' notice by Texaco at the end of any year. The dealers' gasoline and petroleum products supply contracts with Texaco were also on a yearly basis, terminable on 30 days' notice by Texaco. The FTC found this arrangement to be an "unfair method of competition" and ordered Texaco to cease and desist from continuing it.

ISSUE Does Texaco's agreement with Goodrich violate Section 5 of the FTC Act?

DECISION Yes. The Court said that Texaco had dominant economic power over its dealers. Its relationship with them was "inherently coercive," since dealers stood to lose their leases if they incurred Texaco's wrath. The Court concluded that Texaco's arrangement with Goodrich had an adverse effect on the marketing of TBA, since smaller suppliers of TBA had to look to the service station market for sales because five major companies controlled all original equipment TBA sales. Nonsponsored TBA suppliers, the Court noted, could not compete with Goodrich on even terms of price and quality for sales to Texaco dealers, since they also had to overcome Texaco's influence on its dealers. Therefore, the Court concluded that "the anticompetitive tendencies of such a system are clear," and the FTC "was properly fulfilling the task that Congress assigned it in halting this practice in its incipiency."

False advertising and a wide variety of other deceptive practices sometimes used in business have been successfully attacked under the "unfair or deceptive acts or practices" language of the act.

Resort Car Rental System, Inc. v. FTC
518 F.2d 962 (9th Cir. 1975)

FACTS Resort Car Rental controlled several car rental companies, all of which used the term "Dollar-A-Day" in their names. The FTC found that the use of this term was misleading, since the company's actual charges included a mileage charge, minimum mileage requirement, and insurance charges, and it ordered Resort to cease and desist from using the "Dollar-A-Day" term in the future. Resort argued that its use of the term was not deceptive, since customers were informed of all rates and charges before entering a rental contract. It also argued that the FTC had exceeded its authority by ordering the deletion of the "Dollar-A-Day" term, which Resort claimed destroyed valuable goodwill vested in that slogan.

ISSUE Did the FTC act properly in ordering Resort to cease and desist from using the "Dollar-A-Day" slogan?

DECISION Yes. The court observed that the FTC's judgment is entitled to deference in this case because deceptive advertising cases necessarily involve "inference and pragmatic judgment." The FTC Act is violated if a deceptive ad "induces the first contact through deception, even if the buyer later becomes fully informed before entering the contract." The FTC has broad discretion to fashion orders appropriate to prevent unfair trade practices, and its order was not an abuse of that discretion.

The FTC has the power to police the act by using *cease-and-desist orders* (an administrative order similar to an injunction). These orders become final unless they are appealed to the courts, and their violation is punishable by fines of up to $10,000 per day. The FTC also has the power to issue *trade regulation rules,* most of which have been issued in the area of consumer protection. Violations of these rules are also punishable by fines of up to $10,000 per day. This aspect of the FTC's power will be discussed in Chapter 49.

In addition to its responsibilities under Section 5 of the act, the FTC also has broad enforcement responsibilities under other federal statutes. It has joint jurisdiction (with the Department of Justice) over the Clayton Act. It also has jurisdiction over the Webb-Pomerene Act, the Federal Drug and Cosmetic Act, the Flammable Fabrics Act, the Lanham Trademark Act, the Fair Packaging and Labeling Act, and several consumer credit laws.

QUESTIONS AND PROBLEM CASES

1. What factors contributed to the explosion of government regulation of business in the last century?

2. What are the limitations on the power of the states to regulate interstate commerce?

3. What were the factors that contributed to the development of administrative agencies as a device for implementing regulation?

4. The New York Central Railroad was convicted of obstructing a railroad crossing. The applicable state statute allowed a train five minutes to pass; the New York Central took seven minutes. New York Central appealed, claiming that the regulatory statute violated the Commerce Clause of the U.S. Constitution. Is the statute a valid exercise of the state regulatory power?

5. The city of Barre passed an ordinance to license itinerant photographers. Unlike resident photographers, itinerants were required to post a performance bond and pay certain licensing fees. Olan Mills, Inc., a corporation that employs several itinerant photographers, sued the city, claiming that the ordinance was a violation of the Commerce Clause and therefore unconstitutional. Can the city regulate itinerant photographers in this manner?

6. An Illinois state statute provided that any employer who, through advertisements, was seeking to hire employees to replace employees currently on strike had to state in such advertisement that a strike was in progress at that place of business. A violation of this statute was punishable by a fine of not more than $300 for each day of advertising. Federal Tool Company was charged with violating this statute and argued that this state statute has been preempted by the National Labor Relations Act. The NLRA enacted into law by the U.S. Congress covers prohibited employer and employee unfair labor practices. Was the Illinois statute preempted by the NLRA?

7. The lease between a developer landlord, Tyson's Corner Regional Shopping Center, and a tenant, a large department store, gave the store a "sole and absolute" right to disapprove of other tenants' entry into the large suburban center. The Federal Trade Commission charged that these "prior approval provisions" restrained trade in violation of Section 5 of the FTC Act, not only by restricting competition from prospective tenants and competitors,

but also by limiting the floor space available to new entries and prohibiting their use of "discount" advertising and their sale of certain brands of merchandise. How should the court rule on the commission's allegations?

8. Firestone Tire Co., in promoting one of its tire products, used two advertisements. The first claimed that the tires were "safe tires" that were custom built and personally inspected by skilled craftsmen. Firestone's own consumer survey showed that 15.3 percent of a scientifically selected sample of tire purchasers thought the advertisement meant that the tires were absolutely safe and absolutely free from any defects. The second advertisement claimed that the tire "stops 25 percent quicker." Firestone had performed one set of tests on one surface to substantiate this claim. The FTC ordered Firestone to cease and desist the use of these advertisements, saying the first advertisement was deceptive and the second one was unfair and deceptive because it was without substantial scientific test data to support it. Will the FTC order be overturned on appeal?

9. The Colgate-Palmolive Co. marketed and advertised a product called Rapid Shave. Television commercials showed the shaving cream being applied to sandpaper, with a razor immediately shaving the area clean. In actuality, it required 80 minutes for the sandpaper to soak before it could be shaved. Evidence also indicated that the sandpaper as shown on television was in fact plexiglas with sand applied. Colgate claimed that these misrepresentations are not so material as to mislead the public. The FTC claimed that any misrepresentation, if it induces the public to buy, is an illegal deception. The FTC issued a cease-and-desist order. Must Colgate comply?

10. Paint Company advertised and sold paint with a policy that, with the purchase of a gallon or quart of paint, each customer received an equivalent sized can free. Evidence disclosed that Paint Company had no history of selling single cans of paint, but that, with rare exceptions, it always sold two cans of paint at the

advertised price. However, there was no evidence of the company inflating or discounting the single-can price. The FTC enjoined Paint Company's practice essentially on the grounds that, since the company recovers the cost of the second can in the price of the first, the customer "pays" for the second can with the first; and, therefore, the second can is not free. Should the commission's finding be reversed on appeal?

The Antitrust Laws

48

W ith the growth of national markets after the Civil War, the United States witnessed an important development on the economic scene: the growth of large industrial combines and trusts. Many of these huge business entities engaged in practices aimed at destroying their competitors. This behavior led to a public outcry for legislation designed to preserve competitive market structures and prevent the accumulation of great economic power in the hands of a few firms.

Existing law was inadequate to deal with this important problem. The common law had traditionally held that contracts that unreasonably restrain trade were illegal as contrary to public policy, but the only thing the courts could do to enforce this rule was refuse to enforce the contract if one of the parties objected to it. Congress responded by passing the *Sherman Act* in 1890, and later supplemented it with the *Clayton Act* and the *Robinson-Patman Act*.

An examination of developments since the passage of the antitrust laws indicates that they have not been successful in stopping the trend toward concentration in the American economy. The market structure in many industries today is highly *oligopolistic*—consisting of only a few competing firms. It seems fair to assume, however, that antitrust enforcement has at least prevented industry from becoming even more concentrated than it already is.

THE SHERMAN ACT

The Sherman Act makes contracts in restraint of trade and monopolization illegal. It provides criminal penalties for violations of its provisions (up to a $100,000 fine and/or three years in jail for individuals and up to a $1 million fine for corporate violators). It also gives the federal courts broad injunctive powers to remedy antitrust violations. The courts can order convicted defendants to *divest* themselves of the stock or assets of other companies; *divorce* themselves from a functional level of their operations (e.g., order a manufacturer to sell a captive retail chain); or, in extreme cases, order *dissolution*—force the defendant to liquidate its assets and go out of business.

Private individuals who have been injured by antitrust violations have strong incentives to sue. They may recover *treble damages* (three times their actual losses) plus costs and attorneys' fees. This can mean tremendous potential liability for antitrust defendants. A famous antitrust suit against General Electric Company and several other electric equipment manufacturers resulted in awards of more than $200 million in treble damages. Private plaintiffs who seek to recover treble damages must first convince the court that they have *standing* to sue, that is, that they have suffered a *direct injury* as a result of the defendant's claimed antitrust violations. In a recent controversial case, the state of Illinois and several other government entities were denied standing to sue concrete block suppliers they alleged had fixed the price of blocks used in the construction of public buildings.[1] This holding by the U.S. Supreme Court that *indirect purchasers* do not have standing has produced strong efforts in Congress to overturn the Court's decision by corrective legislation.

Since the federal government's power to regulate business flows from the Commerce Clause of the U.S. Constitution, the federal antitrust laws apply only to behavior that substantially affects interstate commerce or international trade. Behavior that affects only intrastate (purely local) commerce is outside the scope of the federal antitrust laws and must be challenged under state antitrust statutes, some of which are not vigorously enforced.

In view of the fact that a large portion of business in the United States is conducted across state lines, it is often relatively easy to show the required impact on interstate commerce. Even behavior that takes place solely within the borders of one state can have an interstate impact in today's economy. For example, an agreement by Oklahoma wholesale liquor distributors to divide up the market in that state was held to violate the Sherman Act because it would result in higher prices for, and therefore lower sales of, liquor purchased in interstate commerce.[2]

---

[1] *Illinois Brick Company v. Illinois*, 429 U.S. 1087 (1977).

[2] *Burke v. Ford*, 389 U.S. 320 (1968).

**Section 1—
Restraints
on Trade**

Section 1 of the Sherman Act provides:

> Every contract, combination in the form or trust or otherwise, or conspiracy, in restraint of trade or commerce among the several states, or with foreign nations is declared to be illegal.

A *contract* is any agreement, express or implied, between two or more persons to restrain competition; a *combination* is a continuing partnership in restraint of trade; and a *conspiracy* occurs when two or more persons join together for the purpose of restraining trade. The purpose of Section 1 is to attack joint action in restraint of trade.

When faced with the difficult problem of deciding what kinds of behavior amounted to a "restraint of trade," the courts concluded that some kinds of behavior always have a negative effect on competition that can never be excused or justified. These kinds of acts are classed as *illegal per se;* they are conclusively presumed to be illegal. Any behavior that has not been classed as illegal per se is judged under the *rule of reason.* Rule of reason trials involve a complex, often lengthy attempt by the court to balance the anticompetitive effects of the defendants' acts against any justifications for their behavior. If the court concludes that the defendants' acts had a significant anticompetitive effect that was not offset by any positive effect on competition or other social benefit, their behavior is held illegal. While per se rules have been criticized as shortcuts that sometimes oversimplify economic realities, they do speed up lengthy trials and provide sure guidelines for business. The following are some of the kinds of behavior that have been held to violate Section 1.

Price-Fixing. The essential characteristic of a free market is that the price of goods and services is determined by the play of forces in the marketplace. Attempts by competitors to interfere with the market and control prices are called *horizontal price-fixing* and are illegal per se under Section 1. Price-fixing may take the form of direct agreements among competitors about what price they will sell a product for or what price they will offer for a product. It may also be accomplished by agreements on the quantities to be produced, offered for sale, or bought. Whether done directly or indirectly, horizontal price-fixing is always illegal and can never be legally justified.

Attempts by manufacturers to control the resale price of their products are also within the scope of Section 1. This kind of behavior is called *vertical price-fixing* or *resale price maintenance.* Manufacturers can lawfully state a "suggested retail price" for their products, since this does not involve a "contract," "combination," or "conspiracy" prohibited by Section 1. If the manufacturer gets the retailer to *agree* to follow the suggested price, however, such an agreement is a contract in restraint of trade and is illegal per se under Section 1.

There are two indirect methods a manufacturer can use lawfully to control resale price: *consignment sales* and *unilateral refusal to deal.* Both these

exceptions are, in effect, "loopholes" resulting from this section's requirement of *joint action,* and their use has been strictly policed by the courts.
A consignment agreement is one in which the owner of goods delivers
them to another who is to act as the owner's agent in selling the goods.
If a manufacturer delivers all goods to its dealers on a consignment basis,
it can lawfully fix the price of those goods, since the goods remain its
property and are not the property of the dealers. In order to be legal
within this exception, the arrangement must be a true consignment: The
manufacturer must retain title to and risk of loss of the goods, and the
dealer must have the right to return unsold goods.

A manufacturer can also lawfully unilaterally refuse to deal with those
who fail to follow its suggested retail price. The idea behind this exception
is that a single firm can deal or not deal with whomever it chooses without
violating Section 1. However, if the manufacturer enlists the aid of others,
like its wholesalers or dealers who are not price-cutting, to help police
price-cutting dealers, or reinstates dealers who have been cut off for price-
cutting, the courts will probably infer that an illegal restraint of trade
has been created.

Division of Markets.   Any agreement among competing firms to divide
up the available market by assigning each other exclusive territories is a
horizontal division of markets and is illegal per se. The idea is that each
firm is given a monopoly in its assigned territory.

A manufacturer can lawfully, as a matter of business policy, unilaterally
assign exclusive dealerships to its dealers or limit the number of dealerships
it grants in any geographic area. Manufacturers who require their dealers
to agree to refrain from selling to customers outside their assigned territories
or to unfranchised dealers inside their assigned territories, however, may
run afoul of Section 1. Such *vertical restraints on distribution* were at one
time considered to be illegal per se when applied to goods that the manufacturer had sold to its dealers (consignment sales being treated under the
"rule of reason").[3] This is not the case today, however, since the U.S.
Supreme Court abandoned the per se rule in the *Continental T.V.* case
in favor of applying the *rule of reason* to most vertical market restraints.

Continental T.V., Inc. v. G.T.E. Sylvania, Inc.
429 U.S. 1070 (U.S. Sup. Ct. 1977)

FACTS   Sylvania, in an attempt to increase its share of the national television sales market
(1 to 2 percent), adopted a franchise plan that limited the number of Sylvania franchises granted in a given area and allowed its franchisees to sell only from specified

---

[3] *U.S. v. Arnold, Schwinn & Co.,* 388 U.S. 365 (1967).

store locations. Continental T.V., a Sylvania franchisee, became dissatisfied when Sylvania appointed one of Continental's competitors in the San Francisco area as a Sylvania franchisee. Continental asked for permission to sell Sylvania televisions in Sacramento, which Sylvania denied. Continental withheld some payments due to Sylvania, and when Sylvania filed suit, Continental counterclaimed, arguing that Sylvania's location restrictions were a per se violation of Section 1 of the Sherman Act.

ISSUE Should location restrictions like Sylvania's be illegal per se under Section 1?

DECISION No. The Court noted that vertical restraints on distribution had been declared illegal per se in the *Schwinn* case. The Court decided, however, that a per se rule was not appropriate for such restraints because per se illegality should be applied only to behavior that always has a negative effect on competition and can never be justified. Vertical market restraints have a mixed potential effect on competition. They harm intrabrand competition between sellers of Sylvania televisions by limiting the number of sellers of a particular product. On the other hand, they can be used to promote interbrand competition between Sylvania and other competing brands by inducing competent and aggressive retailers to market a product, or engage in service or promotional activities that they might not pursue unless given some isolation from intrabrand competition. Therefore, the Court concluded that such vertical market restraints should be judged under the rule of reason.

Group Boycotts and Concerted Refusals to Deal. A single firm can lawfully refuse to deal with certain firms or agree to deal only on certain terms, but any such agreement by two or more firms is a per se violation of Section 1—a *joint* restraint on trade.

Parallel Business Behavior and Section 1. A constant problem that has occurred in the enforcement of Section 1 is when the courts *infer* that a conspiracy or agreement to restraint trade by fixing prices, limiting production, or boycotting competitors exists from the *actions* of firms in the marketplace where there is no evidence of an *overt* agreement. The courts have consistently held that pure "conscious parallelism"—knowing parallel pricing behavior—for example, is not a violation of Section 1.[4] This makes it very difficult to attack *oligopolies* (a few large firms that share one market) under Section 1, since firms in such a market may independently elect to follow a "price leader" firm rather than risk their large market share by competing on price.

Actual agreement among competitors, however, is not required for a violation of Section 1. All that is required is that the court find that the defendant firms were invited to participate in concerted action and that they went along with the proposed scheme.[5] Trade association information

---

[4] *Esco Corp. v. U.S.*, 340 F.2d 1000 (9th Cir. 1965).

[5] *Interstate Circuit, Inc. v. U.S.*, 306 U.S. 208 (1939).

exchanges on matters such as price, costs, inventories, and production have frequently been attacked on this basis.[6]

Other Section 1 Violations. Section 1 has been applied to a wide variety of activities involving joint restraints on trade. Examples include reciprocal buying agreements, the activities of professional associations, some joint ventures by competitors, and agreements by competitors to pool profits or losses or to refrain from advertising prices. Section 1 may also apply in some cases to behavior that is more specifically covered by other sections of the antitrust laws like mergers, acquisitions, tie-in contracts, and exclusive dealing and requirements contracts.

**Section 2—
Monopolization**

When a firm acquires *monopoly power*—the power to fix prices or exclude competitors—in a particular market, the antitrust laws' objective of promoting competitive market structures has been defeated. Monopolists have the power to fix price unilaterally, since they have no effective competition. Section 2 of the Sherman Act was designed to attack monopolies. It provides:

> Every person who shall monopolize, or attempt to monopolize, or combine or conspire with any other person or persons to monopolize any part of trade or commerce among the several states, or with foreign nations shall be deemed guilty of a felony. . . .

The first thing a student should note about the language of Section 2 is that it does not outlaw monopolies. It outlaws the act of "monopolizing." A single firm can be guilty of "monopolizing" or "attempting to monopolize." In order to show a violation of Section 2, the government or a private plaintiff must show not only that the defendant firm has *monopoly power* but also that there is an *intent to monopolize* on the defendant's part.

Intent to Monopolize. Early cases under Section 2 required a showing that the defendant acquired monopoly power by *predatory* or *coercive means* like price-fixing or price discrimination, or *abused* monopoly power in some way like charging unreasonably high prices once it was acquired.[7] This restrictive interpretation hampered enforcement of Section 2 and opened the door to concentration in the American economy.

Courts today look at how the defendant acquired monopoly power. If the defendant intentionally acquired monopoly power or attempted to maintain it after having acquired it, *intent* to monopolize has been shown. Monopolization has been defined as *"the willful acquisition or maintenance of monopoly power in a relevant market as opposed to growth as a consequence of superior product, business acumen, or historical accident."*[8]

---

[6] *U.S. v. Container Corp.*, 393 U.S. 333 (1969).
[7] *Standard Oil Co. of New Jersey v. U.S.*, 221 U.S. 1 (1911).
[8] *U.S. v. Grinnell Corp.*, 384 U.S. 563 (1966).

So the defendant today must convince the court that its monopoly power simply happened and is not the result of a conscious attempt to acquire or maintain it. If the defendant has monopoly power because it "built a better mousetrap," made wise decisions when other competitors did not, or simply was the first entrant or only survivor in a market that can support only one firm of its kind (e.g., the only newspaper in a small town), no violation of Section 2 exists.

Monopoly Power. Monopoly power exists when a firm controls a very high percentage share of the relevant market. The decided cases in this area indicate that a firm must have captured approximately 70 percent or more of the relevant market to have monopoly power. In order to determine the defendant's market share, the court in a Section 2 case must define the *relevant market*. This is a crucial part of the proceedings, since the broader the relevant market is drawn, the smaller the defendant's market share will be. There are two components to a relevant market determination: the geographic market and the product market.

The relevant *geographic market* is determined by economic realities. Where do the sellers of the goods or services in question customarily compete? Transportation cost is often a critical factor that limits geographic market size. It may be a small area for cement but the whole nation for transistors, for example.

The relevant *product market* is composed of those products that are "reasonably interchangeable by consumers for the same purposes" (the *functional interchangeability* test). The idea here is that a firm's power to fix price is limited by the availability of other competing products that buyers find acceptable. So, in a famous case against DuPont for monopolizing the market for cellophane (it had a 75 percent share), the court concluded that the relevant product market was all "flexible wrapping materials," including waxed paper, aluminum foil, and polyethylene, and that DuPont's 20 percent share of that product market was clearly not enough for monopoly power.[9]

United States v. Grinnell Corp.
384 U.S. 563 (U.S. Sup. Ct. 1966)

FACTS Grinnell controlled three companies (AFA, ADT, and Holmes) that jointly controlled 87 percent of the central station protection service market. The central station protection service market includes fire and burglar alarm services that use detection devices to alert a central station staffed by employees who notify the appropriate authorities in the event a burglary or fire is detected. Before acquiring control of the three companies, Grinnel had market division agreements with them, and after acquiring

---

[9] *U.S. v. DuPont*, 351 U.S. 377 (1956).

them, had bought out 30 other companies in the burglar and fire alarm market. At the time suit was filed, Grinnel had offers outstanding to purchase its four largest competitors. Other forms of protective services were available, but subscribers to central station services received substantially greater reductions in their insurance premiums than those subscribing to other forms of protective services.

ISSUE   Is Grinnell guilty of "monopolization" under Section 2 of the Sherman Act?

DECISION   Yes. Grinnell's history of acquisitions clearly demonstrated the intent to monopolize required to violate Section 2. The only question remaining was whether central station services, as opposed to all forms of protective services, could be considered the relevant product market. The Court concluded that central station service was acknowledged to be superior to other forms of protective service and was therefore not functionally interchangeable with them. Therefore, Grinnell clearly had monopoly power, the second element required for a Section 2 violation.

THE CLAYTON ACT

Congress was disappointed with the government's lack of success in the courts in challenging monopolists under the Sherman Act. The Clayton Act was passed in 1914 to supplement the Sherman Act by attacking specific practices that monopolists had historically followed to gain monopoly power. The idea was to "nip monopolies in the bud" before a full-blown restraint of trade or monopoly power was achieved. The Clayton Act was intended to be *preventive* in nature, and in most cases only the *probability* of a significant anticompetitive effect must be shown to establish a violation.

Since it deals with probable harms to competition, there is no criminal liability for Clayton Act violations. Treble damages are available to private plaintiffs, however, and the Federal Trade Commission has the power to enforce the act through the use of cease-and-desist orders.

Section 3

Section 3 of the Clayton Act was basically designed to attack three kinds of anticompetitive behavior: tie-in (or tying) contracts, exclusive dealing contracts, and requirements contracts. Section 3 makes it illegal to lease or sell commodities or to fix a price for commodities on the condition or agreement that the buyer or lessee will not deal in the commodities of the competitors of the seller or lessor if doing so may "substantially lessen competition or tend to create a monopoly in any line of commerce."

Section 3 applies only to *commodities* (goods), so tie-in, exclusive dealing, and requirements contracts that involve services must be attacked under Section 1 of the Sherman Act. Section 3 does not apply to cases where a manufacturer has entered true consignment arrangements with its distributors, since no "sale" or "lease" occurs in such cases. No formal agreement is required for a violation of Section 3; any use by the seller of economic power to stop buyers from dealing with the seller's competitors is enough to satisfy the statute.

Tie-in Contracts. Tie-in (tying) contracts occur when a seller refuses to sell a product (the tie-in or tying product) to a buyer unless the buyer also purchases another product (the tied product) from the seller. So, if Acme Seeds, Inc., refuses to sell its seeds (the tie-in product) to farmers unless they also agree to buy fertilizer (the tied product) from Acme, this is a tie-in contract; the sale of fertilizer is *tied* to the sale of seeds.

The economic harm from such contracts is that Acme's competitors in the sale of fertilizer are foreclosed from competing for sales to Acme's buyers, since Acme has used its power in the seed market to force its buyers to buy its fertilizer. There is no legitimate reason why Acme's buyers would ever want to enter tie-in contracts, and therefore the courts have treated such agreements harshly. Tie-in contracts are illegal under Section 3 if either: (1) the seller has monopoly power in the tie-in product, or (2) the seller has foreclosed competitors from a substantial share of the market in the tied product ($500,000 a year). So, if Acme has monopoly power in its seeds or it has managed to tie-in $500,000 or more a year in fertilizer sales, its tie-in contracts violate Section 3.

Exclusive Dealing and Requirements Contracts. An exclusive dealing contract is created when a buyer agrees to sell only the product lines of his seller. For example, a lawn and garden store agrees to sell only Brand A lawn mowers. A requirements contract is created when a buyer agrees to purchase all its needs in a certain item from one seller, like a candy manufacturer that agrees to buy all the sugar it requires from one sugar refiner. The economic harm of such contracts is that the competitors of the seller are foreclosed from competing for sales to the buyer for the duration of the contract.

These contracts were initially treated like tie-in contracts, with the courts looking at the dollar amount of commerce foreclosed to competition to determine their legality. However, courts today recognize that, unlike tie-in contracts, exclusive dealing and requirements contracts can benefit both the buyer and the seller by reducing selling costs and assuring buyers of a supply of needed items. Therefore, courts today look at the percentage share of the relevant market foreclosed to competition by an exclusive dealing or requirements contract in determining its legality.

Tampa Electric Co. v. Nashville Coal Co.
365 U.S. 320 (U.S. Sup. Ct. 1961)

FACTS   Tampa Electric, a public utility, entered a requirements contract to buy all the coal for its Gannon Station from Nashville Coal for a period of 20 years. A minimum price was set for coal and a cost escalation clause was included. After Tampa Electric had spent $7.5 million preparing to burn coal instead of oil, Nashville Coal notified Tampa that it would not perform, claiming the contract violated Section 3 of the Clayton Act.

ISSUE   Does the parties' contract violate the Clayton Act?

DECISION   No. An exclusive dealing contract does not violate Section 3 unless it is probable that it will foreclose competition in a substantial share of the affected line of commerce in the "area of effective competition." This is the geographic area where the seller operates and the buyer can effectively turn to for supplies. The courts look at the relative strength of the parties and the proportion of volume of commerce involved in the contract in relation to the total volume of commerce in the relevant market area. The dollar amount of commerce involved is ordinarily of little consequence. The Court noted that Nashville Coal had 700 competitors who sold coal mined in Pennsylvania, Virginia, West Virginia, Kentucky, Tennessee, Alabama, Illinois, and Ohio. The proportionate volume of coal preempted by the parties' contract was less than 1 percent, a figure the Court concluded was "quite insubstantial."

Section 7

Section 7 of the Clayton Act was designed to provide a tool for attacking *mergers*—a term broadly used in this section to refer to the acquisition of one company by another. As initially worded, Section 7 was fatally flawed. It applied only to mergers where a firm acquired control of one of its *competitors* (a *horizontal* merger) by purchasing the competitor's *stock*. The courts were powerless to deal with *asset* mergers, where the acquiring company buys all the assets but none of the stock of the acquired company. Section 7 also did not apply to *vertical* (supplier-customer) or *conglomerate* mergers.

Section 7 was amended in 1950 to give it its present wording and make it a much more effective antimerger tool. Section 7 prohibits any corporation engaged in commerce from acquiring all or part of the stock or assets of any other corporation engaged in commerce, unless for investment purposes only, where the effect of the acquisition may be to "substantially lessen competition" or "tend to create a monopoly" in "any line of commerce in any section of the country."

The "line of commerce" and "section of the country" concepts in Section 7 are similar in nature to the relevant product and geographic market concepts in Section 2 of the Sherman Act, but they may be more loosely applied due to the preventative nature of Section 7. Similarly, Section 7 invalidates mergers that involve a *probable* anticompetitive effect at the time of the merger. The fact that economic data after the merger has taken place do not clearly demonstrate an *actual* negative effect on competition is not necessarily fatal to a Section 7 suit.

Horizontal Mergers.   A court seeking to determine the legality of a horizontal merger (between competitors) under Section 7 looks at the market share of the resulting firm. Horizontal mergers that result in a firm with an undue percentage share (roughly 20 percent or more) of the relevant market are presumed illegal if there is no showing by the defendant that the merger is not likely to have an anticompetitive effect.

Mergers involving firms with smaller market shares have, however, frequently been enjoined if other economic or historical factors indicated a probable anticompetitive effect. Some factors that the courts have considered relevant are: a trend toward concentration in the relevant market (a decreasing number of competing firms), the competitive position of the merging firms (Are the defendants dominant firms despite their relatively small market shares?), a past history of acquisitions by the acquiring firm (Are we dealing with a budding "empire builder"?), and the nature of the acquired firm (Is it an aggressive, innovative competitor despite its small market share?).

U.S. v. General Dynamics Corp.
415 U.S. 486 (U.S. Sup. Ct. 1974)

FACTS Material Service Corp., a deep-shaft coal producer with production amounting to 15.1 percent of the Illinois market, acquired effective control of United Electric, an open-pit coal producer with 8.1 percent of the Illinois market. United Electric's coal reserves were very low and they were substantially committed under long-term contracts to large customers. General Dynamics later acquired 100 percent of Material Service's stock and was sued by the government as Material Service's successor.

ISSUE Did Material Service's acquisition of United Electric violate Section 7 of the Clayton Act?

DECISION No. The Court noted a trend toward concentration in the coal-producing industry, but concluded that this was due to a change in the demand for coal, rather than merger activity. United Electric's future ability to compete with other coal producers was much weaker than the government's production statistics indicated, due to the fact that United's reserves were low and substantially committed. Therefore, the Court concluded that allowing Material Service to keep United Electric would not substantially hurt competition and ordering divestiture would not help competition. Past production statistics are relevant only to the extent that they present an accurate picture of a company's future ability to compete.

Vertical Mergers. A *vertical merger* is a supplier-customer merger. Vertical mergers occur when a firm acquires a captive market for its products or a captive supplier of a product it regularly buys, thereby becoming a vertically integrated operation (operating on more than one competitive level). The anticompetitive effect of vertical mergers is that a share of the relevant market is foreclosed to competition. The competitors of a manufacturer who acquires a chain of retail stores are no longer able to compete for sales to the acquired stores. The competitors of a supplier acquired by a larger buyer are no longer able to compete for sales to that buyer.

Courts that seek to determine the legality of a vertical merger look at the share of the relevant market foreclosed to competition and other relevant economic and historical factors. A past history of vertical acquisitions by the defendant or a trend toward vertical integration or concentration in the industry aggravates the potential anticompetitive effects of a vertical merger.

Conglomerate Mergers.   *Conglomerate mergers* are neither horizontal nor vertical. They are a relatively recent phenomenon that emerged after Section 7 was enacted. A conglomerate (a large firm that controls numerous other firms in diverse industries) may acquire a firm in a new product market, or a firm in the same product market as one of its captive firms but in a different geographic market. The economic effects of conglomerate mergers are currently the subject of serious public debate. Proposals may be introduced in Congress to enact legislation to deal specifically with them. Section 7 is not well suited to dealing with conglomerate mergers, although some kinds of conglomerate mergers have been successfully enjoined under its provisions.

Conglomerate mergers that create a potential for reciprocal dealing have been successfully challenged under Section 7. If a conglomerate purchases a firm that produces a product that another member of the conglomerate regularly buys, or buys a product that another member firm regularly sells, the potential for reciprocal buying is obvious. A conglomerate may also acquire a firm that produces products that the conglomerate's suppliers regularly purchase. Suppliers who are eager to continue selling to the conglomerate may therefore be induced to purchase their requirements from the acquired firm.[10]

A conglomerate merger may also mean the elimination of potential competition, if the conglomerate acquires a firm in a product market that it was likely to enter because of its relation to the conglomerate's existing product lines, instead of entering the market by creating a new subsidiary and thereby decreasing concentration in the relevant market.

A conglomerate merger may give the acquired firm an unfair advantage over its small competitors, since it can draw on the financial resources and business expertise of the conglomerate. This may "entrench" the acquired firm in its present market position because its competitors may be discouraged from actively competing with it for fear of retaliation by the conglomerate. Potential entrants may also be afraid to enter the market once the conglomerate has entered.

---

[10] *FTC v. Consolidated Foods*, 380 U.S. 592 (1965).

FTC v. Procter & Gamble Co.
386 U.S. 568 (U.S. Sup. Ct. 1967)

FACTS   Procter & Gamble, a huge, diversified manufacturer of household products (detergents, soaps, cleansers, etc.), acquired Clorox, the leading manufacturer of household liquid bleach (48.8 percent of national sales). The household liquid bleach industry was highly concentrated, and Clorox had a distinct advantage over other competitors because it had plants distributed throughout the nation, allowing it to dominate sales in many parts of the country where it had no effective competition. Procter, the nation's largest advertiser, decided to enter the household bleach market by acquiring Clorox rather than entering independently. The FTC ordered divestiture and Procter appealed.

ISSUE   Did Procter's acquisition of Clorox violate Section 7?

DECISION   Yes. The Court upheld the FTC's findings. The FTC found that substituting Procter with its huge assets and advertising advantages for Clorox would deter new firms from entering the liquid bleach market and discourage existing firms from actively competing with Clorox for fear of retaliation by Procter, thus giving Clorox an unfair advantage over its competitors. The FTC also concluded that the merger would seriously diminish potential competition, since Procter was a likely entrant into the liquid bleach market and as such was a restraining influence on Clorox's exercise of its market power. Also, if Procter had entered independently, Clorox's dominant position would have been eroded and concentration in the industry reduced.

Section 8

If the same people control competing companies, there is a clear danger that anticompetitive behavior like price-fixing or division of markets may result; this could not be attacked under the antitrust laws that have been discussed up to this point. To prevent this from happening, Congress enacted Section 8 of the Clayton Act. Section 8 prohibits a person from being a director of two or more corporations who are or have been competitors if either has aggregate "capital, surplus and undivided profits" of over $1 million, "so that the elimination of competition by agreement between them" would constitute a violation of any of the provisions of the antitrust laws.

Although the enforcement of Section 8 has been historically lax, the FTC recently has stepped up its efforts to enforce Section 8. One major loophole in Section 8 is that the act does not prevent a person from being an officer of two competitors, or an officer of one and a director of another.

THE ROBINSON-PATMAN ACT

Originally, Section 2 of the Clayton Act prohibited local and territorial price discrimination by sellers, a device that had been used frequently by monopolists to destroy their competitors. In the 1930s Congress began to hear complaints that large chain stores were using their buying power to induce manufacturers to sell to them at lower prices than to their small, independent competitors. They also frequently demanded other payments and services that were not available to their smaller competitors. Congress responded by enacting the Robinson-Patman Act in 1936, amending Section 2 of the Clayton Act to deal with these forms of price discrimination.

Direct Price Discrimination

Section 2(a) of the amended Clayton Act prohibits *discriminations in price* between different purchasers of "commodities of like grade and quality" where the effect of the price discrimination may be to "substantially lessen competition or tend to create a monopoly" in any relevant market, or to "injure, destroy, or prevent competition with any person who either grants or knowingly receives the benefits of such discrimination, or with the customers of either of them." To violate Section 2(a), the discriminatory sales must occur roughly within the same period of time and involve goods of like grade and quality. Some substantial physical difference is necessary to justify a different price to competing buyers. So, a manufacturer who sells "house brand" products to a chain store for less than it sells its own brand name products to the chain's competitors has violated Section 2(a) if the only difference between the products is their label.

Defenses to Direct Price Discrimination. A seller who can cost-justify discriminatory prices by showing that the difference in price is solely the product of actual cost savings that result from efficiencies in distributing the goods, like those that sometimes result from volume selling, has a defense under Section 2(a). Sellers can also lawfully discriminate in price where doing so reflects changing conditions in the marketplace that affect the marketability of the goods, like their deterioration or obsolescence. Finally, Section 2(b) allows sellers to meet competition in good faith by granting a discriminatory price where they reasonably believe that doing so is necessary to meet the price offered by one of their competitors if that price is not itself an unlawfully discriminatory price.

Ingram v. Phillips Petroleum Co.
259 F.Supp. 176 (D. N.M. 1966)

FACTS The Ingrams were petroleum jobbers in Clovis, New Mexico. For years Phillips had sold gas to Helton, a jobber in Farwell, Texas, (nine miles east of Clovis) for 0.5 cent per gallon less than Ingrams paid. Helton also sold in Texico, New Mexico, a town across the border from Farwell. In early 1965 price changes by Phillips increased the price differential between Helton and the Ingrams to 1.8 cents per gallon. Ingram filed suit. Phillips argued that Helton was not in competition with the Ingrams, and that oil industry policy was that state boundaries were the appropriate price line. Phillips also argued that since the Ingrams had not lost any customers

ISSUE (they had urged their customers to await the outcome of the suit), no injury to competition had occurred.

ISSUE Did Phillips's discriminatory pricing violate Section 2(a)?

DECISION Yes. The court concluded that the Ingrams and Helton were in competition, since Farwell, Texico, and Clovis were all geographically close, and the evidence indicated that their customers shopped in all three towns and that the state line was not a real trade boundary. The fact that the Ingrams had not lost any sales did not indicate that no injury to competition had resulted, since a loss of profits might occur without a loss of sales. The court also observed that the Ingrams' present customers would probably not stay with them indefinitely and pay higher prices for an identical product, and that all the Ingrams needed to prove was a reasonable possibility of substantial injury in the future. The court rejected Phillips's claim to a "meeting competition in good faith" defense under Section 2(b), since the evidence indicated that Phillips's price reduction to Texas customers followed similar general reductions by Texaco, Shell, and Humble Oil, as reported in the *Oil Daily*. Phillips's reduction was therefore a response to an established pricing system, not a genuine response to an individual competitive situation.

Indirect Price Discrimination

In passing the Robinson-Patman Act, Congress recognized that sellers could indirectly discriminate among competing buyers by making discriminatory payments to them or furnishing them with certain services that were not available to their competitors. Section 2(d) prohibits sellers from making discriminatory payments to competing customers for services, such as advertising or promotional activities, or facilities, such as shelf space furnished by the customers in connection with the marketing of the goods. Section 2(e) prohibits sellers from discriminating in the services they furnish to competing customers. An example of such a service is providing the favored customer with a display case or a demonstration kit.

Sellers may lawfully provide such payments or services only if they are made available to competing customers on proportionately equal terms. This means notifying customers of the availability of such services and distributing them according to some rational basis, such as the quantity of goods the buyer purchases. The seller must also devise a flexible plan that enables various classes of buyers, large chains or small independents, to participate.

Buyer Inducements

Section 2(f) makes it illegal for buyers to knowingly induce or receive a discriminatory price prohibited by Section 2(a). All buyers need to know to violate Section 2(f) is that the price they received is illegally discriminatory. A recent case indicates that buyers who knowingly receive a discriminatory price are not in violation of Section 2(f) if their seller has a good defense to the charge of violating Section 2(a).[11] In that case the seller thought it was meeting a bid by a competitor and so was within the "meeting competition in good faith" defense provided in Section 2(b).

ANTITRUST EXCEPTIONS AND EXEMPTIONS

In 1914 the Clayton Act created a broad exemption to the antitrust laws aimed at allowing the formation of agricultural cooperatives. A similar exemption was made in 1934 for those engaged in commercial fishing. Union activities are now largely exempt from the antitrust laws except where unions combine with or exert economic pressure on business for the purpose of fixing prices or imposing other illegal restraints on competition.

The activities of American exporters engaged in foreign trade are exempted from the antitrust laws by the Webb-Pomerene Act as long as their actions do not artificially or intentionally enhance or depress prices within the United States. This exemption was designed to enable American firms to compete more effectively with the many cartels that operate in foreign markets.

Regulated Industries

Many industries are subject to varying degrees of government regulation in the public interest. Industry activities that have been approved by the appropriate regulatory body are generally held to be exempt from the antitrust laws. The industries that fall within this exception include public utilities, airlines, communications, railroads, shipping, banking, insurance, and the stock exchanges. Movements are afoot to deregulate many of these industries, and the future may provide a return to the idea of allowing competition rather than regulation to promote the public interest.

The Parker Doctrine

In the famous case of *Parker v. Brown*, the Supreme Court held that "state actions" were exempt from the antitrust laws.[12] This exemption embraces the actions of state officials acting under the authority of state law and the actions of private firms or individuals acting under the active supervision of authorized state officials. Recent decisions have apparently narrowed the scope of the *Parker* exemption, casting some doubt on its future as a major exception to the antitrust laws.

The Noerr Doctrine

In 1961 the Supreme Court held that the Sherman Act does not prohibit firms from joining together to restrain competition by lobbying to persuade legislators or administrators to take action that would injure the firms' competitors.[13] This exception was based on the *right of petition* recognized

---

[11] *Great Atlantic & Pacific Tea Co., Inc. v. FTC*, 47 U.S. L.W. 4167 (1979).

[12] 137 U.S. 341 (1943).

[13] *Eastern R.R. President's Conference v. Noerr Motor Freight, Inc.*, 365 U.S. 127 (1961).

656

by the Bill of Rights. Later decisions have recognized a "sham" exception to *Noerr* for activities that are really attempts to interfere with the business activities of a competitor rather than legitimate attempts to petition government.

QUESTIONS AND PROBLEM CASES

1. Why was common law poorly equipped to deal with anticompetitive behavior?

2. Are the antitrust laws well equipped to deal with oligopolies? Explain.

3. How was the original language of Section 7 of the Clayton Act flawed?

4. Page Publishing Company owned and published the *Commercial News*, a general business newspaper serving the Los Angeles area. Page brought an antitrust action against a number of community newspapers that served small neighborhoods in and around Los Angeles and the Los Angeles Newspaper Service Bureau together with several of its officers. The bureau was owned substantially by the defendant newspapers and represented them in the solicitation of legal advertising. Page claimed that collusive and illegal bidding by defendants caused the *Commercial News* to lose printing contracts for the 1951 and 1954 Los Angeles delinquent tax lists. Page argued that newspapers by their nature engage in interstate commerce and therefore are subject to the federal antitrust laws. Is Page correct?

5. The National Society of Professional Engineers (NSPE) created a Code of Ethics, which stated that an engineer "will not compete unfairly with another engineer by attempting to obtain employment . . . by competitive bidding. . . ." The United States attacked this rule as violating Section 1 of the Sherman Act as a conspiracy in restraint of trade. The NSPE urges the application of the rule of reason test to its activities. Will the court apply the rule of reason?

6. Socony-Vacuum Oil Company and several other major oil companies agreed to maintain a purchasing program to absorb the large amounts of "distress" gasoline being marketed as a result of overproduction in the gasoline industry. The plan was effectuated by means of a committee of the various major companies that would designate the distress supplies that each major company would purchase on the open market. The plan, however, was wholly voluntary. Is this a violation of Section 1 of the Sherman Act?

7. IBM leased its punching, sorting, and tabulating machines for a specified rental period upon condition that the lease would terminate if any punch cards not manufactured by IBM were used in the lease machines. IBM maintained that such a provision was necessary since the cards used had to conform to exacting quality specifications concerning the thickness and quality of paper. Is this a valid defense to a charge of a violation of Section 3 of the Clayton Act making unlawful tying clauses that tend to create a monopoly?

8. Ford Motor Co. made a substantial portion of its own parts, although it did not make spark plugs or batteries but purchased these parts from independent companies. The original equipment of new cars, insofar as spark plugs are concerned, is referred to as the "OE." The replacement market is referred to as the "aftermarket." Independent companies, such as Autolite, furnished the auto manufacturers with OE spark plugs at cost or less, intending to recover their losses on OE sales by profitable sales in the aftermarket. Ford was anxious to participate in this aftermarket and so it acquired certain assets of Autolite in 1961. General Motors had already entered the spark plug manufacturing field, making AC brand plugs, whose market share was about 30 percent. When Ford acquired Autolite,

whose market share was 15 percent, only one major competitor was left and that was Champion, whose market share declined from 50 percent in 1960 to just less than 40 percent in 1964 and to about 33 percent in 1966. The government brought a divestiture action under Section 7 of the Clayton Act, claiming that Ford's acquisition of certain of Autolite's assets might have the effect of substantially lessening competition. Was Ford's acquisition permissible?

9. In 1958, Pabst, the nation's tenth largest brewer, acquired Blatz, which ranked 18th. The merger made Pabst fifth largest, with 4.5 percent of the industry's total sales. By 1961, it ranked third, with 5.8 percent of the market. In Wisconsin, before the merger Blatz was the leading seller and Pabst ranked fourth. The merger made Pabst first with 24 percent, and by 1961 this had grown to 27.4 percent. In the three-state area of Wisconsin, Illinois, and Michigan, in 1957 Blatz ranked sixth with 5.8 percent of the market and Pabst was seventh with 5.4 percent. The government sued Pabst, alleging that the acquisition violated Section 7 of the Clayton Act. The district court dismissed the government's case on the ground that it failed to show that the effect of the acquisition ". . . may be substantially to lessen competition or to tend to create monopoly in the continental United States, the only relevant geographic market." Should the decision stand on appeal?

10. The product market of the combined glass and metal container industry was dominated by six firms, with Continental Can ranking second and Hazel-Atlas ranking sixth. In 1956 Continental acquired the assets of Hazel-Atlas, the third largest producer of glass containers, giving the combined firms 25 percent of the combined container market. There was evidence of concentration trends in both the glass and metal container industries. The United States challenged the acquisition under Section 7 and Continental defended on the ground that metal and glass were two separate product lines and hence the acquisition had no potential anticompetitive effect. Is Continental correct?

11. American Can Company granted quantity discounts on a scale ranging from 1 to 5 percent of annual purchases. The 1 percent discount was granted to customers who purchased between $500,000 and $1 million worth of cans annually. Bruce's Juices purchased approximately $350,000 worth of cans per year and received no discount. Two of its competitors had canneries nearby, which used about the same volume of cans, but these customers were permitted to pool their purchases with the result that one qualified for the 5 percent discount and the other for a 4 percent discount. The purchases of 98 percent of the customers of American Can were too small to qualify them for any discount. Only three customers received the 5 percent discount. Bruce's brought an action for treble damages against American Can. Is the discount policy a violation of Section 2(a) of the Robinson-Patman Act?

12. For two years Blass and Cohn, competing department stores, carried Elizabeth Arden Cosmetics. Arden paid Blass an allowance equal to half the salary of a clerk-demonstrator to push Arden products and an allowance equal to the full amount of a demonstrator's salary to Cohn. Sales of Arden's products by the two stores fluctuated; for some periods Blass's sales exceeded Cohn's, although for the full two years Cohn bought $11,251 and Blass $8,788 of Arden's products. Blass sued Arden, alleging violation of Sections 2(d) and 2(e) of the Robinson-Patman Act and asked for treble damages based on the difference in allowances made between Blass and Cohn. Arden argued that Blass had made no showing that its business had been injured as a result of the discrimination. Should Blass recover three times the amount of the difference between the allowances to Blass and those to Cohn?

Consumer Protection Laws

49

For many years, consumers dealt with merchants and providers of services on the basis of *caveat emptor* (let the buyer beware). Buyers were expected to look out for and protect their own interests. In addition, much of the law concerning the sales of goods and extension of credit was structured to protect business interests rather than consumer interests. Beginning in the mid-1960s, at about the same time the law of product liability was changing, many consumers recognized that these sales and credit laws put them at a disadvantage in trying to protect what they thought were their rights. Consumer groups lobbied Congress, state legislatures, and city halls to pass statutes or ordinances changing this law to make it more favorable to consumers.

Many everyday consumer problems are addressed by these new laws. For example, have you ever been denied credit without getting an explanation from the creditor? Have you ever had a department store or charge card company credit your payment to the wrong account or refuse to correct an error in your bill? Have you ever been harassed by a debt collector for a bill you do not owe, or one you have already paid? The laws covering these situations will be discussed in this chapter.

Federal Trade Commission Act

The Federal Trade Commission Act, which is the grandfather of "consumer protection" legislation, was passed in 1914. Under the act the five-member Federal Trade Commission (FTC) has authority to decide whether specific marketing and sales practices are unfair or deceptive, and whether those practices may be harmful to competition among manufacturers, distributors, and sellers. After making such a decision, the FTC may order the company that is engaged in the unlawful conduct to cease and to take corrective action. It may also ask a federal court to award redress, such as giving refunds or damages to injured consumers. The FTC has the power to establish rules that govern conduct in certain industries. It also enforces all the federal consumer protection laws and regulations that are discussed in this chapter.

Warner-Lambert Co. v. F.T.C.
562 F.2d 749 (D.C. Cir. 1977)

FACTS Listerine mouthwash has been on the market since 1879 and its formula has never changed. During this time it has been advertised as being effective against colds and sore throats. The FTC brought an administrative action against the maker of Listerine. The FTC asserted that the advertising claims made by the makers that Listerine would "ameliorate, prevent, and cure colds and sore throats" were false and misleading because Listerine was not beneficial for colds and sore throats. The FTC ordered the maker to cease and desist from representing that Listerine would cure or prevent colds or sore throats. It also ordered Listerine to include in any future advertising (for up to $10 million in cost) the statement that "Contrary to prior advertising, Listerine will not help prevent colds or sore throats or lessen their severity." The maker claimed that the requirement for corrective advertising infringed its right to freedom of speech.

ISSUE Does the FTC have the power to order corrective advertising where it finds ads to be false and misleading?

DECISION The court upheld the FTC's order. It said that the First Amendment does not protect false or misleading advertising claims. The FTC has the power to order corrective advertising, and here the order bore a reasonable relationship to the violation. The $10 million figure was the maker's advertising budget for Listerine for the previous ten years.

CONSUMER CREDIT LAWS

Because of the widespread use of credit by consumers, the federal government and the states have enacted a series of statutes and regulations to govern credit transactions. These credit laws are designed to increase consumers' knowledge before they enter into credit transactions and to give consumers certain rights. They are also intended to assure that consumers are treated fairly and without discrimination throughout the course of a credit transaction.

Consumer Credit Protection Act

In 1969 Congress gave consumers the right to be advised of all the terms of their credit transactions (purchases on credit) at or before the time they sign the credit contract. The Consumer Credit Protection Act, commonly called the *Truth-in-Lending Act,* is intended to furnish the consumer with a better opportunity to shop for credit among merchants, finance companies, credit unions, and banks. A secondary purpose is to enable the consumer to understand all the charges made in connection with credit.

The Truth-in-Lending Act requires that the interest rate be stated clearly in terms of an annual percentage rate. The contract or disclosure form must also show the dollar costs of credit as the "finance charge." The term *finance charge* "includes all costs related to the extension of credit." These costs may include loan fees and fees for credit reports. Charges for life, health, or accident insurance written in connection with the purchase on credit may also be part of the finance charge if the insurance is required for the extension of credit. The Truth-in-Lending Act does not fix or limit interest rates or other credit charges. However, state laws may set a limit on interest rates that can be charged in a credit transaction.

One of the act's most significant protections is the right to cancel the buyer's (debtor's) contract. The act provides a cancelation right, technically called a "right of rescission," for three business days after the purchase or credit or after such time as the creditor makes the required disclosure. The right is limited to cases in which the debtor's home is used as collateral but does not apply to first mortgages that finance the purchase of a home. The creditor must give the purchaser written notice of the right to cancel. If the purchaser cancels, he or she also must give his notice in writing. A typical example of the kind of transaction where the debtor has the right to cancel is major home repair or remodeling on credit. Consumers have the same right if they purchase a furnace or carpeting for their home if the lender takes a security interest or lien on the home.

Because of the cancelation right, the contractor cannot start work until the three days are over. The purchaser may give up the right to cancel and get the work started without the three-day wait by telling the creditor that he or she has an emergency and needs the repairs (and credit) immediately to avoid danger to his or her family or property.

Gardner and North Roofing and Siding Corp. v. Board of Governors
464 F.2d 838 (D.C. Cir. 1972)

FACTS Gardner and North was in the business of renovating, remodeling, and repairing homes in the Syracuse, New York, area. Its salesmen solicited contracts from homeowners for the repair work and credit was extended to them pursuant to a "deferred payment plan." Although the company did not take a mortgage on the homeowner's property, the laws of New York give home improvement contractors a contractor's or mechanic's lien on the customer's home at the time the work is performed. Section 125A of the Truth-in-Lending Act covers consumer credit transactions in which a security interest is retained or acquired in any real property that is expected to be used as the residence of the person to whom credit is extended. The consumer has three days following the receipt of certain information from the creditor to rescind the contract. The creditor must inform the prospective consumer that he has such a right to rescind. The Federal Reserve Board has the responsibility to promulgate regulations to implement the act. The board issued such regulations in which it defined the term *security interest* to include "liens created by operation of law such as mechanic's, materialman's, artisan's, and similar liens."

ISSUE   Was Gardner and North required to give consumers three days to rescind contracts with it for home repair work?

DECISION   The court upheld the Federal Reserve's regulation and held that Gardner and North was required to give the consumer three days to rescind the contracts. The court felt that the same risk was posed to a consumer and his or her property by an artisan's lien as a second mortgage or other consensual-type lien. Congress was concerned about protecting the homeowner against such risks when it passed the Truth-in-Lending Act.

The act also requires disclosure of all credit terms in advertising if the advertiser mentions one or more of the credit terms. An advertisement that states "No down payment" or "12 percent interest" or "No payments until after Christmas" must also include all of the relevant terms. These include the annual percentage rate, the down payment, the number of payments, and the cash price. This requirement helps the consumer put the advertised terms into perspective. Another important feature of the act is that it allows the consumer to sue the creditor for failure to make the required disclosures.

Fair Credit Billing Act

In 1974 Congress supplemented the Truth-in-Lending Act with the *Fair Credit Billing Act*. The Fair Credit Billing Act provides certain protection for users of credit cards. It prescribes the procedures to be followed by both consumers and the department store or bank that issues the credit card. If the credit cardholder thinks the card issuer has made an error on the statement, such as not crediting a payment or showing a charge that was not made by the customer, he or she has 60 days after receiving that statement to report the error to the card issuer. The report must be in writing. The card issuer then has 30 days to tell the cardholder that his or her report has been received. The card issuer must either correct the account or, after investigating the bill, explain why it believes the original bill or statement was accurate. The card issuer has two billing cycles or no more than 90 days to correct the account or notify the cardholder of its accuracy.

The Fair Credit Billing Act also limits the card issuer's freedom to report late payments (delinquencies) to credit reporting agencies, such as credit bureaus. In such cases, the card issuer must inform the cardholder of the persons or companies to whom the card issuer sends its report. The card issuer's failure to comply with the act can cost him the right to collect up to $50. The act also permits the seller to offer discounts if the buyer pays cash for a purchase rather than using a credit card. At the same time it prohibits the seller from imposing a surcharge for noncash purchases made with a credit card.

The Truth-in-Lending Act limits to $50 the amount for which consumers may be liable if there is an unauthorized use of their credit cards.

Martin v. American Express, Inc.
361 So.2d 597 (Ct. Civ. App. Ala. 1979)

FACTS In April 1975, Robert Martin gave his American Express credit card to a business associate, E. L. McBride, to use in a joint business venture they had entered. Martin orally authorized McBride to charge up to $500. However, in June 1975, Martin received a statement from American Express that stated the amount due on his account was approximately $5,300. Martin refused to pay the bill on the grounds that he had not signed any of the credit card invoices. American Express then filed suit against Martin. He claimed that his liability for "unauthorized" use of his credit card was limited to $50 by the Truth-in-Lending Act.

ISSUE Was Martin's liability for McBride's use of his American Express card limited to $50?

DECISION No. The court held that under these facts Martin's liability was not limited to $50 by the Truth-in-Lending Act. When a cardholder, who is under no compulsion by fraud or duress, permits the use of his credit card by another person, the cardholder has "authorized" the use of the card. He is then responsible for any charges as a result of that use. This is true even if he orally requests that other person not to charge over a certain amount. By the term "unauthorized use," Congress intended to protect cardholders only where their card was obtained as a result of loss, theft, or wrongdoing. Thus, the $50 limit does not apply where a person is knowingly permitted to use the card.

Fair Credit Reporting Act

The *Fair Credit Reporting Act* was enacted in 1970. Its purpose is to ensure that information concerning a person's credit background supplied by his or her creditors is both up to date and accurate. It covers credit information supplied to potential creditors, insurers, or employers of that person. A secondary goal of the act is to guard against disclosure of such confidential information to persons who request it for purposes other than those specified in the act. The act offers special protection to persons who have been denied credit, insurance, or employment.

A consumer who is denied credit by the person who received a credit report is entitled to disclosure of the name and address of the credit reporting agency (credit bureau) that made the report. If the consumer asks, the user of the information must disclose free of charge the information contained in the report. The consumer may require the credit reporting agency (as the provider of the information) to reinvestigate information disputed by the consumer and to delete any inaccurate or obsolete information from the file. If the dispute is not resolved at that point (for example, if the consumer still objects to the accuracy of the information), the consumer may give his or her version of the dispute for the credit file. The credit reporting agency is then required by the act to give out the fact that the consumer disputes the information when it gives out the information in the consumer's file. If inaccurate or unverifiable information is deleted from the consumer's file, the consumer may request the reporting agency to contact any person who earlier received the deleted information. Recipients who obtained the credit report for *credit* or *insurance purposes* within six months prior to deletion must be advised of the deletion. If the request for credit information was for *employment purposes* and was made within two years of deletion, then the requestor must be notified of the deletion of the inaccurate or unverifiable information.

The act offers several additional protections to consumers. First, a consumer has the right to have a consumer report withheld from anyone who under the law does not have a legitimate business need for the information. Second, the consumer can sue for damages for willful or negligent violation of the act and to collect attorney's fees and court costs if he or she is successful. Third, the credit reporting agency may not report most adverse information more than seven years old. However the fact that the consumer was declared bankrupt can be reported for 14 years after the bankruptcy.

The act does not apply when an individual applies for commercial, rather than consumer, credit or insurance. It does not give the consumer the right to obtain a copy of his or her report, although some credit reporting agencies voluntarily provide a copy.

Millstone v. O'Hanlon Reports
383 F.Supp. 269 (E.D. Mo. 1974)

FACTS   In August Millstone moved from Washington, D.C., to St. Louis to take a new job. There he obtained a new automobile insurance policy. Shortly afterward, he received a notice saying a personal investigation would be made in connection with the policy. On December 20, he was advised that the policy would be canceled because of a report made to the company by O'Hanlon Reports. Millstone immediately went to O'Hanlon Reports and asked to see what was in his report. Only after repeated efforts was Millstone able to have information from his file read to him.

He was never allowed to see his file and was given only selective information from it. Millstone was told that his former neighbors in Washington disliked him, considered him to be a "hippie type" with long hair and a beard, suggested he was a drug user, and said he had participated in many demonstrations and had housed demonstrators in his house. Millstone protested much of the information in his file. It subsequently turned out that only one former neighbor had given adverse information about Millstone, but O'Hanlon's investigator said he had gotten it from four different neighbors. Millstone brought a lawsuit against O'Hanlon Reports, alleging a violation of the Fair Credit Reporting Act and seeking actual and punitive damages.

ISSUE   Were O'Hanlon Reports' actions a violation of the Fair Credit Reporting Act?

DECISION   Yes. Millstone was awarded a judgment for $2,500 actual damages, $25,000 as punitive damages, and $12,500 for attorney's fees. The court held that O'Hanlon had not used reasonable care to assure maximum possible accuracy of the information about Millstone. It also failed to disclose to him, as required by the act, the nature and substance of all the information contained in its files on Millstone. The court found O'Hanlon Reports had willfully violated the act and evaded its legal responsibilities to Millstone.

Equal Credit Opportunity Act

The *Equal Credit Opportunity Act* prohibits discrimination in credit transactions on grounds of sex or marital status. Amendments to the act effective in 1977 protect credit applicants from discrimination on the additional bases of race, color, religion, national origin, and age.

For example, the Equal Credit Opportunity Act protects the 63-year-old applicant for a mortgage who plans to work five to seven years longer and seeks a 15-year mortgage. The lender could not turn down the application solely because of the applicant's age. The act also assists the widow or divorced woman who has not established her credit worthiness in the past and the young applicant so long as he or she is old enough to enter into a valid contract.

The act applies to banks, finance companies, retail stores, credit card issuers (such as gasoline companies or Diner's Club), and other firms that regularly extend credit. State laws that prohibit separate extensions of credit to each spouse are preempted by the act.

Markham v. Colonial Mortgage Service Co.
— F.2d — (D.C. Cir. 1979)

FACTS   In November 1976 Jerry Markham and Marcia Harris announced their engagement to be married and began looking for a house to buy. In December they signed a contract to buy a house and submitted a joint mortgage application to Colonial

Mortgage Service Company—an agent for Illinois Federal Savings and Loan Association. On February 1, three days before the scheduled closing date for the house, the loan committee of Illinois Federal rejected the loan application. On February 8, the loan committee reconsidered and again rejected the loan application with the statement: "Separate income not sufficient for loan and job tenure." Markham and Harris then filed suit alleging violation of the Equal Credit Opportunity Act.

ISSUE Did Illinois Federal violate the Equal Credit Opportunity Act when it refused, in determining creditworthiness, to aggregate the incomes of an unmarried couple who applied for a joint mortgage.

DECISION Yes. The court held that the Act prohibits discrimination against a credit applicant on the basis of "sex or marital status". The obligations of joint debtors are the same regardless of whether or not they are married to each other. Illinois Federal would have aggregated the incomes had the applicants been married and in this case did not aggregate them because they were not married. Thus, it treated them differently on the basis of their marital status—precisely the kind of discrimination that is barred by the Equal Credit Opportunity Act.

The protections afforded by the act cover all phases of the credit transaction. The creditor may not do any of the following: discourage the application for credit, refuse to grant a separate account to a married woman if she is a credit applicant, or ask the applicant's marital status if a separate account is requested. There are two exceptions to asking marital status. The creditor may do so if security is required for the account or if state laws (such as community property laws) require otherwise.

A typical example of the difference made by the act is as follows: An applicant for credit is a 45-year-old widow. She has just started working after a 15-year absence from the work force. All her credit history was originally reported in her husband's name because all their charge accounts were in his name and their home and car loans were based on his income alone. The widow has assets: her house, car, a savings account, and some investments. Before the Equal Credit Opportunity Act, she would have lacked a credit history and probably would have been denied credit.

The act, however, requires the credit history that she and her deceased husband created be treated as reflecting her history as well as his. To have this right, she must show that the information is an accurate picture of her willingness and ability to repay. This may make the difference between losing all the credit cards she formerly held in his name and keeping them in her own name. It will make that difference only if her financial situation qualifies her for credit. The same is true for a 45-year-old woman whose husband is alive and who wants credit in her own name. The creditor cannot require the husband to sign for the account unless his name is required for security. This might be necessary if the woman was seeking financing for a swimming pool at the house they owned jointly.

The creditor must either accept or reject a credit application within 30 days. If the creditor denies a credit application, it must provide the specific reasons for that denial within a reasonable time or tell the consumer that he or she has the right to specific reasons. Statements that "You didn't meet our minimum standards" or "You didn't receive enough points on our credit scoring system" do not comply with the act.

Carroll v. Exxon
434 F.Supp. 557 (E.D. La. 1977)

FACTS   In August 1976 Kathleen Carroll, a single working woman, applied for an Exxon credit card. Carroll did not have a major credit card, did not list a savings account on her application, had been employed for only one year, and did not have any dependents. On September 14, she was advised by letter that her application for credit was denied, but no reason for the denial was provided. On September 28, she wrote to Exxon and asked to be advised of the specific reasons for the credit denial. In an undated response, she was advised that the credit bureau contacted by Exxon had not responded adversely but had been unable to supply sufficient information concerning her established credit. However, this letter, like the earlier letter, did not contain the name of the credit bureau used by Exxon to investigate her credit. Carroll filed a lawsuit against Exxon, claiming that the Fair Credit Reporting Act and the Equal Credit Opportunity Act had been violated. Only after filing the lawsuit was she given the name and address of the credit bureau.

ISSUE   Did Exxon violate the Fair Credit Reporting Act or the Equal Credit Opportunity Act in denying a credit card to Carroll?

DECISION   Yes. The court held that Exxon had violated both acts. Under the Fair Credit Reporting Act, it was required to disclose the name and address of the credit reporting agency on the basis of whose information the credit was denied. This information should have been given to Carroll when she was notified of the denial of credit. The company also failed to properly give her notice of the reasons for the denial of credit as required by the Equal Credit Opportunity Act. The real reasons were the absence of another major credit card, no savings account, a short job history, and no dependents. No definitive information on these reasons was provided to her.

The consumer is also entitled to have creditors report the credit history of any account shared by a married couple to credit reporting agencies in the names of both spouses. In other words, if Mrs. Ray Hughes shares an account in her husband's name, she may ask the credit agency to retroactively report that account in her name as well as her husband's. The credit experience concerning all accounts that both spouses may use and on which both are liable must be reported by creditors in both names. The act also prohibits a creditor from using unfavorable information about an account that an applicant shared with a spouse or former spouse. To trigger this prohibition, the applicant must show that the bad credit rating does not accurately reflect his or her willingness or ability to pay.

The Equal Credit Opportunity Act does not guarantee credit or unlimited credit to any person. Creditors may still set standards on which they will grant credit. They may not set standards that have the effect of denying credit to a protected class (such as women or the elderly), and they may not apply their standards on a discriminatory basis.

Fair Debt Collection Practices Act

Public concern about harassment by debt collectors, including late-night phone calls and threats of violence, led Congress in 1977 to pass the *Fair Debt Collection Practices Act*. Thirty-seven states had already passed laws aimed at abuses by debt collectors. The federal act allows exemptions for states with debt collection laws similar to the federal law as long as there are adequate provisions for enforcement. The federal act affects only the practices of debt collection agencies that collect bills for creditors other than themselves. It does not cover retail stores, banks, or businesses that collect their own debts.

Among the prohibitions in the Fair Debt Collection Practices Act are the following:

1. Debt collectors may not contact consumers at unusual or inconvenient times, or at all if the consumer is represented by an attorney.
2. Debt collectors may not contact a consumer where he or she works if the employer objects.
3. Debt collectors may not use harassing or intimidating tactics or abusive language against *any* person, not only the debtor.
4. Debt collectors may not use false or misleading tactics, such as posing as a lawyer or a police officer.
5. Debt collectors may not contact third parties—other than a spouse, parent, or financial advisor—about payment of a debt unless authorized by a court, but they may ask where the person lives or works.
6. Debt collectors cannot communicate again with the consumer after receiving the consumer's written refusal to pay the debts except to inform the consumer of actions the collector may take.
7. Debt collectors may not deposit a postdated check prior to the date on it.

The Fair Debt Collection Act is enforced by the Federal Trade Commission. The consumer may sue for violations of the act; however, there are limits on the damages and penalties the consumer may recover from the collection agency. The consumer may recover attorney's fees if he or she wins the suit. If a debt collector brings a suit that is found to be harassing in nature, the winning consumer defendant may also collect attorney's fees.

TransWorld Accounts, Inc. v. FTC
1979-1 CCH Trade Cases (9th Cir. 1979)

FACTS   TransWorld Accounts is a debt collection agency. For a flat rate, TransWorld mailed out a series of five or six form letters to delinquent debtors, encouraging prompt payment to the creditor. The letters, some of which were printed to simulate telegrams, stated that legal action might be taken if payment was not made within a specified period. The letters were sent at prearranged intervals of 10 to 14 days. If the debtor did not respond to one letter in the series, he or she was sent the next letter until the series ran its course. Only then, some days after the last letter was sent, did TransWorld even consider whether legal action would be taken against the debtor.

The FTC brought an administrative action against TransWorld, contending that the forms and content of the debt collection letter series constituted an unfair and deceptive practice.

ISSUE   Were the debt collection letters that resembled telegrams and that represented the imminence of legal action unfair and deceptive?

DECISION   Yes. The court upheld the FTC's finding that the telegram format misrepresented the urgency of the communication. It also agreed that the threat of legal action was deceptive where no decision about suing was made until after the last letter in the series was sent.

FTC Holder in Due Course Rule

Consumers who have purchased defective goods or services on credit have frequently been frustrated when the seller assigns the right to payment (the debt) to a third party. The consumer may face demands for payment from the third party, while at the same time he or she finds the seller is unwilling to correct the defects or has disappeared. In fact the consumer might be obligated to pay the third party even though there is no likelihood that the defective performance will be remedied. This could happen if (1) the consumer signed a negotiable instrument that had been negotiated to a holder in due course (see Chapter 39) or (2) the consumer signed an installment sales contract containing a waiver of defenses clause whereby the consumer agreed to assert any defenses he or she had on the contract against the seller only and not against any assignee of the sales contract.

For example, Harold agrees to pay Ace Improvement $2,500 to put aluminum siding on his house. He signs a promissory note agreeing to pay the note in 24 monthly installments. Ace negotiates the note to a finance company and goes out of business after completing only part of the work on Harold's house. If the finance company can qualify as a holder in due course of the note, it may be able to enforce payment against Harold even though he will not get what he bargained for from Ace Improvement. This results from the basic principle of negotiable instruments law that a holder in due course takes the instrument free of personal defenses (e.g., misrepresentation, nondelivery, nonperformance, breach of warranty) between the original parties to the instrument.

In 1976 the Federal Trade Commission took action to deal with the situation in which a consumer gives a negotiable note or signs an installment credit contract in return for goods or services. Using its authority to regulate unfair trade practices, the FTC adopted a regulation concerning Preservation of Consumer's Claims and Defenses, commonly called the *Holder in Due Course Rule.* The rule performs differently than its common name suggests; it is designed to preserve for consumers in most purchase money credit transactions the right to use claims and defenses against a holder in due course.

The FTC rule makes it an unfair trade practice for a seller, in the course of financing a consumer purchase or lease of goods or services, to use procedures to separate the consumer's duty to pay from the seller's duty to perform. The rule protects the consumer in those situations where: (1) the buyer executes a sales contract that includes a promissory note, (2) the buyer signs an installment sales contract that includes a "waiver of defenses" clause, or (3) the seller arranges with a third-party lender for a direct loan to finance the buyer's purchase. The regulation deals with the first two situations by requiring that the following statement (titled "Notice") be included in bold type in any consumer credit contract signed by the seller and the consumer:

NOTICE

ANY HOLDER OF THIS CONSUMER CREDIT CONTRACT IS SUBJECT TO ALL CLAIMS AND DEFENSES WHICH THE DEBTOR COULD ASSERT AGAINST THE SELLER OF GOODS OR SERVICES OBTAINED PURSUANT HERETO OR WITH THE PROCEEDS HEREOF. RECOVERY HEREUNDER BY THE DEBTOR SHALL NOT EXCEED AMOUNTS PAID BY THE DEBTOR HEREUNDER.

Where the consumer's purchase is financed by a direct loan arranged by the seller, the seller may not accept the proceeds of the loan unless the consumer credit contract between the buyer and the lender contains the following statement in bold type:

NOTICE

ANY HOLDER OF THIS CONSUMER CREDIT CONTRACT IS SUBJECT TO ALL CLAIMS AND DEFENSES WHICH THE DEBTOR COULD ASSERT AGAINST THE SELLER OF GOODS OR SERVICES OBTAINED WITH THE PROCEEDS HEREOF. RECOVERY HEREUNDER BY THE DEBTOR SHALL NOT EXCEED AMOUNTS PAID BY THE DEBTOR HEREUNDER.

The required statement provides that all defenses are available to the purchaser against the seller of the merchandise are also available against the holder in due course. It does this *only* when the consumer's credit contract (promissory note or installment sales contract) contains the required provision. It is treated in the same manner as other written terms and conditions in the agreement. It must appear without qualification. A consumer credit contract that includes the statement in conjunction with other clauses that limit or restrict its application does not satisfy the requirement that the contract "contain the notice."

The FTC rule does not eliminate any rights the consumer may have as a matter of federal, state, or local law. It creates no new claims or defenses. For example, the rule does not create a warranty claim or defense where the product is sold "as is." The rule also does not alter statutes of limitations or other state-created limitations on the consumer's enforcement of claims and defenses. Finally, the claims or defenses relied upon must relate to the sales transaction that is financed; for example, the consumer cannot sue on the grounds of the seller's negligent maintenance of business premises which caused the buyer to break her leg while waiting for warranty service.

The seller's failure to comply with the FTC regulation exposes him or her to a possible fine of $10,000 per violation in a civil action brought by the Federal Trade Commission.

QUESTIONS AND PROBLEM CASES

1. What is the purpose of the Truth-in-Lending Act?

2. Ann, a resident of San Francisco, bought a set of china in Los Angeles to be shipped to her house. She charged the china on her VISA card. The retailer shipped a cheap imitation of the china Ann had selected and now refuses to refund Ann her money or to provide the better china. Ann's current VISA bill contains the charge for the china. What would you advise Ann to do?

3. Raymond buys his daughter a $75 briefcase and charges it on his bank credit card. When Raymond's bill arrives, the same charge is listed twice. He promptly notifies the bank that he has been double-billed, but the bank fails to acknowledge receipt of the complaint within 30 days or to credit his account. What are Raymond's rights against the bank?

4. John J. Smith and his cousin, J. Joseph Smith, live on the same street. Their mail is frequently misdelivered. J. Joseph Smith is a chronic late-payer. His creditors have reported this to the local credit reporting agencies. John J., who believes he has an excellent credit record, applies for a mortgage on a new house and is denied on the basis of a report that states he is a late-payer. What should John J. do?

5. A married woman who has taught school for ten years and has her own checking and savings accounts applies for bank financing for a new car in her own name. Her name does not appear on her husband's credit cards, although she has used them for years. The bank refuses to loan her the money without her husband's signature because she "did not meet our credit criteria." Does the woman have any rights against the bank?

6. Elizabeth worked several years and had an account at a department store during that time. Then she married Ross, who also had an account at the department store. A short time later, the store notified her that it had closed her account. It offered her a new card issued

to "Mr. and Mrs." and demanded the return of her original card. Has the department store violated the Equal Credit Protection Act?

7. John Jones receives a letter from a debt collector about an overdue bill. John does not owe the money and so informs the collector. However, John suspects that his cousin who has the same name does owe the debt. The collector calls John repeatedly over the next two weeks. John again tells the collector that he does not owe the money that is allegedly due. The collector then calls John's employer and tells him that he is going to sue John for not paying the bill. What would you advise John to do?

8. A debt collector, posing as a process server, goes to Isabel's house where no one is at home. The collector then goes to three neighbors asking for Isabel. He tells each of them that he is trying to serve a subpoena on her. In fact, the collector knows that Isabel is at work. Could Isabel successfully sue the collector for violating the Fair Debt Collection Practices Act? Explain.

9. A bank is trying to increase its portfolio of car loans so it solicits referrals of loan customers from a local auto dealer. The dealer suggests a special one-day promotion during which the bank's customers would receive a $200 discount from the sticker price if they finance their purchases through the bank. What do the dealer and the bank have to do to comply with the FTC's Holder-in-Due-Course Rule?

Appendixes

UNIFORM COMMERCIAL CODE

1. General Provisions,
2. Sales,
3. Commercial Paper,
4. Bank Deposits and Collections,
5. Letters of Credit (omitted)
6. Bulk Transfers,
7. Warehouse Receipts, Bills of Lading and Other Documents of Title,
8. Investment Securities (omitted)
9. Secured Transactions: Sales of Accounts and Chattel Paper,
10. Effective Date and Repealer (omitted)

GLOSSARY OF LEGAL TERMS AND DEFINITIONS

Uniform Commercial Code

ARTICLE 1. General Provisions

PART 1
SHORT TITLE, CONSTRUCTION, APPLICATION AND SUBJECT MATTER OF THE ACT

§ 1–101. Short Title.

This Act shall be known and may be cited as Uniform Commercial Code.

§ 1–102. Purposes; Rules of Construction; Variation by Agreement.

(1) This Act shall be liberally construed and applied to promote its underlying purposes and policies.

(2) Underlying purposes and polices of this Act are

    (a) to simplify, clarify and modernize the law governing commercial transactions;

    (b) to permit the continued expansion of commercial practices through custom, usage and agreement of the parties;

    (c) to make uniform the law among the various jurisdictions.

(3) The effect of provisions of this Act may be varied by agreement, except as otherwise provided in this Act and except that the obligations of good faith, diligence, reasonableness and care prescribed by this Act may not be disclaimed by agreement but the parties may by agreement determine the standards by which the performance of such obligations is to be measured if such standards are not manifestly unreasonable.

(4) The presence in certain provisions of this Act of the words "unless otherwise agreed" or words of similar import does not imply that the effect of other provisions may not be varied by agreement under subsection (3).

General note: One asterisk (*) connotates "sections of the U.C.C. where the draftsmen offered the states a choice between several alternative provisions but only one of the alternatives is provided." Two asterisks (**) connotate "those sections of Article 9 which were changed by the 1972 amendments to the Code."

(5) In this Act unless the context otherwise requires
    (a) words in the singular number include the plural, and in the plural include the singular;
    (b) words of the masculine gender include the feminine and the neuter, and when the sense so indicates words of the neuter gender may refer to any gender.

§ 1–103. Supplementary General Principles of Law Applicable.

Unless displaced by the particular provisions of this Act, the principles of law and equity, including the law merchant and the law relative to capacity to contract, principal and agent, estoppel, fraud, misrepresentation, duress, coercion, mistake, bankruptcy, or other validating or invalidating cause shall supplement its provisions.

§ 1–104. Construction Against Implicit Repeal.

This Act being a general act intended as a unified coverage of its subject matter, no part of it shall be deemed to be impliedly repealed by subsequent legislation if such construction can reasonably be avoided.

§ 1–105. Territorial Application of the Act; Parties' Power to Choose Applicable Law.

(1) Except as provided hereafter in this section, when a transaction bears a reasonable relation to this state and also to another state or nation the parties may agree that the law either of this state or of such other state or nation shall govern their rights and duties. Failing such agreement this Act applies to transactions bearing an appropriate relation to this state.

(2) Where one of the following provisions of this Act specifies the applicable law, that provision governs and a contrary agreement is effective only to the extent permitted by the law (including the conflict of laws rules) so specified:
Rights of creditors against sold goods. Section 2–402.
Applicability of the Article on Bank Deposits and Collections. Section 1–102.
Bulk transfers subject to the Article on Bulk Transfers. Section 6–102.
Applicability of the Article on Investment Securities. Section 8–106.
Perfection provisions of the Article on Secured Transactions. Section 9–103.

§ 1–106. Remedies to Be Liberally Administered.

(1) The remedies provided by this Act shall be liberally administered to the end that the aggrieved party may be put in as good a position as if the other party had fully performed but neither consequential or special nor penal damages may be had except as specifically provided in this Act or by other rule of law.

(2) Any right or obligation declared by this Act is enforceable by action unless the provision declaring it specifies a different and limited effect.

§ 1–107. Waiver or Renunciation of Claim or Right After Breach.

Any claim or right arising out of an alleged breach can be discharged in whole or in part without consideration by a written waiver or renunciation signed and delivered by the aggrieved party.

§ 1–108. Severability.

If any provision or clause of this Act or application thereof to any person or circumstances is held invalid, such invalidity shall not affect other provisions or applications of the Act which can be given effect without the invalid provision or application, and to this end the provisions of this Act are declared to be severable

§ 1–109. Section Captions.

Section captions are parts of this Act.

PART 2

GENERAL DEFINITIONS AND PRINCIPLES OF INTERPRETATION

§ 1–201. General Definitions.

Subject to additional definitions contained in the subsequent Articles of this Act which are applicable to specific Articles or Parts thereof, and unless the context otherwise requires, in this Act:

(1) "Action" in the sense of a judicial proceeding includes recoupment, counterclaim, setoff, suit in equity and any other proceedings in which rights are determined.

(2) "Aggrieved party" means a party entitled to resort to a remedy.

(3) "Agreement" means the bargain of the parties in fact as found in their language or by implication from other circumstances including course of dealing or usage of trade or course of performance as provided in this Act (Section 1–205 and 2–208). Whether an agreement has legal consequences is determined by the provisions of this Act, if applicable; otherwise by the law of contracts (Section 1–103). (Compare "Contract.")

(4) "Bank" means any person engaged in the business of banking.

(5) "Bearer" means the person in possession of an instrument, document of title, or security payable to bearer or indorsed in blank.

(6) "Bill of lading" means a document evidencing the receipt of goods for shipment issued by a person engaged in the business of transporting or forwarding goods, and includes an airbill. "Airbill" means a document serving for air transportation as a bill of lading does for marine or rail transportation, and includes an air consignment note or air waybill.

(7) "Branch" includes a separately incorporated foreign branch of a bank.

(8) "Burden of establishing" a fact means the burden of persuading the triers of fact that the existence of the fact is more probable than its non-existence.

(9) "Buyer in ordinary course of business" means a person who in good faith and without knowledge that the sale to him is in violation of the ownership rights or security interest of a third party in the goods buys in ordinary course from a person in the business of selling goods of that kind but does not include a pawnbroker. All persons who sell minerals or the like (including oil and gas) at wellhead or minehead shall be deemed to be persons in the business of selling goods of that kind. "Buying" may be for cash or by exchange of other property or on secured or unsecured credit and includes receiving goods or documents of title under a pre-existing contract for sale but does not include a transfer in bulk or as security for or in total or partial satisfaction of a money debt.

(10) "Conspicuous": A term or clause is conspicuous when it is so written that a reasonable person against whom it is to operate ought to have noticed it. A printed heading in capitals (as: NON-NEGOTIABLE BILL OF LADING) is conspicuous. Language in the body of a form is "conspicuous" if it is in larger or other contrasting

type or color. But in a telegram any stated term is "conspicuous." Whether a term or clause is "conspicuous" or not is for decision by the court.

(11) "Contract" means the total legal obligation which results from the parties' agreement as affected by this Act and any other applicable rules of law. (Compare "Agreement.")

(12) "Creditor" includes a general creditor, a secured creditor, a lien creditor and any representative of creditors, including an assignee for the benefit of creditors, a trustee in bankruptcy, a receiver in equity and an executor or administrator of an insolvent debtor's or assignor's estate.

(13) "Defendant" includes a person in the position of defendant in a cross-action or counterclaim.

(14) "Delivery" with respect to instruments, documents of title, chattel paper or securities means voluntary transfer of possession.

(15) "Document of title" includes bill of lading, dock warrant, dock receipt, warehouse receipt or order for the delivery of goods, and also any other document which in the regular course of business or financing is treated as adequately evidencing that the person in possession of it is entitled to receive, hold and dispose of the document and the goods it covers. To be a document of title a document must purport to be issued by or addressed to a bailee and purport to cover goods in the bailee's possession which are either identified or fungible portions of an identified mass.

(16) "Fault" means wrongful act, omission or breach.

(17) "Fungible" with respect to goods or securities means goods or securities of which any unit is, by nature or usage of trade, the equivalent of any other like unit. Goods which are not fungible shall be deemed fungible for the purposes of this Act to the extent that under a particular agreement of document unlike units are treated as equivalents.

(18) "Genuine" means free of forgery or counterfeiting.

(19) "Good faith" means honesty in fact in the conduct or transaction concerned.

(20) "Holder" means a person who is in possession of a document of title or an instrument or an investment security drawn, issued or indorsed to him or to his order or to bearer or in blank.

(21) To "honor" is to pay or to accept and pay, or where a credit so engages to purchase or discount a draft complying with the terms of the credit.

(22) "Insolvency proceedings" includes any assignment for the benefit of creditors or other proceedings intended to liquidate or rehabilitate the estate of the person involved.

(23) A person is "insolvent" who either has ceased to pay his debts in the ordinary course of business or cannot pay his debts as they become due or is insolvent within the meaning of the federal bankruptcy law.

(24) "Money" means a medium of exchange authorized or adopted by a domestic or foreign government as a part of its currency.

(25) A person has "notice" of a fact when
   (a) he has actual knowledge of it; or
   (b) he has received a notice or notification of it; or
   (c) from all the facts and circumstances known to him at the time in question he has reason to know that it exists.

A person "knows" or has "knowledge" of a fact when he has actual knowledge of it. "Discover" or "learn" or a word or phrase of similar import refers to knowledge rather than to reason to know. The time and circumstances under which a notice or notification may cease to be effective are not determined by this Act.

(26) A person "notifies" or "gives" notice or notification to another by taking such steps as may be reasonably required to inform the other in ordinary course whether or not such other actually comes to know of it. A person "receives" a notice or notification when

(a) it comes to his attention; or

(b) it is duly delivered at the place of business through which the contract was made or at any other place held out by him as the place for receipt of such communications.

(27) Notice, knowledge or a notice or notification received by an organization is effective for a particular transaction from the time when it is brought to the attention of the individual conducting that transaction, and in any event from the time when it would have been brought to his attention if the organization had exercised due diligence. An organization exercises due diligence if it maintains reasonable routines for communicating significant information to the person conducting the transaction and there is reasonable compliance with the routines. Due diligence does not require an individual acting for the organization to communicate information unless such communication is part of his regular duties or unless he has reason to know of the transaction and that the transaction would be materially affected by the information.

(28) "Organization" includes a corporation, government or governmental subdivision or agency, business trust, estate, trust, partnership or association, two or more persons having a joint or common interest, or any other legal or commercial entity.

(29) "Party," as distinct from "third party," means a person who has engaged in a transaction or made an agreement within this Act.

(30) "Person" includes an individual or an organization (see Section 1–102).

(31) "Presumption" or "presumed" means that the trier of fact must find the existence of the fact presumed unless and until evidence is introduced which would support a finding of its nonexistence.

(32) "Purchase" includes taking by sale, discount, negotiation, mortgage, pledge, lien, issue or re-issue, gift or any other voluntary transaction creating an interest in property.

(33) "Purchaser" means a person who takes by purchase.

(34) "Remedy" means any remedial right to which an aggrieved party is entitled with or without resort to a tribunal.

(35) "Representative" includes an agent, an officer of a corporation or association, and a trustee, executor or administrator of an estate, or any other person empowered to act for another.

(36) "Rights" includes remedies.

(37) "Security interest" means an interest in personal property or fixtures which secures payment or performance of an obligation. The retention or reservation of title by a seller of goods notwithstanding shipment or delivery to the buyer (Section 2–401) is limited in effect to a reservation of a "security interest." The term also includes any interest of a buyer of accounts or chattel paper which is subject to Article 9. The special property interest of a buyer of goods on identifica-

tion of such goods to a contract for sale under Section 2–401 is not a "security interest," but a buyer may also acquire a "security interest" by complying with Article 9. Unless a lease or consignment is intended as security, reservation of title thereunder is not a "security interest" but a consignment is in any event subject to the provisions on consignment sales (Section 2–326). Whether a lease is intended as security is to be determined by the facts of each case; however, (a) the inclusion of an option to purchase does not of itself make the lease one intended for security, and (b) an agreement that upon compliance with the terms of the lease the lessee shall become or has the option to become the owner of the property for no additional consideration or for a nominal consideration does make the lease one intended for security.

(38) "Send" in connection with any writing or notice means to deposit in the mail or deliver for transmission by any other usual means of communication with postage or cost of transmission provided for and properly addressed and in the case of an instrument to an address specified thereon or otherwise agreed, or if there be none to any address reasonable under the circumstances. The receipt of any writing or notice within the time at which it would have arrived if properly sent has the effect of a proper sending.

(39) "Signed" includes any symbol executed or adopted by a party with present intention to authenticate a writing.

(40) "Surety" includes guarantor.

(41) "Telegram" includes a message transmitted by radio, teletype, cable, any mechanical method of transmission, or the like.

(42) "Term" means that portion of an agreement which relates to a particular matter.

(43) "Unauthorized" signature or indorsement means one made without actual, implied or apparent authority and includes a forgery.

(44) "Value." Except as otherwise provided with respect to negotiable instruments and bank collections (Sections 3–303, 4–208 and 4–209) a person gives "value" for rights if he acquires them

(a) in return for a binding commitment to extend credit or for the extension of immediately available credit whether or not drawn upon and whether or not a chargeback is provided for in the event of difficulties in collection; or

(b) as security for or in total or partial satisfaction of a pre-existing claim; or

(c) by accepting delivery pursuant to a pre-existing contract for purchase; or

(d) generally, in return for any consideration sufficient to support a simple contract.

(45) "Warehouse receipt" means a receipt issued by a person engaged in the business of storing goods for hire.

(46) "Written" or "writing" includes printing, typewriting or any other intentional reduction to tangible form. As amended 1962 and 1972.

§ 1–202. Prima Facie Evidence by Third Party Documents.

A document in due form purporting to be a bill of lading, policy or certificate of insurance, official weigher's or inspector's certificate, consular invoice, or any other document authorized or required by the contract to be issued by a third party shall be prima facie evidence of its own authenticity and genuineness and of the facts stated in the document by the third party.

§ 1–203. Obligation of Good Faith.

Every contract or duty within this Act imposes an obligation of good faith in its performance or enforcement.

§ 1–204. Time; Reasonable Time; "Seasonably."

(1) Whenever this Act requires any action to be taken within a reasonable time, any time which is not manifestly unreasonable may be fixed by agreement.

(2) What is a reasonable time for taking any action depends on the nature, purpose and circumstances of such action.

(3) An action is taken "seasonably" when it is taken at or within the time agreed or if no time is agreed at or within a reasonable time.

§ 1–205. Course of Dealing and Usage of Trade.

(1) A course of dealing is a sequence of previous conduct between the parties to a particular transaction which is fairly to be regarded as establishing a common basis of understanding for interpreting their expressions and other conduct.

(2) A usage of trade is any practice or method of dealing having such regularity of observance in a place, vocation or trade as to justify an expectation that it will be observed with respect to the transaction in question. The existence and scope of such a usage are to be proved as facts. If it is established that such a usage is embodied in a written trade code or similar writing the interpretation of the writing is for the court.

(3) A course of dealing between parties and any usage of trade in the vocation or trade in which they are engaged or of which they are or should be aware give particular meaning to and supplement or qualify terms of an agreement.

(4) The express terms of an agreement and an applicable course of dealing or usage of trade shall be construed wherever reasonable as consistent with each other; but when such construction is unreasonable express terms control both course of dealing and usage of trade and course of dealing controls usage of trade.

(5) An applicable usage of trade in the place where any part of performance is to occur shall be used in interpreting the agreement as to that part of the performance.

(6) Evidence of a relevant usage of trade offered by one party is not admissible unless and until he has given the other party such notice as the court finds sufficient to prevent unfair surprise to the latter.

§ 1–206. Statute of Frauds for Kinds of Personal Property Not Otherwise Covered.

(1) Except in the cases described in subsection (2) of this section, a contract for the sale of personal property is not enforceable by way of action or defense beyond five thousand dollars in amount or value of remedy unless there is some writing which indicates that a contract for sale has been made between the parties at a defined or stated price, reasonably identifies the subject matter, and is signed by the party against whom enforcement is sought or by his authorized agent.

(2) Subsection (1) of this section does not apply to contracts for the sale of goods (Section 2–201) nor of securities (Section 8–319) nor to security agreements (Section 9–203).

§ 1–207. Performance or Acceptance Under Reservation of Rights.

A party who with explicit reservation of rights performs or promises performance or assents to performance in a manner demanded or offered by the other party does not thereby prejudice the rights reserved. Such words as "without prejudice," "under protest" or the like are sufficient.

§ 1–208. Option to Accelerate at Will.

A term providing that one party or his successor in interest may accelerate payment or performance or require collateral or additional collateral "at will" or "when he deems himself insecure" or in words of similar import shall be construed to mean that he shall have power to do so only if he in good faith believes that the prospect of payment or performance is impaired. The burden of establishing lack of good faith is on the party against whom the power has been exercised.

§ 1–209. Subordinated Obligations.

An obligation may be issued as subordinated to payment of another obligation of the person obligated, or a creditor may subordinate his right to payment of an obligation by agreement with either the person obligated or another creditor of the person obligated. Such a subordination does not create a security interest as against either the common debtor or a subordinated creditor. This section shall be construed as declaring the law as it existed prior to the enactment of this section and not as modifying it.

ARTICLE 2. Sales

PART 1
SHORT TITLE, GENERAL CONSTRUCTION AND SUBJECT MATTER

§ 2–101. Short Title.

This Article shall be known and may be cited as Uniform Commercial Code—Sales.

§ 2–102. Scope; Certain Security and Other Transactions Excluded From This Article.

Unless the context otherwise requires, this Article applies to transactions in goods; it does not apply to any transaction which although in the form of an unconditional contract to sell or present sale is intended to operate only as a security transaction nor does this Article impair or repeal any statute regulating sales to consumers, farmers or other specified classes of buyers.

§ 2–103. Definitions and Index of Definitions.

(1) In this Article unless the context otherwise requires
    (a) "Buyer" means a person who buys or contracts to buy goods.
    (b) "Good faith" in the case of a merchant means honesty in fact and the observance of reasonable commercial standards of fair dealing in the trade.
    (c) "Receipt" of goods means taking physical possession of them.
    (d) "Seller" means a person who sells or contracts to sell goods.

(2) Other definitions applying to this Article or to specified Parts thereof, and the sections in which they appear are:

"Acceptance." Section 2–606.

"Banker's credit." Section 2–325.

"Between merchants." Section 2–104.

"Cancellation." Section 2–106(4).

"Commercial unit." Section 2–105.

"Confirmed credit." Section 2–325.

"Conforming to contract." Section 2–106.

"Contract for sale." Section 2–106.

"Cover." Section 2–712.

"Entrusting." Section 2–403.

"Financing agency." Section 2–104.

"Future goods." Section 2–105.

"Goods." Section 2–105.

"Identification." Section 2–501.

"Installment contract." Section 2–612.

"Letter of Credit." Section 2–325.

"Lot." Section 2–105.

"Merchant." Section 2–104.

"Overseas." Section 2–323.

"Person in position of seller." Section 2–707.

"Present sale." Section 2–106.

"Sale." Section 2–106.

"Sale on approval." Section 2–326.

"Sale or return." Section. 2–326.

"Termination." Section 2–106.

(3) The following definitions in other Articles apply to this Article:

"Check." Section 3–104.

"Consignee." Section 7–102.

"Consignor." Section 7–102.

"Consumer goods." Section 9–109.

"Dishonor." Section 3–507.

"Draft." Section 3–104.

(4) In addition Article 1 contains general definitions and principles of construction and interpretation applicable throughout this Article.

§ 2–104. Definitions: "Merchant"; "Between Merchants"; "Financing Agency."

(1) "Merchant" means a person who deals in goods of the kind or otherwise by his occupation holds himself out as having knowledge or skill peculiar to the practices or goods involved in the transaction or to whom such knowledge or skill may be attributed by his employment of an agent or broker or other intermediary who by his occupation holds himself out as having such knowledge or skill.

(2) "Financing agency" means a bank, finance company or other person who in the ordinary course of business makes advances against goods or documents of title or who by arrangement with either the seller or the buyer intervenes in ordinary course to make or collect payment due or claimed under the contract for sale, as by purchasing or paying the seller's draft or making advances against it or by merely taking it for collection whether or not documents of title company

the draft. "Financing agency" includes also a bank or other person who similarly intervenes between persons who are in the position of seller and buyer in respect to the goods (Section 2–707).

(3) "Between merchants" means in any transaction with respect to which both parties are chargeable with the knowledge or skill of merchants.

§ 2–105. Definitions: Transferability; "Goods"; "Future" Goods; "Lot"; "Commercial Unit."

(1) "Goods" means all things (including specially manufactured goods) which are movable at the time of identification to the contract for sale other than the money in which the price is to be paid, investment securities (Article 8) and things in action. "Goods" also includes the unborn young of animals and growing crops and other identified things attached to realty as described in the section on goods to be severed from realty (Section 2–107).

(2) Goods must be both existing and identified before any interest in them can pass. Goods which are not both existing and identified are "future" goods. A purported present sale of future goods or of any interest therein operates as a contract to sell.

(3) There may be a sale of a part interest in existing identified goods.

(4) An undivided share in an identified bulk of fungible goods is sufficiently identified to be sold although the quantity of the bulk is not determined. Any agreed proportion of such a bulk or any quantity thereof agreed upon by number, weight or other measure may to the extent of the seller's interest in the bulk be sold to the buyer who then becomes an owner in common.

(5) "Lot" means a parcel or a single article which is the subject matter of a separate sale or delivery, whether or not it is sufficient to perform the contract.

(6) "Commercial unit" means such a unit of goods as by commercial usage is a single whole for purposes of sale and division of which materially impairs its character or value on the market or in use. A commercial unit may be a single article (as a machine) or a set of articles (as a suite of furniture or an assortment of sizes) or a quantity (as a bale, gross, or carload) or any other unit treated in use or in the relevant market as a single whole.

§ 2–106. Definitions: "Contract"; "Agreement"; "Contract for Sale"; "Sale"; "Present Sale"; "Conforming" to Contract; "Termination"; "Cancellation."

(1) In this Article unless the context otherwise requires "contract" and "agreement" are limited to those relating to the present or future sale of goods. "Contract for sale" includes both a present sale of goods and a contract to sell goods at a future time. A "sale" consists in the passing of title from the seller to the buyer for a price (Section 2–401). A "present sale" means a sale which is accomplished by the making of the contract.

(2) Goods or conduct including any part of a performance are "conforming" or conform to the contract when they are in accordance with the obligations under the contract.

(3) "Termination" occurs when either party pursuant to a power created by agreement or law puts an end to the contract otherwise than for its breach. On "termination" all obligations which are still executory on both sides are discharged but any right based on prior breach of performance survives.

(4) "Cancellation" occurs when either party puts an end to the contract for breach by the other and its effect is the same as that of "termination" except that the cancelling party also retains any remedy for breach of the whole contract or any unperformed balance.

§ 2–107. Goods to Be Severed From Realty: Recording

(1) A contract for the sale of minerals or the like (including oil and gas) or a structure or its materials to be removed from realty is a contract for the sale of goods within this Article if they are to be severed by the seller but until severance a purported present sale thereof which is not effective as a transfer of an interest in land is effective only as a contract to sell.

(2) A contract for the sale apart from the land of growing crops or other things attached to realty and capable of severance without material harm thereto but not described in subsection (1) or of timber to be cut is a contract for the sale of goods within this Article whether the subject matter is to be severed by the buyer or by the seller even though it forms part of the realty at the time of contracting, and the parties can by identification effect a present sale before severance.

(3) The provisions of this section are subject to any third party rights provided by the law relating to realty records, and the contract for sale may be extended and recorded as a document transferring an interest in land and shall then constitute notice to third parties of the buyer's rights under the contract for sale.

PART 2

FORM, FORMATION AND READJUSTMENT OF CONTRACT

§ 2–201. Formal Requirements; Statute of Frauds.

(1) Except as otherwise provided in this section a contract for the sale of goods for the price of $500 or more is not enforceable by way of action or defense unless there is some writing sufficient to indicate that a contract for sale has been made between the parties and signed by the party against whom enforcement is sought or by his authorized agent or broker. A writing is not insufficient because it omits or incorrectly states a term agreed upon but the contract is not enforceable under this paragraph beyond the quantity of goods shown in such writing.

(2) Between merchants if within a reasonable time a writing in confirmation of the contract and sufficient against the sender is received and the party receiving it has reason to know its contents, it satisfies the requirements of subsection (1) against such party unless written notice of objection to its contents is given within 10 days after it is received.

(3) A contract which does not satisfy the requirements of subsection (1) but which is valid in other respects is enforceable

(a) if the goods are to be specially manufactured for the buyer and are not suitable for sale to others in the ordinary course of the seller's business and the seller, before notice of repudiation is received and under circumstances which reasonably indicate that the goods are for the buyer, has made either a substantial beginning of their manufacture or commitments for their procurement; or

(b) if the party against whom enforcement is sought admits in his pleading, testimony or otherwise in court that a contract for sale was made, but the contract is not enforceable under this provision beyond the quantity of goods admitted; or

(c) with respect to goods for which payment has been made and accepted or which have been received and accepted (Section 2–606).

§ 2–202. Final Written Expression: Parol or Extrinsic Evidence.

Terms with respect to which the confirmatory memoranda of the parties agree or which are otherwise set forth in a writing intended by the parties as a final expression of their agreement with respect to such terms as are included therein may not be contradicted by evidence of any prior agreement or of a contemporaneous oral agreement but may be explained or supplemented

(a) by course of dealing or usage of trade (Section 1–205) or by course of performance (Section 2–208); and

(b) by evidence of consistent additional terms unless the court finds the writing to have been intended also as a complete and exclusive statement of the terms of the agreement.

§ 2–203. Seals Inoperative.

The affixing of a seal to a writing evidencing a contract for sale or an offer to buy or sell goods does not constitute the writing of a sealed instrument and the law with respect to sealed instruments does not apply to such a contract or offer.

§ 2–204. Formation in General.

(1) A contract for sale of goods may be made in any manner sufficient to show agreement, including conduct by both parties which recognizes the existence of such a contract.

(2) An agreement sufficient to constitute a contract for sale may be found even though the moment of its making is undetermined.

(3) Even though one or more terms are left open a contract for sale does not fail for indefiniteness if the parties have intended to make a contract and there is a reasonably certain basis for giving an appropriate remedy.

§ 2–205. Firm Offers.

An offer by a merchant to buy or sell goods in a signed writing which by its terms gives assurance that it will be held open is not revocable, for lack of consideration, during the time stated or if no time is stated for a reasonable time, but in no event may such period of irrevocability exceed three months; but any such term of assurance on a form supplied by the offeree must be separately signed by the offeror.

§ 2–206. Offer and Acceptance in Formation of Contract.

(1) Unless otherwise unambiguously indicated by the language or circumstances

(a) an offer to make a contract shall be construed as inviting acceptance in any manner and by any medium reasonable in the circumstances;

(b) an order or other offer to buy goods for prompt or current shipment shall be construed as inviting acceptance either by a prompt promise to ship or by the prompt or current shipment of conforming or non-conforming goods, but such a shipment of non-conforming goods does not constitute an acceptance if the seller seasonably notifies the buyer that the shipment is offered only as an accommodation to the buyer.

(2) Where the beginning of a requested performance is a reasonable mode of acceptance an offeror who is not notified of acceptance within a reasonable time may treat the offer as having lapsed before acceptance.

§ 2–207. Additional Terms in Acceptance or Confirmation.

(1) A definite and seasonable expression of acceptance or a written confirmation which is sent within a reasonable time operates as an acceptance even though it states terms additional to or different from those offered or agreed upon, unless acceptance is expressly made conditional on assent to the additional or different terms.

(2) The additional terms are to be construed as proposals for addition to the contract. Between merchants such terms become part of the contract unless:

(a) the offer expressly limits acceptance to the terms of the offer;

(b) they materially alter it; or

(c) notification of objection to them has already been given or is given within a reasonable time after notice of them is received.

(3) Conduct by both parties which recognizes the existence of a contract is sufficient to establish a contract for sale although the writings of the parties do not otherwise establish a contract. In such case the terms of the particular contract consist of those terms on which the writings of the parties agree, together with any supplementary terms incorporated under any other provisions of this Act.

§ 2–208. Course of Performance or Practical Construction.

(1) Where the contract for sale involves repeated occasions for performance by either party with knowledge of the nature of the performance and opportunity for objection to it by the other, any course of performance accepted or acquiesced in without objection shall be relevant to determine the meaning of the agreement.

(2) The express terms of the agreement and any such course of performance, as well as any course of dealing and usage of trade, shall be construed whenever reasonable as consistent with each other; but when such construction is unreasonable, express terms shall control course of performance and course of performance shall control both course of dealing and usage of trade (Section 1–205).

(3) Subject to the provisions of the next section on modification and waiver, such course of performance shall be relevant to show a waiver or modification of any term inconsistent with such course of performance.

§ 2–209. Modification, Rescission and Waiver.

(1) An agreement modifying a contract within this Article needs no consideration to be binding.

(2) A signed agreement which excludes modification or rescission except by a signed writing cannot be otherwise modified or rescinded, but except as between merchants such a requirement on a form supplied by the merchant must be separately signed by the other party.

(3) The requirements of the statute of frauds section of this Article (Section 2–201) must be satisfied if the contract as modified is within its provisions.

(4) Although an attempt at modification or rescission does not satisfy the requirements of subsection (2) or (3) it can operate as a waiver.

(5) A party who has made a waiver affecting an executory portion of the contract may retract the waiver by reasonable notification received by the other party that strict performance will be required of any term waived, unless the retraction would be unjust in view of a material change of position in reliance on the waiver.

§ 2–210. Delegation of Performance; Assignment of Rights.

(1) A party may perform his duty through a delegate unless otherwise agreed or unless the other party has a substantial interest in having his original promisor perform or control the acts required by the contract. No delegation of performance relieves the party delegating of any duty to perform or any liability for breach.

(2) Unless otherwise agreed all rights of either seller or buyer can be assigned except where the assignment would materially change the duty of the other party, or increase materially the burden or risk imposed on him by his contract, or impair materially his chance of obtaining return performance. A right to damages for breach of the whole contract or a right arising out of the assignor's due performance of his entire obligation can be assigned despite agreement otherwise.

(3) Unless the circumstances indicate the contrary a prohibition of assignment of "the contract" is to be construed as barring only the delegation to the assignee of the assignor's performance.

(4) An assignment of "the contract" or of "all the rights under the contract" or an assignment in similar general terms is an assignment of rights and unless the language or the circumstances (as in an assignment for security) indicate the contrary, it is a delegation of performance of the duties of the assignor and its acceptance by the assignee constitutes a promise by him to perform those duties. This promise in enforceable by either the assignor or the other party to the original contract.

(5) The other party may treat any assignment which delegates performance as creating reasonable grounds for insecurity and may without prejudice to his rights against the assignor demand assurances from the assignee (Section 2–609).

PART 3
GENERAL OBLIGATION AND CONSTRUCTION OF CONTRACT

§ 2–301. General Obligations of Parties.

The obligation of the seller is to transfer and deliver and that of the buyer is to accept and pay in accordance with the contract.

§ 2–302. Unconscionable Contract or Clause.

(1) If the court as a matter of law finds the contract or any clause of the contract to have been unconscionable at the time it was made the court may refuse to enforce the contract, or it may enforce the remainder of the contract without the unconscionable clause, or it may so limit the application of any unconscionable clause as to avoid any unconscionable result.

(2) When it is claimed or appears to the court that the contract or any clause thereof may be unconscionable the parties shall be afforded a reasonable opportunity to present evidence as to its commercial setting, purpose and effect to aid the court in making the determination.

690

§ 2–303. Allocation or Division of Risks.

Where this Article allocates a risk or a burden as between the parties "unless otherwise agreed," the agreement may not only shift the allocation but may also divide the risk or burden.

§ 2–304. Price Payable in Money, Goods, Realty, or Otherwise.

(1) The price can be made payable in money or otherwise. If it is payable in whole or in part in goods each party is a seller of the goods which he is to transfer.

(2) Even though all or part of the price is payable in an interest in realty the transfer of the goods and the seller's obligations with reference to them are subject to this Article, but not the transfer of the interest in realty or the transferor's obligations in connection therewith.

§ 2–305. Open Price Term.

(1) The parties if they so intend can conclude a contract for sale even though the price is not settled. In such a case the price is a reasonable price at the time for delivery if
   (a) nothing is said as to price; or
   (b) the price is left to be agreed by the parties and they fail to agree; or
   (c) the price is to be fixed in terms of some agreed market or other standard as set or recorded by a third person or agency and it is not so set or recorded.

(2) A price to be fixed by the seller or by the buyer means a price for him to fix in good faith.

(3) When a price left to be fixed otherwise than by agreement of the parties fails to be fixed through fault of one party the other may at his option treat the contract as cancelled or himself fix a reasonable price.

(4) Where, however, the parties intend not to be bound unless the price be fixed or agreed and it is not fixed or agreed there is no contract. In such a case the buyer must return any goods already received or if unable so to do must pay their reasonable value at the time of delivery and the seller must return any portion of the price paid on account.

§ 2–306. Output, Requirements and Exclusive Dealings.

(1) A term which measures the quantity by the output of the seller or the requirements of the buyer means such actual output or requirements as may occur in good faith, except that no quantity unreasonably disproportionate to any stated estimate or in the absence of a stated estimate to any normal or otherwise comparable prior output or requirements may be tendered or demanded.

(2) A lawful agreement by either the seller or the buyer for exclusive dealing in the kind of goods concerned imposes unless otherwise agreed an obligation by the seller to use best efforts to supply the goods and by the buyer to use best efforts to promote their sale.

§ 2–307. Delivery in Single Lot or Several Lots.

Unless otherwise agreed all goods called for by a contract for sale must be tendered in a single delivery and payment is due only on such tender but where the circumstances give either party the right to make or demand delivery in lots the price if it can be apportioned may be demanded for each lot.

§ 2–308. Absence of Specified Place for Delivery.

Unless otherwise agreed
  (a) the place for delivery of goods is the seller's place of business or if he has none his residence; but
  (b) in a contract for sale of identified goods which to the knowledge of the parties at the time of contracting are in some other place, that place is the place for their delivery; and
  (c) documents of title may be delivered through customary banking channels.

§ 2–309. Absence of Specific Time Provisions; Notice of Termination.

(1) The time for shipment or delivery or any other action under a contract if not provided in this Article or agreed upon shall be a reasonable time.

(2) Where the contract provides for successive performances but is indefinite in duration it is valid for a reasonable time but unless otherwise agreed may be terminated at any time by either party.

(3) Termination of a contract by one party except on the happening of an agreed event requires that reasonable notification be received by the other party and an agreement dispensing with notification is invalid if its operation would be unconscionable.

§ 2–310. Open Time for Payment or Running of Credit; Authority to Ship Under Reservation.

Unless otherwise agreed
  (a) payment is due at the time and place at which the buyer is to receive the goods even though the place of shipment is the place of delivery; and
  (b) if the seller is authorized to send the goods he may ship them under reservation, and may tender the documents of title, but the buyer may inspect the goods after their arrival before payment is due unless such inspection is inconsistent with the terms of the contract (Section 2–513); and
  (c) if delivery is authorized and made by way of documents of title otherwise than by subsection (b) then payment is due at the time and place at which the buyer is to receive the documents regardless of where the goods are to be received; and
  (d) where the seller is required or authorized to ship the goods on credit the credit period runs from the time of shipment but post-dating the invoice or delaying its dispatch will correspondingly delay the starting of the credit period.

§ 2–311. Options and Cooperation Respecting Performance.

(1) An agreement for sale which is otherwise sufficiently definite (subsection (3) of Section 2–204) to be a contract is not made invalid by the fact that it leaves particulars of performance to be specified by one of the parties. Any such specification must be made in good faith and within limits set by commercial reasonableness.

(2) Unless otherwise agreed specifications relating to assortment of the goods are at the buyer's option and except as otherwise provided in subsections (1) (c) and (3) of Section 2–319 specifications or arrangements relating to shipment are at the seller's option.

(3) Where such specification would materially affect the other party's performance but is not seasonably made or where one party's cooperation is necessary to the agreed performance of the other but is not seasonably forthcoming, the other party in addition to all other remedies

(a) is excused for any resulting delay in his own performance; and

(b) may also either proceed to perform in any reasonable manner or after the time for a material part of his own performance treat the failure to specify or to cooperate as a breach by failure to deliver or accept the goods.

§ 2–312. Warranty of Title and Against Infringement; Buyer's Obligation Against Infringement.

(1) Subject to subsection (2) there is in a contract for sale a warranty by the seller that

(a) the title conveyed shall be good and its transfer rightful; and

(b) the goods shall be delivered free from any security interest or other lien or encumbrance of which the buyer at the time of contracting has no knowledge.

(2) A warranty under subsection (1) will be excluded or modified only by specific language or by circumstances which give the buyer reason to know that the person selling does not claim title in himself or that he is purporting to sell only such right or title as he or a third person may have.

(3) Unless otherwise agreed a seller who is a merchant regularly dealing in goods of the kind warrants that the goods shall be delivered free of the rightful claim of any third person by way of infringement or the like but a buyer who furnishes specifications to the seller must hold the seller harmless against any such claim which arises out of compliance with the specifications.

§ 2–313. Express Warranties by Affirmation, Promise, Description, Sample.

(1) Express warranties by the seller are created as follows:

(a) Any affirmation of fact or promise made by the seller to the buyer which relates to the goods and becomes part of the basis of the bargain creates an express warranty that the goods shall conform to the affirmation or promise.

(b) Any description of the goods which is made part of the basis of the bargain creates an express warranty that the goods shall conform to the description.

(c) Any sample or model which is made part of the basis of the bargain creates an express warranty that the whole of the goods shall conform to the sample or model.

(2) It is not necessary to the creation of an express warranty that the seller use formal words such as "warrant" or "guarantee" or that he have a specific intention to make a warranty, but an affirmation merely of the value of the goods or a statement purporting to be merely the seller's opinion or commendation of the goods does not create a warranty.

§ 2–314. Implied Warranty: Merchantability; Usage of Trade.

(1) Unless excluded or modified (Section 2–316), a warranty that the goods shall be merchantable is implied in a contract for their sale if the seller is a

merchant with respect to goods of that kind. Under this section the serving for value of food or drink to be consumed either on the premises or elsewhere is a sale.

(2) Goods to be merchantable must be at least such as

    (a) pass without objection in the trade under the contract description; and

    (b) in the case of fungible goods, are of fair average quality within the description; and

    (c) are fit for the ordinary purposes for which such goods are used; and

    (d) run, within the variations permitted by the agreement, of even kind, quality and quantity within each unit and among all units involved; and

    (e) are adequately contained, packaged, and labeled as the agreement may require; and

    (f) conform to the promises or affirmations of fact made on the container or label if any.

(3) Unless excluded or modified (Section 2–316) other implied warranties may arise from course of dealing or usage of trade.

§ 2–315. Implied Warranty: Fitness for Particular Purpose.

Where the seller at the time of contracting has reason to know any particular purpose for which the goods are required and that the buyer is relying on the seller's skill or judgment to select or furnish suitable goods, there is unless excluded or modified under the next section an implied warranty that the goods shall be fit for such purpose.

§ 2–316. Exclusion or Modification of Warranties.

(1) Words or conduct relevant to the creation of an express warranty and words or conduct tending to negate or limit warranty shall be construed wherever reasonable as consistent with each other; but subject to the provisions of this Article on parol or extrinsic evidence (Section 2–202) negation or limitation is inoperative to the extent that such construction is unreasonable.

(2) Subject to subsection (3), to exclude or modify the implied warranty of merchantability or any part of it the language must mention merchantability and in case of a writing must be conspicuous, and to exclude or modify any implied warranty of fitness the exclusion must be by a writing and conspicuous. Language to exclude all implied warranties of fitness is sufficient if it states, for example, that "There are no warranties which extend beyond the description on the face hereof."

(3) Notwithstanding subsection (2)

    (a) unless the circumstances indicate otherwise, all implied warranties are excluded by expressions like "as is," "with all faults" or other language which in common understanding calls the buyer's attention to the exclusion of warranties and makes plain that there is no implied warranty; and

    (b) when the buyer before entering into the contract has examined the goods or the sample or model as fully as he desired or has refused to examine the goods there is no implied warranty with regard to defects which an examination ought in the circumstances to have revealed to him; and

(c) an implied warranty can also be excluded or modified by course of dealing or course of performance or usage of trade.

(4) Remedies for breach of warranty can be limited in accordance with the provisions of this Article on liquidation or limitation of damages and on contractual modification of remedy (Sections 2–718 and 2–719).

§ 2–317. Cumulation and Conflict of Warranties Express or Implied.

Warranties whether express or implied shall be construed as consistent with each other and as cumulative, but if such construction is unreasonable the intention of the parties shall determine which warranty is dominant. In ascertaining that intention the following rules apply:

(a) Exact or technical specifications displace an inconsistent sample or model or general language of description.

(b) A sample from an existing bulk displaces inconsistent general language of description.

(c) Express warranties displace inconsistent implied warranties other than an implied warranty of fitness for a particular purpose.

§ 2–318. Third Party Beneficiaries of Warranties Express or Implied.

A seller's warranty whether express or implied extends to any natural person who is in the family or household of his buyer or who is a guest in his home if it is reasonable to expect that such person may use, consume or be affected by the goods and who is injured in person by breach of the warranty. A seller may not exclude or limit the operation of this section.

§ 2–319. F.O.B. and F.A.S. Terms.

(1) Unless otherwise agreed the term F.O.B. (which means "free on board") at a named place, even though used only in connection with the stated price, is a delivery term under which

(a) when the term is F.O.B. the place of shipment, the seller must at that place ship the goods in the manner provided in this Article (Section 2–504) and bear the expense and risk of putting them into the possession of the carrier; or

(b) when the term is F.O.B. the place of destination, the seller must at his own expense and risk transport the goods to that place and there tender delivery of them in the manner provided in this Article (Section 2–503);

(c) when under either (a) or (b) the term is also F.O.B. vessel, car or other vehicle, the seller must in addition at his own expense and risk load the goods on board. If the term is F.O.B. vessel the buyer must name the vessel and in an appropriate case the seller must comply with the provisions of this Article on the form of bill of lading (Section 2–323).

(2) Unless otherwise agreed the term F.A.S. vessel (which means "free alongside") at a named port, even though used only in connection with the stated price, is a delivery term under which the seller must

(a) at his own expense and risk deliver the goods alongside the vessel in the manner usual in that port or on a dock designated and provided by the buyer; and

   (b) obtain and tender a receipt for the goods in exchange for which the carrier is under a duty to issue a bill of lading.

   (3) Unless otherwise agreed in any case falling within subsection (1) (a) or (c) or subsection (2) the buyer must seasonably give any needed instructions for making delivery, including when the term is F.A.S. or F.O.B. the loading berth of the vessel and in an appropriate case its name and sailing date. The seller may treat the failure of needed instructions as a failure of cooperation under this Article (Section 2–311). He may also at his option move the goods in any reasonable manner preparatory to delivery or shipment.

   (4) Under the term F.O.B. vessel or F.A.S. unless otherwise agreed the buyer must make payment against tender of the required documents and the seller may not tender nor the buyer demand delivery of the goods in substitution for the documents.

§ 2–320. C.I.F. and C.&F. Terms.

   (1) The term C.I.F. means that the price includes in a lump sum the cost of the goods and the insurance and freight to the named destination. The term C.&F. or C.F. means that the price so includes cost and freight to the named destination.

   (2) Unless otherwise agreed and even though used only in connection with the stated price and destination, the term C.I.F. destination or its equivalent requires the seller at his own expense and risk to

   (a) put the goods into the possession of a carrier at the port for shipment and obtain a negotiable bill or bills of lading covering the entire transportation to the named destination; and

   (b) load the goods and obtain a receipt from the carrier (which may be contained in the bill of lading) showing that the freight has been paid or provided for; and

   (c) obtain a policy or certificate of insurance, including any war risk insurance, of a kind and on terms then current at the port of shipment in the usual amount, in the currency of the contract, shown to cover the same goods covered by the bill of lading and providing for payment of loss to the order of the buyer or for the account of whom it may concern; but the seller may add to the price the amount of the premium for any such war risk insurance; and

   (d) prepare an invoice of the goods and procure any other documents required to effect shipment or to comply with the contract; and

   (e) forward and tender with commercial promptness all the documents in due form and with any indorsement necessary to perfect the buyer's rights.

   (3) Unless otherwise agreed the term C.&F. or its equivalent has the same effect and imposes upon the seller the same obligations and risks as a C.I.F. term except the obligation as to insurance.

   (4) Under the term C.I.F. or C.&F. unless otherwise agreed the buyer must make payment against tender of the required documents and the seller may not tender nor the buyer demand delivery of the goods in substitution for the documents.

§ 2–321. C.I.F. or C.&F.: "Net Landed Weights"; "Payment on Arrival"; Warranty of Condition on Arrival.

Under a contract containing a term C.I.F. or C.&F.

(1) Where the price is based on or is to be adjusted according to "net landed weights," "delivered weights," "out turn" quantity or quality or the like, unless otherwise agreed the seller must reasonably estimate the price. The payment due on tender of the documents called for by the contract is the amount so estimated, but after final adjustment of the price a settlement must be made with commercial promptness.

(2) An agreement described in subsection (1) or any warranty of quality or condition of the goods on arrival places upon the seller the risk of ordinary deterioration, shrinkage and the like in transportation but has no effect on the place or time of identification to the contract for sale or delivery or on the passing of the risk of loss.

(3) Unless otherwise agreed where the contract provides for payment on or after arrival of the goods the seller must before payment allow such preliminary inspection as is feasible; but if the goods are lost delivery of the documents and payment are due when the goods should have arrived.

§ 2–322. Delivery "Ex-Ship."

(1) Unless otherwise agreed a term for delivery of goods "ex-ship" (which means from the carrying vessel) or in equivalent language is not restricted to a particular ship and requires delivery from a ship which has reached a place at the named port of destination where goods of the kind are usually discharged.

(2) Under such a term unless otherwise agreed

   (a) the seller must discharge all liens arising out of the carriage and furnish the buyer with a direction which puts the carrier under a duty to deliver the goods; and

   (b) the risk of loss does not pass to the buyer until the goods leave the ship's tackle or are otherwise properly unloaded.

§ 2–323. Form of Bill of Lading Required in Overseas Shipment; "Overseas."

(1) Where the contract contemplates overseas shipment and contains a term C.I.F. or C.&F. or F.O.B. vessel, the seller unless otherwise agreed must obtain a negotiable bill of lading stating that the goods have been loaded on board or, in the case of a term C.I.F. or C.&F., received for shipment.

(2) Where in a case within subsection (1) a bill of lading has been issued in a set of parts, unless otherwise agreed if the documents are not to be sent from abroad the buyer may demand tender of the full set; otherwise only one part of the bill of lading need be tendered. Even if the agreement expressly requires a full set

   (a) due tender of a single part is acceptable within the provisions of this Article on cure of improper delivery (subsection (1) of Section 2–508); and

   (b) even though the full set is demanded, if the documents are sent from abroad the person tendering an incomplete set may nevertheless require payment upon furnishing an indemnity which the buyer in good faith deems adequate.

(3) A shipment by water or by air or a contract contemplating such shipment

is "overseas" insofar as by usage of trade or agreement it is subject to the commercial, financing or shipping practices characteristic of international deep water commerce.

§ 2–324. "No Arrival, No Sale" Term.

Under a term "no arrival, no sale" or terms of like meaning, unless otherwise agreed,

    (a) the seller must properly ship conforming goods and if they arrive by any means he must tender them on arrival but he assumes no obligation that the goods will arrive unless he has caused the non-arrival; and

    (b) where without fault of the seller the goods are in part lost or have so deteriorated as no longer to conform to the contract or arrive after the contract time, the buyer may proceed as if there had been casualty to identified goods (Section 2–613).

§ 2–325. "Letter of Credit" Term; "Confirmed Credit."

(1) Failure of the buyer seasonably to furnish an agreed letter of credit is a breach of the contract for sale.

(2) The delivery to seller of a proper letter of credit suspends the buyer's obligation to pay. If the letter of credit is dishonored, the seller may on seasonable notification to the buyer require payment directly from him.

(3) Unless otherwise agreed the term "letter of credit" or "banker's credit" in a contract for sale means an irrevocable credit issued by a financing agency of good repute and, where the shipment is overseas, of good international repute. The term "confirmed credit" means that the credit must also carry the direct obligation of such an agency which does business in the seller's financial market.

§ 2–326. Sale on Approval and Sale or Return; Consignment Sales and Rights of Creditors.

(1) Unless otherwise agreed, if delivered goods may be returned by the buyer even though they conform to the contract, the transaction is

    (a) a "sale on approval" if the goods are delivered primarily for use, and

    (b) a "sale or return" if the goods are delivered primarily for resale.

(2) Except as provided in subsection (3), goods held on approval are not subject to the claims of the buyer's creditors until acceptance; goods held on sale or return are subject to such claims while in the buyer's possession.

(3) Where goods are delivered to a person for sale and such person maintains a place of business at which he deals in goods of the kind involved, under a name other than the name of the person making delivery, then with respect to claims of creditors of the person conducting the business the goods are deemed to be on sale or return. The provisions of this subsection are applicable even though an agreement purports to reserve title to the person making delivery until payment or resale or uses such words as "on consignment" or "on memorandum." However, this subsection is not applicable if the person making delivery

    (a) complies with an applicable law providing for a consignor's interest or the like to be evidenced by a sign, or

    (b) establishes that the person conducting the business is generally known by his creditors to be substantially engaged in selling the goods of others, or

    (c) complies with the filing provisions of the Article on Secured Transactions (Article 9).

(4) Any "or return" term of a contract for sale is to be treated as a separate contract for sale within the statute of frauds section of this Article (Section 2–201) and as contradicting the sale aspect of the contract within the provisions of this Article on parol or extrinsic evidence (Section 2–202).

§ 2–327. Special Incidents of Sale on Approval and Sale or Return.

(1) Under a sale on approval unless otherwise agreed
    (a) although the goods are identified to the contract the risk of loss and the title do not pass to the buyer until acceptance; and
    (b) use of the goods consistent with the purpose of trial is not acceptance but failure seasonably to notify the seller of election to return the goods is acceptance, and if the goods conform to the contract acceptance of any part is acceptance of the whole; and
    (c) after due notification of election to return, the return is at the seller's risk and expense but a merchant buyer must follow any reasonable instructions.

(2) Under a sale or return unless otherwise agreed
    (a) the option to return extends to the whole or any commercial unit of the goods while in substantially their original condition, but must be exercised seasonably; and
    (b) the return is at the buyer's risk and expense.

§ 2–328. Sale by Auction.

(1) In a sale by auction if goods are put in lots each lot is the subject of a separate sale.

(2) A sale by auction is complete when the auctioneer so announces by the fall of the hammer or in other customary manner. Where a bid is made while the hammer is falling in acceptance of a prior bid the auctioneer may in his discretion reopen the bidding or declare the goods sold under the bid on which the hammer was falling.

(3) Such a sale is with reserve unless the goods are in explicit terms put up without reserve. In an auction with reserve the auctioneer may withdraw the goods at any time until he announces completion of the sale. In an auction without reserve, after the auctioneer calls for bids on an article or lot, that article or lot cannot be withdrawn unless no bid is made within a reasonable time. In either case a bidder may retract his bid until the auctioneer's announcement of completion of the sale, but a bidder's retraction does not revive any previous bid.

(4) If the auctioneer knowingly receives a bid on the seller's behalf or the seller makes or procures such a bid, and notice has not been given that liberty for such bidding is reserved, the buyer may at his option avoid the sale or take the goods at the price of the last good faith bid prior to the completion of the sale. This subsection shall not apply to any bid at a forced sale.

PART 4

TITLE, CREDITORS AND GOOD FAITH PURCHASERS

§ 2–401. Passing of Title; Reservation for Security; Limited Application of This Section.

Each provision of this Article with regard to the rights, obligations and remedies of the seller, the buyer, purchasers or other third parties applies irrespective of title to the goods except where the provision refers to such title. Insofar as situations are not covered by the other provisions of this Article and matters concerning title become material the following rules apply:

(1) Title to goods cannot pass under a contract for sale prior to their identification to the contract (Section 2–501), and unless otherwise explicitly agreed the buyer acquires by their identification a special property as limited by this Act. Any retention or reservation by the seller of the title (property) in goods shipped or delivered to the buyer is limited in effect to a reservation of a security interest. Subject to these provisions and to the provisions of the Article on Secured Transactions (Article 9), title to goods passes from the seller to the buyer in any manner and on any conditions explicitly agreed on by the parties.

(2) Unless otherwise explicitly agreed title passes to the buyer at the time and place at which the seller completes his performance with reference to the physical delivery of the goods, despite any reservation of a security interest and even though a document of title is to be delivered at a different time or place; and in particular and despite any reservation of a security interest by the bill of lading,

    (a) if the contract requires or authorizes the seller to send the goods to the buyer but does not require him to deliver them at destination, title passes to the buyer at the time and place of shipment; but

    (b) if the contract requires delivery at destination, title passes on tender there.

(3) Unless otherwise explicitly agreed where delivery is to be made without moving the goods,

    (a) if the seller is to deliver a document of title, title passes at the time when and the place where he delivers such documents; or

    (b) if the goods are at the time of contracting already identified and no documents are to be delivered, title passes at the time and place of contracting.

(4) A rejection or other refusal by the buyer to receive or retain the goods, whether or not justified, or a justified revocation of acceptance revests title to the goods in the seller. Such revesting occurs by operation of law and is not a "sale."

§ 2–402. Rights of Seller's Creditors Against Sold Goods.

(1) Except as provided in subsections (2) and (3), rights of unsecured creditors of the seller with respect to goods which have been identified to a contract for sale are subject to the buyer's rights to recover the goods under this Article (Sections 2–502 and 2–716).

(2) A creditor of the seller may treat a sale or an identification of goods to a contract for sale as void if as against him a retention of possession by the seller is fraudulent under any rule of law of the state where the goods are situated, except that retention of possession in good faith and current course of trade by a merchant-seller for a commercially reasonable time after a sale or identification is not fraudulent.

(3) Nothing in this Article shall be deemed to impair the rights of creditors of the seller

    (a) under the provisions of the Article on Secured Transactions (Article 9); or

    (b) where identification to the contract or delivery is made not in current course of trade but in satisfaction of or as security for a pre-existing claim for money, security or the like and is made under circumstances which under any rule of law of the state where the goods are situated would apart from this Article constitute the transaction of a fraudulent transfer or voidable preference.

§ 2–403. Power to Transfer; Good Faith Purchase of Goods; "Entrusting."

(1) A purchaser of goods acquires all title which his transferor had or had power to transfer except that a purchaser of a limited interest acquires rights only to the extent of the interest purchased. A person with voidable title has power to transfer a good title to a good faith purchaser for value. When goods have been delivered under a transaction of purchase the purchaser has such power even though

    (a) the transferor was deceived as to the identity of the purchaser, or

    (b) the delivery was in exchange for a check which is later dishonored, or

    (c) it was agreed that the transaction was to be a "cash sale," or

    (d) the delivery was procured through fraud punishable as larcenous under the criminal law.

(2) Any entrusting of possession of goods to a merchant who deals in goods of that kind gives him power to transfer all rights of the entruster to a buyer in ordinary course of business.

(3) "Entrusting" includes any delivery and any acquiescence in retention of possession regardless of any condition expressed between the parties to the delivery or acquiescence and regardless of whether the procurement of the entrusting or the possessor's disposition of the goods have been such as to be larcenous under the criminal law.

(4) The rights of other purchasers of goods and of lien creditors are governed by the Articles of Secured Transactions (Article 9), Bulk Transfers (Article 6) and Documents of Title (Article 7).

PART 5
PERFORMANCE

§ 2–501. Insurable Interest in Goods; Manner of Identification of Goods.

(1) The buyer obtains a special property and an insurable interest in goods by identification of existing goods as goods to which the contract refers even though the goods so identified are non-conforming and he has an option to return or reject them. Such identification can be made at any time and in any manner explicitly agreed to by the parties. In the absence of explicit agreement identification occurs

    (a) when the contract is made if it is for the sale of goods already existing and identified;

    (b) if the contract is for the sale of future goods other than those described in paragraph (c), when goods are shipped, marked or otherwise designated by the seller as goods to which the contract refers;

    (c) when the crops are planted or otherwise become growing crops or the young are conceived if the contract is for the sale of unborn young to be born within twelve months after contracting or for the sale of crops to be harvested within twelve months or the next normal harvest season after contracting whichever is longer.

(2) The seller retains an insurable interest in goods so long as title to or any security interest in the goods remains in him and where the identification is by the seller alone he may until default or insolvency or notification to the buyer that the identification is final substitute other goods for those identified.

(3) Nothing in this section impairs any insurable interest recognized under any other statute or rule of law.

§ 2–502. Buyer's Right to Goods on Seller's Insolvency.

(1) Subject to subsection (2) and even though the goods have not been shipped a buyer who has paid a part or all of the price of goods in which he has a special property under the provisions of the immediately preceding section may on making and keeping good a tender of any unpaid portion of their price recover them from the seller if the seller becomes insolvent within ten days after receipt of the first installment on their price.

(2) If the identification creating his special property has been made by the buyer he acquires the right to recover the goods only if they conform to the contract for sale.

§ 2–503. Manner of Seller's Tender of Delivery.

(1) Tender of delivery requires that the seller put and hold conforming goods at the buyer's disposition and give the buyer any notification reasonably necessary to enable him to take delivery. The manner, time and place for tender are determined by the agreement and this Article, and in particular

    (a) tender must be at a reasonable hour, and if it is of goods they must be kept available for the period reasonably necessary to enable the buyer to take possession; but

    (b) unless otherwise agreed the buyer must furnish facilities reasonably suited to the receipt of the goods.

(2) Where the case is within the next section respecting shipment tender requires that the seller comply with its provisions.

(3) Where the seller is required to deliver at a particular destination tender requires that he comply with subsection (1) and also in any appropriate case tender documents as described in subsections (4) and (5) of this section.

(4) Where goods are in the possession of a bailee and are to be delivered without being moved

    (a) tender requires that the seller either tender a negotiable document of title covering such goods or procure acknowledgment by the bailee of the buyer's right to possession of the goods; but

    (b) tender to the buyer of a non-negotiable document of title or of a written direction to the bailee to deliver is sufficient tender unless the buyer seasonably objects, and receipt by the bailee of notification of the buyer's rights fixes those rights as against the bailee and all third persons; but risk of loss of the goods and of any failure by the bailee to honor the non-negotiable document of title or to obey the direction remains on the seller until the buyer has had a reasonable time to present the document or direction, and a refusal by the bailee to honor the document or to obey the direction defeats the tender.

(5) Where the contract requires the seller to deliver documents
- (a) he must tender all such documents in correct form, except as provided in this Article with respect to bills of lading in a set (subsection (2) of Section 2–323); and
- (b) tender through customary banking channels is sufficient and dishonor of a draft accompanying the documents constitutes non-acceptance or rejection.

§ 2–504. Shipment by Seller.

Where the seller is required or authorized to send the goods to the buyer and the contract does not require him to deliver them at a particular destination, then unless otherwise agreed he must
- (a) put the goods in the possession of such a carrier and make such a contract for their transportation as may be reasonable having regard to the nature of the goods and other circumstances of the case; and
- (b) obtain and promptly deliver or tender in due form any document necessary to enable the buyer to obtain possession of the goods or otherwise required by the agreement or by usage of trade; and
- (c) promptly notify the buyer of the shipment.

Failure to notify the buyer under paragraph (c) or to make a proper contract under paragraph (a) is a ground for rejection only if material delay or loss ensues.

§ 2–505. Seller's Shipment Under Reservation.

(1) Where the seller has identified goods to the contract by or before shipment:
- (a) his procurement of a negotiable bill of lading to his own order or otherwise reserves in him a security interest in the goods. His procurement of the bill to the order of a financing agency or of the buyer indicates in addition only the seller's expectation of transferring that interest to the person named.
- (b) a non-negotiable bill of lading to himself or his nominee reserves possession of the goods as security but except in a case of conditional delivery (subsection (2) of Section 2–507) a non-negotiable bill of lading naming the buyer as consignee reserves no security interest even though the seller retains possession of the bill of lading.

(2) When shipment by the seller with reservation of a security interest is in violation of the contract for sale it constitutes an improper contract for transportation within the preceding section but impairs neither the rights given to the buyer by shipment and identification of the goods to the contract nor the seller's powers as a holder of a negotiable document.

§ 2–506. Rights of Financing Agency.

(1) A financing agency by paying or purchasing for value a draft which relates to a shipment of goods acquires to the extent of the payment or purchase and in addition to its own rights under the draft and any document of title securing it any rights of the shipper in the goods including the right to stop delivery and the shipper's right to have the draft honored by the buyer.

(2) The right to reimbursement of a financing agency which has in good faith honored or purchased the draft under commitment to or authority from the buyer is not impaired by subsequent discovery of defects with reference to any relevant document which was apparently regular on its face.

§ 2–507. Effect of Seller's Tender; Delivery on Condition.

(1) Tender of delivery is a condition to the buyer's duty to accept the goods and, unless otherwise agreed, to his duty to pay for them. Tender entitles the seller to acceptance of the goods and to payment according to the contract.

(2) Where payment is due and demanded on the delivery to the buyer of goods or documents of title, his right as against the seller to retain or dispose of them is conditional upon his making the payment due.

§ 2–508. Cure by Seller of Improper Tender or Delivery; Replacement.

(1) Where any tender or delivery by the seller is rejected because non-conforming and the time for performance has not yet expired, the seller may seasonably notify the buyer of his intention to cure and may then within the contract time make a conforming delivery.

(2) Where the buyer rejects a non-conforming tender which the seller had reasonable grounds to believe would be acceptable with or without money allowance the seller may if he seasonably notifies the buyer have a further reasonable time to substitute a conforming tender.

§ 2–509. Risk of Loss in the Absence of Breach.

(1) Where the contract requires or authorizes the seller to ship the goods by carrier

   (a) if it does not require him to deliver them at a particular destination, the risk of loss passes to the buyer when the goods are duly delivered to the carrier even though the shipment is under reservation (Section 2–505); but

   (b) if it does require him to deliver them at a particular destination and the goods are there duly tendered while in the possession of the carrier, the risk of loss passes to the buyer when the goods are there duly so tendered as to enable the buyer to take delivery.

(2) Where the goods are held by a bailee to be delivered without being moved, the risk of loss passes to the buyer

   (a) on his receipt of a negotiable document of title covering the goods; or

   (b) on acknowledgment by the bailee of the buyer's right to possession of the goods; or

   (c) after his receipt of a non-negotiable document of title or other written direction to deliver, as provided in subsection (4) (b) of Section 2–503.

(3) In any case not within subsection (1) or (2), the risk of loss passes to the buyer on his receipt of the goods if the seller is a merchant; otherwise the risk passes to the buyer on tender of delivery.

(4) The provisions of this section are subject to contrary agreement of the parties and to the provisions of this Article on sale on approval (Section 2–327) and on effect of breach on risk of loss (Section 2–510).

§ 2–510. Effect of Breach on Risk of Loss.

(1) Where a tender or delivery of goods so fails to conform to the contract as to give a right of rejection the risk of their loss remains on the seller until cure or acceptance.

(2) Where the buyer rightfully revokes acceptance he may to the extent of any deficiency in his effective insurance coverage treat the risk of loss as having rested on the seller from the beginning.

(3) Where the buyer as to conforming goods already identified to the contract for sale repudiates or is otherwise in breach before risk of their loss has passed to him, the seller may to the extent of any deficiency in his effective insurance coverage treat the risk of loss as resting on the buyer for a commercially reasonable time.

§ 2–511. Tender of Payment by Buyer; Payment by Check.

(1) Unless otherwise agreed tender of payment is a condition to the seller's duty to tender and complete any delivery.

(2) Tender of payment is sufficient when made by any means or in any manner current in the ordinary course of business unless the seller demands payment in legal tender and gives any extension of time reasonably necessary to procure it.

(3) Subject to the provisions of this Act on the effect of an instrument on an obligation (Section 3–802), payment by check is conditional and is defeated as between the parties by dishonor of the check on due presentment.

§ 2–512. Payment by Buyer Before Inspection.

(1) Where the contract requires payment before inspection non-conformity of the goods does not excuse the buyer from so making payment unless
   (a) the non-conformity appears without inspection; or
   (b) despite tender of the required documents the circumstances would justify injunction against honor under the provisions of this Act (Section 5–114).

(2) Payment pursuant to subsection (1) does not constitute an acceptance of goods or impair the buyer's right to inspect or any of his remedies.

§ 2–513. Buyer's Right to Inspection of Goods.

(1) Unless otherwise agreed and subject to subjection (3), where goods are tendered or delivered or identified to the contract for sale, the buyer has a right before payment or acceptance to inspect them at any reasonable place and time and in any reasonable manner. When the seller is required or authorized to send the goods to the buyer, the inspection may be after their arrival.

(2) Expenses of inspection must be borne by the buyer but may be recovered from the seller if the goods do not conform and are rejected.

(3) Unless otherwise agreed and subject to the provisions of this Article on C.I.F. contracts (subsection (3) of Section 2–321), the buyer is not entitled to inspect the goods before payment of the price when the contract provides
   (a) for delivery "C.O.D." or on other like terms; or
   (b) for payment against documents of title, except where such payment is due only after the goods are to become available for inspection.

(4) A place or method of inspection fixed by the parties is presumed to be exclusive but unless otherwise expressly agreed it does not postpone identification or shift the place for delivery or for passing the risk of loss. If compliance becomes impossible, inspection shall be as provided in this section unless the place or method fixed was clearly intended as an indispensable condition failure of which avoids the contract.

§ 2–514. When Documents Deliverable on Acceptance; When on Payment.

Unless otherwise agreed documents against which a draft is drawn are to be delivered to the drawee on acceptance of the draft if it is payable more than three days after presentment; otherwise, only on payment.

§ 2–515. Preserving Evidence of Goods in Dispute.

In furtherance of the adjustment of any claim or dispute
- (a) either party on reasonable notification to the other and for the purpose of ascertaining the facts and preserving evidence has the right to inspect, test and sample the goods including such of them as may be in the possession or control of the other; and
- (b) the parties may agree to a third party inspection or survey to determine the conformity or condition of the goods and may agree that the findings shall be binding upon them in any subsequent litigation or adjustment.

PART 6
BREACH, REPUDIATION AND EXCUSE

§ 2–601. Buyer's Rights on Improper Delivery.

Subject to the provisions of this Article on breach in installment contracts (Section 2–612) and unless otherwise agreed under the sections on contractual limitations of remedy (Sections 2–718 and 2–719), if the goods or the tender of delivery fail in any respect to conform to the contract, the buyer may
- (a) reject the whole; or
- (b) accept the whole; or
- (c) accept any commercial unit or units and reject the rest.

§ 2–602. Manner and Effect of Rightful Rejection.

(1) Rejection of goods must be within a reasonable time after their delivery or tender. It is ineffective unless the buyer seasonably notifies the seller.

(2) Subject to the provisions of the two following sections on rejected goods (Section 2–603 and 2–604),
- (a) after rejection any exercise of ownership by the buyer with respect to any commercial unit is wrongful as against the seller; and
- (b) if the buyer has before rejection taken physical possession of goods in which he does not have a security interest under the provisions of this Article (subsection (3) of Section 2–711), he is under a duty after rejection to hold them with reasonable care at the seller's disposition for a time sufficient to permit the seller to remove them; but
- (c) the buyer has no further obligations with regard to goods rightfully rejected.

(3) The seller's rights with respect to goods wrongfully rejected are governed by the provisions of this Article on seller's remedies in general (Section 2–703).

§ 2–603. Merchant Buyer's Duties as to Rightfully Rejected Goods.

(1) Subject to any security interest in the buyer (subsection (3) of Section 2–711), when the seller has no agent or place of business at the market of rejection a merchant buyer is under a duty after rejection of goods in his possession or control to follow any reasonable instructions received from the seller with respect to the goods and in the absence of such instructions to make reasonable efforts to sell them for the seller's account if they are perishable or threaten to decline in value speedily. Instructions are not reasonable if on demand indemnity for expenses is not forthcoming.

(2) When the buyer sells goods under subsection (1), he is entitled to reimburse-

ment from the seller or out of the proceeds for reasonable expenses of caring for and selling them, and if the expenses include no selling commission then to such commission as is usual in the trade or if there is none to a reasonable sum not exceeding ten percent on the gross proceeds.

(3) In complying with this section the buyer is held only to good faith and good faith conduct hereunder is neither acceptance nor conversion nor the basis of an action for damages.

§ 2–604. Buyer's Options as to Salvage of Rightfully Rejected Goods.

Subject to the provisions of the immediately preceding section on perishables if the seller gives no instructions within a reasonable time after notification of rejection the buyer may store the rejected goods for the seller's account or reship them to him or resell them for the seller's account with reimbursement as provided in the preceding section. Such action is not acceptance or conversion.

§ 2–605. Waiver of Buyer's Objections by Failure to Particularize.

(1) The buyer's failure to state in connection with rejection a particular defect which is ascertainable by reasonable inspection precludes him from relying on the unstated defect to justify rejection or to establish breach

  (a) where the seller could have cured it if stated seasonably; or
  (b) between merchants when the seller has after rejection made a request in writing for a full and final written statement of all defects on which the buyer proposes to rely.

(2) Payment against documents made without reservation of rights precludes recovery of the payment for defects apparent on the face of the documents.

§ 2–606. What Constitutes Acceptance of Goods.

(1) Acceptance of goods occurs when the buyer

  (a) after a reasonable opportunity to inspect the goods signifies to the seller that the goods are conforming or that he will take or retain them in spite of their nonconformity; or
  (b) fails to make an effective rejection (subsection (1) of Section 2–602), but such acceptance does not occur until the buyer has had a reasonable opportunity to inspect them; or
  (c) does any act inconsistent with the seller's ownership; but if such act is wrongful as against the seller it is an acceptance only if ratified by him.

(2) Acceptance of a part of any commercial unit is acceptance of that entire unit.

§ 2–607. Effect of Acceptance; Notice of Breach; Burden of Establishing Breach After Acceptance; Notice of Claim or Litigation to Person Answerable Over.

(1) The buyer must pay at the contract rate for any goods accepted.

(2) Acceptance of goods by the buyer precludes rejection of the goods accepted and if made with knowledge of a non-conformity cannot be revoked because of it unless the acceptance was on the reasonable assumption that the non-conformity would be seasonably cured but acceptance does not of itself impair any other remedy provided by this Article for non-conformity.

(3) Where a tender has been accepted

    (a) the buyer must within a reasonable time after he discovers or should have discovered any breach notify the seller of breach or be barred from any remedy; and

    (b) if the claim is one for infringement or the like (subsection (3) of Section 2–312) and the buyer is sued as a result of such a breach he must so notify the seller within a reasonable time after he receives notice of the litigation or be barred from any remedy over for liability established by the litigation.

(4) The burden is on the buyer to establish any breach with respect to the goods accepted.

(5) Where the buyer is sued for breach of a wararanty or other obligation for which his seller is answerable over

    (a) he may give his seller written notice of the litigation. If the notice states that the seller may come in and defend and that if the seller does not do so he will be bound in any action against him by his buyer by any determination of fact common to the two litigations, then unless the seller after seasonable receipt of the notice does come in and defend he is so bound.

    (b) if the claim is one for infringement or the like (subsection (3) of Section 2–312) the original seller may demand in writing that his buyer turn over to him control of the litigation including settlement or else be barred from any remedy over and if he also agrees to bear all expense and to satisfy any adverse judgment, then unless the buyer after seasonable receipt of the demand does turn over control the buyer is so barred.

(6) The provisions of subsections (3), (4) and (5) apply to any obligation of a buyer to hold the seller harmless against infringement or the like (subsection (3) of Section 2–312).

§ 2–608. Revocation of Acceptance in Whole or in Part.

(1) The buyer may revoke his acceptance of a lot or commercial unit whose non-conformity substantially impairs its value to him if he has accepted it

    (a) on the reasonable assumption that its non-conformity would be cured and it has not been seasonably cured; or

    (b) without discovery of such non-conformity if his acceptance was reasonably induced either by the difficulty of discovery before acceptance or by the seller's assurances.

(2) Revocation of acceptance must occur within a reasonable time after the buyer discovers or should have discovered the ground for it and before any substantial change in condition of the goods which is not caused by their own defects. It is not effective until the buyer notifies the seller of it.

(3) A buyer who so revokes has the same rights and duties with regard to the goods involved as if he had rejected them.

§ 2–609. Right to Adequate Assurance of Performance.

(1) A contract for sale imposes an obligation on each party that the other's expectation of receiving due performance will not be impaired. When reasonable grounds for insecurity arise with respect to the performance of either party the

other may in writing demand adequate assurance of due performance and until he receives such assurance may if commercially reasonable suspend any performance for which he has not already received the agreed return.

(2) Between merchants the reasonableness of grounds for insecurity and the adequacy of any assurance offered shall be determined according to commercial standards.

(3) Acceptance of any improper delivery or payment does not prejudice the aggrieved party's right to demand adequate assurance of future performance.

(4) After receipt of a justified demand failure to provide within a reasonable time not exceeding thirty days such assurance of due performance as is adequate under the circumstances of the particular case is a repudiation of the contract.

§ 2–610. Anticipatory Repudiation.

When either party repudiates the contract with respect to a performance not yet due the loss of which will substantially impair the value of the contract to the other, the aggrieved party may

(a) for a commercially reasonable time await performance by the repudiating party; or

(b) resort to any remedy for breach (Section 2–703 or Section 2–711), even though he has notified the repudiating party that he would await the latter's performance and has urged retraction; and

(c) in either case suspend his own performance or proceed in accordance with the provisions of this Article on the seller's right to identify goods to the contract notwithstanding breach or to salvage unfinished goods (Section 2–704).

§ 2–611. Retraction of Anticipatory Repudiation.

(1) Until the repudiating party's next performance is due he can retract his repudiation unless the aggrieved party has since the repudiation cancelled or materially changed his position or otherwise indicated that he considers the repudiation final.

(2) Retraction may be by any method which clearly indicates to the aggrieved party that the repudiating party intends to perform, but must include any assurance justifiably demanded under the provisions of this Article (Section 2–609).

(3) Retraction reinstates the repudiating party's rights under the contract with due excuse and allowance to the aggrieved party for any delay occasioned by the repudiation.

§ 2–612. "Installment Contract"; Breach.

(1) An "installment contract" is one which requires or authorizes the delivery of goods in separate lots to be separately accepted, even though the contract contains a clause "each delivery is a separate contract" or its equivalent.

(2) The buyer may reject any installment which is non-conforming if the non-conformity substantially impairs the value of that installment and cannot be cured or if the non-conformity is a defect in the required documents; but if the non-conformity does not fall within subsection (3) and the seller gives adequate assurance of its cure the buyer must accept that installment.

(3) Whenever non-conformity or default with respect to one or more installments substantially impairs the value of the whole contract there is a breach of

the whole. But the aggrieved party reinstates the contract if he accepts a non-conforming installment without seasonably notifying of cancellation or if he brings an action with respect only to past installments or demands performance as to future installments.

§ 2–613. Casualty to Identified Goods.

Where the contract requires for its performance goods identified when the contract is made, and the goods suffer casualty without fault of either party before the risk of loss passes to the buyer, or in a proper case under a "no arrival, no sale" term (Section 2–324) then

(a) if the loss is total the contract is avoided; and

(b) if the loss is partial or the goods have so deteriorated as no longer to conform to the contract the buyer may nevertheless demand inspection and at his option either treat the contract as avoided or accept the goods with due allowance from the contract price for the deterioration or the deficiency in quantity but without further right against the seller.

§ 2–614. Substituted Performance.

(1) Where without fault of either party the agreed berthing, loading, or unloading facilities fail or an agreed type of carrier becomes unavailable or the agreed manner of delivery otherwise becomes commercially impracticable but a commercially reasonable substitute is available, such substitute performance must be tendered and accepted.

(2) If the agreed means or manner of payment fails because of domestic or foreign governmental regulation, the seller may withhold or stop delivery unless the buyer provides a means or manner of payment which is commercially a substantial equivalent. If delivery has already been taken, payment by the means or in the manner provided by the regulation discharges the buyer's obligation unless the regulation is discriminatory, oppressive or predatory.

§ 2–615. Excuse by Failure of Presupposed Conditions.

Except so far as a seller may have assumed a greater obligation and subject to the preceding section on substituted performance:

(a) Delay in delivery or non-delivery in whole or in part by a seller who complies with paragraphs (b) and (c) is not a breach of his duty under a contract for sale if performance as agreed has been made impracticable by the occurrence of a contingency the non-occurrence of which was a basic assumption on which the contract was made or by compliance in good faith with any applicable foreign or domestic governmental regulation or order whether or not it later proves to be invalid.

(b) Where the causes mentioned in paragraph (a) affect only a part of the seller's capacity to perform, he must allocate production and deliveries among his customers but may at his option include regular customers not then under contract as well as his own requirements for further manufacture. He may so allocate in any manner which is fair and reasonable.

(c) The seller must notify the buyer seasonably that there will be delay or non-delivery and, when allocation is required under paragraph (b), of the estimated quota thus made available for the buyer.

§ 2–616. Procedure on Notice Claiming Excuse.

(1) Where the buyer receives notification of a material or indefinite delay or an allocation justified under the preceding section he may by written notification to the seller as to any delivery concerned, and where the prospective deficiency substantially impairs the value of the whole contract under the provisions of this Article relating to breach of installment contracts (Section 2–612), then also as to the whole,

    (a) terminate and thereby discharge any unexecuted portion of the contract; or

    (b) modify the contract by agreeing to take his available quota in substitution.

(2) If after receipt of such notification from the seller the buyer fails so to modify the contract within a reasonable time not exceeding thirty days the contract lapses with respect to any deliveries affected.

(3) The provisions of this section may not be negated by agreement except in so far as the seller has assumed a greater obligation under the preceding section.

PART 7
REMEDIES

§ 2–701. Remedies for Breach of Collateral Contracts Not Impaired.

Remedies for breach of any obligation or promise collateral or ancillary to a contract for sale are not impaired by the provisions of this Article.

§ 2–702. Seller's Remedies on Discovery of Buyer's Insolvency.

(1) Where the seller discovers the buyer to be insolvent he may refuse delivery except for cash including payment for all goods theretofore delivered under the contract, and stop delivery under this Article (Section 2–705).

(2) Where the seller discovers that the buyer has received goods on credit while insolvent he may reclaim the goods upon demand made within ten days after the receipt, but if misrepresentation of solvency has been made to the particular seller in writing within three months before delivery the ten day limitation does not apply. Except as provided in this subsection the seller may not base a right to reclaim goods on the buyer's fraudulent or innocent misrepresentation of solvency or of intent to pay.

(3) The seller's right to reclaim under subsection (2) is subject to the rights of a buyer in ordinary course or other good faith purchaser under this Article (Section 2–403). Successful reclamation of goods excludes all other remedies with respect to them.

§ 2–703. Seller's Remedies in General.

Where the buyer wrongfully rejects or revokes acceptance of goods or fails to make a payment due on or before delivery or repudiates with respect to a part or the whole, then with respect to any goods directly affected and, if the breach is of the whole contract (Section 2–612), then also with respect to the whole undelivered balance, the aggrieved seller may

    (a) withhold delivery of such goods;

    (b) stop delivery by any bailee as hereafter provided (Section 2–705);

    (c) proceed under the next section respecting goods still unidentified to the contract;

    (d) resell and recover damages as hereafter provided (Section 2–706);

    (e) recover damages for non-acceptance (Section 2–708) or in a proper case the price (Section 2–709);

    (f) cancel.

§ 2–704. Seller's Right to Identify Goods to the Contract Notwithstanding Breach or to Salvage Unfinished Goods.

(1) An aggrieved seller under the preceding section may

    (a) identify to the contract conforming goods not already identified if at the time he learned of the breach they are in his possession or control;

    (b) treat as the subject of resale goods which have demonstrably been intended for the particular contract even though those goods are unfinished.

(2) Where the goods are unfinished an aggrieved seller may in the exercise of reasonable commercial judgment for the purposes of avoiding loss and of effective realization either complete the manufacture and wholly identify the goods to the contract or cease manufacture and resell for scrap or salvage value or proceed in any other reasonable manner.

§ 2–705. Seller's Stoppage of Delivery in Transit or Otherwise.

(1) The seller may stop delivery of goods in the possession of a carrier or other bailee when he discovers the buyer to be insolvent (Section 2–702) and may stop delivery of carload, truckload, planeload or larger shipments of express or freight when the buyer repudiates or fails to make a payment due before delivery or if for any other reason the seller has a right to withhold or reclaim the goods.

(2) As against such buyer the seller may stop delivery until

    (a) receipt of the goods by the buyer; or

    (b) acknowledgment to the buyer by any bailee of the goods except a carrier that the bailee holds the goods for the buyer; or

    (c) such acknowledgment to the buyer by a carrier by reshipment or as warehouseman; or

    (d) negotiation to the buyer of any negotiable document of title covering the goods.

(3)(a) To stop delivery the seller must so notify as to enable the bailee by reasonable diligence to prevent delivery of the goods.

    (b) After such notification the bailee must hold and deliver the goods according to the directions of the seller but the seller is liable to the bailee for any ensuing charges or damages.

    (c) If a negotiable document of title has been issued for goods the bailee is not obliged to obey a notification to stop until surrender of the document.

    (d) A carrier who has issued a non-negotiable bill of lading is not obliged to obey a notification to stop received from a person other than the consignor.

§ 2–706. Seller's Resale Including Contract for Resale.

(1) Under the conditions stated in Section 2–703 on seller's remedies, the seller may resell the goods concerned or the undelivered balance thereof. Where the resale is made in good faith and in a commercially reasonable manner the seller may recover the difference between the resale price and the contract price

together with any incidental damages allowed under the provisions of this Article (Section 2–710), but less expenses saved in consequence of the buyer's breach.

(2) Except as otherwise provided in subsection (3) or unless otherwise agreed resale may be at public or private sale including sale by way of one or more contracts to sell or of identification to an existing contract of the seller. Sale may be as a unit or in parcels and at any time and place and on any terms but every aspect of the sale including the method, manner, time, place and terms must be commercially reasonable. The resale must be reasonably identified as referring to the broken contract, but it is not necessary that the goods be in existence or that any or all of them have been identified to the contract before the breach.

(3) Where the resale is at private sale the seller must give the buyer reasonable notification of his intention to resell.

(4) Where the resale is at public sale

(a) only identified goods can be sold except where there is a recognized market for a public sale of futures in goods of the kind; and

(b) it must be made at a usual place or market for public sale if one is reasonably available and except in the case of goods which are perishable or threaten to decline in value speedily the seller must give the buyer reasonable notice of the time and place of the resale; and

(c) if the goods are not to be within the view of those attending the sale the notification of sale must state the place where the goods are located and provide for their reasonable inspection by prospective bidders; and

(d) the seller may buy.

(5) A purchaser who buys in good faith at a resale takes the goods free of any rights of the original buyer even though the seller fails to comply with one or more of the requirements of this section.

(6) The seller is not accountable to the buyer for any profit made on any resale. A person in the position of a seller (Section 2–707) or a buyer who has rightfully rejected or justifiably revoked acceptance must account for any excess over the amount of his security interest, as hereinafter defined (subsection (3) of Section 2–711).

§ 2–707. "Person in the Position of a Seller."

(1) A "person in the position of a seller" includes as against a principal an agent who has paid or become responsible for the price of goods on behalf of his principal or anyone who otherwise holds a security interest or other right in goods similar to that of a seller.

(2) A person in the position of a seller may as provided in this Article withhold or stop delivery (Section 2–705) and resell (Section 2–706) and recover incidental damages (Section 2–710).

§ 2–708. Seller's Damages for Non-Acceptance or Repudiation.

(1) Subject to subsection (2) and to the provisions of this Article with respect to proof of market price (Section 2–723), the measure of damages for non-acceptance or repudiation by the buyer is the difference between the market price at the time and place for tender and the unpaid contract price together with any incidental damages provided in this Article (Section 2–710), but less expenses saved in consequence of the buyer's breach.

(2) If the measure of damages provided in subsection (1) is inadequate to put the seller in as good a position as performance would have done then the measure of damages is the profit (including reasonable overhead) which the seller would have made from full performance by the buyer, together with any incidental damages provided in this Article (Section 2–710), due allowance for costs reasonably incurred and due credit for payments or proceeds of resale.

§ 2–709. Action for the Price.

(1) When the buyer fails to pay the price as it becomes due the seller may recover, together with any incidental damages under the next section, the price

- (a) of goods accepted or of conforming goods lost or damaged within a commercially reasonable time after risk of their loss has passed to the buyer; and
- (b) of goods identified to the contract if the seller is unable after reasonable effort to resell them at a reasonable price or the circumstances reasonably indicate that such effort will be unavailing.

(2) Where the seller sues for the price he must hold for the buyer any goods which have been identified to the contract and are still in his control except that if resale becomes possible he may resell them at any time prior to the collection of the judgment. The net proceeds of any such resale must be credited to the buyer and payment of the judgment entitles him to any goods not resold.

(3) After the buyer has wrongfully rejected or revoked acceptance of the goods or has failed to make a payment due or has repudiated (Section 2–610), a seller who is held not entitled to the price under this section shall nevertheless be awarded damages for non-acceptance under the preceding section.

§ 2–710. Seller's Incidental Damages.

Incidental damages to an aggrieved seller include any commercially reasonable charges, expenses or commissions incurred in stopping delivery, in the transportation, care and custody of goods after the buyer's breach, in connection with return or resale of the goods or otherwise resulting from the breach.

§ 2–711. Buyer's Remedies in General; Buyer's Security Interest in Rejected Goods.

(1) Where the seller fails to make delivery or repudiates or the buyer rightfully rejects or justifiably revokes acceptance then with respect to any goods involved, and with respect to the whole if the breach goes to the whole contract (Section 2–612), the buyer may cancel and whether or not he has done so may in addition to recovering so much of the price as has been paid

- (a) "cover" and have damages under the next section as to all the goods affected whether or not they have been identified to the contract; or
- (b) recover damages for non-delivery as provided in this Article (Section 2–713).

(2) Where the seller fails to deliver or repudiates the buyer may also

- (a) if the goods have been identified recover them as provided in this Article (Section 2–502); or
- (b) in a proper case obtain specific performance or replevy the goods as provided in this Article (Section 2–716).

(3) On rightful rejection or justifiable revocation of acceptance a buyer has a

security interest in goods in his possession or control for any payments made on their price and any expenses reasonably incurred in their inspection, receipt, transportation, care and custody and may hold such goods and resell them in like manner as an aggrieved seller (Section 2–706).

§ 2–712. "Cover"; Buyer's Procurement of Substitute Goods.

(1) After a breach within the preceding section the buyer may "cover" by making in good faith and without unreasonable delay any reasonable purchase of or contract to purchase goods in substitution for those due from the seller.

(2) The buyer may recover from the seller as damages the difference between the cost of cover and the contract price together with any incidental or consequential damages as hereinafter defined (Section 2–715), but less expenses saved in consequence of the seller's breach.

(3) Failure of the buyer to effect cover within this section does not bar him from any other remedy.

§ 2–713. Buyer's Damages for Non-Delivery or Repudiation.

(1) Subject to the provisions of this Article with respect to proof of market price (Section 2–723), the measure of damages for non-delivery or repudiation by the seller is the difference between the market price at the time when the buyer learned of the breach and the contract price together with any incidental and consequential damages provided in this Article (Section 2–715), but less expenses saved in consequence of the seller's breach.

(2) Market price is to be determined as of the place for tender or, in cases of rejection after arrival or revocation of acceptance, as of the place of arrival.

§ 2–714. Buyer's Damages for Breach in Regard to Accepted Goods.

(1) Where the buyer has accepted goods and given notification (subsection (3) of Section 2–607) he may recover as damages for any non-conformity of tender the loss resulting in the ordinary course of events from the seller's breach as determined in any manner which is reasonable.

(2) The measure of damages for breach of warranty is the difference at the time and place of acceptance between the value of the goods accepted and the value they would have had if they had been as warranted, unless special circumstances show proximate damages of a different amount.

(3) In a proper case any incidental and consequential damages under the next section may also be recovered.

§ 2–715. Buyer's Incidental and Consequential Damages.

(1) Incidental damages resulting from the seller's breach include expenses reasonably incurred in inspection, receipt, transportation and care and custody of goods rightfully rejected, any commercially reasonable charges, expenses or commissions in connection with effecting cover and any other reasonable expense incident to the delay or other breach.

(2) Consequential damages resulting from the seller's breach include

    (a) any loss resulting from general or particular requirements and needs of which the seller at the time of contracting had reason to know and which could not reasonably be prevented by cover or otherwise; and

    (b) injury to person or property proximately resulting from any breach of warranty.

§ 2–716. Buyer's Right to Specific Performance or Replevin.

(1) Specific performance may be decreed where the goods are unique or in other proper circumstances.

(2) The decree for specific performance may include such terms and conditions as to payment of the price, damages, or other relief as the court may deem just.

(3) The buyer has a right of replevin for goods identified to the contract if after reasonable effort he is unable to effect cover for such goods or the circumstances reasonably indicate that such effort will be unavailing or if the goods have been shipped under reservation and satisfaction of the security interest in them has been made or tendered.

§ 2–717. Deduction of Damages From the Price.

The buyer on notifying the seller of his intention to do so may deduct all or any part of the damages resulting from any breach of the contract from any part of the price still due under the same contract.

§ 2–718. Liquidation or Limitation of Damages; Deposits.

(1) Damages for breach by either party may be liquidated in the agreement buy only at an amount which is reasonable in the light of the anticipated or actual harm caused by the breach, the difficulties of proof of loss, and the inconvenience or nonfeasibility of otherwise obtaining an adequate remedy. A term fixing unreasonably large liquidated damages is void as a penalty.

(2) Where the seller justifiably withholds delivery of goods because of the buyer's breach, the buyer is entitled to restitution of any amount by which the sum of his payments exceeds

> (a) the amount to which the seller is entitled by virtue of terms liquidating the seller's damages in accordance with subsection (1), or
>
> (b) in the absence of such terms, twenty percent of the value of the total performance for which the buyer is obligated under the contract or $500, whichever is smaller.

(3) The buyer's right to restitution under subsection (2) is subject to offset to the extent that the seller establishes

> (a) a right to recover damages under the provisions of this Article other than subsection (1), and
>
> (b) the amount of value of any benefits received by the buyer directly or indirectly by reason of the contract.

(4) Where a seller has received payment in goods their reasonable value or the proceeds of their resale shall be treated as payments for the purposes of subsection (2); but if the seller has notice of the buyer's breach before reselling goods received in part performance, his resale is subject to the conditions laid down in this Article on resale by an aggrieved seller (Section 2–706).

§ 2–719. Contractual Modification or Limitation of Remedy.

(1) Subject to the provisions of subsections (2) and (3) of this section and of the preceding section on liquidation and limitation of damages,

> (a) the agreement may provide for remedies in addition to or in substitution for those provided in this Article and may limit or alter the measure of damages recoverable under this Article, as by limiting the buyer's remedies to return of the goods and repayment of the price or to repair and replacement of non-conforming goods or parts; and

(b) resort to a remedy as provided is optional unless the remedy is expressly agreed to be exclusive, in which case it is the sole remedy.

(2) Where circumstances cause an exclusive or limited remedy to fail of its essential purpose, remedy may be had as provided in this Act.

(3) Consequential damages may be limited or excluded unless the limitation or exclusion is unconscionable. Limitation of consequential damages for injury to the person in the case of consumer goods is prima facie unconscionable but limitation of damages where the loss is commercial is not.

§ 2–720. Effect of "Cancellation" or "Rescission" on Claims for Antecedent Breach.

Unless the contrary intention clearly appears, expressions of "cancellation" or "rescission" of the contract or the like shall not be construed as a renunciation or discharge of any claim in damages for an antecedent breach.

§ 2–721. Remedies for Fraud.

Remedies for material misrepresentation or fraud include all remedies available under this Article for non-fraudulent breach. Neither rescission or a claim for rescission of the contract for sale nor rejection or return of the goods shall bar or be deemed inconsistent with a claim for damages or other remedy.

§ 2–722. Who Can Sue Third Parties for Injury to Goods.

Where a third party so deals with goods which have been identified to a contract for sale as to cause actionable injury to a party to that contract

(a) a right of action against the third party is in either party to the contract for sale who has title to or a security interest or a special property or an insurable interest in the goods; and if the goods have been destroyed or converted a right of action is also in the party who either bore the risk of loss under the contract for sale or has since the injury assumed that risk as against the other;

(b) if at the time of the injury the party plaintiff did not bear the risk of loss as against the other party to the contract for sale and there is no arrangement between them for disposition of the recovery, his suit or settlement is, subject to his own interest, as a fiduciary for the other party to the contract;

(c) either party may with the consent of the other sue for the benefit of whom it may concern.

§ 2–723. Proof of Market Price: Time and Place.

(1) If an action based on anticipatory repudiation comes to trial before the time for performance with respect to some or all of the goods, any damages based on market price (Section 2–708 or Section 2–713) shall be determined according to the price of such goods prevailing at the time when the aggrieved party learned of the repudiation.

(2) If evidence of a price prevailing at the times or places described in this Article is not readily available the price prevailing within any reasonable time before or after the time described or at any other place which in commercial judgment or under usage of trade would serve as a reasonable substitute for the one described may be used, making any proper allowance for the cost of transporting the goods to or from such other place.

(3) Evidence of a relevant price prevailing at a time or place other than the one described in this Article offered by one party is not admissible unless and until he has given the other party such notice as the court finds sufficient to prevent unfair surprise.

§ 2-724. Admissibility of Market Quotations.

Whenever the prevailing price or value of any goods regularly bought and sold in any established commodity market is in issue, reports in official publications or trade journals or in newspapers or periodicals of general circulation published as the reports of such market shall be admissible in evidence. The circumstances of the preparation of such a report may be shown to affect its weight but not its admissibility.

§ 2-725. Statute of Limitations in Contracts for Sale.

(1) An action for breach of any contract for sale must be commenced within four years after the cause of action has accrued. By the original agreement the parties may reduce the period of limitation to not less than one year but may not extend it.

(2) A cause of action accrues when the breach occurs, regardless of the aggrieved party's lack of knowledge of the breach. A breach of warranty occurs when tender of delivery is made, except that where a warranty explicitly extends to future performance of the goods and discovery of the breach must await the time of such performance the cause of action accrues when the breach is or should have been discovered.

(3) Where an action commenced within the time limited by subsection (1) is so terminated as to leave available a remedy by another action for the same breach such other action may be commenced after the expiration of the time limited and within six months after the termination of the first action unless the termination resulted from voluntary discontinuance or from dismissal for failure or neglect to prosecute.

(4) This section does not alter the law on tolling of the statute of limitations nor does it apply to causes of action which have accrued before this Act becomes effective.

ARTICLE 3. Commercial Paper

PART 1
SHORT TITLE, FORM AND INTERPRETATION

§ 3-101. Short Title.

This Article shall be known and may be cited as Uniform Commercial Code—Commercial Paper.

§ 3-102. Definitions and Index of Definitions.

(1) In this Article unless the context otherwise requires
    (a) "Issue" means the first delivery of an instrument to a holder or a remitter.
    (b) An "order" is a direction to pay and must be more than an authorization

or request. It must identify the person to pay with reasonable certainty. It may be addressed to one or more such persons jointly or in the alternative but not in succession.

(c) A "promise" is an undertaking to pay and must be more than an acknowledgment of an obligation.

(d) "Secondary party" means a drawer or endorser.

(e) "Instrument" means a negotiable instrument.

(2) Other definitions applying to this Article and the sections in which they appear are:

"Acceptance." Section 3–410.

"Accommodation party." Section 3–415.

"Alteration." Section 3–407.

"Certificate of deposit." Section 3–104.

"Certification." Section 3–411.

"Check." Section 3–104.

"Definite time." Section 3–109.

"Dishonor." Section 3–507.

"Draft." Section 3–104.

"Holder in due course." Section 3–302.

"Negotiation." Section 3–202.

"Note." Section 3–104.

"Notice of dishonor." Section 3–508.

"On demand." Section 3–108.

"Presentment." Section 3–504.

"Protest." Section 3–509.

"Restrictive indorsement." Section 3–205.

"Signature." Section 3–401.

(3) The following definitions in other Articles apply to this Article:

"Account." Section 4–104.

"Banking day." Section 4–104.

"Clearing house." Section 4–104.

"Collecting bank." Section 4–105.

"Customer." Section 4–104.

"Depository bank." Section 4–105.

"Documentary draft." Section 4–104.

"Intermediary bank." Section 4–105.

"Item." Section 4–104.

"Midnight deadline." Section 4–104.

"Payor bank." Section 4–105.

(4) In addition Article 1 contains general definitions and principles of construction and interpretation applicable throughout this Article.

§ 3–103. Limitations on Scope of Article.

(1) This Article does not apply to money, documents of title or investment securities.

(2) The provisions of this Article are subject to the provisions of the Article on Bank Deposits and Collections (Article 4) and Secured Transactions (Article 9).

§ 3–104. Form of Negotiable Instruments; "Draft"; "Check"; "Certificate of Deposit"; "Note."

(1) Any writing to be a negotiable instrument within this Article must
    (a) be signed by the maker or drawer; and
    (b) contain an unconditional promise or order to pay a sum certain in money and no other promise, order, obligation or power given by the maker or drawer except as authorized by this Article; and
    (c) be payable on demand or at a definite time; and
    (d) be payable to order or to bearer.
(2) A writing which complies with the requirements of this section is
    (a) a "draft" ("bill of exchange") if it is an order;
    (b) a "check" if it is a draft drawn on a bank and payable on demand;
    (c) a "certificate of deposit" if it is an acknowledgment by a bank of receipt of money with an engagement to repay it;
    (d) a "note" if it is a promise other than a certificate of deposit.
(3) As used in other Articles of this Act, and as the context may require, the terms "draft," "check," "certificate of deposit" and "note" may refer to instruments which are not negotiable within this Article as well as to instruments which are so negotiable.

§ 3–105. When Promise or Order Unconditional.

(1) A promise or order otherwise unconditional is not made conditional by the fact that the instrument
    (a) is subject to implied or constructive conditions; or
    (b) states its consideration, whether performed or promised, or the transaction which gave rise to the instrument, or that the promise or order is made or the instrument matures in accordance with or "as per" such transaction; or
    (c) refers to or states that it arises out of a separate agreement or refers to a separate agreement for rights as to prepayment or acceleration; or
    (d) states that it is drawn under a letter of credit; or
    (e) states that it is secured, whether by mortgage, reservation of title or otherwise; or
    (f) indicates a particular account to be debited or any other fund or source from which reimbursement is expected; or
    (g) is limited to payment out of a particular fund or the proceeds of a particular source, if the instrument is issued by a government or governmental agency or unit; or
    (h) is limited to payment out of the entire assets of a partnership, unincorporated association, trust or estate by or on behalf of which the instrument is issued.
(2) A promise or order is not unconditional if the instrument
    (a) states that it is subject to or governed by any other agreement; or
    (b) states that it is to be paid only out of a particular fund or source except as provided in this section.

§ 3–106. Sum Certain.

(1) The sum payable is a sum certain even though it is to be paid
    (a) with stated interest or by stated installments; or

    (b) with stated different rates of interest before and after default or a specified date; or

    (c) with a stated discount or addition if paid before or after the date fixed for payment; or

    (d) with exchange or less exchange, whether at a fixed rate or at the current rate; or

    (e) with costs of collection or an attorney's fee or both upon default.

(2) Nothing in this section shall validate any term which is otherwise illegal.

§ 3–107. Money.

(1) An instrument is payable in money if the medium of exchange in which it is payable is money at the time the instrument is made. An instrument payable in "currency" or "current funds" is payable in money.

(2) A promise or order to pay a sum stated in foreign currency is for a sum certain in money and, unless a different medium of payment is specified in the instrument, may be satisfied by payment of that number of dollars which the stated foreign currency will purchase at the buying sight rate for that currency on the day on which the instrument is payable or, if payable on demand, on the day of demand. If such an instrument specifies a foreign currency as the medium of payment the instrument is payable in that currency.

§ 3–108. Payable on Demand.

Instruments payable on demand include those payable at sight or on presentation and those in which no time for payment is stated.

§ 3–109. Definite Time.

(1) An instrument is payable at a definite time if by its terms it is payable

    (a) on or before a stated date or at a fixed period after a stated date; or

    (b) at a fixed period after sight; or

    (c) at a definite time subject to any acceleration; or

    (d) at a definite time subject to extension at the option of the holder, or to extension to a further definite time at the option of the maker or acceptor or automatically upon or after a specified act or event.

(2) An instrument which by its terms is otherwise payable only upon an act or event uncertain as to time of occurrence is not payable at a definite time even though the act or event has occurred.

§ 3–110. Payable to Order.

(1) An instrument is payable to order when by its terms it is payable to the order or assigns of any person therein specified with reasonable certainty, or to him or his order, or when it is conspicuously designated on its face as "exchange" or the like and names a payee. It may be payable to the order of

    (a) the maker or drawer; or

    (b) the drawee; or

    (c) a payee who is not maker, drawer or drawee; or

    (d) two or more payees together or in the alternative; or

    (e) an estate, trust or fund, in which case it is payable to the order of the representative of such estate, trust or fund or his successors; or

    (f) an office, or an officer by his title as such in which case it is payable to the principal but the incumbent of the office or his successor may act as if he or they were the holder; or

(g) a partnership or unincorporated association, in which case it is payable to the partnership or association and may be indorsed or transferred by any person thereto authorized.

(2) An instrument not payable to order is not made so payable by such words as "payable upon return of this instrument properly indorsed."

(3) An instrument made payable both to order and to bearer is payable to order unless the bearer words are handwritten or typewritten.

§ 3–111. Payable to Bearer.

An instrument is payable to bearer when by its terms it is payable to

(a) bearer or the order of bearer; or

(b) a specified person or bearer; or

(c) "cash" or the order of "cash," or any other indication which does not purport to designate a specific payee.

§ 3–112. Terms and Omissions Not Affecting Negotiability.

(1) The negotiability of an instrument is not affected by

(a) the omission of a statement of any consideration or of the place where the instrument is drawn or payable; or

(b) a statement that collateral has been given to secure obligations either on the instrument or otherwise of an obligor on the instrument or that in case of default on those obligations the holder may realize on or dispose of the collateral; or

(c) a promise or power to maintain or protect collateral or to give additional collateral; or

(d) a term authorizing a confession of judgment on the instrument if it is not paid when due; or

(e) a term purporting to waive the benefit of any law intended for the advantage or protection of any obligor; or

(f) a term in a draft providing that the payee by indorsing or cashing it acknowledges full satisfaction of an obligation of the drawer; or

(g) a statement in a draft drawn in a set of parts (Section 3–801) to the effect that the order is effective only if no other part has been honored.

(2) Nothing in this section shall validate any term which is otherwise illegal.

§ 3–113. Seal.

An instrument otherwise negotiable is within this Article even though it is under a seal.

§ 3–114. Date, Antedating, Postdating.

(1) The negotiability of an instrument is not affected by the fact that it is undated, antedated or postdated.

(2) Where an instrument is antedated or postdated the time when it is payable is determined by the stated date if the instrument is payable on demand or at a fixed period after date.

(3) Where the instrument or any signature thereon is dated, the date is presumed to be correct.

§ 3–115. Incomplete Instruments.

(1) When a paper whose contents at the time of signing show that it is intended to become an instrument is signed while still incomplete in any necessary respect it cannot be enforced until completed, but when it is completed in accordance with authority given it is effective as completed.

(2) If the completion is unauthorized the rules as to material alteration apply (Section 3–407), even though the paper was not delivered by the maker or drawer; but the burden of establishing that any completion is unauthorized is on the party so asserting.

§ 3–116. Instruments Payable to Two or More Persons.

An instrument payable to the order of two or more persons
   (a) if in the alternative is payable to any one of them and may be negotiated, discharged or enforced by any of them who has possession of it;
   (b) if not in the alternative is payable to all of them and may be negotiated, discharged or enforced only by all of them.

§ 3–117. Instruments Payable With Words of Description.

An instrument made payable to a named person with the addition of words describing him
   (a) as agent or officer of a specified person is payable to his principal but the agent or officer may act as if he were the holder;
   (b) as any other fiduciary for a specified person or purpose is payable to the payee and may be negotiated, discharged or enforced by him;
   (c) in any other manner is payable to the payee unconditionally and the additional words are without effect on subsequent parties.

§ 3–118. Ambiguous Terms and Rules of Construction.

The following rules apply to every instrument:
   (a) Where there is doubt whether the instrument is a draft or a note the holder may treat it as either. A draft drawn on the drawer is effective as a note.
   (b) Handwritten terms control typewritten and printed terms, and typewritten control printed.
   (c) Words control figures except that if the words are ambiguous figures control.
   (d) Unless otherwise specified a provision for interest means interest at the judgment rate at the place of payment from the date of the instrument, or if it is undated from the date of issue.
   (e) Unless the instrument otherwise specifies two or more persons who sign as maker, acceptor or drawer or indorser and as a part of the same transaction are jointly and severally liable even though the instrument contains such words as "I promise to pay."
   (f) Unless otherwise specified consent to extension authorizes a single extension for not longer than the original period. A consent to extension, expressed in the instrument, is binding on secondary parties and accommodation makers. A holder may not exercise his option to extend an instrument over the objection of a maker or acceptor or other party who in accordance with Section 3–604 tenders full payment when the instrument is due.

§ 3–119. Other Writings Affecting Instrument.

(1) As between the obligor and his immediate obligee or any transferee the terms of an instrument may be modified or affected by any other written agreement executed as a part of the same transaction, except that a holder in due course is not affected by any limitation of his rights arising out of the separate written agreement if he had no notice of the limitation when he took the instrument.

(2) A separate agreement does not affect the negotiability of an instrument.

§ 3–120. Instruments "Payable Through" Bank.

An instrument which states that it is "payable through" a bank or the like designates that bank as a collecting bank to make presentment but does not of itself authorize the bank to pay the instrument.

§ 3–121. Instruments Payable at Bank.*

A note or acceptance which states that it is payable at a bank is the equivalent of a draft drawn on the bank payable when it falls due out of any funds of the maker or acceptor in current account or otherwise available for such payment.

§ 3–122. Accrual of Cause of Action.

(1) A cause of action against a maker or an acceptor accrues
    (a) in the case of a time instrument on the day after maturity;
    (b) in the case of a demand instrument upon its date or, if no date is stated, on the date of issue.

(2) A cause of action against the obligor of a demand or time certificate of deposit accrues upon demand, but demand on a time certificate may not be made until on or after the date of maturity.

(3) A cause of action against a drawer of a draft or an indorser of any instrument accrues upon demand following dishonor of the instrument. Notice of dishonor is a demand.

(4) Unless an instrument provides otherwise, interest runs at the rate provided by the law for a judgment
    (a) in the case of a maker, acceptor or other primary obligor of a demand instrument, from the date of demand;
    (b) in all other cases from the date of accrual of the cause of action.

PART 2
TRANSFER AND NEGOTIATION

§ 3–201. Transfer: Right to Indorsement.

(1) Transfer of an instrument vests in the transferee such rights as the transferor has therein, except that a transferee who has himself been a party to any fraud or illegality affecting the instrument or who as a prior holder had notice of a defense or claim against it cannot improve his position by taking from a later holder in due course.

(2) A transfer of a security interest in an instrument vests the foregoing rights in the transferee to the extent of the interest transferred.

(3) Unless otherwise agreed any transfer for value of an instrument not then payable to bearer gives the transferee the specifically enforceable right to have the unqualified indorsement of the tranferor. Negotiation takes effect only when

the indorsement is made and until that time there is no presumption that the tranferee is the owner.

§ 3–202. Negotiation.

(1) Negotiation is the transfer of an instrument in such form that the transferee becomes a holder. If the instrument is payable to order it is negotiated by delivery with any necessary indorsement; if payable to bearer it is negotiated by delivery.

(2) An indorsement must be written by or on behalf of the holder and on the instrument or on a paper so firmly affixed thereto as to become a part thereof.

(3) An indorsement is effective for negotiation only when it conveys the entire instrument or any unpaid residue. If it purports to be of less it operates only as a partial assignment.

(4) Words of assignment, condition, waiver, guaranty, limitation or disclaimer of liability and the like accompanying an indorsement do not affect its character as an indorsement.

§ 3–203. Wrong or Misspelled Name.

Where an instrument is made payable to a person under a misspelled name or one other than his own he may indorse in that name or his own or both; but signature in both names may be required by a person paying or giving value for the instrument.

§ 3–204. Special Indorsement; Blank Indorsement.

(1) A special indorsement specifies the person to whom or to whose order it makes the instrument payable. Any instrument specially indorsed becomes payable to the order of the special indorsee and may be further negotiated only by his indorsement.

(2) An indorsement in blank specifies no particular indorsee and may consist of a mere signature. An instrument payable to order and indorsed in blank becomes payable to bearer and may be negotiated by delivery alone until specially indorsed.

(3) The holder may convert a blank indorsement into a special indorsement by writing over the signature of the indorser in blank any contract consistent with the character of the indorsement.

§ 3–205. Restrictive Indorsements.

An indorsement is restrictive which either
   (a) is conditional; or
   (b) purports to prohibit further transfer of the instrument; or
   (c) includes the words "for collection," "for deposit," "pay any bank," or like terms signifying a purpose of deposit or collection; or
   (d) otherwise states that it is for the benefit or use of the indorser or of another person.

§ 3–206. Effect of Restrictive Indorsement.

(1) No restrictive indorsement prevents further transfer or negotiation of the instrument.

(2) An intermediary bank, or a payor bank which is not the depositary bank, is neither given notice nor otherwise affected by a restrictive indorsement of any person except the bank's immediate transferor or the person presenting for payment.

(3) Except for an intermediary bank, any transferee under an indorsement which is conditional or includes the words "for collection," "for deposit," "pay any bank," or like terms (subparagraphs (a) and (c) of Section 3–205) must pay or apply any value given by him for or on the security of the instrument consistently with the indorsement and to the extent that he does so he becomes a holder for value. In addition such tranferee is a holder in due course if he otherwise complies with the requirements of Section 3–302 on what constitutes a holder in due course.

(4) The first taker under an indorsement for the benefit of the indorser or another person (subparagraph (d) of Section 3–205) must pay or apply any value given by him for or on the security of the instrument consistently with the indorsement and to the extent that he does so he becomes a holder for value. In addition such taker is a holder in due course if he otherwise complies with the requirements of Section 3–302 on what constitutes a holder in due course. A later holder for value is neither given notice nor otherwise affected by such restrictive indorsement unless he has knowledge that a fiduciary or other person has negotiated the instrument in any transaction for his own benefit or otherwise in breach of duty (subsection (2) of Section 3–304).

§ 3–207. Negotiation Effective Although It May Be Rescinded.

(1) Negotiation is effective to transfer the instrument although the negotiation is
    (a) made by an infant, a corporation exceeding its powers, or any other person without capacity; or
    (b) obtained by fraud, duress or mistake of any kind; or
    (c) part of an illegal transaction; or
    (d) made in breach of duty.

(2) Except as against a subsequent holder in due course such negotiation is in an appropriate case subject to rescission, the declaration of a constructive trust or any other remedy permitted by law.

§ 3–208. Reacquisition.

Where an instrument is returned to or reacquired by a prior party he may cancel any indorsement which is not necessary to his title and reissue or further negotiate the instrument, but any intervening party is discharged as against the reacquiring party and subsequent holders not in due course and if his indorsement has been cancelled is discharged as against subsequent holders in due course as well.

PART 3
RIGHTS OF A HOLDER

§ 3–301. Rights of a Holder.

The holder of an instrument whether or not he is the owner may transfer or negotiate it and, except as otherwise provided in Section 3–603 on payment or satisfaction, discharge it or enforce payment in his own name.

§ 3–302. Holder in Due Course.

(1) A holder in due course is a holder who takes the instrument
    (a) for value; and

(b) in good faith; and

(c) without notice that it is overdue or has been dishonored or of any defense against or claim to it on the part of any person.

(2) A payee may be a holder in due course.

(3) A holder does not become a holder in due course of an instrument:

(a) by purchase of it at judicial sale or by taking it under legal process; or

(b) by acquiring it in taking over an estate; or

(c) by purchasing it as part of a bulk transaction not in regular course of business of the transferor.

(4) A purchaser of a limited interest can be a holder in due course only to the extent of the interest purchased.

§ 3–303. Taking for Value.

A holder takes the instrument for value

(a) to the extent that the agreed consideration has been performed or that he acquires a security interest in or a lien on the instrument otherwise than by legal process; or

(b) when he takes the instrument in payment of or as security for an antecedent claim against any person whether or not the claim is due; or

(c) when he gives a negotiable instrument for it or makes an irrevocable commitment to a third person.

§ 3–304. Notice to Purchaser.

(1) The purchaser has notice of a claim or defense if

(a) the instrument is so incomplete, bears such visible evidence of forgery or alteration, or is otherwise so irregular as to call into question its validity, terms or ownership or to create an ambiguity as to the party to pay; or

(b) the purchaser has notice that the obligation of any party is voidable in whole or in part, or that all parties have been discharged.

(2) The purchaser has notice of a claim against the instrument when he has knowledge that a fiduciary has negotiated the instrument in payment of or as security for his own debt or in any transaction for his own benefit or otherwise in breach of duty.

(3) The purchaser has notice that an instrument is overdue if he has reason to know

(a) that any part of the principal amount is overdue or that there is an uncured default in payment of another instrument of the same series; or

(b) that acceleration of the instrument has been made; or

(c) that he is taking a demand instrument after demand has been made or more than a reasonable length of time after its issue. A reasonable time for a check drawn and payable within the states and territories of the United States and the District of Columbia is presumed to be thirty days.

(4) Knowledge of the following facts does not of itself give the purchaser notice of a defense or claim

(a) that the instrument is antedated or postdated;

(b) that it was issued or negotiated in return for an executory promise or

accompanied by a separate agreement, unless the purchaser has notice
that a defense or claim has arisen from the terms thereof;

   (c) that any party has signed for accommodation;

   (d) that an incomplete instrument has been completed, unless the purchaser
   has notice of any improper completion;

   (e) that any person negotiating the instrument is or was a fiduciary;

   (f) that there has been default in payment of interest on the instrument
   or in payment of any other instrument, except one of the same series.

(5) The filing or recording of a document does not of itself constitute notice
within the provisions of this Article to a person who would otherwise be a holder
in due course.

(6) To be effective notice must be received at such time and in such manner
as to give a reasonable opportunity to act on it.

§ 3–305. Rights of a Holder in Due Course.

To the extent that a holder is a holder in due course he takes the instrument
free from

   (1) all claims to it on the part of any person; and

   (2) all defenses of any party to the instrument with whom the holder has
not dealt except

   (a) infancy, to the extent that it is a defense to a simple contract; and

   (b) such other incapacity, or duress, or illegality of the transaction, as renders
   the obligation of the party a nullity; and

   (c) such misrepresentation as has induced the party to sign the instrument
   with neither knowledge nor reasonable opportunity to obtain knowledge
   of its character or its essential terms; and

   (d) discharge in insolvency proceedings; and

   (e) any other discharge of which the holder has notice when he takes the
   instrument.

§ 3–306. Rights of One Not Holder in Due Course.

Unless he has the rights of a holder in due course any person takes the instrument
subject to

   (a) all valid claims to it on the part of any person; and

   (b) all defenses of any party which would be available in an action on a
   simple contract; and

   (c) the defenses of want or failure of consideration, non-performance of
   any condition precedent, non-delivery, or delivery for a special purpose
   (Section 3–408); and

   (d) the defense that he or a person through whom he holds the instrument
   acquired it by theft, or that payment or satisfaction to such holder would
   be inconsistent with the terms of a restrictive indorsement. The claim
   of any third person to the instrument is not otherwise available as a
   defense to any party liable thereon unless the third person himself defends
   the action for such party.

§ 3–307. Burden of Establishing Signatures, Defenses and Due Course.

(1) Unless specifically denied in the pleadings each signature on an instrument
is admitted. When the effectiveness of a signature is put in issue

(a) the burden of establishing it is on the party claiming under the signature; but

(b) the signature is presumed to be genuine or authorized except where the action is to enforce the obligation of a purported signer who has died or become incompetent before proof is required.

(2) When signatures are admitted or established, production of the instrument entitles a holder to recover on it unless the defendant establishes a defense.

(3) After it is shown that a defense exists a person claiming the rights of a holder in due course has the burden of establishing that he or some person under whom he claims is in all respects a holder in due course.

PART 4

LIABILITY OF PARTIES

§ 3–401. Signature.

(1) No person is liable on an instrument unless his signature appears thereon.

(2) A signature is made by use of any name, including any trade or assumed name, upon an instrument, or by any word or mark used in lieu of a written signature.

§ 3–402. Signature in Ambiguous Capacity.

Unless the instrument clearly indicates that a signature is made in some other capacity it is an indorsement.

§ 3–403. Signature by Authorized Representative.

(1) A signature may be made by an agent or other representative, and his authority to make it may be established as in other cases of representation. No particular form of appointment is necessary to establish such authority.

(2) An authorized representative who signs his own name to an instrument

(a) is personally obligated if the instrument neither names the person represented nor shows that the representative signed in a representative capacity;

(b) except as otherwise established between the immediate parties, is personally obligated if the instrument names the person represented but does not show that the representative signed in a representative capacity, or if the instrument does not name the person represented but does show that the representative signed in a representative capacity.

(3) Except as otherwise established the name of an organization preceded or followed by the name and office of an authorized individual is a signature made in a representative capacity.

§ 3–404. Unauthorized Signatures.

(1) Any unauthorized signature is wholly inoperative as that of the person whose name is signed unless he ratifies it or is precluded from denying it; but it operates as the signature of the unauthorized signer in favor of any person who in good faith pays the instrument or takes it for value.

(2) Any unauthorized signature may be ratified for all purposes of this Article. Such ratification does not of itself affect any rights of the person ratifying against the actual signer.

§ 3–405. Impostors; Signature in Name of Payee.

(1) An indorsement by any person in the name of a named payee is effective if

    (a) an impostor by use of the mails or otherwise has induced the maker or drawer to issue the instrument to him or his confederate in the name of the payee; or

    (b) a person signing as or on behalf of a maker or drawer intends the payee to have no interest in the instrument; or

    (c) an agent or employee of the maker or drawer has supplied him with the name of the payee intending the latter to have no such interest.

(2) Nothing in this section shall affect the criminal or civil liability of the person so indorsing.

§ 3–406. Negligence Contributing to Alteration or Unauthorized Signature.

Any person who by his negligence substantially contributes to a material alteration of the instrument or to the making of an unauthorized signature is precluded from asserting the alteration or lack of authority against a holder in due course or against a drawee or other payor who pays the instrument in good faith and in accordance with the reasonable commercial standards of the drawee's or payor's business.

§ 3–407. Alteration.

(1) Any alteration of an instrument is material which changes the contract of any party thereto in any respect, including any such change in

    (a) the number or relations of the parties; or

    (b) an incomplete instrument, by completing it otherwise than as authorized; or

    (c) the writing as signed, by adding to it or by removing any part of it.

(2) As against any person other than a subsequent holder in due course,

    (a) Alteration by the holder which is both fraudulent and material discharges any party whose contract is thereby changed unless that party assents or is precluded from asserting the defense;

    (b) no other alteration discharges any party and the instrument may be enforced according to its original tenor, or as to incomplete instruments according to the authority given.

(3) A subsequent holder in due course may in all cases enforce the instrument according to its original tenor, and when an incomplete instrument has been completed, he may enforce it as completed.

§ 3–408. Consideration.

Want or failure of consideration is a defense as against any person not having the rights of a holder in due course (Section 3–305), except that no consideration is necessary for an instrument or obligation thereon given in payment of or as security for an antecedent obligation of any kind. Nothing in this section shall be taken to displace any statute outside this Act under which a promise is enforceable notwithstanding lack or failure of consideration. Partial failure of consideration is a defense pro tanto whether or not the failure is in an ascertained or liquidated amount.

§ 3–409. Draft Not an Assignment.

(1) A check or other draft does not of itself operate as an assignment of any funds in the hands of the drawee available for its payment, and the drawee is not liable on the instrument until he accepts it.

(2) Nothing in this section shall affect any liability in contract, tort or otherwise arising from any letter of credit or other obligation or representation which is not an acceptance.

§ 3–410. Definition and Operation of Acceptance.

(1) Acceptance is the drawee's signed engagement to honor the draft as presented. It must be written on the draft, and may consist of his signature alone. It becomes operative when completed by delivery or notification.

(2) A draft may be accepted although it has not been signed by the drawer or is otherwise incomplete or is overdue or has been dishonored.

(3) Where the draft is payable at a fixed period after sight and the acceptor fails to date his acceptance the holder may complete it by supplying a date in good faith.

§ 3–411. Certification of a Check.

(1) Certification of a check is acceptance. Where a holder procures certification the drawer and all prior indorsers are discharged.

(2) Unless otherwise agreed a bank has no obligation to certify a check.

(3) A bank may certify a check before returning it for lack of proper indorsement. If it does so the drawer is discharged.

§ 3–412. Acceptance Varying Draft.

(1) Where the drawee's proffered acceptance in any manner varies the draft as presented the holder may refuse the acceptance and treat the draft as dishonored in which case the drawee is entitled to have his acceptance cancelled.

(2) The terms of the draft are not varied by an acceptance to pay at any particular bank or place in the United States, unless the acceptance states that the draft is to be paid only at such bank or place.

(3) Where the holder assents to an acceptance varying the terms of the draft each drawer and indorser who does not affirmatively assent is discharged.

§ 3–413. Contract of Maker, Drawer and Acceptor.

(1) The maker or acceptor engages that he will pay the instrument according to its tenor at the time of his engagement or as completed pursuant to Section 3–115 on incomplete instruments.

(2) The drawer engages that upon dishonor of the draft and any necessary notice of dishonor or protest he will pay the amount of the draft to the holder or to any indorser who takes it up. The drawer may disclaim this liability by drawing without recourse.

(3) By making, drawing or accepting the party admits as against all subsequent parties including the drawee the existence of the payee and his then capacity to indorse.

§ 3–414. Contract of Indorser; Order of Liability.

(1) Unless the indorsement otherwise specifies (as by such words as "without recourse") every indorser engages that upon dishonor and any necessary notice

of dishonor and protest he will pay the instrument according to its tenor at the time of his indorsement to the holder or to any subsequent indorser who takes it up, even though the indorser who takes it up was not obligated to do so.

(2) Unless they otherwise agree indorsers are liable to one another in the order in which they indorse, which is presumed to be the order in which their signatures appear on the instrument.

§ 3–415. Contract of Accommodation Party.

(1) An accommodation party is one who signs the instrument in any capacity for the purpose of lending his name to another party to it.

(2) When the instrument has been taken for value before it is due the accommodation party is liable in the capacity in which he has signed even though the taker knows of the accommodation.

(3) As against a holder in due course and without notice of the accommodation oral proof of the accommodation is not admissible to give the accommodation party the benefit of discharges dependent on his character as such. In other cases the accommodation character may be shown by oral proof.

(4) An indorsement which shows that it is not in the chain of title is notice of its accommodation character.

(5) An accommodation party is not liable to the party accommodated, and if he pays the instrument has a right of recourse on the instrument against such party.

§ 3–416. Contract of Guarantor.

(1) "Payment guaranteed" or equivalent words added to a signature mean that the signer engages that if the instrument is not paid when due he will pay it according to its tenor without resort by the holder to any other party.

(2) "Collection guaranteed" or equivalent words added to a signature mean that the signer engages that if the instrument is not paid when due he will pay it according to its tenor, but only after the holder has reduced his claim against the maker or acceptor to judgment and execution has been returned unsatisfied, or after the maker or acceptor has become insolvent or it is otherwise apparent that it is useless to proceed against him.

(3) Words of guaranty which do not otherwise specify guarantee payment.

(4) No words of guaranty added to the signature of a sole maker or acceptor affect his liability on the instrument. Such words added to the signature of one of two or more makers or acceptors create a presumption that the signature is for the accommodation of the others.

(5) When words of guaranty are used presentment, notice of dishonor and protest are not necessary to charge the user.

(6) Any guaranty written on the instrument is enforcible notwithstanding any statute of frauds.

§ 3–417. Warranties on Presentment and Transfer.

(1) Any person who obtains payment or acceptance and any prior transferor warrants to a person who in good faith pays or accepts that
- (a) he has a good title to the instrument or is authorized to obtain payment or acceptance on behalf of one who has a good title; and
- (b) he has no knowledge that the signature of the maker or drawer is unautho-

rized, except that this warranty is not given by a holder in due course acting in good faith

    (i) to a maker with respect to the maker's own signature; or

    (ii) to a drawer with respect to the drawer's own signature, whether or not the drawer is also the drawee; or

    (iii) to an acceptor of a draft if the holder in due course took the draft after the acceptance or obtained the acceptance without knowledge that the drawer's signature was unauthorized; and

(c) the instrument has not been materially altered, except that this warranty is not given by a holder in due course acting in good faith

    (i) to the maker of a note; or

    (ii) to the drawer of a draft whether or not the drawer is also the drawee; or

    (iii) to the acceptor of a draft with respect to an alteration made prior to the acceptance if the holder in due course took the draft after the acceptance, even though the acceptance provided "payable as originally drawn" or equivalent terms; or

    (iv) to the acceptor of a draft with respect to an alteration made after the acceptance.

(2) Any person who transfers an instrument and receives consideration warrants to his transferee and if the transfer is by indorsement to any subsequent holder who takes the instrument in good faith that

(a) he has a good title to the instrument or is authorized to obtain payment or acceptance on behalf of one who has a good title and the transfer is otherwise rightful; and

(b) all signatures are genuine or authorized; and

(c) the instrument has not been materially altered; and

(d) no defense of any party is good against him; and

(e) he has no knowledge of any insolvency proceeding instituted with respect to the maker or acceptor or the drawer of an unaccepted instrument.

(3) By transferring "without recourse" the transferor limits the obligation stated in subsection (2) (d) to a warranty that he has no knowledge of such a defense.

(4) A selling agent or broker who does not disclose the fact that he is acting only as such gives the warranties provided in this section, but if he makes such disclosure warrants only his good faith and authority.

§ 3–418. Finality of Payment or Acceptance.

Except for recovery of bank payments as provided in the Article on Bank Deposits and Collections (Article 4) and except for liability for breach of warranty on presentment under the preceding section, payment or acceptance of any instrument is final in favor of a holder in due course, or a person who has in good faith changed his position in reliance on the payment.

§ 3–419. Conversion of Instrument; Innocent Representative.

(1) An instrument is converted when

(a) a drawee to whom it is delivered for acceptance refuses to return it on demand; or

(b) any person to whom it is delivered for payment refuses on demand either to pay or to return it; or

(c) it is paid on a forged indorsement.

(2) In an action against a drawee under subsection (1) the measure of the drawee's liability is the face amount of the instrument. In any other action under subsection (1) the measure of liability is presumed to be the face amount of the instrument.

(3) Subject to the provisions of this Act concerning restrictive indorsements a representative, including a depositary or collecting bank, who has in good faith and in accordance with the reasonable commercial standards applicable to the business of such representative dealt with an instrument or its proceeds on behalf of one who was not the true owner is not liable in conversion or otherwise to the true owner beyond the amount of any proceeds remaining in his hands.

(4) An intermediary bank or payor bank which is not a depositary bank is not liable in conversion solely by reason of the fact that proceeds of an item indorsed restrictively (Sections 3–205 and 3–206) are not paid or applied consistently with the restrictive indorsement of an indorser other than its immediate transferor.

PART 5
PRESENTMENT, NOTICE OF DISHONOR AND PROTEST

§ 3–501. When Presentment, Notice of Dishonor, and Protest Necessary or Permissible.

(1) Unless excused (Section 3–511) presentment is necessary to charge secondary parties as follows:

(a) presentment for acceptance is necessary to charge the drawer and indorsers of a draft where the draft so provides, or is payable elsewhere than at the residence or place of business of the drawee, or its date of payment depends upon such presentment. The holder may at his option present for acceptance any other draft payable at a stated date;

(b) presentment for payment is necessary to charge any indorser;

(c) in the case of any drawer, the acceptor of a draft payable at a bank or the maker of a note payable at a bank, presentment for payment is necessary, but failure to make presentment discharges such drawer, acceptor or maker only as stated in Section 3–502(1) (b).

(2) Unless excused (Section 3–511)

(a) notice of any dishonor is necessary to charge any indorser;

(b) in the case of any drawer, the acceptor of a draft payable at a bank or the maker of a note payable at a bank, notice of any dishonor is necessary, but failure to give such notice discharges such drawer, acceptor or maker only as stated in Section 3–502(1) (b).

(3) Unless excused (Section 3–511) protest of any dishonor is necessary to charge the drawer and indorsers of any draft which on its face appears to be drawn or payable outside of the states, territories, dependencies and possessions of the United States, the District of Columbia and the Commonwealth of Puerto Rico. The holder may at his option make protest of any dishonor of any other instrument and in the case of a foreign draft may on insolvency of the acceptor before maturity make protest for better security.

(4) Notwithstanding any provision of this section, neither presentment nor notice of dishonor nor protest is necessary to charge an indorser who has indorsed an instrument after maturity.

§ 3–502. Unexcused Delay; Discharge.

(1) Where without excuse any necessary presentment or notice of dishonor is delayed beyond the time when it is due

    (a) any indorser is discharged; and

    (b) any drawer or the acceptor of a draft payable at a bank or the maker of a note payable at a bank who because the drawee or payor bank becomes insolvent during the delay is deprived of funds maintained with the drawee or payor bank to cover the instrument may discharge his liability by written assignment to the holder of his rights against the drawee or payor bank in respect of such funds, but such drawer, acceptor or maker is not otherwise discharged.

(2) Where without excuse a necessary protest is delayed beyond the time when it is due any drawer or indorser is discharged.

§ 3–503. Time of Presentment.

(1) Unless a different time is expressed in the instrument the time for any presentment is determined as follows:

    (a) where an instrument is payable at or a fixed period after a stated date any presentment for acceptance must be made on or before the date it is payable:

    (b) where an instrument is payable after sight it must either be presented for acceptance or negotiated within a reasonable time after date or issue whichever is later;

    (c) where an instrument shows the date on which it is payable presentment for payment is due on that date;

    (d) where an instrument is accelerated presentment for payment is due within a reasonable time after the acceleration;

    (e) with respect to the liability of any secondary party presentment for acceptance or payment of any other instrument is due within a reasonable time after such party becomes liable thereon.

(2) A reasonable time for presentment is determined by the nature of the instrument, any usage of banking or trade and the facts of the particular case. In the case of an uncertified check which is drawn and payable within the United States and which is not a draft drawn by a bank the following are presumed to be reasonable periods within which to present for payment or to initiate bank collection:

    (a) with respect to the liability of the drawer, thirty days after date or issue whichever is later; and

    (b) with respect to the liability of an indorser, seven days after his indorsement.

(3) Where any presentment is due on a day which is not a full business day for either the person making presentment or the party to pay or accept, presentment is due on the next following day which is a full business day for both parties.

(4) Presentment to be sufficient must be made at a reasonable hour, and if at a bank during its banking day.

§ 3–504. How Presentment Made.

(1) Presentment is a demand for acceptance or payment made upon the maker, acceptor, drawee or other payor by or on behalf of the holder.

(2) Presentment may be made
    (a) by mail, in which event the time of presentment is determined by the time of receipt of the mail; or
    (b) through a clearing house; or
    (c) at the place of acceptance or payment specified in the instrument or if there be none at the place of business or residence of the party to accept or pay. If neither the party to accept or pay nor anyone authorized to act for him is present or accessible at such place presentment is excused.

(3) It may be made
    (a) to any one of two or more makers, acceptors, drawees or other payors; or
    (b) to any person who has authority to make or refuse the acceptance or payment.

(4) A draft accepted or a note made payable at a bank in the United States must be presented at such bank.

(5) In the cases described in Section 4–210 presentment may be made in the manner and with the result stated in that section.

§ 3–505. Rights of Party to Whom Presentment Is Made.

(1) The party to whom presentment is made may without dishonor require
    (a) exhibition of the instrument; and
    (b) reasonable indentification of the person making presentment and evidence of his authority to make it if made for another; and
    (c) that the instrument be produced for acceptance or payment at a place specified in it, or if there be none at any place reasonable in the circumstances; and
    (d) a signed receipt on the instrument for any partial or full payment and its surrender upon full payment.

(2) Failure to comply with any such requirement invalidates the presentment but the person presenting has a reasonable time in which to comply and the time for acceptance or payment runs from the time of compliance.

§ 3–506. Time Allowed for Acceptance or Payment.

(1) Acceptance may be deferred without dishonor until the close of the next business day following presentment. The holder may also in a good faith effort to obtain acceptance and without either dishonor of the instrument or discharge of secondary parties allow postponement of acceptance for an additional business day.

(2) Except as a longer time is allowed in the case of documentary drafts drawn under a letter of credit, and unless an earlier time is agreed to by the party to pay, payment of an instrument may be deferred without dishonor pending reasonable examination to determine whether it is properly payable, but payment must be made in any event before the close of business on the day of presentment.

§ 3–507. Dishonor; Holder's Right of Recourse; Term Allowing Re-Presentment.

(1) An adjustment is dishonored when
    (a) a necessary or optional presentment is duly made and due acceptance or payment is refused or cannot be obtained within the prescribed time or in case of bank collections the instrument is seasonably returned by the midnight deadline (Section 4–301); or

(b) presentment is excused and the instrument is not duly accepted or paid.

(2) Subject to any necessary notice of dishonor and protest, the holder has upon dishonor an immediate right of recourse against the drawers and indorsers.

(3) Return of an instrument for lack of proper indorsement is not dishonor.

(4) A term in a draft or an indorsement thereof allowing a stated time for re-presentment in the event of any dishonor of the draft by nonacceptance if a time draft or by nonpayment if a sight draft gives the holder as against any secondary party bound by the term an option to waive the dishonor without affecting the liability of the secondary party and he may present again up to the end of the stated time.

§ 3–508. Notice of Dishonor.

(1) Notice of dishonor may be given to any person who may be liable on the instrument by or on behalf of the holder or any party who has himself received notice, or any other party who can be compelled to pay the instrument. In addition an agent or bank in whose hands the instrument is dishonored may give notice to his principal or customer or to another agent or bank from which the instrument was received.

(2) Any necessary notice must be given by a bank before its midnight deadline and by any other person before midnight of the third business day after dishonor or receipt of notice of dishonor.

(3) Notice may be given in any reasonable manner. It may be oral or written and in any terms which identify the instrument and state that it has been dishonored. A misdescription which does not mislead the party notified does not vitiate the notice. Sending the instrument bearing a stamp, ticket or writing stating that acceptance or payment has been refused or sending a notice of debit with respect to the instrument is sufficient.

(4) Written notice is given when sent although it is not received.

(5) Notice to one partner is notice to each although the firm has been dissolved.

(6) When any party is in insolvency proceedings instituted after the issue of the instrument notice may be given either to the party or to the representative of his estate.

(7) When any party is dead or incompetent notice may be sent to his last known address or given to his personal representative.

(8) Notice operates for the benefit of all parties who have rights on the instrument against the party notified.

§ 3–509. Protest; Noting for Protest.

(1) A protest is a certificate of dishonor made under the hand and seal of a United States consul or vice consul or a notary public or other person authorized to certify dishonor by the law of the place where dishonor occurs. It may be made upon information satisfactory to such person.

(2) The protest must identify the instrument and certify either that due presentment has been made or the reason why it is excused and that the instrument has been dishonored by nonacceptance or nonpayment.

(3) The protest may also certify that notice of dishonor has been given to all parties or to specified parties.

(4) Subject to subsection (5) any necessary protest is due by the time that notice of dishonor is due.

(5) If, before protest is due, an instrument has been noted for protest by the

officer to make protest, the protest may be made at any time thereafter as of the date of the noting.

§ 3–510. Evidence of Dishonor and Notice of Dishonor.

The following are admissible as evidence and create a presumption of dishonor and of any notice of dishonor therein shown:

    (a) a document regular in form as provided in the preceding section which purports to be a protest;

    (b) the purported stamp or writing of the drawee, payor bank or presenting bank on the instrument or accompanying it stating that acceptance or payment has been refused for reasons consistent with dishonor;

    (c) any book or record of the drawee, payor bank, or any collecting bank kept in the usual course of business which shows dishonor, even though there is no evidence of who made the entry.

§ 3–511. Waived or Excused Presentment, Protest or Notice of Dishonor or Delay Therein.

(1) Delay in presentment, protest or notice of dishonor is excused when the party is without notice that it is due or when the delay is caused by circumstances beyond his control and he exercises reasonable diligence after the cause of the delay ceases to operate.

(2) Presentment or notice or protest as the case may be is entirely excused when

    (a) the party to be charged has waived it expressly or by implication either before or after it is due; or

    (b) such party has himself dishonored the instrument or has countermanded payment or otherwise has no reason to expect or right to require that the instrument be accepted or paid; or

    (c) by reasonable diligence the presentment or protest cannot be made or the notice given.

(3) Presentment is also entirely excused when

    (a) the maker, acceptor or drawee of any instrument except a documentary draft is dead or in insolvency proceedings instituted after the issue of the instrument; or

    (b) acceptance or payment is refused but not for want of proper presentment.

(4) Where a draft has been dishonored by nonacceptance a later presentment for payment and any notice of dishonor and protest for nonpayment are excused unless in the meantime the instrument has been accepted.

(5) A waiver of protest is also a waiver of presentment and of notice of dishonor even though protest is not required.

(6) Where a waiver of presentment or notice of protest is embodied in the instrument itself it is binding upon all parties; but where it is written above the signature of an indorser it binds him only.

PART 6

DISCHARGE

§ 3–601. Discharge of Parties.

(1) The extent of the discharge of any party from liability on an instrument is governed by the sections on

(a) payment or satisfaction (Section 3–603); or

(b) tender of payment (Section 3–604); or

(c) cancellation or renunciation (Section 3–605); or

(d) impairment of right of recourse or of collateral (Section 3–606); or

(e) reacquisition of the instrument by a prior party (Section 3–208); or

(f) fraudulent and material alteration (Section 3–407); or

(g) certification of a check (Section 3–411); or

(h) acceptance varying a draft (Section 3–412); or

(i) unexcused delay in presentment or notice of dishonor or protest (Section 3–502).

(2) Any party is also discharged from his liability on an instrument to another party by any other act or agreement with such party which would discharge his simple contract for the payment of money.

(3) The liability of all parties is discharged when any party who has himself no right of action or recourse on the instrument

(a) reacquires the instrument in his own right; or

(b) is discharged under any provision of this Article, except as otherwise provided with respect to discharge for impairment of recourse or of collateral (Section 3–606).

§ 3–602. Effect of Discharge Against Holder in Due Course.

No discharge of any party provided by this Article is effective against a subsequent holder in due course unless he has notice thereof when he takes the instrument.

§ 3–603. Payment or Satisfaction.

(1) The liability of any party is discharged to the extent of his payment or satisfaction to the holder even though it is made with knowledge of a claim of another person to the instrument unless prior to such payment or satisfaction the person making the claim either supplies indemnity deemed adequate by the party seeking the discharge or enjoins payment or satisfaction by order of a court of competent jurisdiction in an action in which the adverse claimant and the holder are parties. This subsection does not, however, result in the discharge of the liability

(a) of a party who in bad faith pays or satisfies a holder who acquired the instrument by theft or who (unless having the rights of a holder in due course) holds through one who so acquired it; or

(b) of a party (other than an intermediary bank or a payor bank which is not a depositary bank) who pays or satisfies the holder of an instrument which has been restrictively indorsed in a manner not consistent with the terms of such restrictive indorsement.

(2) Payment or satisfaction may be made with the consent of the holder by any person including a stranger to the instrument. Surrender of the instrument to such a person gives him the rights of a transferee (Section 3–201).

§ 3–604. Tender of Payment.

(1) Any party making tender of full payment to a holder when or after it is due is discharged to the extent of all subsequent liability for interest, costs and attorney's fees.

(2) The holder's refusal of such tender wholly discharges any party who has a right of recourse against the party making the tender.

(3) Where the maker or acceptor of an instrument payable otherwise than on demand is able and ready to pay at every place of payment specified in the instrument when it is due, it is equivalent to tender.

§ 3–605. Cancellation and Renunciation.

(1) The holder of an instrument may even without consideration discharge any party

  (a) in any manner apparent on the face of the instrument or the indorsement, as by intentionally cancelling the instrument or the party's signature by destruction or mutilation, or by striking out the party's signature; or

  (b) by renouncing his rights by a writing signed and delivered or by surrender of the instrument to the party to be discharged.

(2) Neither cancellation nor renunciation without surrender of the instrument affects the title thereto.

§ 3–606. Impairment of Recourse or of Collateral.

(1) The holder discharges any party to the instrument to the extent that without such party's consent the holder

  (a) without express reservation of rights releases or agrees not to sue any person against whom the party has to the knowledge of the holder a right of recourse or agrees to suspend the right to enforce against such person the instrument or collateral or otherwise discharges such person, except that failure or delay in effecting any required presentment, protest or notice of dishonor with respect to any such person does not discharge any party as to whom presentment, protest or notice of dishonor is effective or unnecessary; or

  (b) unjustifiably impairs any collateral for the instrument given by or on behalf of the party or any person against whom he has a right to recourse.

(2) By express reservation of rights against a party with a right of recourse the holder preserves

  (a) all his rights against such party as of the time when the instrument was originally due; and

  (b) the right of the party to pay the instrument as of that time; and

  (c) all rights of such party to recourse against others.

PART 7
ADVICE OF INTERNATIONAL SIGHT DRAFT

§ 3–701. Letter of Advice of International Sight Draft.

(1) A "letter of advice" is a drawer's communication to the drawee that a described draft has been drawn.

(2) Unless otherwise agreed when a bank receives from another bank a letter of advice of an international sight draft the drawee bank may immediately debit the drawer's account and stop the running of interest pro tanto. Such a debit and any resulting credit to any account covering outstanding drafts leaves in the drawer full power to stop payment or otherwise dispose of the amount and creates no trust or interest in favor of the holder.

(3) Unless otherwise agreed and except where a draft is drawn under a credit issued by the drawee, the drawee of an international sight draft owes the drawer

no duty to pay an unadvised draft but if it does so and the draft is genuine, may appropriately debit the drawer's account.

PART 8
MISCELLANEOUS

§ 3–801. Drafts in a Set.

(1) Where a draft is drawn in a set of parts, each of which is numbered and expressed to be an order only if no other part has been honored, the whole of the parts constitutes one draft but a taker of any part may become a holder in due course of the draft.

(2) Any person who negotiates, indorses or accepts a single part of a draft drawn in a set thereby becomes liable to any holder in due course of that part as if it were the whole set, but as between different holders in due course to whom different parts have been negotiated the holder whose title first accrues has all rights to the draft and its proceeds.

(3) As against the drawee the first presented part of a draft drawn in a set is the part entitled to payment, or if a time draft to acceptance and payment. Acceptance of any subsequently presented part renders the drawee liable thereon under subsection (2). With respect both to a holder and to the drawer payment of a subsequently presented part of a draft payable at sight has the same effect as payment of a check notwithstanding an effective stop order (Section 4–407).

(4) Except as otherwise provided in this section, where any part of a draft in a set is discharged by payment or otherwise the whole draft is discharged.

§ 3–802. Effect of Instrument on Obligation for Which It Is Given.

(1) Unless otherwise agreed where an instrument is taken for an underlying obligation

    (a) the obligation is pro tanto discharged if a bank is drawer, maker or acceptor of the instrument and there is no recourse on the instrument against the underlying obligor; and

    (b) in any other case the obligation is suspended pro tanto until the instrument is due or if it is payable on demand until its presentment. If the instrument is dishonored action may be maintained on either the instrument or the obligation; discharge of the underlying obligor on the instrument also discharges him on the obligation.

(2) The taking in good faith of a check which is not postdated does not of itself so extend the time on the original obligation as to discharge a surety.

§ 3–803. Notice to Third Party.

Where a defendant is sued for breach of an obligation for which a third person is answerable over under this Article he may give the third person written notice of the litigation, and the person notified may then give similar notice to any other person who is answerable over to him under this Article. If the notice states that the person notified may come in and defend and that if the person notified does not do so he will in any action against him by the person giving the notice be bound by any determination of fact common to the two litigations, then unless after seasonable receipt of the notice the person notified does come in and defend he is so bound.

§ 3–804. Lost, Destroyed or Stolen Instruments.

The owner of an instrument which is lost, whether by destruction, theft or otherwise, may maintain an action in his own name and recover from any party liable thereon upon due proof of his ownership, the facts which prevent his production of the instrument and its terms. The court may require security indemnifying the defendant against loss by reason of further claims on the instrument.

§ 3–805. Instruments Not Payable to Order or to Bearer.

This Article applies to any instrument whose terms do not preclude transfer and which is otherwise negotiable within this Article but which is not payable to order or to bearer, except that there can be no holder in due course of such an instrument.

ARTICLE 4. Bank Deposits and Collections

PART 1
GENERAL PROVISIONS AND DEFINITIONS

§ 4–101. Short Title.

This Article shall be known and may be cited as Uniform Commercial Code—Bank Deposits and Collections.

§ 4–102. Applicability.

(1) To the extent that items within this Article are also within the scope of Articles 3 and 8, they are subject to the provisions of those Articles. In the event of conflict the provisions of this Article govern those of Article 3 but the provisions of Article 8 govern those of this Article.

(2) The liability of a bank for action or non-action with respect to any item handled by it for purposes of presentment, payment or collection is governed by the law of the place where the bank is located. In the case of action or non-action by or at a branch or separate office of a bank, its liability is governed by the law of the place where the branch or separate office is located.

§ 4–103. Variation by Agreement; Measure of Damages; Certain Action Constituting Ordinary Care.

(1) The effect of the provisions of this Article may be varied by agreement except that no agreement can disclaim a bank's responsibility for its own lack of good faith or failure to exercise ordinary care or can limit the measure of damages for such lack or failure; but the parties may by agreement determine the standards by which such responsibility is to be measured if such standards are not manifestly unreasonable.

(2) Federal Reserve regulations and operating letters, clearing house rules, and the like, have the effect of agreements under subsection (1), whether or not specifically assented to by all parties interested in items handled.

(3) Action or non-action approved by this Article or pursuant to Federal Reserve regulations or operating letters constitutes the exercise of ordinary care and, in the absence of special instructions, action or non-action consistent with clearing

house rules and the like or with a general banking usage not disapproved by this Article, prima facie constitutes the exercise of ordinary care.

(4) The specification or approval of certain procedures by this Article does not constitute disapproval of other procedures which may be reasonable under the circumstances.

(5) The measure of damages for failure to exercise ordinary care in handling an item is the amount of the item reduced by an amount which could not have been realized by the use of ordinary care, and where there is bad faith it includes other damages, if any, suffered by the party as a proximate consequence.

§ 4–104. Definitions and Index of Definitions.

(1) In this Article unless the context otherwise requires

    (a) "Account" means any account with a bank and includes a checking, time, interest or savings account;

    (b) "Afternoon" means the period of a day between noon and midnight;

    (c) "Banking day" means that part of any day on which a bank is open to the public for carrying on substantially all of its banking functions;

    (d) "Clearing house" means any association of banks or other payors regularly clearing items;

    (e) "Customer" means any person having an account with a bank or for whom a bank has agreed to collect items and includes a bank carrying an account with another bank;

    (f) "Documentary draft" means any negotiable or non-negotiable draft with accompanying documents, securities or other papers to be delivered against honor of the draft;

    (g) "Item" means any instrument for the payment of money even though it is not negotiable but does not include money;

    (h) "Midnight deadline" with respect to a bank is midnight on its next banking day following the banking day on which it receives the relevant item or notice or from which the time for taking action commences to run, whichever is later;

    (i) "Properly payable" includes the availability of funds for payment at the time of decision to pay or dishonor;

    (j) "Settle" means to pay in cash, by clearing house settlement, in a charge or credit or by remittance, or otherwise as instructed. A settlement may be either provisional or final;

    (k) "Suspends payments" with respect to a bank means that it has been closed by order of the supervisory authorities, that a public officer has been appointed to take it over or that it ceases or refuses to make payments in the ordinary course of business.

(2) Other definitions applying to this Article and the sections in which they appear are:

"Collecting bank." Section 4–105.

"Depositary bank." Section 4–105.

"Intermediary bank." Section 4–105.

"Payor bank." Section 4–105.

"Presenting bank." Section 4–105.

"Remitting bank." Section 4–105.

(3) The following definitions in other Articles apply to this Article:

"Acceptance." Section 3–410.
"Certificate of deposit." Section 3–104.
"Certification." Section 3–411.
"Check." Section 3–104.
"Draft." Section 3–104.
"Holder in due course." Section 3–302.
"Notice of dishonor." Section 3–508.
"Presentment." Section 3–504.
"Protest." Section 3–509.
"Secondary party." Section 3–102.

(4) In addition Article 1 contains general definitions and principles of construction and interpretation applicable throughtout this Article.

§ 4–105. "Depositary Bank"; "Intermediary Bank"; "Collecting Bank"; "Payor Bank"; "Presenting Bank"; "Remitting Bank."

In this Article unless the context otherwise requires:
   (a) "Depositary bank" means the first bank to which an item is transferred for collection even though it is also the payor bank;
   (b) "Payor bank" means a bank by which an item is payable as drawn or accepted;
   (c) "Intermediary bank" means any bank to which an item is transferred in course of collection except the depositary or payor bank;
   (d) "Collecting bank" means any bank handling the item for collection except the payor bank;
   (e) "Presenting bank" means any bank presenting an item except a payor bank;
   (f) "Remitting bank" means any payor or intermediary bank remitting for an item.

§ 4–106. Separate Office of a Bank.*

A branch or separate office of a bank is a separate bank for the purpose of computing the time within which and determining the place at or to which action may be taken or notices or orders shall be given under this Article and under Article 3.

§ 4–107. Time of Receipt of Items.

(1) For the purpose of allowing time to process items, prove balances and make the necessary entries on its books to determine its position for the day, a bank may fix an afternoon hour of 2 P.M. or later as a cut-off hour for the handling of money and items and the making of entries on its books.

(2) Any item or deposit of money received on any day after a cut-off hour so fixed or after the close of the banking day may be treated as being received at the opening of the next banking day.

§ 4–108. Delays.

(1) Unless otherwise instructed, a collecting bank in a good faith effort to secure payment may, in the case of specific items and with or without the approval of any person involved, waive, modify or extend time limits imposed or permitted

by this Act for a period not in excess of an additional banking day without discharge of secondary parties and without liability to its transferor or any prior party.

(2) Delay by a collecting bank or payor bank beyond time limits prescribed or permitted by this Act or by instructions is excused if caused by interruption of communication facilities, suspension of payments by another bank, war, emergency conditions or other circumstances beyond the control of the bank provided it exercises such diligence as the circumstances require.

§ 4–109. Process of Posting.

The "process of posting" means the usual procedure followed by a payor bank in determining to pay an item and in recording the payment including one or more of the following or other steps as determined by the bank:

  (a) verification of any signature;
  (b) ascertaining that sufficient funds are available;
  (c) affixing a "paid" or other stamp;
  (d) entering a charge or entry to a customer's account;
  (e) correcting or reversing an entry or erroneous action with respect to the item.

PART 2

COLLECTION OF ITEMS: DEPOSITARY AND COLLECTING BANKS

§ 4–201. Presumption and Duration of Agency Status of Collecting Banks and Provisional Status of Credits; Applicability of Article; Item Indorsed "Pay Any Bank."

(1) Unless a contrary intent clearly appears and prior to the time that a settlement given by a collecting bank for an item is or becomes final (subsection (3) of Section 4–211 and Sections 4–212 and 4–213) the bank is an agent or subagent of the owner of the item and any settlement given for the item is provisional. This provision applies regardless of the form of indorsement or lack of indorsement and even though credit given for the item is subject to immediate withdrawal as of right or is in fact withdrawn; but the continuance of ownership of an item by its owner and any rights of the owner to proceeds of the item are subject to rights of a collecting bank such as those resulting from outstanding advances on the item and valid rights of setoff. When an item is handled by banks for purposes of presentment, payment and collection, the relevant provisions of this Article apply even though action of parties clearly establishes that a particular bank has purchased the item and is the owner of it.

(2) After an item has been indorsed with the words "pay any bank" or the like, only a bank may acquire the rights of a holder

  (a) until the item has been returned to the customer initiating collection; or
  (b) until the item has been specially indorsed by a bank to a person who is not a bank.

§ 4–202. Responsibility for Collection; When Action Seasonable.

(1) A collecting bank must use ordinary care in

  (a) presenting an item or sending it for presentment; and
  (b) sending notice of dishonor or non-payment or returning an item other

than a documentary draft to the bank's transferor [or directly to the depositary bank under subsection (2) of Section 4–212] *(see note to Section 4–212)* after learning that the item has not been paid or accepted, as the case may be; and

(c) settling for an item when the bank receives final settlement; and

(d) making or providing for any necessary protest; and

(e) notifying its transferor of any loss or delay in transit within a reasonable time after discovery thereof.

(2) A collecting bank taking proper action before its midnight deadline following receipt of an item, notice or payment acts seasonably; taking proper action within a reasonably longer time may be seasonable but the bank has the burden of so establishing.

(3) Subject to subsection (1) (a), a bank is not liable for the insolvency, neglect, misconduct, mistake or default of another bank or person or for loss or destruction of an item in transit or in the possession of others.

§ 4–203. Effect of Instructions.

Subject to the provisions of Article 3 concerning conversion of instruments (Section 3–419) and the provisions of both Article 3 and this Article concerning restrictive indorsements only a collecting bank's transferor can give instructions which affect the bank or constitute notice to it and a collecting bank is not liable to prior parties for any action taken pursuant to such instructions or in accordance with any agreement with its transferor.

§ 4–204. Methods of Sending and Presenting; Sending Direct to Payor Bank.

(1) A collecting bank must send items by reasonably prompt method taking into consideration any relevant instructions, the nature of the item, the number of such items on hand, and the cost of collection involved and the method generally used by it or others to present such items.

(2) A collecting bank may send

(a) any item direct to the payor bank;

(b) any item to any non-bank payor if authorized by its transferor; and

(c) any item other than documentary drafts to any non-bank payor, if authorized by Federal Reserve regulation or operating letter, clearing house rule or the like.

(3) Presentment may be made by a presenting bank at a place where the payor bank has requested that presentment be made.

§ 4–205. Supplying Missing Indorsement; No Notice from Prior Indorsement.

(1) A depositary bank which has taken an item for collection may supply any indorsement of the customer which is necessary to title unless the item contains the words "payee's indorsement required" or the like. In the absence of such a requirement a statement place on the item by the depositary bank to the effect that the item was deposited by a customer or credited to his account is effective as the customer's indorsement.

(2) An intermediary bank, or payor bank which is not a depositary bank, is neither given notice nor otherwise affected by a restrictive indorsement of any person except the bank's immediate transferor.

§ 4–206. Transfer Between Banks.

Any agreed method which identifies the transferor bank is sufficient for the item's further transfer to another bank.

§ 4–207. Warranties of Customer and Collecting Banks on Transfer or Presentment of Items; Time for Claims.

(1) Each customer or collecting bank who obtains payment or acceptance of an item and each prior customer and collecting bank warrants to the payor bank or other payor who in good faith pays or accepts the item that

(a) he has a good title to the item or is authorized to obtain payment or acceptance on behalf of one who has a good title; and

(b) he has no knowledge that the signature of the maker or drawer is unauthorized, except that this warranty is not given by any customer or collecting bank that is a holder in due course and acts in good faith

(i) to a maker with respect to the maker's own signature; or

(ii) to a drawer with respect to the drawer's own signature, whether or not the drawer is also the drawee; or

(iii) to an acceptor of an item if the holder in due course took the item after the acceptance or obtained the acceptance without knowledge that the drawer's signature was unauthorized; and

(c) the item has not been materially altered, except that this warranty is not given by any customer or collecting bank that is a holder in due course and acts in good faith

(i) to the maker of a note; or

(ii) to the drawer of a draft whether or not the drawer is also the drawee; or

(iii) to the acceptor of an item with respect to an alteration made prior to the acceptance if the holder in due course took the item after the acceptance, even though the acceptance provided "payable as originally drawn" or equivalent terms; or

(iv) to the acceptor of an item with respect to an alteration made after the acceptance.

(2) Each customer and collecting bank who transfers an item and receives a settlement or other consideration for it warrants to his transferee and to any subsequent collecting bank who takes the item in good faith that

(a) he has a good title to the item or is authorized to obtain payment or acceptance on behalf of one who has a good title and the transfer is otherwise rightful; and

(b) all signatures are genuine or authorized; and

(c) the item has not been materially altered; and

(d) no defense of any party is good against him; and

(e) he has no knowledge of any insolvency proceeding instituted with respect to the maker or acceptor or the drawer of an unaccepted item.

In addition each customer and collecting bank so transferring an item and receiving a settlement or other consideration engages that upon dishonor and any necessary notice of dishonor and protest he will take up the item.

(3) The warranties and the engagement to honor set forth in the two preceding subsections arise notwithstanding the absence of indorsement or words of guaranty or warranty in the transfer or presentment and a collecting bank remains liable

for their breach despite remittance to its transferor. Damages for breach of such warranties or engagement to honor shall not exceed the consideration received by the customer or collecting bank responsible plus finance charges and expenses related to the item, if any.

(4) Unless a claim for breach of warranty under this section is made within a reasonable time after the person claiming learns of the breach, the person liable is discharged to the extent of any loss caused by the delay in making claim.

§ 4–208. Security Interest of Collecting Banks in Items, Accompanying Documents and Proceeds.

(1) A bank has a security interest in an item and any accompanying documents or the proceeds of either

(a) in case of an item deposited in an account to the extent to which credit given for the item has been withdrawn or applied;

(b) in case of an item for which it has given credit available for withdrawal as of right, to the extent of the credit given whether or not the credit is drawn upon and whether or not there is a right of charge-back; or

(c) if it makes an advance on or against the item.

(2) When credit which has been given for several items received at one time or pursuant to a single agreement is withdrawn or applied in part the security interest remains upon all the items, any accompanying documents or the proceeds of either. For the purpose of this section, credits first given are first withdrawn.

(3) Receipt by a collecting bank of a final settlement for an item is a realization on its security interest in the item, accompanying documents and proceeds. To the extent and so long as the bank does not receive final settlement for the item or give up possession of the item or accompanying documents for purposes other than collection, the security interest continues and is subject to the provisions of Article 9 except that

(a) no security agreement is necessary to make the security interest enforceable (subsection (1) (b) of Section 9–203); and

(b) no filing is required to perfect the security interest; and

(c) the security interest has priority over conflicting perfected security interests in the item, accompanying documents or proceeds.

§ 4–209. When Bank Gives Value for Purposes of Holder in Due Course.

For purposes of determining its status as a holder in due course, the bank has given value to the extent that it has a security interest in an item provided that the bank otherwise complies with the requirements of Section 3–302 on what constitutes a holder in due course.

§ 4–210. Presentment by Notice of Item Not Payable by, Through or at a Bank; Liability of Secondary Parties.

(1) Unless otherwise instructed, a collecting bank may present an item not payable by, through or at a bank by sending to the party to accept or pay a written notice that the bank holds the item for acceptance or payment. The notice must be sent in time to be received on or before the day when presentment is due and the bank must meet any requirement of the party to accept or pay under Section 3–505 by the close of the bank's next banking day after it knows of the requirement.

(2) Where presentment is made by notice and neither honor nor request for compliance with a requirement under Section 3–505 is received by the close of business on the day after maturity or in the case of demand items by the close of business on the third banking day after notice was sent, the presenting bank may treat the item as dishonored and charge any secondary party by sending him notice of the facts.

§ 4–211. Media of Remittance; Provisional and Final Settlement in Remittance Cases.

(1) A collecting bank may take in settlement of an item
   (a) a check of the remitting bank or of another bank on any bank except the remitting bank; or
   (b) a cashier's check or similar primary obligation of a remitting bank which is a member of or clears through a member of the same clearing house or group as the collecting bank; or
   (c) appropriate authority to charge an account of the remitting bank or of another bank with the collecting bank; or
   (d) if the item is drawn upon or payable by a person other than a bank, a cashier's check, certified check or other bank check or obligation.

(2) If before its midnight deadline the collecting bank properly dishonors a remittance check or authorization to charge on itself or presents or forwards for collection a remittance instrument of or on another bank which is of a kind approved by subsection (1) or has not been authorized by it, the collecting bank is not liable to prior parties in the event of the dishonor of such check, instrument or authorization.

(3) A settlement for an item by means of a remittance instrument or authorization to charge is or becomes a final settlement as to both .the person making and the person receiving the settlement
   (a) if the remittance instrument or authorization to charge is of a kind approved by subsection (1) or has not been authorized by the person receiving the settlement and in either case the person receiving the settlement acts seasonally before its midnight deadline in presenting, forwarding for collection or paying the instrument or authorization—at the time the remittance instrument or authorization is finally paid by the payor by which it is payable;
   (b) if the person receiving the settlement has authorized remittance by a non-bank check or obligation or by a cashier's check or similar primary obligation of or a check upon the payor or other remitting bank which is not a kind approved by subsection (1) (b)—at the time of the receipt of such remittance check or obligation; or
   (c) if in a case not covered by sub-paragraphs (a) or (b) the person receiving the settlement fails to seasonably present, forward for collection, pay or return a remittance instrument or authorization to it to charge before its midnight deadline—at such midnight deadline.

§ 4–212. Right of Charge-Back or Refund.

(1) If a collecting bank has made provisional settlement with its customer for an item and itself fails by reason of dishonor, suspension of payments by a bank or otherwise to receive a settlement for the item which is or becomes final, the

bank may revoke the settlement given by it, charge back the amount of any credit given for the item to its customer's account or obtain refund from its customer whether or not it is able to return the items if by its midnight deadline or within a longer reasonable time after it learns the facts it returns the item or sends notification of the facts. These rights to revoke, charge-back and obtain refund terminate if and when a settlement for the item received by the bank is or becomes final (subsection (3) of Section 4–211 and subsections (2) and (3) of Section 4–213).

(2) Within the time and manner prescribed by this section and Section 4–301, an intermediary or payor bank, as the case may be, may return an unpaid item directly to the depositary bank and may send for collection a draft on the depositary bank and obtain reimbursement. In such case, if the depositary bank has received provisional settlement for the item, it must reimburse the bank drawing the draft and any provisional credits for the item between banks shall become and remain final.

(3) A depositary bank which is also the payor may charge-back the amount of an item to its customer's account or obtain refund in accordance with the section governing return of an item received by a payor bank for credit on its books (Section 4–301).

(4) The right to charge-back is not affected by
   (a) prior use of the credit given for the item; or
   (b) failure by any bank to exercise ordinary care with respect to the item but any bank so failing remains liable.

(5) A failure to charge-back or claim refund does not affect other rights of the bank against the customer or any other party.

(6) If credit is given in dollars as the equivalent of the value of an item payable in a foreign currency the dollar amount of any charge-back or refund shall be calculated on the basis of the buying sight rate for the foreign currency prevailing on the day when the person entitled to the charge-back or refund learns that it will not receive payment in ordinary course.

§ 4–213. Final Payment of Item by Payor Bank; When Provisional Debits and Credits Become Final; When Certain Credits Become Available for Withdrawal.

(1) An item is finally paid by a payor bank when the bank has done any of the following, whichever happens first:
   (a) paid the item in cash; or
   (b) settled for the item without reserving a right to revoke the settlement and without having such right under statute, clearing house rule or agreement; or
   (c) completed the process of posting the item to the indicated account of the drawer, maker or other person to be charged therewith; or
   (d) made a provisional settlement for the item and failed to revoke the settlement in the time and manner permitted by statute, clearing house rule or agreement.

Upon a final payment under subparagraphs (b), (c) or (d) the payor bank shall be accountable for the amount of the item.

(2) If provisional settlement for an item between the presenting and payor banks is made through a clearing house or by debits or credits in an account

between them, then to the extent that provisional debits or credits for the item are entered in accounts between the presenting and payor banks or between the presenting and successive prior collecting banks seriatim, they become final upon final payment of the item by the payor bank.

(3) If a collecting bank receives a settlement for an item which is or becomes final (subsection (3) of Section 4–211, subsection (2) of Section 4–213) the bank is accountable to its customer for the amount of the item and any provisional credit given for the item in an account with its customer becomes final.

(4) Subject to any right of the bank to apply the credit to an obligation of the customer, credit given by a bank for an item in an account with its customer becomes available for withdrawal as of right

(a) in any case where the bank has received a provisional settlement for the item—when such settlement becomes final and the bank has had a reasonable time to learn that the settlement is final;

(b) in any case where the bank is both a depositary bank and a payor bank and the item is finally paid—at the opening of the bank's second banking day following receipt of the item.

(5) A deposit of money in a bank is final when made but, subject to any right of the bank to apply the deposit to an obligation of the customer, the deposit becomes available for withdrawal as of right at the opening of the bank's next banking day following receipt of the deposit.

§ 4–214. Insolvency and Preference.

(1) Any item in or coming into the possession of a payor or collecting bank which suspends payment and which item is not finally paid shall be returned by the receiver, trustee or agent in charge of the closed bank to the presenting bank or the closed bank's customer.

(2) If a payor bank finally pays an item and suspends payments without making a settlement for the item with its customer or the presenting bank which settlement is or becomes final, the owner of the item has a preferred claim against the payor bank.

(3) If a payor bank gives or a collecting bank gives or receives a provisional settlement for an item and thereafter suspends payments, the suspension does not prevent or interfere with the settlement becoming final if such finality occurs automatically upon the lapse of certain time or the happening of certain events (subsection (3) of Section 4–211, subsections (1) (d), (2) and (3) of Section 4–213).

(4) If a collecting bank receives from subsequent parties settlement for an item which settlement is or becomes final and suspends payments without making a settlement for the item with its customer which is or becomes final, the owner of the item has a preferred claim against such collecting bank.

PART 3

COLLECTION OF ITEMS: PAYOR BANKS

§ 4–301. Deferred Posting; Recovery of Payment by Return of Items; Time of Dishonor.

(1) Where an authorized settlement for a demand item (other than a documentary draft) received by a payor bank otherwise than for immediate payment over

the counter has been made before midnight of the banking day of receipt the payor bank may revoke the settlement and recover any payment if before it has made final payment (subsection (1) of Section 4–213) and before its midnight deadline it

    (a) returns the item; or

    (b) sends written notice of dishonor or nonpayment if the item is held for protest or is otherwise unavailable for return.

(2) If a demand item is received by a payor bank for credit on its books it may return such item or send notice of dishonor and may revoke any credit given or recover the amount thereof withdrawn by its customer, if it acts within the time limit and in the manner specified in the preceding subsection.

(3) Unless previous notice of dishonor has been sent an item is dishonored at the time when for purposes of dishonor it is returned or notice sent in accordance with this section.

(4) An item is returned:

    (a) as to an item received through a clearing house, when it is delivered to the presenting or last collecting bank or to the clearing house or is sent or delivered in accordance with its rules; or

    (b) in all other cases, when it is sent or delivered to the bank's customer or transferor or pursuant to his instructions.

§ 4–302. Payor Bank's Responsibility for Late Return of Item.

In the absence of a valid defense such as breach of a presentment warranty (subsection (1) of Section 4–207), settlement effected or the like, if an item is presented on and received by a payor bank the bank is accountable for the amount of

    (a) a demand item other than a documentary draft whether properly payable or not if the bank, in any case where it is not also the depositary bank, retains the item beyond midnight of the banking day of receipt without settling for it or, regardless of whether it is also the depositary bank, does not pay or return the item or send notice of dishonor until after its midnight deadline; or

    (b) any other properly payable item unless within the time allowed for acceptance or payment of that item the bank either accepts or pays the item or returns it and accompanying documents.

§ 4–303. When Items Subject to Notice, Stop-Order, Legal Process or Setoff; Order in Which Items May Be Charged or Certified.

(1) Any knowledge, notice or stop-order received by, legal process served upon or setoff exercised by a payor bank, whether or not effective under other rules of law to terminate, suspend or modify the bank's right or duty to pay an item or to charge its customer's account for the item, comes too late to so terminate, suspend or modify such right or duty if the knowledge, notice, stop-order or legal process is received or served and a reasonable time for the bank to act thereon expires or the setoff is exercised after the bank has done any of the following:

    (a) accented or certified the item:

    (b) paid the item in cash;

    (c) settled for the item without reserving a right to revoke the settlement and without having such right under statute, clearing house rule or agreement;

(d) completed the process of posting the item to the indicated account of the drawer, maker or other person to be charged therewith or otherwise has evidenced by examination of such indicated account and by action its decision to pay the item; or

(e) becomes accountable for the amount of the item under subsection (1) (d) of Section 4–213 and Section 4–302 dealing with the payor bank's responsibility for late return of items.

(2) Subject to the provisions of subsection (1) items may be accepted, paid, certified or charged to the indicated account of its customer in any order convenient to the bank.

PART 4
RELATIONSHIP BETWEEN PAYOR BANK AND ITS CUSTOMER

§ 4–401. When Bank May Charge Customer's Account.

(1) As against its customer, a bank may charge against his account any item which is otherwise properly payable from that account even though the charge creates an overdraft.

(2) A bank which in good faith makes payment to a holder may charge the indicated account of its customer according to

(a) the original tenor of his altered item; or

(b) the tenor of his completed item, even though the bank knows the item has been completed unless the bank has notice that the completion was improper.

§–402. Bank's Liability to Customer for Wrongful Dishonor.

A payor bank is liable to its customer for damages proximately caused by the wrongful dishonor of an item. When the dishonor occurs through mistake liability is limited to actual damages proved. If so proximately caused and proved damages may include damages for an arrest or prosecution of the customer or other consequential damages. Whether any consequential damages are proximately caused by the wrongful dishonor is a question of fact to be determined in each case.

§ 4–403. Customer's Right to Stop Payment; Burden of Proof of Loss.

(1) A customer may by order to his bank stop payment of any item payable for his account but the order must be received at such time and in such manner as to afford the bank a reasonable opportunity to act on it prior to any action by the bank with respect to the item described in Section 4–303.

(2) An oral order is binding upon the bank only for fourteen calendar days unless confirmed in writing within that period. A written order is effective for only six months unless renewed in writing.

(3) The burden of establishing the fact and amount of loss resulting from the payment of an item contrary to a binding stop payment order is on the customer.

§ 4–404. Bank Not Obligated to Pay Check More Than Six Months Old.

A bank is under no obligation to a customer having a checking account to pay a check, other than a certified check, which is presented more than six months after its date, but it may charge its customer's account for a payment made thereafter in good faith.

§ 4-405. Death or Incompetence of Customer.

(1) A payor or collecting bank's authority to accept, pay or collect an item or to account for proceeds of its collection if otherwise effective is not rendered ineffective by incompetence of a customer of either bank existing at the time the item is issued or its collection is undertaken if the bank does not know of an adjudication of incompetence. Neither death nor incompetence of a customer revokes such authority to accept, pay, collect or account until the bank knows of the fact of death or of an adjudication of incompetence and has reasonable opportunity to act on it.

(2) Even with knowledge a bank may for 10 days after the date of death pay or certify checks drawn on or prior to that date unless ordered to stop payment by a person claiming an interest in the account.

§ 4-406. Customer's Duty to Discover and Report Unauthorized Signature or Alteration.

(1) When a bank sends to its customer a statement of account accompanied by items paid in good faith in support of the debit entries or holds the statement and items pursuant to a request or instructions of its customer or otherwise in a reasonable manner makes the statement and items available to the customer, the customer must exercise reasonable care and promptness to examine the statement and items to discover his unauthorized signature or any alteration on an item and must notify the bank promptly after discovery thereof.

(2) If the bank establishes that the customer failed with respect to an item to comply with the duties imposed on the customer by subsection (1) the customer is precluded from asserting against the bank

(a) his unauthorized signature or any alteration on the item if the bank also establishes that it suffered a loss by reason of such failure; and

(b) an unauthorized signature or alteration by the same wrongdoer on any other item paid in good faith by the bank after the first item and statement were available to the customer for a reasonable period not exceeding fourteen calendar days and before the bank receives notification from the customer of any such unauthorized signature or alteration.

(3) The preclusion under subsection (2) does not apply if the customer establishes lack of ordinary care on the part of the bank in paying the item(s).

(4) Without regard to care or lack of care of either the customer or the bank a customer who does not within one year from the time the statement and items are made available to the customer (subsection (1)) discover and report his unauthorized signature or any alteration on the face or back of the item or does not within three years from that time discover and report any unauthorized indorsement is precluded from asserting against the bank such unauthorized signature or indorsement or such alteration.

(5) If under this section a payor bank has a valid defense against a claim of a customer upon or resulting from payment of an item and waives or fails upon request to assert the defense the bank may not assert against any collecting bank or other prior party presenting or transferring the item a claim based upon the unauthorized signature or alteration giving rise to the customer's claim.

§ 4-407. Payor Bank's Right to Subrogation on Improper Payment.

If a payor bank has paid an item over the stop payment order of the drawer or maker or otherwise under circumstances giving a basis for objection by the drawer or maker, to prevent unjust enrichment and only to the extent necessary to prevent loss to the bank by reason of its payment of the item, the payor bank shall be subrogated to the rights

(a) of any holder in due course on the item against the drawer or maker; and

(b) of the payee or any other holder of the item against the drawer or maker either on the item or under the transaction out of which the item arose; and

(c) of the drawer or maker against the payee or any other holder of the item with respect to the transaction out of which the item arose.

PART 5

COLLECTION OF DOCUMENTARY DRAFTS

§ 4–501. Handling of Documentary Drafts; Duty to Send for Presentment and to Notify Customer of Dishonor.

A bank which takes a documentary draft for collection must present or send the draft and accompanying documents for presentment and upon learning that the draft has not been paid or accepted in due course must seasonably notify its customer of such fact even though it may have discounted or bought the draft or extended credit available for withdrawal as of right.

§ 4–502. Presentment of "On Arrival" Drafts.

When a draft or the relevant instructions require presentment "on arrival," "when goods arrive" or the like, the collecting bank need not present until in its judgment a reasonable time for arrival of the goods has expired. Refusal to pay or accept because the goods have not arrived is not dishonor; the bank must notify its transferor of such refusal but need not present the draft again until it is instructed to do so or learns of the arrival of the goods.

§ 4–503. Responsibility of Presenting Bank for Documents and Goods; Report of Reasons for Dishonor; Referee in Case of Need.

Unless otherwise instructed and except as provided in Article 5 a bank presenting a documentary draft

(a) must deliver the documents to the drawee on acceptance of the draft if it is payable more than three days after presentment; otherwise, only on payment; and

(b) upon dishonor, either in the case of presentment for acceptance or presentment for payment, may seek and follow instructions from any referee in case of need designated in the draft or if the presenting bank does not choose to utilize his services it must use diligence and good faith to ascertain the reason for dishonor, must notify its transferor of the dishonor and of the results of its effort to ascertain the reasons therefor and must request instructions.

But the presenting bank is under no obligation with respect to goods represented by the documents except to follow any reasonable instructions seasonably received; it has a right to reimbursement for any expense incurred in following instructions and to prepayment of or indemnity for such expenses.

§ 4–504. Privilege of Presenting Bank to Deal With Goods; Security Interest for Expenses.

(1) A presenting bank which, following the dishonor of a documentary draft, has seasonably requested instructions but does not receive them within a reasonable time may store, sell, or otherwise deal with the goods in any reasonable manner.

(2) For its reasonable expenses incurred by action under subsection (1) the presenting bank has a lien upon the goods or their proceeds, which may be foreclosed in the same manner as an unpaid seller's lien.

ARTICLE 6. Bulk Transfers

§ 6–101. Short Title.

This Article shall be known and may be cited as Uniform Commercial Code— Bulk Transfers.

§ 6–102. "Bulk Transfers"; Transfers of Equipment; Enterprises Subject to This Article; Bulk Transfers Subject to This Article.

(1) A "bulk transfer" is any transfer in bulk and not in the ordinary course of the transferor's business of a major part of the materials, supplies, merchandise or other inventory (Section 9–109) of an enterprise subject to this Article.

(2) A transfer of a substantial part of the equipment (Section 9–109) of such an enterprise is a bulk transfer if it is made in connection with a bulk transfer of inventory, but not otherwise.

(3) The enterprises subject to this Article are all those whose principal business is the sale of merchandise from stock, including those who manufacture what they sell.

(4) Except as limited by the following section all bulk transfers of goods located within this state are subject to this Article.

§ 6–103. Transfers Excepted From This Article.

The following transfers are not subject to this Article:

(1) Those made to give security for the performance of an obligation;

(2) General assignments for the benefit of all the creditors of the transferor, and subsequent transfers by the assignee thereunder;

(3) Transfers in settlement of a lien or other security interests;

(4) Sales by executors, administrators, receivers, trustees in bankruptcy, or any public officer under judicial process;

(5) Sales made in the course of judicial or administrative proceedings for the dissolution or reorganization of a corporation and of which is sent to the creditors of the corporation pursuant to order of the court or administrative agency;

(6) Transfers to a person maintaining a known place of business in this State who becomes bound to pay the debts of the tranferor in full and gives public notice of that fact, and who is solvent after becoming so bound;

(7) A transfer to a new business enterprise organized to take over and continue the business, if public notice of the transaction is given and the new enterprise assumes the debts of the transferor and he receives nothing from the transaction except an interest in the new enterprise junior to the claims of creditors;

(8) Transfers of property which is exempt from execution.

Public notice under subsection (6) or subsection (7) may be given by publishing once a week for two consecutive weeks in a newspaper of general circulation where the transferor had its principal place of business in this state an advertisment including the names and addresses of the transferor and transferee and the effective date of the transfer.

§ 6–104. Schedule of Property, List of Creditors.

(1) Except as provided with respect to auction sales (Section 6–108), a bulk transfer subject to this Article is ineffective against any creditor of the transferor unless:

    (a) The transferee requires the transferor to furnish a list of his existing creditors prepared as stated in this section; and

    (b) The parties prepare a schedule of the property tranferred sufficient to identify it; and

    (c) The transferee preserves the list and schedule for six months next following the transfer and permits inspection of either or both and copying therefrom at all reasonable hours by any creditor of the transferor, or files the list and schedule in *(a public office to be here identified)*.

(2) The list of creditors must be signed and sworn to or affirmed by the transferor or his agent. It must contain the names and business addresses of all creditors of the transferor, with the amounts when known, and also the names of all persons who are known to the transferor to assert claims against him even though such claims are disputed. If the transferor is the obligor of an outstanding issue of bonds, debentures or the like as to which there is an indenture trustee, the list of creditors need include only the name and address of the indenture trustee and the aggregate outstanding principal amount of the issue.

(3) Responsibility for the completeness and accuracy of the list of creditors rests on the transferor, and the transfer is not rendered ineffective by errors or omissions therein unless the transferee is shown to have had knowledge.

§ 6–105. Notice to Creditors.

In addition to the requirements of the preceding section, any bulk transfer subject to this Article except one made by auction sale (Section 6–108) is ineffective against any creditor of the transferor unless at least ten days before he takes possession of the goods or pays for them, whichever happens first, the transferee gives notice of the transfer in the manner and to the persons hereafter provided (Section 6–107).

§ 6–106. Application of the Proceeds.

In addition to the requirements of the two preceding sections:

(1) Upon every bulk transfer subject to this Article for which new consideration becomes payable except those made by sale at auction it is the duty of the transferee to assure that such consideration is applied so far as necessary to pay those debts of the transferor which are either shown on the list furnished by the transferor (Section 6–104) or filed in writing in the place stated in the notice (Section 6–107) within thirty days after the mailing of such notice. This duty of the transferee runs to all the holders of such debts, and may be enforced by any of them for the benefit of all.

(2) If any of said debts are in dispute the necessary sum may be withheld from distribution until the dispute is settled or adjudicated.

(3) If the consideration payable is not enough to pay all of the said debts in full distribution shall be made pro rata.

[(4) The transferee may within ten days after he takes possession of the goods pay the consideration into the *(specify court)* in the county where the transferor had its principal place of business in this state and thereafter may discharge his duty under this section by giving notice by registered or certified mail to all the persons to whom the duty runs that the consideration has been paid into that court and that they should file their claims there. On motion of any interested party, the court may order the distribution of the consideration to the persons entitled to it.] (Brackets indicate an optional section.)

§ 6–107. The Notice.

(1) The notice to creditors (Section 6–105) shall state:
- (a) that a bulk transfer is about to be made; and
- (b) the names and business addresses of the transferor and transferee, and all other business names and addresses used by the transferor within three years last past so far as known to the transferee; and
- (c) whether or not all the debts of the transferor are to be paid in full as they fall due as a result of the transaction, and if so, the address to which creditors should send their bills.

(2) If the debts of the transferor are not to be paid in full as they fall due or if the transferee is in doubt on that point then the notice shall state further:
- (a) the location and general description of the property to be transferred and the estimated total of the transferor's debts;
- (b) the address where the schedule of property and list of creditors (Section 6–104) may be inspected;
- (c) whether the transfer is to pay existing debts and if so the amount of such debts and to whom owing;
- (d) whether the transfer is for new consideration and if so the amount of such consideration and the time and place of payment; [and]
- [(e) if for new consideration the time and place where creditors of the transferor are to file their claims.]

(3) The notice in any case shall be delivered personally or sent by registered or certified mail to all the persons shown on the list of creditors furnished by the transferor (Section 6–104) and to all other persons who are known to the transferee to hold or assert claims against the transferor.

§ 6–108. Auction Sales; "Auctioneer."

(1) A bulk transfer is subject to this Article even though it is by sale at auction, but only in the manner and with the results stated in this section.

(2) The transferor shall furnish a list of his creditors and assist in the preparation of a schedule of the property to be sold, both prepared as before stated (Section 6–104).

(3) The person or persons other than the transferor who direct, control or are responsible for the auction are collectively called the "auctioneer." The auctioneer shall:

(a) receive and retain the list of creditors and prepare and retain the schedule of property for the period stated in this Article (Section 6–104);

(b) give notice of the auction personally or by registered or certified mail at least ten days before it occurs to all persons shown on the list of creditors and to all other persons who are known to him to hold or assert claims against the transferor; [and]

[(c) assure that the net proceeds of the auction are applied as provided in this Article (Section 6–106).]

(4) Failure of the auctioneer to perform any of these duties does not affect the validity of the sale or the title of the purchasers, but if the auctioneer knows that the auction constitutes a bulk transfer such failure renders the auctioneer liable to the creditors of the transferor as a class for the sums owing to them from the transferor up to but not exceeding the net proceeds of the auction. If the auctioneer consists of several persons their liability is joint and several.

§ 6–109. What Creditors Protected; Credit for Payment to Particular Creditors.

(1) The creditors of the transferor mentioned in this Article are those holding claims based on transactions or events occurring before the bulk transfer, but creditors who become such after notice to creditors is given (Sections 6–105 and 6–107) are not entitled to notice.

[(2) Against the aggregate obligation imposed by the provisions of this Article concerning the application of the proceeds (Section 6–106 and subsection (3) (c) of 6–108) the transferee or auctioneer is entitled to credit for sums paid to particular creditors of the transferor, not exceeding the sums believed in good faith at the time of the payment to be properly payable to such creditors.]

§ 6–110. Subsequent Transfers.

When the title of a transferee to property is subject to a defect by reason of his non-compliance with the requirements of this Article, then:

(1) a purchaser of any of such property from such transferee who pays no value or who takes with notice of such non-compliance takes subject to such defect, but

(2) a purchaser for value in good faith and without such notice takes free of such defect.

§ 6–111. Limitation of Actions and Levies.

No action under this Article shall be brought nor levy made more than six months after the date on which the transferee took possession of the goods unless the transfer has been concealed. If the transfer has been concealed, actions may be brought or levies made within six months after its discovery.

ARTICLE 7. Warehouse Receipts, Bills of Lading and Other Documents of Title

PART 1
GENERAL

§ 7–101. Short Title.

This Article shall be known and may be cited as Uniform Commercial Code—Documents of Title.

§ 7–102. Definitions and Index of Definitions.

(1) In this Article, unless the context otherwise requires:

    (a) "Bailee" means the person who by a warehouse receipt, bill of lading or other document of title acknowledges possession of goods and contracts to deliver them.

    (b) "Consignee" means the person named in a bill to whom or to whose order the bill promises delivery.

    (c) "Consignor" means the person named in a bill as the person from whom the goods have been received for shipment.

    (d) "Delivery order" means a written order to deliver goods directed to a warehouseman, carrier or other person who in the ordinary course of business issues warehouse receipts or bills of lading.

    (e) "Document" means document of title as defined in the general definitions in Article 1 (Section 1–201).

    (f) "Goods" means all things which are treated as movable for the purposes of a contract of storage or transportation.

    (g) "Issuer" means a bailee who issues a document except that in relation to an unaccepted delivery order it means the person who orders the possessor of goods to deliver. Issuer includes any person for whom an agent or employee purports to act in issuing a document if the agent or employee has real or apparent authority to issue documents, notwithstanding that the issuer received no goods or that the goods were misdescribed or that in any other respect the agent or employee violated his instructions.

    (h) "Warehouseman" is a person engaged in the business of storing goods for hire.

(2) Other definitions applying to this Article or to specified Parts thereof, and the sections in which they appear are:

"Duly negotiate." Section 7–501.

"Person entitled under the document." Section 7–403(4).

(3) Definitions in other Articles applying to this Article and the sections in which they appear are:

"Contract for sale." Section 2–106.

"Overseas." Section 2–323.

"Receipt" of goods. Section 2–103.

(4) In addition Article 1 contains general definitions and principles of construction and interpretation applicable throughout this Article.

§ 7–103. Relation of Article to Treaty, Statute, Tariff, Classification or Regulation.

To the extent that any treaty or statute of the United States, regulatory statute of this State or tariff, classification or regulation filed or issued pursuant thereto is applicable, the provisions of this Article are subject thereto.

§ 7–104. Negotiable and Non-Negotiable Warehouse Receipt, Bill of Lading or Other Document of Title.

(1) A warehouse receipt, bill of lading or other document of title is negotiable

    (a) if by its terms the goods are to be delivered to bearer or to the order of a named person; or

(b) where recognized in overseas trade, if it runs to a named person or assigns.

(2) Any other document is non-negotiable. A bill of lading in which it is stated that the goods are consigned to a named person is not made negotiable by a provision that the goods are to be delivered only against a written order signed by the same or another named person.

§ 7–105. Construction Against Negative Implication.

The omission from either Part 2 or Part 3 of this Article of a provision corresponding to a provision made in the other Part does not imply that a corresponding rule of law is not applicable.

PART 2
WAREHOUSE RECEIPTS: SPECIAL PROVISIONS

§ 7–201. Who May Issue a Warehouse Receipt; Storage Under Government Bond.

(1) A warehouse receipt may be issued by any warehouseman.

(2) Where goods including distilled spirits and agricultural commodities are stored under a statute requiring a bond against withdrawal or a license for the issuance of receipts in the nature of warehouse receipts, a receipt issued for the goods has like effect as a warehouse receipt even though issued by a person who is the owner of the goods and is not a warehouseman.

§ 7–202. Form of Warehouse Receipt; Essential Terms; Optional Terms.

(1) A warehouse receipt need not be in any particular form.

(2) Unless a warehouse receipt embodies within its written or printed terms each of the following, the warehouseman is liable for damages caused by the omission to a person injured thereby:

(a) the location of the warehouse where the goods are stored;
(b) the date of issue of the receipt;
(c) the consecutive number of receipt;
(d) a statement whether the goods received will be delivered to the bearer, to a specified person, or to a specified person or his order;
(e) the rate of storage and handling charges, except that where goods are stored under a field warehousing arrangement a statement of that fact is sufficient on a non-negotiable receipt;
(f) a description of the goods or of the packages containing them;
(g) the signature of the warehouseman, which may be made by his authorized agent;
(h) if the receipt is issued for goods of which the warehouseman is owner, either solely or jointly or in common with others, the fact of such ownership; and
(i) a statement of the amount of advances made and of liabilities incurred for which the warehouseman claims a lien or security interest (Section 7–209). If the precise amount of such advances made or of such liabilities incurred is, at the time of the issue of the receipt, unknown to the warehouseman or to his agent who issues it, a statement of the fact that advances have been made or liabilities incurred and the purpose thereof is sufficient.

(3) A warehouseman may insert in his receipt any other terms which are not contrary to the provisions of this Act and do not impair his obligation of delivery (Section 7–403) or his duty of care (Section 7–204). Any contrary provisions shall be ineffective.

§ 7–203. Liability for Non-Receipt or Misdescription.

A party to or purchaser for value in good faith of a document of title other than a bill of lading relying in either case upon the description therein of the goods may recover from the issuer damages caused by the non-receipt or misdescription of the goods, except to the extent that the document conspicuously indicates that the issuer does not know whether any part or all of the goods in fact were received or conform to the description, as where the description is in terms of marks or labels or kind, quantity or condition, or the receipt or description is qualified by "contents, condition and quality unknown," "said to contain" or the like, if such indication be true, or the party or purchaser otherwise has notice.

§ 7–204. Duty of Care; Contractual Limitation of Warehouseman's Liability.*

(1) A warehouseman is liable for damages for loss of or injury to the goods caused by his failure to exercise such care in regard to them as a reasonably careful man would exercise under like circumstances but unless otherwise agreed he is not liable for damages which could not have been avoided by the exercise of such care.

(2) Damages may be limited by a term in the warehouse receipt or storage agreement limiting the amount of liability in case of loss or damage, and setting forth a specific liability per article or item, or value per unit of weight, beyond which the warehouseman shall not be liable; provided, however, that such liability may on written request of the bailor at the time of signing such storage agreement or within a reasonable time after receipt of the warehouse receipt be increased on part or all of the goods thereunder, in which event increased rates may be charged based on such increased valuation, but that no such increase shall be permitted contrary to a lawful limitation of liability contained in the warehouseman's tariff, if any. No such limitation is effective with respect to the warehouseman's liability for conversion to his own use.

(3) Reasonable provisions as to the time and manner of presenting claims and instituting actions based on the bailment may be included in the warehouse receipt or tariff.

§ 7–205. Title Under Warehouse Receipt Defeated in Certain Cases.

A buyer in the ordinary course of business of fungible goods sold and delivered by a warehouseman who is also in the business of buying and selling such goods takes free of any claim under a warehouse receipt even though it has been duly negotiated.

§ 7–206. Termination of Storage at Warehouseman's Option.

(1) A warehouseman may on notifying the person on whose account the goods are held and any other person known to claim an interest in the goods require payment of any charges and removal of the goods from the warehouse at the termination of the period of storage fixed by the document, or, if no period is fixed, within a stated period not less than thirty days after the notification. If

the goods are not removed before the date specified in the notification, the warehouseman may sell them in accordance with the provisions of the section on enforcement of a warehouseman's lien (Section 7–210).

(2) If a warehouseman in good faith believes that the goods are about to deteriorate or decline in value to less than the amount of his lien within the time prescribed in subsection (1) for notification, advertisement and sale, the warehouseman may specify in the notification any reasonable shorter time for removal of the goods and in case the goods are not removed, may sell them at public sale held not less than one week after a single advertisement or posting.

(3) If as a result of a quality or condition of the goods of which the warehouseman had no notice at the time of deposit the goods are a hazard to other property or to the warehouse or to persons, the warehouseman may sell the goods at public or private sale without advertisement on reasonable notification to all persons known to claim an interest in the goods. If the warehouseman after a reasonable effort is unable to sell the goods he may dispose of them in any lawful manner and shall incur no liability by reason of such disposition.

(4) The warehouseman must deliver the goods to any person entitled to them under this Article upon due demand made at any time prior to sale or other disposition under this section.

(5) The warehouseman may satisfy his lien from the proceeds of any sale or disposition under this section but must hold the balance for delivery on the demand of any person to whom he would have been bound to deliver the goods.

§ 7–207. Goods Must Be Kept Separate; Fungible Goods.

(1) Unless the warehouse receipt otherwise provides, a warehouseman must keep separate the goods covered by each receipt so as to permit at all times identification and delivery of those goods except that different lots of fungible goods may be commingled.

(2) Fungible goods so commingled are owned in common by the persons entitled thereto and the warehouseman is severally liable to each owner for that owner's share. Where because of overissue a mass of fungible goods is insufficient to meet all the receipts which the warehouseman has issued against it, the persons entitled include all holders to whom overissued receipts have been duly negotiated.

§ 7–208. Altered Warehouse Receipts.

Where a blank in a negotiable warehouse receipt has been filled in without authority, a purchaser for value and without notice of the want of authority may treat the insertion as authorized. Any other unauthorized alteration leaves any receipt enforceable against the issuer according to its original tenor.

§ 7–209. Lien of Warehouseman.

(1) A warehouseman has a lien against the bailor on the goods covered by a warehouse receipt or on the proceeds thereof in his possession for charges for storage or transportation (including demurrage and terminal charges), insurance, labor, or charges present or future in relation to the goods, and for expenses necessary for preservation of the goods or reasonably incurred in their sale pursuant to law. If the person on whose account the goods are held is liable for like charges or expenses in relation to other goods whenever deposited and it is stated in the receipt that a lien is claimed for charges and expenses in relation to other goods,

the warehouseman also has a lien against him for such charges and expenses whether or not the other goods have been delivered by the warehouseman. But against a person to whom a negotiable warehouse receipt is duly negotiated a warehouseman's lien is limited to charges in an amount or at a rate specified on the receipt or if no charges are so specified then to a reasonable charge for storage of the goods covered by the receipt subsequent to the date of the receipt.

(2) The warehouseman may also reserve a security interest against the bailor for a maximum amount specified on the receipt for charges other than those specified in subsection (1), such as for money advanced and interest. Such a security interest is governed by the Article on Secured Transactions (Article 9).

(3) (a) A warehouseman's lien for charges and expenses under subsection (1) or a security interest under subsection (2) is also effective against any person who so entrusted the bailor with possession of the goods that a pledge of them by him to a good faith purchaser for value would have been valid but is not effective against a person as to whom the document confers no right in the goods covered by it under Section 7–503.

(b) A warehouseman's lien on household goods for charges and expenses in relation to the goods under subsection (1) is also effective against all persons if the depositor was the legal possessor of the goods at the time of deposit. "Household goods" means furniture, furnishings and personal effects used by the depositor in a dwelling.

(4) A warehouseman loses his lien on any goods which he voluntarily delivers or which he unjustifiably refuses to deliver.

§ 7–210. Enforcement of Warehouseman's Lien.

(1) Except as provided in subsection (2), a warehouseman's lien may be enforced by public or private sale of the goods in block or in parcels, at any time or place and on any terms which are commercially reasonable, after notifying all persons known to claim an interest in the goods. Such notification must include a statement of the amount due, the nature of the proposed sale and the time and place of any public sale. The fact that a better price could have been obtained by a sale at a different time or in a different method from that selected by the warehouseman is not of itself sufficient to establish that the sale was not made in a commercially reasonable manner. If the warehouseman either sells the goods in the usual manner in any recognized market therefor, or if he sells at the price current in such market at the time of his sale, or if he has otherwise sold in conformity with commercially reasonable practices among dealers in the type of goods sold, he has sold in a commercially reasonable manner. A sale of more goods than apparently necessary to be offered to insure satisfaction of the obligation is not commercially reasonable except in cases covered by the preceding sentence.

(2) A warehouseman's lien on goods other than goods stored by a merchant in the course of his business may be enforced only as follows:

(a) All persons known to claim an interest in the goods must be notified.

(b) The notification must be delivered in person or sent by registered or certified letter to the last known address of any person to be notified.

(c) The notification must include an itemized statement of the claim, a description of the goods subject to the lien, a demand for payment within a specified time not less than ten days after receipt of the notification, and a conspicuous statement that unless the claim is paid within that time the goods will be advertised for sale and sold by auction at a specified time and place.

(d) The sale must conform to the terms of the notification.

(e) The sale must be held at the nearest suitable place to that where the goods are held or stored.

(f) After the expiration of the time given in the notification, an advertisement of the sale must be published once a week for two weeks consecutively in a newspaper of general circulation where the sale is to be held. The advertisement must include a description of the goods, the name of the person on whose account they are being held, and the time and place of the sale. The sale must take place at least fifteen days after the first publication. If there is no newspaper of general circulation where the sale is to be held, the advertisment must be posted at least ten days before the sale in not less than six conspicuous places in the neighborhood of the proposed sale.

(3) Before any sale pursuant to this section any person claiming a right in the goods may pay the amount necessary to satisfy the lien and the reasonable expenses incurred under this section. In that event the goods must not be sold, but must be retained by the warehouseman subject to the terms of the receipt and this Article.

(4) The warehouseman may buy at any public sale pursuant to this section.

(5) A purchaser in good faith of goods sold to enforce a warehouseman's lien takes the goods free of any rights of persons against whom the lien was valid, despite noncompliance by the warehouseman with the requirements of this section.

(6) The warehouseman may satisfy his lien from the proceeds of any sale pursuant to this section but must hold the balance, if any, for delivery on demand to any person to whom he would have been bound to deliver the goods.

(7) The rights provided by this section shall be in addition to all other rights allowed by law to a creditor against his debtor.

(8) Where a lien is on goods stored by a merchant in the course of his business the lien may be enforced in accordance with either subsection (1) or (2).

(9) The warehouseman is liable for damages caused by failure to comply with the requirements for sale under this section and in case of willful violation is liable for conversion.

PART 3
BILLS OF LADING: SPECIAL PROVISIONS

§ 7–301. Liability for Non-Receipt or Misdescription; "Said to Contain"; "Shipper's Load and Count"; Improper Handling.

(1) A consignee of a non-negotiable bill who has given value in good faith or a holder to whom a negotiable bill has been duly negotiated relying in either case upon the description therein of the goods, or upon the date therein shown, may recover from the issuer damages caused by the misdating of the bill or the non-receipt or misdescription of the goods, except to the extent that the document indicates that the issuer does not know whether any part or all of the goods in fact were received or conform to the description, as where the description is in

terms of marks or labels or kind, quantity, or condition or the receipt or description is qualified by "contents or condition of contents of packages unknown," "said to contain," "shipper's weight, load and count" or the like, if such indication be true.

(2) When goods are loaded by an issuer who is a common carrier, the issuer must count the packages of goods if package freight and ascertain the kind and quantity if bulk freight. In such cases "shipper's weight, load and count" or other words indicating that the description was made by the shipper are ineffective except as to freight concealed by packages.

(3) When bulk freight is loaded by a shipper who makes available to the issuer adequate facilities for weighing such freight, an issuer who is a common carrier must ascertain the kind and quantity within a reasonable time after receiving the written request of the shipper to do so. In such cases "shipper's weight" or other words of like purport are ineffective.

(4) The issuer may by inserting in the bill the words "shipper's weight, load and count" or other words of like purport indicate that the goods were loaded by the shipper; and if such statement be true the issuer shall not be liable for damages caused by the improper loading. But their omission does not imply liability for such damages.

(5) The shipper shall be deemed to have guaranteed to the issuer the accuracy at the time of shipment of the description, marks, labels, number, kind, quantity, condition and weight, as furnished by him; and the shipper shall indemnify the issuer against damage caused by inaccuracies in such particulars. The right of the issuer to such indemnity shall in no way limit his responsibility and liability under the contract of carriage to any person other than the shipper.

§ 7–302. Through Bills of Lading and Similar Documents.

(1) The issuer of a through bill of lading or other document embodying an undertaking to be performed in part by persons acting as its agents or by connecting carriers is liable to anyone entitled to recover on the document for any breach by such other persons or by a connecting carrier of its obligation under the document but to the extent that the bill covers an undertaking to be performed overseas or in territory not contiguous to the continental United States or an undertaking including matters other than transportation this liability may be varied by agreement of the parties.

(2) Where goods covered by a through bill of lading or other document embodying an undertaking to be performed in part by persons other than the issuer are received by any such person, he is subject with respect to his own performance while the goods are in his possession to the obligation of the issuer. His obligation is discharged by delivery of the goods to another such person pursuant to the document, and does not include liability for breach by any other such persons or by the issuer.

(3) The issuer of such through bill of lading or other document shall be entitled to recover from the connecting carrier or such other person in possession of the goods when the breach of the obligation under the document occurred, the amount it may be required to pay to anyone entitled to recover on the document therefor, as may be evidenced by any receipt, judgment, or transcript thereof, and the amount of any expense reasonably incurred by it in defending any action brought by anyone entitled to recover on the document therefor.

§ 7–303. Diversion; Reconsignment; Change of Instructions.

(1) Unless the bill of lading otherwise provides, the carrier may deliver the goods to a person or destination other than that stated in the bill or may otherwise dispose of the goods on instructions from
    (a) the holder of a negotiable bill; or
    (b) the consignor on a non-negotiable bill notwithstanding contrary instructions from the consignee; or
    (c) the consignee on a non-negotiable bill in the absence of contrary instructions from the consignor, if the goods have arrived at the billed destination or if the consignee is in possession of the bill; or
    (d) the consignee on a non-negotiable bill if he is entitled as against the consignor to dispose of them.

(2) Unless such instructions are noted on a negotiable bill of lading, a person to whom the bill is duly negotiated can hold the bailee according to the original terms.

§ 7–304. Bills of Lading in a Set.

(1) Except where customary in overseas transportation, a bill of lading must not be issued in a set of parts. The issuer is liable for damages caused by violation of this subsection.

(2) Where a bill of lading is lawfully drawn in a set of parts, each of which is numbered and expressed to be valid only if the goods have not been delivered against any other part, the whole of the parts constitute one bill.

(3) Where a bill of lading is lawfully issued in a set of parts and different parts are negotiated to different persons, the title of the holder to whom the first due negotiation is made prevails as to both the document and the goods even though any later holder may have received the goods from the carrier in good faith and discharged the carrier's obligation by surrender of his part.

(4) Any person who negotiates or transfers a single part of a bill of lading drawn in a set is liable to holders of that part as if it were the whole set.

(5) The bailee is obliged to deliver in accordance with Part 4 of this Article against the first presented part of a bill of lading lawfully drawn in a set. Such delivery discharges the bailee's obligation on the whole bill.

§ 7–305. Destination Bills.

(1) Instead of issuing a bill of lading to the consignor at the place of shipment a carrier may at the request of the consignor procure the bill to be issued at destination or at any other place designated in the request.

(2) Upon request of anyone entitled as against the carrier to control the goods while in transit and on surrender of any outstanding bill of lading or other receipt covering such goods, the issuer may procure a substitute bill to be issued at any place designated in the request.

§ 7–306. Altered Bills of Lading.

An unauthorized alteration or filling in of a blank in a bill of lading leaves the bill enforceable according to its original tenor.

§ 7–307. Lien of Carrier.

(1) A carrier has a lien on the goods covered by a bill of lading for charges subsequent to the date of its receipt of the goods for storage or transportation

(including demurrage and terminal charges) and for expenses necessary for preservation of the goods incident to their transportation or reasonably incurred in their sale pursuant to law. But against a purchaser for value of a negotiable bill of lading a carrier's lien is limited to charges stated in the bill or the applicable tariffs, or if no charges are stated then to a reasonable charge.

(2) A lien for charges and expenses under subsection (1) on goods which the carrier was required by law to receive for transportation is effective against the consignor or any person entitled to the goods unless the carrier had notice that the consignor lacked authority to subject the goods to such charges and expenses. Any other lien under subsection (1) is effective against the consignor and any person who permitted the bailor to have control or possession of the goods unless the carrier had notice that the bailor lacked such authority.

(3) A carrier loses his lien on any goods which he voluntarily delivers or which he unjustifiably refuses to deliver.

§ 7–308. Enforcement of Carrier's Lien.

(1) A carrier's lien may be enforced by public or private sale of the goods, in block or in parcels, at any time or place and on any terms which are commercially reasonable, after notifying all persons known to claim an interest in the goods. Such notification must include a statement of the amount due, the nature of the proposed sale and the time and place of any public sale. The fact that a better price could have been obtained by a sale at a different time or in a different method from that selected by the carrier is not of itself sufficient to establish that the sale was not made in a commercially reasonable manner. If the carrier either sells the goods in the usual manner in any recognized market therefor or if he sells at the price current in such market at the time of his sale or if he has otherwise sold in conformity with commercially reasonable practices among dealers in the type of goods sold he has sold in a commercially reasonable manner. A sale of more goods than apparently necessary to be offered to ensure satisfaction of the obligation is not commercially reasonable except in cases covered by the preceding sentence.

(2) Before any sale pursuant to this section any person claiming a right in the goods may pay the amount necessary to satisfy the lien and the reasonable expenses incurred under this section. In that event the goods must not be sold, but must be retained by the carrier subject to the terms of the bill and this Article.

(3) The carrier may buy at any public sale pursuant to this section.

(4) A purchaser in good faith of goods sold to enforce a carrier's lien takes the goods free of any rights of persons against whom the lien was valid, despite noncompliance by the carrier with the requirements of this section.

(5) The carrier may satisfy his lien from the proceeds of any sale pursuant to this section but must hold the balance, if any, for delivery on demand to any person to whom he would have been bound to deliver the goods.

(6) The rights provided by this section shall be in addition to all other rights allowed by law to a creditor against his debtor.

(7) A carrier's lien may be enforced in accordance with either subsection (1) or the procedure set forth in subsection (2) of Section 7–210.

(8) The carrier is liable for damages caused by failure to comply with the requirements for sale under this section and in case of willful violation is liable for conversion.

§ 7–309. Duty of Care; Contractual Limitation of Carrier's Liability.

(1) A carrier who issues a bill of lading whether negotiable or non-negotiable must exercise the degree of care in relation to the goods which a reasonably careful man would exercise under like circumstances. This subsection does not repeal or change any law or rule of law which imposes liability upon a common carrier for damages not caused by its negligence.

(2) Damages may be limited by a provision that the carrier's liability shall not exceed a value stated in the document if the carrier's rates are dependent upon value and the consignor by the carrier's tariffs is afforded an opportunity to declare a higher value or a value as lawfully provided in the tariff, or where no tariff is filed he is otherwise advised of such opportunity; but no such limitation is effective with respect to the carrier's liability for conversion to its own use.

(3) Reasonable provisions as to the time and manner of presenting claims and instituting actions based on the shipment may be included in a bill of lading or tariff.

PART 4
WAREHOUSE RECEIPTS AND BILLS OF LADING: GENERAL OBLIGATIONS

§ 7–401. Irregularities in Issue of Receipt or Bill or Conduct of Issuer.

The obligations imposed by this Article on an issuer apply to a document of title regardless of the fact that
   (a) the document may not comply with the requirements of this Article or of any other law or regulation regarding its issue, form or content; or
   (b) the issuer may have violated laws regulating the conduct of his business; or
   (c) the goods covered by the document were owned by the bailee at the time the document was issued; or
   (d) the person issuing the document does not come within the definition of warehouseman if it purports to be a warehouse receipt.

§ 7–402. Duplicate Receipt or Bill; Overissue.

Neither a duplicate nor any other document of title purporting to cover goods already represented by an outstanding document of the same issuer confers any right in the goods, except as provided in the case of bills in a set, overissue of documents for fungible goods and substitutes for lost, stolen or destroyed documents. But the issuer is liable for damages caused by his overissue or failure to identify a duplicate document as such by conspicuous notation on its face.

§ 7–403. Obligation of Warehouseman or Carrier to Deliver; Excuse.*

(1) The bailee must deliver the goods to a person entitled under the document who complies with subsections (2) and (3), unless and to the extent that the bailee establishes any of the following:
   (a) delivery of the goods to a person whose receipt was rightful as against the claimant;
   (b) damage to or delay, loss or destruction of the goods for which the bailee is not liable, but the burden of establishing negligence in such cases is on the person entitled under the document;

    (c) previous sale or other disposition of the goods in lawful enforcement of a lien or on warehouseman's lawful termination of storage;

    (d) the exercise by a seller of his right to stop delivery pursuant to the provisions of the Article on Sales (Section 2–705);

    (e) a diversion, reconsignment or other disposition pursuant to the provisions of this Article (Section 7–303) or tariff regulating such right;

    (f) release, satisfaction or any other fact affording a personal defense against the claimant;

    (g) any other lawful excuse.

(2) A person claiming goods covered by a document of title must satisfy the bailee's lien where the bailee so requests or where the bailee is prohibited by law from delivering the goods until the charges are paid.

(3) Unless the person claiming is one against whom the document confers no right under Section 7–503 (1), he must surrender for cancellation or notation of partial deliveries any outstanding negotiable document covering the goods, and the bailee must cancel the document or conspicuously note the partial delivery thereon or be liable to any person to whom the document is duly negotiated.

(4) "Person entitled under the document" means holder in the case of a negotiable document, or the person to whom delivery is to be made by the terms of or pursuant to written instructions under a non-negotiable document.

§ 7–404. No Liability for Good Faith Delivery Pursuant to Receipt or Bill.

A bailee who in good faith including observance of reasonable commercial standards has received goods and delivered or otherwise disposed of them according to the terms of the document of title or pursuant to this Article is not liable therefor. This rule applies even though the person from whom he received the goods had no authority to procure the document or to dispose of the goods and even though the person to whom he delivered the goods had no authority to receive them.

PART 5
WAREHOUSE RECEIPTS AND BILLS OF LADING: NEGOTIATION AND TRANSFER

§ 7–501. Form of Negotiation and Requirements of "Due Negotiation."

(1) A negotiable document of title running to the order of a named person is negotiated by his indorsement and delivery. After his indorsement in blank or to bearer any person can negotiate it by delivery alone.

    (2) (a) A negotiable document of title is also negotiated by delivery alone when by its original terms it runs to bearer.

    (b) When a document running to the order of a named person is delivered to him the effect is the same as if the document had been negotiated.

(3) Negotiation of a negotiable document of title after it has been indorsed to a specified person requires indorsement by the special indorsee as well as delivery.

(4) A negotiable document of title is "duly negotiated" when it is negotiated in the manner stated in this section to a holder who purchases it in good faith without notice of any defense against or claim to it on the part of any person and for value, unless it is established that the negotiation is not in the regular course of business or financing or involves receiving the document in settlement or payment of a money obligation.

(5) Indorsement of a non-negotiable document neither makes it negotiable nor adds to the transferee's rights.

(6) The naming in a negotiable bill of a person to be notified of the arrival of the goods does not limit the negotiability of the bill nor constitute notice to a purchaser thereof of any interest of such person in the goods.

§ 7–502. Rights Acquired by Due Negotiation.

(1) Subject to the following section and to the provisions of Section 7–205 on fungible goods, a holder to whom a negotiable document of title has been duly negotiated acquires thereby:

(a) title to the document;
(b) title to the goods;
(c) all rights accruing under the law of agency or estoppel, including rights to goods delivered to the bailee after the document was issued; and
(d) the direct obligation of the issuer to hold or deliver the goods according to the terms of the document free of any defense or claim by him except those arising under the terms of the document or under this Article. In the case of a delivery order the bailee's obligation accrues only upon acceptance and the obligation acquired by the holder is that the issuer and any indorser will procure the acceptance of the bailee.

(2) Subject to the following section, title and rights so acquired are not defeated by any stoppage of the goods represented by the document or by surrender of such goods by the bailee, and are not impaired even though the negotiation or any prior negotiation constituted a breach of duty or even though any person has been deprived of possession of the document by misrepresentation, fraud, accident, mistake, duress, loss, theft or conversion, or even though a previous sale or other transfer of the goods or document has been made to a third person.

§ 7–503. Document of Title to Goods Defeated in Certain Cases.

(1) A document of title confers no right in goods against a person who before issuance of the document had a legal interest or a perfected security interest in them and who neither

(a) delivered or entrusted them or any document of title covering them to the bailor or his nominee with actual or apparent authority to ship, store or sell or with power to obtain delivery under this Article (Section 7–403) or with power of disposition under this Act (Sections 2–403 and 9–307) or other statute or rule of law; nor
(b) acquiesced in the procurement by the bailor or his nominee of any document of title.

(2) Title to goods based upon an unaccepted delivery order is subject to the rights of anyone to whom a negotiable warehouse receipt or bill of lading covering the goods has been duly negotiated. Such a title may be defeated under the next section to the same extent as the rights of the issuer or a transferee from the issuer.

(3) Title to goods based upon a bill of lading issued to a freight forwarder is subject to the rights of anyone to whom a bill issued by the freight forwarder is duly negotiated; but delivery by the carrier in accordance with Part 4 of this Article pursuant to its own bill of lading discharges the carrier's obligation to deliver.

§ 7–504. Rights Acquired in the Absence of Due Negotiation; Effect of Diversion; Seller's Stoppage of Delivery.

(1) A transferee of a document, whether negotiable or non-negotiable, to whom the document has been delivered but not duly negotiated, acquires the title and rights which his transferor had or had actual authority to convey.

(2) In the case of a non-negotiable document, until but not after the bailee receives notification of the transfer, the rights of the transferee may be defeated

    (a) by those creditors of the transferor who could treat the sale as void under Section 2–402; or

    (b) by a buyer from the transferor in ordinary course of business if the bailee had delivered the goods to the buyer or received notification of his rights; or

    (c) as against the bailee by good faith dealings of the bailee with the transferor.

(3) A diversion or other change of shipping instructions by the consignor in a non-negotiable bill of lading which causes the bailee not to deliver to the consignee defeats the consignee's title to the goods if they have been delivered to a buyer in ordinary course of business and in any event defeats the consignee's rights against the bailee.

(4) Delivery pursuant to a non-negotiable document may be stopped by a seller under Section 2–705, and subject to the requirement of due notification there provided. A bailee honoring the seller's instructions is entitled to be indemnified by the seller against any resulting loss or expense.

§ 7–505. Indorser Not a Guarantor for Other Parties.

The indorsement of a document of title issued by a bailee does not make the indorser liable for any default by the bailee or by previous indorsers.

§ 7–506. Delivery Without Indorsement: Right to Compel Indorsement.

The transferee of a negotiable document of title has a specifically enforceable right to have his transferor supply any necessary indorsement but the transfer becomes a negotiation only as of the time the indorsement is supplied.

§ 7–507. Warranties on Negotiation or Transfer of Receipt or Bill.

Where a person negotiates or transfers a document of title for value otherwise than as a mere intermediary under the next following section, then unless otherwise agreed he warrants to his immediate purchaser only in addition to any warranty made in selling the goods

    (a) that the document is genuine; and

    (b) that he has no knowledge of any fact which would impair its validity or worth; and

    (c) that his negotiation or transfer is rightful and fully effective with respect to the title to the document and the goods it represents.

§ 7–508. Warranties of Collecting Bank as to Documents.

A collecting bank or other intermediary known to be entrusted with documents on behalf of another or with collection of a draft or other claim against delivery of documents warrants by such delivery of the documents only its own good faith and authority. This rule applies even though the intermediary has purchased or made advances against the claim or draft to be collected.

PART 6
WAREHOUSE RECEIPTS AND BILLS OF LADING: MISCELLANEOUS PROVISIONS

§ 7–601. Lost and Missing Documents.

(1) If a document has been lost, stolen or destroyed, a court may order delivery of the goods or issuance of a substitute document and the bailee may without liability to any person comply with such order. If the document was negotiable the claimant must post security approved by the court to indemnify any person who may suffer loss as a result of non-surrender of the document. If the document was not negotiable, such security may be required at the discretion of the court. The court may also in its discretion order payment of the bailee's reasonable costs and counsel fees.

(2) A bailee who without court order delivers goods to a person claiming under a missing negotiable document is liable to any person injured thereby, and if the delivery is not in good faith becomes liable for conversion. Delivery in good faith is not conversion if made in accordance with a filed classification or tariff or, where no classification or tariff is filed, if the claimant posts security with the bailee in an amount at least double the value of the goods at the time of posting to indemnify any person injured by the delivery who files a notice of claim within one year after the delivery.

§ 7–602. Attachment of Goods Covered by a Negotiable Document.

Except where the document was originally issued upon delivery of the goods by a person who had no power to dispose of them, no lien attaches by virtue of any judicial process to goods in the possession of a bailee for which a negotiable document of title is outstanding unless the document be first surrendered to the bailee or its negotiation enjoined, and the bailee shall not be compelled to deliver the goods pursuant to process until the document is surrendered to him or impounded by the court. One who purchases the document for value without notice of the process or injunction takes free of the lien imposed by judicial process.

§ 7–603. Conflicting Claims; Interpleader.

If more than one person claims title or possession of the goods, the bailee is excused from delivery until he has had a reasonable time to ascertain the validity of the adverse claims or to bring an action to compel all claimants to interplead and may compel such interpleader, either in defending an action for non-delivery of the goods, or by original action, whichever is appropriate.

ARTICLE 9. Secured Transactions; Sales of Accounts and Chattel Paper

PART 1
SHORT TITLE, APPLICABILITY AND DEFINITIONS

§ 9–101. Short Title.

This Article shall be known and may be cited as Uniform Commercial Code—Secured Transactions.

§ 9–102. Policy and Subject Matter of Article.**

(1) Except as otherwise provided in Section 9–104 on excluded transactions, this Article applies

(a) to any transaction (regardless of its form) which is intended to create a security interest in personal property or fixtures including goods, documents, instruments, general intangibles, chattel paper or accounts; and also

(b) to any sale of accounts or chattel paper.

(2) This Article applies to security interests created by contract including pledge, assignment, chattel mortgage, chattel trust, trust deed, factor's lien, equipment trust, conditional sale, trust receipt, other lien or title retention contract and lease or consignment intended as security. This Article does not apply to statutory liens except as provided in Section 9–310.

(3) The application of this Article to a security interest in a secured obligation is not affected by the fact that the obligation is itself secured by a transaction or interest to which this Article does not apply.

§ 9–103. Perfection of Security Interests in Multiple State Transactions.**

(1) Documents, instruments and ordinary goods.

(a) This subsection applies to documents and instruments and to goods other than those covered by a certificate of title described in subsection (2), mobile goods described in subsection (3), and minerals described in subsection (5).

(b) Except as otherwise provided in this subsection, perfection and the effect of perfection or non-perfection of a security interest in collateral are governed by the law of the jurisdiction where the collateral is when the last event occurs on which is based the assertion that the security interest is perfected or unperfected.

(c) If the parties to a transaction creating a purchase money security interest in goods in one jurisdiction understand at the time that the security interest attaches that the goods will be kept in another jurisdiction, then the law of the other jurisdiction governs the perfection and the effect of perfection or non-perfection of the security interest from the time it attaches until thirty days after the debtor receives possession of the goods and thereafter if the goods are taken to the other jurisdiction before the end of the thirty-day period.

(d) When collateral is brought into and kept in this state while subject to a security interest perfected under the law of the jurisdiction from which the collateral was removed, the security interest remains perfected, but if action is required by Part 3 of this Article to perfect the security interest,

(i) if the action is not taken before the expiration of the period of perfection in the other jurisdiction or the end of four months after the collateral is brought into this state, whichever period first expires, the security interest becomes unperfected at the end of that period and is thereafter deemed to have been unperfected as against a person who became a purchaser after removal;

(ii) if the action is taken before the expiration of the period specified

in subparagraph (i), the security interest continues perfected thereafter;

(iii) for the purpose of priority over a buyer of consumer goods (subsection (2) of Section 9–307), the period of the effectiveness of a filing in the jurisdiction from which the collateral is removed is governed by the rules with respect to perfection in subparagraphs (i) and (ii).

(2) Certificate of title.

(a) This subsection applies to goods covered by a certificate of title issued under a statute of this state or of another jurisdiction under the law of which indication of a security interest on the certificate is required as a condition of perfection.

(b) Except as otherwise provided in this subsection, perfection and the effect of perfection or non-perfection of the security interest are governed by the law (including the conflict of laws rules) of the jurisdiction issuing the certificate until four months after the goods are removed from that jurisdiction and thereafter until the goods are registered in another juris-diction, but in any event not beyond surrender of the certificate. After the expiration of that period, the goods are not covered by the certificate of title within the meaning of this section.

(c) Except with respect to the rights of a buyer described in the next para-graph, a security interest, perfected in another jurisdiction otherwise than by notation on a certificate of title, in goods brought into this state and thereafter covered by a certificate of title issued by this state is subject to the rules stated in paragraph (d) of subsection (1).

(d) If goods are brought into this state while a security interest therein is perfected in any manner under the law of the jurisdiction from which the goods are removed and a certificate of title is issued by this state and the certificate does not show that the goods are subject to the security interest or that they may be subject to security interests not shown on the certificate, the security interest is subordinate to the rights of a buyer of the goods who is not in the business of selling goods of that kind to the extent that he gives value and receives delivery of the goods after issuance of the certificate and without knowledge of the security interest.

(3) Accounts, general intangibles and mobile goods.

(a) This subsection applies to accounts (other than an account described in subsection (5) on minerals) and general intangibles and to goods which are mobile and which are of a type normally used in more than one jurisdiction, such as motor vehicles, trailers, rolling stock, airplanes, ship-ping containers, road building and construction machinery and commer-cial harvesting machinery and the like, if the goods are equipment or are inventory leased or held for lease by the debtor to others, and are not covered by a certificate of title described in subsection (2).

(b) The law (including the conflict of laws rules) of the jurisdiction in which the debtor is located governs the perfection and the effect of perfection or non-perfection of the security interest.

(c) If, however, the debtor is located in a jurisdiction which is not a part of the United States, and which does not provide for perfection of the security interest by filing or recording in that jurisdiction, the law of the jurisdiction in the United States in which the debtor has its major executive office in the United States governs the perfection and the effect of perfection or non-perfection of the security interest through filing. In the alternative, if the debtor is located in a jurisdiction which is not a part of the United States or Canada and the collateral is accounts or general intangibles for money due or to become due, the security interest may be perfected by notification to the account debtor. As used in this paragraph, "United States" includes its territories and possessions and the Commonwealth of Puerto Rico.

(d) A debtor shall be deemed located at his place of business if he has one, at his chief executive office if he has more than one place of business, otherwise at his residence. If, however, the debtor is a foreign air carrier under the Federal Aviation Act of 1958, as amended, it shall be deemed located at the designated office of the agent upon whom service of process may be made on behalf of the foreign air carrier.

(e) A security interest perfected under the law of the jurisdiction of the location of the debtor is perfected until the expiration of four months after a change of the debtor's location to another jurisdiction, or until perfection would have ceased by the law of the first jurisdiction, whichever period first expires. Unless perfected in the new jurisdiction before the end of that period, it becomes unperfected thereafter and is deemed to have been unperfected as against a person who became a purchaser after the change.

(4) Chattel paper.

The rules stated for goods in subsection (1) apply to a possessory security interest in chattel paper. The rules stated for accounts in subsection (3) apply to a non-possessory security interest in chattel paper, but the security interest may not be perfected by notification to the account debtor.

(5) Minerals.

Perfection and the effect of perfection or non-perfection of a security interest which is created by a debtor who has an interest in minerals or the like (including oil and gas) before extraction and which attaches thereto as extracted, or which attaches to an account resulting from the sale thereof at the wellhead or minehead are governed by the law (including the conflict of laws rules) of the jurisdiction wherein the wellhead or minehead is located.

§ 9–104. Transactions Excluded From Article.**

This article does not apply

(a) to a security interest subject to any statute of the United States, to the extent that such statute governs the rights of parties to and third parties affected by transactions in particular types of property; or

(b) to a landlord's lien; or

(c) to a lien given by statute or other rule of law for services or materials except as provided in Section 9–310 on priority of such liens; or

(d) to a transfer of a claim for wages, salary or other compensation of an employee; or

(e) to a transfer by a government or governmental subdivision or agency; or

(f) to a sale of accounts or chattel paper as part of a sale of the business out of which they arose, or an assignment of accounts or chattel paper which is for the purpose of collection only, or a transfer of a right to payment under a contract to an assignee who is also to do the performance under the contract or a transfer of a single account to an assignee in whole or partial satisfaction of a preexisting indebtedness; or

(g) to a transfer of an interest in or claim in or under any policy of insurance, except as provided with respect to proceeds (Section 9–306) and priorities in proceeds (Section 9–312); or

(h) to a right represented by a judgment (other than a judgment taken on a right to payment which was collateral); or

(i) to any right of set-off; or

(j) except to the extent that provision is made for fixtures in Section 9–313, to the creation or transfer of an interest in or lien on real estate, including a lease or rents thereunder; or

(k) to a transfer in whole or in part of any claim arising out of tort; or

(l) to a transfer of an interest in any deposit account (subsection (1) of Section 9–105), except as provided with respect to proceeds (Section 9–306) and priorities in proceeds (Section 9–312).

§ 9–105. Definitions and Index of Definitions.**

(1) In this Article unless the context otherwise requires:

(a) "Account debtor" means the person who is obligated on an account, chattel paper or general intangible;

(b) "Chattel paper" means a writing or writings which evidence both a monetary obligation and a security interest in or a lease of specific goods, but a charter or other contract involving the use or hire of a vessel is not chattel paper. When a transaction is evidenced both by such a security agreement or a lease and by an instrument or a series of instruments, the group of writings taken together constitutes chattel paper;

(c) "Collateral" means the property subject to a security interest, and includes accounts and chattel paper which have been sold;

(d) "Debtor" means the person who owes payment or other performance of the obligation secured, whether or not he owns or has rights in the collateral, and includes the seller of accounts or chattel paper. Where the debtor and the owner of the collateral are not the same person, the term "debtor" means the owner of the collateral in any provision of the Article dealing with the collateral, the obligor in any provision dealing with the obligation, and may include both where the context so requires;

(e) "Deposit account" means a demand, time, savings, passbook or like account maintained with a bank, savings and loan association, credit union or like organization, other than an account evidenced by a certificate of deposit;

(f) "Document" means document of title as defined in the general definitions of Article 1 (Section 1–201), and a receipt of the kind described in subsection (2) of Section 7–201;

(g) "Encumbrance" includes real estate mortgages and other liens on real estate and all other rights in real estate that are not ownership interests;

(h) "Goods" includes all things which are movable at the time the security interest attaches or which are fixtures (Section 9–313), but does not include money, documents, instruments, accounts, chattel paper, general intangibles, or minerals or the like (including oil and gas) before extraction. "Goods" also includes standing timber which is to be cut and removed under a conveyance or contract for sale, the unborn young of animals, and growing crops;

(i) "Instrument" means a negotiable instrument (defined in Section 3–104), or a security (defined in Section 8–102) or any other writing which evidences a right to the payment of money and is not itself a security agreement or lease and is of a type which is in ordinary course of business transferred by delivery with any necessary indorsement or assignment;

(j) "Mortgage" means a consensual interest created by a real estate mortgage, a trust deed on real estate, or the like;

(k) An advance is made "pursuant to commitment" if the secured party has bound himself to make it, whether or not a subsequent event of default or other event not within his control) has relieved or may relieve him from his obligation;

(l) "Security agreement" means an agreement which creates or provides for a security interest;

(m) "Secured party" means a lender, seller or other person in whose favor there is a security interest, including a person to whom accounts or chattel paper have been sold. When the holders of obligations issued under an indenture of trust, equipment trust agreement or the like are represented by a trustee or other person, the representative is the secured party;

(n) "Transmitting utility" means any person primarily engaged in the railroad, street railway or trolley bus business, the electric or electronics communications transmission business, the transmission of goods by pipeline, or the transmission or the production and transmission of electricity, steam, gas or water, or the provision of sewer service.

(2) Other definitions applying to this Article and the sections in which they appear are:

"Account." Section 9–106.
"Attach." Section 9–203.
"Construction mortgage." Section 9–313(1).
"Consumer goods." Section 9–109(1).
"Equipment." Section 9–109(2).
"Farm products." Section 9–109(3).
"Fixture." Section 9–313(1).
"Fixture filing." Section 9–313(1).
"General intangibles." Section 9–106.
"Inventory." Section 9–109(4).
"Lien creditor." Section 9–301(3).
"Proceeds." Section 9–306(1).
"Purchase money security interest." Section 9–107.
"United States." Section 9–103.

(3) The following definitions in other Articles apply to this Article:

"Check." Section 3–104.

"Contract for sale." Section 2–106.
"Holder in due course." Section 3–302.
"Note." Section 3–104.
"Sale." Section 2–106.

(4) In addition Article 1 contains general definitions and principles of construction and interpretation applicable throughout this Article.

§ 9–106. Definitions: "Account"; "General Intangibles."**

"Account" means any right to payment for goods sold or leased or for services rendered which is not evidenced by an instrument or chattel paper, whether or not it has been earned by performance. "General intangibles" means any personal property (including things in action) other than goods, accounts, chattel paper, documents, instruments, and money. All rights to payment earned or unearned under a charter or other contract involving the use or hire of a vessel and all rights incident to the charter or contract are accounts.

§ 9–107. Definitions: "Purchase Money Security Interest."

A security interest is a "purchase money security interest" to the extent that it is

(a) taken or retained by the seller of the collateral to secure all or part of its price; or
(b) taken by a person who by making advances or incurring an obligation gives value to enable the debtor to acquire rights in or the use of collateral if such value is in fact so used.

§ 9–108. When After-Acquired Collateral Not Security for Antecedent Debt.

Where a secured party makes an advance, incurs an obligation, releases a perfected security interest, or otherwise gives new value which is to be secured in whole or in part by after-acquired property his security interest in the after-acquired collateral shall be deemed to be taken for new value and not as security for an antecedent debt if the debtor acquires his rights in such collateral either in the ordinary course of his business or under a contract of purchase made pursuant to the security agreement within a reasonable time after new value is given.

§ 9–109. Classification of Goods; "Consumer Goods"; "Equipment"; "Farm Products"; "Inventory."

Goods are

(1) "consumer goods" if they are used or bought for use primarily for personal, family or household purposes;

(2) "equipment" if they are used or bought for use primarily in business (including farming or a profession) or by a debtor who is a non-profit organization or a governmental subdivision or agency or if the goods are not included in the definitions of inventory, farm products or consumer goods;

(3) "farm products" if they are crops or livestock or supplies used or produced in farming operations or if they are products of crops or livestock in their unmanufactured states (such as ginned cotton, wool-clip, maple syrup, milk and eggs), and if they are in the possession of a debtor engaged in raising, fattening, grazing or other farming operations. If goods are farm products they are neither equipment nor inventory;

(4) "inventory" if they are held by a person who holds them for sale or lease or to be furnished under contracts of service or if he has so furnished them, or if they are raw materials, work in process or materials used or consumed in a business. Inventory of a person is not to be classified as his equipment.

§ 9–110. Sufficiency of Description.

For the purposes of this Article any description of personal property or real estate is sufficient whether or not it is specific if it reasonably identifies what is described.

§ 9–111. Applicability of Bulk Transfer Laws.

The creation of a security interest is not a bulk transfer under Article 6 (see Section 6–103).

§ 9–112. Where Collateral Is Not Owned by Debtor.

Unless otherwise agreed, when a secured party knows that collateral is owned by a person who is not the debtor, the owner of the collateral is entitled to receive from the secured party any surplus under Section 9–502(2) or under Section 9–504(1), and is not liable for the debt or for any deficiency after resale, and he has the same right as the debtor

    (a) to receive statements under Section 9–208;

    (b) to receive notice of and to object to a secured party's proposal to retain the collateral in satisfaction of the indebtedness under Section 9–505;

    (c) to redeem the collateral under Section 9–506;

    (d) to obtain injunctive or other relief under Section 9–507(1); and

    (e) to recover losses caused to him under Section 9–208(2).

§ 9–113. Security Interests Arising Under Article on Sales.

A security interest arising solely under the Article on Sales (Article 2) is subject to the provisions of this Article except that to the extent that and so long as the debtor does not have or does not lawfully obtain possession of the goods

    (a) no security agreement is necessary to make the security interest enforceable; and

    (b) no filing is required to perfect the security interest; and

    (c) the rights of the secured party on default by the debtor are governed by the Article on Sales (Article 2).

§ 9–114. Consignment.**

(1) A person who delivers goods under a consignment which is not a security interest and who would be required to file under this Article by paragraph (3)(c) of Section 2–326 has priority over a secured party who is or becomes a creditor of the consignee and who would have a perfected security interest in the goods if they were the property of the consignee, and also has priority with respect to identifiable cash proceeds received on or before delivery of the goods to a buyer, if

    (a) the consignor complies with the filing provision of the Article on Sales with respect to consignments (paragraph (3)(c) of Section 2–326) before the consignee receives possession of the goods; and

    (b) the consignor gives notification in writing to the holder of the security interest if the holder has filed a financing statement covering the same types of goods before the date of the filing made by the consignor; and

(c) the holder of the security interest receives the notification within five years before the consignee receives possession of the goods; and

(d) the notification states that the consignor expects to deliver goods on consignment to the consignee, describing the goods by item or type.

(2) In the case of a consignment which is not a security interest and in which the requirements of the preceding subsection have not been met, a person who delivers goods to another is subordinate to a person who would have a perfected security interest in the goods if they were the property of the debtor.

PART 2
VALIDITY OF SECURITY AGREEMENT AND RIGHTS OF PARTIES THERETO

§ 9–201. General Validity of Security Agreement.

Except as otherwise provided by this Act a security agreement is effective according to its terms between the parties, against purchasers of the collateral and against creditors. Nothing in this Article validates any charge or practice illegal under any statute or regulation thereunder governing usury, small loans, retail installment sales, or the like, or extends the application of any such statute or regulation to any transaction not otherwise subject thereto.

§ 9–202. Title to Collateral Immaterial.

Each provision of this Article with regard to rights, obligations and remedies applies whether title to collateral is in the secured party or in the debtor.

§ 9–203. Attachment and Enforceability of Security Interest; Proceeds; Formal Requisites.**

(1) Subject to the provisions of Section 4–208 on the security interest of a collecting bank and Section 9–113 on a security interest arising under the Article on Sales, a security interest is not enforceable against the debtor or third parties with respect to the collateral and does not attach unless

(a) the collateral is in the possession of the secured party pursuant to agreement, or the debtor has signed a security agreement which contains a description of the collateral and in addition, when the security interest covers crops growing or to be grown or timber to be cut, a description of the land concerned; and

(b) value has been given; and

(c) the debtor has rights in the collateral.

(2) A security interest attaches when it becomes enforceable against the debtor with respect to the collateral. Attachment occurs as soon as all of the events specified in subsection (1) have taken place unless explicit agreement postpones the time of attaching.

(3) Unless otherwise agreed a security agreement gives the secured party the rights to proceeds provided by Section 9–306.

(4) A transaction, although subject to this Article, is also subject to . . . . ,* and in the case of conflict between the provisions of this Article and any such statute, the provisions of such statute control. Failure to comply with any applicable statute has only the effect which is specified therein.

§ 9–204. After-Acquired Property; Future Advances.**

(1) Except as provided in subsection (2), a security agreement may provide that any or all obligations covered by the security agreement are to be secured by after-acquired collateral.

(2) No security interest attaches under an after-acquired property clause to consumer goods other than accessions (Section 9–314) when given as additional security unless the debtor acquires rights in them within ten days after the secured party gives value.

(3) Obligations covered by a security agreement may include future advances or other value whether or not the advances or value are given pursuant to commitment (subsection (1) of Section 9–105).

§ 9–205. Use or Disposition of Collateral Without Accounting Permissible.**

A security interest is not invalid or fraudulent against creditors by reason of liberty in the debtor to use, commingle or dispose of all or part of the collateral (including returned or repossessed goods) or to collect or compromise accounts or chattel paper, or to accept the return of goods or make repossessions, or to use, commingle or dispose of proceeds, or by reason of the failure of the secured party to require the debtor to account for proceeds or replace collateral. This section does not relax the requirements of possession where perfection of a security interest depends upon possession of the collateral by the secured party or by a bailee.

§ 9–206. Agreement Not to Assert Defenses Against Assignee; Modification of Sales Warranties Where Security Agreement Exists.

(1) Subject to any statute or decision which establishes a different rule for buyers or lessees of consumer goods, an agreement by a buyer or lessee that he will not assert against an assignee any claim or defense which he may have against the seller or lessor is enforceable by an assignee who takes his assignment for value, in good faith and without notice of a claim or defense, except as to defenses of a type which may be asserted against a holder in due course of a negotiable instrument under the Article on Commercial Paper (Article 3). A buyer who as part of one transaction signs both a negotiable instrument and a security agreement makes such an agreement.

(2) When a seller retains a purchase money security interest in goods the Article on Sales (Article 2) governs the sale and any disclaimer, limitation or modification of the seller's warranties.

§ 9–207. Rights and Duties When Collateral Is in Secured Party's Possession.

(1) A secured party must use reasonable care in the custody and preservation of collateral in his possession. In the case of an instrument or chattel paper reasonable care includes taking necessary steps to preserve rights against prior parties unless otherwise agreed.

(2) Unless otherwise agreed, when collateral is in the secured party's possession
  (a) reasonable expenses (including the cost of any insurance and payment of taxes or other charges) incurred in the custody, preservation, use or operation of the collateral are chargeable to the debtor and are secured by the collateral;
  (b) the risk of accidental loss or damage is on the debtor to the extent of any deficiency in any effective insurance coverage;

(c) the secured party may hold as additional security any increase or profits (except money) received from the collateral, but money so received, unless remitted to the debtor, shall be applied in reduction of the secured obligation;

(d) the secured party must keep the collateral identifiable but fungible collateral may be commingled;

(e) the secured party may repledge the collateral upon terms which do not impair the debtor's right to redeem it.

(3) A secured party is liable for any loss caused by his failure to meet any obligation imposed by the preceding subsections but does not lose his security interest.

(4) A secured party may use or operate the collateral for the purpose of preserving the collateral or its value or pursuant to the order of a court of appropriate jurisdiction or, except in the case of consumer goods, in the manner and to the extent provided in the security agreement.

§ 9–208. Request for Statement of Account or List of Collateral.

(1) A debtor may sign a statement indicating what he believes to be the aggregate amount of unpaid indebtedness as of a specified date and may send it to the secured party with a request that the statement be approved or corrected and returned to the debtor. When the security agreement or any other record kept by the secured party identifies the collateral a debtor may similarly request the secured party to approve or correct a list of the collateral.

(2) The secured party must comply with such a request within two weeks after receipt by sending a written correction or approval. If the secured party claims a security interest in all of a particular type of collateral owned by the debtor he may indicate that fact in his reply and need not approve or correct an itemized list of such collateral. If the secured party without reasonable excuse fails to comply he is liable for any loss caused to the debtor thereby; and if the debtor has properly included in his request a good faith statement of the obligation or a list of the collateral or both the secured party may claim a security interest only as shown in the statement against persons misled by his failure to comply. If he no longer has an interest in the obligation or collateral at the time the request is received he must disclose the name and address of any successor in interest known to him and he is liable for any loss caused to the debtor as a result of failure to disclose. A successor in interest is not subject to this section until a request is received by him.

(3) A debtor is entitled to such a statement once every six months without charge. The secured party may require payment of a charge not exceeding $10 for each additional statement furnished.

PART 3

RIGHTS OF THIRD PARTIES; PERFECTED AND UNPERFECTED SECURITY
INTERESTS; RULES OF PRIORITY

§ 9–301. Persons Who Take Priority Over Unperfected Security Interests; Rights of "Lien Creditor."**

(1) Except as otherwise provided in subsection (2), an unperfected security interest is subordinate to the rights of

    (a) persons entitled to priority under Section 9–312;

    (b) a person who becomes a lien creditor before the security interest is perfected;

    (c) in the case of goods, instruments, documents, and chattel paper, a person who is not a secured party and who is a transferee in bulk or other buyer not in ordinary course of business or is a buyer of farm products in ordinary course of business, to the extent that he gives value and receives delivery of the collateral without knowledge of the security interest and before it is perfected;

    (d) in the case of accounts and general intangibles, a person who is not a secured party and who is a transferee to the extent that he gives value without knowledge of the security interest and before it is perfected.

(2) If the secured party files with respect to a purchase money security interest before or within ten days after the debtor receives possession of the collateral, he takes priority over the rights of a transferee in bulk or of a lien creditor which arise between the time the security interest attaches and the time of filing.

(3) A "lien creditor" means a creditor who has acquired a lien on the property involved by attachment, levy or the like and includes an assignee for benefit of creditors from the time of assignment, and a trustee in bankruptcy from the date of the filing of the petition or a receiver in equity from the time of appointment.

(4) A person who becomes a lien creditor while a security interest is perfected takes subject to the security interest only to the extent that it secures advances made before he becomes a lien creditor or within 45 days thereafter or made without knowledge of the lien or pursuant to a commitment entered into without knowledge of the lien.

§ 9–302. When Filing Is Required to Perfect Security Interest; Security Interests to Which Filing Provisions of This Article Do Not Apply.**

(1) A financing statement must be filed to perfect all security interests except the following:

    (a) a security interest in collateral in possession of the secured party under Section 9–305;

    (b) a security interest temporarily perfected in instruments or documents without delivery under Section 9–304 or in proceeds for a 10 day period under Section 9–306;

    (c) a security interest created by an assignment of a beneficial interest in a trust or a decedent's estate;

    (d) a purchase money security interest in consumer goods; but filing is required for a motor vehicle required to be registered; and fixture filing is required for priority over conflicting interests in fixtures to the extent provided in Section 9–313;

    (e) an assignment of accounts which does not alone or in conjunction with other assignments to the same assignee transfer a significant part of the outstanding accounts of the assignor;

    (f) a security interest of a collecting bank (Section 4–208) or arising under the Article on Sales (see Section 9–113) or covered in subsection (3) of this section;

    (g) an assignment for the benefit of all the creditors of the transferor, and subsequent transfers by the assignee thereunder.

(2) If a secured party assigns a perfected security interest, no filing under this Article is required in order to continue the perfected status of the security interest against creditors of and transferees from the original debtor.

(3) The filing of a financing statement otherwise required by this Article is not necessary or effective to perfect a security interest in property subject to

(a) a statute or treaty of the United States which provides for a national or international registration or a national or international certificate of title or which specifies a place of filing different from that specified in this Article for filing of the security interest; or

(b) the following statutes of this state; [list any certificate of title statute covering automobiles, trailers, mobile homes, boats, farm tractors, or the like, and any central filing statute*.]; but during any period in which collateral is inventory held for sale by a person who is in the business of selling goods of that kind, the filing provisions of this article (Part 4) apply to a security interest in that collateral created by him as debtor; or

(c) a certificate of title statute of another jurisdiction under the law of which indication of a security interest on the certificate is required as a condition of perfection (subsection (2) of Section 9–103).

(4) Compliance with a statute or treaty described in subsection (3) is equivalent to the filing of a financing statement under this Article, and a security interest in property subject to the statute or treaty can be perfected only by compliance therewith except as provided in Section 9–103 on multiple state transactions. Duration and renewal of perfection of a security interest perfected by compliance with the statute or treaty are governed by the provisions of the statute or treaty; in other respects the security interest is subject to this Article.

§ 9–303. When Security Interest Is Perfected; Continuity of Perfection.

(1) A security interest is perfected when it has attached and when all of the applicable steps required for perfection have been taken. Such steps are specified in Sections 9–302, 9–304, 9–305 and 9–306. If such steps are taken before the security interest attaches, it is perfected at the time when it attaches.

(2) If a security interest is originally perfected in any way permitted under this Article and is subsequently perfected in some other way under this Article, without an intermediate period when it was unperfected, the security interest shall be deemed to be perfected continuously for the purposes of this Article.

§ 9–304. Perfection of Security Interest in Instruments, Documents, and Goods Covered by Documents; Perfection by Permissive Filing; Temporary Perfection Without Filing or Transfer of Possession.**

(1) A security interest in chattel paper or negotiable documents may be perfected by filing. A security interest in money or instruments (other than instruments which constitute part of chattel paper) can be perfected only by the second party's taking possession, except as provided in subsections (4) and (5) of this section and subsections (2) and (3) of Section 9–306 on proceeds.

(2) During the period that goods are in the possession of the issuer of a negotiable document therefor, a security interest in the goods is perfected by perfecting a security interest in the document, and any security interest in the goods otherwise perfected during such period is subject thereto.

(3) A security interest in goods in the possession of a bailee other than one who has issued a negotiable document therefor is perfected by issuance of a document in the name of the secured party or by the bailee's receipt of notification of the secured party's interest or by filing as to the goods.

(4) A security interest in instruments or negotiable documents is perfected without filing or the taking of possession for a period of 21 days from the time it attaches to the extent that it arises for new value given under a written security agreement.

(5) A security interest remains perfected for a period of 21 days without filing where a secured party having a perfected security interest in an instrument, a negotiable document or goods in possession of a bailee other than one who has issued a negotiable document therefor

   (a) makes available to the debtor the goods or documents representing the goods for the purpose of ultimate sale or exchange or for the purpose of loading, unloading, storing, shipping, transshipping, manufacturing, processing or otherwise dealing with them in a manner preliminary to their sale or exchange, but priority between conflicting security interests in the goods is subject to subsection (3) of Section 9–312; or

   (b) delivers the instrument to the debtor for the purpose of ultimate sale or exchange or of presentation, collection, renewal or registration of transfer.

(6) After the 21 day period in subsections (4) and (5) perfection depends upon compliance with applicable provisions of this Article.

§ 9–305. When Possession by Secured Party Perfects Security Interest Without Filing.**

A security interest in letters of credit and advices of credit (subsection (2) (a) of Section 5–116), goods, instruments, money, negotiable documents or chattel paper may be perfected by the secured party's taking possession of the collateral. If such collateral other than goods covered by a negotiable document is held by a bailee, the secured party is deemed to have possession from the time the bailee receives notification of the secured party's interest. A security interest is perfected by possession from the time possession is taken without relation back and continues only so long as possession is retained, unless otherwise specified in this Article. The security interest may be otherwise perfected as provided in this Article before or after the period of possession by the secured party.

§ 9–306. "Proceeds"; Secured Party's Rights on Disposition of Collateral.**

(1) "Proceeds" includes whatever is received upon the sale, exchange, collection or other disposition of collateral or proceeds. Insurance payable by reason of loss or damage to the collateral is proceeds, except to the extent that it is payable to a person other than a party to the security agreement. Money, checks, deposit accounts, and the like are "cash proceeds." All other proceeds are "non-cash proceeds."

(2) Except where this Article otherwise provides, a security interest continues in collateral notwithstanding sale, exchange or other disposition thereof unless the disposition was authorized by the secured party in the security agreement or otherwise, and also continues in any identifiable proceeds including collections received by the debtor.

(3) The security interest in proceeds is a continuously perfected security interest if the interest in the original collateral was perfected but it ceases to be a perfected security interest and becomes unperfected ten days after receipt of the proceeds by the debtor unless

(a) a filed financing statement covers the original collateral and the proceeds are collateral in which a security interest may be perfected by filing in the office or offices where the financing statement has been filed and, if the proceeds are acquired with cash proceeds, the description of collateral in the financing statement indicates the types of property constituting the proceeds; or

(b) a filed financing statement covers the original collateral and the proceeds are identifiable cash proceeds; or

(c) the security interest in the proceeds is perfected before the expiration of the ten day period.

Except as provided in this section, a security interest in proceeds can be perfected only by the methods or under the circumstances permitted in this Article for original collateral of the same type.

(4) In the event of insolvency proceedings instituted by or against a debtor, a secured party with a perfected security interest in proceeds has a perfected security interest only in the following proceeds:

(a) in identifiable non-cash proceeds and in separate deposit accounts containing only proceeds;

(b) in identifiable cash proceeds in the form of money which is neither commingled with other money nor deposited in a deposit account prior to the insolvency proceedings;

(c) in identifiable cash proceeds in the form of checks and the like which are not deposited in a deposit account prior to the insolvency proceedings; and

(d) in all cash and deposit accounts of the debtor in which proceeds have been commingled with other funds, but the perfected security interest under this paragraph (d) is

(i) subject to any right to set-off; and

(ii) limited to an amount not greater than the amount of any cash proceeds received by the debtor within ten days before the institution of the insolvency proceedings less the sum of (I) the payments to the secured party on account of cash proceeds received by the debtor during such period and (II) the cash proceeds received by the debtor during such period to which the secured party is entitled under paragraphs (a) through (c) of this subsection (4).

(5) If a sale of goods results in an account or chattel paper which is transferred by the seller to a secured party, and if the goods are returned to or are repossessed by the seller or the secured party, the following rules determine priorities:

(a) If the goods were collateral at the time of sale, for an indebtedness of the seller which is still unpaid, the original security interest attaches again to the goods and continues as a perfected security interest if it was perfected at the time when the goods were sold. If the security interest was originally perfected by a filing which is still effective, nothing further is required to continue the perfected status; in any other case, the secured party must take possession of the returned or repossessed goods or must file.

(b) An unpaid transferee of the chattel paper has a security interest in the goods against the transferor. Such security interest is prior to a security interest asserted under paragraph (a) to the extent that the transferee of the chattel paper was entitled to priority under Section 9–308.

(c) An unpaid transferee of the account has a security interest in the goods against the transferor. Such security interest is subordinate to a security interest asserted under paragraph (a).

(d) A security interest of an unpaid transferee asserted under paragraph (b) or (c) must be perfected for protection against creditors of the transferor and purchasers of the returned or repossessed goods.

§ 9–307. Protection of Buyers of Goods.**

(1) A buyer in ordinary course of business (subsection (9) of Section 1–201) other than a person buying farm products from a person engaged in farming operations takes free of a security interest created by his seller even though the security interest is perfected and even though the buyer knows of its existence.

(2) In the case of consumer goods, a buyer takes free of a security interest even though perfected if he buys without knowledge of the security interest, for value and for his own personal, family or household purposes unless prior to the purchase the secured party has filed a financing statement covering such goods.

(3) A buyer other than a buyer in ordinary course of business (subsection (1) of this section) takes free of a security interest to the extent that it secures future advances made after the secured party acquires knowledge of the purchase, or more than 45 days after the purchase, whichever first occurs, unless made pursuant to a commitment entered into without knowledge of the purchase and before the expiration of the 45 day period.

§ 9–308. Purchase of Chattel Paper and Instruments.**

A purchaser of chattel paper or an instrument who gives new value and takes possession of it in the ordinary course of his business has priority over a security interest in the chattel paper or instrument

(a) which is perfected under Section 9–304 (permissive filing and temporary perfection) or under Section 9–306 (perfection as to proceeds) if he acts without knowledge that the specific paper or instrument is subject to a security interest; or

(b) which is claimed merely as proceeds of inventory subject to a security interest (Section 9–306) even though he knows that the specific paper or instrument is subject to the security interest.

§ 9–309. Protection of Purchasers of Instruments and Documents.

Nothing in this Article limits the rights of a holder in due course of a negotiable instrument (Section 3–302) or a holder to whom a negotiable document of title has been duly negotiated (Section 7–501) or a bona fide purchaser of a security (Section 8–301) and such holders or purchasers take priority over an earlier security interest even though perfected. Filing under this Article does not constitute notice of the security interest to such holders or purchasers.

§ 9–310. Priority of Certain Liens Arising by Operation of Law.

When a person in the ordinary course of his business furnishes services or materials with respect to goods subject to a security interest, a lien upon goods in the possession of such person given by statute or rule of law for such materials or services takes priority over a perfected security interest unless the lien is statutory and the statute expressly provides otherwise.

§ 9–311. Alienability of Debtor's Rights: Judicial Process.

The debtor's rights in collateral may be voluntarily or involuntarily transferred (by way of sale, creation of a security interest, attachment, levy, garnishment or other judicial process) notwithstanding a provision in the security agreement prohibiting any transfer or making the transfer constitute a default.

§ 9–312. Priorities Among Conflicting Security Interests in the Same Collateral.**

(1) The rules of priority stated in other sections of this Part and in the following sections shall govern when applicable: Section 4–208 with respect to the security interests of collecting banks in items being collected, accompanying documents and proceeds; Section 9–103 on security interests related to other jurisdictions; Section 9–114 on consignments.

(2) A perfected security interest in crops for new value given to enable the debtor to produce the crops during the production season and given not more than three months before the crops become growing crops by planting or otherwise takes priority over an earlier perfected security interest to the extent that such earlier interest secures obligations due more than six months before the crops become growing crops by planting or otherwise, even though the person giving new value had knowledge of the earlier security interest.

(3) A perfected purchase money security interest in inventory has priority over a conflicting security interest in the same inventory and also has priority in identifiable cash proceeds received on or before the delivery of the inventory to a buyer if

    (a) the purchase money security interest is perfected at the time the debtor receives possession of the inventory; and

    (b) the purchase money secured party gives notification in writing to the holder of the conflicting security interest if the holder had filed a financing statement covering the same types of inventory (i) before the date of the filing made by the purchase money secured party, or (ii) before the beginning of the 21 day period where the purchase money security interest is temporarily perfected without filing or possession (subsection (5) of Section 9–304); and

    (c) the holder of the conflicting security interest receives the notification within five years before the debtor receives possession of the inventory; and

    (d) the notification states that the person giving the notice has or expects to acquire a purchase money security interest in inventory of the debtor, describing such inventory by item or type.

(4) A purchase money security interest in collateral other than inventory has priority over a conflicting security interest in the same collateral or its proceeds if the purchase money security interest is perfected at the time the debtor receives possession of the collateral or within ten days thereafter.

(5) In all cases not governed by other rules stated in this section (including cases of purchase money security interests which do not qualify for the special priorities set forth in subsections (3) and (4) of this section), priority between conflicting security interests in the same collateral shall be determined according to the following rules:

    (a) Conflicting security interests rank according to priority in time of filing or perfection. Priority dates from the time a filing is first made covering the collateral or the time the security interest is first perfected, whichever is earlier, provided that there is no period thereafter when there is neither filing nor perfection.

    (b) So long as conflicting security interests are unperfected, the first to attach has priority.

(6) For the purposes of subsection (5) a date of filing or perfection as to collateral is also a date of filing or perfection as to proceeds.

(7) If future advances are made while a security interest is perfected by filing or the taking of possession, the security interest has the same priority for the purposes of subsection (5) with respect to the future advances as it does with respect to the first advance. If a commitment is made before or while the security interest is so perfected, the security interest has the same priority with respect to advances made pursuant thereto. In other cases a perfected security interest has priority from the date the advance is made.

§ 9–313. Priority of Security Interests in Fixtures.**

(1) In this section and in the provisions of Part 4 of this Article referring to fixture filing, unless the context otherwise requires

    (a) goods are "fixtures" when they become so related to particular real estate that an interest in them arises under real estate law.

    (b) a "fixture filing" is the filing in the office where a mortgage on the real estate would be filed or recorded of a financing statement covering goods which are or are to become fixtures and conforming to the requirements of subsection (5) of Section 9–402.

    (c) a mortgage is a "construction mortgage" to the extent that it secures an obligation incurred for the construction of an improvement on land including the acquisition cost of the land, if the recorded writing so indicates.

(2) A security interest under this Article may be created in goods which are fixtures or may continue in goods which become fixtures, but no security interest exists under this Article in ordinary building materials incorporated into an improvement on land.

(3) This Article does not prevent creation of an encumbrance upon fixtures pursuant to real estate law.

(4) A perfected security interest in fixtures has priority over the conflicting interest of an encumbrancer or owner of the real estate where

    (a) the security interest is a purchase money security interest, the interest of the encumbrancer or owner arises before the goods become fixtures, the security interest is perfected by a fixture filing before the goods become fixtures or within ten days thereafter, and the debtor has an interest of record in the real estate or is in possession of the real estate; or

(b) the security interest is perfected by a fixture filing before the interest of the encumbrancer or owner is of record, the security interest has priority over any conflicting interest of a predecessor in title of the encumbrancer or owner, and the debtor has an interest of record in the real estate or is in possession of the real estate; or

(c) the fixtures are readily removable factory or office machines or readily removable replacements of domestic appliances which are consumer goods, and before the goods become fixtures the security interest is perfected by any method permitted by this Article; or

(d) the conflicting interest is a lien on the real estate obtained by legal or equitable proceedings after the security interest was perfected by any method permitted by this Article.

(5) A security interest in fixtures, whether or not perfected, has priority over the conflicting interest of an encumbrancer or owner of the real estate where

(a) the encumbrancer or owner has consented in writing to the security interest or has disclaimed an interest in the goods as fixtures; or

(b) the debtor has a right to remove the goods as against the encumbrancer or owner. If the debtor's right terminates, the priority of the security interest continues for a reasonable time.

(6) Notwithstanding paragraph (a) of subsection (4) but otherwise subject to subsections (4) and (5), a security interest in fixtures is subordinate to a construction mortgage recorded before the goods become fixtures if the goods become fixtures before the completion of the construction. To the extent that it is given to refinance a construction mortgage, a mortgage has this priority to the same extent as the construction mortgage.

(7) In cases not within the preceding subsections, a security interest in fixtures is subordinate to the conflicting interest of an encumbrancer or owner of the related real estate who is not the debtor.

(8) When the secured party has priority over all owners and encumbrancers of the real estate, he may, on default, subject to the provisions of Part 5, remove his collateral from the real estate but he must reimburse any encumbrancer or owner of the real estate who is not the debtor and who has not otherwise agreed for the cost of repair of any physical injury, but not for any diminution in value of the real estate caused by the absence of the goods removed or by any necessity of replacing them. A person entitled to reimbursement may refuse permission to remove until the secured party gives adequate security for the performance of this obligation.

§ 9–314. Accessions.

(1) A security interest in goods which attaches before they are installed in or affixed to other goods takes priority as to the goods installed or affixed (called in this section "accessions") over the claims of all persons to the whole except as stated in subsection (3) and subject to Section 9–315(1).

(2) A security interest which attaches to goods after they become part of a whole is valid against all persons subsequently acquiring interests in the whole except as stated in subsection (3) but is invalid against any person with an interest in the whole at the time the security interest attaches to the goods who has not in writing consented to the security interest or disclaimed an interest in the goods as part of the whole.

(3) The security interests described in subsections (1) and (2) do not take priority over

(a) a subsequent purchaser for value of any interest in the whole; or

(b) a creditor with a lien on the whole subsequently obtained by judicial proceedings; or

(c) a creditor with a prior perfected security interest in the whole to the extent that he makes subsequent advances

if the subsequent purchase is made, the lien by judicial proceedings obtained or the subsequent advance under the prior perfected security interest is made or contracted for without knowledge of the security interest and before it is perfected. A purchaser of the whole at a foreclosure sale other than the holder of a perfected security interest purchasing at his own foreclosure sale is a subsequent purchaser within this section.

(4) When under subsections (1) or (2) and (3) a secured party has an interest in accessions which has priority over the claims of all persons who have interests in the whole, he may on default subject to the provisions of Part 5 remove his collateral from the whole but he must reimburse any encumbrancer or owner of the whole who is not the debtor and who has not otherwise agreed for the cost of repair of any physical injury but not for any diminution in value of the whole caused by the absence of the goods removed or by any necessity for replacing them. A person entitled to reimbursement may refuse permission to remove until the secured party gives adequate security for the performance of this obligation.

§ 9–315. Priority When Goods Are Commingled or Processed.

(1) If a security interest in goods was perfected and subsequently the goods or a part thereof have become part of a product or mass, the security interest continues in the product or mass if

(a) the goods are so manufactured, processed, assembled or commingled that their identity is lost in the product or mass; or

(b) a financing statement covering the original goods also covers the product into which the goods have been manufactured, processed or assembled.

In a case to which paragraph (b) applies, no separate security interest in that part of the original goods which has been manufactured, processed or assembled into the product may be claimed under Section 9–314.

(2) When under subsection (1) more than one security interest attaches to the product or mass, they rank equally according to the ratio that the cost of the goods to which each interest originally attached bears to the cost of the total product or mass.

§ 9–316. Priority Subject to Subordination.

Nothing in this Article prevents subordination by agreement by any person entitled to priority.

§ 9–317. Secured Party Not Obligated on Contract of Debtor.

The mere existence of a security interest or authority given to the debtor to dispose of or use collateral does not impose contract or tort liability upon the secured party for the debtor's acts or omissions.

§ 9–318. Defenses Against Assignee; Modification of Contract After Notification of Assignment; Term Prohibiting Assignment Ineffective; Identification and Proof of Assignment.**

(1) Unless an account debtor has made an enforceable agreement not to assert defenses or claims arising out of a sale as provided in Section 9–206 the rights of an assignee are subject to

    (a) all the terms of the contract between the account debtor and assignor and any defense or claim arising therefrom; and

    (b) any other defense or claim of the account debtor against the assignor which accrues before the account debtor receives notification of the assignment.

(2) So far as the right to payment or a part thereof under an assignment contract has not been fully earned by performance, and notwithstanding notification of the assignment, any modification of or substitution for the contract made in good faith and in accordance with reasonable commercial standards is effective against an assignee unless the account debtor has otherwise agreed but the assignee acquires corresponding rights under the modified or substituted contract. The assignment may provide that such modification or substitution is a breach by the assignor.

(3) The account debtor is authorized to pay the assignor until the account debtor receives notification that the amount due or to become due has been assigned and that payment is to be made to the assignee. A notification which does not reasonably identify the rights assigned is ineffective. If requested by the account debtor, the assignee must seasonably furnish reasonable proof that the assignment has been made and unless he does so the account debtor may pay the assignor.

(4) A term in any contract between an account debtor and an assignor is ineffective if it prohibits assignment of an account or prohibits creation of a security interest in a general intangible for money due or to become due or requires the account debtor's consent to such assignment or security interest.

PART 4
FILING

§ 9–401. Place of Filing; Erroneous Filing; Removal of Collateral.* **

(1) The proper place to file in order to perfect a security interest is as follows:

    (a) when the collateral is timber to be cut or is minerals or the like (including oil and gas) or accounts subject to subsection (5) of Section 9–103, or when the financing statement is filed as a fixture filing (Section 9–313) and the collateral is goods which are or are to become fixtures, then in the office where a mortgage on the real estate would be filed or recorded;

    (b) in all other cases, in the office of the [Secretary of State].

(2) A filing which is made in good faith in an improper place or not in all of the places required by this section is nevertheless effective with regard to any collateral as to which the filing complied with the requirements of this Article and is also effective with regard to collateral covered by the financing statement against any person who has knowledge of the contents of such financing statement.

(3) A filing which is made in the proper place in this state continues effective even though the debtor's residence or place of business or the location of the collateral or its use, whichever controlled the original filing, is thereafter changed.

(4) The rules stated in Section 9–103 determine whether filing is necessary in this state.

(5) Notwithstanding the preceding subsections, and subject to subsection (3) of Section 9–302, the proper place to file in order to perfect a security interest in collateral, including fixtures, of a transmitting utility is the office of the [Secretary of State]. This filing constitutes a fixture filing (Section 9–313) as to the collateral described therein which is or is to become fixtures.

§ 9–402. Formal Requisites of Financing Statement; Amendments; Mortgage as Financing Statement.**

(1) A financing statement is sufficient if it gives the names of the debtor and the secured party, is signed by the debtor, gives an address of the secured party from which information concerning the security interest may be obtained, gives a mailing address of the debtor and contains a statement indicating the types, or describing the items, of collateral. A financing statement may be filed before a security agreement is made or a security interest otherwise attaches. When the financing statement covers crops growing or to be grown, the statement must also contain a description of the real estate concerned. When the financing statement covers timber to be cut or covers minerals or the like (including oil and gas) or accounts subject to subsection (5) of Section 9–103, or when the financing statement is filed as a fixture filing (Section 9–313) and the collateral is goods which are or are to become fixtures, the statement must also comply with subsection (5). A copy of the security agreement is sufficient as a financing statement if it contains the above information and is signed by the debtor. A carbon, photographic or other reproduction of a security agreement or a financing statement is sufficient as a financing statement if the security agreement so provides or if the original has been filed in this state.

(2) A financing statement which otherwise complies with subsection (1) is sufficient when it is signed by the secured party instead of the debtor if it is filed to perfect a security interest in

(a) collateral already subject to a security interest in another jurisdiction when it is brought into this state, or when the debtor's location is changed to this state. Such a financing statement must state that the collateral was brought into this state or that the debtor's location was changed to this state under such circumstances; or

(b) proceeds under Section 9–306 if the security interest in the original collateral was perfected. Such a financing statement must describe the original collateral; or

(c) collateral as to which the filing has lapsed; or

(d) collateral acquired after a change of name, identity or corporate structure of the debtor (subsection (7)).

(3) A form substantially as follows is sufficient to comply with subsection (1):

Name of debtor (or assignor) _____

Address _____

Name of secured party (or assignee) _____

Address _____

1. This financing statement covers the following types (or items) of property: (Describe) _____

2. (If collateral is crops) The above described crops are growing or are to be grown on:
   (Describe Real Estate) _____

3. (If applicable) The above goods are to become fixtures on[1]
   (Describe Real Estate) _____ and this financing statement is to be filed [for record] in the real estate records. (If the debtor does not have an interest of record) The name of a record owner is _____

4. (If products of collateral are claimed) Products of the collateral are also covered.

(use

whichever _____

is   Signature of Debtor (or Assignor)

applicable) _____

Signature of Secured Party (or Assignee)

(4) A financing statement may be amended by filing a writing signed by both the debtor and the secured party. An amendment does not extend the period of effectiveness of a financing statement. If any amendment adds collateral, it is effective as to the added collateral only from the filing date of the amendment. In this Article, unless the context otherwise requires, the term "financing statement" means the original financing statement and any amendments.

(5) A financing statement covering timber to be cut or covering minerals or the like (including oil and gas) or accounts subject to subsection (5) of Section 9–103, or a financing statement filed as a fixture filing (Section 9–313) where the debtor is not a transmitting utility, must show that it covers this type of collateral, must recite that it is to be filed [for record] in the real estate records, and the financing statement must contain a description of the real estate [sufficient if it were contained in a mortgage of the real estate to give constructive notice of the mortgage under the law of this state]. If the debtor does not have an interest of record in the real estate, the financing statement must show the name of a record owner.

(6) A mortgage is effective as a financing statement filed as a fixture filing from the date of its recording if
   (a) the goods are described in the mortgage by item or type; and
   (b) the goods are or are to become fixtures related to the real estate described in the mortgage; and
   (c) the mortgage complies with the requirements for a financing statement in this section other than a recital that it is to be filed in the real estate records; and
   (d) the mortgage is duly recorded.

No fee with reference to the financing statement is required other than the regular recording and satisfaction fees with respect to the mortgage.

(7) A financing statement sufficiently shows the name of the debtor if it gives the individual, partnership or corporate name of the debtor, whether or not it adds other trade names or names of partners. Where the debtor so changes his

---

[1] Where appropriate substitute either "The above timber is standing on . . ." or "The above minerals or the like (including oil and gas) or accounts will be financed at the wellhead or minehead of the well or mine located on. . . ."

name or in the case of an organization its name, identity or corporate structure that a filed financing statement becomes seriously misleading, the filing is not effective to perfect a security interest in collateral acquired by the debtor more than four months after the change, unless a new appropriate financing statement is filed before the expiration of that time. A filed financing statement remains effective with respect to collateral transferred by the debtor even though the secured party knows of or consents to the transfer.

(8) A financing statement substantially complying with the requirements of this section is effective even though it contains minor errors which are not seriously misleading.

§ 9–403. What Constitutes Filing; Duration of Filing; Effect of Lapsed Filing; Duties of Filing Officer.**

(1) Presentation for filing of a financing statement and tender of the filing fee or acceptance of the statement by the filing officer constitutes filing under this Article.

(2) Except as provided in subsection (6) a filed financing statement is effective for a period of five years from the date of filing. The effectiveness of a filed financing statement lapses on the expiration of the five year period unless a continuation statement is filed prior to the lapse. If a security interest perfected by filing exists at the time insolvency proceedings are commenced by or against the debtor, the security interest remains perfected until termination of the insolvency proceedings and thereafter for a period of sixty days or until expiration of the five year period, whichever occurs later. Upon lapse the security interest becomes unperfected, unless it is perfected without filing. If the security interest becomes unperfected upon lapse, it is deemed to have been unperfected as against a person who became a purchaser or lien creditor before lapse.

(3) A continuation statement may be filed by the secured party within six months prior to the expiration of the five year period specified in subsection (2). Any such continuation statement must be signed by the secured party, identify the original statement by file number and state that the original statement is still effective. A continuation statement signed by a person other than the secured party of record must be accompanied by a separate written statement of assignment signed by the secured party of record and complying with subsection (2) of Section 9–405, including payment of the required fee. Upon timely filing of the continuation statement, the effectiveness of the original statement is continued for five years after the last date to which the filing was effective whereupon it lapses in the same manner as provided in subsection (2) unless another continuation statement is filed prior to such lapse. Succeeding continuation statements may be filed in the same manner to continue the effectiveness of the original statement. Unless a statute on disposition of public records provides otherwise, the filing officer may remove a lapsed statement from the files and destroy it immediately if he has retained a microfilm or other photographic record, or in other cases after one year after the lapse. The filing officer shall so arrange matters by physical annexation of financing statements to continuation statements or other related filings, or by other means, that if he physically destroys the financing statements of a period more than five years past, those which have been continued by a continuation statement or which are still effective under subsection (6) shall be retained.

(4) Except as provided in subsection (7) a filing officer shall mark each statement with a file number and with the date and hour of filing and shall hold the statement or a microfilm or other photographic copy thereof for public inspection. In addition the filing officer shall index the statement according to the name of the debtor and shall note in the index the file number and the address of the debtor given in the statement.

(5) The uniform fee for filing and indexing and for stamping a copy furnished by the secured party to show the date and place of filing for an original financing statement or for a continuation statement shall be $_____ if the statement is in the standard form prescribed by the [Secretary of State] and otherwise shall be $_____, plus in each case, if the financing statement is subject to subsection (5) of Section 9–402, $_____. The uniform fee for each name more than one required to be indexed shall be $_____. The secured party may at his option show a trade name for any person and an extra uniform indexing fee of $_____ shall be paid with respect thereto.

(6) If the debtor is a transmitting utility (subsection (5) of Section 9–401) and a filed financing statement so states, it is effective until a termination statement is filed. A real estate mortgage which is effective as a fixture filing under subsection (6) of Section 9–402 remains effective as a fixture filing until the mortgage is released or satisfied of record or its effectiveness otherwise terminates as to the real estate.

(7) When a financing statement covers timber to be cut or covers minerals or the like (including oil and gas) or accounts subject to subsection (5) of Section 9–103, or is filed as a fixture filing, the filing officer shall index it under the names of the debtor and any owner of record shown on the financing statement in the same fashion as if they were the mortgagors in a mortgage of the real estate described, and, to the extent that the law of this state provides for indexing of mortgages under the name of the mortgagee, under the name of the secured party as if he were the mortgagee thereunder, or where indexing is by description in the same fashion as if the financing statement were a mortgage of the real estate described.

§ 9–404. Termination Statement.**

(1) If a financing statement covering consumer goods is filed on or after _____, then within one month or within ten days following written demand by the debtor after there is no outstanding secured obligation and no commitment to make advances, incur obligations or otherwise give value, the secured party must file with each filing officer with whom the financing statement was filed, a termination statement to the effect that he no longer claims a security interest under the financing statement, which shall be identified by file number. In other cases whenever there is no outstanding secured obligation and no commitment to make advances, incur obligations or otherwise give value, the secured party must on written demand by the debtor send the debtor, for each filing officer with whom the financing statement was filed, a termination statement to the effect that he no longer claims a security interest under the financing statement, which shall be identified by file number. A termination statement signed by a person other than the secured party of record must be accompanied by a separate written statement of assignment signed by the secured party of record complying with subsection (2) of Section 9–405, including payment of the required fee. If

the affected secured party fails to file such a termination statement as required by this subsection, or to send such a termination statement within ten days after proper demand therefor, he shall be liable to the debtor for one hundred dollars, and in addition for any loss caused to the debtor by such failure.

(2) On presentation to the filing officer of such a termination statement he must note it in the index. If he has received the termination statement in duplicate, he shall return one copy of the termination statement to the secured party stamped to show the time of receipt thereof. If the filing officer has a microfilm or other photographic record of the financing statement, and of any related continuation statement, statement of assignment and statement of release, he may remove the originals from the files at any time after receipt of the termination statement, or if he has no such record, he may remove them from the files at any time after one year after receipt of the termination statement.

(3) If the termination statement is in the standard form prescribed by the [Secretary of State], the uniform fee for filing and indexing the termination statement shall be $_____, and otherwise shall be $_____, plus in each case an additional fee of $_____ for each name more than one against which the termination statement is required to be indexed.

§ 9–405. Assignment of Security Interest; Duties of Filing Officer; Fees.**

(1) A financing statement may disclose an assignment of a security interest in the collateral described in the financing statement by indication in the financing statement of the name and address of the assignee or by an assignment itself or a copy thereof on the face or back of the statement. On presentation to the filing officer of such a financing statement the filing officer shall mark the same as provided in Section 9–403(4). The uniform fee for filing, indexing and furnishing filing data for a financing statement so indicating an assignment shall be $_____ if the statement is in the standard form prescribed by the [Secretary of State] and otherwise shall be $_____, plus in each case an additional fee of $_____ for each name more than one against which the financing statement is required to be indexed.

(2) A secured party may assign of record all or part of his rights under a financing statement by the filing in the place where the original financing statement was filed of a separate written statement of assignment signed by the secured party of record and setting forth the name of the secured party of record and the debtor, the file number and the date of filing of the financing statement and the name and address of the assignee and containing a description of the collateral assigned. A copy of the assignment is sufficient as a separate statement if it complies with the preceding sentence. On presentation to the filing officer of such a separate statement, the filing officer shall mark such separate statement with the date and hour of the filing. He shall note the assignment on the index of the financing statement, or in the case of a fixture filing, or a filing covering timber to be cut, or covering minerals or the like (including oil and gas) or accounts subject to subsection (5) of Section 9–103, he shall index the assignment under the name of the assignor as grantor and, to the extent that the law of this state provides for indexing the assignment of a mortgage under the name of the assignee, he shall index the assignment of the financing statement under the name of the assignee. The uniform fee for filing, indexing and furnishing filing data about such a separate statement of assignment shall be $_____ if the statement

is in the standard form prescribed by the [Secretary of State] and otherwise shall be $_____, plus in each case an additional fee of $_____ for each name more than one against which the statement of assignment is required to be indexed. Notwithstanding the provisions of this subsection, an assignment of record of a security interest in a fixture contained in a mortgage effective as a fixture filing (subsection (6) of Section 9–402) may be made only by an assignment of the mortgage in the manner provided by the law of this state other than this Act.

(3) After the disclosure or filing of an assignment under this section, the assignee is the secured party of record.

§ 9–406. Release of Collateral; Duties of Filing Officer; Fees.**

A secured party of record may by his signed statement release all or a part of any collateral described in a filed financing statement. The statement of release is sufficient if it contains a description of the collateral being released, the name and address of the debtor, the name and address of the secured party, and the file number of the financing statement. A statement of release signed by a person other than the secured party of record must be accompanied by a separate written statement of assignment signed by the secured party of record and complying with subsection (2) of Section 9–405, including payment of the required fee. Upon presentation of such a statement of release to the filing officer he shall mark the statement with the hour and date of filing and shall note the same upon the margin of the index of the filing of the financing statement. The uniform fee for filing and noting such a statement of release shall be $_____ if the statement is in the standard form prescribed by the [Secretary of State] and otherwise shall be $_____, plus in each case an additional fee of $_____ for each name more than one against which the statement of release is required to be indexed.

§ 9–407. Information From Filing Officer.* **

(1) If the person filing any financing statement, termination statement, statement of assignment, or statement of release, furnishes the filing officer a copy thereof, the filing officer shall upon request note upon the copy the file number and date and hour of the filing of the original and deliver or send the copy to such person.

(2) Upon request of any person, the filing officer shall issue his certificate showing whether there is on file on the date and hour stated therein, any presently effective financing statement naming a particular debtor and any statement of assignment thereof and if there is, giving the date and hour of filing of each such statement and the names and addresses of each secured party therein. The uniform fee for such a certificate shall be $_____ if the request for the certificate is in the standard form prescribed by the [Secretary of State] and otherwise shall be $_____. Upon request the filing officer shall furnish a copy of any filed financing statement or statement of assignment for a uniform fee of $_____ per page.

§ 9–408. Financing Statements Covering Consigned or Leased Goods.**

A consignor or lessor of goods may file a financing statement using the terms "consignor," "consignee," "lessor," "lessee" or the like instead of the terms specified in Section 9–402. The provisions of this Part shall apply as appropriate to such a financing statement but its filing shall not of itself be a factor in determining whether or not the consignment or lease is intended as security (Section 1–201(37)). However, if it is determined for other reasons that the consignment or lease is so intended, a security interest of the consignor or lessor which attaches to the consigned or leased goods is perfected by such filing.

PART 5
DEFAULT

§ 9–501. Default; Procedure When Security Agreement Covers Both Real and Personal Property.**

(1) When a debtor is in default under a security agreement, a secured party has the rights and remedies provided in this Part and except as limited by subsection (3) those provided in the security agreement. He may reduce his claim to judgment, foreclose or otherwise enforce the security interest by any available judicial procedure. If the collateral is documents the secured party may proceed either as to the documents or as to the goods covered thereby. A secured party in possession has the rights, remedies and duties provided in Section 9–207. The rights and remedies referred to in this subsection are cumulative.

(2) After default, the debtor has the rights and remedies provided in this Part, those provided in the security agreement and those provided in Section 9–207.

(3) To the extent that they give rights to the debtor and impose duties on the secured party, the rules stated in the subsections referred to below may not be waived or varied except as provided with respect to compulsory disposition of collateral (subsection (3) of Section 9–504 and Section 9–505) and with respect to redemption of collateral (Section 9–506) but the parties may by agreement determine the standards by which the fulfillment of these rights and duties is to be measured if such standards are not manifestly unreasonable:

- (a) subsection (2) of Section 9–502 and subsection (2) of Section 9–504 insofar as they require accounting for surplus proceeds of collateral;
- (b) subsection (3) of Section 9–504 and subsection (1) of Section 9–505 which deal with disposition of collateral;
- (c) subsection (2) of Section 9–505 which deals with acceptance of collateral as discharge of obligation;
- (d) Section 9–506 which deals with redemption of collateral; and
- (e) subsection (1) of Section 9–507 which deals with the secured party's liability for failure to comply with this Part.

(4) If the security agreement covers both real and personal property, the secured party may proceed under this Part as to the personal property or he may proceed as to both the real and the personal property in accordance with his rights and remedies in respect of the real property in which case the provisions of this Part do not apply.

(5) When a secured party has reduced his claim to judgment the lien of any levy which may be made upon his collateral by virtue of any execution based upon the judgment shall relate back to the date of the perfection of the security interest in such collateral. A judicial sale, pursuant to such execution, is a foreclosure of the security interest by judicial procedure within the meaning of this section,

and the secured party may purchase at the sale and thereafter hold the collateral free of any other requirements of this Article.

§ 9–502. Collection Rights of Secured Party.**

(1) When so agreed and in any event on default the secured party is entitled to notify an account debtor or the obligor on an instrument to make payment to him whether or not the assignor was theretofore making collections on the collateral, and also to take control of any proceeds to which he is entitled under Section 9–306.

(2) A secured party who by agreement is entitled to charge back uncollected collateral or otherwise to full or limited recourse against the debtor and who undertakes to collect from the account debtors or obligors must proceed in a commercially reasonable manner and may deduct his reasonable expenses of realization from the collections. If the security agreement secures an indebtedness, the secured party must account to the debtor for any surplus, and unless otherwise agreed, the debtor is liable for any deficiency. But, if the underlying transaction was a sale of accounts or chattel paper, the debtor is entitled to any surplus or is liable for any deficiency only if the security agreement so provides.

§ 9–503. Secured Party's Right to Take Possession After Default.

Unless otherwise agreed a secured party has on default the right to take possession of the collateral. In taking possession a secured party may proceed without judicial process if this can be done without breach of the peace or may proceed by action. If the security agreement so provides the secured party may require the debtor to assemble the collateral and make it available to the secured party at a place to be designated by the secured party which is reasonably convenient to both parties. Without removal a secured party may render equipment unusable, and may dispose of collateral on the debtor's premises under Section 9–504.

§ 9–504. Secured Party's Right to Dispose of Collateral After Default; Effect of Disposition.**

(1) A secured party after default may sell, lease or otherwise dispose of any or all of the collateral in its then condition or following any commercially reasonable preparation or processing. Any sale of goods is subject to the Article on Sales (Article 2). The proceeds of disposition shall be applied in the order following to

(a) the reasonable expenses of retaking, holding, preparing for sale or lease, selling, leasing and the like and, to the extent provided for in the agreement and not prohibited by law, the reasonable attorneys' fees and legal expenses incurred by the secured party;

(b) the satisfaction of indebtedness secured by the security interest under which the disposition is made;

(c) the satisfaction of indebtedness secured by any subordinate security interest in the collateral if written notification of demand therefor is received before distribution of the proceeds is completed. If requested by the secured party, the holder of a subordinate security interest must seasonably furnish reasonable proof of his interest, and unless he does so, the secured party need not comply with his demand.

(2) If the security interest secures an indebtedness, the secured party must

account to the debtor for any surplus, and, unless otherwise agreed, the debtor is liable for any deficiency. But if the underlying transaction was a sale of accounts or chattel paper, the debtor is entitled to any surplus or is liable for any deficiency only if the security agreement so provides.

(3) Disposition of the collateral may be by public or private proceedings and may be made by way of one or more contracts. Sale or other disposition may be as a unit or in parcels and at any time and place and on any terms but every aspect of the disposition including the method, manner, time, place and terms must be commercially reasonable. Unless collateral is perishable or threatens to decline speedily in value or is of a type customarily sold on a recognized market, reasonable notification of the time and place of any public sale or reasonable notification of the time after which any private sale or other intended disposition is to be made shall be sent by the secured party to the debtor, if he has not signed after default a statement renouncing or modifying his right to notification of sale. In the case of consumer goods no other notification need be sent. In other cases notification shall be sent to any other secured party from whom the secured party has received (before sending his notification to the debtor or before the debtor's renunciation of his rights) written notice of a claim of an interest in the collateral. The secured party may buy at any public sale and if the collateral is of a type customarily sold in a recognized market or is of a type which is the subject of widely distributed standard price quotations he may buy at private sale.

(4) When collateral is disposed of by a secured party after default, the disposition transfers to a purchaser for value all of the debtor's rights therein, discharges the security interest under which it is made and any security interest or lien subordinate thereto. The purchaser takes free of all such rights and interests even though the secured party fails to comply with the requirements of this Part or of any judicial proceedings

    (a) in the case of a public sale, if the purchaser has no knowledge of any defects in the sale and if he does not buy in collusion with the secured party, other bidders or the person conducting the sale; or

    (b) in any other case, if the purchaser acts in good faith.

(5) A person who is liable to a secured party under a guaranty, indorsement, repurchase agreement or the like and who receives a transfer of collateral from the secured party or is subrogated to his rights has thereafter the rights and duties of the secured party. Such a transfer of collateral is not a sale or disposition of the collateral under this Article.

§ 9–505. Compulsory Disposition of Collateral; Acceptance of the Collateral as Discharge of Obligation.**

(1) If the debtor has paid sixty percent of the cash price in the case of a purchase money security interest in consumer goods or sixty percent of the loan in the case of another security interest in consumer goods, and has not signed after default a statement renouncing or modifying his rights under this Part a secured party who has taken possession of collateral must dispose of it under Section 9–504 and if he fails to do so within ninety days after he takes possession the debtor at his option may recover in conversion or under Section 9–507(1) on secured party's liability.

(2) In any other case involving consumer goods or any other collateral a secured

party in possession may, after default, propose to retain the collateral in satisfaction of the obligation. Written notice of such proposal shall be sent to the debtor if he has not signed after default a statement renouncing or modifying his rights under this subsection. In the case of consumer goods no other notice need be given. In other cases notice shall be sent to any other secured party from whom the secured party has received (before sending his notice to the debtor or before the debtor's renunciation of his rights) written notice of a claim of an interest in the collateral. If the secured party receives objection in writing from a person entitled to receive notification within twenty-one days after the notice was sent, the secured party must dispose of the collateral under Section 9–504. In the absence of such written objection the secured party may retain the collateral in satisfaction of the debtor's obligation.

§ 9–506. Debtor's Right to Redeem Collateral.

At any time before the secured party has disposed of collateral or entered into a contract for its disposition under Section 9–504 or before the obligation has been discharged under Section 9–505(2) the debtor or any other secured party may unless otherwise agreed in writing after default redeem the collateral by tendering fulfillment of all obligations secured by the collateral as well as the expenses reasonably incurred by the secured party in retaking, holding and preparing the collateral for disposition, in arranging for the sale, and to the extent provided in the agreement and not prohibited by law, his reasonable attorneys' fees and legal expenses.

§ 9–507. Secured Party's Liability for Failure to Comply With This Part.

(1) If it is established that the secured party is not proceeding in accordance with the provisions of this Part disposition may be ordered or restrained on appropriate terms and conditions. If the disposition has occurred the debtor or any person entitled to notification or whose security interest has been made known to the secured party prior to the disposition has a right to recovery from the secured party any loss caused by a failure to comply with the provisions of this Part. If the collateral is consumer goods, the debtor has a right to recover in any event an amount not less than the credit service charge plus ten percent of the principal amount of the debt or the time price differential plus ten percent of the cash price.

(2) The fact that a better price could have been obtained by a sale at a different time or in a different method from that selected by the secured party is not of itself sufficient to establish that the sale was not made in a commercially reasonable manner. If the secured party either sells the collateral in the usual manner in any recognized market therefor or if he sells at the price current in such market at the time of his sale or if he has otherwise sold in conformity with reasonable commercial practices among dealers in the type of property sold he has sold in a commercially reasonable manner. The principles stated in the two preceding sentences with respect to sales also apply as may be appropriate to other types of disposition. A disposition which has been approved in any judicial proceeding or by any bona fide creditors' committee or representative of creditors shall conclusively be deemed to be commercially reasonable, but this sentence does not indicate that any such approval must be obtained in any case nor does it indicate that any disposition not so approved is not commercially reasonable.

Glossary of Legal Terms and Definitions

abatement of nuisance Removal of a nuisance by court action.

ab initio From the beginning. A contract that is void ab initio is void from its inception.

absque injuria Without violation of a legal right.

abstract of title A summary of the conveyances, transfers, and other facts relied on as evidence of title, together with all such facts appearing of record that may impair its validity. It should contain a brief but complete history of the title.

abutting owners Those owners whose lands touch.

acceleration The shortening of the time for the performance of a contract or the payment of a note by the operation of some provision in the contract or note itself.

acceptance The actual or implied receipt and retention of that which is tendered or offered. The acceptance of an offer is the assent to an offer that is requisite to the formation of a contract. It is either express or evidenced by circumstances from which such assent may be implied.

accession In its legal meaning it is generally used to signify the acquisition of property by its incorporation or union with other property.

accommodation paper A negotiable instrument signed without consideration by a party as acceptor, drawer, or indorser for the purpose of enabling the payee to obtain credit.

accord and satisfaction The adjustment of a disagreement as to what is due from one person to another, and the payment of the agreed amount.

account stated An account that has been rendered by one to another and that purports to state the true balance due and the balance that is either expressly or impliedly admitted to be due by the debtor.

acknowledgment A form for authenticating instruments conveying property or otherwise conferring rights. It is a public declaration by the grantor that the act evidenced by the instrument is his act and deed. Also an admission or confirmation.

acquit To set free or judicially to discharge from an accusation; to release from a debt, duty, obligation, charge, or suspicion of guilt.

actionable Remedial by an action at law.

action ex contractu An action arising out of the breach of a contract.

action ex delicto An action arising out of the violation of a duty or obligation created by positive law independent of contract. An action in tort.

act of God An occurrence resulting exclusively from natural forces which could not have been prevented or whose effects could not have been avoided by care or foresight.

adjudge To give judgment, to decide, to sentence.

adjudicate To adjudge; to settle by judicial decree; to hear or try and determine, as a court.

ad litem During the pendency of the action or proceeding.

administrator A man appointed by a probate court to settle the estate of a deceased person. His duties are customarily defined by statute.

administratrix A court-appointed woman who settles the estate of a deceased person.

adverse possession Open and notorious possession of real property over a given length of time which denies ownership in any other claimant.

advisement When a court takes a case under advisement it delays its decision until it has examined and considered the questions involved.

affidavit A statement or declaration reduced to writing and sworn or affirmed to before an officer who has authority to administer an oath or affirmation.

affirm To confirm a former judgment or order of a court. Also to declare solemnly instead of making a sworn statement.

agent An agent is the substitute or representative of his principal and derives his authority from him.

aggrieved One whose legal rights have been invaded by the act of another is said to be aggrieved. Also one whose pecuniary interest is directly affected by a judgment, or whose right of property may be divested thereby, is considered a party aggrieved.

alienation The voluntary act or acts by which one person transfers his or her own property to another.

aliquot Strictly, forming an exact proper divisor, but treated as meaning fractional when applied to trusts, etc.

allegation A declaration, a formal averment, or statement of a party to an action in a declaration or pleading of what the party intends to prove.

allege To make a statement of fact, to plead.

amortize In modern usage the word means to provide for the payment of a debt by creating a sinking fund or paying in installments.

ancillary Auxiliary to. An ancillary receiver is one who has been appointed in aid of, and in subordination to, the primary receiver.

answer The pleading of a defendant in which he or she may deny any or all the facts set out in the plaintiff's declaration or complaint.

anticipatory breach The doctrine of the law of contracts that when the promisor has repudiated the contract before the time of performance has arrived the promisee may sue forthwith.

appearance The first act of the defendant in court.

appellant A person who files an appeal.

appellate jurisdiction Jurisdiction to revise or correct the work of a subordinate court.

appellee A party against whom a cause is appealed from a lower court to a higher court, called the "respondent" in some jurisdictions.

applicant A petitioner; one who files a petition or application.

appurtenances An accessory; something that belongs to another thing, e.g., buildings are appurtenant to the land and a bar is appurtenant to a tavern. An easement may be appurtenant to land.

arbitrate To submit some disputed matter to selected persons and to accept their decision or award as a substitute for the decision of a judicial tribunal.

argument The discussion by counsel for the respective parties of their contentions on the law and the facts of the case being tried in order to aid the jury in arriving at a correct and just conclusion.

assent To give or express one's concurrence or approval of something done. Assent does not include consent.

assignable Capable of being lawfully assigned or transferred; transferable; negotiable. Also capable of being specified or pointed out as an assignable error.

assignee A person to whom an assignment is made.

assignment A transfer or setting over of property or some right or interest therein from one person to another. In its ordinary application, the word is limited to the transfer of choses in action, e.g., the assignment of a contract.

assignor The maker of an assignment.

assumpsit An action at common law to recover damages for breach of contract.

attachment Taking property into the legal custody of an officer by virtue of the directions contained in a writ of attachment. A seizure under a writ of a debtor's property.

attest To bear witness to, to affirm, to be true or genuine.

attorney-in-fact A person who is authorized by his or her principal, either for some particular purpose or to do a particular act, not of a legal character.

authentication Such official attestation of a written instrument as will render it legally admissible in evidence.

authority Judicial or legislative precedent; delegated power; warrant.

averment A positive statement of fact made in a pleading.

avoidable Capable of being nullified or made void.

bad faith The term imports a person's actual intent to mislead or deceive another; an intent to take an unfair and unethical advantage of another.

bailee The person to whom a bailment is made.

bailment A delivery of personal property by one person to another in trust for a specific purpose, with a contract, express or implied, that the trust shall be faithfully executed and the property returned or duly accounted for when the special purpose is accomplished, or kept until the bailor reclaims it.

bailor The maker of a bailment; one who delivers personal property to another to be held in bailment.

bankruptcy The state of a person who is unable to pay his or her debts without respect to time; one whose liabilities exceed his or her assets.

bar As a collective noun it is used to include those persons who are admitted to practice law, members of the bar. The court itself. A plea or peremptory exception of a defendant sufficient to destroy the plaintiff's action.

barratry The habitual stirring up of quarrels and suits; a single act does not constitute the offense.

bearer The designation of the bearer as the payee of a negotiable instrument signifies that the instrument is payable to the person who seems to be the holder.

bench A court; the judges of a court; the seat upon which the judges of a court are accustomed to sit while the court is in session.

beneficiary The person for whose benefit an insurance policy, trust, will, or contract is established but not the promisee. In the case of a contract, the beneficiary is called a *third-party beneficiary*. A *donee beneficiary* is one who is not a party to a contract but who receives the promised performance as a gift. A *creditor beneficiary* is one who is not a party to a contract but receives the performance in discharge of a debt owed by the promisee to him.

bequeath Commonly used to denote a testamentary gift of real estate; synonymous with "to devise."

bid To make an offer at an auction or at a judicial sale. As a noun, it means an offer.

bilateral contract A contract in which the promise of one of the parties forms the consideration for the promise of the other; a contract formed by an offer requiring a reciprocal promise.

bill of exchange An unconditional order in writing by one person to another, signed by the person giving it, requiring the person to whom it is addressed to pay on demand or at a fixed or determinable future time a sum certain in money to order or to bearer.

bill of lading A written acknowledgment of the receipt of goods to be transported to a designated place and delivery to a named person or to his or her order.

bill of sale A written agreement by which one person assigns or transfers interests or rights in personal property to another.

binder Also called a binding slip; a brief memorandum or agreement issued by an insurer as a temporary policy for the convenience of all the parties, constituting a present insurance in the amount specified and to continue in force until the execution of a formal policy.

blue sky laws A popular name for statutes that regulate the sale of securities and are intended to protect investors against fraudulent and visionary schemes.

bona fide Good faith.

bond A promise under seal to pay money.

breaking bulk The division or separation of the contents of a package or container.

brief A statement of a party's case; usually an abridgment of either the plaintiff's or defendant's case prepared by his or her attorneys for the use of counsel on a trial at law. Also an abridgment of a reported case.

broker An agent who bargains or carries on negotiations in behalf of the principal as an intermediary between the latter and third persons in transacting business relative to the acquisition of contractual rights, or to the sale or purchase of property the custody of which is not intrusted to him or her for the purpose of discharging the agency.

bulk transfer The sale or transfer of a major part of the stock of goods of a merchant at one time and not in the ordinary course of business.

burden of proof The necessity or obligation of affirmatively proving the fact or facts in dispute on an issue raised in a suit in court.

bylaw A rule or law of a corporation for its government. It includes all self-made regulations of a corporation affecting its business and members that do not operate on third persons or in any way affect their rights.

call A notice of a meeting to be held by the stockholders or board of directors of a corporation. Also a demand for payment. In securities trading, a negotiable option contract granting the bearer the right to buy a certain quantity of a particular security at the agreed price on or before the agreed date.

cancelation The act of crossing out a writing. The operation of destroying a written instrument.

carte blanche A signed blank instrument intended by the signer to be filled in and used by another person without restriction.

case law The law as laid down in the decisions of the courts. The law extracted from decided cases.

cashier's check A bill of exchange, drawn by a bank upon itself, and accepted by the act of issuance.

cause of action A right of action at law arises from the existence of a primary right in the plaintiff, and an invasion of that right by some civil wrong on the part of the defendant, and that the facts which establish the existence of that right and that civil wrong constitute the cause of action.

caveat emptor Let the buyer beware. This maxim expresses the general idea that the buyer purchases at his or her own peril, and that there are no warranties, either express or implied, made by the seller.

caveat venditor Let the seller beware. This tends to be the rule of law in sales of goods today.

certification The return of a writ; a formal attestation of a matter of fact; the appropriate marking of a certified check.

certified check A check that has been "accepted" by the drawee bank and has been so marked or certified that it indicates such acceptance.

cestui que trust The person for whose benefit property is held in trust by a trustee.

champerty The purchase of an interest in a matter in dispute so as to take part in the litigation.

chancellor A judge of a court of chancery.

chancery Equity or a court of equity.

charge To charge a jury is to instruct the jury as to the essential law of the case. The first step in the prosecution of a crime is to formally accuse the offender or charge him with the crime.

charter An instrument or authority from the sovereign power bestowing the right or power to do business under the corporate form of organization. Also the organic law of a city or town, and representing a portion of the statute law of the state.

chattel mortgage An instrument whereby the owner of chattels transfers the title to such property to another as security for the performance of an obligation subject to be defeated on the performance of the obligation. Under the U.C.C., it is called merely a *security interest.*

chattel real Interests in real estate less than a freehold, such as an estate for years.

chattels Goods both movable and immovable except such as are in the nature of freehold or a part of a freehold.

check A written order on a bank or banker payable on demand to the person named or his order or bearer and drawn by virtue of credits due the drawer from the bank created by money deposited with the bank.

chose in action   A personal right not reduced to possession but recoverable by a suit at law.

C.I.F.   An abbreviation for cost, freight, and insurance, used in mercantile transactions, especially in import transactions.

citation   A writ issued out of a court of competent jurisdiction, commanding the person therein named to appear on a day named to do something therein mentioned.

citation of authorities   The reference to legal authorities such as reported cases or treatises to support propositions advanced.

civil action   An action brought to enforce a civil right; in contrast to a criminal action.

class action   An action brought on behalf of the plaintiff and others similarly situated.

close corporation   A corporation in which directors and officers, rather than the shareholders, have the right to fill vacancies in their ranks. Also used to refer to any corporation whose stock is not freely traded and whose shareholders are personally known to each other.

C.O.D.   **"Cash on delivery"**   When goods are delivered to a carrier for a cash on delivery shipment, the carrier must not deliver without receiving payment of the amount due.

code   A system of law; a systematic and complete body of law.

codicil   Some addition to or qualification of one's last will and testament.

cognovit   To acknowledge an action. A cognovit note is a promissory note that contains an acknowledgment clause.

collateral attack   An attempt to impeach a decree, judgment, or other official act in a proceeding that has not been instituted for the express purpose of correcting or annulling or modifying the decree, judgment, or official act.

comaker   A person who with another or others signs a negotiable instrument on its face and thereby becomes primarily liable for its payment.

commercial law   The law that relates to the rights of property and persons engaged in trade or commerce.

commission merchant   A person who sells goods in his own name at his own store, and on commission, from sample. Also one who buys and sells goods for a principal in his own name and without disclosing his principal.

common carrier   One who undertakes, for hire or reward, to transport the goods of such of the public as choose to employ him.

compensatory damages   See **damages.**

complaint   A form of legal process that usually consists of a formal allegation or charge against a party, made or presented to the appropriate court or officer. The technical name of a bill in equity by which the complainant sets out his cause of action.

composition with creditors   An agreement between creditors and their common debtor and between themselves whereby the creditors agree to accept the sum or security stipulated in full payment of their claims.

concurrent   Running with, simultaneously with. The word is used in different senses. In contracts, concurrent conditions are conditions that must be performed simultaneously by the mutual acts required by each of the parties.

condemn   To appropriate land for public use. To adjudge a person guilty; to pass sentence upon a person convicted of a crime.

condition   A provision or clause in a contract that operates to suspend or rescind the principal obligation. A qualification or restriction annexed to a conveyance of lands, whereby it is provided that in case a particular event does or does not happen, or in case the grantor or grantees do or omit to do a particular act, an estate shall commence, be enlarged, or be defeated.

condition precedent   A condition that must happen before either party is bound by the principal obligation of a contract; e.g., one agrees to purchase goods if they are delivered before a stated day. Delivery before the stated day, then, is a condition precedent to one's obligation to purchase.

condition subsequent   A condition that operates to relieve or discharge one from his or her obligation under a contract.

conditional acceptance   An acceptance of a bill of exchange containing some qualification limiting or altering the acceptor's liability on the bill.

conditional sale   The term is most frequently applied to a sale wherein the seller reserves the title to the goods, although the possession is delivered to the buyer, until the purchase price is paid in full.

confession of judgment An entry of judgment upon the admission or confession of the debtor without the formality, time, or expense involved in an ordinary proceeding.

conservator (of an insane person) A person appointed by a court to take care of and oversee the person and estate of an idiot or other incompetent person.

consignee A person to whom goods are consigned, shipped, or otherwise transmitted, either for sale or for safekeeping.

consignment A bailment for sale. The consignee does not undertake the absolute obligation to sell or pay for the goods.

consignor One who sends goods to another on consignment; a shipper or transmitter of goods.

construe To read a statute or document for the purpose of ascertaining its meaning and effect, but in doing so the law must be regarded.

contempt Conduct in the presence of a legislative or judicial body tending to disturb its proceedings or impair the respect due to its authority, or a disobedience to the rules or orders of such a body which interferes with the due administration of law.

contra Otherwise; disagreeing with; contrary to.

contra bonos moris Contrary to good morals.

contribution A payment made by each, or by any, of several having a common interest or liability of his share in the loss suffered, or in the money necessarily paid by one of the parties in behalf of the others.

conversion Any distinct act of dominion wrongfully exerted over another's personal property in denial of or inconsistent with his rights therein. That tort which is committed by a person who deals with chattels not belonging to him in a manner that is inconsistent with the ownership of the lawful owner.

conveyance In its common use it refers to a written instrument transferring the title to land or some interest therein from one person to another. It is sometimes applied to the transfer of the property in personalty.

copartnership A partnership.

corporation An artificial being, invisible, intangible, and existing only in contemplation of law.

It is exclusively the work of the law, and the best evidence of its existence is the grant of corporate powers by the commonwealth.

corporeal Possessing physical substance; tangible; perceptible to the senses.

counterclaim A claim that, if established, will defeat or in some way qualify a judgment to which the plaintiff is otherwise entitled.

counteroffer A cross-offer made by the offeree to the offeror.

covenant The word is used in its popular sense as synonymous with contract. In its specific sense it ordinarily imparts an agreement reduced to writing and executed by a sealing and delivery.

covenantor A person who covenants; the maker of a covenant.

credible As applied to a witness, the word means competent.

cross-action Cross-complaint; an independent action brought by a defendant against the plaintiff.

culpable Blameworthy; denotes breach of legal duty but not criminal conduct.

cumulative voting A method of voting by which an elector who is entitled to vote for several candidates for the same office may cast more than one vote for the same candidate, distributing among the candidates as he chooses a number of votes equal to the number of candidates to be elected.

custody The bare control or care of a thing as distinguished from the possession of it.

d/b/a Doing business as; indicates the use of a trade name.

damages Indemnity to the person who suffers loss or harm from an injury; a sum recoverable as amends for a wrong. An adequate compensation for the loss suffered or the injury sustained.

compensatory Damages that will compensate a party for direct losses due to an injury suffered.

consequential Damages that are not produced without the concurrence of some other event attributable to the same origin or cause.

liquidated Damages made certain by the prior agreement of the parties.

nominal Damages that are recoverable where a legal right is to be vindicated against an invasion that has produced no actual present loss.

special Actual damages that would not necessarily but because of special circumstances do in fact flow from an injury.

date of issue As the term is applied to notes, bonds, etc., of a series, it usually means the arbitrary date fixed as the beginning of the term for which they run, without reference to the precise time when convenience or the state of the market may permit their sale or delivery.

deal To engage in mutual intercourse or transactions of any kind.

debenture A written acknowledgment of a debt; specifically an instrument under seal for the repayment of money lent.

debtor A person who owes another anything, or who is under obligation, arising from express agreement, implication of law, or the principles of natural justice, to render and pay a sum of money to another.

deceit A type of fraud; actual fraud consisting of any false representations or contrivance whereby one person overreaches and misleads another to his hurt.

decision A decision is the judgment of a court, whereas the opinion represents merely the reasons for that judgment.

declaration The pleadings by which a plaintiff in an action at law sets out his cause of action. An admission or statement subsequently used as evidence in the trial of an action.

declaratory judgment One that expresses the opinion of a court on a question of law without ordering anything to be done.

decree An order or sentence of a court of equity determining some right or adjudicating some matter affecting the merits of the cause.

deed A writing, sealed and delivered by the parties; an instrument conveying real property.

de facto In fact; as distinguished from "de jure," by right.

defalcation The word includes both embezzlement and misappropriation and is a broader term than either.

default Fault; neglect; omission; the failure of a party to an action to appear when properly served with process; the failure to perform a duty or obligation; the failure of a person to pay money when due or when lawfully demanded.

defeasible (of title to property) Capable of being defeated. A title to property that is open to attack or may be defeated by the performance of some act.

defend To oppose a claim or action; to plead in defense of an action; to contest an action suit or proceeding.

defendant A party sued in a personal action.

defendant in error Any of the parties in whose favor a judgment was rendered that the losing party seeks to have reversed or modified by writ of error and whom he names as adverse parties.

deficiency That part of a debt that a mortgage was made to secure, not realized by the liquidation of the mortgaged property. Something lacking.

defraud To deprive another of a right by deception or artifice. To cheat; to wrong another by fraud.

dehors Outside of; disconnected with; unrelated to.

de jure By right; complying with the law in all respects.

del credere agent An agent who guarantees his principal against the default of those with whom contracts are made.

deliver To surrender property to another person.

demand A claim; a legal obligation; a request to perform an alleged obligation; a written statement of a claim.

de minimis non curat lex The law is not concerned with trifles. The maxim has been applied to exclude the recovery of nominal damages where no unlawful intent or disturbance of a right of possession is shown, and where all possible damage is expressly disproved.

demurrage A compensation for the delay of a vessel beyond the time allowed for loading, unloading, or sailing. It is also applied to the compensation for the similar delay of a railroad car.

demurrer A motion to dismiss; an allegation in pleading to the effect that even if the facts alleged by the opposing party are true, they are insufficient to require an answer.

de novo, trial Anew; over again; a second time. A trial de novo is a new trial in which the entire case is retried in all its detail.

dependent covenants Covenants made by two parties to a deed or agreement that are such that the thing covenanted or promised to be done on each part enters into the whole consideration for the covenant or promise on the part of the other, or such covenants as are concurrent and to be performed at the same time. Neither party to such a covenant can maintain an action against the other without averring and proving performance on his part.

deposition An affidavit; an oath; the written testimony of a witness given in the course of a judicial proceeding, either at law or in equity, in response to interrogatories either oral or written, and where an opportunity is given for cross-examination.

deputy A person subordinate to a public officer whose business and object is to perform the duties of the principal.

derivative action A suit by a shareholder to enforce a corporate cause of action.

descent Hereditary succession. It is the title whereby a person on the death of his ancestor acquires his estate by right of representation as his heir at law, an heir being one upon whom the law casts the estate immediately at the death of the ancestor, the estate so descending being the inheritance.

detinue A common law action, now seldom used, where a party claims the specific recovery of goods and chattels unlawfully detained from him.

detriment A detriment is any act or forebearance by a promise. A loss or harm suffered in person or property.

dictum The opinion of a judge that does not embody the resolution or determination of the court and is made without argument, or full consideration of the point, and is not the professed deliberation of the judge himself.

directed verdict A verdict that the jury returns as directed by the court. The court may thus withdraw the case from the jury whenever there is no competent, relevant and material evidence to support the issue.

discharge in bankruptcy An order of decree rendered by a court in bankruptcy proceedings, the effect of which is to satisfy all debts provable against the estate of the bankrupt as of the time when the bankruptcy proceedings were initiated.

discount A loan upon an evidence of debt, where the compensation for the use of the money until the maturity of the debt is deducted from the principal and retained by the lender at the time of making the loan.

dismiss To order a cause, motion, or prosecution to be discontinued or quashed.

diverse citizenship A term of frequent use in the interpretation of the federal constitutional provision for the jurisdiction of the federal courts which extends it to controversies between citizens of different states.

divided court A court is so described when there has been a division of opinion between its members on a matter submitted to it for decision.

dividend A gain or profit. A fund that a corporation sets apart from its profits to be divided among its members.

domain The ownership of land; immediate or absolute ownership. The public lands of a state are frequently called the *public domain.*

domicile A place where a person lives or has his home; in a strict legal sense, the place where he has his true, fixed, permanent home and principal establishment, and to which place he has, whenever he is absent, the intention of returning.

dominion (property) The rights of dominion or property are those rights that a person may acquire in and to such external things as are unconnected with his body.

donee A person to whom a gift is made.

donor A person who makes a gift.

dower The legal right or interest that his wife acquires by marriage in the real estate of her husband.

draft A written order drawn upon one person by another, requesting him to pay money to a designated third person. A bill of exchange payable on demand.

drawee A person upon whom a draft or bill of exchange is drawn by the drawer.

drawer The maker of a draft or bill of exchange.

due bill An acknowledgment of a debt in writing, not made payable to order.

dummy One posing or represented as acting for himself, but in reality acting for another. A tool or "straw man" for the real parties in interest.

duress   Overpowering of the will of a person by force or fear.

earnest   Something given as part of the purchase price to bind the bargain.

easement   A liberty, privilege, or advantage in land without profit, existing distinct from the ownership of the soil; the right that one person has to use the land of another for a specific purpose.

edict   A command or prohibition promulgated by a sovereign and having the effect of law.

effects   As used in wills, the word is held equivalent to personal property. It denotes property in a more extensive sense than goods and includes all kinds of personal property but is held not to include real property unless the context discloses an intention on the part of the testator to dispose of his realty by the use of the word.

e.g.   An abbreviation for "exempli gratia," meaning for or by the way of example.

ejectment   By statute in some states, it is an action to recover the immediate possession of real property. At common law, it was a purely possessory action, and as modified by statute, though based on title, it is still essentially a possessory action.

eleemosynary corporation   A corporation created for a charitable purpose or for charitable purposes.

emancipate   To release; to set free. Where a father expressly or impliedly by his conduct waives his right generally to the services of his minor child, the child is said to be emancipated and he may sue on contracts made by him for his services.

embezzlement   A statutory offense consisting of the fraudulent conversion of another's personal property by one to whom it has been entrusted, with the intention of depriving the owner thereof, the gist of the offense being usually the violation of relations of fiduciary character.

encumbrance   An encumbrance on land is a right in a third person in the land to the diminuition of the value of the land, though consistent with the passing of the fee by the deed of conveyance.

endorsement   See **Indorsement**.

entry   Recordation; noting in a record; going upon land; taking actual possession of land. Literally, the act of going into a place after a breach has been effected.

eo nominee   By or in that name or designation.

equity   A system of justice that developed in England separate from the common law courts. Few states in the United States still maintain separate equity courts, though most apply equity principles and procedures when remedies derived from the equity courts are sought. A broader meaning denotes fairness and justice.

escheat   The revision of land to the state in the event there is no person competent to inherit it.

estate   Technically the word refers only to an interest in land.

estate at will   A lease of lands or tenements to be held at the will of the lessor. Such can be determined by either party.

estate for a term   An estate less than a freehold that is in fact a contract for the possession of land or tenements for some determinate period.

estate for life   An estate created by deed or grant conveying land or tenements to a person to hold for the term of his own life or for the life of any other person or for more lives than one.

estate in fee simple   An absolute inheritance, clear of any conditions, limitations, or restrictions to particular heirs. It is the highest estate known to the law and necessarily implies absolute dominion over the land.

estate per autre vie   An estate that is to endure for the life of a person other than the grantee, or for the lives of more than one, in either of which cases the grantee is called the *tenant for life*.

estoppel.   That state of affairs which arises when one is forbidden by law from alleging or denying a fact because of previous action or inaction.

et al.   An abbreviation for the Latin "et alius" meaning "and another", also of "et alii" meaning "and others."

et ux.   An abbreviation for the Latin "et uxor" meaning "and his wife."

eviction   Originally, as applied to tenants, the word meant depriving the tenant of the possession of the demised premises, but technically, it is the disturbance of his possession, depriving him of the enjoyment of the premises demised or any portion thereof by title paramount or by entry and act of the landlord.

evidence That which makes clear or ascertains the truth of the fact or point in issue either on the one side or on the other; those rules of law whereby we determine what testimony is to be admitted and what rejected in each case and what is the weight to be given to the testimony admitted.

exception An objection, a reservation, a contradiction.

ex contractu From or out of a contract.

ex delicto From or out of a wrongful act; tortious; tortiously.

executed When applied to written instruments, the word is sometimes used as synonymous with signed and means no more than that, but more frequently it imports that everything has been done to complete the transaction; that is, that the instrument has been signed, sealed, and delivered. An executed contract is one in which the object of the contract is performed.

execution A remedy in the form of a writ or process afforded by law for the enforcement of a judgment. The final consummation of a contract of sale, including only those acts necessary to the full completion of an instrument, such as the signature of the seller, the affixing of his seal, and its delivery to the buyer.

executor A person who is designated in a will as one who is to administer the estate of the testator.

executory Not yet executed; not yet fully performed, completed, fulfilled, or carried out; to be performed wholly or in part.

executrix Feminine of executor.

exemption A release from some burden, duty, or obligation; a grace; a favor; an immunity; taken out from under the general rule, not to be like others who are not exempt.

exhibit A copy of a written instrument on which a pleading is founded, annexed to the pleading and by reference made a part of it. Any paper or thing offered in evidence and marked for identification.

face value The nominal or par value of an instrument as expressed on its face; in the case of a bond, this is the amount really due, including interest.

factor An agent who is employed to sell goods for a principal, usually in his own name, and who is given possession of the goods.

F.A.S. An abbreviation for the expression "free alongside steamer."

fee simple absolute Same as fee simple. See **estate in fee simple.**

felony As a general rule all crimes punishable by death or by imprisonment in a state prison are felonies.

feme covert A married woman.

feme sole An unmarried woman.

fiction An assumption made by the law that something is true that is or may be false.

fiduciary One who holds goods in trust for another or one who holds a position of trust and confidence.

fieri facias You cause to be made, an ordinary writ of execution whereby the officer is commanded to levy and sell and to "make," if he can, the amount of the judgment creditors demand.

fixture A thing that was originally a personal chattel and has been actually or constructively affixed to the soil itself or to some structure legally a part of such soil; an article that was once a chattel, but by being physically annexed or affixed to the realty has become accessory to it and part and parcel of it.

F.O.B. An abbreviation of "free on board."

forwarder A person who, having no interest in goods and no ownership or interest in the means of their carriage, undertakes, for hire, to forward them by a safe carrier to their destination.

franchise A special privilege conferred by government upon individuals, and which does not belong to the citizens of a country generally, of common right. Also a contractual relationship establishing a means of marketing goods or services giving certain elements of control to the supplier (franchiser) in return for the right of the franchisee to use the supplier's trade name or trademark, usually in a specific marketing area.

fungible goods Goods any unit of which is from its nature or by mercantile custom treated as the equivalent of any other unit.

futures Contracts for the sale and future delivery of stocks or commodities, wherein either party may waive delivery and receive or pay, as the case may be, the difference in market price at the time set for delivery.

garnishee As a noun, the term signifies the person upon whom a garnishment is served, usually a debtor of the defendant in the action. Used as a verb, the word means to institute garnishment proceedings, to cause a garnishment proceedings, to cause a garnishment to be levied on the garnishee.

garnishment A proceeding whereby property, money, or credits of a debtor in possession of another, the garnishee, are applied to the payment of the debts by means of process against the debtor and the garnishee. It is a statutory proceeding based on contract relations and can be resorted to only where it is authorized by statute.

general issue A plea of the defendant amounting to a denial of every material allegation of fact in the plaintiff's complaint or declaration.

going business An establishment that is still continuing to transact its ordinary business, though it may be insolvent.

good faith An honest intention to abstain from taking an unfair advantage of another.

grantee A person to whom a grant is made.

grantor A person who makes a grant.

gravamen Gist, essence, substance. The grievance complained of; the substantial cause of the action.

guarantor A person who promises to answer for the debt, default, or miscarriage of another.

guaranty An undertaking by one person to be answerable for the payment of some debt, or the due performance of some contract or duty by another person, who remains liable to pay or perform the same.

guardian A person (in some rare cases a corporation) to whom the law has entrusted the custody and control of the person, or estate, or both, of an infant, lunatic, or incompetent person.

habeas corpus Any of several common law writs having as their object to bring a party before the court or judge. The only issue it presents is whether the prisoner is restrained of his liberty by due process.

habendum The second part of a deed or conveyance following that part which names the grantee. It describes the estate conveyed and to what use. It is no longer essential and if included in a modern deed is a mere useless form.

hearing The supporting of one's contentions by argument and if need be by proof. It is an absolute right and if denied to a contestant it would amount to the denial of a constitutional rights.

hedging A market transaction in which a party buys a certain quantity of a given commodity at the price current on the date of the purchase and sells an equal quantity of the same commodity for future delivery for the purpose of getting protection against loss due to fluctuation in the market.

heirs Those persons appointed by law to succeed to the real estate of a decedent, in case of intestacy.

hereditaments A larger and more comprehensive word than either "land" or "tenements," and meaning anything capable of being inherited, whether it be corporeal, incorporeal, real, personal, or mixed.

holder in due course A holder who has taken a negotiable instrument under the following conditions: (1) that it is complete and regular on its face; (2) that he became the holder of it before it was overdue, and without notice that it had been previously dishonored, if such was the fact; (3) that he took it in good faith and for value; and (4) that at the time it was negotiated to him he had no notice of any infirmity in the instrument or defect in the title of the person negotiating it.

holding company A corporation whose purpose or function is to own or otherwise hold the shares of other corporations either for investment or control.

homestead In a legal sense the word means the real estate occupied as a home and also the right to have it exempt from levy and forced sale. It is the land, not exceeding the prescribed amount, upon which the dwelling house, or residence, or habitation, or abode of the owner thereof and his family resides, and includes the dwelling house as an indispensable part.

illusory Deceiving or intending to deceive, as by false appearances; fallacious. An illusory promise is a promise that appears to be binding but in fact does not bind the promisor.

immunity A personal favor granted by law, contrary to the general rule.

impanel To place the names of the jurors on a panel; to make a list of the names of those persons who have been selected for jury duty; to go through the process of selecting a jury that is to try a cause.

implied warranty An implied warranty arises by operation of law and exists without any intention of the seller to create it. It is a conclusion or inference of law, pronounced by the court, on facts admitted or proved before the jury.

inalienable Incapable of being alienated, transferred, or conveyed; nontransferrable.

in banc With all the judges of the court sitting.

in camera In the judge's chambers; in private.

incapacity In its legal meaning, it applies to one's legal disability, such as infancy, want of authority, or other personal incapacity to alter legal relationship.

inchoate Imperfect; incipient; not completely formed.

indemnify To hold harmless against loss or damage.

indemnity An obligation or duty resting on one person to make good any loss or damage another has incurred while acting at his request or for his benefit. By a contract of indemnity one may agree to save another from a legal consequence of the conduct of one of the parties or of some other person.

indenture Identures were deeds that originally were made in two parts formed by cutting or tearing a single sheet across the middle in a jagged or indented line, so that the two parts might be subsequently matched; and they were executed by both grantor and grantee. Later the indenting of the deed was discontinued, yet the term came to be applied to all deeds executed by both parties.

independent contractor One who, exercising an independent employment, contracts to do a piece of work according to his or her own methods, and without being subject to the control of the employer except as to result. The legal effect is to insulate the employing party from liability for the misconduct of the independent contractor and his employees.

indictment An accusation founded on legal testimony of a direct and positive character, and the concurring judgment of at least 12 of the grand jurors that upon the evidence presented to them the defendant is guilty.

indorsement Writing on the back of an instrument; the contract whereby the holder of a bill or note transfers to another person his right to such instrument and incurs the liabilities incident to the tranfer.

infant See **Minor.**

information A written accusation of crime presented by a public prosecuting officer without the intervention of a grand jury.

injunction A restraining order issued by a court of equity; a prohibitory writ restraining a person from committing or doing an act, other than a criminal act, that appears to be against equity and conscience. There is also the mandatory injunction, which commands an act to be done or undone and compels the performance of some affirmative act.

in pari delicto Equally at fault in tort or crime; in equal fault or guilt.

in personam Against the person.

in re In the matter; in the transaction.

in rem Against a thing and not against a person; concerning the condition or status of a thing.

insolvency The word has two distinct meanings. It may be used to denote the insufficiency of the entire property and assets of an individual to pay his or her debts, which is its general meaning and its meaning as used in the Bankruptcy Act; but in a more restricted sense, it expresses the inability of a party to pay his debts as they become due in the regular course of his business, and it is so used when traders and merchants are said to be insolvent.

in statu quo In the existing state of things.

instrument In its broadest sense, the term includes formal or legal documents in writing, such as contracts, deeds, wills, bonds, leases, and mortgages. In the law of evidence, it has still a wider meaning and includes not merely documents, but also witnesses and things animate and inanimate that may be presented for inspection.

insurable interest Any interest in property the owner of which interest derives a benefit from the existence of the property or would suffer a loss from its destruction. It is not necessary, to constitute an insurable interest, that the interest is such that the event insured against would necessarily subject the insured to loss; it is sufficient that it might do so.

inter alia Among other things or matters.

interlocutory Something not final but deciding only some subsidiary matter raised while a law suit is pending.

interpleader An equitable remedy applicable where one fears injury from conflicting claims. Where a person does not know which of two or more persons claiming certain property held by him or her has a right to it, filing a bill of interpleader forces the claimants to litigate the title between themselves.

intervention A proceeding by which one not originally made a party to an action or suit is permitted, on his own application, to appear therein and join one of the original parties in maintaining his cause of action or defense, or to assert some cause of action against some or all of the parties to the proceeding as originally instituted.

intestate A person who has died without leaving a valid will disposing of his or her property and estate.

in toto In the whole, altogether; wholly.

In transitu On the journey. Goods are as a rule considered as in transitu while they are in the possession of a carrier, whether by land or water, until they arrive at the ultimate place of their destination and are delivered into the actual possession of the buyer, whether or not the carrier has been named or designated by the buyer.

ipso facto By the fact itself; by the very fact; by the act itself.

joint bank account A bank account of two persons so fixed that they shall be joint owners thereof during their mutual lives, and the survivor shall take the whole on the death of other.

jointly Acting together or in concert or cooperating; holding in common or interdependently, not separately. Persons are "jointly bound" in a bond or note when both or all must be sued in one action for its enforcement, not either one at the election of the creditor.

jointly and severally Persons who find themselves "jointly and severally" in a bond or note may all be sued together for its enforcement, or the creditor may select any one or more as the object of his suit.

joint tenancy An estate held by two or more jointly, with an equal right in all to share in the enjoyments of the land during their lives. Four requisites must exist to constitute a joint tenancy, viz: the tenants must have one and the same interest; the interest must accrue by one and the same conveyance; they must commence at one and the same time; and the property must be held by one and the same undivided possession. If any one of these four elements is lacking, the estate is not one of joint tenancy. An incident of joint tenancy is the right of survivorship.

judgment The sentence of the law upon the record; the application of the law to the facts and pleadings. The last word in the judicial controversy; the final consideration and determination of a court of competent jurisdiction upon matters submitted to it in an action or proceeding.

judgment lien The statutory lien upon the real property of a judgment debtor which is created by the judgment itself. At common law a judgment imposes no lien upon the real property of the judgment debtor, and to subject the property of the debtor to the judgment it was necessary to take out a writ called an *elegit*.

judgment n.o.v. (judgment non obstante veredicto) Judgment notwithstanding the verdict. Under certain circumstances the judge has the power to enter a judgment that is contrary to the verdict of the jury. Such a judgment is a judgment non obstante veredicto.

jurisdiction The right to adjudicate concerning the subject matter in a given case. The modern tendency is to make the word include not only the power to hear and determine, but also the power to render the particular judgment in the particular case.

jury A body of lay persons, selected by lot, or by some other fair and impartial means, to ascertain, under the guidance of the judge, the truth in questions of fact arising in either civil litigation or a criminal process.

kite To secure the temporary use of money by issuing or negotiating worthless paper and then redeeming such paper with the proceeds of similar paper. The word is also used as a noun, meaning the worthless paper thus employed.

laches The established doctrine of equity that, apart from any question of statutory limitation, its courts will discourage delay and sloth in the enforcement of rights. Equity demands conscience, good faith, and reasonable diligence.

law merchant The custom of merchants, or lex mercatorio, that grew out of the necessity and convenience of business, and that, although different from the general rules of the common law, was engrafted into it and became a part of it.

leading case A case often referred to by the courts and by counsel as having finally settled and determined a point of law.

leading questions Those questions which suggest to the witness the answer desired, those which assume a fact to be proved that is not proved, or which, embodying a material fact, admit of an answer by a simple negative or affirmative.

lease A contract for the possession and use of land on one side, and a recompense of rent or other income on the other; a conveyance to a person for life, or years, or at will in consideration of a return of rent or other recompense.

legacy A bequest; a testamentary gift of personal property. Sometimes incorrectly applied to a testamentary gift of real property.

legal According to the principles of law; according to the method required by statute; by means of judicial proceedings; not equitable.

legitimacy A person's status embracing his right to inherit from his ancestors, to be inherited from, and to bear the name and enjoy the support of his parents.

letter of credit An instrument containing a request (general or special) to pay to the bearer or person named money, or sell him or her some commodity on credit or give something of value and look to the drawer of the letter for recompense.

levy At common law a levy on goods consisted of an officer's entering the premises where they were and either leaving an assistant in charge of them or removing them after taking an inventory. Today courts differ as to what is a valid levy, but by the weight of authority there must be an actual or constructive seizure of the goods. In most states, a levy on land must be made by some unequivocal act of the officer indicating the intention of singling out certain real estate for the satisfaction of the debt.

license A personal privilege to do some act or series of acts upon the land of another, without possessing any estate therein. A permit or authorization to do what, without a license, would be unlawful.

lien In its most extensive meaning it is a charge upon property for the payment or discharge of a debt or duty; a qualified right; a proprietary interest that, in a given case, may be exercised over the property of another.

life estate. See **Estate for life.**

lis pendens A pending suit. As applied to the doctrine of lis pendens, it is the jurisdiction, power, or control that courts acquire over property involved in a suit, pending the continuance of the action, and until its final judgment therein.

listing contract A so-called contract whereby an owner of real property employs a broker to procure a purchaser without giving the broker exclusive right to sell. Under such an agreement, it is generally held that the employment may be terminated by the owner at will, and that a sale of the property by the owner terminates the employment.

litigant A party to a lawsuit.

long arm statute A statute subjecting a foreign corporation to jurisdiction although it may have committed only a single act within the state.

magistrate A word commonly applied to the lower judicial officers, such as justices of the peace, police judges, town recorders, and other local judicial functionaries. In a broader sense, a magistrate is a public civil officer invested with some part of the legislative, executive, or judicial power given by the Constitution. The President of the United States is the chief magistrate of the nation.

maker A person who makes or executes an instrument, the signer of an instrument.

mala fides Bad faith.

malfeasance The doing of an act that a person ought not to do at all. It is to be distinguished from misfeasance, which is the improper doing of an act that a person might lawfully do.

malum in se Evil in and of itself. An offense or act that is naturally evil as adjudged by the senses of a civilized community. Acts malum in se are usually criminal acts, but not necessarily so.

malum prohibitum An act that is wrong because it is made so by statute.

mandamus We command. It is a command issuing from a competent jurisdiction, in the name of the state or sovereign, directed to some inferior court, officer, corporation, or person, requiring the performance of a particular duty therein specified, which duty results from the official station of the party to whom it is directed, or from operation of law.

margin A deposit by a buyer in stocks with a seller or a stockbroker, as security to cover fluctuations in the market in reference to stocks that the buyer has purchased, but for which he has not paid. Commodities are also traded on margin.

marshals Ministerial officers belonging to the executive department of the federal government, who with their deputies have the same powers of executing the laws of the United States in each state as the sheriffs and their deputies in such state may have in executing the laws of that state.

mechanic's lien A claim created by law for the purpose of securing a priority of payment of the price of value of work performed and materials furnished in erecting or repairing a building or other structure; as such it attaches to the land as well as to the buildings erected therein.

mens rea A guilty mind, criminal intent.

merchantable Of good quality and salable, but not necessarily the best. As applied to articles sold, the word requires that the article shall be such as is usually sold in the market, of medium quality and bringing the average price.

minor A person who has not reached the age at which the law recognizes a general contractual capacity (called majority), formerly 21 years; recently changed to 18 in many states.

misdemeanor Any crime that is punishable neither by death nor by imprisonment in a state prison.

mistrial An invalid trial due to lack of jurisdiction, error in selection of jurors, or some other fundamental requirement.

mitigation of damages A reduction in the amount of damages due to extenuating circumstances.

moiety One half.

mortgage A conveyance of property to secure the performance of some obligation, the conveyance to be void on the due performance thereof.

motive The cause or reason that induced a person to commit a crime.

movables A word derived from the civil law and usually understood to signify the utensils that are to furnish or ornament a house, but it would seem to comprehend personal property generally.

mutuality Reciprocal obligations of the parties required to make a contract binding on either party.

necessaries With reference to a minor, the word includes whatever is reasonably necessary for his or her proper and suitable maintenance, in view of the income level and social position of the minor's family.

negligence The word has been defined as the omission to do something that a reasonable person, guided by those considerations that ordinarily regulate human affairs, would do, or doing something a prudent and reasonable person would not do.

negotiable Capable of being transferred by indorsement or delivery so as to give the holder a right to sue in his or her own name and to avoid certain defenses against the payee.

negotiable instrument An instrument that may be transferred or negotiated, so that the holder may maintain an action thereon in his own name.

no arrival, no sale A sale of goods "to arrive" or "on arrival," per or ex a certain ship, has been construed to be a sale subject to a double condition precedent, namely, that the ship arrives in port and that when it arrives the goods are on board, and if either of these conditions fails, the contract becomes nugatory.

nolo contendere · A plea in a criminal action that has the same effect as a guilty plea except that it does not bind the defendant in a civil suit on the same wrong.

nominal damages Damages that are recoverable where a legal right is to be vindicated against an invasion that has produced no actual present loss of any kind, or where there has been a breach of a contract and no actual damages whatever have been or can be shown, or where, under like conditions, there has been a breach of legal duty.

non compos mentis Totally and positively incompetent. The term denotes a person entirely destitute or bereft of memory or understanding.

nonfeasance In the law of agency, it is the total omission or failure of an agent to enter upon the performance of some distinct duty or undertaking he or she has agreed with the principal to do.

non obstante veredicto See Judgment non obstante veredicto.

nonsuit A judgment given against a plaintiff who is unable to prove a case, or when the plaintiff refuses or neglects to proceed to trial.

no-par value stock Stock of a corporation that has no face or par value.

noting protest The act of making a memorandum on a bill or note at the time of, and embracing the principal facts attending, its dishonor. The object is to have a record from which the instrument of protest may be written, so that a notary need not rely on memory for the fact.

novation A mutual agreement between all parties concerned for the discharge of a valid existing obligation by the substitution of a new valid obligation on the part of the debtor or another, or a like agreement for the discharge of a debtor to his creditor by the substitution of a new creditor.

nudum pactum A naked promise, a promise for which there is no consideration.

nuisance In legal parlance, the word extends to everything that endangers life or health, gives offense to the sense, violates the laws of decency, or obstructs the reasonable and comfortable use of property.

oath Any form of attestation by which a person signifies that he is bound in conscience to perform an act faithfully and truthfully. It involves the idea of calling on God to witness what is averred as truth, and it is supposed to be accompanied with an invocation of His vengeance, or a renunciation of His favor, in the event of falsehood.

obiter dictum That which is said in passing; a rule of law set forth in a court's opinion, but not involved in the case; what is said by the court outside the record or on a point not necessarily involved therein.

objection In the trial of a case it is the formal remonstrance made by counsel to something that has been said or done, in order to obtain the court's ruling thereon; and when the court has ruled, the alleged error is preserved by the objector's exception to the ruling, which exception is noted in the record.

obligee A person to whom another is bound by a promise or other obligation; a promisee.

obligor A person who is bound by a promise or other obligation; a promisor.

offer A proposal by one person to another that is intended of itself to create legal relations on acceptance by the person to whom it is made.

offeree A person to whom an offer is made.

offeror A person who makes an offer.

opinion The opinion of the court represents merely the reasons for its judgment, whereas the decision of the court is the judgment itself.

option A contract whereby the owner of property agrees with another person that such person shall have the right to buy the property at a fixed price within a certain time. There are two independent elements in an option contract: First, the offer to sell, which does not become a contract until accepted; second, the completed contract to leave the offer open for a specified time.

ordinance A legislative enactment of a county or an incorporated city or town.

ostensible authority Such authority as a principal, either intentionally or by want of ordinary care, causes or allows a third person to believe the agent to possess.

ostensible partners Members of a partnership whose names are made known and appear to the world as partners.

overdraft The withdrawal from a bank by a depositor of money in excess of the amount of money he or she has on deposit there.

overplus That which remains; a balance left over.

owner's risk A term employed by common carriers in bills of lading and shipping receipts to signify that the carrier does not assume responsibility for the safety of the goods.

par Par means equal, and par value means a value equal to the face of a bond or a stock certificate.

parol Oral, verbal, by word of mouth; spoken as opposed to written.

parties All persons who are interested in the subject matter of an action and who have a right to make defense, control the proceedings, examine and cross-examine witnesses, and appeal from the judgment.

partition A proceeding the object of which is to enable those who own property as joint tenants or tenants in common to put an end to the tenancy so as to vest in each a sole estate in specific property or an allotment of the lands and tenements. If a division of the estate is impracticable, the estate ought to be sold and the proceeds divided.

partners Those persons who contribute property, money, or services to carry on a joint business for their common benefit, and who own and share the profits thereof in certain proportions; the members of a partnership.

patent A patent for land is a conveyance of title to government lands by the government; a patent of an invention is the right of monopoly secured by statute to those who invent or discover new and useful devices and processes.

pawn A pledge; a bailment of personal property as security for some debt or engagement, redeemable on certain terms, and with an implied power of sale on default.

payee A person to whom a payment is made or is made payable.

pecuniary Financial; pertaining or relating to money; capable of being estimated, computed, or measured by money value.

per curiam By the court; by the court as a whole.

peremptory challenge A challenge to a proposed juror that a defendant in a criminal case may make as an absolute right, and that cannot be questioned by either opposing counsel or the court.

performance As the word implies, it is such a thorough fulfillment of a duty as puts an end to obligations by leaving nothing to be done. The chief requisite of performance is that it shall be exact.

perjury The willful and corrupt false swearing or affirming, after an oath lawfully administered, in the course of a judicial or quasi-judicial proceeding as to some matter material to the issue or point in question.

per se The expression means by or through itself; simply, as such; in its own relations.

petition In equity pleading, a petition is in the nature of a pleading (at least when filed by a stranger to the suit) and forms a basis for independent action.

plaintiff A person who brings a suit, action, bill, or complaint.

plaintiff in error The unsuccessful party to the action who prosecutes a writ of error in a higher court.

plea A plea is an answer to a declaration or complaint or any material allegation of fact therein, which if untrue would defeat the action. In criminal procedure, a plea is the matter that the accused, on arraignment, alleges in answer to the charge against him.

pledge A pawn; a bailment of personal property as security for some debt or engagement, redeemable on certain terms, and with an implied power of sale on default.

pledgee A person to whom personal property is pledged by a pledgor.

pledgor A person who makes a pledge of personal property to a pledgee.

positive law Laws actually and specifically enacted or adopted by proper authority for the government of a jural society as distinguished from principles of morality or laws of honor.

possession Respecting real property, possession involves exclusive dominion and control such as owners of like property usually exercise over it. The existence of such possession is largely a question of fact dependent on the nature of the property and the surrounding circumstances.

power of attorney A written authorization to an agent to perform specified acts on behalf of his or her principal. The writing by which the authority is evidenced is called a *letter of attorney* and is dictated by the convenience and certainty of business.

precedent A previous decision relied on as authority.

preference The act of a debtor in paying or securing one or more of his creditors in a manner more favorable to them than to other creditors or to the exclusion of such other creditors. In the absence of statute, a preference is perfectly good, but to be legal it must be bona fide, and not a mere subterfuge of the debtor to secure a future benefit to himself or to prevent the application of his property to his debts.

prerogative A special power, privilege, or immunity, usually used in reference to an official or his office.

presumption A term used to signify that which may be assumed without proof, or taken for granted. It is asserted as a self-evident result of human reason and experience.

prima facie At first sight; a fact that is presumed to be true unless disproved by contrary evidence.

privilege A right peculiar to an individual or body.

privity A mutual or successive relationship as, for example, between the parties to a contract.

probate A term used to include all matters of which probate courts have jurisdiction, which in many states are the estates of deceased persons and of persons under guardianship.

process In law, generally the summons or notice of beginning of suit.

proffer To offer for acceptance or to make a tender of.

promisee The person to whom a promise is made.

promisor A person who makes a promise to another; a person who promises.

promissory estoppel An estoppel arising on account of a promise that the promissor should expect to and that does induce an action or forbearance of a substantial nature.

promoters The persons who bring about the incorporation and organization of a corporation.

pro rata According to the rate, proportion, or allowance.

prospectus An introductory proposal for a contract in which the representations may or may not form the basis of the contract actually made; it may contain promises that are to be treated as a sort of floating obligation to take effect when appropriated by persons to whom they are addressed, and amount to a contract when assented to by any person who invests money on the faith of them.

pro tanto For so much; to such an extent.

proximate cause That cause of an injury which, in natural and continuous sequence, unbroken by any efficient intervening cause, produces the injury, and without which the injury would not have occurred.

qualified acceptance A conditional or modified acceptance. In order to create a contract, an acceptance must accept the offer substantially as made; hence, a qualified acceptance is no acceptance at all, is treated by the courts as a rejection of the offer made, and is in effect an offer by the offeree, which the offeror may, if he chooses, accept and thus create a contract.

quantum meruit As much as is deserved. A part of a common law action in assumpsit for the value of services rendered.

quash To vacate or make void.

quasi contract An obligation arising not from an agreement between the parties but from the voluntary act of one of them or some relation between them that will be enforced by a court.

quasi-judicial Acts of public officers involving investigation of facts and drawing conclusions from them as a basis of official action.

quitclaim deed A deed conveying only the right, title, and interest of the grantor in the property described, as distinguished from a deed conveying the property itself.

quo warranto   By what authority. The name of a writ (and also of the whole pleading) by which the government commences an action to recover an office or franchise from the person or corporation in possession of it.

quorum   That number of persons, shares represented, or officers who may lawfully transact the business of a meeting called for that purpose.

ratification   The adoption by one in whose name an unauthorized act has been performed by another upon the assumption of authority to act as his or her agent, even though without any precedent authority whatever, which adoption or ratification relates back, supplies the original authority to do the act, binding the principal so adopting or ratifying to the same extent as if the act had been done in the first instance—by previous authority. The act of a minor upon reaching majority affirming a voidable contract made during infancy and giving it the same force and effect as if it had been valid from the beginning.

rebuttal   Testimony addressed to evidence produced by the opposite party; rebutting evidence.

receiver   An indifferent person between the parties to a cause, appointed by the court to receive and preserve the property or funds in litigation, and receive its rents, issues, and profits, and apply or dispose of them at the direction of the court, when it does not seem reasonable that either party should hold them.

recognizance   At common law, an obligation entered into before some court of record or magistrate duly authorized, with a condition to do some particular act, usually to appear and answer to a criminal accusation. Being taken in open court and entered upon the order book, it was valid without the signature or seal or any of the obligors.

recorder   A public officer of a town or county charged with the duty of keeping the record books required by law to be kept in his or her office and of receiving and causing to be copied in such books such instruments as by law are entitled to be recorded.

redemption   The buying back of one's property after it has been sold. The right to redeem property sold under an order or decree of court is

purely a privilege conferred by, and does not exist independently of, statute.

redress   Remedy, indemnity, reparation.

release   The giving up or abandoning of a claim or right to a person against whom the claim exists or the rights is to be enforced or exercised. It is the discharge of a debt by the act of the party in distinction from an extinguishment that is a discharge by operation of law.

remainderman   One who is entitled to the remainder of the estate after a particular estate carved out of it has expired.

remand   An action of an appellate court returning a case to the trial court to take further action.

remedy   The appropriate legal form of relief by which a remediable right may be enforced.

remittitur   The certificate of reversal issued by an appellate court upon reversing the order or judgment appealed from.

replevin   A common law action by which the owner recovers possession of his or her own goods.

res   The thing; the subject matter of a suit; the property involved in the litigation; a matter; property; the business; the affair; the transaction.

res adjudicata   A matter that has been adjudicated; that which is definitely settled by a judicial decision.

rescind   As the word is applied to contracts, to rescind in some cases means to terminate the contract as to future transactions, while in others it means to annul the contract from the beginning.

residue   All that portion of the estate of a testator of which no effectual disposition has been made by his will otherwise than in the residuary clause.

respondent   The defendant in an action; a party adverse to an appellant in an action that is appealed to a higher court. The person against whom a bill in equity was exhibited.

restitution   Indemnification.

reversion   The residue of a fee simple remaining in the grantor, to commence in possession after the determination of some particular estate granted out by him. The estate of a landlord during the existence of the outstanding leasehold estate.

reversioner   A person who is entitled to a reversion.

right When we speak of a person having a right, we must necessarily refer to a civil right as distinguished from the elemental idea of a right absolute. We must have in mind a right given and protected by law, and a person's enjoyment thereof is regulated entirely by the law that creates it.

riparian Pertaining to or situated on the bank of a river. The word has reference to the bank and not to the bed of the stream.

sanction The penalty that will be incurred by a wrongdoer for the breach of law.

satisfaction A performance of the terms of an accord. If such terms require a payment of a sum of money, then "satisfaction" means that such payment has been made.

scienter In cases of fraud and deceit, the word means knowledge on the part of the person making the representations, at the time when they are made, that they are false. In an action for deceit it is generally held that scienter must be proved.

seal At common law, a seal is an impression on wax or some other tenacious material, but in modern practice the letters "l.s." (locuse sigilli) or the word "seal" enclosed in a scroll, either written or printed, and acknowledged in the body of the instrument to be a seal, is often used as a substitute.

security That which makes the enforcement of a promise more certain than the mere personal obligation of the debtor or promisor, whatever may be his possessions or financial standing. It may be a pledge of property or an additional personal obligation, but it means more than the mere promise of the debtor with property liable to general execution.

security agreement An agreement that creates or provides a security interest or lien on personal property. A term used in the U.C.C. including a wide range of transactions in the nature of chattel mortgages, conditional sales, etc.

seizin In a legal sense, the word means possession of premises with the intention of asserting a claim to a freehold estate therein; it is practically the same thing as ownership; it is a possession of a freehold estate, such as by the common law is created by livery of seizin.

service As applied to a process of courts, the word ordinarily implies something in the nature of an act or proceeding adverse to the party served, or of a notice to that party.

setoff A setoff both at law and in equity is that right which exists between two parties, each of whom, under an independent contract, owes an ascertained amount to the other, to set off their respective debts by way of mutual deduction, so that, in any action brought for the larger debt, the residue only, after such deduction, shall be recovered.

severable contract A contract that is not entire or indivisible. If the consideration is single, the contract is entire; but if it is expressly or by necessary implication apportioned, the contract is severable. The question is ordinarily determined by inquiring whether the contract embraces one or more subject matters, whether the obligation is due at the same time to the same person, and whether the consideration is entire or apportioned.

shareholder It is generally held that one who holds shares on the books of the corporation is a shareholder and that one who merely holds a stock certificate is not. Shareholders may become such by original subscription, by direct purchase from the corporation, or by subsequent transfer from the original holder.

share of stock The right that its owner has in the management, profits, and ultimate assets of the corporation. The tangible property of a corporation and the shares of stock therein are separate and distinct kinds of property and belong to different owners, the first being the property of an artificial person—the corporation, the latter the property of the individual owner.

sight A term signifying the date of the acceptance or that of protest for the nonacceptance of a bill of exchange; for example, ten days after sight.

sinking fund A fund accumulated by an issuer to redeem corporate securities.

situs Location; local position; the place where a person or thing is, is his situs. Intangible property has no actual situs, but it may have a legal situs, and for the purpose of taxation its legal situs is at the place where it is owned and not at the place where it is owed.

specific performance   Performance of a contract precisely as agreed upon; the remedy that arose in equity law to compel the defendant to do what he or she agreed to do.

stare decisis   The doctrine or principle that the decisions of the court should stand as precedents for future guidance.

stated capital   Defined specifically in the Model Business Corporation Act; generally, the amount received by a corporation upon issuance of its shares except that assigned to capital surplus.

status quo   The existing state of things.

stipulation   An agreement between opposing counsel in a pending action, usually required to be made in open court and entered on the minutes of the court, or else to be in writing and filed in the action, ordinarily entered into for the purpose of avoiding delay, trouble, or expense in the conduct of the action.

stockholder   See **Shareholder.**

stoppage in transitu   A right that the vendor of goods on credit has to recall them, or retake them, on the discovery of the insolvency of the vendee. It continues so long as the carrier remains in the possession and control of the goods, or until there has been an actual or constructive delivery to the vendee or some third person has acquired a bona fide right in them.

subpoena   A process the purpose of which is to compel the attendance of a person whom it is desired to use as a witness.

subrogation   The substitution of one person in the place of another with reference to a lawful claim or right, frequently referred to as the doctrine of substitution. It is a device adopted or invented by equity to compel the ultimate discharge of a debt or obligation by the person who in good conscience ought to pay it.

sui generis   Of its own kind; peculiar to itself.

summary judgment   A decision of a trial court without hearing evidence.

summary proceedings   Proceedings, usually statutory, in the course of which many formalities are dispensed with. But such proceedings are not concluded without proper investigation of the facts, or without notice or an opportunity to be heard by the person alleged to have committed the act, or whose property is sought to be affected.

summons   A writ or process issued and served upon a defendant in a civil action for the purpose of securing his or her appearance in the action.

supra   Above, above mentioned, in addition to.

surety   One who by accessory agreement called a *contract of suretyship* binds himself with another, called the *principal,* for the performance of an obligation in respect to which such other person is already bound and primarily liable for such performance.

T/A   Trading as, indicating the use of a trade name.

tacking   The adding together of successive periods of adverse possession of persons in privity with each other, in order to constitute one continuous adverse possession for the time required by the statute, to establish title.

tangible   Capable of being possessed or realized; readily apprenhensible by the mind; real; substantial; evident.

tenancy   A tenancy exists when one has let real estate to another to hold of him as landlord. When duly created and the tenant put into possession, he is the owner of an estate for the time being and has all the usual rights and remedies to defend his possession.

tender   An unconditional offer of payment, consisting in the actual production in money or legal tender of a sum not less than the amount due.

tender offer   An offer to security holders to acquire their securities in exchange for money or other securites.

tenement   A word commonly used in deeds that pass not only lands and other inheritances but also offices, rents, commons, and profits arising from lands. Usually it is applied exclusively to land, or what is ordinarily denominated real property.

tenor   The tenor of an instrument is an exact copy of the instrument. Under the rule that an indictment for forgery must set out in the instrument according to its "tenor," the word means an exact copy—that the instrument is set forth in the very words and figures.

tenure   The manner of holding or occupying lands or offices. The most common estate in land is tenure in *fee simple.* With respect to offices tenure imports time, e.g., "tenure for life" or "during good behavior."

testament A last will and testament is the disposition of one's property to take effect after death.

testator A deceased person who died leaving a will.

testatrix Feminine of testator.

testimony In some contexts the word bears the same import as "evidence," but in most connections it has a much narrower meaning. Testimony is the words heard from the witness in court, and evidence is what the jury considers it worth.

tort An injury or wrong committed, either with or without force, to the person or property of another. Such injury may arise by nonfeasance or by the malfeasance or misfeasance of the wrongdoer.

tort-feasor A person who commits a tort; a wrongdoer.

tortious Partaking of the nature of a tort; wrongful; injurious.

trade fixtures Articles of personal property that have been annexed to the freehold and are necessary to the carrying on of a trade.

transcript A copy of a writing.

transferee A person to whom a transfer is made.

transferor A person who makes a transfer.

treasury shares Shares of stock of a corporation that have been issued as fully paid to shareholders and subsequently acquired by the corporation.

treble damages Three times provable damages, as may be granted to private parties bringing an action under the antitrust laws.

trespass Every unauthorized entry on another's property is a trespass, and any person who makes such an entry is a trespasser. In its widest signification, trespass means any violation of law. In its most restricted sense, it signifies an injury intentionally inflicted by force on either the person or property of another.

trial An examination before a competent tribunal, according to the law of the land, of the facts or law put in issue in a cause, for the purpose of determining such issue. When the court hears and determines any issue of fact or law for the purpose of determining the rights of the parties, it may be considered a trial.

trover A common law action for damages due to a conversion of personal property.

trust A confidence reposed in one person, who is termed *trustee*, for the benefit of another, who is called the *cestui que trust*, respecting property, which is held by the trustee for the benefit of the cestui que trust. As the word is used in the law pertaining to unlawful combinations and monopolies, a trust in its original and typical form is a combination formed by an agreement among the shareholders in a number of competing corporations to transfer their shares to an unincorporated board of trustees, and to receive in exchange trust certificates in some agreed proportion to their shareholdings.

trustee A person in whom property is vested in trust for another.

trustee in bankruptcy The Federal Bankruptcy Act defines the term as an officer, and he is an officer of the courts in a certain restricted sense, but not in any such sense as a receiver. He takes the legal title to the property of the bankrupt and in respect to suits stands in the same general position as a trustee of an express trust or an executor. His duties are fixed by statute. He is to collect and reduce to money the property of the estate of the bankrupt.

ultra vires act An act of a corporation that is beyond the powers conferred upon the corporation.

unilateral contract A contract formed by an offer or a promise on one side for an act to be done on the other, and a doing of the act by the other by way of acceptance of the offer or promise; that is, a contract wherein the only acceptance of the offer that is necessary is the performance of the act.

usury The taking more than the law allows upon a loan or for forbearance of a debt. Illegal interest; interest in excess of the rate allowed by law.

utter As applied to counterfeiting, to utter and publish is to declare or assert, directly or indirectly, by words or action, that the money or note is good. Thus to offer it in payment is an uttering or publishing.

valid Effective; operative; not void; subsisting; sufficient in law.

vendee A purchaser of property. The word is more commonly applied to a purchaser of real property, the word "buyer" being more commonly applied to the purchaser of personal property.

vendor A person who sells property to a vendee. The words "vendor" and "vendee" are more commonly applied to the seller and purchaser of real estate, and the words "seller" and "buyer" are more commonly applied to the seller and purchaser of personal property.

venire The name of a writ by which a jury is summoned.

venue The word originally was used to indicate the county from which the jurors were to come who were to try a case, but in modern times it refers to the county in which a case is to be tried.

verdict The answer of a jury given to the court concerning the matters of fact committed to their trial and examination; it makes no precedent and settles nothing but the present controversy to which it relates. It is the decision made by the jury and reported to the court, and as such it is an elemental entity that cannot be divided by the judge.

verification The affidavit of a party annexed to his pleadings which states that the pleading is true of his own knowledge except as to matters that are therein stated on his information or belief, and as to those matters, that he believes it to be true. A sworn statement of the truth of the facts stated in the instrument verified.

versus Against.

vest To give an immediate fixed right of present or future enjoyment.

void That which is entirely null. A void act is one that is not binding on either party, and is not susceptible of ratification.

voidable Capable of being made void; not utterly null, but annullable, and hence may be either voided or confirmed.

waive To throw away; to relinquish voluntarily, as a right that one may enforce if he chooses.

waiver The intentional relinquishment of a known right. It is a voluntary act and implies an election by the party to dispense with something of value, or to forgo some advantage that he or she might have demanded and insisted on.

warrant An order authorizing a payment of money by another person to a third person. Also an option to purchase a security. As a verb, the word means to defend, to guarantee, to enter into an obligation of warranty.

warrant of arrest A legal process issued by competent authority, usually directed to regular officers of the law, but occasionally issued to private persons named in it, directing the arrest of a person or persons on grounds stated therein.

warranty In the sale of a commodity, an undertaking by the seller to answer for the defects therein is construed as a warranty. In a contract of insurance, as a general rule, any statement or description, or any undertaking on the part of the insured on the face of the policy or in another instrument properly incorporated in the policy, which relates to the risk, is a warranty.

waste The material alteration, abuse, or destructive use of property by one in rightful possession of it that results in injury to one having an underlying interest in it.

watered stock Stock issued by a corporation as fully paid up, when in fact it is not fully paid up.

writ A commandment of a court given for the purpose of compelling a defendant to take certain action, usually directed to a sheriff or other officer to execute it.

Case Index

A

Advance Industrial Div. v. NLRB, 303
Agaliotis v. Agaliotis, 513
Airo Supply Co. v. Page, 611
Allen v. Jordanos', Inc., 142–43
Alphonse Brenner Company, Inc. v. Dickerson, 258
A. Alport & Sons, Inc. v. Hotel Evans, Inc., 505–6
American Trading and Production Corp. v. Shell International Marine, Ltd., 167
Arrow Employment Agency, Inc. v. Seides, 121
Atlantic Insurance Co. v. Massey, 622
Austin Instrument, Inc. v. Loral Corporation, 99
Axelrod v. Wardrobe Cleaners, Inc., 435–36
Axilbund v. McAllister, 291

B

Bacon Estate, 243–44
Bain v. Pulley, 287–88
Bank of Wyandotte v. Woodrow v. Durbin, 532
In re Barnhart, 610
Belcher v. Birmingham Trust Nat'l Bank, 382
Beneficial Finance Co. v. Marshall, 569
Board of Control of Eastern Michigan University v. Burgess, 76
Borel v. Fibreboard Paper Products Corp., 222–23
Bove v. Community Hotel Corp., 403–4
Bowen v. Collins, 566
Brockett v. Kitchen Boyd Motor Co., 52
Brown v. Wichita State University, 157–58
Bunge Corp. v. Williams, 189–90
Burbank v. Lockheed Air Terminal, Inc., 631
In re Burnett Little v. Regency East, 579
Butz v. Glover Livestock Commission Co., Inc., 634–35

C

Carolina Overall Corp. v. East Carolina Linen Supply, Inc., 47
Carroll v. Exxon, 666
Carter v. Conroy, 450–51
Carter v. Reichlin Furriers, 437
Central Credit Collection Control Corp. v. Grayson, 148
Chambers v. Young, 485–86
Chase Manhattan Bank v. Hobbs, 84
Cintrone v. Hertz Truck Leasing & Rental Service, 439
City Mortgage Investment Club v. Beh, 561
Clark v. Allen, 339–40
Clarkson v. Wirth, 162
Coates v. City of Cincinnati, 37
In re Cohen, 604
Cohn v. Fisher, 242
Colley v. Bi-State, Inc., 237
Collier v. B & B Sales, Inc., 204
Continental Bank v. Fitting, 547–48
Continental T.V., Inc. v. G.T.E. Sylvania, Inc., 643–44
E. A. Coronis Associates v. M. Gordon Construction Co., 183
County Trust Co. v. Cobb, 536–37
Cox v. Jones, 338
Credit Bureau of Merced County, Inc. v. Shipman, 345
Cross v. Cross, 492
Cutler Corp. v. Latshaw, 73–74

D

Darvin v. Belmont Industries, Inc., 395
De La Hoya v. Slim's Gun Shop, 247
Desfosses v. Notis, 285

Diaz v. Pan American World Airways, 304
Dudley v. Dumont, 263–64

E

Electro-Voice, Inc. v. O'Dell, 298–99
Elmore v. Blume, 462–63
Escott v. BarChris Construction Corp., 392–93
Estrada v. Darling-Crose Machine Company, Inc., 137–38

F

Fair v. Hamersmith Distributing Co., 254
Filipczak v. I.B.E.W., 474–75
Filler v. Rayex Corp., 213
First Regional Securities, Inc. v. Villella, 101–2
Fisher v. Cattni, 111
Florida Tomato Packers, Inc. v. Wilson, 356
Floyd v. Morristown European Motors, Inc., 290
Frasier v. Carter, 122
Fred Meyer Inc. v. Temco Metal Products, 538–39
FTC v. Procter and Gamble Co., 652
FTC v. Texaco, Inc., 636
Fuqua Homes, Inc. v. Evanston Building and Loan Co., 199

G

Garcia v. Freeland Realty, Inc., 472–73
Garcia v. Villarreal, 120
Gardner and North Roofing and Siding Corp. v. Board of Governors, 660–61
Gay v. Gays Super Markets, Inc., 401
Gebhardt Brothers, Inc. v. Brimmel, 66
General Factors, Inc. v. Beck, 154–55
Gibson v. Hagberg, 585–86
W. T. Grant Co. v. Walsh, 150
Great Atlantic and Pacific Tea Co., Inc. v. Cottrell, 631–32
Griffith v. Byers Construction Co., 97
Griggs v. Duke Power Co., 305
Grissum v. Reesman, 316
Grossman v. Liberty Leasing Co., Inc., 379
Guth v. Loft, Inc., 384–85

H

Hallman v. Federal Parking Services, Inc., 433
Hawkins v. Kourlias, 448
Haydocy Pontiac, Inc. v. Lee, 108
Henningsen v. Bloomfield Motors, 215–16
Hillman v. Hodag Chemical Corporation, 123
Hodgson v. Security National Bank, 306
Hoeflich v. William A. Merrell Co., 240–41
Hollaway v. Forshee, 454–55
Holloway v. Smith, 328–29
Holzman v. de Escamilla, 354
Horn's Crane Service v. Prior, 333–34
Hunt v. Ferguson-Paulus Enterprises, 212
Hunter v. Hayes, 125
Hy-Grade Oil Co. v. New Jersey Bank, 147

I–J

Ingram v. Phillips Petroleum Co., 653–54
Inpaco, Inc. v. McDonald Corp., 361
Jackson v. Steinberg, 425
Jaybe Construction Co. v. Beco, Inc., 79
Jones v. Walsh, 44
Jiffy Markets, Inc. v. Vogel, 54–55

K

Kaufman v. Kaufman's Administrator, 488
Killinger v. Iest, 274–75
Kilpatrick Bros., Inc. v. Poynter, 319
King v. Stoddard, 342
Kole v. Parker Yale Development Co., 164–65
Krasner v. Berk, 112
Krause v. Mason, 364

L

La Gasse Pool Construction Co. v. City of Fort Lauderdale, 166
La Gorga v. Kroger Co., 223–24
Lagniappe of New Orleans, Ltd. v. Denmark, 272
Lange v. National Biscuit Company, 280
Larsen v. General Motors, 221
Lavin v. Ehrlich, 343
Levant v. Kowal, 372
Lieber v. Mohawk Arms, Inc., 424
Liggett v. Lester, 332
Ling and Co. v. Trinity Savings and Loan Ass'n, 407
Locke v. Prudence Mutual Casualty Co., 619
Lowe v. Arizona Power and Light, 350
Lucas v. Whittaker Corp., 130

M

McCarty v. E. J. Korvette, Inc., 210
McDaniel v. Silvernail, 134
McGlynn v. Schultz, 387
Magnavox Employee Credit Union v. Benson, 583
Mahaley v. Colonial Trading Co., 581
Markham v. Colonial Mortgage Service Co., 664
Marsilli v. Pacific Gas and Electric Co., 376
Martin v. American Express, Inc., 662
Massey v. Tube Art Display, Inc., 256
Methodist Mission Home of Texas v. N.A.B., 100
Metropolitan Life Insurance Co. v. Wood, 618
Miller v. American Wonderlands, Inc., 563
Millstone v. O'Hanlon Reports, 663–64
Miron v. Yonkers Raceway, Inc., 232
Misco-United Supply, Inc. v. Petroleum Corporation, 357
Morton v. Young, 95–96
Munchak Corp. v. Cunningham, 153
Murray v. Holiday Rambler, Inc., 233
Myzel v. Fields, 393

N

Naccash v. Naccash, 430
National Cash Register v. Firestone, 594–95
Nationwide Acceptance Corp. v. Henne, 521

Newman v. Manufacturer's National Bank, 508
In re Nicolosi, 580
Ninth Street East, Ltd. v. Harrison, 201

O

Ochoa v. Rogers, /28
O.K. Moving and Storage Co. v. Elgin National Bank, 516–17
O'Keefe v. Lee Calan Imports, Inc., 72

P

Pacific Guano Company v. Ellis, 262
In re Pacific Oil and Metal Co., 606–7
Paloukos v. Intermountain Chevrolet Co., 181
Park City Corp. v. Watchie, 364–65
Parker v. Twentieth Century-Fox Film Corp., 170
Parkin v. Fitzgerald, 476
Pines v. Perssion, 471
H. K. Porter Co. v. NLRB, 301–2
Pravel, Wilson and Matthews v. Voss, 132
Pribil v. Ruther, 89–90

R

Raffa v. Dania Bank, 584
Ramos v. Wheel Sports Center, 202
REA Express, Inc. v. Brennan, 297
Reading Trust Co. v. Hutchinson, 524
Reed's Photo Mart v. Monarch Marking System Co., 103
Reilly v. Rogers Park Prudential Savings and Loan Association, 83
Resort Car Rental System, Inc. v. FTC, 637
Roberts v. American Brewed Coffee, 51–52
Roberts v. Yancy, 447
Robertson v. Robertson, 110
Rose v. Vulcan Materials Co., 155–56
Rosenberger v. Herbst, 315
Rotuba Extruders Inc. v. Ceppos, 530
Ruble Forest Products, Inc. v. Lancer Mobile Homes, Inc., 188
Rushing v. Stephanus, 284
Russello v. Highland National Bank, 549

S

Santee Oil Co., Inc. v. Cox, 404–5
Saperstein v. Holland, McGill & Pasker, 608–9
Schweber v. Rallye Motors, Inc., 248
Scott v. John H. Hampshire, Inc., 55
SEC v. Texas Gulf Sulphur Co., 385
Sherrill v. Frank Morris-Buick-GMC, Inc., 545–46
Smith v. Gentilotti, 506–7
Southern California Acoustics Co. v. C. V. Holder, Inc., 85
Southern Farm Bureau Casualty Co. v. Allen, 276–77
Southwest Drug Stores of Mississippi Inc. v. Garner, 42
Southwest Engineering Co. v. Martin Tractor Co., 196
Spur Industries, Inc. v. Del Webb Development Co., 464
Standard Marine Insurance Co. v. Peck, 624

State v. Ed Cox and Son, 341
State of Alabama v. Delta Airlines, Inc., 197
State Bank of Albany v. Kahn, 597
State of Illinois v. Continental Illinois National Bank, 509–10
State *ex rel* Pillsbury v. Honeywell, Inc., 399–400
Steinberg v. Chicago Medical School, 74
Stender v. Twin City Foods, Inc., 135–36
Sterling Acceptance Co. v. Grimes, 596
Sunshine v. Manos, 78
In re Symons, 589

T

Tampa Electric Co. v. Nashville Coal Co., 648–49
Taylor v. Smith, 426
Terrace Company v. Calhoun, 109
Thomaier v. Hoffman Chevrolet, Inc., 191
Thompson v. Ford Motor Co., 613–14
Town of Lindsay v. Cooke County Electric Cooperative, 86–87
TransWorld Accounts, Inc. v. FTC, 668
Traynor v. Walters, 235
Trentacost v. Brussel, 473
Trisko v. Vignola Furniture, 119
Trout v. Bank of Belleville, 51
Troutman v. Southern Railway Co., 146

U

Umlas v. Acey Oldsmobile, 228
Uniroyal, Inc. v. Chambers Gasket & Mfg. Co., 185
United States v. Grinnell Corp., 646–47
United States v. Park, 40
U.S. v. General Dynamics Corp., 650
Uscian v. Blacconeri, 133

V

Vernon Fire and Casualty Insurance Co. v. Sharp, 169–70
Village of Woodridge v. Bohnen International Inc., 186–87
Vodopich v. Collier County Developers, Inc., 366
Vogel v. W. T. Grant Co., 45
Vrabel v. Acri, 334–35

W–Y

Wallinga v. Johnson, 440
Warner-Lambert v. F.T.C., 659
Watkins v. Sheriff of Clark County, 519
In re Estate of Weir, 484–85
George Whalley Co. v. National City Bank of Cleveland, 551
White v. Brown, 344
Wickard v. Filburn, 632–33
William T. Burton Industries, Inc. v. Cook, 453–54
Wilson v. Kealakekua Ranch Ltd., 145
Wing v. Lederer, 265
Wisconsin Telephone Company v. Lehman, 326
Wood v. United Airlines, Inc., 57
Younger v. Plunkett, 558
Youse v. Employers' Fire Insurance Co., 617

Subject Index

A

Acceptance
  bilateral contract, 83
  communication of, 86–90
    authorized means, 88–90
    stipulated means, 90
  legal power to accept, 85
  nature of, 82
  performance of sales contracts, 231–32
  revocation, 233
  silence, 84
  Uniform Commercial Code, 183–86
  unilateral contracts, 82–83
  written evidence, 85–86
Accession, 427
Accomodation party, 533
Adversary system, 15–16
  judge's function, 16
Adverse possession, 449, 453
Affirmative action plans, 305
After-acquired property, 573, 576, 590
Age Discrimination Act, 306
Agency; see also Agent
  authority to bind principal, 261–67
  basic issues, 258–59
  coupled with an interest, 266
  definition, 253
  ratification, 264–65
  termination, 266–67
Agency law, 254, 258–59
Agent; see also Agency
  apparent, 263
  attorney-in-fact, 257
  broker, 257
  capacity to be agent, 257–58

Agent—Cont.
  definition, 255
  dual agency, 285
  duties to principal, 280–89
  general, 257
  liability, 271–73
    breach of duty to principal, 280–81
    crimes, 281
    torts, 277–81
  professional, 255
  ratification, 264–65
  special, 257
  termination of powers, 266–67
American Arbitration Association, 19–20
American Law Institute, test for insanity, 38
American legal system, 7–13
  adversary system, 15–16
  checks and balances, 8
  common law, 12–13
  constitutional powers, 8
  courts, 12–13
  executive order, 11–12
  federal laws, 9
  regulatory agencies, 10–11, 633–35
  state laws, 9
  statutes, 10
  treaties, 10
Antitrust laws
  Clayton Act, 640, 647–52
  exceptions and exemptions, 655–56
    Noerr doctrine, 655–56
    Parker doctrine, 655
    regulated industry, 655
  Robinson-Patman Act, 640, 652–55
  Sherman Act, 640–47
Appeal courts, 22–23, 25–26

Appeal procedure, 34–35
Arbitration, 19–20
Assault, 41–42
Assignment of contracts
  definition, 152
  duties and rights of assignees, 154–55
  rights and duties of assignors, 155
  Uniform Commercial Code, 229
Assumed name statutes, 334
Assumption of risk, 54–55
Attorney (lawyer), 15–16, 255, 293
Attorney-in-fact, 257
Authority of agent
  apparent, 263
  duty to determine, 263
  express, 261
  implied, 261

B

Bailments
  bailee compensation, 438
  bailee duties, 434–36
  bailee liability, 436–37
  bailor liability, 438
  common carriers, 439–40
  definition, 432
  elements, 432
  hotelkeepers, 440
  involuntary, 441
  safe deposit boxes, 441
  types of, 434
Bank
  duty to pay, 544–45
  paying checks of dead or incompetent customers, 548–49
  relationship with customers, 544
  right to charge to customers account, 547
  stop payment order, 545–47
Bankruptcy
  administration, 602–10
  allowable claims, 606
  bankruptcy consumer debt adjustments, 602, 612–14
    Chapter 13 of Bankruptcy Act, 602, 612–14
  courts, 603
  discharge, 609–11
  exemptions, 604–5
  fraudulent transfers, 608
  involuntary petitions, 602
  nondischargeable debts, 610
  preferential liens, 607–8
  preferential payments, 607
  priority claims, 606
  provable claims, 605–6
  reaffirmation agreements, 609–10
  reorganizations, 601, 611–12
    administration, 611–12
  secured claims, 606
  straight bankruptcy (Chapter 7), 601–11
  trustee, 603, 605
  voluntary petitions, 602

Bankruptcy Act, 600–602, 604, 606, 609–14
  Chapter 11, 611
  Chapter 13, 612–14
Battery, 41
Beneficiary of a trust, 489, 491
Bill of Rights, 9
Blue sky laws, 394
Bona fide occupational qualification (BFOQ), 304, 306
Bond, 371
Breach of contract
  inducement to, 46–47
  remedies for, 168–71
  risk, 202
  sales contract; see Breach of sales contract
  standards of performance, 163
Breach of duty, 51–53
  agent and principal, 280–81, 293
Breach of sales contract
  buyer's remedies, 245–49
  remedies for, 239–40
  seller's remedies, 241–45
  statute of limitations, 240
Brown, Louis M., 30
Bulk transfers, 204–5
Business organization
  business trust, 411
  choosing form, 409–17
  corporation; see Corporation
  joint-stock association, 412
  limited partnership; see Limited partnership
  partnership; see Partnership
  sole proprietorship; see Sole proprietorship
  subchapter S corporation, 411
  types, 313
Business trust, 411

C

C&F (cost and freight), 200
C.I.F. (cost, insurance, and freight), 200
Cardozo, Benjamin N., 14
Causa mortis gift, 425–26
Causation, principles of, 53–54
  proximate cause, 53
Certificate of deposit, 500
Certified check, 548
Charitable trust, 490
Check, 501
  forged or altered, 549–51
Civil procedure; see Court procedure
Civil Rights Act of 1964, Title VII, 303
Clayton Act, 640, 647–53
  conglomerate merger, 651
  exclusive dealing and requirements contracts, 648–49
  horizontal mergers, 649–50
  nature and origin, 647
    Section eight, 652
    Section seven, 649–52
    Section three, 647–49

Clayton Act—*Cont.*
  tie-in contracts, 648
  vertical mergers, 650–51
Code of Federal Regulations, 14
Commerce clause of U.S. Constitution, 630
Commercial paper
  certificates of deposit, 500
  checks, 501
  drafts, 500–501
  promissory note, 498–500
  Uniform Commercial Code, 497
Common carriers, 439–40
Common law, 12–13
Common name statute, 334
Common stock, 370
Community property, 430
Comparative negligence, 54–55
Compensation
  contingent, 289–90
  directors, 379–80
  duty of principal, 289
  insurance commissions, 291–92
  partnerships, 331
  real estate commissions, 290, 454
Condominium ownership, 451
Conflict of laws, 13
Confusion, 427
Consequential damages, 240, 245–47
Consideration
  adequacy, 124
  composition agreements, 120–21
  definition, 115
  exceptions to requirements, 124–25
  forebearance to sue, 121–22
  mutuality of obligation, 122–23
  part payment of debts, 119–20
  past consideration, 121
  preexisting duties, 117–18
  rules of, 117–24
  Uniform Commercial Code, 187–88
Consignment, 203–4
Constitution, U.S., 8
  Bill of Rights, 9
  checks and balances, 8–9
  Commerce Clause, 8, 630
  Due Process Clause; *see* Due Process Clauses of U.S.
    Constitution
  Supremacy Clause, 8, 630
Constructive eviction, 476
Constructive trust, 491
Consumer Credit Protection Act (Truth-in-Lending
  Act), 659–62
Consumer protection laws, 658
  consumer credit laws, 659
  Consumer Credit Protection Act, 659–62
  Equal Credit Opportunity Act, 664–67
  Fair Credit Billing Act, 661–62
  Fair Credit Reporting Act, 662–63
  Fair Debt Collection Practices Act, 667

Consumer protection laws—*Cont.*
  FTC holder in due course rule, 525–26, 668–70
  Truth-in-Lending Act, 659–62
Contract
  acceptance; *see* Acceptance
  bilateral, 64–65
  consideration; *see* Consideration
  contrary to public policy; *see* Contracts contrary to
    public policy
  definition, 61
  disaffirmation, 93, 106–7, 112–13
  divisible, 142
  duress, 98–99
  executed, 65
  executory, 65
  express, 65
  fraud, 96–98
  historical development of law, 62–64
  illegality; *see* Illegality of contracts
  implied, 65
  insane and drunken persons, 111–13
  interpreting, 135–36
  minors, 106
  misrepresentation, 94–96, 107–8
  mistake, 101–3
  offer; *see* Offer
  oral, 128–30
  ratification, 94, 108–11, 264–65
  sales; *see* Sales contract
  third party beneficiaries; *see* Third party beneficiary
    contracts
  unconscionable, 149
  undue influence, 99–100
  unenforceable, 64
  valid, 64–65
  void, 65
  voidable, 64–65
  voluntary consent; *see* Voluntary consent
  written, 128–30
Contracts of adhesion, 149
Contracts contrary to public policy
  exculpatory clauses, 147
  influencing fiduciaries, 146
  injurious to public service, 146
  restraint of trade, 147–48
  unequal bargains, 149
Contractual liability on negotiable instruments, 531–35
Contributory negligence, 54–55
Conversion, 46
  liability for, 279, 540
  liability for conversion of checks, 540
Cooperative ownership, 451–52
Co-ownership
  community property, 430
  condominium, 451
  cooperative, 451
  joint tenancy, 429
  partnership, 314
  tenancy in common, 428
  tenancy by entirety, 429–30

Corporate governance, 380
Corporation, 317–18, 409–10
    as agent, 258
    certificate of incorporation, 360, 366, 368
    close corporation, 318
    doing business, 360–61
    domicile, 360
    financing, 369–71, 414
    formation, 366–69
    freeze-outs, 415
    governmental, 317
    history, 359
    interstate commerce, 360
    jurisdiction of courts, 361
    management; see Management of corporations
    municipal, 317
    nonprofit, 318
    number of, 409–10
    powers, 360, 374–75
    promoters, 363–66
    publicly held, 318
    qualification, 362
    regulation, 362–63
    shares (stock), 369–71
    shareholders; see Shareholder
    Subchapter S corporation, 318, 411
    taxation, 361, 412–14
    termination, 371–72
    ultra vires acts, 375
Course of dealing, 228
Court of chancery, 13
Court procedure
    affirmative defense, 29
    answer, 26, 29–31
    appeal, 34–35
    complaint, 26, 28–29
    criminal cases, 39
    discovery, 32
    pleadings, 31
    pretrial hearing, 32
    reply, 31
    summons, 26–27
    trial, 32–34
Courts
    common law, 12–13
    federal; see Federal courts
    interpretation power, 12
    judicial review, 13
    procedure; see Court procedure
    state; see State courts
Credit
    definition, 555
    secured, 556
    unsecured, 555–56
Crimes, 36–40
    contracts to commit, 142–43
    defendant's capacity, 38
    people in business, 39–40
    prior statutory prohibition, 37

Crimes—Cont.
    proof beyond reasonable doubt, 37–38
    safeguards to defendants, 39
Curtesy, right of, 486

D

Damages, 7
    compensatory, 168–69
    consequential, 169
    duty of mitigate, 170
    liquidated, 169
    nominal, 169
    punitive (exemplary), 7, 169–70
Debenture, 371
Debt securities, 369, 371
Decisional law (common law), 12–13
Deed
    form and execution, 459, 461
    quitclaim, 457–59
    recording, 461
    warranty, 459–61
Deed of trust, 562–63
Defamation, 43
Default
    distribution of proceeds, 585, 598
    liability of creditor, 585
    repossession of collateral, 583
    sale of collateral, 584–85, 598
    Uniform Commercial Code, 583
Destination contracts, 200–201
Director, corporate; see Management of corporations
Discharge, 167–68
Discharge of negotiable instruments, 540–42
Discrimination in employment, 303–6
    state legislation, 306
Dishonor of negotiable instruments, 533–35
Disparagement, 46
Dispute settlement
    arbitration, 19–20
    courts; see Courts
    fact finding, 19
    mediation, 19
    negotiation, 18–19
Dissolution of partnership
    after assignment, 340
    continuation, 343
    by court order, 339
    definition, 337
    distribution of assets, 346–48
    in violation of agreement, 339
    without violation of agreement, 338
    winding up, 340–43
Dividends, 400–403
    directors discretion to pay, 400
    lawsuits by shareholders, 405–6
    legal limits, 402
    liability for, 403, 406
    on preferred stock, 402–3
    record date, 403
    stock, 401–2

Donor, 425–26, 489
Dower right, 486
Draft, 500–501
Drawee
  liability of, 531
Drawer, 500
  liability of, 531–32
Dual agent, 285–86
Due Process Clauses of the U.S. Constitution
  fifth amendment, 9, 37, 634
  fourteenth amendment, 9, 37, 295, 634
Duress, 98–99

E

Easement, 449
Electronic banking, 508–10
Eminent domain, 466
Employee, 255–56, 259
  of agent, 277
  liability for crimes, 281
  liability for torts, 277–80
Employment laws
  collective bargaining and union activities, 300–303
  discrimination, 303–6
  health and safety legislation, 296–99
  history, 295
  pension plans, 307
  Retirement and Income Security Act, 307
  state wage statutes, 299
  wages and hours, 299
Employment Retirement and Income Security Act
  (ERISA), 307
Equal Credit Opportunity Act, 664–67
Equal Employment Opportunity Commission (EEOC),
  304
Equal Pay Act of 1963, 305
Equity, 13
Equity securities, 369
Estate planning, 479–89
  administration of estate, 487
  disposition of property on death of owner, 479–80
  dying intestate, 480–81
  murder disqualification, 481
  probate court, 479
  simultaneous death, 481
  wills; see Wills
Estoppel, 76–77, 124–25
Eviction, 476
Exclusive agency (exclusive listing), 291
Exculpatory clause, 147, 274
Express warranty, 208–10
  limitation, 214
Ex-ship, 200

F

F.A.S. (free alongside), 200
F.O.B. (free on board), 200
Fair Credit Billing Act, 661–62
Fair Credit Reporting Act, 662–63
Fair Debt Collection Practices Act, 667

Fair Labor Standards Act, 299
False imprisonment, 42–43
Federal courts
  appeal courts, 22–23, 25–26
  Bankruptcy Court, 24, 603
  Court of Claims, 24
  Customs Court, 24
  district courts, 22, 24
  judicial circuits, 23
  jurisdiction, 21
  Supreme Court, 23–24
  Tax Court, 24
Federal Mediation and Conciliation Service, 19, 301
Federal Trade Commission (FTC), 11, 635–37, 651
  holder in due course regulations, 525–26, 668–70
  warranty rules, 217
Federal Trade Commission Act, 635–36, 658
Fee simple, 448
Felony, 36
Fictitious payee rule, 539–40
Field warehousing, 591
Financing statement, 577–79, 591
Fixtures, 444–47
  security interest, 582–83, 596–97
Foreclosure, 557
  deed of trust, 563
  land contract, 563
  mortgage, 561
  possessory liens, 558
  strict, 561
Foreign Corrupt Practices Act (1977), 381
Forgery, 549–51
Franchise, 257, 320–22
Fraud, 96–98
  antifraud provisions of Securities Acts, 392–93
  in the inducement, 523
Future advance, 573, 576, 590

G

Garnishment, 299
Gift, 425–26
Good faith, 227
Goodwill, 337
Government regulation
  administrative agencies, 10–11, 633–35
  federal regulation, 8, 632–33
  Federal Trade Commission Act, 635–37
  historical background, 629
  state regulation, 630–32
    intrastate commerce, 630

H

Habitability of leased real property, 470–71
Health and safety legislation
  OSHA, 296–97
  state legislation, 296
  workmen's compensation, 297–99
Holder in due course, 502, 517–26
  FTC rule, 525–26, 668–70
  personal defenses, 522–23

Holder in due course—*Cont.*
  real defenses, 523–24
  requirements, 518–22
  rights, 522–24
  rule changes, 525–26
Holographic will, 485–86
Homestead right, 486
Hotelkeepers, 440
Housing codes, 471–72

I

Illegality of contracts
  contrary to public policy; *see* Contracts contrary to
    public policy
  court enforcement, 140
  crimes, 142
  divisible contracts, 142
  regulatory statutes, 144–45
  rescission before performance, 141
  statutes declaring agreements void, 143–44
  torts, 143
  wagering statutes, 143
Implied warranty, 210–14
  exclusion, 214–15
  fitness for particular purpose, 212–13
  of merchantability, 211
  nature of, 210–11
  title, 213–14
Implied warranty of agents authority, 272
Impossibility of performance, 236
Impostor rule, 539
Independent contractor, 255–56
Individual proprietorship; *see* Sole proprietorship
Indorsement
  blank, 515
  effects, 514
  qualified, 517
  restrictive, 516
  special, 514
Indorser, liability of, 532–33
Inheritance; *see* Estate planning
Injunction, 171
Insanity
  of agent, 266
  checks, 548–49
  of contracting party, 111–13
  of criminal defendant, 34
  defense to criminal charge, 38
  of partners, 326
  of principal, 266, 273
Insurable interest, 202–3
Insurance
  cancelation, 623–24
  coinsurance clause, 617
  fire insurance, 617
  incontestable clause, 620
  insurable interest, 621–22
  lapse, 624
  life insurance, 615–16

Insurance—*Cont.*
  misstatement of age, 620
  notice and proof of loss, 623
  policies as contracts, 618–21
Insurance commissions, 291–92
Intentional torts, 36–47
Inter vivos gift, 425–26
Inter vivos trust, 490
Interstate Commerce Commission (ICC), 11
Interstate Land Sales Full Disclosure Act, 456
Intestacy, 480–81
Intestate succession, 480
Intrastate commerce, 630

J

Joinder, 333
Joint stock association, 412
Joint tenancy, 429
Joint ventures, 355–56
Jury, 33–34

L

Labor Management Relations Act (LMRA), 301–3
Labor Management Reporting and Disclosure Act
  (Landrum-Griffin Act), 301
Laissez faire economic theory, 62
Land contract, 563–65
Landlord
  abandonment, 476
  constructive eviction, 476
  eviction, 476
  habitability, 470
  housing codes, 471
  liability for injuries, 474
  protection of tenants, 473
  rights, 470
  security deposits, 474
  tenant relationship, 468–69
  termination, 475–76
Landrum-Griffin Act, 301
Law
  adaptability, 15
  civil, 7
  criminal, 7
  definition, 5
  functions, 6
  procedural, 6–7
  statutes, 5
  substantive, 6–7
Lawyer (attorney), 15–16, 255, 293
Lease, 469
  abandonment, 476
  assignment, 475
  constructive eviction, 476
  eviction, 476
  sublease, 475
  termination, 475–76
Leasehold, 449
Legal system; *see* American legal system

Liability on negotiable instruments
   contract liability, 531–35
   definition, 528
   fictitious payee rule, 539–40
   impostor rule, 539
   negligence, 538
   signing, 529–30
   warranties, 535–38
Liability of agent, 272–73, 277–81
Liability of corporation, 386–88
Liability of directors and officers, 388
Liability of principal
   acts of subagents, 277
   agent's representations, 273–74
   agent's warranties, 275
   credit contacts, 275
   crimes, 281
   disclosed principal, 270–71
   negotiable instrument, 275
   notice to agent, 276
   partially disclosed principal, 272
   payment to agent, 275
   torts, 277
   undisclosed principal, 270–71
Libel, 43
Lien
   agents, 293
   artisan's and mechanic's, 557–58, 582
   characteristics, 557–58
   common law, 557
   foreclosure of liens on personal property, 558
   mechanic's and materialman's, 565–66
   preferential, 607–8
   statutory, 557
Life estate, 448
Limited partnership
   certificate, 351–53
   definition, 350
   dissolution, 355
   liabilities of partners, 354, 412
   liquidity of investment, 416
   management, 414
   rights of partners, 353
   use of, 351
Liquidated damages, 239–40
Liquidated debt, 119
Living trust, 490
Lockout, 301
Lost property, rights of finder, 423

M

Magnuson-Moss Warranty Act, 217–20
Maker, 488
   liability of, 531
Management of corporations
   board of directors, 377
      committees, 381
      compensation, 379–80
      duties, 377, 383–86
      election, 374

Management of corporations—*Cont.*
   board of directors—*Cont.*
      meetings, 377–79
      powers, 377
      removal, 378
   corporate governance, 380–82
   officers of corporation, 382–83
   Securities Acts violations, 386
   stock trading, 385–86
   torts liability, 386
Marbury v. *Madison*, 13
Marshall, John, 13
Materiality, 94
Mediation, 19
   storefront, 20
Mental distress, recovery for, 45
Mergers, 404, 649–51
   conglomerate, 651
   horizontal, 649–50
   vertical, 650–51
Mining associations, 357
Minors
   agents, 258
   contractual liability, 106–11
   criminal liability, 138
   partners, 258, 326
   principals, 257
Misdemeanors, 36
Mislaid property, rights of finder, 423
Mistake, 101–3
Model Business Corporation Act, 367, 370–72, 375
   corporate management, 376–80, 382
Monopoly
   Sherman Act, 645–46
Mortgage, 559–61
Multiple listing, 291

N

Nader, Ralph, 381
National Labor Relations Act (Wagner Act), 300–301
National Labor Relations Board (NLRB), 11, 300
Negligence, 50
   assumption of risk, 54–55
   breach of duty, 51–53
   causation, principles of, 53
   comparative, 55
   contributory, 54–55
   defenses to, 54–56
   duty, 50
   negotiable instrument, 538
   per se, 52
   product liability, 220
   recklessness, 56
Negotiable instrument
   ambiguous terms, 508
   authority of agents, 275
   basic requirements, 503–4
   commercial paper; *see* Commercial paper
   contractual liability, 531–35
   definition, 497

Negotiable instrument—*Cont.*
  discharge of, 540–42
  pay to order of bearer, 507
  payable on demand or at definite time, 506
  rights of assignee of contract, 502
  rights of holder, 502–3
  signature by authorized agent, 529
  signed, 504
  sum certain, 505–6
  types of; *see* Certificate of deposit; Check; Draft; *and*
    Promissory note
  unauthorized signatures, 530
  unconditional promise or order, 504–5
  in writing, 504
Negotiation, 18–19
Negotiation of commercial paper
  definition, 512
  indorsement; *see* Indorsement
  requirements, 512–13
No arrival, no sale, 201
Noerr doctrine, 655
Nonprofit corporation, 318
Norris-LaGuardia Act, 300
Note, 498–500
Nuisance, 463–64
Nuncupative will, 485

O

Occupational Safety and Health Act (OSHA),
  296–97
Offer
  advertisements, 71
  auctions, 72
  bids, 72
  death of party to contract, 79
  estoppel, 76–77
  insanity of party to contract, 79
  intervening illegality, 79
  terms included, 73, 75
  time lapse, 75
  Uniform Commercial Code, 182
Open (general) listing, 291
Options
  contracts, 75–76
  rights, 370
  securities options, 370
Oral contracts, 128–30

P

Parker doctrine, 655
Parole evidence rule, 129, 136–37
Partner
  authority, 327–28
  compensation, 330, 343
  corporation as, 326
  duties, 331–33, 342
  interest in partnership property, 330
  liability, 325, 348
  minors and insane persons, 326
  powers in winding up, 341

Partner—*Cont.*
  right of noncontinuing partner, 345
  right to wind up, 340
Partnership
  as agent, 258
  articles of partnership, 325
  assignment of partnership interest, 330–31
  authority of partners, 327–29
  definition, 314–16
  dissolution; *see* Dissolution of partnership
  formation, 324–25
  lawsuits by and against, 333–34
  liability for acts of partners, 325, 327–29, 334–35
  life of business, 415
  limited; *see* Limited partnership
  liquidity of investment, 416
  management, 327, 329
  number, 410
  property, 329–30
  taxation, 412–14
  trading and nontrading, 328–29
Pension Benefit Guaranty Corporation, 307
Performance
  condition precedent, 161
  condition subsequent, 161
  constructive condition, 161
  contractual duty, definition of, 161
  discharge, 167–68
  express condition, 161
  material breach of contract, 163
  nonperformance excuses, 165–67
  remedies for breach of contract, 168–71
  sales contracts; *see* Performance of sales contracts
  standards, 162–64
  time, 164
Performance of sales contracts
  acceptance of goods, 231–32, 234
  anticipatory repudiation, 236
  assignment, 229
  assurance, 235–36
  commercial impracticability, 236–37
  course of dealing, 228
  delivery, 229–30
  excuse, 236
  good faith, 227–28
  inspection, 230
  payment, 230–31
  rejection, 234–35
  revocation of acceptance, 232
  usage of trade, 228
  waiver, 228
Periodic tenancies, 469
Personal property
  acquisition of
    abandoned property, 423
    accession, 427
    capture, 423
    confusion, 427
    gift, 425–26

Personal property—*Cont.*
  acquisition of—*Cont.*
    lost property, 423
    mislaid property, 423
    production, 423
    purchase, 423
  community property, 430
  conversion of, 46
  definition, 421–22
  gift, 425–26
  joint tenancy, 429
  ownership, 422
  tenancy in common, 428–29
  tenancy by the entirety, 429–30
  trespass to, 46
Possessory lien, 557–58
Preferential lien, 607–8
Preferential payment, 607
Preferred stock, 370
Preventive law, 3–4
Principal, 257–58, 261
  agent's authority to bind, 261–63
  capacity to be, 257
  disclosed, 270–71
  duties to agent, 289–93
  liability to third party; *see* Liability of principal
  partially disclosed, 271–72
  rights, 271
  undisclosed, 270–71
Privacy, right of, 44
Privilege, absolute or conditional, 43
Privity of contract, 216
Probate court, 479–80
Procedural law, 7
  conflict of laws, 13
Product liability
  definition, 208
  historical development of law, 208
  negligence, 220
  strict liability, 221–25
  warranties; *see* Warranties
Professional associations, 374
Promissory estoppel, 76, 124
Promissory note, 498–500
Property
  definition, 421
  intangible, 422
  ownership, 421–22
  personal; *see* Personal property
  private, 422
  public, 422
  real; *see* Real property
  tangible, 422
Property rights, 46
Proxy voting, 396
Public figures, 44
Public policy, 145
  contracts contrary to, 145–50
Purchase money security interest, 580

Q–R

Quasi contract, 65–66
Quitclaim deed, 457–59
Ratification of contract, 94
  agency, 264–65
  insane persons, 113
  minors, 108–11
Real estate commission, 290–91, 454–55
Real Estate Settlement Procedures Act (RESPA), 455–56
Real property
  acquisition, 452–53
    adverse possession, 453–54
    gift, 452
    purchase, 452, 454–63
    tax sale, 452
    will or inheritance, 452
  condominium ownership, 451
  cooperative ownership, 451–52
  easement, 449
  fee simple, 448
  leasehold, 449
  license, 449
  life estate, 448
  private restrictions, 450–51
  public control of land use, 463–66
    eminent domain, 466
    nuisance control of land use, 463–64
    zoning, 464–66
  sale, 454
    broker, 454–55
    closing statement, 455–57
    contract, 455
    financing purchase, 455, 558–65
  security interests, 558–66
    deeds of trust, 562–63
    land contract, 563–65
    mechanic's and materialmen's liens, 565–66
    mortgage, 559–61
  transfer by deed; *see* Deed
  warranties, 461–63
Recklessness, 56
Regulatory agencies
  Department of Labor, 299, 305–7
  Equal Opportunity Commission, 304
  Federal Trade Commission, 635–37
  generally, 10–11, 633–35
  Interstate Commerce Commission, 11
  National Labor Relations Board, 300–303
  Occupational Safety and Health Administration, 296–97
  Securities and Exchange Commission, 391–93, 396–98, 406, 381, 385
Res ipsa loquitur doctrine, 52–53
Respondeat superior, 279, 334
Restraint of trade, 147–48
  antitrust laws; *see* Antitrust laws
Resulting trust, 490

Risk of loss
  breach of contract, 202
  insurable interest, 202–3
  terms of agreement, 200–201
  Uniform Commercial Code, 199–203
Robinson-Patman Act, 640, 652–55
  buyer inducements, 654–55
  defenses, 653
  price discrimination
    direct, 653
    indirect, 654
Rockefeller, John D., 411
Roosevelt, Franklin D., 11
Rule 10b–5, 385, 393

S

Sales contracts
  acceptances, 183–84
  on approval, 203
  breach; see Breach of sales contract
  bulk transfers, 204–5
  consideration, 187–88
  on consignment, 203–4
  creation of, 180–81
  offers, 182–83
  performance; see Performance of sales contracts
  sale or return, 203
  statute of frauds, 190–91
  terms, 195–96
  unconscionability, 188–90
  Uniform Commercial Code, 178–81
Secured commercial transactions
  buyers in the ordinary course of business, 595
  collateral, 588–89
  default and foreclosure, 598
  fixtures, 596–97
  obtaining security interest, 590
  perfecting security interest, 591–92
  priorities, 593–94
  Uniform Commercial Code, 588
Secured consumer transactions
  attachment, 572–73
  default, 583–85
  fixtures, 582–83
  motor vehicles, 581
  perfection, 577–82
    by attachment, 580–81
    financing statement, 577–78
    by possession, 579
    priorities, 582–83
  Uniform Commercial Code, 571
Securities Act of 1933, 365, 391–92
Securities and Exchange Act of 1934, 386, 391
Securities and Exchange Commission (SEC), 11, 381, 385, 391–93, 396–97, 406
  antifraud rules, 385, 393–94
  proxy rules, 396–98
Security agreement, 573–76, 590
  after-acquired property, 573, 576, 590
  assignment, 576

Security agreement—Cont.
  future advance, 573, 590
  proceeds, 576, 590
Security deposits for rentals, 474
Security interest, 556
  commercial personal property; see Secured commercial transactions
  consumer goods; see Secured consumer transactions
  Uniform Commercial Code, 571, 588
Settlor, 489
Shareholder
  appraisal right, 404
  becoming, 391
  cumulative voting, 398–99
  dividends, 400–403
  functions, 390
  lawsuits, 405–6
  liability, 406
  meetings, 394–99
  petition for dissolution of corporation, 372
  preemptive rights, 400
  proxy voting, 396–97
  right of inspection, 399
  right to vote, 396
Sherman Act, 640–46
  jurisdiction, 641
  monopolization, 645–46
  penalties, 641
  restraints on trade, 642
  Section one, 642–45
  Section two, 645–47
Shipment contracts, 200
Slander, 43
Sole proprietorship, 313, 409–11
  liability, 412
  life of business, 415
  liquidity of investment, 416
  number of, 409–10
  taxation, 413–14
Stare decisis, doctrine of, 12, 14, 16
State courts
  appeal courts, 25
  courts of record, 24
  jurisdiction, 24
  justice of peace, 25
  municipal courts, 25
  probate courts, 25
  small claims, 25
  trial courts, 25
State laws, 9–12
  constitutions, 10
  statutes, 10
Statutes of descent and distribution, 480
Statutes of frauds, 129–35
  contracts covered by, 130–35
  sales contracts, 190–91
  unenforceable oral contracts, 129
  Uniform Commercial Code, 190–91
Statutes of repose, 224

Stock (corporate)
  common, 370
  preferred, 370
  stock split, 402
  stock subscription, 391
  transfer, 406–7
  treasury, 371
Stop payment order, 545–47
Strict foreclosure, 561
Strict liability, 56
  product quality, 221–25
Subagent, 277
Subchapter S corporation, 318, 411
Subleasing, 475
Subrogation, 569
Substantive law, 6
Sum certain in money, 505–6
Sunday laws, 144
Supremacy Clause of the Constitution, 9, 630
Suretyship, 566–69

                      T

Taft-Hartley Act, 301
Tax shelters, 351
Tenancy in common, 428–29
Tenancy by the entirety, 429–30
Tenancy at sufferance, 469
Tenancy at will, 449, 469
Tenant
  abandonment, 476
  assignment, 475
  constructive eviction, 476
  duties, 474
  eviction, 476
  leases, 469–70
  liability, 474
  nature of relationship, 468–69
  protection against criminal conduct, 473
  rights, 474
  security deposits, 474
  subleasing, 475
  termination, 475
Term life insurance, 616
Testator and testatrix, 481
Third party beneficiary contracts
  creditor, 157
  donee, 156–57
  goods in possession of bailee, 201
  incidental, 157
  title, 198–99
Title
  buyer in ordinary course of business, 198
  entrusting rule, 198–99
  implied warranty, 213–14
  transfers, 198
  Uniform Commercial Code, 197
Torts, 7, 40–47
  battery, 41
  contract to commit, 143
  defamation, 43–44

Torts—*Cont.*
  false imprisonment, 42–43
  infliction of mental distress, 45
  interference with contract, 46–47
  invasion of privacy, 44–45
  principal's liability, 277–81
  property rights interference, 46
Treasury stock, 371
Treaties, 10
Trial, 32–34
  jury, 33–34
Trust
  beneficiary, 489, 491
  charitable, 490
  constructive, 491
  definition, 489
  express, 490
  implied, 490–91
  inter vivos, 490
  resulting, 490
  termination and modification, 491
  testementary, 490
Trustee, 489, 491–92
Truth-in-Lending Act (Consumer Credit Protection
  Act), 659–62

                      U

Ultra vires doctrine, 375
Unauthorized signature, 530
Unconscionable contract, 149, 189
Undue influence, 99–100
Unfair labor practices, 301–2
Uniform Commercial Code; see *Appendix*
  acceptance, 183–86
  Article 2, 178–80
  Article 9, 571
  bank's duties, 544
  commercial paper, 497
  consideration, 187–88
  default, 583
  offer, 182
  risk, 199–203
  sales contract, 178–81
  secured commercial transactions, 588
  security interests, 556, 571
  title, 197
  voluntary consent, 188–90
  written contracts, 129, 190–91
Uniform Commercial Credit Code, 503
Uniform Limited Partnership Act (ULPA), 350, 353–
  55
Uniform Partnership Act, 314, 316, 325–29, 331, 333
  continuation, 345
  dissolution, 337–43, 346
Uniform Simultaneous Death Act, 481
Unliquidated debt, 120
U.S. Bankruptcy Court, 24, 603
Usage of trade, 228
Usury laws, 143–44

V

Voluntary consent, 93
    duress and undue influence, 98–100
    fraud, 96–98
    misrepresentation, 94–96
    mistake, 101–3
    Uniform Commercial Code, 188–90
Voting trust, 412

W–Z

Wages and hours laws, 299
Warranties
    availability, 219–20
    express, 208–10
    FTC rules, 217–20
    full, 219
    implied, 208, 210–14
    nonpurchasers, 217
    operation of, 537–38
    presentment, 535–36
    privity of contract, 217
    purchasers, 216

Warranties—Cont.
    transferor's, 535
    unconscionable disclaimers, 215
Warrants, 370
Warranty deed, 459
Watered stock, 369
Whole life insurance, 616
Wills
    codicils, 487
    example of, 482–83
    execution, 481–85
    holographic, 485
    limitation on disposition, 486
    nuncupative, 485
    revocation, 486–87
    right of disposition, 481
Workmen's compensation laws, 297–99
Writ of execution, 168
Writ of garnishment, 168
Written contract, 128–30
    Uniform Commercial Code, 190–91
Zoning, 464–65

This book has been set CAP in 10 and 9 point Avanta (11 set and 10 set), leaded 2 points. Part numbers are 36 point Weiss Roman and part titles are 30 point Weiss Roman bold. Chapter numbers are 60 point Weiss Roman and chapter titles are 24 point Weiss Roman bold. The size of the text area is 28 by 47 picas.